Access 2002 Bible, Gold Edition

Access 2002 Bible, Gold Edition

Michael R. Irwin and Cary N. Prague with Jennifer Reardon

Hungry Minds™

Best-Selling Books • Digital Downloads • e-Books • Answer Networks • e-Newsletters • Branded Web Sites • e-Learning
New York, NY ✦ Cleveland, OH ✦ Indianapolis, IN

Access 2002 Bible, Gold Edition

Published by
Hungry Minds, Inc.
909 Third Avenue
New York, NY 10022
www.hungryminds.com

Library of Congress Control No.: 2001093385

ISBN: 0-7645-3573-0

Printed in the United States of America

10 9 8 7 6 5 4 3 2 1

1P/RX/RQ/QR/IN

Distributed in the United States by Hungry Minds, Inc.

Distributed by CDG Books Canada Inc. for Canada; by Transworld Publishers Limited in the United Kingdom; by IDG Norge Books for Norway; by IDG Sweden Books for Sweden; by IDG Books Australia Publishing Corporation Pty. Ltd. for Australia and New Zealand; by TransQuest Publishers Pte Ltd. for Singapore, Malaysia, Thailand, Indonesia, and Hong Kong; by Gotop Information Inc. for Taiwan; by ICG Muse, Inc. for Japan; by Intersoft for South Africa; by Eyrolles for France; by International Thomson Publishing for Germany, Austria, and Switzerland; by Distribuidora Cuspide for Argentina; by LR International for Brazil; by Galileo Libros for Chile; by Ediciones ZETA S.C.R. Ltda. for Peru; by WS Computer Publishing Corporation, Inc., for the Philippines; by Contemporanea de Ediciones for Venezuela; by Express Computer Distributors for the Caribbean and West Indies; by Micronesia Media Distributor, Inc. for Micronesia; by Chips Computadoras S.A. de C.V. for Mexico; by Editorial Norma de Panama S.A. for Panama; by American Bookshops for Finland.

For general information on Hungry Minds' products and services please contact our Customer Care department within the U.S. at 800-762-2974, outside the U.S. at 317-572-3993 or fax 317-572-4002.

For sales inquiries and reseller information, including discounts, premium and bulk quantity sales, and foreign-language translations, please contact our Customer Care department at 800-434-3422, fax 317-572-4002 or write to Hungry Minds, Inc., Attn: Customer Care Department, 10475 Crosspoint Boulevard, Indianapolis, IN 46256.

For information on licensing foreign or domestic rights, please contact our Sub-Rights Customer Care department at 212-884-5000.

For information on using Hungry Minds' products and services in the classroom or for ordering examination copies, please contact our Educational Sales department at 800-434-2086 or fax 317-572-4005.

For press review copies, author interviews, or other publicity information, please contact our Public Relations department at 650-653-7000 or fax 650-653-7500.

For authorization to photocopy items for corporate, personal, or educational use, please contact Copyright Clearance Center, 222 Rosewood Drive, Danvers, MA 01923, or fax 978-750-4470.

 is a trademark of Hungry Minds, Inc.

Credits

Acquisitions Editor
Greg Croy

Project Editors
Janet Andrews
Erik Schwab
Pat O'Brien

Technical Editors
Maryann Brown
Michael Gibson

Copy Editors
Rebekah Mancilla
Michelle Shaw

Project Coordinator
Regina Snyder

Quality Control Technicians
Valerey Bourke
David Faust
John Greenough
Susan Moritz

Graphics and Production Specialists
Gabrielle McCann
Betty Schulte
Brian Torwelle
Jeremey Unger
Erin Zeltner

Permissions Editor
Carmen Krikorian

Media Development Specialist
Megan DeCraene

Media Development Coordinator
Marisa Pearman

Proofreading and Indexing
TECHBOOKS Production Services

About the Authors

Michael R. Irwin is considered one of the leading authorities on automated database and Internet management systems today. He is a noted worldwide lecturer, a winner of national and international awards, best-selling author, and developer of client/server, Internet, Intranet, and PC-based database management systems.

Mr. Irwin has extensive database knowledge, gained by working with the Metropolitan Police Department in Washington, D.C., as a developer and analyst for the Information Systems Division for over 20 years and assorted Federal Agencies of the United States Government. Since retiring in June 1992, he runs his own consulting firm, named The Irwin Group, and is principal partner in the company - IT in Asia, LLC, specializing in Internet database integration and emphasizing Client/Server and net solutions. With consulting offices in Cincinnati, Ohio; Bangkok, Thailand; and Manila, Philippines, his companies offer Training and Development of Internet and database applications. His company has the distinction of being one of the first Microsoft Solution's Providers (in 1992). His local, national, and international clients include many software companies, manufacturers, government agencies, and international companies.

His range of expertise includes database processing and integration between mainframe, minicomputer, and PC-based database systems, as well as B-2-B and B-2-C integration between back-end databases; he is a leading authority on PC-based databases.

He is one of the top best-selling authors in the computer database management market having authored numerous database books, with several of them consistently on the best-sellers lists. His books, combined, have sold nearly a million copies worldwide. His most recent works include *The OOPs Primer* (Borland Press), *dBASE 5.5 for Windows Programming* (Prentice Hall), *Microsoft Access 2000 Bible, Microsoft Access 2000 Bible, Gold Edition* (co-authored), and *Working with the Internet*. The *Access Bible* series have recently been number one on the Ingram Bestselling Database Titles list and is always in the Amazon.com top 100. He has also written several books on customs and cultures of the countries of Asia (including China, Japan, Thailand, and India). Two of his books have won international acclaim. His books are published in over 24 languages worldwide. He has been a contributing editor and author to many well-known magazines and journals.

He is a frequent speaker at seminars and conferences around the world and has been voted the best speaker by the attendees of several international conferences.

Michael has developed and markets several add-on software products for the Internet and productivity related applications. Many of his productivity applications can be obtained from several of his Internet sites or on many common download sites. Many of his application and systems are distributed as freeware and careware. He has also developed and distributes several development tools and add-ins for a wide range of developer applications.

Cary N. Prague is an internationally best-selling author and lecturer in the database industry. He owns Database Creations, Inc., the world's largest Microsoft Access add-on company. Their products include a line of financial software: Business! for Microsoft Office, a mid-range accounting system; POSitively Business! Point of Sale software; the Inventory Barcode manager for mobile data collection; and the Check Writer and General Ledger. Database Creations also produces a line of developer tools including the appBuilder, an application generator for Microsoft Access; the EZ Access Developer Tools for building great user interfaces; appWatcher for maintaining code bases among several developers; and Surgical Strike, the only Patch Manager for Microsoft Access.

Cary also owns Database Creations Consulting, LLC, a successful consulting firm specializing in Microsoft Access and SQL Server applications. Local and national clients include many Fortune 100 companies including manufacturers, defense contractors, insurance, health-care, and software industry companies. His client list includes Microsoft, United Technologies, ABB, Smith & Wesson Firearms, Pratt and Whitney Aircraft, ProHealth, OfficeMax, Continental Airlines, and other Fortune 500 companies.

Formerly, he has held numerous management positions in corporate information systems, including Director of Managed Care Reporting for MetraHealth, Director of Corporate Finance and Software Productivity at Travelers Insurance where he was responsible for software support for 35,000 end users, and Manager of Information Systems support for Northeast Utilities.

He is one of the top best-selling authors in the computer database management market having written over forty books which have sold over one million copies on software including Microsoft Access, Borland (Ashton-Tate) dBASE, Paradox, R:Base, Framework, and graphics. Cary's books include eleven books in the *Microsoft Access Bible* series (recently number one on the Ingram Bestselling Database Titles list and in the Amazon.com top 100), *Access 97 Secrets, dBASE for Windows Handbook, dBASE IV Programming* (winner of the Computer Press Association's Book of the Year award for Best Software Specific Book), and *Everyman's Database Primer Featuring dBASE IV.* He previously completed three books for Access 2000 including *Weekend Crash Course in Access 2000 Programming.* Cary recently sold a product line named eTools for Microsoft Access to MightyWords, a division of FatBrain.com and Barnes & Noble.

Cary is certified in Access as a Microsoft Certified Professional and has passed the MOUS test in Access and Word. He is a frequent speaker at seminars and conferences around the country. He is on the exclusive Microsoft Access Insider Advisory Board and makes frequent trips to Microsoft headquarters in Redmond, WA. He has been voted the best speaker by the attendees of several national conferences. Recently, he was a speaker for Microsoft sponsored conferences in New Orleans, Hawaii, Phoenix, Chicago, Toronto, Palm Springs, Boston, and Orlando. He has also spoken at Borland's Database Conference, Digital Consulting's Database World, Microsoft's Developer Days, Computerland's Technomics Conference, COMDEX, and COMPAQ Computer's Innovate. He was a contributing editor to *Access Advisor* magazine and has written for the *Microsoft Office Developer's* journal.

Cary holds a master's degree in computer science from Rensselaer Polytechnic Institute, and an M.B.A and Bachelor of Accounting from the University of Connecticut. He is also a Certified Data Processor.

I dedicate this book to the family of Jim and Maria (Minda) Spencer. They have opened their hearts to my family and many others without requesting anything in return. They are dedicated to the true meaning of family (love and support between each other and their three children — Matt, Sara, and Jennifer) and friendship. I pray that all their hardships and suffering from the past, remain in the past and all their future endeavors are filled with joy and happiness.

— *Michael R. Irwin*

This book is dedicated to David Olio, an English teacher at South Windsor High School. David epitomizes everything good in an educator. He is professional, idealistic and most importantly a fantastic teacher and mentor. He is the first teacher to truly motivate my oldest son, helping him to make honors in his sophomore year. For all his work, personal attention, and dedication, I am very grateful.

— *Cary N. Prague*

This book is dedicated to my horse trainers Michele Barnard, Jeff Morse, and Lance Wetmore. They have taught me not simply how to get the job done, but to perform with style and finesse. For it takes skill and enthusiasm to single you apart from the competition, not only in the show ring, but for success in the business world as well.

— *Jennifer Reardon*

Preface

Welcome to the *Access 2002 Bible, Gold Edition* — your personal guide to a powerful, easy-to-use database management system. This book is in its ninth revision and has been totally rewritten for Access 2002.

It examines Access 2002 with more examples than any other Access book ever written. We think that Microsoft Access is an excellent database manager and the best Windows database on the market today. Our goal with this book is to share what we know about Access and, in the process, to help make your work and your life easier.

This book contains everything you need in order to learn Microsoft Access to a mid-advanced level. You'll find that the book starts off with the basics and builds, chapter by chapter, on topics previously covered. In places where it is essential that you understand previously covered topics, we present the concepts again and review how to perform specific tasks before moving on. Although each chapter is an integral part of the book as a whole, each chapter can also stand on its own. You can read the book in any order you want, skipping from chapter to chapter and from topic to topic. (Note that this book's index is particularly thorough; you can refer to the index to find the location of a particular topic you're interested in.)

The examples in this book have been well thought out to simulate the types of tables, queries, forms, and reports most people need to create when performing common business activities. There are many notes, tips, and techniques (and even a few secrets) to help you better understand the product.

This book can easily substitute for the manuals included with Access. In fact, many users do not get manuals today, often relying on just the online help. This book will guide you through each task you might want to do in Access. We even created appendixes to be used as reference manuals for common Access specifications. This book follows a much more structured approach than the Microsoft Access manuals — going into more depth on almost every topic and showing many different types of examples.

Is This Book for You?

We wrote this book for beginning, intermediate, and even advanced users of Microsoft Access 2002. With any product, most users start at the beginning. If, however, you've already read through the Microsoft Access manuals and worked with the Northwinds sample files, you may want to start with the later parts of this book. Note, however, that starting at the beginning of a book is usually a good idea so you don't miss out on the secrets and tips in the early chapters.

We think this book covers Microsoft Access in detail better than any other book currently on the market. We hope you will find this book helpful while working with Access, and that you enjoy the innovative style of a Hungry Minds book (formally IDG books).

Yes — If you have no database experience

If you're new to the world of database management, this book has everything you need to get started with Microsoft Access. It then offers advanced topics for reference and learning.

Yes — If you've used other database managers like dBASE or Paradox

If you're abandoning another database (such as dBASE, Paradox, FoxPro, R:Base, or Alpha Four) or even upgrading from Access 2.0 or Access 95 or 97, this book is for you. You'll have a head start because you're already familiar with database managers and how to use them. With Microsoft Access, you will be able to do all the tasks you've always performed with character-based databases — without programming or getting lost. This book will take you through each subject step by step.

Yes — If you want to learn the basics of Visual Basic Applications (VBA) programming

VBA has replaced the Access Basic language. We know that an entire book is needed to properly cover VBA, but we took the time to put together several introductory chapters that build on what you learn in the macros chapters of this book. The VBA programming chapters use the same examples you will be familiar with by the end of the book.

Conventions Used in This Book

✦ When you are instructed to press a key combination (press and hold down one key while pressing another key), the key combination is separated by a plus sign. Ctrl+Esc, for example, indicates that you must hold down the Ctrl key and press the Esc key; then release both keys.

✦ Point the mouse refers to moving the mouse so that the mouse pointer is on a specific item. Click refers to pressing the left mouse button once and releasing it. Double-click refers to pressing the left mouse button twice in rapid succession and then releasing it. Right-click refers to pressing the right mouse button once and releasing it. Drag refers to pressing and holding down the left mouse button while moving the mouse.

✦ When you are instructed to select a menu, you can use the keyboard or the mouse. To use the keyboard, press and hold down the Alt key (to activate the menu bar) and then press the underlined letter of the menu name; press Alt+E to select the Edit menu, for example. Or you can use the mouse to click on the word Edit on-screen. Then, from the menu that drops down, you can press the underlined letter of the command you want (or click on the command name) to select it.

✦ When you are instructed to select a command from a menu, you will often see the menu and command separated by an arrow symbol. Edit_Paste, for example, indicates that you need to select the Edit menu and then choose the Paste command from the menu.

✦ *Italic type* is used for new terms and for emphasis.

✦ **Bold type** is used for material you need to type directly into the computer.

✦ A special typeface is used for information you see on-screen — error messages, expressions, and formulas, for example.

Icons and Alerts

You'll notice special graphic symbols, or icons, used in the margins throughout this book. These icons are intended to alert you to points that are particularly important or noteworthy. The following icons are used in this book:

 This icon highlights a special point of interest about the topic under discussion.

 This icon points to a useful hint that may save you time or trouble.

 This icon alerts you that the operation being described can cause problems if you're not careful.

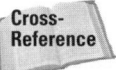 This icon points to a more complete discussion in another chapter of the book.

 This icon highlights information for readers who are following the examples and using the sample files included on the disk accompanying this book.

 This icon calls attention to new features of Access 2002.

Sidebars

In addition to noticing the icons used throughout this book, you will also notice material placed in gray boxes. This material offers background information, an expanded discussion, or a deeper insight about the topic under discussion. Some sidebars offer nuts-and-bolts technical explanations, and others provide useful anecdotal material.

How This Book Is Organized

This book contains 43 chapters divided into seven parts. In addition, the book contains three appendixes.

Part I: First Things First

Part I consists of the first four chapters of the book. In Chapter 1, you receive background information on Microsoft Access and an overview of its features. Chapter 2 covers installation — what you need in terms of hardware and software, as well as how to get Access running properly. You also learn how to start and stop Access, plus several techniques for moving between Access and other applications. Chapter 3 provides a quick hands-on test drive of Access, offering you a quick look at the features of access. Chapter 4 gives an in-depth explanation of database concepts for new users of a database product and is a case study of the upfront design that is necessary to properly implement a database system; otherwise, you must go through many false starts and redesigns when creating an application. You will design on paper the tables, forms, queries, reports, and menus necessary for creating the application.

Part II: Creating the Objects

The next six chapters make up Part II. You learn how to create a database table in Chapter 5, and you also examine how to change a database table, including moving and renaming fields without losing data. You will also learn about the new data types in Access, including the new Internet data types. In Chapter 6 you will learn about creating many tables and relating tables and using the Relationship builder tool in Access. In Chapter 7, you learn how to enter, display, change, and delete data. Chapter 8 teaches the basics of creating data-entry forms and using Wizards to simplify the creation process; using data-entry forms is also discussed. In Chapter 9, you examine the concept of queries; then you create several queries to examine how data can be rearranged and displayed. Chapter 10 covers the basics of report creation and printing.

Part III: Using Access in Your Work

Part III contains 11 chapters that go into more depth on creating and using forms, queries, and reports. In Chapter 11 you examine the meanings of operators, functions, and expressions. This chapter also covers many of the more common functions and expressions you will use in Access. You will also learn how to create the expressions and built-in functions that are so important in forms and reports. In Chapter 12, you learn how to create relations and joins in queries. Chapter 13 discusses basic selection queries, using many examples and pictures. In Chapter 14, you examine the concepts of controls and properties, and then learn how to manipulate controls in a form. Chapter 15 examines in detail how to create and use data-entry forms. Chapter 16 covers how to use visual effects to create great-looking forms and reports that catch the eye and increase productivity. In Chapter 17, you learn how to add complex data validation to tables and data-entry forms. Chapter 18 explains the use of pictures, graphs, sound, video, and other OLE objects. Chapters 19, 20, and 21 cover reports — from simple controls to complex calculations, summaries, printing, and desktop publishing.

Part IV: Advanced Access Database Topics

This part contains six chapters that present advanced topics on each of the basic tasks of Access. Chapter 22 examines how to import, export, and attach external files, and how to copy Access objects to other Access databases. Chapter 23 discusses advanced select query topics, including total, cross-tabulation, top-value, and union queries. Chapter 24 covers action queries, which change data rather than simply displaying records. Chapter 25 is a compendium of advanced query topics that will leave you amazed at the power of Access. Creating forms and subforms from multiple tables is the subject of Chapter 26; this chapter examines how to create the one-to-many relationship found in many database systems. Part IV ends with Chapter 27, which offers a look at additional types of reports not previously covered, including mail-merge reports and mailing labels.

Part V: Access Application Tools

This part contains five chapters and looks at Access as an application environment. Chapter 28 covers the concept of event-driven software and how Access uses macros to automate manual processes. This chapter also examines what a macro is, how macros are created, and how to debug them. Chapter 29 demonstrates how to use Macros in Forms and Reports. In Chapter 30 and 31 you work with Visual Basic for Applications (VBA) in Access with focus on using VBA in forms and reports; it explains data manipulation, including posting totals and filling in data-entry fields. In Chapter 32, you learn how to create button menus known as switchboards, as well as traditional pull-down menus, custom toolbars, and dialog boxes using the new Access Tab Control. In Access 2002, you will also learn about the new command bars used to build menus and toolbars.

Part VI: Access and the External World

The four chapters of Part VI focus on using Access to work SQL Server, Access projects and Data Access Pages, XML, and the Internet. In Chapter 33, you will learn about client/server topics including installing, starting, connecting to, and building Access Data Projects using the new Microsoft Database Engine. It also focuses on moving from the local Jet engine to the Microsoft Database Engine and SQL Server, focusing on the issues surrounding the two different engines and how to use tables in SQL Server. Chapter 34 shows how to work with Access Projects and the advantage of using them. Chapters 35 and 36 cover the World Wide Web and Access. Chapter 35 shows how to create and maintain HTML documents from Access Objects. Chapter 36 is dedicated to Data Access Pages and XML and how they are used for creating live data links to intranet web pages and the other incredible web capabilities of Access 2002.

Part VII: Advanced Topics in Access 2002

This final part presents seldom-discussed topics for advanced use. Chapter 37 offers important techniques for making Access faster and bypassing some of the software's perceived limitations (there are none). Chapter 38 delves into permissions, workgroups, and the Access security module — even preventing users from seeing or changing design screens and VBA code. Chapter 39 shows how to add real help systems to your Access applications. Chapter 40 introduces the Office XP Developers Edition, which creates standalone installation routines and applications. In Chapter 41, we explain how Access data integrates with Word, Excel, and other Microsoft Office applications. The most difficult components of replication are discussed in Chapter 42, while add-ins, wizards, and external libraries end the book in Chapter 43.

Appendixes and Reference Material

Three appendixes are included in this book. Appendix A presents a series of tables listing Access specifications, including maximum and minimum sizes of many of the controls in Access. Appendix B displays a database diagram of the many database tables used in this book so you can create your own system. Appendix C describes the CD-ROM.

Acknowledgments

When we first saw Access in July of 1992, we were instantly sold on this new-generation database management and access tool. Both of us have spent the last nine years using Access daily. In fact, we eat, breathe, live, and sleep Access! The fact that we can earn a living from our work on principally one product is a tribute to the designers of Microsoft Access. This product has changed the productivity of corporations and private citizens of the world. More people use this product to run their businesses, manage their affairs, track the most important things in their lives, and manage data in their work and play than any other product ever written. It is indeed a privilege to be part of this worldwide community. We have found readers in every country on the map and a few countries we never heard of. The global Internet age has allowed readers in emerging countries, in the Himalayan mountains, in Siberia, and even in Antarctica to contact us this year.

Now we have completely rewritten this book for all the incredible new features in Access 2002. We've covered every new feature we could think of for the beginning user and especially enhanced our programming section. Over 500,000 copies of our *Access Bibles* have been sold for all versions of Microsoft Access; for this we thank all of our loyal readers.

Our first acknowledgment is to all the users of Access who have profited and benefited beyond everyone's wildest dreams.

There are many people who assisted us in writing this book. We'd like to recognize each of them.

To Kim Manzone, an employee of Database Creations, who helped write several of the chapters on forms and reports. To Diana Reid, also an employee of Database Creations, who had assisted in previous versions of this book (on programming and forms chapters) and was the technical editor for several of the previous versions of this book. To her we offer an additional and special thank you. Thanks to Jennifer Reardon, one of Cary's top developers, for stepping in as always and for writing the Visual Basic for Application chapters. To John S. Dranchak for designing the reports so long ago, used in Chapters 19 and 21, and creating the logo for Mountain Animal Hospital. It still lives!!!!!

To all the people who really made this book possible. To Andy Cummings at Hungry Minds Inc., formerly IDG Books Worldwide, who pushes us beyond our limits. The word NO is not in his vocabulary! He challenges us daily with impossible tasks and deadlines (I don't care if the software doesn't work yet—write the book anyway, use your imagination—we must get this book out first). Cary thinks he wants us to get started on the Access 2004 Bible next month, although the software won't be in beta for another 18 months.

Special acknowledgments go to our technical editors Janet Andrews and Pat O'Brien. Janet edited the first half of the book and found bugs, problems, misspellings, and more that have eluded us and her predecessors for years. She had some very insightful comments throughout the editing process and didn't mind that she had to edit the entire book twice. She is a seasoned professional and we found her to be one of the best editors we have ever worked with in over 20 years of writing books. A special thank you to Pat O'Brien, and all the other unnamed editors, who were brought in at the last minute to edit the second half of the book — they had to do the same amount of work as Janet, but had less than half the time. What a terrific job and dedication — another truly seasoned professional. A special thank you must also go to Kyle Looper, Editorial Manager, also from Hungry Minds. When things started getting crazy with deadlines and trying to make Access work as expected with non-released product, he was the one that was there to bring calm to the trouble. He was more than just a coordinator between the authors, tech editors, and wordsmiths. He was the one person that kept everything on an even playing field and got everyone to work together cohesively.

To the best literary agents in the business, Matt Wagner and Bill Gladstone, and all the folks at Waterside Productions for helping us negotiate our fairest advance ever and for keeping the screaming down at the flying pig company (Hungry Minds new logo).

We would be remiss if to not thank several people at Microsoft, especially David Gainer, Microsoft Access Product Manager; Rich Dickinson, Microsoft Development Manager; and Lucille Pan, the Access Product Manager. These folks were incredibly helpful in supplying us with beta builds and information not publicly available. They kept us informed about last-minute changes and sent us new CDs when our examples didn't work. Thanks to Microsoft and these wonderful people, we were able to deliver a quality book to our readers.

Michael R. Irwin and Cary N. Prague

To the people of Database Creations who let me miss all my deadlines while I worked on this book. To Kim, Jerry, Larry, Diana, Julie, Phuc, Nate, Tom, Debbie, Karen, and especially Dick James for handling all my technical support calls. To Vic, my golfing partner, thanks for dragging me to Las Vegas after I finished most of the book. Kaching!

—CNP

First to all our clients who let me get away and spend four months solely on re-writing this book. Although my telephone bills seem to reflect the opposite — I am so grateful to them for not insisting that I personally appear to solve their 'critical' problems. To my family, Arni, Richard, Joseph, and David, who had to put up with the long months away from me while I dedicated myself to this book and organizing it into the best Access Bible yet. Even worse, having to be away, in a country (13,000 miles away), literally on the other side of the world, for three of the four months it took to solely focus on this book.

I also want to thank Dave Gainer and Clint Covington of Microsoft who offered many suggestions for the Data Access Pages section of this book. Data Access Pages have been greatly enhanced and things were being added and cut from this section so rapidly it was impossible to figure out what was going to be in the final build. Without Dave and Clint's help, these sections may have missed some items and put others in that were pulled.

—MRI

Contents at a Glance

Preface ix
Acknowledgments xv

Part I: First Things First 1
Chapter 1: What Is Access 2002? 3
Chapter 2: Installing and Running Access 2002 23
Chapter 3: A Hands-on Tour of Access 2002 55
Chapter 4: Database Concepts and Design 81

Part II: Creating the Objects 117
Chapter 5: Creating Database Tables 119
Chapter 6: Setting Relationships Between Tables 165
Chapter 7: Working with Information in Tables 211
Chapter 8: Creating and Using Simple Data-Entry Forms 249
Chapter 9: Understanding and Creating Simple Queries 269
Chapter 10: Creating and Working with Simple Reports 295

Part III: Using Access in Your Work 315
Chapter 11: Using Operators, Functions, and Expressions 317
Chapter 12: Creating Relations and Joins in Queries 343
Chapter 13: Working with Select Queries 369
Chapter 14: Understanding Form Controls 395
Chapter 15: Creating and Customizing Data-Entry Forms 423
Chapter 16: Creating Great Looking Forms 471
Chapter 17: Adding Data-Validation Controls to Forms 493
Chapter 18: Using OLE Objects, Graphs, Pivot Tables/Charts,
and ActiveX Controls 519
Chapter 19: Creating and Customizing Reports 571
Chapter 20: Presentation-Quality Reports and Printing 623
Chapter 21: Creating Calculations and Summaries in Reports 655

Part IV: Advanced Access Database Topics 689
Chapter 22: Working with External Data 691
Chapter 23: Working with Advanced Select Queries 741
Chapter 24: Working with Action Queries 773

Chapter 25: Advanced Query Topics 801
Chapter 26: Working with Subforms 833
Chapter 27: Creating Mail Merge and Label Reports 863

Part V: Access Application Tools **891**
Chapter 28: Working with Macros and Events 893
Chapter 29: Using Macros in Forms and Reports 917
Chapter 30: Working with Visual Basic in Access 2002 961
Chapter 31: Using Visual Basic in Forms and Reports 993
Chapter 32: Creating Switchboards, Command Bars,
Menus, Toolbars, and Dialog Boxes 1049

Part VI: Access and the External World **1111**
Chapter 33 Moving from Jet to the SQL Server 2000 Desktop Engine 1113
Chapter 34: Working with Access Projects 1151
Chapter 35: Using and Creating Access Objects
for Intranets and the Internet 1179
Chapter 36: Building Web Applications, Data Access Pages, and XML 1217

Part VII: Advanced Topics in Access 2002 . . . . **1273**
Chapter 37: Optimizing Performance 1275
Chapter 38: Securing an Access Application 1319
Chapter 39: Creating Help Systems in Access 2002 1367
Chapter 40: Using the Microsoft Office XP Developer 1401
Chapter 41: Integrating with Microsoft Office XP 1437
Chapter 42: Exploring Replication 1463
Chapter 43: Exploring Add-Ins and Libraries 1499

Appendix A: Access 2002 Specifications 1533
Appendix B: Mountain Animal Hospital Tables 1539
Appendix C: What's on the CD-ROM 1547

Index 1557
Hungry Minds, Inc. End-User License Agreement 1616
CD-ROM Installation Instructions 1618

Contents

● ●

Preface ix

Acknowledgments xv

Part I: First Things First   1

Chapter 1: What Is Access 2002? 3

Access Is 3
What Access Offers 7
    True relational database management 7
    Context-sensitive Help and the Office Assistant 8
    Ease-of-use Wizards 9
    Importing, exporting, and linking external table files 9
    WYSIWYG forms and reports 10
    Multiple-table queries and relationships 11
    Business graphs and charts 13
    DDE and OLE capabilities 14
    The Internet is also accessible 14
True Client/Server for Everyone 15
    Built-in functions 15
    Macros: Programming without programming 16
    Modules: Visual Basic for Applications —
        database programming 16
Information for Database Users 17
    The Windows environment 18
    GUI environment 18
    Event-driven environment 19
    Programming by exception 19
Information for Spreadsheet Users 20
    Database manipulation 21

Chapter 2: Installing and Running Access 2002 23

Determining What You Need 23
    Hardware requirements 24
    Software requirements 24
Upgrading to Access 2002 from Access 2.0, 95, 97, or 2000 25
Installing Access 2002 or Office XP 25
Activating Your Product 35
    Activating by using the Internet 36
    Activating by using the telephone 38

Converting Access 1.x, 2.0, 95, 97, and 2000 Files 39
Troubleshooting 42
Getting Started with Access 2002 42
    Starting from the Windows Start menu 42
    Starting from an Access shortcut icon 43
    Starting Access from the Start menu 43
    Starting from an Access icon created in the Office folder 44
    Starting from Windows Explorer 45
    Options for starting Access 46
Exiting Access 48
Getting Help 49
    Office Assistant 49
    Using the new Menu bar Help 51
    Standard Help 52
    Screen Tips (What's This?) 53
    Web-based resources on the Microsoft Web site 53
    Sample databases 54

Chapter 3: A Hands-on Tour of Access 2002 55
Touring the Access Window 55
    Using the mouse and the keyboard 55
    The Access window 55
    The Database window 58
    Design windows 60
A Simple Access Session 62
    Opening a database 64
    Opening a table 65
    Displaying and moving around in a datasheet 66
    Viewing a table design 70
    Displaying a form 72
    Creating a query 74
    Displaying a report 78
Ready for More? 80

Chapter 4: Database Concepts and Design 81
The Database Terminology of Access 82
    What Is a Database? 82
    Databases, tables, records, fields, and values 83
Using More Than One Table 85
    Working with multiple tables 85
    Why You Should Create Multiple Tables 86
Access Database Objects and Views 87
    Datasheets 87
    Queries and dynasets 87
    Data-entry and display forms 88
    Reports 89
    Designing the Systems Objects 89
    The Seven-Step Design Method 89

Step 1: The Overall Design — From Concept to Reality 90
    Conceptual design 91
    Interviewing the user 91
    The Process of prototyping 92
Step 2: Report Design — Placing Your Fields 93
    Laying out fields in the report 93
    The Pets and Owners Directory 94
    The Monthly Invoice Report 95
Step 3: Data Design — What Fields Do You Have? 97
    Determining customer information 98
    Determining pet information 98
    Determining visit information 99
    Combining the data 100
Step 4: Table Design and Relationships 103
    Database Normalization 103
    The four primary tables of the system 106
    Relating the four primary tables of the system to each other 107
Step 5: Field Design Data-Entry Rules and Validation 108
    Designing field names, types, and sizes 108
    Designing data-entry rules 109
    Designing lookup tables 109
    Creating test data 111
Step 6: Form Design — Input 111
    Designing data-entry screens 111
    The Customer form 112
    The Pets form 113
    The General Visits form 114
    The Visit Details form 114
Step 7: Automation Design — Menus 115

Part II: Creating the Objects   **117**

Chapter 5: Creating Database Tables **119**
Creating the Pets Table 119
Creating a Database 120
    Templates dialog box 121
    Blank database 123
The Database Window 125
    Objects menu bar 126
    Groups menu bar 127
    The Database window toolbar buttons 128
    The Access window toolbar 128
Creating a New Table 129
    The table design process 130
    The New Table dialog box 130
    Creating a new table with a Datasheet view 132

The Table Design Window 135
    Using the Table Design window toolbar 135
    Working with fields 135
Completing the Pets Table 139
Changing a Table Design 141
    Inserting a new field 141
    Deleting a field 141
    Changing a field location 142
    Changing a field name 142
    Changing a field size 142
    Changing a field data type 143
Understanding Field Properties 144
    Entering field-size properties 146
    Using formats 147
    Entering formats 151
    Entering input masks 152
    The Input Mask Wizard 154
    Entering decimal places 154
    Creating a caption 155
    Setting a default value 155
    Working with validation 155
    Understanding the Lookup Property window 157
Determining the Primary Key 158
    Creating a unique key 158
    Creating the primary key 159
    The Indexes window 160
    The Table Properties window 160
Printing a Table Design 161
Saving the Completed Table 162
Manipulating Tables in a Database Window 162
    Renaming tables 162
    Deleting tables 163
    Copying tables in a database 163
    Copying a table to another database 164

Chapter 6: Setting Relationships Between Tables 165
Tables Used in the Mountain Animal Hospital Database 165
Understanding Keys 168
    Deciding on a primary key 169
    Benefits of a primary key 170
    Creating a primary key 172
    Understanding foreign keys 173
Understanding Relations Between Tables 174
    A review of relationships 174
    Understanding the four types of table relationships 174
Understanding Referential Integrity 177

Creating Relationships 177
    Using the Relationship window 178
    Creating relationships between tables 180
    Specifying relationship options in the Edit Relationships
        dialog box 181
    Saving the relationships between tables 184
    Adding another relationship 184
    Deleting an existing relationship 184
    Join lines in the Relationships window 184
    Creating the relationships for the Mountain Animal Hospital
        system 185
Using the Access Table Analyzer 186
    Starting the Table Analyzer 187
    Selecting a table to analyze 189
    Analyzing the table 189
    Changing the table and field definitions 192
    Changing the key fields 194
    Searching for typos and duplicate key data 196
    Completing Table Analyzer 197
Using the Lookup Wizard in the Table Designer 199
Using Subdatasheets 205
    Setting up subdatasheets 207

Chapter 7: Working with Information in Tables **211**

Understanding Datasheets 211
The Datasheet Window 213
    Moving within a datasheet 214
    The Navigation buttons 214
    The Datasheet toolbar 215
Opening a Datasheet 218
Entering New Data 218
    Saving the record 220
    Understanding automatic data-type validation 220
    Understanding how properties affect data entry 221
Navigating Records in a Datasheet 224
    Moving between records 225
    Finding a specific value 225
Changing Values in a Datasheet 228
    Replacing an existing value manually 228
    Changing an existing value 229
    Fields that you can't edit 230
Using the Undo Feature 230
Copying and Pasting Values 231
Replacing Values 231
Adding New Records 232
Deleting Records 233

Adding, Changing, and Deleting Columns 234
    Deleting a column from a datasheet 234
    Adding a column to a datasheet 234
    Changing a field name (column header) 234
Displaying Records 235
    Changing the field order 235
    Changing the field display width 236
    Changing the record display height 237
    Displaying cell gridlines 238
    Changing display fonts 239
    Hiding and unhiding columns 241
    Freezing columns 241
    Saving the changed layout 241
    Saving a record 242
Sorting and Filtering Records in a Datasheet 242
    Using the QuickSort feature 242
    Using Filter by Selection 243
    Using Filter by Form 244
Printing Records 245
    Printing the datasheet 246
    Using the Print Preview window 246

Chapter 8: Creating and Using Simple Data-Entry Forms 249

Understanding Data-Entry Forms 249
    What are the basic types of forms? 250
    How do forms differ from datasheets? 252
    Creating a form with AutoForm 252
Creating a Form with Form Wizards 254
    Creating a new form 254
    Selecting the New Form type and data source 255
    Choosing the fields 255
    Choosing the form layout 257
    Choosing the style of the form 258
    Creating a form title 259
    Completing the form 259
Changing the Design 260
Using the Form Window 262
    The Form toolbar 262
    Navigating between fields 262
    Moving between records in a form 263
Displaying Your Data with a Form 263
    Working with pictures and OLE objects 264
    Memo field data entry 265
    Switching to a datasheet 265
Saving a Record and the Form 266
Printing a Form 266
Using the Print Preview Window 266

Chapter 9: Understanding and Creating Simple Queries 269

Understanding Queries 269
    What is a query? 270
    Types of queries 271
    Query capabilities 272
    How dynasets work 273
Creating a Query 274
    Selecting a table 275
    Using the Query window 275
    Navigating the Query Design window 276
    Using the Query Design toolbar 277
    Using the QBE pane of the Query Design window 278
Selecting Fields 278
    Adding a single field 278
    Adding multiple fields 280
    Adding all table fields 281
Displaying the Dynaset 282
    Working with the datasheet 283
    Changing data in the query datasheet 283
    Returning to the query design 283
Working with Fields 283
    Selecting a field 283
    Changing field order 284
    Resizing columns in design mode 285
    Removing a field 286
    Inserting a field 286
    Changing the field display name 286
    Showing table names 287
    Showing a field 287
Changing the Sort Order 288
    Specifying a sort 288
    Sorting on more than one field 289
Displaying Only Selected Records 290
    Understanding record criteria 290
    Entering simple character criteria 291
    Entering other simple criteria 292
Printing a Query Dynaset 293
Saving a Query 294

Chapter 10: Creating and Working with Simple Reports 295

Understanding Reports 295
    What types of reports can you create? 295
    The difference between reports and forms 298
    The process of creating a report 298
Creating a Report with Report Wizards 301
    Creating a new report 302
    Choosing the data source 303
    Choosing the fields 303

Selecting the grouping levels 304
Defining the group data 305
Selecting the sort order 305
Selecting summary options 306
Selecting the layout 306
Choosing the style 308
Opening the report design 308
Using the Print Preview window 309
Viewing the Report Design window 310
Printing a Report 311
Saving the Report 312
Creating a Report with AutoReport 312

Part III: Using Access in Your Work   315

Chapter 11: Using Operators, Functions, and Expressions 317

What Are Operators? 317
Types of operators 317
When are operators used? 318
Mathematical operators 318
Relational operators 321
String operators 323
Boolean (logical) operators 326
Miscellaneous operators 329
Operator precedence 330
What Are Functions? 331
Using functions in Access 331
Types of functions 333
What Are Expressions? 336
The parts of an expression 336
Creating an expression 337
Special identifier operators and expressions 339

Chapter 12: Creating Relations and Joins in Queries 343

Adding More than One Table to a Query 343
Working with the Table/Query Pane 345
The join line 345
Manipulating the Field List window 346
Resizing the Table/Query pane 347
Moving a table 348
Removing a table 349
Adding more tables 349
Resizing a Field List window 349
Creating a database diagram 350

Adding Fields from More than One Table 351
    Adding a single field 351
    Viewing the table names 352
    Adding multiple fields at the same time 353
    Adding all table fields 353
Understanding the Limitations of Multiple-Table Queries 354
    Updating limitations 354
    Overcoming query limitations 356
Creating and Working with Query Joins 357
    Joining tables 358
    Deleting joins 360
Understanding Types of Table Joins 360
    Inner joins (Equi-joins) 361
    Changing join properties 362
    Inner and outer joins 363
    Creating a Cartesian product 367

Chapter 13: Working with Select Queries **369**
Moving Beyond Simple Queries 369
    Using query comparison operators 370
    Understanding complex criteria selection 371
    Using functions in select queries 375
    Referencing fields in select queries 375
Entering Single-Value Field Criteria 375
    Entering character (Text or Memo) criteria 376
    The Like operator and wildcards 377
    Specifying non-matching values 380
    Entering numeric (Number, Currency, or Counter) criteria 381
    Entering Yes/No (logic) criteria 382
    Entering a criterion for an OLE object 382
Entering Multiple Criteria in One Field 383
    Understanding an Or operation 383
    Specifying multiple values for a field using the Or operator 383
    Using the Or: cell of the QBE pane 385
    Using a list of values with the In operator 385
    Understanding an And query 386
    Specifying a range using the And operator 386
    Using the Between...And operator 387
    Searching for Null data 388
Entering Criteria in Multiple Fields 389
    Using And and Or across fields in a query 389
    Specifying And criteria across fields of a query 390
    Specifying Or criteria across fields of a query 391
    Using And and Or together in different fields 391
    A complex query on different lines 392
    A complex query on one line 393
Creating a New Calculated Field in a Query 393

Chapter 14: Understanding Form Controls **395**

What Is a Control? 396
  The different control types 396
  Understanding bound, unbound, and calculated controls 399
Standards for Using Controls 400
  Label controls 401
  Text box controls 402
  Toggle buttons, option buttons, and check boxes 402
  Option groups 404
  Buttons in rectangles 405
  List boxes 406
  Combo boxes 407
  Tab controls 407
Creating New Controls 408
  The two ways to add a control 409
  Dragging a field name from the Field List window 410
  Creating unbound controls with the toolbox 412
Selecting Controls 413
  Deselecting selected controls 413
  Selecting a single control 414
  Selecting multiple controls 414
Manipulating Controls 415
  Resizing a control 415
  Moving a control 415
  Aligning controls 417
  Sizing controls 419
  Grouping controls 419
  Deleting a control 420
  Attaching a label to a control 421
  Copying a control 421

Chapter 15: Creating and Customizing Data-Entry Forms **423**

Creating a Standard Data-Entry Form 423
  Assembling the data 424
  Creating a new blank form and binding it to a query 426
  Defining the form display size 427
Understanding Properties 429
  Working with control properties 430
  Working with form properties 434
Placing Bound Fields on the Form 444
  Displaying the field list 444
  Selecting the fields for your form 444
  Dragging fields onto your form 445
Working with Label Controls and Text Box Controls 447
  Creating unattached labels 447
  Modifying the text in a label or text control 447
  Modifying the format of text in a control 448
  Sizing a text box control or label control 449

Moving label and text controls 450
Modifying the appearance of multiple controls 451
Changing the control type 452
Setting the tab order 452
Adding multiple-line text box controls for Memo fields 453
Adding a bound object frame to the form 455
Using Fields from Multiple Tables in a Form 457
Adding fields from a second table 457
Working with attached label and text controls 459
Creating a calculated field 460
Changing the updatability of a multiple-table form 462
Creating a Multiple-Page Form 463
Why use multiple-page forms? 464
Adding a page break 465
Using Form and Page Headers and Footers 467
The different types of headers and footers 467
Creating a form header and footer 468
Printing a Form 469
Converting a Form to a Report 470

Chapter 16: Creating Great Looking Forms 471

Making a Good Form Look Great 471
Understanding WYSIWYG 472
Using the formatting windows and toolbar 472
Creating special effects 474
Changing the form's background color 476
Enhancing Text-Based Controls 477
Enhancing label and text box controls 477
Creating a text shadow 477
Changing text to a reverse video display 479
Displaying label or text box control properties 479
Displaying Images in Forms 483
Working with Lines and Rectangles 485
Emphasizing Areas of the Form 486
Adding a shadow to a control 486
Changing the header dividing line 487
Adding a Background Bitmap 487
Using AutoFormat 489
Customizing and adding new AutoFormats 491
Copying individual formats between controls 491

Chapter 17: Adding Data-Validation Controls to Forms 493

Creating Data-Validation Expressions 493
Table-level validation 494
Form-level validation 495
Entering a validation expression 496

Creating Choices with Option Buttons 496
    Creating option groups 497
    Creating an option group box 497
Creating Yes/No Options 501
    Creating check boxes 502
    Creating visual selections with toggle buttons 504
    Adding a bitmapped image to the toggle button 504
Working with List Boxes and Combo Boxes 505
    The differences between list boxes and combo boxes 505
    Settling real-estate issues 506
    Creating a single-column list box 506
    Understanding list box properties 508
    Creating a multiple-column list box 510
    Hiding a column in a list box 512
    Creating multi-selection list boxes 512
Creating and Using Combo Boxes 512
    Creating a single-column combo box 513
    Creating a multiple-column combo box from a query 515

**Chapter 18: Using OLE Objects, Graphs,
Pivot Tables/Charts, and ActiveX Controls 519**
Understanding Objects 519
    Types of objects 520
    Using bound and unbound objects 520
    Linking and embedding 521
Embedding Objects 523
    Embedding an unbound object 523
    Embedding bound objects 528
    Adding a bound OLE object 528
    Adding a picture to a bound object frame 529
    Editing an embedded object 530
Linking Objects 531
    Linking a bound object 531
Creating a Graph or Chart 534
    The different ways to create a graph 534
    Customizing the Toolbox 535
Embedding a Graph in a Form 535
    Assembling the data 536
    Adding the graph to the form 536
Customizing a Graph 543
    Understanding the Graph window 543
    Working with attached text 544
    Changing the graph type 548
    Changing axis labels 549
    Changing a bar color, pattern, and shape 550
    Modifying gridlines 551
    Manipulating three-dimensional graphs 552

Integration with Microsoft Office 554
    Checking the spelling of one or more fields and records 555
    Correcting your typing automatically when entering data 556
    Using OLE automation with Office 2002 557
    Creating an Excel type Pivot Table 557
    Creating a Pivot Chart 564
Using the Calendar ActiveX Control 566

Chapter 19: Creating and Customizing Reports **571**

Starting with a Blank Form 571
The Design Window Toolbar 573
Banded Report Writer Concepts 574
    How sections process data 575
    The Report Writer sections 577
Creating a New Report 581
    Eleven tasks to creating a great report 583
    Designing the report 583
    Assembling the data 584
    Creating a new report and binding it to a query 586
    Defining the report page size and layout 587
    Placing fields on the report 589
    Resizing a section 592
    Working with unattached label controls and text 593
    Working with text boxes and their attached label controls 595
    Changing label and text box control properties 607
    Formatting the display of text controls 609
    Growing and shrinking text box controls 610
    Sorting and grouping data 611
    Adding page breaks 617
    Saving your report 621

Chapter 20: Presentation-Quality Reports and Printing **623**

Making Reports Presentation Quality 623
Understanding WYSIWYG Printing 626
Enhancing Text-Based Controls 628
    Enhancing label controls 628
    Working with multiple-line text box controls 632
Adding New Controls 633
    Displaying values with option groups and option buttons 634
    Creating the option group 634
    Creating an option group with a calculated control 636
    Displaying Yes/No values with check boxes 640
    Displaying values as toggle buttons 641
    Displaying bound OLE objects in reports 643
    Displaying an image in a report 643

Working with Lines and Rectangles 644
Emphasizing Areas of the Report 646
    Adding background shading 646
    Sinking controls 646
    Etched controls 647
    Creating a shadow on a rectangle 647
    Changing text to a reverse video display 647
Seeing Your Output in Different Ways 648
    Using the Print Preview window 648
    Using layout previews 651
    Printing a report 651

Chapter 21: Creating Calculations and Summaries in Reports . . . 655

Designing a Multilevel Grouping Report with Totals 655
    Designing the Invoice Report 657
    Designing and creating the query for the report 659
    Designing test data 662
Creating a Multilevel Grouping Report with Totals 663
    Creating the sorting orders 664
    Creating the detail section 666
    Creating the detail section controls 666
    Testing the detail section 668
    Creating the Pet ID header and footer sections 669
    Creating the Pet ID header controls 670
    Creating the Pet ID footer controls 671
    Creating the Customer Number header and footer sections 675
    Creating the Customer Number header controls 676
    Creating the Customer Number footer controls 678
    Creating the Visit Date header 681
    Creating the page header controls 682
    Creating the page footer controls 684
    Calculating percentages using totals 685
    Calculating running sums 686
    Creating a title page in a report header 687
    Using the report footer 688

Part IV: Advanced Access Database Topics   689

Chapter 22: Working with External Data 691

Access and External Data 691
    Types of external data 691
    Methods of working with external data 692
    Should you link to or import data? 693

Linking External Data 696
    Types of database management systems 696
    Linking to other Access database tables 699
    Linking to dBASE and FoxPro databases (tables) 700
    Linking to Paradox tables 703
    Linking to non-database tables 705
    Splitting an Access database into two linked databases 709
Working with Linked Tables 712
    Setting view properties 712
    Setting relationships 713
    Setting links between external tables 713
    Using external tables in queries 714
    Renaming tables 716
    Optimizing linked tables 716
    Deleting a linked table reference 717
    Viewing or changing information for linked tables 717
Importing External Data 718
    Importing other Access objects 719
    Importing non-Access PC-based database tables 720
    Importing spreadsheet data 722
    Importing from word-processing files 725
    Importing text file data 725
    Importing HTML tables 736
    Modifying imported table elements 736
    Troubleshooting import errors 736
Exporting to External Formats 738
    Exporting objects to other Access databases 738
    Exporting objects to other external databases or
        to Excel, HTML, or text files 739

Chapter 23: Working with Advanced Select Queries **741**

Creating Queries That Calculate Totals 742
    Showing and hiding the Total: row in the QBE pane 742
    The Total: row options 743
    Performing totals on all records 746
    Performing totals on groups of records 748
    Specifying criteria for a total query 751
    Creating expressions for totals 754
Creating Crosstab Queries 757
    Understanding the crosstab query 757
    Creating the crosstab query 758
    Entering multiple-field row headings 760
    Specifying criteria for a crosstab query 761
    Specifying fixed column headings 765
    The Crosstab Query Wizard 766

Creating a Parameter Query 767
  Understanding the parameter query 768
  Creating a single-parameter query 768
  Running a parameter query 768
  Creating a multiple-parameter query 770
  Specifying parameter order 771

Chapter 24: Working with Action Queries 773

About Action Queries 773
  Types of action queries 773
  Uses of action queries 774
  The process of action queries 775
  Viewing the results of an action query 775
  Reversing action queries 776
Creating Action Queries 777
  Creating an update action query to change values 777
  Creating a new table using a make-table query 781
  Creating a query to append records 785
  Creating a query to delete records 790
  Creating other queries using the Query Wizards 794
  Saving an action query 798
  Running an action query 799
Troubleshooting Action Queries 799
  Data-type errors in appending and updating 799
  Key violations in action queries 799
  Record-locked fields in multi-user environments 800
  Text fields 800

Chapter 25: Advanced Query Topics 801

Using Lookup Tables and Joins 801
Using Calculated Fields 805
Finding the Number of Records in a Table or Query 809
Finding the Top (n) Records in a Query 811
SQL-Specific Queries 813
  Creating union queries 813
  Creating pass-through queries 815
  Creating data definition queries 816
  Creating SQL subqueries in an Access query 817
How Queries Save Field Selections 817
  Hiding (not showing) fields 818
  Renaming fields in queries 819
  Hiding and unhiding columns in the QBE pane 820
Query Design Options 821
Setting Query Properties 823
Understanding SQL 826
  Viewing SQL statements in queries 826
  An SQL primer 827

Chapter 26: Working with Subforms 833

What Is a Subform? 833
Creating Subforms with the Form Wizard 835
    Creating the form and selecting the Form Wizard 835
    Choosing the fields for the main form 835
    Selecting the table or query that will be the subform 836
    Choosing the fields for the subform 837
    Selecting the form data layout 838
    Selecting the subform layout 839
    Selecting the form style 839
    Selecting the form title 840
    Displaying the form 840
    Displaying the main form design 842
    Displaying the subform design 843
Creating a Simple Subform Without Wizards 845
    Creating a form for a subform 846
    Adding the subform to the main form 849
    Linking the form and subform 851
    Adding lookup tables to the subform fields 852
    Creating totals in subforms 859

Chapter 27: Creating Mail Merge and Label Reports 863

Creating Mailing Labels Using the Label Wizard 863
    Selecting the label size 864
    Selecting the font and color 865
    Creating the mailing-label text and fields 866
    Sorting the mailing labels 867
    Displaying the labels in the Print Preview window 869
    Modifying the label design in the Report Design window 870
    Printing labels 872
Creating Snaked Column Reports 873
    Creating the report 874
    Defining the page setup 875
    Printing the snaked column report 876
Creating Mail Merge Reports 877
    Assembling data for a mail merge report 879
    Creating a mail merge report 880
    Creating the page header area 880
    Working with embedded fields in text 882
    Printing the mail merge report 884
Using the Access Mail Merge Wizard for Microsoft Word 884

Part V: Access Application Tools   891

Chapter 28: Working with Macros and Events 893

Understanding Macros 893
    What is a macro? 894
    When to use a macro 894
The Macro Window 895
    The Action pane 896
    The Argument pane 896
Creating a Macro 897
    Entering actions and arguments 898
    Adding multiple actions to a macro 901
    Rearranging macro actions 902
    Deleting macro actions 903
    Editing existing macros 903
    Copying entire macros 904
    Renaming macros 904
Running Macros 904
    Running a macro from the Macro window 904
    Running a macro from the Database window 905
    Running a macro from any window in the database 905
    Running a macro from another macro 905
    Running a macro automatically when you open a database . . . 905
Macro Groups 906
    Creating macro groups 907
    Running a macro in a macro group 908
Supplying Conditions for Actions 909
    What is a condition? 909
    Activating the Condition column in a macro 909
    Specifying a condition for a single action 910
    Specifying a condition for multiple actions 912
    Controlling the flow of actions 913
Troubleshooting Macros 913
    Single-step mode 913
    The Action Failed dialog box 914
Understanding Events 915
    What is an event? 915
    How do events trigger actions? 915
    Where to trigger macros 916

Chapter 29: Using Macros in Forms and Reports 917

Types of Macros 917
    Macros for forms 919
    Macros for reports 921
    Macros for importing and exporting 921
    Macros for Keyboard accelerators 921

Form-Level Event Macros 922
    Attaching macros to forms 922
    Opening a form with a macro 925
    Attaching a macro to a form 926
    Synchronizing two forms with On Current 927
    Running a macro when closing a form 930
    Confirming a delete with On Delete 932
Control Event Macros 936
    Attaching macros to controls 936
Working with Macros on Forms 938
    Validating data 938
    Setting values 939
    Navigating in forms and records 941
    Filtering records 942
    Finding records 944
Report Event Macros 947
    Opening a report with a macro 948
    Deactivating a section of a report with a macro 948
    Creating a Report Snapshot macro 949
Report Section Macros 951
    Using On Format 952
    Using On Print 952
    Using On Retreat 952
Report Properties 953
    Using Format Count 953
    Using Print Count 953
    Working with macros in reports 954
    Underlining data in a report with a macro 954
    Hiding data in a report with a macro 957
    Filtering records for a report with a macro 957
Macros for Importing and Exporting 957
    Using command buttons to import or export 957
Creating Keyboard Accelerators (Hot Keys) 958
    Creating a hot-key combination 959

Chapter 30: Working with Visual Basic in Access 2002 . . . . **961**

Instant Applications Using the Access 2002 Database Wizard 961
    Getting started 962
    Working with tables and fields 964
    Selecting AutoFormat styles 965
    Customizing by selection 966
    Using the switchboard system 967
    Customizing the switchboards 968
Creating Programs in Visual Basic for Applications 970
    Understanding events and event procedures 970
    Creating a new module 972

Migrating from Macros to Visual Basic 983
    When to use macros and when to use Visual Basic procedures . . . 983
    Converting existing macros to Visual Basic 985
    Using the Command Button Wizard to create Visual Basic code . . . 989

Chapter 31: Using Visual Basic in Forms and Reports 993

Understanding Modules 993
    Form and report modules 994
    Standard modules 995
Using Variables 996
    Naming variables 997
    Declaring variables 997
Working with Data Types 1001
Understanding Visual Basic Logical Constructs 1003
    Conditional processing 1003
    Repetitive looping 1009
Planning for Runtime Errors 1014
    Adding error-handling code to a procedure 1014
    Displaying meaningful runtime error messages 1017
    Trapping for specific error codes 1018
Filtering Records in Procedures 1018
    Displaying a dialog box for selecting a record 1019
    Selecting a set of records to print 1023
    Printing records by using selection criteria 1025
Working with Combo-Box and List-Box Controls 1027
    Handling a combo box entry that is not in the list 1028
    Handling MultiSelect list boxes 1031
Creating Programs to Update a Table 1035
    Updating fields in a record using ADO and DAO 1036
    Updating a total field for a record 1041
    Adding a new record 1044
    Deleting a record 1046

Chapter 32: Creating Switchboards, Command Bars, Menus, Toolbars, and Dialog Boxes 1049

Switchboards and Command Buttons 1049
    Using a switchboard 1050
    Creating the basic form for a switchboard 1051
    Working with command buttons 1051
    Creating command buttons 1053
    Linking a command button to a macro 1058
    Adding a picture to a command button 1062
Creating Custom Menu Bars, Toolbars, and Shortcut Menus 1065
    Understanding command bars 1066
    Creating custom menu bars with command bars 1066
    Changing existing menus and toolbars 1068
    Creating a new menu bar 1069
    Attaching the menu bar to a form 1076
    Creating shortcut menus 1078

Creating and using custom toolbars 1082
Attaching the toolbar to a form 1084
Adding control tips to any form control 1085
Running a macro automatically when you start Access 1086
Controlling options when starting Access 1086
Creating a Print Report Dialog Box Form and Macros 1087
Creating a form for a macro 1088
Creating the option group 1089
Creating command buttons 1090
Creating a list box on the print report form 1091
Creating the print macros 1093
Creating the Print macro group 1093
Using the Access 2002 Tab Control 1103
Creating a new form with the Access 2002 tab control 1103
Access 2002 Tab control properties 1106

Part VI: Access and the External World   1111

Chapter 33: Moving from Jet to the SQL Server 2000 Desktop Engine 1113

Understanding SQL Server 2000 Desktop Engine 1113
Comparing SQL Server 2000 Desktop Engine and Jet 1114
Choosing the right database engine 1115
Installing SQL Server 2000 Desktop Engine 1117
Hardware requirements 1117
Software requirements 1117
Running the SQL Server 2000 Desktop Engine
Installation Program 1117
Customizing the installation of SQL Server 2000
Desktop Engine 1118
Starting the SQL Server 2000 Desktop Engine 1119
Creating a SQL Server 2000 Desktop Engine Database 1121
Creating a project 1121
Understanding projects 1126
Project objects 1127
Creating a New Table 1128
Working with fields in the Table Design window 1128
The Table Properties window 1131
Working with Database Diagrams 1138
Using the Upsizing Wizard 1142
Before upsizing an application 1143
Starting the Upsizing Wizard 1143

Chapter 34: Working with Access Projects 1151

Upsizing to an Access Project 1152
Starting the Upsizing Wizard 1152
Using the Upsizing Wizard to create a
client/server application 1154

Understanding Project Queries 1158
    Creating views 1158
    Creating stored procedures 1161
    Creating user-defined functions 1165
Using Unbound Forms 1166
    Working with unbound forms 1167
    Creating an unbound form 1168
    Displaying data on the form 1170
    Updating data 1173
    Finding a record 1176

Chapter 35: Using and Creating Access Objects for Intranets and the Internet 1179

Using the Web Toolbar with Access 2002 1181
    The Web toolbar 1182
Types of Web Pages That Access Can Create 1184
    Data access pages 1184
    Working with dynamic and static views of Web-based data 1185
Exporting Tables, Queries, Forms, and Reports to Web Pages 1189
    Exporting an Access table to static HTML format 1190
    Exporting an Access query datasheet to static HTML format 1192
    Exporting an Access form datasheet to static HTML format 1194
    Changing Page Setup properties for datasheets 1198
    Exporting a datasheet to dynamic HTML format 1198
    Exporting a form to dynamic HTML format 1200
    Processing an IDC/HTX file on the Web server 1201
    Processing ASP files on the Web server 1202
    Exporting a report to static HTML format 1202
    HTML template files 1205
Importing and Linking (Read-Only) HTML Tables and Lists 1208
    Importing an HTML table 1208
    Linking to an HTML table 1210
Using Hyperlinks to Connect Your Application to the Internet 1210
    Using the Hyperlink data type 1211
    Adding a hyperlink to a form, report, or datasheet 1212
    Creating a label using the Insert Hyperlink button 1214
Browsing Web Pages with the Web Browser Control 1215

Chapter 36: Building Web Applications, Data Access Pages, and XML 1217

Working with the Data Access Pages 1217
    What is a data access page? 1218
    Creating a single table data access page 1221
    Working with multiple tables and grouped pages 1230
    Changing some key properties on data access pages 1244
    Saving other Access objects as data access pages 1255

XML Data and Access 1265
    Understanding XML 1266
    Exporting to XML 1267
    Importing XML data 1270

Part VII: Advanced Topics in Access 2002   1273

Chapter 37: Optimizing Performance 1275

Understanding Module Load on Demand 1276
    Organizing your modules 1276
    Access 2002 prunes the call tree 1276
Using the Access 2002 Database File Format 1279
Distributing .MDE Files 1279
Understanding the Compiled State 1282
    Putting your applications code into a compiled state 1283
    Losing the compiled state 1284
    Distributing applications in a compiled or uncompiled state 1285
Improving Absolute Speed 1289
    Tuning your system 1291
    Getting the most from your tables 1292
    Getting the most from your queries 1294
    Getting the most from your forms and reports 1296
    Getting the most from your modules 1298
    Increasing network performance 1303
Improving Perceived Speed 1303
    Using a splash screen 1304
    Loading and keeping forms hidden 1305
    Using the hourglass 1305
    Using the built-in progress meter 1305
    Creating a Progress Meter with a Pop-up Form 1308
    Speeding up the Progress Meter display 1310
Working with Large Program Databases in Access 2002 1310
    How databases grow in size 1311
    Simply compiling and compacting may not be enough 1312
    Rebooting gives you a clean memory map 1312
    Repair does nothing if the database is not corrupt 1313
    You can fix a single corrupt form by removing
        the record source 1313
    Create a new database and import all of the objects 1313
    The undocumented decompile option in Access 2002 1314
    Summary — six steps to large database success 1315
    An interface for detecting an uncompiled database
        and automatically recompiling 1316
    Making small changes to large databases —
        one word — export 1317

Chapter 38: Securing an Access Application 1319

Understanding Jet Security 1319
    Understanding workgroup files 1320
    Understanding permissions 1320
    Understanding security limitations 1321
Choosing a Security Level to Implement 1322
Creating a Database Password 1322
Using the /runtime Option 1325
Using a Database's Startup Options 1328
Distributing a Database as an .MDE File 1330
Using the Jet User-Level Security Model 1332
    Enabling security 1333
    Working with workgroups 1333
    Working with users 1337
    Working with groups 1341
    Securing objects by using permissions 1345
Using the Access Security Wizard 1353
Encrypting a Database 1360
Decrypting a Database 1362
Manipulating Security Objects Using DAO 1362
    Creating a user account by using DAO 1362
    Changing a user's password by using DAO 1363
    Creating a group account using DAO 1363
    Changing an object's owner by using DAO 1364
    Assigning object permissions by using DAO 1364

Chapter 39: Creating Help Systems in Access 2002 1367

Understanding the Windows Help Structure 1367
    The Help Viewer 1368
    The Contents tab 1369
    The Topic pane 1370
Creating a Windows Help System 1371
    Creating Help topics 1372
    Creating a Help project file 1373
    Creating a Table of Contents 1383
    Creating a Help index 1387
Integrating a Help File with Your Application 1392
    Displaying form-level help 1392
    Displaying control-level help 1393
    Mapping a Help Context ID to a Help topic 1394
    Testing the HTMLHelp API 1397
    Testing Help in Access 1398
    What's this? Help 1399
Third-Party Help Tools 1399

Chapter 40: Using the Microsoft Office XP Developer 1401

Preparing Your Application for Distribution 1401
    Defining the startup parameters of the application 1402
    Testing the application before distribution 1405
    Polishing your application 1406
    Creating comprehensive and intuitive menus and toolbars 1412
    Bulletproofing an application 1412
    Separating the code objects from the tables in the application . . . 1413
    Documenting the application 1414
    Creating a help system 1414
    Implementing a security structure 1414
Using Visual Basic Productivity Tools to Streamline the Development
    Environment 1414
    What is Office XP Developer? 1415
    Installing the Visual Basic productivity tools 1416
    Creating distribution disks using the Office XP
        Developer Packaging Wizard 1418

Chapter 41: Integrating with Microsoft Office XP 1437

Using Automation to Integrate with Office 1437
    Creating Automation references 1438
    Creating an instance of an Automation object 1441
    Getting an existing object instance 1442
    Working with Automation objects 1443
    Closing an instance of an Automation object 1444
An Automation example using Word 2002 1444
    Creating an instance of a Word object 1449
    Making the instance of Word visible 1449
    Creating a new document based on an existing template 1450
    Using bookmarks to insert data 1450
    Activating the instance of Word 1450
    Moving the cursor in Word 1451
    Closing the instance of the Word object 1451
    Inserting pictures by using bookmarks 1451
    Using Office's Macro Recorder 1452
Programming the Office Assistant 1455
    Hiding and showing the Office Assistant 1456
    Keeping the Office Assistant out of the way 1456
    Enabling and disabling the Assistant's sounds 1457
    Displaying an Assistant animation 1457
    Displaying information and getting user
        input by using balloons 1458

Chapter 42: Exploring Replication 1463

The Components of Replication 1464
    Nonreplicable database 1464
    Making a database replicable 1465
    Design Master 1466

Creating a Replica 1470
    Access replication 1471
    Briefcase replication 1473
    Replication in an Access project 1474
    Replication programmatically using JRO 1474
    Replication using DAO 1474
    Replication Manager 4.0 utility 1478
Synchronizing Replicas 1486
    Synchronizing with Access 1486
    Synchronizing from the Briefcase 1487
    Synchronizing with DAO 1487
    Synchronizing with Replication Manager 1489
Resolving Conflicts 1490
    Resolving conflicts in Access 1491
    Resolving conflicts with DAO 1493
Building a New Design Master 1497

Chapter 43: Exploring Add-Ins and Libraries **1499**

Understanding Types of Add-Ins 1499
Understanding Libraries 1501
    Referencing library databases 1501
    Calling functions in Dynamic Link Libraries 1502
An Overview of a Few Access 2002 Add-Ins 1505
    Using the Switchboard Manager 1505
    Using the Form Wizard 1508
    Using the Command Button Wizard 1512
Creating Your Own Add-Ins 1513
    Considering the add-in purpose and type 1514
    Designing the add-in user interface and flow of control 1515
    Coding your add-in 1517
    Coding on the run 1519
    Preparing your add-in for installation 1524

Appendix A: Access 2002 Specifications **1533**

Appendix B: Mountain Animal Hospital Tables **1539**

Appendix C: What's on the CD-ROM **1547**

Index 1557

Hungry Minds, Inc. End-User License Agreement 1616

CD-ROM Installation Instructions 1618

First Things First

In This Part

Chapter 1
What Is Access
2002?

Chapter 2
Installing and
Running Access
2002

Chapter 3
A Hands-on Tour of
Access 2002

Chapter 4
Database Concepts
and Design

What Is Access 2002?

✦   ✦   ✦   ✦

In This Chapter

Examining what
Access is

Looking at some of
the capabilities of
Access

Working with Access
if you are already a
database user

Working with Access
if you are already a
spreadsheet user

✦   ✦   ✦   ✦

Before you begin to use a software product, it is important to understand its capabilities and the types of tasks that it's designed to perform. Microsoft Access 2002 (also known simply as Access) is a multifaceted product; its uses are bounded only by your imagination.

Access Is . . .

Essentially, Access is a *database management system* (DBMS). Like other products in this category, Access stores and retrieves information (often referred to as *data*), presents requested information, and automates repetitive tasks (such as maintaining accounts payable or a personnel system, and performing inventory control and scheduling). With Access you can create easy-to-use input forms like the one shown in Figure 1-1. You can display your information in any way that you want and run powerful reports.

Access is also a powerful Windows database application — probably the best end-user/developer product ever written. Microsoft Access brings the productivity of database management to the usability and consistency of Microsoft Windows. Because both Windows and Access are from Microsoft, the two products work very well together. Access runs on the Windows 95, Windows 98, Windows ME, Windows 2000, or Windows NT platforms, so all the advantages of Windows are available in Access. You can cut, copy, and paste data from any Windows application to and from Access. You can also create a form design in Access and paste it into the report designer.

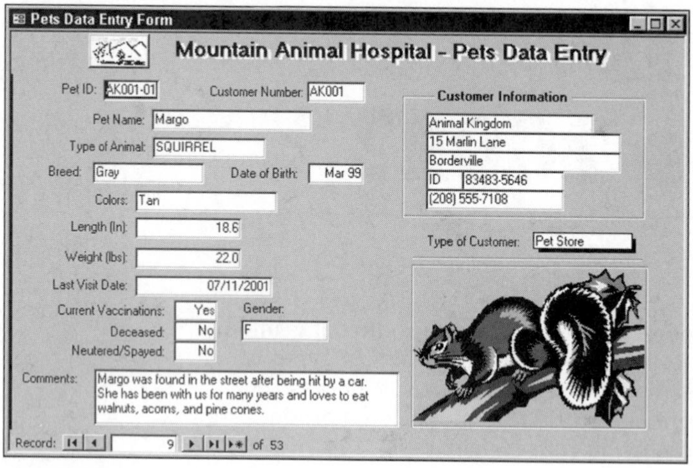

Figure 1-1: A typical Access data-entry form

Using *OLE* (Object Linking and Embedding) objects in Windows and Microsoft Office products (Excel, Word, PowerPoint, and Outlook), you can extend Access's ability to incorporate viewable objects of these Microsoft products — without the need to copy their contents and paste them into Access. This ability enables you to work with the actual data already included in these products without the need to duplicate the information. By using OLE, you can actually change the information in the underlying form object (Excel, Word, etc.). With the Internet extensions in Access, you can create forms that interact with data directly from the World Wide Web and then translate your forms directly into data access pages for corporate intranets that work directly with your Internet browser.

Note   The data access pages feature of Access 2002 enables you to create browser-based forms to view and edit live data on a corporate intranet or across the Internet. In Access 2000, data access pages only work with Microsoft Internet Explorer 5.0. In version 2002, however, data access pages work with any browser that supports XML 1.1 — including Netscape Navigator 6.x. Browsers that don't support this standard include older versions of Netscape (4.x or earlier) or Internet Explorer (3.x or earlier).

Access is more than just a local database manager. As a *relational* database manager, it allows users to access information from more than one database table at a time — even linking database tables to create a new table. It can reduce the complexity of your data and make your job easier to finish. You can connect your Access tables with mainframe or server data — you can even use a table created in dBASE or Excel. You can easily combine the results of the link with an Excel worksheet.

Access's ability to link to outside data (stored in other database formats) makes it a very robust program. Access can be used in a network environment to connect to a wide range of tables from other databases — both locally (on the same machine) and remotely (even to a mainframe computer's database, such as Oracle or DB2). Access can link directly to these "outside" tables or import them for local use. Once outside tables are linked or imported, you can create forms and reports to work with the information — to make changes or to view or print the information for later use.

Figure 1-2 shows the original Microsoft marketing concept for Access. This simple figure conveys the message that Access is usable at all levels.

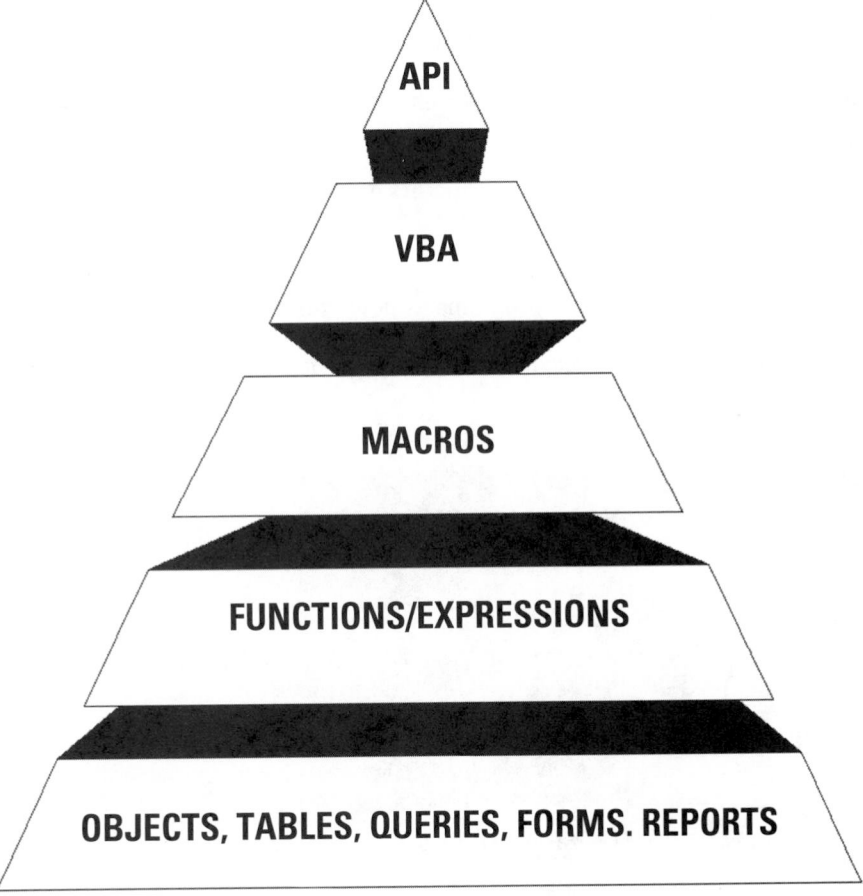

Figure 1-2: The Access usability hierarchy

Beginning at the lowest level of the hierarchy and moving up, you see *objects* listed first; these give the end user the capability of creating tables, queries, forms, and reports easily. You can perform simple processing by using *expressions* to validate data, enforce a business rule, or simply display a number with a currency symbol. Following the chart, you see that you can use the built-in *macros* to perform relatively complex tasks without the need for creating a formal program.

However, Access also lets you build professional quality programs by using *VBA* (Visual Basic for Applications), which is a code written by the programmer/developer to let the database perform complex processes repetitively. Finally, by using Windows *API* (Application Programming Interface) calls to functions or DLLs (Dynamic Link Libraries) written in other languages, such as C, Java, or Visual Basic, a programmer can write interfaces to other programs and data sources — using the existing functions built into Windows or other applications.

Access has a complete set of tools for end-user database management. Access has a table creator, a form designer, a query manager, a Data Access Page Creator, and a Report Writer. Access also offers a powerful environment for developing complete database applications. As Figure 1-2 points out, you can use macros or modules to automate tasks and create user-oriented applications as powerful as the applications created with programming languages — complete with buttons, menus, and dialog boxes, as shown in Figure 1-3. By programming in Visual Basic for Applications, you can create programs as powerful as Access itself. In fact, many of the tools in Access (such as Wizards and Builders) are written in VBA. The power and usability of Access make it, by far, the best database management software on the market.

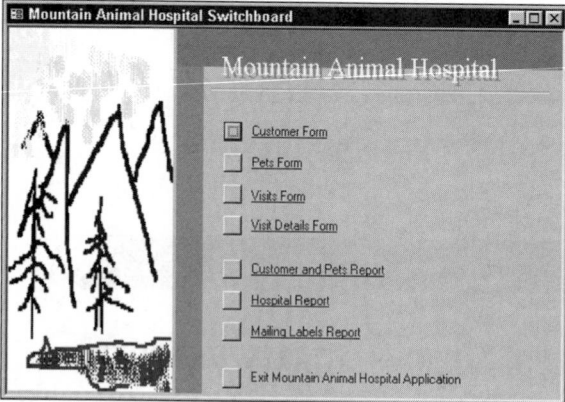

Figure 1-3: A macro switchboard

Simply telling you about what Access can do, however, doesn't begin to cover the material in this book. In the first 500 pages, you learn to use Access from an end user's point of view. In the next 500 pages, you learn to use Access from the power user's point of view. In the remaining pages, you learn the basics of VBA, the Internet, and the client/server. This book offers you the ability to examine many topics to a depth that your reference manuals can only begin to touch.

What Access Offers

The following sections briefly describe some of Access's key features and prepare you for some of the subjects covered in this book.

True relational database management

Access provides a true *relational database management system*. It allows you to build a system consisting of multiple tables that you store in a single container. After these tables are created, they can be linked together to display information from several tables in a single common view. This simply means that when you create and store your information you aren't required to duplicate information in a single table.

For instance, you may need a birthday and Christmas card table that contains the names of all the people that you send cards each year. You may only send birthday cards to some people and you may only send Christmas cards to others. You may also want to track gifts that you send. You can create a single table with a lot of fields for each person — for instance, his or her name and address, whether you sent a birthday card or Christmas gift, and what type of gift you sent. You would probably have to create one table with up to 25 fields in each record, or you can create two tables — one for personal information and the other for the card and gift information.

The first example — one single table — is prone to all sorts of problems. For example, each year you have to re-enter the names and addresses of the people you sent gifts and cards to (thus, you have a lot of duplicate information about their names and addresses, which is prone to error). In addition, you may be tempted to add even more fields to the single table — card2 field or gift2 field, for example — making it even larger and more prone to error. The second method of employing two tables is more efficient. The first table can contain all of the person's personal information; and the second table can include many records for each person about the gifts and cards sent. These two tables can then be linked together using a common field that allows you to display information from both tables.

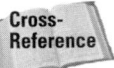 **Cross-Reference** Database design is covered more in-depth in Chapters 4 and 6.

As we pointed out earlier in this chapter, Access is a true relational database management system and includes the ability to define *primary* and *foreign* keys that support full referential integrity at the database engine level (which prevents inconsistent updates or deletions). In addition, tables in Access have data-validation rules to prevent entry of inaccurate data, regardless of how data is entered, and every field in a table has format and default definitions for more productive data entry. Access supports all the necessary field types, including Text, Number, AutoNumber (counter), Currency, Date/Time, Memo, Yes/No, Hyperlink, and OLE objects. If values are missing in special processing, Access provides full support for null values.

The relational processing in Access fills many needs with its flexible architecture. It can be used as a stand-alone database management system, in a file-server configuration, or as a front-end client to products like a SQL server. Access also features *ODBC* (Open DataBase Connectivity), which permits connection to many external formats, such as SQL/Server, Oracle, Sybase, or mainframe IBM DB/2.

Access provides complete support for transaction processing, ensuring the integrity of transactions. In addition, user-level security provides control over assigning user and group permissions to view and modify database objects.

Context-sensitive Help and the Office Assistant

The Microsoft Help feature is still the industry's best for beginners and experienced users alike. Access provides context-sensitive Help — pressing the F1 key instantly brings up help information about the item that you're working on. Access Help also has an easy-to-use table of contents, a search facility, a history log, and bookmarks.

Access 2002 goes further by using the *Office Assistant* and *Screen Tips*. As Figure 1-4 shows, the Office Assistant responds when you ask for help.

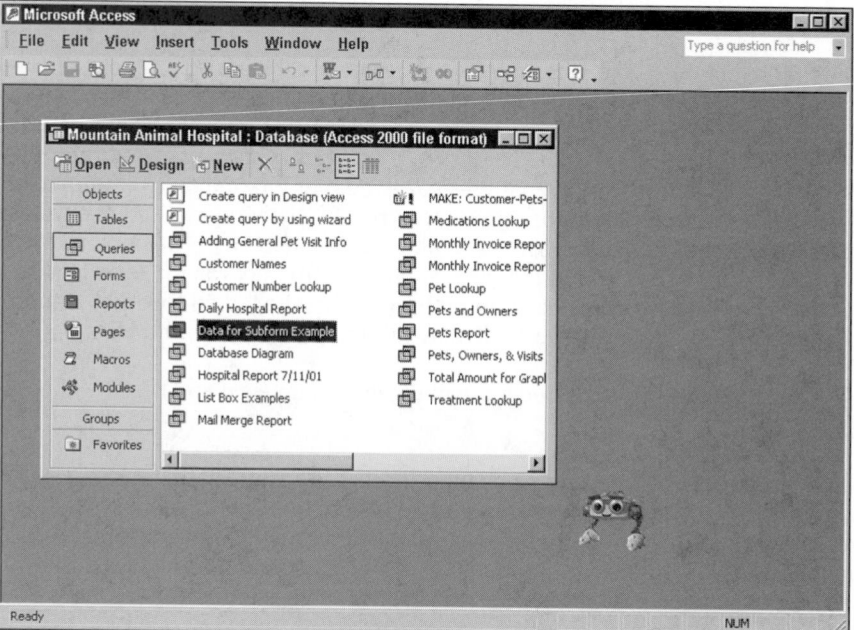

Figure 1-4: The Access 2002 Office Assistant

Screen Tips (also known as *What's This?*) give you brief, on-screen explanations of what the cursor is pointing to. You can choose from a gallery of ten different assistants. You can also turn them off at any time if they become annoying.

Ease-of-use Wizards

A wizard can turn hours of work into minutes. Figure 1-5 shows a Form Wizard screen. You can customize wizards for use in a variety of tasks.

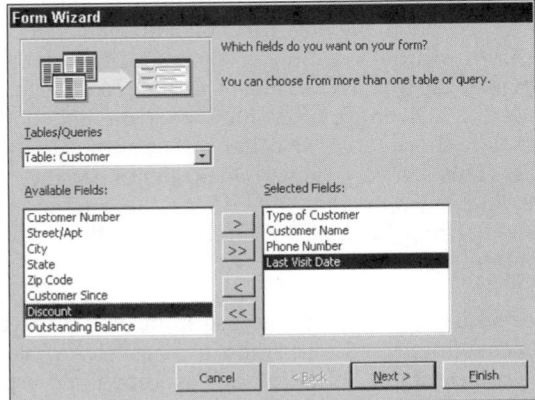

Figure 1-5: A typical Form Wizard screen

Wizards ask questions about content, style, and format, and then they automatically build the object that you requested. Nearly 100 Wizards design databases, applications, tables, forms, reports, graphs, mailing labels, controls, and properties.

Importing, exporting, and linking external table files

Access lets you import from or export to many common database formats, including dBASE, FoxPro, Excel, SQL Server, Oracle, Btrieve, many ASCII text formats (including fixed width and delimited), as well as data in HTML (HyperText Markup Language) format. Importing creates an Access table; exporting an Access table creates a file in the native file format that you are exporting to.

Note   In addition to importing tables from external files, you can import any object from other Access databases. This means you can import tables, forms, queries, reports, macros, and/or modules.

You can import information from many sources, including another Access database, an Excel spreadsheet, a Lotus spreadsheet, text files, Paradox tables, dBase tables, HTML files, Outlook, Exchange, or any ODBC-compliant database table (these include SQL Server, Oracle, FoxPro, Sybase, and many others).

You can also export information to a wide range of sources, including another Access database, Excel or Lotus spreadsheets, text (simple text and Rich Text Format — .rtf) and HTML files, Paradox and dBase tables, Microsoft's IIS and Active Server Pages, or ODBC-supported database tables.

In addition to importing and exporting data, Access supports linking data in other tables to the database that is currently open. *Linking* (formally known as *attaching*) means that external data can be used without creating an Access table. You can link to dBASE files, Paradox files, Excel, ASCII Text, HTML files, Outlook, Exchange, and other ODBC-compliant tables (such as SQL data). After you have established a link to external tables, you can then relate these tables to other tables, either in the system or also linked through Access. This is a very powerful capability because you can link to several Access tables, an Excel spreadsheet, a dBASE file, and an SQL server table — all at the same time in order to display related information that's stored in these different types of tables and files.

Note Some import or export types require purchasing a license from their respective vendors while some are available from Microsoft's Web site as a free download. Today, the Web is a valuable source of free software, such as import and export engines, along with valuable tips and techniques.

When linking external information, Access uses its built-in query engine as the tool to link and display the information from the different sources.

WYSIWYG forms and reports

The Form and Report Design windows share a common interface and power. You design your form or report in a WYSIWYG (What You See Is What You Get) environment. As you add each control, you can visually see the form take shape.

You can add labels, text data fields, option buttons, tab controls, check boxes, lines, boxes, colors, shading — even pictures, graphs, subforms, or subreports — to your forms and reports. In addition, you have complete control over the style and presentation of data in a form or report, as shown in Figure 1-6. Forms can have multiple pages; reports can have many levels of groupings and totals.

After you create your form or report, you can view it in *page preview* mode, which allows you to zoom out for a bird's-eye view. You can also view your report with sample data while you design it — so you don't waste valuable time waiting for a large data file to be processed.

The Report Writer is a very powerful tool because it allows up to ten levels of aggregation and sorting. To accomplish this, the Report Writer performs two passes on the data, allowing you to create reports that show the row percentage of a group total, which can be done only by having a calculation based on a calculation that requires two passes through the data. You can create many types of reports that include mailing labels and mail-merge reports.

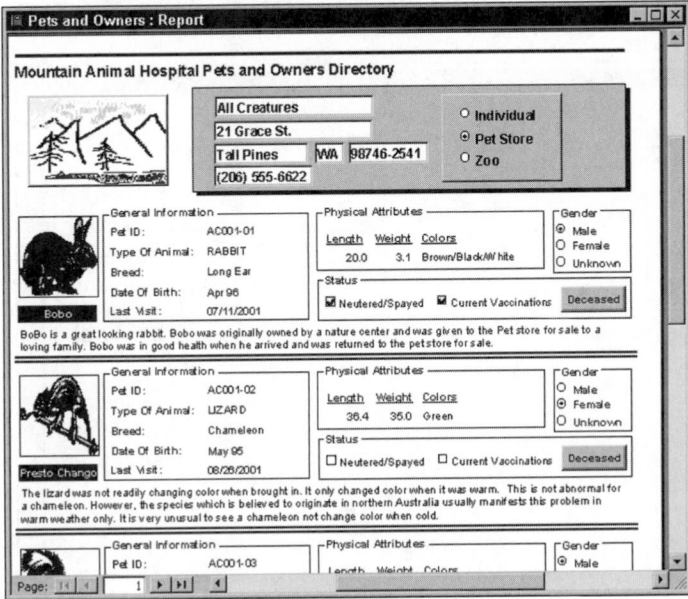

Figure 1-6: A database-published report

Multiple-table queries and relationships

One of the most powerful features in Access is also one of the most important — the query engine and Access's queries.

After you store information in the system, you will inevitably need new ways to view the information. With previous editions, you had to contact someone, or have the personal knowledge and expertise, to build a new program to examine and work with the data in this new form. Access's query engine allows you to build very complex queries by using a graphical and visual environment and drag-and-drop tools. With this powerful tool, users can quickly build views (queries) of the information that is stored in one or many tables by linking them together.

As Figure 1-7 shows, the tables in this relationship were built by using the Relationship tool. The links in these tables were created by using drag-and-drop methods and are displayed in an easy-to-understand graphical way. As we pointed out earlier in this chapter, you can even link tables of different file types (such as an Access table and a dBASE table).

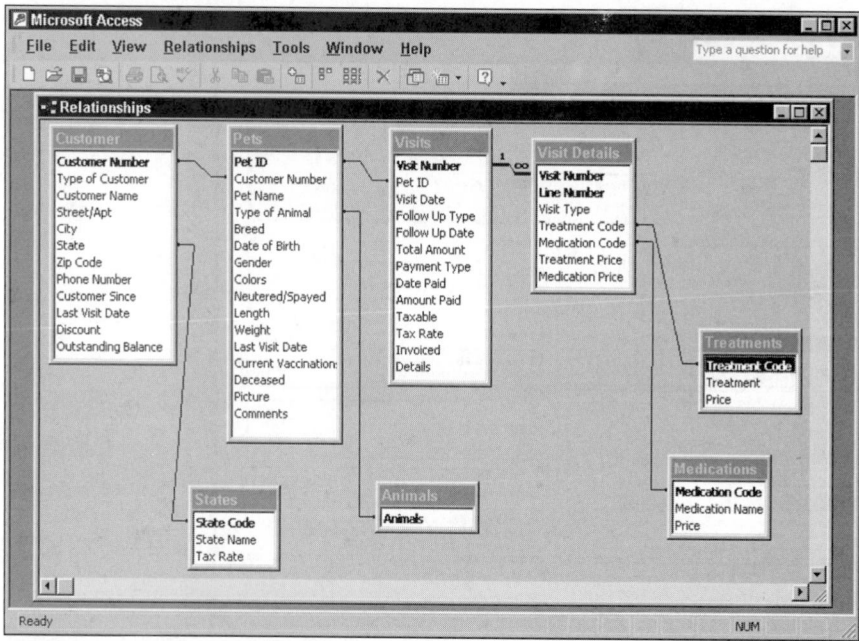

Figure 1-7: A relationship window

When linked, your tables act as a single table, which you can use to view and manipulate your information—even change the contents of the data shown in the query.

You can select specific fields, define sorting orders, create calculated expressions, and enter criteria to select desired records. The results of a query can be displayed and used in a datasheet, form, or report. Although you can pre-define or build relationships between tables, you don't have to set relationships in advance. Rather than set your relationships permanently, you can use a query window to set relationships when you need them for a specific purpose, such as a report.

Tip   If you are working in an environment where people are using several different versions of Access (2002, 2000, 97, 95, and 2) you can attach to MDB files of different versions and update data without any problems. This way, the people who only have Access 2 or Access 97 can continue to use that version and those who have upgraded to Access 2002 can use their data for reporting.

Queries have other uses as well. You can create queries to calculate totals and display cross-tabs and then make new tables from the results. You can even use a query to update data in tables, delete records, or append one table to another. Figure 1-8 shows a cross-tab query that a user can create very quickly.

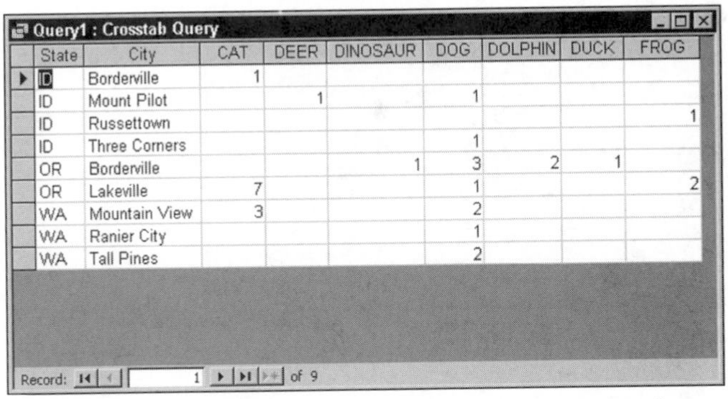

State	City	CAT	DEER	DINOSAUR	DOG	DOLPHIN	DUCK	FROG
ID	Borderville	1						
ID	Mount Pilot		1		1			
ID	Russettown							1
ID	Three Corners				1			
OR	Borderville			1	3	2	1	
OR	Lakeville	7			1			2
WA	Mountain View	3			2			
WA	Ranier City				1			
WA	Tall Pines				2			

Record: I◀ ◀ [1] ▶ ▶I ▶* of 9

Figure 1-8: The results of a cross-tab query built using the Query Tool

Queries and the ability to easily create them make Access one of the most powerful databases available today — especially from a productivity standpoint.

Business graphs and charts

The same graph application that is found in Microsoft Word, Excel, PowerPoint, and Project is built into Access. You can create hundreds of types of business graphs and customize the display to meet your every business need. You can create bar charts, column charts, line charts, pie charts, area charts, and high-low-close charts — in two and three dimensions. You can add free-form text, change the gridlines, adjust the color and pattern in a bar, display data values on a bar or pie slice, and rotate the viewing angle of a chart from within the Graph program.

Although these graphs can be built by hand — and often require a lot of training to build them — you can use the built-in Graph Wizards to build them quickly and accurately.

In addition, you can link your graph with a form to get a powerful graphic data display that changes from record to record in the table. Figure 1-9 is an example of linking a graph to a form.

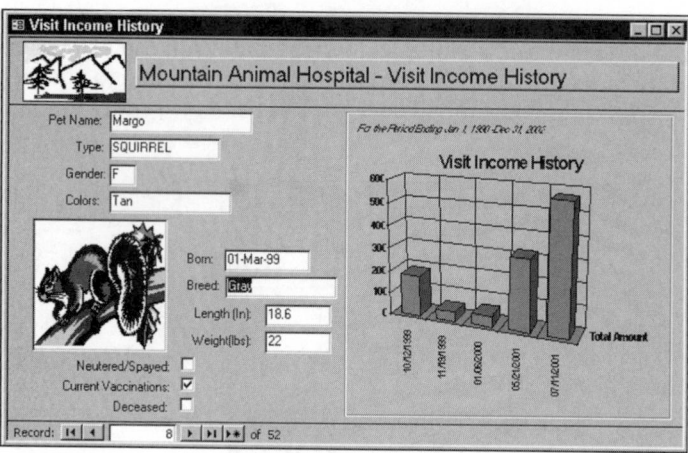

Figure 1-9: A typical form linked to a graph

DDE and OLE capabilities

Through the capabilities of *DDE* (Dynamic Data Exchange) and *OLE* (Object Linking and Embedding), you can use objects from other applications and third-party tools in your Access forms and reports. The objects that you can add include sound, pictures, graphs, and video clips. You can embed OLE objects (such as a bitmap picture) or documents from word processors (such as Word or WordPerfect), or link to a range of cells in an Excel spreadsheet. By linking these objects to records in your tables, you can create dynamic database forms and reports and share information between Windows applications. These forms and reports can display the most up-to-date information every time they are used — by obtaining the data dynamically.

The Internet is also accessible

Access is full of features that allow you to easily make your applications Internet/intranet-ready. With just a click of the mouse, you can save tables, queries, reports, and form datasheets as HTML files.

The data access pages feature lets you create complex forms for a corporate intranet, or for use across the Internet, that link with live data on your network. Even a novice can create live data pages on the Web. Hyperlinks allow you and others to access your published data (and other published data) as hypertext links, directly from your Access forms.

Many people feel that the process of publishing data to the Web is something to be left to a Webmaster. Access turns this idea into a myth. When you create a data access page (DAP), the DAP Wizard walks you through the steps of creating the form, linking to your data, and even placing the generated HTML on your Web site. As Figure 1-10 shows, with the Wizard you can create dynamic forms!

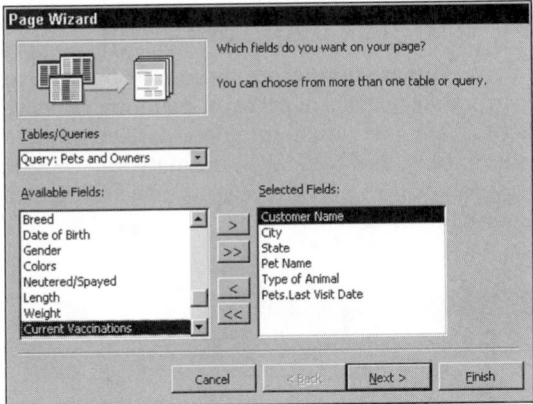

Figure 1-10: Creating a Data Access Page

True Client/Server for Everyone

In previous versions of Microsoft Access, a true Client/Server environment was very difficult to achieve. First you had to have an expensive copy of SQL Server. This required owning a high-end computer capable of running Windows NT Server, plus a high-priced consultant to install and maintain it. Access 2002 comes with the Microsoft Database Engine (MSDE, also known as the SQL Server 2000 Desktop Engine). This allows you to create true client/server-based applications on your desktop, which you can relatively easily upsize to the more robust SQL Server Enterprise Edition when you're ready.

Access 2002, like its predecessors, still comes with the Jet engine. Jet is the original Access Database Engine — it handles the creation and storage of your tables and it runs your queries. Though not as powerful or as fast as SQL Server, it is quite satisfactory for smaller applications of 20 workstations or less, and up to about 30-50MB of data (although some say only up to 10-20MB of data). Unless you have hundreds of thousands of data records, Jet is quite satisfactory for your needs.

Built-in functions

Access contains more than 200 *functions* (small built-in programs that return a value) that perform tasks in a wide variety of categories. Access includes database, mathematics, business, financial, date, time, and string functions. You can use them to create calculated expressions in your forms, reports, and queries. They add versatility to your forms and reports. For example, functions can display a date field in a different format (like 12/12/2001 to 12 December 2001) or return and display a new date (like a warranty expiration date of 60 days from the day of purchase), without needing to store it in the database.

Macros: Programming without programming

Macros are available for those of you who are nonprogrammers (or power users who simply don't want to program). Macros let you perform common tasks without user intervention. Nearly 50 macro actions let you manipulate data, create menus and dialog boxes, open forms and reports, and basically automate any task that you can imagine. Macros can probably solve 50-75 percent of your processing problems. Figure 1-11 shows a macro being created in Access.

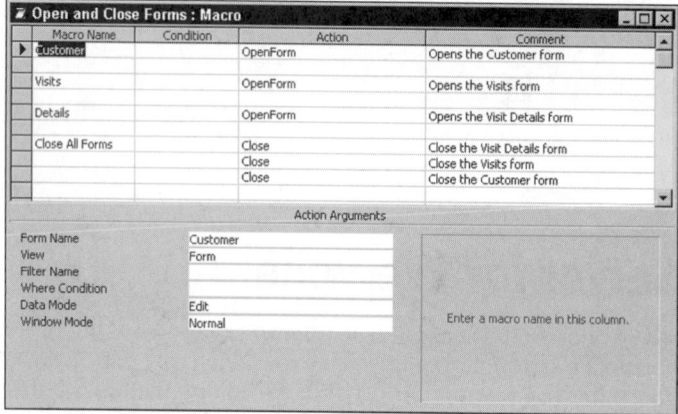

Figure 1-11: Creating a macro in Access

Modules: Visual Basic for Applications – database programming

Access is a serious development environment with a full-featured programming language.

The Visual Basic Application edition (VBA, for short, and formerly known as Access Basic) features an event-driven programming model that lets you do more than you can with just forms and reports. VBA is a powerful structured programming language; it's also fully extensible, featuring API call routines in any *dynamic link library* (DLL) for the Windows 95, Windows 98, Windows ME, Windows 2000, and Windows NT operating systems.

The full-featured development environment allows multiple windows for color-coded editing and debugging, automatic syntax checking, watch points, breakpoints, single-step execution, and even syntax help that displays each possible commands option as you type. Figure 1-12 shows a simple program being developed in Access 2002.

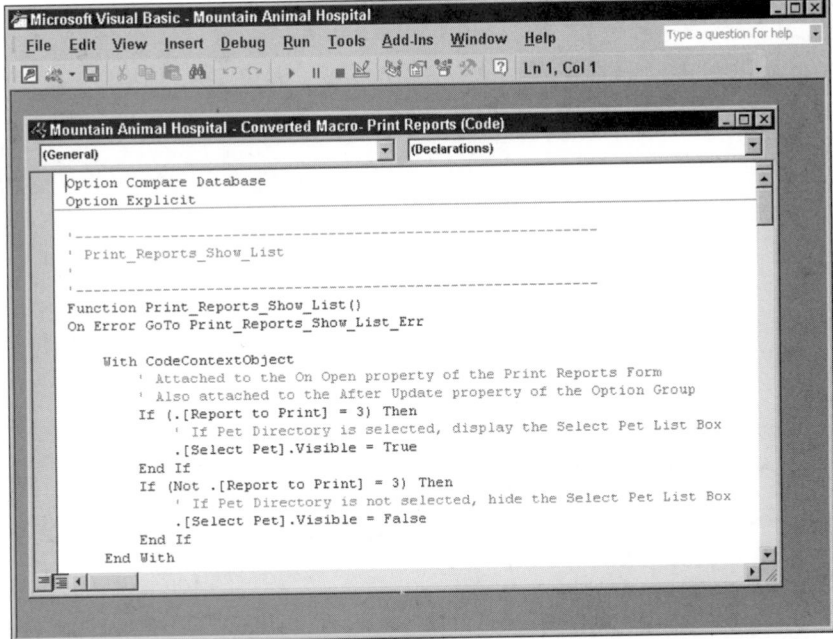

Figure 1-12: Creating a VBA program in the Development Environment

Information for Database Users

If you're already a database user, chances are you're ready to jump right in and start using Access. A word of warning: *This is not your father's database.* You may be an expert in relational database management software, such as dBASE, FoxPro, or Paradox, but you may never have used a database under Windows.

You should be familiar with Windows software before you jump into a database package. Play with Windows Paint and experiment with Word or Excel. Learn how to use the mouse to click, double-click, select, drag, and drop. Create a graph in Excel, use a Wizard, and try the Help system. Knowing how to perform these tasks will make your learning experience much faster with Access.

You also need to get used to some new terminology. Table 1-1 lists the Access terminology and its dBASE/FoxPro and Paradox equivalents.

Table 1-1
Access, dBASE/FoxPro, and Paradox Terminology

Microsoft Access	dBASE/FoxPro	Paradox
Database	Catalog	Directory of related files
Table	Database file	Table
Datasheet	BROWSE command	View command
Table Design	MODIFY STRUCTURE	Modify Restructure
Text data type	Character data type	Alphanumeric data type
Primary key	Unique Index	Key field
Index	Index	Tools QuerySpeed
Validation rule	PICTURE/VALID Clause	ValChecks
Query	Query, QBE, View	Query
Form	Screen	Forms
Subform	Multiple File Screen	Multiple-record selection
Open a form	SET FORMAT TO, EDIT	Image PickForm
Find command	LOCATE AND SEEK	Zoom
Data-entry command	APPEND	Modify DataEntry
List box, combo box	Pick list	Lookup
Exclusive/shared access	SET EXCLUSIVE ON/OFF	Edit/Co-edit mode
Module	Program file	Script

The Windows environment

In addition to understanding the terminology, you need to understand that Access works in an event-driven and graphical-user interface (GUI) environment — Microsoft Windows. This environment offers the database programmer exciting new challenges and eliminates many of the ways that you programmed in the past.

GUI environment

Using the graphical tools built into Access, you can quickly create great-looking graphical-oriented forms and reports — consisting of labels, text data fields, option buttons, tab controls, check boxes, lines, boxes, colors, shading, pictures, and graphs. Forms become an extension of your creativity because they allow you to work with your data in a way never offered before in a text-based environment. Using the Form and Report Wizards you can quickly create very powerful graphical objects (forms and reports).

Event-driven environment

Building these types of objects comes with a price — you must learn the concept of objects and their properties and events. Although many of the chapters on forms and reports dedicate a lot of space to their properties and events, you should be aware of the fact that Access is a Windows program that relies on the event model of Windows.

An *event-driven environment*, such as Windows, is one that simply responds to *events* (user- or program-directed actions). In its simplest form, an event is some action that occurs. In Windows, for example, if the user types the key combination **Ctrl+Esc,** the Windows Task List dialog box appears and lets the user move to another active Windows program. The event in this scenario is the actual key-combination being pressed. Windows and Access look for events and then respond to those events (if programmed to do so) by taking some action.

You must understand this concept of an event-driven environment because you will rely upon it for all Access programs.

Programming by exception

If you aren't familiar with these concepts and you expect to just start writing code to develop your application — then you are in for a surprise. Access' object- and event-driven models require a bit of re-thinking about the work that you do with tables, forms, reports, and queries.

For instance, the concept of a dBASE *dot prompt* and issuing single or multiple com-mands in sequence through a command window simply doesn't exist in Access. However, you can use an immediate window to verify a command before attaching it to an event or in a program. This means that you won't be able to immediately access information from your database in the manner that you're used to in dBASE or FoxPro.

The good news is that it takes considerably less time to develop an Access applica-tion than is required to create older database applications, such as dBASE, Cobol, Paradox, and others. This is especially true considering the fact that these applica-tions have become more complex — from the UI to the methods used to access the information. You will find that you can solve complex development issues much faster and more efficiently by using Access. This speed and efficiency is due, in part, to the concept of *programming by exception*. In traditional programming, you have to program all actions that the user could possibly perform — including actions that you don't want them to do (such as pressing the wrong keys [and if they do press it, you must program what to do about it]). In Access, you simply program the actions that you want the user to perform, such as pressing a specific button or key and then ignoring all the rest. In other words, this is a program by exception—Access and Windows will simply ignore all other actions. This concept will become clearer as you use Access and create forms, queries, and reports.

Finally, you still create code with Access, but now you will create "snippets" of code and attach them to events in your tables, queries, forms, and reports. This code can be in the form of accessing a built-in function or writing your own function in VBA. You won't write code to create your forms and reports, however; rather, you will build these objects by using the tools found in Access. You can even use the Query tool to allow Access to create your queries for you—or write your own SQL statements. You can use these queries in other queries, forms, and reports to limit or specify what records to view, edit, update, or add.

Information for Spreadsheet Users

If you are an Excel expert, you find that many things about Access are like Excel. Both programs are Windows products, so you should already have experience using the Windows-specific conventions that are used in Access. Access has a spreadsheet view of the table or query data that is known as a *datasheet*. You can resize the rows and columns in much the same way as you can within Excel worksheets. In fact, Access 2002 has a data-entry mode exactly like Excel's. Simply enter data and define column headings, and then Access automatically creates a table (see Figure 1-13).

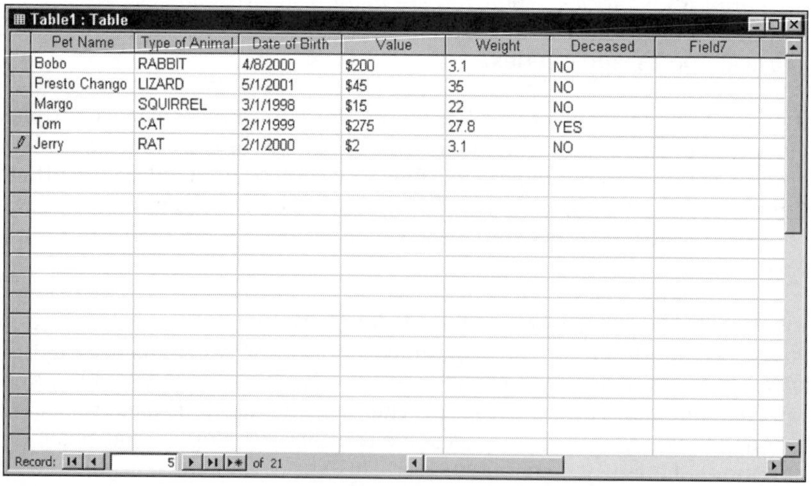

Pet Name	Type of Animal	Date of Birth	Value	Weight	Deceased	Field7
Bobo	RABBIT	4/8/2000	$200	3.1	NO	
Presto Chango	LIZARD	5/1/2001	$45	35	NO	
Margo	SQUIRREL	3/1/1998	$15	22	NO	
Tom	CAT	2/1/1999	$275	27.8	YES	
Jerry	RAT	2/1/2000	$2	3.1	NO	

Figure 1-13: Creating a new table using an Access datasheet

Access has a WYSIWYG drawing capability like that of Excel, and it shares the same graph application. Thus, you can create the same types of graphs in both programs and annotate the graphs in the same way. Also, Access uses Graph Wizards that you may have already used in Excel.

Access 2002 also contains a Pivot Table Wizard just like Excel's; in fact, it can create Excel pivot tables. You can also drag-and-drop information from an Access database to an Excel spreadsheet and link Access databases to Excel spreadsheets. You can query and sort data in both products, using a common query interface. (If you've used Excel menu options for queries and sorting, you're already familiar with these concepts.) Access is interoperable with all Microsoft Office 2002 products.

Database manipulation

Unlike Excel and other spreadsheet programs, working with data in new ways is much easier with Access. Although you're probably familiar with the methods to sort records in Excel, you can quickly sort and even limit which records you use in Access. This is due to the powerful, simple-to-use, Graphical User Interface of the Access query engine — you can drag-and drop-field names (column titles in Excel) onto a field row in the lower pane of the Query Design view. Then you can specify sort order and even specify criteria to limit which records are displayed. In addition, by using the powerful Query and Report building tools, you can create dynamic forms and reports that can display individual records in any way that you want to look at them — formatting how they look on the screen and in the report. You can quickly and easily toggle between single record and multi-record views.

✦   ✦   ✦

Installing and Running Access 2002

✦   ✦   ✦   ✦

In This Chapter

Getting to know the hardware and software necessary for running Access or Office

Determining how to install and run Access successfully on your computer

Installing the Access 2002 upgrade

Converting Access 2.x, 95, 97, and 2000 databases

Handling problems that occur during installation

Starting Access 2002 in several different ways

Using open options in the Access command line

Exiting Access

Using the various Help options

✦   ✦   ✦   ✦

Access 2000 must be installed on your computer before you can use it. Because the majority of copies of Microsoft Access are now purchased through the Microsoft Office suite, you use the Office CD to install the Access 2002 programs on your computer. You can install one of the Microsoft Office 2002 suites that include Access (the Professional, Premium, and Developer Editions), or the stand-alone version of Access 2002. Regardless of which way you choose, the installation routines are the same — after you get to the portion of the setup routine that lets you select the Access 2002 options.

You install Access 2002 in a manner similar to other Windows 95, 98, ME, 2000, or NT software products. If your company has a special person or team designated to install and troubleshoot software, you may want to have this person or team install Access for you so that your system is installed following the company's software standards.

If you are installing an upgrade version of Access or Office 2002, the older program must already be installed on your machine. New installations of Access 2002 don't require a previous version to be already installed on your machine.

Determining What You Need

Access 2002 requires specific hardware and software in order to run. Before you install Access, check to see that your computer meets the minimum requirements needed to run it.

Hardware requirements

To use Access 2002 successfully, you need an IBM (or compatible) personal computer with a Pentium III 133 Mhz or higher processor and 64MB of RAM. If you plan on using the voice recognition features of Office 2002, or will be running more than one Office application, simultaneously, you need, at a minimum, a Pentium III 250 MHz or faster machine with 128MB of memory. To get really good performance from Access 2002, a Pentium III 350 MHz or faster computer with at least 128MB of RAM is recommended. With more memory and a faster processor, you can run more applications simultaneously, and increase overall performance. A fast video card is also recommended to display pictures and graphs.

You also need between 260MB and 550MB of hard drive space for a typical installation of Microsoft Office 2002. If you are installing only Access 2002, you still need, at a minimum, about 140MB (or 200MB to install all Access options and the necessary Office shared components) because many of the Office shared files are used by Access and are included in the stand-alone version. Keep in mind that you also need additional space to store your database files when you create them.

If space is a problem, Office 2002 provides some useful options, including the ability to run various options from the CD, such as Office Clip Art, or open various large-templates. You can also receive an automatic prompt from each Office application to install a feature on first use. This way, if you or one of your users will never need a certain feature, such as WordPerfect support, it will never be loaded. Using the custom installation, you can decide which features are installed, and you can even choose to exclude individual features or entire applications. You can perform a partial installation, or you can delete unwanted files from your hard drive to free up space that's needed for the installation. Access needs a VGA monitor as a minimum requirement, but we recommend an SVGA (or better) display. This configuration allows you to view more information at one time at a sharper resolution.

A mouse or some other compatible pointing device (trackballs and pens also work) is mandatory for you to use Access 2002.

If you're planning to print from Access, you need a printer. Any printer that is supported by Windows 98, 95, ME, Windows 2000, or Windows NT works.

Software requirements

Access requires that Microsoft Windows 2000 (formerly named Windows NT), 98, 95, ME, or Windows NT be installed on your computer. Windows doesn't come with Access; it must be purchased separately. If Windows 2000 (NT), 98, 95, or ME isn't installed on your computer, you must install it before you can install Access or Office 2002. Microsoft Office 2002 doesn't run on OS/2 or Windows 3.1.

Upgrading to Access 2002 from Access 2.0, 95, 97, or 2000

If you are upgrading to Access 2002 from earlier versions of Access, you should consider a few points. Earlier versions of Access databases must be converted to the Access 2000 format before they are usable, because the default file format for Access 2002 is Access 2000. To take advantage of the Access 2002 database enhancements, however, you need to convert your tables to Access 2002 format. After you convert an Access 2.0, Access 95, Access 97, and Access 2000 database to Access 2002 format, it becomes unusable by Access 2.0, 95, 97, or 2000. You can, however, save an Access 2002 database back to an Access 2000 or Access 97 format. As an Access 2002 user, you can open and work with Access 2.0, 95, or 97 data by linking to them as external tables in the database, but you can't modify any of the objects (forms, reports, queries, etc.) you find in them. Because the default file format of Access 2002 is Access 2000, you can work with Access 2000 databases in their native structure — even modifying and saving any of the objects.

If you share data files with people who use older versions of Access, consider leaving the older version of Access on your machine so you can make files in Access 2002 but use Access 2.0, 95, 97, or 2000 with files that are shared with others.

Tip   Access 2002 uses Access 2000 databases in their native format — you can create and modify Objects (such as forms and reports). You can use Access 2002 in a network with Access 2000 users and leave data files in the Access 2000 format.

Installing Access 2002 or Office XP

To install Office XP or Access 2002, insert your CD-ROM into your CD-ROM drive. A startup screen for the install displays automatically.

Tip   If the startup screen doesn't display automatically, select Run from the Windows Start menu. Windows displays the Run dialog box. In the Open box, type **D:\SETUP** (use the letter that corresponds to the drive containing your installation CD-ROM), as shown in Figure 2-1. Click OK to begin the installation. This procedure works for both new installations and upgrades to Access 2002.

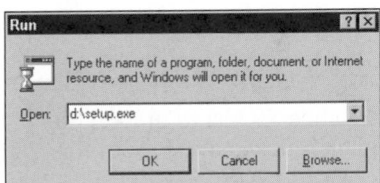

Figure 2-1: The Run dialog box

Because some Windows programs interfere with the setup program, Access or Office may warn you to shut down any applications that are currently running. If you get this warning, you can simply click the Continue button to continue the setup, or you can click the Exit Setup button to cancel the installation. Then, shut down the applications and restart the setup. The install program begins, and if it needs to update Windows and Office components, it displays the window shown in Figure 2-2, which states:

> Microsoft Office XP requires newer Windows system components not detected on your computer. . . . After installing this update, Setup will automatically resume with Office installation.

If you get this message, simply click the Next button to review the End User License Agreement. Click the Agree button and the program begins to update your Windows components. A new screen appears, and you see a status bar moving as the program files are being updated.

After the new system files are installed, you are prompted to shut down your computer to complete setup of Office XP. Re-start your computer by clicking the Yes button.

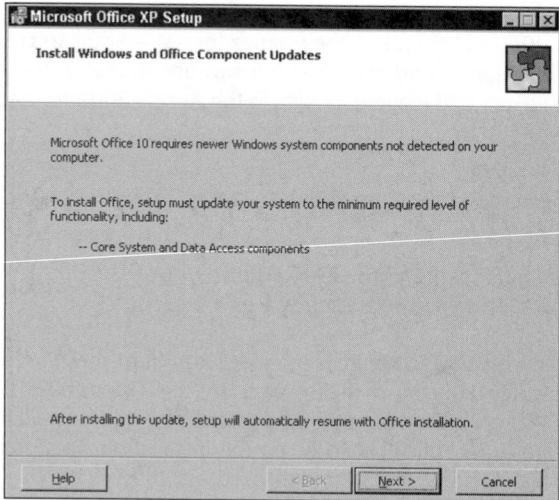

Figure 2-2: The Office XP Install window that *may* display if you need to update Windows and Office components before installing Access 2002 or Office XP

After the system reboots, you may be told that Office XP has to update the Window's installer program. If this screen displays, click Yes to reboot the computer a second time.

At this point, you see the first setup screen, as shown in Figure 2-3.

The setup program now requires some information from you. The first screen contains text boxes for your name, initials, company, and the Office 2002 Product Key from your CD. The Product Key refers to the Office Product Key number that can be found on the back of the CD case; it consists of five sets of five letter/number combinations. If you have previously installed any Microsoft Office component, you see your name, initials, and company from your previous installation in the text box. Microsoft Office stores these entries in the Windows registry for use by all Office components.

Tip   You can always find your Product Key and the software version number in any Microsoft product by selecting Help ⇨ About. You can also find technical support options and help on the Web from the Help menu.

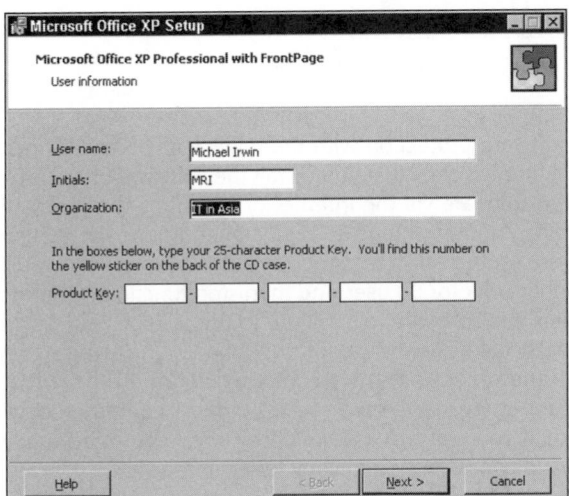

Figure 2-3: The Office 2002 Install first screen. This screen prompts you for your name, initials, and Product Key.

After you enter your license information (Product Key) and click Next, you have to agree to Microsoft's licensing. As you can see in Figure 2-4, this is a very intimidating screen.

You can read all of the text, or have your lawyer read it for you. Basically, you have no choice but to select the "I accept the terms in the license agreement" option. Even though this obligates you to give all the money you ever make to Microsoft, you must accept the terms of the agreement before you can click Next. Well, maybe not all your money—just the amount left over after the IRS takes it all.

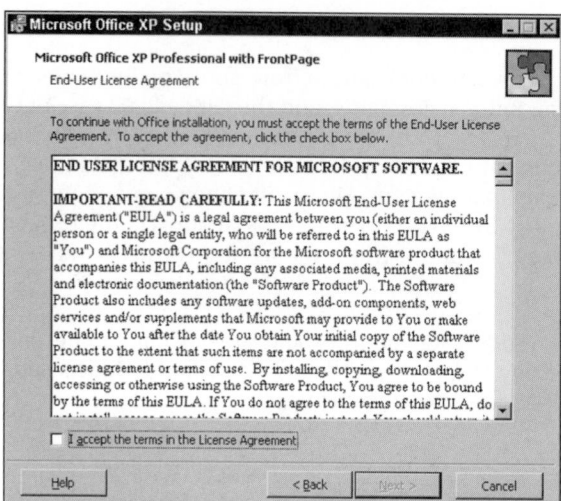

Figure 2-4: The Office XP License Agreement screen

Tip   Microsoft has instituted software protection with the release of Office XP (including Access 2002). This scheme requires that you install the software on your computer and then register the software via the Internet or by calling the registration information in and obtaining another unique 25 digit alphanumeric key that must be entered for your software (automatic if registering via the Internet). If you fail to do so, the programs will only work for 50 uses and then stop functioning correctly. After that you must 'register' the software to continue to use it. This 'new' key that is created is unique to each computer. Microsoft will allow you to register two copies of the software — one on your primary computer and the other on your portable computer. You cannot register it on a second primary computer, only on a portable computer. Should you want to install Office on another machine, you need to purchase another copy of Office (one copy for each machine).

Setup now gives you two broad choices for installing Microsoft Office or Access. As you can see in Figure 2-5, the choices depend on which components you want to install:

✦ **Upgrade Now.** If you have any version of an Office product on your computer, this option automatically removes older versions of Office before installing the new version using your current configuration.

If you choose an install type, you must choose between:

- **Typical (New Users).** This option installs each Office product with the most commonly used set of components. It makes all the choices for you, including the location of the Office files, which are installed in C:\Program Files\Microsoft Office.

- **Complete.** This option is for users who want to install all of Microsoft Office on your computer, including all optional components and tools.

- **Custom.** This option lets you decide how Office is installed, including where files are placed, and which specific product features, options, shared Office components, sample files, and even Help systems are installed. You can also decide which older products in the Office family you want to keep or remove.

Note
Regardless of which option you choose, the new technology in Microsoft Office XP prompts you to insert your Office CD if you need to use a feature that wasn't installed. Although this may be annoying for the first few weeks you use Office, it may save you a lot of hard drive space and registry entries that you may otherwise never need. As an added bonus, you won't have to know where the feature is located on the install disk — you simply click OK.

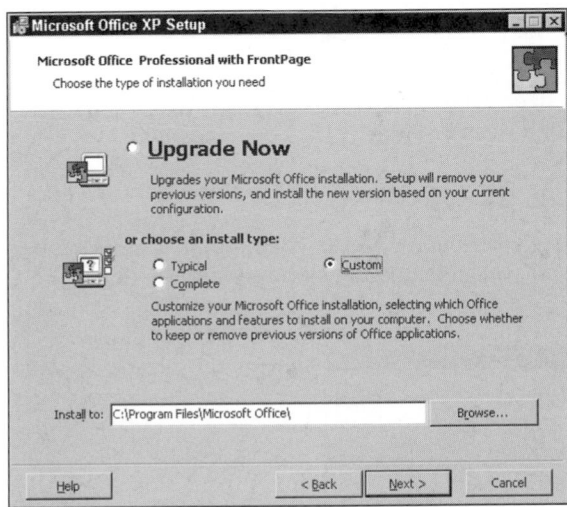

Figure 2-5: Selecting how to install Office 2002

In this example, you step through a custom installation. Office lets you specify where you want to install the files — notice that it is at the bottom of the screen, as shown in Figure 2-5. You can use the default subdirectory, which is usually C:\Program Files\Microsoft Office\, or click the Browse button to change the default location.

Note
If this is your first time installing a Microsoft Office Product, your screen will differ from the one shown in Figure 2-5. It will offer you three choices, Install Now (or choose an install type), Complete, or Custom. Figure 2-6 shows this install screen. If this is your first time installing you should select 'Custom' to continue.

If you are installing the Microsoft Office suite, the default location of C:\Program Files\Microsoft Office is satisfactory for this example. If you want to change the location, type the new drive and folder name. To install Microsoft Office in a folder called *Office* on your E drive, type *E:\OFFICE*. If you type the name of a folder that doesn't exist, one is created for you. Some shared Office components must reside on your C drive (or the hard drive where Windows or the System Registry is installed).

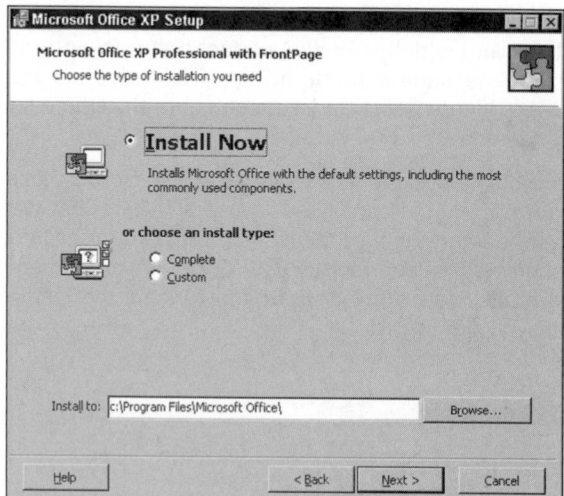

Figure 2-6: The install screen for a clean install, versus upgrading as in Figure 2-5

Click Next to display the screen where you choose which application(s) you want to install, as shown in Figure 2-7 (the selected check boxes are the default).

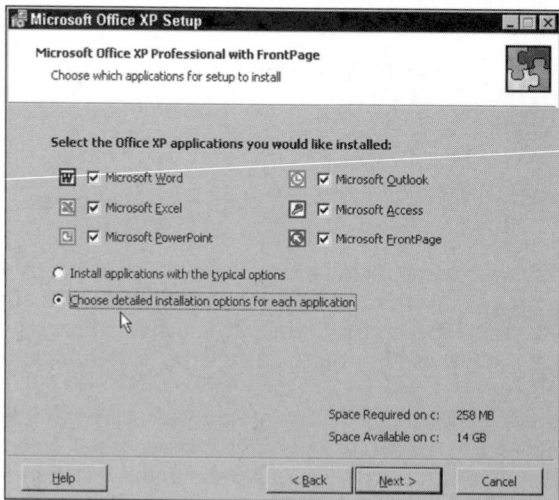

Figure 2-7: Choosing detailed installation options

You must also choose whether you want to install "Typical" options (default) or "Choose to install detailed options (as in Figure 2-7) for each application." The installer also checks your hard drive for space and reports how much space is initially needed. If you choose not to install certain options, this number may later change.

The default option for installing office Applications is "Install applications with the typical options." If you decide to install using detailed installation options you should click on the "Choose detailed installation options for each application" option button as shown in Figure 2-7.

This screen shows the Choose detailed installation options for each application chosen. The only difference between choosing the "Install applications with the typical options" or the "Choose detailed installation options for each application" option button is the screens that appear, prompting you to choose installation options for each product of Office, as shown in Figure 2-8 and Figure 2-9.

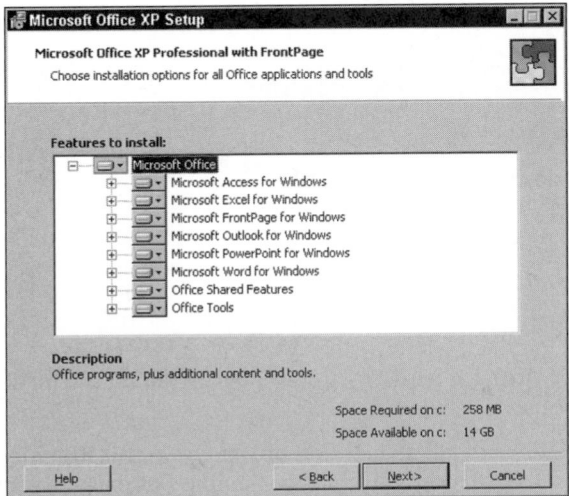

Figure 2-8: The "Choose detailed installation options" button for each Microsoft Office product. You can click on the plus sign (+) to expand the options beneath each application.

Figure 2-8 shows what is perhaps the most important screen because it lets you choose which Office features to install and how each of them will run. As you can see in Figure 2-8, this screen shows a tree view of all the products. Each application is listed with a plus sign next to its name. Clicking the plus sign expands the offering into more and more levels. Although most icons are white, indicating the options to be installed, some icons are gray, meaning that some options still haven't been selected for installation.

In Figure 2-9, you can see that Microsoft Access for Windows and Sample Databases have been expanded and that the Northwind Database feature's icon (small hard drive figure with a yellow one to the left of it and a down arrow to its right) has been clicked to show four different icon choices. Each icon represents a different option.

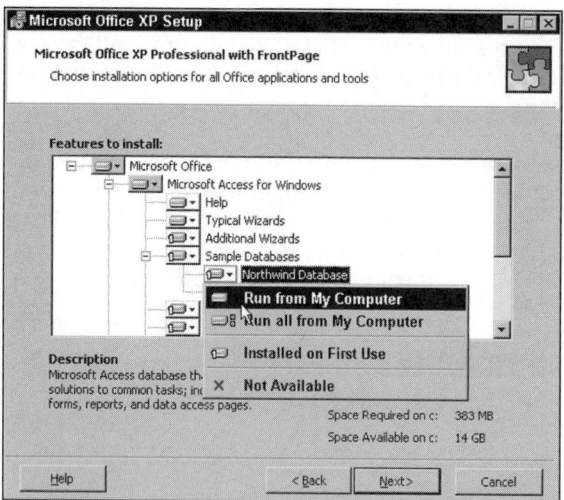

Figure 2-9: The Access for Windows program is expanded and the Sample Database is further expanded. Clicking Northwind Database displays the possible options.

These installation options are:

✦ **Run from My Computer/ Run all from My Computer.** Install on the local or server hard drive previously specified

✦ **Run all from My Computer.** Install all included objects from this item down through its tree. If you select this option from the Sample Database object, both Sample database will automatically be selected.

✦ **Installed on First Use.** Install on your computer the first time you try to use the feature or product. This is the default option for the Sample Databases.

✦ **Not Available.** The feature or product can't be used without re-running the Office Setup program.

If you want to use the Northwind Database, you should select the Run from My Computer option—this installs the Northwind Database on your computer for later use. In addition, you may want to select Run from My Computer for the Database Replication and the Snapshot Viewer features under the Access for Windows application.

If you want to take the quick hands-on tour of Access in the next chapter, you need to install the CD that comes with the Access 2002 Bible, although you can use the Northwind Database to do the same hands-on tour.

If you click on the plus sign (+) to expand the Office Tools, you see that most options are set to be Installed on First Use.

After you choose all the items you need, press Next. Now the installer checks to see which previous version of Office components are installed on your machine. As you can see in Figure 2-10, this author's computer has previous versions of Microsoft Excel and Word on the machine.

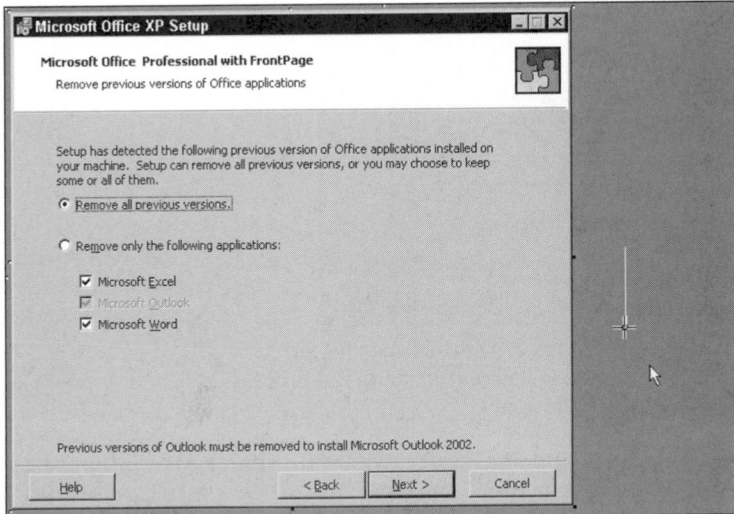

Figure 2-10: When installing, you can choose to remove all previous versions, keep all previous versions, or simply keep specific applications.

 Note   This is the screen that displays if you choose to use the "Typical" options, as shown in Figure 2-7. From this point on in the process, both the typical and detailed installations are the same.

You are given three choices in this screen. The first choice is to simply "Remove all previous versions of the products," which is the default. The second choice is to "Keep all previous older versions." The third choice is to "Remove only the following applications" by selecting their check boxes.

 Note   Microsoft Office XP products can coexist with Office 97 or 2000 versions, or even Access 2.0, with almost no problem.

 Note   If you are installing Office XP on a clean machine — one that has not had a copy of office installed before — you will not see this screen.

In this case, you can select "Remove all previous versions" and click Next. This takes you to a screen that displays a review of all actions that you selected for installing Microsoft Office, as shown in Figure 2-11.

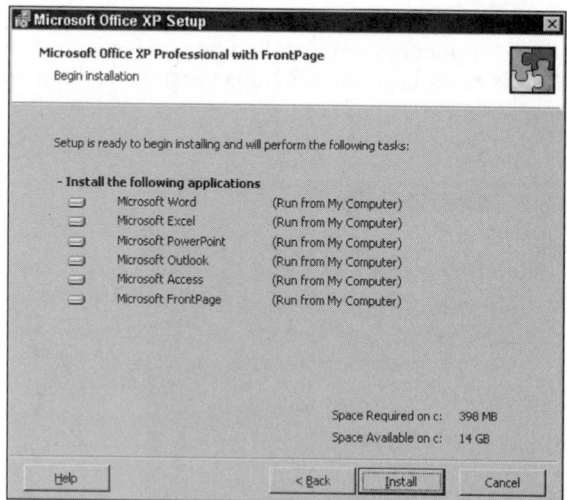

Figure 2-11: The final screen before Office is installed on your computer. Clicking on the Install button starts the process.

Clicking Install takes you to the final screen where the installation progresses; placing Microsoft Office XP on your computer. This process takes some time — approximately 20 to 120 minutes for a complete installation — depending on your processor speed, CD-ROM drive speed, and hard drive speed.

After the installation is complete, you will see a final dialog box appear like the one in Figure 2-12. It informs you that the configuration changes made to Microsoft Office XP Professional will not take effect until your computer has been restarted. Then it asks if you want to restart the computer. You can select Yes or No.

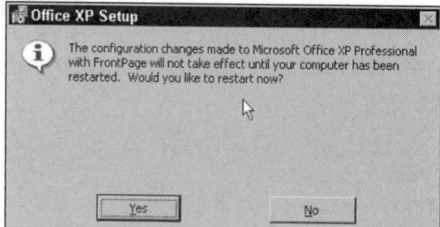

Figure 2-12: The information screen that appears after Office XP has been installed

You can answer Yes and have Office re-boot your computer to update the Registry with the changes made by Microsoft Office XP installation. If you answer No, you can have the Registry updated the next time your start Windows. You should answer Yes and have it done immediately so that you don't forget to do it and have unexpected results occur.

If you installed the stand-alone version of Access, a new program shortcut named Microsoft Access appears in your Start menu. If you installed the entire Office suite, you see an entry for each Office product. You can run Access by either choosing Start ➪ Microsoft Access or by locating the Microsoft Access folder on the desktop or in Windows Explorer, and then finding the Access icon and double-clicking it. If the Office XP shortcut bar is present, you can start Access by pressing the Access (key) icon.

Activating Your Product

One you have installed Office XP or stand-alone Access, you are *required* to register it with Microsoft. This is a new "feature" added by Microsoft. The registration is actually not for registration purposes, rather to activate the software or disable the new software protection scheme built into the product.

Office XP has a copy-protection scheme that only allows you to run the application 50 times before you must "activate" it. If you do not register the application by the fiftieth time, it will be handicapped. You will be unable to create or modify any objects, only read them. For instance, Access will continue to be capable of opening tables and using forms and reports but not capable of making changes to them.

Every time you start any Office application (Word, Excel, Access, and others) your counter decrements by one until you have opened the applications a total of 50 times.

To assist you in activating your product, Office will automatically start an *Activation Wizard* each time you start an Office application. Figure 2-13 shows this wizard.

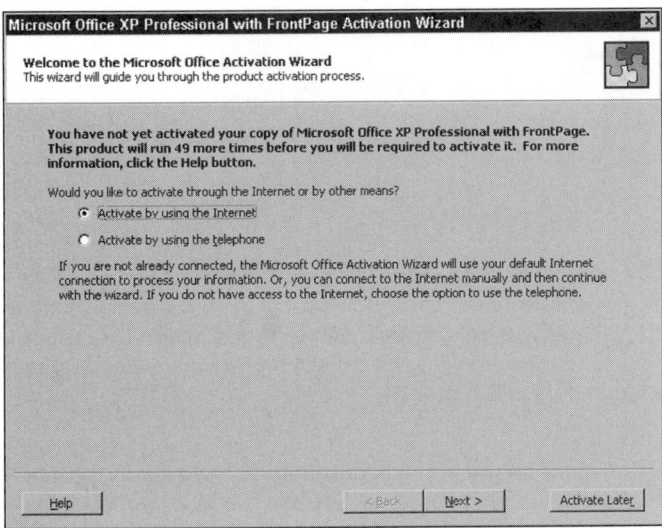

Figure 2-13: This is the first screen of the Activation Wizard.

If you click on the Activate Later button (lower right-hand corner) you can continue to use the Office application without registration until the counter reaches a total of 50 uses. After 50 uses, all Office products will cease to work properly until you activate the product.

As Figure 2-13 shows you can register your product one of two ways — either by using the Internet or by using the telephone.

This is the first screen of the Activation Wizard. The default method of activation is by using the Internet.

Activating by using the Internet

To activate your product via the Internet, make sure that the choice "Activate by using the Internet" is selected and press the Next button (as shown in Figure 2-13).

Once you click on the Next button you are taken to another screen that tells you that it is connecting to the Internet. It should look similar to the one in Figure 2-14.

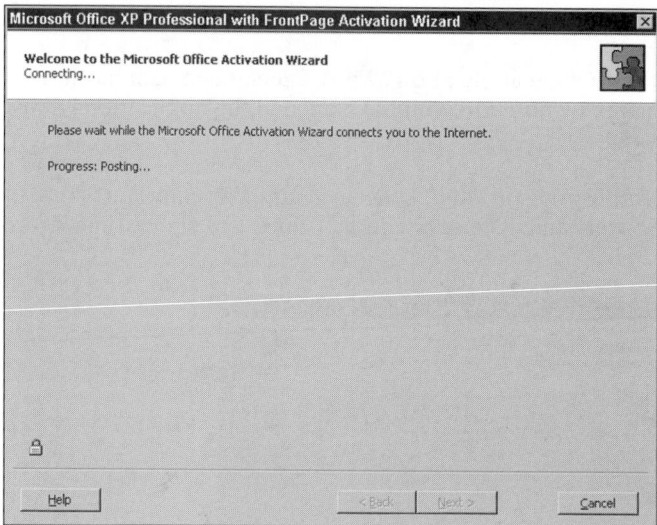

Figure 2-14: Connecting to Internet screen for activating Office XP

Caution   To register via the Internet you have to first connect to the Internet via your dialer program. If you fail to connect first, the Wizard will report an error and return you to the first screen as shown in Figure 2-13.

Once a connect has been established you will automatically be taken to the next screen of the activation process. This screen describes the Microsoft Office Privacy Policy and informs you that the only information you must give is the country where the product will be used. Figure 2-15 shows this screen.

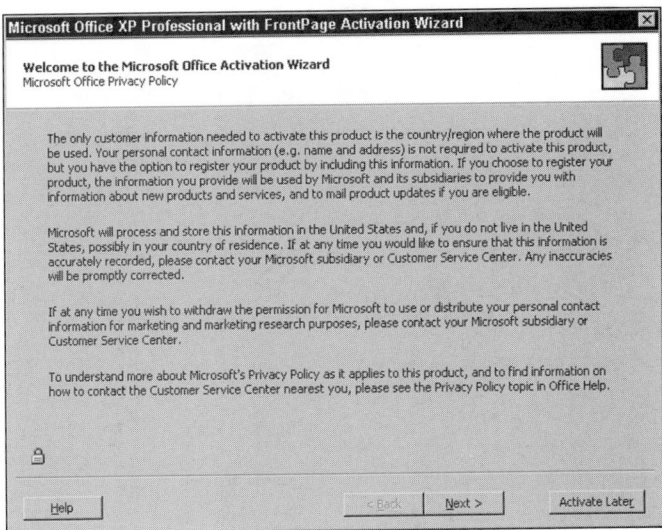

Figure 2-15: The Office Privacy Policy for activating Office XP

Click on next to move to the next screen in the process. This takes you to the screen seen in Figure 2-16. The only field that you must fill in is the first one.

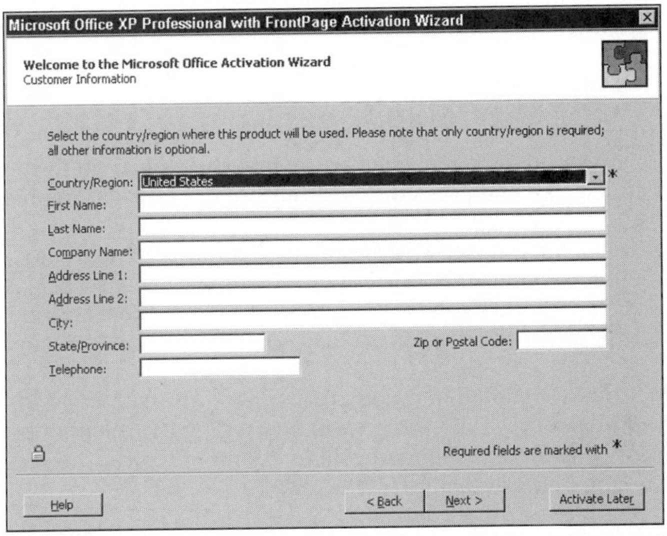

Figure 2-16: The Customer Information Screen for activating Office XP

Clicking on the Next button takes you to the next screen of the Wizard, which asks you if you want to receive offers from Microsoft or other third-party products and update information. If you do, you will need to supply an e-mail address. Figure 2-17 shows this screen.

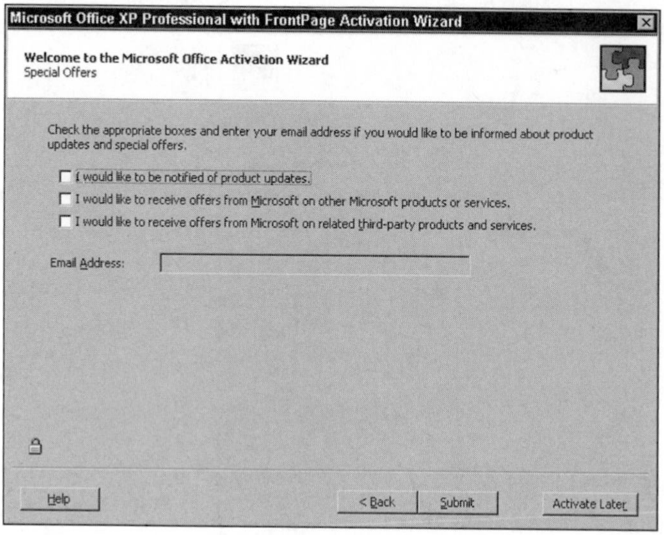

Figure 2-17: The Special Offers screen that appears when activating Office XP via the Net

Finally, when you click on the Next button, you will be taken to the final screen, which informs you that activation has been completed. This screen is shown in Figure 2-19. Click on the finish button to return to the application you were running when the Activation Wizard started.

Activating by using the telephone

To activate your product via the telephone, make sure that the choice "Activate by using the Telephone" is selected and press the Next button (as shown in Figure 2-13).

Once the Next button has been pressed you are taken to another screen that informs you about Microsoft's Office Privacy Policy. This is the same screen as shown in Figure 2-15. It also informs you that you must only give them the country where you are registering the product. Click on Next to go to the next screen.

Figure 2-18 shows you the next screen that you are taken to. This screen is comprised of four parts — the country the product will be used in, the telephone number to call to register, specific information you will be required to give the service agent, and the area to type in the activation code.

First you need to go to the first section and select the country where you will use the product. Once this is done, the second section will display the telephone number to call to activate your copy of Office XP. At this point you simply call the telephone number and talk with the Microsoft customer service agent and give them the information that is on your screen in section 3. Section 3 has the Install date and a series of numbers that are unique to this individual computer (in the case of Figure 2-18, nine groups of numbers — eight with six digits, and one with two digits).

After you give the representative these numbers they will give you 35 (seven groups of five) additional alpha-numeric values (letters and numbers) to enter into the final section — section 4. You should enter these values into the area while you are still on the telephone with the representative to make sure you have them correct.

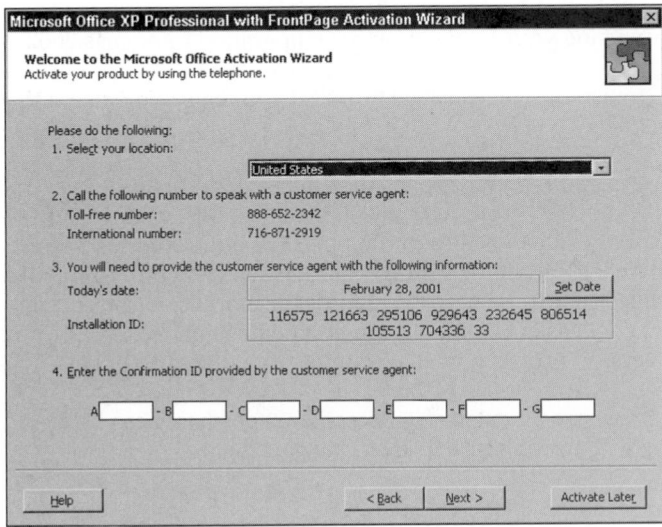

Figure 2-18: The activating your Office XP by telephone registration screen

Once this is done, simply click on the next button and you will be taken to the last page. Click on the Finish button to return to the office product that you were using.

Converting Access 1.x, 2.0, 95, 97, and 2000 Files

New Feature

Access 2002 introduces a new file format for table files (MDB). This new format offers little externally to the user or developer. However, it does offer a smarter method of OLE storage in MDB files and lets the developer more easily create MDE files that support the new properties, methods, and functions introduced in Access 2002.

Interestingly, Access 2002 is the first version of Access that supports working with two different file formats — Access 2000 and 2002 formats; offering the greatest back-version compatibility with Access 2000 users.

Access 2002 works just fine with the Access 2000 file format — if you are not quite ready to convert. In fact, the default setting for Access 2002 is to create Access 2000 files so that both Access 2000 and 2002 users can work on the same file by default. To change the default file format, select Tools ➪ Options ➪ Advance and change the Default File Format to Access 2002.

You may want to consider converting to the Access 2002 file format for very definite reasons. You should use the new Access 2002 file format in any of these situations:

✦ You need to create MDE/ADE files using Access 2002.

✦ All users that are using your application have upgraded to Access 2002.

You should continue to use the Access 2000 format if you have some users that will still be using Access 2000.

Access 2002 can convert and read databases that were created in older versions of Access (Access 2.0, 95, and 97). From Access 2002 you can add, change, and delete data from older versions. You can even run the older version's queries, forms, reports, macros, and Access BASIC or VBA modules. However, you cannot change any objects (tables, queries, forms, reports, macros, or modules). To redesign an older version's object (Access 2000 objects can still be designed in 2002), you must either use the older version program itself or convert the object to Access 2002.

> **Tip** Unlike Access 2.0, 95, and 97 databases, Access 2000 databases can be used directly — working with the objects and even changing them.

The first time you attempt to open a database that was created in a previous version of Microsoft Access (2.0, 95, or 97), you are given the option to convert it or open it in read-only mode, as shown in Figure 2-19.

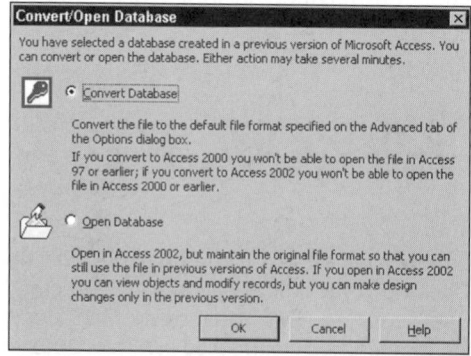

Figure 2-19: Converting an Access 97 database the first time you open it

Caution
The option to convert the database is only offered the first time you attempt to open a non-2002 Access database — every time thereafter you are simply given a message window like the one in Figure 2-20.

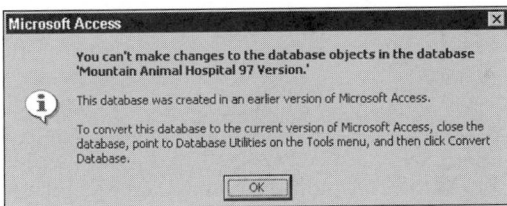

Figure 2-20: Opening a non-2002 database the second and subsequent times displays this message, letting you know that you can't make changes to the objects in the database — only the data in it.

You can also convert older Access databases by selecting Tools ➪ Database Utilities ➪ Convert Database ➪ To (three options here — To Access 97, To Access 2000, or To Access 2002 File Format). You can convert the Access database while it is open by using this method.

If the file being converted is in Access 97 file format, this option is dimmed (not available) — this is also true for versions 2000 and 2002. If you select a conversion type from 97 to 2002, a standard Windows file-selector dialog box appears. You select the database to be converted and give it a new name. The database is then converted.

Note
Although Access 2002 only lets you convert back to Access 97 and 2000, if you decided to convert other previous versions, Access 2.0 and 95 to Access 2002, you will receive the same file selection dialog box.

If you use Microsoft Access security, you must own the database or be a member of the Admins group that was in effect when the database was created.

Caution
If you try to convert the database and save it to the same path and name, you get an error message and the conversion does not take place.

You can also convert a database, to any of three versions, without opening it first. Simply select Tools ➪ Database Utilities ➪ Convert Database ➪ To (three choices: Access 97, 2000, or 2002) and a dialog box appears, asking "Database to Convert From?" Select the name of the database that you want to convert, and click Convert.

Note
If you attempt to convert a database from the same version that you want to save it to, a Message box displays, stating "The database you tried to convert was either created in or was already converted to the requested version of Microsoft Access."

After you select a database name and click Convert, or double-click on the file name, the "Convert Database Into" dialog box displays. Now type the new name that you want to assign to the database to be saved, click Save, and the file is converted.

Note   If any errors occur during compilation, Access reports them via a dialog box.

Troubleshooting

If you run into problems while installing Office or Access, setup displays a message telling you what the problem may be. Some common problems include lack of hard drive space and problems reading the CD-ROM.

If you receive a message stating that an error occurred during setup, you may have run out of hard drive space. You need to delete some files before proceeding with the installation. You can delete files from the hard drive. Remember to be careful not to delete important files. If you find that you have plenty of available hard drive space, then something else has failed in the installation. You should contact Microsoft Product Support for help.

If your CD-ROM or floppy disk drive has problems reading the installation disks, you may have a problem with your drive. You may want to contact someone in your company's MIS or tech-support department to check the drive for you. Then, if you still receive this message and can't find the problem, call Microsoft Product Support for help in troubleshooting the problem.

Getting Started with Access 2002

After you've installed Access successfully, you are ready to learn the various ways to start the Access database program.

You can start Access in several ways:

✦ From the Windows Start menu

✦ From an Access shortcut icon

✦ From the Access icon in a folder

✦ From the Windows Explorer

Starting from the Windows Start menu

If you use Windows to install Access 2002, Windows automatically adds Access to the Start menu's Programs selection. A simple way to start Access is to click on the

Start menu, select the Programs submenu, and then select Microsoft Access. This starts Microsoft Access and displays the initial Access screen.

Starting from an Access shortcut icon

If you've gotten the hang of Windows, you've probably learned how valuable a *short-cut* can be. Figure 2-21 shows the Windows desktop that belongs to one of the authors.

Note that a copy of the Access 2002 icon is located on the desktop (right margin in the center). You can create a shortcut for Access by dragging it to the Windows desktop from the Office folder that contains Office 2002. You can start Access 2002 quickly by clicking on this icon.

Figure 2-21: The Windows desktop, showing a shortcut to Access

Starting Access from the Start menu

If you install Access as part of the Microsoft Office, you can quickly find the program by pressing the Start button and selecting Programs ➪ Microsoft Access 2002 — Figure 2-22 shows how you can run Access from the Start menu.

Tip

If you're using Windows 98, 98 SE, ME, or Windows 2000, you can create a desktop icon for Access by selecting the program name from the Start button, programs menu. Then, instead of clicking on the Access icon to run the program, simply press and hold the Ctrl key to highlight the Access program icon and drag a copy of the icon from the menu list (an arrow appears, which is a small box icon with a plus sign below it, as you move to the desktop), you can drop it on the desktop, automatically creating a new Access icon for use on the desktop.

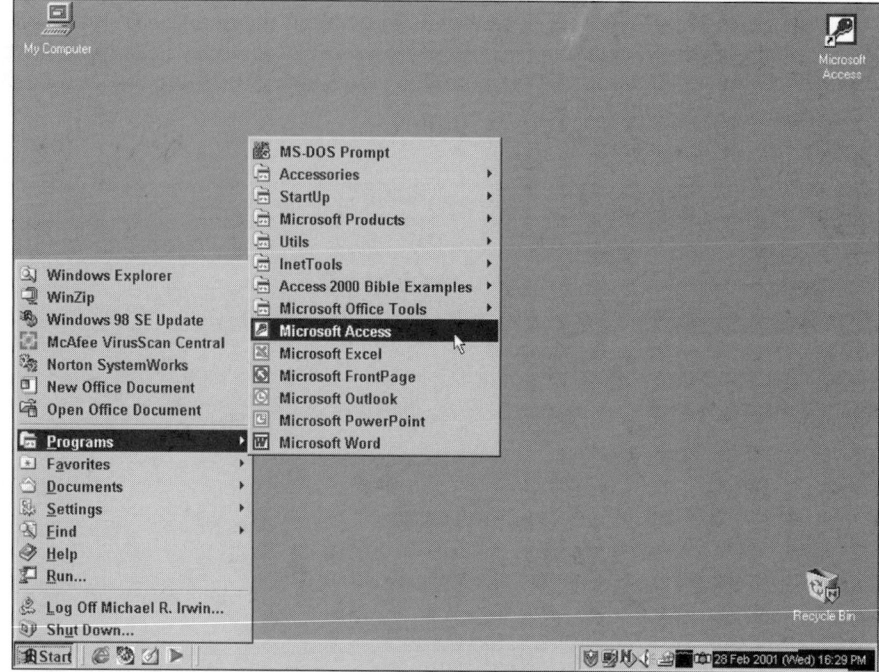

Figure 2-22: Starting Access from the Start menu

Starting from an Access icon created in the Office folder

You can also create an Access icon by displaying the folder that holds the Microsoft Office suite. If you purchased Access as part of Microsoft Office XP and installed it using the default settings, then one of your folders in Windows is probably the OfficeXP folder (or, as shown in Figure 2-23, C:\Program Files\Microsoft Office\ OfficeXP). Inside that folder you should find an icon to launch Access 2002 and each Office product. This is the actual Access program file, named MSACCESS.EXE — clicking on this icon launches Access 2002. You can start Access by double-clicking on this icon. You can create a Desktop shortcut icon that refers to this file by following these steps:

1. Right-click on the desktop.

2. Select New from the menu.

3. Select Shortcut from the menu.

4. Click the Browse button.

5. Navigate to the C:\Program Files\Microsoft Office\OfficeXP\ folder (or where to put the Office files).

6. Select the file name MSACCESS and click Open.

7. Click the Next button.

8. Click the Finish button.

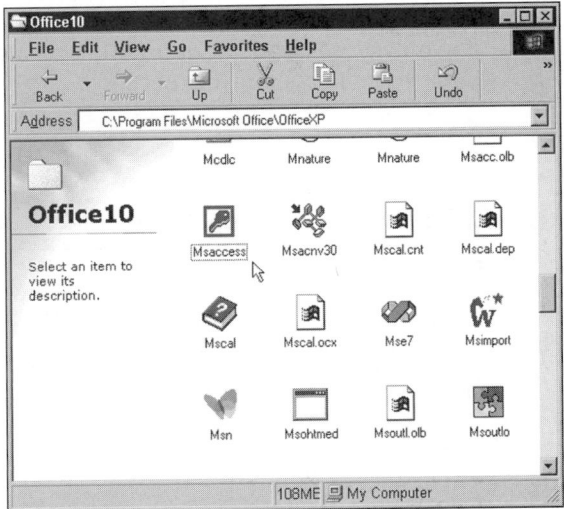

Figure 2-23: Starting Access by clicking on the Access program in the C:\Program Files\Microsoft Office\Office\ folder

Starting from Windows Explorer

You can also start Access from Windows Explorer (which has basically replaced Program Manager and File Manager) by selecting the MDB database file that you want to load. After you find the database file that you want to load, double-click on the filename. Windows then starts the version of Access that you last installed and defined in the System Registry and opens the database that you selected. If this isn't the correct version of Access, the database file may not run or you may be asked to convert it to the current version of Access.

If you are not sure which file you should choose, check to see that it has a proper file extension. Microsoft Access database files normally have the file extension MDB. Because Microsoft Access is a registered application in Windows, Access launches whenever you select a file with the .MDB extension. You may also find files with an .MDA or .MDE file extension; these also launch Access. MDA files are library files that typically contain add-ins or wizards. MDE files are Access databases that contain preprogrammed applications in which all the module source code has been removed. You can run the application, but you can't see any of the modules.

Note   If you already have Access running and you double-click on a file in Windows Explorer, another copy of Access starts, which loads the file that you selected. You may want to do this if you want more than one database open at a time. (Access doesn't let you open multiple databases at a time in only one occurrence of Access.)

Options for starting Access

You can customize how Access starts by adding options to the MSACCESS command line from the properties of a shortcut icon. For example, you can have Access open a database, execute a macro, or supply a user name or password — all automatically. Table 2-1 identifies the options available for starting Access.

Table 2-1
Command-Line Options for Starting Access

Option	Effect
<database>	Opens the specified database. Include a path if necessary.
/Excl	Opens the specified database for exclusive access. To open the database for shared access in a multiuser environment, omit this option.
/RO	Opens the specified database for read-only access.
/User <user name>	Starts Microsoft Access using the specified user name.
/Pwd <password>	Starts Microsoft Access using the specified password.
/Profile <user profile>	Starts Microsoft Access using the options in the specified user profile instead of the standard Windows Registry settings (created when you installed Microsoft Access). This replaces the /ini option used in previous versions of Microsoft Access to specify an initialization file. However, the /ini option will still work for user-defined .INI files from earlier versions of Microsoft Access.

Option	Effect
/Compact <target database>	Compacts the database specified before the /Compact option and then closes Microsoft Access. If you omit a target database name following the /Compact option, Access compacts the database using the original database name. To compact to a different name, specify a target database.
/Repair	Repairs the specified database and then closes Microsoft Access.
/Convert <target database>	Converts a database in an earlier version (2.0, 95, or 97) to a Microsoft Access 2000database with a new name and then closes Microsoft Access. Specify the source database before using the /Convert option
/X <macro>	Starts Microsoft Access and runs the specified macro. Another way to run a macro when you open a database is to use an AutoExec macro or the Database Startup properties.
/Cmd	Specifies that what follows on the command line is the value that will be returned by the Command function. This option must be the last option on the command line. You can use a semicolon (;) as an alternative to /Cmd.
/Nostartup	Starts Microsoft Access without displaying the Startup dialog box (the second dialog box you see when you start Microsoft Access).

Tip

To run a VBA procedure when you open a database, use the RunCode action in a command-line macro or the AutoExec macro, or use the Access 2002 Startup dialog box. You can also run a VBA procedure when you open a database by creating a form with a VBA procedure defined for its On Open event. Designate this as the startup form by using the right mouse button to click in the database window, click Startup, and then enter that form in the Display Form box.

For example, to have Access automatically execute a macro called MYMACRO, you enter the following parameter in the Shortcut Properties section of an Access shortcut. (You may find the command MSACCESS.EXE preceded by its path.)

MSACCESS.EXE /X MYMACRO

You can also use a special option that Access runs automatically when you first open a Microsoft Access database (you learn more about this in Part V). This is the *startup form*. You can use it to open certain tables or forms every time you enter a database or to perform complex processing, change the menus, change the title bar, hide the database window, or do just about anything you can think of.

Note   In previous versions of Access, you created a macro named Autoexec to do this. In Access 2002, the startup form is an easier way to run a program automatically when you open a database.

Tip   To prevent a startup form from running automatically, hold down Shift as you open the database.

Exiting Access

When you're finished using Access (or any application), you should always exit gracefully. It bears repeating: Simply turning off your system is not a good method and can cause problems. Windows and your other applications use many files while they are running — some of which you may not be aware of. Turning off your system can cause these files to not close properly, which can result in hard drive problems in the future.

Another reason for exiting gracefully is to ensure that all your data is saved before you exit the application. If you have spent quite a bit of time entering data and then you turn off your system — accidentally forgetting to save your work — all this unsaved data will be lost! Access does save records as you edit them — more specifically, Access saves it when you leave the record.

However, it is possible to corrupt your database by simply turning off the computer while Access and your database are open. At a minimum, you can lose all the work on an object that you're designing — or a report or form that you have not saved yet from the design window. If you simply turn off the machine, all that hard work is probably gone forever — Access can't attempt to save it if you don't close Access properly. Save yourself time and grief by exiting your applications the correct way.

You can exit Access in several safe ways:

✦ Click the Close button on the Title bar.

✦ Double-click the Control icon on the Access title bar.

✦ From the Access menu, select File ➪ Exit.

✦ Press Alt+F4.

✦ Display the taskbar and select Microsoft Access. Then right-click and select Close. You can use this method to close Access from within another application.

When you exit Access by using one of these methods, you may see a message displayed on-screen that prompts you to save any changes you may have made. You can select Yes to save the changes and exit Access. By selecting No, you exit Access without saving the changes you made. Selecting Cancel stops Access from closing, and you are returned to Access. You can also choose Help for more information on exiting Access.

Getting Help

After you know how to start Access, you may need some help in learning how to use the software. After you have started Access, you can choose from any of the Help options that are available. Some of these include

✦ Office Assistant

✦ Standard Windows Help (Contents, Index, and Find tabs)

✦ Screen Tips (What's This?)

✦ Web-based resources on the Microsoft Web site

✦ Northwinds database

✦ Solutions database

Office Assistant

In previous versions of Access, when you pressed F1 to request help, Access automatically displayed the Office Assistant; this has changed in Access 2002. The default action in Access now is to show standard help only. If you want to use the Office Assistant you need to turn it on by selecting Help ➪ Show the Office Assistant.

The default assistant is Clippit, your guide to help. Figure 2-24 shows F1 the robot. As you can see in the figure, the Office Assistant provides you with a blank text box where you can type a question. You can type a request in standard English (or whatever language you use), get helpful tips and hints, or select options to change the Office Assistant character. You can choose from several different assistants, including Clippit, The Dot, F1 the robot, the Office Logo, Links, Rocky the dog, Mother Nature, and others.

After you type a question, the Assistant displays a series of possible solutions that you can select to review. Figure 2-25 shows the answers to the question "How do I secure a database table?"

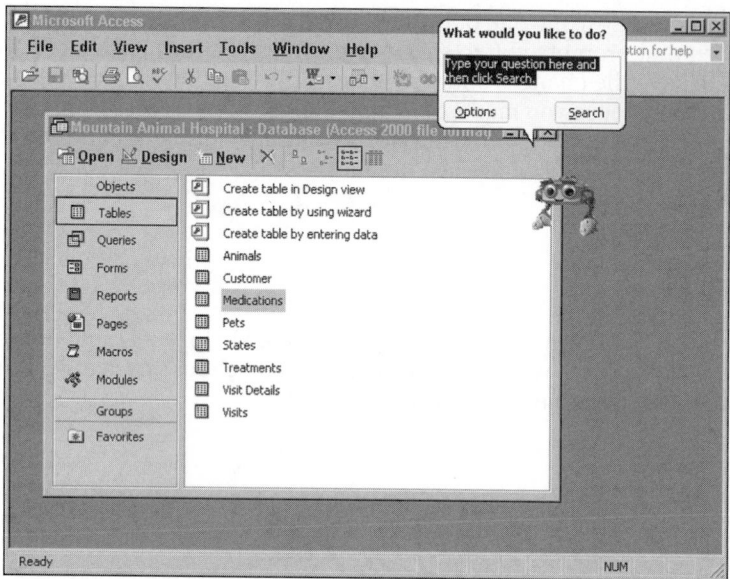

Figure 2-24: The Office Assistant. You can type a question in plain English to get assistance. In this case the author typed, "How do I secure a database table?"

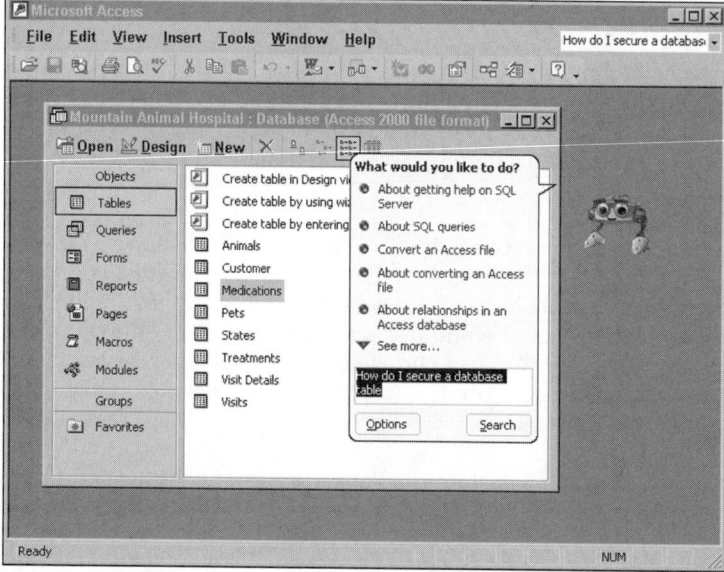

Figure 2-25: The Office Assistant responding with possible solutions to your question

Tip Right-click on the Assistant and select Animate. You are then treated to an amazing show. Each character comes with between 10 and 30 different shows.

If you have access to the Microsoft Web site, you can use a variety of other characters in the Office pages.

Tip You can turn the Office Assistant off by selecting Options from the Assistant menu or right-click and select Options. (Make sure the Options tab is active and de-select the Use the Office Assistant check box.) After the assistant is deactivated, you can reactivate it by following the same steps you used to turn it on. If you select Help ➪ Hide the Office Assistant, it will not turn it off, simply hide it. The next time you call help, it will appear.

Using the new Menu bar Help

Access 2002 and Office XP give you a new way to request Help—simply type your question in English in the Help text box on the right side of the menu bar and press Enter. Figure 2-26 shows a question that has been typed in the Help text box on the right side of the menu bar.

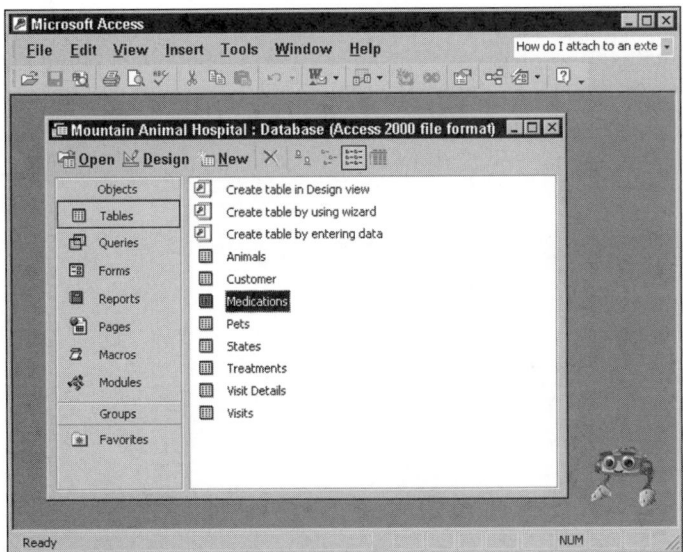

Figure 2-26: Typing a question in the Help menu bar text box

Help responds with several possible answers, as shown in Figure 2-27, for the question "How do I attach to an external database?"

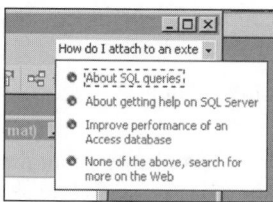

Figure 2-27: The possible answers to the question entered in the Help text box on the menu bar

Standard Help

With the Office Assistant turned off (default value), you are presented with Standard Windows Help when you press the F1 key or select Help ➪ Microsoft Access Help from the Access menu. When you press F1 with the assistant turned off, Access presents you with a tabbed dialog box (as shown in Figure 2-28). This dialog box provides several ways to help you get started using Access. You have three options to choose from (tabs across the top of the box):

✦ **Contents.** As shown in Figure 2-28, the Table of Contents lists major topics grouped by task. When you select a topic, a menu of subtopics appears and leads you to various Help screens.

✦ **Answer Wizard.** (The default tab) Enables you to type a question into an area and then evaluates the words you type and displays a list of matching Help topics. This is like using the Office Assistant — but not as annoying.

✦ **Index.** This displays an alphabetical list of Help topics. Type the first few letters of the Help topic that you're searching for or scroll through the list.

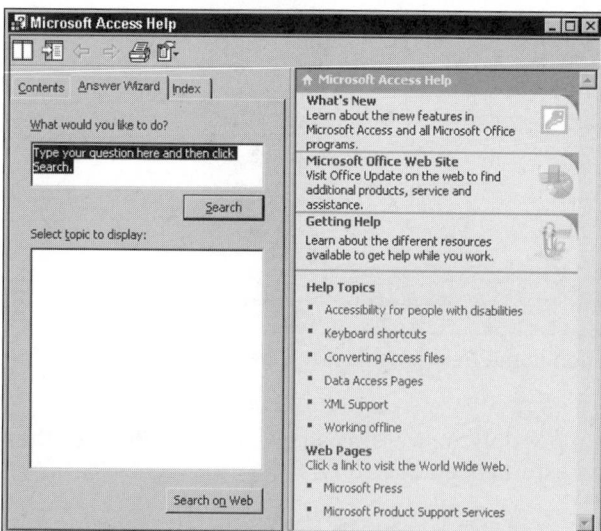

Figure 2-28: The Access 2002 Help Topics dialog box. The Contents tab is selected and you are shown a series of topics to select from.

Screen Tips (What's This?)

Screen Tips are a type of help found in all Microsoft Office products. They give you short explanations of tasks in the various products. They are text-only explanations and are generally displayed in a small rectangle. Although standard toolbar ToolTips display only a word or two, Screen Tips display a paragraph. When you select Help ⇨ What's This?, the mouse pointer changes to an arrow with a question mark. You can then click on various parts of an Access screen and receive a short explanation of the task or function that you clicked on. You can also press Shift+F1 for the same effect. For example, if you press Shift+F1 and then click on the Tables tab in the Database window, you see a Screen Tip explaining what you can do with a table, as shown in Figure 2-29.

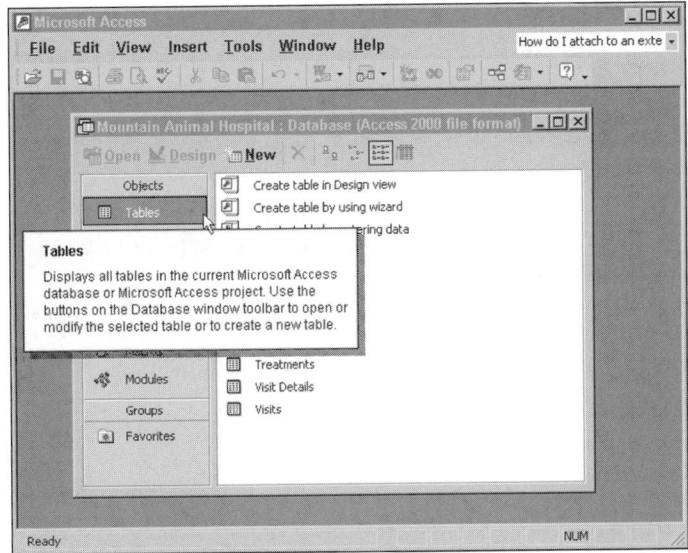

Figure 2-29: An Access 2002 Screen Tip. You activate this by pressing Shift+F1 and clicking on the Tables tab in the Database window.

Tip   You can create your own Screen Tips in your applications, using the same techniques that create standard Access 2002 Help.

Web-based resources on the Microsoft Web site

The Access Help menu contains a group of options to give you access to the Microsoft Web site and many free resources to help you use Microsoft products. All the options launch the Microsoft Internet Explorer Web browser and take you to the appropriate page on the Microsoft Web site. This page includes Free Stuff, Product News, the Access Developer Forum, FAQs (Frequently Asked Questions), and Online

Support. The options at the bottom also let you go to the Office Home Page, send Feedback to Microsoft, go to a list of the best Web sites, search the Web, take a tutorial about using the Web, and go to the general Microsoft Home Page.

Sample databases

You should be aware of one more place you can get help. The Office Samples directory contains two special databases: Northwind.MDB (the Northwinds example file used throughout the Access documentation) and NorthwindCS.ADP (the Northwinds example file used for Client/Server and Data Access pages). The objects in these two databases can be worked with to see how things work in Access 2002.

Help in Access is always a keystroke away. You can get help in many easy ways:

✦ Press the F1 key to get the Assistant (if it's active), and then ask a question or select a Help suggestion.

✦ Press Shift+F1 or choose Help ➪ What's This? on the menu to get Screen Tips help.

✦ Select Help from the Access menu and then choose Microsoft Access Help (if the Office Assistant is deactivated) to get standard help with three tabs — Contents, Answer Wizard, or Index.

✦ Type a question into the new Help text box (on the right side of the menu bar.

Help is available for every aspect of Access — commands, menus, macros, Access terms and concepts, and even programming topics.

✦   ✦   ✦

A Hands-on Tour of Access 2002

✦ ✦ ✦ ✦

In This Chapter

Navigating the screen by using the mouse, the keyboard, or a combination of the two

Surveying the basic components of the Access screen

Touring Access 2002, including opening a database, using a table, displaying a form, creating and using a query, and displaying a report

✦ ✦ ✦ ✦

Throughout this book, we discuss many Access windows and dialog boxes, and we use many specific terms to describe them. So it's a good idea to become familiar with these terms. If you used another database software package before Access, you need to translate the terms that you already know into the words that Microsoft Access uses to refer to the same task or action.

Touring the Access Window

The first stop on our tour of Access is a look at the two major windows in Access and how to navigate them by using the mouse and the keyboard.

Using the mouse and the keyboard

You can navigate the Access screen by using the mouse, the keyboard, or a combination of both. The best way to get around in Access is by using a mouse or another pointing device. The keyboard is useful for entering data and for moving around the various data-entry areas. You won't be productive, however, if you use only the keyboard when designing new forms, queries, or reports.

In this book, you learn to complete tasks by using both the keyboard and the mouse. In most cases, using the mouse is preferable.

The Access window

When you first open Access, you see the *Access window* showing a title bar with the Microsoft Access caption and its menu bar and toolbar. The Access window is the center of activity for everything that you can do in Access. From this window, you can open many other windows simultaneously; each window displays a different view of your data. Figure 3-1 shows the Access window with a Database window open. The title bar of the Database window displays the title of the database followed by the word *Database*.

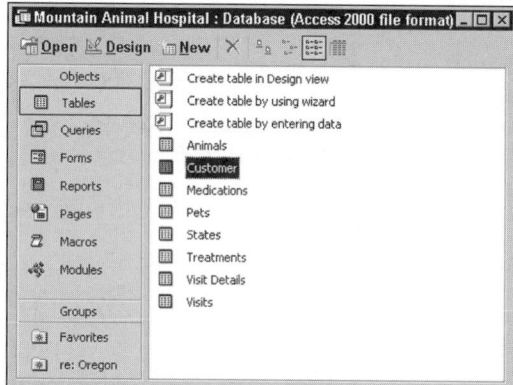

Figure 3-1: The Microsoft Access window with the Mountain Animal Hospital Database window open

Here are some Access window features that you should be familiar with:

✦ **Title bar.** You can tell which program is currently active by the name of the program that you see displayed on the title bar. The title bar displays the name Microsoft Access, the Control menu, and the Minimize, Restore/Maximize, and Close buttons. The title bar displays the text

Options That Change How Access Looks

You may notice when following along in this book that some of your screens look slightly different from the screen pictures in the book. Microsoft Access lets you or your company decide how Access works and how the screens look. You can display or hide various toolbars by right-clicking any of the toolbars or the toolbar area and then selecting or deselecting the toolbar that you want to view or hide.

You may also notice the New Object shortcuts in the Database window. These appear before the other database objects, such as table, form, or report names. New Object shortcuts appear with an Access gold and red key icon in front of them, along with descriptive text, such as Create table in Design view, as shown in Figure 3-1. You can turn this feature off by clicking Tools ⇨ Options and deselecting New object shortcuts from the View tab.

'Microsoft Access' by default. When you are viewing a table, form, or other object, the title bar also displays the name of the object in brackets and the object type if the window is maximized; for example, Microsoft Access — [Pets: Table].

Tip If you are writing a custom application, you may not want the user to see the Access text. You can change the title bar display by entering a different application title in the Startup dialog box, which you can display by right-clicking in the gray area of the Database window and selecting Startup.

✦ **Control menu button.** This button is found in the upper-left corner of the title bar. When you click this button, a menu appears that lets you perform certain tasks, including moving, sizing, minimizing, or closing the current application window. When you double-click the Control button, you automatically exit the application.

✦ **Minimize button.** This is the first of a set of three buttons on the right side of the title bar; it shows a dash at the bottom of the box. Clicking this button reduces Access to an icon on the Windows taskbar. Access continues to run, and you can redisplay it by clicking the icon on the taskbar.

✦ **Restore/Maximize.** This middle button takes on two looks: Two overlapping boxes when you maximize the window or a square with a dark top when you restore the window to its previous size.

✦ **Close button.** This right-most button has an X on it and closes Access when you click it.

✦ **Menu bar.** The menu bar contains commands. When you click a name, a list drops down, offering a selection of commands. Depending on what you are working on, the items on the menu bar and the choices found on each menu vary. The pictures on the menus correspond to pictures on the toolbar. In Access, you can completely customize the menu bars and toolbars.

✦ **Toolbar.** The toolbar is a group of picture buttons just below the menu bar; it provides shortcuts for running commands. The buttons on the toolbar vary depending on what you are working on. You can resize and move the toolbar by clicking between buttons and moving it around the screen. You can also select View ⇨ Toolbars to show, hide, define new, or customize different toolbars; you can use the same command to select large or small buttons, turn off tooltips, and even display monochrome buttons.

✦ **Status bar.** The left side of the status bar, at the bottom of the window, displays helpful information about what you are currently doing. In Figure 3-1, the status bar simply says Ready. The right side of the status bar tells you whether certain keyboard settings are active. For example, if you have the Caps Lock feature turned on, the word *CAPS* appears in the status bar.

✦ **Database window.** This window appears whenever a database is open; it is the control center of your database. You use the Database window to open the

Understanding What an Access Database Is

Access creates a single container that is used to work with your information. This container, called an Access database, contains all the data, information, and all the related tools — forms, reports, queries, macros, and code modules. All these objects, parts of the database, are stored in a single file that usually has the file name extension of **MDB** — although other extensions are possible (more on this later). When you open an Access database you open a single container that has object button bar buttons (like tabs) along the left side of the container that, when pressed, open each section — revealing the objects for that object bar button. Tables are separated from forms and reports separated from queries, and on and on. Figure 3-1 and 3-2 show the database container (or window opened).

objects within a database, including tables, queries, forms, reports, macros, and modules.

Tip   You can change the words on the title bar in the Startup dialog box. You display this by selecting Tools ⇨ Startup ⇨ Application Title from the Database window.

The Database window

The name of the open database always displays on the title bar of the Database window. In Figure 3-1, for example, you see the *Mountain Animal Hospital: Database (Access 2000 file format)* on the title bar. The Mountain Animal Hospital database is on the CD-ROM that comes with this book; it contains all the tables, forms, and other objects demonstrated in this book.

Note   The Database window consists of three basic parts: A set of seven object buttons in a vertical row on the left side, a set of eight toolbar buttons along the top of the window, and a list of object names in the right pane.

✦ **Object buttons.** These buttons are located in a vertical row along the left side of the Database window. Using these buttons, you can select the type of object you want to work with. For example, selecting the Form button displays a list of forms created for that database. Selecting this button also lets you create a new form or redesign an existing one.

✦ **Toolbar buttons.** You use the toolbar buttons, which are located along the top of the Database window, to change a database object in a different window or view. These buttons let you create, open, or design a database object and view certain details about those database objects.

✦ **Object list.** This list displays existing objects for the database object that you select. You can choose a name from the list to display or redesign the object. You can also select what type of view you want for these objects. For example, you can view the details about your database objects, such as description, date modified, date created, and type.

You can change the view of the objects in the Object list by selecting View from the Access window menu bar or by using the buttons on top of the database window (the last four buttons on the right side of the database window). You have four choices:

- ✦ **Large Icons.** Displays a large icon with the object type and the object name

- ✦ **Small Icons.** Displays a small icon with the object type and the object name

- ✦ **List.** The default view, as shown in Figure 3-1

- ✦ **Details.** Lists the object name, description, date last modified and date created, and type (see Figure 3-2)

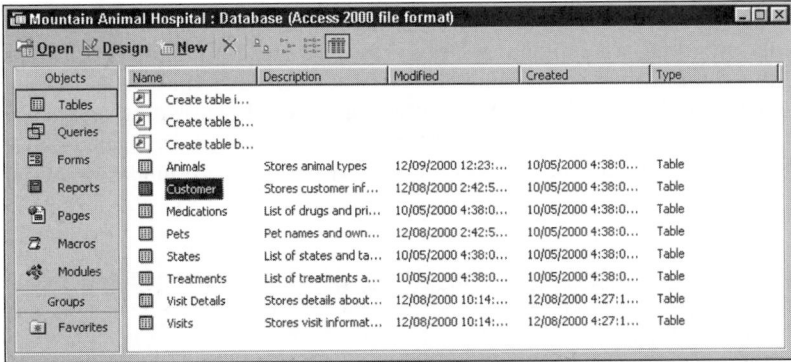

Figure 3-2: The Microsoft Access Database window in Details view showing (1) the list of objects — in this case, tables, (2) their description, assigned to the Properties of the table, (3) the date modified, and (4) the date created

As Figure 3-2 shows, Details view displays more information about each object. The most important information is the date last modified. If you are trying to maintain different versions of a database, this is a great way to see which database contains your latest version. Of course, you can also use the Briefcase replication features in Access 2002 to keep multiple databases synchronized.

You can click the column headers in the Database window and re-sort the data by the value in the column. Each time you click on a column, you change the order of the sort. For example, clicking on the Name column sorts the data by Name in ascending order. Clicking the Name column again sorts the data by Name in descending order. You can sort the details of the Database window objects by any of the columns. You can change a column's width by placing your mouse pointer on the divider between column names and then dragging it to the right or the left. Drag to the right to make a column wider and drag to the left to make the column narrower.

Tip   You can enter a description for an object by right-clicking on the object name and then selecting Properties or selecting View ⇨ Properties from the Access Menu bar. You can enter a long description for the object or you can hide the object.

Design windows

The Database window is just one of several windows that you use in Access. Several other commonly used windows are the *object design windows*, which let you design objects, such as tables, queries, forms, reports, pages, macros, and modules, and the windows that enable you to view or edit your data in datasheets, forms, and report previews.

Figure 3-3 shows the Database window minimized in the bottom-left corner of the Access window, along with the Form Design window (titled Animals: Form, located in the center right of the screen) and several other windows that assist in the design of forms and reports. These windows are generally known as *design windows*. The Form window is shown with several fields displayed. The form you see in the figure, Animals, can be used for displaying information about each pet in the Pets table.

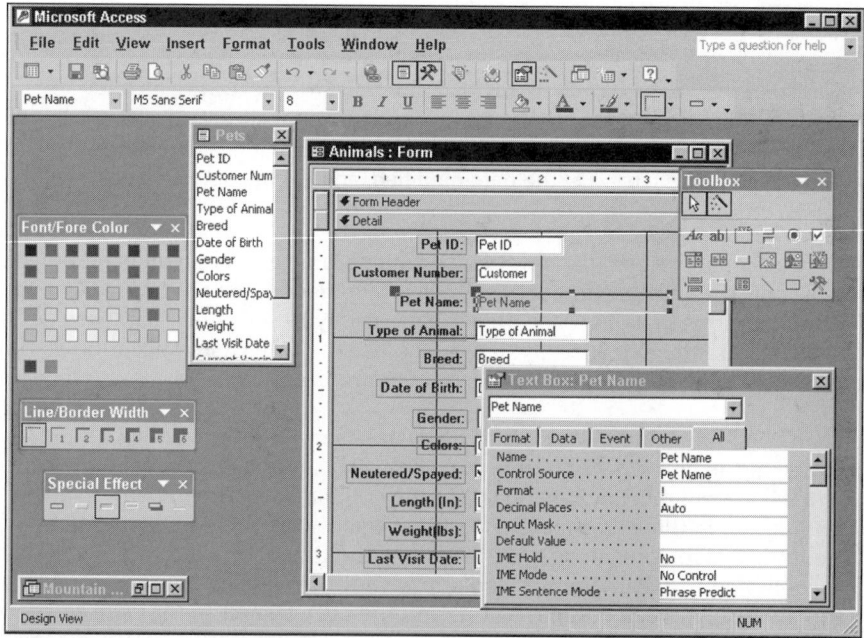

Figure 3-3: Several design windows opened in Microsoft Access, which you can use to select objects to work with in the actual Form Design window

Figure 3-3 displays the most common design windows (start from the top left and go clockwise) – the Font/Fore Color window, the field list (titled Pets), the Form Design window (titled Animals: Form), the Toolbox, the Properties window (titled Text Box: Pet Name), the Database window (titled Mountain ...), the Special Effect window, and the Line/Border Width window. Because the Form window is active, the title bar is a darker color than the other windows.

Access 2002 features tear-off windows on the Form Design and Formatting toolbars. After you display a window from the toolbar, you can drag it anywhere on the desktop by using its title bar and then you can resize it. In fact, Figure 3-3 shows the Toolbox, Special Effect, and Line/Border Width windows as they appear when resized from their default sizes. You can use several design windows that are open at the same time to select objects to work with in the actual Form Design window. For instance, you can select an object to place on the form design surface from the toolbox or change the font color by choosing a color in the Font/Fore Color window.

 Tip   After you have resized a window, it retains its sizing until the next time you re-size it. You can close and open the window, like the Toolbox window, and it retains its last size setting.

The Toolbox

Figure 3-3 displays the Toolbox in the top-right portion of the screen. You can use the Toolbox to design a form or report. The Toolbox is similar to a toolbar, but the Toolbox is initially arranged vertically and can be moved around. The Toolbox contains toggle buttons that you can select to add objects to a form or report, such as labels, text boxes, option group boxes, and so on — as shown in Figure 3-3. You can move the Toolbox or close it when you don't need it. You can also resize it by clicking and dragging its border. You can also anchor it with other toolbars by dragging it to an edge of the screen.

Color, Special Effect, and Border windows

The *Font/Fore Color window* is shown on the left side of Figure 3-3. You can also see a background (Fill/Back) color window and a border (Line/Border) color window, which can be dragged from the Form/Report Formatting toolbar and opened in their own windows. Also in the figure are the Special Effect and Line/Border Width windows.

You use the Font/Fore Color, Fill/Back Color, and Line/Border Color windows to change the colors of objects, such as text (foreground), background, and borders of a control. The Line/Border Width window allows you to change the thickness of lines, rectangles, and borders. You use the Special Effect window to give the objects a three-dimensional look (sunken or raised, for example), add a shadow, or add the chiseled look of Windows. As with the Toolbox, many of these palettes are resizable. The Border Width window lets you change the thickness of lines, rectangles, and control borders.

The Field List window

The *Field List* window (titled Pets and located at the top and center left in Figure 3-3) displays a list of fields from the currently open table or query dynaset. You use Field List windows in Query Design, Form Design, and Report Design windows. You select fields from this window by clicking on them and then dragging the fields onto a query, form, or report. You can select fields individually, or you can select ranges or groups of fields to drag onto the form by using the Ctrl key or Shift key. If you first select a control type in the Toolbox and then drag a field from the Field List, a control is created (using the selected control type) that is automatically bound to the data field in the Field List.

The Property window

In a form or report, each field (called a *control* in Access) has *properties* that further define the characteristics of the control. The form or report and sections of the form or report also have properties. In the lower-right area of Figure 3-3, you see a Property window displaying some of the properties for a form. Usually, a Property window displays only a portion of the properties available for a specific control, so a tabbed dialog box and a vertical scrollbar in the window let you scroll through the complete list. You can also resize a Property window and move it around the screen.

Having many windows open at once and resizing and rearranging them on-screen helps you use information productively as you create objects (such as forms and reports) and use Access's features. Each of the windows is described in detail in their appropriate chapters in this book.

A Simple Access Session

Your goal for this session is to open an existing database and then perform such simple steps as opening and navigating through a table, using an existing query, creating a simple query using the query design window, displaying and using a form, and displaying and using a report. These actions will be preformed using the Mountain Animal Hospital database that came with this book (Mountain Animal Hospital.MDB).

After you become familiar with the two main Access window types — the Database window and the Design windows — you can go through a simple Access session even before you know much about Access. Before proceeding, make sure that you are ready to follow along on your own computer. Your computer should be on, and Access should be installed.

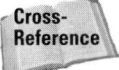

Cross-Reference   Chapter 2 covers installing and starting Access in detail.

If you have not done so already, perform these steps to get ready for this session:

1. Start your computer and Windows 95/98/ME or Windows 2000.

2. Start Access 2002 from the Start menu or double-click the Access 2002 icon or shortcut. (See Chapter 2 if you need more help starting Access.) Access begins with a blank screen except for the New File dialog box on the right side, as shown in Figure 3-4. You can turn the New File dialog box off by de-selecting the check box at the bottom of the dialog box titled "Show at startup."

3. Remove the New File dialog box by clicking the Close button on the right side of the title bar. This leaves Access 2002 running without a database open.

4. If the Restore/Maximize button (middle button on right side of title bar) in the title bar shows two rectangles, Access is already maximized, and you can go on to the next section. If only one square is visible, click the Restore/Maximize button to maximize the Access screen. Your screen should look like the one shown in Figure 3-4.

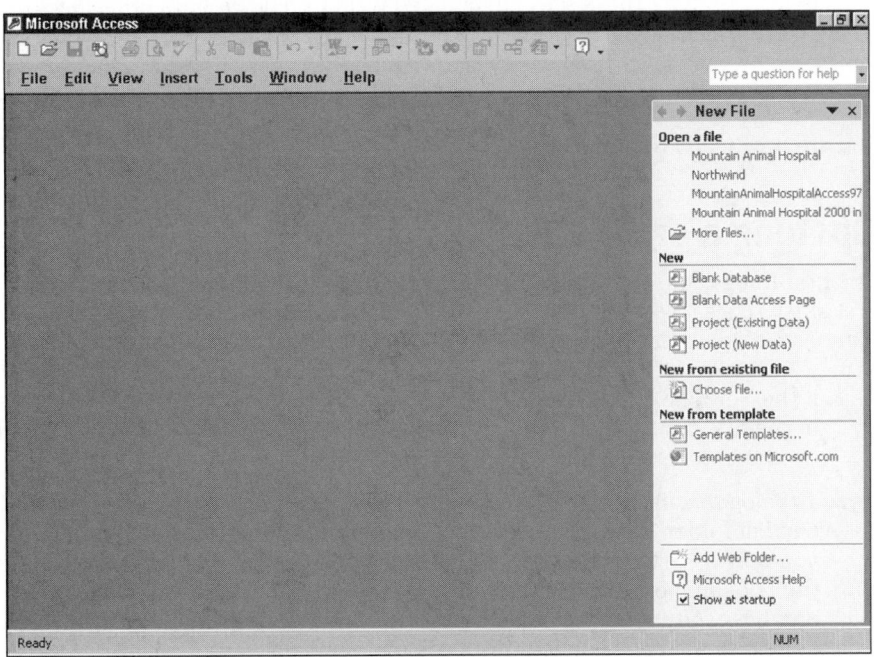

Figure 3-4: The initial Access window as it appears when first opened, showing the New File dialog box along the right side of the window

The CD-ROM at the Back of This Book

At the back of this book is a CD-ROM containing several database files that you use throughout this book, as well as some other files that you can use for practicing importing other file types (see Chapter 22 for more information) and a variety of other goodies. To use this CD-ROM, follow the directions at the back of the book on the pages opposite the CD-ROM envelope. The two main database files used in this book are:

Mountain Animal Hospital.MDB: A database that contains all the tables, queries, forms, reports, and macros used in this book.

Mountain Animal Start.MDB: A file that contains only tables and one Query.

Beginning with Chapter 5, you can use the Mountain Start database file to create your own queries, forms, and reports. You can use the Mountain Animal Hospital database file to see how the final application is created and used.

If you haven't yet used this book's CD-ROM, now is a good time to take it out and run the setup in order to copy the files to the Access folder or another folder (perhaps named Bible2002) on your hard drive. Updates to this CD are periodically posted on either of two Official Access 2002 Bible Web sites, which are run by the authors—Cary Prague's at `http://www.databasecreations.com/accessbible2002`. Michael Irwin's Web site is located at `http://dbintegrators.com/accessbible2002` (or simply `dbintegrators.com/accessbible2002`) These sites are updated with any known bugs or reader suggestions and contain news about Microsoft Access and many free goodies to download.

You are now ready to move on.

Opening a database

The first thing to do is to open the Mountain Animal Hospital database. When you first start Access, you can open an existing database, or you can create a new database, data access page, or project. To open the database, follow these steps:

1. If the New File dialog box is open, close it by clicking on the Close button (X) in the title bar of the New File window. After it's closed, Select File ⇨ Open from the Access menu.

2. A dialog box like the one in Figure 3-5 lists all the databases available in the current folder. If you don't see the Mountain Animal Hospital database listed, you may have to change the folder that Access is looking in. To do so, go to the Look in: box and select the drive and folder in which you stored this database. After you tell Access where to find the database, the name should appear in the File List window of the dialog box.

3. Click Mountain Animal Hospital.MDB and click Open.

Access opens the database. You should find Mountain Animal Hospital at the top of the Database window.

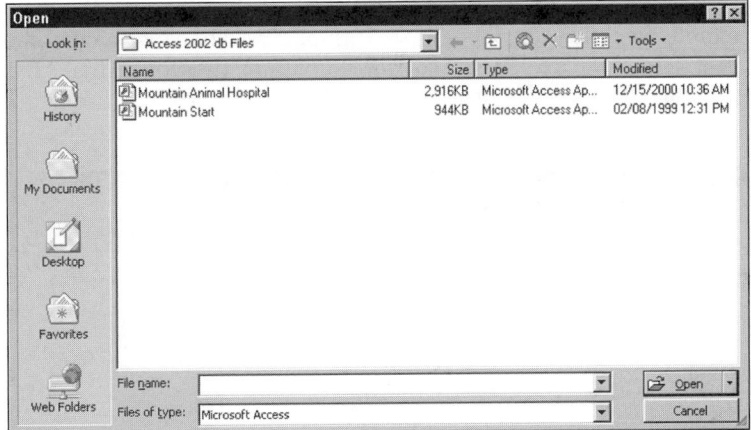

Figure 3-5: The Open dialog box showing two database files in the folder—Mountain Animal Hospital and Mountain Start. You need to use the Mountain Animal Hospital database.

Opening a table

In this session, you open the Pets table to view some of the data stored in the Mountain Animal Hospital database. This table contains information about the pets that are treated at the hospital, including the pet number, customer identification (instead of a number it shows the actual customer name, which you can find by using a lookup function attached to the field), type of animal, pet name, breed, gender, height, weight, and so on. Follow these steps to open the Pets table:

1. Click the Tables button in the Database window if it isn't already selected.

2. Select the Pets table.

3. Select the Open toolbar button in the top part of the Database window.

4. Maximize the window by clicking the Maximize button in the title bar at the top-right of the window.

Access opens the Pets table in Datasheet view, as shown in Figure 3-6. Notice that the displayed information is shown in column and row format. Each column is a single field and each row is a single record. If you look down any given column you can see that each cell holds the same type of information—thus, it's a field. In contrast, each row holds a collection of all the fields with information about one specific pet—thus, it's a record. The top row holds the Field Names for each column—Pet ID, Customer Number, Pet Name, etc.The Pets table contains additional fields beyond those shown in Figure 3-6. You can see the other fields by moving the horizontal scroll bar on the bottom right of the Datasheet (display of records).

You can move the vertical scroll bar up and down to scroll through the other records in the table. Because this table deals with pets and because a customer may own several pets, you can see that the table contains two Johnathan Adams records (one for Patty the pig, the other for Rising Sun the horse).

Pet ID	Customer Number	Pet Name	Type of Animal	Breed	Date of Birth	Gender	Color
AC001-01	All Creatures	Bobo	RABBIT	Long Ear	Apr 96	M	Brown/Black/Whi
AC001-02	All Creatures	Presto Chango	LIZARD	Chameleon	May 95	F	Green
AC001-03	All Creatures	Stinky	SKUNK		Aug 99	M	Black/White
AC001-04	All Creatures	Fido	DOG	German Shepherd	Jun 95	M	Brown
AD001-01	Johnathan Adams	Patty	PIG	Potbelly	Feb 99	F	Brown
AD001-02	Johnathan Adams	Rising Sun	HORSE	Palomino	Apr 97	M	Black/White
AD002-01	William Adams	Dee Dee	DOG	Mixed	Feb 99	F	White/Grey/Brown
AK001-01	Animal Kingdom	Margo	SQUIRREL	Gray	Mar 99	F	Tan
AK001-02	Animal Kingdom	Tom	CAT	Tabby	Feb 96	M	Tan/White
AK001-03	Animal Kingdom	Jerry	RAT	Hooded	Feb 98	M	Brown
BA001-01	Borderville Aquarium	Swimmy	DOLPHIN	Bottlenose	Jul 96	F	Grey
BA001-03	Borderville Aquarium	Daffy	DUCK	Mallard	Sep 99	M	Black
BA001-05	Borderville Aquarium	Jake	DOLPHIN	Bottlenose	Apr 92	M	Grey
BR001-01	Stephen Brown	Suzie	DOG	Mixed	Jan 00	M	Brown
BR002-01	James Brown	John Boy	DOG	Mixed	Apr 98	M	Brown/Grey
EP001-01	Exotic Pets	Mikos	WOLF	Timber	Nov 97	M	Grey
EP001-02	Exotic Pets	Museum Rm 7	DINOSAUR	Stegosauras		U	Brown
GR001-01	George Green	Adam	FROG	Bullfrog	Apr 99	M	Green
GR001-02	George Green	Killer	SNAKE	Ball Python	Mar 97	F	Brown/White/Gree
GR001-03	George Green	Slither	SNAKE	Boa Constrictor	May 98	M	Brown/Grey
GR001-04	George Green	Sammie	SNAKE	Boa Constrictor	May 99	F	Brown/Grey
GR002-01	Wanda Greenfield	Sammie Girl	DOG	Spitz	May 97	F	White
IR001-01	Petra Irish	D.C.	CAT	Tabby	Apr 99	F	White/Brown/Grey
IR001-02	Petra Irish	Jimeny	CAT	Siamese	Mar 97	M	White/Grey/Black
IR001-03	Petra Irish	Shadow	CAT	Long Hair	Mar 96	M	White/Grey
IR001-04	Petra Irish	Romeo	CAT	Mouser	Oct 99	F	Black/Grey
IR001-05	Petra Irish	Ceasar	CAT	Domestic	Oct 99	M	Grey
IR001-06	Petra Irish	Jameo	CAT	Tabby	Oct 99	F	Black/Grey
IR001-07	Petra Irish	Tigger	CAT	Barn	Feb 98	M	Black/Grey/white
JO001-01	Michael Johnson	Rover	DOG	Terrier	Jun 93	M	Grey

Record: 1 of 52

Pet ID is entered as AA###-## (Customer Number-Sequence Number)

Figure 3-6: The Pets table opened and maximized in Datasheet view. The figure only shows a portion of the records and fields.

Tip   You can also open a table by double-clicking the table name in the Database window or by right-clicking the table name and clicking Open from the shortcut menu.

You can open a table in Datasheet view or you can open a table in Design view to change its design structure. To do so, click the table to select it and then click the Design button You can also press the New button, and the New Table dialog box opens, where you can create a new table using either a Wizard or Design view.

Displaying and moving around in a datasheet

As shown in Figure 3-6, when you open the Pets table, you see a worksheet-like view called *Datasheet view*. This datasheet displays all of the data stored in the Pets table. The data is displayed in column-and-row format. You can move around the datasheet to view the different types of data that is stored. Table 3-1 lists the

The Difference Between an Access Database and Table

An *Access database* is simply the complete container of all parts of a database—the tables, queries, forms, reports, modules, macros, and data access pages (pointers to the Web HTML documents).

In contrast, *tables* are the actual containers where the related information is stored. For example, in the Mountain Animal Hospital database Customer information is stored in one table, and Pets information is stored in another table. Each table is composed of records and fields. For spreadsheet users, the fields are simply the column headings in a worksheet. The cells below these headings always contain the same type of information—for example, if a field is named Customer Name, all the information stored in each cell of this column will always be a Customer's name. The records are the rows of a worksheet. Each row is composed of all the fields—that is, one row contains one of each field. If you have a table with three fields—(1) Customer Name, (2) Address, and (3) Telephone Number, each record contains all three of these fields. Each record normally contains information about one customer only. Thus, one row holds all information for Michael Irwin, while another row holds all information for Cary Prague (each row represents a single record). This is a very simplistic view of tables and is covered more in-depth in later chapters.

keyboard commands used to move around the table window. You can also use the mouse to navigate throughout the table. Simply click any cell to move the cursor to that cell. You can also use the mouse to move the scroll bars to navigate around the table.

If you look closely at the table displayed in Figure 3-6, you see the gray frame on the left side of the datasheet. This is the *record selector column*. The column shown in Figure 3-6 displays a right-pointing triangle beside the first record of the table, indicating that it is the selected record. If you use the down arrow to move down through the records you will observe that the pointer follows to the new row where you have moved. This column can be used to select a series of records that you want to take some action on, such as deleting them.

Caution Be very careful when using the record selector column to select records. You may accidentally press the Delete key with several records highlighted, and if you then press YES to delete, these records are deleted forever—and you can't reverse this action.

You can also move through the records in a table with the mouse by using the Navigation buttons found in the bottom-left corner of the Datasheet window. (These are sometimes called *VCR buttons*, although the official name is *navigation buttons*.) The arrows located at the left and right ends with a vertical line next to them move you to the first or last record of the table. The two arrows to the inside of the outer two arrows move you to the preceding or the next record. The right-pointing arrow with the asterisk moves you to a new record area.

Table 3-1
Keyboard Techniques for Moving Around the Window

Keyboard Keys	Where It Moves
Left- (←) and right-arrow (→)	Left or right one column at a time
Up- (↑) and down-arrow (↓)	Up or down one row at a time
PgUp and PgDn	Up or down one screen at a time
Ctrl+PgUp and Ctrl+PgDn	Left or right one screen at a time
Home	To the first column of the row the insertion point is in
End	To the last column of the row the insertion point is in
Tab	Right one column at a time
Shift+Tab	Left one column at a time
Ctrl+Home	To the first column of the first record in the table
Ctrl+End	To the last column of the last record in the table

Between these arrows is a rectangle that displays the current record number. The total number of records displays to the right of the arrows. If you know which record you want to move to, you can get there quickly by clicking the mouse on the record number (or by pressing F5), typing the number of the record that you want to move to, and pressing Enter.

Tip   You can also use the GoTo command (found on the Edit menu) to go to the First, Last, Next, Previous, or New record.

Caution   When in Datasheet view, you can change the information in records, delete records, or even add records to the table. Datasheet view provides live access to the information being stored in the Pets table. If you make changes, they are permanent — so you should be careful when working with information in Datasheets.

Drilling down into the records of the Datasheet.

In the column to the right of the gray Record Selector you find a column of plus signs beside each record. Clicking on this plus sign opens a "mini" view of another table — the Visits table. This table is related or associated with each pet in the Pets table. Each pet can visit the vet many times, and for each visit, a single record is created in the Visits table.

If you click the plus sign (+) in the second column of the fifth record (Johnathan Adams's pig named Patty), that record expands to show you a "mini" datasheet of all records from the Visits table that are associated with Patty the pig. Figure 3-7 shows Patty's record expanded to show all her Visits records. When you expand a record, the plus symbol changes to a minus sign.

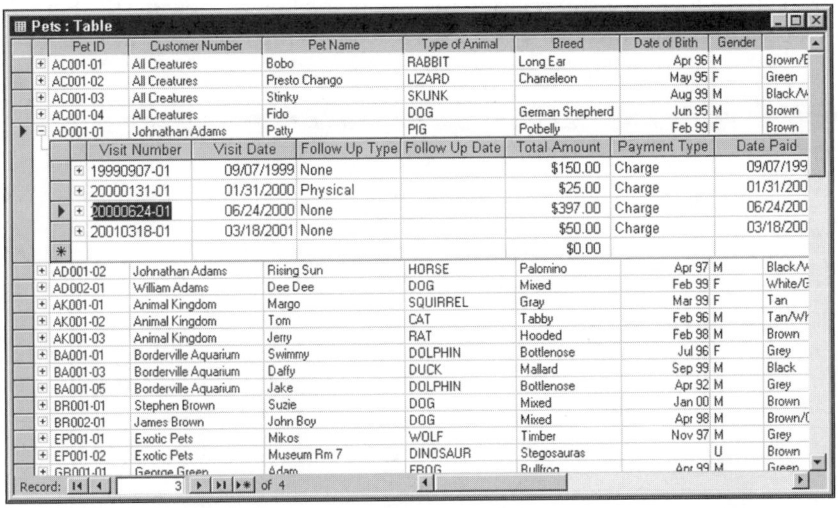

Figure 3-7: The Pets table opened to Patty the pig's record expanded to show all her Visits records

Notice that the "mini" datasheet in Figure 3-7 shows four visit records for this animal. The records also have plus signs next to them, and the records can be further expanded to display all Visits Detail records associated with each visit. Remember that the pet may visit the vet and require several treatments — thus, several Visits Detail records may be associated with each visit.

This process of going deeper and deeper into the records associated with a specific record is known as *drilling down* through the data.

You can close any sub view by simply clicking on the drill down/up button (a negative sign when expanded).

Viewing a table design

After you're familiar with what kind of information is contained in the Pets table and how to navigate around the datasheet, you can look at the table's structure in Design view.

Note If you have closed the Pets table, you may want to reopen it for this next section.

To move to Design view of the Pets table, simply click the Design button on the tool-bar; it is the left-most button on the Access toolbar and displays a triangle, ruler, and pencil and has an arrow next to it. If you press the down-arrow beside the Design button, four icons appear that represent the possible views of the data. These icons are Design, Datasheet, Pivot Table, and Pivot Chart. When you click the Design button or the Design View selection from the menu, the Design view for the Pets table replaces the Pets Datasheet view. Figure 3-8 displays the Pets table Design view.

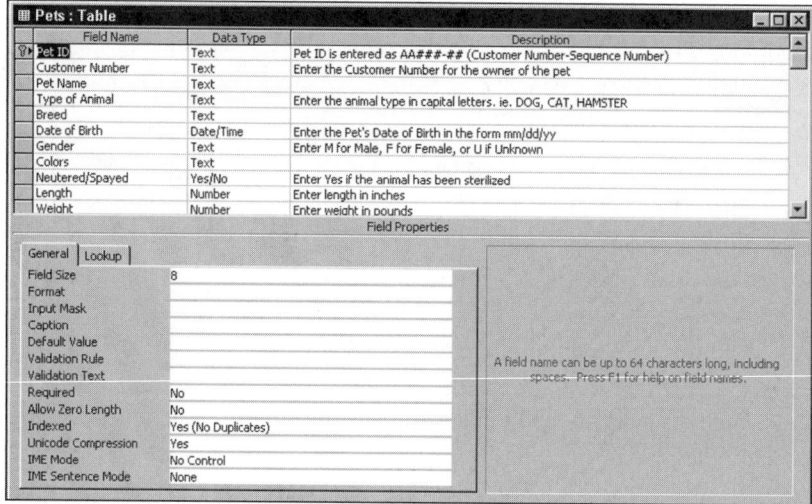

Figure 3-8: The Pets table Design view is composed of two parts—the upper part (or pane) shows the field names, the type of data, and a description. The bottom part shows Field Properties, such as formatting and validation information.

Design view shows how the fields for the Pets table are defined. Depending on the type of information to be entered in each field, a specific data type is assigned to each field. Some of the data types that you can use are Text, Currency, Date/Time, and Memo. An area is also provided for a description of the type of data that the field contains.

The Design window consists of two parts. The top half of the window, known as a *pane*, lists the field names, field types, and descriptions for each field of the Pets table, as shown in Figure 3-8. Moving around this portion of the window is similar to moving around the Pets datasheet.

The bottom half of the Pets Design window displays the field properties for the currently selected field. Different properties can be defined for each field in the table. You can use the mouse or the F6 key to move between the top and bottom panes of the Design window.

You can add fields to the Pets table or specify specific rules about the fields in the table in Design view. For instance, notice that the first field, Pet ID, has a KEY symbol next to it. This indicates that this field is the primary key (or sort) field for the table. If you look at the bottom pane of the record in Figure 3-8 you also see that the *Indexed* value says *YES (No DUPLICATES)*. This simply means that each record of this table must have a unique Pet ID number. If you click the Lookup tab of the Pet ID and most of the other fields, you see that only one property—Display Control and its value, *Text Box*.

To see some of the power of this design mode, move down to the Customer Number field and examine it closely. First notice that this field is also indexed (sorted); however, it can contain duplicate records. This makes sense because one owner can own more than one pet. Now click the Lookup tab in the lower pane. Here you see many values for these properties. Figure 3-9 shows the active Lookup tab and the associated field properties for the Customer Number.

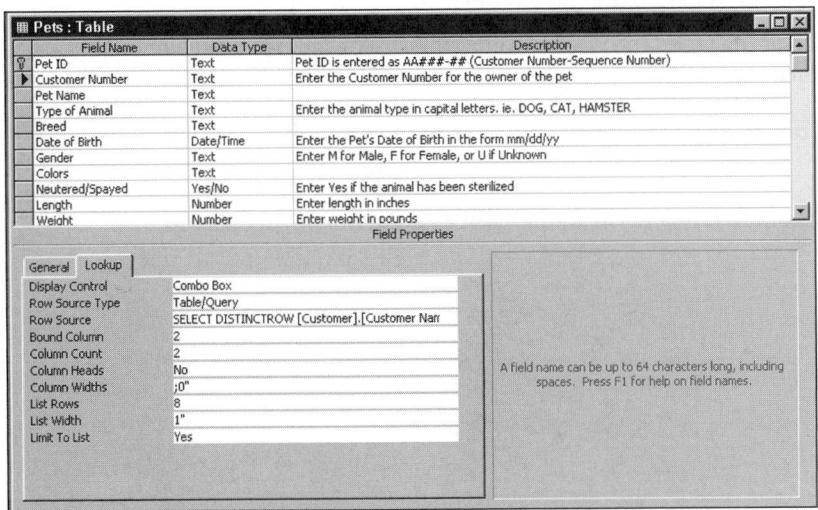

Figure 3-9: The Pets table Design window Field Properties pane (lower) for the Customer Number field with the Lookup tab pressed. Notice that many new properties are listed and each has a value associated with it.

As Figure 3-9 shows, the Customer Number field has the Display Control property set to *Combo Box*—versus Text Box for the Pet ID. By setting the value to Combo box, you can specify that the name of the Customer is displayed instead of the Customer's ID number every time the Pets table is opened and the records are displayed. If you set this value back to Text Box, then the display shows a Customer ID Number instead of the Customer Name in this field.

Caution   You should *not* change the Display Control value in the Pets table. If you do, you have to reload this table from the CD because the remaining chapters of this book require the value to be Combo Box.

The next object to display is a form. Close the Design window by clicking File ⇨ Close, which closes the Table Design window and returns you to the Database window. Of course, you can also close it by clicking the Close button on the right side of the title bar. If you are asked to SAVE changes to the table, say NO.

Displaying a form

The steps for displaying a form are similar to the steps for opening a table. You are just opening a different type of database object. Follow these steps to open the Pets form:

1. Click the Forms button in the Database window.

2. Select the Pets Data Entry Form.

3. Click the Open toolbar button at the top of the Database window to open the form.

Tip   You can also double-click any name to open a form.

The Pets Data Entry Form should look like the one in Figure 3-10.

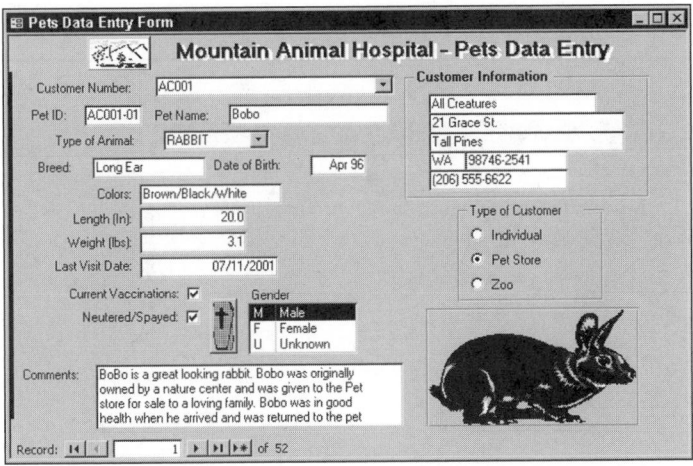

Figure 3-10: The Pets Data Entry Form open and pointing to record number 1

A *form* provides another way of displaying or changing data—usually one record at a time. The Pets form, as shown in Figure 3-10, is an example of a simple form. You enter information in each text box just as you enter information in a table. Using a form instead of a datasheet comes with many advantages; in a form, you can view more fields on-screen at one time, and you can use many data-entry and validation shortcuts. You can also view the picture of each animal on a form and the contents of the Comments Memo field. A datasheet can't display the picture of each animal or the contents of the Comments Memo field.

To see how the Pets form was created, click the Design button located on the Access toolbar (the first button on the left with the triangle, ruler, and pencil) or select View ➪ Design View from the Access menu. Your form should look like the one shown in Figure 3-11.

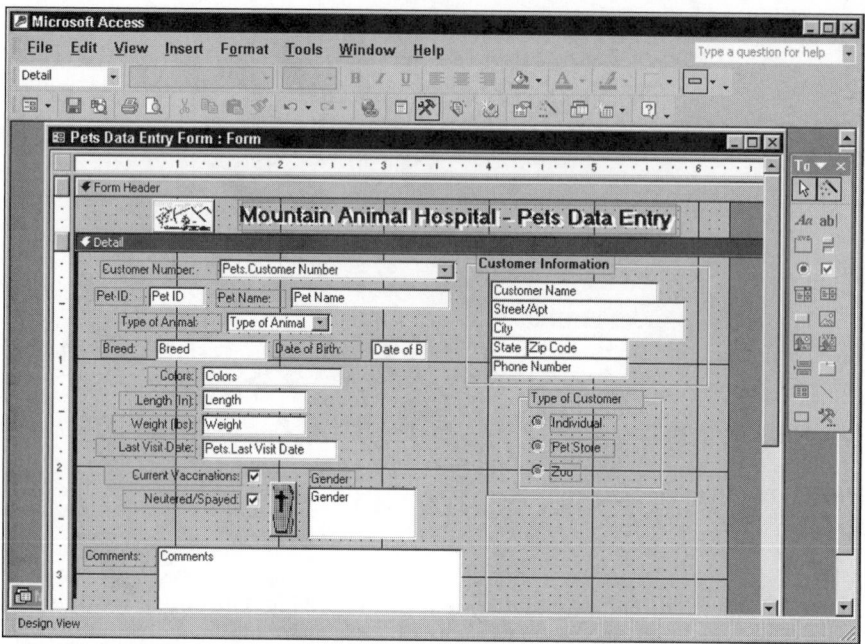

Figure 3-11: The Pets Data Entry Form in Design view. Notice that the toolbox is located to the right of the Design window (titled Pets Data Entry Form: Form).

In Figure 3-11, on the right side of the form, you see a long, rectangular box that contains several buttons. This is the Form Toolbox window. You can move the toolbox anywhere on-screen. The toolbox lets you add controls to the form. A *control* is a graphical object, such as a label, text box, check box, or command button like the ones on this form that is used to display data from a field or enhance the look of the form.

After you are familiar with the two different methods of entering data — datasheets and forms — you should be ready to work with the information, or data, that is actually stored in the Pets table. For example, you may want to look at only records for Dogs or have some other question answered. You can find the answers to your questions by using queries. Before creating a query, you should close the form by selecting File ➪ Close, or by clicking on the Close button on the form. This selection closes both the form and the Form Toolbox and returns you to the Database window. If you made any changes to the form, Access prompts you to save your changes before closing the form. You may want to avoid making changes to the form at this time.

Creating a query

A *query* lets you ask all sorts of questions about the information that is stored in your database. The information, or data, produced by the query can be saved in its own table for future use or can be printed as a report. In the following section, you learn to create a simple query by using the Pets table.

Suppose that you want to see only the records in the Pets table in which the type of animal is a dog and that you only want to see the pet name, type of animal, and breed. To do this, you need to create a query and in that query only use the Pets table. You can add as many tables as you want to a query, but for this example you add only the Pets table. To create the query and add the Pets table, follow these steps:

1. Select the Queries button from the Database window.

2. Click New to create a new query. Access displays a list of all available Query Wizards. Design View should be highlighted.

3. Click the OK button. The Show Table tabbed dialog box appears, showing three tabs — Tables, Queries, or Both, as shown in Figure 3-12.

4. Select Pets by clicking the table name in the Show Table dialog box.

5. Click Add (or simply double-click the Pets table name).

6. Click Close.

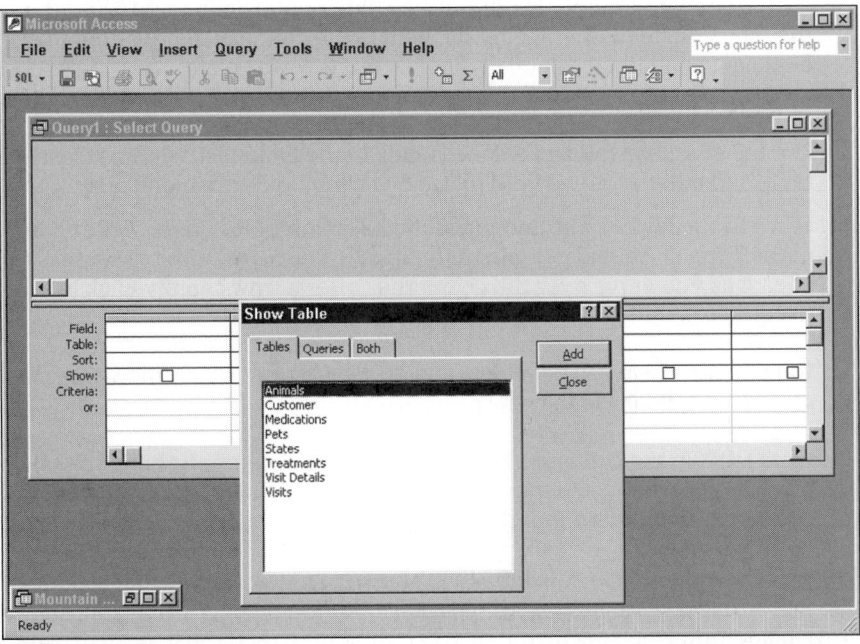

Figure 3-12: The Query Design window of Access with the Show Table dialog box open, where you can select the tables or queries that you want to use in your new query

Tip If you closed the Show Table window before adding the Pets table, you can re-open it by selecting Query ⇨ Show Table from the Access menu or by right-clicking while in the upper pane of the Design window and selecting Show Table from the menu. If you accidentally placed two tables in the upper pane of the Design window, simply click on one and press the Delete key to remove it.

You should now see a Query window with a single table — Pets — in it.

The query design window has two panes. The top pane contains the record source for the query, in this case the Field List for the Pets table — the small window, known as a Field List Window with the table name 'Pets' on the titlebar. Use the Field List window to select the fields that you want in the query datasheet. The bottom part of the query screen contains rows and columns. Use this pane to specify fields from your tables by dragging them from the Field List Window into the individual columns. You can also specify a sort order and any specific conditions (criteria) you want to against these fields. These criteria are used to display the contents of the fields in the datasheet. Follow these steps to view the Pet Name, Type of Animal, and Breed fields and select only the records where the value of Type of Animal is DOG:

1. Click the Pet Name field from the Pets table Field List window and drag it down to the first empty Field: cell (left side of bottom pane) to add the field to the query. Instead of dragging the field down, you can simply double-click the field name and it automatically moves to the lower pane.

2. Add the Type of Animal field to the query.

3. Use the scrollbar to display more fields in the Field List Window of the Pets table and add the Breed field to the query by double-clicking on it.

4. Move to the lower pane and place the insertion point on the Criteria: row of the Type of Animal column of the query. The arrow cursor changes to an I-beam as you move over the cell of the Criteria: row. Simply click in the Criteria: cell under the name of Type of Animal.

Tip You can move between panes by pressing the F6 key or simply moving the mouse pointed and clicking in the new pane.

5. Type **DOG** in the cell and move away from the field by pressing the tab key (or by clicking somewhere else in the window). Access automatically encloses the word *DOG* in quotation marks.

Your query should now look like the one shown in Figure 3-13. You have added three fields that you are interested in seeing in the Datasheet when you run the query. In addition, you specified that you only want to see those records where the type of animal is a dog. Placing DOG in the criteria range tells Access to find only records where the value of Type of Animal is DOG.

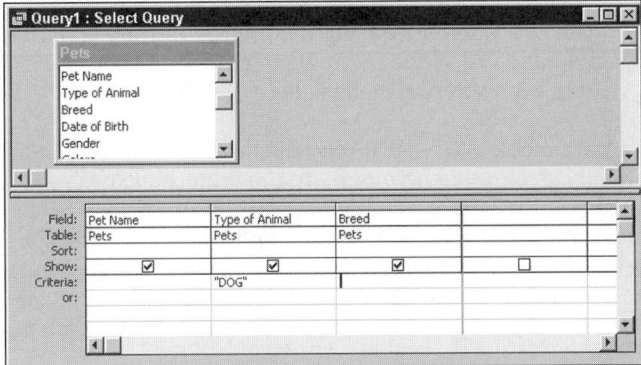

Figure 3-13: The completed Query Design window showing three fields in the lower pane of the Design window. The Type of Animal column has the word *DOG* specified in the Criteria row.

To run the query, click the Run button on the toolbar (it's the button that looks like an exclamation point and is located in the center of the Query Design toolbar). After you click the Run button, Access processes your query and displays the results in what is called a *dynaset*. Your dynaset should look like the one in Figure 3-14. The dynaset displays the Pet Name, Type of Animal, and Breed for each pet that is a dog.

Pet Name	Type of Animal	Breed
Rex	DOG	Boxer
Caesar	DOG	Boxer
Fido	DOG	German Shepherd
Brutus	DOG	German Shepherd
Cleo	DOG	German Shepherd
Dee Dee	DOG	Mixed
Suzie	DOG	Mixed
John Boy	DOG	Mixed
Fi Fi	DOG	Poodle
Sammie Girl	DOG	Spitz
Rover	DOG	Terrier

Record: ⏮ ◀ 1 ▶ ⏭ ▶✳ of 11

Figure 3-14: The Query dynaset showing the three fields that you requested by searching only those records where the value of Type of Animal is DOG

Tip You can experiment with this query by adding more fields or more criteria (for instance you may want to add CAT in the OR: row under DOG to show records of only Cats and Dogs), or to even sort one of the fields.

A dynaset is similar to a datasheet; however, it only displays those fields and records that you specifically ask for when you create the underlying query.

After you create the query, its definition can be saved and used for creating a report that you can view or print. It can even be used for a form or for any other purpose that you use a table for. The query definition can even be used by another query to further limit the records viewed — or to perform specific calculations against.

Before moving on to the next section, you may want to close this query. It isn't necessary to save it, so answer NO to the question "Do you want to save changes to the query: Query1?"

The next section explains how to display a report. Select File ➪ Close to close the query. Click NO because you don't want to save the query.

Displaying a report

Queries and tables can be formatted and placed in a *report* for output to a printer. To view and print an existing report of all the pets in the Pets table, follow these steps:

1. Click the Reports button in the Database window.

2. Select Pet Directory from the list of reports.

3. Click the Preview button (or double-click the report name). The report is displayed in the zoomed preview mode. You can display the entire page by clicking the mouse pointer anywhere on the report when the pointer is shaped like a magnifying glass.

4. Click anywhere on-screen again to redisplay the entire page.

5. Click the two-page icon (fifth from the left) on the toolbar to see two pages.

The report should look like the one shown in Figure 3-15.

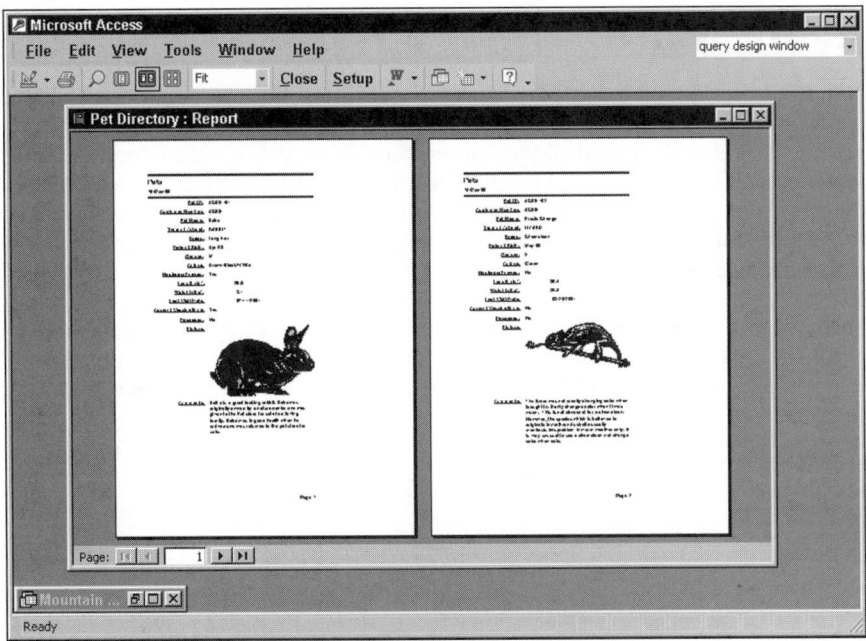

Figure 3-15: The Pets report in Print Preview mode. If you click anywhere on either page of the report it enlarges for a better view.

Tip   You can see up to six pages at a time by clicking on the four-page icon located to the right of the two-page icon, then selecting any combination up to six pages.

Figure 3-15 shows all the fields from the first two records of the Pets table. Use the Page Down key or the navigation buttons in the bottom-left corner of the window to see other pages of the report. The report can also be sent to a printer that has been set up in Windows, or you can switch to the Design window to enhance the report. Click the Close button to return to the Database window.

Ready for More?

You have experienced many of Access's capabilities. If you had problems with this chapter, start again from the beginning. Follow the directions exactly and don't move on to the next step until you understand what you need to do. Don't be afraid to experiment. You can reload the files from the CD-ROM at the back of this book. You can't hurt Access or your computer. After you have a basic understanding of the various database objects in Access, you are ready to create your own tables, forms, queries, and reports.

Before moving on to Part II, however, you need to understand how to design a database system. In upcoming chapters, you learn how to design some of the tables, forms, queries, reports, and macros. This design is implemented throughout the book.

✦   ✦   ✦

Database Concepts and Design

♦ ♦ ♦ ♦

In This Chapter

Understanding what a database is

Examining the differences between databases, tables, records, fields, and values

Learning why multiple tables are used in a database

Looking at database objects

Learning the seven-step design method

Using the Mountain Animal Hospital example

Creating the overall design of a system

Creating reports

Extracting report fields to perform data design

Designing database tables and relationships

Understanding the Normalization Process

Designing data-entry rules and validation

Designing input forms

Designing menus

♦ ♦ ♦ ♦

In this chapter, you learn the concepts and terminology of databases and how to design the tables that will be used by your forms and reports.

Before you begin to use a database software package, you must understand several basic concepts. The most important concept is that the data is stored in a "black box" known as a *table* and that by using the tools of the database system, you can retrieve, display, and report the data in any format you want.

After you understand the basic concepts and terminology, the next important lesson to learn is good database design. Without a good design, you constantly rework your tables, and you may not be able to extract the information you want from your database. Throughout this book, you learn how to use queries, forms, and reports and how to design each of these objects before you create one. The Mountain Animal Hospital case study provides invented examples, but the concepts are not fictitious.

This chapter is not easy to understand; some of its concepts are complex. If your goal is to get right into Access, you may want to read this chapter later. If you are fairly familiar with Access but new to designing and creating tables, you may want to read this chapter before starting to create tables.

Cross-Reference   To jump right into using Access, skip to Chapter 5.

The Database Terminology of Access

Before examining the actual table examples in this book, it's a good idea to have a firm understanding of the terminology that is used when working with databases—especially Access databases.

What Is a Database?

Generally, the word *database* is a computer term for a collection of information concerning a certain topic or business application. Databases help you organize this related information in a logical fashion for easy access and retrieval.

Figure 4-1 is a conceptual view of a typical manual filing system that consists of people, papers, and filing cabinets. This lighthearted view of a manual database makes the point that paper is the key to a manual database system. In a real manual database system, you probably have in/out baskets and some type of formal filing method. You access information manually by opening a file cabinet, taking out a file folder, and finding the correct piece of paper. You use paper forms for input, perhaps by using a typewriter. You find information by sorting the papers manually or by copying desired information from many papers to another piece of paper (or even into a computer spreadsheet). You may use a calculator or a computer spreadsheet to analyze the data further or to report it.

Figure 4-1: A typical manual filing system. The keys to a manual database are paper records.

A computer database is nothing more than an automated version of the filing and retrieval functions of a manual paper filing system. Computer databases store information in a structured format that you define. They can store data in a variety of forms, from simple lines of text (such as name and address) to complex data structures that include pictures, sounds, or video images. Storing data in a precise, known format enables a database management system (DBMS) to turn the data into useful information through many types of output, such as queries and reports.

In an automated database management system such as Access, you use a computer to access the information or data stored in tables — entering data in the tables through data-entry forms and retrieving it by using a query. You can create and use queries to obtain a specific portion of data from the tables. Then a report outputs the data to the screen or a printer. Macros and modules allow you to automate this process and to create new menus and dialog boxes.

A relational database management system (RDBMS), such as Access, stores data in many related tables. You can ask complex questions, using queries, from one or more of these related tables, with the answers returning as forms and reports.

Databases, tables, records, fields, and values

Microsoft Access follows traditional database terminology. The terms *database*, *table*, *record*, *field*, and *value* indicate a hierarchy from largest to smallest.

Databases

In Access, a *database* is the overall container for the data and associated objects. It is more than the collection of tables; rather, it includes all objects. Database *objects* include tables, queries, forms, reports, data access pages, macros, and modules. In some computer software products, the database is the object that holds the actual data; in Access, this is called a *table*. Other products refer to the database as the collection of all tables related to the system.

Access can work with only one database at a time. Within a single Access database, however, you can have hundreds of tables, forms, queries, reports, pages, macros, and modules — all stored in a single file with the file extension .MDB (multiple database) or .ADP if you are using SQL Server.

 **Cross-Reference** Chapters 33 and 34 cover SQL server and Access projects in detail.

Tables

The table is the container for raw information (called *data*). When you enter data in Access, a table stores it in logical groupings of similar data (the Pets table, for example, contains data about pets) and the table's design organizes the information into rows and columns.

You create these tables after careful analysis of the type of information that you want to store, as discussed in the "Designing field names, types, and sizes" section later in this chapter. After you create a table, you can view the table in a spreadsheet-like form, called a *datasheet*, comprising rows (records) and columns (fields). Figure 4-2 shows a simple datasheet of the Pets table.

	Pet ID	Customer Numb	Pet Name	Type of Animal	Breed	Date of Birth	Gender
	AC001-01	AC001	Bobo	RABBIT	Long Ear	04/01/1996	M
	AC001-02	AC001	Presto Chango	LIZARD	Chameleon	05/01/1995	F
	AC001-03	AC001	Stinky	SKUNK		08/01/1999	M
	AC001-04	AC001	Fido	DOG	German Shephe	06/01/1995	M
	AD001-01	AD001	Patty	PIG	Potbelly	02/01/1999	F
	AD001-02	AD001	Rising Sun	HORSE	Palomino	04/01/1997	M
	AD002-01	AD002	Dee Dee	DOG	Mixed	02/01/1999	F
	AK001-01	AK001	Margo	SQUIRREL	Gray	03/01/1999	F
	AK001-02	AK001	Tom	CAT	Tabby	02/01/1996	M
	AK001-03	AK001	Jerry	RAT	Hooded	02/01/1998	M
	BA001-01	BA001	Swimmy	DOLPHIN	Bottlenose	07/01/1996	F
	BA001-03	BA001	Daffy	DUCK	Mallard	09/01/1999	M
	BA001-05	BA001	Jake	DOLPHIN	Bottlenose	04/01/1992	M
	BR001-01	BR001	Suzie	DOG	Mixed	01/01/2000	M
	BR002-01	BR002	John Boy	DOG	Mixed	04/01/1998	M
	EP001-01	EP001	Mikos	WOLF	Timber	11/01/1997	M

Record: ⏮ ◀ 1 ▶ ⏭ ▶* of 53

Figure 4-2: A Database displayed in a datasheet

Records and fields

As Figure 4-2 shows, the datasheet is divided into rows called *records* and columns called *fields*, with the first row (heading on top of each column) containing the names of the fields in the database. The data shown in the table has columns of similar information, such as Pet Name, Customer Number, Breed, or Date of Birth; these columns of data items are fields. Each field is identified as a certain type of data (Text, Number, Date, and so on) and has a specified length. Each field has a name that identifies its category of information.

The rows of data within a table are its records. Each row of information is considered a separate entity that can be accessed or sequenced as desired, and each record is made up of fields. Each record has all the fields (one each) of the database structure. For example, looking at Figure 4-2, Row 1 has a Pet ID field with the value of "AC001-01," a Customer Number of "AC001," a Pet Name of "Bobo," and the remaining fields. Row 2 has a Pet ID field with the value of "AC001-02," a Customer Number of "AC001," a Pet Name of "Presto Chango," and the other fields. Each row and record has all the fields of the database with a value in each (some of the values may be blank or empty, known as *null*). All the fields of information concerning a certain pet are contained within a specific record.

Values

At the intersection of a row (record) and a column (field) is a *value* — the actual data element. For example, Bobo, the Pet Name in the first record, represents one data value. Questions you may ask – How do you identify the first record? It's sitting in the first row of the datasheet and is the record with the rabbit. But what if you have more than one rabbit in your database? Whereas fields are known by the field name, records are usually identified by some unique characteristic or value within one or more of the fields of the record. This unique value makes each record different from all the other records. In the Pets table, the field that makes each record unique is the Pet ID; fields like the Pet Name or Type of Animal are not unique because you may have two pets named Fido or more than one Dog in the table.

Sometimes it takes more than one field to find a unique value. You can use Customer Number and Pet Name, but it's possible for one customer to have two pets with the same name. You can use the fields Customer Number, Pet Name, and Type of Animal. Again, theoretically, you can have a customer come in and say, "Hi, my name's Larry — this is my pet snake Darryl, and this is my other pet snake Darryl." Creating a unique identifier (such as Pet ID) helps distinguish one record from another without having to look through all the values.

Using More Than One Table

A database contains one or more tables (that is, logical groupings of similar data). Most applications that are developed in Access have several related tables to present the information efficiently. An application that uses multiple tables can usually manipulate data more efficiently than it can with one large table.

Working with multiple tables

Multiple tables simplify data entry and reporting by decreasing the input of redundant data. By defining two tables for an application that uses customer information, for example, you don't need to store the customer's name and address every time the customer purchases an item.

After you've created the tables, they need to be related to each other. For example, if you have a Customer table and a Pets table, you must relate the Customer table to the Pets table in order to see all the pets owned by the customer. If you had only one table, you would have to repeat the customer name and address for each pet record. Two tables let you look up information in the Customer table for each pet by using the common field Customer Number. This way, when a customer changes address (for example), it changes only in one record in the Customer table; when the pet information is on-screen, the correct customer address is always visible.

Separating data into multiple tables within a database makes the system easier to maintain because all records of a given type are within the same table. By taking the time to segment data properly into multiple tables, you experience a significant reduction in design and work time. This process is known as *normalization*.

It's also a good idea to create a separate database for just your tables. By separating your design objects (queries, forms, reports, pages, macros, and modules) and the tables into two different databases, it's easier to maintain your application.

Later in this chapter, you have the opportunity to work through a case study for the Mountain Animal Hospital that consists of eight tables

Cross-Reference   For more information about the Access Application Splitter, see Chapter 6.

Why You Should Create Multiple Tables

The prospect of creating multiple tables always scares beginning database users. Normally, they want to create one simple table that contains information — in this instance, a Customer table with all the pets owned by the customer and their visit information. So they create a single table containing all the fields, including fields for the personal information for the animal (type of animal, name, date of birth, etc.) and the visit information for the animal. Before you know it, the table has 50 fields or more. You add more fields as you think of more things that need to be captured.

As you can see, the table design begins to take on a life of its own. After you've created the single table, it becomes even more difficult to maintain. You begin to realize that you have to put in customer information for every pet that the customer owns (repeating the information, over and over). The same is true for the visits that each pet makes to the vet — which is usually more than one visit (thus duplicate information again). This makes the system more inefficient and prone to mistakes. The information that is actually in the table becomes inefficiently maintained — many fields may not be appropriate for each record, and the table ends up with a lot of empty fields.

So, as you can see, it's important to create tables that hold the minimum of information while still making the system easy to use and flexible enough to grow. To accomplish this, you need to consider making more than one table, with each table containing records with fields that are only related to the focus of that table. Then, after you create the tables, you can link them together by some means that will let you glean useful information from them. Although this sounds extremely complex, the actual implementation is relatively easy. This process of creating multiple tables from a single table is known as normalization — or normalizing your tables.

Cross-Reference Normalization is covered in more detail later in this chapter under Table Design and Relationships.

Access Database Objects and Views

If you are new to databases (or even if you're an experienced database user), you need to understand some key Access concepts before starting to use the program. The Access database contains seven objects, which consist of the data and tools that you need to use Access:

✦ **Table.** Holds the actual data (uses a *datasheet* to display the raw data)

✦ **Query.** Lets you search, sort, and retrieve specific data

✦ **Form.** Lets you enter and display data in a customized format

✦ **Report.** Lets you display and print formatted data, including calculations and totals

✦ **Pages.** Lets you publish live forms to a corporate intranet

✦ **Macro.** Gives you easy-to-use commands to automate tasks without programming

✦ **Module.** Program written in VBA

Datasheets

Datasheets are one of the many ways by which you can view data. Although not a database object, a datasheet displays a list of records from a table in a format commonly known as a *browse screen* or *table view*. A datasheet displays data as a series of rows and columns (comparable to a spreadsheet). A datasheet simply displays the information from a table in its raw form. This spreadsheet format is the default mode for displaying all fields for all records.

You can scroll through the datasheet using the directional keys on your keyboard. You can also display related records in other tables while in a datasheet. In addition, you can make changes to the displayed data. However, use caution when making any changes or allowing a user to make any modifications in this format. When a datasheet record is changed, the data in the underlying table is the data actually being changed.

Queries and dynasets

You use a query to extract information from a database. A query can select and define a group of records that fulfill a certain condition. You can use queries before printing a report so that only the desired data is printed. You can also use a query with forms so that only certain records (that meet the desired criteria) appear on-screen. You can also use queries within procedures to change, add, or delete database records.

An example of a query is when a doctor at Mountain Animal Hospital says, "Show me which of the pets that we treat are dogs or cats located in Idaho. Show them to me sorted by customer name and then by pet name." Instead of asking the question in actual English, the doctor uses a method known as *QBE*, which stands for *Query by Example*. When you enter instructions into the QBE Design window, the query translates the instructions and retrieves the desired data. In this example, the query first combines data from both the Customer and Pets tables, using the related field Customer Number (the common link between the tables). Then it retrieves the fields Customer Name, Pet Name, Type of Animal, and State. Access then filters the records, selecting only those in which the value of State is ID and the value of Type of Animal is dog or cat. It sorts the resulting records first by Customer Name and then by Pet Name within the customer names that are alike. Finally, the records appear on-screen in a datasheet.

These selected records are known as a *dynaset*—a dynamic set of data that can change according to the raw data in the original tables.

After you run a query, the resulting dynaset can be used in a form that can be displayed on-screen in a specified format or printed on a report. In this way, user access can be limited to the data that meets the criteria in the dynaset.

Data-entry and display forms

Data-entry forms help users get information into a database table quickly, easily, and accurately. Data-entry and display forms provide a more structured view of the data than what a datasheet provides. From this structured view, database records can be viewed, added, changed, or deleted. Entering data through the data-entry forms is the most common way to get the data into the database table.

You can use data-entry forms to restrict access to certain fields within the table. You can also use these forms to check the validity of your data before you accept it into the database table.

Most users prefer to enter information into data-entry forms rather than datasheet tables; data-entry forms can be made to resemble familiar paper documents. Forms make data entry self-explanatory by guiding the user through the fields of the table being updated.

Display-only screens and forms are solely for inquiry purposes. These forms allow for the selective display of certain fields within a given table. Displaying some fields and not others means that you can limit a user's access to sensitive data while allowing inquiry into other fields.

Reports

Reports present your data in printed format. You can create several different types of reports within a database management system. For example, your report can list all records in a given table, such as a customer table. You can also create a report that lists only the customers who meet a given criterion, such as all those who live in the state of Washington. You do this by incorporating a query into your report design. The query creates a dynaset consisting of the records that contain the state code WA.

Your reports can combine multiple tables to present complex relationships among different sets of data. An example of this is printing an invoice. You access the customer table to obtain the customer's name and address (and other pertinent data) and the sales table to print the individual line-item information for the products ordered. You can then have Access calculate the totals and print them (in a specific format) on the form. Additionally, you can have Access output records into an invoice report, a table that summarizes the invoice.

When you design your database tables, keep in mind all the types of information that you want to print. Doing so ensures that the information you require in your various reports is available from within your database tables.

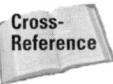

Cross-Reference

For descriptions of the remaining database objects (pages, macros, and modules), see the appropriate chapters (pages are 35 and 36, macros are 28, and modules are 30 and 31).

Designing the Systems Objects

To create database objects, such as tables, forms, and reports, you first complete a series of tasks known as *design*. The better your design is, the better your application will be. The more you think through your design, the faster you can complete any system. Design is not some necessary evil, nor is its intent to produce voluminous amounts of documentation. The sole intent of design is to produce a clear-cut path to follow as you implement it.

The Seven-Step Design Method

Figure 4-3 is a version of the design method that is modified especially for use with Access. This is a top-down approach, starting with the Overall System Design and ending with the Menu Design, and consists of seven steps.

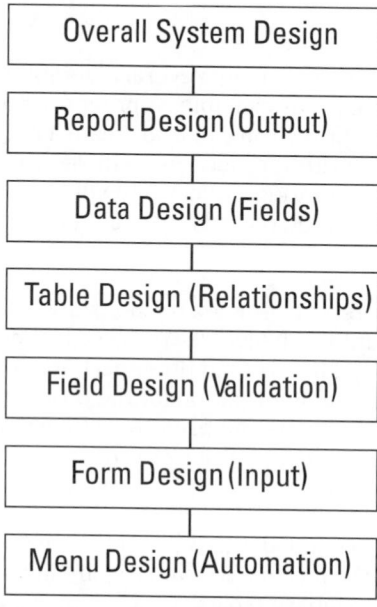

Figure 4-3: The seven-step design flowchart. This design methodology is one that has been modified specifically for use with Access databases.

These seven design steps, along with the database system illustrated by the examples in this book, teach a great deal about Access and provide a great foundation for creating database applications — including databases, tables, queries, forms, data pages, reports, macros, and simple VBA (Visual Basic for Applications) modules.

As you read through each step of the design process, *always* look at the design in terms of outputs and inputs. Although you see actual components of the system (customers, pets, visits, and visit details), remember that the focus of this chapter is how to design each step. As you watch the Mountain Animal Hospital system being designed, pay attention to the design process, not the actual system.

This process is often referred to as performing a *needs analysis*.

Step 1: The Overall Design — From Concept to Reality

All software developers and end users face similar problems, the first of which is determining what will meet the needs of the end user (typically your client, your coworker, or yourself). It's important to understand the overall needs that the system must meet before you begin to zero in on the details.

The seven-step design method shown in Figure 4-3 helps you to create the system that you need, at a price (measured in time or dollars) that you can afford. The Mountain Animal Hospital, for example, is a medium-sized animal hospital that services individuals, pet stores, and zoos across three states. The Mountain Animal Hospital needs to automate several tasks:

✦ Entering and maintaining customer information — name, address, and financial history

✦ Entering and maintaining pet information — pet name, type, breed, length, weight, picture, and comments

✦ Entering and maintaining visit information — details of treatments performed and medications dispensed

✦ Viewing information from all the tables — Customers, Pets, and Visit Information

✦ Asking all types of questions about the information in the database

✦ Producing a current Pets and Owners directory

✦ Producing a monthly invoice report

✦ Producing mailing labels and mail-merge reports

Conceptual design

These eight tasks are conceptual at this point; they are the ones that you have been told about by the client. You may need to consider other tasks as you start the design process.

The design process is a repetitious procedure; as you finish each step, you need to look at all the previous steps again to make sure that nothing in the basic design has changed. For example, if you are creating a data-entry rule and decide that you need another field (that's not already in the table) to validate a field you've already defined, you have to go back and follow each previous step needed to add the field. You have to be sure to add the new field to each report in which you want to see it. You also have to make sure that the new field is on an input form that uses the table the field is in. Only then can you use this new field in your system.

Interviewing the user

Most of the information that is necessary to build the system comes from the people that you are building the system for. This means that you need to sit down with them and learn about how the existing manual process works. To accomplish this you need to do a thorough *needs analysis* of the user or client's current system and how you anticipate automating it.

One way to accomplish this is to sit down and prepare a series of questions that can give you insight of how the client currently performs their business. For example, when considering automating a veterinary system, you may consider asking these questions:

✦ What reports and forms are currently used?

✦ How are records currently kept on the pets?

✦ How are the manual records/charts filed of the customers and their pets?

✦ What happens when a customer doesn't come back for a year or more?

✦ What do they do with the records when a pet dies?

✦ How are billing and appointments processed?

As you ask these questions and others, the client will probably remember other things about their business that you should know.

A walk-through of the manual process is also necessary to get a "feel" for the business. You will probably have to go back several times to watch the manual process and how the employees work.

When you prepare to follow the remaining steps, keep the client involved — let them know what you are doing and ask for their input as to what you want to accomplish — making sure it is within the scope of their needs.

The Process of prototyping

You may want to create a *prototype system* for the client to look at and play with, to give you further input about what needs to be added to make the system functional for them.

In its simplest terms, a prototype is a working sample system. It comprises one or more tables that are used to demonstrate the forms and reports of the system. A prototype is made up of the visual parts of the system — as opposed to the logical underlying structure of the system.

A prototype is only the visual representation of how the system will look and function after it's complete. Often you can build a prototype in a few days and give it to the client for their comments. This allows the user to see a working prototype demonstrating the data display and data access techniques through forms and reports.

Prototypes can be very stress-inducing. Essentially, they are an attempt to visualize the future and plan for change, and are often undertaken without a clear vision of what the end result will be. Remember that a prototype is a working sample of the final system — it will need to be changed.

So why build one? Prototypes can help you visualize a strategy or direction, describe functionality or form, and demonstrate a proof of concept. You can use them to gauge customer reaction, explore system functionality, and test the system's concepts and directions.

Because of these reasons, prototyping offers a highly valuable tool in the overall building of your database system.

To build a prototype of the overall system, you have to quickly define the major components of your database from your specifications that you gathered during the initial meetings with the client. A prototype shouldn't become the final working system — it is only a sample system. Keeping this in mind, you shouldn't spend weeks and months on building one. Here's a good analogy to keep in mind: Think of a prototype system as the house fronts that are built for a street scene in a movie. They look great, but the moment you open the front door to the building, you find yourself in a vacant lot; it's all make-believe!

Basically, a good prototype saves time and significantly reduces the cost of the overall project.

Step 2: Report Design — Placing Your Fields

After you've defined Mountain Animal Hospital's overall systems in terms of what must be accomplished, you can begin report design.

Design work should be broken into the smallest level of detail, based on your knowledge of the current system. Start each new step by reviewing the overall design objectives. In the case of Mountain Animal Hospital, your objectives are to track customers, track pets, keep a record of visits and treatments, produce invoices, create a directory of pets and owners, and produce mailing labels.

Laying out fields in the report

When you see the reports that you will create in this section, you may wonder, "Which comes first — the chicken or the egg?" Does the report layout come first, or do you first determine the data items and text that make up the report? Actually, these items are conceived together.

It isn't important how you lay out the fields in this conception of a report. The more time you take now, however, the easier it will be when you actually create the report. Some people go so far as to place gridlines on the report so that they will know the exact location they want each field to occupy. In this example, you can just do it visually.

The Pets and Owners Directory

Mountain Animal Hospital begins with the task of tracking customers and pets. The first report that you need to develop should show important information about pets and their owners and should be sorted by customer number. Each customer's name and address should appear with a listing of the pets that the customer has brought into the Mountain Animal Hospital.

The hospital staff has already decided on some of the fields for the customer file. First, of course, is the customer's name (individual or company), followed by address (the customer's street, city, state, and ZIP code), and phone number.

The last visit date is another field that the hospital wants to maintain on file and use on the report. This field lets the Mountain Animal Hospital staff know when it's time to remove a pet from the Pets table; in this case, a pet is to be removed if it hasn't been in for a visit in the last three years. The plan is to purge the Pets table each year, and recording the last visit is a good way to find this information. This field also alerts the Mountain Animal Hospital staff as to when an animal is due for its yearly checkup so that they can send out reminder notices.

With that information in mind, the Mountain Animal Hospital people create the report form design shown in Figure 4-4.

Cross-Reference If you want to learn to implement this report, see Chapter 20. If you want to learn to complete this report with advanced database-publishing enhancements, see Chapter 21.

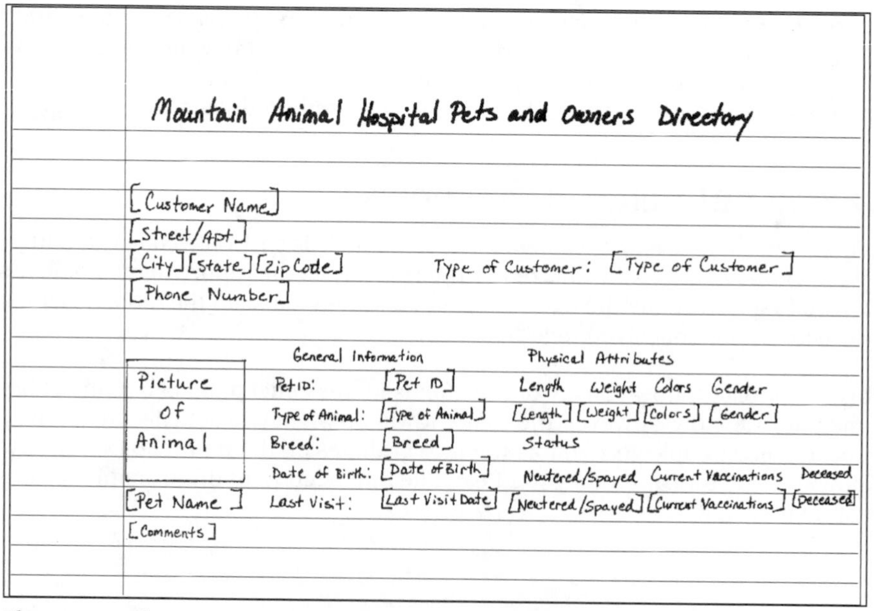

Mountain Animal Hospital Pets and Owners Directory

[Customer Name]
[Street/Apt]
[City][State][Zip Code]   Type of Customer: [Type of Customer]
[Phone Number]

General Information   Physical Attributes
Picture   Pet ID: [Pet ID]   Length Weight Colors Gender
of   Type of Animal: [Type of Animal]   [Length][Weight][Colors][Gender]
Animal   Breed: [Breed]   Status
           Date of Birth: [Date of Birth]   Neutered/Spayed Current Vaccinations Deceased
[Pet Name] Last Visit: [Last Visit Date] [Neutered/Spayed][Current Vaccinations][Deceased]
[Comments]

Figure 4-4: The Pets and Owners Directory report design

Figure 4-5 shows how the final hard-copy printout of this report will look; it also illustrates the capabilities of Access. Notice that only part of the page is shown. The report shows one customer at the top of the page and the pets that are owned by that customer. If the customer has more pets than can fit on a single page, another page is created with the additional pets (and the top of the second page repeats the customer information).

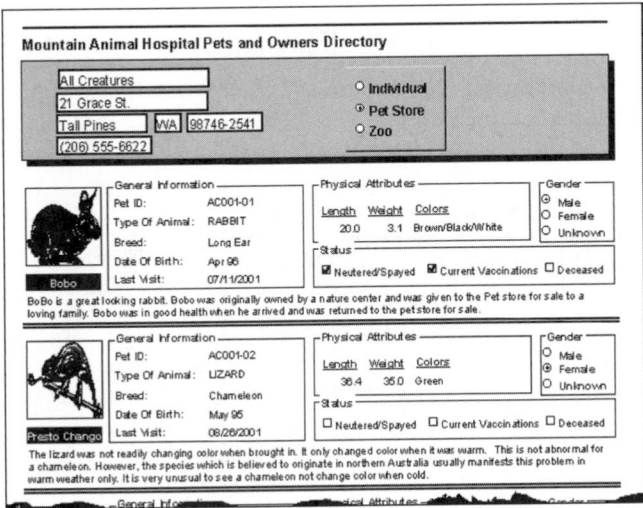

Figure 4-5: The completed Pets and Owners Directory report

The Monthly Invoice Report

Whereas the Pets and Owners Directory concentrates on information about customers and pets, the Monthly Invoice Report displays information about the individual visits of specific customers and pets. Mountain Animal Hospital needs to produce a monthly report that lists all the daily visits by each customer and the customer's pets. Figure 4-6 shows the design of this report.

The design of this report shows customer information at the top and data about each visit in the middle. The middle block appears as many times as each customer had visits on the same date. If a customer brings three pets to the hospital on the same day, the report shows the middle block of data three times — once for each pet. The prices are totaled for each line; the sum of these line totals appears at the bottom of the block.

Figure 4-6: The design for the Monthly Invoice Report

All the data items in the bottom block are summarized and calculated fields. (Because these fields can be calculated whenever necessary, they are not stored in a table.) After subtracting the discount from the subtotal, the report shows a taxable amount. If the customer's visit is subject to tax, the report calculates it at the current tax rate and then displays it. Adding the tax to the taxable amount gives the total for the invoice; the customer pays this amount. Figure 4-7 shows the final report (created in Chapter 21).

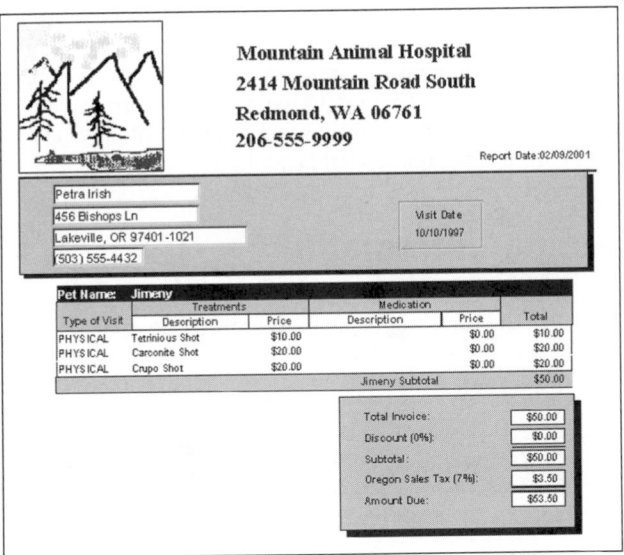

Figure 4-7: The final Mountain Animal Hospital Invoice Report

In reality, you will probably design many more reports. In the interest of time and pages, however, the preceding two report designs suffice.

Step 3: Data Design — What Fields Do You Have?

After you've decided what you want for output, it's time to think about how to organize your data into a system to make it available for the reports that you've already defined (as well as for any ad hoc queries). The next step in the design phase is to take an inventory of all the information or data fields that you need to create the desired output — reports and forms. One of the best methods is to list the data items in each report. As you do so, take careful note of items that are in more than one report. Make sure that you keep the same name for a data item that is in more than one report because the data item is really the same item.

Another method is to see whether you can separate the data items into some logical arrangement. Later, these data items are grouped into logical table structures and then mapped on data-entry screens that make sense. You should enter customer data, for example, as part of a customer table process — not as part of a visit entry.

This process of grouping common information is known as *normalizing* your database. The actual process of normalizing is covered in the "Step 4: Table Design and Relationships" section later in this chapter; however, as you conceptually work with the data items (or fields) you should group them together into logical groups (the customer-related fields, the pet-related fields, and on and on).

Determining customer information

First, look at each report. For the Mountain Animal Hospital customer reports, start with the customer data and list the data items, as shown in Table 4-1.

Table 4-1	
Customer-Related Data Items Found in the Reports	
Pets and Owners Directory Report	*Monthly Invoice Report*
Customer Name	Customer Name
Street	Street
City	City
State	State
ZIP Code	ZIP Code
Phone Number	Phone Number
Type of Customer	Discount
Last Visit Date	

As you can see, most of the data fields pertaining to the customer are found in both reports. The table shows only the fields that are used. Fields appearing on both reports appear on the same lines in the table, which allows you to see more easily which items are in which reports. You can look across a row instead of looking for the same names in both reports. Because the related row and the field names are the same, it's easy to make sure that you have all the data items. Although locating items easily is not critical for this small database, it becomes very important when you have to deal with large tables.

Determining pet information

After extracting the customer data, you can move on to the pet data. Again, you need to analyze the two reports for data items that are specific to the pets. Table 4-2 lists the fields in the two reports that contain information about the animals. Notice that only one field in the Monthly Invoice Report contains pet information.

Table 4-2	
Pet Data Items Found in the Reports	
Pets and Owners Directory Report	*Monthly Invoice Report*
Pet ID	
Pet Name	Pet Name
Type of Animal	
Breed	
Date of Birth	
Last Visit Date	
Length	
Weight	
Colors	
Gender	
Neutered/Spayed	
Current Vaccinations	
Deceased	
Picture	
Comments	

Determining visit information

Finally, you need to extract information about the visits from the Monthly Invoice Report, as shown in Table 4-3. You use only this report because the Pets and Owners Directory report doesn't deal with visit information.

Table 4-3
Extracting Visit Information
Visit Data Items
Visit Date
Type of Visit
Treatment

Continued

Table 4-3 *(continued)*
Visit Data Items
Treatment Price
Medication
Discount
Tax Rate
Total Amount
Medication Price
Line Total

The table doesn't list some of the calculated fields, but you can re-create them easily in the report.

Tip Unless a field needs to be specifically stored in a table, simply recalculate it when you run the report (or form). You should avoid creating fields in your tables that can be created based on other fields, because these calculation fields can be created and displayed in a form or report—therefore, you don't waste storage space, not to mention your valuable time!

Combining the data

Now for the difficult part: You must determine what fields that you need to create for the tables that make up the reports. When you examine the multitude of fields and calculations that make up the many documents you have, you begin to see which fields actually belong to the different tables. (You already did some preliminary work by arranging the fields into logical groups.) For now, include every field you extracted. You will need to add others later (for various reasons), although certain fields won't appear in any table.

After you have used each report to display all the data, it's time to consolidate the data by function—and then compare the data across functions. To do this step, first you look at the customer information and combine all its different fields to create one set of data items. Then you do the same thing for the pet information and the visit information. Table 4-4 compares data items from these three groups of information.

Table 4-4
Comparing the Data Items from the Three Groups

Customer Data Items	Pet Data Items	Visit Data Items
Customer Name	Pet ID	Visit Date
Street	Pet Name	Type of Visit
City	Type of Animal	Treatment
State	Breed	Treatment Price
ZIP Code	Date of Birth	Medication
Phone Number	Last Visit Date	Medication Price
Type of Customer	Length	Discount
Last Visit Date	Weight	Tax Rate
Discount	Colors	Total Amount
	Gender	
	Neutered/Spayed	
	Current Vaccinations	
	Deceased	
	Picture	
	Comments	

Consolidating and comparing data is a good way to start creating the table definitions for Mountain Animal Hospital, but you have much more to do. First, as you learn more about how to perform a data design, you also learn that the information in the Visits column must be split into two columns. Some of these items are used only once for the visit; other items are used for each detail line in the visit. It is necessary to separate these two types of items — an example of the *normalization* part of the design process. For example, one customer has one pet, which has one visit with many visit details. The customer and pet data items each represent one customer or one pet, but a visit may require multiple detail lines.

Table 4-5 divides the Visits column into two columns. The visit date is no longer a unique field for the second table, which contains multiple items for each visit. You have to add another field (which is shown in Table 4-6).

When you look at Table 4-5, you may wonder how to link these two files together so that Access knows which visit-detail information goes with which visit. A unique field (often an identification number or code) can do this job. By adding the same field to each group of information, you can keep similar information together. You can create a field called Visit Number, for example, and use a consistent methodology to assign values to it. If you use a numeric sequence of year, the day number of the year, and a sequence number, then the third pet to visit on January 12, 2001 becomes 2001012-03. The first four digits record the year, the next three digits tell you the Julian number or number of days since January 1, and a hyphen separates the date from a sequence number. After you have added this field to both columns for the Visits and Visit Details tables, you can tie the two files together.

Table 4-5
Dividing the Visits Information

Visits	Visit Details
Visit Date	Visit Date
Discount	Type of Visit
Tax Rate	Treatment
Total Amount	Treatment Price
	Medication
	Medication Price

You have one more identification number to assign. The Visit Details table doesn't have a unique identifier, although it does have a partially unique identifier. The Visit Number identifier is unique for an individual visit, but not for a visit that has multiple detail lines. A common practice is to assign a sequential number (such as 001, 002, 003, and so on) for each visit detail.

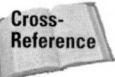
Cross-Reference   In a one-to-many type of relationship, you usually need more than one field to make a record unique. See Chapter 11 for a complete discussion of keys and relationships.

Table 4-6 lists the original data items and the reworked items for the Visits and Visit Details tables.

Table 4-6
A Final Design of Data Items

Customer	Pets	Visits	Visit Details
Customer Number	Pet ID	Visit Number	Visit Number
Customer Name	Pet Name	Visit Date	Line Number
Street	Type of Animal	Discount	Type of Visit

Customer	Pets	Visits	Visit Details
City	Breed	Tax Rate	Treatment
State	Date of Birth	Total Amount	Treatment Price
ZIP Code	Last Visit Date		Medication
Phone Number	Length		Medication Price
Type of Customer	Weight		
Last Visit Date	Colors		
Discount	Gender		
	Neutered/Spayed		
	Current Vaccinations		
	Deceased		
	Picture		
	Comments		

These are not the final fields that are to be used in the Mountain Animal Hospital database. You will make many more changes as the design is examined and enhanced.

Step 4: Table Design and Relationships

You have identified the core of the four primary tables for your system, as reflected in Table 4-6. This is the general, or first, cut toward the final table designs.

Taking time to properly design your database and the tables contained within it is arguably the most important step in developing a database-oriented application. By designing your database efficiently, you maintain control of the data—eliminating costly data-entry mistakes and limiting your data entry to essential fields.

Although this book is not geared toward teaching Database Theory and all its nuances, this is a good point to briefly describe the art of *Database Normalization*.

Database Normalization

Database Normalization can essentially be defined as the process of optimizing how you store and use the information in your tables. E. F. Codd, an employee of IBM, first proposed the normalization process back in 1972 (*Normalized Data Structure: A Brief Tutorial*, 1971, and *Relational Completeness of Data Base Sublanguages*, 1972). Codd proposed that a person should take the *relational schema* (the system of tables that are all interrelated) and put it through a series of tests to "certify" whether or not it belonged to a certain *normal form*. He initially proposed three normal forms, which he named *first, second,* and *third normal form.* Later, E.F. Codd, with Mr. Boyce, created an even stronger definition, known as *Boyce-Codd normal form* (BCNF). Even later, they proposed a *fourth* and *fifth normal form*, based on more obscure concepts of dependencies (multi-valued and join).

Simply put, these "normal forms" are based on the functional dependencies of the fields within a table and how they interrelate with the other tables of the database system. Using normalization, you can ensure that the information in your tables is being utilized and stored efficiently.

Normalizing to Third Normal Form

In order for normalization to work, you must separate your tables into the focused groups that you've already started. After you separate the tables, you are ready to look at each table separately and determine if you can optimize them better. This is accomplished via a process known as normalizing to *Third Normal Form* (3NF). Third Normal Form requires three steps.

Often you perform these steps *after* you create all the fields that you need in your tables.

> **Note**
>
> When learning Normal Forms, you'll hear a lot of buzzwords, such as lossless joins, tuples, superkey (minimal), candidate keys, primary keys, foreign keys, domains, atomic values, nonkey attributes, nontransitive dependence, transitive dependencies, functional dependencies, determinants, entities, and relationships. With the exception of relationships, primary and foreign keys, you can safely avoid these terms here. If you are interested in learning 3NF or 4NF—or even 5NF—in detail, many excellent books on the topic are available. You can find out more about relationships, primary and foreign keys in Chapter 6.

The reasons you want to consider making your tables conform to 3NF is two-fold:

✦ **Eliminating Data Redundancy.** The repetition of typing data creates two problems: First, it consumes more space and resources than necessary. Second, entry of repetitive information is prone to typographical errors.

✦ **Unforeseen Scalability Issues.** The database tends to continue to grow and take on a life of its own after creation. If you fail to normalize your tables, you run the risk of "hard coding" in fields that later need to be expanded. For example, you may have two telephone fields in your system (one for home, one for business). Later you realize that you need to also capture cellular phone numbers and perhaps beeper numbers. Going back and changing the structure to accommodate this new information is cumbersome at best. Or perhaps the opposite can be true; for example, you have a student system that allows for five classes per student, but the administration has decided that they can only be allowed to take three classes. The system needs to be able to quickly adapt to these growth issues.

You can eliminate these types of problems by building your tables following the three basic steps of normalizing to Third Normal Form.

First normal form (1NF)

Converting a table to the first normal form is relatively simple. The first rule calls for the elimination of any repeating groups of data—moving repeating data into their own tables.

Here's a practical rule to follow:

Eliminate Repeating Groups—that is, move fields that are of a repeating nature to their own table.

 Tip A critical part of 1NF is to assign each table a primary key. An index, created from one or more fields in the table, makes each record unique.

For example, looking at the Customer table you see that you have a repeating group in the table of the City and State names. In reality, you should move these fields to another table and link it back to the Customer table via the zip code (only if, in America, you use the nine-digit zip code instead of the traditional five-digit one). For this exercise, we acknowledge that it should be done. For simplicity, however, we will leave it in the database, allowing people to enter the five-digit code or other country codes.

Second normal form (2NF)

Converting a table to second normal form takes a bit more thought. It relies on each table having a defined primary key.

 **Cross-Reference** For more information on primary keys, see Chapter 6.

Here's a practical rule to follow:

Eliminate Redundant Data—that is, any field in the table that is redundant, or will always be the same, based on another field's value, should be removed to a separate table.

For example, using Table 4-6 as a guide, we see that the Visits Details table has a field for Treatments and Treatment price and another for Medications and Medication price. Because these data elements will probably be repeated over and over (and the price is always the same for each different Treatment and Medication—i.e., redundant) they should be moved to their own tables. Then you can add a treatment code field and a medication code field to the Visits Details table to link the actual Medications and Treatment names to the Pets coming to the hospital.

Third Normal Form (3NF)

The final step in the 3NF model is a bit more difficult. It relies on each table having all the fields in the table *directly* related to the primary key field.

Here's a practical rule to follow:

Eliminate Columns (fields) not Dependent on the Key—that is, any field in the table that is not directly related to the primary key field should be removed to a separate table.

For example, using Table 4-6 as a guide, we see that the Visits table has three fields unrelated to the Visits table directly—Discount, Tax Rate, and Total Amount. These fields should also be moved to a more appropriate table or to their own tables and linked back to the Visits table. For the purposes of this book, several of the fields will remain in this table—making it only 2NF.

In summary, when creating your tables you should consider building them to 3NF. This greatly enhances both the accuracy and performance of your system.

The four primary tables of the system

With normalization in mind—and having completed the general data design (as in Table 4-6)—the next step is the final organization of the data into tables. Figure 4-8 shows the final design for the four primary tables and two lookup tables (Treatments and Medications); it's a database diagram found in Microsoft Access.

Cross-Reference   In Chapter 5, you create a table in Access. Creating the final set of tables is easy if you have lots of experience. If you don't, that's all right too, because Access lets you change a table definition after you've created it—without losing any data.

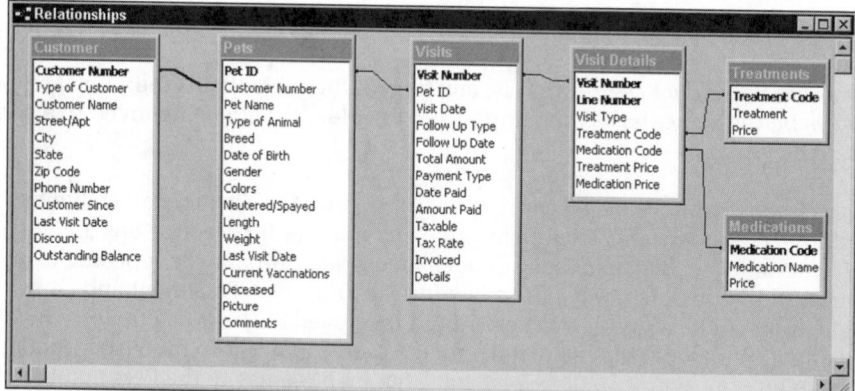

Figure 4-8: The final design of the primary tables of the Mountain Animal Hospital System, separating the data by function

Relating the four primary tables of the system to each other

Figure 4-8 shows the relationships that join one table to another. Notice the relationship between customers and pets, which is created by adding the Customer Number field to the Pets table. Each pet has a link to its owner (the customer) through this field. The same method can be used to establish a relationship between pets and visits. When you add the Pet ID field to the Visits table, each visit itself involves a pet in the Pets table. The Visit Number field establishes a similar relationship between Visits and Visit Details.

Cross-Reference In Chapter 6, you learn all about using multiple tables and how to set relations in Access. For now, a brief discussion of this topic shows how to design the relations between the various tables that you've identified.

Tables are related to each other so that information in one table is accessible to another. Usually, systems designed with Access contain several tables that are all related to one another. You establish these relations by having fields in the various tables that share a common value. The field names in these tables need not be the same; only the values have to match. In the Pets table, for example, you have the customer number. By relating the customer number in the Pets table to the customer number in the Customer table, you can retrieve all you need to know about the customer.

This saves you from storing the data in two places, and it is the first reason to have a relation — for a table lookup. A field in one table can look up data in another table. Another example: You can use the Pet ID field to create a table-lookup relation from the Visits table to the Pets table. Then, as you enter each item, Access passes data about the item (such as pet name, type of animal, breed, and date of birth) from the Pets table to the Visits table.

You may want to set a relation for a second reason, however. As you decide how to relate the tables that you've already designed, you must also decide how to handle multiple occurrences of data. In this system design, you may have multiple occurrences of visit details for each visit. For example, each treatment or medication is entered on a separate detail line. When this happens, you should split the table into two tables. In this design, you need to place the visit number of the visit in a separate table from the single-occurrence visit. This new Visit Details table is related by the Visit Number field found in the Visits table.

The Visits and Visit Details tables are the central focus of the system. The Visits table needs to be related not only to the Pets table but also to the Customer table, so you can retrieve information from it for the invoice report. Even so, you don't have to link the Visits table directly to the Customer table; you can go through the Pets table to get there. Figure 4-6 shows these chain link relationships graphically in an actual Access screen (the Query window), where you can set relations between tables.

In the course of a visit, the Pet ID field would be entered, linking the pet information to the Visits table. The Pets table uses the Customer Number field to retrieve the customer information (such as name and address) from the Customer table. Although the name and address are not stored in the Visits table itself, this information is needed to confirm that a pet in for a visit belongs to a particular customer.

Step 5: Field Design Data-Entry Rules and Validation

The next step is to define your fields and tables in greater detail. You also need to determine data-validation rules for each field and to define some new tables to help with data validation.

Designing field names, types, and sizes

First, you must name each field. The name should be easy to remember, as well as descriptive, so that you recognize the function of the field by its name. It should be just long enough to describe the field but not so short that it becomes cryptic. Access allows up to 64 characters (including spaces) for a field name.

You must also decide what type of data each of your fields will hold. In Access, you can choose any of several data types:

- ✦ **Text.** Alphanumeric characters; up to 255 characters
- ✦ **Memo.** Alphanumeric characters; long strings up to 64,000 characters
- ✦ **Number.** Numeric values of many types and formats
- ✦ **Date/Time.** Date and time data
- ✦ **Currency.** Monetary data
- ✦ **AutoNumber.** Automatically incremented numeric counter
- ✦ **Yes/No.** Logical values, Yes/No, True/False
- ✦ **OLE object.** Pictures, graphs, sound, video, word processing, and spreadsheet files

The Lookup Wizard is not actually a data type but is, instead, a way of storing a field one way and displaying a related value in another table. Generally, these are text fields, but they can also be numeric. For example, you can store 1, 2, or 3 for the Type of Customer and then look up and display the values Individual, Pet Store, and Zoo instead.

Note The AutoNumber data type was called Counter in Access 2.0.

One of these data types must be assigned to each of your fields (Part II explains data types in more detail). You must also specify the length of the text fields.

Designing data-entry rules

The last major design decision concerns data validation, which becomes important when you enter data. You want to make sure that only good data gets into your system — data that passes certain defined tests. You have to deal with several types of data validation. You can test for known individual items, stipulating that the Gender field can accept only the values Male, Female, or Unknown, for example. Or, you can test for ranges, specifying that the value of Weight must be between 0 and 1,500 pounds. Finally, you can test for compound conditions, such as whether the Type of Customer field indicates an individual (in which case the discount is 0 percent), a pet store (the discount field must show 20 percent), or a zoo (the discount is 50 percent). In the next chapter, you learn where you can enter conditions to perform data validation.

Designing lookup tables

Sometimes you need to design entire tables to perform data validation or just to make it easier to create your system; these are called *lookup tables*. For example, because Mountain Animal Hospital needs a field to determine the customer's tax rate, you decide to use a lookup table that contains the state code, state name, and state tax rate. This also allows you to enter no more than a two-digit state code in the Customer table and then look up the state name or tax rate when necessary. The state code then becomes the field that relates the tables. Because the tax rate can change, Access looks up the current tax rate whenever a visit record is created. The tax-rate value is stored in the Visits table to capture the tax rate for each visit because it is time-dependent data.

Tip This is the perfect time to use a Lookup Wizard in the Customer table — to look up and display the state instead of the state code.

Although you can create a field on a data-entry form that limits the entry of valid genders to Male, Female, and Unknown, too many animal types are allowable to create a field for animal type in a form. Instead, you create a table with only one field — Type of Animal — and use the Type of Animal field in the Pets table to link to this field in the Animals lookup table.

Note   You create a lookup table in exactly the same way as you create any other table, and it behaves in the same way. The only difference is in the way you use the table.

In Figure 4-9, four lookup tables have been added to the design, including the two that you created when you normalized your system. The States lookup table is necessary for determining an individual's tax rate. The Animals lookup table is added to ensure that standard animal types are entered into the Pets table (for the sake of consistency). The Animals lookup table is designed as an alphabetized listing of valid animal types.

The two tables on the far right, Treatments and Medications, are added for several reasons. The last thing you want is to require that doctors enter a long name to complete the Treatment or Medication fields after an animal's visit. Doctors should be able to choose from a list or enter a simple code. Then the code can be used to look up and retrieve the name of the treatment or medication along with its current price. The price that the doctor looks up must be stored in the Visit Details table because prices can change between the time of the visit and the time the invoice is sent out. The Treatments lookup table is added to store a list of treatments and their associated prices. Similarly, a Medications table is added for keeping a list of available medications and their associated prices.

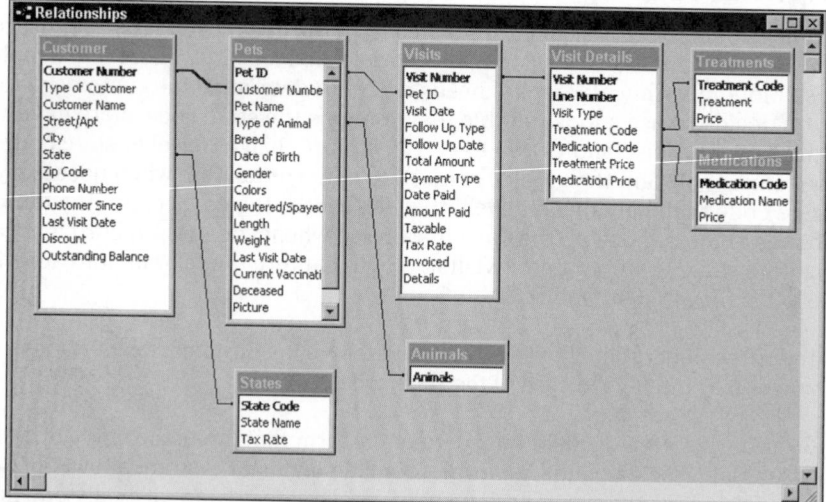

Figure 4-9: The final database diagram, with lookup tables added for the Mountain Animal Hospital System

Creating test data

After you define your data-entry rules and how the database should look, it's time to create test data. You should prepare this data scientifically (in order to test many possible conditions), and it should serve various purposes. For example, it should let you test the process of data entry: Do all the conditions that you created generate the proper acceptance or error messages? In addition, it may lead you to some conditions that you should test for that you hadn't considered. What happens, for example, when someone enters a blank into a field? How about numbers in a character field? Access automatically traps items such as bad dates or characters in Date and Numeric fields, but you must take care of the rest yourself.

The first type of test data you want to create is simply data that allows you to *populate*, or fill, the databases with meaningful data. This is the initial good data that should end up in the database and then be used to test output. Output consists mainly of your reports. The second type of test data you want to create is for testing data entry. This includes designing data with errors that display every one of your error conditions, along with good data that can test some of your acceptable conditions.

Test data should let you test routine items of the type you normally find in your data. You should also test for limits. Enter data that is only one character long for some fields, and use every field. Create several records that use every position in the database (and thereby every position in the data-entry screen and in the reports).

Create some "bad" test data. Enter data that tests every condition. Try to enter a customer number that already exists. Try to change a customer number that's not in the file. These are a few examples of what to consider when testing your system. Testing your system begins, of course, with the test data.

Step 6: Form Design — Input

After you've created the data and established table relationships, it's time to design your forms. Forms are made up of the fields that can be entered or viewed in edit mode. If at all possible, your screens should look much like the forms that you use in a manual system. This setup makes for the user-friendliest system.

Designing data-entry screens

When you're designing forms, you need to place three types of objects on-screen:

- ✦ Labels and text box data-entry fields
- ✦ Special controls (multiple-line text boxes, option buttons, list boxes, check boxes, business graphs, and pictures)

✦ Graphical objects to visually enhance them (color, lines, rectangles, and three-dimensional effects)

When designing a form, place your fields (text boxes, check boxes, list boxes, and radio buttons) just where you want them on the form. Ideally, if the form is being developed from an existing printed form, the Access data entry form should resemble the printed form. The fields should be in the same relative place on the screen as they are in the printed counterpart.

After you have placed your fields on the form, you can check the order of the fields. In other words, when you fill in a field and tab to the next field — which field does the cursor move to next? The tab order for data entry normally moves from top to bottom and from left to right when you fill in the fields (text boxes and special controls). However, you can tell Access to use a different order for moving from one field to another. When placing the fields, be sure to leave as much space around them as is needed. A calculated field, such as a total that is used only for data display, can also be part of a data-entry form.

You can use labels to display messages, titles, or captions. Text boxes provide an area where you can type or display text or numbers that are contained in your database. Check boxes indicate a condition and are either unchecked or checked (selected). Other types of controls available with Access include list boxes, combo boxes, option buttons, toggle buttons, and option groups.

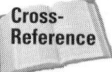

Cross-Reference

Chapter 14 covers the various types of controls available in Access. Access also provides a tool called *Microsoft Graph* that can be used to create a wide variety of graphs. Pictures can also be displayed using an OLE (Object Linking and Embedding) object stored in a database table, as you learn in Chapter 18.

In this book, you create several basic data-entry forms:

✦ Customer

✦ Pets

✦ Visits general information

✦ Visit Details

The Customer form

The Customer data-entry form shown in Figure 4-10 is the simplest of the data-entry forms that you create in this book. It is straightforward, simply listing the field descriptions on the left and the fields themselves on the right. The unique key field (primary key) is Customer Number. At the top of the form is the main header, a title that identifies this data-entry form by type: the Customer data-entry form.

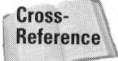

Cross-Reference

You can create this simple form by using a Form Wizard. See Chapter 8 for details.

Figure 4-10: The Customer data-entry form

The Pets form

The Pets data-entry form is more complex. It contains several types of controls, including option buttons, a list box, several combo boxes, check boxes, a picture, and a memo field. As shown in Figure 4-11, the form contains two sections: One section contains pet information, and the other contains customer information.

Cross-Reference: You learn how to create this form in Chapter 15 and to modify it in Chapters 16 through 18.

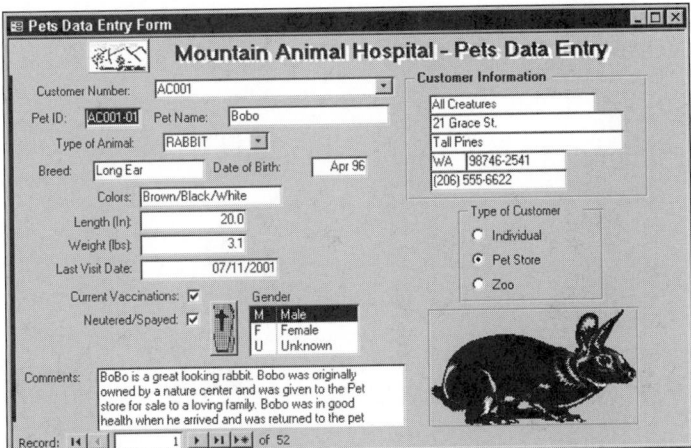

Figure 4-11: The Pets data-entry form for viewing and adding Pet and Customer information

The General Visits form

As shown in Figure 4-12, the next data-entry form combines data from several tables to provide general information about visits. This form contains information about customers, pets, and visits; its primary purpose is to allow a user to enter this type of information into the database. Visit Number is the key field for this form.

The Visit Details form

The final form in this book (shown in Figure 4-13) is for adding the details of individual visits. (You create this form in Chapter 26.) This form contains a subform so that many visit details can be seen at once. Many types of subforms can be linked to a form; you can even have a graph as a subform, as you discover in Chapter 18.

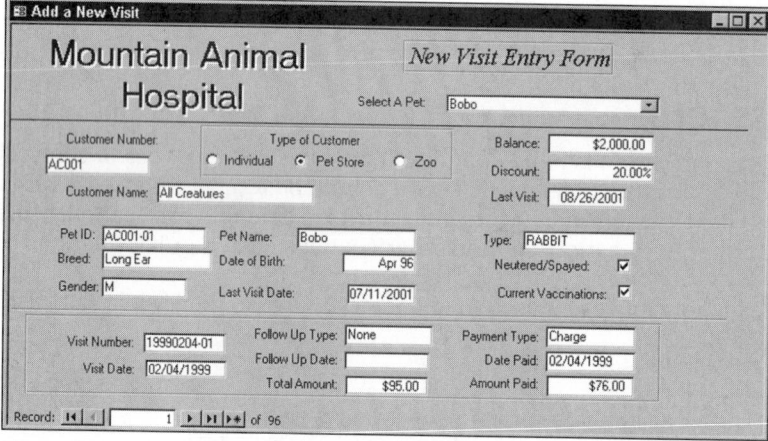

Figure 4-12: The General Visits data-entry form

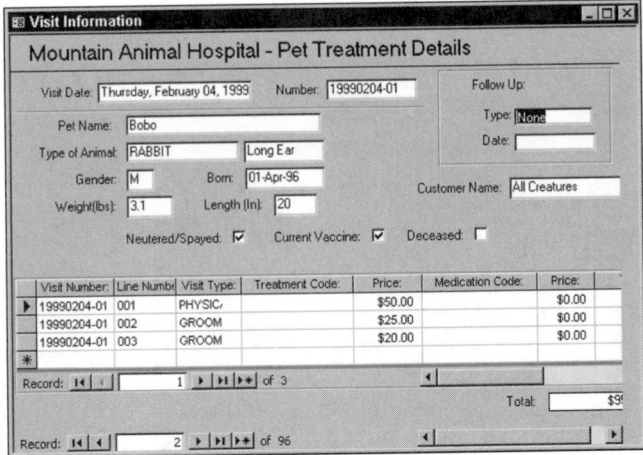

Figure 4-13: The Visit Details data-entry form

Step 7: Automation Design – Menus

After you've created your data, designed your reports, and created your forms, it's time to tie them all together using switchboards and menus. Figure 4-14 is a switchboard form that also contains a custom menu bar. Switchboards are graphical menus, which are usually built with command buttons with text or pictures on them. Menus refer to the lists of commands at the top of a window.

Menus are the key to a good system. A user must be able to follow the system to understand how to move from place to place. Usually each form or report is also a choice on a menu. This means that your design must include decisions on how to group the commands. When you examine the overall design and look at all your systems, you begin to see a distinct set of combinations.

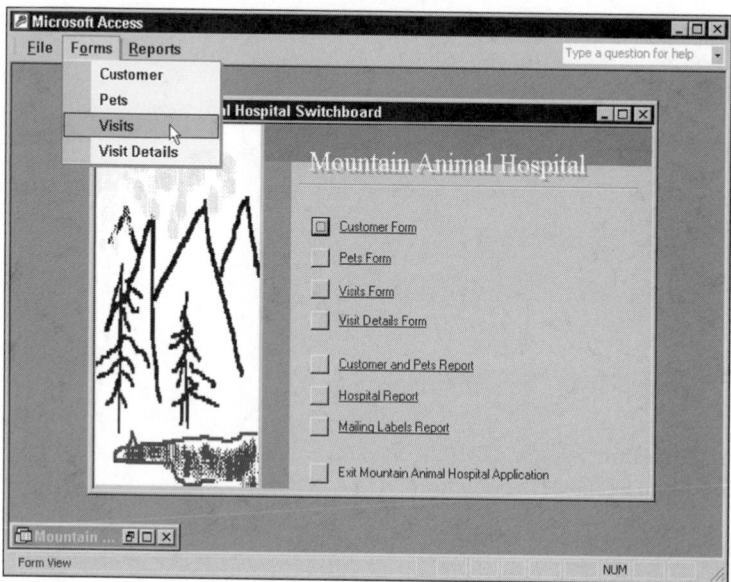

Figure 4-14: A switchboard and menu for Mountain Animal Hospital

You can use Access macros to create a menu on the top menu bar of the switch-board. This menu gives the user the choice of using pull-down menus or switchboard buttons. You create this switchboard, along with the menus and a complicated dialog box, in Chapter 32.

✦   ✦   ✦

Creating the Objects

◆   ◆   ◆   ◆

In This Part

Chapter 5
Creating Database
Tables

Chapter 6
Setting Relationships
Between Tables

Chapter 7
Working with
Information in Tables

Chapter 8
Creating and Using
Simple Data-Entry
Forms

Chapter 9
Understanding and
Creating Simple
Queries

Chapter 10
Creating and
Working with Simple
Reports

◆   ◆   ◆   ◆

Creating Database Tables

In this chapter, you learn to start the process of database and table creation. You create a database container to hold the tables, queries, forms, reports, and macros that you create as you learn Access. You also create the Pets database table, which stores data about the pets treated by the Mountain Animal Hospital.

Creating the Pets Table

The Pets table is one of the best table examples in the Mountain Animal Hospital database because it illustrates the major field types used by Access. In most tables, the majority of fields are *text fields*. Most data in the world is either numbers or text. The Pets table contains many text fields used to fully describe each animal, but it also contains several *numeric fields* for storing the animal's length and weight. Another common field type is *date and time*; the Pets table uses a date/time field for storing the date of birth. The Pets table also contains several *yes/no fields* for storing a single choice. Examples of this field are Neutered and Current Vaccination. Large amounts of text are stored in *memo fields*; for example, notes about the animal, such as special customer preferences or known allergies. Another field type is the *OLE field*, which is used for storing sound, pictures, or video. In the Pets example, this field will be used to store a picture of the animal.

Before you can create a table, however, you must first create the overall database container.

♦   ♦   ♦   ♦

In This Chapter

Creating a database

Creating a table

Navigating in the Table window

Entering field names and descriptions

Selecting a field data type

Entering field properties

Changing a table design

Creating a primary key

Saving and printing your table design

Renaming, copying, and deleting tables

Using groups

♦   ♦   ♦   ♦

Creating a Database

The Database window displays all the various object files from your database that you may create while using Access. Actually, a database is a single file. As you create new *object files*, they are stored within the database file. They are not DOS files in themselves; instead, they are stored objects. The database file starts at about 94,000 bytes (92K) and grows as you create new objects — tables, queries, forms, reports, macros, and modules. Adding data to an Access database also increases the size of the file.

There are many ways to create a new database file. When you start Microsoft Access 2002 you will see the New File dialog box open in the Database window as shown in Figure 5-1. You can also display this dialog box by selecting File ➪ New from the main Access menu, or by clicking on the New button (the first button in the toolbar). It looks like a sheet of paper with the right top corner bent down.

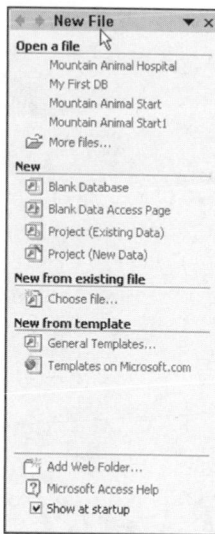

Figure 5-1: The New File dialog box opens along the right-hand side of the Access window showing three general categories for creating a new database.

The New File dialog box shows several groupings. These are

> ✦ **Open a file.** This lets you open an existing database file. The last four databases opened are displayed. Clicking on the *More files* choice opens the Open dialog box, which enables you to browse through your hard drive for the existing database you want to open.

> ✦ **New.** Lets you open a blank Database, a blank Data Access Page, a Project (Existing Data) or a Project (New Data).

✦ **New from existing file.** Select *Choose file* to open the Open dialog box, which enables you to select an existing database. It will then make a copy of that database and name it by the same name with a number 1 attached to the end of the name — for example, 'Mountain Animal.mdb' will be copied and the new database file name will be "Mountain Animal1.mdb".

✦ **New from template.** This group enables you to choose from *General templates* or *Templates on Microsoft.com*'s web site.

Templates dialog box

In addition to using the New section to create a blank database, you can select the first choice in the "New from template" section of the New File dialog box — General Templates — and it will open the Templates dialog box, as shown in Figure 5-2. This Templates dialog box was what would open automatically in previous versions of Access — 2000, 97, and backward.

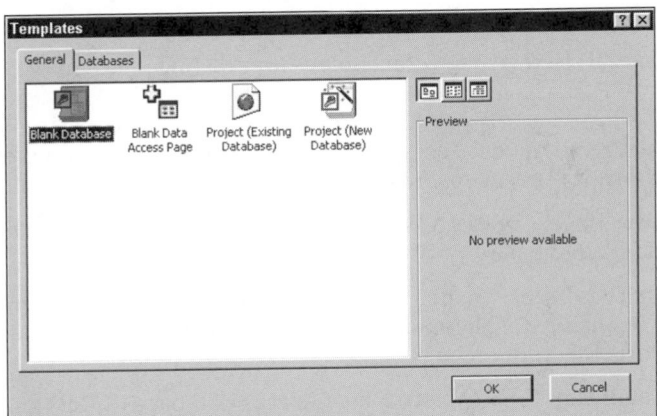

Figure 5-2: The Templates dialog box is activated by selecting the General Templates choice from the New Files dialog box. This is the same as the old New dialog box that Access presented in previous versions.

The Templates dialog box has two tabs. These are

✦ **General.** Create new Access databases, data access pages, or Access databases connected to SQL Server projects.

✦ **Databases.** Lets you use the Database Wizard to create a simple ready-to-run database created for Access 2002 including Asset Tracking, Contact Management, Event Management, Expenses, Inventory Control, Ledger, Order Entry, Resource Scheduling, Service Call Management, and Time and Billing. Figure 5-3 shows these selections.

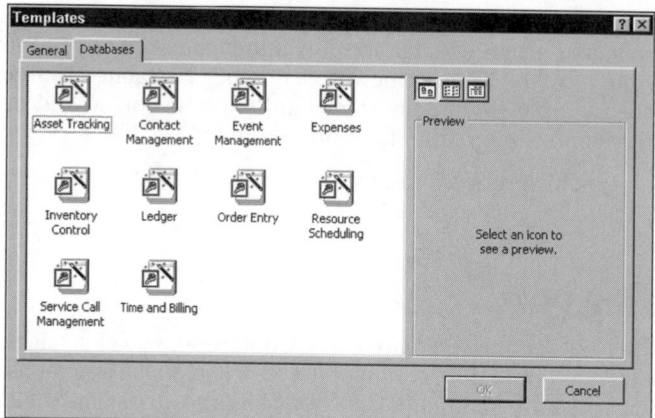

Figure 5-3: The Databases page, showing the included database wizards. You can view these by selecting the Database tab of the Templates dialog box.

Click the first tab (General) to reveal several choices for creating new empty databases.

✦ **Blank Database.** Creates a new Access .MDB file to enable you to you create tables, queries, forms, reports, macros, and modules.

✦ **Blank Data Access Page.** Creates a Web-based (intranet) form with live links to an Access or SQL database.

✦ **Project (Existing Database).** Creates a new SQL Server project (.ADP file) to hold the table data using the Microsoft Database Engine but uses an existing Access .MDB file as the front-end.

✦ **Project (New Database).** Creates both a new Access database (.MDB) and a new SQL Server project (.ADP) to hold the data tables.

New Feature

Data Access Pages were new in Access 2000 and are essentially live data forms that you publish to a corporate intranet. Access 2002 has added many new features to Data Access Pages. It still requires Internet Explorer 5.x or later and works best in version 5.5 or better.

Project (Existing Database) creates a new SQL Server project using either SQL Server 6.5, SQL Server 7.x Enterprise Edition, or SQL Server 2000 Desktop (new in Version 2002) and Microsoft Database Engine. When you create a project, you are creating a database file with an .ADP extension that only contains tables and queries. You must also have an Access .MDB data file to contain your user interface objects (forms, reports, macros, and modules).

Project (New Database) creates a new SQL Server project using either SQL Server 6.5, SQL Server 7.x Enterprise Edition, SQL Server 2000 Desktop, or the Microsoft

Database Engine. It will create a database file with the .ADP extension that will contain the tables and queries. The interface objects will be stored in a standard Access .MDB database.

Note If you have the Templates dialog box open, close it at this time to continue with "Creating a new database."

Blank database

Creating a database is a very simple matter. Just follow the steps below:

1. Click New (the first toolbar button) if the New File dialog box is *not open* already. You should see the New File dialog box as shown in Figure 5-1

2. Click 'Blank Database' under the New category.

3. The File New Database dialog box opens, as shown in Figure 5-4. You can see any existing .MDB files in the file list part of the window. The Save in: combo box may initially open to the My Documents folder. Navigate to the folder you want to place your new database file in — in the case of the author it is a folder named "Access 2002 db Files."

4. A default name of *db1.mdb* will appear in the File name text box at the bottom of the window — simply type over this default name with the name **My Mountain Animal Hospital**, or any other name you want to give the database. (Typing the extension, *.mdb*, is optional, because Access will automatically supply it if you do not.)

5. Click the Create button.

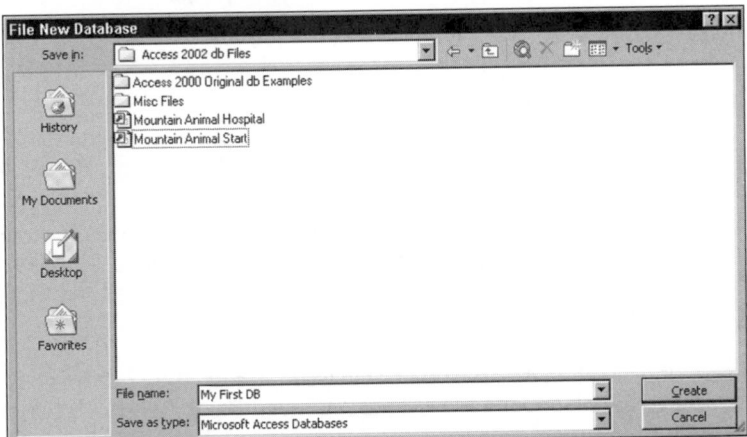

Figure 5-4: The File New Database dialog box, where you will specify a name for the new database. In this case type **My Mountain Animal Hospital.**

Once the new database is created, Access will automatically open it for you.

Understanding How Access Works with Data

There are many ways that Microsoft Access 2002 works with data. For simplicity, you will see the data stored in local tables in the examples of this book. A local table is a table stored within the Access .MDB file This is how you have seen examples so far.

In many professionally developed Microsoft Access applications, the actual tables are in their own database while the other interface objects (forms, reports, queries, pages, macros, and modules) are stored in another database. The reason for this is usually maintainability. By separating the data and their tables into another database you can easily do maintenance work on them (building new indexes, repairing the tables, etc.) without affecting the remainder of the system. In contrast, you may be working with a multi-user system and find a problem with a form or report object in the system. If you have all the data and interface objects in the same database, you would have to shut down the system while repairing the broken form or report — others could not be using the system while you repair one object. Instead, by separating the data from the other objects, you can fix the erring object while others are still working with the data. Once you fixed the problem, you can deliver the new changes to the others and they can import it into their local database system. In addition, there is a more critical reason to separate your data from the interface objects — security. By maintaining the data separately in its own database, either locally or in a remote location, as in a multi-user environment, you can maintain better control over the information. Thus, the solution is to consider separating your tables, and their stored data, from the rest of the application.

While you may want to first develop your application with the tables within the .MDB database, later you can use the Database Splitter wizard to automatically move the tables in your .MDB file to a separate Access .MDB file and then attach the tables. You can also attach your tables to the Microsoft Database Engine or the larger SQL Server database. You can also attach to non-Microsoft servers such as Oracle, Informix, or Sybase.

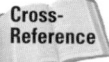

Cross-Reference   You will learn more about file attaching in Chapter 22.

Caution   An Access 2002 database cannot be used by previous versions of Access. However, Access 2002 can use previous formats of Access databases — 2.0, 95, 97, and 2000. Since the default version is 2000 you can use these files with Access 2000 or Access 2002.

Tip   You can save or convert an Access 2002 Database in Access 2000 or Access 97 format by selecting Tools ➪ Database Utilities ➪ Convert Database ➪ To Access 97 or Access 2000 File Format.

Caution   If you enter a file extension other than MDB, Access saves the database file but does not display it when you open the database later. By default, Access searches for and displays only those files with an MDB file extension.

If you are following the examples in this book, note that we have chosen the name *My Mountain Animal Hospital* for the name of the database you create as you complete the chapter. This database is for our hypothetical business, the Mountain Animal Hospital. After you enter the filename, Access creates the empty database. The CD-ROM that comes with your book contains two primary database files named *Mountain Animal Hospital Start* (only the database tables), and *Mountain Animal Hospital* (the completed application, including tables, forms, queries, reports, macros, and modules).

The Database Window

The Database window is shown in Figure 5-5. It comprises three basic parts. First is the Object menu bar on the left side of the window and below it a Groups menu bar. Along the top of the window is the second part, the toolbar with the buttons Open, Design, and New. Finally, the third part is the open pane to the right and center that is used to show all of the objects of the type selected (Tables, Queries, and so on).

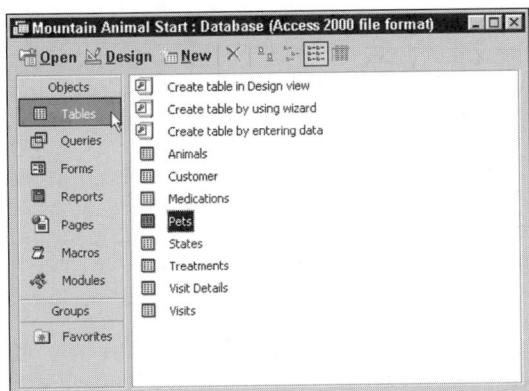

Figure 5-5: The Database window. This window, or container, has three basic parts — the Menu bars on the left side, the toolbar along the top, and the open pane.

The Database window can be thought of as a container that holds all the different objects that make up the database itself. When you click any of the object menu items (Tables, Forms, etc.), the open pane on the right of the menu bar will display the appropriate objects. For instance, Figure 5-5 shows all the Table objects because the Table button is selected (it is also the default selection). If you click on the Forms button you will see all the forms that you have built in the open pane.

The menu bar comprises two different groups of menus — Object types and Groups. The Object type menu references all the object types that are used to make up the entire database. The Groups menu is used to store and retrieve different object types by use of a shortcut — it can contain any type of object.

Objects menu bar

The Database window contains seven buttons on the vertical Objects menu bar; using them, you can quickly select any of these objects that are available in Access:

✦ Tables

✦ Queries

✦ Forms

✦ Reports

✦ Pages

✦ Macros

✦ Modules

As you create new objects, the names of the files appear in the open pane of the Database window. You see only the files for the particular type of object selected. You can select an object type to view by clicking one of the object buttons.

In addition to the new objects that you create, the Database window will show several new object shortcuts for each object type selected. For instance in Figure 5-5 you see three new object shortcuts at the top of the object pane — "Create table in Design view," "Create table by using wizard," and "Create table by entering data."

Only the Tables, Queries, Forms, Reports, and Pages objects have new objects shortcuts. Queries, Forms, and Reports each have two and the Tables and Pages have three. To see the two for Forms, simply click on the Forms button and the first two choices in the window pane are the new object shortcuts — "Create form in Design view" and "Create form by using wizard."

Tip   Inside the object window pane are two or three create icons and their new object shortcut labels. These can help you get started and are provided for each type of object. You can turn off this new feature by clicking Tools ➪ Options and deselecting New object shortcuts.

There are four buttons on the right side of the toolbar that can change how you look at the objects in the database object pane — one to see Large Icons of objects, one for Small Icons, one for List of objects (default) and the last for Details listing of objects.

Figure 5-5 shows the default (List) Database window view. In it you only see the object names, for instance, table names — Animals, Customers, Medications, Pets, and more. You can switch to the Details view of the object files in the Database window by clicking the last button on the toolbar — a button that looks like a series of lines in a box. This shows information such as a description, the date modified, date created, and type of object. You can also view this detailed information by clicking View from your Access menu bar and then clicking Details.

Groups menu bar

The Groups menu has one default button under it — Favorites. Groups are used to store shortcuts to the different database objects, so that they can be accessed quickly from one place. For instance you may want to add a shortcut for the Customer table and the Customer form, or other different types of objects.

Tip When you place your database objects into a group, this creates a shortcut to that object. For example, assume you are working with a fairly large database with several hundred objects but that you are currently working with only three of those objects. Instead of switching between the seven database objects and browsing for the individual object names, you can store shortcuts to all the objects you use in a group you create. As shown in Figure 5-6, there are shortcuts to a table, a query, a macro, and a form showing in the default Favorites Group.

The objects must already have been created to add them to a group. This figure uses objects that you create later and are not yet in this database.

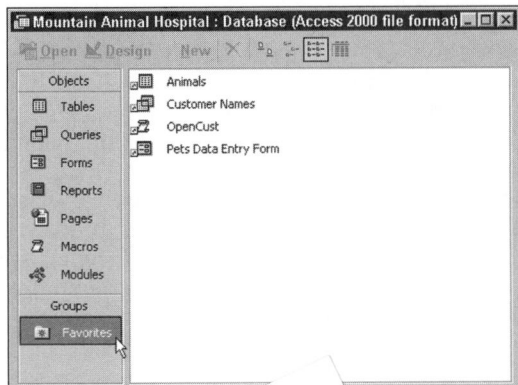

Figure 5-6: The A~ ~stomer Names query, OpenCust m~ ~try Form shortcuts are located ~ ~named Favorites.

~roup. You can create your own groups menu
~o create a new group, right-click on the
~This will display a dialog box where you can
~ed in the group name, click OK and the

~ in your groups, click and drag the object into
~olbar buttons appear for the different objects as
~y command you can't perform when you are in a group is
~ct (Table, Query, Form, Report, Pages, Macro, or Module). The
~ are described in the next section.

The Database window toolbar buttons

The toolbar buttons in the Database window enable you to 'Open' an existing object that is highlighted (selected); display "Design" mode for the current high-lighted object; create a "New" object; or "Delete" (the X button) the currently high-lighted object. When a button is clicked, the appropriate action is taken. Before clicking Open or Design, you should select an object name by highlighting it. When you select New, the type of the new object that will be created depends on the object type button you have selected in the Objects menu bar (Form, Table, Query or others). If you chose the Tables type, a new table is created. When you select some of the other object types, the toolbar buttons may change. When you select the Reports type, for example, the three available toolbar buttons are Preview, Design, and New.

The Access window toolbar

The toolbar shown in Figure 5-7 enables you to perform tasks quickly without using the menus. (Tools that are not available appear in light gray.)

If you place the cursor on a button without clicking and wait a short time (a second or two), a Help prompt known as a *Tool Tip* appears just below the button. If you want even more help, press Shift+F1, and then move the cursor to the object you want more information about and click it. You will see *What's This?* help: A small rectangle with a paragraph explaining the use of the selected object. Figure 5-7 shows the What's This? information box for the Spelling button. Another way of get-ting Help is to select the Office Assistant button at the far right of the toolbar (it has a question mark inside a bubble), and then type a question in the Office Assistant box. Finally you can type in your question directly in the new Help combo box along the right-most side of the menu bar of Access.

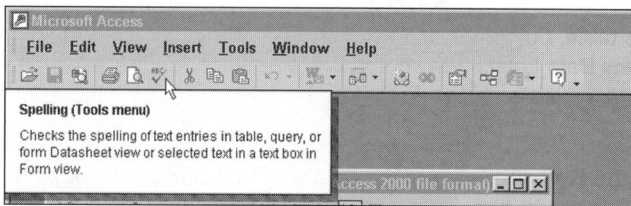

Figure 5-7: The Database window toolbar. Notice that it also shows the Shift-F1 information box that is displayed for the Spelling button.

Starting from the left you see the following toolbar buttons:

✦ **Open.** Open a database (an open file folder)

✦ **Save.** Save an object (a floppy disk)

✦ **Search.** Search the disk for a file (the Windows logo over a piece of paper with magnifying glass)

✦ **Print.** Print an object to the printer (printer)

✦ **Print Preview.** View an object as it will look printed (piece of paper with magnifying glass)

✦ **Spelling.** Check the spelling (check mark "ABC")

✦ **Cut.** Remove the selection (scissors)

✦ **Copy.** Copy the selection (two pieces of paper)

✦ **Paste.** Insert from the clipboard (clipboard with piece of paper)

✦ **Undo.** Undo the last action (an arrow rotating counterclockwise and menu selection arrow)

✦ **Office Links.** Display the links to Word and Excel (icon of a large W and envelope and menu selection arrow)

✦ **Analyze.** Display the Analyze commands (Table picture with two table icons and a menu selection arrow)

✦ **Code.** Displays the Code window (rectangle with red, blue, and yellow boxes on it) — Optional and only visible if loaded

✦ **Microsoft Script Editor.** Displays the Script Editor window (an eight inside another eight on its side) — Optional and only visible if loaded. The editor is used to create VBScript or JScript for data access pages.

✦ **Properties.** Displays the Properties window (a hand holding a piece of paper)

✦ **Relationships.** Displays the Relationships window (three tables with lines between them)

✦ **New Object.** Displays the New Object choices (a starburst over top left corner of a table icon and a menu selection arrow)

✦ **Help.** Displays the Microsoft Access Help window (a cartoon caption box with a question mark inside)

✦ **Toolbar Options.** Allows you to add or remove toolbar buttons (a Menu selection arrow — pointing down)

Creating a New Table

After you design your table on paper, you need to create the table design in Access. Although you can create the table interactively without any forethought, carefully planning a database system is a good idea. You can make any changes later, but doing so wastes time; generally the result is a system that is harder to maintain than one that is well planned from the beginning. Before you get started, you should understand the table design process.

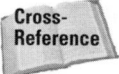

Cross-Reference   To refresh your knowledge on how to design your tables for the database, refer to Chapter 4.

The table design process

Creating a table design is a multi-step process. By following the steps in order, your table design can be created readily and with minimal effort:

✦ Create a new table.

✦ Enter each field name, data type, and description.

✦ Enter properties for each defined field.

✦ Set a primary key.

✦ Create indexes for necessary fields.

✦ Save the design.

You can use any of these four methods to create a new table design:

✦ Click the New toolbar button in the Database window.

✦ Select Insert ⇨ Table from the menus.

✦ Select New Table from the New Object button in the Access toolbar.

✦ Select Create table in Design view (first object in Tables pane of Database window) if the New object shortcuts option is turned on.

Tip   If you create a new table by clicking the 'New' command button in the Database window, make sure that the Table object button is selected first from the Objects menu bar.

Select the New command button in the Database window to begin creating a new table.

The New Table dialog box

Figure 5-8 shows the New Table dialog box as Access displays it.

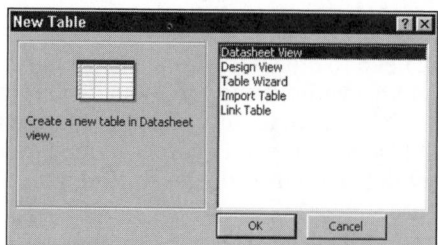

Figure 5-8: The New Table dialog box

Using the Table Wizard

When you create a new table, you can type in every field name, data type, size, and other table property information, or you can use the Table Wizard (as shown in Figure 5-9) to select from a long list of predefined tables and fields. Unlike the Database Wizard (which creates a complete application), the Table Wizard creates only a table and a simple form.

Wizards can save you a lot of work; they are meant to save you time and make complex tasks easier. Wizards work by taking you through a series of screens that ask what you want. You answer these questions by clicking on buttons, selecting fields, entering text, and making yes/no decisions.

In the Table Wizard, first you choose between the lists of Business or Personal tables. Some of the Business tables are Mailing List, Contacts, Employees, Products, Orders, Suppliers, Payments, Invoices, Assets, and Students. The Personal list includes Guests, Recipes, Exercise Log, Plants, Wine List, Photographs, Video Collection, and more.

When you select a table, a list appears and shows you all the fields that you might want in the table. Select only the fields you want. Although they are all predefined for data type and size, you can rename a field once it's selected. Once you've chosen your fields, another screen uses input from you to create a primary key automatically. Other screens help you to automatically link the primary key to another table and establish relationships. Finally, the Wizard can display the table, enable you to enter records into a datasheet, or even create an automatic form for you. The entire process of creating a simple table and form can take less than one minute! Whenever you need to create a table for an application on the Wizard's list, you can save a lot of time by using the Wizard.

You use this dialog box to select one of these five ways to create a new table:

✦ **Datasheet View.** Enter data into a spreadsheet

✦ **Design View.** Create a table in Design view

✦ **Table Wizard.** Select a pre-built table that is complete with generic field definitions

✦ **Import Table.** Import external data formats into a new Access table

✦ **Link Table.** Link to an existing external data source

Access 2002 provides several ways to create a new table. You can design the structure of the table (such as field names, data types, and size) first, and then add data. Another method is to use the Table Wizard to choose from a list of predefined table designs. Access also gives you three new ways to create a new table easily. First, you can enter the data into a spreadsheet-like form known as Datasheet view; Access will create the table for you automatically. Second, you can use the Import Table Wizard to select an external data source and create a new table containing a copy of the data found in that source; the Wizard takes you through the import process. Third, you can use the Link Table Wizard, which is similar to the Import Table Wizard except the data stays in the original location and Access links to it from the new table.

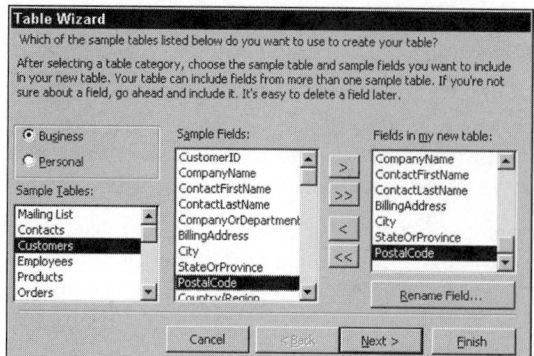

Figure 5-9: This is the first screen of the Table Wizard.
It enables you to select an example type table (Customers
in this figure) then select fields to add to the table to be created.

To create your first table, the Datasheet view is a great method for getting
started; then you can use the table's Design view to make any final changes
and adjustments.

Cross-Reference   The Import Table and Link Table are covered in Chapter 22.

Select New from the Database window, then select Datasheet View and click on the
OK button to display a blank datasheet with which you can create a new table.

Creating a new table with a Datasheet view

The empty datasheet appears, ready for you to enter data and create a new record.
You begin by entering a few records into the datasheet. Each column will become a
field and each row will become a record in the table. You will learn more about
these terms later in this chapter. For now, all you have to do is add data. The more
records you add, the more accurately Access can tell what type of data you want
for each field, and the approximate size of each data item.

When you first see the datasheet, it's empty. The column headers that will become
field names for the table are labeled *Field1, Field2, Field3,* and so on. You can
change the column header names if you want; they become the field names for the
table design. You can always change the field names after you have finished creating the table. The table datasheet is initially named *Table* followed by a number. If
there are no other tables named Table with a number, Access uses the name *Table1*;
the next table is named *Table2*, and so forth. You can always change this name
when you save the table.

Add the five records as shown in Figure 5-10, and then change the column headers to the names shown by double-clicking on the field name (Field1, etc.).

Note You can change a column name by double-clicking the column name and editing the value. When you're done, press Enter to save the new column header. If you enter a column header name that is wider than the default column width, adjust the column width by placing the cursor on the line between the column names and dragging the line to the right to make it wider or to the left to make it narrower.

Pet Name	Type of Animal	Date of Birth	Value	Weight	Deceased	Field7
Bobo	RABBIT	4/8/2000	$200	3.1	NO	
Presto Chango	LIZARD	5/1/2001	$45	35	NO	
Margo	SQUIRREL	3/1/1998	$15	22	NO	
Tom	CAT	2/1/1999	$275	27.8	YES	
Jerry	RAT	2/1/2000	$2	3.1	NO	

Record: 5 of 21

Figure 5-10: A partially completed Datasheet view of the data used to create a new Table. Notice that the first six fields have had their field names changed and that each column holds the same type of data.

Tip The Access 2002 and Microsoft Excel spreadsheet Datasheet windows work similarly. Many techniques are the same for both products; even many menus and toolbar buttons are the same.

Once you have finished entering the data, save the table and give it a name — Pets. To close the table and save the data entered, either choose Close from the File menu or click the Close button in the upper-right corner of the Table window (the button with the X on it). You can also click the Save button on the toolbar, but this only saves the table; you still have to close it.

Clicking the Close button in the window will activate a dialog box that asks whether you want to save changes to Table1. You have three choices — "Yes" to save the table and give it a name, "No" to forget everything, or "Cancel" to return to the table to enter more data.

For this example, select "Yes" to continue the process to save the table. The Save As dialog box appears prompting you for a new name for the table. It shows you the default table name of Table1.

Enter "Pets" and click OK to continue to save the table. Yet another dialog box appears, asking whether you want to create a primary key — a unique identifier for each record, which you learn about later in the chapter. For now, just select No.

Access saves the table and returns you to the Database window. Notice that the table name "Pets" now appears in the table object list. If you did everything correctly, you have successfully created a table named Pets that has five fields and five records. The next step is to edit the table design and create the final table design you saw in Chapter 4.

To open the Pets table in Design View, select it, and then click the Design button. Figure 5-11 shows the Pets Table Design window with the design that was automatically created by the data you entered in the Datasheet view. Notice the field names that you created by entering their names in the first row of each column. Also notice the data types that Access automatically assigned to each field. It looked at the information that you typed into each column and attempted to determine the type of data you entered. For instance it figured out that you wanted a Date/Time type field for the Date of Birth column, and Currency for the Value field. In the next part of this chapter, you learn about these field types.

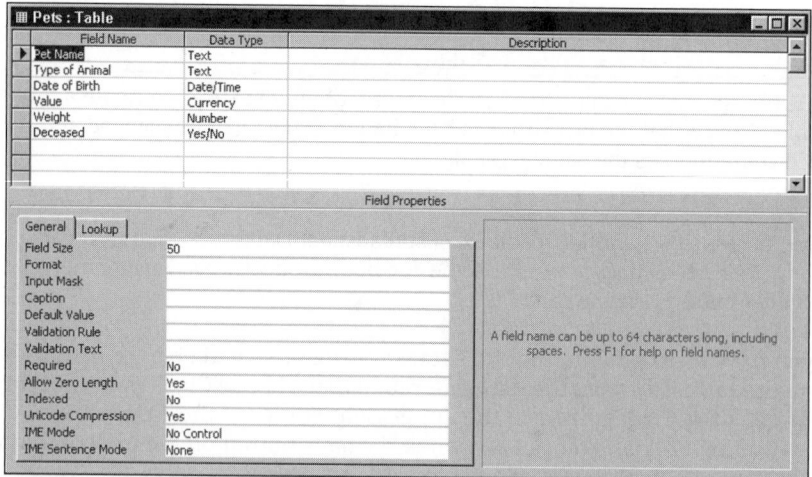

Figure 5-11: The Table Design window contains the Field Names and Data types in the top pane and Field Properties for the current field in the bottom pane — in this case the properties for the Pet Name field.

The Table Design Window

The Table Design window consists of two areas:

✦ The field entry area

✦ The field properties area

The *field entry area* is for entering each field's name and data type; you can also enter an optional description. The *property area* is for entering more options, called *properties,* for each field. These properties include field size, format, input mask, alternate caption for forms, default value, validation rules, validation text, required, zero length for null checking, index specifications, and unicode compression. You learn more about these properties later in the book.

 Tip   You can switch between areas (also referred to as panes) by clicking the mouse when the pointer is in the desired pane or by pressing F6.

Using the Table Design window toolbar

The Table Design window toolbar, shown in Figure 5-12, contains many buttons that assist in creating a new table definition.

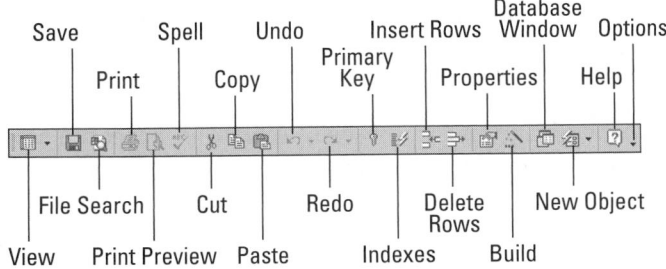

Figure 5-12: The Table Design window toolbar

Working with fields

Fields are created by entering a *field name* and a *field data type* in each row of the field entry area of the Table Design window. The *field description* is an option to identify the field's purpose; it appears in the status bar during data entry. After you enter each field's name and data type, you can further specify how each field is used by entering properties in the property area. Before you enter any properties, however, you should enter all your field names and data types for this example. You have already created some of the fields you will need.

Naming a field

A *field name* should be clear enough to identify the field to you, the user of the system, and to Access. Field names should be long enough to quickly identify the purpose of the field, but not overly long. (Later, as you enter validation rules or use the field name in a calculation, you'll want to save yourself from typing long field names.)

To enter a field name, position the pointer in the first row of the Table Design window under the Field Name column. Then type a valid field name, observing these rules:

- ✦ Field names can be from 1 to 64 characters.

- ✦ Field names can include letters, numbers, and many special characters.

- ✦ Field names cannot include a period (.), exclamation point (!), brackets ([ ]), or accent grave (`).

- ✦ You can't use low-order ASCII characters, for example Ctrl-J or Ctrl-L (ASCII values 0 to 31).

- ✦ You can't start with a blank space.

- ✦ You can't use a double quotation mark (") in the name of a Microsoft Access project file.

You can enter field names in upper-, lower-, or mixed case. If you make a mistake while typing the field name, position the cursor where you want to make a correction and type the change. You can change a field name at any time — even if it's in a table and the field contains data — for any reason.

 Caution   Once your table is saved, however, if you change a field name that is also used in queries, forms, or reports, you have to change it in those objects as well.

Specifying a data type

After you name a field, you must decide what type of data the field will hold. Before you begin entering data, you should have a good grasp of the data types that your system will use. Ten basic types of data are shown in Table 5-1; some data types (such as numbers) have several options.

<table>
<tr><td colspan="3" align="center">Table 5-1
Data Types Available in Microsoft Access</td></tr>
<tr><td>*Data Type*</td><td>*Type of Data Stored*</td><td>*Storage Size*</td></tr>
<tr><td>Text</td><td>Alphanumeric characters</td><td>0–255 characters</td></tr>
<tr><td>Memo</td><td>Alphanumeric characters</td><td>0–65,536 characters</td></tr>
</table>

Data Type	Type of Data Stored	Storage Size
Number	Numeric values	1, 2, 4, or 8 bytes, 16 bytes for Replication ID (GUID)
Date/Time	Date and time data	8 bytes
Currency	Monetary data	8 bytes
AutoNumber	Automatic number increments	4 bytes, 16 bytes for Replication ID (GUID)
Yes/No	Logical values: Yes/No, True/False	1 bit (0 or −1)
OLE Object	Pictures, graphs, sound, video	Up to 1GB (disk space limitation)
HyperLink	Link to an Internet resource	0–64,000 characters
Lookup Wizard	Displays data from another table	Generally 4 bytes

Figure 5-13 shows the Data Type drop-down list. It is used to select the choice for the type of data you want to save in the field you just created. When you move the pointer into the Data Type column, a down arrow (↓) appears in the text-entry box. To open this drop-down list, move the cursor into the Data Type column and click on the down arrow (↓).

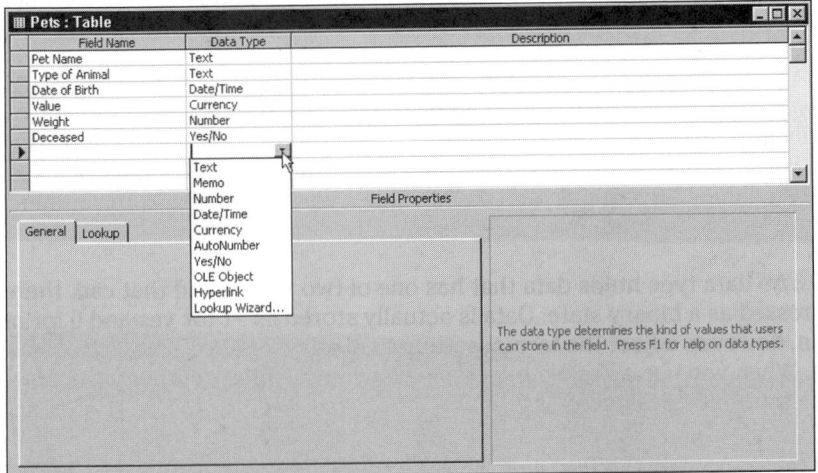

Figure 5-13: The Data Type drop-down list. You can quickly select the type of data you want to store in a field by clicking on the list and selecting from it. You can also type in the name of the data type.

Text data is any type of data that is simply characters. Names, addresses, and descriptions are all text data — as are numeric data that are not used in a calculation (such as telephone numbers, Social Security numbers, and ZIP codes). Although you specify the size of each text field in the property area, you can enter no more than 255 characters of data in any text field. Access uses variable length fields to store its data. If you designate a field to be 25 characters wide and you only use 5 characters for each record, then that is all the space you will actually use in your database container. You will find that the .MDB database file can get large quickly but text fields are not the cause. However, rather than allow Access to create every text field with the default 50 characters or the maximum 255 characters, it is good practice to limit text field widths to the maximum you believe they will be used for. Names are tricky because some cultures have long names. However, it is a safe bet that a postal code might be less than 12 characters wide while a U.S. state abbreviation is always 2 characters wide. By limiting the size of the text width, you also limit the number of characters the user can type when the field is used in a form.

The *Memo* data type holds a variable amount of data, from 0 to 65,536 characters for each record. Therefore, if one record uses 100 characters, another requires only 10, and yet another needs 3,000, you only use as much space as each record requires.

The *Number* data type enables you to enter *numeric* data; that is, numbers that will be used in mathematical calculations. (If you have data that will be used in monetary calculations, you should use the *Currency* data type, which enables you to specify many different currency types.)

The *Date/Time* data type can store dates, times, or both types of data at once. Thus, you can enter a date, a time, or a date/time combination. You can specify many types of formats in the property entry area and then display date and time data as you prefer.

The *AutoNumber* data type stores an integer that Access increments (adds to) automatically as you add new records. You can use the AutoNumber data type as a unique record identification for tables having no other unique value. If, for example, you have no unique identifier for a list of names, you can use an AutoNumber field to identify one John Smith from another.

The *Yes/No* data type holds data that has one of two values and that can, therefore, be expressed as a binary state. Data is actually stored as –1 for yes and 0 for no. You can, however, adjust the format setting to display Yes/No, True/False, or On/Off. When you use a Yes/No data type, you can use many of the form controls that are especially designed for it.

The *OLE Object* data type provides access for data that can be linked to an OLE server. This type of data includes bitmaps (such as Windows Paint files), audio files (such as WAV files), business graphics (such as those found in Access and Excel), and even full-motion video files. Of course, you can play the video files only if you have the hardware and necessary OLE server software.

The *Hyperlink* data type field holds combinations of text and numbers stored as text and used as a hyperlink address. It can have up to three parts: (1) the visual text that appears in a field (usually underlined); (2) the Internet address — the path to a file (UNC, or Universal Naming Convention, path) or page (URL or Uniform Resource Locator); and (3) any sub-address within the file or page. An example of a sub-address is the name of an Access 2000 form or report. Each part is separated by the pound symbol (#).

The *Lookup Wizard* data type creates a field that enables you to use a combo box to choose a value from another table or from a list of values. This is especially useful when you are storing key fields from another table in order to link to data from that table. Choosing this option in the Data Type list starts the Lookup Wizard, with which you define the data type and perform the link to another table. You learn more about this field type later.

Entering a field description

The *field description* is completely optional; you use it only to help you remember a field's uses or to let another user know its purpose. Often you don't use the description column at all, or you use it only for fields whose purpose is not readily recognizable. If you enter a field description, it appears in the status bar whenever you use that field in Access — in the datasheet or in a form. The field description can help clarify a field whose purpose is ambiguous, or give the user a fuller explanation of the values valid for the field during data entry.

Completing the Pets Table

Table 5-2 shows the completed field entries for the Pets table. If you are following the examples, you should modify the table design now for these additional fields. Enter the field names and data types exactly as shown. You also need to rearrange some of the fields and delete the Value field you created. You may want to study the next few pages to understand how to change existing fields (which includes rearranging the field order, changing a field name, and deleting a field).

Table 5-2		
Structure of the Pets Table		
Field Name	**Data Type**	**Description**
Pet ID	Text	Pet ID is entered as AA###-## (Customer # Sequence).
Customer Number	Text	Enter the Customer Number for the owner of the pet.

Continued

Table 5-2 *(continued)*

Field Name	Data Type	Description
Pet Name	Text	
Type of Animal	Text	Enter the animal type in capital letters, for example, DOG, CAT.
Breed	Text	
Date of Birth	Date/Time	Enter the Pet's Date of Birth in the form mm/dd/yy.
Gender	Text	Enter M for Male, F for Female, or U if Unknown.
Colors	Text	
Neutered/Spayed	Yes/No	Enter Yes if the animal has been sterilized.
Length	Number	Enter length in inches.
Weight	Number	Enter weight in pounds.
Last Visit Date	Date/Time	Do not enter this field. It is automatically filled in.
Current Vaccinations	Yes/No	Do not enter this field. It is automatically filled in.
Deceased	Yes/No	Enter Yes if pet has died.
Picture	OLE Object	Copy this in from the photograph scanner or picture library.
Comments	Memo	

The steps for adding fields to a table structure are

1. Place the cursor in the Field Name column in the row where you want the field to appear.

2. Enter the field name and press Enter or Tab.

3. In the Data Type column, click the down arrow and select the data type.

4. Place the pointer in the Description column and type a description (optional).

Repeat each of these steps to complete the Pets data entry for all fields. You can press the down-arrow (↓) key to move between rows, or simply use the mouse and click on any row.

Tip You can also type in the name of the data type or the first unique letters. The type is validated automatically to make sure it's on the drop-down list. A warning message appears for an invalid type.

Changing a Table Design

As you create your table, you should be following a well-planned design. Yet, changes are sometimes necessary, even with a plan. You may find that you want to add another field, remove a field, change a field name or data type, or simply rearrange the order of the field names. You can make these changes to your table at any time. After you enter data into your table, however, things get a little more complicated. You have to make sure that any changes made don't affect the data entered previously.

In older versions of Access (versions 95 and earlier), changes to the table design could be made only in the Table Design window. Since Access 97, including Access 2002, you can make changes to the table design in a datasheet, including adding fields, deleting fields, and changing field names.

New Feature In previous versions of Access, changing a field name usually meant that any queries, forms, reports, macros, or modules that referenced that field name would no longer work and had to be manually found and changed. Access 2002 automatically seeks out most occurrences of the name and changes it for you.

Inserting a new field

To insert a new field, in the Table Design window, place your cursor on an existing field and select Insert ⇨ Row or click the Insert Row button in the toolbar. A new row is added to the table, and any existing fields are pushed down. You can then enter a new field definition. Inserting a field does not disturb other fields or existing data. If you have queries, forms, or reports that use the table, you may need to add the field to those objects as well.

Deleting a field

There are three ways to delete a field:

  ✦ Select the field by clicking the row selector and pressing Delete.
  ✦ Select the field and choose Edit ⇨ Delete Row.
  ✦ Select the field and click the Delete Row button on the toolbar.

When you delete a field containing data, a warning that you will lose any data in the table for this field displays. If the table is empty, you won't care. If your table contains data, however, make sure that you want to eliminate the data for that field (column). You will also have to delete the same field from queries, forms, and reports that use the field name.

Tip   When you delete a field, you can immediately select the Undo button and return the field to the table. But you must do this step before you save the changed table's definition.

Tip   If you attempt to delete a field that is part of a relationship (primary or secondary key field), Access will inform you that you cannot delete it until you delete the reference in the Relationships window.

If you delete a field, you must also delete all references to that field throughout Access. Because you can use a field name in forms, queries, reports, and even table-data validation, you must examine your system carefully to find any instances where you may have used the specific field name.

Changing a field location

One of the easiest changes to make is to move a field's location. The order of your fields, as entered, determines the initial display sequence in the datasheet that displays your data. If you decide that your fields should be rearranged, click on a field selector twice and drag the field to a new location.

Changing a field name

You can change a field name by selecting an existing field name in the Table Design screen and entering a new name; Access updates the table design automatically. As long as you are creating a new table, this process is easy.

Caution   If you used the field name in any forms, queries, or reports, however, you must also go to each object that references the field name and change it in them. (Remember that you can also use a field name in validation rules and calculated fields in queries, as well as in macros and module expressions — all of which must be changed.) As you can see, it's a good idea not to change a field name; it creates more work.

Changing a field size

Making a field size larger is simple in a table design. However, only text and number fields can be increased in size. You simply increase the Field Size property for text fields or specify a different field size for number fields. You must pay attention to the decimal-point property in number fields to make sure that you don't select a new size that supports fewer decimal places than you currently have.

When you want to make a field size smaller, make sure that none of the data in the table is larger than the new field width. (If it is, the existing data will be truncated.) Text data types should be made as small as possible to take up less storage space.

> **Tip** Remember that each text field uses only the number of characters actually entered in the field. You should still try to make your fields only as large as the largest value so that Access can stop someone from entering a value that may not fit on a form or report.

Changing a field data type

You must be very careful when changing a field's data type if you want to preserve your existing data. Such a change is rare; most data types limit (by definition) what kind of data you can input. Normally, for example, you cannot input a letter into a Numeric field or a Date/Time field.

Some data types do, however, convert readily to others. For example, a Numeric field can be converted to a Text data type, but you lose the understanding of mathematics in the value because you can no longer perform mathematical calculations with the values. Sometimes you might accidentally create a phone number or ZIP code as a Numeric and want to redefine the data type correctly as Text. Of course, you also have to remember the other places where you've used the field name (for example, queries, forms, or reports).

> **Caution** The OLE data type cannot be converted to any other format.

You need to understand four basic conversion types as you change from one data type to another. The paragraphs that follow describe each of these types.

To Text from other data types

Converting to Text is easiest; you can convert practically any other data type to Text with no problems. Number or Currency data can be converted with no special formatting (dollar signs or commas) if you use the General Number format; the decimal point remains intact. Yes/No data converts as is; Date/Time data also converts as is if you use the General Date format (mm/dd/yy hh:mm:ss AM/PM). Hyperlink data easily converts to Text. The displayed text loses its underline but the remaining Internet resource link information is visible.

From Text to Number, Currency, Date/Time, Yes/No, or Hyperlink

Only data stored as numeric characters (0, 1, 2, 3, 4, 5, 6, 7, 8, 9) or as periods, commas, and dollar signs can be converted to Number or Currency data from the Text data type. You must also make sure that the maximum length of the text string is not larger than the field size for the type of number or currency field you use in the conversion.

Text data being converted to Date data types must be in a correct date or time format. You can use any legal date or time format (such as 10/12/2001, 12-Oct-00, or October 1999), or any of the other date/time formats.

You can convert text fields to either a Yes or No value, depending on the specification in the field. Access recognizes Yes, True, or On as Yes values, and No, False, or Off as No values.

> **Tip** Access can also convert Number data types to Yes/No values. Access interprets Null values as Null, 0 as No, and any nonzero value as Yes.

A text field that contains correctly formatted hyperlink text converts directly to hyperlink format — displaying text and address.

From Currency to Number

You can convert data from Currency to Number data types as long as the receiving field can handle the size and number of decimal places. Remember that the Field Size property in numeric fields determines the size (in bytes) of the storage space and the maximum number of decimal places. Anything can be converted to Double, which holds 8 bytes and 15 decimals, whereas Single holds only 4 bytes and 7 decimal places. (For more information, refer to "Entering Field-Size Properties" later in this chapter and to Table 5-2.)

From Text to Memo

You can always convert from Text to Memo data types because the maximum length of a text field is 255 characters, whereas a memo field can hold up to 65,536 characters. You can convert from Memo to Text, however, only if every value in the memo fields is less than the text field size — that is, no more than 255 characters. Values longer than the field size are truncated.

Understanding Field Properties

After you enter the field names, data types, and field descriptions, you may want to go back and further define each field. Every field has properties, and these are different for each data type. In the Pets table, you must enter properties for several data types. Figure 5-14 shows the property area for the field named Length; ten options are available in the General section of the property area.

> **Tip** Figure 5-14 shows 13 property options available for the text field named Pet Name. Other types, such as Numeric or Yes/No, will show more or fewer options.

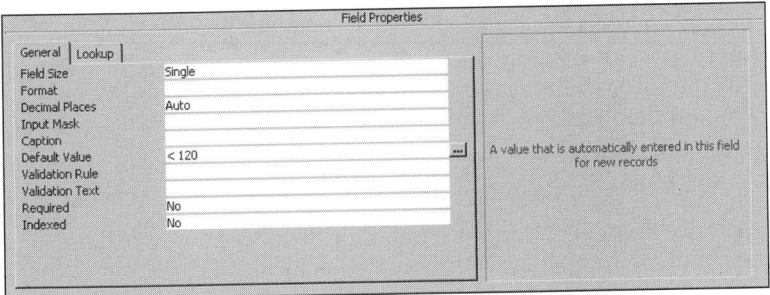

Figure 5-14: Property area for the Numeric field named Pet Name. Notice that there are two tabs on the property box — General and Lookup. Lookup will be discussed later.

Pressing F6 switches between the field entry pane and the property pane. You can also move between panes by clicking the desired pane. Some properties display a list of possible values, along with a downward-pointing arrow, when you move the pointer into the field. When you click the arrow, the values appear in a drop-down list.

Here is a list of all the general properties (note that they may not all be displayed, depending on which data type you chose):

✦ **Field Size.** Text: limits size of the field to the specified number of characters (1–255); default is 50.

✦ **Numeric.** Allows specification of numeric type.

✦ **Format.** Changes the way data appears after you enter it (uppercase, dates, and so on).

✦ **Input Mask.** Used for data entry into a predefined and validated format (Phone Numbers, ZIP Codes, Social Security numbers, Dates, Custom IDs).

✦ **Decimal Places.** Specifies number of decimal places (Numeric/Currency only).

✦ **Caption.** Optional label for form and report fields (replacing the field name).

✦ **Default Value.** The value filled in automatically for new data entry into the field.

✦ **Validation Rule.** Validates data based on rules created through expressions or macros.

✦ **Validation Text.** Displays a message when data fails validation.

✦ **Required.** Specifies whether you must enter a value into a field.

✦ **Allow Zero Length.** Determines whether you may enter the value " " into a text field type to distinguish it from a null value.

✦ **Indexed.** Speeds up data access and (if desired) limits data to unique values.

✦ **Unicode Compression.** Used for multi-language applications. Requires about twice the data storage but enables Office documents including Access reports to be displayed correctly no matter what language or symbols are used.

✦ **IME Mode.** Also known as the Kanji Conversion Mode property, is used to show whether the Kanji mode is maintained when the control is lost.

✦ **IME Sentence Mode.** Used to determine the Sequence Mode of fields of a table or controls of a form that switch when the focus moves in or out of the field.

IME Mode and IME Sequence Mode are available only if international support for Simplified Chinese, Traditional Chinese, or Japanese is enabled through Microsoft Office Language Settings. IME stands for Input Method Editor.

Entering field-size properties

Field size has two purposes. For text fields, it simply specifies the storage and display size. For example, the field size for the Pet ID field is 8 bytes. You should enter the size for each field with a Text data type. If you don't change the default field size, Access will use a 50-byte size for each text field in every record. You should limit the size to the value equal to the largest number of characters.

For Numeric data types, the field size enables you to further define the type of number, which in turn determines the storage size. There are seven possible settings in the Numeric Field Size property, as described in Table 5-3.

You should make the field size the smallest one possible; Access runs faster with smaller field sizes. Note that the first three settings don't use decimal points but allow increasingly larger positive or negative numbers. Single and Double permit even larger numbers: Single gives you 7 decimal places, and Double allows 15. Use the Double setting when you need many decimal places or very large numbers.

Table 5-3 Numeric Field Settings			
Field Size Setting	*Range*	*Decimal Places*	*Storage Size*
Byte	0 to 255	None	1 byte
Integer	-32,768 to 32,767	None	2 bytes
Long Integer	-2,147,483,648 to 2,147,483,647	None	4 bytes
Double	-1.797×10^{308} to 1.797×10^{308}	15	8 bytes
Single	-3.4×10^{38} to 3.4×10^{38}	7	4 bytes
Replication ID	N/A	N/A	16 bytes

Tip   Use the Currency data type to define data that stores monetary amounts.

Tip   The replication ID data type should be used for AutoNumber fields that are used in databases that will be replicated and more than 100 records are routinely added. This is also true for any numeric field where the field is the primary key. When two copies of a table are synchronized, it is possible to get duplicate fields in the numeric values *unless* the field type is set to Replication ID. This will produce a 128-bit value that will require more disk space.

Using formats

Formats enable you to display your data in a form that differs from the actual keystrokes used to enter the data originally. Formats vary, depending on the data type you use. Some data types have predefined formats, others have only user-defined formats, and some data types have both. Formats affect only the way your data appears, not how it is actually stored in the table or how it should be entered.

Text and Memo data-type formats

Access uses four user-defined format symbols in Text and Memo data types:

@	Required text character (character or space)
&	Text character not required
<	Forces all characters to lowercase
>	Forces all characters to uppercase

The symbols @ and & work with individual characters that you input, but the < and > characters affect the whole entry. If you want to make sure that a name is always displayed as uppercase, for example, you enter > in the Format property. If you want to enter a phone number and allow entry of only the numbers, yet display the data with parentheses and a dash, you enter the following into the Format property: (@@@)@@@-@@@@. You can then enter 2035551234 and have the data displayed as (203) 555-1234.

You can also specify your own Custom Format for Text and Memo fields. To specify a Custom format you would create a format specific for the field that you want to show. The example above for telephone numbers is a type of Custom Format; however, you have a bit more flexibility than suggested by the telephone example.

When creating a custom format you can specify two sections for the format, separated by a semicolon (;). The first section is the format for the fields with text, the second is the format for fields with a *zero-length* value and a *null* value. To specify a custom format you can use the @ (required), & (optional), < (convert to lowercase for display), or >(convert to all uppercase for display) symbols for the first part of the format and any text you wish to specify for the second part (surrounded by quotation marks). For instance the format — **@@@-@@;"Unknown"[Red]** — will display the data with a dash without you having to type a dash, and it will display the word *Unknown* (colored Red) if the field is left blank.

Number and Currency data type formats

You can choose from six predefined formats for Numeric or Currency formats and many symbols for creating your own custom formats. The predefined formats are as shown in Table 5-4, along with a column that shows how to define custom formats.

Table 5-4			
Numeric Format Examples			
Format Type	*Number As Entered*	*Number As Displayed*	*Format Defined*
General	987654.321	987654.3	######.#
Currency	987654.321	$987,654.32	$###,##0.00
Fixed	987654.321	987654.32	######.##
Standard	987654.321	987,654.32	###,###.##
Percent	.987	98.7%	###.##%
Scientific	987654.321	9.88E+05	###E+00
Euro	987654.321	¤987,654.32	¤###,###.##

All of the formats above are the default formats based on setting the Decimal places property to AUTO.

Table 5-4 also shows the default format that would be built internally when selecting any of the built-in format definitions. However, you can also specify your own Custom format in this field by typing your example data. Numeric custom formats have four parts that can be specified — (1) for positive numbers, (2) for negative numbers, (3) for Zero values, and (4) for Null values. You can even specify a specific color to display for each section. For instance you could create a custom format for Currency that may look like this — **$#,##0.00[Green]; ($#,##0.00)[Red]; "zero";"Null"** — this format uses all four sections. It will display all values that are positive in green, values that are negative in red; any field that contains a 0 will show the word "zero," and any field that has not had a value entered will show "Null."

The symbols you can use in a numeric field custom format are period (.), comma (,), 0 (digit place holder that shows a digit or 0), # (digit place holder that shows the digit or nothing), $ (show the literal $), % (show % sign), E- or e- (minus sign next to scientific notation), and E+ or e+ (displays a minus sign next to negative numbers and a plus sign next to positive numbers). A final Currency example could be #,##0.00; (#,##0.00);; "Null". This This will show the numbers displaying negatives in parentheses, a minimum of 0.00 and the word "Null" in fields with a null value. Note that the 0 section was not used because the minimum valued displayed was already 0.00.

Date/Time data-type formats

The Date/Time data formats are the most extensive of all, providing these seven predefined options:

✦ **General Date.** (Default) Display depends on the value entered; entering only a date will display only a date; entering only time will result in no date displayed; standard format for date and time is 2/10/01 10:32 PM

✦ **Long Date.** Taken from Windows Regional Settings Section Long Date setting; example: Wednesday, February 10, 2001

✦ **Medium Date.** Example: 10-Feb-01

✦ **Short Date.** Taken from Windows Regional Settings Section Short Date setting; example: 2/10/01

Tip
For the best Year 2000 compliancy, define all of your dates as Short Dates. When the Windows Regional Settings are changed to display four digit years, so will all of your date fields.

Note
Office 2002 automatically treats all two-digit dates before 30 as 2000–2029. Other dates are treated as 1930–1999.

✦ **Long Time.** Taken from Windows Regional Settings Section Time setting; example: 10:32:15 PM

✦ **Medium Time.** Example: 10:32 PM

✦ **Short Time.** Example: 22:32

You can also use a multitude of user-defined date and time settings, including these:

: (colon)	Time separator; taken from Windows Regional Settings Section Separator setting
/	Date separator
c	Same as General Date format
d, dd	Day of the month — one or two numerical digits (1–31)
ddd	First three letters of the weekday (Sun–Sat)

dddd	Full name of the weekday (Sunday–Saturday)
ddddd	Same as Short Date format
dddddd	Same as Long Date format
w	Day of the week (1–7)
ww	Week of the year (1–53)
m, mm	Month of the year — one or two digits (1–12)
mmm	First three letters of the month (Jan–Dec)
mmmm	Full name of the month (January–December)
q	Date displayed as quarter of the year (1–4)
y	Number of the day of the year (1–366)
yy	Last two digits of the year (01–99)
yyyy	Full year (0100–9999)
h, hh	Hour — one or two digits (0–23)
n, nn	Minute — one or two digits (0–59)
s, ss	Seconds — one or two digits (0–59)
ttttt	Same as Long Time format
AM/PM or A/P	Twelve-hour clock with AM/PM in uppercase as appropriate
am/pm or a/p	Twelve-hour clock with am/pm in lowercase as appropriate
AMPM	Twelve-hour clock with forenoon/afternoon designator, as defined in the Windows Regional Settings Section forenoon/afternoon setting

You can also specify custom formats for Data/Time types; however, they will be displayed based on the settings specified in the *Regional Settings Properties* dialog box in the Windows Control Panel. You can add a comma or other separator to your custom format, but you must enclose the separator in quotation marks. For instance the following format will use the comma — mmm dd", " yyyy — will display February 04, 1999 for the date 02/04/99.

Yes/No data-type formats

Access stores Yes/No data in a manner different from what you might expect. The Yes data is stored as a –1, whereas No data is stored as a 0. You'd expect it to be stored as a 0 for No and 1 for Yes, but this isn't the case. Without a format setting, you must enter –1 or 0, and it will be stored and displayed that way. With formats, you can store Yes/No data types in a more recognizable manner. The three predefined format settings for Yes/No data types are

✦ **Yes/No.** (Default) Displays –1 as Yes, 0 as No

✦ **True/False.** Stores –1 as True, 0 as False

✦ **On/Off.** Stores –1 as On, 0 as Off

You can also enter user-defined custom formats. User-defined Yes/No formats can contain up to three sections. The first section has no effect on the Yes/No data type but must always be a semicolon (;). The second section is used to display a value for the On or True values (literally stored as a –1). The third section is used to specify a value for the Off or False values (literally stored as a 0). If, for example, you want to use the values *Neutered* for Yes and *Fertile* for No, you enter ;"Neutered";"Fertile". You can also specify a color to display different values. To display the Neutered value in red and the Fertile value in green, you enter;"Neutered" [Red]; "Fertile[Green]".

Caution

There are two problems when changing the table level format property of a logical, Yes/No, field. First, if you enter a customer format like in the above example you need to also change the default Lookup Display Control property from checkbox to Text box to see the new format. Second, one the format is assigned and the text box is the display method, the user will only be able to enter a 0 for –1. The format property only affects how the value is displayed not entered into the table.

Hyperlink data-type format

Access also displays and stores Hyperlink data in a manner different from what you would expect. The format of this type is composed of up to three parts:

✦ **Display Text.** The visual text that is displayed in the field or control

✦ **Address.** The path to a file (UNC) or page (URL) on the Internet

✦ **Sub-Address.** A specific location within a file or page

The parts are separated by pound signs. The Display Text is visible in the field or control, while the address and subaddress are hidden. For example, **Microsoft Net Home Page#http://www.msn.com.**

Entering formats

The Pets table uses several formats. The Gender text field has a > in the Format property to display the data entry in uppercase. The Date of Birth field has an mmm yy format to display the date of birth as the short month name, a space, and a two-digit year (Feb 01). The Neutered/Spayed field has a format of Yes/No.

Numeric custom formats can vary, based on the value. You can enter a four-part format into the Format property. The first part is for positive numbers, the second for negatives, the third if the value is 0, and the last if the value is null; for example, #,##0; (#,##0);"- -";"None".

Table 5-5 shows several formats.

<table>
<tr><td colspan="3" align="center">Table 5-5
Format Examples</td></tr>
<tr><td>*Format Specified*</td><td>*Data as Entered*</td><td>*Formatted Data As Displayed*</td></tr>
<tr><td>></td><td>Adam Smith</td><td>ADAM SMITH</td></tr>
<tr><td>#,##0;(#,##0);
"-0-";"None"</td><td>15 -15 0 No Data</td><td>15 (15) -0- None</td></tr>
<tr><td>Currency</td><td>12345.67</td><td>$12,345.67</td></tr>
<tr><td>"Acct No." 0000</td><td>3271</td><td>Acct No. 3271</td></tr>
<tr><td>mmm yy</td><td>9/11/99</td><td>Sep 99</td></tr>
<tr><td>Long Date</td><td>9/11/99</td><td>Friday, September 11, 1999</td></tr>
</table>

Entering input masks

Input masks enable you to have more control over data entry by defining data-validation placeholders for each character that you enter into a field. Another way of thinking about this is that the Input mask property lets you design a pattern that will be used to *input* information into the field. This pattern, or input mask, is what the users will see when they begin to enter the data. This pattern or mask is NOT saved in the underlying data. This is different from how the field will be displayed–controlled by the format property.

For example, if you set the input mask property to (999)000-0000, parentheses and hyphens appear as shown when entering data, and an underscore (_) appears in place of each 9 or 0 of this phone number template. You would see (_) in your data entry field. Access will automatically add a \ character before each placeholder; for example, \(999\)000\-0000. You can also enter a multi-part input mask, such as !(999)000-0000;0;" ". The input mask can contain up to three parts separated by semicolons.

The first section of a multi-part mask defines the input mask itself (for example, !(999)000-0000). The ! is used to fill the input mask from right to left when optional characters are on the left side. The second section specifies whether Microsoft Access stores the literal display characters in the table when you enter data. If you enter a 0 for this part, all literal display characters (for example, the parentheses and hyphen) are stored with the value; if you enter 1 or leave this part blank, only characters typed into the text box are stored. The third part specifies the character that Microsoft Access displays for spaces in the input mask. You can use any character; the default is an underscore. If you want to display a space, use a space enclosed in quotation marks (" ").

Note   When you have defined an input mask and set the Format property for the same data, the Format property takes precedence when Access displays the data. This means that even if you've saved an input mask with data, it is ignored when data is formatted.

Some of the characters that can be used are shown in Table 5-6.

Table 5-6
Input Mask Characters

Character	Description
0	Digit (0–9; entry required; plus [+] and minus [–] signs not allowed).
9	Digit or space (entry not required; [+] and [–] not allowed).
#	Digit or space (entry not required; blanks converted to spaces; [+] and [-] allowed).
L	Letter (A–Z, entry required).
?	Letter (A–Z, entry optional).
A	Letter or digit (entry required).
a	Letter or digit (entry optional).
&	Any character or a space (entry required).
C	Any character or a space (entry optional).
<	Converts all characters that follow to lowercase
>	Converts all characters that follow to uppercase.
!	Causes input mask to fill from right to left, rather than from left to right, when characters on the left side of the input mask are optional. You can include the exclamation point anywhere in the input mask.
\	Displays the character that follows as the literal character (for example, appears as just A).
. , : ; - /	Decimal placeholder, thousands, and date time separator determined by Regional Settings section of the Control Panel.

Tip   Setting the Input Mask property to the word **Password** creates a password entry text box. Any character typed in the text box is stored as the character, but appears as an asterisk (*).

The Input Mask Wizard

Although you can enter an Input Mask manually, you can easily create an input mask for text or date type fields by using the Input Mask Wizard. When you click the Input Mask property, the builder button (three periods) appears. You can click the Build button to start the Wizard. Figure 5-15 shows the first screen of the Input Mask Wizard.

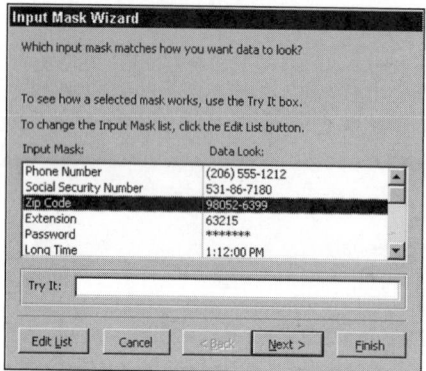

Figure 5-15: The Input Mask Wizard for creating input masks for text and date field types

The Wizard shows not only the name of each predefined input mask, but also an example for each name. You can choose from the list of predefined masks; click the Try It text box to see how data entry will look. After you choose an input mask, the next Wizard screen enables you to customize it and determine the placeholder symbol. Another Wizard screen enables you to decide whether to store any special characters with the data. When you complete the Wizard, Access places the actual input mask characters in the property sheet.

You can enter as many custom masks as you need. You can also determine the international settings so that you can work with multiple country masks.

Entering decimal places

Decimal places are valid only for Numeric or Currency data. The number of decimal places can be from 0 to 15, depending on the field size of the numeric or currency field. If the field size is Byte, Integer, or Long Integer, you can have 0 decimal places. If the field size is Single, you can enter from 0 to 7 for the Decimal Places property. If the field size is Double, you can enter from 0 to 15 for the Decimal Places property. If you define a field as Currency (or use one of the predefined formats, such as General, Fixed, or Standard), Access sets the number of decimal places to 2 automatically. You can override this setting by entering a different value into the Decimal Places property.

Creating a caption

You use *captions* when you want to display an alternative to the field name on forms and reports. Normally, the label used to describe a field in a form or a report is the field name. Sometimes, however, you want to call the field name one thing while displaying a more (or less) descriptive label. You should keep field names as short as possible to make them easier to use in calculations. You may then want a longer name to be used for a label in forms or reports. For example, you may use the field name Length but want the label *Length (in)* on all forms.

Setting a default value

A *default value* is the value Access displays automatically for the field when you add a new record to the table. This value can be any value that matches the data type of the field. A default is no more than an initial value; you can change it during data entry. To enter a default value, simply enter the desired value into the Default Value property setting. A default value can be an expression, as well as a number or a text string. Chapter 11 explains how to create expressions.

Note   Numeric and Currency data types are set automatically to 0 when you add a new record.

Working with validation

Data validation enables you to limit the values that are accepted in a field. Validation may be automatic, such as the checking of a numeric field for text or a valid date. Validation can also be user-defined. User-defined validation can be as simple as a range of values (such as those found in the Length or Weight fields), or it can be an expression like the one found in the Gender field.

Figure 5-14 (shown earlier) displays the property area for the Length field. Notice the validation options for the Length field. The Validation Rule <120 specifies that the number entered must be less than 120. The Validation Text Length must be less than 120" (120 inches) appears in a warning dialog box (see Figure 5-16) if a user tries to enter a length greater than 120.

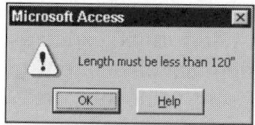

Figure 5-16: A data-validation warning box. This appears when the user enters a value in the field that does not match the rule specified in the design of the table.

Caution

The dialog box shown in Figure 5-16 will not display if you have the "Show Office Assistant" value turned on for Help. Rather, the message will be displayed in amessage box shown by the assistant, as shown in Figure 5-17.

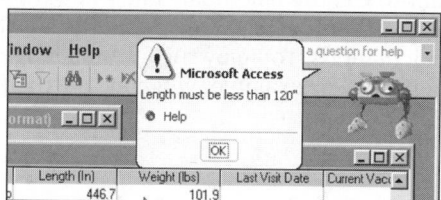

Figure 5-17: The warning displayed by the Assistant that a value was entered outside of the range of the values accepted

You can also use Date values with Date/Time data types in range validation. Dates are surrounded, or *delimited*, by pound signs when used in data-validation expressions. If you want to limit the Date of Birth data entry to dates between January 1, 1970, and December 31, 2001, you enter Between #1/1/70# and #12/31/01#.

If you want to limit the upper end to the current date, you can enter a different set of dates, such as Between #1/1/70# and Date( ).

The Gender field contains a validation rule based on an expression. The Gender field validation rule limits the data entry to three values: M for Male, F for Female, and U for Unknown. The validation rule for this is InStr("MFU",[Gender])>0. The expression InStr means Access must validate that the entry is in the string specified.

Following the design in Table 5-7, you can now complete all the property settings in the Pets table. Note that the design only shows the critical fields that must have their properties defined. You can also find this table (and the others in this book) in the Mountain Animal Start and Mountain Animal Hospital databases on the CD-ROM that accompanies this book.

Table 5-7
Properties for the Pets Table

Field Name	Properties
Pet ID:	Field Size –8, Input Mask — AA###-##, Required — Yes, Indexed — Yes (No Duplicates).
Customer Number:	Field Size — 5, Input Mask — AA###, Required — Yes.
Date of Birth:	Format — mmm yy, Validation Rule — Between #01/01/70# And Date(), Validation Text — The Date of Birth is Invalid, Required — Yes.
Gender:	Field Size — 1, Format - >@, Validation Rule — InStr("MFU",[Gender])>0, Validation Text — Value must be M, F, or U.
Neutered/Spayed:	Default Value — No.
Length:	Field Size — Single, Format — Standard, Decimal Places — 1, Caption — Length (In), Default Value — 0, Validation Rule — <120, Validation Text — Length must be less than 120".
Weight:	Field Size — Single, Decimal Places — 1, Caption — Weight (lbs), Default Value — 0, Validation Rule - Between 0 And 1500, Validation Text — Weight must be between 0 and 1500.

Understanding the Lookup Property window

The Field Properties pane of the Table Design window has a second tab — the Lookup tab. After clicking on this tab you may see a single property — the Display Control property. This property is used for Text, Number, and Logical fields.

Figure 5-18 shows the Lookup Property window for a Yes/No field where Display Control is the only property. This property has three choices: Text Box, Check Box, and Combo Box. Choosing one of these determines which control type is used when a particular field is added to a form. Generally, all controls are created as text boxes except Yes/No fields, which are created as a check box. For Yes/No data types, however, use the default Check Box setting. If you know a certain text field can only be one of a few combinations, use a combo box. When you select the combo-box control type as a default, the properties change so that you can define a combo box.

Cross-Reference   You learn about combo boxes in Chapter 17.

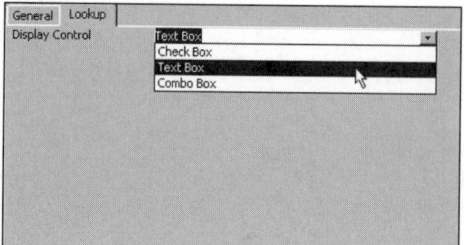

Figure 5-18: The Lookup properties for a field

Note   The properties for a Lookup field are different for each data type. The Yes/No data type fields differ from text fields or numeric fields. Because a Lookup field is really a combo box (you learn more about these later), the standard properties for a combo box are displayed when you select a Lookup field data type.

Determining the Primary Key

Every table should have a *primary key* — one or more fields with a unique value for each record. (This principle is called *entity integrity* in the world of database management.) In the Pets table, the Pet ID field is the primary key. Each pet has a different Pet ID value so that you can identify one from the other. If you don't specify a primary key (unique value field), Access can create one for you.

Creating a unique key

Without the Pet ID field, you'd have to rely on another field for uniqueness. You couldn't use the Pet Name field because two customers could have pets with the same name. You could use the Customer Number and Pet Name fields as a multiple-field key, but theoretically it's possible a customer could have two pets, each with the exact same name and even some of the same characteristics (such as Type of Animal and Breed).

Cross-Reference   Multiple-field primary keys are discussed in Chapter 6.

If you don't designate a field as a primary key, Access creates an AutoNumber field and adds it to the beginning of the table. This field contains a unique number for each record in the table, and Access maintains it automatically. For several reasons, however, you may want to create and maintain your own primary key:

  ✦ A primary key is an index.

  ✦ Indexes maintain a presorted order of one or more fields that greatly speeds up queries, searches, and sort requests.

✦ When you add new records to your table, Access checks for duplicate data and doesn't allow any duplicates for the primary key field.

✦ Access displays your data in the order of the primary key.

By designating a field such as Pet ID as the unique primary key, you can see your data in an understandable order. In our example, the Pet ID field is composed of the owner's customer number followed by a dash and a two-digit sequence number. If the Adams family, for example, is the first customer on the list of those whose last name begins with AD, its customer number is AD001. If they have three pets, their Pet IDs are designated AD001-01, AD001-02, and AD001-03. This way, the Pet ID field shows the data in the alphabetical order of customers by using the first two letters of their last name as a customer number.

Creating the primary key

The primary key can be created in any of four ways:

✦ Select the field to be used as the primary key and choose Edit ➪ Primary Key.

✦ Select the field to be used as the primary key and select the Primary Key button (the key icon) in the toolbar.

✦ Right-click the mouse to display the shortcut menu and select Primary Key.

✦ Save the table without creating a primary key, and Access automatically creates an AutoNumber field.

Before you click the Primary Key button or select the menu choice, you must click the gray area in the far-left side of the field that you want as the primary key. A right-pointing triangle appears. After you select the primary key, a key appears in the gray area to indicate that the primary key has been created.

Since a primary key must contain a unique value, and that value cannot be a blank, you will need to first empty the Pets table of My Mountain Animal Hospital database and then assign the primary key. Follow these steps to empty the table and create a primary key:

1. Select and open the table named Pets in the Database window.

2. Select all the fields by clicking in the first (selector) field and while holding the mouse button drag across all five records. The records should be highlighted.

3. Press the Delete key and Answer YES to the dialog box that appears and says "You are about to delete 5 record(s)."

4. Click on the Design button to move to the design window.

5. Select the Pet ID field.

6. Click the Primary Key button to make the Pet ID field the primary key.

7. Save the file.

The Indexes window

A primary key is really an *index*. The key icon beside the Pet ID field indicates that this field is the primary key for the table. You can also see the primary key by looking at the Indexes window. (Figure 5-19 shows a primary key in the Indexes window.) You can display or hide this window by toggling the Indexes button on the toolbar.

Using the Indexes window, you can determine whether an index is a primary key, whether or not it is unique, and whether null values should be ignored. Notice that the window in Figure 5-19 shows a complex index named CustPetID. Unlike the other two indexes, which only use a single field to build the index, CustPetID uses two fields — first Customer Number in Ascending Order and then Pet ID also in Ascending Order. This index is only used as an example of how the Indexes window will show multi-field indexes. The index is actually redundant since the Pet ID already has the Customer number built into it.

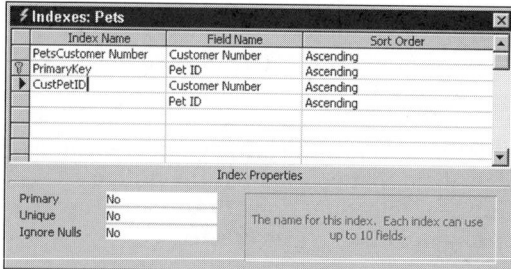

Figure 5-19: The Indexes window that shows all the indexes built for the Pets table. You can add more indexes directly into this window.

The Table Properties window

Just as each field has a property area, the overall table has one, too. While in the Table Design window, right-click while the cursor is inside the design area and choose *Properties* or click the Properties button (hand with a piece of paper) on the Table Design toolbar to display the Table Properties window.

Cross-Reference

Figure 5-20 shows the Table Properties window. Here you can enter the validation rule and message that are to be applied to the overall record that will be enforced when you save a record. You can set up a default sorting order (other than by primary key), and even a default filter to show only a subset of the data. This is also where you can set up your subdatasheets.

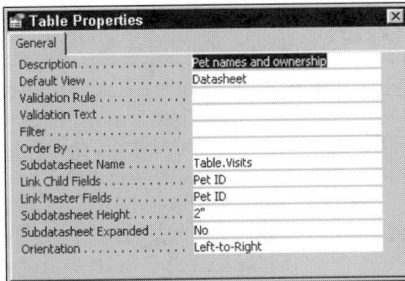

Figure 5-20: Setting general Table properties

Printing a Table Design

You can print a table design by using Tools ➪ Analyze ➪ Documenter. The *Database Documenter* is an Access 2002 tool that makes it easy to document your database objects. When you select this command, Access shows you a dialog box that lets you select objects to print. In Figure 5-21, there is only one object, the Pets table. You can select it by clicking the check box next to the table name.

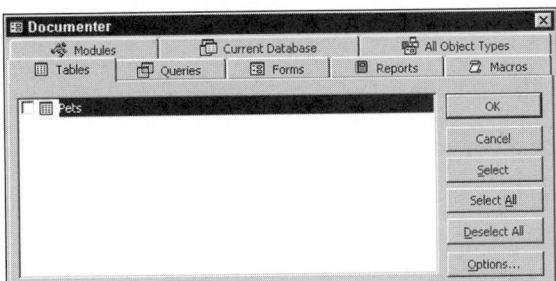

Figure 5-21: The Access Documenter dialog box

You can also set various options for printing. When you click on the Options button, a dialog box appears that enables you to select which information from the Table Design to print. You can print the various field names, all their properties, the indexes, and even network permissions.

After you select which data you want to view, Access generates a report; you can view it in a Print Preview window or send the output to a printer.

Tip   The Database Documenter creates a table of all the objects and object properties you specify. You can use this utility to document such database objects as forms, queries, reports, macros, and modules.

Saving the Completed Table

You can save the completed table design by choosing File ➪ Save or by clicking the Save button on the toolbar. If you are saving the table for the first time, Access asks for the name of the table; enter it and click OK. Table names can be up to 64 characters long and follow standard Access field-naming conventions. If you have saved this table before and want to save it with a different name, choose File ➪ Save As and enter a different table name. This creates a new table design and leaves the original table with its original name untouched. If you want to delete the old table, select it in the Database window and press Delete. You can also save the table when you close it.

Manipulating Tables in a Database Window

As you create many tables in your database, you may want to use them in other databases or copy them for use as a history file. You may want to copy only the table structure. You can perform many operations on tables in the Database window, including

- ✦ Renaming tables
- ✦ Deleting tables
- ✦ Copying tables in a database
- ✦ Copying a table from another database

You can perform these tasks by direct manipulation or by using menu items.

Renaming tables

You can rename a table with these steps:

1. Select the table name in the Database window.

2. Click once on the table name.

3. Type the name of the new table and press Enter.

You can also rename the table by selecting Edit ➪ Rename or by right-clicking a table and selecting Rename from the shortcut menu. After you change the table name, it appears in the Tables list, which re-sorts the tables in alphabetical order.

Caution   If you rename a table, you must change the table name in any objects where it was previously referenced, including queries, forms, and reports.

Deleting tables

You can delete a table by selecting the table name and pressing the Delete key. Another method is to select the table name and select Edit ⇨ Delete or by right-clicking a table and selecting Delete from the shortcut menu. Like most delete operations, you have to confirm the delete by selecting Yes in a Delete Table dialog box.

Copying tables in a database

By using the Copy and Paste options from the Edit menu or the toolbar buttons, you can copy any table in the database. When you paste the table back into the database, you can choose from three option buttons:

✦ Structure Only

✦ Structure and Data

✦ Append Data to Existing Table

Selecting the Structure Only button creates a new table design with no data. This enables you to create an empty table with all the same field names and properties as the original table. This option is typically used to create a temporary table or a history structure to which you can copy old records.

When you select Structure and Data, a complete copy of the table design and all its data is created.

Selecting the button Append Data to Existing Table adds the data of one table to the bottom of another. This option is useful for combining tables, as when you want to add data from a monthly transaction table to a yearly history table.

Follow these steps to copy a table:

1. Select the table name in the Database window.

2. Select Edit ⇨ Copy.

3. Select Edit ⇨ Paste.

4. Type the name of the new table.

5. Choose one of the Paste Options.

6. Click OK to complete the operation.

Figure 5-22 shows the Paste Table As dialog box, where you make these decisions. To paste the data, you have to select the type of paste operation and type the name of the new table. When you are appending data to an existing table, you must type the name of an existing table.

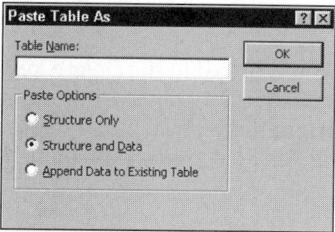

Figure 5-22: Pasting a table will activate this dialog box. You can paste only the structure, the data and structure, or even paste the data to an existing table.

Copying a table to another database

Just as you can copy a table within a database, you can copy a table to another database. There are many reasons why you may want to do this. Possibly you share a common table among multiple systems, or you may need to create a backup copy of your important tables within the system.

When you copy tables to another database, the relationships between tables are not copied; Access copies only the table design and the data. The method for copying a table to another database is essentially the same as for copying a table within a database. To copy a table to another database, follow these steps:

1. Select the table name in the Database window.

2. Select Edit ⇨ Copy.

3. Open another database.

4. Select Edit ⇨ Paste.

5. Type the name of the new table.

6. Choose one of the Paste Options.

7. Click OK to complete the operation.

✦   ✦   ✦

Setting Relationships Between Tables

◆   ◆   ◆   ◆

In This Chapter

Reviewing the Mountain Animal Hospital database tables

Understanding keys

Looking at the benefits of using primary keys

Creating a multiple-field primary key

Understanding what a foreign key is

Examining the types of relationships

Learning how referential integrity works

Creating relationships

Deleting relationships

Using the Table Analyzer Wizard

Using lookup fields in a table

Using subdatasheets

◆   ◆   ◆   ◆

So far, you have learned to create a simple table, to enter its data, and to display it in either a datasheet or a form. You have also learned to use simple queries and reports. All these techniques were demonstrated using only a single table. The Pets table has been an excellent sample of a single table; it contains many different data types that lend themselves to productive examples.

It's time now to move into the real world of relational database management.

Tables Used in the Mountain Animal Hospital Database

Figure 6-1 diagrams the database of the Mountain Animal Hospital system. There are eight tables in the figure, each of which requires its own table design, complete with field names, data types, descriptions, and properties.

On the CD-ROM

If you're following the examples, you can use the Mountain Animal Start.mdb files on the CD-ROM that accompanies this book or create these tables yourself in a database of your own naming. If you want to create each of these tables, you can use Appendix B as a reference for each table's description; then use the steps you learned in Chapter 4 to create each table.

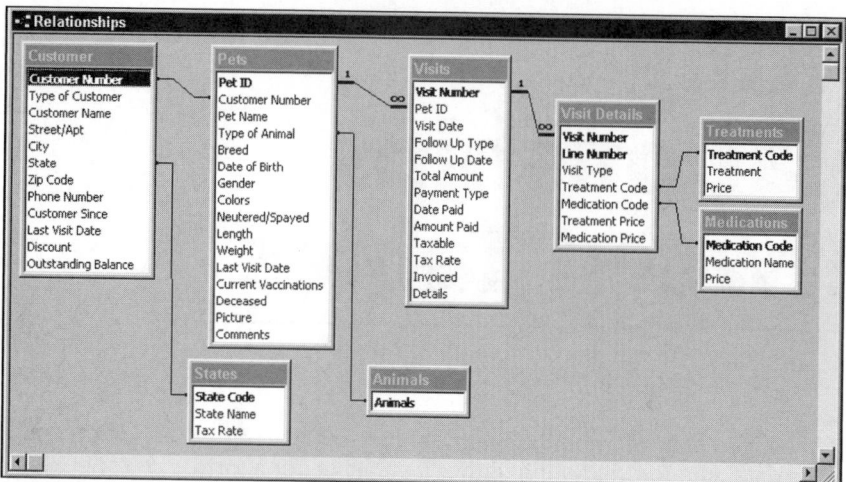

Figure 6-1: The database diagram for the Mountain Animal Hospital system. This diagram shows all eight tables that are used in the system and how they relate to each other.

Cross-Reference

Figure 6-1 shows lines joining the tables. These are the relationship lines between the tables. Each line indicates a separate relationship between two tables; these are established either at the table level (using the Relationship window of Access) or by using a query (Chapter 12 shows how to establish relationships in a query). In this chapter, you learn to use the Relationship window to establish a relationship at the table level.

If you closely look at the lines between the tables in Figure 6-1 you will observe that some of the lines (relations) between the tables have writing above them.

For instance, the line between the Pets and Visits tables shows a darkened, thicker line near both tables and a light line connecting them. The one near the Pets table shows the number 1 above it and the one near the Visits table show the infinity symbol (∞ next to it (a sideways 8). This simply means that there are *many* visits (the infinity symbol) for every *one* pet. You can specifically tell Access that this is the case when you create the relationship diagram of all tables in your system. This will be discussed more later in this chapter.

Of the eight tables in the database diagram, four hold data about Mountain Animal Hospital and four are used for *lookups*.

A lookup table is simply a table that is used to hold secondary information that is related to the overall system. Lookup tables are good for holding common information that will be used over and over in a system — like the State Code lookup table holds the actual state names, their tax rates, and the state abbreviation. This table is used by the system to verify that the users enter an accurate State Code (WA for Washington, ID for Idaho) in the Customer table, as well as supplying secondary information (like Tax Rates) that can be used to expand the capabilities of the system (in reports and forms). You can eliminate the lookup tables and still use the system if you want, although some of the value of the system may be lost. The four main tables are listed below:

- ✦ **Customer.** Contains information about each customer (one customer can own several pets)
- ✦ **Pets.** Contains information about each animal (each pet can have many visits to the doctors)
- ✦ **Visits.** Contains information about each visit (each visit can be for more than one purpose)
- ✦ **Visit Details.** Contains records about the details of each visit

The four lookup tables are listed below:

- ✦ **States.** Used by the Customer table to retrieve state name and tax rate
- ✦ **Animals.** Used by the Pets table to retrieve a list of valid animal types
- ✦ **Treatments.** Used by the Visit Details table to retrieve treatment name and price
- ✦ **Medications.** Used by the Visit Details table to retrieve medication name and price

To set relations between tables, you must first establish a link between fields, known as *key fields*, that contain some common information. The fields themselves do not need to have the same name (like the common link between the Animals table and the Pets table — Type of Animal versus Animals).

However, the contents in the linked fields must be of the same data type and length. Most importantly, the information contained within both fields (one value in each table) for any specific record must be the same in both tables for the link to work. Generally, a relationship is established by linking *key fields* between tables — the *primary* key in one table (the senior table, like Customer is primary to Pets and Pets is primary to Visits) to a *foreign* key in another table (the junior or secondary table — Pets is secondary to Customer). A table can have both a *primary* key and a *foreign* key in it — as is the case with the Pets table, *Pet ID* is a primary key (used to link to the Visits table) and *Customer Number* is a foreign key (used to link back to the Customer table).

A table can even have more than one primary or foreign key. It is easy to identify the primary key of any table when you look at its structure in the Query Design window or in the Relationship window — it will be in bold. It is more difficult to identify foreign keys, because they have no specific font formatting.

In Figure 6-1, each table has one or more fields in bold. These are the fields that define each table's primary key.

Understanding Keys

When you create your tables, as in those created in Chapter 4, you should assign each table a *primary key*—one or more fields whose contents are unique to each record. This key is a way to make sure that the table records contain only one unique value; for example, you may have several Customers named Michael Irwin, and you may even have more than one living at the same address. So in a case like this you have to decide on how you can create a record in the Customer database that will let you identify each Michael Irwin separately. That is what a primary key field can do for you. For example, the Customer Number field (a unique number that you assign to each Customer that comes into your office) is the primary key in the Customer table—each record in the table has a different Customer Number. (No two records have the same number.) This is important for several reasons — (1) you do not want to have two records in your database for the same customer — this can make updating the customer's record virtually impossible; (2) you want to be assured that each record in the table is accurate, thus the information extracted from the table is accurate; and (3) you do not want to make the table (and its records) any bigger than necessary.

The capability to assign a single, unique value to each record makes the table "clean" and reliable. This is known as *entity integrity* in the world of database management. By having a different primary key value in each record (such as the Customer Number in the Customer table), you can tell two records (in this case, customers) apart. This is important because you can easily have two individual customers named Fred Smith (or pet stores named Animal Kingdom) in your table.

Theoretically, you could use the customer name and the customer's address, but two people named Fred D. Smith could live in the same town and state, or a father and son (Fred David Smith and Fred Daniel Smith) could live at the same address. The goal of setting primary keys is to create individual records in a table that will *guarantee* uniqueness.

If you don't specify a primary key when creating Access tables, Access asks whether you want one. If you say yes, Access creates a primary key for you as an AutoNumber data type. It places a new sequential number in the primary key field for each record automatically. Table 6-1 lists tables and their primary keys.

Note
In Access, you can specify that a field be created that is an AutoNumber data type — a field that Access will automatically put a unique value in every time you add a new record to the table. It is important to note that you cannot use an AutoNumber data field in both tables to enforce referential integrity (more on this topic later) between tables. Therefore, it is important to specify another data type — such as Text or Numeric — for the primary key. (More about this topic later in this chapter.)

Table	Primary Key
	Table 6-1
	Tables and Primary Keys
Customer	Customer Number
Pets	Pet ID
Visits	Visit Number
Visit Details	Visit Number; Line Number
States	State Code
Animals	Animals
Treatments	Treatment Code
Medications	Medication Code

Deciding on a primary key

As you learned previously, a table normally has a unique field (or combination of fields) — the primary key for that table — which makes each record unique; often it's an ID field that uses the Text data type. To determine the contents of this ID field, you specify a method for creating the value in the field. Your method can be as simple as using the first letter of the real value you are tracking along with a sequence number (such as A001, A002, A003, B001, B002, and so on). The method may rely on a random set of letters and numbers for the field content (as long as each field has a unique value), or a complicated calculation based on information from several fields in the table.

Table 6-2 lists the Mountain Animal Hospital tables and explains the plan for deriving the primary key values in each table.

As Table 6-2 shows, it doesn't take a great deal of work (or even much imagination) to derive a plan for key values. Any rudimentary scheme with a good sequence number always works. Access automatically tells you when you try to enter a duplicate key value. To avoid duplication, you can simply add the value of 1 to the sequence number. You may think that all these sequence numbers make it hard to look up information in your tables. Just remember that *normally* you never look up information by an ID field. Generally, you look up information according to the *purpose* of the table. In the Customer table, for example, you would look up information by Customer Name. In some cases, the Customer Name is the same, so you can look at other fields in the table (ZIP code, phone number) to find the correct customer. Unless you just happen to know the Customer Number, you'll probably never use it in a search for information.

Table 6-2
Deriving the Primary Key

Table	Derivation of Primary Key Value
Customer	Individuals: first two letters of last name, three-digit sequence number
	Pet Stores: first letter of first two major words, three-digit sequence number
	Zoos: first letter of first two major words, three-digit sequence number
Pets	Customer Number, a hyphen (–), and a two-digit sequential number
Visits	Eight-digit date in the format of YYYYMMDD with a dash and two-digit sequence number
Visit Details	Visit Number and another field that holds a three-digit sequence number (Line Number field)
States	Two-alpha characters — state abbreviation
Animals	Type of animal spelled out using multiple alpha characters
Treatments	Four-digit unique number (arbitrarily selected)
Medications	Four-digit unique number (arbitrarily selected)

Benefits of a primary key

Have you ever placed an order with a company for the first time and then decided the next day to increase your order? You call the people at the order desk. Sometimes they ask you for your customer number. You tell them that you don't know your customer number. This happens all the time. So they ask you for some other information — generally, your ZIP code or telephone area code. Then, as they narrow down the list of customers, they ask your name. Then they tell you your customer number. Some businesses use phone numbers as a unique starting point.

Database systems usually have more than one table, and these tend to be related in some manner. For example, the Customer table and Pets table are related to each other via a link field called Customer Number in both tables. The Customer table always has one record for each customer, and the Pets table has a record for each pet the customer owns. Because each customer is *one* physical person, you only need one record for the customer in the Customer table. Each customer can own several pets, however, which means you need to set up another table to hold information about each pet — thus the Pets table. Again, each pet is *one* physical animal (a dog, a cat, a bird, and so on). Each animal has one record in the Pets table. Of course, you need to have some way to relate the Customer to his pets in the Pets table. This is accomplished by using a common field that is in both tables. In this case, the field is the Customer Number (which is in both tables).

When linking tables, you link the primary key field from one table (the Customer Number in the Customer table) to a field in the second table that has the same structure and type of data in it (the Customer Number in the Pets table). If the link field in the second table is not the primary key field (and usually it isn't), it's known as a *foreign* key field (discussed later in this chapter).

Besides being a common link field between tables, a primary key field in Access has these advantages:

✦ A primary key field is one that is used to create an index for the table that greatly speeds up queries, searches, and sort requests.

✦ When you add new records, you must enter a value in primary key field(s). Access will not allow you to enter Null values, which guarantees that you'll have only valid records in your table.

✦ When you add new records to a table that has a primary key, Access checks for duplicate data and doesn't enable you to enter duplicates for the primary key field — thus it maintains its integrity.

✦ By default, Access displays your data in the order of the primary key.

Tip An index is a special internal file that is created to put the records in a table in some specific order. For instance, the primary key field in the Customer table is an index that puts the records in order by Customer ID. Using an indexed table, Access can display records in a specific manner and quickly find any record within the table using the index.

If you define a primary key based on part of the data in the record, you can have Access automatically place your data in an understandable order. In the example, the Pet ID field is composed of the owner's Customer Number, followed by a hyphen and a two-digit sequence number. If Johnathan Adams is the first customer on the list whose last name begins with AD, the customer's number is AD001. If this customer brings in three pets, the Pet IDs are designated AD001-01, AD001-02, and AD001-03. This way, the Pet ID field provides you with data in the order of customers displayed alphabetically.

Tip Primary key fields should be made as short as possible (built using as few characters and fields as possible), because they can affect the speed of operations in a database.

Creating a primary key

As discussed in Chapter 4, a primary key is created by selecting the field (or fields) that you want to use as a primary key and clicking on the Primary Key button on the toolbar (the button with the key on it). If you are specifying more than one field, you specify the fields that you want for the primary key and again click the Primary Key button. Selecting each field while holding down the Ctrl key specifies the fields.

When you're specifying multi-field primary keys, the selection order is important. Therefore, check your selection by clicking the Indexes button on the toolbar and looking at the field order. Figure 6-2 shows the two-field index for the Visit Details table. Notice that the Visit Number field is before the Line Number field in the Indexes: Visit Details dialog box.

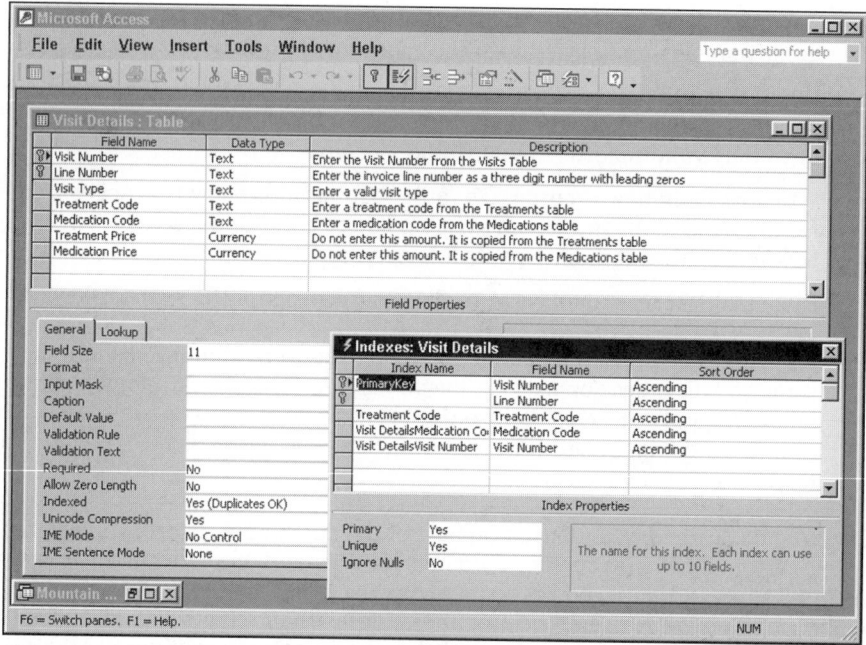

Figure 6-2: The Indexes: Visit Details dialog box showing a two-field primary key

The Indexes: Visit Details dialog box shown in the bottom right-hand corner of Figure 6-2 is opened by opening a table in Design View and selecting View ➪ Indexes from the Access menu or clicking on the Indexes button (center of the toolbar with a series of parallel lines and a lighting bolt along side of them — to the right of the Key button). Once open it shows you all of the Indexes in that table — including primary, foreign keys, and other indexes for sorting. Notice that it ONLY shows the word PrimaryKey in the Visit Number field, although it still shows the graphical key (for primary key) to the left of both fields. This simply means that both fields together make up the primary key.

The order of these fields is critical; if you reverse them and make the Line Number field the first part of the primary key, it will not work correctly — you may create a situation where you do not have a viable way to create unique records in the table.

Note There are three additional index names in the Indexes: Visit Details dialog box. These are not keys, but indexes used to speed sorts used in these tables. If you regularly sort data in tables by the same field or fields, you should create an index for that field. An index is an internal table of values that maintains the order of the records. This way, when you need to sort data or find a piece of data instantly, Access can search through the index keys in a known order, rather than sequentially through the data.

Caution Creating indexes slows data entry; each new record, deleted record, or change to the indexed field requires a change to the index. Use the index fields only when you actually need them; for example, when you need to speed sorting your application for later use. You will have to balance the display and reporting speed with the need of data-entry speed.

Understanding foreign keys

Primary keys guarantee uniqueness in a table, and you use the primary key field in one table to link to related records in another table (the Pets owned by a specific Customer). The common link field in the other table (records that are associated with a record in the primary table) may not be (and usually isn't) the primary key in the other table.

The *common link field* is a field or fields that hold the same type of data (matching the content of the field exactly) as in the primary key of the link table. This common link field, or combination of fields, is known as a *foreign key* field. Like a primary key, which must be created in a special way, a *foreign key* must be created using the same structure; however, it can be any field(s) in any order of the structure of the table. You are not limited to a specific field order when you create the table's structure. By matching the same values (from a primary key field in a record in the primary key table to the values in a specific field of one or more records in a foreign key table) in both tables, you can relate records between tables.

In the relationship diagram of Figure 6-1, you saw a relationship between the Customer and Pets tables. The primary key of Customer, Customer Number, is related to the Customer Number field in Pets. In Pets, Customer Number is the foreign key because it is the key of a related "foreign" table.

An example would be George Green in the Customer table with the Customer ID of GR001. The one record in the Customer table with the Customer ID GR001 is linked to four records in the Pets table — one record of a frog named Adam (Pet ID GR001-01) and three Snakes named Killer (Pet ID GR001-02), Slither (Pet ID GR001-03), and Sammie (Pet ID GR001-04). Thus there is one record in the Customer table with GR001 in the Customer Field and three records in the Pets table Customer Number field with the number GR001.

A relation also exists between the States and Customer tables. The primary key of States, State Code, is related to the State field in the Customer table. In the Customer table, State is the foreign key because it is the key of a related foreign table.

Understanding Relations Between Tables

At the beginning of this chapter, you saw eight tables in the Mountain Animal Hospital database and seven relationships. Before you learn to create these relationships, it is important to understand them.

A review of relationships

First, you can create relationships between tables at two places — (1) in the Relationship window that will relate them at a table level, and (2) when you create queries to display information from those tables — known as the query level.

Relationships established at the table level take precedence over those established at the query level. If you specify a relationship between tables at the table level (in the Relationship window), Access will recognize it automatically when you create a multiple-table query that uses fields from more than one table.

With that said, it is now important to understand that there are four types of relationships that you can set between two tables:

✦ One-to-one

✦ One-to-many

✦ Many-to-one

✦ Many-to-many

Understanding the four types of table relationships

When you physically join two tables (by connecting fields with like information), you create a relationship that Access recognizes. Figure 6-3 shows the relationships between all the tables in the Mountain Animal Hospital system.

The relationship that you specify between tables is important. It tells Access how to find and display information from fields in two or more tables. The program needs to know whether to look for only one record in a table or to look for several records on the basis of the relationship. The Customer table, for example, has a *one-to-many* relationship to the Pets table. There will *always* be one record in the Customer table for *at least* one record in the Pets table; there could be *many* related records in the Pets table. So Access knows to find only one record in the Customer table and to look for any in the Pets table (one or more) that have the same Customer Number.

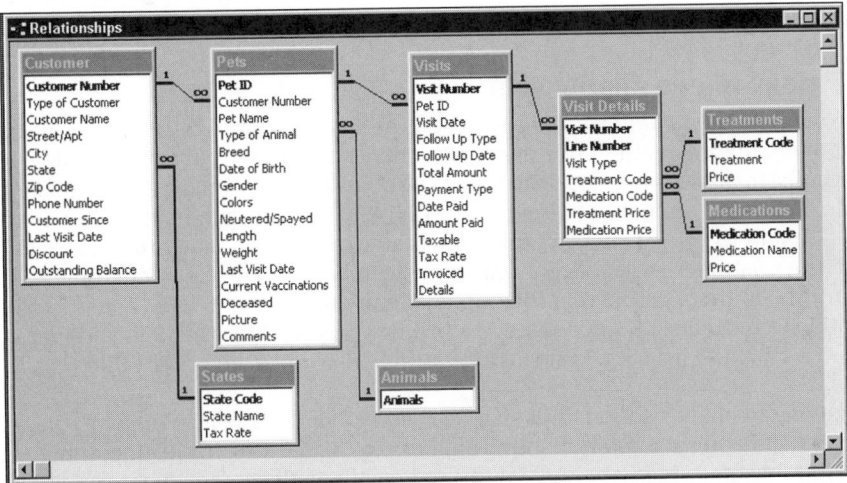

Figure 6-3: The Mountain Animal Hospital tables relationships. This shows that there are three one-to-many relationships between the primary tables and four many-to-one relationships between the primary tables and the lookup tables.

The one-to-one relationship

The *one-to-one relationship*, though rarely used in database systems, can be a very useful way to link two tables together.

A good example of a one-to-one relationship occurs in most billing systems; a billing file is created to allow additional information necessary to invoice customers at a location other than their listed addresses. This file usually contains the customer number and another set of address fields.

Only a few customers would have a separate billing address, so you wouldn't add this information to the main customer table. A one-to-one relationship between a customer table and billing table may be established to retrieve the billing address for those customers who want to have a separate address for billing purposes and one for catalogs or other uses. Although all the information on one table could be added to the other, the tables are maintained separately for efficient use of space.

The one-to-many relationship

The *one-to-many relationship* is used to relate one record in a table with many records in another. Examples are one customer to many pets or one pet to many visits. Both of these examples are one-to-many relationships. The Customer-Pets relationship links the customer number (the primary key of the Customer table) to the customer number in the Pets table (which becomes the foreign key of the Customer table).

The many-to-one relationship

The *many-to-one relationship* (often called the *lookup table relationship*) tells Access that many records in the table are related to a single record in another table. Normally, many-to-one relationships are not based on a primary key field in either table. Mountain Animal Hospital has four lookup tables, each having a many-to-one relationship with the primary table. The States table has a many-to-one relationship with the Customer table; each state record can be used for many customers. Although (in theory) this relationship is one-to-one, it is known as a many-to-one relationship because it does not use a primary key field for the link, and many records from the primary table link to a single record in the other table.

Some one-to-many relationships can be reversed and made into many-to-one relationships. If you set a relationship from Pets to Customers, for example, the relationship becomes many-to-one; many pets can have the same owner. So relationships depend on how the information in your tables is used and interpreted. Thus, one-to-many and many-to-one relationships can be considered the same — just viewed from opposite perspectives.

The many-to-many relationship

The *many-to-many relationship* is the hardest to understand. Think of it generally as a pair of *one-to-many relationships* between two tables, with a special table created (called a *junction* table) that is used to link them together. The junction table is comprised of a minimum of two fields — the foreign keys from both tables it is linking together. These two fields are subsequently used to create the primary key in the junction table. This *junction* table could easily be created in the case of the tables Pets and Visits Details in the Mountain Animal Hospital database — with the Visits table, by simply making the primary key a combination of the Visit Number and Pet ID.

A pet can be serviced at the hospital on many dates, so you see a one-to-many relationship between Pets and Visits Details. On the other hand, each medication or type of treatment can be given or performed on many Pets; this is also a one-to-many relationship. Thus a pair of separate, two-way, one-to-many relationships creates a many-to-many relationship — for a true many-to-many relationship between these two tables, the Visits table (acting as a junction table) would have to have a primary key of Pet ID and Visit Number in the junction table.

Understanding Referential Integrity

In addition to specifying relationships between tables in an Access database, you can also set up some rules that will help in maintaining a degree of accuracy, or *Referential Integrity,* between the tables. For example, you would not want to delete a customer record in your Customer table if there are related pet records in the Pets table. If you did delete a customer record without first deleting the customer's pets, you would have a system that has pets without an owner. This type of problem could be catastrophic.

Imagine being in charge of a bank that tracks loans in a database system. Now imagine that this system has *no* rules that say, "Before deleting a customer's record, make sure that there is no outstanding loan." It would be disastrous! So a database system needs to have rules that specify certain conditions between tables — rules to enforce the integrity of information between the tables. These rules are known as *referential integrity*; they keep the relationships between tables intact in a relational database management system. Referential integrity prohibits you from changing your data in ways that invalidate the links between tables.

Referential integrity operates strictly on the basis of the tables' key fields; it checks each time a key field, whether primary or foreign, is added, changed, or deleted. If a change to a value in a key field creates an invalid relationship, it is said to violate referential integrity. Tables can be set up so that referential integrity is enforced automatically.

When tables are linked, one table is usually called the *parent* and the other (the table it is linked to) is usually called the *child*. This is known as a *parent-child relationship* between tables. Referential integrity guarantees that there will never be an *orphan*, a child record without a parent record.

Cross-Reference   If you connect to an SQL Server back end database or use the Microsoft Database Engine and create an Access Data Project, the relationship window is different. This is discussed in Chapter 34.

Creating Relationships

Unless you have a reason for not wanting your relationships always to be active, create your table relationships at the table level using the *Relationship window*. The table relationships can be overridden later, in a query, if necessary. For normal data entry and reporting purposes, however, having your relationships defined at the table level makes it much easier to use your database system.

Access 2002 has a very powerful Relationship window. With it you can add tables, use drag-and-drop methods to link tables, easily specify the type of link, and set any referential integrity between tables.

Using the Relationship window

You begin creating relationships in the Database window. From this window, you can select Tools ➾ Relationships or click the Relationships button on the toolbar (usually the third button from the right side — three little squares, one on the left and two on the right, with blue tops and lines from the left one to the other two). The main Relationships window appears, which lets you add tables and create links between them.

Figure 6-4 shows the Relationships window with the eight tables that you will add below. Notice the toolbar associated with it — it has two options specific to the Relationship window — Show Direct Relationships and Show All Relationships (center right of toolbar). When first opened, the Relationships window is a blank surface. Tables are added to the window by using one of these methods:

✦ Add the tables before entering the Relationship window from the Show Tables dialog box that's first displayed.

✦ Click the Show Tables button on the toolbar.

✦ Click Relationships ➾ Show Table from the menu bar.

✦ While in the Relationships window, click the right mouse button (which displays the shortcut menu) and select Show Table from the menu.

To start the Relationship window and add the Mountain Animal Hospital tables to the Relationships window, follow these steps:

1. Click the Relationships button on the toolbar. Access opens the Show Table dialog box.

2. Select all the tables (Customer, Pets, Visits, Visit Details, States, Animals, Medications, and Treatments) by clicking Animals, holding Shift, and clicking Visits. Then click Add

3. Click the Close button on the Show Table dialog box. Your screen should look similar to the one in Figure 6-4. Notice that Access has placed each table in the Relationships window. Each table is in its own box; the title of the box is the name of the table. Inside the table box are the names of the fields for each table. Currently, there are no relationships, or lines, between the tables. Now you are ready to set relationships between them.

Note If you select a table by mistake, it can be removed from the window by clicking in it and pressing the Delete key.

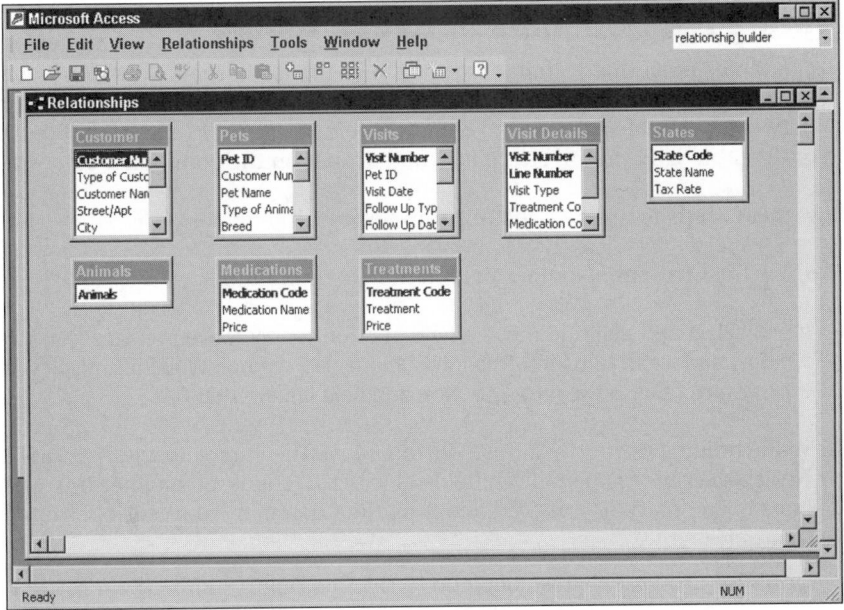

Figure 6-4: The Relationships window with eight tables added

 Tip   You may want to resize each table window to see all the fields, as shown in Figure 6-5.

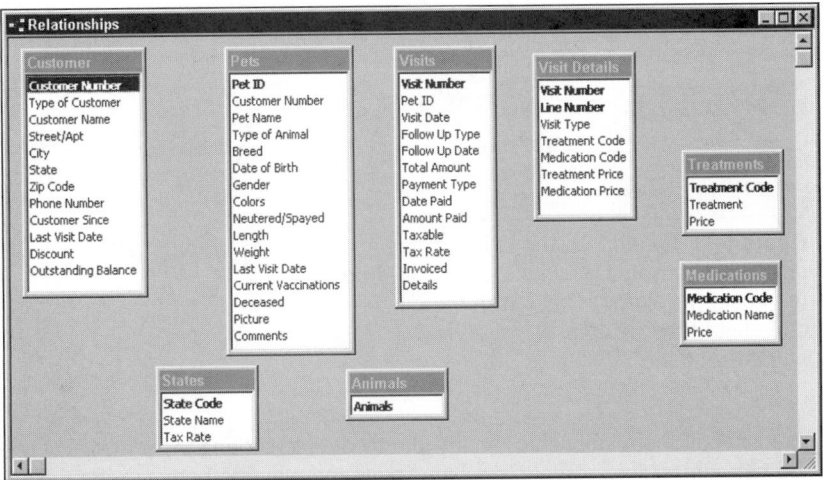

Figure 6-5: The Relationships window with tables sized and repositioned, ready to create the relationships between them

Creating relationships between tables

With the tables positioned similar to those in Figure 6-5 in the Relationships window, you are ready to create relationships between the tables. To create a relationship between two tables, select the common field in one table and drag it to the field in the table you want to relate it to and drop it on the common field.

Follow these steps to create a relationship between the tables:

1. Click the Customer Number field of the Customer table.

> **Note**   If you select and begin to move a field in error, simply move the field icon to the window surface; it turns into the international No symbol. While it is displayed as this symbol, release the mouse button and field linking stops.

2. While holding down the mouse button, move the cursor to the Pets table. Notice that Access displays a field-select icon (small rectangular box with lines inside of it) as you hold and drag the Customer Number field from the Customer table.

3. Drag-and-drop the field-select icon to the Customer Number field of the Pets table. Access displays the Edit Relationships dialog box as seen in Figure 6-6.

4. Click the Create button to create the relationship. Access closes the dialog box and places a join line between the Customer and Pets table.

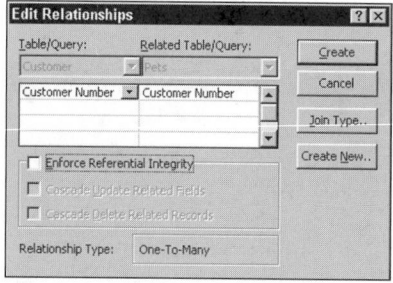

Figure 6-6: The Edit Relationships dialog box that is activated when you drag-and-drop the Customer Number field from the Customer table onto the Customer Number field of the Pets table

> **Note**   You can edit the relationship for any join by double-clicking the join line between the two tables. For example, double-clicking the join line between the Customer and Pets table reactivates the Edit Relationships dialog box for that link.

Tip Access automatically tries to determine the type of link between the two tables by looking at the data in the records of both tables and displays it at the bottom of the Relationships dialog box. Figure 6-6 shows the type of relationships between the Customer and Pets table is a One-to-Many type. However, it does not physically display the type of link between the tables in the Relationship window unless Enforce Referential Integrity is checked on.

Specifying relationship options in the Edit Relationships dialog box

The Edit Relationships dialog box has several options for the relationship between the Customer and Pets tables. Figure 6-6 shows the dialog box and all the options. The Edit Relationships dialog box tells you which table is the primary table for the relationship (the one on the left side of the dialog box — Customer) and whether referential integrity is enforced (a check box below the names of the related fields on the left side). The dialog box also tells you the type of relationship (one-to-one or one-to-many — at the bottom of the dialog box) and lets you specify (after selecting Enforce Referential Integrity) whether *cascading* updates and *deletes* (automatically fix key changes or deletions in related records) between related tables are allowed.

Note For the following sections, activate the Edit Relationships dialog box for the link between the Customer and Pets tables. To do so, double-click the join line between the tables.

Checking the primary table

The top of the dialog box has two table names — Customer on the left and Pets on the right. The Customer table is considered the primary table for this relationship. The dialog box shows the related fields for each table in a separate box immediately below the table names. Make sure that the correct table name is in both boxes (Customer and Pets) and that the correct field is specified.

Caution If you relate two tables incorrectly, simply click the Cancel button in the Edit Relationships dialog box. Access closes the dialog box and erases the join line, and you can begin again.

Tip If you relate two tables by the wrong field, simply select the correct field for each table by using the combo box under each table name.

Enforcing referential integrity

After specifying the relationship and verifying the table and related fields, you can set referential integrity between the tables by clicking the Enforce Referential Integrity check box below the table information. If you choose not to enforce referential integrity, you can add new records, change key fields, or delete related records without worrying about referential integrity — thus making it possible to change critical fields without being warned or prevented from doing so. With no integrity active you can create tables that have orphans (Pets without a Customer) or parents without children. With normal operations (such as data entry or changing information), referential integrity rules should be enforced. By setting this option, you can specify several additional options.

Clicking the check box in front of the option Enforce Referential Integrity activates the two Cascading choices (Update and Delete) in the dialog box.

You might find, when you specify Enforce Referential Integrity and click the Create button (or the OK button if you've reopened the Edit Relationship window to edit a relationship), that Access will not allow you to create a relationship and enforce referential integrity. The reason probably is that you are asking Access to create a relationship supporting referential integrity between two tables that have records that *violate* referential integrity rules, such as a child table with orphans in it. In such a case, Access warns you by displaying a dialog box similar to that shown in Figure 6-7. The warning happens in this example because there is a Pet record in the database with no Customer record, known as an *orphan record.*

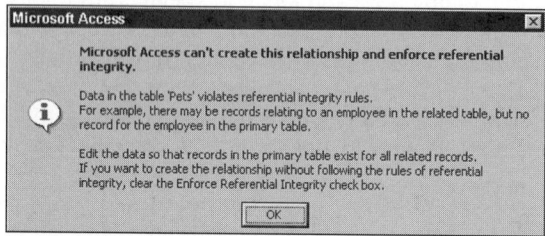

Figure 6-7: A dialog box warning that referential integrity cannot be created between two tables due to violations in some of the records between the two tables — one or more Pets without a Customer is probably the problem

Access returns you to the Relationships window after you click the OK button; you need to deselect the Enforce Referential Integrity check box before saving your work.

Tip   To solve any conflicts between existing tables, you can create a Find Unmatched query by using the Query Wizard to find the records in the many-side table (in this case the Pets table) that violate referential integrity. Then you can convert the Unmatched query to a Delete query to delete the offending records. You learn how to do this in Chapter 12.

Caution   When selecting Enforce Referential Integrity, Access does not check to see if you have Customers without Pets. This is not an issue with referential integrity. You can have multiple Customers that have no pets, known as *widow* records. However, these records do not violate integrity; thus they are not checked for by Access. Even with enforcement on, you can still create a parent record without children (a Customer without any Pets). However, you can create a Find Unmatched query to delete these records. This will be covered in Chapter 12.

You could remove the offending records and return to the Relationships window and set referential integrity between the two tables. However, you should not do this. The offending records are needed in Chapter 12, when they will be removed.

Choosing the Cascade Update Related Fields option

If you specify Enforce Referential Integrity in the Edit Relationships dialog box, Access activates a check box option labeled Cascade Update Related Fields. This option tells Access that a user can change the contents of a related field (the primary key field in the primary table — Customer Number, for example).

When the user changes the contents of the primary key field in the primary table, Access verifies that the change is to a unique value (because there cannot be duplicate records in the primary table) and then goes through the related records in the many table and changes the foreign key value from the old value to the new value. Suppose you code your customers by the first two letters of their last names, and one of your customers gets married and changes the name that Access knows to look for. You could change the Customer Number, and all changes would ripple through other related records in the system.

If this option is not selected, you cannot change the primary key value in the primary table that is used in a relationship with another table.

Note   If the primary key field in the primary table is a related field between several tables, this option must be selected for all related tables or it will not work.

Choosing the Cascade Delete Related Records option

Similarly, if you specify Enforce Referential Integrity in the Edit Relationships dialog box, Access activates the Cascade Delete Related Records check box. By selecting this option, you tell Access that if a user attempts to delete a record in a primary table that has child records, first it must delete all the related child records and then delete the primary record.

This can be very useful for deleting a series of related records. For example, if you have chosen Cascade Delete Related Records and you try to delete a particular customer (who moved away from the area), Access first deletes all the related records from the related tables — Pets, Visits, and Visit Details — then deletes the customer record. In other words, Access deletes all the records in the Visit Details for each visit for each pet owned by the customer, the visit records, the associated pet records, and the customer record, with one step.

If you do not specify this option, Access will not enable you to delete a record that has related records in another table. In cases like this, you must delete all related records in the Visit Details table first, then delete related records in the Visits table, then delete related records in the Pets table, and finally delete the customer record in the Customer table.

Tip

To use this option, you must specify Cascade Delete Related Records for all of the table's relationships in the database. If you do not specify this option for all the tables in the chain of related tables, Access will not allow cascade deleting.

Caution

Use this option with caution! Access does not warn that it is going to do a cascade delete when you build a Delete query. The program just does it. Later you may wonder where all your records went. However, if you delete a record in a form that has a subform with related records in it, Access will display a message saying it will delete 'this record and all its related records.'

Saving the relationships between tables

The easiest way to save the relationships you created between the tables is to click the Save button on the toolbar and then close the window. Another method is to close the window and answer *Yes* to the Save Relationships dialog box that appears.

Adding another relationship

After you specify all the tables, the fields, and their referential integrity status, you can add tables to the Relationships window by clicking the Relationships button on the toolbar and adding new tables.

Again, if there is data in a new table that violates referential integrity between it and a related table, you must fix the offending table by removing the records before you can set referential integrity between the tables.

Deleting an existing relationship

To delete an existing relationship, open the Relationships window, right-click the join line you want to delete, and select Delete from the Menu. In previous versions of Access you could simply press the Delete key, and answer Yes to the question *Are you sure you want to delete the selected relationship?*

Join lines in the Relationships window

When you create a relationship between two tables, Access automatically creates a thin join line from one table to another. Figure 6-8 shows a simple join line between several tables; for example, between States and Customer, Pets and Animals, and Visit Details and Treatments or Medications.

If you specify that you want to enforce referential integrity, however, Access changes the appearance of the join line. It becomes thicker at each end (alongside the table). It also has either a 1 or the infinity symbol (∞ over the thick bar of the line (on each side of the join line) as between Pets and Visits tables, or the Visits table and Visits Detail table.

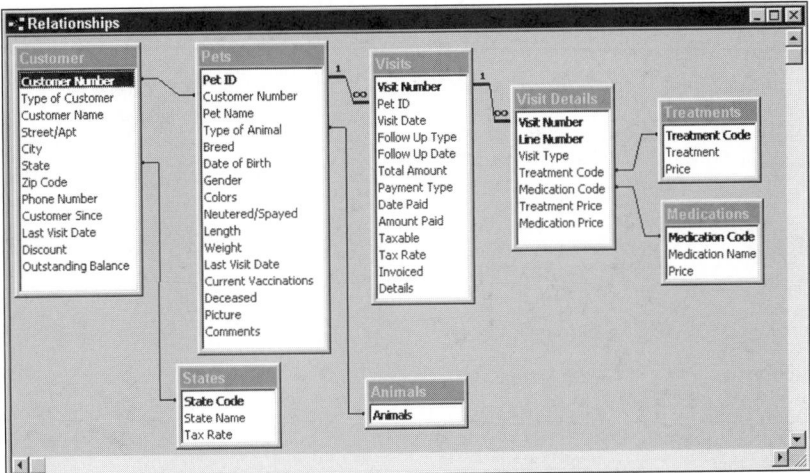

Figure 6-8: The relationships in the Mountain Animal Hospital system. Notice that there are plain thin lines between Customer and States and Pets and Animals. In contrast, the lines between the Pets and Visits tables and the Visits and Visits Details tables show a join line with a 1 and the infinity symbol at either end.

Creating the relationships for the Mountain Animal Hospital system

Table 6-3 shows the relationships between all the tables in the system. Referential integrity is set between three of the four primary tables. In addition to having referential integrity, each of the four main tables has the Cascade Delete Related Records option set.

Table 6-3			
Relationships in the Mountain Animal Hospital System			
Primary Table/Field	*Related Table/Field*	*Referential Integrity*	*Cascade Delete*
Customer	Pets		
Customer Number	Customer Number	No*	No*
Pets	Visits		
Pet ID	Pet ID	Yes	Yes
Visits	Visit Details		

Continued

Table 6-3 (continued)			
Primary Table/Field	**Related Table/Field**	**Referential Integrity**	**Cascade Delete**
Visit Number	Visit Number	Yes	Yes
State	Customer		
State Code	State	No	No
Animals	Pets		
Animals	Type of Animal	No	No
Medications	Visit Details		
Medication Code	Medication Code	No	No
Treatments	Visit Details		
Treatment Code	Treatment Code	No	No

*These will be changed in Chapter 12 after orphan records are deleted.

Printing a report of the relationships

Once you have defined the relationships for your tables, you can create a graphical report of the relationships of the tables by selecting File ➪ Print Relationships from the Access menu while the Relationships window is open.

Using the Access Table Analyzer

Everything that you have read in this chapter assumes that your tables are designed and that the relationships are normalized in the entire database. With many new systems, however (and especially with new developers), this is not the case. Sometimes you might start by importing an Excel spreadsheet file into Access, or by importing a large mainframe file (commonly known as *flat files* because all the data is contained in a single file). When imported into Access, a flat file becomes one single table.

Caution   Although you can obtain some useful information about your tables from the Analyzer, you should not rely on it totally. In fact, it can often give wrong advice.

Access 2002 contains a tool called Table Analyzer that analyzes a single table and attempts to determine whether it is normalized.

A Brief Understanding of Normalization

In Database parlance, *Normalization* is a formal process that you can use to analyze the information stored in a single table and determine if any of the data in that table should be moved to another table that can be linked to this table — thus making the system more efficient and accurate. There are several degrees of normalization that you can perform on information stored in a table. Most professionals will *"normalize"* their tables to what is known as third-level normalization (although there are many more levels of the process). However, for the purpose of this book, simply think of normalization as a process by which you remove any primary information that is repeated over and over in a single table — moving it to its own table — in a single record that is then linked back to the original table. By doing this you could create two types of new tables — those containing multiple records — like the Pets table is to the Customer table, or a lookup table, like the States table is the Customer table.

This Table Analyzer tool, when used, will make suggestions for splitting the data into related tables. It creates both primary and foreign keys, searches for misspellings of commonly used data, and suggests corrections.

If, for example, you have a flat file that contains both sales items and customers, you might have the customer information (name, address, and so on) repeated over and over. Where the customer name *Animals R Us* is found many times, it might be listed as *Animals R Us Inc.* or *Animals R Us Company* or *Animals are Us* or even misspelled as *Aminals R Us*. The Table Analyzer attempts to split your data into two or more tables and suggests corrections to the data — thus finding all these different spellings and suggesting that they are the same company.

On the CD-ROM

To test this tool, you can use the database named "Table Analyzer DB" included on the CD-ROM. There is a special table named Customer-Pet-Visit in that database. (You can also create this table by running a special query named 'MAKE Customer-Pets-Visits' in the Mountain Animal Start databases named MAKE: Customer-Pets-Visits, if you feel comfortable enough with running a query.) If you use the Mountain Animal Start database, simply run this query to create the Customer-Pet-Visit table. Either way, the Customer-Pet-Visit table will be used to learn how Table Analyzer tool works. The Table Analyzer DB.mdb does have three records that are deliberately different to be caught by the Analyzer (these records are not in the Mountain Animal Start,mdb so they will not be found if you build the tables using this database).

Starting the Table Analyzer

You can start the Table Analyzer by selecting Tools ⇨ Analyze ⇨ Table from any design screen. This displays the first window of the Table Analyzer Wizard, as shown in Figure 6-9.

Caution   If the Table Analyzer Wizard is not already installed on your computer, Access will prompt you to install it at the time you first run it — now. To do this, you will need to have your original Office XP CD available. Access will prompt you to put your CD into the drive and it will automatically install it for you.

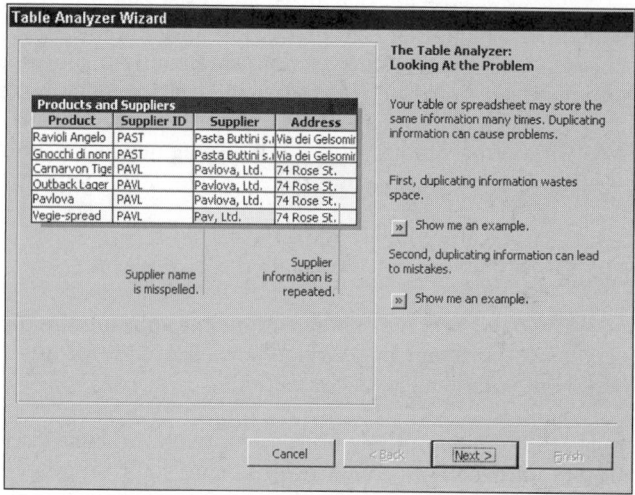

Figure 6-9: Using the Table Analyzer. This is the first window, titled Looking At the Problem.

Note   If you have already used the Analyzer, you may not see the introductory screens shown in Figures 6-9 and 6-10.

This first window shown in Figure 6-9 is actually the first of two introductory windows. These introductory windows have no function other than to offer Help text. This first screen introduces the concepts performed by Table Analyzer. You can click the Show me arrows in the right center of the screen to get a further explanation of why you should not duplicate information in a table.

Once you finish looking at that window for the first time, click the Next button to move to the next screen. This screen tells you how Table Analyzer solves the potential problems you have in your table (Figure 6-10). The first window's title is Looking At the Problem; the second window's title is Solving the Problem. Figure 6-10 also has Show me arrows to click for more detailed explanations about data normalization. Click the Next button to continue.

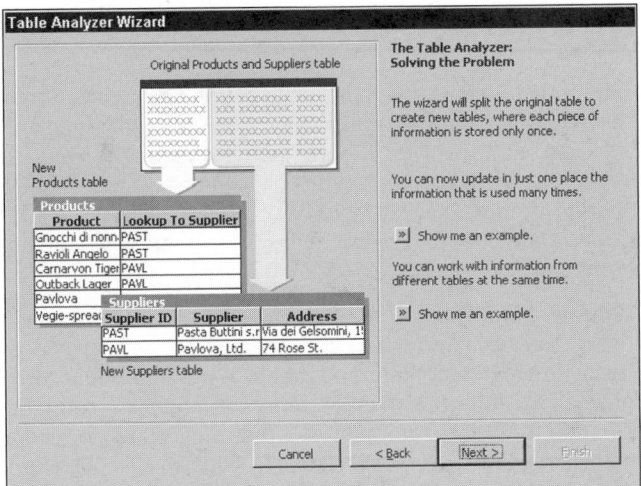

Figure 6-10: The Table Analyzer's second introductory window, titled Solving the Problem

Selecting a table to analyze

After the introductory screens, Table Analyzer displays another screen. This screen is used to select the table to analyze. If you are following this example, select *Customer-Pet-Visit* from the list of tables, as shown in Figure 6-11.

Tip

Only tables can be analyzed, not queries. This Analyzer will not enable you to analyze a query. It relies on the use of tables that need to be Normalized — a query is simply a view of existing tables.

You don't have to look at the introductory screens each time you run Table Analyzer. As Figure 6-11 shows, there is a check box to turn the introductory screens on the next time you run Table Analyzer. The default is to turn it off once you have used the wizard once.

Analyzing the table

Once the table is selected, click the Next button to move on. The next window asks whether you want Access to analyze the tables and make decisions for you, or whether you want to make your own decisions. If you prefer to make your own choices, Access takes you to the Table Analyzer screen in a special version of the Relationships window. There you can drag and drop fields to create a new table, or drag fields from a related table into a parent table to undo a relationship. You learn about this screen later in this section.

Analyzing a Flat-File Table

The following figure shows part of the Customer-Pet-Visit table in Datasheet View. The data was created via a Make Table query that combined information from three tables and eliminated the primary and foreign keys and many of the unimportant fields. The fields used from the Customer table are as follows: Customer Number, Customer Name, Street/Apt, City, State, ZIP Code, and Phone Number. The Pet table fields are as follows: Pet ID, Pet Name, Type of Animal, Breed, and Date of Birth. Finally, the fields from the Visit table are as follows: Visit Date and Total Amount.

If you study the information in the table, you will see repeating groups. For instance, the Customer information and individual Pet information are repeated across many records. The Table Analyzer should recognize this repetition and create a separate table for customers, pets, and visits because all the information is the same for multiple records. Table Analyzer can recognize information that is or is not part of a repeating group. When Table Analyzer looks at the Customer Name, Street/Apt, City, State, ZIP Code, and Phone Number fields, it finds many records with exactly the same data, City and State for example, and moves this information into its own table.

Analyzing a flat-file table

In addition to recognizing reoccurring information, Table Analyzer will also attempt to compare data for misspellings. If it finds misspellings, it reports them during the process of analyzing the table.

Before you use Table Analyzer, you may want to place your information in a sorted order. This will aid Table Analyzer in normalizing your data. For instance, the information stored in the table in the above figure is in order by Customer (Customer Number) first and then pet (Pet ID) second.

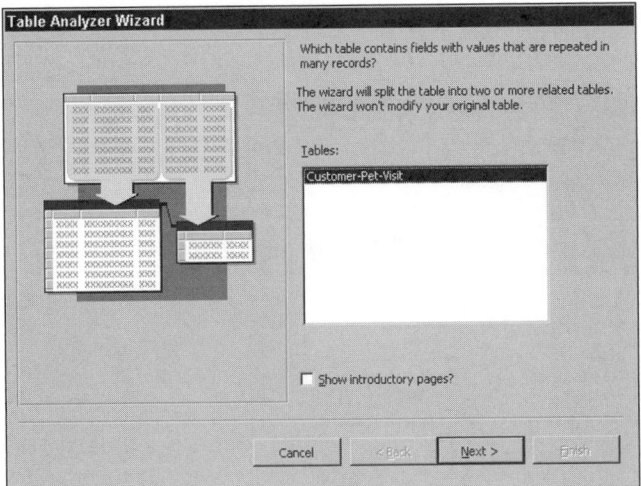

Figure 6-11: Selecting the table to be analyzed. Notice that the table Customer-Pet-Visit is highlighted (selected). You can de-select showing the introductory pages by clicking on the check box below the table names.

At this point, accept the default value of Yes, and then click the Next button. When you select *Yes, let the wizard decide*, Table Analyzer performs a multistep analysis of your data, possibly displaying several progress meters onscreen. When the process is complete, the next Wizard screen appears automatically. It shows the proposed structure of the tables, their relationships, and the primary and foreign keys (Figure 6-12).

As Figure 6-12 shows, Table Analyzer has done a great job in splitting the flat file into several tables. The first table (named Table1) contains data about the Visit. The second table (named Table2) contains Pet information. The third table (Named Table3) contains Customer information, and the final table (named Table4) contains City/State information. Each table has been built based on repeating and similar type of information in the fields from the flat table. Each table has a primary key assigned: the Pets and Customer tables have an existing field; the other two are assigned a Generated Unique Key. The relationships are already created between suggested tables.

Changing the table and field definitions

In Figure 6-12, the fourth table has City and State information in it. Although Table Analyzer related it to the Pets table, you know that it is really related to the Customer table. At this point, you can interactively work with Table Analyzer. You can rename the tables, move fields from table to table, and even delete or create tables from fields in the tables displayed.

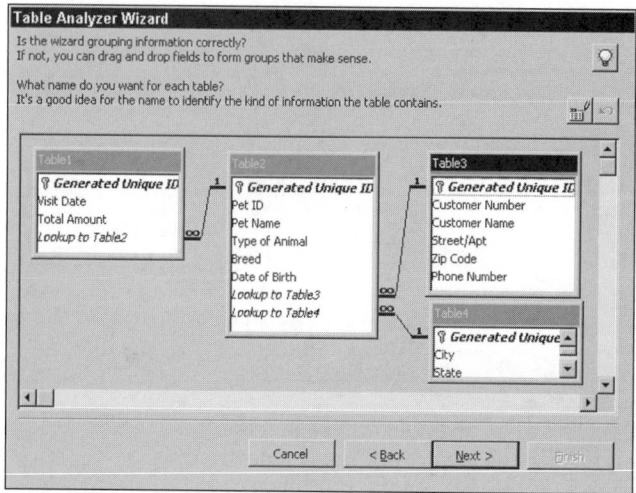

Figure 6-12: The Table Analyzer's Relationships window. It suggested breaking the file into four unique tables. Only one of these seems a bit fuzzy — pets table to city/state versus customer to city/state.

All three of the main tables appear to have been split correctly (Visits [Table1], Pets [Table2], and Customer [Table3]), and to have been assigned the correct primary key fields (or to have created one). However, Table4 seems to have some problems. Following normalization rules, you could create a separate table that holds City, State, and ZIP Code information, and link it to a table that looks up cities according to the ZIP Code. To guarantee uniqueness of cities, you must use the U.S. Postal Service 9-digit ZIP Code system. If you use 5-digit ZIP codes, it is possible to have multiple cities with the same ZIP Code. So for purposes of this session, you should move the two fields from the fourth table into Table3 (the customer information table). You can move a field from one table to another by dragging it from one table to another. (You will do this in the next series of steps.) For example you could highlight the City and State fields in Table4 and click and drag them to Table3, between Street/Apt and ZIP Code. As you move them, the multifield icon appears and a horizontal crossbar appears between the Street/Apt and ZIP Code fields. Because all the fields except the Generated Unique ID field are moved out of the table, Table4 is automatically removed from the screen.

Note Likewise, you can drag a field back from one table to another. You can also create a new table by dragging a field from one table to an empty area of the screen. This creates a new table, a primary key for the new table, and a new foreign key in the original table you dragged the field from. You can also change the order of the fields by selecting one and dragging it above or below other fields in the table.

To drag the City and State fields from Table 4, follow these steps:

1. Click on the field named City in Table 4.

2. While holding the mouse button down, drag the field icon to Table 3 and drop it in the field list above the Zip Code field.

3. Repeat this process for the State field.

Once you have completed this, the structure for Table 4 should disappear from the Wizard window.

With three tables now left in Table Analyzer, you should rename each of the tables. Logically, you would rename them Customer, Pets, and Visits. However, these tables already exist, so instead give them the same name with the word "Analyze" before them — rename them from *Table1* to *Analyze Visit*, from *Table2* to *Analyze Pet*, and from *Table3* to *Analyze Customer*.

Note Although you can rename the table in Table Analyzer, you cannot rename any fields, such as the new primary and foreign key fields. You can rename the new key primary and foreign fields in the tables only by using the standard Table Design screen after the Wizard is complete.

To rename the tables, follow these steps:

1. Select Table1 by clicking on the title bar or any field in the table.

2. Either double-click the title bar of the table or click the Rename Table button that looks like a pencil with a table (second row, second button from the right along the top of the Wizard window in Figure 6-12). This displays the Table Analyzer Wizard, Table Name dialog box.

3. Type the name "Analyze Visit" in the text box.

4. Click the OK button.

5. Repeat Steps 1 through 5 for Table2, renaming it Analyze Pets.

6. Repeat Steps 1 through 5 for Table3, renaming it Analyze Customer. Having completed this, the window should now look similar to the one in Figure 6-13.

7. Click Next to move to the next Wizard window.

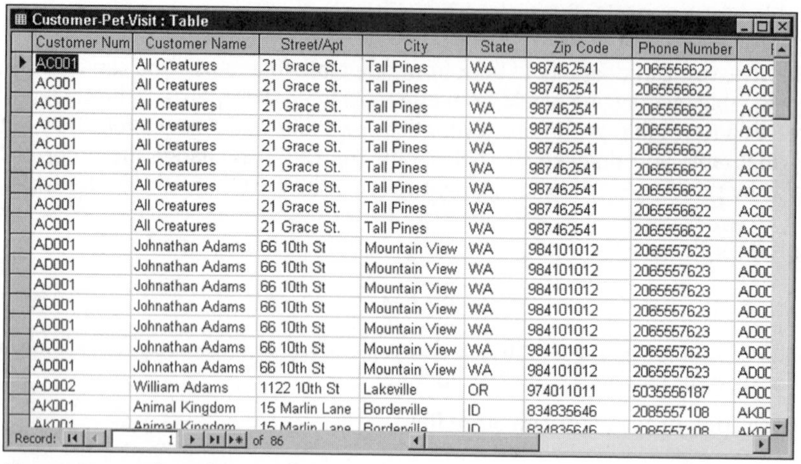

Figure 6-13: The Table Analyzer

Changing the key fields

This window enables you to change which fields are the key fields that Table Analyzer has created. Figure 6-14 shows this screen with the three tables created and renamed. On the right side of the window there are four buttons — one by itself (a light bulb) and three below it. The three buttons below the top one are used to work with the primary keys.

If you need to create a new primary key, or to change a primary key to an existing field, this is where to do it. To keep a new unique key, one generated by Access, you don't have to do anything — it is already done for you in each table. Notice in Figure 6-13 that each table has a key symbol and the word "Generated Unique" as the first field of the table — this is a new unique key. If you need to change the assigned primary key field, click the correct field that should be the primary field and then click the Set Unique Identifier button. This cancels the previously created primary key assignment. If the previous field was a generated field, it is removed from the table.

To assign the correct primary key fields in the Pets and Customer table, follow these steps:

1. Select Analyze Pets table and highlight the Pet ID field.

2. Click on the Set Unique Identifier icon (third button from the right) to set it as the primary key field.

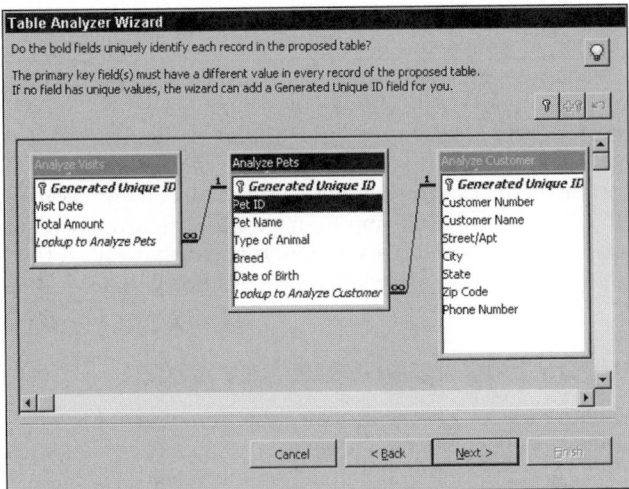

Figure 6-14: The Table Analyzer's Relationships window with the tables renamed. This window is where you can create a primary key or change a primary key.

3. Select the Analyze Customer table and highlight the Customer Number field.

4. Click on the Set Unique Identifier icon (third button from the right) to set it as the primary key field.

The "Generate Unique ID" fields were removed automatically from the tables as you assigned new primary keys. If you accidentally assigned the primary key to the wrong field, you can simply select the correct field and click on the button. If you need to reassign a Generated Unique ID key to the table instead, simply click on the second button of the series — a key with a plus sign. This will add the "Generated Unique ID" field to the table and make it the primary key.

Click the Next button to continue to the next step of Table Analyzer.

Once you have changed the primary key fields in the Analyze Pets and Analyze Customer tables and you click on the Next button, you will receive a Warning dialog box that says "The fields in the proposed table 'Analyze Pets' don't all appear to be related. Do you want to proceed with the spilt anyway?" Answer Yes to move to the next screen. This is referring to the link field of "Lookup to Analyze Customer" in the Analyze Pets table that is now linked to "Customer Number." It originally had the link based on the Generated Unique ID field.

Caution If the link field value in the Analyze Pets tables does not match the value in the Customer Number field, Access will attempt to correct this problem, linking the tables correctly by building an SQL statement in the table lookup property of the field. Should the correction be wrong, you may have to manually fix these records afterwards.

This warning dialog box will only appear if you make changes to the Primary Key fields (Set Unique Identifier). After answering yes to the warning dialog box, Access begins a search for aberrant data. Misspellings and inconsistencies in like data are the most common types of problem data Table Analyzer can find.

If you examine Figure 6-14, you will see that it has found 19 records that may have similar information as other records in the system. For instance, if you now click on the first record AC001-03, Stinky the Skunk, and then click on the proposed similar records field (Correction) you will be given a series of records that asks if this record is really one of them. Figure 6-15 shows this process being done.

Searching for typos and duplicate key data

If during the process of searching for aberrant data, Table Analyzer finds what it believes are inconsistencies or misspellings, it displays a series of screens that enable you to correct those apparent errors. You may see screens that make no sense, because Table Analyzer may make a wrong assumption about what to analyze. It might, for example, do some analysis on duplicate key data. The screens depend totally on the analysis of the data.

If Access does not find any data that appears to be in error, it will skip this series of screens.

Continuing with the example, Access did find an error in the data from the Customer-Pet-Visit flat file table. Figure 6-15 shows the next screen. The Analyzer found that there was a record that had the Type of Animal as CATS instead of Cat.

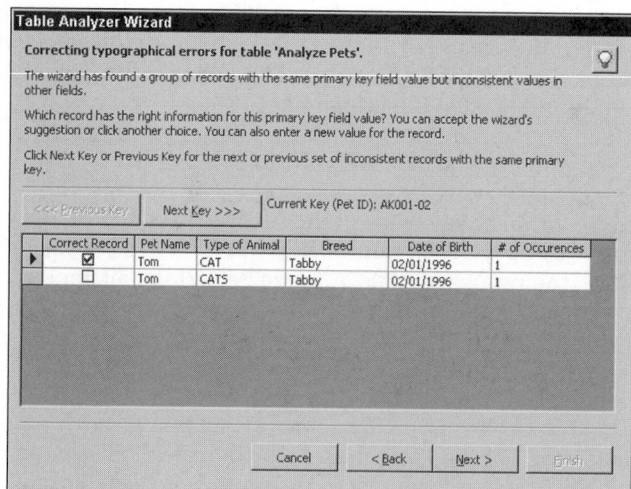

Figure 6-15: Screen showing what Access believes is an error in the table

If you examine Figure 6-15 you will see that it has two buttons in the center —
<<< Previous Key (which is grayed out) and Next Key >>>. These buttons are used
to go through the series of records that Access believes are in error. Below the
buttons is an open space that displays two records — the first is a record with corrections Access believes should be made to the record, the second is the original
record and its contents. Both records have a check box in them under a field name
of "Correct Record" and the first box is checked (the default value). Actually, this is
a radio button type control — only one box can be checked. Examining these two
records, you see that the suggested new record has the Type of Animal of CAT
instead of CATS. This is correct, so you can simply accept the change to record.

You should go through all the Next Key >>> records that Access finds to make sure
that the records found do in fact need to be changed. Clicking on the Next Key >>>
button, you will see another record where the Type of Animal is DOF instead of
DOG. These are the only two records that the Analyzer found in this table.

Once all the records have been examined, you are ready to continue on to the next
part of the Analyzer. Click on the Next button.

Once the typos are corrected, and you click the Next button, you are taken to the
final screen of Table Analyzer.

Note If Table Analyzer finds no apparent typos, you are immediately taken to the next,
and final, screen.

Completing Table Analyzer

The final screen (Figure 6-16) lets you complete the analysis process. Notice that
Table Analyzer offers to create a query using the original name of your table and
rename the original table. If you accept this choice, any forms and reports that
work with the old flat file table will continue to work. This gives you the best of
both worlds — you can start to work with the normalized tables while still being
able to work with the old table. If you decide to accept this choice, you should NOT
continue to add records to the old table!

Caution One problem the Table Analyzer can cause is to render existing queries, forms,
reports, and macros inoperable because all these objects are tied to specific table
and field names. When you change the table name or field names within a table,
Access reports an error when you try to run the form, report, or macro; they cannot automatically adjust. A solution is to create a new query (with the same name
as the original table) that uses the new tables and creates a view identical to the
original table.

This screen also has a check box labeled "Display Help on working with the new
tables or queries?" The default value is on (checked). You can turn this off if you do
not want to see help on working with the tables after they are completed — just
click the check box off.

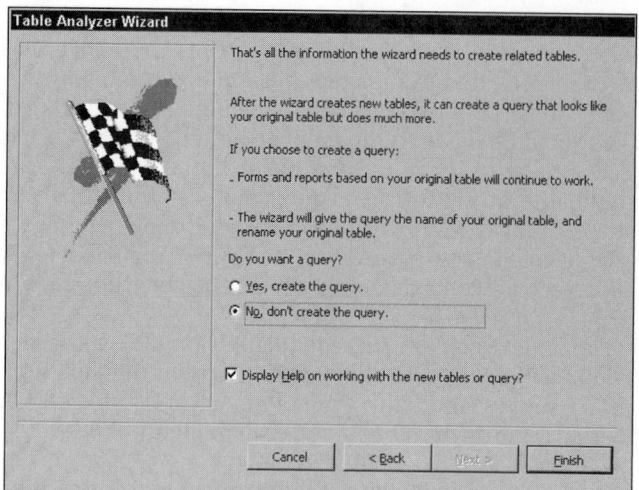

Figure 6-16: Completing the Table Analyzer process. This is the final screen of the Table Analyzer Wizard.

For the purpose of this exercise, select the choice *No, don't create the query,* and then click the Finish button.

Clicking the Finish button closes the Table Wizard, and a tiled view of all the new tables appears, with a dialog box that says "Here are the tables produced by the Wizard." Click on the OK button to continue. (If you left the check box for help on, you will see the Help file automatically open to the topic Analyzer Wizard.)

If you go through the Analyze Pets table, you will see that the Analyzer did not find and suggest a change to the Type of Animal from DOGGIE to DOG. (This record is 11 — Suzie, DOGGIE, Mixed, born 1/1/2000.) You can now change the record by editing it and changing the value to DOG.

Working with the tables, you will also see that the Pets and Visits tables have some additional things you may want to fix — the lookup value of the link field "Lookup to Analyze Customer" in Pets, the "ID" field values in the Visits table, and the "Lookup to Analyze Pets" in Visits. You cannot change the values in any of these fields — the ID field has been made an AutoNumber field, and the other two have a lookup table associated with them. To change them, you will have to accept the changes as made, go into the individual tables and modify their structures, and then work with the data. However, looking at the tables you can see that the records are *correctly* linked from child to parent.

When you are finished looking at the new tables, close them.

If you want to change the names of any of the fields, you can open each table in Design view and rename any field names. Although the Table Wizard is not perfect, it is one way to normalize a table with little effort.

You have completed working with the Table Analyzer. At this point, close the Table Analyzer DB.mdb and open the Mountain Animal Start.mdb.

Using the Lookup Wizard in the Table Designer

Note   The remainder of this chapter uses the Mountain Animal Start database.

When you view one table that is related to another table, the table often contains a foreign key — generally the primary key of the other table. The foreign key field is often cryptic when looked at through the related table. Until you relate the two tables and look at the data from a Query view, you cannot tell the real value of the field.

For example, Figure 6-17 shows the Pets table sorted by Type of Animal and Breed. Notice the cryptic value in the Customer Number field. In earlier versions of Access (versions 2.0 and earlier), the only way to see the Customer Name was to create a query and look at the resulting dynaset. In Access 2002, you can display the Customer Name in a table that contains only a foreign key lookup to the Customer table. This means that you can display, select, and immediately see a Customer Name, such as All Creatures, while in the Pets table, instead of using a foreign name such as AC001.

To do this you need to change the display nature of the field from showing actual content (Customer Number) to showing a lookup value from another table or list (the Customer's Name) by redefining the properties of the field. For instance, to change the display of the Customer Number field in the Pets table so that it displays the actual Customer Name, you change some properties at the database level of the Pets table.

To start the process of showing the actual Customer name instead of the Customer number, follow these steps:

1. Open the Pets table.

2. Switch to Design view.

3. Select the data type of the Customer Number field.

    You may want to click on the Lookup and see that the display control type is currently a Text Box, the default value. Then click on the General tab to continue.

4. Click the down-arrow to display the data type list.

Pet ID	Customer Number	Pet Name	Type of Animal	Breed	Date of Birth	Gender	
MZ001-01	MZ001	Ben	BEAR	Black	Oct 92	M	Blac
RZ001-01	RZ001	Moose	BEAR	Brown	Jan 87	M	Brow
ON001-04	ON001	Martin	BEAR	Northern	Apr 86	M	Brow
RW001-03	RW001	Pirate	BIRD	Blackbird	Apr 88	M	Blac
RW001-01	RW001	Bobby	BIRD	Bobwhite	Apr 86	F	Brow
BL001-04	BL001	Yellow Jacket	BIRD	Canary	Mar 83	F	Yellc
BL001-02	BL001	Carlos	BIRD	Cockatoo	Jan 91	M	Whit
WL001-03	WL001	Rosey	BIRD	Cockatoo	Nov 86	F	Whit
BL001-03	BL001	Ming	BIRD	Humming	Feb 88	F	Brow
WL001-02	WL001	Indigo	BIRD	Parakeet	Oct 89	F	Yellc
BL001-06	BL001	Mickey	BIRD	Parrot	May 91	M	Blue
BL001-07	BI001	Sally	BIRD	Parrot	Jul 85	F	Yellc
WL001-01	WL001	Tweety	BIRD	Parrot	Dec 87	F	Blue
GB001-01	GB001	Strutter	BIRD	Peacock	May 85	M	Blue
BL001-05	BL001	Red Breast	BIRD	Robin	Jun 90	M	Gree
BL001-01	BL001	Tiajuana	BIRD	Toucan	Sep 90	F	Blue
RW001-02	RW001	Tiger	BIRD	Wren	Feb 87	M	Brow
IR001-07	IR001	Tiger	CAT	Barn	Feb 88	M	Blac
GP001-02	GP001	Delilah	CAT	Burmese	Feb 90	F	Blac
WI001-01	WI001	Flower	CAT	Burmese	Apr 89	F	Brow
WI002-02	WL002	Lightning	CAT	Burmese	Jul 87	M	Blac
IR001-05	IR001	Ceasar	CAT	Domestic	Oct 89	M	Grey
WI001-02	WI001	Shadow	CAT	Domestic	May 87	F	Blac
CM001-02	CM001	Mule	CAT	House	Sep 89	M	Blac

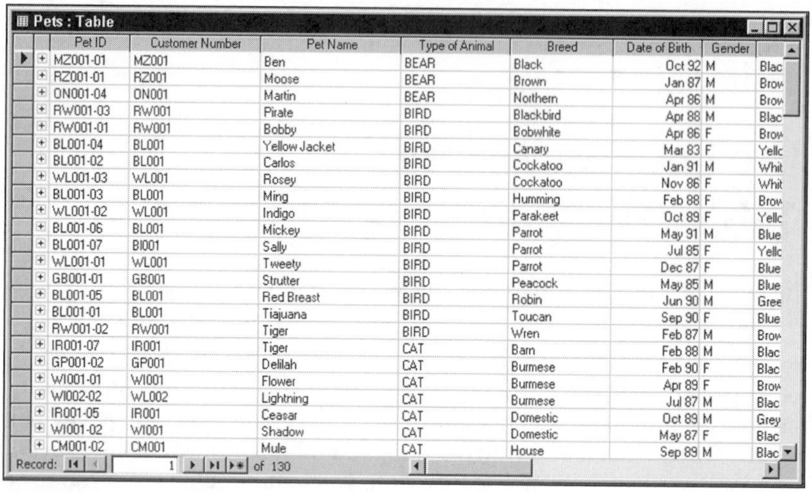

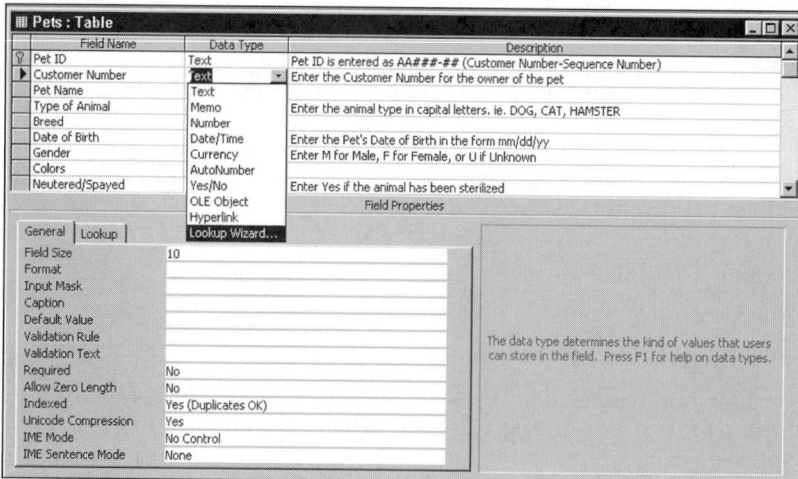

Figure 6-17: The Customer Number is displayed in the Pets table rather that the Customer Name. This number is difficult to remember for all your customers, so it would be better if you could see the actual name of the Customer instead of the Customer Number.

5. Notice the last item in the list is Lookup Wizard (as shown in Figure 6-18).

   This is actually not a data type, of course, but rather a way of changing the Lookup properties.

6. Select the Lookup Wizard data type.

Figure 6-18: Creating a Lookup field in a table. You can select Lookup Wizard from the Data Type list as shown here.

Caution

If you have already set relations between the Pets table and Customer table (as you did earlier in this chapter), you will see a warning box appear, as in Figure 6-19. It simply says that you cannot change the content of the data type field without first breaking (removing) the relationship between this table and the one it is related to (Customer) in the Relationships window. You can click OK to return to the Design window and then select Tools ⇨ Relationships from the menu and delete the selected relationship between the Pets and Customer table (highlight the link and press the Delete key). Then close the Relationship window and return to the Design surface to start again. You can then return to the Relationship window to reset the relationship after you have used the Wizard.

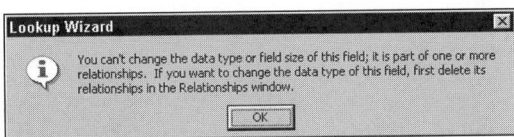

Figure 6-19: A warning that appears if you have a relationship set between two tables, one of which you want to change the data type to Lookup.

Once you click on the Lookup Wizard and it is accepted, the Wizard starts. The Wizard takes you through a series of windows that help you create a lookup to another table instead of displaying the field value itself.

Figure 6-20 shows the first Lookup Wizard window. There are two choices. The first choice lets you use data from another related table as the displayed value in the field.

The second option lets you type in a list of values. Use this option only when you enter a code, such as the Type of Customer field in the Customer table. Later you learn how to change the Lookup properties of that field to display *Individual* if the code entered is 1, *Pet Store* if the code entered is 2, and *Zoo* if the code entered is 3.

In this example, you want to display the Customer Name from the Customer table in the Customer Number field in the Pets table. Select the first choice and click Next.

Note

Creating a lookup does not change the stored value in the Pets table for the Customer Number field. Only the display of the value is changed.

The next window asks *Which table or query contains the fields for the lookup?* and lets you choose the table or query to use for the lookup. This is the standard table-selection Wizard window that is used in most Wizards. Select the Customer table and click the Next button.

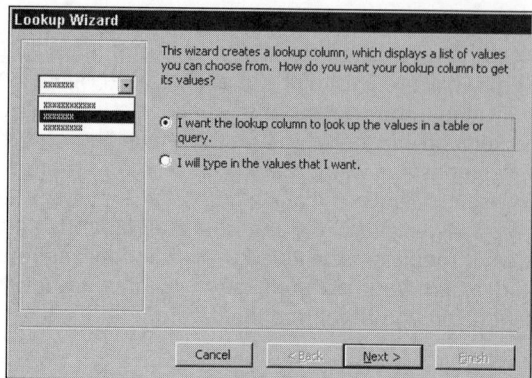

Figure 6-20: Selecting the type of lookup to create from the Lookup Wizard's first window

The next Wizard screen displays a list of all of the fields in the Customer table and enables you to select the fields to use in the lookup. The lookup Wizard will actually build a combo box that will be used by this field (Customer Number of the Pets table). The combo box will have all the valid values (in this case Customer names) that can be found in the parent table. Only the correct value will be shown for each pet. However, this same field can be used to assign a new Customer to the pet.

You can select any number of fields that you want to use in the combo box.

At a minimum, you need to select two fields from the Customer table. One field is the field used to relate to the Pets table, and the other is the field that you want to be displayed in the Pets table. Select the Customer Number and the Customer Name fields. Remember to click the > button (or double-click the field name) after you select each field (which copies it from the Available Fields list to the Selected Fields list).

> **Tip** In Access 2002, the field selection order is NOT important. The Wizard automatically determines which field is the link field and which is the display field.

After you do this and click the Next button, the display and size screen shown in Figure 6-21 appears.

A list of the data is displayed from the Customer table. As Figure 6-21 shows, the only field visible is the Customer Name. The Customer Number field is hidden from view. If you want to see the hidden field, turn the *Hide key column* check box off. (Be sure to turn it back on before continuing.)

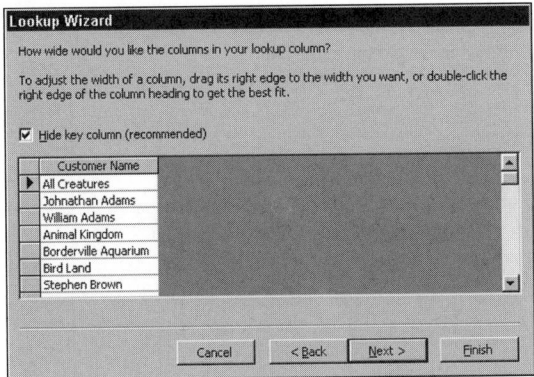

Figure 6-21: This window shows you the actual data that will be displayed in the Customer Number field of the Pets table (instead of the Customer Number) — in this case the Customer name. You can now resize the field so that all the content is fully visible.

Resize the Customer Name field to display all of its contents. When done, click the Next button.

The final screen asks what name to display as the column head when the table is viewed. The default name is the original name of the column. Accept the default name of Customer Number and click the Finish button to complete the Wizard. The Wizard displays a dialog box (Figure 6-22) telling you that the table must be saved before the relationship between the two tables (Customer and Pets) can be created. Accept the default action of Yes and the lookup table reference is created.

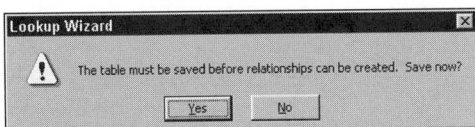

Figure 6-22: Message box to save the table changes before a relationship can be set between the Pets and Customers tables

Once the Lookup Wizard is done, you are returned to the Table designer. To see what type of Lookup the Wizard built, click on the Lookup tab in the bottom pane of the Table Design window. Figure 6-23 shows the new settings in the Pets: Table design window, in the fields set in the Field Properties Lookup tab sheet (bottom half of screen).

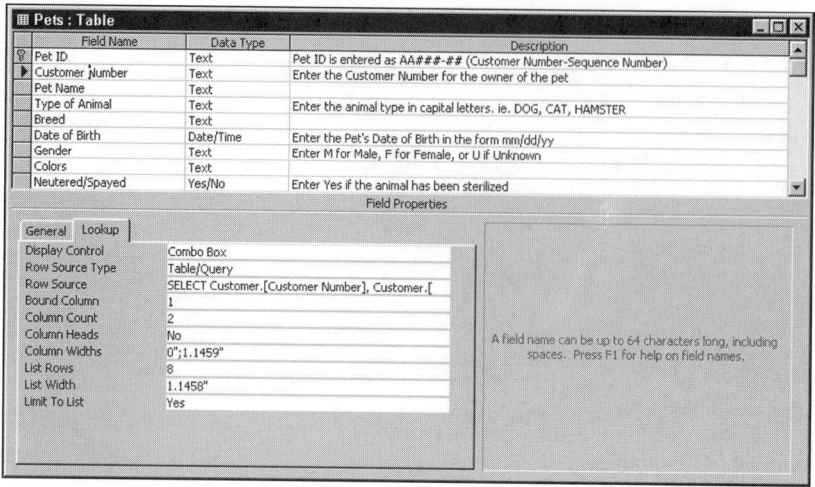

Figure 6-23: Showing the Lookup properties tab. Now there is a Combo Box that will display the Customer Name instead of the Customer Number.

The properties under the Lookup tab have changed significantly. The first property tells you that the field will now appear as a combo box (default is text box) whenever it is displayed in a table, or by default when it is placed on a form. The data type, specified in the top pane, for the Customer Number field is still Text. Even though you chose the Lookup Wizard from the Data Type list, it still creates a Text data type. The Lookup Wizard merely changes the Lookup properties.

The next two Lookup properties define the type of data for the record. In this case, the source of the data in the record is a table or query. Other choices are Value List (you type them into the Row Source property, separated by semicolons) and Field List (a list of fields in a table).

The Row Source displays a statement in SQL (Standard Query Language), an internal language that Access translates all queries into. You can see only a portion of the SQL statement in Figure 6-23. To see the entire SQL statement, open the Zoom window by pressing Shift-F2.

The entire statement is

SELECT [Customer].[Customer Number], [Customer].[Customer Name] FROM [Customer];

This command tells Access to use the Customer Name and Customer Number fields from the Customer table. The remaining values tell Access 2002 how many columns to use from the Customer table, which field to display (Customer Name, field 0), and which one is used for a link.

When you display the Pets table in a Datasheet view (as shown in Figure 6-24), Customer Name is shown in the Customer Number column instead of Customer Number. Using this method, you can display and limit the selection of any coded field in a table. You can even use fields found in only one table, such as the Gender field in the Pets table. Rather than display an M, F, or U, you can select from Male, Female, or Unknown and still store the correct code in the field.

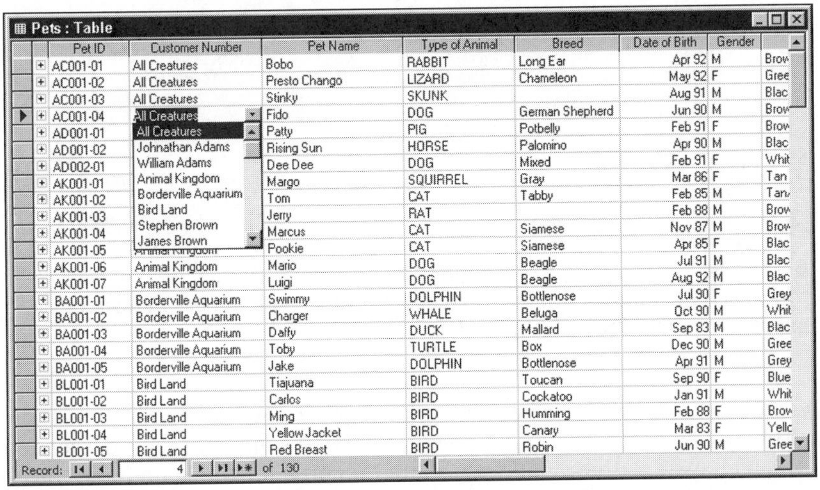
Pets : Table

Pet ID	Customer Number	Pet Name	Type of Animal	Breed	Date of Birth	Gender	
AC001-01	All Creatures	Bobo	RABBIT	Long Ear	Apr 92	M	Brow
AC001-02	All Creatures	Presto Chango	LIZARD	Chameleon	May 92	F	Gree
AC001-03	All Creatures	Stinky	SKUNK		Aug 91	M	Blac
AC001-04	All Creatures	Fido	DOG	German Shepherd	Jun 90	M	Brow
AD001-01	All Creatures	Patty	PIG	Potbelly	Feb 91	F	Brow
AD001-02	Johnathan Adams	Rising Sun	HORSE	Palomino	Apr 90	M	Blac
AD002-01	William Adams	Dee Dee	DOG	Mixed	Feb 91	F	Whit
AK001-01	Animal Kingdom	Margo	SQUIRREL	Gray	Mar 86	F	Tan
AK001-02	Borderville Aquarium	Tom	CAT	Tabby	Feb 85	M	Tan
AK001-03	Bird Land	Jerry	RAT		Feb 88	M	Brow
AK001-04	Stephen Brown	Marcus	CAT	Siamese	Nov 87	M	Brow
AK001-05	James Brown	Pookie	CAT	Siamese	Apr 85	F	Blac
AK001-06	Animal Kingdom	Mario	DOG	Beagle	Jul 91	M	Blac
AK001-07	Animal Kingdom	Luigi	DOG	Beagle	Aug 92	M	Blac
BA001-01	Borderville Aquarium	Swimmy	DOLPHIN	Bottlenose	Jul 90	F	Grey
BA001-02	Borderville Aquarium	Charger	WHALE	Beluga	Oct 90	M	Whit
BA001-03	Borderville Aquarium	Daffy	DUCK	Mallard	Sep 83	M	Blac
BA001-04	Borderville Aquarium	Toby	TURTLE	Box	Dec 90	M	Gree
BA001-05	Borderville Aquarium	Jake	DOLPHIN	Bottlenose	Apr 91	M	Grey
BL001-01	Bird Land	Tiajuana	BIRD	Toucan	Sep 90	F	Blue
BL001-02	Bird Land	Carlos	BIRD	Cockatoo	Jan 91	M	Whit
BL001-03	Bird Land	Ming	BIRD	Humming	Feb 88	F	Brow
BL001-04	Bird Land	Yellow Jacket	BIRD	Canary	Mar 83	F	Yellc
BL001-05	Bird Land	Red Breast	BIRD	Robin	Jun 90	M	Gree

Record: 4 of 130

Figure 6-24: Displaying a lookup field in a datasheet. Notice that the Customer Name has replaced the Customer Number.

Using Subdatasheets

Sometimes when viewing information in datasheets, you want to see a table's related records that are in a different table.

Note

Access 2002 has the capability to view hierarchical data in the Datasheet view. You can set up the subdatasheets manually in the design of the table or you can have the database automatically determine them based on the relationships between tables. The subdatasheets can be viewed with a table, query, form, and subform datasheets.

You will know that there has been a relationship with another table set up when you view records in a datasheet, because there will be a new column added to the left-hand side of the datasheet with a + next to each row, as shown in Figure 6-25.

Figure 6-25: Displaying a datasheet that has related tables. Notice the plus sign field next to each Customer Number. Clicking this will expand a new datasheet (subdatasheet) of related records in the Pets table.

When you click the + sign for a row, the related records in the subdatasheet are shown. The tables that are set up to be subdatasheets may have subdatasheets for them, which allow the viewing of both related records for the main table that you are in and related records for the subdatasheet. Figure 6-26 is an example of this. It shows records from three different tables related to this one record in the Customers table.

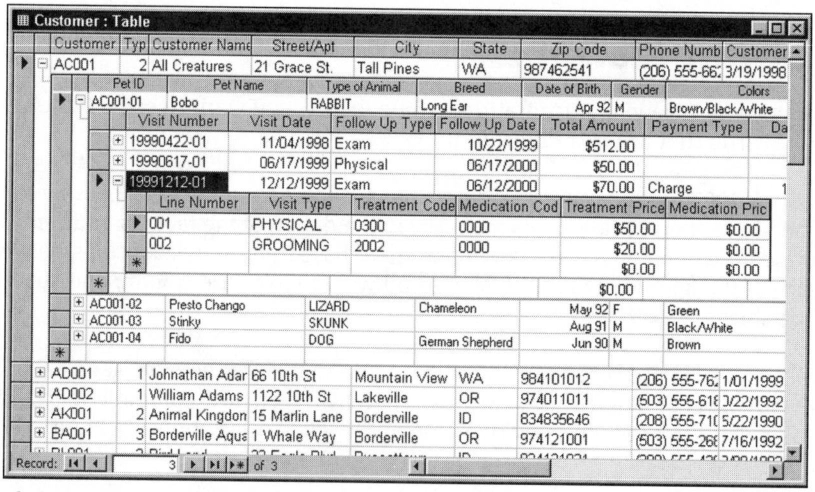

Figure 6-26: Displaying four levels of subdatasheets in Datasheet view for a specific customer, pet, visit date, and visit details

Setting up subdatasheets

You can set up subdatasheets in the design view of a table by clicking View ⇨ Properties from the Access menu bar, or by clicking the Properties button on your toolbar. This displays the Table Properties dialog box as shown in Figure 6-27.

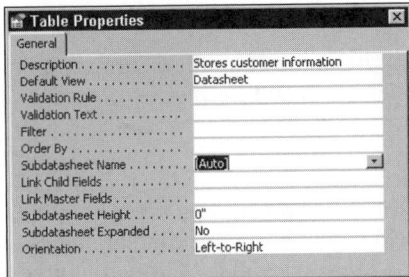

Figure 6-27: Table Properties

Selecting a subdatasheet name

If you are moving directly from Access 97 to Access 2002, you will notice that five new properties have been added to the Table Properties dialog box. All of these properties are related to subdatasheets. Also notice the value entered for Subdatasheet Name, Auto. Auto automatically assigns the subdatasheet name based on relationships set up in the database. To display a list of Tables and Queries in the database, click anywhere in the Subdatasheet Name field and a combo box displays, as shown in Figure 6-28.

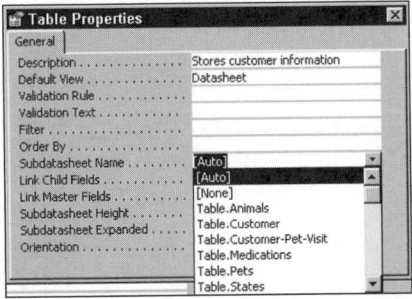

Figure 6-28: Displaying Table and Query names that may be linked to the Customer table

Entering the Link Child Fields and the Link Master Fields

The Link Child Fields and Link Master Fields property settings must have the same number of fields and must represent data of the same type. For example, if the Customer table and the Pets table both have Customer ID fields (one each) that contain the same type of data, enter Customer ID for both properties. The subform automatically displays all the pets found for the customer identified in the main table's Customer ID field.

Although the data must match, the names of the fields can differ. For example, the Customer ID field from the Customer table can be linked to the Customer Number field from the Pets table.

If you select the table or query that you would like to have related records displayed as, the Link Master Field and Link Child Field properties are automatically filled in if the linked fields have the same field name. If the linked field names are different, then these properties are left blank for you to fill in. If you are entering *Table.Pets* as the subdatasheet, the field Customer Number is in both tables, so this is the field that will be used for both the Link Master Field and the Link Child Field.

If you change the name of the field Customer Number in the Customers table (which we don't recommend that you do) to Customer ID, and leave the Customer Number field in the Pets table, you will have to enter these field names into the correct property.

To create the link in this example (of different field names for the same value), you would first Enter **Customer Number** in the Link Child Fields property and then enter **Customer ID** in the Link Master Fields property.

Without the link fields entered, no records will be displayed when you try to display your subdatasheet for the Pets table because Access doesn't know what fields to automatically link (they would have to be the same name).

Entering a subdatasheet height

The property for the subdatasheet height has a default value of 2 inches. This will show you the related records in a sheet that is 2 inches high. If the records don't fit in this space, scroll bars permit a view of all the records.

To change the height to a smaller or larger number, type in your preferred height in inches.

Expanding the subdatasheet

The Subdatasheet Expanded field is a Yes/No field. If you have Yes entered in this field, the subdatasheets are expanded, as shown in Figure 6-29.

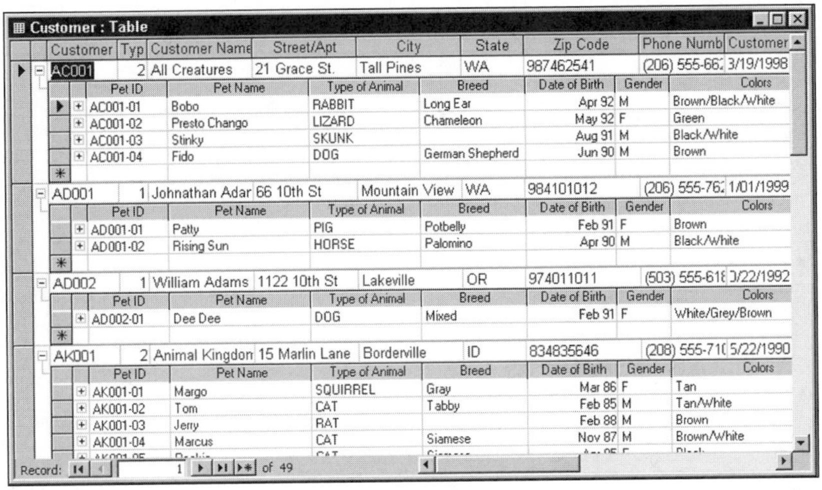

Figure 6-29: Subdatasheet Expanded option set to Yes in the Table Properties from the Table Design window

✦   ✦   ✦

Working with Information in Tables

In This Chapter

Displaying a datasheet

Navigating within a Datasheet window

Opening a new datasheet

Adding, changing, and deleting records

Using special data-entry techniques

Finding and replacing specific values

Hiding, freezing, and rearranging datasheet columns

Sorting or filtering records in a database

Saving and printing datasheets

In this chapter, you use a datasheet to enter data into a Microsoft Access table. This method enables you to see many records at once, as well as many of your fields. Using the Pets table that you create in an earlier chapter, you learn to add, change, and delete data, and you learn about features for displaying data in a datasheet.

Understanding Datasheets

Using a datasheet is one of the many ways that you can view data in Access. Datasheets display a list of records, in a format commonly known as a *browse screen,* in dBASE, a table view in Paradox, and a spreadsheet in Excel or Lotus 1-2-3. It is also referred to as a *browse table* or *table view.*

A datasheet is like a table or spreadsheet because data is displayed as a series of rows and columns. Figure 7-1 is a typical datasheet view of data. Like a table or spreadsheet, a datasheet displays data as a series of rows and columns. Each row represents a single record and each column represents a single field in the table. By scrolling up or down in the datasheet, you can see records that don't fit on-screen at that moment, and by scrolling left or right, you can see more columns or fields.

Datasheets are completely customizable, so you can view your data in many ways. By changing the font size, you can see more or less of your table on-screen. You can rearrange the order of the records or the fields. You can hide columns, change the displayed column width or row height, and lock several columns in position so that they continue to be displayed as you scroll around other parts of your datasheet.

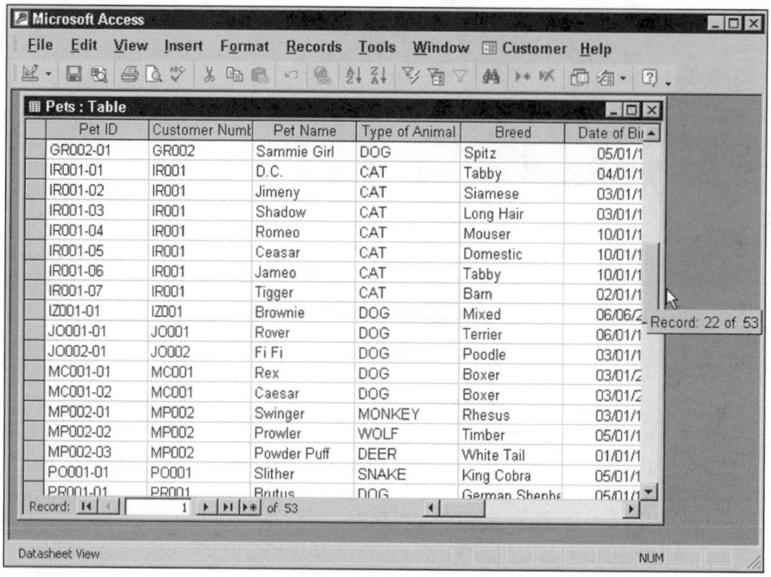

Figure 7-1: A typical datasheet view of data. Each column holds the common information that is found in a single field (like the Customer Number or Pet Name). Each row represents a single record in the table.

Quick Review of Records and Fields

As you recall, a *table* is a container for entering related information—recipes, card (Birthday/Xmas/Holiday) list, birthday reminders, payroll information, pets table, patient records, and on and on. Each table has a formal structure comprising fields. Each field, when displayed in a datasheet (two-dimensional sheet of information) has similar information stored in each column, called a *field*. Each field is identified as a specific type of data— text, numeric, date type, and so on. Each field has a unique name that is used to categorize the information stored in it. The table is composed of records, where each record stores information about a single entity (like a single pet or a single customer) in the fields of the table. One record is made up of information stored in all the fields of the table structure. For example, if a table has three fields—name, address, and phone number—then record one has one name, one address, and one phone number in it. Record two also has only one name, one address and one phone number in it. All three fields can be found in each record—only the contents of those fields change. That is why a datasheet is an ideal way of looking at the contents of a table all at once—you can see the individual field contents by looking down any column (field). You can also review a single record's values by finding the row (record) that holds the information that you want to review and simply looking across the row to see all values for that specific record.

You can sort the datasheet quickly into any order by using one toolbar button. You can filter the datasheet for specific records — making other records invisible. You can also import records directly to the datasheet, or export formatted records from the datasheet directly to Word, Excel, or other applications that support OLE (Object Linking and Embedding) 2.x.

The Datasheet Window

The Datasheet window is similar to other object windows in Access. The actual Datasheet window is open within the Access Window. At the top of the Access window, you see the title bar (displaying Microsoft Access), the menu bar, and the toolbars.

At the bottom of the Access window, you see the status bar. The status bar displays assorted information in the datasheet; for example, it may contain field description information (like in Figure 7-1 'Pet ID is entered as AA####-## (Customer Number-Sequence Number)'), error messages, and warnings. If the field was given a Description when it was created, the Field Description that you enter for each field is displayed here. If a specific field doesn't have a Field Description, Access displays the words *Datasheet View*. Generally, error messages and warnings appear in dialog boxes in the center of the screen rather than in the status bar. If you need help understanding the meaning of a button in the toolbar, move the mouse over the button and a tooltip appears with a one- or two-word explanation, while the status bar displays a more comprehensive explanation.

In the center of the Access window is another window — the actual Datasheet window. This Datasheet window displays the data in rows and columns. Each record occupies one row, and each column — headed by a field name (in the first row or field title area of the browse window) — contains that field's values. The display arranges the records initially by primary key and the fields by the order of their creation in the table design.

The right side of the window contains a scrollbar for moving quickly between records (up and down). As you scroll between records, a Scroll Tip (shown in Figure 7-1) tells you precisely where the scrollbar takes you. In Access 2002, the size of the scrollbar thumb gives you a proportional look at how many of the total number of records are being displayed. In Figure 7-1, the scrollbar thumb takes up about 15 percent of the scroll area, and 24 of 130 records are shown on-screen. You also have a proportional scrollbar at the bottom of the window for moving among fields (left to right and back). Also located at the bottom of the Datasheet window are the Navigation buttons (along the left side of the bottom of the frame). You can also use these buttons to move between records.

Moving within a datasheet

You can move easily in the Datasheet window by using the mouse pointer to indicate where you want to change or add to your data: Just click a field and record location. In addition, the menus, toolbars, scrollbars, and navigation buttons make it easy to move among fields and records. You can think of a datasheet as a spreadsheet without the row numbers and column letters. Instead, your columns have field names, and your rows are unique records that have identifiable values in each cell.

Table 7-1 lists the navigational keys that you can use for moving within a datasheet.

Table 7-1 Navigating in a Datasheet	
Navigational Direction	*Keystrokes*
Next field	Tab
Previous field	Shift+Tab
First field of current record	Home
Last field of current record	End
Next record	Down arrow (↓)
Previous record	Up arrow (↑)
First field of first record	Ctrl+Home
Last field of last record	Ctrl+End
Scroll up one page	PgUp
Scroll down one page	PgDn
Go to record number box	F5

The Navigation buttons

The *Navigation buttons* (shown in Figure 7-2) are the six controls located at the bottom of the Datasheet window, which you click to move between records. The two leftmost controls move you to the first record or the previous record in the datasheet (table). The three rightmost controls position you on the next record, last record, or new record in the datasheet (table). If you know the record number (the row number of a specific record), you can click the record number box, enter a record number, and press Enter.

Figure 7-2: The Navigation buttons of
a datasheet

Note If you enter a record number greater than the number of records in the table, an error message appears stating that you can't go to the specified record.

The Datasheet toolbar

The Datasheet toolbar (shown in Figure 7-3) provides a way to work with the datasheet. The toolbar has many familiar objects on it, as well as some new ones.

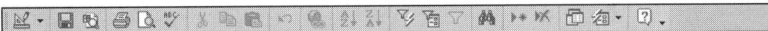

Figure 7-3: The Datasheet toolbar

The first icon is the View button, which allows you to switch between Table Design View, Datasheet View, PivotTable View, and PivotChart View. You can see all four choices by clicking on the button's down-arrow (triangle pointing down). Clicking Design View permits you to make changes to the design of your table. You can then click the Datasheet View to return to the datasheet.

Note If you originally displayed a data-entry form, this icon has three primary choices: Table Design, Datasheet, and Form, as well as the PivotTable and PivotChart views.

The next icon, Save, looks like a floppy disk. Click this icon to save any layout changes to the datasheet.

Caution Save does not allow you to roll back changes to the data. As you move from record to record, the data is forever changed.

You can use the next icon, Search, to activate the Advanced Search dialog box (default) as shown in Figure 7-4. You can use this icon to search for specific files on your hard drive or network drive. You can switch to the Basic Search by selecting it at the bottom of the Advance Search box.

Figure 7-4: The dialog box of the new toolbar button, Search. This new tool lets you search for a specific file on your hard drive.

The next set of three icons includes Print (which looks like a printer and sends the datasheet information to your printer in a quick, two-dimensional table report) and Print Preview (which looks like a printed page with a magnifying glass and shows on-screen how your datasheet looks when printed). The third icon lets you spell-check your data using the standard Microsoft Office spell-checking feature.

Following the printer and spelling grouping are the editing buttons — Cut, Copy, and Paste — that are represented by these icons, respectively: scissors, two sheets of paper, and a clipboard. These three buttons allow you to remove a value, copy a value, and paste a value to the table. The objects that can be copied, removed, or pasted include a single value, a datasheet row, a column, or a range of values. You can copy and paste objects to and from other programs (such as Microsoft Word or Excel), but the Format Painter is not available in a datasheet.

The next icon, which looks like an arrow pointing counter-clockwise, lets you Undo a change to a record, or, more globally, undo formatting.

The next icon is the Internet icon that enables you to insert a hyperlink.

The next two icons are the QuickSort icons. They are easy to identify — one is the letter A on top of the letter Z with the arrow pointing down (to represent alphabetical sort order), and the other icon is the reverse, Z to A (representing reverse sort order). You can select one or more columns and click on one of these buttons to sort the data instantly, in ascending or descending order, using the selected columns as the sorting criteria.

The next three icons in this toolbar look like funnels. They let you determine and display only selected records. The first icon, Filter by Selection, lets you filter records to match a specific highlighted value in a given field. Each time you highlight a value, you add the selection to the filter. This additive process continues until the filter is cleared. (See the detailed discussion of this filter later in this chapter.)

The second icon, Filter by Form, turns each column of data into a combo box where you can select a single value from the datasheet and filter for matching records. Figure 7-5 illustrates how this works. A special window appears with the name of the table, which is Pets, and the Filter by Form title.

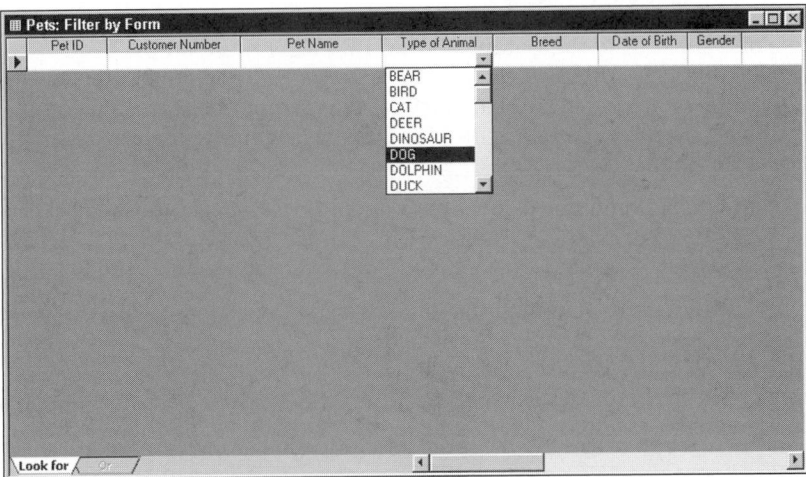

Figure 7-5: The Filter by Form window for filtering records via a series of field values. You simply select the value that you want from one or more columns and click on the filter button.

You use the last icon in the group to turn any filter on or off; it is a toggle button. The first time you press it, you activate the search specified in the Filter by form or Filter by selection.

The Find Specified Text icon is a pair of binoculars; clicking it displays a dialog box that lets you search for a specific value in a specific field.

The next two icons allow you to add a new record or delete an existing record. To create a new record, click the icon with the arrow and asterisk, and a new record row is added at the bottom of the datasheet. To delete an existing record, click anywhere in the record row that you want to delete and click the icon with the arrow and X. A message displays, warning you that you are about to delete a record and that you won't be able to undo your change; select Yes to continue or No to save the record.

The next icon is the Database Window icon, which displays the Database window. Next is the New Object icon, which contains a pull-down menu that gives you choices so that you can create new objects, such as tables, queries, forms, reports, macros, and modules. Two interesting choices are the first two — AutoForm and AutoReport. When you click on either of these, you immediately create a single record form or report that can be used without any further formatting.

The last icon is the Help icon. When you click it, either Small Card Help or Office Assistant appears.

Opening a Datasheet

To open a datasheet from the Database window, follow these steps:

1. Using the My Mountain Animal Start database from Chapter 5, click the Table button on the Object menu bar of the Database window (in this case, My Mountain Animal Hospital).

2. Click the table name that you want to open. (In this example, *Pets*.)

3. Click Open.

An alternative method for opening the datasheet is to double-click on the *Pets* table name.

 Tip   If you are in any of the design windows, you can click on the Datasheet button and view your data in a datasheet.

Entering New Data

When you open a datasheet, all the records in your table are visible; if you just created your table design, however, the new datasheet doesn't yet contain any data. Figure 7-6 is an empty datasheet. When the datasheet is empty, the record pointer on the first record is displayed as a right-pointing triangle.

Pet ID	Customer Numb	Pet Name	Type of Animal	Breed	Date of Birth	Gender	C

Record: ⏮ ◀ 1 ▶ ⏭ ▶* of 1

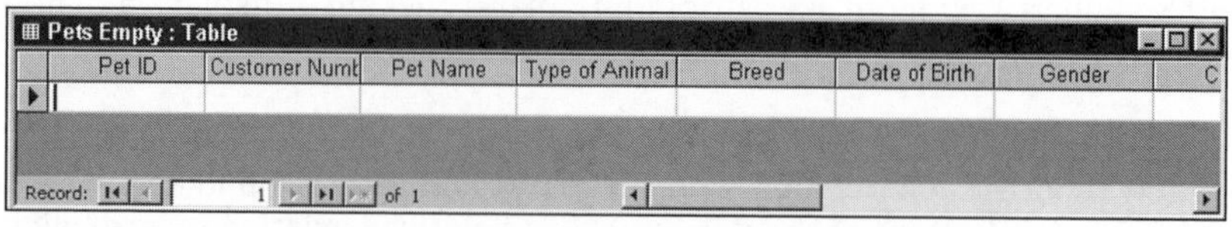

Figure 7-6: An empty datasheet. Notice that the first record is blank and the record pointer, a right-pointing triangle, is shown in the left-most column.

You can enter a record into a datasheet by moving the cursor to the first field, typing the value, moving to the next field, etc. As you begin to enter the record, the record pointer turns into a pencil, indicating that the record is being edited. A second row also appears as you begin to enter the first record; this row contains an asterisk in the record-pointer position, which indicates a new record. The new-record pointer always appears in the last row of the datasheet; after you enter a record, it is inserted at the bottom of the table, immediately before the last row (a new blank record).

The cursor generally starts in the first field of the table for data entry.

If you performed the steps in Chapter 5, using the My Mountain Animal Hospital database, you already have five partial records. If not, you have an empty datasheet. To enter or edit the first record in the Pets table, follow the steps below. Figure 7-7 is an example of a record being entered into the datasheet.

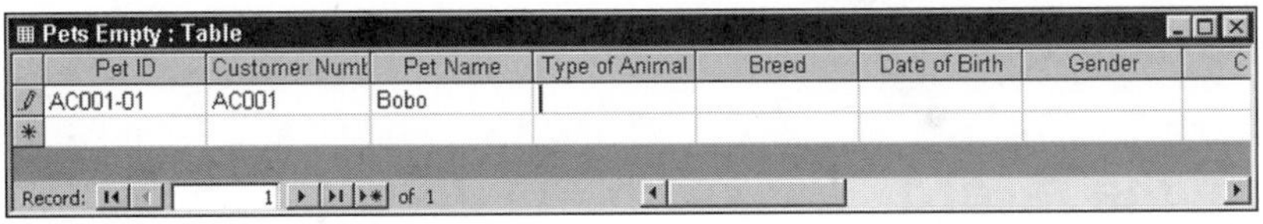

Figure 7-7: Entering a record into the datasheet of the My Mountain Animal Hospital Database (which you can create in Chapter 5)

1. Move the cursor to the Pet ID field, by clicking the New Record button.

2. Type **AC001-01** and press Tab to move to the Customer Number field.

3. Type **AC001** and press Tab to move to the Pet Name field.

4. Type **Bobo** and press Tab to move to the Type of Animal field.

5. Type **RABBIT** and press Tab to move to the Breed field.

6. Type **Long Ear** and press Tab to move to the Date of Birth field.

7. Type **4/8/2000** and press Tab to move to the Gender field.

8. Press M and press Tab to move to the Colors field.

9. Type **Brown/Black/White** and press Tab to move to the Neutered/Spayed field.

10. Press Tab to move to the Length field (because the default No is acceptable).

11. Type **20.0** and press Tab to move to the Weight field.

12. Type **3.1** and press Tab twice to move to the Current Vaccination field.

13. Type **Yes** (over the default No) and press Tab three times to move to the Comments field.

14. When you get to the Comments field, press Shift+F2 to open the Zoom window.

15. In the Zoom window, type "**Bobo is a great looking rabbit. He was originally owned by a nature center and was given to the pet store for sale to a loving family. Bobo was in good health when he was returned to the pet store to sell.**"

16. Press Enter or Tab to move to the Pet ID field of the next record.

You can continue to add records, but you should probably stop at this point.

When adding or editing records, you may see four different record pointers:

✦ Current record

✦ Record being edited

✦ Record is locked (multiuser systems)

✦ New record

Saving the record

After you have entered all the values in the record, normally you move to the next record. This action saves the record. Any time you move to a different record or close the table, the last record you worked on is written to the database and the record pointer changes from a pencil to a right-pointing triangle.

To save a record, you must enter a valid value into the primary key field. The primary key is validated for data type, uniqueness, and any validation rules that you have entered into the Validation Rule property.

Tip   The Undo Current Field/Record icon in the toolbar can only undo changes to the current record. After you move to the next record, you must use the regular Undo icon. This only works for a single record. After you change a second record, you cannot undo the first record.

Tip   You can save the record to disk without leaving the record by selecting Records ➪ Save Record or by pressing Shift+Enter.

After you've entered a record, you understand what happens as you enter the first record. Next you learn how Access validates your data as you make entries into the fields.

Understanding automatic data-type validation

Access validates certain types of data automatically. Therefore, you don't have to enter any data-validation rules for these data types when you specify table properties. The data types that Access validates automatically include

✦ Number/Currency

✦ Date/Time

✦ Yes/No

Number or Currency fields allow only valid numbers to be entered into the field. Initially, Access lets you enter a letter into a Number field. When you move off the field, however, a dialog box appears with the message, *The value you entered isn't valid for this field.* The same is true of any other inappropriate characters. If you try to enter more than one decimal point, you get the same message. If you enter a number too large for a certain Number data type, you also get this message.

Date and Time fields are validated for valid date or time values. If you try to enter a date such as 14/45/00, a time such as 37:39:12, or a single letter in a Date/Time field, a dialog box appears with the error message, *The value you entered isn't valid for this field.*

Yes/No fields require that you enter one of these defined values: Yes, True, -1, or a number other than 0 (it displays as a -1) for Yes; or No, False, Off, or 0 for No. Of course, you can also define your own acceptable values in the Format property for the field, but generally these are the only acceptable values. If you try to enter an invalid value, the dialog box appears with the usual message to indicate an inappropriate value.

Understanding how properties affect data entry

Because field types vary, you use different data-entry techniques for each type. Previously in this chapter, you learned that some data-type validation is automatic. Designing the Pets table, however, means entering certain user-defined format and data-validation rules. The following sections examine the types of data entry.

Standard text data entry

The first five fields that you enter in the Pets table are Text fields. You simply enter each value and move on. The Pet ID field uses an input mask (AA###-##;0;_ or you can use LL000-00;0;_) for data entry. You don't use any special formatting for the other fields. If you enter a value in lowercase in the gender field, it displays in uppercase. You can validate text for specific values, and you can display it with format properties.

Tip   Sometimes you want to enter a Text field on multiple lines. You can press Ctrl+Enter to add a new line. This is useful, for example, in large text strings for formatting a multiple-line address field. It is also useful in Memo fields for formatting multiple-line entries.

Date/Time data entry

The Date of Birth field is a Date/Time data type, which uses a format value of mmm yy. This simply means that no matter how you type in the birth date—using month and year, day month year, or month day year, it always displays as the Month and Year in the form of mmm yy or Apr 01. So even if you type 4/8/01, Access displays the value Apr 01 when you leave the field. The value 4/8/2001 is really stored in the table; you can display it whenever the cursor is in the Date of Birth field. Alternatively, you can enter the value in the format specified; that is, you can enter Apr 01 in the field and the value Apr 2001 is stored in the table.

Date of Birth also has the validation rule *Between #1/1/70# And Date()*, which means that you can enter Date of Birth values only between January 1, 1970, and the current date. Of course, if the pet is a mynah bird that is 60 years old you may have to wait a few years before you can enter the bird's birthday.

Tip Formats affect only the display of the data. They do not change storage of data in the table.

Text data entry with data validation

The Gender field of the Pets table has a data-validation rule entered for it in the Validation Rule property. This rule limits valid entries to M, F, or U. If you try to enter a value other than M, F, or U into the Gender field, a dialog box appears with the message, *Value must be M, F, or U*, as shown in Figure 7-8. The message comes from the Validation Text property that you entered into the Pets table Gender field.

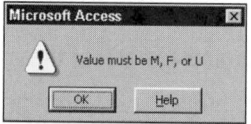

Figure 7-8: The data validation message for the Pets Gender field appears anytime the user fails to enter an M, F, or U in the field.

Numeric data entry with data validation

The Length and Weight fields both have validation rules. The Length field has a Validation Rule property to limit the size of the animal to a realistic length below 120 inches (10 feet). The Weight field has a Validation Rule property to limit the weight of the animal to below 1,500 pounds. If either of the rules is violated, a dialog box appears with the validation text entered for the field. If an animal arrives that weighs more than 1,500 pounds or is more than 10 feet long, the validation rule can simply be changed in the table design.

OLE object data entry

You can enter the OLE (Object Linking and Embedding) data-type Picture field into a datasheet, even though you don't see the picture of the animal. An OLE field can hold many different item types, including

✦ Bitmap pictures

✦ Sound files

✦ Business graphs

✦ Word or Excel files

✦ Web page or Hyperlink

Any object that an OLE server supports can be stored in an Access OLE field. OLE objects are generally entered into a form so you can see, hear, or use the value. When OLE objects appear in datasheets, you see text that tells what the object is (for example, you may see Paintbrush Picture in the OLE field). You can enter OLE objects into a field in two ways:

✦ Pasting from the Clipboard

✦ Inserting into the field from the Insert ➪ Object menu dialog box

Cross-Reference   For thorough coverage of using and displaying OLE objects, see Chapter 19.

Memo field data entry

The last field in the table is Comments, which is a Memo data type. This type of field allows up to 65,536 characters of text for each field. Recall that you entered a long string (about 260 characters) into the Memo field. As you entered the string, however, you saw only a few characters at a time. The rest of the string scrolled out of sight. By pressing Shift+F2, you can display a Zoom box with a scrollbar (see Figure 7-9) that lets you see about 1,000 characters at a time.

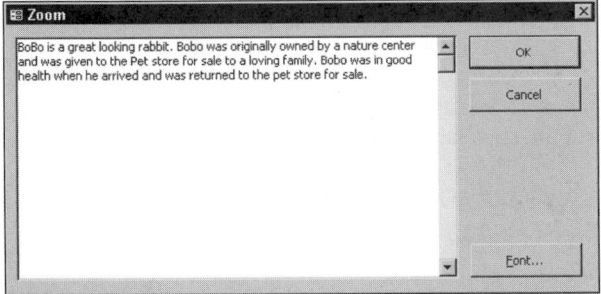

Figure 7-9: The Zoom box for a memo field. Notice that you can now see a lot more of the note in the memo field — not all 65,526 characters, but still quite a lot.

Note   When you first display text in a zoomed window, all the text is selected and highlighted in reverse video. You can de-select the text by pressing the Home key.

New Feature   In the Zoom box, you see a Font button at the bottom. When you press this button, the dialog box in Figure 7-10 displays.

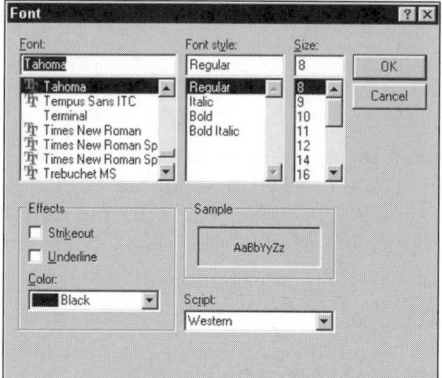

Figure 7-10: The Font dialog box of the Zoom box. Here you can change the Font Type, Style, and Size, and add Effects such as Strikeout and Script for the memo field from this dialog box.

Note When you change the font for the text in a memo field, all of the text is affected. You can't change the format of a single word or sentence.

Navigating Records in a Datasheet

On the CD-ROM If you are following the examples, you may want to use the Mountain Animal Start database file now. For the remainder of this section, you work with the data in the Pets table.

It's not unusual to want to make changes to records after you've entered them. You may want to change records for several reasons:

✦ You receive new information that changes existing values

✦ You discover errors that change existing values

✦ You need to add new records

When you decide to edit data in a table, the first step is to open the table — if it isn't already open. From the Database window, open the Pets datasheet by double-clicking Pets in the list of tables.

Note If you are in any of the Design windows, you can click the Datasheet button to make changes to the information within the table.

When you open a datasheet in Access 2002 that has related tables, a column with a plus sign (+) is added to access the related records, or subdatasheets, and is displayed as the first column. Subdatasheets are thoroughly explained in Chapter 6.

Moving between records

You can move to any record by scrolling through the records and positioning your cursor on the desired record. When your table is large, however, you want to get to a specific record as quickly as possible.

You can use the vertical scrollbar to move between records. The scrollbar arrows, however, move the record pointer only one record at a time. To move through many records at a time, you must use the scrollbar elevator (known as a *scroll box* in Windows 95/98/NT) or click the area between the scrollbar elevator and the scrollbar arrows.

The Edit ➪ GoTo menu, shown open in Figure 7-11, has several choices to help you quickly move around the worksheet.

You can also use the five Navigation buttons, located along the bottom of the Datasheet window (also shown in Figure 7-11), for moving between records. You simply click these buttons to move to the desired record. If you know the record number (row number of a specific record), you can click on the record number box, enter a record number, and press Enter. You can also press F5 to move to the record number box.

Tip   Watch the Scroll Tips when you use scrollbars to move to another area of the datasheet. Access does not update the record number box until you click on a field.

Finding a specific value

Although you can move to a specific record (if you know the record number) or to a specific field in the current record, usually what you really want to find is a certain value in a record. You can use one of three methods for locating a value in a field:

 ✦ Select Edit ➪ Find
 ✦ Select the Find button in the toolbar (a pair of binoculars)
 ✦ Press Ctrl+F

Choosing any of these methods displays the Find and Replace dialog box (shown in Figure 7-12). To limit the search to a specific field, make sure your cursor is on the field that you want to use in the search before you open the dialog box. You can also choose to search the entire table for the specified record by clicking on the Look In combo box and selecting the table.

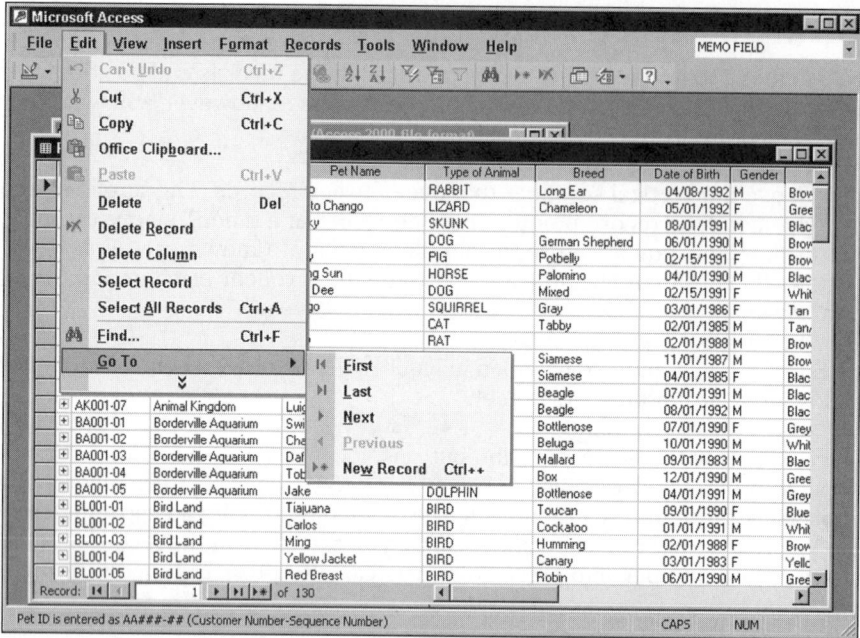

Figure 7-11: Moving between records using the GoTo menu. You can do the same thing by using the Navigation buttons along the bottom of the window.

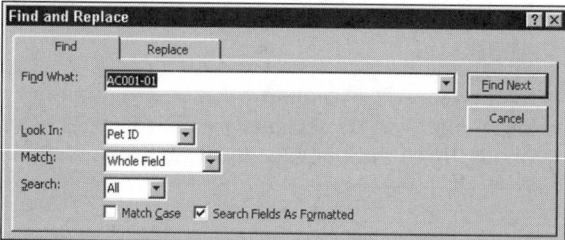

Figure 7-12: The Find and Replace dialog box. The fastest way to activate it is to simply press the Ctrl+F key combination.

Tip   If you highlight the entire record by clicking on the record selector (the small gray box next to the record), Access 2002 automatically searches through all fields.

The Find and Replace dialog box lets you control many aspects of the search. In the Find What text box, you enter the value to be searched for. You can also display and choose from a list of items that you have previously searched for in this database. You can enter the value just as it appears in the field, or you can use three types of wildcards:

* (any number of characters)

? (any one character)

(any one number)

To look at how these wildcards work, first suppose that you want to find any value beginning with AB; for this, you type **AB***. Then suppose that you want to search for values ending with 001, so you type ***001**. To search for any value that begins with AB, ends with 001, and contains any two characters in between, you type **AB??001**. If you want to search for any street number that ends in th, you can type **#th** to find 5th or 8th. To find 5th or 125th, you can type ***th**.

The Match drop-down list contains three choices:

✦ Any Part of Field

✦ Whole Field

✦ Start of Field

The default is Whole Field. This option finds only the whole value you enter. For example, the Whole Field option finds the value SMITH only if the value in the field being searched is exactly SMITH. If you select Any Part of Field, Access searches to see whether the value is contained anywhere in the field; this search finds the value SMITH in the field values SMITHSON, HAVERSMITH, and ASMITHE. A search for SMITH using the Start of Field option searches from the beginning of the field, returning only values like SMITHSON or SMITHVILLE. You can choose one of three search direction choices (Up, Down, All) in the Search combo box.

In addition to these combo boxes, you can use two check boxes at the bottom of the Find and Replace dialog box—Match Case and Search Fields As Formatted. Match Case determines whether the search is case-sensitive. The default is not case-sensitive (not checked). A search for SMITH finds smith, SMITH, or Smith. If you check the Match Case check box, you must then enter the search string in the exact case of the field value. (The data types Number, Currency, and Date/Time do not have any case attributes.)

If you have checked Match Case, Access does not use the value Search Fields as Formatted (the second check box), which limits the search to the actual values displayed in the table. (If you format a field for display in the datasheet, you should check the box.) In the Date of Birth field, for example, you can accomplish a search for an animal born in April 1999 by checking the box and entering **Apr 99**. Without this entry, you must search for the exact date of birth, which may be 4/8/99.

The Search Fields as Formatted check box, the selected default, finds only text that has the same pattern of uppercase and lowercase letters as the text you specified in the Find What box. Clear this box to find text regardless of case.

Using Search Fields as Formatted may slow the search process.

When you click the Find Next button, the search begins. If Access finds the value, the cursor highlights it in the datasheet. To find the next occurrence of the value, you must click the Find Next button again. You can also select the Find Next button to find the first occurrence. The dialog box remains open so that you can find multiple occurrences. When you find the value that you want, select the Close command button to close the dialog box.

Changing Values in a Datasheet

Usually, you change values by moving to the value that you want to change or edit and making the change.

If the field that you are in has no value, you can type a new value into the field. When you enter new values into a field, follow the same rules as for a new-record entry.

Replacing an existing value manually

Generally, you enter a field with either no characters selected or the entire value selected. If you use the keyboard to enter a field, normally you select the entire value. (You know that the entire value is selected when it is displayed in reverse video.) When you begin to type, the new content replaces the selected value automatically.

To select the entire value with the mouse, use any of these methods:

✦ Click just to the left of the value when the cursor is shown as a large plus sign.

✦ Select any part of the value and double-click the mouse button. (This usually works unless the text contains a space.)

✦ Click to the left of the value, hold down the left mouse button, and drag the mouse to select the whole value.

✦ Select any part of the value and press F2.

You may want to replace an existing value with the default from the Default Value table property. To do so, select the value and press Ctrl+Alt+Spacebar. If you want to replace an existing value with that of the same field from the preceding record, you can press Ctrl+' (single quote mark). You can press Ctrl+; (semicolon) to place the current date in a field as well.

Caution   Pressing Ctrl+– (hyphen) deletes the current record.

Changing an existing value

If you want to change an existing value instead of replacing the entire value, you can use the mouse and click in front of any character in the field. When you position the mouse pointer in front of an individual character, you activate Insert mode; the existing value moves to the right as you type the new value. If you press Insert, your entry changes to Overstrike mode; you replace one character at a time as you type. You can use the arrow keys to move between characters without disturbing them. Erase characters to the left by pressing Backspace, or to the right of the cursor by pressing Delete.

Table 7-2 lists editing techniques.

Table 7-2 Editing Techniques	
Editing Operation	**Keystrokes**
Move the insertion point within a field	Press the right(→) and left-arrow(←) keys
Insert a value within a field	Select the insertion point and type new data
Select the entire field	Press F2 or double-click the mouse button
Replace an existing value with a new value	Select the entire field and type a new value
Replace a value with the value of the previous field	Press Ctrl+' (single quote mark)
Replace the current value with the default value	Press Ctrl+Alt+Spacebar
Insert a line break in a Text or Memo field	Press Ctrl+Enter
Save the current record	Press Shift+Enter or move to another record
Insert the current date	Ctrl+; (semicolon)
Insert the current time	Ctrl+: (colon)

Continued

Table 7-2 *(continued)*	
Editing Operation	*Keystrokes*
Add a new record	Ctrl++ (plus sign)
Delete the current record	Ctrl+– (minus sign)
Toggle values in a check box or option button	Spacebar
Undo a change to the current record	Press Esc or click the Undo button

Fields that you can't edit

Some fields can't be edited, such as

✦ **AutoNumber fields.** Access maintains AutoNumber fields automatically, calculating the values as you create each new record. AutoNumber fields can be used as the primary key.

✦ **Calculated fields.** Access creates calculated fields in forms or queries; these values are not actually stored in your table.

✦ **Locked or disabled fields.** You can set certain properties in a form to disallow entry for a specific field. You can lock or disable a field when you designate Form properties.

✦ **Fields in multiuser locked records.** If another user locks the record, you can't edit any fields in that record.

Using the Undo Feature

The Undo button is often dimmed in Access so that it can't be used. As soon as you begin editing a record, however, you can use this button to undo the typing in the current field. You can also undo a change with the Esc key; pressing Esc cancels either a changed value or the previously changed field. Pressing Esc twice undoes changes to the entire current record.

Several Undo menu commands and variations are available to undo your work. The following list explains how you can undo your work at various stages of completion:

✦ **Edit ➪ Can't Undo.** Undo is not available.

✦ **Edit ➪ Undo Typing.** Cancels the most recent change to your data.

✦ **Edit ➪ Undo Current Field/Record.** Cancels the most recent change to the current field. Cancels all changes to the current record.

✦ **Edit ➪ Undo Saved Record.** Cancels all changes to last saved record.

As you type a value into a field, you can select Edit ➪ Undo or use the toolbar Undo button to undo changes to that value. After you move to another field, you can undo the change to the preceding field's value by selecting Edit ➪ Undo Current Field/Record or by using the Undo button. You can also undo all the changes to an unsaved current record by selecting Edit ➪ Undo Current Field/Record. After you save a record, you can still undo the changes by selecting Edit ➪ Undo Saved Record. However, after the next record is edited, changes are permanent.

Copying and Pasting Values

Copying or cutting data to the Clipboard is a Microsoft Windows task; it is not actually a specific function of Access. After you cut or copy a value, you can paste into another field or record by using Edit ➪ Paste or the Paste button in the toolbar. You can cut, copy, or paste data from any Windows application or from one task to another in Access. Using this technique, you can copy entire records between tables or databases, and you can copy datasheet values to and from Microsoft Word and Excel.

Replacing Values

To replace an existing value in a field, you can manually find the record to update or you can use the Find and Replace dialog box. You can display the Find and Replace dialog in four ways:

✦ Select Edit ➪ Find

✦ Select the Find button in the toolbar (a pair of binoculars)

✦ Press Ctrl+F

✦ Select Edit ➪ Replace

This dialog box allows you to do a find and replace in the current field or in the entire datasheet. You can find a certain value and replace it with a new value in every place in the table that you are in.

After the Find and Replace dialog box is active, you should first click on the Replace tab and type in the value that you want to find in the *Find What:* text box, as shown in Figure 7-12. After you have selected all of the remaining search options (turn off

Search Fields As Formatted for example), click on the *Find Next* button. You are taken to the first occurrence of what you want to find. After you get there, if you want to change the value of the current found item (under the cursor), click on the Replace button, and it replaces the selected value. For example, Figure 7-13 shows that you want to find the value DOLPHIN in the Type of Animal field and change it to the value DOG.

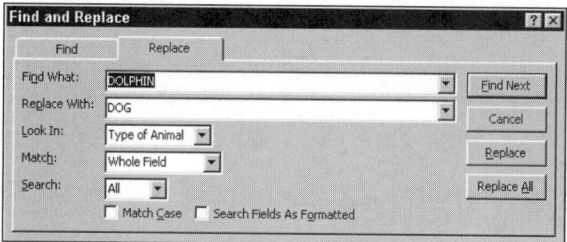

Figure 7-13: Find and Replace dialog box with the Replace tab showing. In this case you want to replace the value DOLPHIN with DOG.

You can select your search options in the Find tab and then click on the Replace tab to continue the process. However, it is far easier to simply do the entire process using the Replace tab. Enter what you want to find and the value that you want to use to replace the existing value. After you have completed the dialog box with all the correct information, select one of the command buttons on the side.

✦ **Find Next.** Finds the next field that has the value in the Find What field.

✦ **Cancel.** Closes the form and performs no find and replace.

✦ **Replace.** Must use the Find Next button first. When you click on Replace it replaces the value in the current field only.

✦ **Replace All.** Finds all the fields with the Find What value and automatically replaces them with the Replace with value.

Tip   Use the Find Next and Replace commands if you aren't sure about changing all the fields with the Find What value. When you use this command, you can pick the fields that you want to replace and the fields that you want to leave with the same value.

Adding New Records

You can add records to the datasheet by positioning the cursor on the datasheet's last line (where the record pointer is an asterisk) and entering the new record. You can go to a new record in many ways: You can select Insert ➪ New Record, or you can go directly to a new record by using the new-record button in the toolbar, the navigation button area, or the menu selection Edit ➪ GoTo ➪ New. Another way to move quickly to the new record is to go to the last record and press the down-arrow (↓) key.

Sometimes you want to add several new records and make all existing records temporarily invisible. The menu item Records ➪ Data Entry clears the screen temporarily of all records while you are editing new records. When you want to restore all records, select Records ➪ Remove Filter/Sort.

Deleting Records

You can delete any number of records by selecting the record(s) and pressing the Delete key. You can also select the records and choose Edit ➪ Delete or place your cursor in a record and select Edit ➪ Delete Record. When you press Delete or choose the menu selection, a dialog box asks you to confirm the deletion (see Figure 7-14). If you select Yes, the records are deleted. If you select Cancel, no changes are made.

Caution The Default value for this dialog box is Yes. Pressing the Enter key automatically deletes the records. If you accidentally erase records using this method, the action can't be reversed.

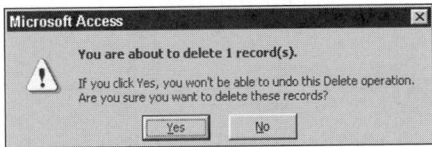

Figure 7-14: The Delete Record dialog box warns you that you are about to delete x number of records — the DEFAULT response is YES (OK to delete) so be careful when deleting records.

Caution If you have relations set between tables and *Enforce Referential Integrity* is checked — for example, the Customer table is related to the Pets table — then you can't delete a record unless the Cascade Delete check box is also checked and you are attempting to delete from the lowest child in the relationship builder (Pets vs. Customer). Otherwise you receive an error message dialog box that reports *The record can't be deleted or changed because the table '<tablename>' includes related records*.

You can select multiple contiguous records. To do so, click the record selector of the first record that you want to select and drag the record-pointer icon (right-pointing arrow) to the last record that you want to select.

Adding, Changing, and Deleting Columns

A very dangerous feature in Access 2002 is the capability to add, delete, and rename columns in a datasheet. This feature actually changes the data design. When you go to the Table Design screen and make changes, you know that you are changing the underlying structure of the data because you can see yourself do it. Within a datasheet, however, you may not realize the consequences of the changes that you are making. Any field name that is changed may cause any query, form, report, macro, or module that uses that name to no longer function. If you are creating applications for others, you should not allow users to use a datasheet to make the changes described in this part of the book.

Deleting a column from a datasheet

You can delete columns from a datasheet by selecting one column at a time and selecting Edit ➪ Delete Column. When you take this action, a dialog box warns that you will be deleting all the data in this column, as well as the field itself, from the table design. More importantly, if you have used this field in a data-entry form or a report, you get an error message the next time you use any object that references this field name. You can't delete more than one column at a time.

Adding a column to a datasheet

You can add new columns to a datasheet by selecting Insert ➪ Column, which creates a new column to the left of the column that your insertion point was in. The new column is labeled Field1. You can then add data to the records for the column.

Adding a new column also adds the field to the table design. When you save the datasheet, Access writes the field into the table design, using the characteristics of the data for the field properties.

Changing a field name (column header)

When you add a new field, you want to change the column name before you save the datasheet. You can change a column header by double-clicking the column header and editing the text in the column header. When you save the datasheet, this column header text is used as a field name for the table design.

Caution When you change a column header, you are changing the field name in the table. If you have used this field name in forms, reports, queries, macros, or modules, they no longer work until you change them in the other objects. This is a dangerous way to change a field name; only experienced users should use it.

Displaying Records

A number of mouse techniques and menu items can increase your productivity when you add or change records. Either by selecting from the Format menu or by using the mouse, you can change the field order, hide and freeze columns, change row height or column width, change display fonts, and change the display or remove gridlines.

Changing the field order

By default, Access displays the fields in a datasheet in the same order that they appear in a table or query. Sometimes, however, you need to see certain fields next to each other in order to better analyze your data. To rearrange your fields, select a column (as shown in Figure 7-15) and drag the column to its new location.

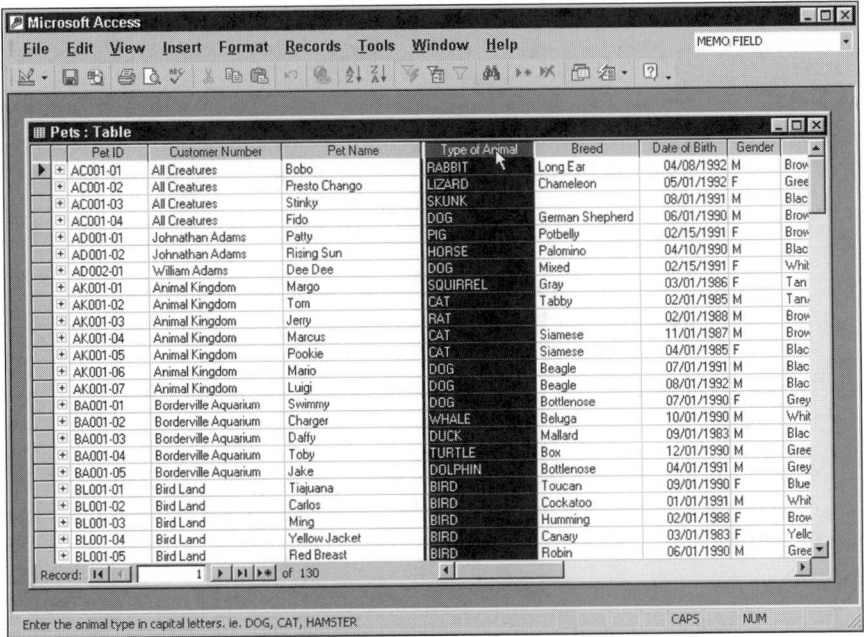

Figure 7-15: Selecting a column to change the field order

You can select and drag columns one at a time, or you can select multiple columns to drag. Suppose you want the fields Pet Name and Type of Animal to appear first in the datasheet. Use the following steps to make this change:

1. Position the mouse pointer on the Pet Name field (column) name. The cursor changes to a down arrow.

2. Click to select the column and hold down the mouse button. The entire Pet Name column is now highlighted.

3. Drag the mouse to the right to highlight the Type of Animal column.

4. Release the mouse button; the two columns should now be highlighted.

5. Click the mouse button again; the pointer changes to an arrow with a box under it.

6. Drag the two columns to the left edge of the datasheet.

7. Release the mouse button; the two columns now move to the beginning of the datasheet.

With this method, you can move any individual field or contiguous field selection. You can move the fields left or right or past the right or left boundary of the window.

Note   Moving fields in a datasheet does not affect the field order in the table design.

Changing the field display width

You can change the *field display width* (column width) either by specifying the width in a dialog box (in number of characters) or by dragging the column border. When you drag a column border, the cursor changes to the double-arrow symbol.

To widen a column or to make it narrower, follow these two steps:

1. Place the mouse pointer between two column names on the field separator line. The mouse pointer turns into a small line with arrows pointing to the left and right — if you have it in the correct location.

2. Drag the column border to the left to make the column smaller or to the right to make it larger.

Tip   You can resize a column instantly to the best fit (based on the longest data value) by double-clicking on the right column border after the cursor changes to the double arrow.

Note   Resizing the column doesn't change the number of characters allowed in the table's field size. You are simply changing the amount of viewing space for the data contained in the column.

Alternatively, you can resize a column by choosing Format ⇨ Column Width or by right-clicking on the column header and selecting Column Width from the menu. When you click Column Width, the dialog box in which you enter column width in number of characters displays, as shown in Figure 7-16. You can also return the column to its default size by checking the Standard Width check box.

You can create an icon on your toolbar for Column Width. To do this, click the down arrow next to the Help button on the toolbar and select Add or Remove Buttons. Select the Table Datasheet choice, and finally select the Column Width button. This button becomes the last button on that toolbar. To remove it, just repeat the process.

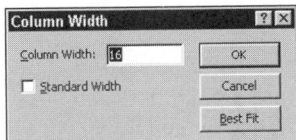

Figure 7-16: The Column Width dialog box

Caution   You can hide a column if you drag the column gridline to the gridline of the next column to the left. This also happens if you set the column width to 0 in the Column Width dialog box. If you do this, you must use Format ⇨ Unhide Columns to redisplay the columns.

Changing the record display height

You can change the record (that is, row) height of all rows by dragging a row's border to make the row height larger or smaller, or you can select Format ⇨ Row Height. Sometimes you may need to increase the row height to accommodate larger fonts or text data displays of multiple lines.

You can also create an icon on your toolbar for Row Height. To do this, click the down arrow next to the Help button and select Add or Remove Buttons. Select the Table Datasheet choice, and finally select the Row Height button. This button becomes the last button on that toolbar. To remove it, just repeat the process.

When you drag a record's border, the cursor changes to the vertical two-headed arrow that you see at the left edge of Figure 7-17. The two-headed arrow is visible in Figure 7-17.

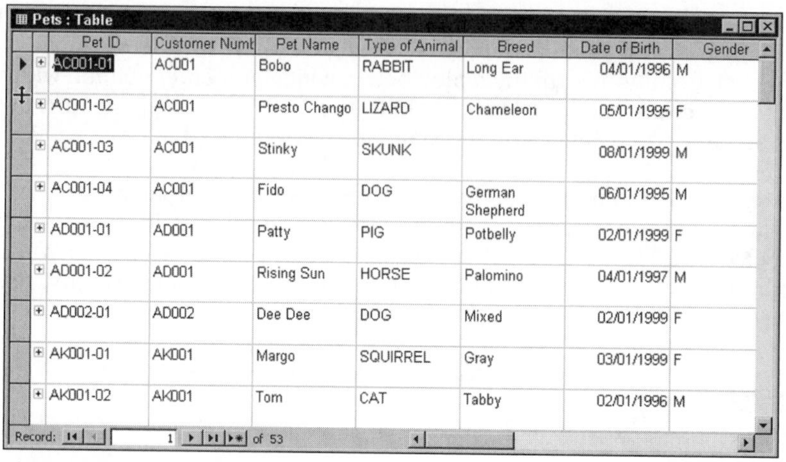

Pets : Table							_ □ ×
Pet ID	Customer Numb	Pet Name	Type of Animal	Breed	Date of Birth	Gender ▲
AC001-01	AC001	Bobo	RABBIT	Long Ear	04/01/1996	M
AC001-02	AC001	Presto Chango	LIZARD	Chameleon	05/01/1995	F
AC001-03	AC001	Stinky	SKUNK		08/01/1999	M
AC001-04	AC001	Fido	DOG	German Shepherd	06/01/1995	M
AD001-01	AD001	Patty	PIG	Potbelly	02/01/1999	F
AD001-02	AD001	Rising Sun	HORSE	Palomino	04/01/1997	M
AD002-01	AD002	Dee Dee	DOG	Mixed	02/01/1999	F
AK001-01	AK001	Margo	SQUIRREL	Gray	03/01/1999	F
AK001-02	AK001	Tom	CAT	Tabby	02/01/1996	M

Record: ◄◄ ◄ [1] ► ►I ►✳ of 53

Figure 7-17: Changing a row's height. Simply put the mouse pointer between two rows. When the mouse pointer changes to arrows pointing up and down, drag the height to what you want.

To increase or decrease a row's height, follow these steps:

1. Place the mouse pointer between two rows on the gray record selector. The cursor changes to the double pointing arrow (up and down).

2. Drag the row border upward to shrink all row heights. Drag the border downward to increase all row heights.

Note The procedure for changing row height changes the row size for all rows in the datasheet.

You can also resize rows by choosing Format ➪ Row Height. A dialog box appears so that you can enter the row height in point size. You can also return the rows to their default point size by checking the Standard Height check box.

Caution If you drag a record's gridline up to meet the gridline immediately above it in the previous record, all rows are hidden. This also occurs if you set the row height close to 0 (for example, a height of 0.1) in the Row Height dialog box. In that case, you must select Format ➪ Row Height and reset the row height to a larger number to redisplay the rows.

Displaying cell gridlines

Normally gridlines appear between fields (columns) and between records (rows). By selecting Format ➪ Datasheet, you can determine whether to display gridlines and how they look. Figure 7-18 shows the Cells Effects dialog box that you use.

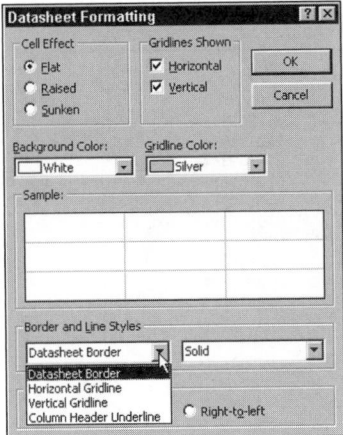

Figure 7-18: Changing cell gridlines

The Datasheet Formatting dialog box gives you complete control over gridlines. Using the Gridlines Shown check boxes, you can eliminate both Horizontal and Vertical gridlines. If you choose to keep the gridlines, you can change both the Gridline Color and the Background Color. A sample shows you what the effect you have chosen looks like. You can also determine whether the gridlines are Flat (default white background with silver gridlines), Raised (default silver background with gray gridlines), or Sunken (default silver background with white gridlines).

Caution   You can also determine the Border and Line Styles for each of the different datasheet borders. You can determine a different border for the Datasheet Border, Horizontal Gridline, Vertical Gridline, and Column Header Underline. To select a different border style for each border in the datasheet, first select the Border that you want to update from the left combo box and then the Line Style from the combo box on the right. Repeat the process for each border. Each border in Figure 7-19 has a different line style.

The different line styles that you can use for the different datasheet borders include

Transparent Border	Short Dashes	Dash-Dot
Solid	Dots	Dash-Dot-Dot
Dashes	Sparse Dots	Double Solid

Changing display fonts

You can resize the row height and column width automatically by changing the display font. By default, Access displays all data in the datasheet in the MS Sans Serif 8-point Regular font. You may find that this font does not print correctly because MS Sans Serif is only a screen font. Arial 8-point Regular is a good match. Select Format ⇨ Font to change the font type style, size, and style.

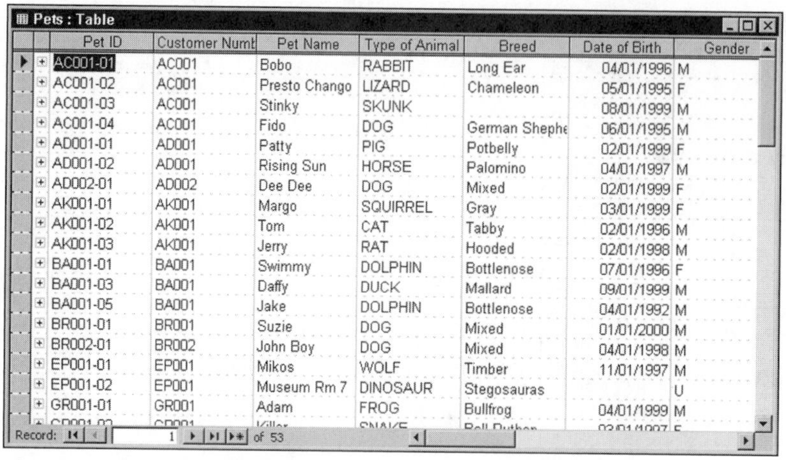

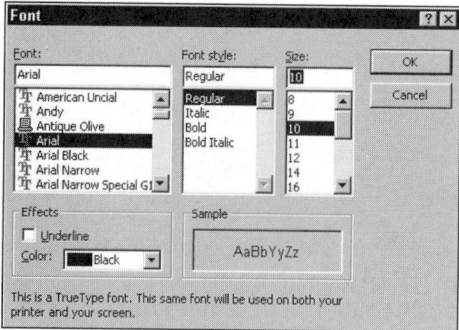

Figure 7-19: Different line styles are used for the different borders in the datasheet. In this case, the cell effect has been changed to change the Gridline Color and remove the Horizontal lines from the grid.

Setting the font display affects the entire datasheet. If you want to see more data on the screen, you can use a very small font. You can also switch to a higher-resolution display size if you have the necessary hardware. If you want to see larger characters, you can increase the font size.

To change the font to Arial 10-point bold, follow these steps:

1. Select Format ➪ Font. A dialog box appears.

2. Select Arial from the Font combo box, as shown in Figure 7-20.

3. Select Bold from the Font style combo box.

4. Enter **10** into the text box area of the Size combo box.

5. Click OK.

Figure 7-20: Changing to a different font and font size in the datasheet

As you change font attributes, a sample appears in the Sample area. This way, you can see the changes that you are making before you make them. You can also change the font color if you want.

Hiding and unhiding columns

You can hide columns by dragging the column gridline to the preceding field or by setting the column size to 0. You can also use the Hide Columns dialog box to hide one or more columns. To hide a single column, follow these steps:

1. Position the cursor anywhere within the column that you want to hide.
2. Select Format ⇨ Hide Columns. The column disappears. Actually, the column width is simply set to 0. You can hide multiple columns by first selecting them and then selecting Format ⇨ Hide Columns.

After you've hidden a column, you can redisplay it by selecting Format ⇨ Unhide Columns. This action displays a dialog box that lets you hide or unhide columns selectively by checking off the desired status of each field. When you are finished, click Close; the datasheet appears, showing the desired fields.

Freezing columns

When you want to scroll among many fields but want to keep certain fields from scrolling out of view, you can use Format ⇨ Freeze Columns. With this selection, for example, you can keep the Pet ID and Pet Name fields visible while you scroll through the datasheet to find the animals' lengths and weights. The columns that you want to keep visible remain frozen on the far-left side of the datasheet; other fields scroll out of sight horizontally. The fields must be contiguous if you want to freeze more than one at a time. (Of course, you can first move your fields to place them next to each other.) When you're ready to unfreeze the datasheet columns, simply select Format ⇨ Unfreeze All Columns.

Tip   When you unfreeze columns, the column doesn't move back to its original position. You must move it manually.

Saving the changed layout

When you close the datasheet, you save all your data changes, but you lose all your layout changes. As you make all these display changes to your datasheet, you probably won't want to make them again the next time you open the same datasheet. By default, however, Access does not save the datasheet's layout changes. If you want your datasheet to look the same way the next time you open it, you can select File ⇨ Save; this command saves your layout changes with the datasheet. You can also click the Save icon on your toolbar (the icon with the floppy disk on it).

Caution   If you are following the example, don't save the changes to the Pets table.

Saving a record

As you move off a record, Access saves it. You can press Shift+Enter to save a record without moving off it. A third way to save a record is to close the table. Yet another way to save a record is to select Records ➪ Save.

Sorting and Filtering Records in a Datasheet

Finding a value lets you display a specific record and work with that record. If you have multiple records that meet a find criteria, however, you may want to display just that specific set of records. Using the Filter and Sort toolbar icons (or the Records menu option Sort), you can display just the set of records that you want to work with. You can also sort selected records instantly into any order that you want: Use the two QuickSort buttons to sort the entire table, or use the three filter buttons to select only certain records.

Using the QuickSort feature

Sometimes you may simply want to sort your records into a desired order. The QuickSort buttons on the toolbar let you sort selected columns into either ascending or descending order. The toolbar contains a different button for each order. Before you can click on either the Ascending (A-Z) or Descending (Z-A) QuickSort buttons, you must select the fields that you want to use for the sort.

You select a field to use in the sort by placing your cursor in the field in any record. After the cursor is in the column that you want to use in the sort, click the QuickSort button. The data redisplays instantly in the sorted order.

If you want to sort your data on the basis of values in multiple fields, you can highlight more than one column: Highlight a column (as previously discussed), hold down the Shift key, and drag the cursor to the right. These steps select multiple contiguous fields. When you select one of the QuickSort buttons, Access sorts the records into major order (by the first highlighted field) and then into orders within orders (based on subsequent fields). If you need to select multiple columns that aren't contiguous (next to each other), you can move them next to each other, as discussed earlier in this chapter.

Tip   If you want to redisplay your records in their original order, use Records ➪ Remove Filter/Sort.

Cross-Reference   You learn more about sorting in Chapter 9.

Using Filter by Selection

Filter by Selection is a technology within Access 2002 that lets you select records instantly on the basis of the current value that you selected. For example, suppose you move your cursor to the Type of Animal column and click the Sort Ascending button. Access sorts the data by type of animal. Now highlight any of the records with the value DOG. When you press the Filter by Selection button, Access selects only the records where the Type of Animal is DOG. The Pets table contains 53 records. After you have selected DOG and pressed the Filter by Selection button, only 12 records are shown and all have the value DOG in the Type of Animal field.

The navigation button area of the Datasheet window tells you whether the database is currently filtered; in addition, the Apply Filter/Remove Filter icon (third filter icon that looks like a large funnel) is depressed, indicating that a filter is in use. When you toggle this button, it removes all filters or sorts. The filter specification does not go away; it is simply turned off.

Filter by Selection is additive. You can continue to select values, each time pressing the Filter by Selection button.

Tip   You can also right-click on the field content that you want to filter by and then select Filter by Selection from the menu choices.

If, for example, you place your cursor in the Gender column in a record (with the male dogs already filtered) where the value of Gender is M and press the Filter by Selection button, only eight records are displayed—the male dogs. If you then place your cursor in the Colors column in a record where the value of Colors is Brown and press the Filter by Selection button, only three records are displayed—the brown male dogs.

If you want to further specify a selection and then see everything that doesn't match that selection (not equal to German Shepherd), move the cursor to the field that you want to say *doesn't match* and right-click on the datasheet and select Filter Excluding Selection. For example, when filtering by selection, move the cursor to the Breed column and select one of the German Shepherd fields and right-click to select Filter Excluding Selection. You are now left with two records. This selects everything but the German Shepherd records that are Brown and Male.

Imagine using this technique to review sales by salespeople for specific time periods or products. Filter by Selection provides incredible opportunities to drill down into successive layers of data. As you add to Filter by Selection and Filter Excluding Selection, it continues to add to its own internal query manager (also known as

Query by Example). Even when you click the Remove Filter icon to redisplay all the records, Access still stores the query specification in memory. If you click the icon again (now called Apply Filter), only the two records return (DOG, M, Brown, not German Shepherd). Figure 7-21 shows this Filter by Selection screen in a Datasheet.

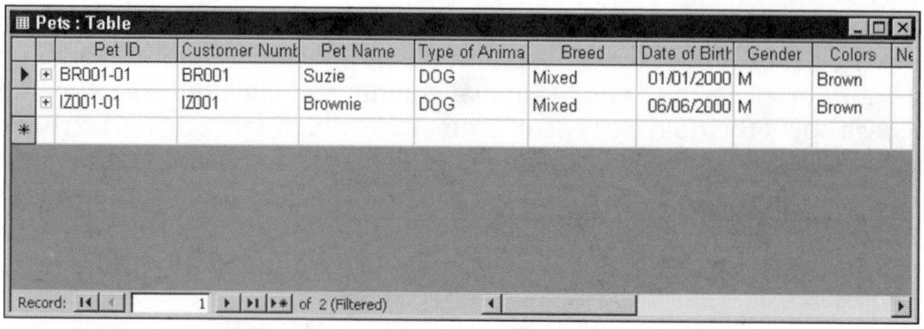

Figure 7-21: Using Filter by Selection. In this case you see all records for DOGS that are Male, Brown, and not German Shepherd.

Filter by Selection has some limitations. Most importantly, all of the choices are added together (i.e., DOG, Male, Brown, and not German Shepherd). This means that the only operation you can perform is a search for records that meet all of the specified conditions. Another option, Filter by Form, lets you create more complex analyses.

If you want to use the Filter by Selection but can't find the selection that you want to use, but you know the value, right-click on the field that you want to apply the filter to and select Filter For. This option allows you to type in the selection to filter for.

Using Filter by Form

Filter by Selection is just one way to filter data in Access 2002. Another way is Filter by Form. Selecting the second filter icon changes the datasheet to a single record; every field becomes a combo box that enables you to select from a list of all values for that field. As Figure 7-22 shows, the bottom of the form lets you specify the *OR* conditions for each group of values that you specify.

In Figure 7-22, you can see four conditions created in the Filter by Selection example (described previously) in the single line of the Filter by Form screen. If you click the Or tab, you can enter a second set of conditions. Suppose you want to see non-German Shepherd male dogs or any male ducks. You already have the specification for non-German Shepherd male brown dogs. You would click on the Or tab and then select DUCK from the now-empty Type of Animal combo box and M from the Gender column. When you click on the Apply Filter button (the large funnel), three records display.

Figure 7-22: Using Filter by Form lets you set multiple conditions for filtering at one time.

You can have as many conditions as you need. If you need even more advanced manipulation of your selections, you can choose Records ⇨ Filter ⇨ Advanced Filter/Sort and get an actual QBE (Query by Example) screen that you can use to enter more complex queries.

Cross-Reference

Later chapters explain more advanced concepts of queries.

Printing Records

You can print all the records in your datasheet in a simple row-and-column layout. Later you learn to produce formatted reports. For now, the simplest way to print is to select File ⇨ Print or use the Print icon in the toolbar. This selection displays the standard Print dialog box, as shown in Figure 7-23.

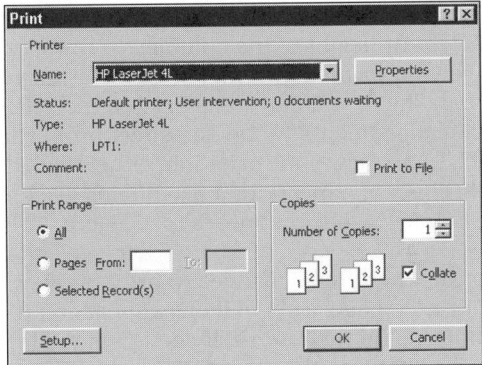

Figure 7-23: The Print dialog box

Assuming that you set up a printer in Microsoft Windows, you can select OK to print your datasheet in the font that you selected for display (or the nearest printer equivalent). The printout reflects all layout options that are in effect when the datasheet is printed. Hidden columns don't print. Gridlines print only if the cell gridline properties are on. The printout also reflects the specified row height and column width.

Only so many columns and rows can fit on a page; the printout takes up as many pages as required to print all the data. Access breaks up the printout as necessary to fit on each page. For example, the Pets table printout is six pages. Three pages across are needed to print all the fields in the Pets table; each record requires three pages in length.

Printing the datasheet

You can also control printing from the Print dialog box, selecting from several options:

- ✦ **Print Range.** Prints the entire datasheet or only selected pages or records.
- ✦ **Copies.** Determines the number of copies to be printed.
- ✦ **Collate.** Determines whether multiple copies are collated.

You can also click on the Properties button and set options for the selected printer or select the printer itself to change the type of printer. The Setup button allows you to set margins and print headings.

Using the Print Preview window

Although you may have all the information in the datasheet ready to print, you may be unsure of whether to change the width or height of the columns or rows, or whether to adjust the fonts to improve your printed output. For that matter, you may not want to print out the entire datasheet; you may need printed records from only pages 3 and 4. Before making such adjustments to the datasheet properties, you should view the report on-screen. To preview your print job, either click the Print Preview button on the toolbar (a sheet of paper with a magnifying glass) or select File ➪ Print Preview. The Print Preview window appears (see Figure 7-24).

After you select the Print Preview button, the screen changes to print preview mode. You see an image of your first printed page; a set of icons appears on the toolbar. You can use the Navigation buttons (in the lower-left section of the Print Preview window) to change pages, just as you use them to select records in a datasheet.

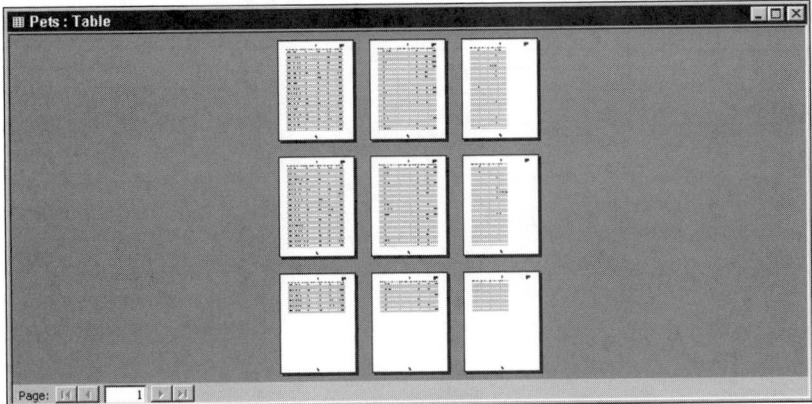

Figure 7-24: Print preview of a datasheet. You can specify up to 12 pages to view at one time.

The toolbar buttons provide quick access to printing tasks:

✦ **Close Window.** Returns to Datasheet view

✦ **Print.** Displays the Print dialog box, which is accessible when you select File ⇨ Print from the menu bar

✦ **One Page.** Toggles in and out to make the Print Preview show a single page

✦ **Two Pages.** Shows two pages in the Print Preview

✦ **Zoom Control.** Adjusts the Print Preview screen to show more or less detail

> **Tip**   You can view more than two pages by selecting View ⇨ Pages and selecting 1, 2, 4, 8, or 12.

If you are satisfied with the datasheet after examining the preview, select the Print button on the toolbar to print the datasheet. If you are not satisfied, select the Close button to return to datasheet mode to make further changes to your data or layout.

✦   ✦   ✦

Creating and Using Simple Data-Entry Forms

◆ ◆ ◆ ◆

In This Chapter

Understanding the
types of forms that
you can create

Looking at the
difference between a
form and a datasheet

Creating a form with
a Form Wizard

Using the Form
window

Displaying data with
a form

Entering pictures and
data into OLE fields
and Memo fields

Switching to
Datasheet view from
a form

Finding and
replacing data in a
form

Making simple form
design changes

Saving a form

Printing a form

◆ ◆ ◆

Forms provide the most flexible way for viewing, adding, editing, and deleting your data. In this chapter, you learn to use Form Wizards as the starting point for your form. You also learn how forms work and the types of forms that you can create with Access.

Understanding Data-Entry Forms

Although you can view your data in many ways, a form provides the most flexibility for viewing and entering data. A form lets you view one or more records at a time while viewing all of the fields. A datasheet also lets you view several records at once, but each record is displayed as a row so you can see only a limited number of fields at a time.

When you use a form, you can see all your fields at once, or at least as many as you can fit on a screen. By rearranging your fields in a form, you can easily get 20, 50, or even 100 fields on one screen. You can also use forms to create tabbed dialog boxes or main (graphical button) menus known as *switchboards*. Forms are useful for viewing data in a formatted display, as well as for entering, changing, or deleting data. You can also print forms with the visual effects that you create.

What are the basic types of forms?

These are the six basic types of forms:

✦ Columnar (also known as full-screen) forms, which are used for data entry or switchboards

✦ Datasheets, which display many records at a time like a spreadsheet in rows and columns

✦ Tabular forms, which display more than one formatted record at a time

✦ Main/subforms, which display data that include parent/child relationships

✦ Pivot table forms (like those found in Microsoft Excel), which display cross-tabs

✦ Graphs, including bar charts, pie charts, line graphs, and other chart types

Figure 8-1 shows a *columnar form*; the fields are arranged as columns. The form can occupy one or more screen pages. Generally, this type of form simulates the hard-copy entry of data; the fields can be arranged any way that you want. Most standard Windows controls are available with Access forms to simplify data entry. Lines, boxes, colors, and special effects (such as shadows or three-dimensional looks) enable you to make great looking, easy-to-use forms.

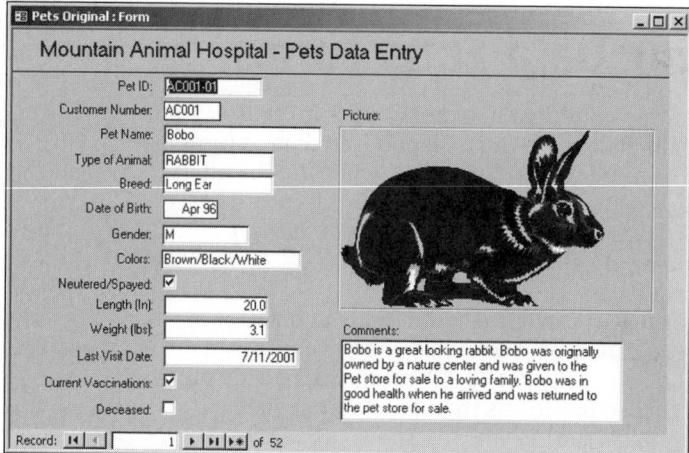

Figure 8-1: A full-screen (columnar) form showing a sample data record

Figure 8-2 shows a tabular form that displays several records at one time. You can format any part of a tabular form; your column headers can span lines and be for-matted separately from the records (datasheets don't allow you to customize the column headers). Tabular forms can have multiple rows per record, as in Figure 8-2. You can add special effects (such as shadows) to the fields. Field controls can be option buttons, command buttons, and text boxes.

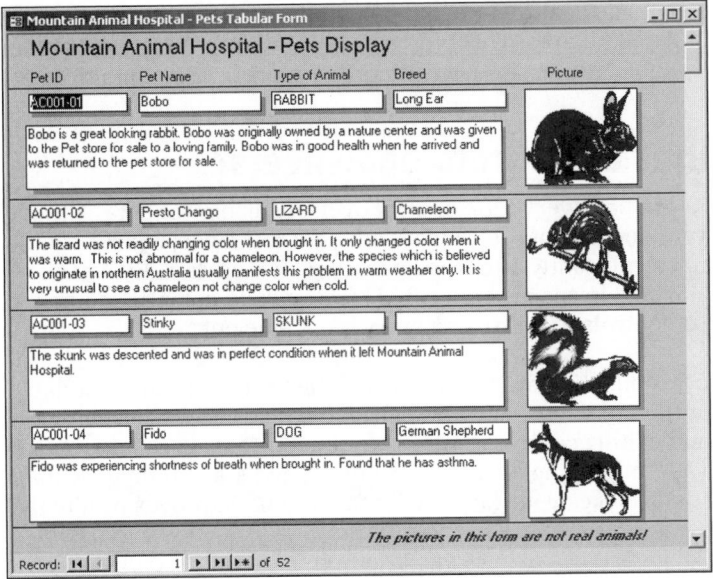

Figure 8-2: A tabular form

Figure 8-3 shows a main/subform, which is commonly used to display data with one-to-many relationships. The main form displays the main table; the subform is often a datasheet or tabular form that displays the many side tables of the relationship.

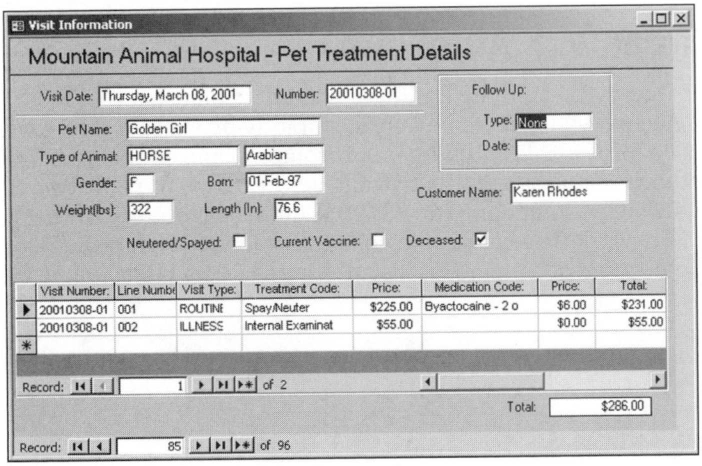

Figure 8-3: A main/subform

In Figure 8-3, the visit information for each pet appears once, while the subform shows many visit detail records. This type of form combines the benefits of forms and datasheets. A subform can show one record or more, each on multiple lines.

How do forms differ from datasheets?

With a datasheet, you have very little control over the display of data. Although you can change the type and size of the display font, and rearrange, resize, or hide columns, you can't significantly alter the appearance of the data. By using forms, you can place each field in an exact specified location, add color or shading to each field, and add text controls to make data entry more efficient.

A form has more flexibility in data entry than a datasheet. You can input data to multiple tables at the same time, and add calculated fields as well as enhanced data-validation and editing controls (such as option buttons, check boxes, and pop-up list boxes) to a form. Adding lines, boxes, colors, and static bitmaps enhances the look of your data, makes your form easier to use, and improves productivity.

In addition, OLE objects (such as pictures or graphs) are visible *only* in a form or report. Additionally, although you can increase a datasheet's row size to see more of a Memo field, using a form makes it easier to display large amounts of text in a scrollable text box.

 **Tip**   After you create a form with editing or enhanced data validation controls, you can still switch into Datasheet view, which lets you use data-validation rules and controls, such as combo boxes, in the datasheet.

Creating a form with AutoForm

From the Table or Query object in the Database window, a datasheet, or most design screens in Access, you can create a form instantly by clicking the New button on the toolbar (a form with a lightning bolt through it) and choosing AutoForm icon. Another method is to use Insert ⇨ Form and select one of the AutoForm choices from the dialog box that appears. With the AutoForm button, the form appears with no more work. You can create columnar, tabular, or datasheet forms with AutoForm. To create a columnar AutoForm using the Pets table, follow these steps:

1. From the Mountain Animal Hospital database window, click the Table object button.

2. Select Pets.

3. Click the New Object button on the main Microsoft Access toolbar (not the Database window toolbar).

4. Select AutoForm.

The form instantly appears, as shown in Figure 8-4. Your screen resolution and the size of your monitor may show more or less of the form than in this figure.

5. Close the form and don't save it.

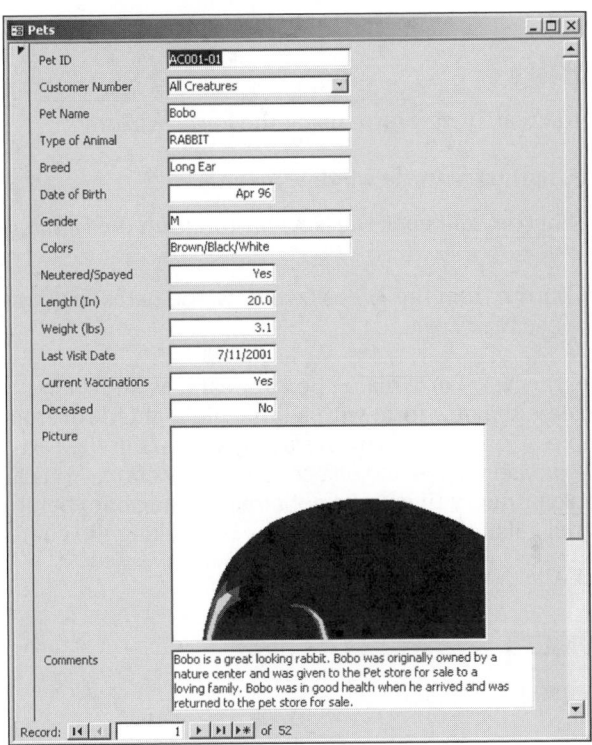

Figure 8-4: The AutoForm form

Some values are not properly displayed in different areas of the form. For example, if you looked at the picture of the rabbit (yes, it's the hindquarter of a rabbit) in the first record, you saw only a portion of the rabbit. Later in this chapter you learn how to fix this, as well as how to customize the form.

Using AutoForm is the quickest way to create a form. Generally, however, you want more control over your form creation. Other Form Wizards can help you create a more customized form from the outset.

Creating a Form with Form Wizards

Form Wizards simplify the layout process for your fields. A Form Wizard visually walks you through a series of questions about the form that you want to create and then creates it for you automatically. This chapter creates single-column forms with a Form Wizard, starting from the columnar form to create a full-screen form.

Creating a new form

You have several methods to create a new form using the Form Wizard:

✦ Select Insert ⇨ Form from the Database window menu.

✦ Select the Form object button and click the New button from the Database window.

✦ Select the New object button from the Access window, the datasheet, or the Query toolbar, and choose New Form.

Whichever method you use, the New Form dialog box appears, as shown in Figure 8-5. If you begin to create the new form with a table highlighted (or from a datasheet or query), the table or query that you are using appears in the text box labeled *Choose the table or query where the object's data comes from*. You can enter the name of a valid table or query (if you are not already using one) before continuing—just choose from a list of tables and queries by clicking the combo box's selection arrow.

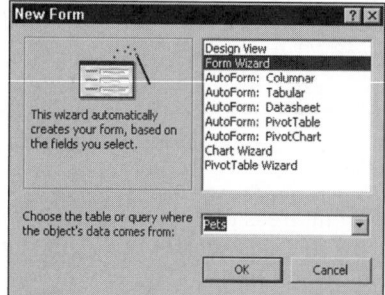

Figure 8-5: The New Form dialog box

Selecting the New Form type and data source

The New Form dialog box provides nine choices for creating a form:

✦ **Design View.** Displays a completely blank form to start with in Form design

✦ **Form Wizard.** Creates a form with one of four default layouts: columnar, tabular, datasheet, or justified using data fields that you specify in a step-by-step process that lets you customize the form creation process

✦ **AutoForm: Columnar.** Instantly creates a columnar form

✦ **AutoForm: Tabular.** Instantly creates a tabular form

✦ **AutoForm: Datasheet.** Instantly creates a datasheet form

✦ **AutoForm: PivotTable.** Instantly creates a pivot table form

✦ **AutoForm: PivotChart.** Instantly creates a pivot chart form

✦ **Chart Wizard.** Creates a form with a business graph

✦ **PivotTable Wizard.** Creates an Excel Pivot Table form

The picture at the left of the dialog box shows your selection.

To start the Form Wizard follow the next steps:

1. With the Form object selected, click New. From the New Form dialog box choose the Form Wizard option.

2. Select the Pets table in the table/query combo box at the bottom of the New Form window

3. Click OK

Choosing the fields

After you select Form Wizard, the field-selection window appears, as shown in Figure 8-6. The field-selection dialog box has three work areas. The first area lets you choose multiple tables or queries, so you can create many types of forms, including those with subforms. As you select each table or query, Available Fields list displays the possible fields, and Selected Fields displays the selected fields.

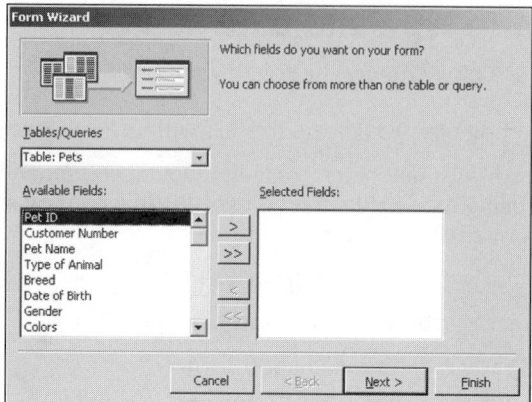

Figure 8-6: Choosing the fields for the form

The field-selection area consists of two list boxes and four buttons. The Available Fields: list box on the left displays all fields from the selected table/query that was used to create the form. The Selected Fields: list box on the right displays the fields that you have selected for this form. You can select one field, all the fields, or any combination of fields. The order in which you add the fields to the list box on the right is the order in which the fields appear in the form. You can use the buttons to place or remove fields in the Selected Fields: box. Here is a description of these buttons:

>   Add selected field

>>   Add all fields

<   Remove selected field

<<   Remove all fields

When you highlight a field in the Available Fields: list box and click >, the field name appears in the Selected Fields: list box. You can add each field that you want to the list box. If you add a field by mistake, you can select the field in the Selected Fields: list box and click < to remove it from the selection. If you decide that you want to change the order in which your fields appear in the form, you must remove any fields that are out of order and reselect them in the proper order.

Note   You can also double-click any field in the Available Fields: list box to add it to the Selected Fields: list box.

At the bottom of the form, you can see a series of buttons to use when the field selection is completed. The types of buttons available here are common to most Wizard dialog boxes:

✦ **Cancel.** Cancel form creation and return to the starting point

✦ **Back.** Return to the preceding dialog box

✦ **Next.** Go to the next dialog box

✦ **Finish.** Go to the last dialog box (usually the form title)

Note   If you click Next > or Finish without selecting any fields, Access tells you that you must select fields for the form before you can continue.

1. Select all of the fields by clicking the >> button.

2. Click the Next button to display the dialog box from which to choose a form layout.

Choosing the form layout

After you have chosen the fields, you must choose the type of layout. As Figure 8-7 shows, you can choose from six types of layouts:

✦ Columnar

✦ Tabular

✦ Datasheet

✦ Justified

✦ Pivot Table

✦ Pivot Chart

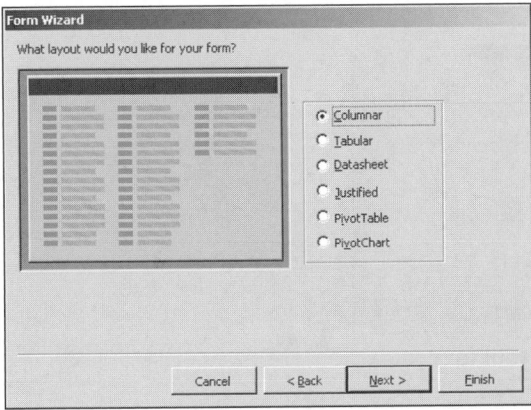

Figure 8-7: Choosing the type of layout for the form

As you click through the button choices, the display on the left changes to show how the form will look if you use that choice.

1. Select the Columnar layout.

2. After you choose the type of layout, you can click the Next button to display the choices for style of the form as shown in Figure 8-8.

Choosing the style of the form

You have many choices, which you can access by clicking the desired name in the list box. When you select a style, the display on the left changes to illustrate the special effect used to create the look.

The default look uses the Standard style, which creates a dark gray background and sunken controls. Figure 8-8 shows the Expedition style selected.

1. Select Expedition for the first form that you create in this chapter.

2. Click Next.

After you select the form's style, you are ready to create a title and view the form. The style that you select is used as the default the next time you use the Wizard.

Tip   You can customize the style by changing a form and then using the AutoFormat function in the Form design screen.

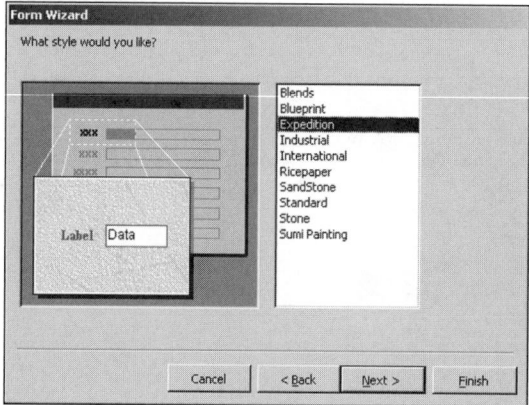

Figure 8-8: Choosing the style of your form

Creating a form title

The form title dialog box is usually the last dialog box in a Form Wizard. It always has a checkered flag that lets you know you've reached the finish line. By default, the text box for the form title contains the name of the table or query used for the form's data. You can accept the entry for the form title, enter your own, or erase it and have no title. The title in Figure 8-9 is Pets, which is the name of the table as long as you don't already have another form named Pets. If you do, a number is added to the end of the name.

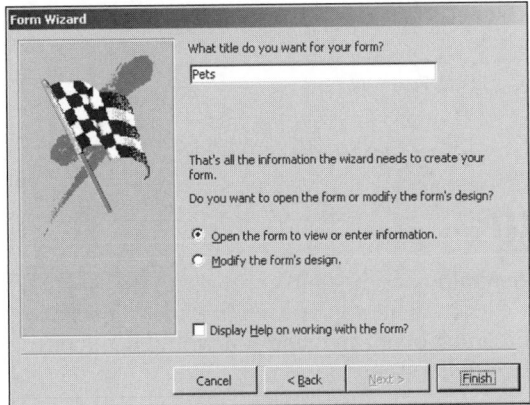

Figure 8-9: Choosing a form title

Completing the form

After you complete all the steps to design your form, you open the new form by selecting one of these two options:

✦ Open the form to view or enter information

✦ Modify the form's design

1. Select Open the form to view or enter information.

2. Click the Finish button.

After you click the Finish button, the form appears in the Form View window (as shown in Figure 8-10).

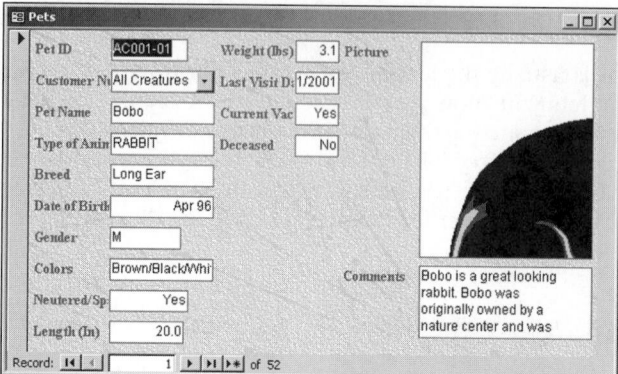

Figure 8-10: A form design created with a Form Wizard

Changing the Design

To demonstrate how easy it is to manipulate the field controls, in this section you learn how to change the way the Picture field appears. Figure 8-10 shows a lovely view of the hind part of the rabbit going over the fence—it would be nicer to see the whole rabbit. To fix this, follow these steps:

1. Click the Design button to open the form in the Form Design window.

2. Click the Picture field (the large, empty rectangle next to the Picture label).

3. Click the Property icon in the toolbar (picture of a hand and a sheet of paper, the fifth icon from the right).

4. Click the Size Mode property and change it from Clip to Stretch (as shown in Figure 8-11).

Tip   If you don't like the Grid or Ruler being displayed (as shown in Figure 8-11), you can turn them off by selecting View ➪ Ruler and/or View ➪ Grid.

After you complete the move, click the Form button to redisplay the form. The whole rabbit is displayed, as shown in Figure 8-12.

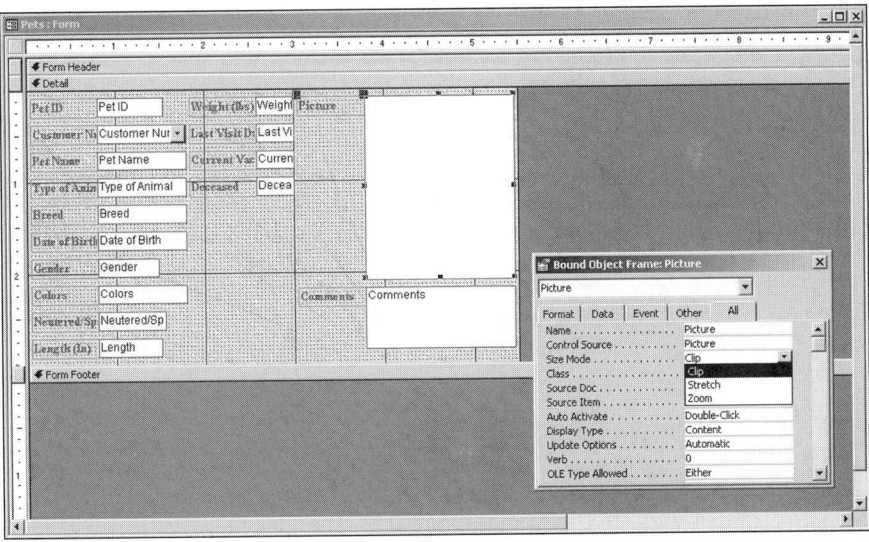

Figure 8-11: Changing a control property

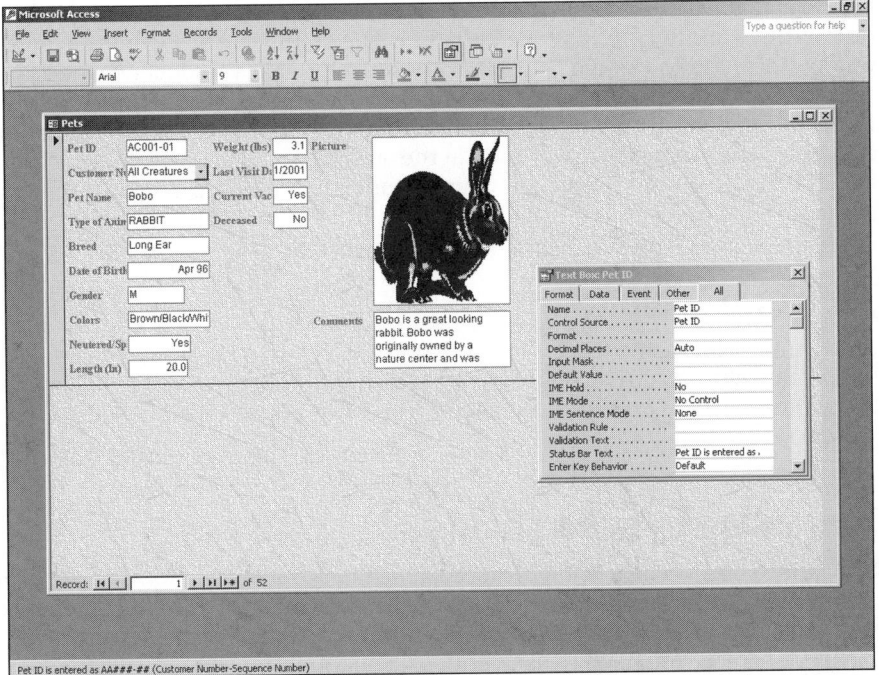

Figure 8-12: The form redisplayed to show the full picture of the rabbit

Chapters 14–18 teach you how to completely customize a form. In these chapters, you learn how to use all the controls in the toolbox, add special effects to forms, create forms with graphs and calculated fields, and add complex data validation to your forms.

As you can see in Figure 8-12, the Property window is displayed while the form is in Form view. This is a major new feature in Access 2000 and 2002 and allows you to make property changes while the form is displayed. In previous versions of Microsoft Access, you had to make all property changes in Design view and then display the form to see the result of your changes. This new feature makes it much easier to make property changes.

Using the Form Window

The window shown in Figure 8-12 is very similar to the Datasheet window. At the top of the screen you see the title bar, menu bar, and toolbars. The center of the screen displays your data, one record at a time, in the Form window (unless you have the Form window maximized). If the form contains more fields than can fit on-screen at one time, Access 2002 automatically displays a horizontal and/or vertical scrollbar that can be used to see the remainder of the record. You can also see the rest of the record by pressing the PgDn key. The status bar, at the bottom of the window, displays the active field's Field Description that you defined when you created the table. If no Field Description exists for a specific field, Access displays the words Form View. Generally, error messages and warnings appear in dialog boxes in the center of the screen (rather than in the status bar). The navigation buttons are found at the bottom of the screen. This feature lets you move quickly from record to record.

The Form toolbar

The Form toolbar — the top toolbar, as shown in Figure 8-12 — is almost identical to the Datasheet toolbar. The only difference is that the first icon contains five selections: Design View, Form View, Datasheet View, PivotTable View, and PivotChart View.

Navigating between fields

Navigating a form is nearly identical to navigating a datasheet. You can easily move around the Form window by clicking the field that you want and making changes or additions to your data. Because the Form window displays only as many fields as can fit on-screen, you need to use various navigational aids to move within your form or between records.

Table 8-1 displays the navigational keys used to move between fields within a form.

Table 8-1 Navigating in a Form	
Navigational Direction	**Keystrokes**
Next field	Tab, right-arrow (→) or down-arrow (↓) key, or Enter
Previous field	Shift+Tab, left-arrow (←), or up-arrow (↑)
First field of current record	Home or Ctrl+Home
Last field of current record	End or Ctrl+End
Next page	PgDn or Next Record
Previous page	PgUp or Previous Record

If you have a form with more than one page, a vertical scrollbar displays. You can use the scrollbar to move to different pages on the form. You can also use the PgUp and PgDn keys to move between form pages. You can move up or down one field at a time by clicking the scrollbar arrows. With the scrollbar button, you can move past many fields at once.

Moving between records in a form

Although you generally use a form to display one record at a time, you still need to move between records. The easiest way to do this is to use the navigation buttons.

The navigation buttons offer the same five controls at the bottom of the screen that you see in the datasheet. You can click these buttons to move to the desired record.

Pressing F5 moves you instantly to the record number box.

You can also press Ctrl+PgDn to move to the current field in the next record, or Ctrl+PgUp to move to the current field in the preceding record.

Displaying Your Data with a Form

In Chapter 7, you learn techniques to add, change, and delete data within a table by using a datasheet. These techniques are the same ones you use within a form. Table 8-2 summarizes these techniques.

Table 8-2
Editing Techniques

Editing Technique	Keystrokes
Move insertion point within a field	Press the right (→) and left-arrow (←) keys
Insert a value within a field	Move the insertion point and type the new data
Select the entire field	Press F2 or double-click the mouse button
Replace an existing value with a new value	Select the entire field and type a new value
Replace value with value of preceding field	Press Ctrl+' (single quotation mark)
Replace current value with default value	Press Ctrl+Alt+Spacebar
Insert current date into a field	Press Ctrl+; (semicolon)
Insert current time into a field	Press Ctrl+: (colon)
Insert a line break in a Text or Memo field	Press Ctrl+Enter
Insert new record	Press Ctrl++ (plus sign)
Delete current record	Press Ctrl+– (minus sign)
Save current record	Press Shift+Enter or move to another record
Undo a change to the current record	Press Esc or click the Undo button

Working with pictures and OLE objects

In a datasheet, you can't view a picture or any OLE object without accessing the OLE server. In a form, however, you can size the OLE control area to be large enough to display a picture, business graph, or visual OLE object. You can also size the Memo controls on forms so that you can see the data within the field — you don't have to zoom in on the value, as you do with a datasheet field. Figure 8-12 shows both the picture and the Memo data displayed in the form. Each of these controls can be resized.

In Chapter 7, we discuss that any object supported by an OLE server can be stored in an Access OLE field. OLE objects are entered into a form so that you can see, hear, or use the value. As with a datasheet, you have two ways to enter OLE fields into a form:

✦ Paste them in from the Clipboard from the Edit menu.

✦ Insert them into the field from the Insert ➪ Object menu.

Chapter 19 covers using and displaying OLE objects in forms in more detail.

Memo field data entry

The last field in the form shown in Figure 8-12 (in the right-most column) is a Memo data type. This type of field allows up to 65,536 bytes of text for each field. You can see the first two sentences of data in the Memo field. When you move the cursor (also known as the *insertion point*) into the Memo field, a vertical scrollbar appears (see Figure 8-13). Using this scrollbar, you can view the rest of the data in the field. Better yet, you can resize the Memo control in the Form Design window if you want to make it larger to see more data. You can also press Shift+F2 and display a Zoom dialog box in the center of the screen, which lets you view about 12 lines at a time.

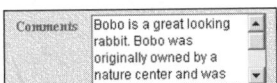

Figure 8-13: A vertical scrollbar appears in a Memo field when it contains the text cursor.

Switching to a datasheet

While in the form, you can display a Datasheet view of your data by using one of two methods:

✦ Click the Datasheet View button in the toolbar.

✦ Select View ➪ Datasheet View.

The datasheet is displayed with the cursor on the same field and record that it occupied in the form. If you move to another record and field and then redisplay the form, the form appears with the cursor on the field and with the record it last occupied in the datasheet.

To return to the form from a datasheet, you can use either of these two methods:

✦ Click the Form button in the toolbar.

✦ Select View ➪ Form View.

Saving a Record and the Form

As you move off each record, Access automatically saves any changes to the record. You can also press Shift+Enter to save a record without moving off of it. The final way to save a record is to close the form. You can save any changes to the current record by selecting Records ➪ Save Record. This action saves any changes and keeps the form open. When you are ready to close a form and return to the Database window (or to your query or datasheet), you can select File ➪ Close. If you made any changes to the form design, you are asked whether you want to save the design.

Printing a Form

You can print one or more records in your form exactly as they appear on-screen. (You learn how to produce formatted reports in chapters 19, 20, and 21, later in the book.) The simplest way to print is to use the File ➪ Print selection or the Print toolbar button. Selecting File ➪ Print displays the Print dialog box.

Assuming that you have set up a printer in Microsoft Windows, you can select OK to print your form. Access then prints your form, using the font that you selected for display or using the nearest printer equivalent. The printout contains any formatting that you specified in the form (including lines, boxes, and shading), and converts colors to grayscale if you are using a monochrome printer.

The printout includes as many pages as necessary to print all the data. If your form is wider than a single printer page, you need multiple pages to print your form. Access breaks up the printout as necessary to fit on each page.

Using the Print Preview Window

You may find that you have all the information in your form, but you aren't sure whether that information will print on multiple pages or fit on one printed page. Maybe you want to see whether the fonts need adjustment, or you need only the printed records from pages 3 and 4. In cases like this, view the report on-screen before printing to make these adjustments to the form design.

To preview your printout, you either click the Print Preview button on the toolbar (a sheet of paper with a magnifying glass on top) or select File ➪ Print Preview. Figure 8-14 shows the Print Preview window; it works exactly like the datasheet Print Preview window that you learn about in Chapter 7.

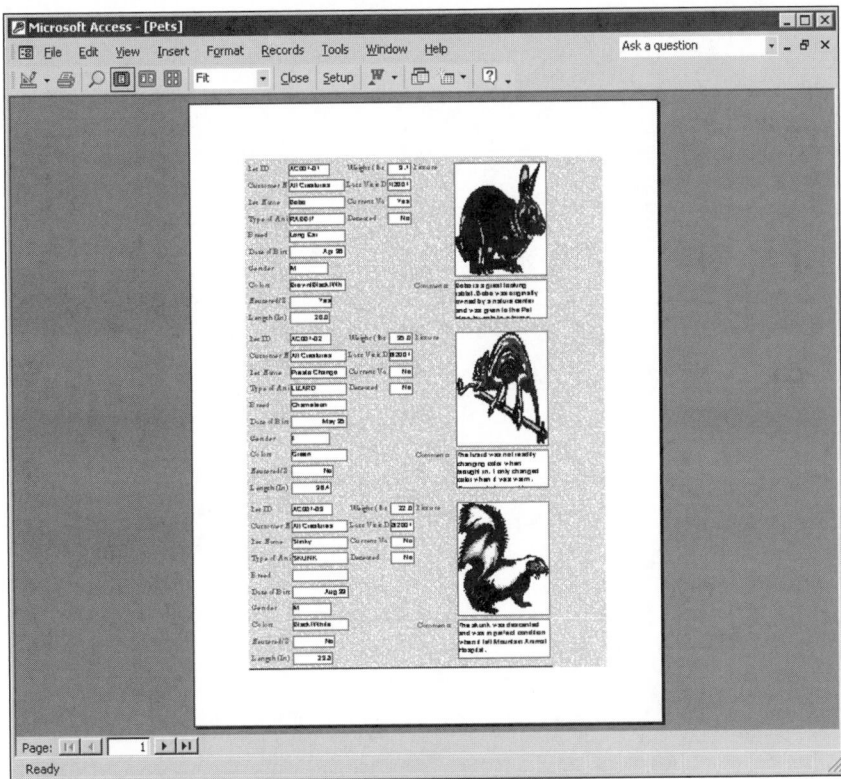

Figure 8-14: The Print Preview window

If you are satisfied with the form after examining the preview, select the Print button on the toolbar to print the form. If you are not satisfied, click the Close button to return to the form in order to make changes to the data or design.

✦   ✦   ✦

Understanding and Creating Simple Queries

✦   ✦   ✦   ✦

In This Chapter

Understanding the different types of queries

Creating queries

Selecting tables and fields for queries

Displaying information in queries

Sorting information in queries

Selecting specific records in queries

Printing the results of queries

✦   ✦   ✦   ✦

In this chapter, you learn what a query is and about the process of creating queries. Using the Pets table, you create several types of queries for the Mountain Animal Hospital database.

Understanding Queries

A database's primary purpose is to store and extract information. Information can be obtained from a database immediately after you enter the data or years later. Of course, obtaining information requires knowledge of how the database is set up.

For example, reports may be filed manually in a cabinet, arranged first by order of year and then by a *sequence number* that indicates when the report was written. To obtain a specific report, you must know its year and sequence number. In a good manual system, you may have a cross-reference book to help you find a specific report. This book may have all reports categorized alphabetically by type of report (rather than topic). Such a book can be helpful, but if you know only the report's topic and approximate date, you still may have to search through all sections of the book to find out where to obtain the report.

Unlike manual databases, computer-automated databases can easily obtain information to meet virtually any criteria you specify.

This is the real power of a database—the capacity to examine the data any way you want to look at it. Queries, by definition, ask questions about the data stored in the database. After you create a query, you can use its data for reports, forms, and graphs.

What is a query?

The word *query* is from the Latin word *quærere*, which means to ask or inquire. Over the years, the word "query" has become synonymous with quiz, challenge, inquire, or question. Therefore, you can think of a query as a question or inquiry posed to the database about information found in its tables.

A Microsoft Access query is a question that you ask about the information stored in your Access tables. The way you ask questions about this information is by using the query tools. Your query can be a simple question about information stored in a single table, or it can be a complex question about information stored in several tables. After you ask the question, Microsoft Access returns only the information you requested.

Using queries this way, you can ask the Mountain Animal Hospital database to show you only the dogs that are named within it. To see the dogs' names, you need to retrieve information from the Pets table. Figure 9-1 is a typical Query Design window.

After you create and run a query, Microsoft Access can return and display the set of records you asked for in a datasheet. This set of records is called a *dynaset*, which is the set of records selected by a query. As you've seen, a datasheet looks just like a spreadsheet, with its rows of records and columns of fields. The datasheet can display many records simultaneously.

You can query information from a single table easily using the Search and Filter capabilities of the datasheet view of a table (Filter by Selection and Filter by Form, as you did in Chapter 6). In addition to viewing information from one table, you can create a query and view common information from two or more tables at the same time. Many database queries, however, require information from several tables.

Suppose, for example, that you want to send a reminder to everyone living in a certain state, of a tri-state area, that their dog or cat is due for its annual vaccination. This type of query requires getting information from two tables: Customer and Pets.

Cross-Reference

You may want Access to show you a single datasheet of all customers and their pets that meet your specified criteria. Access can retrieve customer names and cities from the Customer table and then pet names, animal type, and current vaccination status from the Pets table. Access then takes the information that's common to your criteria, combines it, and displays all the information in a single datasheet. This datasheet is the result of a query that draws from both the Customer and Pets tables. The database query performed the work of assembling all the information for you.

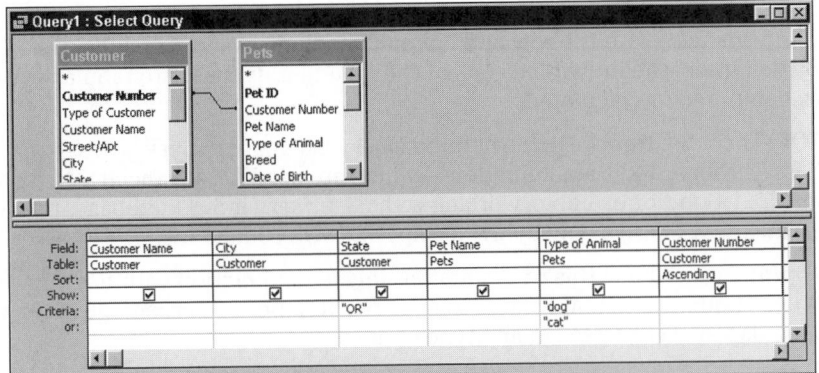

Figure 9-1: A typical two-table select query. This query will display the customer and pet names for all customers who live in Oregon and whose pets are a dog or cat.

If you click the datasheet button on the toolbar you will see that the query shows 15 records that match the query that was designed in Figure 9-1. This is a relatively easy query to design once you understand how the query design tool works. This query design has many of the elements present that show the power of the Access query engine — sorting a resulting dynaset, specifying multi-field criteria, and even using a complex Or condition in one of those fields.

Cross-Reference In this chapter, you work with only a single table — the Pets table; Part III covers multiple tables.

Types of queries

Access supports many different types of queries. They can be grouped into six basic categories:

✦ **Select.** These are the most common types of query. As its name implies, the select query selects information from one or more tables (based on specific criteria), creating a dynaset and displaying this information in a datasheet that you can use to view and analyze specific data; you can make changes to your data in the underlying tables.

✦ **Total.** These are special versions of select queries. Total queries provide the capability to sum or produce totals (such as count) in a select query. When you select this type of query, Access adds a Total row in the QBE (Query by Example) pane.

✦ **Action.** These queries enable you to create new tables (Make Tables) or change data (delete, update, and append) in existing tables. When you make changes to records in a select query, the changes must be made one record at a time. In action queries, changes can be made to many records during a single operation.

✦ **Crosstab.** These queries can display summary data in cross-tabular form like a spreadsheet, with the row and column headings based on fields in the table. By definition, the individual cells of the resultant dynaset are tabular — that is, computed or calculated.

✦ **SQL.** There are three SQL (Structured Query Language) query types — Union, Pass-Through, and Data Definition — which are used for advanced SQL database manipulation (for example, working with client/server SQL databases). You can create these queries only by writing specific SQL commands.

✦ **Top(n).** You can use this query limiter only in conjunction with the other five types of queries. It enables you to specify a number or percentage of the top records you want to see in any type of query.

Query capabilities

Queries are flexible. They provide the capability of looking at your data in virtually any way you can think of. Most database systems are continually evolving, developing more powerful and necessary tools. The original purpose they are designed for changes over time. You may decide that you want to look at the information stored in the database in a different way. Because information is stored in a database, you should be able to look at it in this new way. Looking at data in a way that's different from its intended manner is known as performing *ad hoc* queries. Querying tools are among the most powerful and flexible features of your Access database. Here is a sampling of what you can do:

✦ **Choose tables.** You can obtain information from a single table or from many tables that are related by some common data. Suppose you're interested in seeing the customer name along with the type of animals each customer owns. This sample task takes information from the Customer and Pets tables. When using several tables, Access returns the data in a combined single datasheet.

✦ **Choose fields.** You can specify which fields from each table you want to see in the resultant dynaset. For example, you can look at the customer name, customer ZIP code, animal name, and animal type separated from all the other fields in the Customer or Pets table.

✦ **Choose records.** You can select the records to display in the dynaset by specifying criteria. For example, you may want to see records for dogs only.

✦ **Sort records.** You may want to see the dynaset information sorted in a specific order. You may need, for example, to see customers in order by last name and first name.

✦ **Perform calculations.** You can use queries to perform calculations on your data. You may be interested in performing such calculations as averaging, totaling, or simply counting the fields.

✦ **Create tables.** You may need another database table formed from the combined data resulting from a query. The query can create this new table based on the dynaset.

✦ **Create forms and reports based on a query.** The dynaset you create from a query may have just the right fields and data that you need for a report or form. When you base your form or report on a query, every time you print the report or open the form, your query will retrieve the most current information from your tables.

✦ **Create graphs based on queries.** You can create graphs from the data in a query, which you can then use in a form or report.

✦ **Use a query as a source of data for other queries (subquery).** You can create additional queries based on a set of records that you selected in a previous query. This is very useful for performing ad hoc queries, where you may repeatedly make small changes to the criteria. The secondary query can be used to change the criteria while the primary query and its data remain intact.

✦ **Make changes to tables.** Access queries can obtain information from a wide range of sources. You can ask questions about data stored in dBASE, Paradox, Btrieve, and Microsoft SQL Server databases.

How dynasets work

Access takes the records that result from a query and displays them in a datasheet, in which the actual records are called a dynaset. Physically, a dynaset looks like a table; in fact, it is not a table. The dynaset is a *dynamic* (or virtual) set of records. *This dynamic set of records is not stored in the database.*

Note

When you close a query, the query dynaset is gone; it no longer exists. Even though the dynaset itself no longer exists, the data that formed the dynaset remains stored in the underlying tables.

When you run a query, Access places the resultant records in the dynaset. When you save the query, the information is not saved; only the structure of the query is saved — the tables, fields, sort order, record limitations, query type, and so forth. Consider these benefits of *not* saving the dynaset to a physical table:

✦ A smaller amount of space on a storage device (usually a hard disk) is needed.

✦ The query uses updated versions of any records changed since the query was last run.

Every time the query is executed, it reads the underlying tables and recreates the dynaset. Because dynasets themselves are not stored, a query automatically reflects any changes to the underlying tables made since the last time the query was executed — even in a real-time, multi-user environment.

Creating a Query

After you create your tables and place data in them, you are ready to work with queries. To begin a query, follow these steps:

1. From the Database window, click the Queries Objects button.

2. Click the New button, third button from left.

   The New Query dialog box appears, as shown in Figure 9-2. You select from the five choices. The first choice displays the Query Design window.

3. Select Design View and click the OK button.

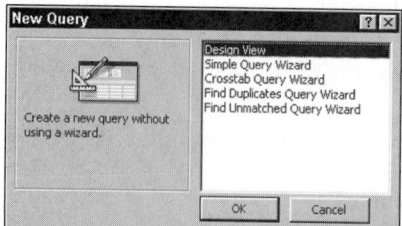

Figure 9-2: The New Query dialog box is activated by clicking the New button in the query container.

Figure 9-3 shows two windows. The underlying window is the Query Design window. The accompanying Show Table dialog box is *nonmodal*, which means that you must do something in the dialog box before continuing with the query. Before you continue, you should add tables for the query to work with; in this case, the Pets table is highlighted to be added.

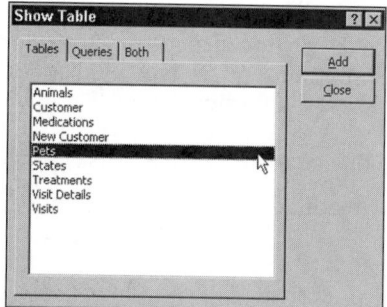

Figure 9-3: The Show Table dialog box in the Query Design window

Selecting a table

The Show Table dialog box shown in Figure 9-3 displays all tables and queries in your database. Whether you are using the Mountain Animal Hospital or Mountain Animal Start databases, you should see all the tables in the Mountain Animal Hospital database. You can add the Pets table to the query design with these steps:

1. Select the Pets table from the Show Table dialog box.

2. Click the Add button to add the Pets table to the Query Design window. Or you can double-click the table name instead of pressing the Add button.

3. Click the Close button.

   When starting a new query, you can alternatively click the New Object button on the toolbar of the Database window (when the Query container is active) and choose Query. If you have already selected and opened a table or query before you start a new query, Access will assume you want to use the table or query already opened and load the selected table or query automatically.

While in Query Design mode, you can activate the Show Table dialog box to add more tables at any time; select Query ⇨ Show Table or click the Show Table button (picture of table with plus sign).

Tip You can also add tables by moving the mouse to any empty place in the top-half of the window (the Table/Query pane) and clicking the right mouse button to activate the shortcut menu. Then select Show Table.

When you want to delete a table from the Table/Query pane, click the table name in the query/table entry pane (the upper portion of the window shown in Figure 9-4 — currently containing a single table — Pets) and either click Delete or select Query ⇨ Remove Table.

Tip You also can add a table to the Query/Table Pane by selecting the Database window and dragging and dropping a table name from the Table window into the Query window.

Using the Query window

The Query window has two main views, the Design View and the Datasheet View. The difference between them is self-explanatory: The Design View is where you create the query, and the Datasheet View is where you display the query's dynaset.

The Query Design window should now look like Figure 9-4, with the Pets table displayed in the top half of the Query Design window.

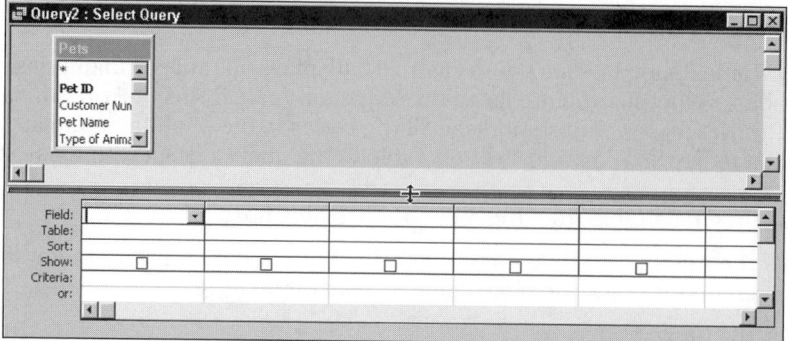

Figure 9-4: The Query Design window with the Pets table in the upper pane and the bottom pane currently empty. Notice that the bar between the two panes is dark: this is the pane-resizing bar that has been clicked to activate it.

The Query Design window is currently in the Design View; it consists of two panes:

✦ The table/query entry pane

✦ The Query by Example (QBE) design pane (also called the QBE grid)

The table/query entry pane, the upper pane, is where tables and/or queries and their design structures are displayed. The visual representation of the table is a small window inside the table/query entry pane. It shows the table name in the title bar of this small window and displays all the fields in the listbox of the window. This window can be resized by clicking on the edges and dragging it right or down to make it wider or longer.

The Query by Example (QBE) pane, the lower pane, is used for holding the field names that will be displayed and any criteria that will be used by the query. Each column in the QBE design pane contains information about a single field from a table or query in the upper pane.

Navigating the Query Design window

The title bar at the top of the Query Design window bears information about a particular window, the type of query, and the query name. Any new query is named Query1. Note that the title bar in Figure 9-4 displays the query type and name as Query1: Select Query.

The two windowpanes are separated horizontally by a pane-resizing bar. This bar, the dark line between the panes in Figure 9-4, is used to resize the panes. To enlarge the upper pane, click the bar and drag it down or drag the bar up to enlarge the lower pane. When you move the mouse pointer over the pane-resizing bar, the pointer turns into a small line with an arrow pointing up and another pointing down.

You switch between the upper and lower panes either by clicking the desired pane or by pressing F6 to move to the other pane. Each pane has scrollbars to help you move around.

Tip   If you make the Pets design structure longer, you can see more fields at one time. If you make it wider, you can see more of a field's name. To see more fields, first make the top pane larger; then size the Pets structure vertically.

You write the query by dragging fields from the upper pane to the lower pane of the Query window. After placing fields on the QBE pane (lower pane), you can set their display order by dragging a field from its current position to a new position in the pane.

Using the Query Design toolbar

The toolbar in the Query Design window contains several buttons specific to building and working with queries, as shown in Figure 9-5.

Figure 9-5: The default Query Design toolbar, with 21 buttons

This toolbar has many buttons that can be helpful when designing your queries. Although they will be used and explained as they are used in the query chapters of this book, the primary buttons that will be used are listed below:

✦ **View (first button).** This button is used to switch between the Datasheet View and Design View of the query. It also enables you to display the underlying SQL statement that was created in the Query (more on this later).

✦ **Save (second button).** This button is used to save the query as you are working on it. It is a good idea to save your work often, especially when creating complex queries.

✦ **Query Type (twelfth button).** The button with two datasheets overlapping each other with a pull-down menu arrow, is the Query type menu. It can be found underneath the Window menu item on the menu bar. It is used to specify the type of query you want to create.

✦ **Run (thirteenth button, an exclamation point).** This button is used to run a query. When working with Select Queries, as in this chapter, it simply displays the datasheet — serving the same function as the View button (first button). However, when working with action queries that will be covered in later chapters, it will actually run the series of actions specified by the user in the query.

✦ **Show Table (fourteenth button).** This button will activate the Show Table dialog box and enable you to add additional tables to the query.

The remaining buttons are used for more advanced queries, create quick reports and forms, show the database window, print the contents of the query, or copy/paste actions.

Using the QBE pane of the Query Design window

As you saw earlier, Figure 9-4 displays an empty Query Design pane (QBE grid), which has six named rows:

✦ **Field.** This row is where field names are entered or added.

✦ **Table.** This row shows the table the field is from (useful in queries with multiple tables).

✦ **Sort.** This row enables you to enter sort directives for the query.

✦ **Show.** This check box determines whether to display the field in the resulting dynaset.

✦ **Criteria.** This row is where you enter the first line of criteria to limit the record selection.

✦ **or.** This row is the first of a number of rows to which you can add multiple values to be used in criteria selection.

You learn more about these rows as you create queries in this chapter.

Selecting Fields

There are several ways to add fields to a query. You can add fields one at a time, select and add multiple fields, or select and add all fields. You can use your keyboard or mouse to add the fields.

Adding a single field

You can add a single field in several ways. One method is to double-click the field name in the field list (also called a table window); the field name will immediately appear in the first available column in the QEB pane. You can also add a field graphically to the QEB pane by following these steps:

1. Highlight the field name in the table window located in the table/query entry area, in this case the Pet Name.

2. Click the Pet Name field, and while holding the pointer down, drag the Field icon, which appears as you move the mouse, toward the QBE Design pane.

3. Drop the Field icon in the desired column of the QBE Design pane.

The Field icon looks like a small rectangle when it is inside the Pets table. As the mouse is dragged outside the Pets table, the icon changes to a circle-with-slash (the international symbol for "no"), which means that you cannot drop the Field icon in that location. When this icon enters any column in the QBE column, the field name appears in the Field: row. Figure 9-6 shows the Field icon (it looks like a small rectangle) being added to the second column of the QBE pane. If you drop the Field icon between two other fields, it appears between those fields and pushes all existing fields to the right.

Figure 9-6: Adding fields in the QBE Design pane (grid). In the first column of the QBE pane, lower half, clicking the down arrow reveals a drop-down list from which you can select a field. The second column shows the Field icon as it is being dragged from the Table field list in the upper pane of the window.

Tip   If you select a field accidentally, you can deselect it by releasing the mouse button while the icon is the No symbol.

Another way to add fields to the QBE Design pane is to click an empty Field: cell in the QBE Design pane and then type the field name in the field cell. Another method is to select the field you want from the drop-down list that appears when you click the down arrow button in the Field: cell of the QBE pane. Figure 9.6 shows selecting the Pet ID field from the drop-down list.

After you have selected your fields, you can run your query to see the results. To run the query, click the Datasheet button on the toolbar (the first icon from the left). When you are finished, click the Design button on the toolbar (the first one on the left) to return to design mode. You can also run the query by clicking the Run icon on your toolbar with the exclamation point on it, or by selecting Query ➪ Run. To return to the design window, click the Design View button on your toolbar (the first icon from the left).

Figure 9-6 is actually a conglomerate of two different actions — selecting a field using the Field icon, as in column two, and using the drop-down list in column one. These actions are mutually exclusive — in other words, you will not be able to duplicate this figure by doing both actions. Each action is independent of the other.

Adding multiple fields

You can add more than one field at a time by selecting the fields you want to place in the query and then dragging and dropping the selection in the QBE pane. The selected fields do not have to be contiguous (one after the other). Figure 9-7 illustrates the process of adding multiple fields. Notice that three of the fields are contiguous and the fourth is further down in the table structure.

Figure 9-7: Selecting several fields graphically to move to the QBE Design pane. Notice that the field icon comprises three fields — this tells you that you are adding more than one field to the QBE pane.

To add ***multiple contiguous fields***, follow these steps:

1. Remove any existing fields in the QBE pane by selecting Edit ➪ Clear Grid from the menu.

2. Highlight in the table/query entry area the first field name that you want to add — in this case Pet Name.

3. Hold the Shift key down and click the last field that you want to select — in this case Breed. (All the fields in-between will be selected as well.)

4. Click the selected fields and drag the Multiple Field icon, which appears as you move the mouse. The icon appears as a group of three field icons.

5. Drop the Multiple Field icon in the desired column of the QBE Design pane.

To add *multiple noncontiguous fields* to the query, follow these steps:

1. Remove any existing fields in the QBE pane by selecting Edit ⇨ Clear Grid from the menu.

2. Highlight in the table/query entry area the first field name that you want to add; for this example, click the Pets ID field.

3. Hold the Ctrl key down and click each field that you want to select. (Only the fields you select are highlighted.) For this example, click the Pet Name, Breed, and Date of Birth fields.

4. Click the selected fields and drag the Multiple Field icon, which appears as you move the mouse. The icon appears as a group of three field icons.

5. Drop the Multiple Field icon in the desired column of the QBE Design pane.

Notice that in the second example you selected two fields that were contiguous — using the non-contiguous method. You can select any field using the Ctrl key — contiguous or non-contiguous — but you can select only one field at a time.

Adding all table fields

In addition to adding fields (either in groups or individually), you can move all the fields to the QBE pane at once. Access gives you two methods for choosing all fields: dragging all fields as a group or selecting the all-field reference tag — the asterisk (*).

Dragging all fields as a group

To select all the fields of a table, perform these steps:

1. Remove any existing fields in the QBE pane by selecting Edit ⇨ Clear Grid from the menu.

2. Double-click the title bar of the table to select all the fields.

3. Point to any of the selected fields with the mouse.

4. Drag the Multiple Field icon to the QBE pane.

This method fills in each column of the QBE pane automatically. All the fields are added to the QBE pane from left to right, based on their field order in the Pets table. By default, Access displays only the fields that can fit in the window. You can change the column width of each field to display more or fewer columns.

Selecting the all-field reference tag

The first object (above the field names) in the Pets table is an asterisk, which appears at the top of the field list. When you select all fields by using the asterisk, you don't see the fields in the QBE Design pane; Pets.* in the Field: row indicates that all Pets table fields are selected. (This example assumes that the QBE Design pane is empty when you drag the asterisk from the Pets table to the QBE Design pane.)

The asterisk places the fields in a single Field: cell. Dragging multiple fields with the first technique added actual table field names to the Query Design window; each field is in a separate Field: cell across the QBE pane. If you change the table design later, you must change the design of the query, too. By using the asterisk for selecting all fields, you won't have to change the query later if you add, delete, or rename fields in the underlying table or query. (Access automatically adds or removes fields that change in the underlying table or query.)

To add the all-fields reference tag to the Query Design pane, follow these steps:

1. Remove any existing fields in the QBE pane by selecting Edit ➪ Clear Grid from the menu.

2. Click the asterisk (*) in the Pets table to select this field.

3. Click the selected field and drag the Field icon to the first cell in the QBE Design pane.

The all-fields reference tag is in the QBE pane. This query displays the Pets fields.

Displaying the Dynaset

With the all fields reference tag (asterisks) selected, display the resultant dynaset by selecting either View ➪ Datasheet or the Datasheet button on the toolbar. The datasheet should look like Figure 9-8. You can also display the dynaset by clicking the explanation point icon or selecting Query ➪ Run from your Access menu.

Pet ID	Customer Number	Pet Name	Type of Animal	Breed	Date of Birth
AC001-01	AC001	Bobo	RABBIT	Long Ear	04/01/1996
AC001-02	AC001	Presto Chango	LIZARD	Chameleon	05/01/1995
AC001-03	AC001	Stinky	SKUNK		08/01/1999
AC001-04	AC001	Fido	DOG	German Shepherd	06/01/1995
AD001-01	AD001	Patty	PIG	Potbelly	02/01/1999
AD001-02	AD001	Rising Sun	HORSE	Palomino	04/01/1997
AD002-01	AD002	Dee Dee	DOG	Mixed	02/01/1999
AK001-01	AK001	Margo	SQUIRREL	Gray	03/01/1999
AK001-02	AK001	Tom	CAT	Tabby	02/01/1996
AK001-03	AK001	Jerry	RAT	Hooded	02/01/1998
BA001-01	BA001	Swimmy	DOLPHIN	Bottlenose	07/01/1996
BA001-03	BA001	Daffy	DUCK	Mallard	09/01/1999
BA001-05	BA001	Jake	DOLPHIN	Bottlenose	04/01/1992
BR001-01	BR001	Suzie	DOG	Mixed	01/01/2000
BR002-01	BR002	John Boy	DOG	Mixed	04/01/1998
EP001-01	EP001	Mikos	WOLF	Timber	11/01/1997

Record: ◄◄ ◄ [1] ► ►► ►* of 53

Figure 9-8: The datasheet of the Pets table with all the fields selected for the query using the asterisks, or all-field reference tag (*)

Working with the datasheet

Access displays the dynaset (resulting view of records of the query) in a datasheet. The techniques for navigating a query datasheet, as well as for changing its field order and working with its columns and rows, are exactly the same as for the other datasheets you worked with in Chapter 7.

Access 2002 enables you to sort and filter the results of a datasheet created by a query. All data in Access 2002 is editable all the time.

Changing data in the query datasheet

The query datasheet offers you an easy and convenient way to change data quickly. You can add and change data in the dynaset, and it will be saved to the underlying tables.

When you're adding or changing data in the datasheet, all the table properties defined at the table level are in effect. For example, you cannot enter a gender of X for any animal (only M, F, or U are accepted).

Returning to the query design

To return to the query design mode, select the Design View button on the toolbar (the first button on the left).

Tip   You can also toggle between the design and datasheet mode by selecting View ⇨ Datasheet View or View ⇨ Design View from the Query menu.

Caution   Clear the query grid by selecting Edit ⇨ Clear Grid. Next, add all the fields to the query grid by double-clicking the Pets data structure title bar and dragging all the selected fields to the query grid.

Working with Fields

There are times when you want to work with the fields you've already selected — rearranging their order, inserting a new field, or deleting an existing field. You may even want to add a field to the QBE pane without showing it in the datasheet.

Selecting a field

Before you can move a field's position, you must first select it. To select it you will work with the *field selector row*.

The field selector row is the narrow gray row above the Field: row of each column. This row is approximately half the size of the others; it's important to identify this row because this is where you select columns, either single or multiple columns. Recall that each column represents a field. To select the Pet Name field, move the mouse pointer until a small selection arrow (in this case, a dark downward arrow) is visible in the selector row and then click the column. Figure 9-9 shows the selection arrow above the Pet Name column just before it is selected.

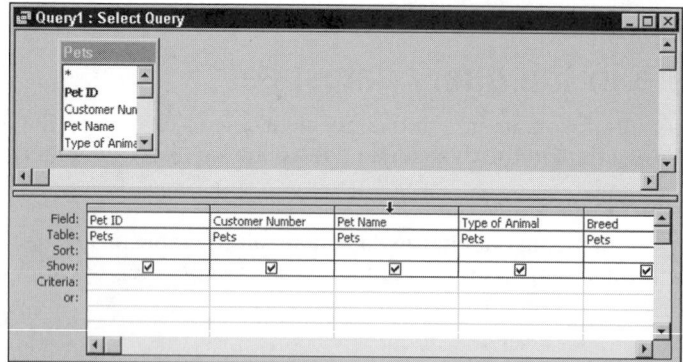

Figure 9-9: Selecting a column in the QBE pane. The pointer changes to a down-pointing arrow when you move over the selection row. After the arrow changes, you can click the selection row and the entire column will be highlighted.

Tip

You can select multiple contiguous fields by clicking the first field you wish to select and then dragging across the field selector bars of the other fields.

Caution

Extend mode will also enable you to chose more than one contiguous field in the QBE pane. If extend mode (F8) is on, you must first move the cursor into the column of the field that you wish to select (by clicking in any field) This moves the insertion point (I cursor) into the row whose column you want to select. If the insertion point is in an adjacent column and you select a column, you will select the adjacent column (containing the insertion point) as well. To deactivate extend mode (EXT), press the Esc key. You can see that EXT mode is active by looking at the bottom frame of Access — the letters EXT will be active on the right side of the frame (about a quarter of the way in).

Changing field order

After your fields are selected, you can move them. (Of course you could delete all the fields and conditions and start the query over — although this method can be bothersome.) With the fields selected, you can move the fields on the QBE design by simply dragging them, as you have learned to move columns in a datasheet. Follow these steps to move a field:

1. Add several fields to the QBE pane.

2. Select the field you want to move (Pet Name) by clicking the field selector above the field name. The column is highlighted — as the Pet Name field is in Figure 9-10.

3. Click and hold the field selector again; the QBE Field icon, a small graphical box, appears under the arrow.

4. While holding down the left mouse button, drag the column to its new position (in this case, to the left of Customer Name).

5. Release the left mouse button to drop the field in its new position.

Figure 9-10 shows the Pet Name field highlighted (selected). As you move the selector field to the left, the column separator between the fields Pet ID and Customer Number changes (gets wider) to show you where Pet Name will go.

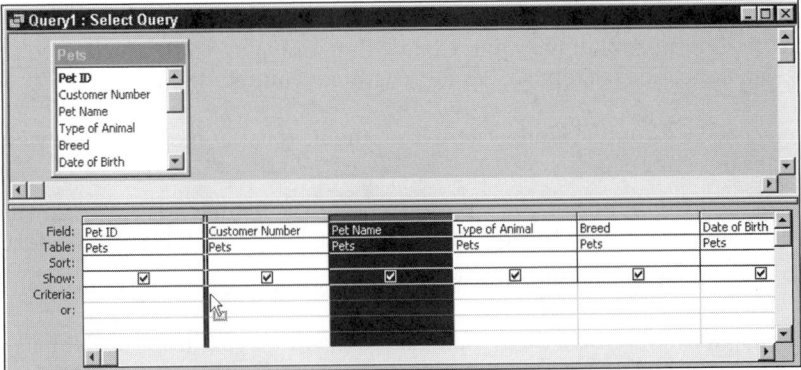

Figure 9-10: Moving the Pet Name field to between Pet ID and Customer Number. Notice the QBE field icon below the arrow near the Customer Number column.

Resizing columns in design mode

The QBE pane generally shows about 5 or 6 field columns in the viewable area of your screen — the remaining fields can be viewed by moving the horizontal scroll bar along the bottom of the window.

There are times that you may want to show more fields than those visible on the screen. You can resize the width of the field columns to make them smaller (or larger to show less) by moving the mouse pointer between the field selectors of the fields you want to adjust. After you have moved it between the two field selectors, the pointer turns into a thick vertical bar with arrows pointing to the left and right. With the sizing pointer you can drag left or right to adjust the width of the column.

Removing a field

You can remove a field from the QBE Design pane. Select the field or fields to be deleted in the QBE Design pane, and then press Delete or select Edit ⇨ Delete. To remove the Customer Number field from the QBE Design pane, follow these steps:

1. Select the Customer Number field (or any other field) by clicking the field selector above the field name.

2. Press Delete.

Tip   If the field is not selected but the insertion point is in it, you can select Edit ⇨ Delete Column. You can delete all the fields in the QBE Design pane in a single operation: Select Edit ⇨ Clear Grid from the Query Design window's menu bar.

Inserting a field

You insert fields from the table/query entry pane in the QBE Design pane by selecting field(s) from the table/query entry pane, then dragging your selection to the QBE Design pane. These steps insert the Customer Number field:

1. Select the Customer Number field from the field list in the table/query entry pane (top pane).

2. Drag the field to the column where you want the field. If it is to go between two columns, put it to the left side of the column you want it to go before.

3. Drop the field by releasing the left mouse button.

Dragging a field to the QBE Design pane inserts it where you drop the field. If you drop it on another field, it is inserted before that field. Double-clicking the field in the table/query entry pane appends the field to the Field: list in the QBE Design pane.

Changing the field display name

To make the query datasheet easier to read, you can rename the fields in your query. The new names become the tag headings in the datasheet of the query. To rename the field Breed to Lineage, follow these steps:

1. Click to the left of the B in Breed in the Field: row of the QBE Design pane.

2. Type Lineage and a colon (:) between the new name and the old field name.

The heading now is Lineage:Breed. When the datasheet appears, you see *Lineage*.

Note   Changing the datasheet caption changes *only* the name of the heading for that field in the datasheet. It does *not* change the field name in the underlying table.

Showing table names

Multiple tables can make it difficult to determine where a field has come. That's why the Table: row automatically shows where a field came from.

When you select a field for display in the QBE pane, the name of the source table is shown in the row directly below the field name. If you want to hide this row, click View ➪ Table Names as shown in Figure 9-11. The row with the table names disappears. To view the tables, follow the same procedure to turn it on.

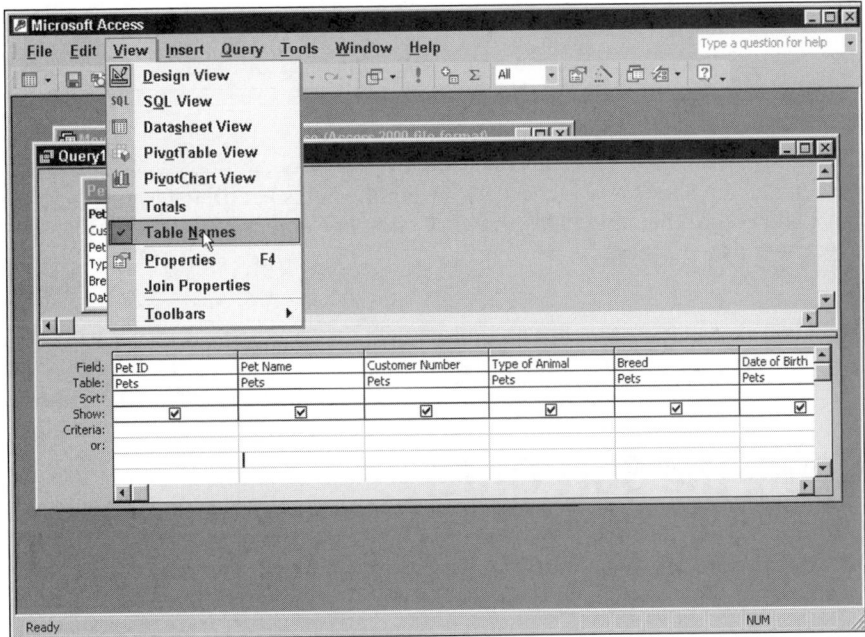

Figure 9-11: View/Hide Table: Row. You can hide the Table: row by selecting View ➪ Table Names from the Access Menu.

Showing a field

While performing queries, you may want to temporarily show only some of the fields. Suppose, for example, that you want to show only the fields Pet ID, Pet Name, and Breed. You can delete all other fields (and restore them when you're done with the dynaset), or you can simply indicate which fields you want to see in the datasheet.

When you select fields, Access automatically makes every field a displayed field. Every Show: property is displayed with a check mark in the box.

To deselect a field's Show: property, simply click the field's Show: box. The box clears, as you see in Figure 9-12. To reselect the field later, simply click the Show: box again.

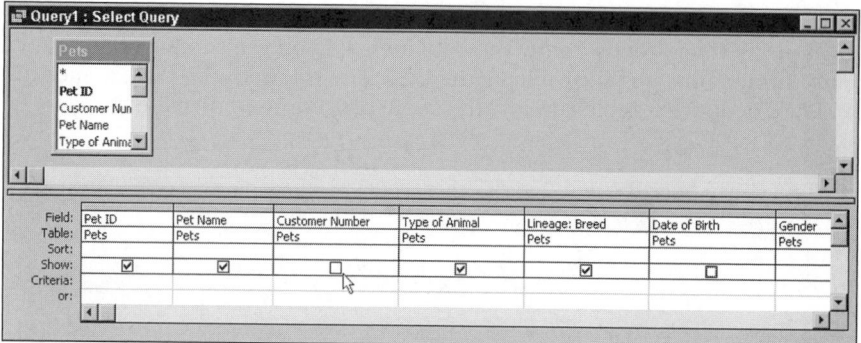

Figure 9-12: The Show: row is checked only for the fields Pet ID, Pet Name, Type of Animal and Breed. The other fields shown, Customer Name, and Date of Birth have the Show: check box unchecked.

Caution

If you save a query that has an unused field (its Show: box is unchecked), Access eliminates the field from the query pane.

Changing the Sort Order

When viewing a dynaset, you may want to display the data in a sorted order. You may want to sort the dynaset to make it easier to analyze the data (for example, to look at all the pets in order by Type of Animal).

Sorting places the records in alphabetical or numeric order. The sort order can be ascending (0 to 9 and A to Z) or descending (9 to 0 and Z to A).

Just as Access has a Show: property row for fields, there is a Sort: property row for fields in the QBE Design pane. In the following section, you learn to set this property.

Specifying a sort

To sort the records in the datasheet by Type of Animal in ascending order, perform these steps:

1. Using the same query in Figure 9-12, click the Sort: cell for the Type of Animal field. An arrow appears in the cell.

2. Click the down arrow at the right of the cell.

3. Select Ascending from the list.

Figure 9-13 shows the QBE pane with the Type of Animal field selected for sorting by ascending order. Notice that the word Ascending is being selected in the field's Sort: cell.

Note   You *cannot* sort on a Memo or an OLE object field.

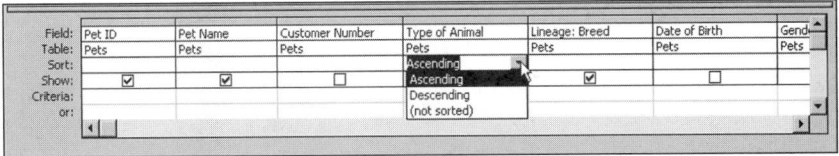

Figure 9-13: The Type of Animal field has been selected to sort by Ascending order (0 to 9, A to Z).

Sorting on more than one field

Access gives you the capability of sorting on multiple fields. You may, for example, want a primary sort order by Type of Animal and a secondary sort order by Breed. To create this query, start with the query illustrated in Figure 9-13. Notice that the Breed field (Lineage: Breed) is after the Type of Animal field (to the right). Finally, add a sort to the Breed field by selecting Ascending in the Sort: cell.

Access always sorts the leftmost sort field first — this is known as *sort order precedence*. To make sure that Access understands how you want to sort your data, you must arrange the fields in order from left to right according to sort-order precedence. You can easily change the sort order by selecting a sort field and moving it relative to another sort field. Access corrects the sort order automatically.

That's all there is to it. Now the dynaset is arranged in order by two different fields. Figure 9-14 shows the multiple-field sort criteria. The sort order is controlled by the order of the fields in the QBE pane (from left to right); therefore, this dynaset is displayed in order first by Type of Animal and then by Breed, as shown in Figure 9-15. Also note that Breed has been renamed Lineage in the column header of the datasheet in Figure 9-15. This was done earlier in the section titled "Change the field name display."

Field:	Pet ID	Pet Name	Customer Number	Type of Animal	Lineage: Breed	Date of Birth	Gend-
Table:	Pets	Pets	Pets	Pets	Pets	Pets	Pets
Sort:				Ascending	Ascending		
Show:	☑	☑	☐	☑	☑	☐	
Criteria:							
or:							

Figure 9-14: Multiple-field sort criteria. The order of the fields is critical. It will sort first by the left-most field and then sub-sort by the next field to the right.

Query1 : Select Query

Pet ID	Pet Name	Type of Animal	Lineage	Gender	Colors
R001-07	Tigger	CAT	Barn	M	Black/Grey/white
WI001-01	Flower	CAT	Burmese	F	Brown
IR001-05	Ceasar	CAT	Domestic	M	Grey
WI001-02	Shadow	CAT	Domestic	F	Black
IR001-03	Shadow	CAT	Long Hair	M	White/Grey
IR001-04	Romeo	CAT	Mouser	F	Black/Grey
PR001-03	Little Bit	CAT	Mouser	F	Mixed
IR001-02	Jimeny	CAT	Siamese	M	White/Grey/Black
AK001-02	Tom	CAT	Tabby	M	Tan/White
IR001-06	Jameo	CAT	Tabby	F	Black/Grey
IR001-01	D.C.	CAT	Tabby	F	White/Brown/Gre
MP002-03	Powder Puff	DEER	White Tail	F	Brown
EP001-02	Museum Rm 7	DINOSAUR	Stegosauras	U	Brown
MC001-01	Rex	DOG	Boxer	M	Brown/white

Record: ◄◄ ◄ 1 ► ►► ►* of 53

Figure 9-15: A dynaset sorted — first by Type of Animal and then by Breed (Lineage)

Displaying Only Selected Records

So far, you've been working with all the records of the Pets table. There are times when you may want to work only with selected records in the Pets table. For example, you may want to look only at records where the value of Type of Animal is DOG. Access makes it easy for you to specify a record's criteria.

Tip   If you are following along with the examples, start a new query using the Pets table and select all the fields before continuing.

Understanding record criteria

Record criteria are simply some rule or rules that you supply for Access to follow. These criteria tell Access which records you want to look at in the dynaset. A typical criterion could be "all male animals," or "only those animals that are not currently vaccinated," or "all animals that were born before January 2000."

In other words, with record criteria, you create limiting filters to tell Access which records to find and which to leave out of the dynaset.

You specify criteria starting in the Criteria: property row of the QBE pane. Here you designate criteria with an expression. The expression can be simple example data or can take the form of complex expressions using predefined functions.

As an example of a simple data criterion, type DOG in the Criteria: cell of Type of Animal. The datasheet displays only records for dogs.

Entering simple character criteria

Character-type criteria are entered into fields that accommodate the Text data type. To use such criteria, type in an example of the data contained within the field. To limit the record display to DOG, follow these steps:

1. Click the Criteria: cell in the Type of Animal column in the QBE Design pane.

2. Type DOG in the cell.

3. Click the Datasheet button.

Only the dogs are displayed — in this case 12 records. Observe that you did not enter an equal sign or place quotes around the sample text, yet Access added double quotes around the value. Access, unlike many other applications, automatically makes assumptions about what you want. This is an illustration of its flexibility. You could enter the expression in any of these other ways:

✦ Dog

✦ = Dog

✦ "Dog"

✦ = "Dog"

In Figure 9-16, the expression "DOG" is entered under Type of Animal; the double quote marks were placed around the example DOG automatically by Access.

Figure 9-16 is an excellent example for demonstrating the options for various types of simple character criteria. You could just as well type Not Dog in the criteria column, to say the opposite. In this instance, you would be asking to see all records for animals that are not dogs, adding only Not before the example text Dog.

Generally, when dealing with character data, you enter equalities, inequalities, or a list of values that are acceptable.

With either of these examples, Dog or Not Dog, you entered a simple expression in a Text-type field. Access took your example and interpreted it to show you all records that equal the example data you placed in the Criteria: cell.

Field:	Pet ID	Customer Number	Pet Name	Type of Animal	Breed	Date of Birth
Table:	Pets	Pets	Pets	Pets	Pets	Pets
Sort:						
Show:	☑	☑	☑	☑	☑	☑
Criteria:				"DOG"		
or:						

Figure 9-16: Specifying character criteria. You can type an example of the type of records you want to view. In this case, all DOGs — so you type DOG in the criteria field of the Type of Animal field.

This capability is a powerful tool. Consider that you have only to supply an example and Access not only interprets it but also uses it to create the query dynaset. This is exactly what Query by Example means: You enter an example and let the database build a query based on this data.

To erase the criteria in the cell, select the contents and press Delete, or select the contents and select Edit ➪ Delete from the Query Design window's menu bar. You can also select Edit ➪ Undo Cell Edit to revert to the previous content (in this case a blank cell).

On the CD-ROM If you are following the examples, delete the criterion (DOG) in the Type of Animal field before continuing.

Entering other simple criteria

You can also specify criteria for Numeric, Date, and Yes/No fields. Suppose, for example, that you want to look only at records for animals born after January 1, 1993. To limit the display to records where the value of Date of Birth is greater than June 30, 1999, follow these steps:

1. Remove any existing fields in the QBE pane by selecting Edit ➪ Clear Grid from the menu.

2. Add the following fields: Pet Name, Type of Animal, Breed, and Date of Birth to the QBE grid.

3. Click the Criteria: cell in the Date of Birth column in the QBE Design pane.

4. Type > 06/30/99 in the cell.

5. Click the Datasheet button.

Access displays records of pets that were born after 6/30/1999 — in this example it will display 13 records.

Access also compares Date fields to a value by using comparison operators, such as less than (<), greater than (>), equal to (=), or a combination thereof. Notice that Access automatically adds pound-sign (#) delimiters around the date value. Access recognizes these delimiters as differentiating a Date field from Text fields. It's the same as entering text data examples; however, you don't have to enter the pound signs. Access understands what you want (based on the type of data entered in the field), and it converts the entry format for you.

Printing a Query Dynaset

After you create your query, you can quickly print all the records in the dynaset. Although you can't specify a type of report, you can print a simple matrix-type report (rows and columns) of the dynaset that your query created.

You do have some flexibility when printing a dynaset. If you know that the datasheet is set up just as you want, you can specify some options as you follow these steps:

1. Use the datasheet you just created for pets born after 6/30/1999.

2. Switch to the query datasheet mode by clicking the Datasheet button on the toolbar.

3. Select File ⇨ Print from the Query Datasheet window's menu bar.

4. Specify the print options that you want in the Print dialog box.

5. Click the OK button in the Print dialog box.

Tip In Step 3 above, you could have also pressed the Print button on the toolbar to immediately create a report of the datasheet and send it to the default Windows printer. If you print the datasheet this way, you will not have to do Steps 4 or 5.

Access now prints the dynaset for you if have set up a default printer in Microsoft Windows. Your dataset prints out in the font selected for display or in the nearest equivalent your printer offers. The printout also reflects all layout options in effect when you print the dataset. Hidden columns do not print; gridlines print only if the Gridlines option is on. The printout does reflect the specified row height and column width.

Cross-Reference Refer to Chapter 7 to review printing fundamentals. Chapter 7 covers printing the datasheet and using the Print Preview functions.

Saving a Query

To save a query while working in design mode, follow this procedure:

1. Select File ⇨ Save from the Query Design window or click the Save button on the toolbar.

2. If this is the first time you're saving the query, enter a new query name in the Save As dialog box.

To save a query while working in datasheet mode, follow this procedure:

1. Select File ⇨ Save from the Datasheet File menu.

2. If this is the first time you're saving the query, enter a new query name in the Save As dialog box.

Tip   The F12 key is the Save As key in Access. You can press F12 to save your work and continue working on your query.

Both of these methods save the query and return you to the mode you were working in. Occasionally, you will want to save and exit the query in a single operation. To do this, select File ⇨ Close from the query or the datasheet and answer Yes to the question Save changes to Query 'query name'? If this is your first time saving the query, Access prompts you to supply a query name and asks whether you want to save the query to the current database or to an external file or database.

You can leave the Query window at any time by any one of these ways:

✦ Select File ⇨ Close from the Query menu.

✦ Select Close from the Query window control box.

✦ Press Ctrl+F4 while inside the Query window.

All three of these methods activate an Access dialog box that asks, Save changes to Query 'Query1'?

✦   ✦   ✦

Creating and Working with Simple Reports

✦ ✦ ✦ ✦

In This Chapter

Understanding the types of reports you can create

Knowing the differences between a report and a form

Understanding the process of creating reports

Creating reports with a Report Wizard

Viewing reports onscreen

Printing reports

Saving reports

✦ ✦ ✦ ✦

Reports provide the most flexible way for viewing and printing summarized information. Reports display information with the desired level of detail, while enabling you to view or print your information in almost any format. You can add multilevel totals, statistical comparisons, and pictures and graphics to a report. In this chapter, you learn to use Report Wizards as a starting point. You also learn how to create reports and what types of reports you can create with Access.

Understanding Reports

Reports are used for presenting a customized view of your data. Your report output can be viewed onscreen or printed to a hard-copy device. Reports provide the capability to control summarization of the information. Data can be grouped and sorted in any order and then presented in the order of the groupings. You can create totals that add numbers, calculate averages or other statistics, and display your data graphically. You can print pictures and other graphics as well as Memo fields in a report. If you can think of a report you want, Access can probably create it.

What types of reports can you create?

Four basic types of reports are used by businesses:

 ✦ **Tabular reports.** These print data in rows and columns with groupings and totals. Variations include summary and group/total reports.

- **Columnar reports.** These print data as a form and can include totals and graphs.
- **Mail-merge reports.** These create form letters.
- **Mailing labels.** These create multicolumn labels or snaked-column reports.

Tabular reports

Figure 10-1 is a typical tabular-type report in the Print Preview window. *Tabular reports* (also known as *groups/totals reports*) are generally similar to a table that displays data in neat rows and columns. Tabular reports, unlike forms or datasheets, usually group their data by one or more field values; they calculate and display subtotals or statistical information for numeric fields in each group. Some groups/totals reports also have page totals and grand totals. You can even have *snaked columns* so that you can create directories (such as telephone books). These types of reports can use page numbers, report dates, or lines and boxes to separate information. They can have color and shading and can display pictures, business graphs, and Memo fields, like forms. A special type of tabular report, *summary reports,* can have all the features of a tabular report but not print the detail records.

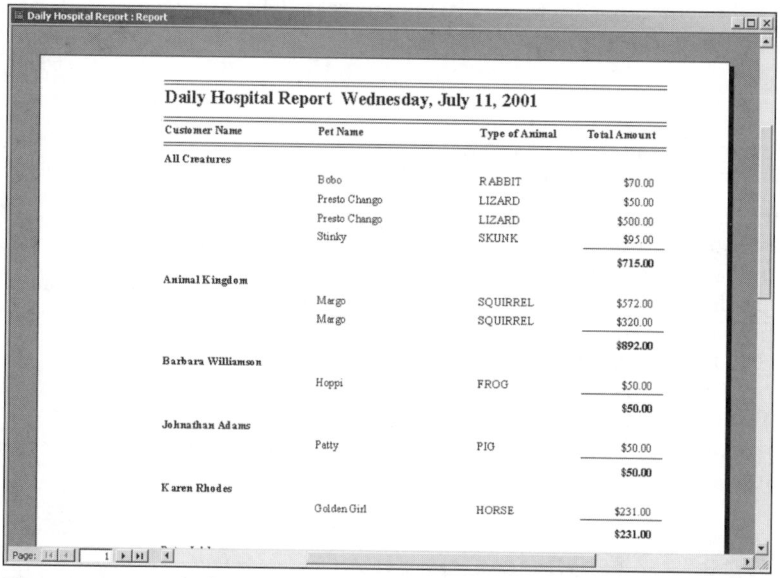

Customer Name	Pet Name	Type of Animal	Total Amount
All Creatures			
	Bobo	RABBIT	$70.00
	Presto Chango	LIZARD	$50.00
	Presto Chango	LIZARD	$500.00
	Stinky	SKUNK	$95.00
			$715.00
Animal Kingdom			
	Margo	SQUIRREL	$572.00
	Margo	SQUIRREL	$320.00
			$892.00
Barbara Williamson			
	Hoppi	FROG	$50.00
			$50.00
Johnathan Adams			
	Patty	PIG	$50.00
			$50.00
Karen Rhodes			
	Golden Girl	HORSE	$231.00
			$231.00

Figure 10-1: A tabular report in the Print Preview window of Access 2002

Columnar reports

Columnar reports (also known as *form reports*) generally display one or more records per page, but do so vertically. Column reports display data very much as a data-entry form does, but the report is used strictly for viewing data and not for entering data. An invoice is a typical example. This type of report can have sections that display only one record and at the same time have sections that display multiple records from the *many* side of a one-to-many relationship — and even include totals. Figure 10-2 is part of a typical column report from the Mountain Animal Hospital database system in the Print Preview window.

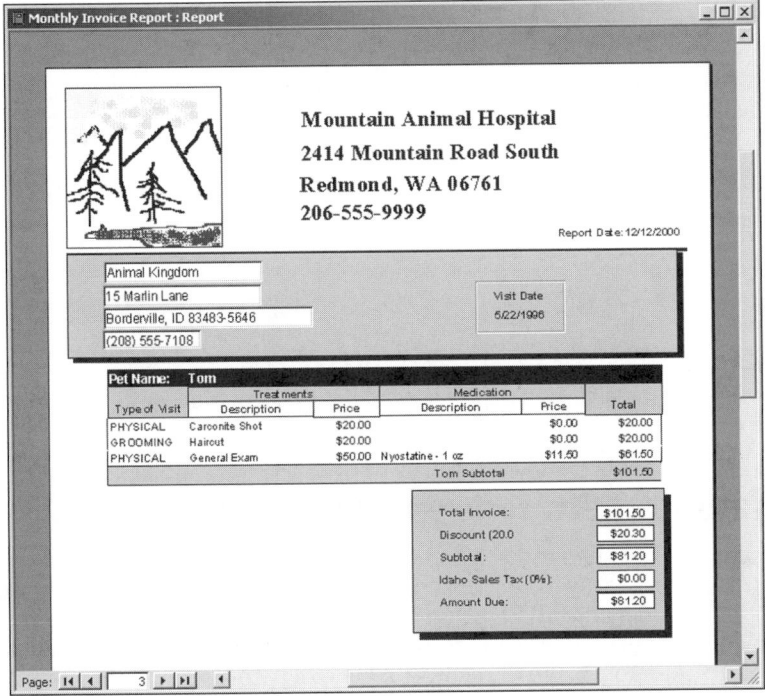

Figure 10-2: The primary part of a form report (columnar) showing multiple records

Mailing labels

Mailing labels are also a type of report. You can easily create mailing labels, shown in Figure 10-3, using the Label Wizard to create a report in Access. The Label Wizard enables you to select from a long list of Avery label (and other vendors) paper styles, after which Access correctly creates a report design based on the data you specify to create your label. After the label is created, you can open the report in design mode and customize it as needed.

Mailing labels are covered in detail in Chapter 27.

Figure 10-3: A typical mailing-label report in the Print Preview window

The difference between reports and forms

The main difference between reports and forms is the purpose of the output. Whereas forms are primarily for data entry, reports are for viewing data (either onscreen or in hard-copy form). Calculated fields can be used with forms and can calculate an amount based on the fields in the record. With reports, you calculate on the basis of a common group of records, a page of records, or all the records processed during the report. Anything you can do with a form—except data input—can be duplicated by a report. In fact, you can save a form as a report and then customize the form controls in the Report Design window.

The process of creating a report

Planning a report begins long before you actually create the report design. The report process begins with your desire to view your data in a table, but in a way that differs from datasheet display. You begin with a design for this view; Access begins with raw data. The purpose of the report is to transform the raw data into a meaningful set of information. The process of creating a report involves several steps:

> ✦ Defining the report layout
>
> ✦ Assembling the data

✦ Creating the report design using the Access Report Design window

✦ Printing or viewing the report

Defining the report layout

You should begin by having a general idea of the layout of your report. You can define the layout in your mind, on paper, or interactively using the Access Report Design window. Figure 10-4 is a report layout created using the Access Report Designer. This report was first laid out on paper, showing the fields needed and the placement of the fields.

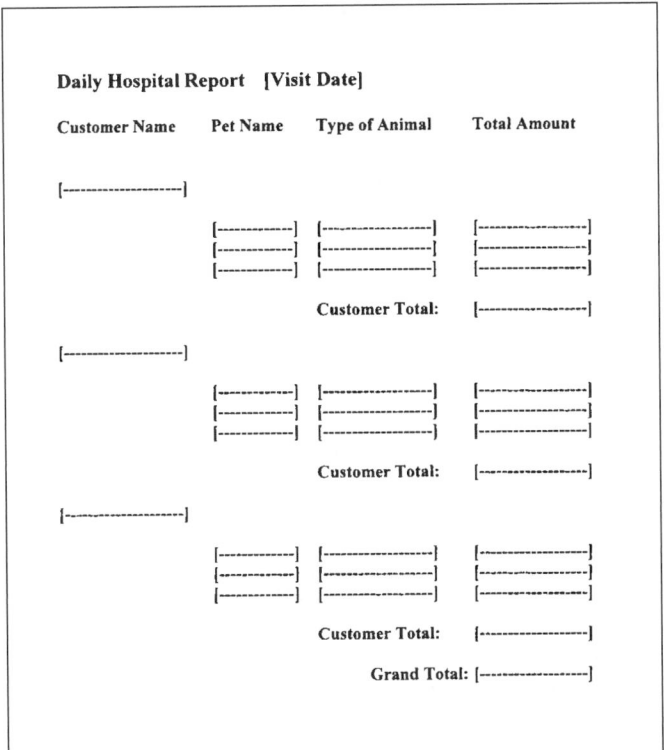

Figure 10-4: A sample report layout

Assembling the data

After you have a general idea of your report layout, you should assemble the data needed for the report. A report can use data from a single database table or from the results of a query dynaset. You can link many tables with a query and then use the result of the query (its dynaset) as the record source for your report. A dynaset appears in Access as if it were a single table. As you learned, you can select the fields, records, and sort order of the records in a query. Access treats this dynaset data as a single table (for processing purposes) in datasheets, forms, and reports. The dynaset becomes the source of data for the report and Access processes each record to create the report. The data for the report and the report *design* are entirely separate. In the report design, the field names to be used in the report are specified. Then, when the report is run, Access matches data from the dynaset or table against the fields used in the report and uses the data available at that moment to produce the report.

Consider the layout shown in Figure 10-4. You want to create a report that shows a daily total of all the pets the hospital treated during a specific day, called the Daily Hospital Report. Looking at the layout, you see that you need to assemble these fields:

✦ **Visit Date from the Visits table.** Used to select the visit date as a criterion in a query

✦ **Customer Name from the Customer table.** Displays and groups customers on the report

✦ **Pet Name from the Customer table.** Displays the pet name on the report table

✦ **Type of Animal from the Customer table.** Displays the type of animal on the report

✦ **Total Amount from the Visits table.** Displays and calculates totals for amounts charged

You begin the report by creating a query, as shown in Figure 10-5; notice the three tables linked together and the appropriate fields chosen for the report. The Visit Date field is limited to values of 7/11/2001, indicating that this specific view of your data will be limited to customers who visited on July 11, 2001. The Customer Name field shows a sort into ascending sequence in the QBE grid. This will cause the data to be sorted by Customer Name when the report is run and makes it easier for the report to be grouped by customer name.

Figure 10-6 shows the results of this query. The datasheet shown in this figure is the dynaset created when you run the Daily Hospital Report query for 7/11/2001. After assembling the data, you create the report design.

On the CD-ROM   If you are following the examples, you may want to create a query and name it Hospital Report 7/11/2001.

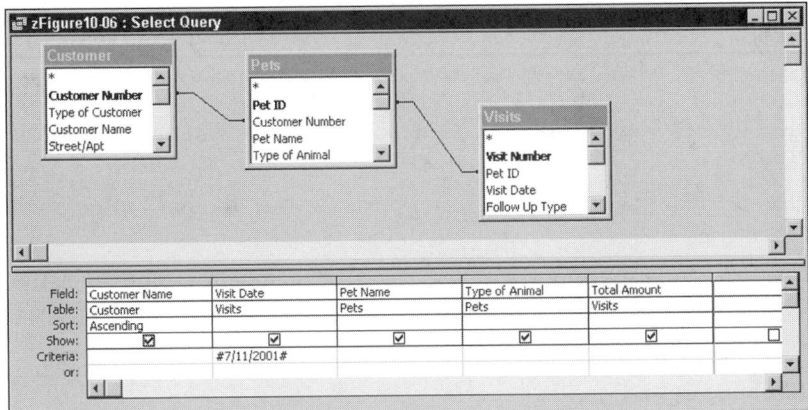

Figure 10-5: Creating a query for a report

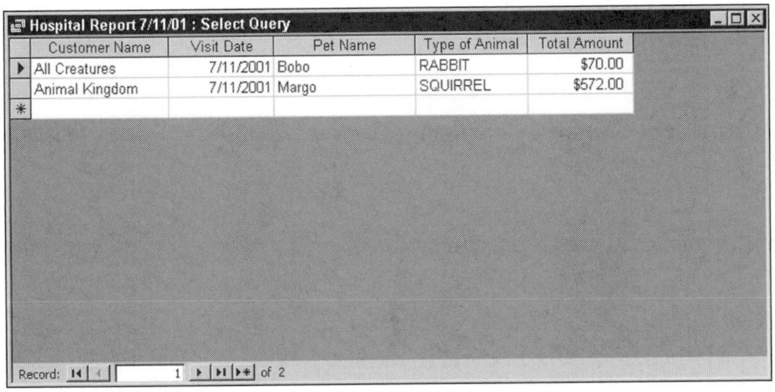

Figure 10-6: The Daily Hospital Report dynaset datasheet

Creating a Report with Report Wizards

With Access, you can create virtually any type of report. Some reports, however, are more easily created than others, when a Report Wizard is used as a starting point. Like Form Wizards, Report Wizards give you a basic layout for your report, which you can then customize.

Report Wizards simplify the layout process of your fields by visually stepping you through a series of questions about the type of report that you want to create and then automatically creating the report for you. In this chapter, you use Report Wizards to create both tabular and columnar reports.

Creating a new report

You can choose from many ways to create a new report, including the following:

✦ Select Insert ⇨ Report from the main menu when the database window is selected.

✦ Select the Reports object button and press the New toolbar button on the Database window.

✦ From the Database window, the datasheet, or the query toolbar click the New Object down-arrow and select Report.

Regardless of how you start a new report, the New Report dialog box shown in Figure 10-7 appears.

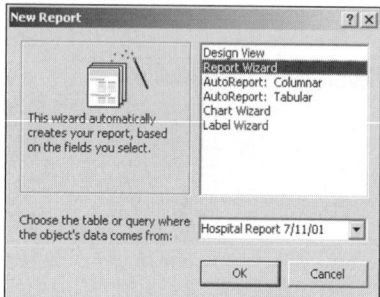

Figure 10-7: The New Report dialog box

The New Report dialog box enables you to choose from among six ways to create a report:

✦ **Design View.** Displays a completely blank Report Design window for you to start with

✦ **Report Wizard.** Helps you create a tabular report by asking you many questions

✦ **AutoReport: Columnar.** Creates an instant columnar report

✦ **AutoReport: Tabular.** Creates an instant tabular report

✦ **Chart Wizard.** Helps you create a business graph

✦ **Label Wizard.** Helps you create a set of mailing labels

To create a new report using a Report Wizard, follow these steps:

For the example below, use the Mountain Animal Hospital database file.

1. Create a new report by first selecting the Reports object button and then pressing the New toolbar button.

2. In the New Report dialog box, select Report Wizard.

3. Select the query Hospital Report 7/11/01 and click OK.

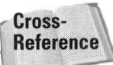

Cross-Reference
Chapter 19 discusses creating a new report without using a wizard.

Choosing the data source

Tip
If you begin creating a report in Design View, you don't need to specify a table or query in the New Report dialog box because you can select the Record Source later on from the Properties sheet.

Choosing the fields

After you select the Report Wizard and click the OK button, a *field selection box* appears. This box is virtually identical to the field selection box used in Form Wizards (see Chapter 8 for detailed information). In this example, select all the fields except Visit Date, as shown in Figure 10-8.

1. Click the All Fields button (>>) to place all the fields in the Selected Fields: area.

2. Select the Visit Date field and click the Remove Field button (<) to remove the field. Click the Next button when you are through to move to the next wizard screen

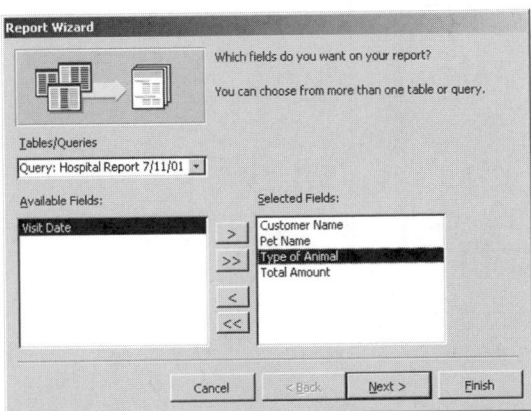

Figure 10-8: Selecting report fields

You can continue to select other tables or queries by using the Tables/Queries: combo box in this Wizard screen; you can also display fields from additional tables or queries. As long as you have specified valid relationships so that Access can link the data, these fields are added to your original selection and you can use them on the report. If you choose fields from tables that don't have a relationship, a dialog box will ask you to edit the relationship and join the tables. Or you can return to the Report Wizard and remove the fields.

Once you have selected your data, click the Next button to go to the next Wizard dialog box.

Selecting the grouping levels

The next dialog box enables you to choose which field(s) you want to use for a grouping. In this example, Figure 10-9 shows Customer Name selected as the only group field. This step designates the field(s) to be used to create group headers and footers. Using the Report Wizard, you can select up to four different group fields for your report; you can change their order by using the Priority buttons. The order you select for the group fields is the order of the grouping hierarchy.

Select the Customer Name field as the grouping field and click (>). Notice that the picture changes to graphically show Customer Name as a grouping field.

After you select the group field(s), click the Grouping Options button at the bottom of the dialog box to display another dialog box, which enables you to further define how your report will use the group field.

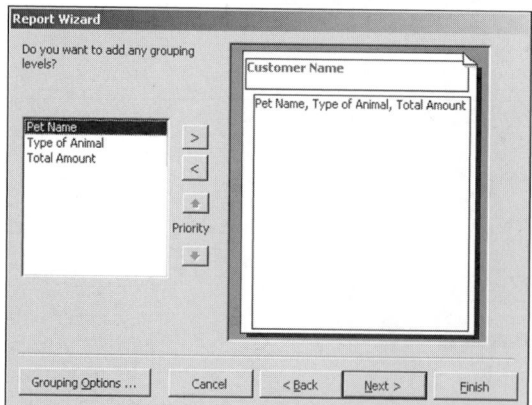

Figure 10-9: Selecting report group fields

Defining the group data

The Grouping Options dialog box enables you to further define the grouping. This selection can vary in importance, depending on the data type.

The list box displays different values for the various data types:

✦ **Text.** Normal, First Letter, 2 Initial Letters, 3 Initial Letters, 4 Initial Letters, and so on

✦ **Numeric.** Normal, 10s, 50s, 100s, 500s, 1000s, 5000s, 10000s, 50000s, 100000s, 500000s

✦ **Date.** Normal, Year, Quarter, Month, Week, Day, Hour, Minute

Normal means that the grouping is on the entire field. In this example, use the entire Customer Name field. By selecting different values of the grouping, you can limit the group values. For example, suppose you are grouping on the Pet ID field. A typical Pet ID value is AP001-01. The first five characters represent the owner; the two after the hyphen represent the pet number for that owner. By choosing the Pet ID field for the grouping and then selecting 5 Initial Letters as the grouping data, you can group the pets by customer instead of by pet.

In this example, the default text-field grouping option of Normal is acceptable.

Click the OK button to return to the Grouping levels dialog box, and then click the Next button to move to the Sort order dialog box.

Selecting the sort order

Access sorts the Group record fields automatically in an order that helps the grouping make sense. The additional sorting fields specify fields to be sorted in the detail section. In this example, Access is already sorting the data by Customer Name in the group section. As Figure 10-10 shows, the data is also to be sorted by Pet Name so that the pets appear in alphabetical order in the detail section.

The sort fields are selected by the same method that is used for grouping fields in the report. You can select fields that you have not already chosen to group and use these as sorting fields. The fields chosen in this dialog box do not affect grouping; they affect only the sorting order in the detail section fields. You can determine whether the order is ascending or descending by clicking the button to the right of each sort field, which toggles between Ascending and Descending.

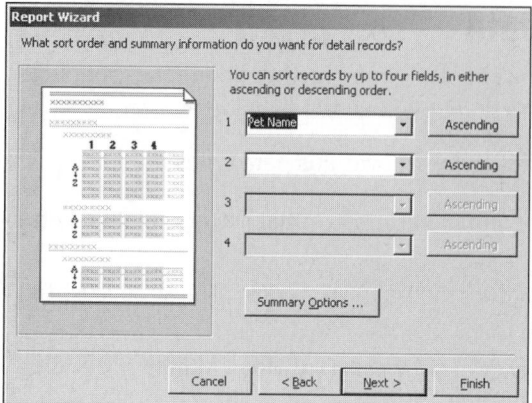

Figure 10-10: Selecting the field sorting order

Selecting summary options

At the bottom of the sorting dialog box is a button named Summary Options. Clicking this button displays the dialog box shown in Figure 10-11. This dialog box provides additional options for numeric fields. As you can see, the Field Total Amount is to be summed. Additionally, you can display averages, minimums, and maximums.

Sum should be checked.You can also decide whether to show or hide the data in the detail section. If you select Detail and Summary, the report shows the detail data; selecting Summary Only hides the detail section and shows only totals in the report.

Finally, checking the box labeled Calculate percent of total for sums adds the percentage of the entire report that the total represents below the total in the group footer. If, for example, you had three customers and their totals were 15, 25, and 10, respectively, they would show 30%, 50%, and 20% below their total (that is, 50) — indicating the percentage of the total sum (100%) represented by their sum.

Clicking the OK button in this dialog box returns you to the sorting dialog box. There you can click the Next button to move to the next Wizard dialog box.

Selecting the layout

Two more dialog boxes affect the look of your report. The first (shown in Figure 10-12) enables you to determine the layout of the data. The Layout area provides six layout choices; these tell Access whether to repeat the column headers, whether to indent each grouping, and whether to add lines or boxes between the detail lines. As you select each option, the picture on the left changes to show the effect.

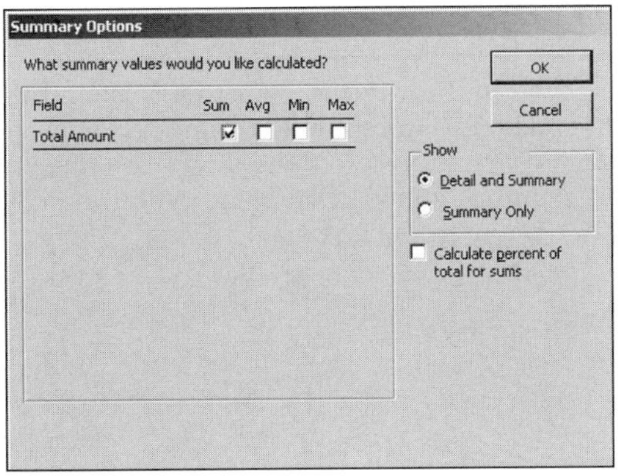

Figure 10-11: Selecting the summary options

The Orientation area enables you to choose between a Portrait (up-and-down) and a Landscape (across-the-page) layout. This choice affects how it prints on the paper. Finally, the check mark next to Adjust field width so that all fields fit on a page enables you to cram a lot of data into a little area. (Magnifying glasses may be necessary!)

For this example, choose Stepped and Portrait, the default values, as shown in Figure 10-12. Then click on the Next button to move to the next dialog box.

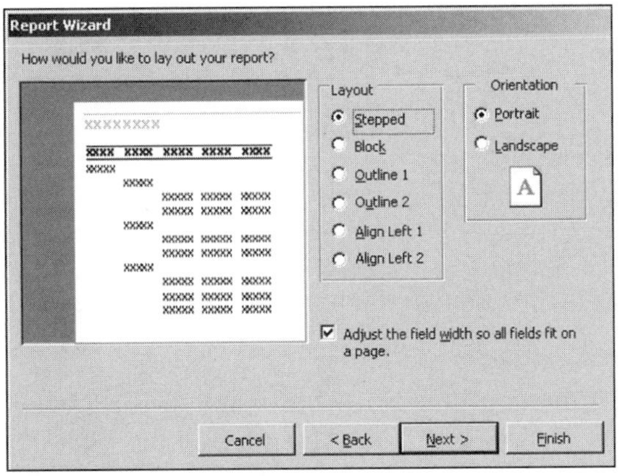

Figure 10-12: Selecting the page layout

Choosing the style

After you choose the layout, you can choose the style of your report from the dialog box shown in Figure 10-13. Each style has different background shadings, font size, typeface, and other formatting. As each is selected, the picture on the left changes to show a preview. For this example, choose Compact (as shown in Figure 10-13). Finally, click the Next button to move to the last dialog box.

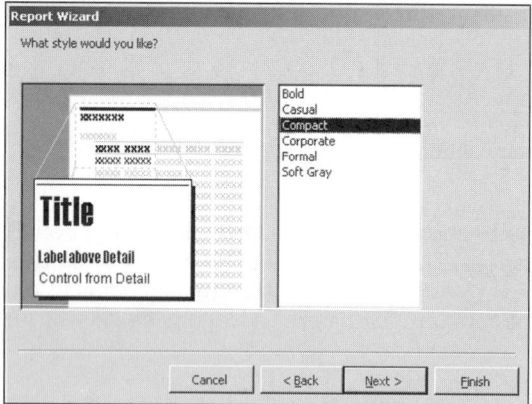

Figure 10-13: Choosing the style of your report

Tip You can customize the styles, or add your own, by using the AutoFormat option from the Format menu of the Report Design window and choosing Customize.

Opening the report design

Figure 10-14 is the final Report Wizard dialog box. The checkered flag lets you know that you're at the finish line. The first part of the dialog box enables you to enter a title for the report. This title will appear once at the beginning of the report, not at the top of each page. The default is the name of the table or query you used initially.

Next you can choose one of the option buttons at the bottom of the dialog box:

✦ Preview the report

✦ Modify the report's design

For this example, leave the default selection intact to preview the report. When you click the Finish button, your report is displayed in the Print Preview window.

Click Finish to complete the Report Wizard and view the report.

Using the Print Preview window

Figure 10-14 displays the Print Preview window in a zoomed view. This view displays your report with the actual fonts, shading, lines, boxes, and data that will be on the printed report. When the Print Preview mode is in a zoomed view, pressing the mouse button changes the view to a *page preview* that shows the entire page.

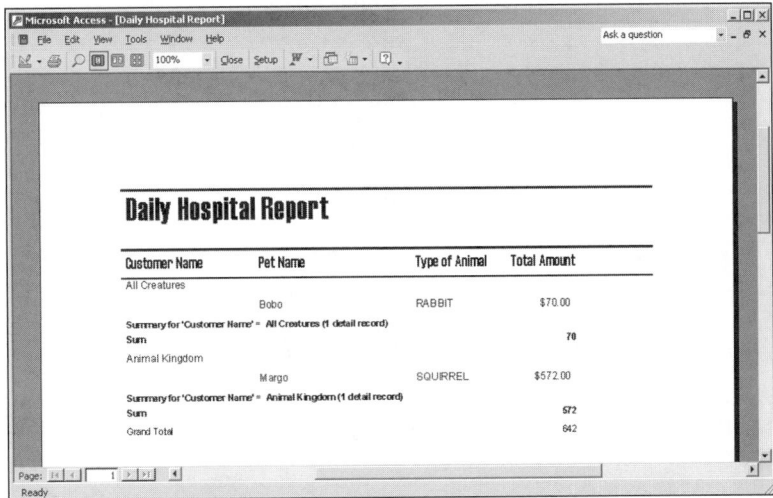

Figure 10-14: Displaying a report in the zoomed preview mode

You can move around the page by using the horizontal and vertical scrollbars. Use the Page controls (at the bottom-left corner of the window) to move from page to page. These controls include VCR-like navigation buttons to move from page to page or to the first or last page of the report. You can also go to a specific page of the report by entering a value in the text box between the previous and next controls.

Figure 10-15 shows a whole page of the report in the page preview mode of Print Preview. The magnifying glass mouse pointer selects part of the page to zoom in. In Figure 10-15, you can see a representation of the printed page. Use the navigation buttons (in the lower-left section of the Print Preview window) to move between pages, just as you would to move between records in a datasheet. The Print Preview window has a toolbar with commonly used printing commands.

If, after examining the preview, you are satisfied with the report, select the Printer button on the toolbar to print the report. If you are dissatisfied, select the Close button to return to the design window; Access takes you to the Report Design window to make further changes.

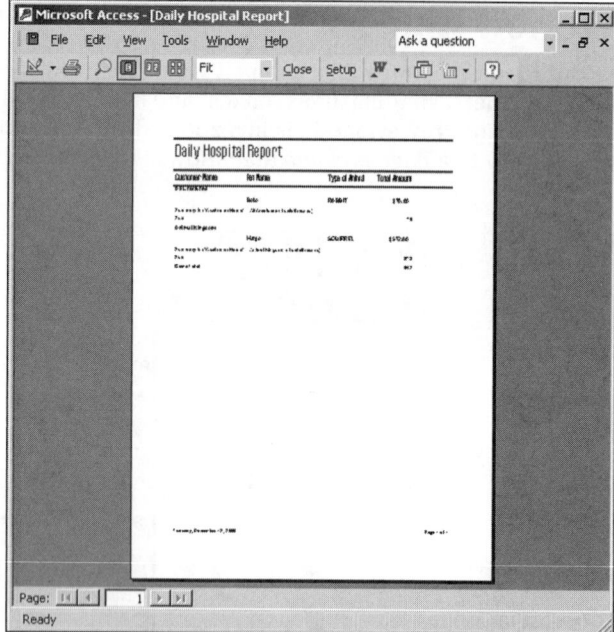

Figure 10-15: Displaying a report in Print Preview's page preview mode

Viewing the Report Design window

When you click Design View (the left-most button on the toolbar), Access takes you to the Report Design window, which is similar to the Form Design window. The major difference is in the sections that make up the report design. As shown in Figure 10-16, the report design reflects the choices you made using the Report Wizard.

Cross-Reference

You may also see the Toolbox, Sorting and Grouping dialog box, property sheet, and Field List window, depending on whether you pressed the toolbar buttons to see these tools. You learn to change the design of a report in Chapters 19 and 20.

You can return to the Print Preview mode by selecting the Print Preview button on the Report Design toolbar or by selecting the Print Preview option on the File menu. You can also select Print or Page Setup from the File menu. This menu also provides options for saving your report.

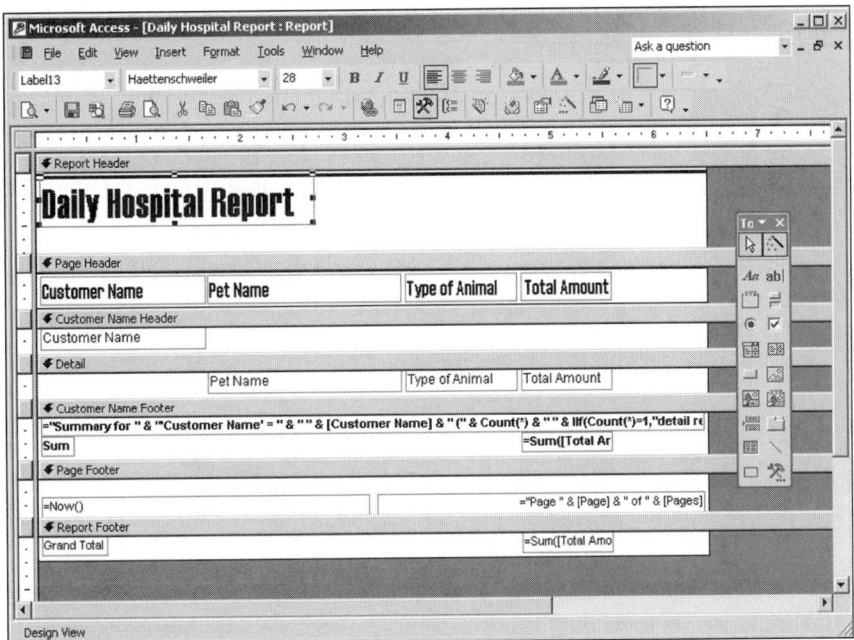

Figure 10-16: The Report Design window

Printing a Report

You can print one or more records in your report, exactly as they look onscreen, using one of these methods:

✦ Click File ⇨ Print in the Report Design window

✦ Click the Print button in the Preview window

✦ Click File ⇨ Print in the Database window (with a report highlighted)

If you select File ⇨ Print, a standard Microsoft Windows Print dialog box appears. You can select the print range, number of copies, and print properties. If you click the Print button, the report goes immediately to the currently selected printer without displaying a Print dialog box.

Cross-Reference For a complete discussion of printing, see Chapter 20.

Saving the Report

You can save the report design at any time by selecting File ➪ Save, or File ➪ Save As, or File ➪ Export from the Report Design window, or by clicking the Save button on the toolbar. The first time you save a report (or any time you select Save As or Export), a dialog box enables you to select or type a name. The text box initially displays the default name from the Report Wizard, *Report1*.

On the CD-ROM Remember that Access saves only the report design, not the data or the actual report. You must save your query design separately if you created a query to produce your report. You can recreate the dynaset at any time by running the report that automatically reruns the query.

Creating a Report with AutoReport

From a table, datasheet, form, or nearly any design screen in Access, you can create a columnar report instantly. Just click the New Object drop-down arrow and select AutoReport. Another method is to use the Insert ➪ Report command and then click one of the two AutoReport selections from the dialog box that appears. When you use the AutoReport button, the report appears instantly with no additional work from you. To create an AutoReport using the Pets table, follow these steps:

1. From the Mountain Animal Hospital or Mountain Animal Start database, click the Table button.

2. Select Pets.

3. Click the New Object button on the toolbar and select AutoReport.

The report instantly appears, as shown in Figure 10-17. Actually, the Picture property of the OLE control has been changed to Stretch to show the whole rabbit. (This was done in the Report Design screen, using the techniques you learned in Chapter 8.)

Using AutoReport is the quickest way to create a report. Generally, however, you want more control over the process. Other Report Wizards are available to help you create more customized reports.

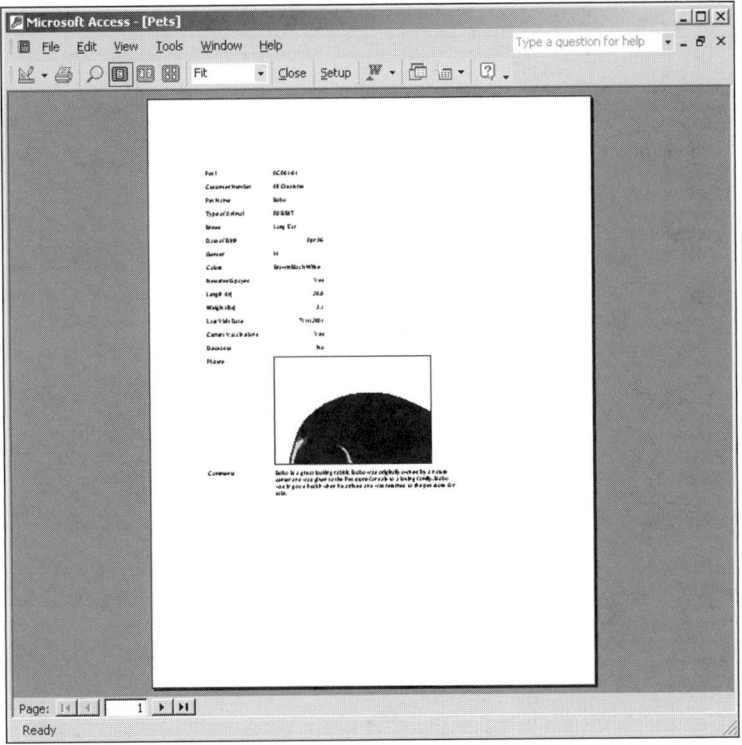

Figure 10-17: The AutoReport report

✦   ✦   ✦

Using Access in Your Work

◆　　◆　　◆　　◆

In This Part

Chapter 11
Using Operators,
Functions, and
Expressions

Chapter 12
Creating Relations and
Joins in Queries

Chapter 13
Working with Select
Queries

Chapter 14
Understanding Form
Controls

Chapter 15
Creating and Custom-
izing Data-Entry Forms

Chapter 16
Creating Great Looking
Forms

Chapter 17
Adding Data-Validation
Controls to Forms

Chapter 18
Using OLE Objects,
Graphs, Pivot Tables/
Charts, and ActiveX
Controls

Chapter 19
Creating and
Customizing Reports

Chapter 20
Presentation-Quality
Reports and Printing

Chapter 21
Creating Calculations
and Summaries in
Reports

◆　　◆　　◆　　◆

Using Operators, Functions, and Expressions

◆ ◆ ◆ ◆

In This Chapter

Understanding what
operators, functions,
and expressions are
and how they are
used

Reviewing types of
operators

Looking at types of
functions

Learning how to
create an expression

Examining special
identifier operators
and expressions

◆ ◆ ◆ ◆

Operators, functions, and expressions are the fundamental building blocks for Access operations. You use them
in such as criteria in queries to specify which records to display, calculated fields in forms to show calculated information
or to display data in a different format, and summary controls
in reports to show totals and subtotals.

What Are Operators?

Operators let you add numbers, compare values, put text
strings together, and create complex relational expressions.
You use operators to inform Access that a specific operation
is to be performed against one or more items.

Types of operators

The types of operators discussed in this chapter are listed
below:

- ◆ Mathematical (arithmetic) operators
- ◆ Relational operators
- ◆ String operators
- ◆ Boolean (logical) operators
- ◆ Miscellaneous operators

When are operators used?

You find yourself using operators all the time. In fact, you use them every time you create an equation in Access. For example, operators specify data-validation rules in table properties, create calculated fields in forms, and specify criteria in queries.

Operators indicate that an operation needs to be performed on one or more items. Some common examples of operators are

=

&

And

Like

+

Mathematical operators

There are seven basic mathematical operators. These are also known as arithmetic operators, because they are used for performing arithmetic calculations:

*	Multiply
+	Add
−	Subtract
/	Divide
\	Integer Divide
^	Exponentiation
Mod	Modulo

By definition, you use mathematical operators to work with numbers. When you work with mathematical operators, numbers can be any numeric data type. The number can be an actual number (constant value), or the value of a memory variable, or a field's contents. Furthermore, the numbers can be used individually or combined to create complex expressions. Some of the examples in this section are quite complex, but don't worry if you don't usually work with sophisticated mathematics. This chapter shows you how to work with mathematical formulas in Access.

The * (multiplication) operator

A simple example of when to use the *multiplication operator* is to calculate the total price of purchasing several items. You could design a form for entering the number of items purchased and the per-item price. Then you could use a calculated field to calculate and display the total price for that number of items. In this case, the calculated field would contain the formula [Price] * [Quantity]. The standard notation for dealing with field names in an expression is to enclose them in square brackets.

The + (addition) operator

If you want to create a calculated field in the same form for adding the values in fields, such as Gross Amount and Tax, you would use the expression [Gross Amount] + [Tax]. This simple formula uses the *addition operator* to add the contents of both fields and display the result in the object that contains the formula.

Besides adding two numbers, the *addition operator* can be used for concatenating two character strings – putting two text-based strings together forming a single text string. For example, you may want to combine the fields First Name and Last Name to display them as a single field. This expression is

[First Name] + [Last Name]

Caution   Although you can concatenate (put two strings together) text strings by using the addition operator, you should use the ampersand (&). The reason for this appears in the section "String operators," later in this chapter.

The – (subtraction) operator

An example of using the *subtraction operator* on the same form is to calculate the final invoice amount minus a discount. The formula to determine the Net Invoice Amount would be as follows:

[Gross Amount] – ([Gross Amount]*[Discount]).

Note   Although parentheses are not mathematical operators, they play an integral part in working with operators, as discussed later, in the section "Operator precedence."

The / (division) operator

You can use the *division operator* to divide two numbers and (as with the previous operators) display the result wherever you need it. Suppose, for example, that a pool of 212 people win the $1,000,000 lottery this week. The formula to determine each individual's payoff is 1,000,000 / 212, resulting in $4,716.98 per person.

Tip   Using Access's Immediate window that is built into the Visual Basic Window, you can determine the values of mathematical formulas. To activate the immediate window, press the Ctrl+G key combination. Once active, you can perform any calculation and have it display the results by placing a question mark in front of the calculation — for example, typing **? 1000000 / 212** and pressing Enter will result in an answer of 4716.9811. To close this window, close the Microsoft Visual Basic window.

The \ (integer division) operator

Should you ever need to take two numbers, round them both to integers, divide the two rounded integers, and receive a non-rounded integer, the *integer division operator* does it in one step. Here is an example:

Normal Division   **Integer Conversion Division**

100 / 6 = 16.667   100 \ 6 = 16

100.9 / 6.6 = 15.288   100.9 \ 6.6 = 14

Tip   Access has the round function for rounding fractional numbers to whole numbers. You can also use the integer division operator to round any number. Just integer-divide (\) the number you want to round by 1, as in 125.6 \ 1 = 126.

Note   Access rounds numbers based on the greater-than-.5 rule: Any number with a decimal value of x.5 or less rounds down; greater than x.5 rounds up to the next whole number. This means that 6.5 becomes 6, but 6.51 and 6.6 become 7.

What Are Integer Values?

Integers are whole numbers (numbers that have no decimal places), which in Access are the values between –32768 and +32767. They have no fractional part (after the dot — for example, 7.2 is not an integer, because it has a fractional part — .2; 7 is the integer number!). Examples are 1, 722; 33; –5460; 0; and 22. They include all whole positive and negative numbers and 0. When you use the Int() function or the integer divide operator (\), to determine the integer part of any number, simply drop any decimal values. For example, the integer value of 45.123 is 45; for 2.987, the integer is 2; and so forth.

The integer divide operator can be a confusing operator until you understand just what it does. If you enter the following print statements in the Immediate window of Access, it should become clear:

✦ 101 / 6 results in 16.833.

✦ 101.9 / 6.6 results in 15.439.

✦ 102 / 7 results in 14.571.

✦ INT(102 / 7) results in 14.

✦ 101.9 \ 6.6 results in 14.

The last entry uses the integer divide sign (\) and is equivalent to rounding both numbers in the division operation (101.9 = 102 and 6.6 = 7), dividing 102 by 7, and converting the answer to an integer. In other words, it is equivalent to the following:

INT((101.9 \ 1) / (6.6 \ 1)) or INT(round(101.9)/ round(6.6))

The ^ (exponentiation) operator

The *exponentiation operator* (^) raises a number to the power of an exponent. Raising a number simply means indicating the number of times that you want to multiply a number by itself. For example, multiplying the value 4 x 4 x 4 (that is, 4-cubed) is the same as entering the formula 4^3.

The Mod (Modulo) operator

The *modulo operator* (mod), or remainder operator, takes any two numbers (number1 and number2) and divides the first by the second (number1 / number2), returning only the remainder. For example, if you type in the following examples in the Immediate window of Access it should become clear:

✦ 10 Mod 5 results in 0 (10 divided by 5 is 2 with a remainder of 0)

✦ 10 Mod 4 results in 2 (10 divided by 4 is 2 with a remainder of 2)

All numbers, if they are not integers, are first rounded to integers before the Mod operator is performed. For example

✦ 22.24 Mod 4 results in 2 (22 divided by 4 is 5 with a remainder of 2)

✦ 22.51 Mod 4 results in 3 (23 divided by 4 is 5 with a remainder of 3)

✦ 21 Mod 5.49 results in 1 (21 divided by 5 is 4 with a remainder of 1)

Relational operators

There are six basic relational operators (also known as comparison operators). They compare two values or expressions via an equation. The relational operators include the following:

=	Equal
<>, !=	Not equal
<	Less than
<=, !<	Less than or equal to
>	Greater than
>=, !>	Greater than or equal to

The expression build from relational operators always return either a logical value or Null; the value they return says Yes (True), No (not True; that is, False), or it is a Null (unknown/no value).

Note Access actually returns a numeric value for relational operator equations. It returns a −1 (negative 1) for True and a 0 (zero) for False.

If either side of an equation is a Null value, the resultant will always be a Null.

The = (equal) operator

The *equal operator* returns a logical True if the two expressions being compared are the same. Here are two examples of the equal operator:

[Type of Animal] = "Cat"	Returns a True if the animal is a cat; False is returned for any other animal.
[Date of Birth] = Date()	Returns a True if the date in the Date of Birth field is today.

The <> (not-equal) operator

The *not-equal operator* is exactly the opposite of the equal operator. In this example, the cat example is changed to not-equal:

[Type of Animal] <> "Cat"	Returns a True if Type of Animal is anything but a cat.
[Type of Animal] != "Dog"	Returns a True if Type of Animal is anything but a dog.

Notice that you have two different ways to express not equal to: the <> or != symbols both mean exactly the same thing.

The < (less-than) operator

The *less-than operator* returns a logical True if the left side of the equation is less than the right side, as in this example:

[Weight] < 10	Returns a True if the Weight field contains a value of less than 10.

The <= (less-than-or-equal-to) operator

The *less-than-or-equal-to operator* returns a True if the left side of the equation is either less than or equal to the right side, as in this example:

[Weight] <= 10	Returns a True if the value of Weight equals 10 or is less than 10.
[Weight] !> 10	Returns a True if the value of Weight equals 10 or is less than 10.

Notice in the second example you got the same results using the operator !> (not greater than). In other words, equal to or less than can be expressed using either operator <= or !>.

Note   Access is not sensitive to the order of the operators. Access accepts either of these forms as the same: (<=) or (=<).

The > (greater-than) operator

The *greater-than operator* is the exact opposite of the less-than operator. This operator returns a True when the left side of the equation is greater than the right side, as in this example:

[Length (In)] > 22	Returns True if the value of Length (In) is greater than 22

The > = (greater-than-or-equal-to) operator

The *greater-than-or-equal-to operator* returns a True if the left side of the equation is either equal to or greater than the right side; for example:

[Weight (lbs)] >= 100	Returns a True if the field Weight (lbs) contains a value equal to or greater than 100.
[Weight (lbs)] !< 100	Returns a True if the field Weight (lbs) contains a value equal to or greater than 100.

Notice in the second example you got the same results using the operator !< (not less than). In other words, equal to or greater than can be expressed using either operator, >= or !<.

String operators

Access has two *string operators*, also know as text operators. Unlike the other operators, these work specifically with the Text data type:

&	Concatenation
Like	Similar to . . .
NOT Like	Not similar to . . .

The & (concatenation) operator

The *concatenation operator* connects or links (concatenates) two or more objects into a resultant string. This operator works similarly to the addition operator. Unlike the addition operator, however, the & operator always forces a string concatenation. For instance, this example produces a single string:

[First Name] & [Last Name]

However, in the resultant string, no spaces are automatically added. If [First Name] equals "Fred" and [Last Name] equals "Smith," concatenating the field contents yields FredSmith. To add a space between the strings, you must concatenate a space string between the two fields. To concatenate a space string between first and last name fields, you enter a formula such as this:

[First Name] & " " & [Last Name]

This operator can easily concatenate a string object with a number- or date-type object. Using the & eliminates the need for special functions to convert a number or date to a string.

Suppose, for example, that you have a Number field, which is House Number, and a Text field, which is Street Name, and that you want to build an expression for a report of both fields. For this, you can enter the following:

[House Number] & " " & [Street Name]

If House Number has a value of 1600 and Street Name is "Pennsylvania Avenue N.W.," the resultant concatenation of the number and string is as follows:

"1600 Pennsylvania Avenue N.W."

Perhaps you want to have a calculated field in a report that prints the operator's name and the date and time the report was run. This can be accomplished using syntax similar to the following:

"This report was printed " & Now( ) & " by " & [operator name]

If the date is March 21, 2001, and the time is 4:45 p.m., this concatenated line prints something like this:

This report was printed 3/21/01 4:45:40 PM by Michael R. Irwin

Notice the spaces at the end or the beginning of the strings. Knowing how this operator works makes maintenance of your database expressions easier. If you always use the concatenation operator for creating concatenated text strings, you won't have to be concerned with the data types of the concatenated objects. Any formula that uses the & operator converts all the objects being concatenated to a string data type for you.

Note

Using the & with Nulls: If both objects are Null, the result is also a Null. If only one of the two objects is Null, Access converts the object that is Null to a string type with a length of 0 and builds the concatenation.

The Like (similar to) operator

The Like operator, and its opposite, the NOT Like operator, are used to compare two string objects by using wildcards. This operator determines whether one object matches, or doesn't match, the pattern of another object. The resultant value of the comparison is a True, False, or Null.

The Like operator uses the following basic syntax:

expression object Like *pattern object*

Like looks for the *expression object* in the *pattern object*; if it is present, the operation returns a True. (The Like operator is discussed in more detail in Chapter 13.)

Note   If either object in the Like formula is a Null, the resultant is a Null.

This operator provides a powerful and flexible tool for string comparisons. The pattern object can use wildcard characters to increase flexibility (see the sidebar "Using Wildcards").

Tip   If you want to match one of the wildcard characters in the Like operation, the wildcard character must be enclosed in brackets in the pattern object. In the example

"AB*Co" Like "AB[*]C*"

the [*] in the third position of the pattern object will look for the asterisk as the third character of the string.

Following are some examples that use the Like operator:

[Last Name] Like "M[Cc]*"	Returns a True for any last name that begins with "Mc" or "MC." "McDonald," "McJamison," "MCWilliams" are all True; "Irwin" and "Prague" are False.
[Answer] Like "[!e-zE-Z]"	Returns a True if the Answer is A, B, C, D, a, b, c, or d. Any other letter is False.
"AB1989" Like "AB####"	Results in True because the string begins with the letters *AB* and is followed by any four numbers.
"#10 Circle Drive" Like "[#]*Drive"	Results in True because the first character is the pound sign (#) and the last part is the word *Drive*.
[Answer] NOT Like "[!e-zE-Z]"	Returns a False if the Answer is A, B, C, D, a, b, c, or d. Any other letter is TRUE.
[Last Name] NOT Like "M[Cc]*"	Is True for any last name that DOES NOT begin with "Mc" or "MC." "McDonald," "McJamison," "MCWilliams" are all FALSE; "Irwin" and "Prague" are TRUE.

Using Wildcards

Access lets you use these five wildcards with the Like operator:

Character	Matches
?	A single character (A to Z, 0 to 9)
*	Any number of characters (0 to n)
#	Any single digit (0 to 9)
[list]	Any single character in the list
[!list]	Any single character not in the list

Both [list] and [!list] can use the hyphen between two characters to signify a range.

Boolean (logical) operators

Access uses six *Boolean operators*. Also referred to as *logical operators*, these are used for setting conditions in expressions. Boolean operators are used to create complex multiple-condition expressions. Like relational operators, these always return either a logical True or False or a Null. Boolean operators include the following:

And	Logical and
Or	Logical inclusive or
Eqv	Logical equivalence
Imp	Logical implication
Xor	Logical exclusive or
Not	Logical not

The And operator

You use the *And operator* to perform a logical conjunction of two objects; the operator returns the value True if both conditions are true. The general syntax of an And operation is

object expression 1 And *object expression 2*

Here is an example:

[State] = "MN" And [Zip Code] = "12345"   Is True only if both conditions are True.

If the conditions on both sides of the And operator are True, the result is a True value. Table 11-1 demonstrates the results.

Table 11-1 And Operator Resultants		
Expression 1	**Expression 2**	**Return Resultant**
True	True	True
True	False	False
True	Null	Null
False	True	False
False	False	False
False	Null	False
Null	True	Null
Null	False	False
Null	Null	Null

The Or operator

The *Or operator* is used to perform a logical disjunction of two objects; the operator returns the value True if either condition is true. The general syntax of an Or operation is

object expression 1 Or *object expression 2*

The following two examples show how the Or operator works:

[Last Name] = "Williams" Or [Last Name] = "Johnson"   Is True if Last Name is either Williams or Johnson.

[Animal Type] = "Frog" Or [Animal Color] = "Green"   Is True if the animal is a frog or any animal that is green (a snake, bird, and so forth).

If the condition of either side of the Or operator is True, a True value is returned. Table 11-2 demonstrates the results.

	Table 11-2	
	Or Expression Resultants	
Expression 1	**Expression 2**	**Return Resultant**
True	True	True
True	False	True
True	Null	True
False	True	True
False	False	False
False	Null	Null
Null	True	True
Null	False	Null
Null	Null	Null

The Not operator

The *Not operator* is used for negating a numeric object; the operator returns the value True if the condition is not true. This operator reverses the logical result of the expression.

The general syntax of a Not operation is

> Not *numeric object expression*

The following example shows how to use the Not operator:

> Not [Final Sales Amount] >= 1000   Is true if Final Sales Amount is less than 1000.

If the numeric object is Null, the resulting condition is Null. Table 11-3 demonstrates the results.

	Table 11-3
	Not Operator Resultants
Expression	**Return Resultant**
True	False
False	True
Null	Null

Miscellaneous operators

Access has three very useful miscellaneous operators:

Between . . . And	Range
In	List comparison
Is	Reserved word

The Between . . . And operator

You can use the *Between . . . And operator* to determine whether an object is within a specific range of values. This is the general syntax:

> *object expression* Between *value 1* And *value 2*

If the value of the object expression is between *value 1* and *value 2*, the result is True; otherwise, it is False.

The following is an example of the Between . . . And operator that uses the IIF function for a calculated control:

> IIF([Amount Owed] Between 0 And 250, "Due 30 Days", "Due NOW")

This displays a 30-day-past due notice for values of $250 or less, and due-now notices for values over $250.

The In operator

The *In operator* is used to determine whether an object is equal to any value in a specific list. This is the general syntax:

> *object expression* In *(value1, value2, value3, . . .)*

If the object expression is found in the list, the result is True; otherwise, the result is False.

The following example also uses the IIF function. Here, the In operator is used for a control value in a form:

> IIF([Animal Type] In ("Cat," "Dog"), "Common Pet", "Unusual Pet")

This displays the message Common Pet if Animal Type is a cat or dog, otherwise it displays Unusual Pet.

The Is (reserved word) operator

The *Is operator* is used only with the keyword *Null* to determine whether an object has nothing in it. This is the general syntax:

object expression Is Null, *value 1*

This example is a validation-check message in a data-entry form to force entry of a field:

IIF([Customer Name] Is Null, "Name Must be Entered"," ")

Operator precedence

When you work with complex expressions that have many operators, Access must determine which operator to evaluate first, and then which is next, and so forth. To do this, Access has a built-in predetermined order, known as *operator precedence*. Access always follows this order unless you use parentheses to specify otherwise.

Parentheses are used to group parts of an expression and override the default order of precedence. Operations within parentheses are performed before any operations outside of them. Inside the parentheses, Access follows the predetermined operator precedence.

Precedence is determined first according to category of the operator. The operator rank by order of precedence is

1. Mathematical
2. Comparison
3. Boolean

Each category contains its own order of precedence, which is explained next.

The mathematical precedence

Within the general category of mathematical operators, this order of precedence is in effect:

1. Exponentiation
2. Negation
3. Multiplication and/or division (left to right)
4. Integer division
5. Modulo
6. Addition and/or subtraction (left to right)
7. String concatenation

The comparison precedence

Comparison operators observe this order of precedence:

1. Equal

2. Not equal

3. Less than

4. Greater than

5. Less than or equal to

6. Greater than or equal to

7. Like

The Boolean precedence

The Boolean category follows this order of precedence:

1. Not

2. And

3. Or

4. Xor

5. Eqv

6. Imp

What Are Functions?

Functions are small programs that always, by definition, return a value based on some calculation, comparison, or evaluation that the function performs. The value returned can be string, logic, or numeric, depending on the type of function. Access provides hundreds of common functions that are used in tables, queries, forms, and reports. You can also create your own user-defined functions (UDFs) using the Access Visual Basic language.

Using functions in Access

Functions perform specialized operations that enhance the utility of Access. Many times you find yourself using functions as an integral part of Access. The following are examples of the types of tasks functions can accomplish:

Precedence Order

Simple mathematics provides an example of order of precedence. Remember that Access performs operations within parentheses before operations that are not in parentheses. Also remember that multiplication and division operations are performed before addition or subtraction operations.

For example, what is the answer to this simple equation?

X=10+3*4

If your answer is 52, you need a better understanding of precedence in Access. If your answer is 22, you're right. If your answer is anything else, you need a calculator!

Multiplication is performed before addition by the rules of mathematical precedence. Therefore, the equation 10+3*4 is evaluated in this order:

3*4 is performed first, which yields an answer of 12. 12 is then added to 10, which yields 22.

Look at what happens when you add parentheses to the equation. What is the answer to this simple equation?

X=(10+3)*4

Now the answer is 52. Within parentheses, the values 10 and 3 are added first; then the result (13) is multiplied by 4, which yields 52.

✦ Define a default value in a table

✦ Place the current date and time on a report

✦ Convert data from one type to another

✦ Perform financial operations

✦ Display a field in a specific format

✦ Look up and return a value based on another

✦ Perform an action upon the triggering of an event

Access functions can perform financial, mathematical, comparative, and other operations. Therefore, functions are used just about everywhere — in queries, forms, reports, validation rules, and so forth.

Many Access functions evaluate or convert data from one type to another; others perform an action. Some Access functions require use of parameters; others operate without them.

Note   A parameter is a value that you supply to the function when you run it. The value can be an object name, a constant, or a quantity.

Access functions can be quickly identified because they always end with parentheses. If a function uses parameters, the parameters are placed inside the parentheses immediately after the function name.

Examples of Access functions are

Now( )	Returns the current date and time
Rnd( )	Returns a random number
Ucase( )	Returns the uppercase of an object
Format( )	Returns a user-specified formatted expression

Types of functions

Access offers several types of functions. They can be placed in the following general categories:

✦ Conversion

✦ Date/Time

✦ Financial (SQL)

✦ Financial (monetary)

✦ Mathematical

✦ String manipulation

✦ Domain

Conversion

Conversion functions change the data type from one type to another. A few common functions are listed here:

Str()	Returns a numeric as a string: Str(921.234) returns "921.234".
Val()	Returns a numeric value from a string: Val("1234.56") returns 1234.56. Val("10 Farmview Ct") returns 10.
Format()	Returns an expression according to the user-specified format: Format("Next",">") returns NEXT. Format("123456789","@@@-@@-@@@@") returns 123-45-6789. Format(#12/25/93#,"d-mmmm-yyyy") returns 25-December-1993.

What Is a Program?

A program is a series of defined steps that specify one or more actions the computer should perform. A program can be created by the user or can already exist in Access; all Access functions are already created programs. For example, a Ucase() function is a small program. If you employ Ucase () on a string, such as "Michael R. Irwin," Access creates a new string from the existing string, converting each letter to uppercase. The program starts at the left-most letter, first converting M to M and then i to I, and so forth, until the entire string is converted. As it converts each letter, the program concatenates it to a new string.

Date/Time

Date/Time functions work with date and time expressions. The following are some common Date/Time functions:

Now()	Returns the current date and time: 3/4/99 12:22:34 PM.
Time()	Returns the current time in 12-hour format: 12:22:34 PM.
Date()	Returns the current date (vs. Now() which returns date and time): 3/4/99.
DateDiff()	Returns a number based on a specific time interval between two different dates. The syntax is

DateDiff("d", date1, date2)

For example DateDiff("d", date, #01/01/1999#) will return the negative number of days between today and 1/1/1999. You can specify the number of days, weeks, months, quarters, years, and other intervals for this function.

Financial (SQL)

Financial (SQL) functions perform aggregate financial operations on a set of values. The set of values is contained in a field. The field can be in a form, report, or query. Two common SQL functions are listed below:

Avg()	An example is Avg([Scores]).
Sum()	An example is Sum([Gross Amount] + [Tax] + [Shipping]).

Financial (monetary)

Financial (monetary) functions perform financial operations. Two monetary functions are listed below:

NPV()	Is the net present value, based on a series of payments and a discount rate. The syntax is

NPV(discount rate, cash flow array())

DDB()   Is the double-declining balance method of depreciation return. The syntax is

DDB(initial cost, salvage value, life of product, period of asset depreciation)

Mathematical

Mathematical functions perform specific calculations. The following are some mathematical functions, with examples of how to use them.

Int()   Determines the integer of a specific value:

Int(1234.55) results in 1234.

Int(-55.1) results in -56.

Fix()   Determines the correct integer for a negative number:

Fix(-1234.55) results in -1234.

Sqr()   Determines the square root of a number:

Sqr(9) returns 3.

Sqr(14) returns 3.742.

String manipulation

String functions manipulate text-based expressions. Here are some common uses of these functions:

Right()   Returns the rightmost characters of a string:

Right("abcdefg",4) returns "defg."

Len()   Returns the length of a string:

Len("abcdefgh") results in 8.

Lcase()   Returns the lowercase of the string:

Lcase("Michael R. Irwin") Returns michael r. irwin.

Domain

A *domain* is a set of records contained in a table, a query, or an SQL expression. A query dynaset is an example of a domain. Domain aggregate functions determine specific statistics about a specific domain. If you need to perform statistical calculations in code, it must be done using domain aggregate functions. Domain aggregate functions can also be used to specify a criteria, update values, or even create calculated fields in a query expression.

Two examples of domain functions are listed below:

DAvg()   Returns the arithmetic mean (average) of a set of values.

                DAvg("[Total Amount]","Visits") Determines the average billing for patients.

DCount()   Returns the number of records specified.

What Are Expressions?

In general, an *expression* is the means used to explain or model something to someone or something. In computer terms, an expression is generally defined as a combination of a symbol, sign, figure, or set of symbols that presents or represents an algebraic fact as a quantity or operation. The expression is a representative object that Access can use to interpret something and, based on that interpretation, to obtain specific information. Simply put, an expression is a term or series of terms controlled by operators. Expressions are a fundamental part of Access operations. They are used to perform a calculation, manipulate characters, or test data.

You can use expressions in Access to accomplish a variety of tasks. You can use an expression as a property setting in SQL statements, in queries and filters, or in macros and actions. Expressions can set criteria for a query, filter, or control macros, or perform as arguments in user-defined functions.

Access evaluates an expression each time it is used. If an expression is in a form or report, Access calculates the value every time the form refreshes (as with changing records and so forth). This ensures accuracy of the results. If an expression is used as a criterion in a query, Access evaluates the expression every time the query is executed, thereby ensuring that the criterion reflects any changes, additions, or deletions to records since the last execution of the query. If an expression is used in the table design as a validation rule, Access executes the evaluation each time the field is trespassed to determine whether the value is allowed in the field; this expression may be based on another field's value!

To give you a better understanding of expressions, consider the examples that follow — all are examples of expressions:

=[Customer First Name] & " " & [Customer Last Name]

=[Total Amount] - ([Total Amount] * [Discount])<25

[Deceased]=Yes

[Animal Type] = "Cat" And [Gender] = "M"

[Date of Birth] Between 1/91 And 12/93

Each is a valid expression. Access can use them as validation rules, query criteria, calculated controls, control sources, and control-source properties.

The parts of an expression

As the examples in the preceding section demonstrated, expressions can be simple or complex. They can include a combination of operators, object names, functions, literal values, and constants.

Remembering that expressions don't need to contain all these parts, you should understand each of the following uniquely identifiable portions of an expression:

Operators: >, =, *, And, Or, Not, Like, and so on.

Operators indicate what type of action (operation) will be performed on one or more elements of an expression.

Object names: Forms![Add a Customer & Pets], [Customer Address], [Pet Name]

Object names, also known as *identifiers*, are the actual objects: tables, forms, reports, controls, or fields.

Functions: Date(), DLookUp(), DateDiff()

Functions always return a value. The resultant value can be created by a calculation, a conversion of data, or an evaluation. You can use a built-in Access function or a user-defined function that you create.

Literal values: 100, Jan. 1, 1993, "Cat," "[A-D]*"

These are actual values that you supply to the expression. Literal values can be numbers, strings, or dates. Access uses the values exactly as they are entered.

Constants: Yes, No, Null, True, False

Constants represent values that do not change.

The following example illustrates the parts of an expression:

[Follow Up Date] = Date() + 30 where:

[Follow Up Date] is an object name or identifier.

= is an operator.

Date() is a function.

+ is an operator.

30 is a literal.

Creating an expression

Expressions are commonly entered in property windows, action arguments, and criteria grids. As you create expressions, the area is scrolled so that you can continue to enter the expression. Although you can enter an expression in this manner, it is usually desirable to see the entire expression as you enter it. This is especially true when you are working with long, complex expressions. Access has a Zoom box that you can use to change how much of the expression you see as you enter it. Open this box by clicking where you want to enter your expression and pressing Shift+F2.

As you enter expressions, Access may insert certain characters for you when you change focus. Access checks your syntax and automatically inserts these characters:

✦ Brackets ([]) around control names that have no spaces or punctuation in the name

✦ Pound signs (#) around dates it recognizes

✦ Quotation marks (" ") around text that contains no spaces or punctuation in the body

Note   The term *changing focus* refers to the movement of the insertion point out of the location where you are entering the expression, which is accomplished by pressing Tab or by moving the mouse and clicking another area of the screen.

Caution   Access reports an error when it changes focus when Access doesn't understand the date form entered, the name of the control contains spaces, a control is not placed in brackets, or an end parenthesis is missing in a function, and on and on.

Entering object names

Object names are identified by placing brackets ([]) around the element. Access requires the use of brackets when the object contains a space or punctuation in its name. If these conditions are not present, you can ignore the brackets — Access inserts them automatically. The following expressions are syntactically identical:

Breed + [Type of Animal]

[Breed] + [Type of Animal]

Notice that in both cases the brackets are placed around Type of Animal because this object name contains spaces.

Although it isn't necessary to enter brackets around objects such as Breed in the second example, it is good programming practice to always surround object names with brackets for consistency in entry.

Entering text

Placing quotation marks around the text element of an expression identifies text. Access automatically places the quotation marks for you if you forget to add them.

As an example, you can type Cat, Dog, and Frog into separate criteria cells of a query, and Access automatically adds the quotation marks around each of these three entries. Access recognizes these as objects and helps you.

Entering date/time values

Placing pound signs (#) around the date/time element identifies date/time data. Access will evaluate any valid date/time format automatically and place the pound signs around the element for you.

Expression Builder

Access has added an *Expression Builder* tool to help you build complex expressions. You can use it anywhere you can build an expression (such as creating a calculated field on a form or report). You can activate the builder tool in two ways:

✦ Press the Build button on the toolbar (the button with the ellipsis on it).

✦ Click the *right* mouse button and select Build from the shortcut menu.

Special identifier operators and expressions

Access has two special *identifier operators*: the dot (.) and the exclamation point (!). Access tables provide many ways to display and access objects. You can use fields and their contents, and any field object can be reused repeatedly. You can display the field object in numerous forms and reports by using the same reference, the field object name, in every form and report.

For example, the field Pet Name from the Pets table can be used in seven different forms. When you want to use the Pet Name field in an expression for a comparison, how do you tell Access which copy of the field Pet Name it should use for the expression? Because Access is a Windows database, it is possible to have several different forms open in the same session on the same computer. In fact, it is possible to have multiple copies of Access running the same data and forms.

With all this repetition, there must be a way to tell Access which Pet Name field object you want the expression to use. That is the purpose of the dot and exclamation point as operator identifiers. These symbols clarify which field to use.

The ! (exclamation) identifier operator

The exclamation mark (!) is used in conjunction with several reserved words. One such reserved word is Forms. When this word is followed by !, Access is being told that the next object name is the form object name that you want to refer to.

A Few Words About Controls and Properties

When you create a form or report, you place many different objects on the form—fields in text boxes, text labels, buttons, check boxes, combo boxes, lines, rectangles, and so on.

As you select and place these objects on a form, each object is assigned a control name. Access supplies the control name according to predefined rules. For example, control names for fields default to a control-source name of the field name. The field name appears in the text box on the form. The label for the text box is assigned the control name Text, with a sequence number attached to it (for example, Text11 or Text12). The sequence number is added to make each control name unique.

After all objects are placed on the form, you can identify any object on the form (line, button, text box, and so on) by its unique control name. This control name is what you use to refer to a specific table field (or field on a form). You can change the name of the control that Access assigned to the object if you want. The only requirement for the new control name is that it must be unique to the form or report that contains it.

Every object on the form (including the form itself) has associated properties. These are the individual characteristics of each object; as such, they are accessible by a control name. Properties control the appearance of the object (color, size, sunken, alignment, and so forth). They also affect the structure, specifying format, default value, validation rules, and control name. In addition, properties designate the behavior of a control; for instance, whether the field can grow or shrink and whether you can edit it. Behaviors also affect actions specified for the event properties, such as On Enter and On Push.

As an example, say that you have a Date of Birth field that is in two forms—[Customer & Pets] and [Pet Specifics]. (These two form names are objects; you need to use square brackets to refer to them.) You want to refer to the Date of Birth field in the [Pet Specifics] form. The way to specify this form is by use of the ! and the *Forms* reserved word:

    Forms![Pet Specifics]

Now that the form is specified, further refine the scope to add the field Date of Birth.

Note   Although Chapter 14 covers controls and properties, by this point you should have a partial understanding of what properties and controls are (for a refresher, see the preceding sidebar).

Actually, what you are specifying is a control on the form. That control will use the field you need, which is Date of Birth. The control has the same name as the field. Therefore, you access this specific object by using the following expression:

    Forms![Pet Specifics]![Date of Birth]

The second exclamation mark specifies a control on a form — one identified by the reserved word *Forms*.

By following the properties of each object, starting with the object Forms, you can trace the control source object back to a field in the original table.

In summary, the exclamation-point identifier is always followed by an object name. This object name is defined by using the name of a form, report, field, or other control name that was created in the database. If you don't use the existing name for the desired object, you can change the default value name of the source.

The . (dot) identifier operator

The . (dot) is also a key symbol that is used in conjunction with expression identification operators. Normally it is placed immediately after a user-defined object. Unlike the !, the . (dot) usually identifies a property of a specific object. Therefore, if you want to determine the value of the Visible property of the same control you worked with before, you specify it as follows:

Forms![Pet Specifics]![Date of Birth].Visible

This gives the value for the Visible property of the specific field on the specific form.

Note

Normally the . (dot) identifier is used to obtain a value that corresponds to a property of an object. Sometimes, you can use it between a table name and a field name when you access a value associated with a specific field in a specific table, such as: [Pets].[Pet Name]

A thorough analysis of the two special identifier operators is beyond the scope of this book. Even so, you'll find that these identifiers enable you to find any object and the values associated with its properties.

✦   ✦   ✦

Creating Relations and Joins in Queries

◆ ◆ ◆ ◆

In This Chapter

Adding more than
one table to a query

Manipulating the
Table/Query pane

Determining which
table a field is from
in a query

Moving and resizing
the Field List windows

Creating a database
diagram

Adding single fields
to a query

Adding multiple fields
to a query

Working around
query limitations

Understanding types
of joins

Changing the type of
join

Creating an inner
join and an outer join

◆ ◆ ◆ ◆

In Chapter 9, you worked with simple single-table queries using the Pets table. Using a query to obtain information from a single table is common; often, however, you need information from several related tables. For example, you may want to obtain a customer's name and the type of pets the customer owns. In this chapter, you learn how to use more than one table to obtain information.

Adding More than One Table to a Query

In Chapter 6, you learned about the different tables in the Mountain Animal Hospital database system and how they relate to each other through their relationships. This system is composed of four primary tables and four lookup tables. You learned about primary and foreign table keys and their importance for linking two tables together. You learned how to create relationships between two tables at the table level by using the Tools ➪ Relationships command from the Database window. Finally, you learned how referential integrity rules affect data in tables.

After you create the tables for your database and decide how the tables are related to one another, you are ready to begin creating multiple-table queries to obtain information from several tables at the same time.

By adding more than one table to a query and then selecting fields from the tables in the query, you can view information from your database just as though the information from the several tables was in one table. As an example, suppose you need to send a letter to all owners of snakes who have not brought their pets in for a visit in the past six months. The data you need to get this information is in three separate tables: Pets, Customer, and Visits. You can get this information by creating a query using the Pets, Customer, and Visits tables for all animals where the Type of Animal field equals snake and where Visit Date falls between today's date and today's date minus six months. The relationship between the Pets and Customer tables gives access to the customer information for each snake, permitting you to create a report form using the related information from the tables Pets, Visits, and Customer. The same is true for the relationship between the Pets and Visits table.

Note For this chapter and subsequent query chapters you should be using the Mountain Animal Start database.

The first step in creating a multiple-table query is to open each table in the Query window. The following steps show how to open the Pets, Customer, and Visits tables in a single query:

1. Click the Query object in the Database window.

2. Click the New toolbar button to create a new query.

3. Select Design View and click the OK button in the New Query dialog box.

4. Select the Pets table (in the Show Table dialog box) by double-clicking the table name.

5. Select the Customer table by double-clicking the table name.

6. Select the Visits table by double-clicking the table name.

7. Click the Close button in the Show Table dialog box.

Note You can also add each table by highlighting the table in the list separately and clicking Add.

Figure 12-1 shows the top pane of the Query Design window with the three tables you just added: Pets, Customer, and Visits.

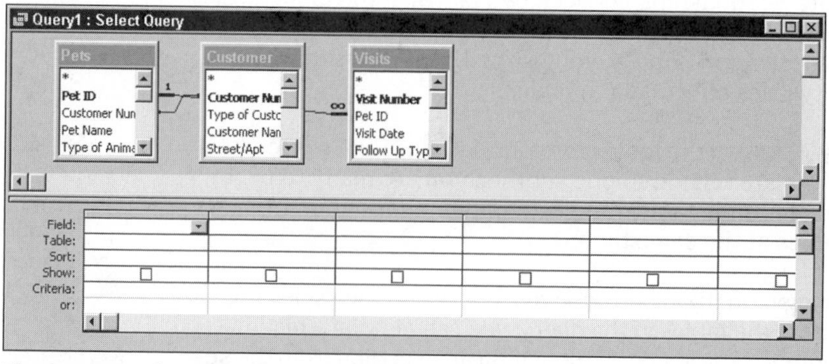

Figure 12-1: The Query Design window with three tables added. Notice the join lines are already present.

Note You can add more tables by selecting Query ➪ Show Table from the Query Design window or by clicking the Show Table button.

Working with the Table/Query Pane

As Figure 12-1 shows, a single line is present between tables, going from the primary key field to the foreign key field, which signifies a connection between the tables. Actually, on your screen it probably looks as if two lines connect Pets to Customer and a single line runs from Customer to Visits. Later you learn how to move the field list so that the lines appear correctly.

Cross-Reference These lines were pre-drawn because you already set the relationships between the tables earlier in Chapter 6.

The join line

When Access displays each set of related tables, it places a line between the two tables. This line is known as a join line. A *join line* is a graphical line that represents the relationship between two tables. In this example, the join line goes from the Pets table to the Customer table to connect the two Customer Number fields. A join line also runs from Pets to Visits, connecting the Pet ID fields in these two tables.

This line is created automatically because a relationship was set in the Relationship builder. If Access already knows what the relationship is, it automatically creates the line for you when the tables are added to a query. The relationship is displayed as a join line between two tables.

If Referential Integrity was set in the relationship between two tables, Access displays a thick portion of the line right at the table window similar to the line in Figure 12-2. The line starts heavy and becomes thin between Pets and Visits (heavy on both ends). This line variation tells you that Referential Integrity has been set between the two tables in the Relationship Builder. If a one-to-many relationship exists, the many relationship is denoted by an infinity symbol (sideways 8 — ∞).

The upper Query pane in Figure 12-2 has been re-sized and the tables moved around to better show the visual connection between the two tables. To resize the pane, simply click on the *pane resizing bar* and drag it down to enlarge the upper pane. After the pane has been resized, you can move the tables around to match those in Figure 12-2. Resizing the pane and moving tables are covered after this section.

Cross-Reference Chapter 9 has more information on how to work with the Query window and its two panes.

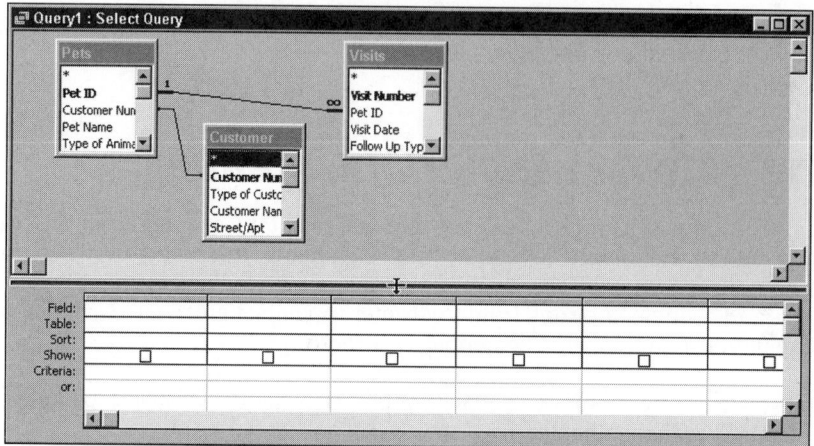

Figure 12-2: Resizing the Query Design panes. Note that the Table/Query pane is larger. The *pane-resizing bar* is highlighted (dark) between the two tables and the mouse pointer has changed to a small bar with up and down arrows to let you know that the panes are being resized.

Note   If you have not specified a relationship between two tables and the following conditions are true, Access 2002 automatically joins the tables:

1. Both tables have a field with the same name.

2. The field with the same name in both tables has the same data type (text, numeric, and so on).

3. The field is a *primary key* field in one of the tables.

Tip   Access 2002 automatically attempts to join the tables if a relationship exists. It will not attempt to set the referential integrity — only the join. However, you can turn this property off by deselecting the default Enable AutoJoin option from the global Access options tabbed dialog box. To display this option, select Tools ⇨ Options, click the Tables/Queries tab in the options box, and deselect the Enable AutoJoin option (under the Query design section).

Manipulating the Field List window

Each Field List window begins at a fixed size, which shows approximately four fields and 12 characters for each field. Each Field List window is a true window and behaves like one; it can be resized and moved. If you have more fields than will show in the Field List window, a scroll bar displays to enable you to scroll through the fields in the Field List window.

Note After a relationship is created between tables, the join line remains between the two fields. As you move through a table selecting fields, the graphical line will move relative to the linked fields. For example, if the scroll box moves down (toward the bottom of the window) in the Customer table, the join line moves up with the customer number, eventually stopping at the top of the table window.

When you're working with many tables, these join lines can become visually confusing as they cross or overlap. If you move through the table, the line eventually becomes visible, and the field it is linked to becomes obvious.

Resizing the Table/Query pane

When you place Field Lists on the Table/Query pane, they appear in a fixed size with little spacing between tables. When you add a table to the top pane, it initially shows five fields. If more fields are in the table, a scroll bar is added to the box (right side). The table window may show only part of a long field name, the rest being truncated by the window size. You can move the tables around the pane and resize them to show more field names or more of the field name. The first step, however, is to resize the pane itself. The Query Design window has two panes. The top pane displays your Field Lists, whereas the bottom QBE (Query by Example) pane below enables you to enter fields, sort orders, and define criteria. Often you will want the top pane to be larger than the bottom pane so that you can see more field names. The Query window's title bar tells you that you are creating a Select query (Query1: Select Query). If you change the query to another type of query (which you do in later chapters), the title bar changes to let you know what type of query you are creating.

You can resize the Table/Query pane by placing your mouse pointer on the thick line between the two panes. This is the *window split bar*, also known as the pane-resizing bar. The pointer changes to a small, thick bar with double vertical arrows (up and down), as shown in Figure 12-2, which enables you to drag the split bar up or down. To resize the panes, follow these steps:

1. Place the pointer on the window split bar.

2. Hold down the mouse button and drag the split bar down.

3. Release the bar when it is two lines below the QBE row "or."

The top pane is now much larger; the bottom pane is smaller but it still displays the entire QBE Design area. If the QBE Design area shows insufficient area, simply resize the entire window by selecting the bottom border of the window and then click and drag the window down — making it larger. You now have space to move the Field Lists around and properly view the Table/Query pane.

Note You can build a database diagram, as you did in Chapter 6, so that you view only the Field Lists by moving the split bar to the bottom of the screen and then positioning the Field Lists as you want within the full-screen area.

Moving a table

You can move Field Lists in the Table/Query pane by placing the mouse pointer on the title bar of a Field List (where the name of the table is) and dragging the table to a new location. You may want to move the Field Lists for a better working view or to clean up a confusing database diagram (like the one shown in Figure 12-2). To move Field Lists, follow these steps:

1. Place the mouse pointer on the title bar of the Customer table on the name *Customer*.

2. Drag the Customer table design straight down until the top of the table design appears where the bottom was when you started.

The window should now look like Figure 12-3. You can see that each line is now an individual line that goes from one table's primary key to the foreign key in another table.

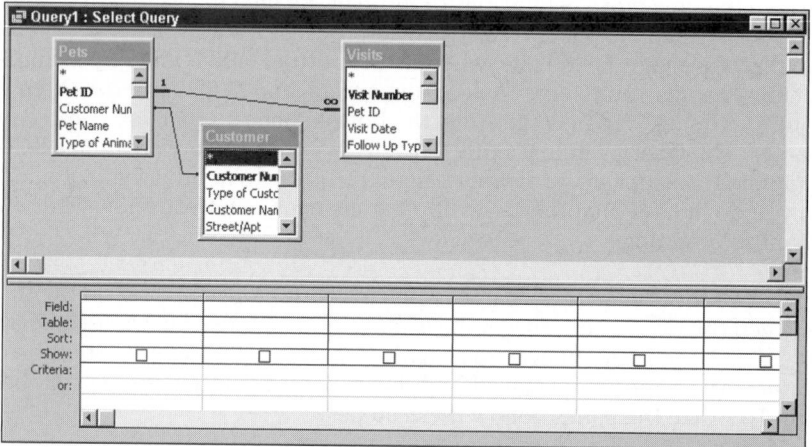

Figure 12-3: The repositioned Pets, Customer, and Visits tables. Note the join lines are now clearly visible between the Pets and Customer tables and between the Pets and Visits tables.

You can move the Field Lists anywhere in the top pane. You can spread them out by moving the Field Lists farther apart. You can also rearrange the Field Lists. You may want to place the Customer table first, followed by the Pets table and then the Visits table.

In this exercise you want to view the snakes that have not been in for a visit in the past six months so that you can send a letter to the customer. So the table sequence of Pets, Customer, and Visits makes sense. You generally want to view your diagram with a particular business purpose in mind. The Pets table (where you find records when Type of Animal is a snake) is the main table in this business example because it is needed to retrieve information from both the Visits and Customer tables.

Removing a table

There are times when you need to remove tables from a query. Any table can be removed from the Query window. Follow these steps to delete the Visits table; remember, you can bring it back later:

1. Select the Visits table in the top pane of the Query window by clicking either the table or a field in the table.

2. Press the Delete key or select Edit ⇨ Delete.

> **Note**   Only one table can be removed at a time from the Query window. The menu choice Edit ⇨ Clear Grid does not remove all tables; it removes all fields from the QBE pane. You can also remove a table by right-clicking a table and selecting Remove Table from the shortcut menu.

When you delete a table, any join lines to that table are deleted as well. When you delete a table, there is no warning or confirmation dialog box. The table is simply removed from the screen.

Adding more tables

You may decide to add more tables to a query or you may accidentally delete a table and need to add it back. You can accomplish this task by either selecting Query ⇨ Show Table or by clicking the *right* mouse button and selecting Show Table from the shortcut menu that appears. When you use either of these methods, the Show Table dialog box that appeared when you created the query is redisplayed. To restore the Visits table to the screen, follow these steps:

1. Move the mouse pointer to the top pane (outside of any existing tables) and press the right mouse button. Select Show Table from the menu.

2. Select the Visits table by double-clicking the table name.

3. Click the Close button in the Show Table dialog box.

Access adds the Visits table to the Query window and redisplays the join line.

Resizing a Field List window

You can also resize each of the Field Lists by placing the cursor on one of the Field List borders. The Field List is nothing but a window; thus, you can enlarge or reduce it vertically, horizontally, or diagonally by placing the cursor on the appropriate border. When you enlarge the Field List vertically, you can see more fields than the default number (five). By making the Field List larger horizontally, you can see the complete list of field names. Then, when you resize the Table/Query pane to take up the entire window, you can create a database diagram.

Creating a database diagram

Figure 12-4 is a database diagram for the three tables — Pets, Customers, and Visits. Notice that it displays all the fields of these tables. The more tables and relationships there are, the more important a database diagram is to viewing the data graphically with the proper relationships visible. In upcoming chapters, many different database diagrams are displayed as queries are written to assemble the data for various forms and reports.

In Figure 12-4, the Table/Query pane is expanded to almost its full size and the QBE pane is displayed (800 x 600 resolution). It's OK if you can't see any of the QBE pane on your screen. You can get to the QBE pane by using the split bar to resize. When working with fields in the QBE pane, keep the screen split so that both panes are visible.

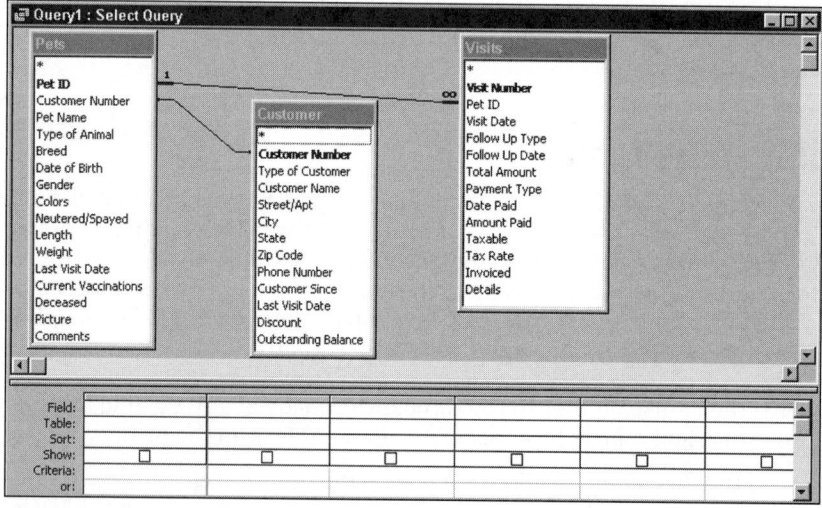

Figure 12-4: A database diagram using the three tables — Pets, Customers, and Visits

 **Caution**   You can switch panes by pressing F6, but you can't see where the insertion point is in the QBE pane while the Table/Query pane is displayed in full-screen size and the QBE pane is not visible.

 **Caution**   If you move the cursor to the outside of the panes — for example, clicking on the resizing bar and then pressing F6 — it will *not* move the cursor between panes. You must have the cursor active in one of the two panes of the Query Design window.

Tip

If you are following the examples in this chapter, resize the panes so that you can see both the Field List pane and the QBE pane.

Adding Fields from More than One Table

You add fields from more than one table to the query in exactly the same way as when you're working with a single table. You can add fields one at a time, many fields grouped together, or all the fields from one or all tables.

Cross-Reference

Adding fields from a single table is covered in detail in Chapter 9; this chapter covers the topic in less detail, but focuses on the differences between single- and multiple-table field selection.

Adding a single field

You can add a single field from any table to the QBE pane by several methods:

✦ Double-click a field name in the Table/Query pane.

✦ Click a field name in the Table/Query pane and drag it to the QBE pane.

✦ Click an empty Field cell in the QBE pane and type a field name.

✦ Click an empty Field cell and select the field from the drop-down list.

Caution

If you type a field name in an empty Field cell that is in both tables, Access enters the field name from the first table that it finds containing that field. Access searches the tables, starting from the left side in the top pane.

If you select the field from the drop-down list in the Field cell, you see the name of the table first, followed by a period and the field name. For example, the field Pet ID in the Pets table is displayed as *Pets.Pet ID*. This helps you select the right field name. Using this method, you can select a common field name from a specific table.

The easiest way to select fields is still to double-click the field names while in the query/table design pane. To do so, you may have to resize the Field Lists to see the fields that you want to select. To select Customer Name, Pet Name, Type of Animal, and Visit Date, follow these steps:

1. Double-click Customer Name in the Customer table.

2. Double-click Pet Name in the Pets table.

3. Double-click Type of Animal in the Pets table.

4. Double-click Visit Date in the Visits table.

Viewing the table names

When you're working with two or more tables, the field names in the QBE pane can become confusing. You may find yourself asking, for example, just which table the field Customer Number is from.

Access automatically maintains the table name that is associated with each field displayed in the QBE pane. The default is to display the table name below the name of the field. If you do not want to show the table name of each field in the QBE pane, select View ➪ Table Names and the toggle will be turned off (unchecked).

This command controls the display of table names immediately below the corresponding field name in the QBE pane. Figure 12-5 shows the QBE pane with the Table row below the Field row. It contains the name of the table for each field.

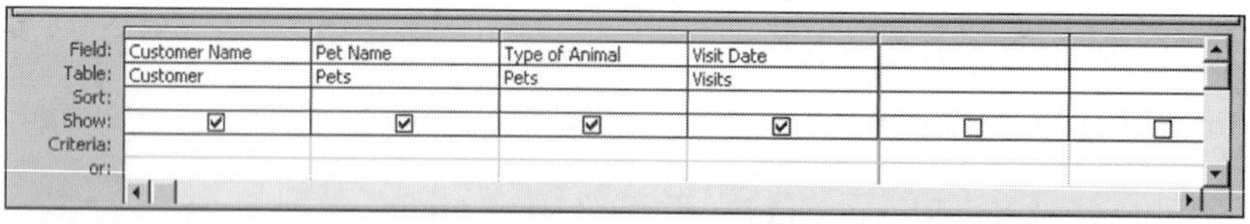

Field:	Customer Name	Pet Name	Type of Animal	Visit Date		
Table:	Customer	Pets	Pets	Visits		
Sort:						
Show:	☑	☑	☑	☑	☐	☐
Criteria:						
or:						

Figure 12-5: The QBE pane with table names displayed. Notice that the second row (Table) shows the Customer table name, then two Pets table names, and the Visits table name.

After you add fields to a query, you can view your resultant data at any time. Although you eventually limit the display of data to snakes that have not visited you during the past six-month period, you can view all the data now by selecting the Datasheet icon. Figure 12-6 displays the data as currently selected. The fields have been resized to show all the data values.

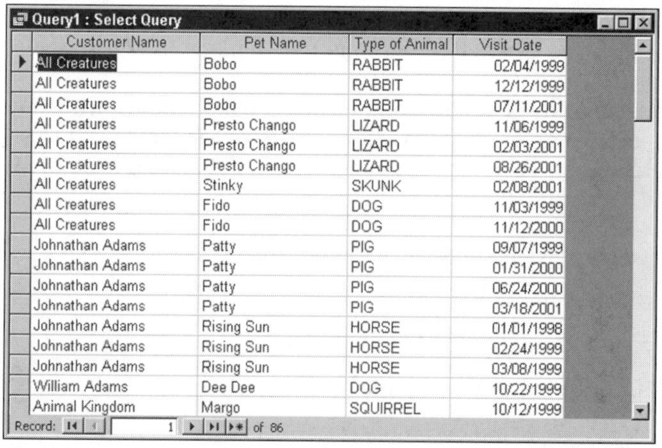

Customer Name	Pet Name	Type of Animal	Visit Date
All Creatures	Bobo	RABBIT	02/04/1999
All Creatures	Bobo	RABBIT	12/12/1999
All Creatures	Bobo	RABBIT	07/11/2001
All Creatures	Presto Chango	LIZARD	11/06/1999
All Creatures	Presto Chango	LIZARD	02/03/2001
All Creatures	Presto Chango	LIZARD	08/26/2001
All Creatures	Stinky	SKUNK	02/08/2001
All Creatures	Fido	DOG	11/03/1999
All Creatures	Fido	DOG	11/12/2000
Johnathan Adams	Patty	PIG	09/07/1999
Johnathan Adams	Patty	PIG	01/31/2000
Johnathan Adams	Patty	PIG	06/24/2000
Johnathan Adams	Patty	PIG	03/18/2001
Johnathan Adams	Rising Sun	HORSE	01/01/1998
Johnathan Adams	Rising Sun	HORSE	02/24/1999
Johnathan Adams	Rising Sun	HORSE	03/08/1999
William Adams	Dee Dee	DOG	10/22/1999
Animal Kingdom	Margo	SQUIRREL	10/12/1999

Record: ◄◄ ◄ 1 ► ►► ►* of 86

Figure 12-6: Datasheet view of data from multiple tables. This resulting dynaset, from the query, contains 86 records.

The display of the table name is only for your information. Access always maintains the table name associated with the field names.

Adding multiple fields at the same time

The process of adding multiple fields at the same time is identical to adding multiple fields in a single table query. When you're adding multiple fields from several tables, you must add them from one table at a time. The easiest way to do this is to select multiple fields and drag them together down to the QBE pane.

You can select multiple contiguous fields by clicking the first field of the list, then clicking the last field while holding down the Shift key (as you click the last field that you want to add). You can also select non-contiguous fields in the list by holding down the Ctrl key while clicking individual fields with the mouse.

Adding all table fields

To add all table fields at the same time, select which table's fields you want to add, and then select the fields to be added. You can select all the fields by either double-clicking the title bar of the table name or by selecting the Asterisk (*) field. These two methods, however, produce very different results.

Selecting all fields using the title bar method

One method of selecting all the fields is to double-click the title bar of the table whose fields you want to select.

This method automatically selects all the fields (except the Asterisk). Once selected, all the fields can be dragged to the QBE pane. The fields are added in the order of their position in the table, from left to right (based on their field order in the table). By default, Access displays only the first five full fields in the QBE pane (lower pane). You can change the column width of each field to display more or fewer columns.

Selecting all fields using the Asterisk (*) method

The first object in each table is an asterisk (at the top of the field list), which is known as the *all-field reference tag*. When you select and drag the asterisk to the QBE pane, all fields in the table are added to the QBE pane, but there is a distinct difference between this method and the double-clicking method referred to previously: When you add the all-field reference tag (*), the QBE pane shows only one cell with the name of the table and an asterisk. For example, if you select the * in the Pets table, you see *Pets.* * displayed in one field row cell.

Unlike selecting all the fields, the asterisk places a reference to all the fields in a single column. When you drag multiple columns, as in the preceding example, you drag actual table field names to the query. If you later change the design of the table, you also have to change the design of the query. The advantage of using the asterisk for selecting all fields is that the query doesn't need to be changed if you add, delete, or rename fields in the underlying table or query. Changing fields in the underlying table or query automatically adds fields to or removes fields from the query.

Caution

Selecting the * does have one drawback: You cannot perform criteria conditions on the asterisk column itself. You have to add an individual field from the table and enter the criterion. If you add a field for a criterion (when using the *), the query displays the field twice — once for the * field and a second time for the criterion field. Therefore, you may want to deselect the Show cell of the criterion field.

Understanding the Limitations of Multiple-Table Queries

When you create a query with multiple files, there are limitations to what fields can be edited. Generally, you can change data in a query dynaset, and your changes are saved to the underlying tables. A primary key field normally cannot be edited if referential integrity is in effect and if the field is part of a relationship (unless Cascade Updates is set to Yes).

To update a table from a query, a value in a specific record in the query must represent a single record in the underlying table. This means that you cannot update fields in a Crosstab or Totals query because they both group records together to display grouped information. Instead of displaying the actual underlying table data, they display records of data that are calculated and stored in a virtual (nonreal) table called a *snapshot*.

Updating limitations

In Access, the records in your tables may not always be updateable. Table 12-1 shows when a field in a table is updateable. As Table 12-1 shows, queries based on one-to-many relationships are updateable in both tables (depending on how the query was designed). Any query that creates a *snapshot*, however, is not updateable.

Table 12-1
Rules for Updating Queries

Type of Query or Field	Updateable	Comments
One Table	Yes	
One-to-One relationship	Yes	
Results contains Memo field	Yes	Memo field updateable
Results contain Hyperlink	Yes	Hyperlink updateable
Results contain an OLE object	Yes	OLE object updateable
One-to-Many relationship	Mostly	Restrictions based on design methodology (see text)
Many-to-One-to-Many	No	Can update data in a form or data access page if RecordType = Dynaset
Two or more tables with NO join line	No	Must have a join to determine updateability
Crosstab	No	Creates a snapshot of the data
Totals Query (Sum, Avg, etc.)	No	Works with Grouped data creating a snapshot
Unique Value property is Yes	No	Shows unique records only in a snapshot
SQL-specific queries	No	Union & Pass-through work with ODBC data
Calculated field	No	Will recalculate automatically
Read-only fields	No	If opened read-only or on read-only drive (CD-ROM)
Permissions denied	No	Insert, Replace, or Delete are not granted
ODBC Tables with no Primary Key	No	A primary key (unique index) must exist
Paradox Table with no Primary Key	No	A primary key file must exist
Locked by another user	No	Cannot be updated while a field is locked by another

Overcoming query limitations

Table 12-1 shows that there are times when queries and fields in tables are not updateable. As a general rule, any query that does aggregate calculations or is an ODBC (Open DataBase Connectivity)-based SQL (Structured Query Language) query (SQL-specific query) is not updateable. All others can be updated. When your query has more than one table and some of the tables have a one-to-many relationship, there may be fields that are not updateable (depending on the design of the query).

Updating a unique index (primary key)

If a query uses two tables that have a one-to-many relationship, the one side of the join must have a unique (primary key) index on the field that is used for the join. If not, the fields from the one side of the query cannot be updated.

Replacing existing data in a query with a one-to-many relationship

Normally, all the fields in the many-side table are updateable in a one-to-many query; the one-side table can update all the fields *except* the primary key (join) field. Normally, this is sufficient for most database application purposes. Also, the primary key field is rarely changed in the one-side table because it is the link to the records in the joined tables.

At times, however, you may need to change the link-field contents in both tables (make a new primary key in the one table and have the database program change the link field in all the related records from the *many* table). Access 2002 enables you to do this by defining a relationship between the two tables and using referential integrity. If you define a relationship and enforce referential integrity in the Relationship Builder, two selections are activated. If you want to enable changes (updates) to the primary key field, check the Cascade Update Related Fields box, as shown in Figure 12-7. By selecting this option, you can change the primary key field in a relationship; Access automatically updates the link field to the new value in all the other related tables.

To display the Edit Relationships dialog box as shown in Figure 12-7, right-click anywhere in the top pane and select Relationships from the shortcut menu (or Select Tools ⇨ Relationships). The Relationships window appears. Right-click on the one-to-many link between the Pets and Visits tables and select Edit Relationships to activate the Edit Relationships dialog box.

Design tips for updating fields in queries

✦ If you want to add records to both tables of a one-to-many relationship, include the join field from the *many-side* table and show the field in the datasheet. After doing this, records can be added starting with either table. The *one* side's join field is copied automatically to the *many* side's join field.

✦ If you do not want any fields to be updateable, set the Allow Edits property of the form to No.

✦ If you do not want to update some fields on a form, set the Tab Stop property for the control (field) to No for these fields.

✦ If you want to add records to multiple tables in a form (covered in later chapters), remember to include all (or most) of the fields from both tables. Otherwise, you will not have a complete record of data in your form.

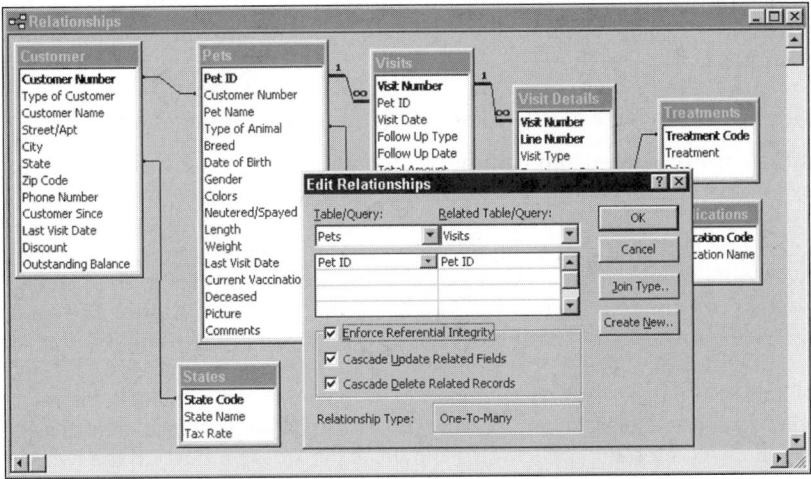

Figure 12-7: The Relationships dialog box with referential integrity in effect between the Pets and Visits table

Temporary inability to update in a one-to-many relationship

When updating records on the one side of a one-to-many query, you will *not* be able to change the many-side *join* field until you save changes to the one side. You can quickly save changes to the one side by pressing Shift+Enter or selecting File ➪ Save Record. Once the one-side changes are saved, the join field in the *many*-side record can be changed.

Creating and Working with Query Joins

You can create joins between tables in these three ways:

✦ By creating relationships between the tables when you design the database (Select Tools ➪ Relationships from the Database window or click the Relationships button on the toolbar.)

✦ By selecting two tables for the query that have a field that has the same data type and name in both tables and is a primary key field in one of the tables

✦ By creating joins in the Query window at the time you create a query

The first two methods are automatic in the Query design window. If you create relationships when designing the tables of your database, Access displays join lines based on those relationships automatically when you add the related tables to a query. It also creates an automatic join between two tables that have a common field, provided that field is a primary key in one of the tables and the Enable AutoJoin choice is selected (default) in the Options dialog box.

If relationships are set in the relationship builder, there may be times when you add a table to a query and it will not automatically be related to another table, as in these examples:

✦ The two tables have a common field, but it is not the same name.

✦ A table is not related and cannot be logically related to the other table (for example, the Customer table cannot directly join the Treatments table).

If you have two tables that are not automatically joined and you need to relate them, you join them in the Query Design window. Joining tables in the Query Design window does *not* create a permanent join between the tables. Rather, the join (relationship) will apply only to the tables for the query you are working on.

Caution   All tables in a query should be joined to at least one other table. If, for example, you place two tables in a query and do not join them, Access creates a query based on a Cartesian product (also known as the cross product) of the two tables. This subject is discussed later in this chapter. For now, note that a Cartesian product means that if you have five records in table 1 and six records in table 2, then the resulting query will have 30 records (5 x 6) that will probably be useless.

Joining tables

Figure 12-8 shows the joined Pets and Customer tables. They're joined automatically.

Note   When the two tables are brought in, Access automatically joined them. For this exercise, delete the join line by clicking on it to highlight it; then press the delete key or select delete from the right mouse click menu. If you have problems, refer to the next section, Deleting Joins, and then return to this one.

Note   Tables are not joined automatically in a query if they are not already joined at the table level, if they do not have a common named field for a primary key, or if the AutoJoin option is off.

With the Pets and Customer's tables no longer joined, you will need to re-join them. To join the Pets and Customer tables, follow the steps below:

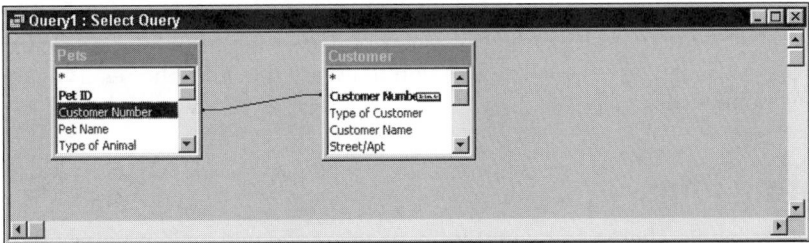

Figure 12-8: Joining tables in the Table/Query pane. Notice that in this figure, BOTH the join line and the Field icon (over the Customers table Customer number field) are present. This figure shows both processes being performed — selecting the fields to join and the resulting join line. As you move the Field icon from table to table, the line will not be there until you drop the field icon on the second table's field.

1. Select the Customer Number field in the Customer Table in the Table/Query pane.

2. Drag the highlighted field to the Pets table (as you drag the field, the Field icon appears).

3. Drop the Field icon on the Customer Number field in the Pets table (the Field icon disappears and a join line appears connecting the two tables via the fields specified).

Figure 12-8 shows the new join line after it is created. Notice that the field icon is also shown. When you perform this action (joining one field to another) the icon disappears *before* the join line is displayed. After selecting the field (Customer Number), the Field icon first appears in the Customer Number field of the Customer table; then it moves to the Pets table. As it moves between tables, the Field icon changes to the symbol that indicates the icon cannot be dropped in the area between the tables. When the icon is over the Customer Number field, it changes back to the Field icon, indicating that it can be dropped in that location. When you release the mouse button over the Customer Number field of the Customer table, the join line appears.

Of course, you can also create joins that make no sense, but when you view the data, you will get less-than-desirable results. If two joined fields have no values in common, you will have a datasheet in which no records are selected.

Caution If you fail to create a join line between tables, the resulting dynaset, viewed in the datasheet, will be a Cartesian product in which each and every record is joined with each and every record in the second table. If one table has 100 records and the other has 200 records, the Cartesian join will create a table with 20,000 records and the results will make no sense.

Note You can select either table first when you create a join.

You would never want to create a meaningless join. For example, you would not want to join the City field from the Customer table to the Date of Birth field in the Pets table. Although Access will enable you to create this join, the resulting dynaset will have no records in it.

Deleting joins

To delete a join line between two tables, you select the join line and press the Delete key. You can select the join line by placing the mouse pointer on any part of the line and clicking once. To practice, create a new query by adding the Customer and Pets tables, and then follow these steps to delete the join line between the Pets and Customer tables:

1. Select the join line between the Customer Number field in the Pets table and the Customer table by clicking the line with the mouse button.

2. With the join line highlighted, press the Delete key.

After Step 2, the line should disappear. If you delete a join line between two tables that have a relationship set at the database level, the broken join is effective only for the query in which you broke the join. When you exit the query, the relationship between the two tables remains in effect for other operations, including subsequent queries.

You can also delete a join by selecting it and choosing Edit ➪ Delete.

Caution   If you delete a join between two tables and the tables remain in the Query window unjoined to any other tables, the solution will have unexpected results because of the Cartesian product that Access creates from the two tables. The Cartesian product is effective for only this query. The underlying relationship remains intact.

Note   Access enables you to create multiple-field joins between tables (more than one line can be drawn). The join must be between two fields that have the same data and data type; if not, the query will not find any records from the datasheet to display.

Understanding Types of Table Joins

In Chapter 6, you learned about table relationships and relating two tables by a common field. Access understands all types of table and query relations, including these:

✦ One-to-one

✦ One-to-many

✦ Many-to-one

✦ Many-to-many

When you specify a relationship between two tables, you establish rules for the type of relationship, not for viewing the data based on the relationship.

To view data in two tables, they must be joined through a link that is established via a common field (or group of fields) between the two tables. The method of linking the tables is known as *joining*. In a query, tables with established relationships are shown already joined. Within a query, you can create new joins or change existing joins; just as there are different types of relationships, there are different types of joins. In the following sections, you learn about these types of joins:

✦ Equi-joins (inner joins)

✦ Outer joins

✦ Self-joins

✦ Cross-product joins (Cartesian joins)

Inner joins (Equi-joins)

The default join in Access is known as an *inner join* or *equi-join*. It tells Access to select all records from both tables that have the same value in the fields that are joined.

> **Note**
>
> The Access manuals refer to the default join as both an equi-join and inner join (commonly referred to as an inner join in database relational theory). The Access Help system refers to it as an inner join. The terms equi-join and inner join are interchangeable; however, in the remainder of this chapter they shall be referred to as inner joins.

If records are found in either table that do not have matching records in the other table, they are excluded from the resultant dynaset and will not be shown in the datasheet. Thus an inner join between tables is simply a join where records are selected when matching values exist in the joined field of both tables.

Recall the Customer and Pets tables for an example of an inner join. Remember that you are looking for all records from these two tables with matching fields. The Customer Number fields are common to both, so the inner join does not show any records for customers that have no pets or any pets that do not relate to a valid customer number. The rules of referential integrity prevent pet records that are not tied to a customer number from being saved. Of course, it's possible to delete all pets from a customer or to create a new customer record with no pet records, but a pet should always be related to a valid customer. Referential integrity should keep a customer number from being deleted or changed if a pet is related to it.

It's possible to have a customer in the Customer table who has no pets. It's less likely, but still theoretically possible, to have a pet with no owner. If you create a query to show customers and their pets, any record of a customer without a pet or a pet record without a matching customer record will not be shown in the resulting dynaset.

It can be important to find these lost records. One of the features of a query is to perform several types of joins.

Tip   Access can help find lost records between tables by using a Query Wizard to build a Find Unmatched Query (these are covered in Chapter 24).

Changing join properties

With the Customer and Pets tables joined, certain join behaviors (or *properties*) exist between the tables. The join property is a rule that says to display all records (for the fields you specify) that correspond to the characters found in the Customer Number field of the Customer table and in the corresponding Customer Number field of the Pets table.

To translate this rule into a practical example, this is what happens in the Customer and Pets tables:

   ✦ If a customer's record in the Customer table has a Customer Number that is not found in any of the records of the Pets table, then that Customer record is not shown.

   ✦ If a record in the Pets table has a number for a customer number that is not related to any Customer in the Customer table, then that Pets record is not shown.

This makes sense, at least most of the time. You don't want to see records for customers without pets — *or do you?*

A join property is a rule that is enforced by Access. This rule tells Access how to interpret any exceptions (possible errors) between two tables. For example, as you saw earlier, should the non-corresponding records be shown?

Access has several types of joins, each with its own characteristics or behaviors. Access enables you to change the type of join quickly by changing its properties. You can change join properties by selecting the join line between tables and double-clicking the line, or right mouse clicking and select Join Properties from the menu. When you do so, a Join Properties dialog box appears. If you double-click the join line between the Customer and Pets table, the dialog box in Figure 12-9 displays.

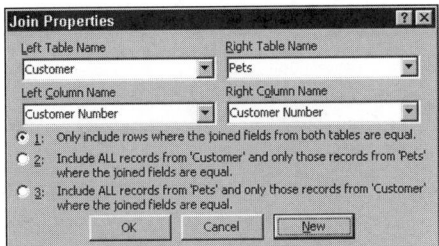

Figure 12-9: The Join Properties dialog box for the Customer and Pets tables. Notice that the first option button is selected (for the inner join).

The Join Properties dialog box has two parts: the four combo boxes and three option buttons. For now you focus on the three options buttons:

1. Only include rows where the joined fields from both tables are equal. (This is the default.)

2. Include ALL records from "Customer" and only those records from "Pets" where the joined fields are equal.

3. Include ALL records from "Pets" and only those records from "Customer" where the joined fields are equal.

The first choice is commonly known as an *inner join,* and the other two are known as *outer joins*. These joins control the behavior of Access as it builds the dynaset from the query.

Inner and outer joins

At this point you should delete the Visits table for the remainder of the exercises. The Query Design window should now display two tables in the top pane of the Query window — Customer and Pets. (If the query has other tables, delete them.) If your query window does not have these two tables, create a new query and add them. The following sections use these tables as examples to explain how inner and outer joins operate.

Displaying an inner join

To display an inner join, follow this procedure: In the QBE pane, select the fields Customer Number and Customer Name from the Customer table and the fields Pet Name and Type of Animal from the Pets table. Then display the dynaset by selecting the Datasheet button on the toolbar. The datasheet should now look like Figure 12-10, displaying each customer, all the customers' pets, and the type of animal for each pet. Scroll through the records until you reach the bottom of the datasheet.

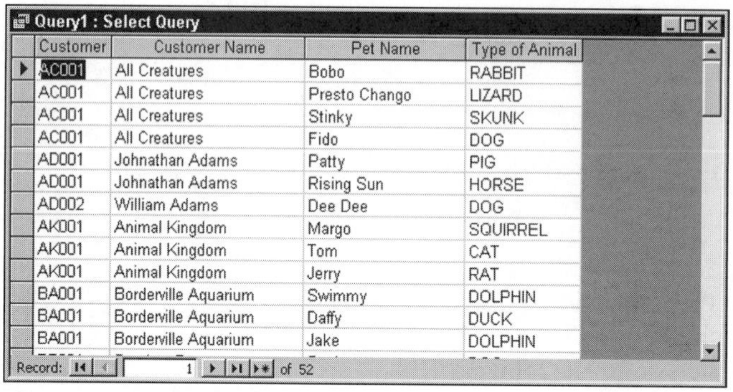

Query1 : Select Query

Customer	Customer Name	Pet Name	Type of Animal
AC001	All Creatures	Bobo	RABBIT
AC001	All Creatures	Presto Chango	LIZARD
AC001	All Creatures	Stinky	SKUNK
AC001	All Creatures	Fido	DOG
AD001	Johnathan Adams	Patty	PIG
AD001	Johnathan Adams	Rising Sun	HORSE
AD002	William Adams	Dee Dee	DOG
AK001	Animal Kingdom	Margo	SQUIRREL
AK001	Animal Kingdom	Tom	CAT
AK001	Animal Kingdom	Jerry	RAT
BA001	Borderville Aquarium	Swimmy	DOLPHIN
BA001	Borderville Aquarium	Daffy	DUCK
BA001	Borderville Aquarium	Jake	DOLPHIN

Record: 1 of 52

Figure 12-10: The datasheet for an inner join between the Customer and Pets tables

Notice that each of the 52 records has entries in all four fields. This means that every record displayed from the Customer table has a corresponding record or records in the Pets table.

Return to query design mode by clicking the Design icon on the toolbar. When you double-click the join line between the Customer and Pets tables, you see that the join property for these two tables becomes the first selection shown in the Join Properties dialog box (see Figure 12-9). This is an inner join, or *equi-join*, the most common type. These joins show only the records that have a correspondence between tables.

Creating a right outer join

Unlike inner joins (equi-joins), *outer joins* are used for showing all records in one table while showing common records in the other. The table or query that does not have a matching record will simply display empty cells in the datasheet when the dynaset is displayed.

When you have created an outer join, the join line will point graphically to one of the tables. If displaying the join property, it says to show all records from the main table (the one missing the arrow) while showing only matching records in the table being pointed to. For a further explanation, follow these instructions:

1. Return to the query design and again double-click the join line between Customer and Pets.
2. Select the second choice from the Join Properties dialog box, which includes *all* records from the Customer table and only those records from Pets where the joined fields are equal. (This may be the third choice if you have the Pets table to the left of the Customer table and no relationship built between the Customer and Pets tables.) Then click the OK button. Notice that the join line now has an arrow at one end, pointing rightward to the Pets table. This is known in database terminology as a *right outer join*. (If the Pets table is to the left of the Customers table, move it to the right and the arrow will point right — remember the relationship is that one customer can own many pets).

3. Click the Datasheet button to display this dynaset. Everything looks the same as before, except now there are 53 records instead of 52. Now move down the page until you can see record number 32. You should see a record for Customer Number JO003, Carla Jones, but no corresponding entries in the fields Pet Name or Type of Animal (see Figure 12-11). This record results from selecting the join property that specifies "include all records from Customer table."

Customer	Customer Name	Pet Name	Type of Animal
IR001	Petra Irish	Shadow	CAT
IR001	Petra Irish	Romeo	CAT
IR001	Petra Irish	Ceasar	CAT
IR001	Petra Irish	Jameo	CAT
IR001	Petra Irish	Tigger	CAT
JO001	Michael Johnson	Rover	DOG
JO002	Adam Johnson	Fi Fi	DOG
JO003	Carla Jones		
MC001	Margaret McKinley	Rex	DOG
MC001	Margaret McKinley	Caesar	DOG
MP002	Mount Pilot Zoo	Swinger	MONKEY
MP002	Mount Pilot Zoo	Prowler	WOLF
MP002	Mount Pilot Zoo	Powder Puff	DEER

Record: 32 of 53

Figure 12-11: A datasheet with a right outer join. It shows all Customers, including those with no pets.

There are now 53 records, with the extra record being displayed in a record in the Customer table. This person does not own any of the pets that have been entered into the tables.

Unlike inner joins, outer joins show all corresponding records between two tables and records that do *not* have a corresponding record in the other table. In the preceding example, there was a record for Carla Jones but no corresponding record for any pet she owns.

Caution　If you've changed the display order of the tables since adding them to the Query window, Access does not follow the new table order you set up; rather, it uses the original order in which you selected the tables. Because the information is normally the same in either table, it doesn't make a difference which field is selected first.

Tip　You may want to break the joins between tables that you have moved around and recreate the joins once you have put them in the order that you want. Now Access will accept your changes.

Select the Design button on the toolbar to return to the Query Design window. When you created the outer join for the Customer table with the Pets table, Access changed the appearance of the graphical join line to show an arrow at one end. As

Figure 12-12 shows, the arrow is pointing toward the Pets table, which tells you that Access has created an outer join and will show all records in the Customer table but only those that match in the Pets table.

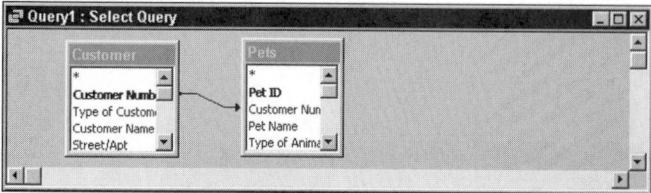

Figure 12-12: The Table/Query pane shows a right outer join.

Creating a left outer join

Once in the query design, again double-click the join line between the Customer and Pets tables. Select the third choice from the Join Properties dialog box, which asks to "include all records from Pets." Then click the OK button. The join line now has an arrow pointing to the Customer table, as shown in Figure 12-13. This is known as a *left outer join*. (If the arrow points to the right in the top pane, the join is known as a right outer join; if the arrow points to the left, it's a left outer join.)

Select the Datasheet button to display this dynaset. Move down the page until you see record number 30, as shown in Figure 12-14. A record should be empty in the fields Customer Number and Customer Name. All you see is Animal Name (Brownie) and the fact that it's a dog. This record results from selecting the join property to include all records from Pets (a *left outer join* in database terminology).

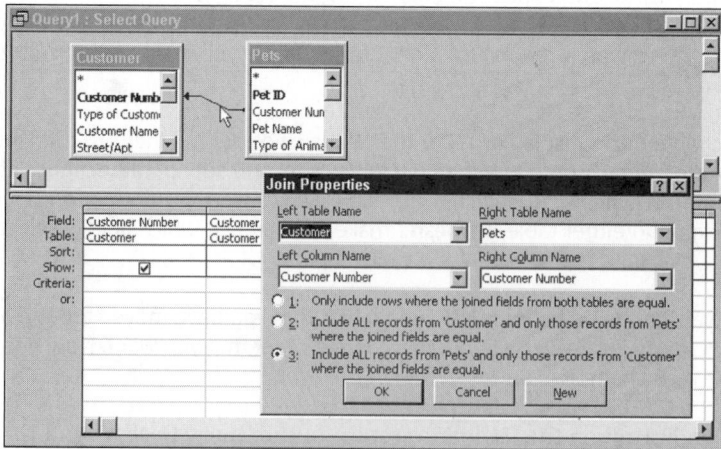

Figure 12-13: The Table/Query pane shows a left outer join between the Pets table and Customers. Notice the arrow is pointing to Customer from Pets.

Again, there are 53 records in this dynaset. However, the extra record is not from the Customer table. This record is in the Pets table, but no Customer owns it. It is an *orphan* record. Referential integrity can't be set in the Relationships window because of this record. Remove this record to set up referential integrity between the tables.

Cross-Reference Removing unwanted, unrelated records is detailed in Chapter 24.

Customer	Customer Name	Pet Name	Type of Animal
GR002	Wanda Greenfield	Sammie Girl	DOG
IR001	Petra Irish	D.C.	CAT
IR001	Petra Irish	Jimeny	CAT
IR001	Petra Irish	Shadow	CAT
IR001	Petra Irish	Romeo	CAT
IR001	Petra Irish	Ceasar	CAT
IR001	Petra Irish	Jameo	CAT
IR001	Petra Irish	Tigger	CAT
		Brownie	DOG
JO001	Michael Johnson	Rover	DOG
JO002	Adam Johnson	Fi Fi	DOG
MC001	Margaret McKinley	Rex	DOG
MC001	Margaret McKinley	Caesar	DOG
MP002	Mount Pilot Zoo	Swinger	MONKEY
MP002	Mount Pilot Zoo	Prowler	WOLF
MP002	Mount Pilot Zoo	Powder Puff	DEER
PO001	Tyrone Potter	Slither	SNAKE
PR001	William Primen	Brutus	DOG

Record: 30 of 53

Figure 12-14: Datasheet with left outer join. The record being pointed to has no Customer Name.

Creating a Cartesian product

If you add both the Customer and Pets tables to a query, but don't specify a join between the tables, Access combines the first Customer record with all the Pets records; then it takes the second record and combines it with all the Pets records and continues until all the Customer records have been combined with all of the Pets records. Combining each record in one table with each record in the other table results in a Cartesian product (cross-product) of both tables. Since the Customer table has 24 records and the Pets table has 53, the resulting dynaset has 1,272 records.

✦   ✦   ✦

Working with Select Queries

In previous chapters, you work with queries using criteria on a single field. You also get experience adding multiple tables to a query and joining the tables together. This chapter focuses on extracting information from multiple tables in select queries.

Moving Beyond Simple Queries

Select queries are the most common type of query used; they select information (based on a specific criterion) from one or more related tables. With these queries, you can ask questions and receive answers about information that's stored in your database tables. In previous chapters, you work with queries that use simple criteria on a single field in a table with operators, such as equal (=) and greater-than (>).

Knowing how to specify criteria is critical to designing and writing effective queries. Although queries can be used against a single table for a single criterion, most queries extract information from several tables using more complex criteria.

Because of this complexity, your queries are able to retrieve only the data you need, in the order that you need it. You may, for example, want to select and display data from the Mountain Animal Hospital database to answer these questions:

- ✦ All owners of horses or cows or pigs
- ✦ All animals that were given a specific medication in a specific week last year

✦   ✦   ✦   ✦

In This Chapter

Creating and using Text expressions as criteria

Using the Like and Not operators and wildcards

Creating and using Memo, Date, and Numeric expressions as criteria

Using the And/Or operators in single-field criteria

Using the In and Between...And operators

Searching for Null data

Using the And/Or operators across several fields

Using functions as expressions for criteria

Creating and using a calculated field

✦   ✦   ✦   ✦

✦ All owners whose dogs or cats had blood work in the past four months

✦ Only the first animal of each type that you have treated

✦ Any animal that has the word *color* in the Memo field comments

As your database system evolves, you will ask questions like these about the information stored in the system. Although the system was not originally developed specifically to answer these questions, you can find the information needed to answer them stored in the tables. Because the information is there, you find yourself performing ad hoc queries, which can be very simple or quite complex, against the database. You perform ad hoc queries by using select queries.

Select queries are the easiest way to obtain information from several tables without resorting to writing programs.

Using query comparison operators

When working with select queries, you may need to specify one or more *criteria* to limit the scope of information shown. You specify criteria by using *comparison operators* in equations and calculations. The categories of operators are mathematical, relational, logical, and string. In select queries, operators are used in either the Field: or Criteria: cell of the QBE (Query by Example) pane.

Here's a good rule of thumb to observe:

Use mathematical and string operators for creating calculated fields; use relational and logical operators for specifying scope criteria.

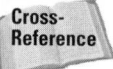
Cross-Reference   We discuss calculated fields later in this chapter. You can find an in-depth explanation of operators in Chapter 11.

Table 13-1 shows most of the common operators that are used with select queries.

Table 13-1				
Common Operators Used in Select Queries				
Mathematical	*Relational*	*Logical*	*String*	*Miscellaneous*
* (multiply)	= (equal)	And	& (concatenate)	Between...And
/ (divide)	<> (not equal)	Or	Like	In
+ (add)	> (greater than)	Not		Is Null / Not Null
– (subtract)	< (less than)			

Using these operators, you can ferret out groups of records like these:

✦ Pet records that have a picture associated with them

✦ A range of records, such as all patients seen between November and January

✦ Records that meet both And *and* Or criteria, such as all pets that are dogs and are not either neutered or have a current vaccination

✦ All records that do *not* match a value, such as any animal that is not a cat

When you add a criterion to a query, you use the appropriate operator with an *example* of what you want. In Figure 13-1, the example is *PIG*. The operator is equal (=). Notice that the equal sign is *not* shown in the figure. The equal sign is the default operator for selection criteria.

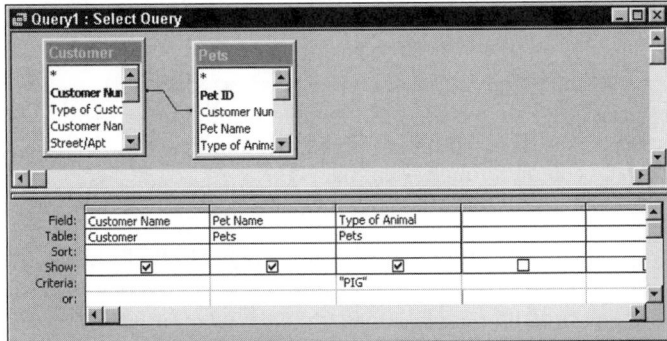

Figure 13-1: The QBE pane shows a simple criterion asking for all animals where the Type of Animal is a Pig.

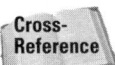

Cross-Reference   Chapter 9 gives an in-depth explanation of working with queries.

Understanding complex criteria selection

As Table 13-1 shows, you can use several operators to build complex criteria. To most people, complex criteria consist of a series of Ands and Ors, as in these examples:

✦ State must be Idaho *or* Oregon

✦ City must be Borderville *and* state must be Washington

✦ State must be Idaho *or* Washington *and* city must be Borderville

These examples demonstrate the use of both logical operators: *And/Or*. Many times, you can create complex criteria by entering example data in different cells of the QBE pane. Figure 13-2 demonstrates how to create complex And/Or criteria without entering the operator keywords And/Or at all. This example displays all the customers and their pets that satisfy these criteria:

Live in the city of Borderville and live in either the state of Washington or the state of Idaho and whose pet is not a dog.

Note   You learn how to create this type of complex query later in this chapter.

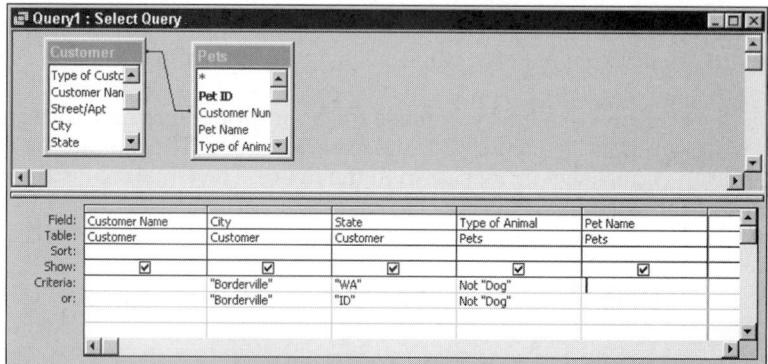

Figure 13-2: Creating complex And/Or criteria by example without using the And/Or operators. This Query uses both the Criteria row and the Or row to combine the And/Or criteria through example.

Access takes your graphical query and creates a single SQL SELECT statement to actually extract the information from your tables. You can see this SQL statement by selecting View ⇨ SQL View from the Database menu. This action opens a new window named Query1: Select Query to display the actual SQL statement that was built. Figure 13-3 shows the statement that Access based on what you built with the example data in Figure 13-2. This is the same query in its written SQL format.

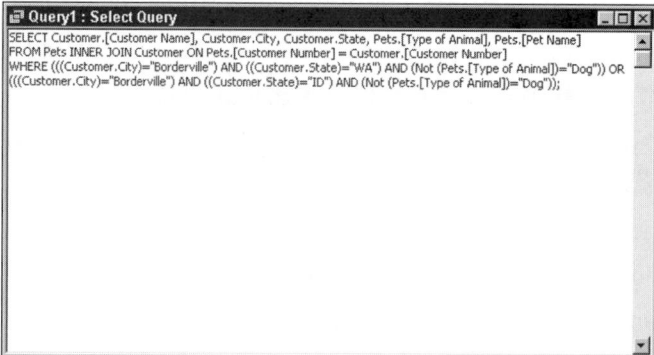

Figure 13-3: The SQL window for the same query built in Figure 13-2. Notice that it contains a single OR statement and four AND statements.

Cross-Reference

SQL statements in queries are covered in Chapter 25.

Note

Sometimes you see a field name referred to first by the table name and then by the field name, as shown in the SQL statement in Figure 13-3. When you see this kind of reference, it will have a dot (.) between the two names, such as Customer.[Customer Name]. This nomenclature tells you which table a field belongs to. This is especially critical when you're describing two fields that have the same name but are contained in different tables. In a multiple-table query, you see this format in the field list when you add a field to the QBE pane by clicking an empty column. You also see this format when you create a multiple table form by using the field list. The general format is Table Name.Field Name. If the field name or table name has spaces in it, you must surround the name with brackets [ ]; for example, Pets.[Type of Animal] and Customer.[Customer Name].

Tip

We use spaces in table and field names for better readability, but it's a really good idea to not use spaces at all. This way, you don't have to use brackets around your field or object names. For example, you can reference Customer.[Customer Name] without a space between the names as Customer.CustomerName — thus eliminating the need for using brackets. To do this, you need to create your table fields without using spaces.

If you build a mathematical formula for this query (not the SQL statement), it looks similar to this example :

((Customer.City="Borderville") **AND** (Customer.State="WA") **AND** (Not Pets.[Type of Animal]="DOG")) **OR** ((Customer.City= "Borderville") **AND** (Customer.State="ID") **AND** (Not Pets.[Type of Animal]="DOG"))

You must enter the city and pet example for each state line in the QBE pane, as shown in Figure 13-2. Later, you learn to use the And/Or operators in a Criteria: cell of the query, which eliminates the need for redundant entry of these fields.

Tip

In this example, you looked for all animals that were not Dogs. To find records that match a value, drop the use of the Not operator with the value. For example, enter the expression **Not Dog** to find all animals except dogs, enter **Dog** to find all dogs.

The And/Or operators are the most commonly used operators when working with complex criteria. The operators consider two different formulas (one on each side of the And/Or operators) and then determine individually whether they are True or False. Then the operators compare the results of the two formulas against each other for a logical True/False answer. For example, take the first And statement in the formula given in the preceding paragraph:

(Customer.City="Borderville") AND (Customer.State="WA")

The first half of the formula, Customer.City = "Borderville", converts to a True if the city is Borderville (False if a different city; Null if no city was entered in the field).

Then the second half of the formula, Customer.State = "WA", is converted to a True if the state is Washington (False if a different state; Null if no state was entered). Then the And compares the logical True/False from each side against the other side to give a resultant True/False answer.

Note A field has a Null value when it has no value at all; it is the lack of entry of information in a field. Null is neither True nor False; nor is it equivalent to all spaces or zero — it simply has no value. If you never enter a city name in the City field and just skip it, Access leaves the field empty. This state of emptiness is known as Null.

When the result of an And/Or is True, the overall condition is True, and the query displays those records meeting the True condition. Table 13-2 reviews the True and False conditions for each operator.

Table 13-2 **Results of Logical Operators And/Or**			
Left Side Is	*Operator Is*	*Right Side Is*	*Resultant Answer Is*
True	AND	True	True
True	AND	False	False
False	AND	True	False
False	AND	False	False
True	OR	True	True
True	OR	False	True
False	OR	True	True
True	OR	Null	True
Null	OR	True	True
False	OR	False	False
False	OR	Null	False
Null	OR	False	False

Notice that the And operator is True only when both sides of the formula are True, whereas the Or operator is True when either side of the formula is True. In fact, one side can be a Null value, and the Or operator will still be True if the other side is True. This is the difference between And/Or operators.

Cross-Reference   Refer to Chapter 11 for further details about logical operators.

Using functions in select queries

When you work with queries, you may want to use built-in Access functions to display information. For example, you may want to display items such as

✦ The day of the week (Sunday, Monday, and so forth) for visit dates

✦ All customer names in uppercase

✦ The difference between two date fields

You can display all this information by creating calculated fields for the query. We discuss calculated fields in depth later in this chapter.

Referencing fields in select queries

When you work with a field name in queries, as you do with calculated fields or criteria values, you should enclose the field name in square brackets ([]). Access requires brackets around any field name that is in a criterion and around any field name that contains a space or punctuation. An example of a field name in brackets is the criterion [Visit Date] + 30. You can find more examples like this later in the chapter.

Caution   If you omit the brackets ([ ]) around a field name in the criterion, Access automatically places quotes around the field name and treats it as text instead of a field name.

Entering Single-Value Field Criteria

You'll encounter situations in which you want to limit the query records returned on the basis of a single field criterion, such as in these queries:

✦ Customer information for customers living in the state of Washington

✦ Animals you have treated from the local zoos in the area

✦ Customers and animals you treated during the month of January

Each of these queries requires a *single-value criterion*. Simply put, a single-value criterion is the entry of only one expression in a field. That expression can be example data, such as "WA," or a function, such as DatePart ("m", [Visit Date])=1. Criteria expressions can be specified for any data type: Text, Numeric, Date/Time, and so forth. Even OLE Object and Counter field types can have criteria specified.

Cross-Reference   For a full explanation of expressions, operators, identifiers, literals, and functions, see Chapter 11.

Note   All the examples in this chapter rely on several tables: Customer, Pets, and Visits. The Mountain Start database contains the tables used in this chapter. The majority of these examples use only the Customer and Pets tables. If you want to follow the examples, create a new query and add the Customer and Pets tables.

Each series of steps in this chapter tells you which tables and fields make up the query. For most examples, you should clear all previous criteria. Each example focuses on the criteria line of the QBE pane. You can also view each figure to make sure you understand the correct placement of the criteria in each example. Only a few dynasets are shown, but you can follow along and view the data.

Entering character (Text or Memo) criteria

You use character criteria for Text or Memo data-type fields. These are either examples or data about the contents of the field. To create a text criterion to display customers who own birds, for example, follow these steps:

1. Add Customer Name from the Customer table to the QBE pane and then add Pet Name and Type of Animal from the Pets table.

2. Click the Criteria: cell for Type of Animal.

3. Type **WOLF** in the cell.

Your query should look similar to the query shown in Figure 13-4. Notice that only two tables are open and only three fields are selected. You can click the Datasheet button to see the results of this query.

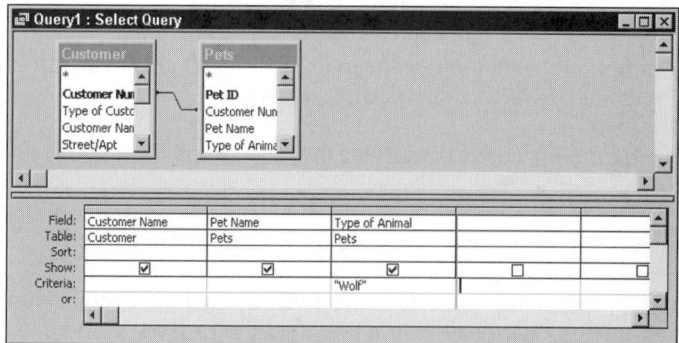

Figure 13-4: The Query Design window showing two tables that were automatically linked. You see the example data WOLF in the Criteria row under the Type of Animal field.

Tip
When specifying example-type criteria, it isn't necessary to match capitalization. Access defaults to case-insensitive when working with queries. Entering WOLF, wolf, or WoLf provides the same results.

You don't have to enter an equal sign before the literal word *wolf* because Access uses the equal operator as the default operator. To see all animals except wolf, you must enter either the <> (not equal) or the Not operator before the word *wolf*.

You also don't have to type quotes around the word *wolf*. Access assumes that you are using an example literal *WOLF* and adds the quotes for you automatically.

Tip
You should use the double quotation mark to surround literals. Access normally uses the single quotation mark as a remark character in its programming language. However, when you use the single quotation mark in the Criteria: cell, Access interprets it as a double quotation mark.

The Like operator and wildcards

In previous sections, you worked with *literal* criteria. You specified the exact field contents for Access to find, which was "Wolf" in the previous example. Access used the literal to find the specific records. Sometimes, however, you know only a part of the field contents, or you may want to see a wider range of records on the basis of a pattern. For example, you may want to see all pet visits for pets that begin with the letter *g*; so you need to check gerbils, goats, and so forth. Here's a more practical example: Suppose you have a customer who owns a pig that was born Siamese. You remember making a note of it in the Comments field, but you don't, however, remember which pig it was. To do this, you are required to use a wildcard search against the Memo field to find any records that contain the word *Siamese*.

Access uses the string operator Like in the Criteria: cell of a field to perform wildcard searches against the field's contents. Access searches for a pattern in the field; you use the question mark (?) to represent a single character or the asterisk (*) for several characters. (This works just like filenames at the DOS level.) In addition to the two characters (?) and (*), Access uses three other characters for wildcard searches. Table 13-3 lists the wildcards that the Like operator can use.

The question mark (?) stands for any single character located in the same position as the question mark in the example expression. An asterisk (*) stands for any number of characters in the same position in which the asterisk is placed. Unlike the asterisk at DOS level, Access can use the asterisk any number of times in an example expression. The pound sign (#) stands for any single digit found in the same position as the pound sign. The brackets ([]) and the list they enclose stand for any single character that matches any one character of the list located within the brackets. Finally, the exclamation point (!) inside the brackets represents the Not word for the list — that is, any single character that does not match any character in the list within the brackets.

Table 13-3
Wildcards Used by the Like Operator

Wildcard	Purpose
?	A single character (0-9, Aa-Zz)
*	Any number of characters (0 to n)
#	Any single digit (0-9)
[list]	Any single character in the list
[!list]	Any single character not in the list

These wildcards can be used alone or in conjunction with each other. They can even be used several times within the same expression. The examples in Table 13-4 demonstrate how you can use the wildcards.

To create an example using the Like operator, let's suppose that you want to find the record of the Siamese pig. You know that the word *Siamese* is used in one of the records in the Comments field. To create the query, follow these steps:

1. Remove the criterion field contents ("wolf") under the Type of Animal field.
2. Double-click the Comments field in the Pets table to add it to the QBE pane.
3. Click the Criteria: cell of the Comments field.
4. Type ***Siamese*** in the cell (be sure to put asterisks before and after Siamese).

Table 13-4
Using Wildcards with the Like Operator

Expression	Field Used In	Results of Criteria
Like "Re?"	Pets.Pet Name	Finds all records of pets whose names are three letters long and begin with "Re", examples: Red, Rex, and Ren
Like "*Siamese*"	Pets.Comments	Finds all records with the word "Siamese" anywhere within the Comments field

Expression	Field Used In	Results of Criteria
Like "G*"	Pets.Type of Animal	Finds all records for animals of a type that begin with the letter G
Like "1/*/93"	Visits.Visit Date	Finds all records for the month of January 1993
Like "## Main St."	Customer.Street/Apt	Finds all records for houses with house numbers between 10 and 99 inclusively; examples: 10, 22, 33, 51
Like "[RST]*"	Customer.City	Finds all records for customers who live in any city with a name beginning with R, S, or T
Like "[!EFG]*"	Pets.Type of Animal	Finds all records for animals of types that do not begin with the letters E, F, or G; all other animals are displayed

When you click outside the Criteria: cell, Access automatically adds the operator Like and the quotation marks around the expression. Your query QBE pane should look similar to the one shown in Figure 13-5.

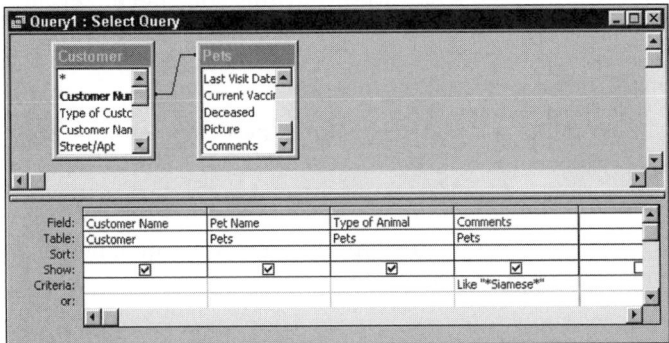

Figure 13-5: Using the Like operator with a select query in a Memo field. In this case, the query looks for the word *Siamese* in the Comments field.

Access automatically adds the Like operator and quotation marks if you meet these conditions:

✦ Your expression contains no spaces

✦ You use only the wildcards ?, *, and #

✦ You use brackets ([ ]) inside quotation marks " "

If you use the brackets without quotation marks, you must supply the operator Like and the quotation marks.

Using the Like operator with wildcards is the best way to perform pattern searches through Memo fields.

Caution   The Like operator and its wildcards can be used only against three types of fields: Text, Memo, and Date. Using these with any other type can result in an error.

Clicking on the Datasheet button on the toolbar, you see that one record matches your query request — a Pig named Rosie, owned by William Price. Return to the query design mode by clicking on the Design button.

Specifying non-matching values

To specify a non-matching value, you simply use either the Not or the <> operator in front of the expression that you don't want to match. For example, you may want to see all customers and their pets for all states, but you want to exclude Washington. Follow these steps to see how to specify this non-matching value:

1. Click Edit ➪ Clear Grid to remove the field names and criteria from the QBE pane and leave the Customer and Pets tables.

2. Select the Customer Name and State fields from the Customer table and Pet Name from Pets.

3. Click in the Criteria: cell of State.

4. Type **Not WA** in the cell. Access automatically places quotation marks around WA if you don't do so before you leave the field.

The query should look similar to the one shown in Figure 13-6. The query selects all records *except* those for customers who live in the state of Washington.

Note   You can use the <> operator instead of Not in Step 4 of the previous instructions to exclude Washington. The resultant dynaset is the same with either operator. These two operators are interchangeable except with the use of the keyword Is. You cannot say Is <> Null. Rather, you must say Not Is Null or more accurately Is Not Null.

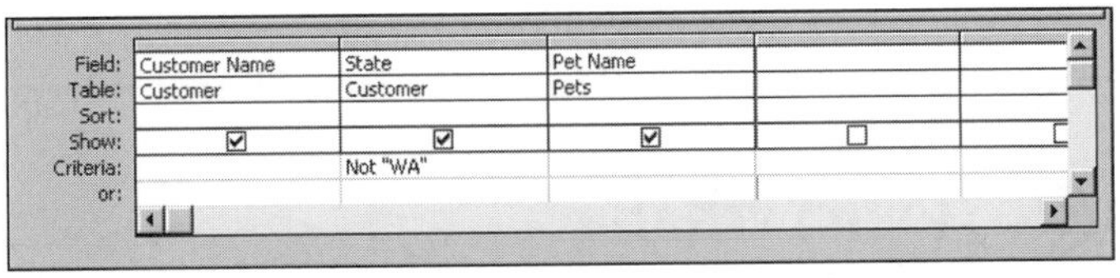

Figure 13-6: Using the Not operator in criteria. Entering **Not WA** in the State field displays all records except those where the State is WA (Washington).

Entering numeric (Number, Currency, or Counter) criteria

You use numeric criteria with Number, Currency, or Counter data-type fields. You simply enter the numbers and the decimal symbol — if required — following the mathematical or comparison operator. For example, you may want to see all animals that weigh over 100 pounds. To create a query like this, follow these steps:

1. Start with a new query using the Customer and Pets tables.

2. Select the Customer Name in the Customer table, and select Pet Name, Type of Animal, and Weight in the Pets table.

3. Click in the Criteria: cell for Weight.

4. Type **>100** in the cell.

When you follow these steps, your query looks similar to the query shown in Figure 13-7. When working with numeric data, Access doesn't enclose the expression with quotes, as it does with string criteria.

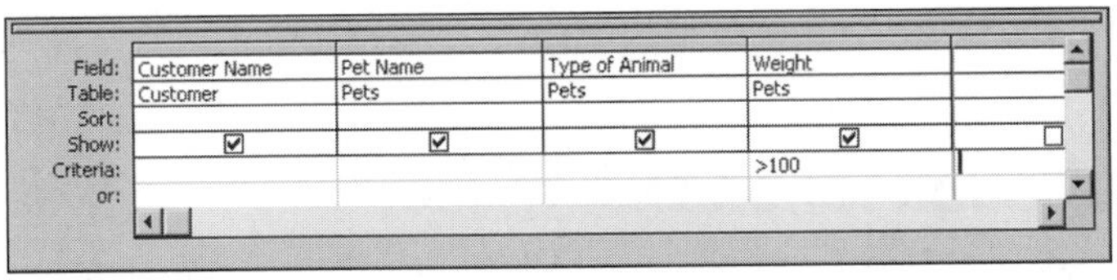

Figure 13-7: Criteria set for weight of animals. Here the criteria is greater than (>)100.

Numeric fields are generally compared to a value string that uses comparison operators, such as less than (<), greater than (>), or equal to (=). If you want to specify a comparison other than equal, you must enter the operator as well as the value. Remember that Access defaults to equal when an operator is not specified in criteria. That is why you needed to specify greater than (>) 100 in the previous example query for animals over 100 pounds.

Working with Currency and Counter data in a query is exactly the same as working with Numeric data; you simply specify an operator and a numeric value.

Entering Yes/No (logic) criteria

Yes/No criteria are used with Yes/No type fields. The example data that you supply in the criteria can be for only Yes or No states. You can also use the Not and the <> operators to signify the opposite, but the Yes/No data also has a Null state that you may want to check for. Access recognizes several forms of Yes and No. Table 13-5 lists all the positive and negative values that you can use.

Thus, instead of typing Yes, you can type any of these in the Criteria: cell: On, True, Not No, <> No, <No, or -1.

Tip   In Access 2002, you can enter any number except 0 to represent TRUE or Yes.

Note   A Yes/No field can have only three criteria states: Yes, No, and Null. Null only occurs when no default value was set in a table and the value has not yet been entered. Checking for "Is Null" displays only records with no value, and checking for "Is Not Null" always displays all Yes or No records. After a Yes/No field check box is checked (or checked and then deselected) it can never be null. It must be either Yes or No (-1 or 0).

Table 13-5						
Positive and Negative Values Used in Yes/No Fields						
Yes	True	On	Not No	<> No	<No	-1
No	False	Off	Not Yes	<>Yes	>Yes	0

Entering a criterion for an OLE object

You can even specify a criterion for OLE objects: Is Not Null. For example, suppose you don't have pictures for all the animals and you want to view only those records that have a picture of the animal—that is, those in which the picture Is Not Null. You specify the Is Not Null criterion for the Picture field of the Pets table. After you do this, Access limits the records to those that have a picture in them.

Although Is Not Null is the correct syntax, you can also type Not Null and Access supplies the Is operator for you.

Entering Multiple Criteria in One Field

In previous sections of this chapter, you worked with single-condition criteria on a single field. As you learned in those sections, you can specify single-condition criteria for any field type. In this section, you work with multiple criteria based on a single field. For example, you may be interested in seeing all records in which the type of animal is either a cat or a squirrel, or perhaps you want to view the records of all the animals that came to the vet between March 1 and December 15, 2000.

The QBE pane has the flexibility to solve these types of problems. You can specify several criteria for one field or for several fields in a select query. Using multiple criteria, for example, you can determine which customers and pets are from Idaho or Washington ("ID" or "WA") or which animals you saw for general examinations in the past 90 days (Between Date( ) and Date( )-90).

You use the And and the Or operators to specify several criteria for one field.

Understanding an Or operation

You use an Or operation in queries when you want a field to meet either of two conditions. For example, you may want to see the customer and pet names of all rabbits and squirrels. In other words, you want to see all records where a customer owns a rabbit or a squirrel, or both. The general formula for this operation is

[Type of Animal] = "Rabbit" Or [Type of Animal] = "Squirrel"

If either side of this formula is True, the resulting answer is also True. To clarify this point, consider these conditions:

✦ Customer 1 owns a rabbit but does not own a squirrel — the formula is True.

✦ Customer 2 owns a squirrel but does not own a rabbit — the formula is True.

✦ Customer 3 owns a squirrel and a rabbit — the formula is True.

✦ Customer 4 does not own a rabbit and does not own a squirrel — the formula is False.

Specifying multiple values for a field using the Or operator

The Or operator is used to specify multiple values for a field. For example, you use the Or operator if you want to see all records of owners of fish or frogs or ducks. To do this, follow these steps:

1. Create a new query using the Customer and Pets tables.

2. Select the Customer Name field from the Customer table and then select Pet Name and Type of Animal from the Pets table.

3. Click in the Criteria: cell of Type of Animal.

4. Type **Fish Or Frog Or Duck** in the cell.

Your QBE pane should resemble the one shown in Figure 13-8. Access automatically placed quotation marks around your example data — Fish, Frog, and Duck.

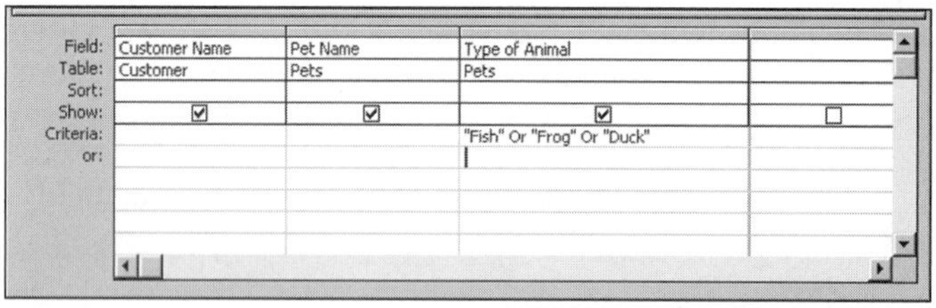

Figure 13-8: Using the Or operator. Notice the two Or operators under the Type of Animal field — Fish OR Frog OR Duck.

Figure 13-9 shows the resulting dynaset of this query in the datasheet. Notice that the only records selected contain FISH, FROG, or DUCK in the Type of Animal column. Actually, the table contained no fish, so they weren't displayed. If the table had contained fish, they would have also been displayed.

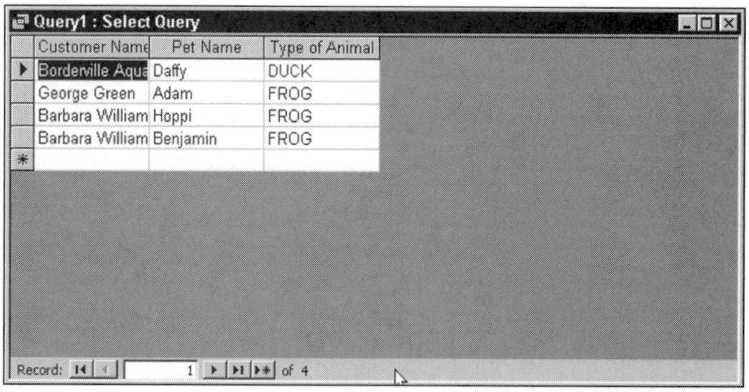

Figure 13-9: Displaying the records matching a criteria using the Or operator. These four records match the request in the query built in Figure 13-8.

Using the Or: cell of the QBE pane

Besides using the literal Or operator in a single statement on the Criteria row under the Type of Animal field, you can supply individual criteria for the field on separate rows of the QBE pane. To do this, enter the first criterion example in the Criteria: cell of the field. Then enter the second criterion example in the Or: cell of the same field. Enter the next criterion in the cell directly beneath the Or: example; and continue entering examples vertically down the column. This is exactly equivalent to typing the Or operator between examples. Using the example in which you queried for fish, frogs, or ducks, change your QBE pane to look like the one in Figure 13-10. Notice that each type of animal is on a separate row in the query.

Field:	Customer Name	Pet Name	Type of Animal	
Table:	Customer	Pets	Pets	
Sort:				
Show:	☑	☑	☑	☐
Criteria:				
or:			"Fish"	
			"Frog"	
			"Duck"	

Figure 13-10: Using the Or: cell of the QBE pane. You can place each example data on its own row in the Or: cells.

Tip   Access allows up to nine (depending upon the resolution that you are using — 640 x 480, etc.) Or: cells for each field. If you need to specify more Or conditions, use the Or operator between conditions (for example: Cat Or Dog Or Pig).

Using a list of values with the In operator

You can use yet another method for specifying multiple values of a single field. This method uses the In operator. The In operator finds a value that is one of a *list of values*. For example, type the expression **IN(Frog, Snake, Lizard)** under the Type of Animal field. This action creates a list of values, where any item in the list becomes an example criterion. Your query should resemble the query shown in Figure 13-11.

In this example, quotation marks have been automatically added by Access around Frog, Snake, and Lizard.

Note   When you work with the In operator, each value (example data) must be separated from the others by a comma.

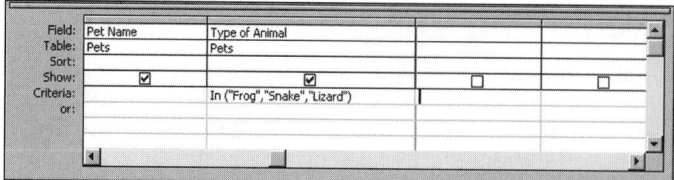

Figure 13-11: Using the In operator to find all records for Type of Animal that is a Frog, a Snake, or a Lizard.

Understanding an And query

You use And operators in queries when you want a field to meet both of two conditions that you specify. For example, you may want to see records of pets that had a visit date between October 1, 2000 and March 31, 2001. In other words, the animal had to be a patient during the last quarter of the year 2000 and first quarter of 2001. The general formula for this example is

[Visit Date] >= 10/1/00 And [Visit Date] <= 3/31/01

Unlike the Or operator (which has several conditions under which it is True), the And operator is True only when both sides of the formula are True. When both sides are True, the resulting answer is also True. To clarify use of the And operator, consider these conditions:

✦ Visit date (9/22/2000) is not greater than 10/01/00, but it is less than 3/31/01 — the formula is False.

✦ Visit date (4/11/2002) is greater than 10/01/00, but it is not less than 3/31/01 — the formula is False.

✦ Visit date (11/22/2000) is greater than 10/01/00, and it is less than 3/31/01 — the formula is True.

Both sides of the operation must be True for the And operation to be True.

An And operation can be performed in several ways against a single field in Access.

Specifying a range using the And operator

The And operator is frequently used in fields that have Numeric or Date/Time data types. It is seldom used with Text data types, although it can be. For example, you may be interested in viewing all animals whose names start with the letters *d*, *e*, or *f*. The And operator can be used here (> "Cz" and <"G"), although the Like operator is better (Like" [DEF]*"). Using an And operator with a single field sets a range of acceptable values in the field. Therefore, the key purpose of an And operator in a single field is to define a range of records to be viewed. For example, you can use the And operator to create a range criterion to display all animals that weigh between 100 and 300 pounds, inclusively. To create this query, follow these steps:

1. Create a new query using the Customer and Pets tables.

2. Select the Customer Name field from the Customer table, and select the Pet Name, Type of Animal, and Weight from the Pets table.

3. Click in the Criteria: cell of Weight.

4. Type **>=100 And <=300** in the cell.

The query should resemble the one shown in Figure 13-12. You can change the formula to >99 And <301 with identical results.

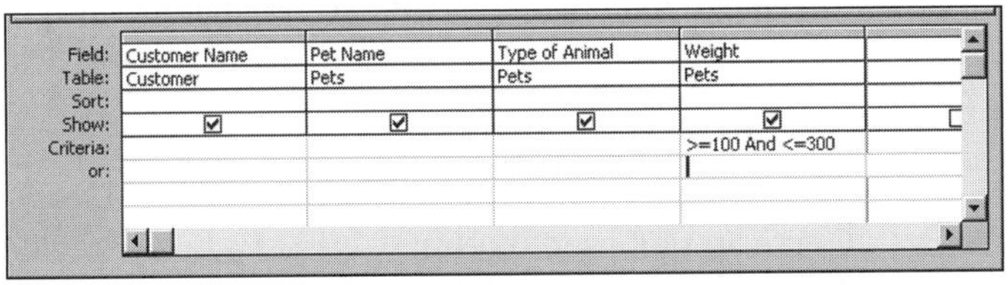

Figure 13-12: Using the And operator with numeric fields. Notice that this query shows all records equal to or greater than a weight of 100 *and* less than or equal to 300.

Using the Between...And operator

You can request a range of records from a single field by using another method — the Between...And operator. With the Between...And operator, you can find records that meet a range of values — for example, all pets Between Dog And Pig. Using the example of animals weighing between 100 and 300 pounds, create the query using the Between...And operator, as shown in Figure 13-13.

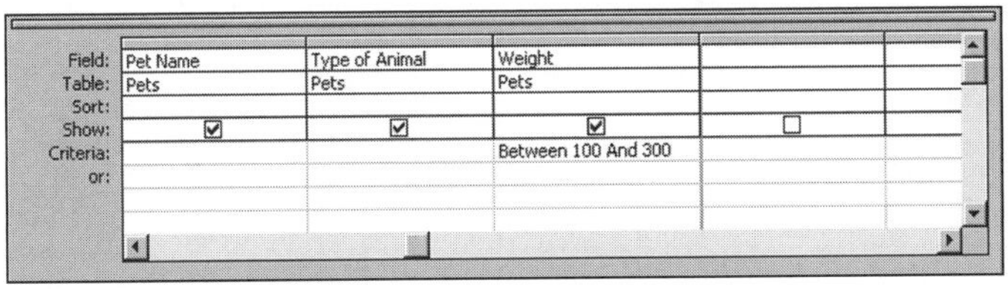

Figure 13-13: Using the Between...And Operator. The resulting datasheet shows the same records as shown in the query in Figure 13-12.

Caution   When you use the Between...And operator, the values entered in the Criteria field (in this example 100 and 300) are (if they match) included in the resulting dynaset.

Searching for Null data

A field may have no contents for several reasons: For example, perhaps the value wasn't known at the time of data entry, or the person who did the data entry simply forgot to enter the information, or the field's information was removed. Access does nothing with this field; it simply remains an empty field. (A field is said to be *null* when it's empty.)

Logically, a Null is neither True nor False. A Null field is not equivalent to all spaces or to zero. A Null field simply has no value.

Access lets you work with Null value fields by means of two special operators:

Is Null

Is Not Null

You use these operators to limit criteria based on Null values of a field. Previously in this chapter, you learned that a Null value can be used to query for animals having a picture on file. In the next example, you look for animal records that don't specify gender. To create this query, follow these steps:

1. Create a new query using the Customer and Pets tables.

2. Select the Customer Name field from the Customer table, and select Pet Name, Type of Animal, and Breed field from the Pets table.

3. Click in the Criteria: cell of Breed.

4. Type **Is Null** in the cell.

Your query should look like the query shown in Figure 13-14. Select the Datasheet button to see that you have four records without a breed. If you add a record in the database and don't enter a value in this field, that record shows in the resulting dynaset of this query as a null value.

Field:	Customer Name	Pet Name	Type of Animal	Breed	
Table:	Customer	Pets	Pets	Pets	
Sort:					
Show:	☑	☑	☑	☑	☐
Criteria:				Is Null	
or:					

Figure 13-14: Using the Is Null operator. If the database has any records with the Gender field missing a value (the user clicked past the field), they will be shown as blanks in the dynaset when the datasheet button is pressed. Their actual value is defined as Null — or no value entered (versus a blank space).

Tip When using the Is Null and Is Not Null operators, you can enter Null or Not Null and Access automatically adds the Is to the Criteria field.

Entering Criteria in Multiple Fields

Previously in this chapter, you worked with single and multiple criteria specified in single fields. In this section, you work with criteria across several fields. When you want to limit the records based on several field conditions, you do so by setting criteria in each of the fields that will be used for the scope. Suppose you want to search for all dogs in Idaho. Or, suppose you want to search for dogs in Idaho or Washington. Or, suppose you want to search for all dogs in Washington or all cats in Oregon. Each of these queries requires placing criteria in multiple fields and on multiple lines.

Using And and Or across fields in a query

To use the And operator and the Or operator across fields, place your example or pattern data in the Criteria: cells (for the And operator) and the Or: cells of one field relative to the placement in another field. When you want to use And between two fields, you place the example or pattern data across the same row. When you want to use Or between two fields, you place the example or pattern data on different rows in the QBE pane. Figure 13-15 shows the QBE pane and a conceptual representation of this placement.

Field:	Exp1: [Field 1]	Exp2: [Field 2]	Exp3: [Field 3]	Exp4: [Field 4]	Exp5: [Field 5]	
Table:						
Sort:						
Show:	☑	☑	☑	☑	☑	☐
Criteria:	"Ex1"	"Ex2"	"Ex3"			
or:				"Ex4"		
					"Ex5"	

Figure 13-15: The QBE pane with And/Or criteria between fields using the Criteria: and or: rows

Figure 13-15 shows that if the only criteria fields present were Ex1, Ex2, and Ex3 (with Ex4 and Ex5 removed), all three would be Anding between the fields. If only the criteria fields Ex4 and Ex5 were present (with Ex1, Ex2, and Ex3 removed), the two would be Oring between fields. As it is, the selection for this example is (EX1 AND EX2 AND EX3) OR EX4 OR EX5. Therefore, this query is True if a value matches any of these criteria:

EX1 AND EX2 AND EX3 (all must be True) or

EX4 (this can be True and either/both of the other two lines can be False) or

EX5 (this can be True and either/both of the other two lines can be False)

As long as one of these three criteria are True, the record is selected.

Specifying And criteria across fields of a query

The most common type of condition operator between fields is the And operator. You use the And operator to limit records on the basis of several field conditions. For example, you may want to view only the records of customers who live in the state of Washington and own rabbits. To create this query, follow these steps:

1. Create a new query using the Customer and Pets tables.

2. Select the Customer Name and State fields from the Customer table and then select Pet Name and Type of Animal fields from the Pets table.

3. Click the Criteria: cell of State.

4. Type **WA** in the cell.

5. Click the Criteria: cell for Type of Animal.

6. Type **RABBIT** in the cell.

Your query should look like the query shown in Figure 13-16. Notice that both example data are in the same row.

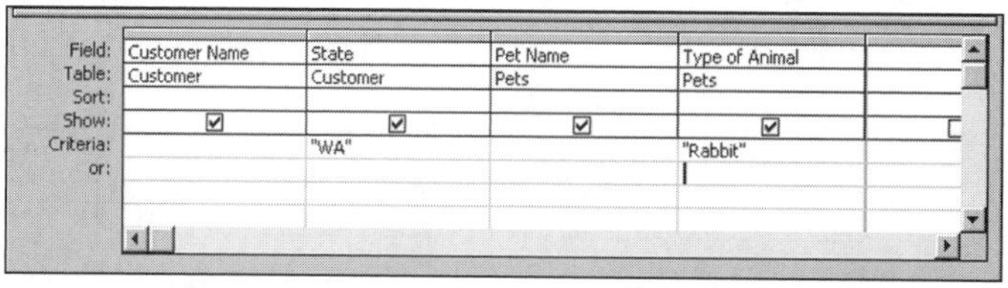

Figure 13-16: An And operator performing a mathematical operation based on two fields — WA in State and Rabbit in Type of Animal

Because you placed data for both criteria on the same row, Access interprets this as an And operation — where both conditions must be True. If you click on the Datasheet button, you see that you only have one record in the resulting dynaset.

Specifying Or criteria across fields of a query

Although the Or operator isn't used across fields as commonly as the And operator, occasionally Or is very useful. For example, you may want to see records of any animals in Washington or you may want to see records on all rabbits, regardless of the state they live in. To create this query, follow these steps:

1. Use the query from the previous example, emptying the two criteria cells first.

2. Click the Criteria: cell of State.

3. Type **WA** in the cell.

4. Click in the Or: cell for Type of Animal (one line below the WA example).

5. Type **RABBIT** in the cell.

Your query should resemble the query shown in Figure 13-17. Notice that the criteria entered this time are not in the same row for both fields.

When you place the criterion for one field on a different line from the criterion for another field, Access interprets this as an Or between the fields. If you click on the Datasheet button, you see that you now have 19 records in the resulting dynaset. This is because you gave a criteria that stated "Show me all records where the State is WA," or the Type of Animal is a "Rabbit." Either condition is True — thus more than one record meets the condition.

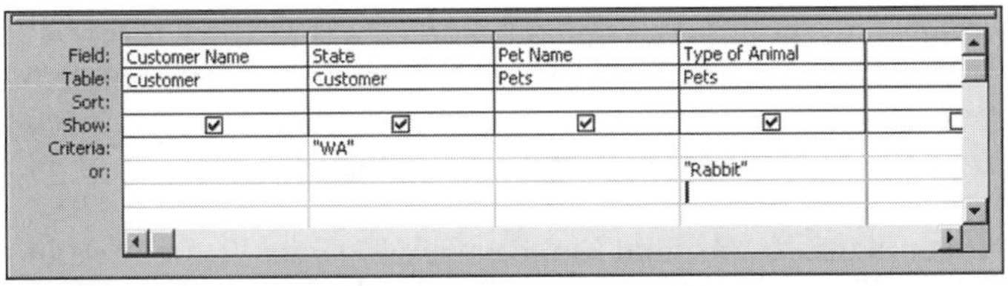

Field:	Customer Name	State		Pet Name	Type of Animal	
Table:	Customer	Customer		Pets	Pets	
Sort:						
Show:	☑	☑		☑	☑	
Criteria:		"WA"				
or:					"Rabbit"	

Figure 13-17: Using the Or operator between fields. Either condition must be True — either from the State of WA or the Type of Animal is a Rabbit.

Using And and Or together in different fields

After you've worked with And and Or separately, you're ready to create a query using And and Or in different fields. In the next example, you want to display information for all rabbits in Washington and all snakes in Idaho. To create this query, follow these steps:

1. Use the query from the previous example, emptying the two criteria cells first.

2. Click the Criteria: cell of State.

3. Type **WA** in the cell.

4. Click the Or: cell of State.

5. Type **ID** in the cell.

6. Click the Criteria: cell for Type of Animal.

7. Type **RABBIT** in the cell.

8. Click the Or: cell for Type of Animal.

9. Type **SNAKE** in the cell.

Figure 13-18 shows how the query should look. Notice that WA and Rabbit are in the same row; ID and Snake are in another row. This query represents two Ands across fields, with an Or in each field.

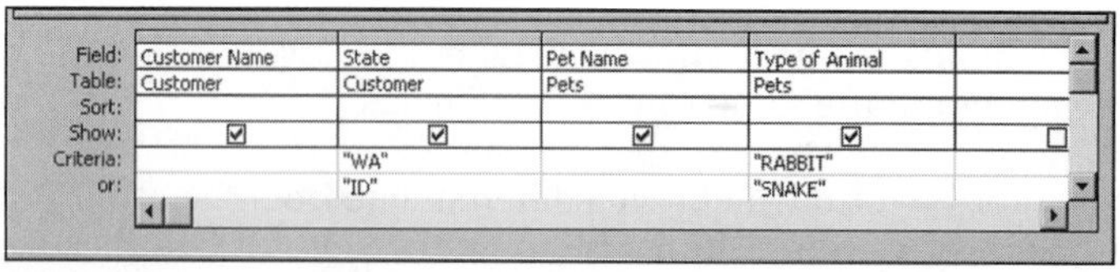

Field:	Customer Name	State	Pet Name	Type of Animal	
Table:	Customer	Customer	Pets	Pets	
Sort:					
Show:	☑	☑	☑	☑	☐
Criteria:		"WA"		"RABBIT"	
or:		"ID"		"SNAKE"	

Figure 13-18: Using Ands and Ors across fields to select all Rabbits that live in WA or all Snakes that live in ID

A complex query on different lines

Suppose you want to view all records of squirrels and rats that were brought in by Animal Kingdom between July 1, 1999, and August 1, 2001. In this example, you use three fields for setting criteria: Customer.Customer Name, Pets.Type of Animal, and Visits.Visit Date. Here's the formula for setting these criteria:

(Customer.[Customer Name] = "Animal Kingdom" AND (Pets.[Type of Animal] = "SQUIRREL" OR Pets.[Type of Animal]="RAT") AND (Visits.[Visit Date] >= #7/1/99# AND <= #8/1/01#)

You can display this data by creating the query shown in Figure 13-19.

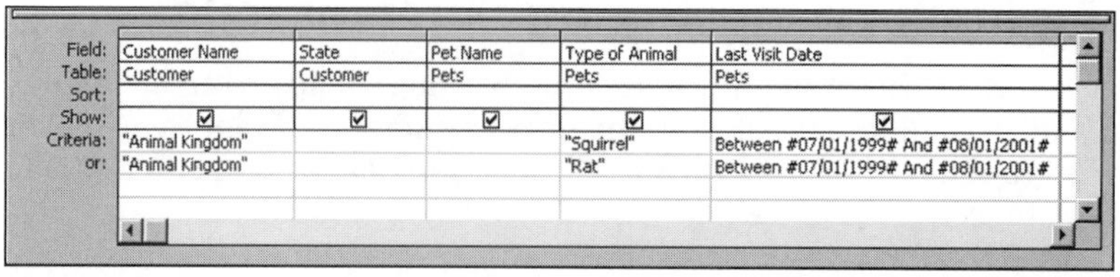

Field:	Customer Name	State	Pet Name	Type of Animal	Last Visit Date
Table:	Customer	Customer	Pets	Pets	Pets
Sort:					
Show:	☑	☑	☑	☑	☑
Criteria:	"Animal Kingdom"			"Squirrel"	Between #07/01/1999# And #08/01/2001#
or:	"Animal Kingdom"			"Rat"	Between #07/01/1999# And #08/01/2001#

Figure 13-19: Using multiple Ands and Ors across fields. This is a rather complex Select query that can be built on a single line.

 **Note** You can enter the date 8/1/2001 instead of 8/1/01 and Access 2002 processes the query exactly the same. Access 2002 is Year 2000 (Y2K) compliant. All Microsoft Office 2002 products process two-digit years from 00 to 30 as 2000 to 2030, while all two-digit dates between 31 and 99 are processed as 1931 to 1999.

A complex query on one line

Notice in Figure 13-19 that the Customer Name Animal Kingdom is repeated on two lines, as is the Visit Date of Between #6/30/99# And #8/1/01#. This is necessary because the two lines actually form the query:

> Animal Kingdom AND SQUIRREL AND Between #6/30/99# And #8/1/01# OR
>
> Animal Kingdom AND RAT AND Between #6/30/99# And #8/1/01#

You can rewrite the query so that you don't have to repeat Animal Kingdom in a query like this. Figure 13-20 shows another approach.

Field:	Customer Name	State	Pet Name	Type of Animal	Last Visit Date	
Table:	Customer	Customer	Pets	Pets	Pets	
Sort:						
Show:	☑	☑	☑	☑	☑	
Criteria:	"Animal Kingdom"			"Squirrel" Or "Rat"	Between #07/01/1999# And #08/01/2001#	
or:						

Figure 13-20: Using multiple Ands and Ors across fields on one line. Notice that the Squirrel Or Cat has been added to a single line in the Criteria: cell.

Notice that the criteria in Figure 13-19 have duplicate information in the Or: cell of the Customer Name and Visit Date fields. Only the Type of Animal Field has different criteria—"SQUIRREL" or "RAT." By combining the Type of Animal information into a single criterion (using the Or), the Customer Name and Visit Date criteria only have to be entered once, which creates a more efficient query.

Creating a New Calculated Field in a Query

Fields in a query are not limited to the fields from the tables in your database. You can also create *calculated fields* to use in a query. For example, you can create a calculated field named *Discount Amount* that displays the result of multiplying the value of Discount times Outstanding Balance in the Customer table.

To create this calculated field, follow these steps:

1. Create a new query using the Customer table.

2. Select the Customer Name, Discount, and Outstanding Balance fields in the Customer table.

3. Click the first empty Field: cell.

4. Type the following Discount Amount: **[Discount]*[Outstanding Balance]** and click in another cell.

Your query should look like the one shown in Figure 13-21. The expression has changed to Discount Amount:[Discount]*[Outstanding Balance]. The name of the calculated field is now "discount amount." If you didn't type the name in Step 4 above, then Expr1: precedes the calculation.

Note   For two reasons, a calculated field has a name (supplied either by the user or by an Access default). The name is needed as a label for the datasheet column, and the name is necessary for referencing the field in a form, a report, or another query.

Notice that the general format for creating a calculated field is as follows:

Calculated Field Name: Expression to build calculated field

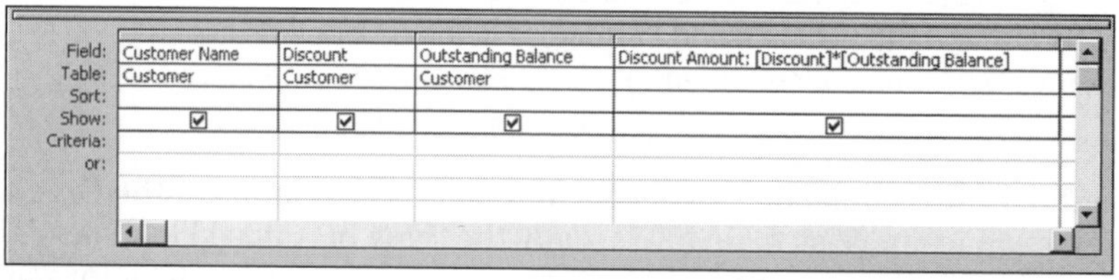

Field:	Customer Name	Discount	Outstanding Balance	Discount Amount: [Discount]*[Outstanding Balance]
Table:	Customer	Customer	Customer	
Sort:				
Show:	☑	☑	☑	☑
Criteria:				
or:				

Figure 13-21: A calculated field, Discount Amount, was created using two fields Discount and Outstanding Balance from the Customer Table.

✦   ✦   ✦

Understanding Form Controls

T his is one of many chapters in Part III that examine forms and reports in detail. Forms are the basic interface to an Access system. You learned earlier that you use forms to input, edit, and view data. However forms can be much more. They can help make input easier by allowing the user to select from a list. They can calculate and display important information. They can navigate you through the database as menus.

Forms are probably the most important type of object in any application. Forms allow you to display your raw data in a user-friendly format, to validate data entry, and to display your data in a nicely formatted window. You can use Microsoft Access forms to create any Windows interface. Although Autoforms serve as great starting points, Access's Forms Designer lets you create any imaginable design and then display it as a form.

Controls and properties form the basis of forms and reports. It is critical to understand the fundamental concepts of controls and properties before you begin to apply them to custom forms and reports.

On the CD-ROM This chapter uses the Pets table in the Mountain Animal Hospital database as the example to follow. This chapter explains each control by examining one or more fields in the Pets table.

To create the first form you need for this chapter, follow these steps:

1. Open the Mountain Animal Start database.

2. Select Insert ⇨ Form.

3. Select Design View from the New Form dialog box.

4. Select the Pets table from the combo box in the New Form dialog box.

In This Chapter

Understanding controls

Creating a new blank form

Looking at the three types of controls: bound, unbound, and calculated

Learning standards for using controls

Creating a new control

Using the Field List window

Using the Toolbox

Selecting controls

Manipulating controls

5. Click OK to display the Form Design window.

6. Maximize the form by clicking the maximize button in the top-right corner of the window.

7. Expand the light gray area of the form to the full-window size by dragging the bottom-right corner of the light gray area to the bottom-right corner of the window. Figure 14-1 shows this blank form design.

Before continuing with this form, it is important to understand the basic concepts of controls.

What Is a Control?

A *control* has many definitions in Access. Generally, a control is any object on a form or report, such as a label or text box. These are the same controls that you use in any Windows application, such as Access, Excel, or Web-based HTML forms, or that are used in any language, such as Visual Basic or C++. Although each language or product has different file formats and different properties, a text box in Access is the same as a text box in any other Windows product.

You enter data into controls and display data using controls. A control can be bound to a table field, but it can also be an object, such as a line or rectangle. Calculated fields are also controls, as are pictures, graphs, option buttons, check boxes, and objects. Some controls that aren't part of Access are developed separately—these are ActiveX controls. ActiveX controls extend the base feature set of Access 2002 and are available from a variety of vendors. Many ActiveX controls are shipped with Access 2002.

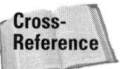
Cross-Reference   ActiveXcontrols are covered in Chapter 18.

Whether you're working with forms or reports, essentially the same process is followed to create and use controls. In this chapter, we explain controls from the perspective of a form.

The different control types

Forms and reports contain many different control types. You can add some of these controls to forms by using the Toolbox shown in Figure 14-1. In this book, you learn to add and use the controls that are used most often (these are listed in Table 14-1). In this chapter, you learn when to use each control and you also learn how these controls work.

Table 14-1
Controls You Can Create in Access Forms and Reports

Basic Controls

Label	Literal text is displayed in a label control.
Text box	Data is typed into a text box.

Enhanced Data Entry and Data Validation Controls

Option group	This group holds multiple option buttons, check boxes, or toggle buttons.
Toggle button	This is a two-state button, up or down, which usually uses pictures or icons instead of text to display different states.
Option button	Also called a radio button, this button is displayed as a circle with a dot when the option is on.
Check box	This is another two-state control, shown as a square that contains a check mark if it's on and an empty square if it's off.
Combo box	This box is a pop-up list of values that allows entries not on the list.
List box	This is a list of values that is always displayed on the form or report.
Command button	Also called a push button, this button is used to call a macro or run a Basic program to initiate an action.
Subform/Subreport	This control displays another form or report within the original form or report.
Tab control	This control can display multiple pages in a file folder type interface.

Graphic and Picture Controls

Image	Displays a bitmap picture with very little overhead.
Unbound object frame	This frame holds an OLE object or embedded picture that is not tied to a table field and can include graphs, pictures, sound files, and video.
Bound object frame	This frame holds an OLE object or embedded picture that is tied to a table field.
Line	This is a single line of variable thickness and color, which is used for separation.
Rectangle	A rectangle can be any color or size or can be filled in or blank; the rectangle is used for emphasis.
Page break	This is usually used for reports and denotes a physical page break.

Note   If the toolbox isn't displayed, you can display it by selecting View ⇨ Toolbox or by clicking the toolbox icon.

Tip   You can move, resize, and anchor the toolbox on the window. You can anchor it to any border, grab it, and resize it in the middle of the window.

Figure 14-1 shows the resulting new form. This is the design grid where you place the controls you will want on the form. You can also see the Field List window on the form ready for you to select the fields from the Pets table to use in your form.

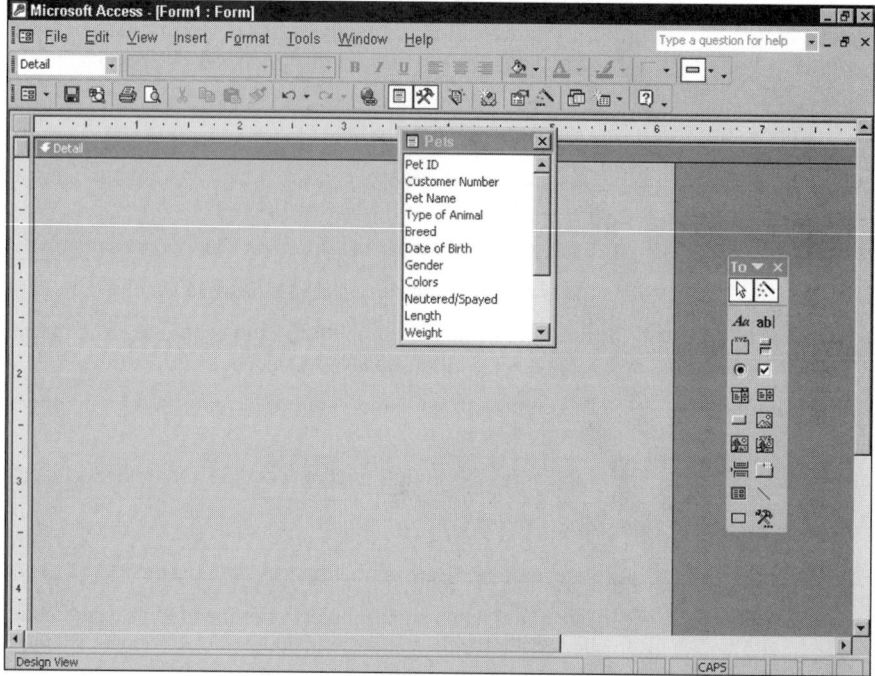

Figure 14-1: A new blank form, the Field List window, and the toolbox

The Control Wizard icon, located in the upper-right corner of the toolbox, does not add a control to a form; rather, it determines whether a Wizard is automatically activated when you add certain controls. The option group, combo box, list box, subform/subreport, object frame, and command button controls all have Wizards that Access starts when you add a new control. You can use the More Controls icon to display a list of ActiveX controls, which you can add to Access 2002.

Understanding bound, unbound, and calculated controls

Here are the three basic types of controls:

✦ Bound controls

✦ Unbound controls

✦ Calculated controls

Bound controls are controls that are bound to a table field. When you enter a value into a bound control, Access automatically updates the table field in the current record. Most of the controls that let you enter information can be bound; these include OLE (Object Linking and Embedding) fields. Controls can be bound to most data types, including text, dates, numbers, Yes/No, pictures, and memo fields.

Unbound controls retain the entered value, but they don't update any table fields. You can use these controls for text display, for values to be passed to macros, lines, and rectangles, or for holding OLE objects (such as bitmap pictures) that aren't stored in a table but on the form itself. Unbound controls are also known as *variables* or *memory variables*.

Calculated controls are based on expressions, such as functions or calculations. Calculated controls are also unbound because they don't update table fields. An example of a calculated control is =[Medication Price] + [Treatment Price]; this control calculates the total of two table fields for display on a form.

Figure 14-2 shows examples of these three control types. The picture of the mountain, which is the company's logo, and the company name, *Mountain Animal Hospital,* are examples of unbound controls. Below the name and logo are examples of bound controls (they contain field names) including the picture. The animal's age is an example of a calculated control. The function DateDiff is being used to calculate the number of years from the *Date of Birth* bound control to the current date supplied by the Now ( ) function.

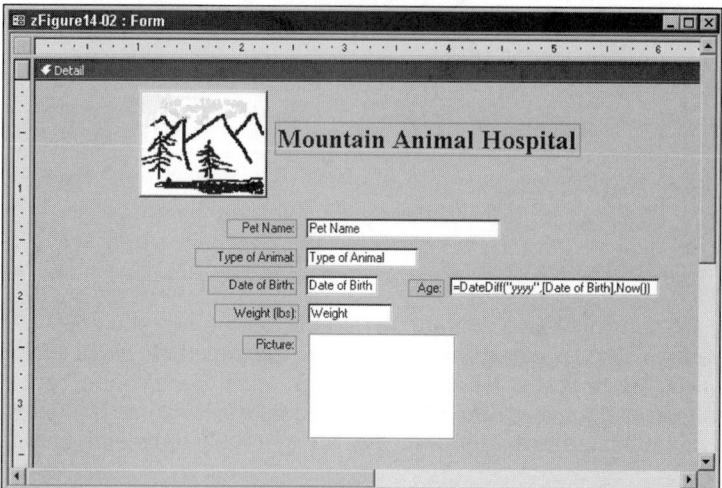

Figure 14-2: Examples of the three control types: Unbound, bound, and calculated

Standards for Using Controls

Most of you reading this book have used Microsoft Windows. You have probably used other applications in Windows as well, such as word processing applications (Word for Windows, WordPerfect for Windows, or WordPad) or spreadsheet applications (Excel, 1-2-3 for Windows, or Quattro Pro). Using a Windows application and designing a Windows application, however, are two different stories.

The controls in Access 2002 have specific purposes. The uses of these controls, however, are not decided by whim or intuition — a scientific method determines which control should be used for each specific situation. Experience shows you that correct screen and report designs lead to more usable applications.

Tip   In fact, you may learn that Office developers use the fonts and colors that Microsoft Office uses. Some of the simplest guidelines include using the Tahoma font for all form controls that are 12 points or smaller and the Verdana font for all font sizes above 12 point. Other Office standards include using only etched line rectangles (never sunken or raised), gray form backgrounds, flat label controls, and sunken text box controls with white backgrounds for data entry. The only item that should be raised on a form is a button that you can click. Finally, no control text is bolded except for an occasional label at the top of the form.

Label controls

You use a *label control* to display descriptive text (such as a title, a caption, or instructions) on a form or report. Labels can be separate controls, which is common when they are used for titles or data-entry instructions. When labels are used for field captions, they are often attached to the control that they describe.

You can display labels on a single line or on multiple lines. Labels are unbound controls that accept no input; you use them strictly for one-way communication (they are read-only). You can use them on many types of controls. Figure 14-3 shows many uses of labels, including titles, captions, button text, and captions for buttons and boxes. You can use different font styles and sizes for your labels, and you can boldface, italicize, and underline them.

You should capitalize the first letter of each word in a label, except for articles and conjunctions, such as *the, an, and, or*, and so on. You should follow several guidelines when you use label controls with other controls. The following list explains some of these placement guidelines, which are shown Figure 14-3:

✦ **Command buttons.** Inside the button

✦ **Checkboxes.** To the right of the check box

✦ **Option buttons.** To the right of the option button

✦ **Text box.** Above or to the left of the text box

✦ **List or combo box.** Above or to the left of the box

✦ **Group box.** On top of and replacing part of the top frame line

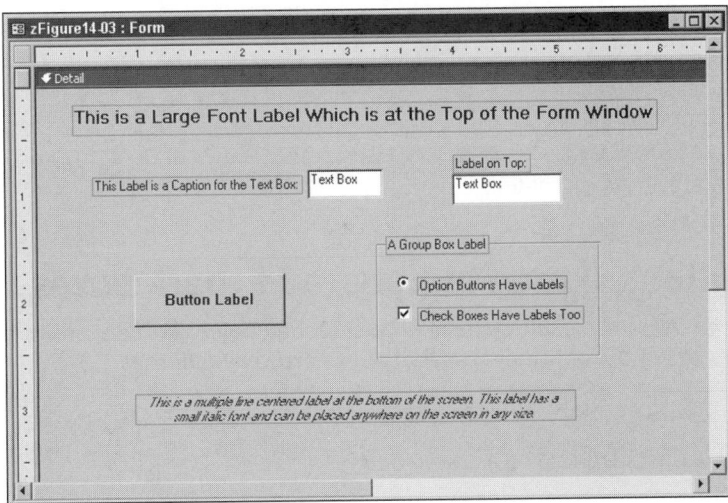

Figure 14-3: Sample label controls alone and with other controls

Text box controls

Text boxes are controls that display data or allow the user to enter or edit information. In a text box, you can accept the current text, edit it, delete it, or replace it. You can use text boxes with most data types, including Text, Number, Date/Time, Yes/No, and Memo — and they can also be used as bound or unbound controls. You can use text box fields from tables or queries, or the text box can contain calculated expressions. A text box is the most-used control because editing and displaying data are the main purposes of any database system.

Every text box needs an associated label to identify its purpose. Text boxes can contain multiple lines of data and often do (you use one to display Memo field data, for example). Data that is too long for the width of the text field wraps automatically within the field boundaries. Figure 14-4 shows several different text boxes in Form view. Notice how the different data types vary in their alignment within the text boxes. The Comments text box displays multiple lines in the resized text box, which also has a scrollbar.

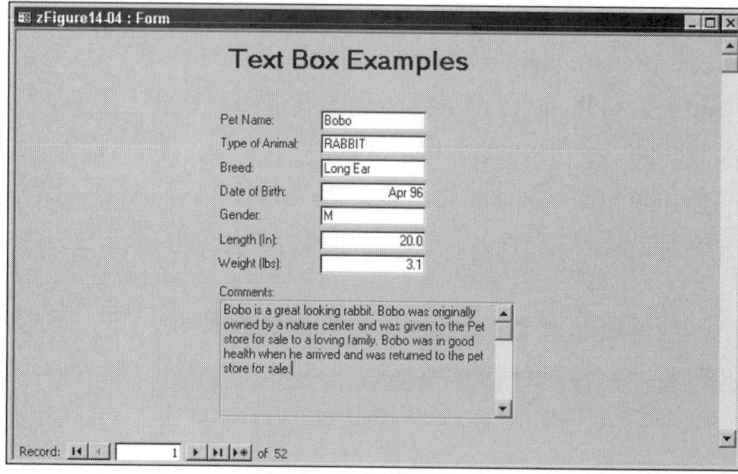

Figure 14-4: Sample text box controls

Toggle buttons, option buttons, and check boxes

Button or *check box* controls allow the user to select a choice. Three types of buttons act in the same way, but their visual displays are very different:

  ✦ Toggle buttons

  ✦ Option buttons (also known as *radio buttons*)

  ✦ Check boxes

These controls are used with Yes/No data types. You can use each control individually to represent one of two states: Yes or No, On or Off, or True or False. Table 14-2 describes the appearance of these controls in both states.

Toggle buttons, option buttons, and check boxes return a value of -1 to the bound table field if the button value is Yes, On, or True; they return a value of 0 if the button is No, Off, or False. You can enter a default value to display a specific state. The control is initially displayed in a Null state if no default is entered and no state is selected. The Null state's visual appearance is the same as that of the No state.

Although you can place Yes/No data types in a text box, it's better to use one of these controls. The values that are returned to a text box (-1 and 0) are very confusing, especially because Yes is represented by -1 and No is represented by 0.

Table 14-2
Button Control Visual Displays

Button Type	State	Visual Description
Toggle button	True	Button is sunken
Toggle button	False	Button is raised
Option button	True	Circle with a large solid dot inside
Option button	False	Hollow circle
Check box	True	Square with a check in the middle
Check box	False	Empty square

Note   As Figure 14-5 shows, using the special effects options from the Formatting toolbar can change the look of the option button or check box. See Chapter 16 for more details.

Tip   You can format the display of the Yes/No values in Datasheet or Form view by setting the Format property of the text box control to Yes/No, On/Off, or True/False. If you don't use the Format property, the datasheet displays -1 or 0. Using a default value also speeds data entry, especially if the default is the value selected most often.

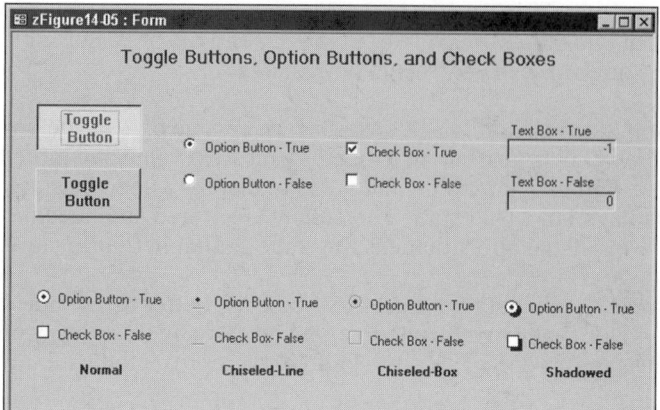

Figure 14-5: Sample toggle buttons, option buttons, and check boxes

Option groups

An *option group* can contain multiple toggle buttons, option buttons, or check boxes. When these controls are inside an option group box, they work together rather than individually. Instead of representing a two-state Yes/No data type, controls within an option group return a number based on the position in the group. You can select only one control within an option group at a time; the maximum number of buttons in such a group should be four. If you need to exceed that number, switch to a drop-down list box (unless you have plenty of room on your screen).

An option group is generally bound to a single field or expression. Each button inside it passes a different value back to the option group, which in turn passes the single choice to the bound field or expression. The buttons themselves are not bound to any field; instead, they are bound to the option group box.

Figure 14-6 shows three types of buttons; two of these types are shown in option group boxes. In the Toggle Buttons option group, the second choice is selected; the same is true of the Option Buttons option group. Notice, however, that the first and third choices are selected in the Check Boxes rectangle; the check boxes are independent and are not part of an option group. When you make a new selection in an option group, the current selection is deselected. For example, if you click on Option Button 3 in the option group box in the middle of Figure 14-6, the solid dot appears to move to the third circle, and the second circle becomes hollow.

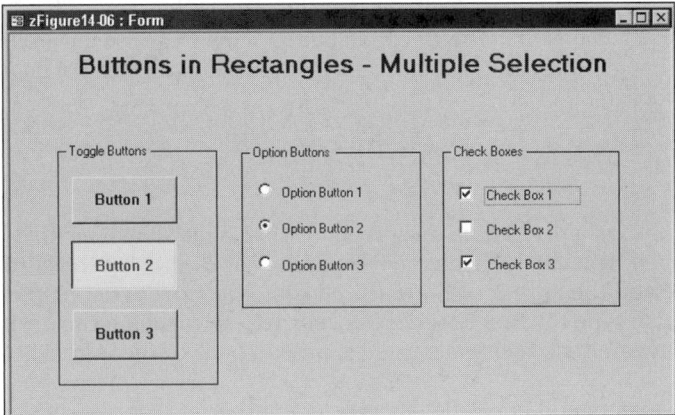

Figure 14-6: Three types of option groups

Buttons in rectangles

The three types of buttons act very differently, depending on whether they are used individually or in an option group. You can create buttons that look like a group but that do not function as a single entity. Figure 14-7 shows a multiple-selection group. Notice that check boxes 2 and 3 are simultaneously selected. This is not an option group; rather, this is a group of controls enclosed in a box. They act independently, so that they don't have to be in the same box; each control passes either a -1 (True) or a 0 (False) to the field, expression, or control to which it is bound. A common use for this type of grouping is to let a user select from a list of nonexclusive options, such as a list of reports or a list of days on which a process should occur.

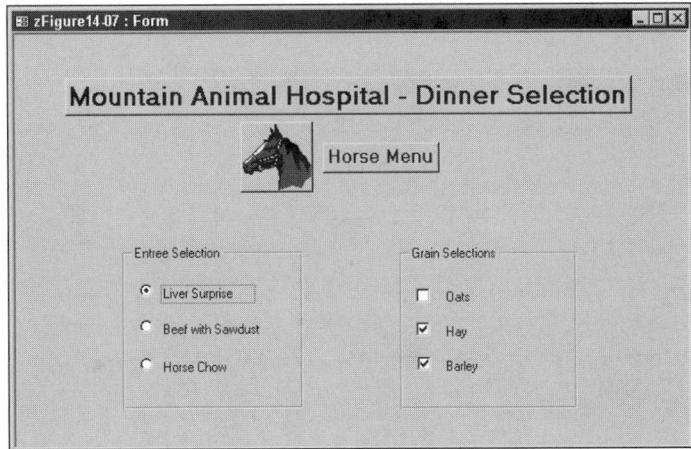

Figure 14-7: A multiple-selection group for selecting a meal

Tip

You may want to create groups of buttons that look like option groups but have multiple selections. Rather than use an option button, simply enclose the group of buttons in a rectangle. Each button remains an individual entity instead of becoming part of a group.

List boxes

A *list box* control displays a list of data on-screen just like a pull-down menu, but the list box is always open. You can highlight an item in the list by moving the cursor to your desired choice and then pressing Enter (or clicking the mouse) to complete the selection. You can also type the first letter of the selection to highlight the desired entry. After you select an item, the item's value is passed back to the bound field.

List boxes can display any number of fields and any number of records. By sizing the list box, you can make it display more or fewer records.

Note

List boxes have a feature called Multi-Select property that allows you to select more than one item at a time. The results are stored in a type of array and must be used with the VBA programming language.

List boxes are generally used when you have plenty of room on-screen and you want the operator to see the choices without having to click on a drop-down arrow. A vertical — and horizontal — scrollbar is used to display any records and fields not visible when the list box is in its default size. The highlighted entry is the one that is currently selected. If no entries are highlighted, either a selection has not been made or the selected item is not currently in view. You can select only the items in the list.

You also have a choice of whether to display the column headings in list boxes. Figure 14-8 displays list boxes with three layout schemes.

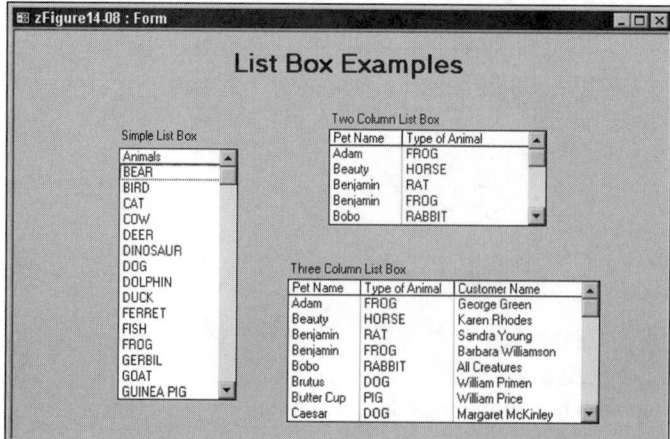

Figure 14-8: Sample list boxes

Combo boxes

In Access, *combo boxes* differ from list boxes in two ways:

✦ The combo box is initially displayed as a single row with an arrow that opens the box to the normal size.

✦ As an option, the combo box lets you enter a value that is not on the list.

You see a list box and a combo box (shown both open and closed) in Figure 14-9.

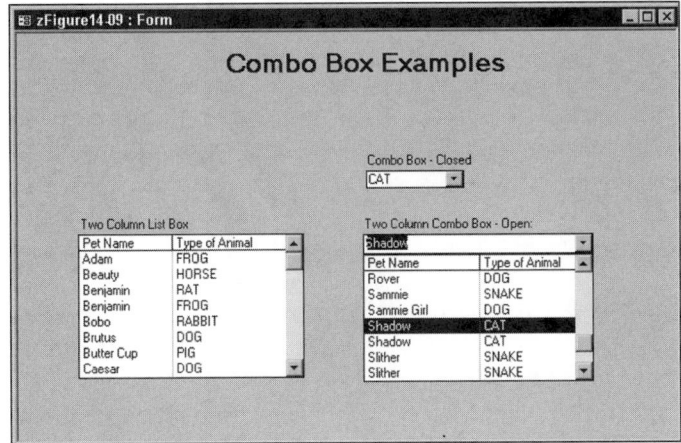

Figure 14-9: An example of the differences between combo boxes and list boxes

Tab controls

The *tab control* is one of the most important controls because it allows you to create completely new interfaces by using the tabbed dialog box look and feel.

Cross-Reference   Chapter 33 teaches you how to use the tabbed dialog box when creating a print dialog box example for Mountain Animal Hospital.

Most serious Windows applications now contain tabbed dialog boxes. Tabbed dialog boxes look very professional. They allow you to have many screens of data in a small area by grouping similar types of data and using tabs to navigate between the areas.

The tab control gets its name from the fact that it looks like the tabs on a file folder when you use it. Figure 14-10 shows the Access 2002 Tab Control icon and a tab control under construction on the design screen. As you can see, the tab control looks like the tabs seen in Form view.

You create a new tab control in the same way that you create any Access control. You select the tab control, as shown in Figure 14-10, and then you draw a rectangle to indicate the size of the control. When the tab control is initially shown, it is displayed with two tab pages. The tab control contains pages. Each tab that you define creates a separate page. As you choose each tab in Design view, you see a different page. You can place other controls on each page of the tab control. The control can have many pages; in fact, you can have multiple rows of tabs, each having its own page. You can place new controls on a page or copy and paste them from other forms or other pages. You can't drag and drop between pages of a tab control. To change the active page for the tab control, click the page that you want and it becomes active (even in design mode).

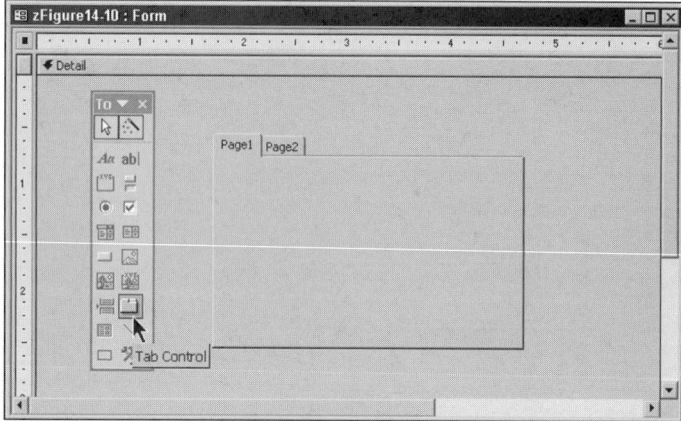

Figure 14-10: Designing a tab control

You can insert new pages by right-clicking a tab and then choosing the Insert command. The new page is inserted before the selected page. You can delete pages by right-clicking a tab and choosing the Delete command. This deletes the active page and all the controls on it.

You can size the tab control but not individual pages. Individual pages don't have visual appearance properties — they get these from the tab control itself. You select the border of the tab control by clicking it — clicking directly on a page selects that page. As with an Access detail section, you can't size the tab control smaller than the control in the rightmost part of the page. You must move controls before resizing.

Creating New Controls

After you learn about the controls that you can use on a form or report, you can learn how to add controls to a form and how to manipulate them in the Form Design window. Although the Form Wizard can quickly place your bound controls in the Design window, you still may need to add more controls to a form, such as for calculated fields.

The two ways to add a control

You add a control to a form in either of two ways:

✦ Dragging a field from the Field List window to add a bound control

✦ Clicking a button in the toolbox and then adding a new unbound control to the screen

Using the Field List window

The Field List window shown in Figure 14-11 displays all the fields in the open table/query that you used to create a form. This window is movable and resizable and displays a vertical scrollbar if it contains more fields than can fit in the window.

Figure 14-11: The Field List window sized to show all the fields in the Pet's table

When you first create a new form in Design View, the Field List window is open and available to use. Later on, however, it may be closed. If it's closed, you can display it in the Field List window by using one of two methods:

✦ Click the Field List button on the toolbar (this button looks like an Access table).

✦ Select View ⇨ Field List from the Form menu bar.

Note   After you resize or move the Field List window, it remains that size for all forms, even if toggled off or if the form is closed. Only if you exit Access is the window set to its default size.

Generally, dragging a field from the Field List window adds a bound text box to the Form Design window. If you drag a Yes/No field from the Field List window, you add a check box. If you drag a field that has a Lookup property, you add a list or combo box control. If you drag an OLE field from the Field List window, you create a bound object frame. Optionally, you can select the type of control by selecting a control from the toolbox and dragging the field to the Form Design window.

Caution When you drag fields from the Field List window, the first control is placed where you release the mouse button. Make sure that you have enough space to the left of the control for the labels. If you don't have sufficient space, the labels slide under the controls.

You gain several distinct advantages by dragging a field from the Field List window:

✦ The control is bound automatically to the field that you dragged it to.

✦ Field properties inherit table-level formats, status-bar text, and data-validation rules and messages.

✦ The label control and label text are created with the field name as the caption.

✦ The label control is attached to the field control so they move together

Using the toolbox

By using the *toolbox buttons* to add a control, you can decide which type of control to use for each field. If you don't create the control by dragging it from the Field List window, the field is *unbound* (or, not attached to the data in a table field) and has a default label name like Field3 or Option11. After you create the control, you can decide what field to bind the control to, enter text for the label, and set any properties.

The deciding factor of whether to use the field list or the toolbox is this: Does the field exist in the table/query or do you want to create an unbound or calculated expression? By using the Field List window and the toolbox together, you can create bound controls of nearly any type. You will find, however, that some data types don't allow all the control types found in the toolbox. For example, if you select the Chart control type from the toolbox and drag a single field to the form, a text box control is added instead of a chart control.

In Access 2002, you can change the type of control after you create it; then you can set all the properties for the control. For example, suppose that you add a field as a text box control and you want to change it to list box. You can use Format ➪ Change To and change the control type. However, you can change only from some types of controls to others. You can change anything to a text box control; option buttons, toggle buttons, and check boxes are interchangeable, as are list and combo boxes.

Dragging a field name from the Field List window

The easiest way to create a text box control is to drag a field from the Field List window. When the Field List window is open, you can click an individual field and drag it to the Form Design window. This window works in exactly the same way as a Table/Query window in QBE. You can also select multiple fields and then drag them to the screen together by using these techniques:

✦ Select multiple contiguous fields by holding down the Shift key and clicking the first and last fields that you want.

✦ Select multiple noncontiguous fields by holding down the Ctrl key and clicking each field that you want.

✦ Double-click the table/query name in the window's title bar to select all the fields.

After selecting one or more fields, drag the selection to the screen.

Drag the Pet Name, Type of Animal, Date of Birth, and Neutered/Spayed fields from the Field List window to the form. If you haven't created a new form, create one first and resize the form as instructed at the beginning of this chapter. When you complete these steps successfully, your screen should look like the one shown in Figure 14-12.

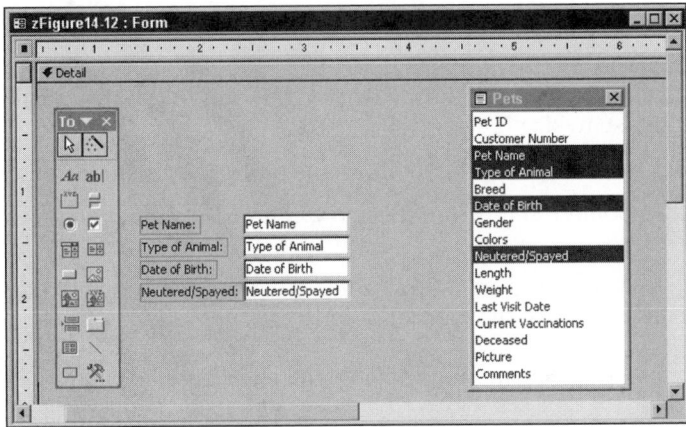

Figure 14-12: Fields dragged from the Field List window

You can see four controls in the Form Design window — each one consists of a label control and a text box control (Access attaches the label control to the text box automatically). You can work with these controls as a group or independently, and you can select, move, resize, or delete them. Notice that each control has a label with a caption matching the field name, and the text box control displays the bound field name used in the text box. If you want to resize just the control and not the label, you must work with the two controls separately.

You can close the Field List window by clicking the Field List button on the toolbar or the close button on the Field List window.

Creating unbound controls with the toolbox

You can add one control at a time by using the toolbox. You can add any of the controls listed in the toolbox. Each control becomes an unbound control that has a default label and a name.

To create three different unbound controls, perform these steps:

1. Click the Text Box button on the toolbox (the button appears with a box around it).

2. Place the mouse pointer in the Form Design window (the cursor changes to the Text Box button).

3. Click and hold down the mouse button where you want the control to begin, and drag the mouse to size the control.

4. Click the Option Button on the toolbox (this button appears sunken).

5. Place the mouse pointer in the Form Design window (the cursor changes to an Option button).

6. Click and hold down the mouse button where you want the control to begin, and drag the mouse to size the control.

7. Click the Check Box button on the toolbox (the button appears sunken).

8. Place the mouse pointer in the Form Design window (the cursor changes to a check box).

9. Click and hold down the mouse button where you want the control to begin, and drag the mouse to size the control.

When you are done, your screen should resemble the one shown in Figure 14-13.

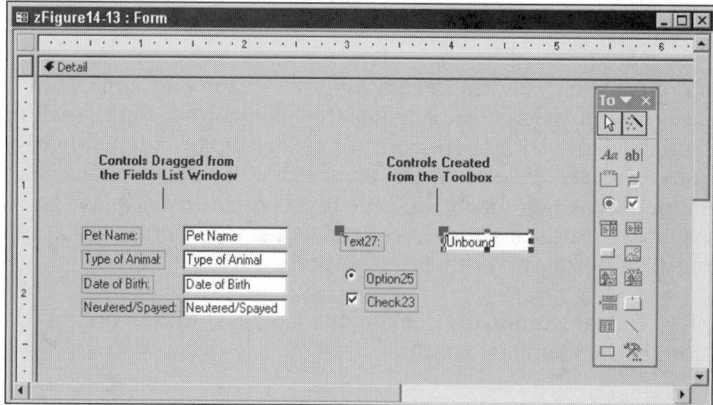

Figure 14-13: Three additional new unbound controls added by using the toolbox

> **Tip** If you just click the Form Design window, Access creates a default-sized control.

In Figure 14-13, notice the difference between the controls that were dragged from the Field List window and the controls that were created from the toolbox. The Field List window controls are bound to a field in the Pets table and are appropriately labeled and named. The controls created from the toolbox are unbound and have default names. The default names are automatically assigned a number according to the type of control.

Later you learn how to change the control names, captions, and properties. Using properties speeds the process of naming controls and binding them to specific fields. If you want to see the differences between bound and unbound controls, display the form in Form view by pressing the Form button in the toolbar or by selecting View ⇨ Form View. You can see that the Pet Name, Type of Animal, Date of Birth, and Neutered/Spayed bound controls display data. The other three controls don't display data because they aren't bound to any data source. After you view the data, display the form in Design view again.

Selecting Controls

After a control is on the Form Design window, you can work with it; for example, you can resize it, move it, or copy it. The first step is to select one or more controls. Depending on its size, a selected control may show from four to eight *handles* (small squares called *moving and sizing handles*) around the control — at the corners and midway along the sides. The handle in the upper-left corner is larger than the other handles and you use it to move the control. You use the other handles to size the control. Figure 14-14 displays some selecting controls and their moving and sizing handles.

The Select Objects tool (top leftmost icon) on the toolbox must be on for you to select a control. The pointer always appears as an arrow pointing diagonally toward the upper-left corner. If you use the toolbox to create a single control, Access automatically reselects the pointer as the default.

Deselecting selected controls

It's a good practice to deselect any selected controls before you select another control. You can deselect a control by clicking an unselected area of the screen that doesn't contain a control. When you do so, the handles disappear from any selected control.

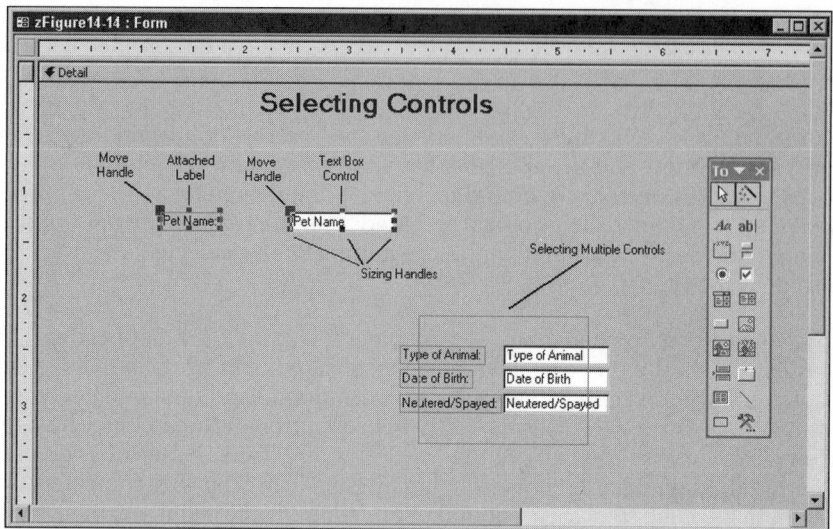

Figure 14-14: A conceptual view of selecting controls and their moving and sizing handles

Selecting a single control

You can select any single control by clicking anywhere on the control. When you click a control, all the handles appear. If the control has an attached label, the handle for moving the label also appears. If you select a label control that is part of an attached control, all the handles for the label control are displayed, and only the *Move handle* (the largest handle) is displayed in the attached control.

Selecting multiple controls

You can select multiple controls in these two ways:

✦ Click each desired control while holding down the Shift key.

✦ Drag the pointer through or around the controls that you want to select.

Figure 14-14 shows selecting the multiple bound controls graphically. When you select multiple controls by dragging the mouse, a light gray rectangle appears as the mouse is dragged. When you select multiple controls by dragging the pointer through the controls, be careful to select only the controls that you want to select. Any control that is touched by the line or enclosed within it is selected. If you want to select labels only, you must make sure that the selection rectangle encloses only the labels.

Tip

When you click on a ruler, an arrow appears and a line is displayed across the screen. You can drag the mouse to widen the line. Each control that the line touches is selected.

Tip If you find that controls are not selected when the rectangle passes through the control, you may have the Selection behavior global property set to fully enclosed. This means that a control is selected only if the selection rectangle completely encloses the entire control. The normal default for this option is partially enclosed. You can change this option by first selecting Tools ⇨ Options and then selecting the Forms/Reports tab in the Options dialog box. The option Selection behavior should be set to partially enclosed.

By holding down the Shift key, you can select several noncontiguous controls. This lets you select controls on totally different parts of the screen, cut them, and then paste them together somewhere else on-screen.

Manipulating Controls

Creating a form is a multi-step process. The next step is to make sure that your controls are properly sized and moved to their correct positions.

Resizing a control

You can *resize* controls by using any of the smaller handles on the control. The handles in the control corners let you make the field larger or smaller — in both width and height — and at the same time. You use the handles in the middle of the control sides to size the control larger or smaller in one direction only. The top and bottom handles control the height of the control; the handles in the middle change the control's width.

When the mouse pointer touches a corner handle of a selected control, the pointer becomes a diagonal double arrow. You can then drag the sizing handle until the control is the desired size. If the mouse pointer touches a side handle in a selected control, the pointer changes to a horizontal or vertical double-headed arrow. Figure 14-15 shows the Pet Name control after being resized. Notice the double-headed arrow in the corner of the Pet Name control.

Tip You can resize a control in very small increments by pressing the Shift key and pressing the arrow keys. This also works with multiple controls selected. Using this technique, a control changes by only one pixel at a time (or moves to the nearest grid line if Snap to Grid is selected in the Format menu).

Moving a control

After you select a control, you can easily move it, using either one of these methods:

✦ Select the control and, with the hand icon displayed, drag it to a new location.

✦ Select the control and place your mouse on the move handle in the upper-left corner of the control. With the index finger icon displayed, drag it to a new location.

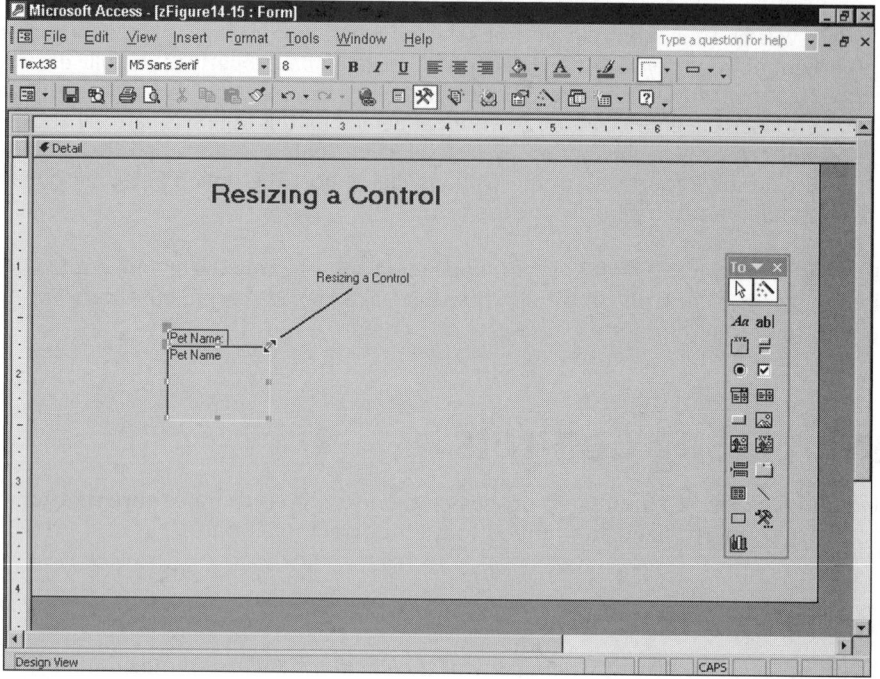

Figure 14-15: Resizing a control

If the control has an attached label, you can move both label and control with either method. It doesn't matter whether you click the control or the label; they move together.

You can move a control separately from an attached label by pointing to the move handle of the control and then dragging it. You can also move the label control separately from the other control by pointing to the move handle of the label control and dragging it separately.

Figure 14-16 shows a label control that has been separately moved to the top of the text box control. The hand icon indicates that the controls are ready to be moved together. To see the hand, the control(s) must already be selected.

Tip   You can move a control in small increments with the keyboard by pressing the Ctrl key and pressing the arrow keys after you select a control or group of controls.

You can restrict the direction in which a control is moved so that it maintains alignment within a specific row or column by holding down the Shift key as you press and holding down the mouse button to select and move the control. The control moves only in the direction that you first move it, either horizontally or vertically.

You can cancel a move or a resizing operation by pressing Esc before you release the mouse button. After a move or resizing operation is complete, you can click the Undo button or select Edit ➪ Undo Move or Edit ➪ Undo Sizing to undo the changes.

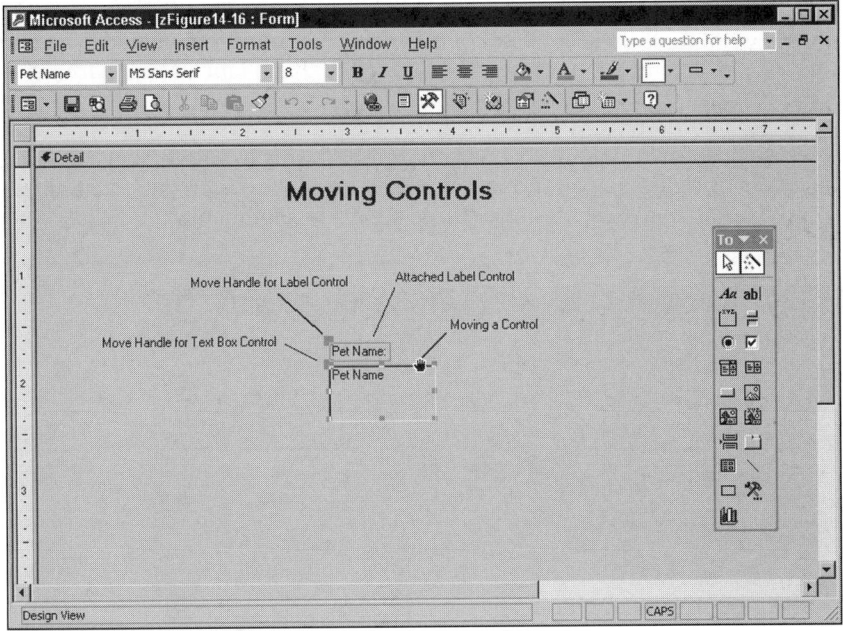

Figure 14-16: Moving a control

Aligning controls

You may want to move several controls so that they are all *aligned* (lined up). The Format ➪ Align menu has several options, as shown in Figure 14-17, and are described in the following list:

- ✦ **Left.** Aligns the left edge of the selected controls with that of the leftmost selected control

- ✦ **Right.** Aligns the right edge of the selected controls with that of the rightmost selected control

- ✦ **Top.** Aligns the top edge of the selected controls with that of the topmost selected control

- ✦ **Bottom.** Aligns the bottom edge of the selected controls with that of the bottommost selected control

- ✦ **To Grid.** Aligns the top-left corners of the selected controls to the nearest grid point

You can align any number of controls by selecting from this menu. When you choose one of the options, Access uses the control that is the closest to the desired selection as the model for the alignment. For example, suppose that you have three controls and you want to left-align them. They are aligned on the basis of the control farthest to the left in the group of the three controls.

Figure 14-17 shows several sets of controls. The first set of controls is not aligned. The label controls in the second set of controls have been left-aligned. The text box controls in the second set have been right-aligned. Each label, along with its attached text box, has been bottom-aligned.

Each type of alignment must be done separately. In this example, you can left-align all the labels or right-align all the text boxes at once. However, you must align each label and its text control separately (three separate alignments).

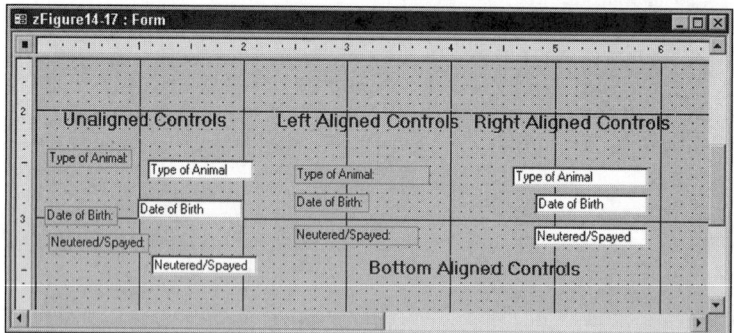

Figure 14-17: An example of unaligned and aligned controls on the grid

The series of dots in the background of Figure 14-17 is the *grid*. The grid can assist you in aligning controls. You can display the grid by selecting View ➪ Grid.

You can use the Format ➪ Snap to Grid option to align new controls to the grid as you draw or place them on a form. It also aligns existing controls when you move or resize them.

When Snap to Grid is on from the Format menu, and you draw a new control by clicking on the form and dragging to size the control, Access aligns the four corners of the control to points on the grid. When you place a new control by clicking the control in the field list and then dragging it to the form, only the upper-left corner is aligned.

As you move or resize existing controls, Access 2002 lets you move only from grid point to grid point. When Snap to Grid is off, Access 2002 ignores the grid and lets you place a control anywhere on the form or report.

Tip

You can turn Snap to Grid off temporarily by pressing the Ctrl key before you create a control (or while creating or moving it).

You can change the grid's *fineness* (number of dots) from form to form by using the GridX and GridY Form properties. The grid is invisible if its fineness is greater than 16 units per inch horizontally or vertically. (Higher numbers indicate greater fineness.)

Another pair of alignment commands can make a big difference when you have to align the space between multiple controls. The Format ⇨ Horizontal Spacing and Vertical Spacing change the space between controls on the basis of the space between the first two selected controls. If the controls are across the screen, use horizontal spacing. If they are down the screen, use vertical spacing.

 Tip   Aligning controls aligns the control boxes only. If you want to align the text itself within the controls (also known as *justifying the text*) you must use the form's formatting toolbar and select the Left, Right, or Center icons

Sizing controls

The Size command on the Format menu has several options that help size controls based on the value of the data, the grid, or other controls. The Size menu options are:

✦ **To Fit.** Adjusts control height and width for the font of the text they contain

✦ **To Grid.** Moves all sides of selected controls in or out to meet the nearest points on the grid

✦ **To Tallest.** Makes selected controls the height of the tallest selected control

✦ **To Shortest.** Makes selected controls the height of the shortest selected control

✦ **To Widest.** Makes selected controls the width of the widest selected control

✦ **To Narrowest.** Makes selected controls the height of the narrowest selected control

 **Tip**   You can access most of the Format commands by right-clicking after selecting multiple controls. When you right-click on multiple controls, a shortcut menu displays—this is similar to the Format menu on the Access menu bar. This is a quick way to resize or align your controls.

Grouping controls

 Tip   Access 2002 can group controls. When controls are grouped, you can select and format many controls at once. While you can select multiple controls and format them, grouping is like a permanent selection. When you click on any of the grouped controls, they all are instantly selected and can then be formatted.

To group multiple controls, select the controls by holding down the Shift key and clicking them. After the desired controls are selected, select Format ⇨ Group from the Access menu bar, as shown in Figure 14-18.

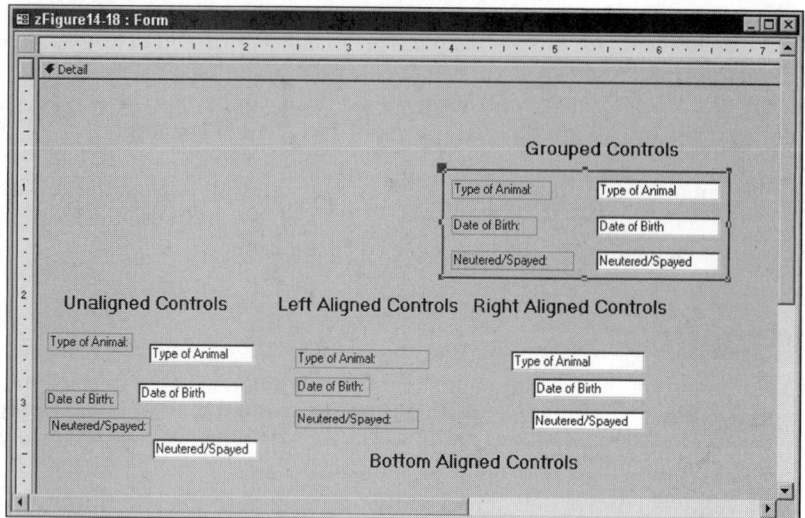

Figure 14-18: Grouping multiple controls together

After you have grouped the objects together, whenever you click any of the fields inside the group, the entire group is selected. If you click again, just the field is selected. To resize the entire group, put your mouse on the side you want to resize. After the double arrow is displayed, click and drag until you reach the desired size.

To remove a group, select the group by clicking any field inside the group and then select Format ➪ UnGroup from the Access menu bar. This ungroups the controls.

Deleting a control

No longer want a specific control on the Form Design window? Delete it by selecting the control and pressing Delete. You can also select Edit ➪ Delete to delete a selected control or Edit ➪ Cut to cut the control to the Clipboard.

You can delete more than one control at a time by selecting multiple controls and pressing one of the Delete key sequences. You can delete an entire group of controls by selecting the group and pressing Delete or by selecting Edit ➪ Delete. If you have a control with an attached label, you can delete only the label by clicking the label itself and then selecting one of the delete methods. If you select the control, both the control and the label are deleted. To delete only the label of the Pet Name control, follow the next set of steps (this example assumes that you have the Pet Name text box control in your Form Design window):

1. Select the Pet Name label control only.
2. Press Delete.

The label control is removed from the window.

Attaching a label to a control

If you accidentally delete a label from a control, you can reattach it. To create and then reattach a label to a control, follow these steps:

1. Click the Label button on the toolbox.
2. Place the mouse pointer in the Form Design window (the mouse pointer becomes the Text Box button).
3. Click and hold down the mouse button where you want the control to begin; drag the mouse to size the control.
4. Type **Pet Name:** and click outside the control.
5. Select the Pet Name label control.
6. Select Edit ➪ Cut to cut the label control to the Clipboard.
7. Select the Pet Name text box control.
8. Select Edit ➪ Paste to attach the label control to the text box control.

Copying a control

You can create copies of any control by duplicating it or by copying it to the Clipboard and then pasting the copies where you want them. If you have a control for which you have entered many properties or specified a certain format, you can copy it and revise only the properties (such as the control name and bound field name) to make it a different control. This capability is useful with a multiple-page form when you want to display the same values on different pages and in different locations.

✦　　✦　　✦

Creating and Customizing Data-Entry Forms

In Chapter 14, you learned about the tools necessary to create and display a form—Design view, bound and unbound controls, Toolbox, etc. In this chapter, you learn about properties and then use all your newly acquired skills to create several types of data-entry and display forms.

You will use the Customer and Pets tables in the Mountain Animal Start database to create several types of simple forms. Each control is explained in more depth as you are adding the fields to the forms.

Creating a Standard Data-Entry Form

The first form you will create is a data-entry form that uses two tables. In Chapter 8, you created a simple Pets data-entry form using a Form Wizard. Now, you will create a more complex form shown in Figure 15-1. Generally, the more features you add to a form, the easier it is to use. This form demonstrates the use of label and text box controls from multiple tables as well as embedded pictures. You will continue to modify this form in the next several chapters, adding more complex controls and features, making the form increasingly more powerful and functional.

In This Chapter

Creating a multiple-file query to be used for the form

Creating a blank form bound to the query

Learning about properties

Modifying controls on a form

Setting the tab order of a form

Creating controls for Memo and OLE fields

Creating a form using two tables

Creating a multiple-page form

Learning how to use form and page headers and footers

Printing a form

Converting a form to a report

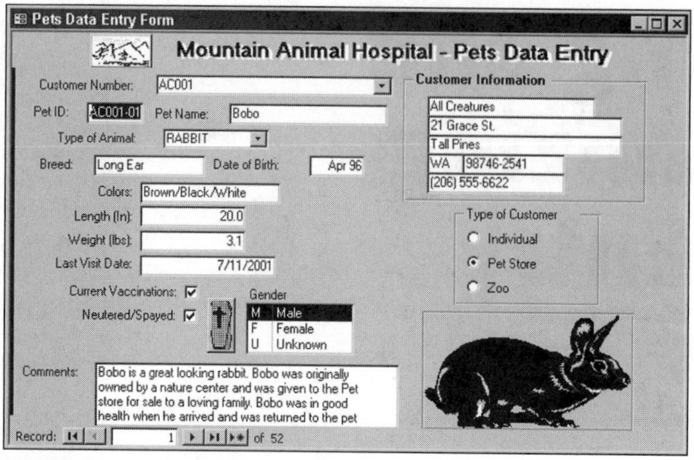

Figure 15-1: A complex data-entry form

Assembling the data

To create this form, fields from both the Customer and Pets tables are needed. So, the first thing you need to do is to assemble the data. Table 15-1 lists the necessary fields and their table locations.

To assemble this data, you will write a query called Pets and Owners that includes all the fields from both tables, even though you aren't going to use all the fields. These extra fields in the query give you the flexibility to add a field later to the form without changing the query. You may need another field in the form, for example, to derive a calculated control.

Table 15-1
Fields Needed for the Pets Data-Entry Form

Fields from Pets Table	Fields from Customer Table
Pet ID	Customer Name
Customer ID	Street/Apt
Pet Name	City
Type of Animal	State
Breed	Zip Code
Date of Birth	Phone Number
Colors	Type of Customer

Fields from Pets Table	Fields from Customer Table
Length	
Weight	
Last Visit Date	
Current Vaccinations	
Deceased	
Neutered/Spayed	
Gender	
Comments	
Picture	

In this example, you will sort the data by the Pet ID. It's always a good idea to arrange your data into some known order. When you display a form, the data is listed in its physical order unless it is sorted.

To create the Pets and Owners query, follow these steps:

1. Click the Queries button on the Object bar and then click the New button to start a new query.

2. Select Design View from the New Query dialog box and click OK. The Show Table dialog box appears.

3. Add the Customer table.

4. Add the Pets table.

5. Close the Show Table dialog box.

6. Drag the asterisk (*) from the Customer field list to the first column in the QBE (Query by Example) design pane.

7. Drag the asterisk (*) from the Pets field list to the second column in the QBE design pane.

8. Drag the Pet ID field from the Pets field list to the third column in the QBE pane.

9. Click the Pet ID Show: box to turn it off.

10. Change the Sort to Ascending in the Pet ID field, as shown in Figure 15-2.

11. Click Save and name the query Pets and Owners. Run the query to see that all the fields from both tables display. Close the query.

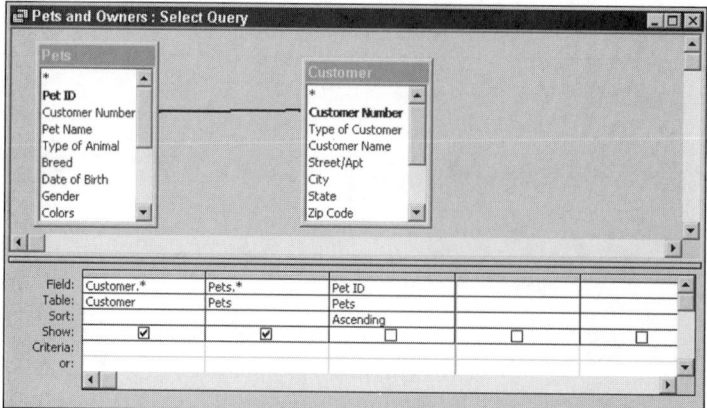

Figure 15-2: The Pets and Owners query

Note The asterisk (*) is used to select all fields from each table.

Creating a new blank form and binding it to a query

Now that you've created the Pets and Owners query, you need to create a new blank form and bind it to the query. Later you will add the controls. Follow these steps to continue this process:

1. Close the query to display the Database window if it is not already displayed.

2. Click the Forms button on the Object bar then click the New button to start a new form.

3. Select Design View in the New Form dialog box, then choose the Pets and Owners query from the combo box at the bottom of the dialog box.

4. Click the OK button to create the new form.

5. Maximize the Form window.

Note If the Toolbox and Property windows are not open along with the Field List window, as they are in Figure 15-3, you can open them by selecting them from the View menu or the toolbar.

You now see a blank Form Design View window, as shown in Figure 15-3. The form is bound to the query Pets and Owners as shown in the Property window on the screen. This means that the fields from the query are available for use in the form design, and they appear in the Field List window. Data from the query will be displayed when the form is viewed or printed.

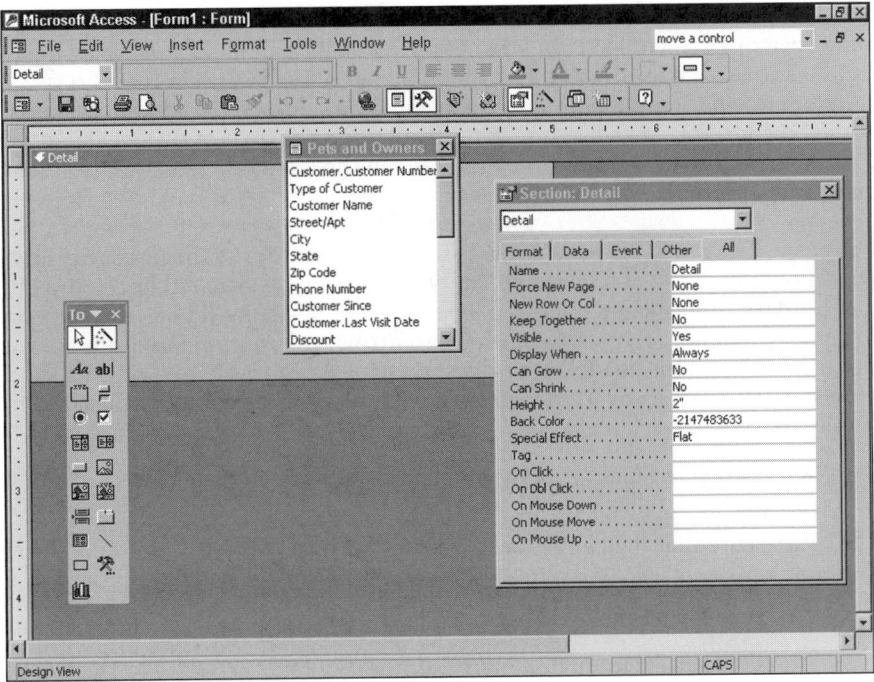

Figure 15-3: The blank Form Design View window

If you need to create a form that contains no bound controls, you would create a blank form that is not bound to a query. This is done by not selecting a table/query when you select Design View in the New Form dialog box.

Defining the form display size

Next you must resize the form's workspace. In Figure 15-3, the light gray background is the *workspace*. If you place controls in the dark gray area surrounding it, the workspace expands automatically until it is large enough to hold the controls you placed there. The workspace size you need depends on the design of your form. If you want the form to fill the screen, make it the size of your screen; however, that depends on your screen resolution. More data can fit onscreen if you are using a Super VGA screen size of 800 x 600 or 1024 x 768 than will fit if you are using the standard VGA size of 640 x 480. Because many users may use a form you create, you should stay with the smallest size of any anticipated user.

A maximized standard VGA screen set to 800 x 600 in Microsoft Windows 98 or above can display a full-screen size of approximately 7½ inches by 5¼ inches. This includes the space for the title bar, menu bar, and toolbar at the top; the vertical scrollbar down the right side; and the navigation buttons/scrollbar and status line at the bottom. You can set form properties to control most of these elements. If you want to have the record pointer column down the left side, decrease the 7½-inch margin by approximately ⅛-inch.

The easiest way to set the form size is to grab the border of the light gray area with your mouse and drag it to the size that you want. If you grab either the top or bottom borders, your mouse pointer becomes a double-arrow. If you grab the corner, the mouse pointer becomes a four-headed arrow and you can size both sides at the same time. (The four-headed arrow is shown in Figure 15-4.) Next, you will set the form size to 6¼ inches by 3¾ inches, using Figure 15-4 as a guide. At this size, form scrollbars should not appear.

Follow these steps to change the form size:

1. Make sure that the ruler is displayed; if needed, select it from the View menu.

2. Place the mouse pointer at the bottom-right corner of the light gray workspace.

3. When the mouse pointer changes to a four-headed arrow, drag the workspace until the size is exactly 6¼ inches by 3¾ inches.

4. Release the mouse button to accept the new size.

If controls are added beyond the right border, you have to scroll the form to see these controls. This is generally not acceptable in a form. If controls are added beyond the bottom border, you have to scroll the form to see these controls as well; this is acceptable because the form becomes a multiple-page form. Later in this chapter, you learn to control multiple-page forms.

Note If you change to Form View and see a horizontal scroll bar along the bottom, either resize the right margin or turn the Record Selector property off for the form. This topic is covered later.

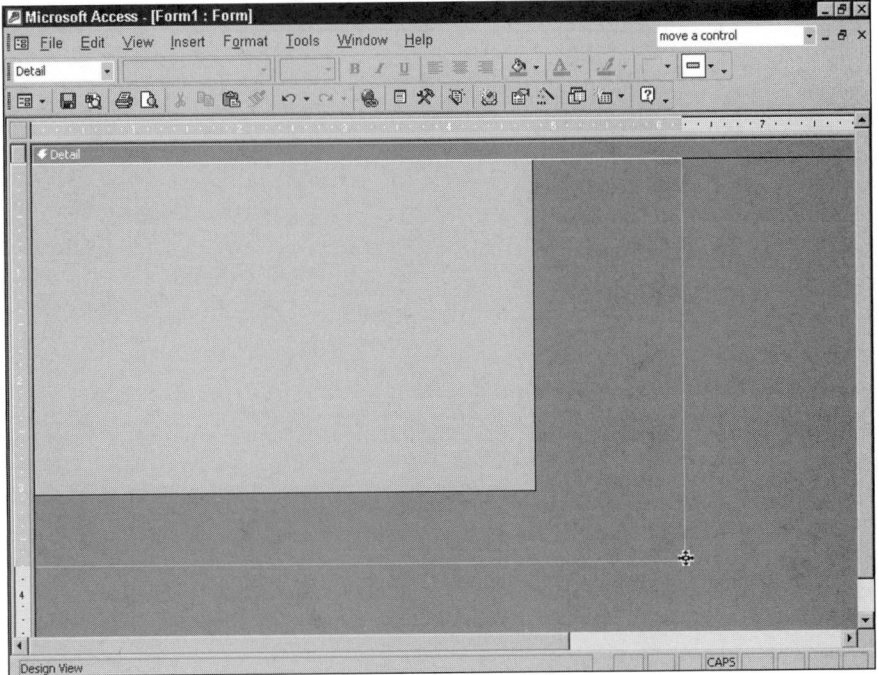

Figure 15-4: Resizing the workspace using the four-headed arrow

Understanding Properties

Properties are named attributes of controls, fields, or database objects that are used to modify the characteristics of a control, field, or object. Examples of these attributes are the size, color, appearance, or name of an object. A property can also modify the behavior of a control, determining, for example, whether the control is read only or editable and visible or not visible.

Properties are used extensively in forms and reports to change the characteristics of controls. Each control on the form has properties. The form itself also has properties, as does each of its sections. The same is true for reports; the report itself has properties, as does each report section and individual control. The label control also has its own properties, even if it is attached to another control.

Properties are displayed in a Property sheet (also called a Property window because it is an actual window). Figure 15-5 shows the Property sheet for the Date of Birth text box. The first column lists the property names; the second column is where you enter or select property settings or options.

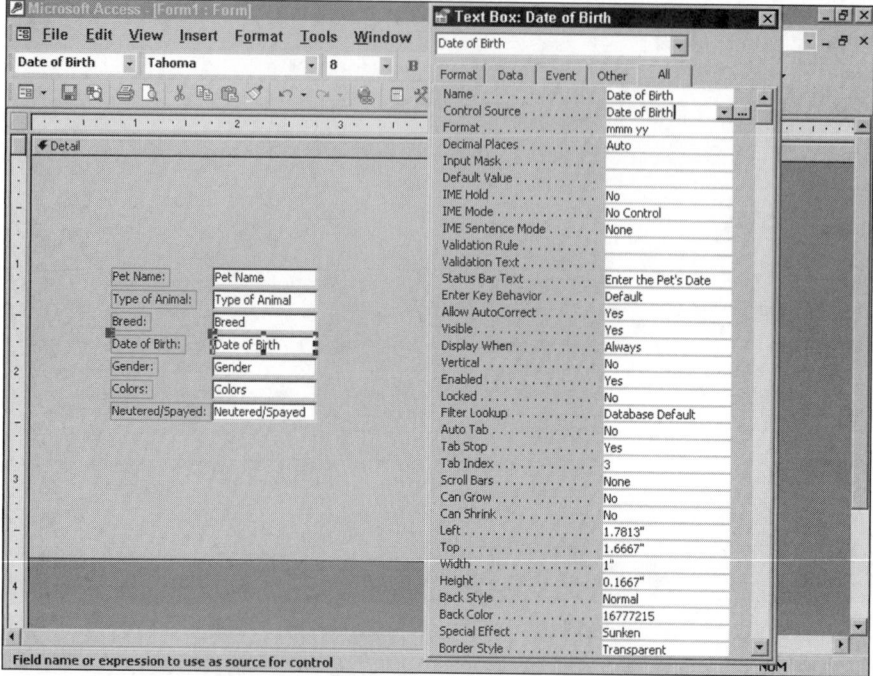

Figure 15-5: The Property sheet for the Date of Birth text box

Working with control properties

You use control properties to change the way controls look and behave. There are several ways to display a control's Property sheet:

- ✦ Select a control and click View ➪ Properties from the menu bar.
- ✦ Select a control and click the Properties button on the toolbar.
- ✦ Double-click any control.
- ✦ Right-click any control and select Properties from the menu.

To display the Property sheet for the Date of Birth text box control, follow the steps below. First close the current form and don't save it. You will be creating a new blank form.

1. Drag the fields Pet Name through Neutered/Spayed from the Field List window to the Form Design window.

2. Click the Date of Birth text box control to select it.

3. Click the Properties button on the toolbar.

A partial property sheet is displayed. In Figure 15-5, the Property sheet has been sized to be larger. By widening the property sheet, you can see more of its values; by increasing the length, you can see more controls at one time. The vertical scrollbar lets you move between various properties. Only the text box control has more properties than can fit onscreen at one time. Because the Property sheet is a true window, it can be moved anywhere onscreen and resized. It does not, however, have Maximize or Minimize buttons.

The Property window has an All tab that lets you see all the properties for a control. Or you can choose another tab to limit the view to a specific group of properties. The specific tabs and groups of properties are:

✦ **Format.** These properties determine how a label or value looks: font, size, color, special effects, borders, and scrollbars.

✦ **Data.** These properties affect how a value is displayed and the data source it is bound to: control source, input masks, validation, default value, and other data type properties.

✦ **Event.** Event properties are named events, such as clicking a mouse button, adding a record, pressing a key for which you can define a response (in the form of a call to a macro or a VBA procedure), and so on.

✦ **Other.** Other properties show additional characteristics of the control, such as the name of the control or the description that displays in the status bar.

Cross-Reference

The number of properties available in Access has increased greatly since early versions of Access. The most important new properties are described in various chapters of this book. For a discussion of new Event properties and Event procedures, see Chapters 30–33.

The properties displayed in Figure 15-5 are the specific properties for Date of Birth text box. The first two properties, Name and Control Source, show the field name Date of Birth.

The Name is simply the name of the control itself. When a control is bound to a field, Access automatically assigns it the bound field name. Unbound controls are given names such as Field11 or Button13. However, you can give the control any name you want.

With bound controls the Control Source's setting is the name of the table field to which the control is bound. In this example, Date of Birth refers to the field with the same name in the Pets table. An unbound control has no control source, whereas the control source of a calculated control is the actual expression for the calculation, as in the example =[Weight] * .65.

The following properties always inherit their settings from the field's table definition. Figure 15-5 shows some of these properties and the settings that have been inherited from the Pets table:

✦ Format

✦ Decimal Places

✦ Status Bar Text (from the field Description)

✦ Input Mask

✦ Default Value

✦ Validation Rule

✦ Validation Text

Note   Changes made to a control's properties don't affect the field properties in the source table.

Each type of control has a different set of properties, as do objects such as forms, reports, and sections within forms or reports. In the next few chapters, you learn about many of these properties as you use each of the control types to create more complex forms and reports.

Changing a control's property setting

There are many different methods for changing property settings, including

✦ Entering or selecting the desired value in a Property sheet

✦ Changing a property directly by changing the control itself such as changing its size

✦ Using inherited properties from the bound field or the control's default properties

✦ Entering color selections for the control by using the toolbar options

✦ Changing label text style, size, color, and alignment by using the toolbar buttons

You can change a control's properties by clicking a property and typing the desired value.

In Figure 15-5 you can see a down-arrow and a button with three dots to the right of the Control Source property-entry area. Some properties display the arrow in the property-entry area when you click in the area. This tells you that Access has a list of values from which you can choose. If you click the down-arrow in the Control Source property, you find that the choices are a list of all fields in the data source.

Some properties have a list of standard values such as Yes or No; others display varying lists of fields, forms, reports, or macros. The properties of each object are determined by the object itself and what the object is used for.

A feature in Access 2002 is the capability of cycling through property choices by repeatedly double-clicking on the choice. For example, double-clicking on the Display When property alternately selects Always, Print Only, and Screen Only.

Three dots on a button constitute the Builder button, which opens one of the many Builders in Access. This includes the Macro Builder, the Expression Builder, and the Module Builder. When you open a builder and make some selections, the property will be filled in for you. You will learn about them later in this book.

Default control properties

The property values shown in a specific control's property window are for that specific control. You can click on a control to see its properties. You can also create a set of default properties for a specific type of control for all forms in the database by clicking the toolbar button for that control type. For example, to view or change the default properties for a text box in the current form, follow these steps:

1. Make sure that the property sheet is displayed.
2. Click the Text Box button on the Toolbox.

Figure 15-6 shows some of the default properties for a text box. You can set these properties; from then on, each new text box that you create will have these properties as a starting point. This set of default properties can determine the color and size for new controls, the font used, the distance between the attached label and the control, and most other characteristics.

Customized forms can be created much more quickly by changing the default property settings than by changing every control.

Access provides many tools for customizing your data-entry and display forms and your reports. In addition, you can apply the default properties to existing controls and save a set of default controls as a template. You can then use the template as the basis for a new form. Learning these techniques can save you even more time when you create new forms and reports.

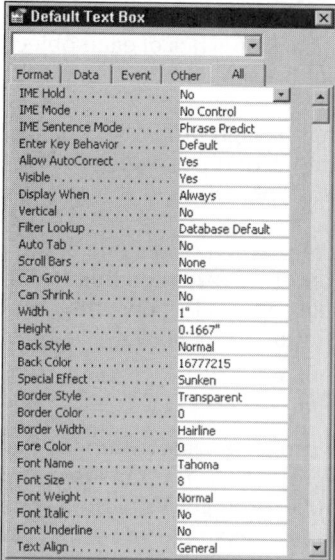

Figure 15-6: Displaying default properties

Working with form properties

You use form properties to change the way the entire form is displayed. This includes properties such as the forms background color or picture, the form's width, etc. Table 15-2 (in "Eliminating the Record Selector Bar" later in this chapter) discusses some of the most important properties. Changing default properties is relatively easy: you select the property in the Property sheet and set a new value. Following are some of the more important form properties.

Changing the title bar text with the Caption property

Normally the title bar displays the name of the form after it is saved. By changing the Caption property, you can display a different title on the title bar when the form is run. To change the title bar text, follow these steps. First close the current form and don't save it. You will be creating a new blank form.

1. Erase the fields you added to the form so the form is blank again. Remember, this form uses the Pets and Owners query. (Resize the form if necessary.)

2. Display the Property window if it is not already displayed and click the Format tab to show the Format properties.

3. Click the Caption property in the Format sheet of the Property window.

4. Type **Pets Data Entry Form**.

5. Click any other property or press Enter.

You can display the blank form by clicking the Form View button on the toolbar to check the result. The caption you enter here overrides the name of the saved form.

Specifying how to view the form

In previous versions of Access, two properties determined how your form displays records: *Default View* and *Views Allowed*. Because of the addition of two new properties, Access 2002 handles each property individually, instead of grouping them within the Views Allowed property. While the Default Views property still exists, Access 2002 now lists four additional properties in Yes/No format.

Formerly, the Views Allowed property had three settings: Form, Datasheet, and Both. To replace these properties, there are now four separate properties: Allow Form View, Allow Datasheet View, Allow Pivot Table View, and Allow Pivot Chart View. The default settings are Yes to all of these properties, which lets you switch between Form and Datasheet view, as well as Pivot table and Pivot Chart view. If you set the Allow Datasheet property to No, the Form button and the View ➪ Form menu selections cannot be selected; the data can be viewed only as a datasheet. If you set the Allow Form View property to No, the Datasheet button and the View ➪ Datasheet menu selections cannot be selected; the data can be viewed only as a form.

A PivotTable form can display a field's values horizontally or vertically, and then calculate the total of the row or column. Similar to this is the Pivot Chart, which displays a graphical analysis of data stored in a table, query, or form.

The Default View property is different; it determines how the data is displayed when the form is first run. Five settings are possible: Single Form, Continuous Forms (showing more than one record at a time), Datasheet (which is a simple row and column view like a spreadsheet or the standard query datasheet view), Pivot Table, and Pivot Chart. Single Form is the default and displays one record per form page, regardless of the form's size. Continuous Forms tells Access to display as many detail records as will fit on-screen. Normally you would use this setting to define the height of a very small form and to display many records at one time. Figure 15-7 shows such a form. The records have a small enough height that you can see a number of them at once. The Datasheet setting displays the form as a standard datasheet when run. Change this property setting to Single Form.

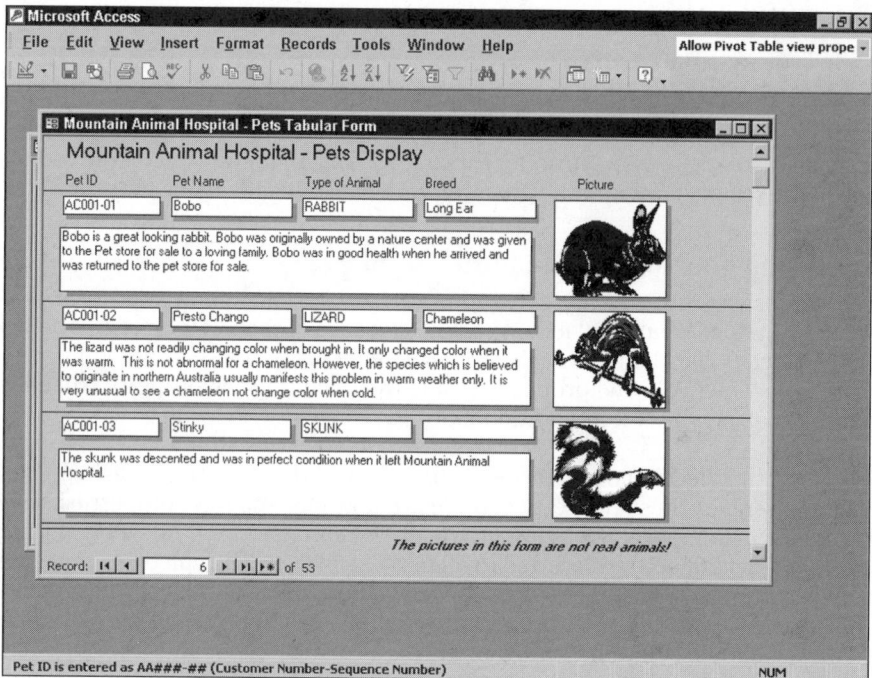

Figure 15-7: The Continuous Forms setting of the Default View property

Eliminating the record selector bar

The Record Selectors property determines whether the Record Selector Bar (the vertical bar on the left side of the form) is visible. The Record Selector Bar is very important in multiple-record forms or datasheets because a right-pointing triangle indicates the current record and a Pencil indicates that the record is being edited. Though the Record Selector Bar is important for datasheets, you probably won't want it for a single record form. To eliminate it, simply change the form's Record Selector property from Yes to No. Go ahead and set the Record Selector property to No for your form.

The table below lists the most commonly used properties and offers brief descriptions of each. As many of these are used in examples throughout the chapters you will learn more about them.

Table 15-2
Form Properties

Property	Description and Options	Option Definition
Format properties		
Caption	Displayed on the title bar of the displayed form	
Default View	Determines the type of view when the form is run	
	Single Form	One record per page
	Continuous Forms	As many records per page as will fit (Default)
	Datasheet	Standard row and column datasheet view
	PivotTable	Displays a field's values horizontally or vertically, then calculates the total of the row or column
	PivotChart	Graphical analysis of data
Allow Form View	Form view allowed (Yes/No)	
Allow Datasheet View	Datasheet view allowed (Yes/No)	
Allow Pivot Table View	Pivot Table view allowed (Yes/No)	
Allow Pivot Chart View	Pivot Chart allowed (Yes/No)	
Scroll Bars	Determines whether any scroll bars are displayed	
	Neither	No scrollbars are displayed
	Horizontal Only	Displays only horizontal scrollbar
	Vertical Only	Displays only vertical scrollbar
	Both	Displays both horizontal and vertical scrollbars
Record Selectors (Yes/No)	Determines whether vertical record selector bar is displayed	

Continued

Table 15-2 *(continued)*

Property	Description and Options	Option Definition
Navigation Buttons	Determines whether navigation buttons are visible (Yes/No)	
Dividing Lines	Determines whether lines between form sections are visible (Yes/No)	
Auto Resize	Form is opened to display a complete record (Yes/No)	
Auto Center	Centers form on-screen when it's opened (Yes/No)	
Border Style	Determines form's border style	
	None	No border or border elements (scrollbars, navigation buttons)
	Thin	Thin border, not resizable
	Sizable	Normal form settings
	Dialog	Thick border, title bar only, cannot be sized; use for dialog boxes
Control Box	Determines whether control menu (Restore, Move Size) is available (Yes/No)	
Min Max Buttons		
	None	No buttons displayed in upper-right corner of form
	Min Enabled	Minimize button only is displayed
	Max Enabled	Maximize button only is displayed
	Both Enabled	Minimize and Maximize buttons are displayed
Close Button	Determines whether to display Close button in upper-right corner and a close menu item on the control menu (Yes/No)	
What's This Button	Determines whether Screen Tips appear when user presses Shift+F1 for Help	

Property	Description and Options	Option Definition
Width	Displays the value of the width of the form; can be entered or Access fills it in as you adjust the width of the work area	
Picture	Enter the name of a bitmap file for the background of the entire form	
Picture Type	Determines whether picture is embedded or linked	
	Embedded	Picture is embedded in the form and becomes a part of the database file
	Linked	Picture is linked to the form. Access stores the location of the picture and retrieves it every time the form is opened.
Picture Size Mode	Determines how picture is displayed	
	Clip	Displays the picture at its actual size
	Stretch	Fits picture to form size (nonproportional)
	Zoom	Fits picture to form size (proportional); this may result in the picture not fitting in one dimension (height or width)
Picture Alignment	Determines picture alignment	
	Top Left	The picture is displayed in the top-left corner of the form, report window, or image control
	Top Right	The picture is displayed in the top-right corner of the form, report window, or image control
	Center	(Default) The picture is centered in the form, report window, or image control

Continued

Table 15-2 *(continued)*

Property	Description and Options	Option Definition
Picture Alignment *(continued)*	Bottom Left	The picture is displayed in the bottom-left corner of the form, report window, or image control
	Bottom Right	The picture is displayed in the bottom-right corner of the form, report window, or image control
	Form Center	The form's picture is centered horizontally in relation to the width of the form and vertically in relation to the topmost and bottommost controls on the form
Picture Tiling	Used when you want to overlay multiple copies of a small bitmap; for example, a single brick can become a wall (Yes/No)	
Grid X	Displays setting for number of points per inch when X grid is displayed	
Grid Y	Displays setting for number of points per inch when Y grid is displayed	
Layout for Print	Determines whether form uses screen fonts or printer fonts	
	Yes	Printer Fonts
	No	Screen Fonts
Subdatasheet Height	Determines the height of a subdatasheet when expanded	
Subdatasheet Expanded	Determines the saved state of all subdatasheets in a table or query	Yes – The saved state of subdatasheets is expanded No – The saved state of subdatasheets is closed

Property	Description and Options	Option Definition
Orientation	Determines the View Orientation	
	Right to Left	Appearance and functionality move from right to left
	Left to Right	Appearance and functionality move from left to right
Moveable	Determines whether the form can be moved (Yes/No)	
Data properties		
Record Source	Determines where the data to be displayed in the form is coming from, or where the data is going when you create a new record. Can be a table or a query.	
Filter	Used to specify a subset of records to be displayed when a filter is applied to a form. Can be set in the form properties, a macro, or in Visual Basic.	
Order By	Allows you to specify a field to sort the data in the display	
Allow Filters	Determines whether a user will be able to display a filtered form (Yes/No)	
Allow Edits	Prevents or allows editing of data, making the form read-only for saved records	
	Yes/No	You can/cannot edit saved records
Allow Deletions	Used to prevent records from being deleted	
	Yes/No	You can/cannot delete saved records
Allow Additions	Used to determine whether new records can be added	
	Yes/No	You can/cannot add new records

Continued

	Table 15-2 *(continued)*	
Property	**Description and Options**	**Option Definition**
Data Entry	Used to determine whether form displays saved records	
	Yes/No	Only new records are displayed/All records are displayed
Recordset Type	Used to determine whether multi-table forms can be updated; replaces Access 2.0's Allow Updating property	
	Dynaset	Only default table field controls can be edited
	Dynaset	All tables and fields are editable (Inconsistent Update)
	Snapshot	No fields are editable (Read Only in effect)
Record Locks	Used to determine multiuser record locking	
	No Locks	Record is locked only as it is saved
	All Records	Locks entire form records while using the form
	Edited Record	Locks only current record being edited
Other properties		
Pop Up	Form is a pop-up that floats above all other objects (Yes/No)	
Modal	For use when you must close the form before doing anything else. Disables other windows; when Pop Up set to Yes, Modal disables menus and toolbar, creating a dialog box (Yes/No).	

Property	Description and Options	Option Definition
Cycle	Determines how Tab works in the last field of a record	
	All Records	Tabbing from the last field of a record moves to the next record
	Current Record	Tabbing from the last field of a record moves to the first field of that record
	Current Page	Tabbing from the last field of a record moves to the first field of the current page
Menu Bar	Used to specify an alternate menu bar	
Toolbar	Use this property to specify the toolbar to use for the form. You can create a toolbar for your form by selecting the Customize option under the Toolbar command in the View menu.	
Shortcut Menu	Determines whether shortcut menus are active	
Shortcut Menu Bar	Used to specify an alternate shortcut menu bar	
Fast Laser Printing	Prints rules instead of lines and rectangles (Yes/No)	
Help File	Name of compiled Help file to assign custom help to the form	
Help Context Id	ID of context-sensitive entry point in the help file to display	
Tag	Use this property to store extra information about your form	
Has Module	Use this property to show if your form has a class module. Setting this property to No can improve the performance and decrease the size of your database.	
Allow Design Changes	Determines when design edits can be made	
	Design View	Allows design edits in design view of the form only
	All Views	Allows design edits in all views.

Placing Bound Fields on the Form

The next step is to place the necessary fields on the form. When you place a field on a form, it is called a *control* and it is bound to another field (its *control source*). Therefore, the terms *control* and *field* are used interchangeably in this chapter.

As you've learned, the process of placing controls on your form consists of three basic tasks:

✦ Display the Field List window by clicking the Field List button on the toolbar.

✦ Click the desired Toolbox control to determine the type of control that is created.

✦ Select each of the fields that you want on your form and drag them to the Form Design window.

Displaying the field list

To display the Field List window, click the Field List button on the toolbar (the icon that looks like a list sheet). The Field List window can be resized and moved around. The enlarged window (shown in Figure 15-6) displays all the fields in the Pets and Owners query dynaset.

Notice, in Figure 15-8, that the fields Customer.Customer Number and Pets.Customer Number, as well as Customer.Last Visit Date and Pets.Last Visit Date have the table name as a prefix. This prefix distinguishes fields of the same name that come from different tables within a query.

You can move the Field List window by clicking its title bar and dragging it to a new location.

Selecting the fields for your form

The method for selecting a field in the Field List window is the same as selecting a field from a query field list. The easiest way to select a field is to click it, which highlights it; then you can drag it to the Form window.

To highlight *contiguous* (adjacent) fields in the list, click the first field you want in the field list and move the mouse pointer to the last field you want; hold down the Shift key as you click the last field. The block of fields between the first and last fields is displayed in reverse video as you select it. Drag the block to the Form window.

Tip   You can highlight noncontiguous fields in the list by clicking each field while holding down the Ctrl key. Each field is then displayed in reverse video and can be dragged (as part of the group) to the Form Design window. One way this method differs from using the query Field List is that you cannot double-click a field to add it to the Form window.

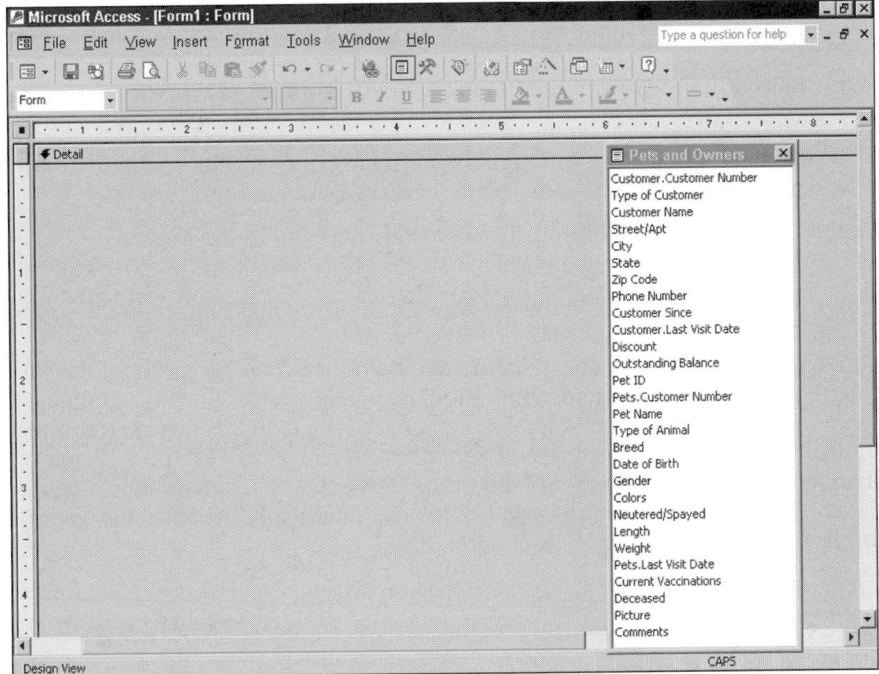

Figure 15-8: The Field List window resized so you can see all the fields

You will begin by selecting the Pets table fields for the Detail section. To select the fields you need for the Pets Data Entry form, follow these steps:

1. Click on the Pet ID field.

2. Scroll down the field list until the Deceased field is visible.

3. Hold down the Shift key and click on the Deceased field.

The block of fields from Pet ID to Deceased should be highlighted in the Field List window.

Dragging fields onto your form

After you select the proper fields from the Pets table, drag the fields onto the form. Depending on whether you choose one or several fields, the mouse pointer changes to reflect your selection. If you select one field, you see a Field icon (a box containing text). If you select multiple fields, you see a Multiple Field icon instead. These are the same mouse pointer icons you saw on the Query Design screens.

To drag the Pets table fields onto the Form Design window, follow these steps:

1. Click within the highlighted block of fields in the Field List window.

2. Without releasing the mouse button, drag the mouse pointer onto the form, placing it under the 1½-inch mark on the horizontal ruler at the top of the screen and the ½-inch mark of the vertical ruler along the left edge.

3. Release the mouse button. The fields now appear in the form, as shown in Figure 15-9.

4. Close the Field List window by clicking the Field List button on the toolbar.

Notice that there are two controls for each field that you dragged onto the form. When you use the drag-and-drop method for placing fields, Access automatically creates a label control that displays the name of the field; it's attached to the text control that the field is bound to. If you followed along with Chapter 12, you changed the Customer Number field in the Pets table to a lookup field. Figure 15-9 shows this field displayed as a combo box (automatically because it is one of the properties that was changed in Chapter 10).

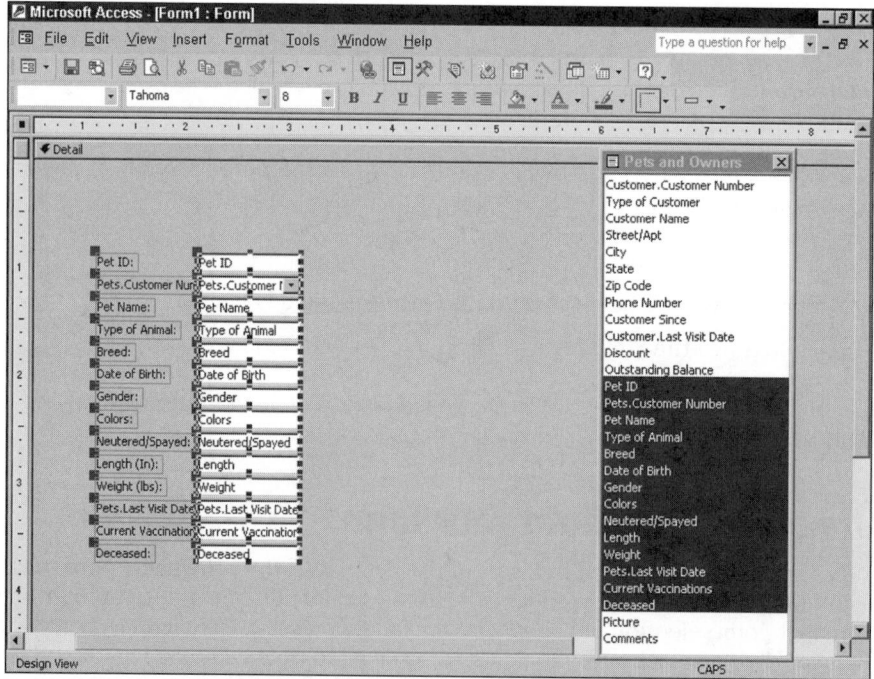

Figure 15-9: Bound fields from the Pet's table after they have been dragged to the form

Working with Label Controls and Text Box Controls

Attached label controls are automatically added to a form when you drag a field from the Field List. Sometimes, however, you want to add text label controls by themselves to create headings or titles for the form.

Creating unattached labels

To create a new, unattached label control, you must use the Toolbox unless you copy an existing label. The next task in the example is to add the text header *Mountain Animal Hospital Pets Data Entry* to your form. This task is divided into segments to demonstrate adding and editing text. To create an unattached label control, follow these steps:

1. Display the Toolbox.
2. Click the Label button on the Toolbox.
3. Click just to the right of and above the label that says Pet ID and drag the pointer to make a small rectangle about 3 inches long and ¼-inch high.
4. Type Pets Data.
5. Press Enter.

To create a multiple-line label, press Ctrl+Enter to force a line break in the text.

Modifying the text in a label or text control

To modify the text in a control, click inside the label and the mouse pointer changes to the standard Windows insertion point, an I-beam. You can now edit the text. Also notice that the Formatting toolbar icons become grayed out and cannot be selected. This is because you cannot apply specific formatting to individual characters. You can only apply formatting to the control (all of the text).

If you drag across the entire selection so that it is highlighted, anything new you type replaces the selected text. Another way to modify the text is to edit it from the control's Property window. The second property in a label's Property window is Caption. In the Caption property, you can edit the contents of a label control by clicking the value box and typing new text. If you want to edit or enter a caption that is longer than the space in the Property window, the contents will scroll as you type. Or you can press Shift+F2 to open a zoom box with more space to type.

In the next exercise you will edit the text in the label control not in the Property window. To edit the label so that it contains the proper text, follow these steps:

1. Click in front of the *P* in *Pets Data* in the label control.

2. Type Mountain Animal Hospital - before *Pets Data*. (Don't forget to type the dash too).

3. Type Entry after *Pets Data*.

4. Press Enter.

The form title would look better if it were larger.

Modifying the format of text in a control

To modify the formatting of text within a control, select the control by clicking its border (not in it). Then select a formatting style to apply to the label. Just click the appropriate button on the toolbar. To add visual emphasis to the title, follow these steps:

1. Click on the newly created form heading label.

2. Click on the Bold button on the Formatting toolbar.

3. Click on the drop-down arrow of the Font-Size list box.

4. Select 14 from the Font-Size drop-down list.

The label control now needs to be resized to display all the text.

The Formatting Toolbar

Access 2002 features a second toolbar known as the Formatting toolbar (which is described more fully in Chapter 16). Toolbars are really windows. You can move any toolbar by dragging it from its normal location to the middle of a form, and you can change its size and shape. Most toolbars can be docked to any edge of the screen (such as the left, right, or bottom).

The Formatting toolbar contains objects found in most Office toolbars The first area of the Formatting toolbar (on the left side) selects a control or Form section, such as the Form or Page headers or footers, Detail, or the form itself. When you have multiple pages of controls and you want (for example) to select a control that's on page 3 or behind another control, this combo box makes it easy. The next few objects on the Formatting toolbar change text properties. Two more combo boxes let you change the font style and size. (Remember, you may have fonts others do not have. Do not use an exotic font if the user of your form does not have the font.) After the Font Style and Size combo boxes are icons for making a text control Bold, Italic, and Underlined. Beyond those are alignment icons for Left, Center, and Right text alignment. The last five pull-down icons change color properties, line types and styles, and special effects. See Chapter 16 for more complete descriptions.

Sizing a text box control or label control

When you select a control, from three to seven sizing handles appear depending on the size. One appears on each corner except the upper left, and one appears on each side. When the pointer moves over one of the sizing handles, the mouse pointer changes into a double-headed arrow. When this happens, click and drag the control to the size you want. As you drag, a dotted outline appears, indicating how large the label will be when the mouse button is released.

When you double-click on any of the sizing handles, Access usually resizes a control to a *best fit* for the text in the control. This is especially handy if you increase the font size and then notice that the text is cut off either at the bottom or to the right. For label controls, note that this *best-fit* sizing adjusts the size vertically and horizontally, though text controls are resized only vertically. This is because when Access is in form-design mode, it can't predict how much of a field to display — the field name and field contents can be radically different. Sometimes, however, label controls are not resized correctly and must be manually adjusted.

In the example, the text no longer fits within the label control, but you can resize the text control to fit the enhanced font size. To do this, follow these steps:

1. Click the *Mountain Animal Hospital - Pets Data Entry* label control.

2. Move the mouse pointer over the control. Notice that the mouse pointer changes shape as it moves over the sizing handles.

3. Double-click one of the sizing handles.

The label control size may still need readjustment. If so, place the mouse pointer in the bottom-right corner of the control so that the diagonal arrow appears and drag the control until it is the correct size. You also need to move some of the controls down to make room to center the label over the form. You can select all the controls and move them down using the techniques you learned in the previous chapter.

You can also select Format ➪ Size ➪ To Fit to change the size of the label control text automatically.

As you create your form, you should test it frequently by selecting the Form View button on the toolbar. Figure 15-10 shows the form in its current state of completion.

Now that you've dragged the Pets fields to the form design and added a form title, you can move the text box controls into the correct position. You then need to size each control to display the information properly within each field.

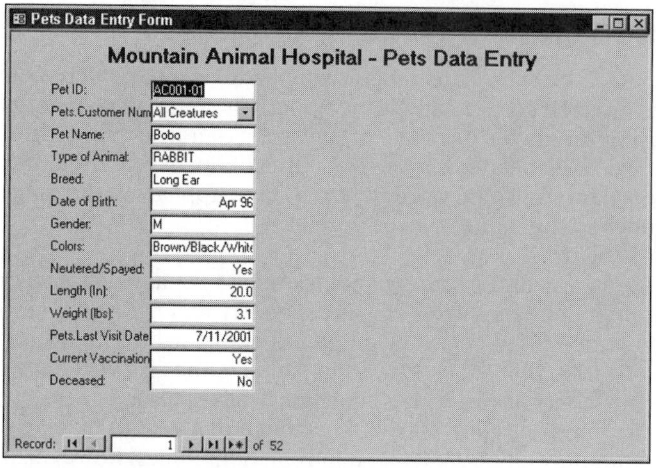

Figure 15-10: The form with bound and unbound controls

Moving label and text controls

Before you move the label and text controls, it is important that you are reminded of a few differences between attached and unattached controls. When an attached label is created automatically with a text control, it is called a *compound control* — that is, whenever one control in the set is moved, the other control in the set is also moved.

To move both controls in a compound control, select one of the pair by clicking anywhere on it. Move the mouse pointer over either of the objects. When the pointer turns into a hand, you can click the controls and drag them to their new location.

Now go ahead and place the controls in their proper position to complete the form layout, using Figure 15-11 as a guide. Remove the Pets. prefix from the Customer Number and Last Visit Date attached labels. The Gender control's label has been moved to a position above the text box control and some of the text labels are updated. Remember that you can do this by selecting the attached label control and then using the Move handle (big box in the upper-left corner) to move only the label. Also notice that some formatting was added, which you will do in the next section.

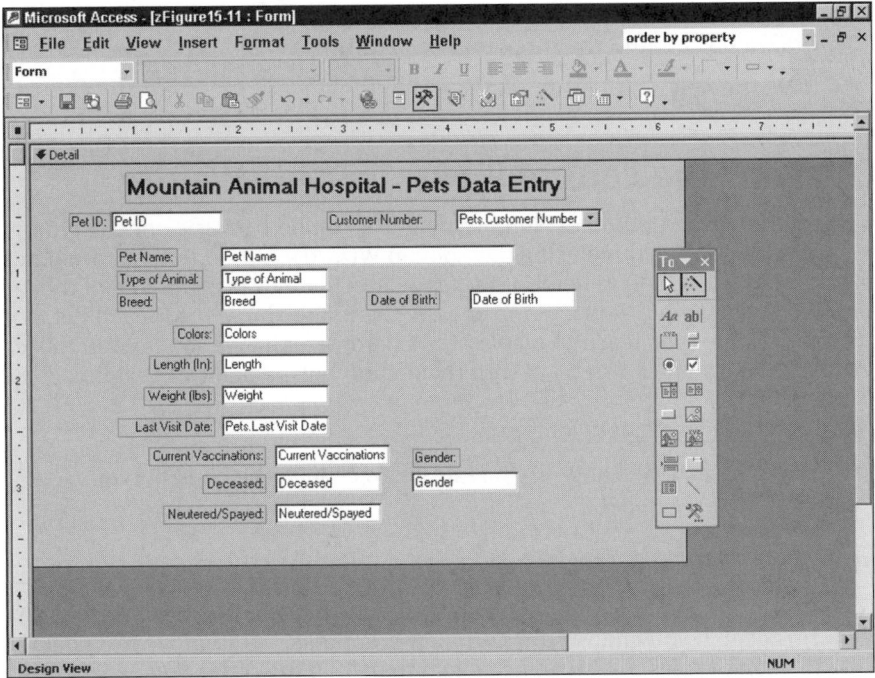

Figure 15-11: Repositioned text box and label controls in the Detail section

Modifying the appearance of multiple controls

Although the standard is to leave the attached labels with their default format, you can change them to make your form unique. The following steps guide you through the process of formatting the label controls to be bold.

1. Select all the attached label controls in the form by clicking on them individually while holding down the Shift key. There are 14 label controls to select, as shown in Figure 15-11.

2. Click the Bold button on the toolbar.

3. Select Format ⇨ Size ⇨ To Fit to resize all the labels.

You could have selected the label controls by using the drag-and-surround method. However do not drag the rectangle through the text boxes because that method also selects all the text boxes and you only wanted to bold and resize the labels.

If you change to Form View now, the Length, Width, and Last Visit Date data items are all right-aligned within the text controls. You want to left-align these controls so that values appear left-aligned next to the label. To make this change, follow these steps:

1. Select the Length, Weight, and Last Visit Date text box controls only (drag to draw a box around the three text box controls).

2. Click the AlignLeft button on the toolbar.

Changing the control type

In Figure 15-11, the Customer Number field is a combo box (the control type you defined earlier in the table using the Lookup Wizard). Although there are times you may want to use a lookup field to display related data, this is not one of those times. In this example, you need to see the Customer Number for each Pet, not the Customer Name (you learn to display the Customer information later in this chapter). For now, use these steps to turn the combo box back into a text box control:

1. Select the Customer Number field.

2. Select Format ⇨ Change To ⇨ Text Box to change the control type.

Setting the tab order

Now that you've completed moving all your controls into position, you should test the form again. If you change to Form View and press Tab to move from field to field, the cursor does not move from field to field in the order you expect. It starts out in the first field, *Pet ID*, and then continues vertically from field to field until it reaches the *Date of Birth* field. Then the insertion point jumps down to *Gender*, back up to *Colors*, and then down again to *Neutered/Spayed*. This route may seem strange, but that is the original order in which the fields were added to the form.

This is called the *tab order* of the form. The form's *default tab order* is always the order in which the fields were added to the form. If you don't plan to move the fields around, this is all right. If you do move the fields around, however, you may want to change the order. After all, although you may make heavy use of the mouse when designing your forms, the average data-entry person still uses the keyboard to move from field to field.

When you need to change the tab order of a form, you can do so in either one of two ways. In Design View you may select the View ⇨ Tab Order menu option or you may right-click any control and select Tab Order to change the order to match your layout. To change the tab order of the form, follow the next set of steps (make sure that you are in Design View before continuing):

1. Select View ⇨ Tab Order or right-click any control and select Tab Order.

2. Click the Gender row Selection bar in the Tab Order dialog box (gray bar to the left of the field names).

3. Click again and drag the row to the bottom of the dialog box to a point below the Deceased row, as shown in Figure 15-12.

4. Click the Neutered/Spayed Selection bar in the dialog box.

5. Click the Neutered/Spayed row again; drag the row to the bottom of the dialog box between the Deceased and Gender rows.

6. Click the OK button to complete the task.

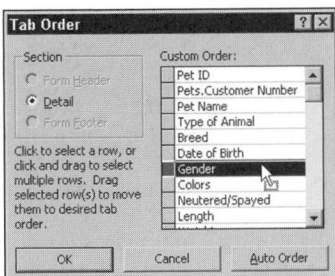

Figure 15-12: The Tab Order dialog box

The Tab Order dialog box lets you select either one row or multiple rows at a time. Multiple contiguous rows are selected by clicking the first Selection bar and dragging down to select multiple rows. After the rows are highlighted, the selected rows can be dragged to their new positions.

The Tab Order dialog box has several buttons at the bottom of the box. The Auto Order button places the fields in order from left to right and from top to bottom, according to their position in the form. This button is a good place to start when you have significantly rearranged the fields.

Each control has two properties that interact with this screen. The Tab Stop property determines whether pressing the Tab key lands you on the field. The default is Yes; changing the Tab Stop property to No removes the field from the tab order. When you set the tab order, you are setting the Tab Index property values. In this example, the first field (*Pet ID*) is set to 1, *Customer Number* is set to 2, and so on. Moving the fields around in the Tab Order dialog box changes the Tab Index properties of those (and other) fields.

Adding multiple-line text box controls for Memo fields

Multiple-line text box controls are used for Memo data types such as the Comments field in the Pets table. When adding a Memo field to a form, make sure that there is plenty of room in the text box control to enter a large amount of text. There are several ways to make certain that you've allowed enough space.

The first method is to resize the text box control until it's large enough to accommodate any text you may enter into the Memo field, but this is rarely possible.

Usually the reason you create a Memo field is to hold a large amount of text; that text can easily take up more space than the entire form.

The default property for a text box control is to display a vertical scrollbar when it is not large enough for all the text. By allowing scrollbars on the Memo field's text box control, you can accommodate for any amount of data. To create a Memo field text box control, follow these steps:

1. Display the Field List window.

2. Drag the Comments field to the bottom-left corner of the form below the Neutered/Spayed field.

3. Resize the Comments text box control so that the bottom of the control is about ½-inch high, and put the right side of the control just past the right side of the Gender text box control (as shown in Figure 15-13).

4. Close the Field List window.

The Comments text box by default displays a vertical scrollbar if the text in the box is larger than the display area. If you do not want to display a scrollbar, you can set the Scroll Bars property in the Property window to None.

Figure 15-13 shows the added Comments control.

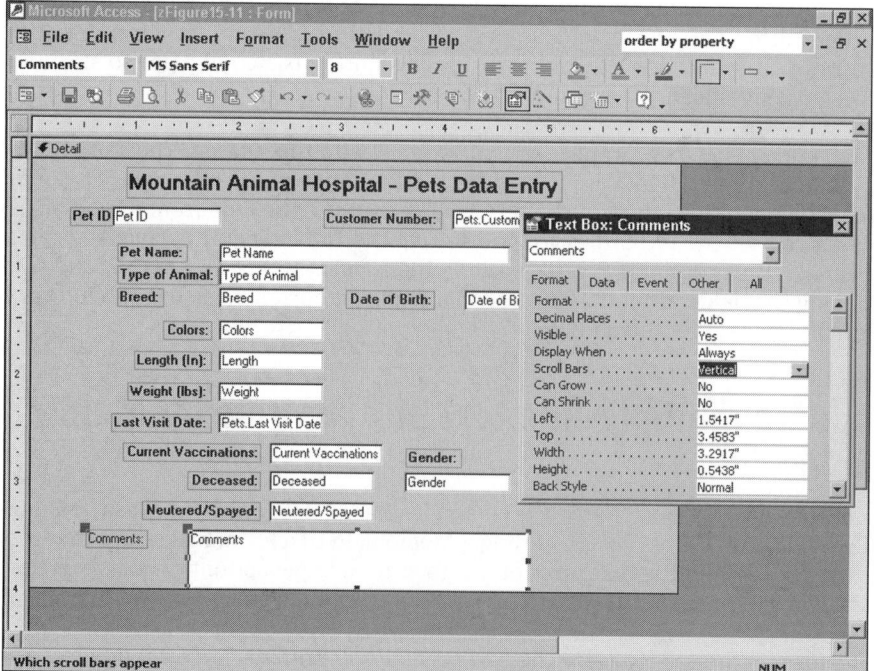

Figure 15-13: The form with a multiple-line text box control

When you display the form in Design View, the scrollbar appears when you move into the Comments field.

Adding a bound object frame to the form

When you drag a field that uses the OLE data type to a form, Access creates a bound object frame automatically. This control can be resized and moved the same as any control. To add the Picture OLE field to the form, follow these steps:

1. Display the Field List window.

2. Drag the Picture field to the center right area of the form.

3. Select the Picture attached label control by clicking the move box in the top-left corner of the text area.

4. Press Delete to delete the attached label control.

5. Move the left edge of the bound object frame just to the right of the Comments text box.

Note

One problem you may have when adding controls is that their default size exceeds the form's borders. When this happens, you must resize the control and also resize the border. If you don't resize the border, the form becomes scrollable outside the normal screen boundaries. This may work, but it doesn't create a well-displayed form.

To resize the bound object frame control and the form's border, follow these steps:

1. Select the Picture bound object frame.

2. Resize the control so that the right edge is just inside the original form border at 6⅛ inches on the top border. As you resize the control, you can follow the illustration in Figure 15-14.

3. Resize the form borders to make sure that they are at 6¼ inches and 3¾ inches.

When you're done, the design should look like Figure 15-14. Before you complete the OLE field, there is one more task to perform. The default value for the Size Mode property of a bound object frame is Clip. This means that a picture displayed within the frame is shown in its original size and truncated to fit within the frame. In this example, you need to display the picture so that it fits completely within the frame. Two property settings let you do this:

✦ **Zoom.** Keeps picture in its original proportion but may result in extra white space

✦ **Stretch.** Sizes picture to fit exactly between the frame borders

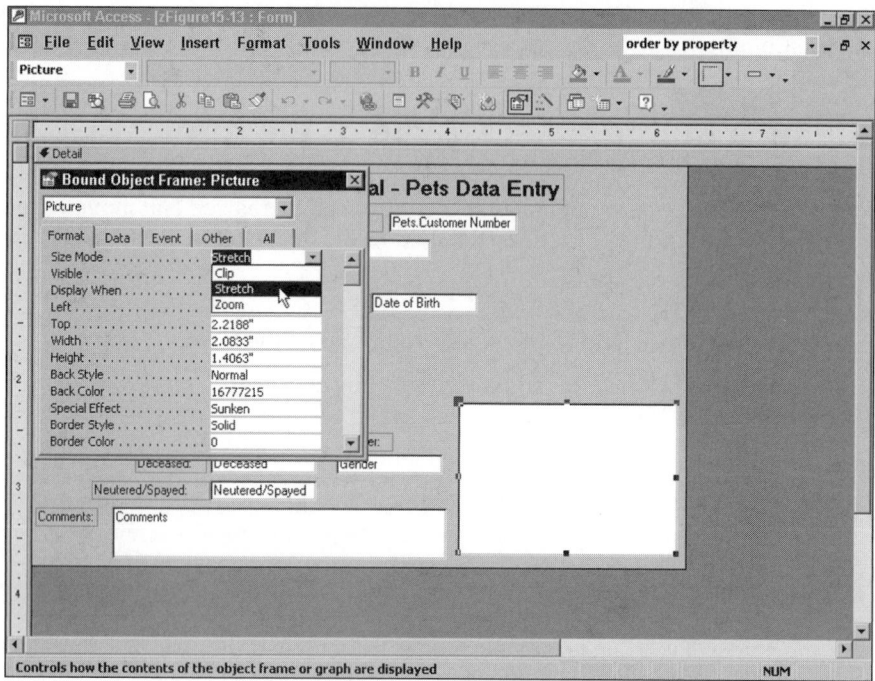

Figure 15-14: Adding an OLE field in a bound object frame control

Although the Zoom setting displays the picture more correctly, the Stretch setting looks better, unless the picture's proportions are important to viewing the data. To set the Size Mode property of a bound object frame, follow these steps:

1. Select the Picture bound object frame.
2. Display the Property window.
3. Select the Size Mode property.
4. Select Stretch.

Figure 15-14 shows the form in Design View in its current stage of completion. Notice the Property window for the bound object frame control. The Size Mode property is being set to Stretch.

When you complete this part of the design, you should save the form and then display it. You can now name this form Pets Data Entry if you want. Figure 15-15 shows the form.

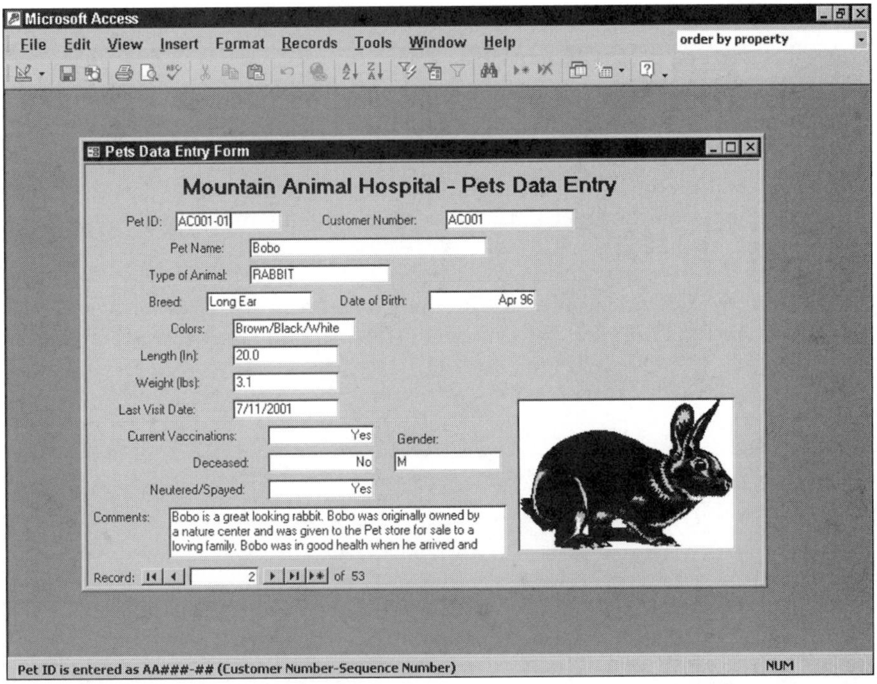

Figure 15-15: The form with a Memo and OLE field

So far, you've created a blank form and added several types of controls to the form, but only fields from the Pets table are on the form. Originally, you created a query that linked the Pets and Customer tables. The Customer table can serve as a lookup table for each Pet record, which allows you to display customer information for each pet.

Using Fields from Multiple Tables in a Form

When you create a form from a single table, you use fields from the one table. When you create a form from multiple tables, fields from the second table are used as lookup fields to display additional information. In this section, you learn how to display the customer information.

Adding fields from a second table

You will now add the fields from the Customer table to the Pets form to display the customer name and address along with the Type of Customer field. These fields will be placed in the upper-right portion of the form. Follow these steps to add the customer fields to the form:

1. Display the Field List window.

2. Click the Type of Customer field.

3. Hold down the Shift key and click the Phone Number field.

4. Click within the highlighted block of fields in the Field List window.

5. Without releasing the mouse button, drag the fields to the form under the 5-inch mark on the ruler at the top of the screen and the ½-inch mark of the ruler along the left edge.

At this point, your form should look similar to Figure 15-16. Now all the fields needed for the Pets Data Entry form are in the form. You may have to adjust some of the other fields to make it look correct.

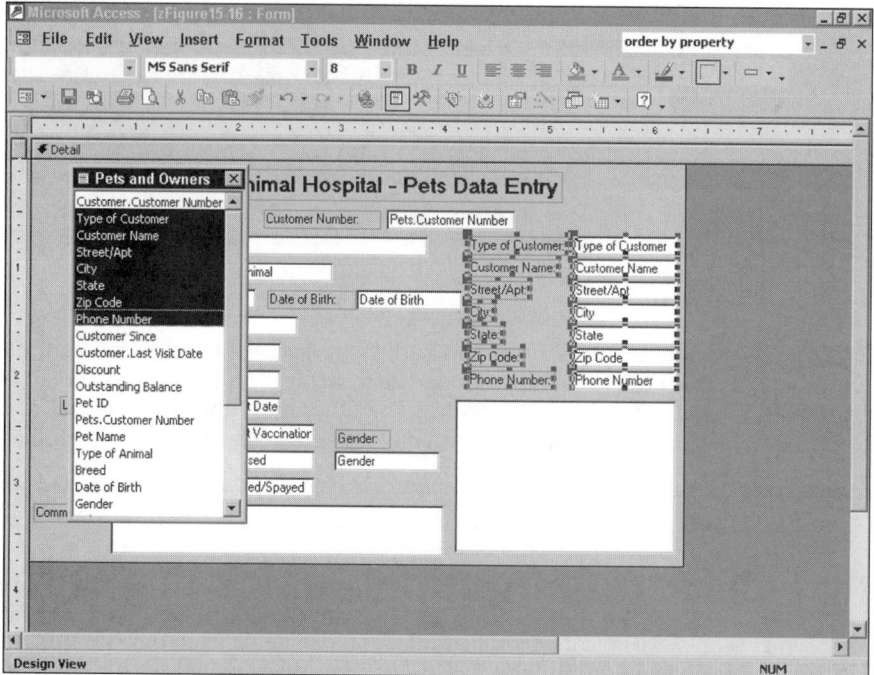

Figure 15-16: Adding the Customer fields

As Figure 15-16 shows, the new fields begins with the Type of Customer field. Actually, you want that field separated from the others because you change it to a calculated field later. You can use Figure 15-17 as a guide for the final placement of the field.

To move the Type of Customer control below the other customer controls, follow these steps:

1. Deselect all the selected controls by clicking any empty area of the form.

2. Select just the Type of Customer text box control and its attached label.

3. Move the control just below the Phone Number control so that it's just above the Picture bound object frame control.

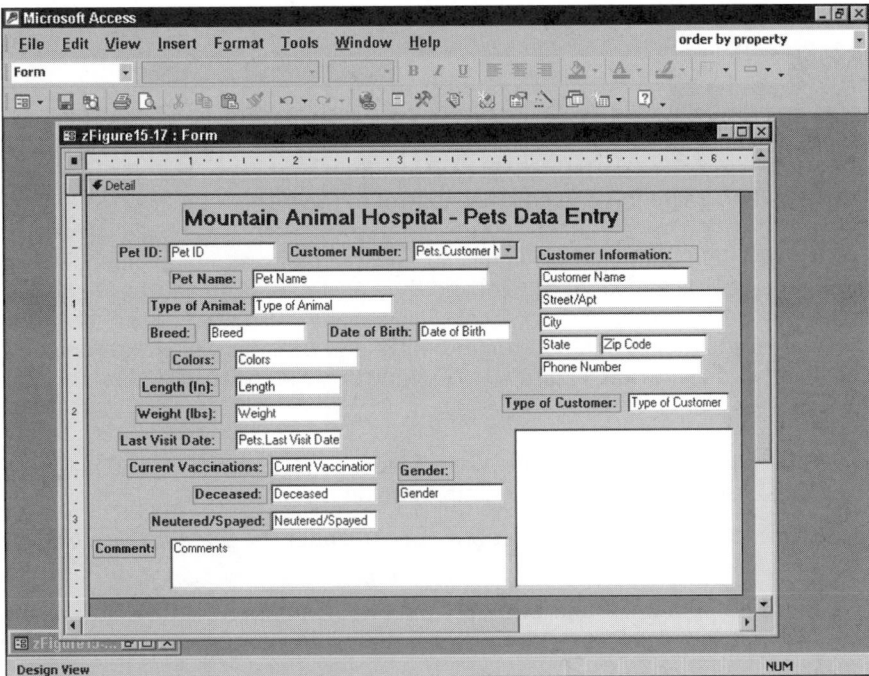

Figure 15-17: Customer fields in the Pets form

Working with attached label and text controls

As Figure 15-17 shows, the remaining customer fields are displayed in a very small area of the screen with no labels other than the label control Customer Information. It is very easy to delete one or more attached label controls in a form. Simply select the label control (or controls) to delete and press Delete. When deleting attached controls, there are two choices:

✦ Delete only the label control.

✦ Delete both the label control and the field control.

If you select the label control and press Delete, only the label control is deleted. If you select the field control and press Delete, both the label control and the field control are deleted. To delete only the Customer label controls (that is, the attached label controls), follow these steps:

1. Draw a box that surrounds only the six label controls from Customer Name through Phone Number.

2. Verify that only the label controls are selected (sizing handles are displayed in all the label controls; only the Move handle is displayed in the text box controls).

3. Press Delete.

If you want to delete the field control yet keep the attached label control, first select the label control and click Edit ⇨ Copy. Then select the field control and press Delete to delete both the field control and the label control. Finally, choose Edit ⇨ Paste to paste the copied label control to the form.

As you learned in Chapter 14, a label can be attached to an unlabeled control by cutting the unattached label control and then pasting it onto another control.

The final task is to move the customer controls to their final positions and add a label control, as shown in Figure 15-17. Follow these steps to complete this part of the form:

1. Rearrange the controls in the page header to resemble a typical mailing label's address format with State and Zip Code on the same line.

2. Move the Phone Number text box control under the State and Zip Code text box controls.

3. Move the block of name, address, and phone number controls into position so that it resembles Figure 15-17. Notice that all the control lines need to touch one another.

   You can use the new Format ⇨ Vertical Spacing ⇨ Make Equal option to line up all the controls above each other. If there is still space between them, use the Decrease option.

4. Create a label control with the text Customer Information, as shown in Figure 15-17.

Creating a calculated field

The field Type of Customer is a numeric field that displays a 1 if the customer is an individual, 2 if the customer is a pet store, and 3 if the customer is a bird sanctuary, aquarium, or municipal zoo. Rather than have the number displayed, you can transform the value into a more recognizable text expression.

The easiest way to do this is to replace the original Type of Customer control with a calculated expression. In Chapter 11, you used the function called Immediate IF (IIF) that lets you transform one value to another. In this example, the expression uses two IIF functions together.

The expression must transform the value of 1 to "Individual," the value of 2 to "Pet Store," and the value of 3 to "Zoo." This is the complete expression:

> =IIF([Type of Customer]=1,"Individual",IIF([Type of Customer]=2,"Pet Store","Zoo"))

The first IIF function checks the value of the Type of Customer field; if the value is 1, the value of the calculated control is set to *Individual*. If the value is not 1, another IIF checks to see whether the value of Type of Customer is 2. If the value is 2, the value of the calculated control is set to *Pet Store*. If not 2, the value of the calculated control is set to the only other possibility, which is *Zoo*. To create this new calculated control, follow these steps:

1. Select the Type of Customer text box control.

2. Display the Property window and click the Other tab to display the Other properties.

3. Change the Name property to Calculated Type of Customer.

4. Click the Data tab and click the Control Source property.

5. Press Shift+F2 to display the Zoom box.

6. In the Control Source property, type the following:

> =IIF([Type of Customer]=1,"Individual",IIF([Type of Customer]=2,"Pet Store","Zoo"))

7. Click OK.

8. Close the Property window.

Note The Lookup Wizard for Access 2002 will help you create a control to display a different value from the value used in the control. You could use the Lookup Wizard in the Customer table and build a combo box to display Individual, Pet Store, or Zoo but store the values 1, 2, or 3. In Chapter 17, you create an option group, but this method is better for now.

Now that the form is complete, you can test it. Change to Form View and observe that the customer information is now displayed as you see the third record in Figure 15-18.

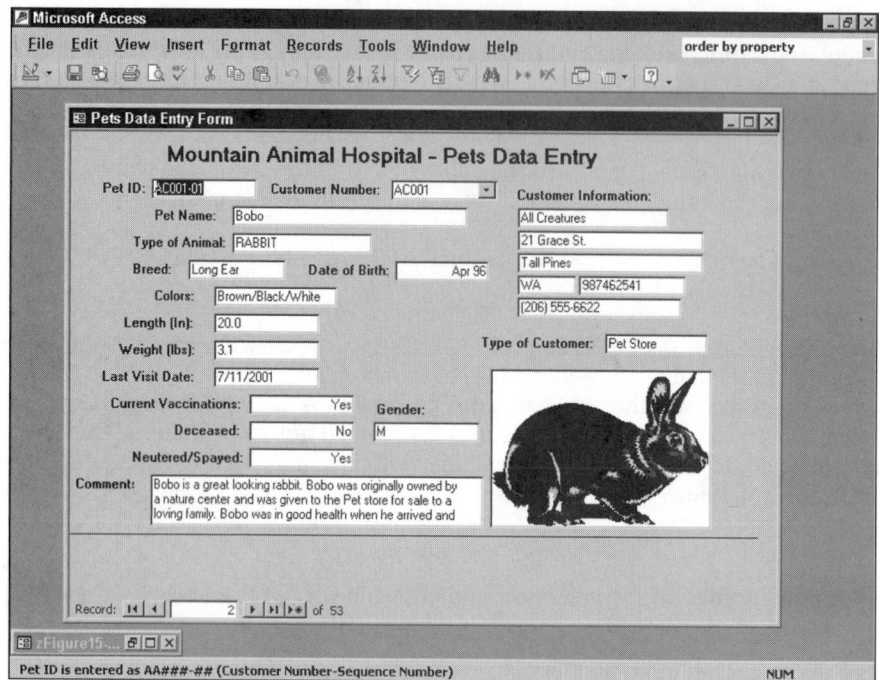

Figure 15-18: The Pets Data Entry form with customer information

Changing the updatability of a multiple-table form

When you use the form you just created, you can edit the existing pet data or add new pet records. As you enter a new pet's valid customer number, the customer information is automatically displayed because it is already in the customer table. In this form you can also change the customer information. Because changing customer information affects all pets for this customer, you have decided not to allow changes to the customer fields.

You can use the Locked property to prevent changes to the customer information fields. Select all the fields under Customer information. Change the Locked property, found under the Data tab of the Property window, to Yes.

Updating a field such as Customer Name (which is on the one side of a one-to-many relationship) changes the value for all records of pets owned by that customer.

Figure 15-19 shows the Locked property being changed to Yes for the Customer information in the Pets Data Entry form.

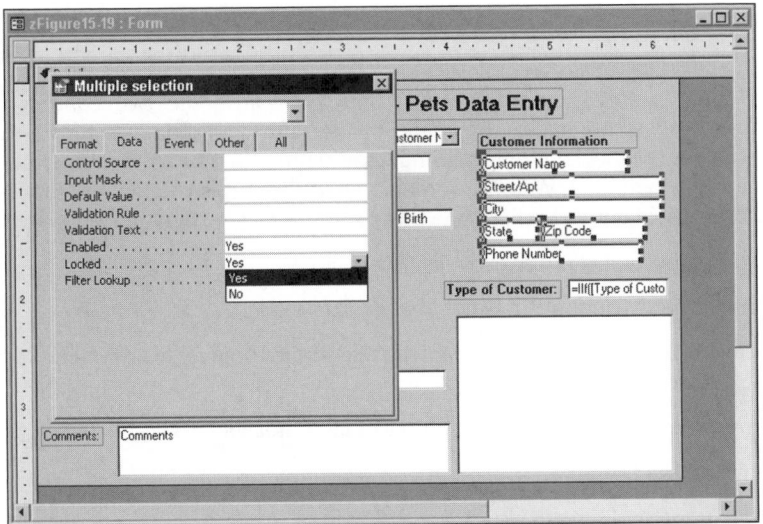

Figure 15-19: Locking the customer data from changes

You should save this form with all the changes currently made. Later if you have had any problems with this chapter there is also a form named Pets Data Entry Form - Without Formatting in the Mountain Animal Hospital.mdb database file containing the work on the form up until now in its final form. This form is used later in this chapter and again in the next few chapters, starting with the form in its current state.

Creating a Multiple-Page Form

Suppose that you want to add more information to the form. There is little room to add more fields or labels, but you may want to see a larger picture of the animal and the ability to see all the comments at once in the multiple-line text box. Without a larger form, you can't do that. You can't just make the screen bigger unless you change to a higher screen resolution, which means getting the necessary hardware. One solution is to create a *multiple-page* form.

Cross-Reference
Another and possibly better solution is to use a Tab control to display multiple pages of data on one form. Tab controls are discussed in Chapter 32. Another option is to open other forms as you need them by clicking a button. This requires using a macro or Visual Basic for Applications.

Changing Default Settings for Attached Labels

Attached label controls are called compound controls because the two controls are attached. You can disable this feature by changing the AutoLabel default setting. When AutoLabel is set to Yes, a label control is automatically created that bears the name of the field the text control is bound to. With AutoLabel in effect, a label is created automatically every time you drag a field onto a form. Follow these steps to change the AutoLabel default:

1. Display the Toolbox if it is not already displayed.

2. Display the Property window if it is not already displayed.

3. Click the Text Box button on the Toolbar. The title of the Property window should be Default Text Box.

4. Under the Format tab scroll down until you see the AutoLabel property.

5. Click the AutoLabel text box.

6. Change the property setting to No.

The next property, AutoColon, is related because if set to Yes a colon automatically follows any text in a new label. Two other properties control where the attached label appears relative to the control itself. These are the Label X and Label Y properties. Label X controls the horizontal position of the label control relative to the text box control. The default setting is −1 (to the left of the text box control). As you make the value a smaller negative number, for example −0.5, you decrease the space from the attached label to the control. If you want the label to the right of the control (as you may for an option button), set the Label X property to a positive number, such as 1.5.

Label Y controls the vertical position of the label control relative to the text box control. The default setting is 0, which places the label on the same line as the text box control. If you want to place the label above the control, change the Label Y setting to −1 or a larger negative number.

The Label Align property lets you control the alignment of the text within the label.

If you changed the AutoLabel property setting to No and you now drag fields from the Field List window to the form, no labels will be attached. The AutoLabel property setting is only in effect for this form. Because you don't need to add further labeled fields to this form, you can leave AutoLabel set to No.

Why use multiple-page forms?

You use multiple-page forms when all your information won't fit on one page or when you want to segregate specific information on separate pages. Multiple-page forms allow you to display less information on a page so that a complicated form looks less cluttered. You can also place data items that are not always necessary on the second (or even the third) page, which makes data entry on the first page easier for the user.

You can have as many pages as you need on a form, but the general rule is that more than five pages make the form very tedious. There is also a 22-inch size limitation in the form. After you add pages to a form, you can move between them by using the PgUp and PgDn keys or you can use macros or Visual Basic for Applications to program navigation keys.

You can create a multiple-page form only when the Default View property of the form is set to Single Form.

Adding a page break

You can add *page breaks* to a form by adding a Page Break control (which is third from the bottom-left of the Toolbox). You can use Figure 15-20 as a guide as you change the Pets Data Entry form to add a separate page for larger Picture and Comments controls.

Follow these steps to add a new page and a page break:

1. Increase the length of the form to 7½ inches.
2. Move and resize the Comments text box control as shown in Figure 15-20.
3. Move and resize the Picture text box control.
4. Select the Pet Name text box control in the upper area of the control, and then select Edit ➪ Copy.
5. Select Edit ➪ Paste and move the copy to the second page of the form.
6. Display the Toolbox.
7. Click the Page Break button in the Toolbox.
8. Move the mouse pointer to the left corner of the intersection of the two pages (3¼ inches).
9. Click the mouse to add the page break.

Figure 15-20 shows the completed design.

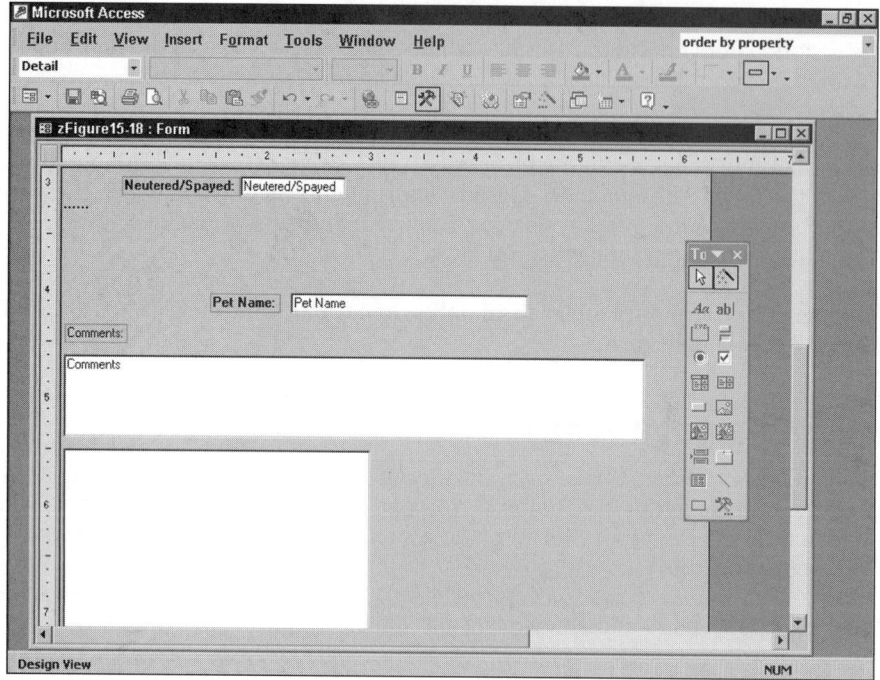

Figure 15-20: Adding a new page and a page break

You copied the *Pet Name* control and moved it to the second page. This was for display-only purposes. Unless you change the properties of the second Pet Name control, you can also edit its value. When working with forms that require multiple pages, you may want to place controls that are used as headers in a form header section so they will display on both pages. If you are working with numeric data, you may also want to add a form footer section to display totals.

Figure 15-21 shows the second page of the form for the first record in the table.

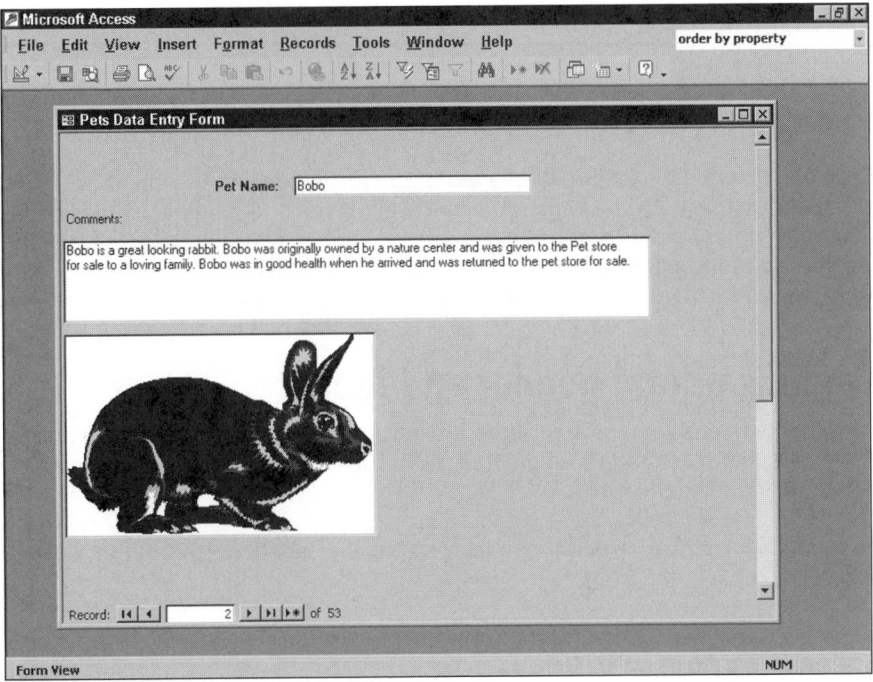

Figure 15-21: The second page of the form

Do not save this last set of changes to create a multiple-page form. Reopen the form you saved or the form sets Data Entry Form - Without Formatting.

Using Form and Page Headers and Footers

The most common use of a page or form header is to repeat identification information. In the Pets Data Entry form, for example, the text header is part of the form itself. When you have a second page, you don't see the text header. In Access forms, you can add both form and page sections. Sections include *headers* (which come before the detail controls) and *footers* (which come after the detail controls).

The different types of headers and footers

Several types of headers and footers can appear in a form:

- ✦ **Form header.** Displayed at the top of each page when viewed and at the top when the form is printed

- ✦ **Page header.** Displayed only when the form is printed; prints after the form header

✦ **Page footer.** Appears only when the form is printed; prints before the form footer

✦ **Form footer.** Displayed at the bottom of each page when viewed and at the bottom of the form when the form is printed

Form headers and footers are displayed in the form; you can use them optionally in a printed form. *Page headers and footers* are displayed only when a form is printed. Generally, unless you are printing the form as a report, you won't use the page headers or footers. Because you can create reports easily in Access (and even save a form as a report), you won't find much use for page headers and footers.

Creating a form header and footer

Form headers and footers are created by clicking View ➪ Form Header/Footer. When this menu command is selected, both the form header and form footer sections are added to the form.

To create a form header and move the text header label control into it, follow these steps:

1. Open the original Pets Data Entry Form - Without Formatting form in Design view.

2. Select View ➪ Form Header/Footer to display the form header and footer.

3. Select the label control Mountain Animal Hospital - Pets Data Entry.

4. Move the label control straight up from the Detail section to the Form Header section.

5. Resize the Form Header to fit the label control properly, as shown in Figure 15-22.

6. Close the Form Footer section by dragging the Form Footer bottom border to meet the top border.

When you display a form with an added header or footer, the equivalent amount of space is lost from the Detail section. The size of your Detail section must be adjusted to compensate for this lost space.

In this example, you might need to move the other controls up and make the height of the Detail section smaller because you moved the text label control to the Form Header section. You are not using the Form Footer section, so it is best to close it.

The size of a section can be changed by placing the mouse pointer on the bottom border of the section, where it turns into a double-headed arrow, and dragging the section border up or down. You can only drag a section up to the bottom of the lowest control in the section.

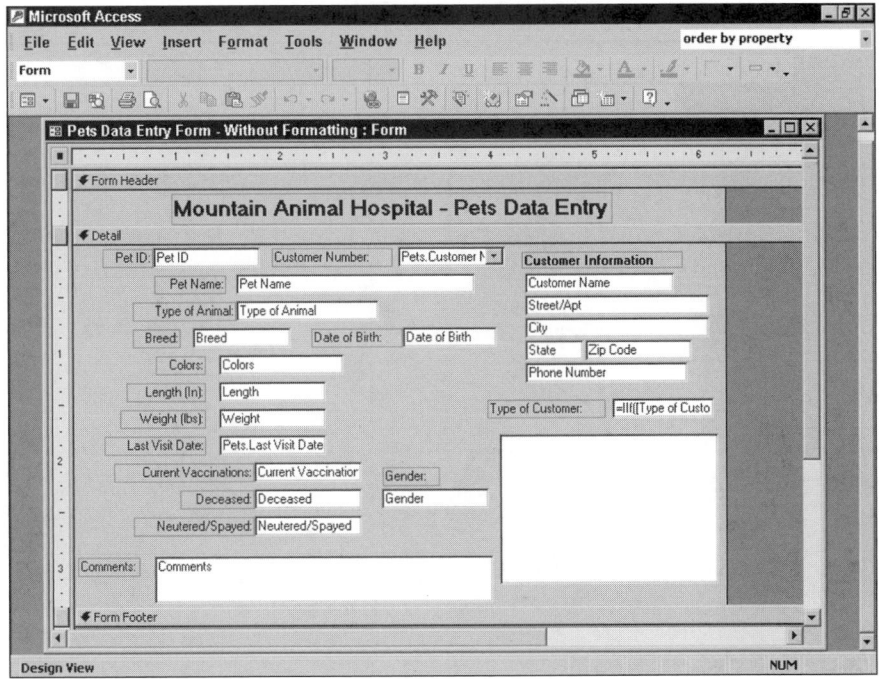

Figure 15-22: Adding a form header

When you display a form with a header or footer section, the sections are separated from the detail section by a line. The form headers and footers are literally anchored in place. If you create a scrollable or a multiple-page form, the headers and footers remain where they are while the data in the detail section moves.

After completing the form, save it.

Printing a Form

You can print a form by selecting the File ⇨ Print command and entering the desired information in the Print dialog box. Printing a form is like printing anything else; you are in a WYSIWYG ("What You See Is What You Get") environment, so what you see on the form is essentially what you get in the printed hard copy. If you added Page Headers or Page Footers, they are printed at the top or bottom of the page.

You can also preview the printout by clicking the File ⇨ Print Preview menu command. This displays a preview of the printed page, as shown in Figure 15-23.

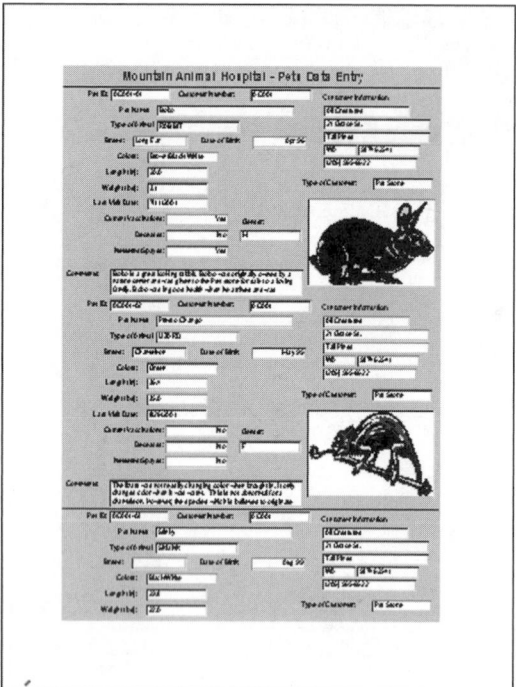

Figure 15-23: A preview of a form

Converting a Form to a Report

By right-clicking a form name in the Database window and selecting Save As Report, you can save the form design as a report. The entire form is placed in the report form. If the form has form headers or footers, these are placed in the report header and report footer sections. If the form has page headers or page footers, these are placed in the page header and footer sections in the report. After the design is in the Report Design window, it can be enhanced using the report design features. This allows you to add group sections and additional totaling in a report without having to recreate a great layout!

✦   ✦   ✦

Creating Great Looking Forms

◆ ◆ ◆ ◆

In This Chapter

Enhancing the font
size and style of text
control

Applying special
display effects to
forms

Adding lines and
rectangles to a form

Adding color or
shading to a form

Adding a
background picture
to a form

Copying formatting
properties between
controls

Using AutoFormat
and the Format
Painter

◆ ◆ ◆ ◆

In Chapter 15, you build a form that starts with a blank
Form Design view screen. That form had no special formatting other than some label and text box controls. The most
exciting object on the form was the picture of the rabbit. By
using the various formatting windows and the Formatting
toolbar, the line and rectangle controls, background pictures,
and your own imagination, you can create great-looking forms
with a small amount of work.

In this chapter, you learn to format the data-entry form that
you create in Chapter 15 to make it more readable and interesting to look at.

Making a Good Form Look Great

Just as you can use a desktop publishing package to enhance
a word-processing document to make it more readable, you
can use the tools in Form Design view to enhance a database
form to make it more usable. One way that you can make your
database form more usable is to draw attention to areas of the
form that you want the reader to notice. Just as a headline in
a newspaper calls your attention to the news, an enhanced
section of a form makes the information that it contains stand
out.

The Access form designer has a number of tools to make the
form controls and sections more visually striking, such as

- ◆ Lines and rectangles
- ◆ Color and background shading
- ◆ Three-dimensional effects (raised, sunken, etched, chis-
  eled, shadowed)
- ◆ Background pictures
- ◆ Form headers and footers

In this chapter, you learn to use special formatting to add shading, shadows, lines, rectangles, and three-dimensional effects. Figure 16-1 shows the form as it appears after some special effects have been added.

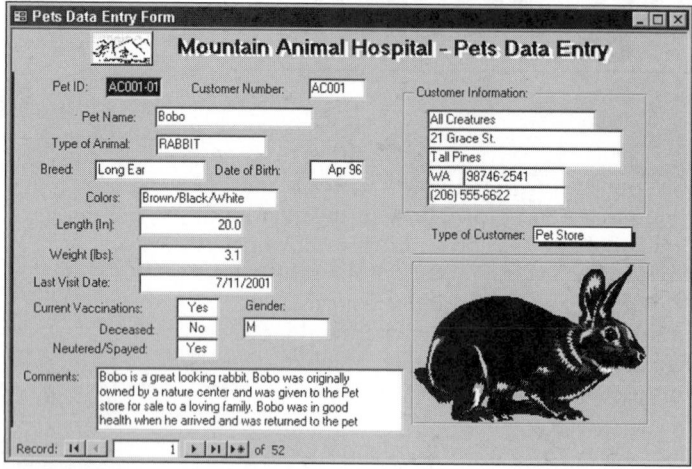

Figure 16-1: The enhanced form

Understanding WYSIWYG

Access has a WYSIWYG (What You See Is What You Get) form designer called *Form Design view*. As you add controls on-screen, you see instantly what they look like in your form. If you want to see what the data looks like during the form design process, the on-screen preview mode lets you see the actual data in your form design without using a hard-copy device such as a printer.

The Access form designer lets you add color and shading to form text and controls. You can also display them in reverse video, which shows white letters on a black background. You can even color or shade the background of form sections. As you specify these effects, you see each change instantly on the Design screen.

Using the formatting windows and toolbar

The most important tools for enhancing a form are the formatting windows and the Formatting toolbar. You can choose from five formatting windows, including

✦ Fill/Background color for shading

✦ Font/Foreground color for text

✦ Line/Border Color for lines, rectangles, and control borders

✦ Line/Border Width for lines, rectangles, and control borders

✦ Special Effect, such as raised, sunken, etched, chiseled, or shadowed

Note   You can display or remove the Formatting toolbar from the screen by selecting View ↪ Toolbars and selecting Formatting, or by right-clicking on the toolbar area and selecting Formatting. Figure 16-2 shows the five formatting windows pulled off of the toolbar and opened. You can use these windows to format the different controls in a form.

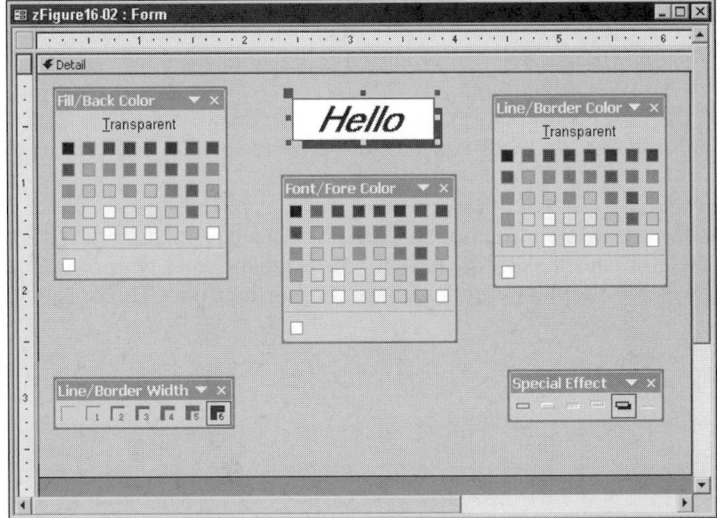

Figure 16-2: The five formatting windows

Tip   You can tell the selected color in the three color windows (Fill/Back Color, Font/Fore Color, and Line/Border Color) by looking at the small colored rectangle just below the three picture icons (Fill/Back Color, Font/Fore Color, Line/Border Color) in the toolbar.

A *formatting window* is a window similar to the toolbox or the Field List. You can move a formatting window around the screen, but you can't anchor it in the way that you can dock a toolbar to a window border. To open the window and place it on the surface, click the formatting tool icon's down-arrow and then click the title bar and drag it to where you want it. A formatting window can remain on-screen all the time; you can use it to change the options for one or more controls. To close a formatting window, click the Close button or reselect its icon on the Formatting toolbar.

You can modify the appearance of a control by using a formatting window. To modify the appearance of a control, select it by clicking it, and then click the formatting window that you need to change the control's appearance. (Refer to Figure 16-2 to see all five formatting windows.)

The Font/Fore Color (foreground text) and Fill/Back Color (background color) windows change the color of the text or background of a control. You can make a control's background transparent by selecting the Transparent button in the Fill/Back Color window. The Line/Border Color window changes the color of control's borders, lines, and rectangles. Clicking the Transparent button in the Line/Border Color window makes the border on any selected control invisible.

The Line/Border Width window changes the thickness of control borders, standalone lines, and rectangles. You can select the thickness of a line by using the thickness buttons. Available thicknesses (in points) are hairline, 1 point, 2 points, 3 points, 4 points, 5 points, and 6 points.

Note   A point (approximately $\frac{1}{72}$ inch) is a unit of measure for text and rule heights.

The Special Effect window lets you choose from flat, raised, sunken, etched, shadowed, and chiseled appearances for a control. The Special Effect window also provides a control property that lets you designate the border style. The border styles include

✦ Transparent

✦ Solid

✦ Dashes

✦ Short Dashes

✦ Dots

✦ Sparse Dots

✦ Dash Dot

✦ Dash Dot Dot

After you have finished using a formatting window, you can close it by clicking the Close button in the upper-right corner.

Creating special effects

Figure 16-3 shows some of the special effects that can easily be created for controls with the Special Effect window. In the figure, you see that controls with gray as a background color display special effects much better than controls with white as a background color. In fact, a form background in gray or a dark color is almost mandatory to make certain special effects easy to see. The following sections describe each of these effects; you will use some of them later to modify the Pets Data Entry form.

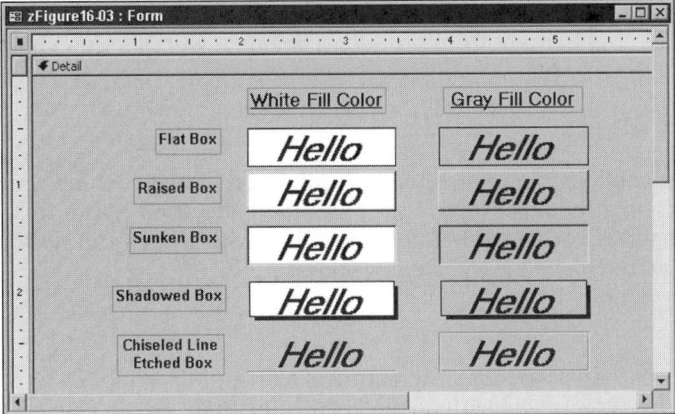

Figure 16-3: Special effects

You can apply special effects to rectangles, label controls, text box controls, check boxes, option buttons, and option group boxes. Anything that has a box or circle around it can be raised, sunken, etched, chiseled, or shadowed.

By simply selecting the control and adding the special effect, you can make your forms look much better and draw attention to their most important areas.

Flat

In Figure 16-3, the first pair of labels exhibits the Flat special effect. The flat box stands out better when set against the gray background.

Tip You can also use the Border Width window to increase the width of the border lines, which makes the box more prominent. The Border Color window lets you change the color of the border. A thick white border also stands out.

Raised

The raised box is best used to set off a rectangle that surrounds other controls or for label controls. This box gives the best effect in a dark color against a dark background. As Figure 16-3 shows, the raised box is difficult to see with a white fill color. By increasing the width of the box, you can give the control the appearance of being higher than the surface of the on-screen background. You can achieve the raised three-dimensional effect by contrasting the white left and top borders with the black right and bottom borders.

Sunken

The sunken special effect is the most dramatic and most often used; it's the standard format for text box (data entry) controls in the Form Wizard. As Figure 16-3 shows, either the white or the gray fill color looks very good on a gray form background. You can also increase the width of the border to give the effect of a deeper impression. You achieve the sunken three-dimensional effect by using black left and top borders and white right and bottom borders. The effect works well with check boxes and option buttons.

Shadowed

The shadowed special effect places a solid, dark-colored rectangle behind the original control, which is slightly offset to give the shadowed effect. As Figure 16-3 shows, the black shadow works well behind a box filled with white or gray. You can change the border color to change the shadow color.

Etched

The etched effect is perhaps the most interesting of all the special looks. Essentially, it's a sunken rectangle with no sunken inside area.

Tip   Current Microsoft Windows standards make heavy use of etched rectangles. Sunken rectangles around groups are a Windows 3.1 standard and should only be used for text box controls. Option groups or rectangles around controls should use the etched look.

Chiseled

The chiseled effect adds a chiseled line underneath a selected control.

On the CD-ROM   In this chapter, you modify the form that you create in Chapter 15 so that it looks like Figure 16-1. If you are following the examples, you should have the Pets Data Entry Form—Without Formatting form open in the Form Design window or the form you complete in Chapter 15.

Changing the form's background color

If your form is primarily intended for on-screen viewing (instead of print), it may be beneficial to color the background. A light gray background (the Microsoft Windows default) seems to be the best neutral color in all types of lighting and visual conditions. However, you may want to have a different color for the form's Header and Footer sections. To change the background for the form header or detail sections, select the desired section by clicking on the section's top border and then select the appropriate background color.

Tip   When you change the background color of form sections, also change the background of individual label controls for a more natural look. A label control generally doesn't look good if its background doesn't match the background of the form itself.

Enhancing Text-Based Controls

Generally, you should ensure the accuracy of your label text and data before you start enhancing display items with shading or special effects. When your enhancements include label and text box control changes, begin with them.

Enhancing label and text box controls

You can enhance label and text box controls in several ways:

✦ Change the text font type (Arial, Times New Roman, Wingdings)

✦ Change the text font size (4–200)

✦ Change the text font style (bold, italic, underline)

✦ Change the text color (using a formatting window)

✦ Add a shadow

Tip   The Windows standards call for text to be non-bold 8-point Tahoma font for all label and text controls and 12-point non-bold Verdana for large header labels.

Cross-Reference   In Chapter 15, you change the title's text in the label control. You then change the text's font size and font style. In the next section, you learn how to add a text shadow to the label control.

Creating a text shadow

Text shadows give text a three-dimensional look by making the text seem to float above the page while its shadow stays on the page. This effect uses the same basic principle as a shadowed box. Use this process to create text shadows:

✦ Duplicate the text.

✦ Offset the duplicate text from the original text.

✦ Change the duplicate text to a different color (usually a lighter shade).

✦ Place the duplicate text behind the original text.

✦ Change the original text's background color to Clear.

To create a shadow for the title's text, follow these steps:

1. Select the *Mountain Animal Hospital — Pets Data Entry* label control.

2. Click Edit ➪ Duplicate.

3. Click the Font/Fore Color down-arrow and choose white to change the duplicate text's color to white.

4. Drag the duplicate text up and to the right of the original text to create an off-set from the text.

5. Click Format ➪ Send to Back.

You may have to move the text or its shadow to be in the best position. You also may have to decrease the Form Header section. The text now appears to have a shadow, as shown in Figure 16-4.

Tip   To move the selected control a very small distance, press Ctrl+arrow key; the control moves slightly in the direction of the arrow key that you use.

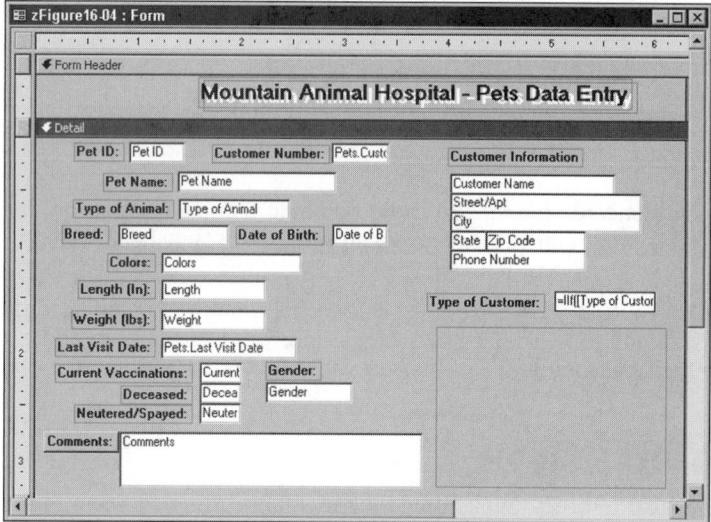

Figure 16-4: The text with a shadow and reverse video

Note   If you don't see the shadow, select the original text and then select the Transparent option on the Fill/Back Color Formatting toolbar.

Tip   The box around the label control is not visible when the form is displayed because the Transparent button in the Border Color window is depressed.

When you duplicate the original text, the duplicate is automatically offset below the original text. When you place the duplicate text behind the original, it's hidden. You can redisplay it by placing the original text in front. If the offset (the distance from the other copy) is too large, the effect doesn't look like a shadow. You can perfect the shadowed appearance by moving one of the label controls slightly.

Although the shadow appears correct on-screen and looks great, it won't print correctly on most monochrome laser printers if you decide to save the form as a report or simply print the form. What you normally see is two lines of black text, which look horrible. If you plan to print your forms and don't have a printer that prints text in color (or prints many shades of gray by using graphics rather than text fonts), avoid using shadowed text on a form.

Changing text to a reverse video display

Text really stands out when you create white text on a black background. This setup is called *reverse video*; it's the opposite of the usual black letters on white. You can convert text in a label control or text box to reverse video by changing the Back Color to black and the Fore Color to white. To change the Pet ID text control to reverse video, follow these steps:

1. Select the Pet ID text box control (not the label control).

2. Select Black from the Fill/Back Color formatting window.

3. Select White from the Font/Fore Color formatting window.

To make it more dramatic, you may want to set the font to Bold and resize the control.

With some laser printers you may not see reverse video if you print your form because the printer's drivers can't print it.

Displaying label or text box control properties

As you change appearances of a label control or text box control using a formatting window, you are actually changing the control's properties. Figure 16-5 displays the Property window for the text box control that you just modified. As Figure 16-5 shows, a formatting window can affect many properties. Table 16-1 shows the various properties (and their possible values) for both label and text box controls.

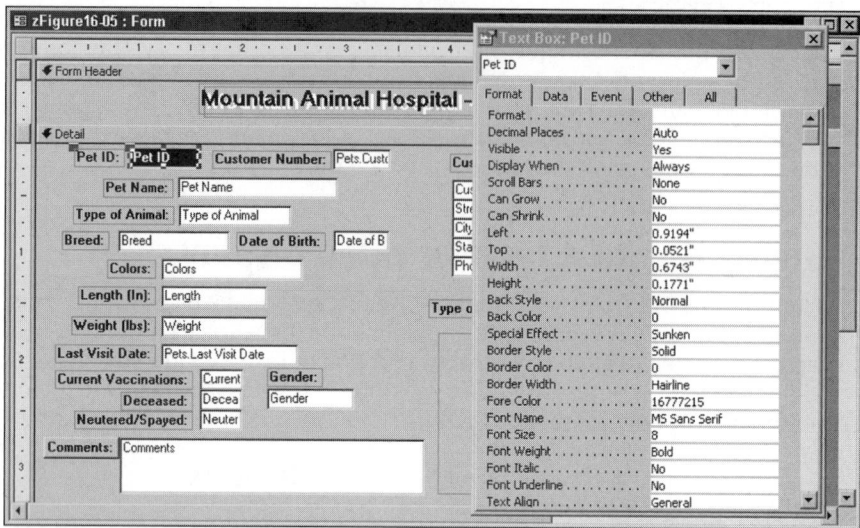

Figure 16-5: Text Box control properties

Table 16-1
Label or Text Box Format Properties

Property	Options	Description
Format	Various Numeric and Date Formats	Determines how the data is displayed.
Decimal Places	Auto, 1-15	Determines how many decimal places, if any, you want to apply to this control.
Visible	Yes/No	Yes: Control is displayed normally No: Control is invisible when displayed.
Display When	Always, Print Only, Screen Only	Determines when the control is displayed.
Scrollbars	None, Vertical, Horizontal, Both	Specifies when scrollbars are displayed.
Can Grow	Yes/No	If multiple lines of text are in the control, does the text box get larger?
Can Shrink	Yes/No	If fewer lines of text are in the control than in its initial size, does the text box height get smaller?

Property	Options	Description
Left	Position of the left corner of the control in the current measure (include an indicator, such as centimeters or inches, if you use a different unit of measurement)	Specifies the position of an object on the horizontal axis.
Top	Position of the top corner of the control in the current measure	Specifies the position of an object on the vertical axis.
Width	The width of the control in the current unit of measure	Specifies the width of an object.
Height	The height of the control in the current unit of measure	Specifies the height of an object.
Back Style	Transparent, Normal	Determines whether a control's background is opaque or transparent.
Back Color	Any available background color	Specifies the color for the interior of the control or section.
Special Effect	Flat, Raised, Sunken, Shadowed, Etched, Chiseled	Determines whether a section or control appears flat, raised, sunken, shadowed, etched, or chiseled.
Border Style	Transparent or Solid, Dashes, Dots (Lines/Boxes Only)	Determines whether a control's border is opaque or transparent.
Border Color	Any available border color	Specifies the color of a control's border
Border Width	Hairline, 1pt, 2pt, 3pt, 4pt, 5pt, 6pt	Specifies the width of a control's border.
Fore Color	Any selection from a formatting window	Specifies the color for text in a control or the printing and drawing color.
Font Name	Any system font name that appears on the toolbar; depends on fonts installed	Specifies the name of the font used for text or a control.
Font Size	Any size available for a given font	Specifies the size of the font used for text or a control.
Font Weight	Extra Light, Light, Normal, Medium, Semi-Bold, Bold, Extra Bold, Heavy	Specifies the width of the line Windows uses to display and print characters.
Font Italic	Yes/No	Italicizes text in a control.

Continued

Table 16-1 *(continued)*

Property	Options	Description
Font Underline	Yes/No	Underlines text in a control.
Text Align	General (default), Left, Center, Right	Sets the alignment for text in a control.
Reading Order	Context, Left-To-Right, Right-To-Left	Determines the reading order of the letters based on the language.
Keyboard Language	System, English	Determine the keyboard language for entry into the control.
Scroll Bar Align	System, Right, Left	Scroll bars can be placed on the left or right side of a control based on the language.
Numeral Shapes	System, Arabic, National, Context	Used for Arabic and Hindi languages for the shapes of numbers.
Left Margin		Used to set margins on a control. Enter in inches for the left margin. Can only be used for text box and label controls.
Right Margin		Used to set margins on a control. Enter in inches for the right margin. Can only be used for text box and label controls.
Top Margin		Used to set margins on a control. Enter in inches for the top margin. Can only be used for text box and label controls.
Bottom Margin		Used to set margins on a control. Enter in inches for the bottom margin. Can only be used for text box and label controls.
Line Spacing		Used to specify line spacing for a control. Enter in inches for the amount of space between lines. Can only be used for text box and label controls.
Is Hyperlink	Yes, No	Used to specify if control is a hyperlink. If you select Yes, the text is blue and underlined. Can be used for a direct link to the Internet and for text box and label controls.

Although you can set many of these controls from the property sheet, it's much easier to drag the control to set the Top, Left, Width, and Height properties or to use a formatting window to set the other properties of the control.

Displaying Images in Forms

You can display a picture on a form by using *an image control*. This method is different from the way you use a bound OLE (Object Linking and Embedding) control. Normally, you store an OLE object (sound, video, Word, or Excel document) with a data record or with an unbound OLE object that is used specifically for storing OLE objects (those same sound, video, Word, or Excel documents) on a form.

Image controls in Access 2002 are used only for non-OLE objects, such as Paintbrush (.BMP) pictures. Image controls offer a distinct advantage: Unlike OLE objects (which can be edited but use huge amounts of resources), the image control adds only the size of the bitmap picture to your computer's overhead. Using too many OLE objects in Access causes resource and performance problems. New and existing applications should use image controls only when you need to display pictures that don't change or don't need to be edited within Access.

Tip

In previous versions of Access, you may have learned to select an unbound OLE object picture and then select Edit ➪ Save As Picture. This technique broke the OLE connection but did not fix the resource problem.

On the CD-ROM

You can add an image control to your form by either pasting a bitmap from the Clipboard or embedding a bitmap file. For example, you may want to add a logo for Mountain Animal Hospital. On the CD that accompanies this book, you can find a bitmap file called *MTN.BMP*. In this section, you add this bitmap to the page header section of the form.

You can display an image object in one of three ways:

✦ **Clip.** Displays picture in its original size

✦ **Stretch.** Fits the picture into the control regardless of size; often displayed out of proportion

✦ **Zoom.** Fits the picture into the control (either vertically or horizontally) and maintains proportions; often results in white space on top or right side

To add the logo to the form, follow these steps:

1. Display the toolbox by selecting View ➪ Toolbox.

2. Click the Image control on the toolbox.

3. Click in the Form Header's left corner above the title; drag the box so that it is sized as shown in Figure 16-1. The Insert Picture dialog box appears, as shown in Figure 16-6.

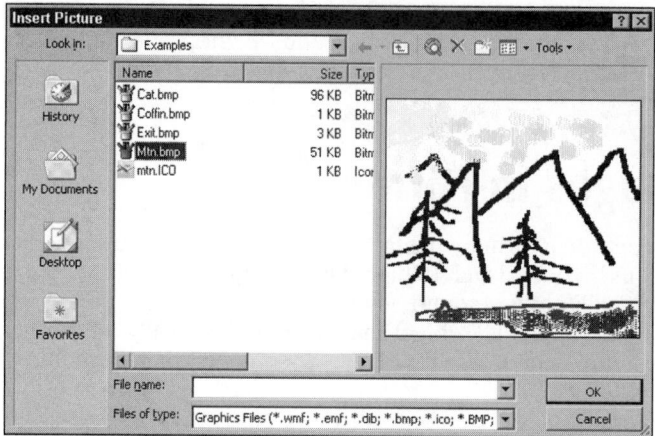

Figure 16-6: The Insert Picture dialog box

Note From this dialog box, you can select the type of picture object that you want to insert into your form. The dialog box supports many picture formats, including .BMP, .TIF, .WMF, .PCX, .ICO, .WPG, JPG, .PCT, as well as any other picture format that your copy of Microsoft Windows supports.

Tip If you don't see a preview of the picture, select Insert Picture ⇨ Views ⇨ Preview.

4. Select Mtn.bmp and click OK. Notice that when you click on a file, it is first displayed in the Preview area on the right part of the dialog box before the picture is inserted.

If the file doesn't already exist and you want to create a new object (such as a Paintbrush picture), you must add an unbound OLE frame rather than an image control.

After you complete Step 4, Access returns you to the Form Design View window, where the picture is displayed. You must still change the Size Mode property to Stretch.

5. Display the property sheet.

6. Change the Size Mode property to Stretch. Now, you have to change the Border property so that the picture does not blend in with the background because it contains so much white. You make this modification by changing the border color to black or by making the border three-dimensional, which you can do by selecting the Raised toggle button in the Special Effect formatting window.

7. Display the Special Effect formatting window and click the Raised toggle button.

The image control is complete and should look like the one in Figure 16-1.

Working with Lines and Rectangles

You can use lines or rectangles (commonly called *boxes*), to make certain areas of the form stand out and attract attention. In Figure 16-1, several groups of lines and rectangles are being used for emphasis. In the next exercise, you need to add the lines and the rectangle. You can use Figure 16-7 as a guide for this procedure.

To create the rectangle for the customer information block, follow these steps:

1. Select the Rectangle control on the toolbox.

2. Click to the left of the *Customer Information* text so that the rectangle encompasses the Customer fields and cuts through the middle of the *Customer Information* text.

3. Drag the rectangle around the entire set of Customer text box controls and release the mouse button.

Tip If the default rectangle is not transparent, then Select Format ⇨ Send to Back or choose Fill/Back Color and select Transparent to redisplay the text boxes.

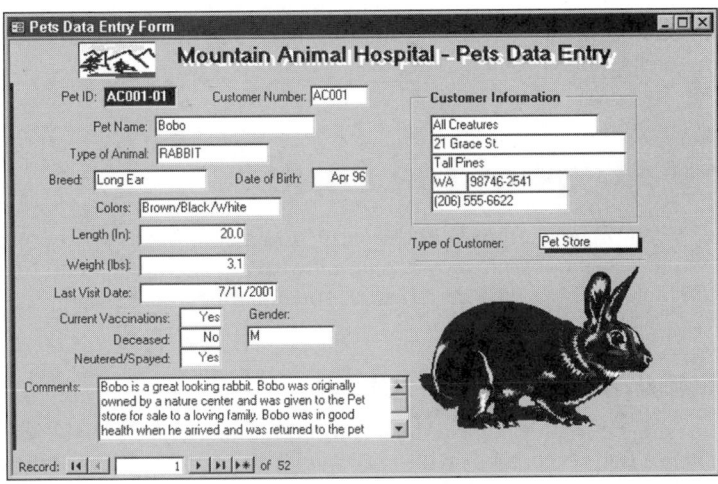

Figure 16-7: Completing the rectangles and lines

Tip When you create a rectangle, the controls beneath it are blocked out. Sending the rectangle to the background makes the controls reappear.

Select the etched effect in the Special Effect formatting window if it isn't already selected.

Tip You can also redisplay the controls behind the rectangle by checking the Transparent button of the Background Color option in a formatting window. This method, however, doesn't allow you to add other shading effects. For a rectangle, you should always select Format ⇨ Send to Back.

You still need to add several lines to the form. You need to add a single horizontal line just above the title and a thick vertical line down the left side of the form (beginning with Pet ID and ending to the left of the Comments field). To add these lines, complete these steps (use Figure 16-7 as a guide):

1. Click the Line control in the toolbox.

2. Create a new horizontal line just above the image control.

3. Select the chiseled special effect.

4. Create a new vertical line, starting just to the left of the Pet ID field. To keep the line vertical, hold down the Shift key as you drag the line to just left of the Comments field, as shown in Figure 16-7.

5. Select the 3 button in the Border Width formatting window to make the line thicker.

Tip If you hold down the Shift key while creating the line, the line remains perfectly straight, either horizontally or vertically, depending on the initial movement you make when drawing the line.

Emphasizing Areas of the Form

If you really want to emphasize an area of the form, add a shadow to any control. The most common types of controls to add a shadow to are rectangles and text boxes. You can create shadows with the Shadow special effect.

Adding a shadow to a control

If the background is light or white, use a dark-colored rectangle. If the background is dark or black, use a light-colored or white rectangle. To create a shadow for the Type of Customer text box, follow these steps:

1. Select the Type of Customer control.

2. Select the Shadow special-effects button.

If you want to give the form a Microsoft Windows look and feel, you need to change some other objects. The first object that you need to change is the rectangle around the bound OLE object (displaying the rabbit in the first record). A Microsoft Windows look and feel has an etched gray rectangle rather than a sunken white one. Figure 16-7 shows this change.

Changing the header dividing line

Form headers and footers are automatically separated from the Detail section by a solid black line. In Access 2002, you can remove this line by setting the Dividing Lines form property to No. This action removes the line and makes the form appear seamless. This is especially important if you have a background bitmap on the entire form, if you're using form headers or footers, and if you want a single look.

Figure 16-7 shows the form in Form View. Notice both the etched rectangle around the Customer information and the two new lines. Also notice that the Mountain Animal Hospital logo appears in the form header.

Figure 16-8 shows the final form in the Form Design View window.

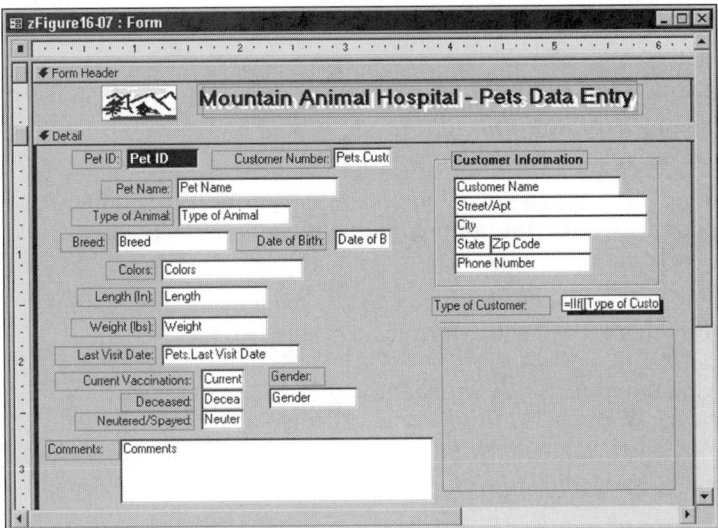

Figure 16-8: The final form

On the CD-ROM

You use this final form in the next chapter, so save it now. Select File ⇨ Save As/Export and name the form *Pets Data Entry – With Formatting*.

Adding a Background Bitmap

To add a really fun effect, you can add a background bitmap to any form, just as you added one control behind another. In Access 2002, you can do this by using the form's Picture properties. You have five properties to work with:

✦ **Picture.** The name of the bitmap picture; it can be any image-type file.

✦ **Picture Type.** Embedded or linked. You can save the picture in the database or you can just save the location (pointer) of the picture.

✦ **Picture Size Mode.** Clip, Stretch, or Zoom. Clip displays the picture only at its actual size starting at the Picture Alignment property. Stretch and Zoom fill the entire form from the upper-left corner of any header to the lower-right corner of any footer.

✦ **Picture Alignment.** Top-Left, Top-Right, Center, Bottom-Left, Bottom-Right, and so on. Use this property only when you use the Clip option in Picture Size mode.

✦ **Picture Tiling.** Yes/No. When you use a small bitmap with Clip mode, this repeats the bitmap across the entire form. For example, a brick becomes a brick wall.

For this example, you can add Mtn.bmp to the background of the form. Use these steps to add a background bitmap:

1. Select the form itself by clicking in the upper-left corner of the intersection of the two design rulers or by selecting Form from the combo box at the left margin of the Formatting toolbar.

2. Display the Properties window; click the Picture property that's on the Format sheet of the property window.

3. Enter **C:\ACCESS\MTN.BMP** (or the path to where you have placed your bitmap on the disk). When you move to another property, the Mountain Animal Hospital logo (or your bitmap) appears in the upper-left corner of the form background.

4. Click the Picture Size Mode property and change it from Clip to Stretch. The picture now occupies the entire form background.

If you are following the example, notice that the gray box for the Customer Information is still gray, the fields themselves still have white backgrounds, and the bitmap does not show through. If the bitmap doesn't show through, check the Transparent background color of any control; the background then shows through the form.

You can do this by choosing Edit ➪ Select All to select all the controls and then selecting Transparent from the Fill Back Color formatting window. This action produces the effect shown in Figure 16-9. As Figure 16-9 shows, the white background of the picture (along with the thick, black lines) makes it difficult to see the fields.

Tip   Using background bitmaps adds some interesting capabilities to your form. For example, you can take this process a step further and incorporate the bitmap into your application. A bitmap can have buttons tied to macros (or Visual Basic for Applications code placed in the right locations). To help the office staff search for a patient, for example, you can create a form that has a map with three states behind it. By adding invisible buttons over each state, you can give the staff the choice of clicking a state to select the patient records from that state.

You can also scan a paper form into your computer and use that image as the form background. You do this by placing fields on top of the scanned form itself, which spares you from spending a great deal of time recreating the form (which gives the phrase *filling out a form* a whole new meaning).

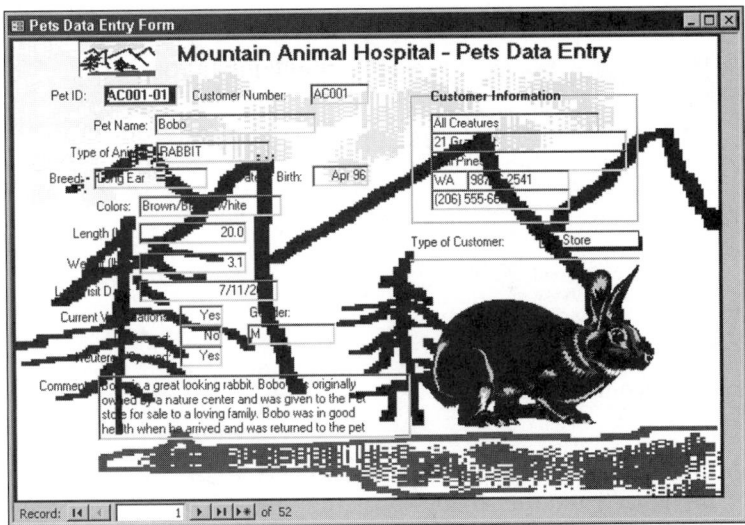

Figure 16-9: A bitmap picture behind a form

Using AutoFormat

You can change the format of an entire form by using the AutoFormat feature in Access 2002. This is the first menu option on the Format menu. AutoFormat lets you make global changes to all fonts, colors, borders, background bitmaps, and to virtually all other properties on a control-by-control basis. This feature works instantly and completely and is totally customizable.

When you select Format ⇨ AutoFormat, a dialog box appears, as shown in Figure 16-10. This window lets you select from the standard AutoFormats or any formats that you have created. The figure is shown after you click on the Options button. It lets you apply only fonts, colors, or border style properties separately.

In this example, you can choose the Blends AutoFormat type to change the style of the control fonts and colors and to change the background bitmap. As you select the different AutoFormats, you can see an example in the preview area to the right of the selections.

For this example, click the Options button and deselect the check box for color (turn it off). Then click OK. You receive a message that asks if you want to change the Image in the Form Header section. Select Leave each image unchanged and press OK.

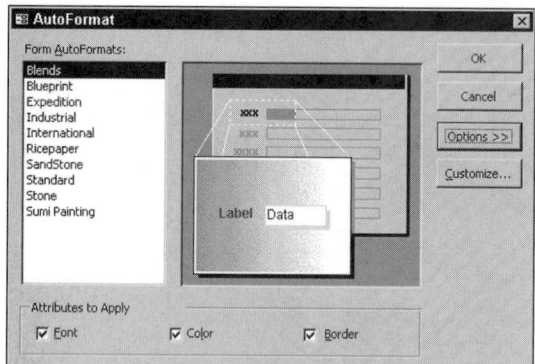

Figure 16-10: Selecting AutoFormat

After you're finished, the controls appear, as shown in Figure 16-11. Notice that the title text size has changed and the shadow box around the Type of Customer has been removed. The reason is that the defaults for these controls are different from what you were using.

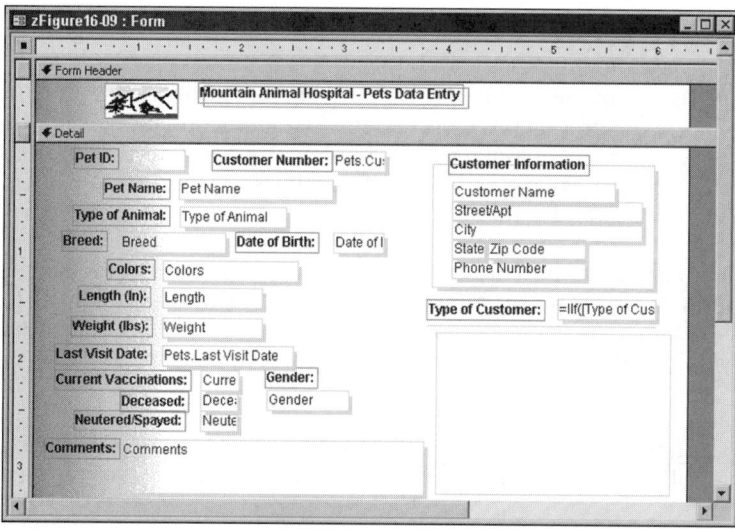

Figure 16-11: Pets Data Entry form using the Blends format

Customizing and adding new AutoFormats

You can modify existing AutoFormats — or define new ones — by creating a form, setting various form properties, and starting AutoFormat. Although AutoFormat changes the look of your form totally, it does its job on one control type at a time. This means that it can format a label different from a text box and different from a line or rectangle. This capability also lets you define your own formats for every control type, including the background bitmap.

After you have created a form that you want to use as a basis for an AutoFormat, select AutoFormat and click the Customize button, as shown in Figure 16-10. Another window appears, as shown in Figure 16-12. This window allows you to create a new format, update the selected format, or delete the selected format.

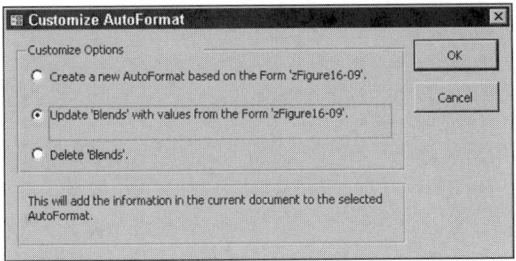

Figure 16-12: Creating your own AutoFormat

Copying individual formats between controls

A subset of the AutoFormat technology is the Format Painter. This tool allows you to copy formatting properties from one individual control to another. To use the Format Painter, first select the control whose properties you want to use. Then click the Format Painter icon on the toolbar (the picture of a paintbrush, next to the Paste icon). Your mouse pointer changes to a paintbrush. Click the control that you want to update; Access copies the properties from the control that you first selected to the newly selected control.

✦   ✦   ✦

Adding Data-Validation Controls to Forms

◆   ◆   ◆   ◆

In This Chapter

Creating data-validation expressions

Using the Option Group Wizard

Working with option buttons

Creating Yes/No check boxes

Making visual selections with toggle buttons

Using the List Box Wizard

Working with list boxes

Using the Combo Box Wizard

Working with combo boxes

◆   ◆   ◆   ◆

In the preceding three chapters, you learned to create a basic form and to enhance it with visual effects to make data entry and display easier. In this chapter, you learn techniques for creating several *data-validation* controls; these controls help ensure that the data being entered (and edited) in your forms is as correct as possible.

On the CD-ROM

In this chapter, you modify your form from Chapter 16 to look like the one in Figure 17-1. If you are following the examples, open either the form you created in Chapter 16 (Pets Data Entry—With Formatting) or the Pets Data Entry Form—Without Validation form in the Mountain Animal Hospital.mdb database file on the CD-ROM that comes with this book.

Creating Data-Validation Expressions

Expressions can be entered into table design properties or a form control's property sheet to limit input to specific values or ranges of values. The limit is effective when a specific control or form is used.

In addition, a status line message can be displayed that advises users how to enter the data properly when they move the insertion point into a particular field. Access can also show an error message if a user makes an invalid entry. These expressions can be entered in a table design or in a form.

Expressions entered in a table design are automatically inherited or used by any form that uses the table. If the expression is entered only in a form, only that form will do the validation check.

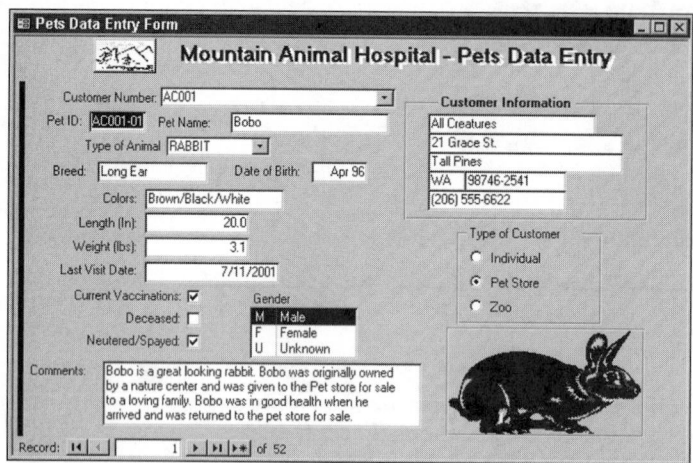

Figure 17-1: The Pets Data Entry form after adding validation controls

Table-level validation

Several types of validation text can be entered into a table design, as shown in Table 17-1. When the user of a form or datasheet moves the cursor into the field, messages appear in the status line at the lower-left corner of the screen. In your table design, you enter these messages into the Description column, as shown in Figure 17-2. In this example, the status line message displays *Enter M for Male, F for Female, or U if Unknown* when the insertion point is in the Gender field.

Table 17-1		
Types of Validation Entered into a Table Design		
Type of Validation	*Stored in*	*Displayed in Form*
Status line message	Description/Status Bar Text	Status bar
Validation expression	Validation Rule	Not displayed
Error message	Validation Text	Dialog box
Input mask	Input Mask	Control text box

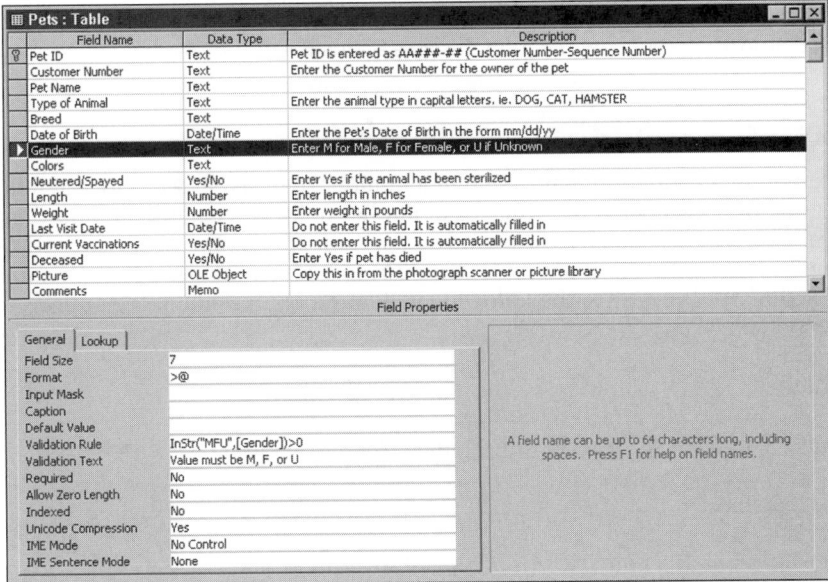

Figure 17-2: The validation properties for the Gender field in the table design

Figure 17-2 is a table design with the Gender field selected in the Pets table. The only properties that are displayed are for the highlighted field, although you can see all the descriptions in the upper part of the Table Design window. *Validation expressions* are the rules the data must follow. Any type of expression can be entered into the Validation Rule property box (found in the Field Properties pane of the table design). In Figure 17-2, the expression InStr("MFU",[Gender])>0 limits the entry to the three letters M, F, or U.

You can also display your own error message in a dialog box when data entry does not pass the validation rule. This text is entered into the Validation Text property box also found in the Field Properties pane of the table design. In this example, the dialog box will display *Value must be M, F, or U.*

Form-level validation

You can enter the same types of validation text into a form's property sheet. When you create a form, the table validation properties are copied into each bound field's validation properties in the form. This way, if you enter validation expressions at the table level, you don't have to enter them again for each form. If you want to override them for a particular form, you can do so here by simply entering a new value for any of the properties.

Note Similarly, when you enter status bar instructions into a table design's Description column, they appear in the form design's Status Bar Text property.

Entering a validation expression

You can enter a validation expression in a number of different ways for each field in your table or control in your form. For a number field, you can use standard mathematical expressions such as *less than*, *greater than*, or *equal to*, using the appropriate symbols (<, >, =). For example, if you want to limit a numerical field to numbers greater than 100, you enter the following validation expression in the appropriate property box:

> 100

To limit a date field to dates before January 2002, you enter

< #1/1/2002#

If you want to limit a numeric or date value to a range, you can enter

Between 0 And 1500

or

Between #1/1/70# And Date( )

Cross-Reference You can use a series of the functions included within Access to validate your data. In Figure 17-2, Access interprets the validation expression used to limit the input in the Gender field as "allow only the letters M, F, or U." The Access function InStr means in string. Access will search the Gender input field and allow only those entries. Chapter 11 details the functions available for validation purposes.

Creating Choices with Option Buttons

Sometimes you don't want to enable a user to enter anything at all—only to pick a valid entry from a list. You can limit input on your form in this way by using an *option button* (also known as a *radio button*), a control that indicates whether a situation is True or False. The control consists of a string of text and a button that can be turned on or off by clicking the mouse. The Type of Customer field in Figure 17-1 shows three option buttons. When you click the button, a black dot appears in its center, indicating that the situation is True; otherwise, the situation is False.

Generally, you use an option button when you want to limit data entry but more than two choices are available. You should limit the number of choices to four, however, when using option buttons. If you have more than four choices, use a list or combo box (described later in this chapter). If there is only one choice, true or false, use a check box.

Option buttons can increase flexibility in validating data input. For example, when an option group control is created for the Type of Customer field it will display a number: 1 means individual, 2 means pet store, and 3 means zoo. It is much more meaningful to users if all these choices are displayed onscreen. Figure 17-1 shows the numerical field input for the control changed to an option group box that shows the three choices available to users.

Only one of the option buttons can be made True for any given record. This approach also ensures that no other possible choices can be entered on the form. In an option group, the option group box itself is bound to a field or expression. In Figure 17-1 all three option buttons and the surrounding box make up the option group. Each button passes a different value back to the option group box, which in turn passes a single value to the field or expression. Each option button is bound to the option group box rather than to a field or expression.

Caution   Only fields with a Numeric data type can be used for an option group in a form. In a report, you can transform nonnumeric data into numeric data types for display-only option buttons (see Chapter 21). You can also display an alternative value by using the Lookup Wizard in the Table design window and displaying a combo box.

To create an option group with option buttons, you must do two things:

✦ Create the option group box and bind it to a field.

✦ Create each option button and bind each one to the option group box.

Creating option groups

In Access 2002, the easiest and most efficient way to create option groups is with the Option Group Wizard. You can use it to create *option groups* with multiple option buttons, toggle buttons, or check boxes. When you're through, all your control's property settings are correctly set. This Wizard greatly simplifies the process and enables you to create an option group quickly, but you still need to understand the process.

Creating an option group box

When you create a new option group, the Option Group Wizard is triggered automatically. Clicking the Option Group tool on the Toolbox and drawing the control box rectangle starts the process. Another method is to click the Option Group button and then drag the appropriate field from the Field List window.

Caution   To start any of the Wizards that create controls, you must first have the Control Wizards button on the Toolbox selected.

Before you create the option group for the Type of Customer field, select the current field and press the Delete key to delete it. You may also want to reduce the height of the picture so that the option group box will have enough room. Use the completed option group in Figure 17-1 as a guide. If the Toolbox and Field List are not open, open them now.

After you have deleted the existing Type of Customer text box control, you can create the Type of Customer option group box by following these steps:

1. Click the Option Group button on the Toolbox. When you release the mouse button, the Option Group button will remain depressed.

2. Select and drag the Type of Customer field from the Field List window to the space under the Customer Information box.

   The first screen of the Option Group Wizard should be displayed (as shown, completed, in Figure 17-3). You enter the label name for each option button, check box, or toggle button that will be in your option group on this screen. You enter each entry as you would in a datasheet. You can press the down-arrow (↓) or tab key to move to the next row.

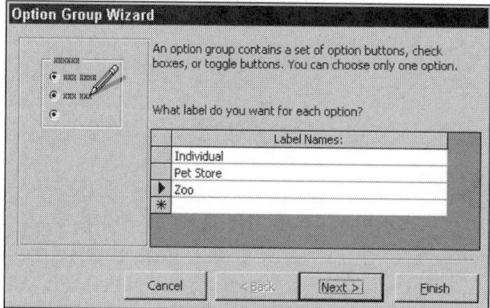

Figure 17-3: Entering the option group labels

3. Enter Individual, Pet Store, and Zoo, pressing the down-arrow (↓) key between choices.

4. Click the Next button to move to the second Wizard screen.

   You use the second screen to select which control will be the default selection. The Wizard starts with the first option as the default. If you want to make a different option button the default, select the *Yes, the default choice is* option button and then select the default value from the combo box that lists your choices. In this example, you want the first option, *Individual*, to be the default.

5. Click the Next button to move to the third Wizard screen used for assigning values.

This screen (shown in Figure 17-4) displays a default set of numbers that will be used to store the selected value in the bound option group field (in this example, the Type of Customer field) along with the actual values you entered. The screen looks like a datasheet with two columns. Your first choice, *Individual*, is automatically assigned a 1, *Pet Store* a 2, and *Zoo* a 3. This means that when Pet Store is selected, a 2 is stored in the Type of Customer field.

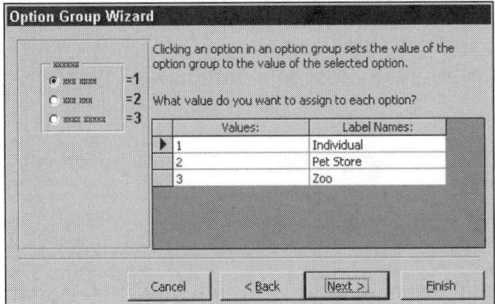

Figure 17-4: Assigning the value of each option button

In this example, the default values are acceptable. Sometimes, however, you may want to assign values other than 1, 2, 3, etc. You may want to use 100, 200, and 500 for some reason. As long as you use unique numbers, you can assign any values you want.

6. Click the Next button to move to the next Wizard screen.

In this screen, you tell Access whether the option group itself is bound to a form field or unbound. The first choice in the Wizard — *Save the value for later use* — creates an unbound field. You use this choice if you're going to put the option group in a dialog box and use the selected value to make a decision. However, you want to store the value in a table field, thus in this example you want the second value — *Store the value in this field.* The Wizard automatically selected it because you started with the Type of Customer field. If you wanted to bind the option group value to a different table field, you could select from a list of all form fields. Again, in this example, the default is acceptable.

7. Click the Next button to move to the option group style Wizard screen.

The upper half of this Wizard screen enables you to choose which type of buttons you want; the lower half enables you to choose the style for the option group box and the type of group control. The style affects the option group rectangle. If you choose one of the special effects (such as Etched, Shadowed, Raised, or Sunken), that value is applied to the Special Effect property of the option group. For this example (as shown in Figure 17-5), again you want to accept the default selections of Option buttons and Etched style. Notice that your actual values are used as a sample.

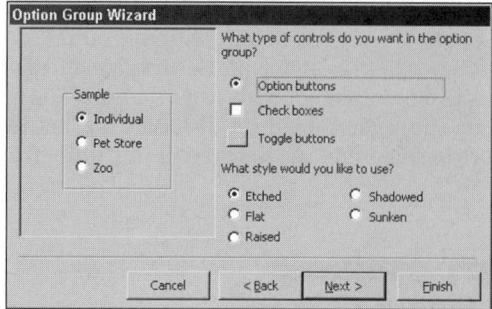

Figure 17-5: Selecting the type and look of your buttons

Note   As you change your selections, the Sample changes to show how it will look.

8. Click the Next button to move to the final Option Group Wizard screen.

   This screen enables you to give the option group control itself a label that will appear in the option group border. Then you can add the control to your design and (optionally) display Help to additionally customize the control.

9. Check that Type of Customer is entered as your caption for the Option Group.

   Click the Finish button to complete the Wizard.

   You may want to switch to form view and test your option group by moving from one record to the next. Watch how the option button changes from one record to the next based on the data that is already in the table. When you are through, switch back to design view.

Your Wizard work is now complete. Eight new controls appear on the design screen: the option group, its label, three option buttons, and their labels. However, you may still have some work to do. You may want to move the option buttons closer together, or change the shape of the option group box as shown in Figure 17-6, or change the Special Effect property of some controls. As you learned, you can do this using the property sheet for the controls.

Figure 17-6 shows the option group controls and the property sheet for the first option button. Notice that the Option Value property is set to 1, the value you accepted in the third Wizard screen. Only controls that are part of an option group have an Option Value property.

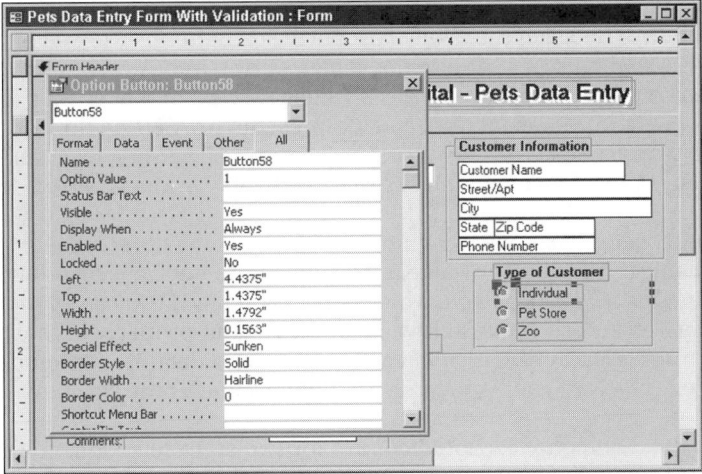

Figure 17-6: The option group controls and property sheet

If you want to create an option group manually, the best advice is *don't*. If you must, however, the steps are the same as for creating any control. First create the option group box and then create each button inside it manually. You'll have to manually set all data properties, palette properties, and specific option group or button controls.

Caution   If you create the option buttons outside the option group box and then drag or copy them into the option group box, they will not work. The reason is that the automatic setting of the Option Value for buttons is left undone, and the option button control has not been bound to the option group box control.

After you finish studying this process, you can turn your attention to the next subject, Yes/No controls.

Creating Yes/No Options

There are three ways to show data properly from Yes/No data types:

✦ Display the values *Yes* or *No* in a text box control, using the Yes/No Format property.

✦ Use a check box.

✦ Use a toggle button.

Although you can place values from Yes/No data types in a text box control and then format the control by using the Yes/No property, it's better to use one of the other controls. Yes/No data types require the values –1 or 0 to be entered into them. An unformatted text box control returns values (–1 and 0) that seem confusing, especially because –1 represents Yes and 0 represents No. Setting the Format property to Yes/No or True/False to display those values helps, but a user still needs to read the text *Yes/No* or *True/False*. A visual display is much better.

Toggle buttons and check boxes work with these values *behind the scenes* — returning –1 to the field if the button value is on and 0 if the button is off — but they display these values as a box or button, which is faster to read. You can even display a specific state by entering a default value in the Default property of the form control. The control is displayed initially in a Null state if no default is entered and no state is selected. The Null state appears visually the same as the No state.

The check box is the commonly accepted control for two-state selection. Toggle buttons are nice (they can use pictures rather than a text caption to represent the two states) but not always appropriate. Although you could also use option buttons, they would never be proper as a single Yes/No control.

Creating check boxes

A *check box* is a Yes/No control that acts the same as an option button but is displayed differently. A check box consists of a string of text (to describe the option) and a small square that indicates the answer. If the answer is True, a check mark is displayed in the box. If the answer is False, the box is empty. The user can toggle between the two allowable answers by clicking on the mouse with the pointer in the box.

Generally, any Yes/No field you create will automatically appear as a check box when you create a form. Sometimes, you want to create a check box to use with numeric or text type data fields. For this example, the Pets Data Entry without Validation form has no check boxes as a starting point.

The Pets Data Entry form contains three fields that have Yes/No data types. These are Current Vaccinations, Deceased, and Neutered/Spayed. The choices are easier to understand if they are shown as a check box (rather than as a simple text box control). To change these fields to a check box, first delete the original text box controls. The following steps detail how to create a check box for each of the Yes/No fields after you have deleted the original controls:

1. Click the Check Box tool in the Toolbox.

2. While holding down the Ctrl key, select Current Vaccinations, Deceased, and Neutered/Spayed from the Field List window.

3. Using Figure 17-7 as a guide, drag these fields just below the Last Visit Date control. (This process adds each of the check boxes and automatically sets the Control Source property to the proper bound field.)

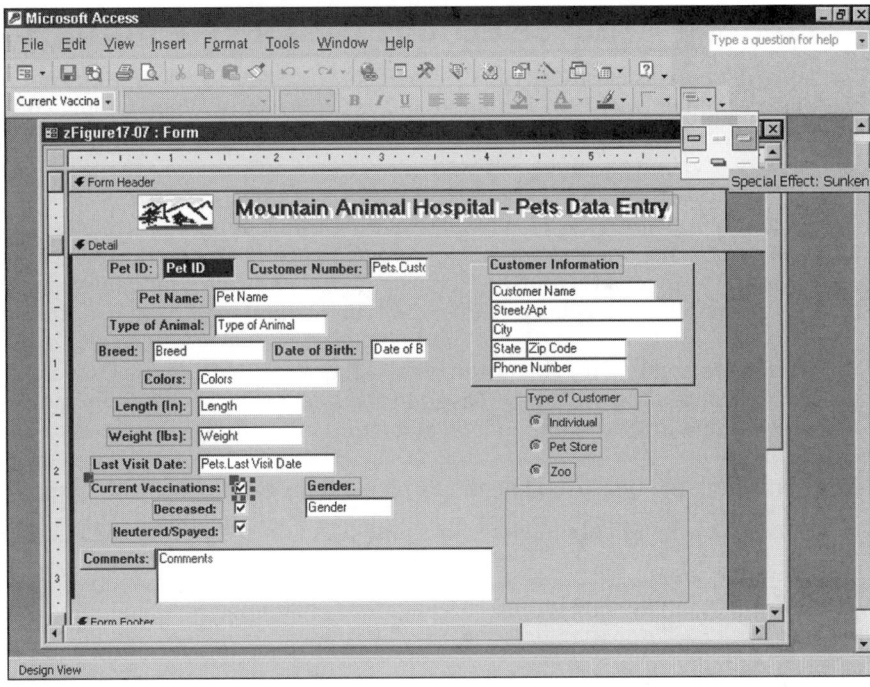

Figure 17-7: Creating check boxes

4. Rearrange the fields so that they look like Figure 17-7. (Move the check boxes to be on the right side of the labels.)

5. Select each label control and modify it by changing the style to bold, adding a colon to the end of the label, and then sizing the controls to fit and align as necessary.

Tip

While you can set the Display Control option of the Lookup tab in the Table Design to Check Box for any field with a Yes/No data type, you don't really need to. A check box is automatically created whenever you add a Yes/No field to a form. You can always change it to another type of control if you want.

Note

Before creating the check box controls, you could change the Default Check Box Label X property to a negative value; this would automatically place the check boxes to the right of the labels when they are created. The value to enter depends on the length of the labels. To save several steps when creating a group of similar-looking controls, change the Add Colon property to Yes to add a colon automatically and change the Special Effect property to Sunken.

The completed check boxes are shown in Figure 17-7.

Creating visual selections with toggle buttons

A *toggle button* is another type of True/False control. Toggle buttons act like option buttons and check boxes but are displayed differently. When a toggle button is set to True (in *pushed* mode), the button appears onscreen as depressed. When it is set to False, the button appears raised.

Toggle buttons provide a capability that the other button controls do not offer. That is you can set the size and shape of a toggle button, and you can display text or pictures on the face of the button to illustrate the choice a user can make. This additional capability provides great flexibility in making your form user-friendly.

To learn to create a toggle button, follow these steps using the Deceased Yes/No field (this example will not be saved in the final form as it takes up more space then we want and no one wants to look at a coffin on a form!):

1. Select the Deceased check box label control and delete the label.

2. Select the Deceased check box and select Format ➪ Change To ➪ Toggle Button.

3. Resize the toggle button to the desired size.

4. Type the text Deceased for display on the face of the button and press Enter.

5. Using the keyboard arrows keys, change the size of the button to fit the text (or select Format ➪ Size ➪ To Fit) and move it below the other check boxes.

Adding a bitmapped image to the toggle button

As mentioned earlier, you can display a picture on a toggle button rather than text. For example, you can modify the button you just created in the preceding steps, changing it to display a picture (included in the sample files). Use the following steps to modify the button for the Deceased field (this exercise assumes that you completed the prior steps to create the toggle button):

1. Select the toggle button.

2. Open the properties sheet and select the Picture property.

3. Click the Builder button (the button with three dots next to the property setting).

   The Picture Builder dialog box appears, which provides more than 100 predefined pictures. In this example, select the bitmap named COFFIN.BMP that came with your *Access 2002 Bible* disk; it should be in the same directory your Access book files were copied to (the example assumes that it's C:\ACCESS2002).

4. Click the Browse button in the Picture Builder dialog box.

5. Select COFFIN.BMP from the C:\ACCESS2002 directory; click the OK button. A sample of the picture appears in the Picture Builder dialog box, as shown in Figure 17-8.

6. Click the OK button to add the picture to the toggle button. The coffin appears on the toggle button on the design screen. You may need to move it on the screen to make it fit between other controls.

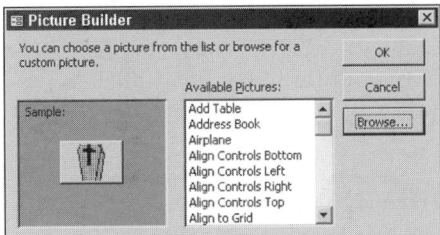

Figure 17-8: The Picture Builder dialog box

Although option buttons, check boxes, and toggle buttons are great for handling a few choices, they are not a good idea when many choices are possible. Access has other controls that make it easy to pick from a list of values.

Working with List Boxes and Combo Boxes

Access has two types of controls that enable you to show lists of data from which a user can select. These controls are *list boxes* and *combo boxes*.

The differences between list boxes and combo boxes

The basic difference between a list box and a combo box is that the list box is always open ready for selection, whereas the combo box has to be clicked to open the list for selection. Another difference is that the combo box enables you to enter a value that is not on the list.

Cross-Reference Chapter 14 contains details on these controls. Review Figures 14-8 and 14-9 if you are not familiar with list boxes and combo boxes.

A closed combo box appears as a single text box field with a downward-pointing arrow on its far right side. A list box, which is always open, can have one or more columns, from one to as many rows as will fit onscreen, and more than one item to be selected. An open combo box displays a single-column text box above the first row, followed by one or more columns and as many rows as you specify on the property sheet. Optionally, a list box or combo box can display column headers in the first row.

Settling real-estate issues

Note   You have to consider the amount of space that is available on the form before deciding between a list box and combo box. If only a few choices are allowed for a given field, a list box is sufficient. However, if there is not enough room on the form for the choices, use a combo box (a list box is always open, but a combo box is initially closed). When you use a list box, a user cannot type any new values, but instead must choose from the selection list.

When designing a list box, you must decide exactly which choices will be allowed for the given field and select an area of your form that has sufficient room for the open list box to display all selections.

Creating a single-column list box

List boxes and combo boxes can be more difficult to create than option groups, especially when a combo box uses a query as its source and contains multiple columns. However, as with the combo box, the List Box Wizard and Combo Box Wizard in Access make the process much easier. This first exercise uses the List Box Wizard to create a simple list box for the Gender field.

To create the single-column list box, follow these steps:

1. Delete the existing Gender text box field control and its label.

2. Click the List Box icon in the toolbox.

3. Display the field list and drag the Gender field to the right of the recently created check boxes.

   The List Box Wizard starts automatically, as shown in Figure 17-9. The first screen enables you to tell Access whether the values will come from a table/query, you will type a list of values, or Access will create a query-by-form list box to display all the unique values in the current table. Depending on your answer, you either select the number of columns (and type in the values) or select the fields to use from the selected table/query.

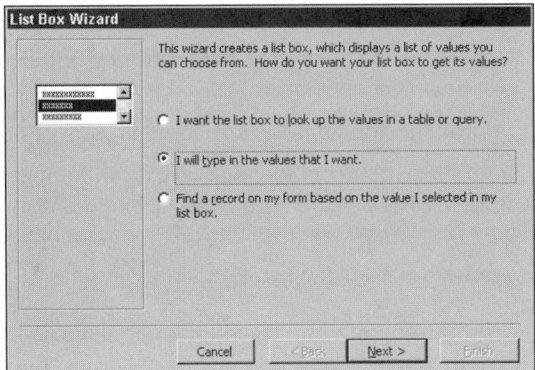

Figure 17-9: Selecting the data source for the list box

4. Select the second option, *I will type in the values that I want*, and click the Next button.

In the second Wizard screen, enter the number of columns to be in the list box and enter the values you want to display in the list. You can also resize the column widths, just as in any datasheet. In this example, you will enter three values in a single column — M, F, and U — as shown in Figure 17-10.

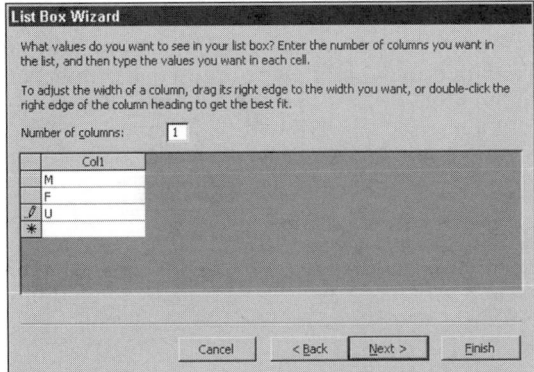

Figure 17-10: Entering the choices for the list box

5. Enter 1 in the box that specifies Number of columns; then click in the first row under the Col1 header.

6. Enter M, press the down arrow (↓), enter F, press the down arrow (↓), and then enter U.

7. Resize the width of the column to match the single-character entry.

You can double-click the right side of the column list to size the column automatically.

8. Click the Next button to move to the next screen.

You use the third Wizard screen to specify the field that you will be bound to. It should currently say *Gender*. Accept this value.

9. Click the Next button to move to the final Wizard screen.

You use this screen to give the list box control a label that will appear with your list box. When you click the Finish button, your control is added to your design; you can optionally display Help if you want to continue customizing the control.

10. Click the Finish button to complete the Wizard.

Your work with the Wizard is now complete and the control appears on the design screen. You need to move the label control and resize the list box rectangle because the Wizard does not do a good job of sizing the box to the number of entries.

Figure 17-11 shows the list box control and the property sheet settings for the list box.

Understanding list box properties

As Figure 17-11 shows, several properties were set to define the list box. The Wizard takes care of these for you (except for the Column Heads property, which adds the name of the column at the top of the list box). Begin by setting the Row Source properties; the first of these is Row Source Type (shown later in this chapter), which specifies the source of the data type.

The Row Source properties are the first two properties that have to be set. Row Source Type determines the data type. Valid Row Source Type property options are listed in Table 17-2.

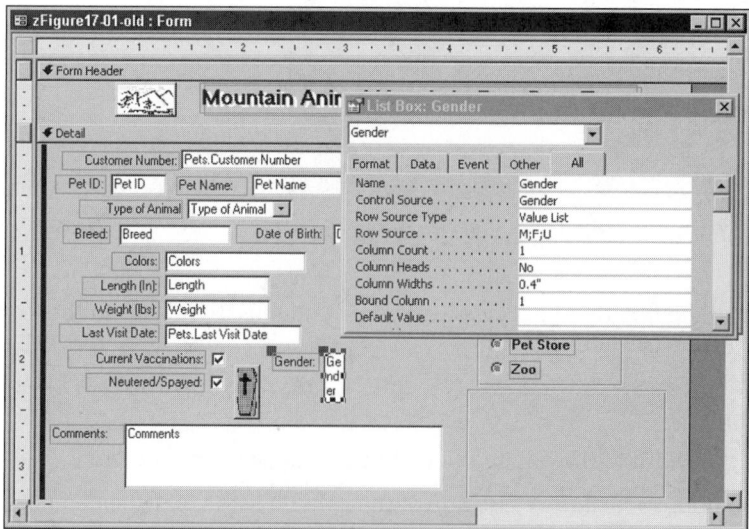

Figure 17-11: The list box control and property sheet

Table 17-2
Row Source Type Settings

Row Source Type	Source of the Data Type
Table/Query	(Default setting) Data is from a table or is the result of a query or SQL statement
Value List	List of items specified by the Row Source setting
Field List	List of field names from the Table/Query named by the Row Source setting

The Row Source property settings depend on the source type specified by Row Source Type.

The method used to specify the Row Source property settings, as listed in Table 17-3, depends on the type of source (which you specified by setting the Row Source Type).

Table 17-3
Row Source Property Settings

Row Source Type	Method of Setting the Row Source Property
Table/Query	Enter the name of a table, a query, or an SQL statement
Value List	Enter a list of items separated by semicolons
Field List	Enter the name of a table or query

In this exercise, you entered values in the Wizard screen. Therefore, the Row Source Type was set to Value List, and the Row Source was set to "M";"F";"U." As you can see, semicolons separate the entered values.

When Table/Query or Field List is specified as the Row Source Type, you can pick from a list of tables and queries for the Row Source. The table or query must already exist. This list box would display fields from the table or query according to the order they follow in their source. Other settings in the property sheet determine the number of columns, their size, whether there are column headers, and which column is bound to the field's control source.

A description of these settings include the following:

✦ **Column Count.** The number of columns to be displayed.

✦ **Column Heads.** Yes or No. Yes displays the field names as the first row. No just displays the data.

✦ **Column Widths.** The width of each column. Each value is separated by a semicolon.

✦ **Bound Column.** The column that passes the value back to the control source field.

Suppose that you want to list Pet Name, Type of Animal, and Breed, returning Pet Name to the field control. You could enter Table/Query in the Row Source Type and Pets in the Row Source. You would then enter 3 for the Column Count, 1.5;1;1 in the Column Width, and 1 for the Bound Column.

Following are valid entries for the Row Source property of a list box with the Value List Row Source Type:

For a one-column list with three rows (Column Count = 1):

M;F;U

For a two-column list with three rows (Column Count = 2):

M;Male;F;Female;U;Unknown

For a two-column list with five rows of data and a column header (Column Count = 2, Column Heads = Yes):

Pet Name;Type of Animal;Bobo;Rabbit;Fido;Dog;Daffy;Duck;Patty; Pig;Adam;Frog

Tip   If you want to use noncontiguous table/query fields in the list box, you should use an SQL statement rather than a list of field names. The Wizard can do this for you automatically. The following is an example of an SQL statement for a two-column list, drawn from the Pets table in the Mountain Animal Hospital database:

SELECT [Pet Name], [Type of Animal] FROM [Pets] ORDER BY [Pet ID];

Creating a multiple-column list box

It's easy to create a list box with multiple columns of data. You could easily go back and run the Wizard again to create a two-column list box, but it's just as easy to modify the list box you already have on the design screen. Follow these steps to modify the list box control to change it to a two-column list:

1. Change the Row Source property to M;Male;F;Female;U;Unknown.

2. Set the Column Count property to 2.

3. Enter the Column Widths property as .25;.75.

4. Set the Bound Column property to 1.

5. Resize the list box control to fit the new column widths.

By changing the Number of Columns property to 2 and setting the Column Widths to the size of the data, you can display multiple columns. As Figure 17-12 shows, there are now multiple columns. The first column's value (specified by the Bound Column property) is passed back to the Gender field.

Note   You enter the column widths as decimal numbers; Access adds the abbreviation for inches (in) automatically. You can also change it to cm or any other unit of measurement.

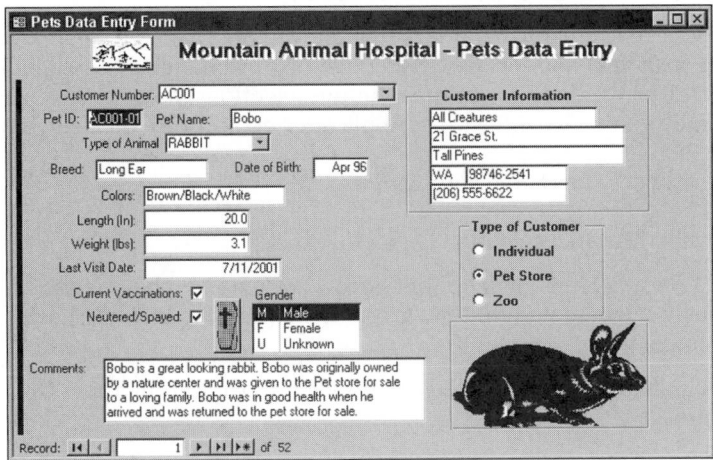

Figure 17-12: Creating a two-column list box

Caution   If you don't size the list box wide enough to match the sum of the column widths, a horizontal scrollbar appears at the bottom of the control. If you don't size the list box deep enough to display all the items in the list (including the horizontal scrollbar), a vertical scrollbar appears.

When looking at this list box, you may wonder, "Why display the single-letter code at all?" You may think that you need it to pass the single-letter code back to the Gender field. That *is* the reason, in fact, for the first column, but there is no need to display it. Data in hidden *or* displayed columns can be used as a bound column.

Hiding a column in a list box

When you create a multiple-column list box, Access enables you to *hide* any column you don't want displayed. This capability is especially useful when a list box is bound to a field that you don't want displayed. You can hide the first column in the list box you just created by following these steps:

1. Display the Properties sheet for the list box.

2. Change the Column Widths property to 0;.75.

3. Resize the list box control to the new width.

When you display the list box, only the one column is visible; the hidden column is used as the bound column. You can bind a list box to a field that isn't even displayed on-screen.

Creating multi-selection list boxes

An option in Access 2002 creates list boxes that allow more than one selection. You can build such a *multi-selection* (or *multi-select*) list box by changing the Multi-Select property of a standard list box. To use the multiple selections, however, you must define a program by using Visual Basic for Applications to capture the selections.

The Multi-Select property has three settings:

✦ **None.** (Default) Multiple selection isn't allowed.

✦ **Extended.** Pressing Shift+click or Shift+arrow key extends the selection from the previously selected item to the current item. Pressing Ctrl+click selects or deselects an item.

✦ **Simple.** Multiple items are selected or deselected by choosing them with the mouse or pressing the spacebar.

Creating and Using Combo Boxes

As mentioned earlier, a *combo box* is very similar to a list box; it's a combination of a normal entry field and a list box. The operator can enter a value directly into the text area of the combo box or else click the directional arrow (in the right portion of the combo box) to display the list. In addition, the list remains hidden from view unless the arrow is activated, conserving valuable space on the form. A combo box is useful when there are many rows to display. A vertical scrollbar gives users access to the records that are out of sight.

In this next exercise, you will change the Type of Animal control from a text box to a combo box by using the Combo Box Wizard.

Creating a single-column combo box

To create a single-column combo box using the Wizard, follow these steps:

1. Delete the existing Type of Animal text box field control and its label.

2. Click the Combo Box tool in the Toolbox.

3. Display the field list and drag the Type of Animal field to the area below Pet Name.

   The Combo Box Wizard starts automatically; its first screen is exactly the same as the first list box screen. You decide whether the values will come from a table or query, or whether you want to type in a list of values. In this example, the values come from a table.

4. Select the first option, *I want the combo box to look up the values in a table or query*; then click the Next button.

   As shown in Figure 17-13, the second Wizard screen enables you to choose the table from which to select the values. By using the row of option buttons under the list of tables, you can view all the Tables, Queries, or Both tables and queries.

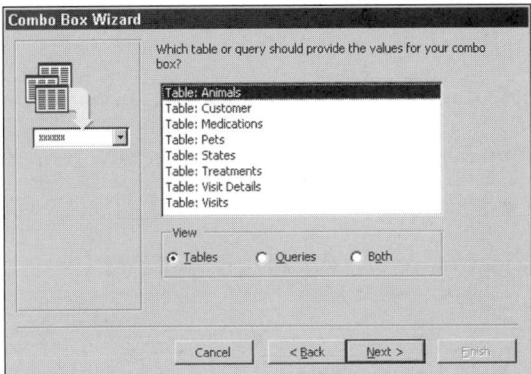

Figure 17-13: Selecting the table for the row source of the combo box

5. Select the Animals table and click the Next button.

   The third Wizard screen enables you to pick the fields you want to use to populate the combo box. You can pick any field in the table or query and select the fields in any order; Access creates the necessary SQL statement for you. The Animals table has only one field (Animals), a list of valid animals, so it is the only field in the Available Fields list.

6. Select the Animals field; click the right-pointing arrow to add it to the Selected Fields list.

7. Click the Next button to move to the next Wizard screen.

In this screen, a list of the actual values in your selected field appears (as shown in Figure 17-14). Here you can adjust the width of any columns for their actual display.

The rest of the Wizard screens are like the list box Wizard screens. First, you accept or change the name of the bound field; then, the last screen enables you to enter a label name, and the Wizard creates the combo box.

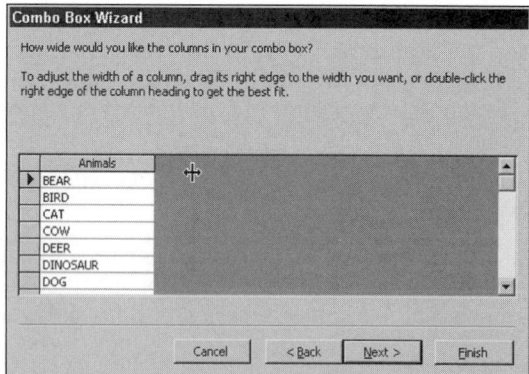

Figure 17-14: Adjusting the column width of the selection

8. Click Finish to complete the entries with the default choices.

Figure 17-15 shows the combo box control in design view and the property sheet for the combo box.

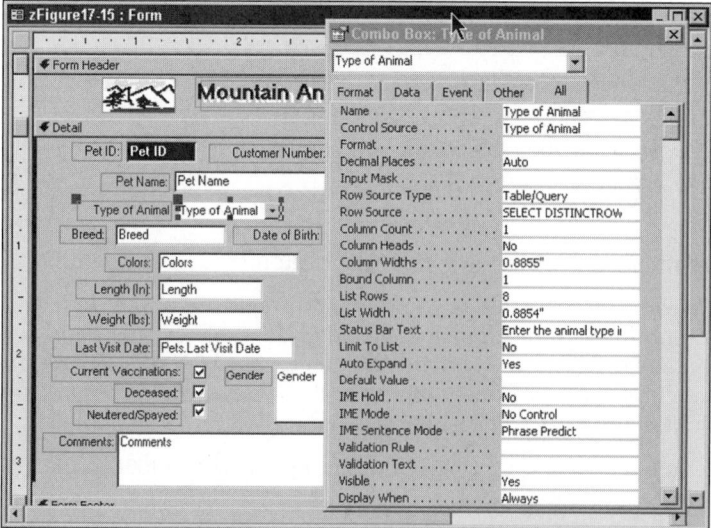

Figure 17-15: The combo box control and property sheet

The Row Source Type property was set to Table/Query. The Row Source property was set to the SQL statement *Select Distinctrow [Animals] From [Animals].* This statement selects the Animal field from the Animals table and limits it to unique values. There are two ways to display the animals in a sorted order: either enter the data into the Animals table in a sorted order or create a simple query to sort the data into the desired order and then use the query as the basis for the combo box. You can also add sorting directives to the SQL statement by adding *Order By [Animals].*

The List Rows property was set to 8. It controls the number of rows that display when the combo box is opened, but the Wizard does not enable you to select this. The property, Limit To List, determines whether you can enter a value into the Pets table that is not in the list; this property is another one the Wizard does not enable you to set. You must set these directly in the property sheet. The default No value for Limit To List says that you can enter new values because you are not limiting the entry to the list.

Tip Setting the AutoExpand property to Yes enables the user to select the combo box value by entering text into the combo box that matches a value in the list. As soon as Access finds a unique match, it displays the value without having to display the list. The default value is Yes for the AutoExpand property. To change it to No, you must do so in the property sheet.

Creating a multiple-column combo box from a query

Just as with list boxes, combo boxes can have multiple columns of information. These columns are displayed when the operator activates the field list. Unless you are extracting fields from a single table — in the order in which they appear in the table — use a query as the data source.

Figure 17-16 shows the combo box you will create next. Notice that this combo box displays the Customer Number and Customer Name in the order of the Customer Name. You will use a query to help you accomplish this task. Also notice (in Figure 17-16) that the Customer Number and Customer Name heads are displayed.

To understand the selection criteria of a multiple-column combo box, you will first create the query to select the proper fields.

Before continuing, minimize the form that you are working on and create a new query after selecting the Query object button in the Database window. The query you want to create is shown in Figure 17-17. After the query is created, save it as Customer Number Lookup. Note that the Customer table is related to the Pets table; the Customer Name field is selected to be used as the query's sorting field. When used for the combo box, this query selects the Customer Name from the Customer table, matches it with the Customer Number in the Customer table, and passes it to the Customer Number in the Pets table. When a Customer is selected, the Customer Number in the Pets table is updated and the correct name is displayed in the Customer area of the form. Thus, you can reassign the ownership of a pet or (more usefully) add a new pet to the system and correctly choose the pet's owner.

Figure 17-16: The multi-column combo box

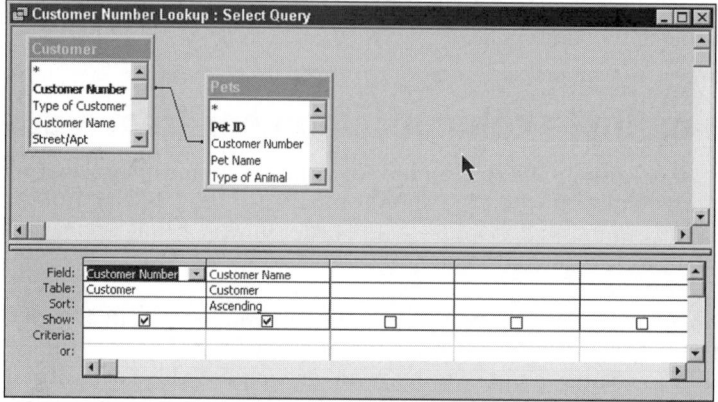

Figure 17-17: Customer Number Lookup query

The query shown in Figure 17-17 is the basis for a multiple-column combo box for the Pets.Customer Number field on the form. Before beginning, maximize the form to work on it. These steps describe how to create this new combo box without using the Wizard:

1. Select the Pets.Customer Number text box, and then select Format ➪ Change To ➪ Combo Box from the menu.

2. Move the original Pet ID and Pet Name controls, as shown in Figure 17-18. Also, resize the new Customer Number combo box control.

3. Select the Data sheet (Data tab) in the Property window. If the Property window is not open, open it.

4. Enter Pets.Customer Number in the Control Source property.

5. Select Table/Query in the Row Source Type property.

6. Set the Row Source property to the query Customer Number Lookup.

7. Set the Bound Column property to 1.

8. Select the Format tab to activate the Format sheet.

9. Enter 2 in the Column Count property.

10. Set the Column Heads property to Yes.

11. Set the Column Widths property to 1;1.25.

If you have followed the preceding steps properly, your Form design should resemble Figure 17-18, and the Form view should look like Figure 17-16.

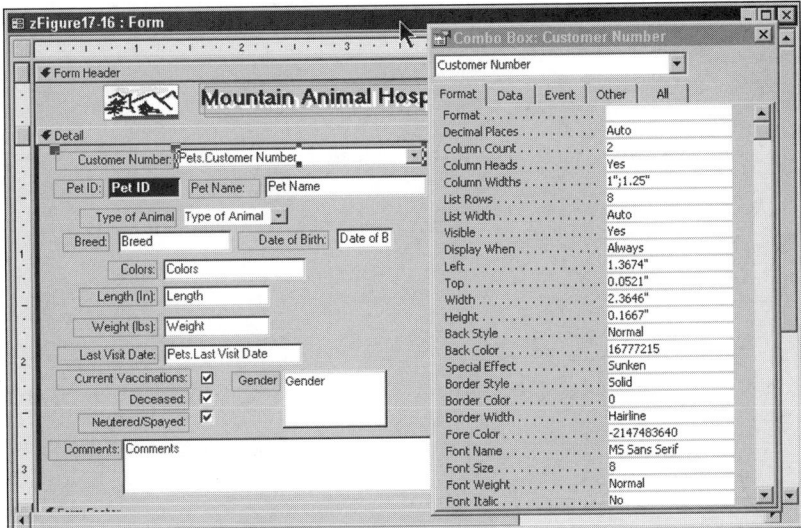

Figure 17-18: A multiple-column combo box in design view

✦   ✦   ✦

Using OLE Objects, Graphs, Pivot Tables/Charts, and ActiveX Controls

✦   ✦   ✦   ✦

In This Chapter

Understanding the differences between bound and unbound objects

Reviewing the differences between linking and embedding

Learning the different ways of storing these objects

Modifying an existing OLE object from your form design

Creating a graph and linking it to a form

Customizing a graph

Using Office integration in Access 2002

Creating an Excel Pivot Table

Creating an Excel Pivot Chart

Using ActiveX custom controls

✦   ✦   ✦   ✦

Access provides many powerful tools for enhancing your forms and reports. These tools let you add pictures, graphs, sound — even video — to your database application. Chart Wizards make it easy to build business graphs and add them to your forms and reports. ActiveX controls extend the power of Access 2002; new features borrowed from Microsoft Office 2002 make using Access forms more productive than ever. In this chapter, you learn about the different types of graphical and ActiveX objects you can add to your system. You also learn how to manipulate them to create professional, productive screen displays and reports. You will also learn how to use some of the new Office 2002 tools that work with Access 2002 forms.

Understanding Objects

Access 2002 gives you the capability of embedding pictures, video clips, sound files, business graphs, Excel spreadsheets, and Word documents; you can also link to any OLE (Object Linking and Embedding) object within forms and reports. Therefore, Access lets you not only use objects in your forms but also edit them directly from within your form.

Types of objects

As a general rule, Access can add any type of picture or graphic object to a form or report. You can interact with OLE objects with great flexibility. For example, you can link to an entire spreadsheet, a ranges of cells, or even an individual cell.

Access can embed and store any binary file within an object frame control, including even sound and full-motion video. As long as you have the software driver for the embedded object, you can play or view the contents of the frame.

These objects can be bound to a field in each record (*bound*) or to the form or report itself (*unbound*). Depending on how you want to process the OLE object, you may either place (*embed*) the copy directly in the Access database or tell Access where to find the object (*link*) and place it in the bound or unbound object frame in your form or report. The following sections describe the different ways to process and store both bound and unbound objects by using embedding and linking.

Using bound and unbound objects

A *bound object* is an object displayed (and potentially stored) within a field of a record in a table. Access can display the object on a form or print it on a report.

A bound object is bound to an OLE object data type field in the table. If you use a bound object in a form, you can add and edit pictures or documents record by record, the same way you can edit other data. To display a bound OLE object, you use a *Bound Object Frame* control. In Figure 18-1, the picture of the pig is a bound object. Each record stores a photograph of the animal in the field named Picture in the Pets table. You can enter a different picture for each record.

An *unbound object* is not stored in a table; it is placed on the form or report. An unbound object control is the graphic equivalent of a label control. These are generally used for OLE objects in the form or report itself; they don't belong to any of the record's fields. Unbound objects don't change from record to record.

An *image control* that displays a picture is another example of an unbound object. Although an unbound OLE object frame allows you to edit an object by double-clicking on it and launching the source application (Paint, Word, Excel, a sound or video editor or recorder, and so on), an image control only displays a bitmap picture (usually in .BMP, .JPG, or .GIF format) that cannot be edited.

Tip Always use an image control for unbound pictures; it uses far fewer computer resources than an OLE control and significantly increases performance.

In Figure 18-1, the picture of the mountain is an image control. The pig is a bound OLE object; the graph is an unbound object. Though the graph is unbound, there is a data link from the graph template to the data on the form. This means the graph is updated each time data in the record changes.

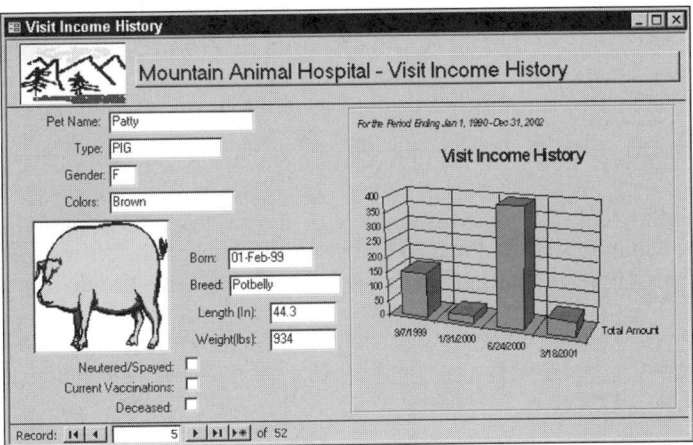

Figure 18-1: Bound and unbound objects

Linking and embedding

The basic difference between linking and embedding objects within a form or report is that *embedding* the object stores a copy of it within your database. *Linking* an object from another application does not store the object in your database; instead, the external location of the object is stored.

Linking an object gives you two benefits:

✦ You can make changes to the object using the source application, without opening Access.

✦ The Access MDB database only uses space for the file path and file name to the external reference.

Caution   If the external file is moved to another directory (or if the file is renamed), the link to Access is broken. Therefore opening the Access form that is linked to the object will result in an error message.

One benefit of embedding is that you don't have to worry about someone changing the location or name of the linked file. Because it is embedded, the file is part of the Access MDB database file. Embedding does have its costs, however. The first is that it takes up space in your database—sometimes a great deal of it (some pictures can take several megabytes). In fact, if you embed an .AVI video clip of just 30 seconds in your database for one record, it can use ten or more megabytes of space. Imagine the space 100 records with video could use.

After the object is embedded or linked, you can use the source application (such as Excel or Paintbrush) to modify the object directly from the form. To make changes to these objects, you need only display the object in Access and double-click on it. This automatically launches the source application and lets you modify the object.

When you save the object, it is saved within Access.

Suppose that you've written a document management system in Access and have embedded a Word file in an Access form. When you double-click on the image of the Word document, Word is launched automatically and you can edit the document.

 **Note**   When you use a linked object, the external application is started, and when you modify the object the changes are made to the external file, not within your database as they are with an embedded file.

 **Note**   To edit an OLE object, you must have the associated OLE application installed in Windows. If you have embedded an Excel .XLS file but don't own Excel, you can view the spreadsheet (or use its values), but you won't be able to edit or change it.

 **On the CD-ROM**   In the next section of this chapter, you use the form shown in Figure 18-2. You can find the form in the Mountain Animal Hospital database file, named Pet Picture Creation - Empty.

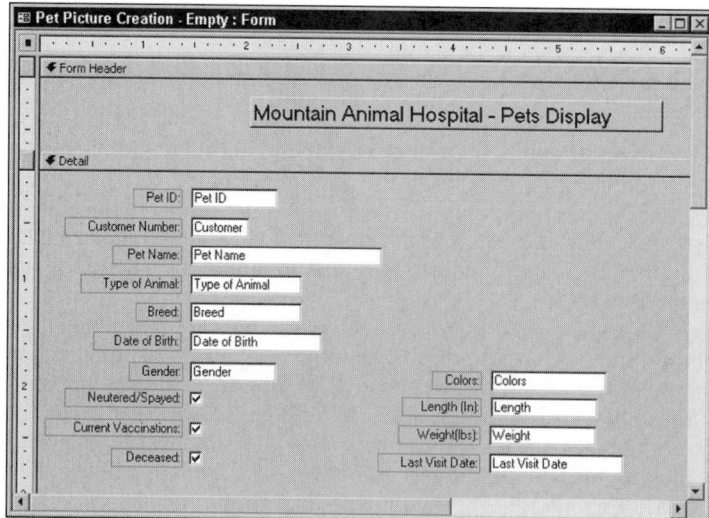

Figure 18-2: The Pet Picture Creation - Empty form

Embedding Objects

You can embed objects in both unbound and bound object frames as well as in image frames. Embedding places the object in the Access database, where it is stored in the form, the report, or a record of a table.

Embedding an unbound object

Access provides two methods you can use to embed an unbound object in a form or report:

✦ You can simply paste an object on the form or report. Access adds an image or unbound object frame that contains the object.

✦ You can add an unbound object frame or image frame and then insert the object or picture into the frame.

Pasting an unbound object

If the object you want to insert is not an OLE object, you *must* first copy in the source application and then paste the object on the form. Generally today most applications include OLE technology and can be recognized by the Insert menu option. Sometimes, you may just want to select an image using Windows Explorer and copy and paste the object to an Access form. As an example, to cut or copy an object and then paste it into an image or unbound object frame, follow these steps:

1. Create or display any object by using any source application like Word, Excel, or Paint.

2. Select the object and choose Edit ➪ Cut or Edit ➪ Copy.

3. Display the Access form or report in Design View and click Edit ➪ Paste.

This process automatically adds an unbound object frame for an OLE object (such as Word or Excel) or an Image control for a Paint picture and then embeds the pasted object in it.

If the object you paste into a form is an OLE object and you have the OLE application loaded, you can still double-click on the object to edit it. For example, you can highlight a range of cells in an Excel worksheet and paste the highlighted selection into an Access form or report. You can use the same highlight-and-paste approach with a paragraph of text in Word and paste it on the Access form or report. You can paste both OLE and non-OLE objects on a form or report with this method, but you'll see that there are other ways to add an OLE object.

Inserting an image-type object

You can also use the second method to embed OLE objects or pictures into an unbound object frame or image frame like you did in Chapter 16. Suppose that you want to embed a file containing a Paint picture. In Figure 18-1, the picture of the mountain appears on the form in the form header in an *image control*. You can embed the picture by either pasting it into the image control or by inserting the object into the image frame (the rectangle that contains and displays the picture). Follow these steps to add an image control:

1. Open the form Pet Picture Creation-Empty in Design View.

2. Select the Image Frame tool on the Toolbox.

3. Draw a rectangle in the Form Header, as shown in Figure 18-3, to add the image frame.

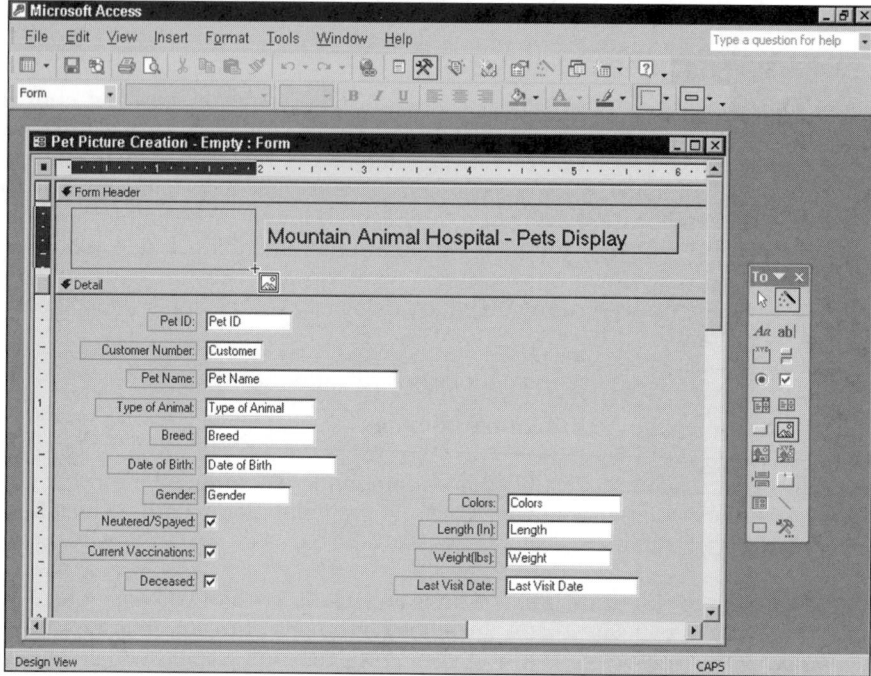

Figure 18-3: Creating an image frame

When you add an image frame, the Insert Picture dialog box appears. This dialog box, shown in Figure 18-4, displays the image objects you have on your system. As you click on each file, a preview of the image appears to the right of the file selection list. If you don't see the preview, select Preview from the View menu in the Insert Picture toolbar.

To embed the existing Paintbrush file MTN.BMP in the image frame, follow these steps:

4. Using the standard file navigation dialog box, select MTN.BMP from the folder in which your other database files reside. (This file was installed when you installed files from the *Access 2002 Bible* CD-ROM.)

5. Click on OK after the filename appears in the Insert Picture dialog box.

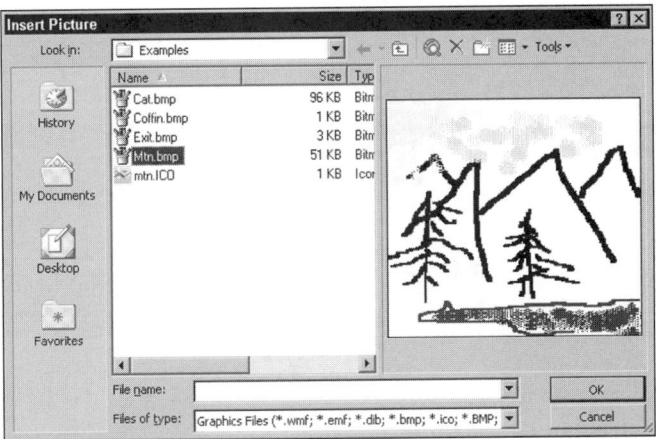

Figure 18-4: The Insert Picture dialog box

Access embeds and displays the picture in the unbound object frame, as you can see in Figure 18-5. Notice that in this figure the picture of the mountain does not seem to be displayed correctly. You can correct this by using the Size Mode property.

Figure 18-5 also shows some of the other properties of the Image control. The Picture property is set to the path and filename of the image you selected. The Picture Type property below has two choices. The default is Embedded and saves a copy of the bitmap picture in the database container in a compressed form. When you save the form and have chosen Embedded, the Picture property will change to (bitmap) rather than the name of the path and file for the original location of the picture. The other Picture Type option is Linked. This setting will maintain a link to the original picture. However, if you move the bitmap, the picture will no longer be displayed and the link will be broken.

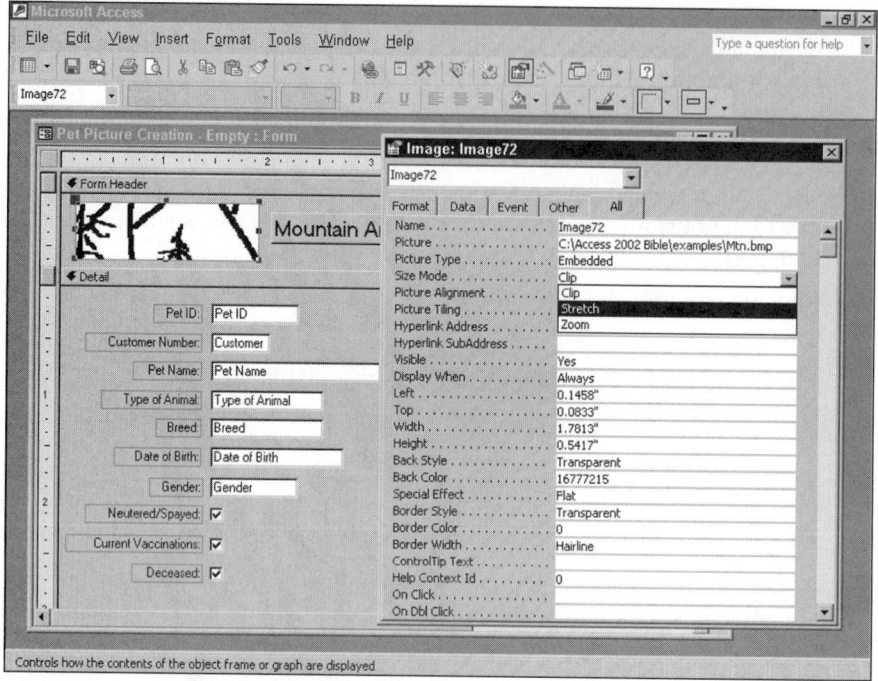

Figure 18-5: The image frame property sheet

Changing the display of an image

After you add an image to a form or a report, you may want to change the size of the object or the object frame. If you embed a small picture, you may want to adjust the size of the object frame to fit the picture. Similarly, you might want to reduce the size of the picture to fit a specific area on your form or report.

To change the appearance and proportions of the object you embedded, you must change the size of the image frame and set the Size Mode property. In Figure 18-6, you see the result of the three choices for the Size Mode property as well as the correct view of the picture:

✦ **Clip.** Shows the picture at its the actual size, truncating both the right and bottom

✦ **Stretch.** Fits the picture within the frame, distorting the picture's proportions

✦ **Zoom.** Fits the picture proportionally within the frame, possibly resulting in extra white space

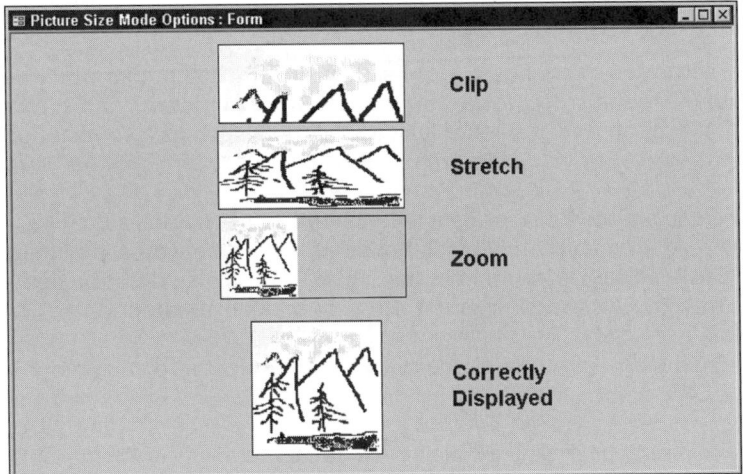

Figure 18-6: Results of using the various scaling options

You should use Clip option only when the frame is the exact size of the picture or when you want to crop the picture. Stretch is useful when you can accept a slight amount of distortion in the picture. Although using Zoom fits the picture to the frame and maintains the original proportions, it may leave empty space in the frame. To change the Size Mode setting for the MTN.BMP file on the Pets form, follow these steps:

1. Select the image frame in Design View.
2. Display the property sheet.
3. Change the Size Mode setting to Stretch.

If you want to return the selected object to its original size, select it and choose Format ⇨ Size ⇨ To Fit.

When you have added a picture whose frame (border) is much larger than the picture itself and you have selected a Size Mode of Clip, the picture normally is centered within the frame. You can control this by using one of the Picture Alignment options, which are Center, Top Left, Top Right, Bottom Left, and Bottom Right. These options are also the same ones used when placing a picture in the background of a form using the form's Picture property. Using the Picture Tiling property, you can instruct Access to display many copies of a picture within a frame. For example, a brick wall is made up of many bricks. You can specify one brick (BRICKS.BMP) in your Windows system directory and then set the Picture Tiling option to Yes to build a wall within your frame. Access copies the bitmap as many times as it needs to fit within the frame.

Embedding bound objects

You can store pictures, spreadsheets, word-processing documents, or other objects as data in a table. You can store (for example) a Paintbrush picture, an Excel worksheet, or an object created in any other OLE application, such as a sound clip, an HTML document, or even a video clip from a movie.

You store objects in a table by creating a field in your table that uses the OLE Object data type. After you create a blank bound object frame, you can bind its Control Source to the OLE Object field in the table. You can also drag the field to the form from the Field List window and it will automatically be bound.

You can then use the bound object frame to embed an object into each record of the table.

 **Note**   You can also insert objects into a table from the Datasheet view of a form, table, or query, but the objects cannot be displayed in a view other than Form. When you switch to Datasheet view, you'll see text describing the OLE class of the embedded object. For example, if you insert a .BMP picture into an OLE object field in a table, the text Picture or Paintbrush Picture appears in Datasheet view.

Adding a bound OLE object

To add an embedded OLE object in a new bound object frame, follow these steps:

1. Select the Bound Object Frame button from the Toolbox.

2. Drag and size the frame, as shown in Figure 18-7.

3. Display the properties sheet.

4. Type Picture in the Control Source property. This is the name of the OLE field in the Pets table that contains pictures of the animals.

5. Set the Size Mode property to Zoom so that the picture will be zoomed proportionally within the area you define.

6. Select and delete only the bound object frame label (OLEBoundxx:).

7. Close and save the changes to this form.

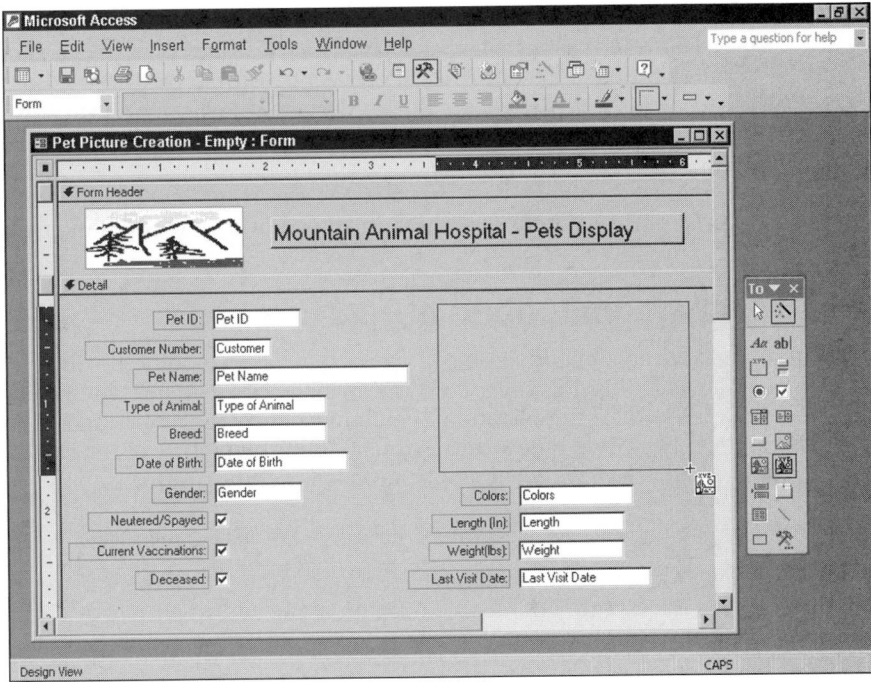

Figure 18-7: Creating a bound object frame

Adding a picture to a bound object frame

After you define the bound object frame control and place it on a form, you can add pictures to it in several ways. You can paste a picture into a record or insert a file object into the frame. You insert the file object for a bound frame in nearly the same way you would insert an unbound object or image frame. The only difference is that where an unbound image frame has a picture inserted in the design screen, a bound object frame contains a picture that is stored in a table, and therefore the picture is inserted in Form view like any other data

To insert a picture or other object into a bound object frame, display the form in Form view, move to the correct record (each record can have a different picture or object), select the bound object frame, and then choose Insert ⇨ Object from the Form menu. The dialog box is a little different. Because you can insert any OLE object (in this example, a picture), you first have to select Create from File and then choose the first option, Bitmap Image. You can then select the actual picture. When you're through, the picture or object appears in the bound object frame in the form.

> **Note** If you create the object (rather than embed an existing file), some applications display a dialog box asking whether you want to close the connection and update the open object. If you choose Yes, Access embeds the object in the bound object frame or embeds the object in the datasheet field along with text (such as Paintbrush Picture) that describes the object.

After you embed an object, you can start its source application and edit it from your form or report. Simply select the object in Form view and double-click on it.

Editing an embedded object

After you have an embedded object, you may want to modify the object itself. You can edit an OLE object in several ways. Normally, you can just double-click on it and launch the source application; then you can edit the embedded OLE object. As an example, you could follow these steps to edit the picture of the cat in Windows Paint or whatever your default application is for editing bitmaps:

1. Display the form Pets Picture Creation — Empty in Form view.

2. Move to record 9 (or whichever record contains Tom the Cat record) and select the Picture bound object frame of the cat.

3. Double-click on the picture. The screen changes to an image-editing environment with Windows Paint (or your default bitmap editor) menus and functions available.

   If you get the message *The OLE object was changed to a picture or the link was broken*, it just means that our pictures may not be compatible with your system. Insert your own picture and try again.

> **Note** As you can see in Figure 18-8, Windows supports full in-place editing of OLE objects. Rather than launch a different program, it changes the look of the menus and screen to match Windows Paint, temporarily adding that functionality to Access. Notice the different menus in Figure 18-8.

4. Make any changes you want to the picture.

5. Click on any other control in the form to close Paint.

If you make any changes, you will be prompted to update the embedded object before continuing.

> **Caution** In most cases you can modify an OLE object by double-clicking on it. When you attempt to modify either a sound or video object, however, double-clicking on the object causes it to use the player instead of letting you modify it. For these objects, you must use the Edit menu; select the last option, which changes (according to the OLE object type) to let you edit or play the object. You can also convert some embedded OLE objects to static images, which breaks all OLE links and simply displays a picture of the object.

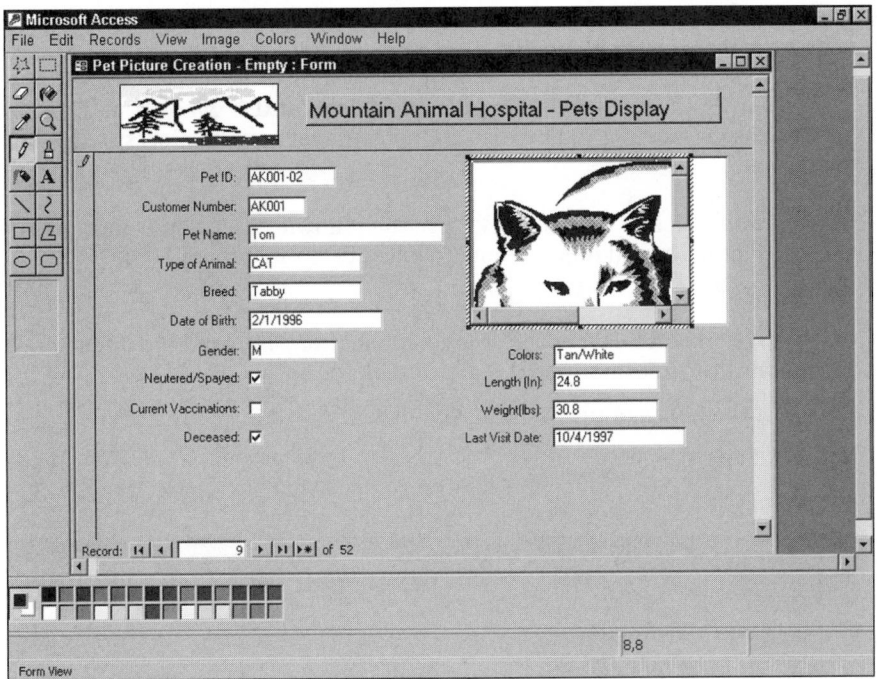

Figure 18-8: Editing the embedded object

Linking Objects

Besides embedding objects, you can link them to external application files in much the same way as you would embed them. As you learned earlier, the difference is the object itself is not stored in the form, the report, or the database table. Instead, Access stores the file name and path to the object, saving valuable space in the MDB file. This feature also allows you to edit the object in its source application without having to go through Access.

Linking a bound object

When you create a link from a file in another application (for example, Microsoft Excel) to a field in a table, the information is still stored in its original file.

Suppose that you decide to use the OLE object field to store an Excel file containing additional information about the animal. If the Excel file contains history about the animal, you might want to link the information from the Pet record to this file.

Before linking information in a file to a field, however, you must first create and save the file in the source application.

On the CD-ROM

On your CD-ROM should be a file named TomCat.XLS, which is an Excel 2002 worksheet. However, you can use any spreadsheet or word-processing file in this example.

To link information to a bound object, use the following steps showing you how to use the Picture bound object frame to link a Pets table record to an Excel worksheet:

1. Open Microsoft Excel or the source application, and load the document that contains the information you want to link to.

2. Select the information you want to link, as shown in Figure 18-9.

3. Click Edit ➪ Copy.

	A	B	C
1	Pet Name	Visit Date	Total Amount
2	Tom	8/23/2000	$180.50
3	Tom	3/2/2001	$40.00
4	Tom	7/12/2001	$50.00
5	Tom	11/23/2001	$572.00

Figure 18-9: Copying a range from Microsoft Excel

After you copy the range to the Clipboard, you can paste it into the bound object frame in the Access form by using the Paste Special option of the Edit menu.

4. Switch to Access and open the Pet Picture Creation - Empty form in Form view.

5. Go to record number 9 in the Access form or the record that contains Tom the cat.

6. Select the bound object frame that you have been using at the top right of the form.

7. Click Edit ➪ Paste Special.

   You may have to first click on the double down arrows at the bottom of the Edit menu to display Paste Special.

   The Paste Special dialog box displays and asks you to choose whether you want to Paste or Paste Link the worksheet. The Paste option lets you embed the worksheet either as a static worksheet (the numbers never change until you double-click on the bound OLE frame to redisplay the worksheet), a picture, or a bitmap (you see the image of the numbers but it's just a picture and has no real data.

8. Select Paste Link and then choose Microsoft Excel Worksheet.

The linked Excel worksheet appears in the bound object frame, as shown in Figure 18-10. Access creates the link and displays the object in the bound object frame or it links the object to the datasheet field, displaying text (such as Microsoft Excel) that describes the object. When you double-click on the picture of the worksheet, Excel is launched and you can edit the data.

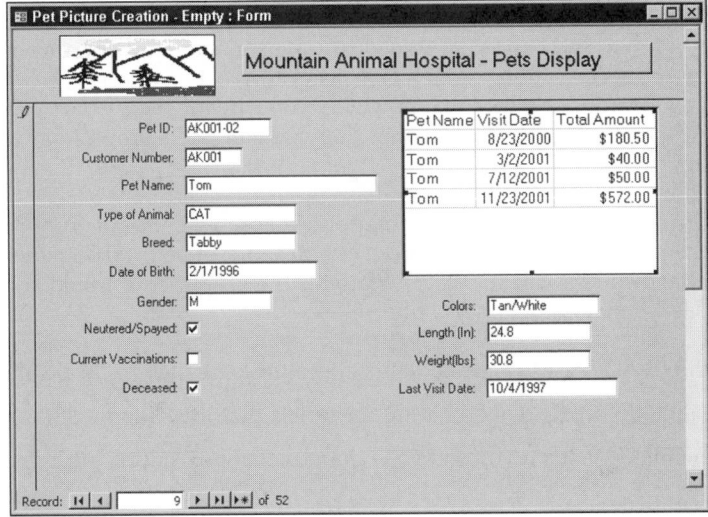

Figure 18-10: The linked worksheet

Creating a Graph or Chart

You can use Microsoft Graph to chart data from any of your database tables or data stored within other applications (such as Microsoft Excel). You can create graphs in a wide variety of styles — bar graphs, pie charts, line charts, and others. Because Graph is an embedded OLE application, it does not work by itself; you have to run it from within Access.

Note   The terms Graph and Chart are used interchangeably in this chapter. Technically, you use Microsoft Graph to create a chart. There are many chart types that Microsoft Access cannot create. These have little to do with data, and include organization charts and flow charts. Since Microsoft Access creates data charts known as graphs, the term graph will be used throughout the chapter.

After you embed a graph, you can treat it as any other OLE object. You can modify it from the Design view of your form or report by double-clicking on the graph itself. You can edit it from the Form or Datasheet view of a form. The following sections describe how to build and process graphs that use data from within an Access table as well as from tables of other OLE applications.

The different ways to create a graph

Access provides several ways to create a graph and place it on a form or a report. Using the Graph form or report wizard, you can create a graph as a new form or report, add it to an existing form or report, or add it to an existing form and link it to a table data source. (To use this third method, in form Design View click on the Unbound Object frame tool on the Toolbox and then choose Microsoft Graph 2002 Chart.) Unless you are already an experienced Graph user, familiar with it from previous versions of Access or Excel, you'll find it easier to create a new graph from the Toolbox. If you examine the Toolbox, however, you will not see a Chart Wizard icon. You must first customize the Toolbox so that you can add a graph to an existing form by using the Chart Wizard.

As a general rule (for both types of graph creation), before you enter a graph into a form or report that will be based on data from one or more of your tables, you must specify which table or query will supply the data for the graph. You should keep in mind several rules when setting up your query:

✦ Make sure that you've selected the fields containing the data to be graphed.

✦ Be sure to include the fields containing the labels that identify the data.

✦ Include any linking fields if you want the data to change from record to record.

Customizing the Toolbox

You may notice the Chart Wizard button is missing from the Access Toolbox. This is an optional item, left for you to add. Fortunately, as with toolbars, the Toolbox can be customized.

The easiest way to customize the Toolbox is to right-click on it, display the shortcut menu, and choose Customize. The Customize Toolbars dialog box appears. Click on the Commands tab. You can then select Toolbox from the list of toolbars and then (as shown in Figure 18-11) click on the Chart command and drag it to the Toolbox. This adds the missing icon permanently. You can rearrange Toolbox icons by clicking on an icon and dragging it to the desired location in the Toolbox.

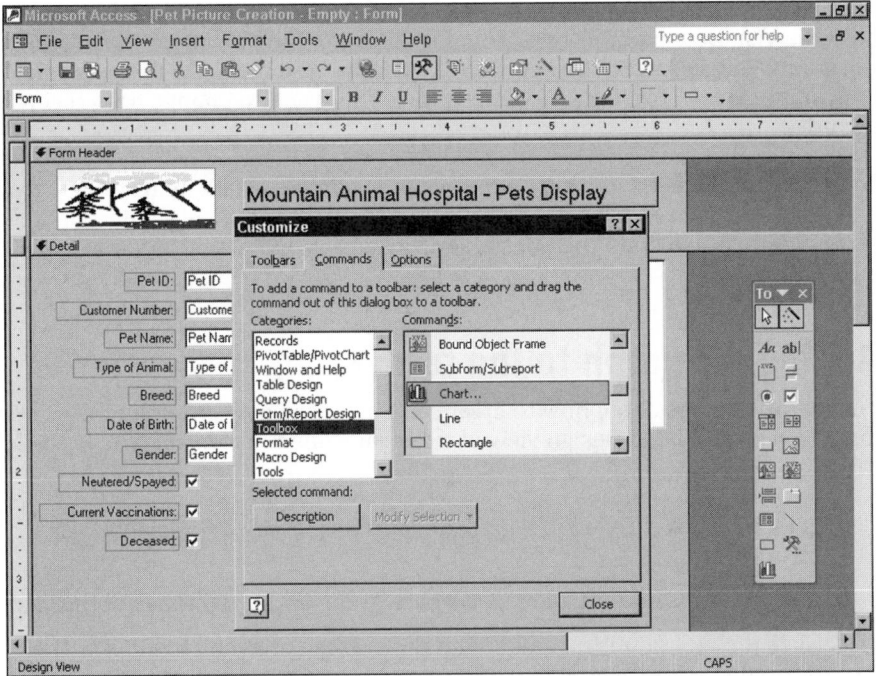

Figure 18-11: Customizing the Toolbox toolbar

Embedding a Graph in a Form

As you learned earlier in this chapter, you can both link and embed objects in your Access tables, and you can create and display objects on your Access forms. Next you create and display a graph based on the Mountain Animal Hospital data and then display it in a form.

This graph (which was shown in Figure 18-1) will show the dates a pet visited the hospital and the dollars received for each visit. When you move through the records in the Pets table, the form will display the data in graph format for each pet's visits. You'll use a form that already exists but doesn't contain the graph: *Visit Income History - Without Graph.*

The form *Visit Income History - Without Graph* is in the Mountain Animal Hospital.MDB database, along with the final version (called Visit Income History) that contains the completed graph.

Assembling the data

As a first step in embedding a graph, make sure that the query associated with the form provides the information you need for the graph. In this example, you need both the Visit Date and the Total Amount fields from the Visits table as the basis of the graph. You also need the Pet ID field from the Visits table to use as a link to the data on the form. This link allows the data in the graph to change from record to record.

Sometimes you'll need to create a query when you need data items from more than one table. In this example, you can select all the data you need right from the Wizard; Access will build the query (actually an SQL statement) for you automatically.

Adding the graph to the form

The following steps detail how to create and place the new graph on the existing form (you should be in Design view of the form named *Visit Income History - Without Graph*):

1. Select the Insert Chart tool you added to the Toolbox, or select Chart from the Insert menu.

2. Position the cursor at about 3-½ inches in the upper-right side of the form.

3. Click the mouse button and hold it down while dragging the box to the desired size for the graph.

   Access 2002 displays the Chart Wizard dialog box you will use to embed a graph in the form. As shown in Figure 18-12, the first Chart Wizard screen lets you select the table or query with the data for the chart. By using the row of option buttons under the list of tables, you can view all the Tables, all the Queries, or Both.

   The following steps take you through the Wizard to create the desired graph and link it to your form:

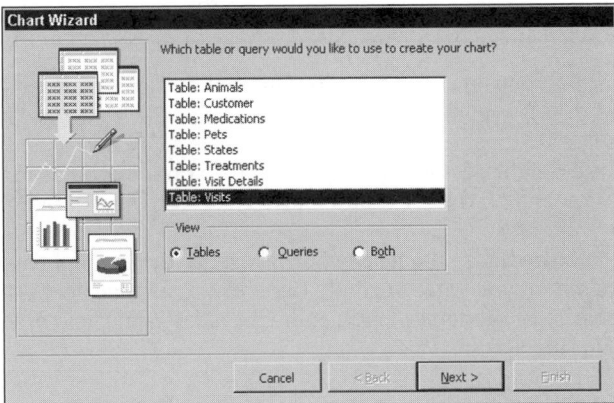

Figure 18-12: Selecting the table for the source of data for the graph

4. Choose *Table: Visits* as the data source for the graph as shown in Figure 18-12.

5. Click on Next to go to the next Wizard screen.

   The second screen of the Chart Wizard lets you select fields to include in your graph.

6. Select the Visit Date and Total Amount fields by double-clicking on them to move them to the Fields for Chart box.

7. Click on Next to go to the next Wizard screen.

   The third Chart Wizard screen (Figure 18-13) lets you choose the type of graph you want to create and determine whether the data series are in rows or columns. In this example, select a column chart; you'll customize it later using the graph options. As you click on each of the graph types, an explanation appears in the box in the lower-right corner of the screen.

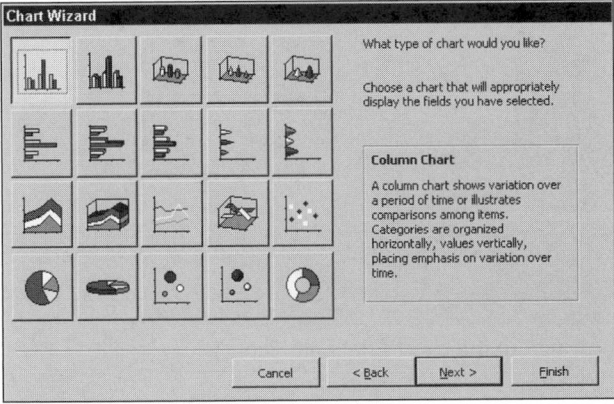

Figure 18-13: Selecting the type of chart

8. Select the Column Chart (as shown in Figure 18-13), and then click on Next to go to the next Wizard screen. (The Column Chart is easiest to work with.)

The next Wizard screen, shown in Figure 18-14, shows the choices Access has made for you but lets you change the assumptions. The Visit Date field has been used for the x-axis and the Total Amount field has been used in the y-axis to determine the height of the bars. If you want to change the assumptions, drag the field buttons on the right side of the screen to simulated graph area.

Note It is important to only choose the fields you will use for the graph if you want the wizard to figure out for you what to graph. Generally, a numeric field will become the y-axis variable as you generally graph amounts. A date/time field or text field is generally used for the x-axis.

For this example, the assumptions made by Access are fine. You may notice (in Figure 18-14) that each of the fields on the <u>left</u> side of the screen is actually a button. When you double-click on one, you can further define how the data is used in the graph.

Note There is a button on the top-left corner of the Chart Wizard that lets you preview that chart at any time. This way you can see the results of your selections.

Generally, the x-axis variable is either a date or a text field. The y-axis field is almost always a number (though it can be a count of values). Only numeric and date fields (such as the y-axis variable Total Amount) can be further defined.

9. Double-click on the Total Amount field on the left side of the screen, and the dialog box shown in Figure 18-15 appears; it lets you define options for summarizing the field. Remember that there may be many records for a given summary; in this example, many pets may have visits in a specific month.

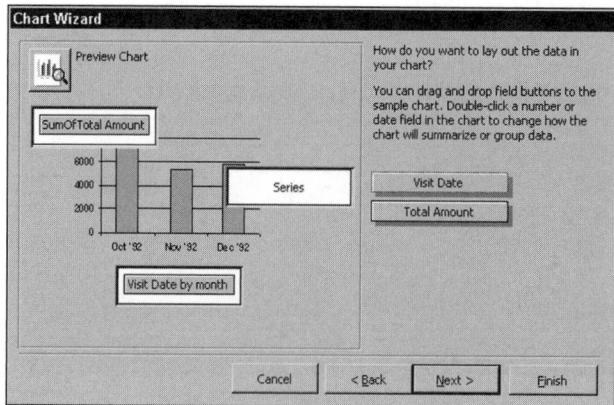

Figure 18-14: Laying out the chart's data elements

Tip

If you had several numeric fields, you could drag them (or any multiple fields) to the left side for a multiple series; these would appear in a legend and display more than one bar or lines in the graph. You can also drag the same field to both the x-axis and the Series indicator, as long as you're grouping differently. For example, you could group the Visit Date by month and use it again in the Series grouped by year. Without using the Visit Date field a second time as the series variable, you would have one bar for each month in sequential order—for example, Jan01, Feb01, Mar01... Dec01, Jan02, Feb02.... By adding the Visit Date as a series variable and grouping it by year, you could get pairs of bars. Multiple bars can be created for each month, each a different color and representing a different year and a legend for each year.

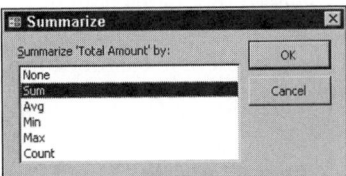

Figure 18-15: Selecting options to summarize the y-axis numeric field

10. As you can see in Figure 18-15, Sum has been chosen as the summarization type. You could change it to Average to graph the average amount of a visit instead of summing all the visit amounts. Click Cancel to accept Sum.

Caution

You must supply a numeric variable for all the selections except Count, which can be any data type.

11. Double-click Visit Date by month, and the dialog box shown in Figure 18-16 appears to let you choose the date hierarchy from larger to smaller roll-ups. The choices include Year, Quarter, Month, Week, Day, Hour, and Minute. If you have data for many dates within a month and want to roll it up by month, you would choose Month. In this example, you want to see all the detail data. Since the data is in Visits by date (mm/dd/yy), you would select Day to view all the detail records. For this example, change the default selection from Month to Day and click OK.

12. After you change the group options from Month to Day for the Visit Date field, click on Next to go to the next Wizard screen.

Figure 18-17 shows the Field Linking box. If you run the Chart Wizard from inside an existing form, you have the option to link a field in the form to a field in the chart. Even if you don't specify the field when you select the chart fields, you can make the link as long as the field exists in the selected table.

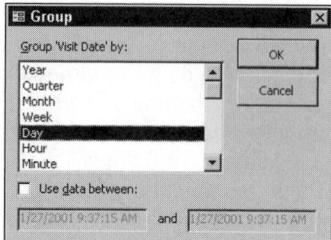

Figure 18-16: Choosing group options for a date field

In this example, Access has correctly selected the Pet ID field from both the Visit Income History form and the Visits table. This way, as you move from record to record (keyed by Pet ID) in the Visit Income History form, the graph changes to display the data for that pet.

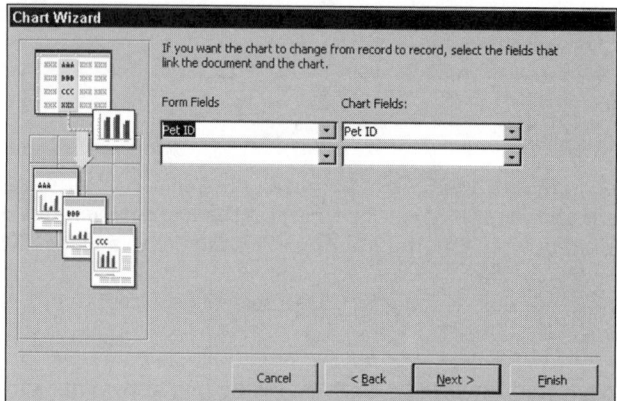

Figure 18-17: Linking fields between the form and the graph

13. Click Next to move to the last Wizard screen.

    The last Chart Wizard screen, shown in Figure 18-18, lets you enter a title and determine whether a legend is needed. You won't need one for this example because you have only one data series.

14. Enter Visit Income History for the graph title.

15. Select the button next to the text *No, don't display a legend* and click Finish to complete the Wizard.

    The sample chart appears in the graph object frame on the design screen (as shown in Figure 18-19). Until you display the form in Form view, the link to the individual pet is not established and the graph is not recalculated to show the visits for a specific pet's record.

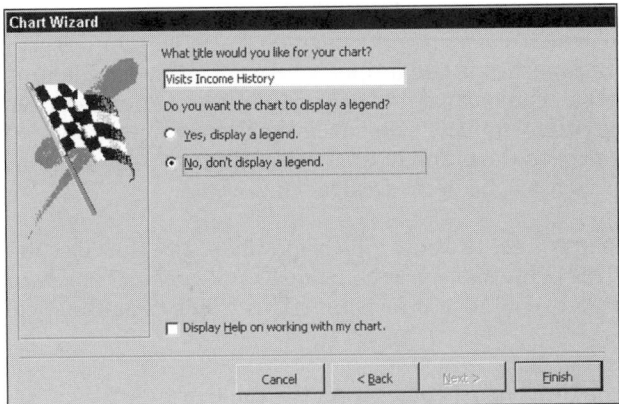

Figure 18-18: Specifying a chart title and legend

In fact, the graph shown is a sample preview; it doesn't use any of your data. If you were worried about where that strange-looking graph came from, don't be.

16. Click the Form View button on the toolbar to display the Visit Income History form and recalculate the graph. Figure 18-20 shows the final graph in Form view.

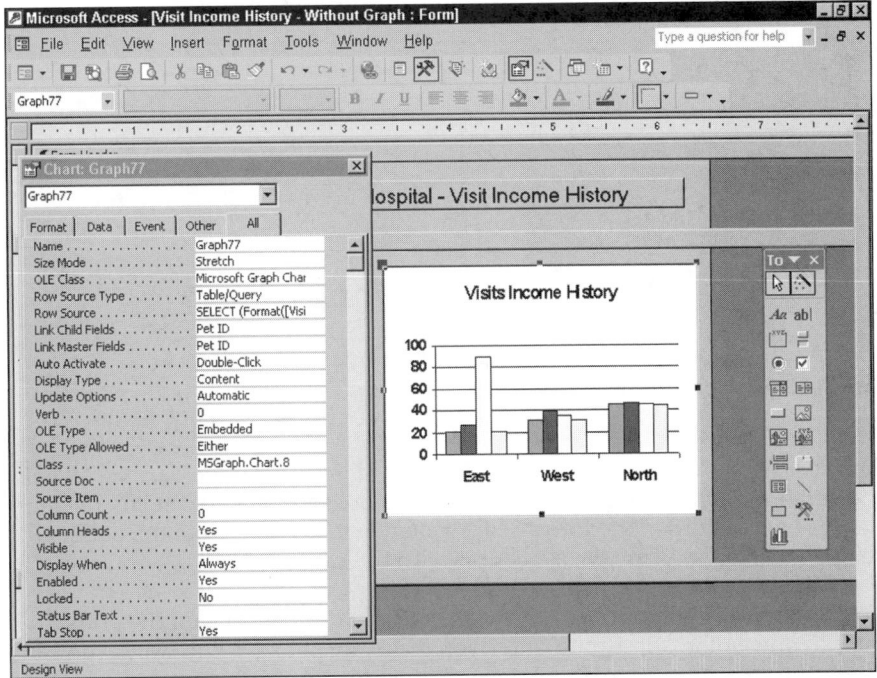

Figure 18-19: The graph in the Form Design window

In Figure 18-19, you saw the graph and the property sheet. You display a graph by using a *graph frame*, which shows its data in either Form view or Design view. Now take a look at some properties in the property sheet. The Size Mode property is initially set to Stretch. You can change this to Zoom or Clip, although the graph should always be displayed proportionally. You can size and move the graph to fit on your form. When you work with the graph in the Graph window, the size of the graph you create is the same size it will be in the Design window.

The OLE Class property is set to Microsoft Graph Chart and the class itself is set to MSGraph.Chart.8. This is the same graph engine as in Access 97 and hasn't been changed in several Microsoft Access revisions. This is linked automatically by the Chart Wizard.

The Row Source property setting comes from the table or query you used with the graph, but it appears as an SQL statement that is passed to the Graph. The SQL statement (more on this later) created for this graph is

SELECT Format([Visit Date], "DDDDD"), SUM([Total Amount]) AS [SumOfTotalAmount] FROM [Visits] GROUP BY Int([Visit Date]), Format([Visit Date], "DDDDD");

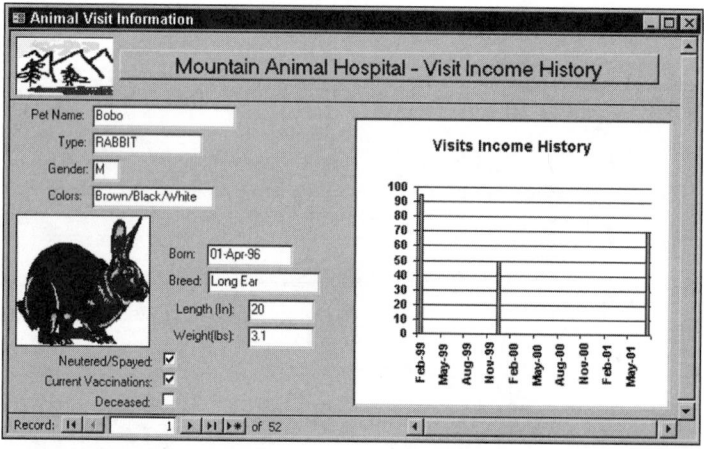

Figure 18-20: Recalculating the graph in Form view

The next two properties, Link Child Fields and Link Master Fields, control linking of the data to the form data itself. Using the link properties, you can link the graph's data to each record in the form. In this example, the Pet ID from the current Pets record is linked to Visit Details records with the same Pet ID.

To change the appearance of the graph, you can double-click on the graph in Design view to open Microsoft Graph. After you make the changes you want, you can select File ⇨ Exit, return to Microsoft Access, and go back to Design view.

Customizing a Graph

After you create a graph within Access, you can enhance it by using the tools within Microsoft Graph. As demonstrated in the preceding section, just a few mouse clicks will create a basic graph. The following section describes a number of ways to make your graph a powerful presentation and reporting tool.

In many cases, the basic chart you create presents the idea you want to get across. In other cases, however, it may be necessary to create a more illustrative presentation. You can accomplish this by adding any of these enhancements:

✦ Entering free-form text to the graph to highlight specific areas of the graph

✦ Changing attached text for a better display of the data being presented

✦ Annotating the graph with lines and arrows

✦ Changing certain graphic objects with colors and patterns

✦ Moving and modifying the legend

✦ Adding gridlines to reflect the data better

✦ Manipulating the 3-D view to show your presentation more accurately

✦ Adding a bitmap to the graph for a more professional presentation

✦ Changing the graph type to show the data in a different graphic format, such as Bar, Line, or Pie

✦ Adding or modifying the data in the graph

After the graph appears in the Graph application, you can begin to modify it.

Understanding the Graph window

The Graph or Chart window, shown in Figure 18-21, lets you work with and customize the graph. As you can see, the *graph* itself is highlighted and each object of the graph is active including titles, axis labels, and even the bars themselves. The data last displayed is shown in the graph. A *datasheet* containing the data for the last record used is also displayed. In Figure 18-21, there are three visit records for the graph.

✦ **Datasheet.** A spreadsheet of the data used in the graph

✦ **Graph or Chart.** The displayed chart of the selected data

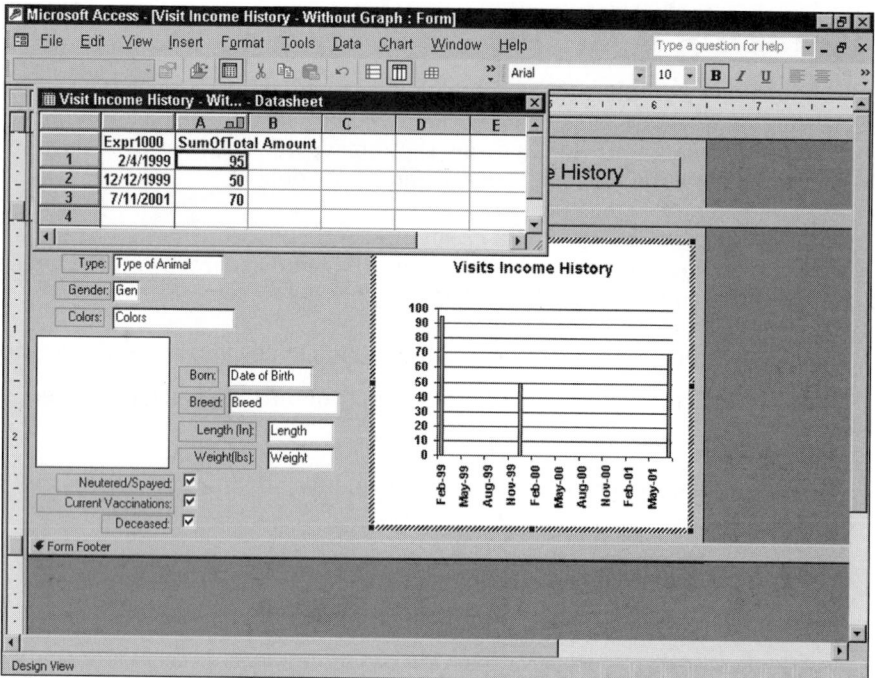

Figure 18-21: The Graph window

In the datasheet, you can add, change, or delete data. Any data you modify this way is reflected immediately in the graph. After you change the datasheet in the Graph window, you can even tell Access whether to include each row or column when the graph is drawn.

Changing data in a linked record will change data in the graph for only as long as you are on that record. After you move off it, the changes are discarded.

More important, you can use the Chart portion of the Graph window to change the way the graph appears. By clicking on objects such as attached text (or on areas of the graph such as the columns), you can modify these objects. You can customize an object by double-clicking on an object to display a dialog box or by making selections from the menus at the top of the window.

Working with attached text

Text generated by the program is called attached text. These graph items are attached text:

✦ Graph title

✦ Value of y-axis

✦ Category of x-axis

✦ Data series and points

✦ Overlay value of y-axis

✦ Overlay value of x-axis

After the initial graph appears, you can change this text. Click on a text object to change the text itself, or double-click on any text item in the preceding list and then modify its properties.

You can choose from three categories of settings to modify an attached text object:

✦ **Patterns.** Background and foreground colors, borders, and shading

✦ **Font.** Text font, size, style, and color

✦ **Alignment.** Alignment and orientation

Note   You can change attributes from the Format menu too.

The Font options let you change the font assignment for the text within the text object, as shown in Figure 18-22.

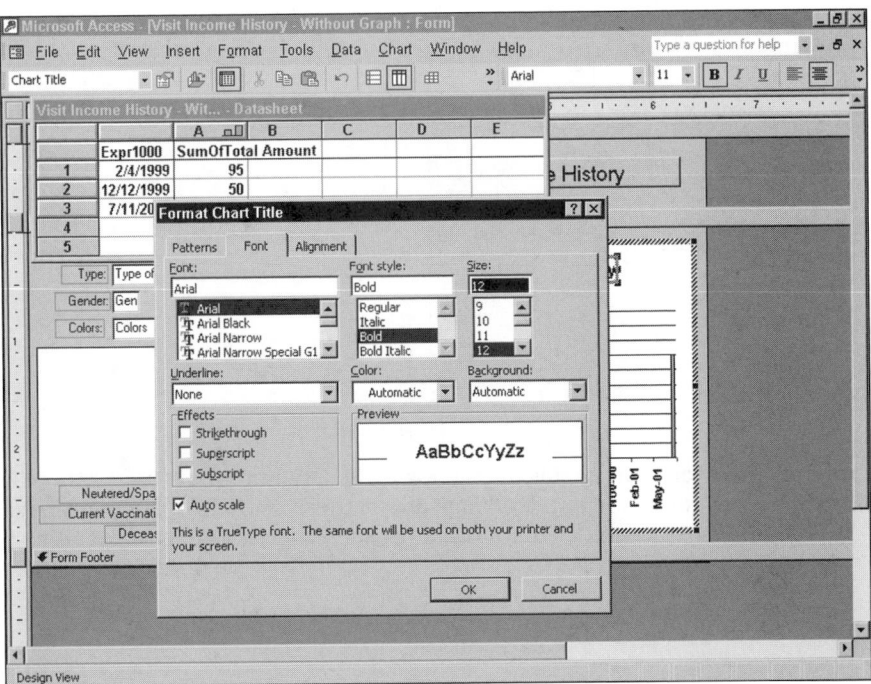

Figure 18-22: The chart fonts dialog box

The chart fonts dialog box is a standard Windows font-selector box. Here you can select Font, Size, Font Style, Color, and Background effects. To change the text, follow these steps:

1. Double-click on the chart title *Visit Income History*.

2. Select the Font tab from the Format Chart Title dialog box.

3. Select Arial in the Font list box. (This is probably the default.)

4. Select Bold in the Font Style list box.

5. Select 12 in the Size list box.

6. Click on OK to complete the changes.

As you make the font changes, a sample of each change appears in the Preview box.

The Alignment tab in the dialog box lets you set the horizontal alignment (left, center, right, or justify), the vertical alignment (top, center, bottom, or justify), and the orientation (a control that lets you rotate your text on a compass).

Figure 18-23 shows the Alignment tab and the options available.

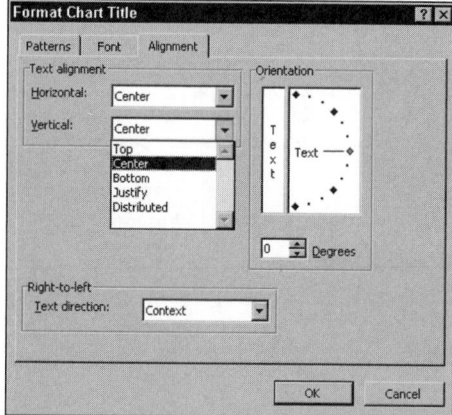

Figure 18-23: The Alignment tab

The most important part of this dialog box is the Orientation setting. Although for some titles it is not important to change any of these settings, it becomes necessary to change them for titles that normally run vertically (such as axis titles).

Sometimes you may need to add text to your graph to present your data better. This text is called *free-form* (or *unattached*) text. You can place it anywhere on your graph and combine it with other objects to illustrate your data as you want. Figure 18-24 shows free-form text being entered on the graph, as well as the changes you previously made to the graph title.

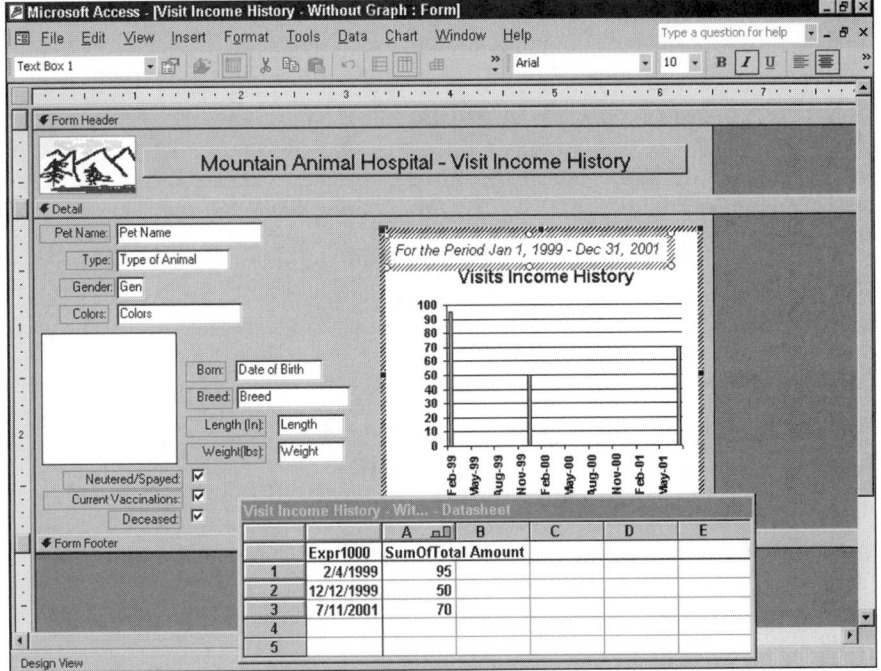

Figure 18-24: Free-form text on a graph

In the next steps, you see how to add free-form text to the graph:

1. Type **For the Period Jan 1 1999 - Dec 31, 2001** anywhere on the graph, as shown in Figure 18-24.

   Microsoft Graph positions the text near the middle of the graph. The text is surrounded by handles so that you can size and position the text.

2. Drag the text to the upper-left corner of the graph.

3. Right-click on the text, select Format ➪ Text Box, and change the font to Arial, 10 point, italic.

Changing the graph type

After you create your initial graph, you can experiment with changing the graph type to make sure that you selected the type that best reflects your data. Microsoft Graph provides a wide range of graphs to select from; a few mouse clicks can change the type of graph.

Table 18-1 shows the different types of graphs you can select:

Table 18-1 Types of Charts	
Two-Dimensional Charts	*Three-Dimensional Charts*
Column	3-D Column
Bar	3-D Bar
Line	3-D Line
Pie	3-D Pie
XY (Scatter)	3-D Area
Area	3-D Surface
Doughnut	3-D Cylinder
Radar	3-D Cone
Surface	3-D Pyramid
Bubble	
Stock	
Cylinder	
Cone	
Pyramid	

To select a different type of graph, select Chart ➪ Chart Type from the menu bar of the Chart window to display the various chart types. When you select any of the graph options, a window opens (as shown in Figure 18-25) to display all the different graphing options available within the selected graph type. Click on one of them to select your new graph type.

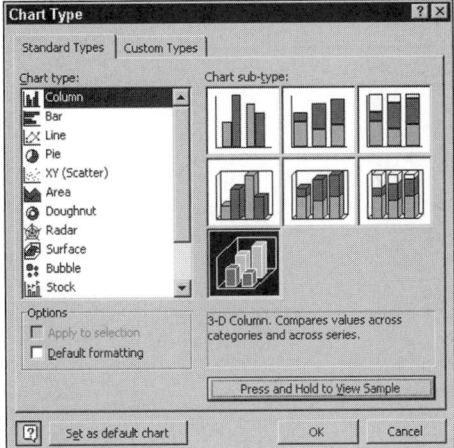

Figure 18-25: The chart types

To display some different graph types, follow these steps:

1. Select Chart ➪ Chart Type, as shown in Figure 18-25.

2. Select Column from the Standard Types tab and select the 3-D Column type.

3. Click on OK to return to the Graph window.

Changing axis labels

You may want to change the text font of the x-axis so that you can see all the labels. Follow these steps to change axis labels:

1. Double-click on the x-axis (the bottom axis with the dates on it). You can see the Format Axis tabbed dialog box showing the Pattern tab in Figure 18-26.

2. Select the Font tab from the Format Axis dialog box.

3. Change the Size setting to 9 points by entering 9 in the Font Size box.

4. Click on OK to return to the chart.

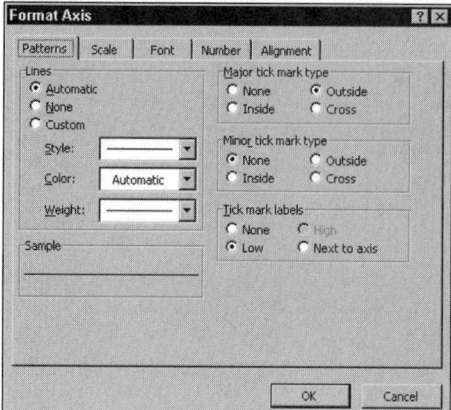

Figure 18-26: The Format Axis dialog box
Pattern tab

Changing a bar color, pattern, and shape

If you are going to print the graph in monochrome, you should always adjust the patterns so that they are not all solid colors. You can change the color or pattern of each bar by double-clicking on any bar in the category you want to select.

The Format Data Series dialog box is displayed. You can change the patterns and color of the bars from the first tab. If you press the Shape tab, as shown in Figure 18-27, you can select from cubes, pyramids, cylinders, or cones.

1. Double-click on any bar.

2. Click the Shape tab, select 4 – Cylinders for the bar shape and click OK.

3. Change to Form View and display Fido the Dog record (should be record number 4) to see the graph change and view the cylinders better. If the graph doesn't change, press F5 to refresh the screen.

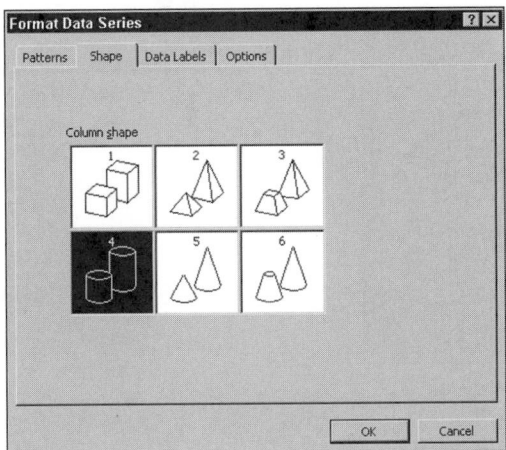

Figure 18-27: The Format Data Series dialog box showing the Shape tab

Modifying gridlines

Gridlines are lines that extend from the axis across the plotting area of the graph to help you read the graph properly. You can add them for the x-axis and y-axis of your graph; if it's three-dimensional, an additional gridline is available for the z-axis. You can add gridlines for any axis on the graph. The *z-axis gridlines* appear along the back and side walls of the plotting area. The *x-* and *y-axis gridlines* appear across the base and up the walls of the graph.

1. Select the graph again, double-click and then click Chart ⇨ Chart Options to begin working with gridlines.

2. Click the Gridlines tab, as shown in Figure 18-28.

Here, you can define which gridlines are shown. The y-axis gridlines are shown on the left wall; the z-axis gridlines are shown on the back wall; and the x-axis gridlines are shown on the floor. You can change the line type by double-clicking on the gridlines when you're in the normal Design view of the graph and working with the Format Gridlines dialog box to change the Patterns and Scale.

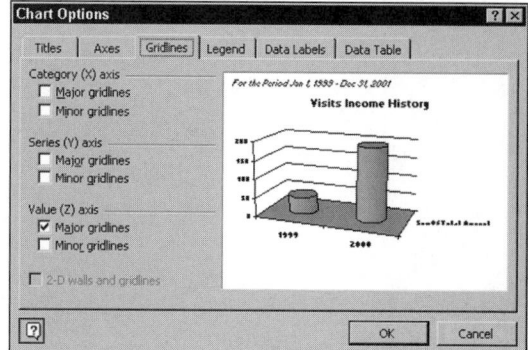

Figure 18-28: The Chart Options dialog box showing the Gridlines tab options

Manipulating three-dimensional graphs

In any of the three-dimensional chart options, you can modify the following graph-display characteristics:

✦ Elevation

✦ Perspective (if the Right angle axes option is turned off)

✦ Rotation

✦ Scaling

✦ Angle and height of the axes

1. Click Chart ⇨ 3-D View to change the 3-D view. The dialog box shown in Figure 18-29 appears. You can enter the values for the various settings or use the six buttons to rotate the icon of the graph in real time. When you see the view you like, click on OK and your chart will change to that perspective.

Note   The Elevation buttons control the height at which you view the data. The elevation is measured in degrees; it can range from –90 to 90 degrees.

An elevation of zero displays the graph as if you were level with the center of the graph. An elevation of 90 degrees shows the graph as you would view it from above center. A –90-degree elevation shows the graph as you would view it from below its center.

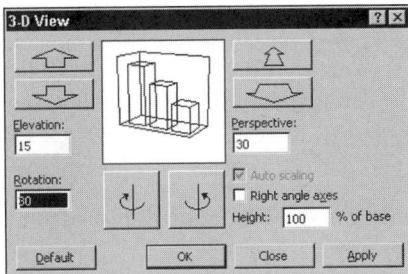

Figure 18-29: The 3-D View dialog box

The Perspective buttons control the amount of perspective in your graph. Adding more perspective makes the data markers at the back of the graph smaller than those at the front of the graph. This option provides a sense of distance; the smaller data markers seem farther away. If your graph contains a large amount of data, you may want to use a larger perspective value (the ratio of the front of the graph to the back of the graph). This value can range from 0 to 100.

A perspective of 0 makes the back edge of the graph equal in width to the front edge. You can experiment with these settings until you get the effect you need.

The Rotation buttons control the rotation of the entire plotting area. The rotation is measured in degrees, from 0 to 360. A rotation of 0 displays your graph as you view it from directly in front. A rotation of 180 degrees displays the graph as if you were viewing it from the back. (This setting visually reverses the plotting order of your data series.) A rotation of 90 degrees displays your graph as if you were viewing it from the center of the side wall.

2. Change the rotation from 20 to 30 degrees by pressing the left rotation button once.

The Auto scaling check box lets you scale a three-dimensional graph so that its size is closer to that of the two-dimensional graph using the same data. To activate this option, click on the Auto scaling check box so that the X appears in the box. When this option is kept activated, Access will scale the graph automatically whenever you switch from a two-dimensional to a three-dimensional graph.

Two options within the 3-D View dialog box pertain specifically to display of the axes. The Right angle axes check box lets you control the orientation of the axes. If the check box is on, all axes are displayed at right angles to each other.

Caution   If the Right angle axes check box is selected, you cannot specify the perspective for the three-dimensional view.

The Height box contains the height of the z-axis and walls relative to the width of the graph's base. The height is measured as a percentage of the x-axis length. A height of 100 percent makes the height equal to the x-axis. A height of 50 percent makes the height half the x-axis length. You can set this height percentage at more than 100 percent; by doing so, you can make the height of the z-axis greater than the length of the x-axis.

Caution   If you change the Height setting, your change will not be displayed in the sample graph shown in the 3-D View dialog box.

After you have made the desired changes, you can select File ➪ Exit and then select Return to (which will bring you back to the Form Design screen). You may just see the buttons OK, Close, or Apply, which will do the same thing.

You might want to make one more change: A graph frame is really an unbound object frame, and you can change its border type and background (as you can for any unbound object frame). Figure 18-30 shows the final graph after the border has been changed to an etched special effect, and the background colored light gray or made transparent to match the background of the form. This allows the graph to stand out more than it would if you used a sunken white background. Figure 18-30 shows the Flower the Cat record.

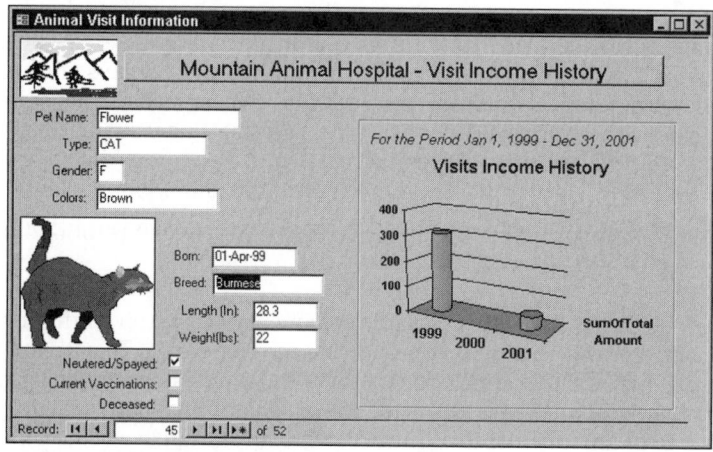

Figure 18-30: The final graph

Integration with Microsoft Office

Access 2002 is not only integrated with Windows, it now shares many major components with Microsoft Office 2002. (If you are an Excel 2002 or Word 2002 user, you will be especially thrilled.) Access 2002 has an integrated Spell Checker that is used to make sure that the data stored in Access 2002 tables and database objects is spelled correctly. The dictionary is shared across all Office 2002 applications. There are also specific technical dictionaries for legal, medical, and foreign languages and also several custom dictionaries that you can maintain to store your own technical words. Access 2002 also shares the Office 2002 AutoCorrect features to fix errors while you type.

Checking the spelling of one or more fields and records

You can check the spelling of your data in either Form or Datasheet view. In Form view, you can spell-check only a single record — and field within the record — at a time. To check the spelling of data in Form view, you would select the field or text containing spelling you want to check, and then click on the Spell Check toolbar button (the icon with the check mark and the small letters ABC above it).

When you click on the icon, Access checks the field (or selected text within the field) for spelling, as shown in Figure 18-31.

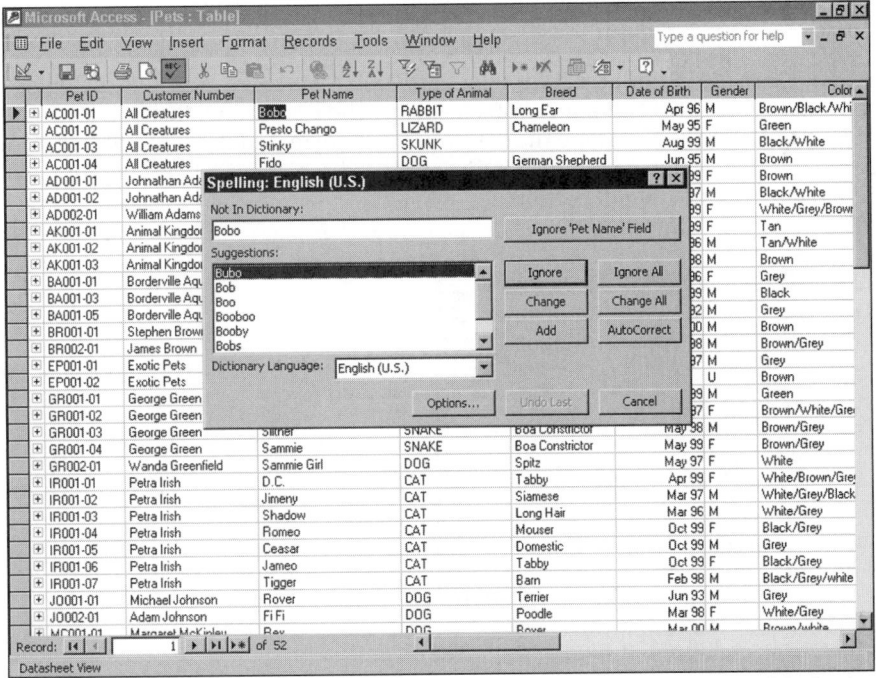

Figure 18-31: Spell-checking in Access

In the Spelling dialog box that appears, you can click on Add if you want to add the word in the Not In Dictionary: box to the custom dictionary.

You can select only one field at a time in Form view. You'll probably want to use only Form view to spell-check selected memo data. To select multiple fields or records, you must switch to Datasheet view. To check the spelling of data in Datasheet view, you would select the records, columns, fields, or text within a field containing spelling you want to check and then click on the Spell Check icon.

You can also check the spelling in a table, query, or form in the Database window by clicking on the table, query, or form object containing spelling you want to check.

You only spell-check the data inside the objects. Access 2002 cannot spell-check control names.

Correcting your typing automatically when entering data

You can use the AutoCorrect feature to provide automatic corrections to text you frequently mistype and to replace abbreviations with the long names they stand for (also automatically). For example, you can create an entry "mah" for Mountain Animal Hospital. Whenever you type mah followed by a space or punctuation mark, Microsoft Access replaces *mah* with the text *Mountain Animal Hospital*.

You can activate AutoCorrect by selecting Tools ➪ AutoCorrect. The dialog box shown in Figure 18-32 appears. You can select the Replace text as you type check box. In the Replace box, type the text you want corrected. In the With box, type the corrected text. When you click on Add, the word replacement combination will be added to the AutoCorrect dictionary.

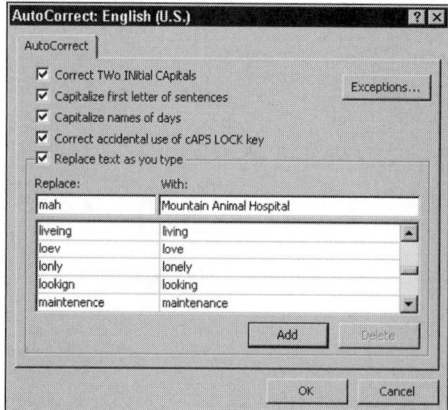

Figure 18-32: Using AutoCorrect in Access 2002

AutoCorrect won't correct text that was typed before you selected the Replace text as you type check box.

Using OLE automation with Office 2002

Access 2002 takes advantage of drag and drop; you can do it from a Datasheet view across Excel and Word. You can instantly create a table in a Word document (or add a table to an Excel spreadsheet) by simply copying and pasting (or dragging and dropping) data from an Access datasheet to a Word document or an Excel spreadsheet. (Obviously, you must have Word or Excel to take advantage of these features.)

Creating an Excel type Pivot Table

Access 2002 contains a PivotTable Wizard to create Excel PivotTables based on Access tables or queries. A *PivotTable* is like a cross-tabulation of your data; you can define the data values for rows, columns, pages, and summarization. Figure 18-33 shows a conceptual figure of a PivotTable.

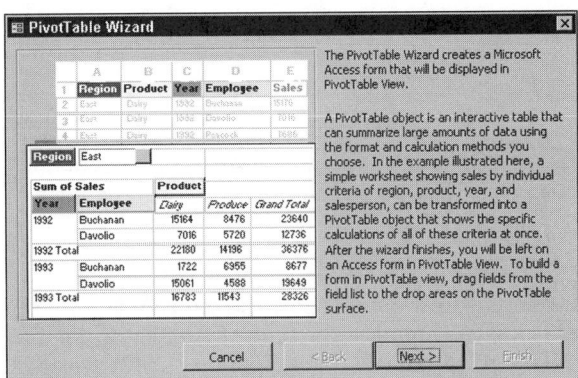

Figure 18-33: A conceptual view of a PivotTable displayed when you start the form PivotTable Wizard

A PivotTable can have multiple levels of rows, columns, and even pages. As you can see in the conceptual figure, the center of the table contains numeric data; the rows and columns form a hierarchy of unique data. In this figure, dates and employees are the row hierarchies, along with multiple levels of subtotals. The column headers are types of products, and each page of the PivotTable is a different region.

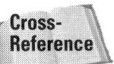
Cross-Reference   A PivotTable is like a cross-tab query (see Chapter 23) but much more powerful.

Before you begin creating a pivot table, you should make sure you can display a simple datasheet containing the data you want to analyze. Figure 18-34 shows a query using the Customers, Pets, Visits, and Visits Details tables in order to create an analysis of sales.

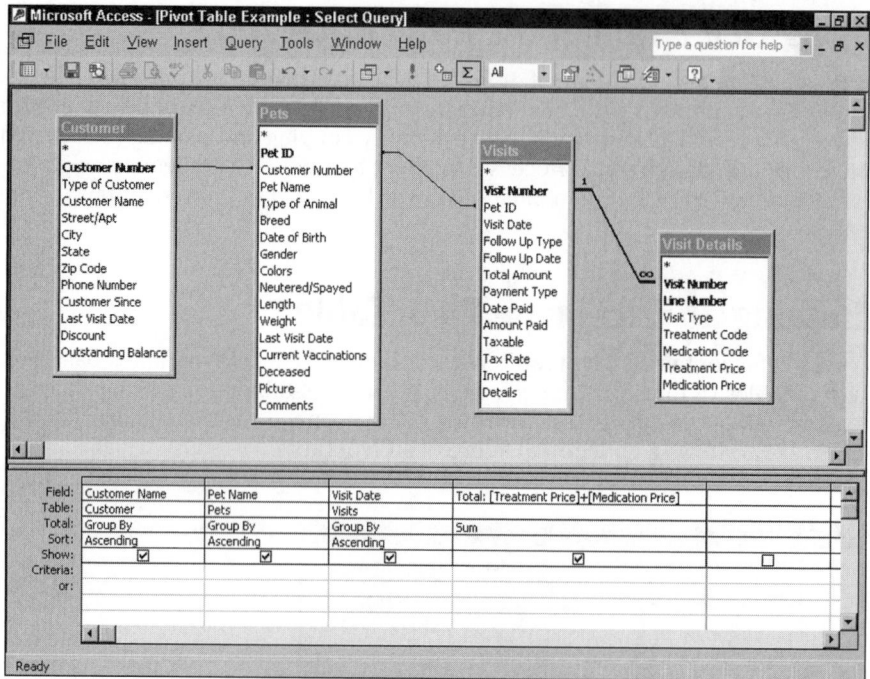

Figure 18-34: A query combining data from the Customers, Pets, Visits, and Visits Details tables

Once you have created your query, you should display the datasheet to make sure the data you expect to see is displayed and that the type of data lends itself to Pivot Table analysis. Since the idea of a pivot table is to manipulate or pivot various categorization data, there should be many different groupings of data. As you can see in Figure 18-35, the data is perfect for pivot table analysis. There are many customers, each having several parts, who each have several visits where there is a total charge for the treatment and medication of each visit.

Once the data is reviewed, you can create your pivot table. You start creating a PivotTable from the New Form dialog box using the PivotTable Wizard selection from the list of standard Wizards you can select as you can see in Figure 18-36. Notice the query you just created, *Pivot Table Example,* has been selected as the data source.

Customer Name	Pet Name	Visit Date	Total
▶ Adam Johnson	Fi Fi	5/9/1999	$167.80
All Creatures	Bobo	2/4/1999	$95.00
All Creatures	Bobo	7/11/2001	$120.00
All Creatures	Fido	11/3/1999	$45.00
All Creatures	Fido	11/12/2000	$197.00
All Creatures	Presto Chango	11/6/1999	$20.00
All Creatures	Presto Chango	2/3/2001	$501.00
All Creatures	Presto Chango	8/26/2001	$50.00
All Creatures	Stinky	2/8/2001	$95.00
Animal Kingdom	Jerry	3/2/1999	$32.00
Animal Kingdom	Jerry	5/7/1999	$17.00
Animal Kingdom	Jerry	7/28/1999	$109.00
Animal Kingdom	Margo	10/12/1999	$180.50
Animal Kingdom	Margo	11/19/1999	$40.00
Animal Kingdom	Margo	1/6/2000	$50.00
Animal Kingdom	Margo	5/21/2001	$320.00
Animal Kingdom	Margo	7/11/2001	$572.00
Animal Kingdom	Tom	5/22/1996	$101.50
Animal Kingdom	Tom	10/4/1997	$26.00
Anita Zimmerman	Midnight	2/22/1998	$50.00
Barbara Williamson	Benjamin	4/22/1999	$50.00
Barbara Williamson	Hoppi	3/1/2001	$50.00
George Green	Adam	8/13/1999	$50.00
George Green	Adam	10/23/1999	$130.00

Record: I◄ ◄ | 1 | ► ►I ►* of 76

Figure 18-35: A datasheet displaying data from the Customers, Pets, Visits, and Visits Details tables

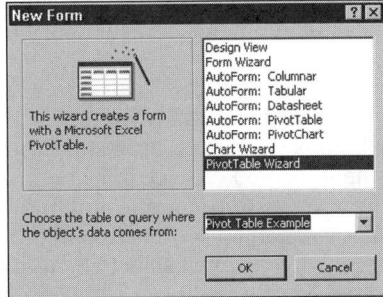

Figure 18-36: The New Form dialog box showing the PivotTable Wizard selected and the Pivot Table Example query being used as the data source

After you begin the PivotTable Wizard process, you will first see an introductory screen explaining how a PivotTable works (Figure 18-33). After you view this screen, press the Next button. Figure 18-37 displays the table/queries dialog box. You have already selected the *Query: Pivot Table Example*. In this example, since the query only selected the four fields you want to use for the PivotTable, you can select all of the fields in the *Available Fields* list box which moves them to the *Fields Chosen for Pivoting* list box.

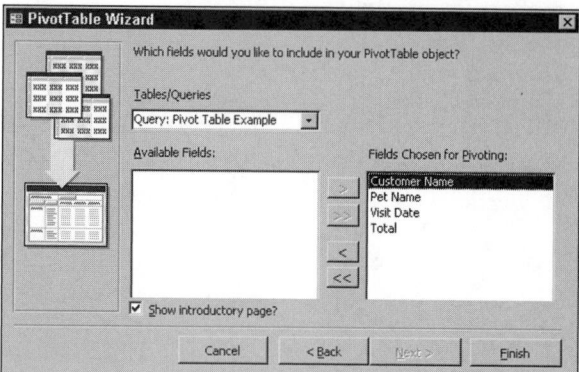

Figure 18-37: Selecting the Table/Query to supply data for the Pivot Table and the fields to be used for pivoting

Once you have selected the data, you can press the Finish button to complete the process. The blank Pivot Table type form is displayed in Figure 18-38. If you were a user of the Access or Excel 2000 Pivot Tables, you will see a huge improvement. This layout screen now features live data links. The way it works is that you drag your fields for the Pivot Table onto the form from the Pivot Table field list shown at the bottom-right corner of the form. You can move the field list around and expand and collapse the data lists displayed. It will automatically group date type fields by week or month. You can also create your own calculated fields and summary fields at any level.

In this example, you are going to be using all of the fields for the pivot table. Starting in the upper-left corner of the form, which is where you drag and drop Filter Fields, you will drag the *Customer Name* field. As you can see in Figures 18-39 and 18-40, this will create a combo box with the text Customer Name and initially displays all of the customers in the data sample. You can click on the combo box and filter the data for any or all of the customers. You can even select any number of customers using the check boxes you can see in Figure 18-40.

The *Pet Name* field will be used for the Row Field, and the *Visit Date* field will be used for the Column Field. When you complete dragging and dropping these field names from the Pivot Table Field List to the drop area, the live data appears along the top (Column Fields) or side (Row Fields). Instantly you can see your column headers, and the first row data appear like a data sheet. When you drag the *Total* field to the Total or Detail Fields area, data is filled in like a cross-tab query. Figure 18-39 shows this data after the fields are dragged to the form from the Field List.

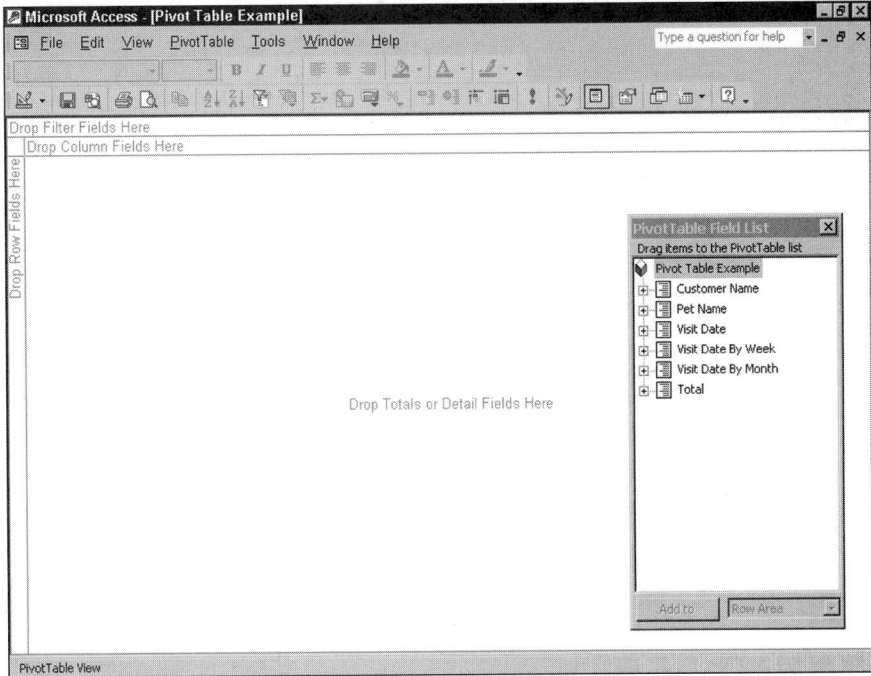

Figure 18-38: The Layout window of the PivotTable Wizard

The intersection of a row and a column displays a data value. For example, in Figure 18-39 you can see the value $80.00 where Cleo and 8/4/1998 intersect. This means that Cleo, the Pet had a visit to the veterinarian on 8/4/1998 and the total charges was $80.00. If you filtered the Customer Name, you could see who owns Cleo.

Once your fields are dragged to the form and your data is displayed in the form you can begin to manipulate the data. If you notice the data elements in either the rows or the column headers, you can see there are + and – signs on very small buttons next to each element. If you click on the – button, the data row or column is hidden. You can click on the + sign to redisplay the data from that column or row.

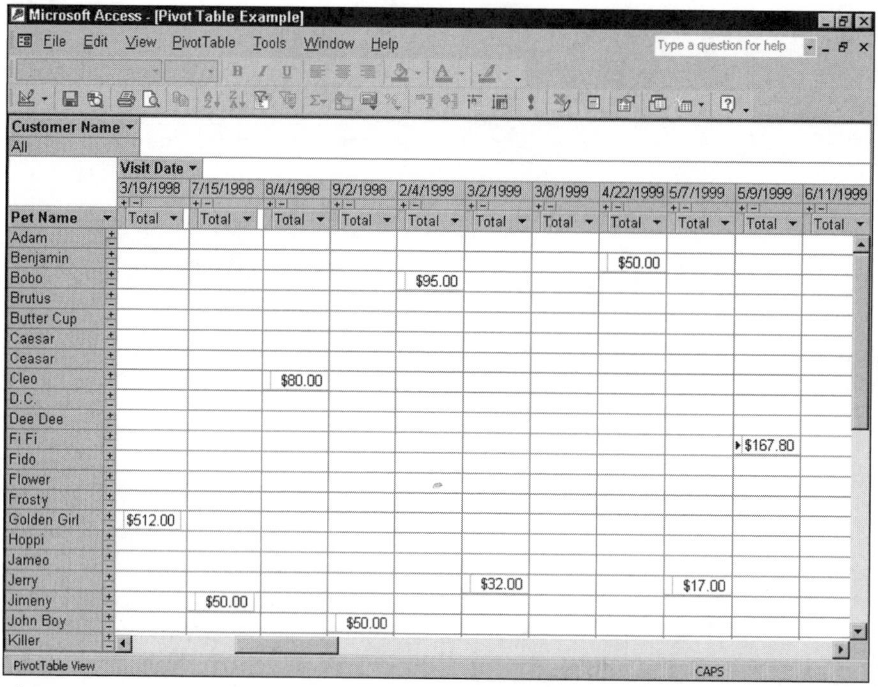

Figure 18-39: Data displayed in the PivotTable Wizard

Remember, the real value of a pivot table view is to pivot the data. You can also move row fields to the column area and column fields to the row area. You can filter by any of the selections. The three major filters Pet Name, Visit Date, and Customer Name each have a downward pointing arrow in the rectangle that contains the name. Figure 18-40 shows what happens when you press the down arrow on the Customer Name field.

A type of list box with a series of check boxes is displayed. If you click on the (All) selection, all of the customers below are either selected or all deselected. If you deselect all of the options, you will have no data displayed. You can then select the Customers you want to include in the selection. You can select one, two, twenty, or as many as are displayed. When you press the OK button at the bottom of the list, the pivot table is filtered.

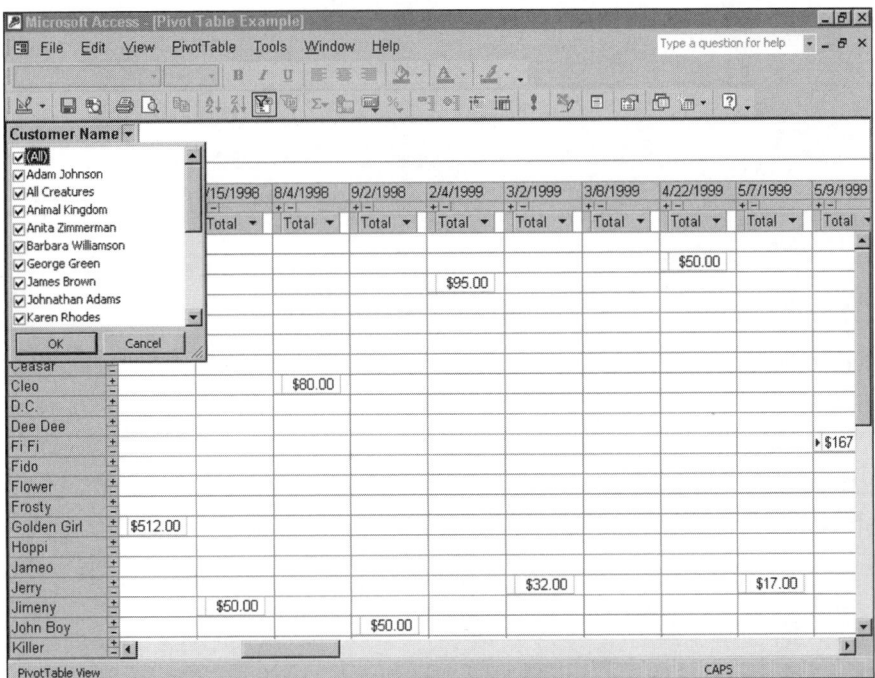

Figure 18-40: Changing a filter in the PivotTable Wizard

Pivot tables are very powerful. You can switch the row and columns by simply dragging the column or row designator to the other dimension. For example, you could move the Visit Date from being a column field to being a row field. That could show you dates by Pet. There is no limit to the number of ways you can manipulate the data.

Figure 18-41 shows the PivotTable menu. This helps you create subtotals, calculated fields and totals, and to do many things the individual buttons can do such as expanding and collapsing levels and hiding or showing details. You can also Export the data directly to Microsoft Excel and create a PivotTable on a worksheet. Pivot Tables provide a great way to view hierarchical data in many ways. It can be much easier to use a pivot table than to create a multitude of reports.

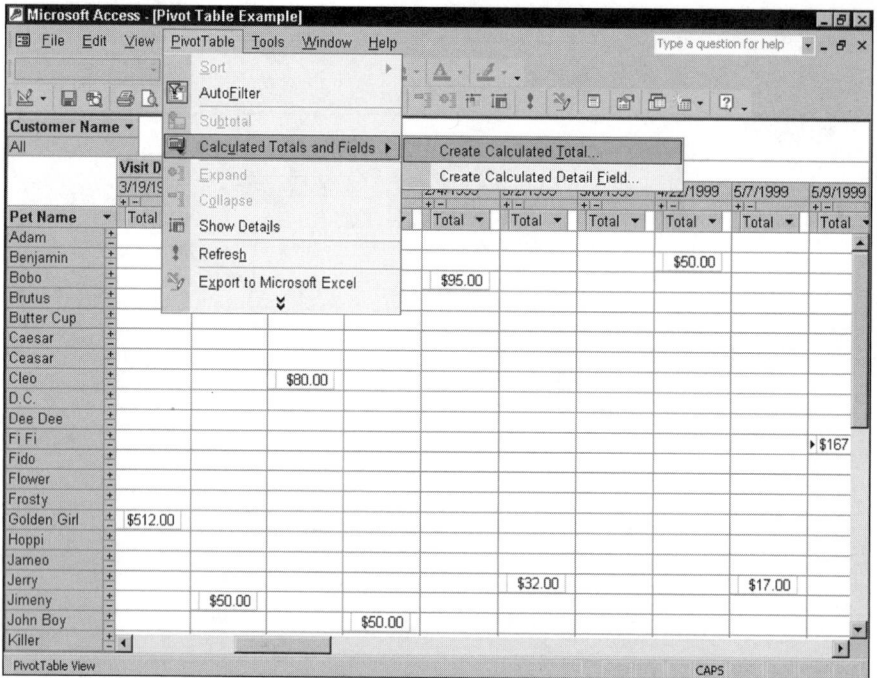

Figure 18-41: Using the PivotTable menu

Creating a Pivot Chart

Just as the PivotTable lets you display data, a Pivot Chart lets you represent data graphically. You begin by creating a new form and selecting the AutoForm: PivotChart. There is no specific PivotChart wizard like there is a PivotTable Wizard. In Figure 18-42, you can see the New Form dialog box with the same query, Pivot Table Example, selected that was used in the last example for the PivotTable wizard.

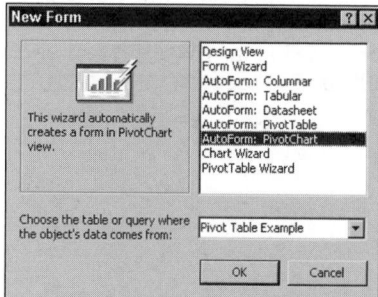

Figure 18-42: Creating a new Pivot Chart using the AutoForm: PivotChart selection

After selecting the AutoForm: PivotChart and clicking OK, you will see a screen similar to the PivotTable design screen except that an empty chart is shown (see Figure 18-43). The Chart Field List is identical to the Pivot Table field list. You drag and drop fields to the chart areas in the same ways as the Pivot Table.

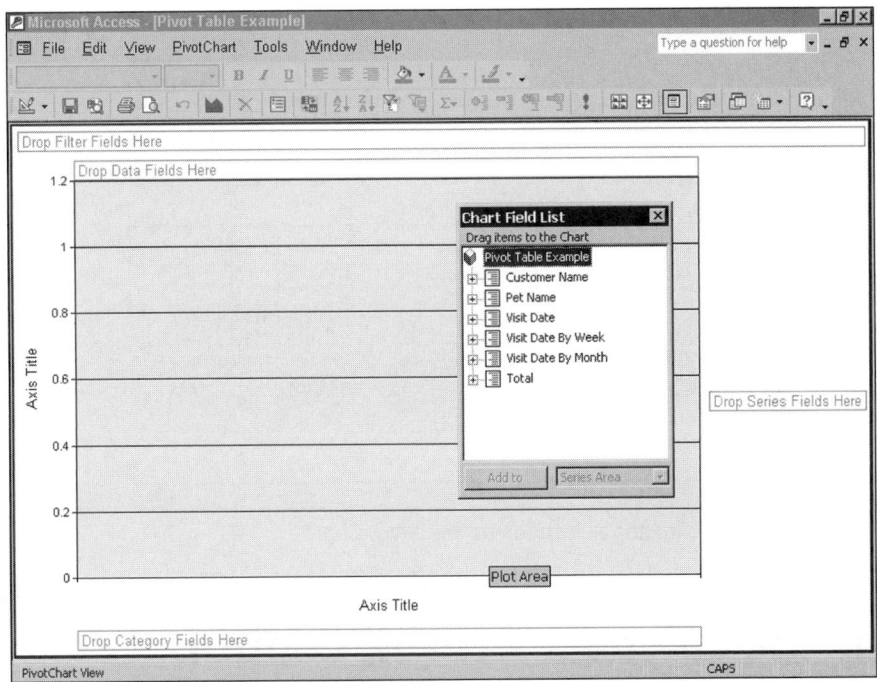

Figure 18-43: Creating a new Pivot Chart using the AutoForm: PivotChart selection

You can drag the Customer Name field as the overall Filter Field at the top of the screen. The Series would be what separates the various lines. The Pet Name would be appropriate for the Series. The Category field is usually time or dates and the Visit Date field can be dragged to the Category area. Finally, the Total can be dragged to the Data Field area.

After you drag these fields, the chart appears with data as shown in Figure 18-44. You can manipulate the data and change the look of the graph, chart type, axes lines, and any standard chart options.

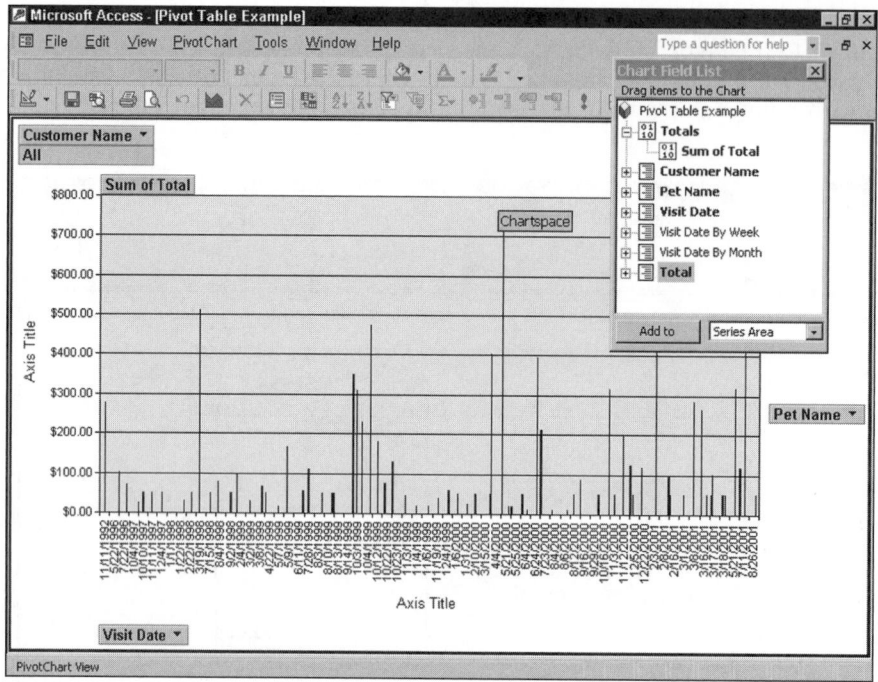

Figure 18-44: Viewing the selections on the Pivot Chart

Using the Calendar ActiveX Control

ActiveX controls (also known as OCX controls) are not new to Access. Custom controls extend the number of controls already found in Access. Some of the more popular controls are Calendars, Tab Dialog box controls, Progress Meters, Spin Box, Sliders, and many others. Though they existed in early versions of Access they were seldom used; they required separate sets of properties and were not totally stable. Access for Windows 95 introduced support for the new 32-bit controls, and Access 2002 continues their popularity. Access 2002 comes with several ActiveX controls. One of the most often used is the Calendar control. If you have Office 2002, you have many ActiveX controls from the new Microsoft Forms collection used to create Office forms without Access. There are many ActiveX controls from third parties for Access 2002. See the CD appendix for several demos of the best ActiveX controls that are compatible for Microsoft Access.

The Office Developers Edition is a separate product from Microsoft that allows you to create a run-time application that runs Microsoft Access applications without having Access on the computer. It also includes the Help compiler, a printed-language reference manual, the Windows Setup Wizard, many other ActiveX controls, and many new tools for Access 2002 and Office 2002 developers, including many Internet tools.

You can select Insert ➪ ActiveX Control or select the More Tools icon from the Toolbox to see a list of all your ActiveX controls.

If you don't have the Office Developer's Edition or the full Office 2002, you probably will see only the Calendar control. You add a custom control as you would to any unbound OLE control. To add a Calendar custom control to a new blank form, follow these steps:

1. Open a new form in Design view and display the Toolbox. Don't select any table in the New Form dialog box.

2. Select Insert ➪ ActiveX Control... or choose the More Tools icon from the Toolbox.

3. Select Calendar Control 10.0 and click on OK.

The Calendar control appears on the new form. The calendar can be resized like any unbound control, and (of course) it has properties. Figure 18-45 shows the Calendar control and its basic properties.

The Property window shows the properties specific to a Calendar control. These are the properties displayed by the Other tab. With these properties, you can change some of the display characteristics of the calendar, including the following:

✦ **DayLength.** System (Sunday, Monday, Tuesday), System Medium (Sun, Mon, Tue, . . .)

✦ **FirstDay.** First day of week displayed (Mon, Tue, Wed, Thu, etc., default is Sun)

✦ **GridCellEffect.** Flat, Raised, Sunken

✦ **MonthLength.** System (January, February, . . .), System Medium (Jan, Feb, . . .)

✦ **ShowDateSelectors.** Display a combo box for month and year in Form view

Many other properties control the various colors and fonts of the calendar components. A number of value properties affect the display of the calendar and the selected date. Four properties change the display of the calendar data:

✦ **Day.** The day of the current month (19 in this example)

✦ **Month.** The month of the current date (6 in this example)

✦ **Year.** The year being displayed (2001 in this example)

✦ **Value.** The date displayed (6/19/2001 in this example)

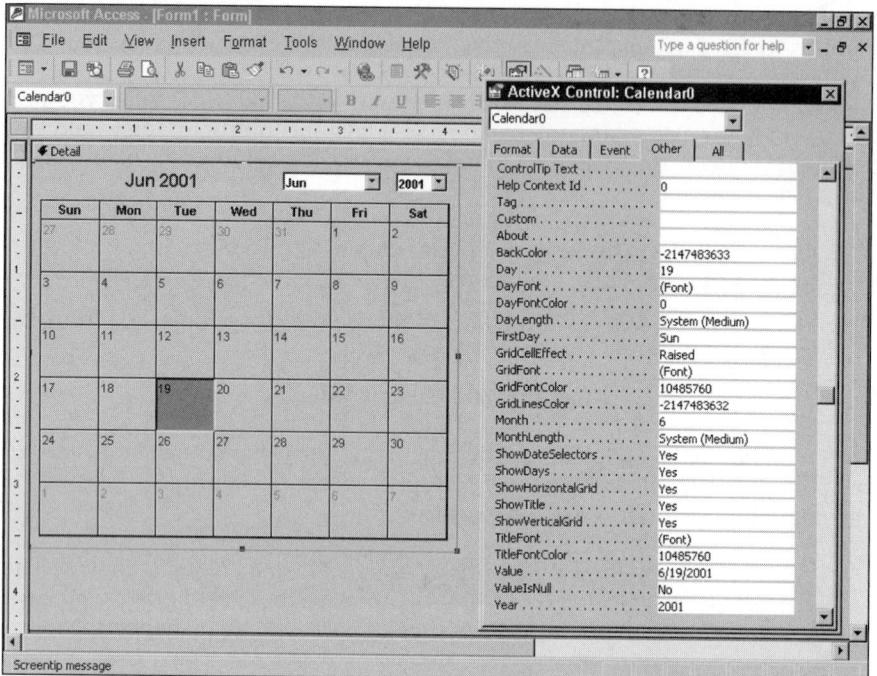

Figure 18-45: The Calendar control and the standard and additional Access properties

Cross-Reference

The values can be changed in several ways. You can click on a date in the calendar in Form view, which changes the Value property. When the Value property changes, so do the Day, Month, and Year properties. You can also change these properties in the Property window or programmatically from a macro or Visual Basic for Applications.

Another way to change properties in a custom control is to display the Calendar Properties dialog box, as shown in Figure 18-46. This provides combo-box access to certain control properties. You can display this dialog box by selecting Edit ⇨ Calendar Object ⇨ Properties or by right-clicking on the Calendar control and selecting Calendar Object ⇨ Properties from the shortcut menu.

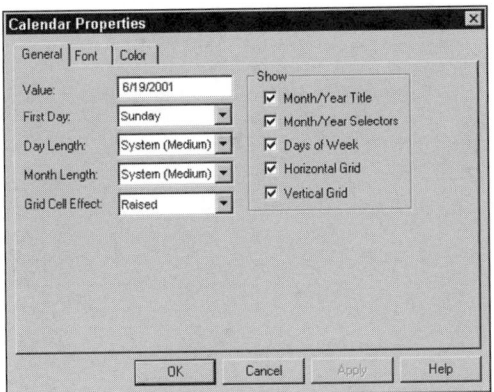

Figure 18-46: The Calendar Properties dialog box

When you display the calendar in Form view, you can also display combo boxes (using the ShowDateSelectors property) to change the month or year because you can only click on a day in the calendar. These are the Month/Year Selectors in the Property dialog box.

The calendar's real power is that you can link it to a field. When the calendar is changed, the field value changes. Likewise, if the field value changes, the calendar display changes. You can easily do this by linking the calendar to a field by using its Control Source property.

✦   ✦   ✦

Creating and Customizing Reports

In This Chapter

Understanding the 11 tasks necessary to create a great report

Creating a report from a blank form

Sorting and grouping data

Adding label and text controls to your report

Modifying the appearance of text and label controls

Adding page breaks

Copying an existing report

In previous chapters, you learned to create a report from a single table by using a Wizard. You also learned to create multiple-table queries and work with controls. In this chapter, you combine and build on these concepts. While the wizards give you a good start, it is sometimes better to start with a blank report. This chapter teaches you to create — from scratch — a report that enables you to view data from multiple tables, group the data, and sort it in meaningful ways. In subsequent chapters, you learn to create more powerful reports and different types of reports, including reports that summarize and help analyze data, presentation reports with fancy formatting and graphics, and mail merge and labels created with reports.

Cross-Reference In Chapter 10, you learned to create a report using an Access Report Wizard with a single table as the data source. Wizards are great for creating quick and simple reports, but they are fairly limited and give you little control over field type or placement. Although there are advantages to creating a report with a Wizard and then modifying the report, this chapter focuses on creating a report from a blank form without the help of the Wizards. If you haven't read Chapter 10, now is a good time to read or review it, because the basic report concepts presented there are necessary to understand this chapter. You also need to be familiar with the basic controls and properties used in forms and reports presented in Chapter 14.

Starting with a Blank Form

Previous chapters about forms introduced you to all the tools available in the Report Design window. When you create reports, you use some of these tools in a slightly different manner from the way they are used to create forms. Therefore, it is important to review some of the unique report menus and toolbar buttons.

Note　Because the Report Design window is set to a width of eight inches, most of the screen printouts in this chapter were taken with a screen driver of 800 x 600 resolution. This resolution enables you to see almost the entire screen in the screen figures. Some report print previews were also created in 1024 x 768 or higher resolutions to help you see more of the report in the book.

You can view a report in three different views: Design View, Layout Preview, and Print Preview. You can also print a report to the hard-copy device defined for Microsoft Windows. You have already seen the preview windows in previous chapters. This chapter focuses on the Report Design window.

The Report Design window is where you create and modify reports. The empty Report Design window, shown in Figure 19-1, contains various tools, including the Toolbox.

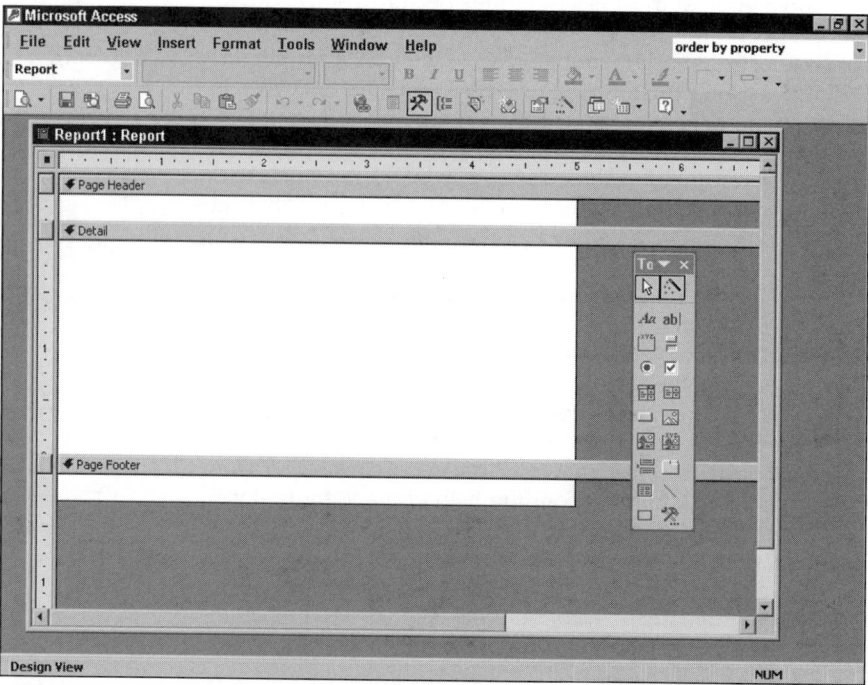

Figure 19-1: The Report Design window showing the Toolbox

The Design Window Toolbar

The Report Design toolbar is shown in Figure 19-2. You click the button you want for quick access to such design tasks as displaying different windows and activating Wizards and utilities. Table 19-1 summarizes what each item on the toolbar does. (The table defines each tool from left to right on the toolbar.)

Figure 19-2: The Report Design toolbar

The Report Design toolbar is distinct from the Format toolbar. To make such changes as font selection and justification, you must first make sure that the Format Form/Report Design toolbar is displayed.

Table 19-1 The Design View Toolbar	
Toolbar Item	**Description**
Report View button	Drop-down box displays the three types of views available
Save button	Saves the current report design
Search button	Finds text within a database or your computer
Print button	Prints a form, table, query, or report
Print Preview button	Toggles to print preview mode
Cut button	Removes selection from the document and adds it to the Clipboard
Copy button	Copies the selection to the Clipboard
Paste button	Copies the Clipboard contents to the document
Format Painter button	Copies the style of one control to another
Undo button	Undoes previous commands
Redo button	Redoes previously undone commands
Insert Hyperlink button	Inserts hyperlink
Field List button	Displays or hides the Field List window
Toolbox button	Displays or hides the Toolbox
Sorting and Grouping button	Displays or hides the Sorting and Grouping box
AutoFormat button	Applies a predefined format to a form or report

Continued

Table 19-1 (continued)	
Toolbar Item	**Description**
Code button	Displays or hides the module window
Properties button	Displays the properties sheet for the selected item
Build button	Displays the Builder or Wizard for selected control or item
Database window button	Displays the Database window
New Object button	Creates a new object
Help button	Displays Access Help

Note   The tools on the Report Design screen are virtually identical to the Form Design tools.

Banded Report Writer Concepts

In a report, your data is processed one record at a time. Depending on how you create your report design, each data item is processed differently. Reports are divided into sections, known as *bands* in most report-writing software packages. (In Access, these are simply called *sections*.) Access processes each data record from a table or dynaset, processing each section in order and deciding (for each record) whether to process fields or text in each section. For example, the report footer section is processed only after the last record is processed in the dynaset.

A report is made up of groups of *details*—for example as shown in Figure 19-3, all the animals William Price brought to the hospital on a certain day and how much he paid. Each group must have an identifying *group header*, which in this case is customer William Price. Each group also has a footer where you can calculate the total amount paid by each customer. For William Price, this amount is $315. The *page header* contains column descriptions; the *report header* contains the report title. Finally, the *report footer* contains grand totals for the report, and the *page footer* prints the page number.

The Access sections are listed below:

✦ **Report header.** Prints only at the beginning of the report; used for title page

✦ **Page header.** Prints at the top of each page

✦ **Group header.** Prints before the first record of a group is processed

✦ **Detail.** Prints each record in the table or dynaset

✦ **Group footer.** Prints after the last record of a group is processed

✦ **Page footer.** Prints at the bottom of each page

✦ **Report footer.** Prints only at the end of a report after all records are processed

How sections process data

Most sections are triggered by changes in the values of the data. Table 19-2 shows the records that make up the dynaset for the Daily Hospital Report (*Yes* indicates that a section is triggered by the data).

Table 19-2
Processing Report Sections

Customer Name	Pet Name	Report Header	Page Header	Customer Name Header	Detail	Customer Name Footer	Page Footer	Report Footer
All Creatures	Bobo	Yes	Yes	Yes	Yes	No	No	No
All Creatures	Presto Chango	No	No	No	Yes	No	No	No
All Creatures	Presto Chango	No	No	No	Yes	No	No	No
All Creatures	Stinky	No	No	No	Yes	Yes	No	No
Animal Kingdom	Margo	No	No	Yes	Yes	No	No	No
Animal Kingdom	Margo	No	No	No	Yes	Yes	No	No
Barbara Williamson	Hoppi	No	No	Yes	Yes	Yes	No	No
Jonathan Adams	Patty	No	No	Yes	Yes	Yes	No	No
Karen Rhodes	Golden Girl	No	No	Yes	Yes	Yes	No	No
Petra Irish	Ceasar	No	No	Yes	Yes	Yes	No	No
Petra Irish	D.C.	No	No	No	Yes	Yes	No	No
Sandra Williams	Flower	No	No	Yes	Yes	Yes	No	No
William Price	Butter Cup	No	No	Yes	Yes	No	No	No
William Price	Rosie	No	No	No	Yes	Yes	No	No
William Primen	Brutus	No	No	Yes	Yes	Yes	Yes	Yes

Figure 19-3 shows these sections superimposed on a report.

Daily Hospital Report Wednesday, July 11, 2001

Customer Name	Pet Name	Type of Animal	Total Amount
All Creatures			
	Bobo	RABBIT	$70.00
	Presto Chango	LIZARD	$50.00
	Presto Chango	LIZARD	$500.00
	Stinky	SKUNK	$95.00
			$715.00
Animal Kingdom			
	Margo	SQUIRREL	$572.00
	Margo	SQUIRREL	$320.00
			$892.00
Barbara Williamson			
	Hoppi	FROG	$50.00
			$50.00
Johnathan Adams			
	Patty	PIG	$50.00
			$50.00
Karen Rhodes			
	Golden Girl	HORSE	$231.00
			$231.00
Petra Irish			
	Ceasar	CAT	$50.00
	D.C.	CAT	$26.00
			$76.00
Sandra Williams			
	Flower	CAT	$50.00
			$50.00
William Price			
	Butter Cup	PIG	$265.00
	Rosie	PIG	$50.00
			$315.00
William Primen			
	Brutus	DOG	$50.00
			$50.00
		Grand Total :	**$2,429.00**

Report Printed on : 12/25/2000

Page: 1 of 1

Figure 19-3: Typical Report Writer sections

As you can see, Table 19-2 shows fifteen records. Nine groups of records are grouped by the customer name. All Creatures has four records; Animal Kingdom, Petra Irish, and William Price have two; and the rest have one. Each record in the table has corresponding columns for each section in the report. Yes means that the record triggers processing in that section; No means that the section is not processed for that record. This report is only one page, so it is very simple.

The report header section is triggered by only the first record in the dynaset. This section is always processed first, regardless of the data. The report footer section is triggered only after the last record is processed, regardless of the data.

Access processes the page header section after the report header section for the first record and then every time a new page is started. The page footer section is processed at the bottom of each page and after the report footer section of the last page.

Group headers are triggered only by the first record in a group. Group footers are triggered only by the last record in a group. Notice that the Barbara Williamson record triggers both a group header and a group footer because it is the only record in a group. If three or more records are in a group, only the first or the last record can trigger a group header or footer; the middle records trigger only the detail section.

Access always processes each record in the detail section (which is always triggered, regardless of the value of a data item). Most reports with a large amount of data have many detail records and significantly fewer group header or footer records. This small report has as many group header and footer records as it has detail records.

The Report Writer sections

Figure 19-4 shows what a report design looks like in Access. It is the Report Design window for the Daily Hospital Report. As you can see, the report is divided into seven sections. The group section displays data grouped by Customer Name, so you see the sections Customer Name Header and Customer Name Footer. Each of the other sections is also named for the type of processing it performs.

You can place any type of text or field controls in any section, but Access processes the data one record at a time. It also takes certain actions (based on the values of the group fields, the location of the page, or placement in the report) to make the bands or sections active. The example in Figure 19-4 is typical of a report with multiple sections. As you learned, each section in the report has a different purpose and different triggers.

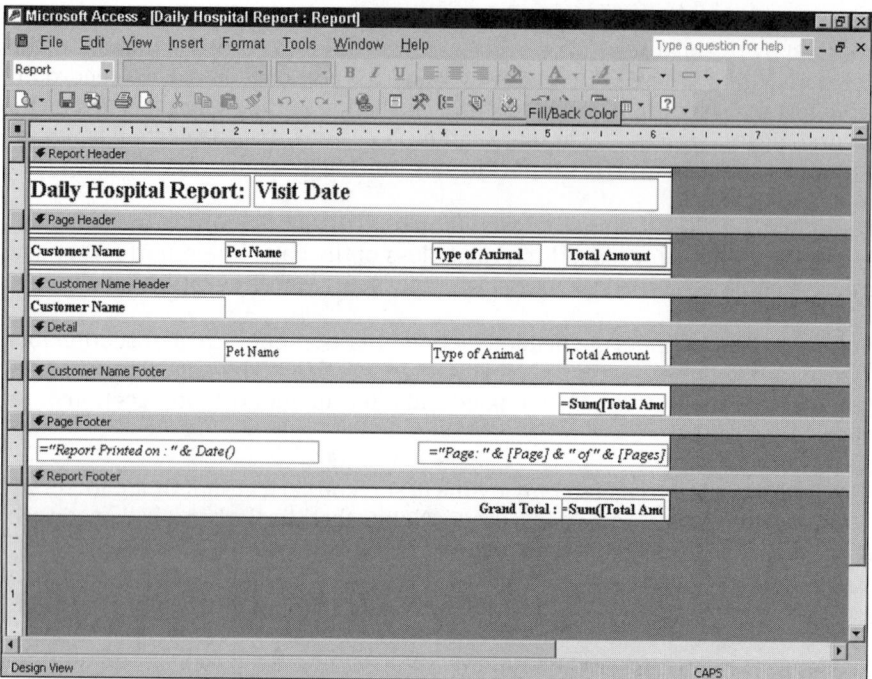

Figure 19-4: The Report Design window

Note   Page and report headers and footers must be added as pairs. To establish one without the other, simply resize the section you don't want to a height of zero; then set its Visible property to No.

Caution   If you remove a header or footer section, you also lose the controls in those sections.

Report header section

Controls in the *report header section* are printed only once at the beginning of the report. In Figure 19-3 the report header section contains a text control that displays the words *Daily Hospital Report* in a large font size only on the first page at the top of the report. The report header also contains the field control *Visit Date* that displays the value of the visit date from the first record, *Wednesday, July 11, 2001*. It has been formatted using the long date format.

The report header section also has a double line placed before the text and field controls. You can place lines, boxes, shading, color, and special effects in any section. (You learn more about formatting and special effects in later chapters.)

You can also have controls in the report header section print on a separate page, which enables you to create a title page and include a graphic or picture in the section. A common use of a report header section is as a cover page or a cover letter.

Note   Only data from the first record can be placed in a report header.

Page header section

Text or field controls in the *page header section* normally print at the top of every page. If a report header on the first page is not on a page of its own, the information in the page header section prints just below the report header information. Typically, page headers serve as column headers in group/total reports; they can also contain a title for the report. In this example, placing the Daily Hospital Report title in the report header section means that the title appears on only the first page; move it into the page header section if you want it to appear on every page.

The page header section seen in Figure 19-4 also has double lines above and below the text controls. Each of the text controls is separate and each can be moved or sized individually. You can also change special effects (such as color, shading, borders, line thickness, font type, and font size) for each text control.

Both the page header and page footer sections can be set for one of four settings (this setting can be found in the report's properties):

✦ **All Pages.** Both the page header and page footer print on every page.

✦ **Not with Report Header.** Neither the page header nor footer prints on a page with the report header.

✦ **Not with Report Footer.** The page header does not print with the report footer. The report footer prints on a new page.

✦ **Not with Report Header/Footer.** Neither the page header nor the footer prints on a page with the report header or footer.

Group header

Group headers sections normally display the name of the group. Access knows when all the records in a group have been displayed in a detail section when the group name changes. In this example, the detail records are about animals and the cost of their treatments. The group header field control Customer Name tells you that these animals are owned by the customer who appears in the group header section. Group header sections immediately precede detail sections.

It is possible to have multiple levels of group headers and footers. In this report, for example, the data is only for July 11, 2001. The detail data is grouped by the field Customer Name. If you want to see one report for the entire month of July 2001, you can change the query and add a second group section to the report. In this second group section, you can group the data by date—and then, within each date, by customer. You can have many levels of groupings, but you should limit the number to between three and six; reports with too many levels become impossible to read. You don't want to defeat the purpose of the report, which is to show information clearly in a summarized format.

Note To set group-level properties such as Group On, Group Interval, Keep Together, or something other than the default, you must first set the Group Header and Group Footer property (or both) to Yes for the selected field or expression.

Detail section

The *detail section* processes *every* record in the record set and is where each value is printed. The detail section frequently contains a calculated field such as a price extension that is the result of multiplying quantity times the price. In this example, the detail section simply displays the Pet Name, Type of Animal, and Total Amount (which is the cost of the treatments). Each record in the detail section *belongs* to the same group header Customer Name.

Tip You can tell Access whether you want to display a section in the report by changing the section's Visible property in the Report Design window. Turning off the display of the detail section (or by excluding selected group sections) displays a summary report with no detail or with only certain groups displayed.

Group footer

You use the *group footer section* to calculate summaries for all the detail records in a group. In the Daily Hospital Report, the expression =Sum([Total Amount]) adds all the Total Amount fields for a specific customer. In the Animal Kingdom group, this expression sums the two Total Amount records ($572.00 and $320.00) and produces the value $892.00. This type of field is automatically reset to 0 every time the group changes. (You learn more about expressions and summary fields in later chapters.)

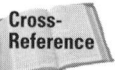

Cross-Reference You can change the way summaries are calculated by changing the Running Sum property of the field box in the Report Design window.

Page footer

The *page footer section* usually contains page numbers or control totals. In very large reports, you may want page totals as well as group totals (such as when you have multiple pages of detail records with no summaries). For the Daily Hospital Report, the page number is printed by combining the text and page number controls to show Page x of y where x is the current page number and y is the total number of pages in the report:

="Page: " & [Page] & " of " & [Pages]

(which keeps track of the page number in the report).

You can also print the date and the time printed. Figures 19-3 and 19-4 show the date printed in the Page Footer section as well as the page numbers.

Report footer

The *report footer section* is printed once at the end of the report after all the detail records and group footer sections are printed. Report footers typically display grand totals or other statistics (such as averages or percentages) for the entire report. The report footer for the Daily Hospital Report uses the expression =Sum([Total Amount]) to add the Total Amount fields for all records. This expression, when used in the report footer, is not reset to 0, as it is in the group footer, because it is used only for a grand total.

When there is a report footer, the page footer section is printed after the report footer.

The Report Writer in Access is a *two-pass report writer*, capable of preprocessing all records to calculate the totals (such as percentages) needed for statistical reporting. This capability enables you to create expressions that calculate percentages as Access processes those records that require foreknowledge of the grand total.

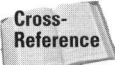

Cross-Reference   Chapter 21 covers calculating percentages.

Creating a New Report

Fundamental to all reports is the concept that a report is another way to view the records in one or more tables. It is important to understand that a report is bound to either a single table or a query that brings together data from one or more tables. When you create a report, you must select which fields from the query or table you want to see in your report. Unless you want to view all the records from a single table, bind your report to a query. Even if you are accessing data from a single table, using a query lets you create your report on the basis of a particular search criterion and sorting order. If you want to access data from multiple tables, you have almost no choice but to bind your report to a query. In the examples in this chapter, all the reports are bound to a query (even though it is possible to bind a report to a table).

Note   Access lets you create a report without first binding it to a table or query, but you will have no fields on the report. This capability can be used to work out page templates, which can serve as models for other reports. You can add fields later by changing the underlying control source of the report.

Throughout this chapter and the next chapter, you learn the tasks necessary to create the Mountain Animal Hospital Pets and Owners Directory (the first hard-copy page is shown in Figure 19-5). In this chapter, you design the basic report, assemble the data, and place the data in the proper positions. In Chapter 20, you enhance the report by adding lines, boxes, and shading so that certain areas stand out. You will also add enhanced controls (such as option buttons and check boxes) to make the data more readable.

As with almost every task in Access, there are many ways to create a report without Wizards. It is important, however, to follow some type of methodology, because creating a good report involves a fairly scientific approach. You should create a checklist that is a set of tasks that will result in a good report every time. As you complete each task, check it off your list. When you are done, you will have a great-looking report. The following section outlines this approach.

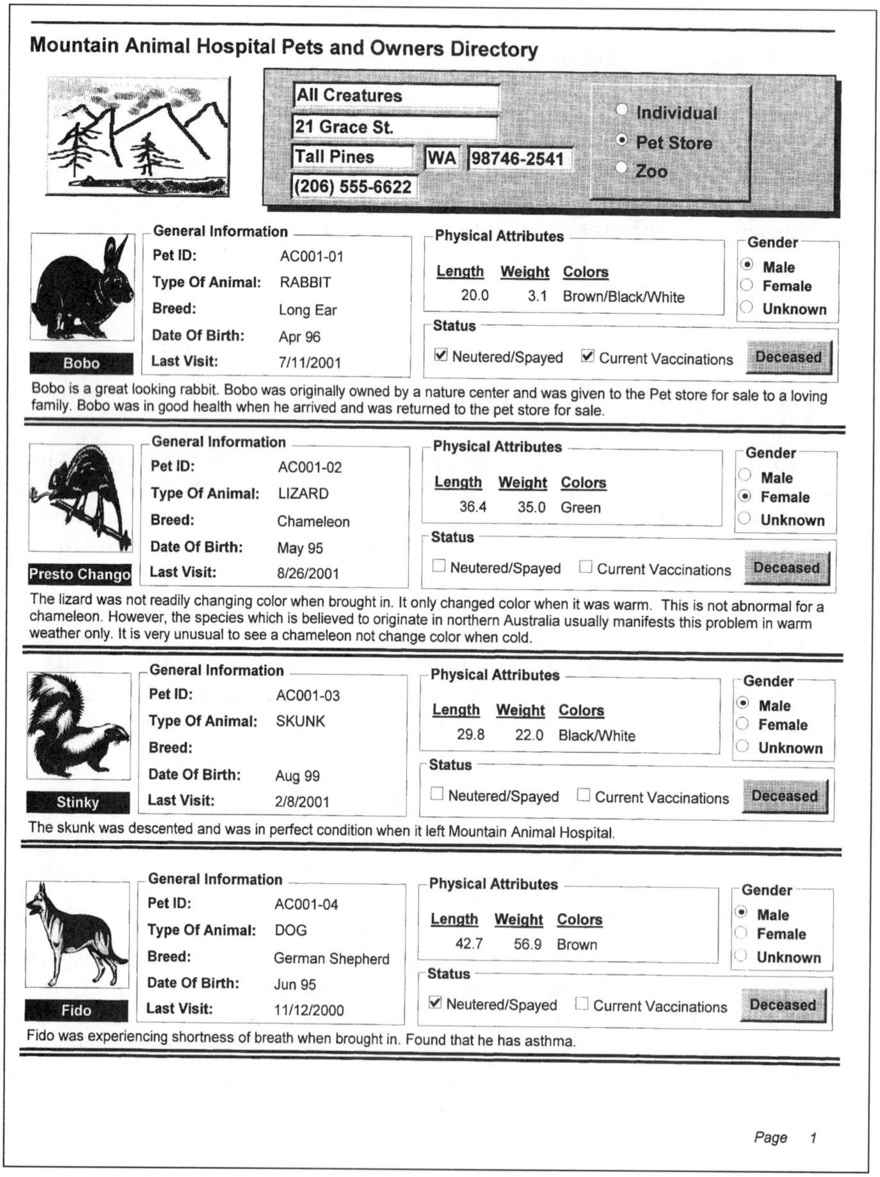

Figure 19-5: The Mountain Animal Hospital Pets and Owners Directory — first page

Eleven tasks to creating a great report

To create a good report, perform these 11 steps:

1. Design your report.
2. Assemble the data.
3. Create a new report and bind it to a query.
4. Define your page layout properties.
5. Place the fields on the report using text controls.
6. Add other label and text controls as necessary.
7. Modify the appearance, size, and location of text, text controls, and label controls.
8. Define your sorting and grouping options.
9. Save your report.
10. Enhance your report by using graphics and other control types.
11. Print your report.

Cross-Reference

This chapter covers tasks 1 through 9. Chapter 20 discusses task 10 and 11 — using other controls, such as group boxes, option buttons, and memo fields, as well as methods to enhance your report visually. It also covers printing and the use of images and graphical elements in your reports to give them a professional quality.

Designing the report

The first step in this process is to design the report. By using clues from the report name, Mountain Animal Hospital Pets and Owners Directory, you can surmise that you want to create a report that contains detailed information about both the customer and the customer's pets. You want to create a report that lists important customer information at the top of a page followed by detailed information about each of the customer's pets, including their pictures. You want only one customer on a page. If a customer has more than one pet, you want to see as many pets as possible on the same page. If a customer has more pets than will fit on one page, you want to duplicate the customer details at the top of each page. (The grouping section of this chapter discusses this task.)

Figure 19-6 shows a hand-drawn design of the layout for this report. This is not the complete report shown in Figure 19-5; rather, it is a plan for only the major data items, placed roughly where you want them to appear in the report. You can sketch a design for your report by hand on paper or use any good word processor or drawing tool (such as Microsoft Visio or Microsoft PhotoDraw or even Microsoft Word or Excel) to lay out the basic design. Because Access has a WYSIWYG (What You See Is What You Get) report writer, you can also use that to lay out your report. (Personally, I like the pencil-and-paper approach to good design.)

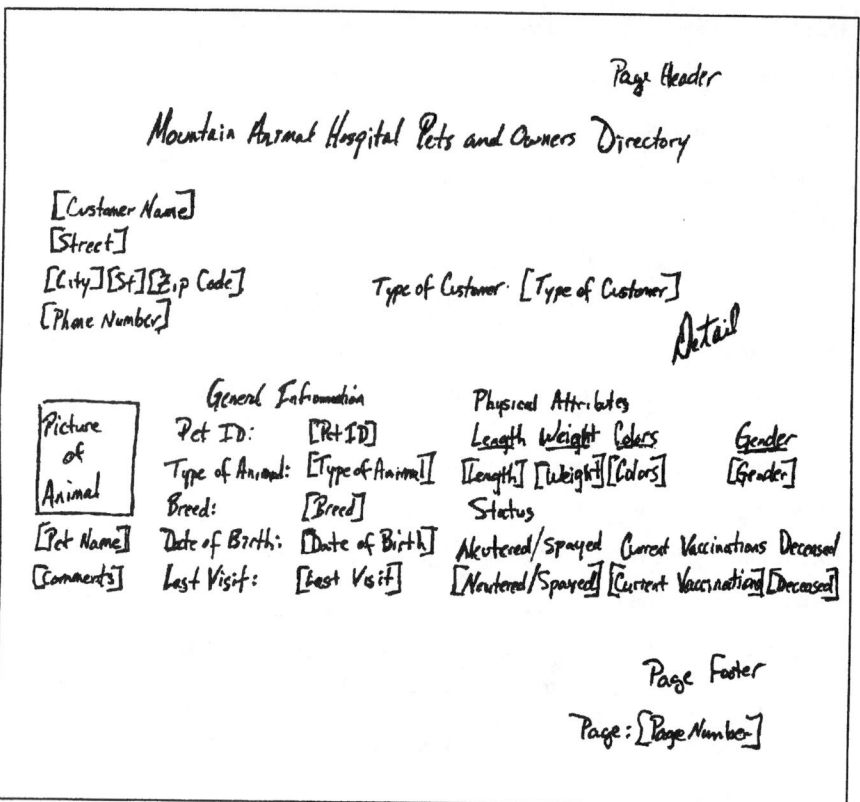

Figure 19-6: The report layout design for the Mountain Animal Hospital Pets and Owners Directory

The report layout design is created only to lay out the basic data elements with no special formatting. Although this design may seem rudimentary, it is, nevertheless, a good starting point. This layout represents the report you will create in this chapter.

Assembling the data

With this design in mind, you now have the information to determine what data you need to assemble for the report. To create this report, you need fields from two tables: Customer and Pets. Table 19-3 lists the necessary fields and identifies the tables that contain them.

Table 19-3	
Tables and Fields Needed for the Pets and Owners Directory	
Fields from Pets Table	*Fields from Customer Table*
Pet ID	Customer Number
Picture	Customer Name
Pet Name	Type of Customer
Type of Animal	Street/Apt
Breed	City
Date of Birth	State
Last Visit Date	ZIP Code
Length	Phone Number
Weight	
Colors	
Gender	
Neutered/Spayed	
Current Vaccinations	
Deceased	
Comments	

To assemble this data, you need to create a query that you will call Pets and Owners. This query will include *all* the fields from both tables, even though you won't use all of them in the report. Some of the fields that don't appear in the report itself may be used later to derive other fields. Some fields may be used merely to sort the data, although the fields themselves are not displayed on the report. In this example, you will sort the data by Pet ID. It is always a good idea to arrange your data in some known order, otherwise when reports are run, the data is listed in its *physical* order.

If you don't already have the Pets and Owners query, follow Figure 19-7. You can find this completed in the Mountain Animal Hospital.mdb database file.

Note You use the asterisk (*) to select all fields from each table.

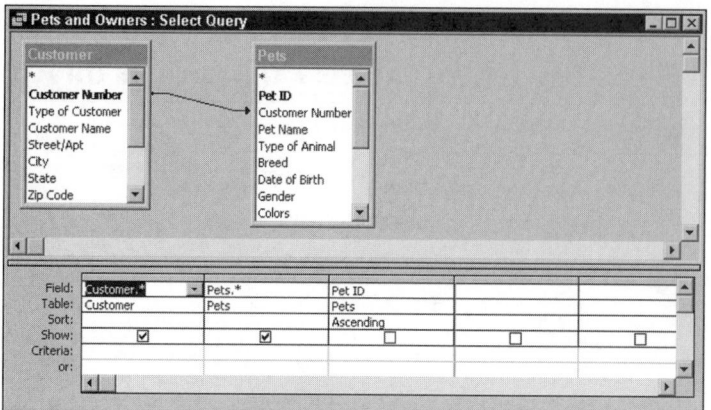

Figure 19-7: The Pets and Owners query

Creating a new report and binding it to a query

Now that you have created the Pets and Owners query, you need to create a new report and bind it to the query. Follow these steps to complete this process:

1. Press F11 to display the Database window if it is not already displayed.

2. Click the Reports object button.

3. Click the New toolbar button. The New Report dialog box appears.

4. Select Design View.

5. Click the combo box labeled Choose a table or query. A drop-down list of all tables and queries in the current database appears.

6. Select the Pets and Owners query.

7. Click OK.

8. Maximize the Report window.

A blank Report Design window appears (see Figure 19-8). Notice the three sections in the screen display: Page Header, Detail, and Page Footer. The report is bound to the query Pets and Owners. This means that the fields from the query are available for use in the report design and that they appear in the Field List window. It also means that the data from that query will be displayed when the report is viewed or printed.

Note There are two options for the AutoReport: Columnar and Tabular.

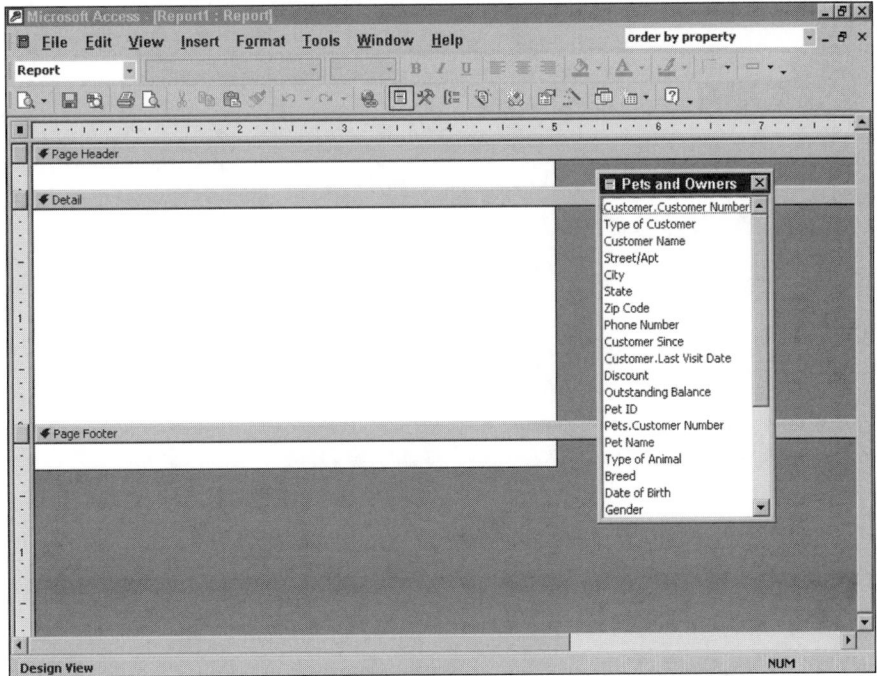

Figure 19-8: A blank Report Design window

Defining the report page size and layout

As you plan your report, consider the page-layout characteristics as well as the kind of paper and printer you want to use for the output. If you use a dot-matrix printer with a wide-carriage feed, you design your report differently than for printing on a laser printer with 8½ x 11-inch paper. After you make these decisions, you use several dialog boxes and properties to make adjustments; these items work together to create the desired output. You learn to use these tools in the next several chapters.

First, you need to select the correct printer and page-layout characteristics by selecting File ➪ Page Setup. The Page Setup dialog box, shown in Figure 19-9, enables you to select your printer and set printer options.

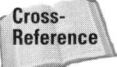

Cross-
Reference

Chapter 21 discusses Page Setup options in detail.

Figure 19-9: The Page Setup dialog box showing the Page tab

The Page Setup dialog box has three tabs: Margins, Page, and Columns. The information under the Page tab is divided into three sections:

✦ **Orientation.** Select the page orientation you want

✦ **Paper.** Select the paper size and paper source you want

✦ **Printer.** Select the printer you want

Note   If you click the Printer button, the Page Setup dialog box for the selected printer appears. Clicking Properties will then display a more extensive dialog box with all the applicable options.

The design for the Pets and Owners report is to be a *portrait* report, which is taller than it is wide. You want to print on letter size paper that is 8½ x 11 inches, and you want the left, right, top, and bottom margins all set to 0.250.

Follow these steps to create the proper report setup for the Pets and Owners report:

1. Open the Page Setup dialog box and select the Page tab.

2. Click the Portrait option button.

   Next to the Orientation buttons are two sheet-of-paper icons with the letter A pictured on them. The picture of the sheet is an indication of its setting.

3. Click the Margins tab.

4. Click the Top margin setting and change the setting to 0.250.

5. Click the Bottom margin setting and change the setting to 0.250.

6. Click the Left margin setting and change the setting to 0.250.

7. Click the Right margin setting and change the setting to 0.250.

8. Click OK to close the Page Setup dialog box.

Tip

Access displays your reports in Print Preview view by using the driver of the active printer. If you don't have a good-quality laser available for printing, install the driver for a PostScript printer so that you can view any graphics that you create (and see the report in a high-resolution display). Later, you can print to your ink jet or other available printer and get the actual hard copy in the best resolution your printer offers.

Caution

Figure 19-9 shows the option buttons in the bottom-left corner of the Page tab. If you are going to give your database or report to others, you should always select the first option, Default Printer. This way, if you have selected a printer the recipient doesn't have, the report will use their default printer. If you have selected the second option (Use Specific Printer), those who don't have that printer will get an error message and will not be able to use the report.

After you define your page layout in the Page Setup dialog box, you need to define the size of your report (which is not necessarily the same as the page definition).

To define the report size, place the mouse pointer on the rightmost edge of the report (where the white page meets the gray background). The pointer changes to a double-headed arrow. Drag the pointer to change the width of the report. As you drag the edge, a vertical line appears in the ruler to let you know the exact width if you release the mouse at that point. Be careful not to exceed the width of the page you defined in the Page Setup dialog box.

When you position the mouse pointer at the bottom of the report, it changes to a double-headed arrow similar to the one for changing width. Dragging will change the height of the page footer section or other specified bottom section not of the whole page. (Predefining a page length directly in the report section doesn't really make sense because the detail section will vary in length, based on your groupings.) Remember that the Report Design view shows only a representation of the various report sections, not the actual report.

To set the right border for the Pets and Owners report to 8 inches, follow these steps:

1. Click the rightmost edge of the report body (where the white page meets the gray background). The mouse pointer changes to a double-headed arrow.

2. Drag the edge to the 8-inch mark.

3. Release the mouse button.

Note

You can also change the Width property in the report's property sheet.

Placing fields on the report

Access takes full advantage of Windows' drag-and-drop capabilities. The method for placing fields on a report is no exception. As with forms when you place a field on a report, it is no longer called a field; it is called a *control*. A control has a *control source* (a specific field) that it is bound to, so the terms *control* and *field* are used interchangeably in this chapter.

To place controls on your report:

✦ Display the Field List window by clicking the Field List toolbar button.

✦ Click the desired Toolbox control to determine the type of control that will be created if they are to be different from the default control types for the fields.

✦ Select each of the fields that you want on your report and then drag them to the Report Design window.

Displaying the field list

To display the Field List window, click the Field List button on the toolbar. A small window with a list of all the fields from the underlying query appears. This window is called a *modeless* dialog box because it remains on-screen even while you continue with other work in Access. The Field List window can be resized and moved around the screen. The enlarged Field List window is illustrated in Figure 19-10, showing all the fields in the Pets and Owners query dynaset.

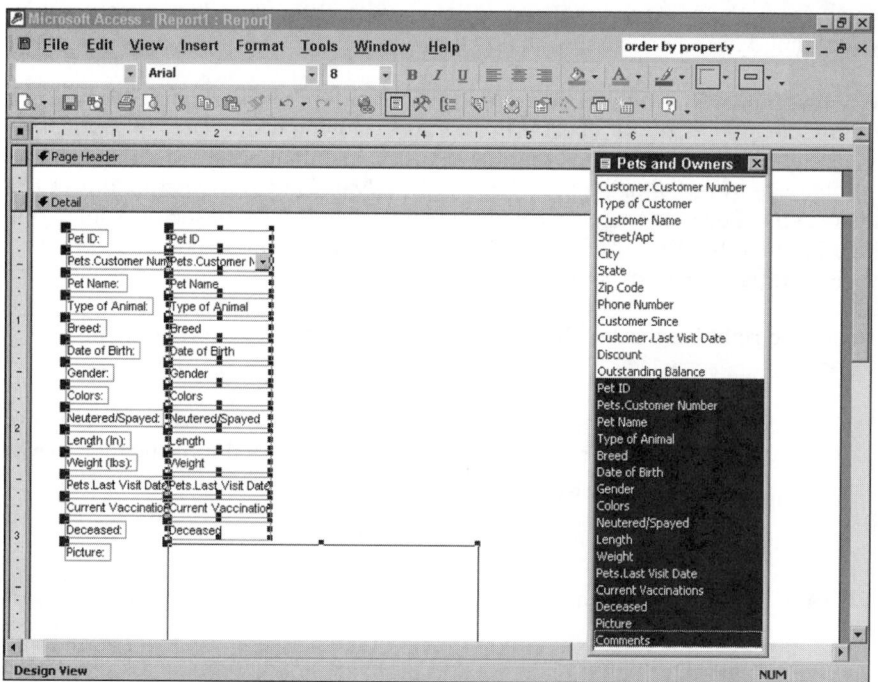

Figure 19-10: Dragging fields to the Design window

Notice that in Figure 19-10 the fields Customer.Customer Number and Pets.Customer Number as well as Customer.Last Visit Date and Pets.Last Visit Date use the table name as a prefix. This nomenclature is necessary to distinguish fields of the same name that come from different tables used in the query.

Tip You can move the Field List window by simply clicking on the title bar and dragging it to a new location.

Selecting the fields for your report

Selecting a field in the Report field list is the same as selecting a field in the Query field list. The easiest way to select a field is simply to click it. When you click a field, it becomes highlighted. After a field is highlighted, you can drag it to the Report window.

You can highlight *contiguous* (adjacent) fields in the list by following these steps:

+ Click the first field you want in the field list.

+ Move the mouse pointer to the last field you want from the list.

+ Hold down the Shift key and click the last field you want.

The block of fields between the first and last field you selected is displayed in reverse video indicating it is selected. You can then drag the block of fields to the Report window.

You can highlight noncontiguous fields in the list by clicking each field while holding down the Ctrl key. Each selected field will be displayed in reverse video; then you can drag the fields as a group to the Report Design window.

Note Unlike the Query field list, you cannot also double-click a field to add it to the Report window.

You can begin by selecting the Pets table fields for the detail section. To select the fields needed for the detail section of the Pets and Owners report, follow these steps:

1. Click the Pet ID field.

2. Scroll down the field list until the Comments field is visible.

3. Hold down the Shift key and click the Comments field.

The block of fields from Pet ID to Comments should be highlighted in the Field List window, as shown in Figure 19-10.

Dragging fields onto your report

After you select the proper fields from the Pets table, all you need to do is drag them to the detail section of your report. Depending on whether you choose one or several fields, the mouse pointer changes shape to represent your selection. If you select one field, you see a Field icon, which shows a single box with some unreadable text inside. If you select multiple fields, you see a set of three boxes. These are the same icons you saw when you were using the Query Design screens.

To drag the selected Pet table fields into the detail section of the Report Design window, follow these steps:

1. Click within the highlighted block of fields in the Field List window. You may need to move the horizontal scroll bar back to the left before starting this process.

2. Without releasing the mouse button, drag the mouse pointer into the detail section; place the icon under the 1½-inch mark on the horizontal ruler at the top of the screen and next to the 0-inch mark of the vertical ruler along the left edge of the screen.

3. Release the mouse button.

The fields appear in the detail section of the report, as shown in Figure 19-10. Notice that for each field you dragged onto the report there are two controls. When you use the drag-and-drop method for placing fields, Access automatically creates a label control with the field name attached to the text control the field is bound to.

Note   Notice the Bound Object Frame control for the field named Picture. Access always creates a Bound Object Frame control for an OLE-type object found in a table. Also notice that the detail section automatically resizes itself to fit all the controls. Below the Bound Object Frame control is the control for the memo field Comments.

You also need to place the desired field controls for the customer information you need in the page header section. Before you do this, however, you need to resize the page header frame to leave room for a title you will add later.

Resizing a section

To make room on the report for both the title and the Customer table fields in the page header, you must resize it. You can resize a section by placing the mouse pointer at the bottom of the section you want to resize. The pointer turns into a vertical double-headed arrow; drag the section border up or down to make the section smaller or larger.

Resize the page header section to make it larger by following these steps:

1. Move the mouse pointer between the bottom of the page header section and the top of the detail section.

2. When the pointer is displayed as a double-sided arrow, hold down the left mouse button.

3. Drag the page header section border down until it intersects the detail section's ruler at the 1½-inch mark.

4. Release the button to enlarge the page header section.

Now place the Customer table fields in the page header section by following these steps:

1. Click the Customer.Customer Number field.

2. Scroll down the field list until the Phone Number field is visible.

3. Hold down the Shift key and click the Phone Number field.

4. Click within the highlighted block of fields in the Field List window.

5. Without releasing the mouse button, drag the pointer into the page header section; place the icon under the 1½-inch mark on the horizontal ruler at the top of the screen and next to the ⅝-inch mark of the vertical ruler along the left edge of the screen.

6. Release the mouse button; the fields now appear in the page header section of the report, as shown in Figure 19-11.

7. Close the Field List window by clicking the Field List toolbar button.

The page header section expanded to fit the fields that were dragged into the section. At this point, your report should look like Figure 19-11. All the fields needed for the Pets and Owners report are now placed in their appropriate sections.

Working with unattached label controls and text

When you drag a field from the Field List window to a report, Access creates not only a data control but also a label control that is attached to the data control. At times, you will want to add label controls by themselves to create headings or titles for the report.

Creating unattached labels

To create a new, unattached label control, you must use the Toolbox (unless you copy an existing label). The next task in the current example is to add the text header *Mountain Animal Hospital Pets and Owners Directory* to your report. This task demonstrates adding and editing text.

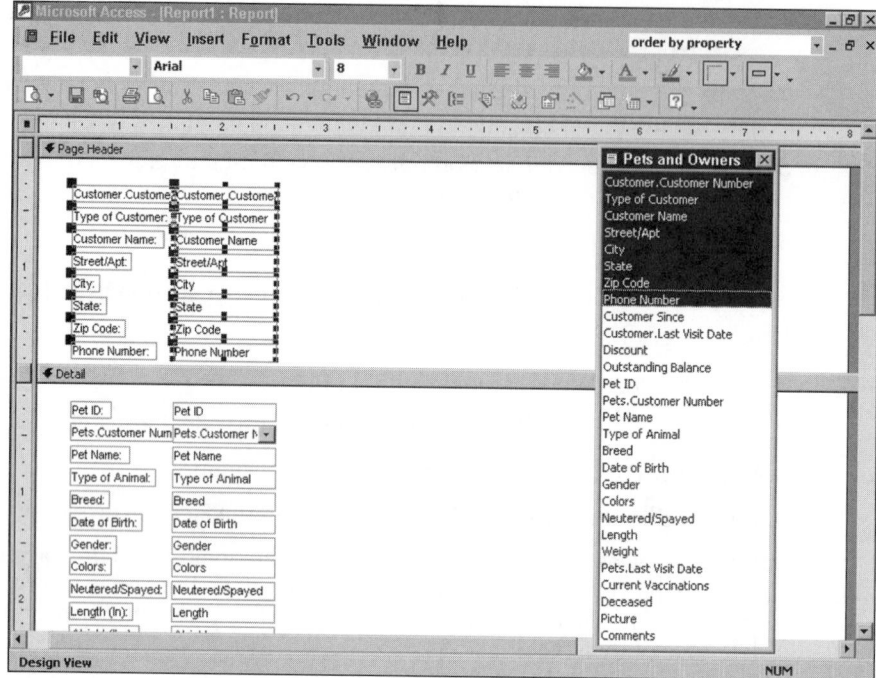

Figure 19-11: The Report Design window for Pets and Owners with all fields shown

To begin creating an unattached label control, follow these steps:

1. Display the Toolbox.

2. Click the Label tool in the Toolbox.

3. Click near the top-left edge of the page header at about the 1-inch mark on the ruler; then drag the mouse pointer downward and to the right to make a small rectangle about 2½-inches wide and ½-inch high.

4. Type Mountain Animal Hospital Pets and Owners Directory.

5. Press Enter.

Tip   To create a multiple-line label entry, press Ctrl+Enter to force a line break where you want it in the control.

Tip   If you want to edit or enter a caption that is longer than the space in the property window, the contents will scroll as you type. Otherwise, open a Zoom box that gives you more space to type by pressing Shift+F2.

Modifying the appearance of text in a control

To modify the appearance of the text in a control, select the control by clicking its border (not in the control itself). You can then select a formatting style to apply to the label by clicking the appropriate button on the Formatting toolbar.

To make the title stand out, follow these steps to modify the appearance of label text:

1. Click the newly created report heading label.
2. Click the Bold button on the Formatting toolbar.
3. Click the arrow beside the Font-Size drop-down box.
4. Select 18 from the Font-Size drop-down list box.

To display all the text, you need to resize it (which you do later in this chapter).

Working with text boxes and their attached label controls

So far you have added controls bound to fields in the tables and unbound label controls used to display titles in your report. There is another type of text box control that is typically added to a report: unbound text boxes that are used to hold expressions such as page numbers, dates, or a calculation.

Creating and using text box controls

In reports, text box controls serve two purposes. First, they enable you to display stored data from a particular field in a query or table. Second, they display the result of an expression. Expressions can be calculations that use other controls as their operands, calculations that use Access functions (either built-in or user-defined), or a combination of the two. You have learned how to use a text box control to display data from a field and how to create that control. Next, you learn how to create new text box controls that use expressions.

Entering an expression in a text control

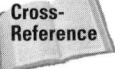
Cross-
Reference

Expressions enable you to create a value that is not already in a table or query. They can range from simple functions (such as a page number) to complex mathematical computations. Chapters 11 and 21 cover expressions in greater detail; for the example in this chapter, you use an expression that is necessary for the report.

A *function* is a small program that when run returns a single value. The function can be one of many built-in Access functions or it can be user-defined. For example, to facilitate page numbering in reports, Access has a function called Page that returns the value of the current report page. The following steps show you how to use an unbound text box to add a page number to your report:

1. Select the Text Box tool on the Toolbox.

2. Scroll down to the page footer section by using the vertical scroll bar.

3. Click in the middle of the page footer section, and then create a text box about three-quarters of the height of the section and about ½-inch wide by resizing the default text box control.

4. Click the label control to select it. (It should say something similar to Text25.)

5. Click the beginning of the label control text, drag over the default text in the label control, and type Page: or double-click the text to highlight it and then replace it.

6. Click twice on the text box control (it says "Unbound"); type =Page and press Enter. (Notice that the Control Source property changes on the data sheet of the Property window to =Page, as shown in Figure 19-12. If the Property window is not open, you may want to open it to see the change.)

7. Click the Page label control's Move handle (upper-left corner); move the label closer to the =Page text box control until the right edge of the label control touches the left edge of the text box control. (Later, you will move the entire control to the right side of the page.)

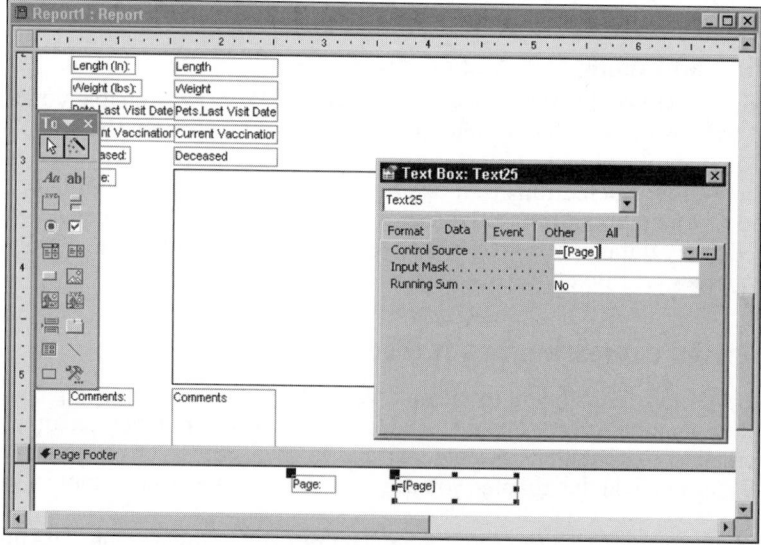

Figure 19-12: Adding a page-number expression in a text box control

Tip   You can always check your result by clicking the Print Preview button on the toolbar and zoom in on the page footer section to check the page number.

Sizing a text box control or label control

You can select a control by simply clicking it. Depending on the size of the control, from three to seven sizing handles will appear — one on each corner except the upper-left corner and one on each side. When you move the mouse pointer over one of the sizing handles, the pointer changes into a double-headed arrow. When the pointer changes, click the control and drag it to the size you want. Notice that, as you drag, an outline appears; it indicates the new size the label control will be when you release the mouse button.

If you double-click any of the sizing handles, Access resizes a control to the best fit for the text in the control. This feature is especially handy if you increase the font size and then notice that the text is cut off, either on the bottom or to the right. Note that for label controls, this *best-fit sizing* resizes both vertically and horizontally, though text controls can resize only vertically. The reason for this difference is that in the report design mode, Access doesn't know how much of a field you want to display; the field name and field contents might be radically different. Sometimes label controls are not resized correctly, however, and have to be adjusted manually.

Changing the size of a label control

Earlier in this chapter (in the steps that modified the appearance of label text), you changed the characteristics of the Pets and Owners label; the text changed, but the label itself did not adjust. The text no longer fits within the label control. You can resize the label control, however, to fit the enhanced font size by following these steps:

1. Click the Mountain Animal Hospital Pets and Owners Directory label control.

2. Move your mouse pointer over the control. Notice how the pointer changes shape over the sizing handles.

3. To size the control automatically, double-click one of the sizing handles. The label control size may still need to be readjusted.

4. Place the pointer in the bottom-right corner of the label control so that the diagonal double-arrow appears.

5. Hold down the left mouse button and drag the handle to resize the label control until it correctly displays all of the text (if it doesn't already).

Tip You can also select Format ⇨ Size ⇨ To Fit to change the size of the label control text automatically.

Before continuing, you should check how the report is progressing. You should do this frequently as you create a report. You can send a single page to the printer or view the report in print preview. Figure 19-13 is a zoomed print preview of how the report currently looks. The customer information is at the top of the page; the pet information is below that and offset to the left.

Note Depending on how you created the Pets and Owners query you may see a differ-ent first record. If you created a right outer join between Customers and Pets, the first customer record Carla Jones has no pets and will appear as in Figure 19-13 with no pet data. If you created the Pets and Owners query with an inner join, the first record will be All Creatures and the Carla Jones record is not displayed. You can tell if the Pets and Owners query contains an inner join or a right outer join by the arrow as shown in Figure 19-7. The arrow signifies an outer join and tells you that all Customer records will be displayed even if there are no related Pet records.

Notice the title at the top of the page. You can see the page number at the bottom if you click the magnifying glass button to zoom out and see the entire page. Only one record per page appears on the report because of the vertical layout. In the next section, you move the fields around and create a more horizontal layout.

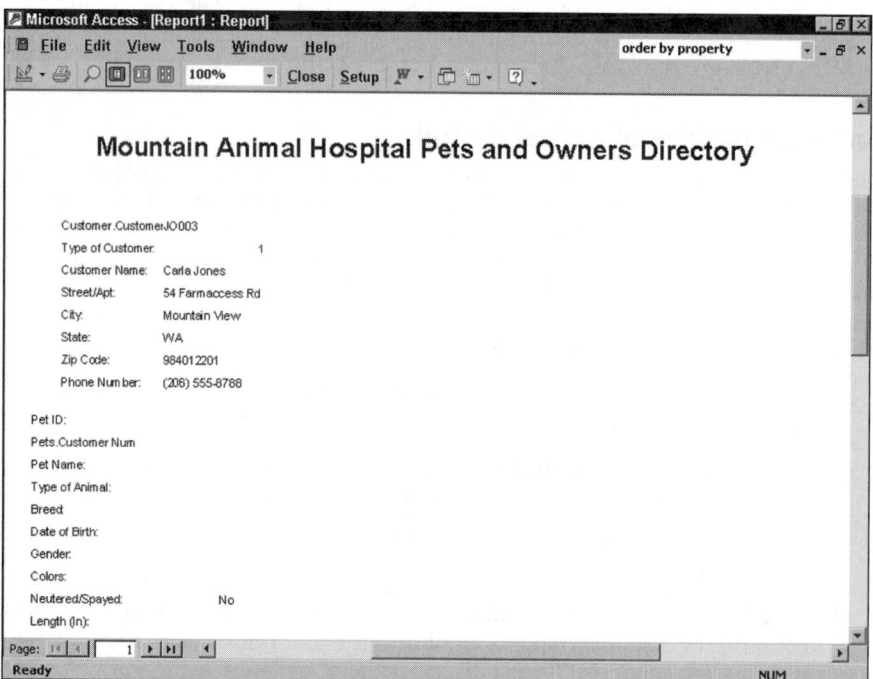

Figure 19-13: A print preview of the report

Deleting attached label and text controls

As Figure 19-13 shows, the report begins with the Customer Number field. The origi-nal design in Figure 19-6 did not have the Customer Number field on the report. After talking to the report design's architect (who is usually yourself), you find that the Customer Number field is not wanted on the report, either in the page header section or the detail section. It's very easy to delete one or more attached controls in a report. Simply select the desired controls and press Delete. When deleting attached controls, there are two choices:

✦ Delete only the label control.

✦ Delete both the label control and the field control.

If you select the label control and press Delete, only the label control is deleted. If you select the field control and press Delete, both the label control and the field control are deleted. To delete an attached control (in this case, the Customer Number controls and their attached label), follow these steps:

1. Click the Close button on the toolbar to exit print preview mode. Select the Customer.Customer Number control in the page header.

2. Press Delete.

3. Select the Pets.Customer Number control in the detail section.

4. Press Delete.

If you accidentally selected the label control that precedes the text box control, the text box control was not removed. Simply click the control and press Delete.

Tip   If you want to delete only the field control and keep the attached label control, first select the label control and then select Edit ⇨ Copy. Next, to delete both the field control and the label control, select the field control and press Delete. Finally, select Edit ⇨ Paste to paste only the copied label control to the report.

Moving label and text controls

Before discussing how to move label and text controls, it is important to review a few differences between attached and unattached controls. When an attached label is created automatically with a text control, it is called a *compound control*. In a compound control, whenever one control in the set is moved, the other control moves as well. With a text control and a label control, whenever the text control is moved, the attached label is also moved. Likewise, whenever the label control is moved, the text control is also moved.

To move both controls in a compound control, select one of the pair by clicking the control. Move the mouse pointer over either of the objects. When the pointer turns into a hand, click the controls and drag them to their new location. As you drag an outline for the compound control moves with your pointer.

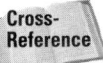

Cross-Reference   The concepts of moving controls are covered visually and in more detail in Chapter 14.

To move only one of the controls in a compound control, drag the desired control by its *Move handle* (the large square in the upper-left corner of the control). When you click a compound control, it looks like both controls are selected, but if you look closely, you see that only one of the two controls is selected (as indicated by the presence of both moving and sizing handles). The unselected control displays only a moving handle. A pointing finger indicates that you have selected the Move handles and can now move only one control. To move either control individually, select the control's Move handle and drag it to its new location.

Cross-Reference   To move a label that is not attached, simply click any border (except where there is a handle) and drag it. You can also move groups of controls with the selection techniques you learned in Chapter 14.

To make a group selection, click with the mouse pointer anywhere outside a starting point and drag the pointer through (or around) the controls you want to select. A gray, outlined rectangle is displayed that shows the extent of the selection. When you release the mouse button, all the controls the rectangle surrounds are selected. You can then drag the group of controls to a new location.

Tip   The global option Tools ➪ Options – Form/Reports tab – Selection Behavior is a property that controls the enclosure of selections. You can enclose them fully (the rectangle must completely surround the selection) or partially (the rectangle must only touch the control), which is the default.

In the next steps, you begin to place the controls in their proper position to complete the report layout as designed (see Figures 19-5 and 19-6). You want this first pass at rearranging the controls to look like Figure 19-14. You will make a series of block moves by selecting several controls and then positioning them close to where you want them. Then, if needed, you fine-tune their position. This is the way most reports are done. Follow these steps to begin placing the controls where they should be.

To roughly position the page header controls:

1. Move the Type of Customer control to the right and down so that the top of the control intersects 1-inch on the vertical ruler and the left edge is under the *P* in *Pets* in the title.

2. Still in the page header, delete (only) the attached labels from all the text controls except Type of Customer.

3. Rearrange the controls in the page header to resemble a typical mailing-label address format; City, State, and ZIP Code should be on the same line.

4. Move the Phone Number text box control under the City text box control.

5. Move the block of name, address, and phone number controls into position so that the top of the block intersects the ½-inch mark on both the vertical and horizontal rulers.

6. Resize the page header section so that it intersects the 1½-inch mark on the left vertical ruler.

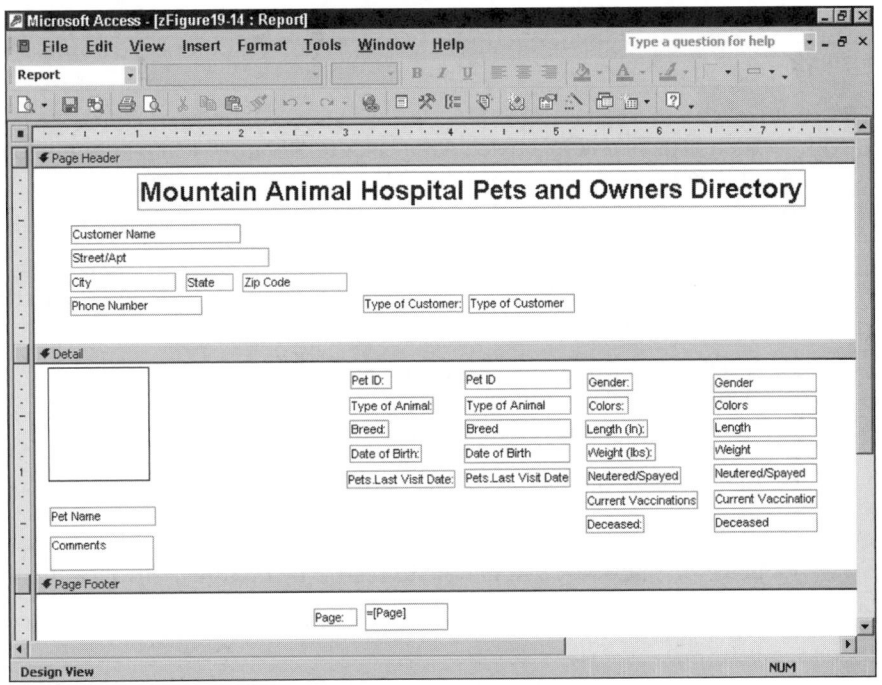

Figure 19-14: Rearranging the controls on the report

Note   Some fields, such as Customer Name, Street/Apt, and Phone Number, may need to be adjusted. You can adjust them now or later.

To roughly position the detail controls:

1. Select the Pet ID, Type of Animal, Breed, Date of Birth, and Last Visit Date controls (and their attached labels) by clicking each text control while holding down the Shift key.

2. Drag the block of controls to the right so that the left edge intersects 3 inches on the top ruler.

3. Select (only) the Last Visit Date control and its attached label.

4. Drag the Last Visit Date control up so that it is just under the Date of Birth control. Make sure all the controls are under the Pet ID control as shown in Figure 19-14.

5. Select the Gender control and its attached label.

6. Drag the control to the right so that the left edge of the label intersects the 5-inch mark on the top ruler and its top is the same as the Pet ID field's top.

7. Select the Colors, Length, and Weight controls and their attached labels by clicking on each text control while holding down the Shift key.

8. Drag the block of controls to the right so that the left edge intersects the 5-inch mark on the top ruler and the top of the Colors controls is the same as the top of the Type of Animal control.

9. Select the Neutered/Spayed, Current Vaccinations, and Deceased controls and their attached labels by clicking each text control while holding down the Shift key.

10. Drag the block of controls to the right so that they are just under the most recently moved block.

11. Select the Current Vaccinations and Deceased controls and their attached labels by clicking each text control while holding down the Shift key.

12. Drag the block of controls upward so that they are just under the Neutered/Spayed control.

13. Delete (only) the Pet Name label control.

14. Delete (only) the Picture label control.

15. Delete (only) the Comments label control.

16. Select the bottom-right handle to resize the Picture control to 1 inch × 1 inch.

17. Move the Picture control to ⅛ inch × ⅛ inch on the rulers (top-left corner) of the detail section.

18. Move the Pet Name text box control under the picture so that the bottom intersects the left ruler at the 1½-inch mark.

19. Move the Comments text box control under the Pet Name text box so that it intersects the left ruler just above the 2-inch mark.

20. Resize the detail section so that it intersects the 2-inch mark on the left ruler.

At this point, you are about halfway done. The screen should look like Figure 19-14. (If it doesn't, adjust your controls until your screen matches the figure.) Remember that these screen pictures are taken with the Windows screen driver set at 800 × 600. If you are using 640 × 480 or large fonts, you'll have to scroll the screen to see the entire report.

The next step is to refine the design to get as close as possible to the design shown in Figures 19-5, and 19-6. The page header section is complete for now. Later in this chapter, you reformat the controls to change the font size and style. In the following steps, you'll complete the detail section's layout:

1. Group select all the fields starting with Pet ID through Last Visit date (in a column).

2. Select and drag that block to the right of the Picture OLE control, as shown in Figure 19-15.

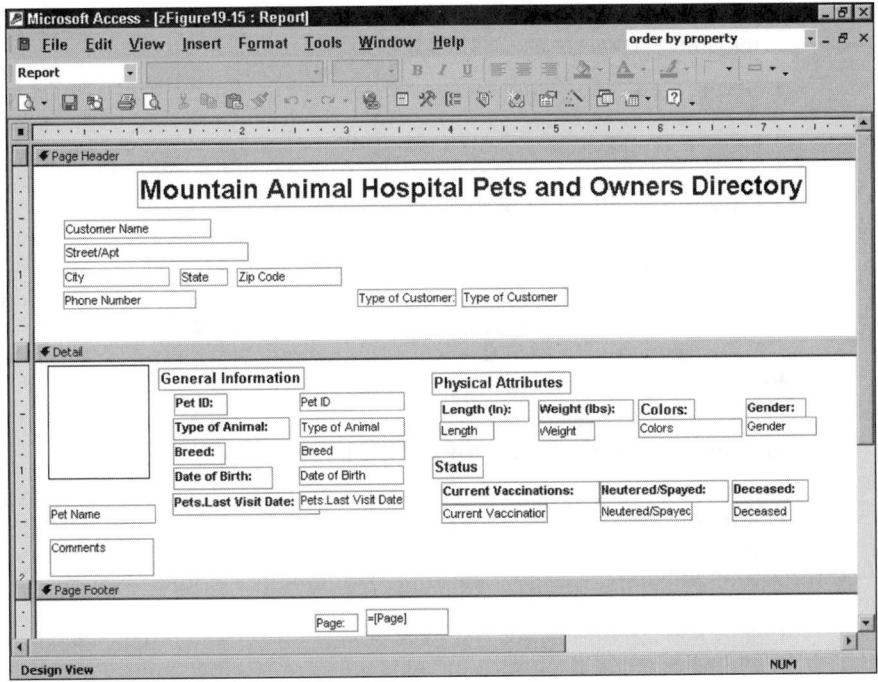

Figure 19-15: The resized label control in the detail section

3. Drag the controls Neutered/Spayed, Current Vaccinations, and Deceased away from other controls to allow space to move the label controls above the text box controls, as shown in Figure 19-15.

4. Drag each of the label controls to locations above the text box controls by grabbing each Move handle individually and then moving the controls above the text box controls.

5. Select all three label controls and align them by selecting Format ⇨ Align ⇨ Bottom.

6. Repeat Steps 3 and 4 for the Length, Weight, Colors, and Gender controls, moving them into position as shown in Figure 19-15.

Again, you may have to resize some of the controls to match the ones shown in Figure 19-15. If you compare the design shown in Figure 19-6 to your screen, you can see that you still need to add some label controls to define the groups. To add the label controls, follow these steps:

1. Double-click the Label Control button in the Toolbox so that you can add more than one label control.

2. Create a new label control above the Pet ID field and enter General Information. Make sure that you press Enter after entering the text of each

label control so that the control is sized automatically to fit the text. You still may have to resize the label if it is bigger than the text.

3. Create a new label control above the Length field and enter Physical Attributes.

4. Create a new label control above the Neutered/Spayed field and enter Status.

5. Click the Pointer tool in the Toolbox to unlock the Toolbox.

These steps complete the rough design for this report. There are still properties, fonts, and sizes to change. When you make these changes, you'll have to move fields around again. Use the design in Figure 19-6 only as a guideline. How it looks to *you*, as you refine the look of the report in the Report window, determines the real design.

Modifying the appearance of multiple controls

The next step is to format all the label controls in the detail section to be bold with a 10-point font size. This will help to differentiate between label controls and text controls, which currently have the same formatting. The following steps guide you through modifying the appearance of text in multiple label controls:

1. Select all label controls in the detail section by individually clicking them while holding down the Shift key. There are 15 label controls to select, as shown in Figure 19-15.

2. Click the Bold button on the toolbar.

3. Click the down-arrow in the Font Size drop-down box.

4. Select 10 from the Font Size drop-down list.

5. Select Format ➪ Size ➪ To Fit to resize all the labels.

Note   You cannot select all the label controls in the preceding steps by using the drag-and-surround method. This method would also select all the text boxes; you want only to bold and resize the labels.

You also need to make all the text box controls bold and increase their font size to 12 points in the page header section. To modify the appearance of text box controls, follow these steps:

1. Select all the controls except the title in the page header section by clicking the mouse pointer in the top-left corner of the section and then dragging the pointer to surround all the controls. Include the Type of Customer label control.

2. Click the Bold button on the toolbar.

3. Click the Font Size box drop-down arrow.

4. Select 12 from the Font Size drop-down list.

5. Select Format ➪ Size ➪ To Fit to resize all the text box controls.

Caution Notice that the text box controls do not display the entire field name. Remember that sizing to fit works only on the vertical height of a control. It is impossible to know how wide a field's value will be — you have to adjust these values manually. You can use the Print Preview window (shown in Figure 19-16) to check your progress.

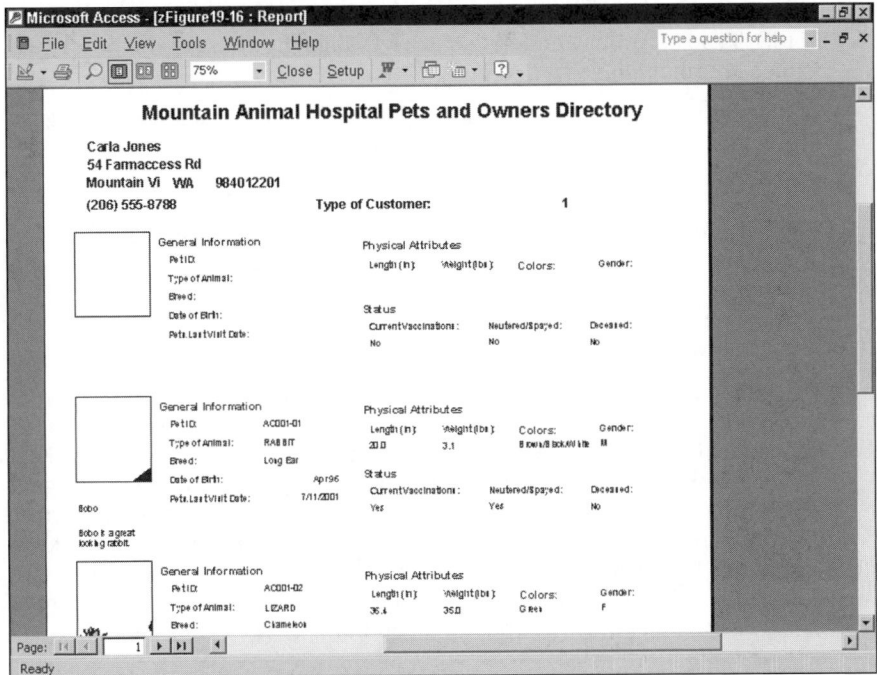

Figure 19-16: Previewing the report

Looking at the print preview may show some minor problems. If you haven't already made any cosmetic changes, you should notice that these changes have to be made (some or all of these may need to be fixed on your form):

Page header section:

- ✦ The City text box is not wide enough.
- ✦ There is too much space after the State text box before the ZIP Code.
- ✦ The Zip Code field is not formatted for ten-digit ZIP codes.
- ✦ The City and State and ZIP Code controls are not aligned.
- ✦ The Phone Number text box is not wide enough.
- ✦ The Type of Customer label needs to be longer.
- ✦ The Type of Customer text box value needs to be left aligned.

Detail section:

- ✦ None of the text boxes in the detail section is 10-point; all are 8-point.
- ✦ The Pet Name needs to be bolded, centered, and moved closer to the picture.
- ✦ The data under General Information is not lined up properly.
- ✦ The Pets.Last Visit Date label needs to have the prefix Pets deleted.
- ✦ Pet ID, Type of Animal, and Breed are left aligned, whereas the other two values are right aligned.
- ✦ The Length and Weight values under Physical Attributes are right aligned and don't line up with the labels above them.
- ✦ The Gender control doesn't quite fit.
- ✦ The Picture bound object frame control is not correctly displayed.

Page footer section:

- ✦ The Page Number control needs to be moved to the right edge of the page.
- ✦ The page number needs to be left aligned; both controls should be italicized.

Tip   Remember that you may have looked at the data for only two records. Make sure that you look at data for many records before completing the report design, and watch the maximum sizes of your data fields. Another suggestion is to create a dummy record to use only for testing; it should contain values that use each position of the field. For example, a great name to test a 24-character field is Fred Rumpelstiltskin III. (Of course, with proportional fonts, you really can't count characters because an i uses less space than an m.)

Another and perhaps the most important problem is that there are two records displayed. Notice the first record for Carla Jones has no pet information. This is because she has no pets, as previously discussed. However, a second record is shown for the Pet ID AC001-01. This is actually Bobo the rabbit, which belongs to All Creatures. This report needs a Customer Number header to show the different customer names and handle the display each time a different customer record is encountered. This will be done later in the chapter.

The problems listed above need to be fixed before this report is considered complete. You can fix many of them easily with the techniques you've already learned. Complete the changes as outlined in the list on the preceding pages. When you're through, your screen should look like Figure 19-17.

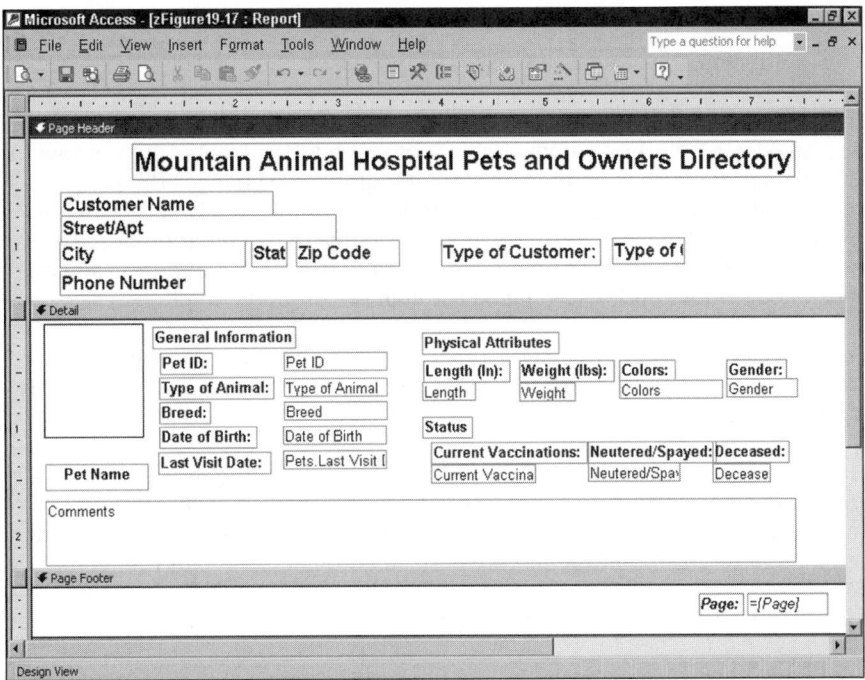

Figure 19-17: The final design layout

After you make the final modifications, you are finished, except for fixing the picture control. To do this, you need to change properties, which you do in the next section. This may seem to be an enormous number of steps because the procedures were designed to show you how laying out a report design can be a slow process. Remember, however, that when you click away with the mouse, you don't realize how many steps you are doing as you design the report layout visually. With a WYSIWYG layout like that of the Access report designer, you may need to perform many tasks, but it's still easier and faster than programming. Figure 19-17 shows the final version of the design layout as seen in this chapter. In the next chapter, you continue to improve this report layout.

Changing label and text box control properties

To change the properties of a text or label control, you need to display the control's property sheet. If it is not already displayed, perform one of these actions to display it:

✦ Double-click the border of the control (anywhere except a sizing handle or Move handle).

✦ Click the Properties button on the toolbar.

✦ Select View ⇨ Properties.

✦ Right-click the mouse and select Properties.

The *property sheet* enables you to look at a control's property settings and provides an easy way to edit the settings. Using tools such as the formatting windows and text-formatting buttons on the Formatting toolbar also changes the property settings of a control. Clicking the Bold button, for example, really sets the Font Weight property to Bold. It is usually much more intuitive to use the toolbar (or even the menus), but some properties are not accessible this way. In addition, sometimes objects have more options available through the property sheet.

The Size Mode property of an OLE object (bound object frame), with its options of Clip, Stretch, and Zoom, is a good example of a property that is available only through the property sheet.

The Image control, which is a bound object frame, presently has its Size Mode property set to Clip, which is the default. With Clip, the picture is displayed in its original size and may be too large to fit in the frame. In this exercise you will change the setting to Stretch so that the picture is sized automatically to fit the picture frame.

Cross-Reference   Chapter 18 covers the use of pictures, OLE objects, and graphs.

To change the property for the bound object frame control that contains the picture, follow these steps:

1. Click the frame control of the picture bound object.
2. Click the Size Mode property.
3. Click the arrow to display the drop-down list box.
4. Select Stretch.

These steps complete the changes so far to your report. A print preview of a single record appears in Figure 19-18. If you look at the second record for BoBo the rabbit, notice how the picture is now properly displayed and the Comments field now appears across the bottom of the detail section. The City field also has more space to display its data.

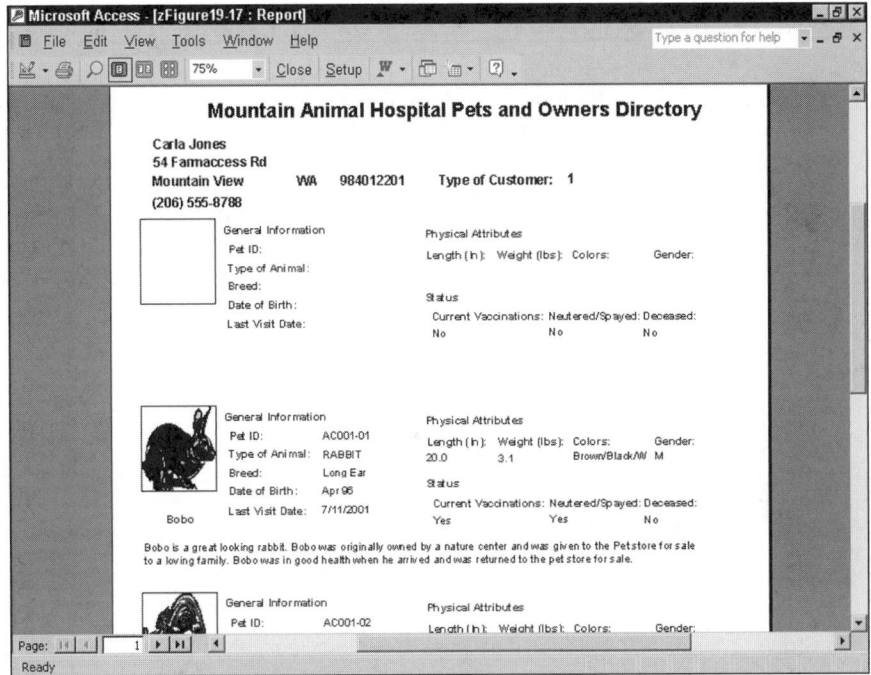

Figure 19-18: The final report print preview

Formatting the display of text controls

Using the Formatting toolbar you can change the appearance of a control and its text. For example, you can make a control's value bold or change its font size. In addition, you can make changes by using the property sheet. Depending on the type of field a text box is bound to — or on whether it contains an expression — you can use various types of format masks. You can type the > character to capitalize all letters, or you can create an input mask to add parentheses and hyphens to a phone number. For numeric and date-formatting properties, you can select from a drop-down list box, which enables you to add dollar signs to a number or format a date in a more readable way. If you want the data to always appear a certain way when used in all forms and reports, apply the format in the table design screen when you create the field.

Note   Access 2002 has the capability to add margins and line spacing to your text box and label controls in both forms and reports. This capability provides greater flexibility in how reports look. You can set up margins for these types of controls in the control's property sheet.

Growing and shrinking text box controls

When you print or print-preview fields that can have variable text lengths, Access provides options for enabling a control to grow or shrink vertically, depending on the exact contents of a record. The option Can Grow determines whether a text control adds lines to fit additional text if the record contains more lines of text than the control can display. The option Can Shrink determines whether a control deletes blank lines if the record's contents use fewer lines than the control can display. Although these properties are usable for any text field, they are especially helpful for memo field controls.

Table 19-4 explains the acceptable values for these two properties.

Table 19-4		
Text Control Values for Can Grow and Can Shrink		
Property	**Value**	**Description**
Can Grow	Yes	If the data in a record uses more lines than the control is defined to display, the control resizes to accommodate additional lines.
Can Grow	No	If the data in a record uses more lines than the control is defined to display, the control does not resize; it truncates the data display.
Can Shrink	Yes	If the data in a record uses fewer lines than the control is defined to display, the control resizes to eliminate blank lines.
Can Shrink	No	If the data in a record uses fewer lines than the control is defined to display, the control does not resize to eliminate blank lines.

To change the Can Grow settings for a text control, follow these steps:

1. Select the Comments text control.

2. Display the property sheet.

3. Click the Can Grow property; then click the arrow and select Yes.

 Note   The Can Grow and Can Shrink properties are also available for report sections. Use a section's property sheet to modify these values.

As previously discussed, you may see a problem with the report: The animals owned by All Creatures are listed under Carla Jones on page 1. What's wrong? The problem is that you haven't told Access how to group your data.

Sorting and grouping data

You have now completely designed the layout of your report. You may think that you're done, but some tasks still remain; one of these is sorting.

Sorting enables you to determine the order in which the records are viewed in a datasheet, form, or report, based on the values in one or more fields. This order is important when you want to view the data in your tables in a sequence other than that of your input. For example, new customers are added to the Customer table as they become clients of the hospital; the physical order of the database reflects the date and time a customer is added. Yet, when you think of the customer list, you probably expect it to be in *alphabetical* order, and you want to sort it by Customer Number or Customer Name. By sorting in the report itself, you don't have to worry about the order of the data. Although you can sort the data in the query, it is more advantageous to do it in the report. This way, if you change the query, the report is still in the correct order.

You can take this report concept even further by *grouping*; that is, breaking related records into groups. Suppose that you want to list your customers first by Customer Name and then by Pet Name within each Customer Name group. To do this, you must use the Customer Number field to sort the data. Groupings that can create group headers and footers are sometimes called *control breaks* because changes in data trigger the report groups.

Before you can add a grouping, however, you must first define a *sort order* for at least one field in the report using the Sorting and Grouping dialog box, which is shown completed in Figure 19-19. In this example, you use the Customer.Customer Number field to sort on first and then the Pet ID field as the secondary sort.

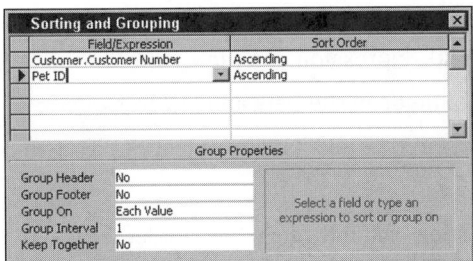

Figure 19-19: The Sorting and Grouping box

To define a sort order based on Customer Number and Pet ID, follow these steps:

1. Click the Sorting and Grouping button on the toolbar to display the Sorting and Grouping box.

Part III ✦ Using Access in Your Work

The Customer Name and Customer Number Fields

You may have noticed that the Customer Name field is not in last name/first name order and that the Customer Number is generally in a sorted order by the customer's last name. The Customer Number field begins with the first two characters of a customer's last name if the customer is an individual (Type of Customer = 1). If the customer is a pet store (Type of Customer = 2) or zoo (Type of Customer = 3), the Customer Number field begins with the first two logical characters of the pet store or zoo name.

For an illustration, examine the following list, which shows Type of Customer, Customer Name, and Customer Number for five records in the Customer table:

Type of Customer	Customer Name	Customer Number
2 - Pet Store	**Al**l **C**reatures	AC001
1 - Individual	Johnathan **Ad**ams	AD001
1 - Individual	William **Ad**ams	AD002
2 - Pet Store	**A**nimal **K**ingdom	AK001
3 - Zoo	**B**orderville **A**quarium	BA001

2. Click in the first row of the Field/Expression column of the Sorting and Grouping box. A downward-pointing arrow appears.

3. Click the arrow to display a list of fields in the Pets and Owners query.

4. Click the Customer.Customer Number field in the field list. Notice that Sort Order defaults to Ascending.

5. Click in the second row of the Field/Expression column.

6. Click the arrow to display a list of fields in the Pets and Owners query.

7. Scroll down to find the Pet ID field in the field list and select Pet ID. The Sort Order defaults to Ascending.

Tip

To see more of the Field/Expression column, drag the border between the Field/Expression and Sort Order columns to the right (as shown in Figure 19-19).

Note

You can drag a field from the Field List window into the Sorting and Grouping box Field/Expression column rather than enter a field or choose one from the field list in the Sorting and Grouping box Field/Expression column.

Although in this example you used a field, you can alternatively sort (and group) by using an expression. To enter an expression, click in the desired row of the Field/Expression column and enter any valid Access expression, making sure that it begins with an equal sign, as in =[Length]*[Weight].

To change the sort order for fields in the Field/Expression column, simply click the Sort Order column and click the down arrow to display the Sort Order list; then select Descending.

Creating a group header or footer

Now that you have added instructions to sort by the Customer Number and Pet ID, you will also need to create a group header for Customer Number to force a page break before each new customer page. This way, a customer page will display pet records for only that customer; customers who have more pets than will fit on one page will continue to generate new pages, with only the customer information and pets for that customer. You don't need a group footer in this example because there are no totals by customer number or other reasons to use a group footer.

To create a group header that enables you to sort and group by Customer Number, follow these steps:

1. Click the Sorting and Grouping button on the toolbar if the Sorting and Grouping box is not displayed. The field Customer.Customer Number should be displayed in the first row of the Sorting and Grouping box; it should indicate that it is being used as a sort in Ascending order.

2. Click Customer.Customer Number in the Field/Expression column.

3. Click the Group Header property in the bottom pane; an arrow appears.

4. Click the arrow on the right side of the text box; a drop-down list appears.

5. Select Yes from the list. (A header section bar appears on the report.)

After you define a header or footer, the row selection bar changes to the grouping symbol shown in Figure 19-20. This is the same symbol as in the Sorting and Grouping button on the toolbar. Figure 19-20 shows both the grouping row symbol and the newly created report section. The Customer.Customer Number header section appears between the page header and detail sections. If you define a group footer, it appears below the detail section. If a report has multiple groupings, each subsequent group becomes the one closest to the detail section. The groups defined first are farthest from the detail section.

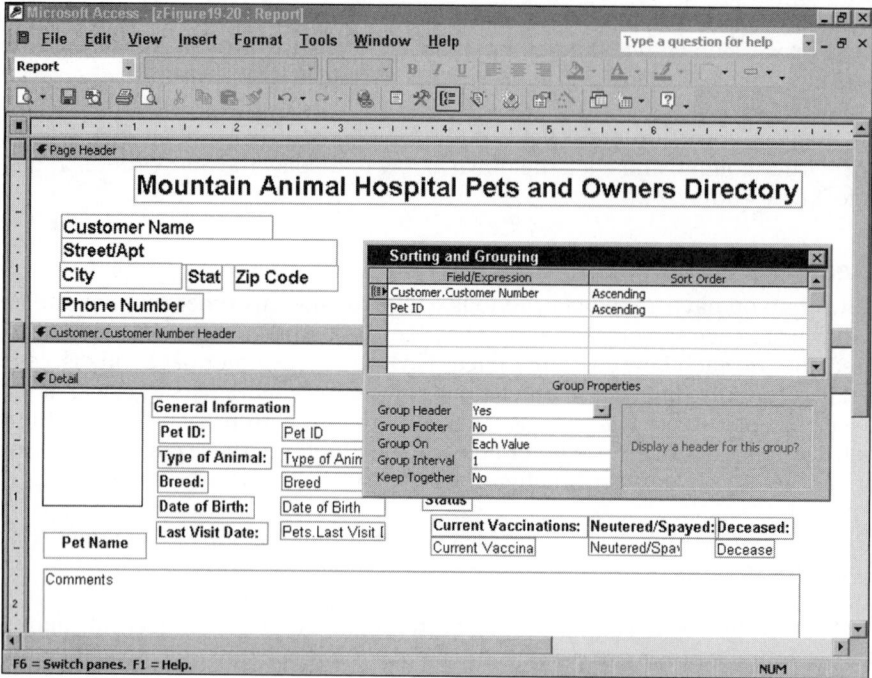

Figure 19-20: The group header definition

The Group Properties pane (displayed at the bottom of the Sorting and Grouping box) contains these properties:

> ✦ **Group Header.** Yes creates a group header. No removes the group header.

> ✦ **Group Footer.** Yes creates a group footer. No removes the group footer.

> ✦ **Group On.** Specifies how you want the values grouped. The options you see in the drop-down list box depend on the data type of the field on which you're grouping. If you group on an expression, you see all the options. Group On has more choices to make.

For Text data types, there are two choices:

> ✦ **Each Value.** The same value in the field or expression

> ✦ **Prefix Characters.** The same first *n* number of characters in the field

For Date/Time data types, there are additional options:

> ✦ **Each Value.** The same value in the field or expression

> ✦ **Year.** Dates in the same calendar year

> ✦ **Qtr.** Dates in the same calendar quarter

✦ **Month.** Dates in the same month

✦ **Week.** Dates in the same week

✦ **Day.** Dates on the same date

✦ **Hour.** Times in the same hour

✦ **Minute.** Times in the same minute

AutoNumber, Currency, or Number data types provide three options:

✦ **Each Value.** The same value in the field or expression

✦ **Interval.** Values falling within the interval you specify

✦ **Group Interval.** Specifies any interval that is valid for the values in the field or expression you're grouping on

✦ **Keep Together.** This option controls what's known as widows and orphans in the word processing world so you don't have a header at the bottom of a page with no detail until the next page

✦ **Whole Group.** Prints header detail and group footer on one page

✦ **With First Detail.** Prevents the contents of the group header from printing without any following data or records on a page

✦ **No.** Do not keep together

On the CD-ROM

After you create the Customer Number group header, you are done with the Sorting and Grouping box for this report. You may need to make additional changes to groupings as you change the way a report looks; the following three sections detail how to make these changes. You should not make any of these changes, however, if you are following the examples. If you want to practice these skills, you can save the report before practicing and then retrieve the original copy of the report you saved. After the next three sections, you will have to size the group header section and change its properties.

Changing the group order

Access enables you to easily change the Sorting and Grouping order without moving all the individual controls in the associated headers and footers. Here are the general steps to change the sorting and grouping order:

1. Click the selector bar of the field or expression you want to move in the Sorting and Grouping window.

2. Click the selector again and hold down the left mouse button.

3. Drag the row to a new location.

4. Release the mouse button.

Removing a group header or footer

To remove a page or report header/footer section, use the View ➪ Page Header/Footer and View ➪ Report Header/Footer toggles. To remove a group header or footer while leaving the sorting intact, follow these steps:

1. In the Sorting and Grouping window, click the selector bar of the field or expression that you want to remove from the grouping.

2. Click the Group Header text box.

3. Change the value to No.

4. Press Enter.

To remove a group footer, follow the same steps, but click Group Footer in Step 2.

To permanently remove both the sorting and grouping for a particular field (and thereby remove the group header and footer sections), follow these steps:

1. Click the selector of the field or expression you want to delete.

2. Press Delete. A dialog box appears asking you to confirm the deletion.

3. Click OK.

Hiding a section

Access also enables you to hide headers and footers so that you can break data into groups without having to view information about the group itself. You can also hide the detail section so that you see only a summary report. To hide a section, follow these steps:

1. Click the section you want to hide.

2. Display the section property sheet.

3. Click the Visible property's text box.

4. Click the drop-down list arrow on the right side of the text box.

5. Select No from the drop-down list box.

Note   Sections are not the only objects in a report that can be hidden; controls also have a Visible property. This property can be useful for expressions that trigger other expressions.

On the CD-ROM   If you are following the examples, complete the steps in the following section.

Sizing a section

Now that you have created the group header, you must decide what to do with it. Its only purpose in this example is to trigger a page break before a new customer record is displayed. (You learn how to do this later in this chapter.) For this example, you don't need to place any controls within the section. Unless you want to see the empty space on the report that is the height of the group header section, you should close the section. You can do this by resizing the section height to 0.

To modify the height of a section, drag the border of the section below it. If, for example, you have a report with a page header, detail section, and page footer, change the height of the detail section by dragging the top of the page footer section's border. You can make a section larger or smaller by dragging the bottom border of the section. For this example, change the height of the group header section to zero with these steps:

1. Move your mouse pointer to the bottom of the Customer.Customer Number section. The pointer changes to a horizontal line split by two vertical arrows.

2. Select the top of the detail section band.

3. Drag the selected band until it meets the bottom of the header Customer.Customer Number. The gray line indicates where the top of the border will be when you release the mouse button.

4. Release the mouse button.

Caution   If every even-numbered page is blank, you accidentally widened the report past the 8-inch mark. If you move a control to brush up against the right page-margin border or exceed it, the right page margin increases automatically. When it is past the 8-inch mark, it can't display the entire page on one physical piece of paper. The blank page you get is actually the right side of the preceding page. To correct this, make sure that all your controls are within the 8-inch right margin; then drag the right page margin back to 8 inches.

Adding page breaks

Access enables you to add page breaks based on group breaks; you can also insert forced breaks within sections, except in page header and footer sections.

In some report designs, it's best to have each new group begin on a different page. A design criteria for the Pets and Owners report created in this chapter, is that no more than one customer will appear on a page (though a customer can appear on more than one page). You can achieve this effect easily by using the Force New Page property of a group section, which enables you to force a page break every time the group value changes.

The four Force New Page property settings are listed below:

✦ **None.** No forced page break (the default)

✦ **Before Section.** Starts printing the current section at the top of a new page every time there is a new group

✦ **After Section.** Starts printing the next section at the top of a new page every time there is a new group

✦ **Before & After.** Combines the effects of Before Section and After Section

To create the report you want, you must force a page break before the Customer Number group by using the Force New Page property in the Customer Number header. To change the Force New Page property on the basis of groupings, follow these steps:

1. Click anywhere in the Customer.Customer Number header.

2. Display the Property sheet.

3. Select the Force New Page property.

4. Click the drop-down list arrow on the right side of the edit box.

5. Select Before Section from the drop-down list box.

Figure 19-21 shows this property sheet.

If you run the report now, you'll see that page 2 has correctly printed only the last record from All Creatures. Page 3 now contains the two pets owned by Johnathan Adams.

Tip   Alternatively, you can create a Customer Number footer and set its Force New Page property to After Section.

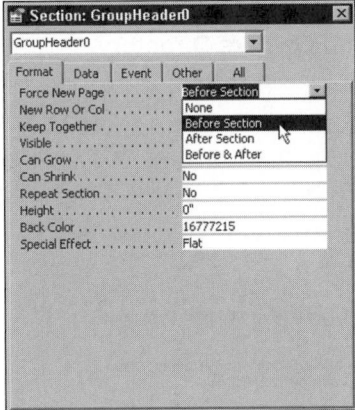

Figure 19-21: Forcing a page break in a group header

Sometimes you don't want to force a page break on the basis of a grouping, but still want to force a page break. For example, you may want to split a report title across several pages. The solution is to use the Page Break tool from the Toolbox; just follow these steps:

1. Display the Toolbox.

2. Click the Page Break tool.

3. Click in the section where you want the page break to occur.

4. Test the results by using Print Preview.

 Note   Be careful not to split the data in a control. Place page breaks above or below controls; do not overlap them.

As you near completion of testing your report design, you should also test the printing of your report. Figure 19-22 shows a hard copy of the first page of the Customer and Pets report. You can see three pet records displayed for the Customer named All Creatures.

Mountain Animal Hospital Pets and Owners Directory

All Creatures
21 Grace St.
Tall Pines   **WA**   **987462541**

Type of Customer: **2**

(206) 555-6622

Bobo

General Information

Pet ID:	AC001-01
Type of Animal:	RABBIT
Breed:	Long Ear
Date of Birth:	Apr 96
Last Visit Date:	7/11/2001

Physical Attributes

Length (In):	Weight (lbs):	Colors:	Gender:
20.0	3.1	Brown/Black/W	M

Status

Current Vaccinations:	Neutered/Spayed:	Deceased:
Yes	Yes	No

Bobo is a great looking rabbit. Bobo was originally owned by a nature center and was given to the Pet store for sale to a loving family. Bobo was in good health when he arrived and was returned to the pet store for sale.

Presto Chango

General Information

Pet ID:	AC001-02
Type of Animal:	LIZARD
Breed:	Chameleon
Date of Birth:	May 95
Last Visit Date:	8/26/2001

Physical Attributes

Length (In):	Weight (lbs):	Colors:	Gender:
36.4	35.0	Green	F

Status

Current Vaccinations:	Neutered/Spayed:	Deceased:
No	No	No

The lizard was not readily changing color when brought in. It only changed color when it was warm. This is not abnormal for a chameleon. However, the species which is believed to originate in northern Australia usually manifests this problem in warm weather only. It is very unusual to see a chameleon not change color when cold.

Stinky

General Information

Pet ID:	AC001-03
Type of Animal:	SKUNK
Breed:	
Date of Birth:	Aug 99
Last Visit Date:	2/8/2001

Physical Attributes

Length (In):	Weight (lbs):	Colors:	Gender:
29.8	22.0	Black/White	M

Status

Current Vaccinations:	Neutered/Spayed:	Deceased:
No	No	No

The skunk was descented and was in perfect condition when it left Mountain Animal Hospital.

General Information

Pet ID:	AC001-04
Type of Animal:	DOG
Breed:	German Sheph
Date of Birth:	Jun 95
Last Visit Date:	11/12/2000

Fido

Physical Attributes

Length (In):	Weight (lbs):	Colors:	Gender:
42.7	56.9	Brown	M

Status

Current Vaccinations:	Neutered/Spayed:	Deceased:
No	Yes	No

Fido was experiencing shortness of breath when brought in. Found that he has asthma.

Page: 1

Figure 19-22: The final report's hard-copy printout

Saving your report

After all the time you spent creating your report, you'll want to save it. It is good practice to save your reports frequently, starting as soon as you create them. This prevents the frustration that can occur when you lose your work because of a power failure or human error. Save the report as follows:

1. Select File ⇨ Save. If this is the first time you have saved the report, the Save As dialog box appears.

2. Type a valid Access object name. For this example, type Pets and Owners - Unformatted.

3. Click OK.

If you already saved your report, Access saves your file with no message about what it is up to.

✦   ✦   ✦

Presentation-Quality Reports and Printing

◆ ◆ ◆ ◆

In This Chapter

Understanding "presentation quality" and "WYSIWYG"

Enhancing text controls by controlling font size and style

Working with multi-line text controls

Applying special display effects to reports

Using a set of option buttons rather than a text box control

Using check boxes and toggle buttons to display Yes/No fields

Adding lines and rectangles to a report

Adding color or shading to a report

Adding three-dimensional effects to a report

Reviewing the Print and Page Setup dialog boxes

◆ ◆ ◆ ◆

In Chapter 19, you build a report from a blank form. That report is fairly simple. You work with only label and text box controls, and the report had no special formatting. There are no lines or boxes and no shading to emphasize any areas of the report. Although the report displays all the necessary data, you can make the data more readable by using check boxes, option buttons, and toggle buttons to display certain fields.

In this chapter, you learn to complete the formatting of the report you created in the preceding chapter, enhancing it to make it more readable and presentable.

Making Reports Presentation Quality

Once you create a report that provides the correct data in a proper format, you can continue to format the report to make it presentation quality. The term presentation quality generally refers to the process of enhancing a report from a database by using special effects that desktop publishing packages provide. The Access Report Writer can accomplish with data, reports, and forms what any good desktop publishing package can do with words. Just as a desktop publishing application can enhance a word-processing document to make it more readable, a good report writer can enhance a database report to make it more usable.

You can, for example, draw attention to special areas of the report that you want the reader to notice. Just as a headline in a newspaper screams the news, an enhanced section of the report screams the information.

Note   You accomplish database publishing in reports with a variety of controls and by enhancing the controls with color, shading, or other means of emphasis. However, you use a somewhat different process to add and enhance these controls in a report. One major difference is the ultimate viewing medium. Because the output of these controls is usually viewed on paper, you have design concerns that differ from those of creating a design to be viewed onscreen. Another difference is the use of each data control. In a form, you input or edit the data; in a report, you just view it.

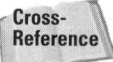

Cross-Reference   To learn about adding controls to a form (many of the controls that you work with in this chapter), see Chapters 16, 17, and 18.

Figure 20-1 shows the hard copy of the final report that you create in this chapter. The report has been significantly enhanced with the addition of special effects and more control types than mere labels or text boxes. For example, important information, such as the type of customer, gender, and current vaccinations, is easily understood because readers only need to glance at an option button or check box versus a numeric code or text.

The Access Report Writer offers a number of tools to make the report controls and sections stand out visually. These tools enable you to create special effects such as the following:

✦ Lines and rectangles

✦ Color and background shading

✦ Three-dimensional effects (raised, sunken, shadowed, flattened, etched, and chiseled)

In this chapter, you use all these features as you change many of the text box controls into option buttons, toggle buttons, and check boxes. You also enhance the report with special text options: shading, shadows, lines, rectangles, and three-dimensional effects.

Caution   When you add shading to a report, you can increase printing time dramatically. Shading can also make data hard to read on all but the best black and white printers. Reverse video (white on black) looks great but can also increase printing time. Also, avoid adding colors unless you plan to print on a color printer.

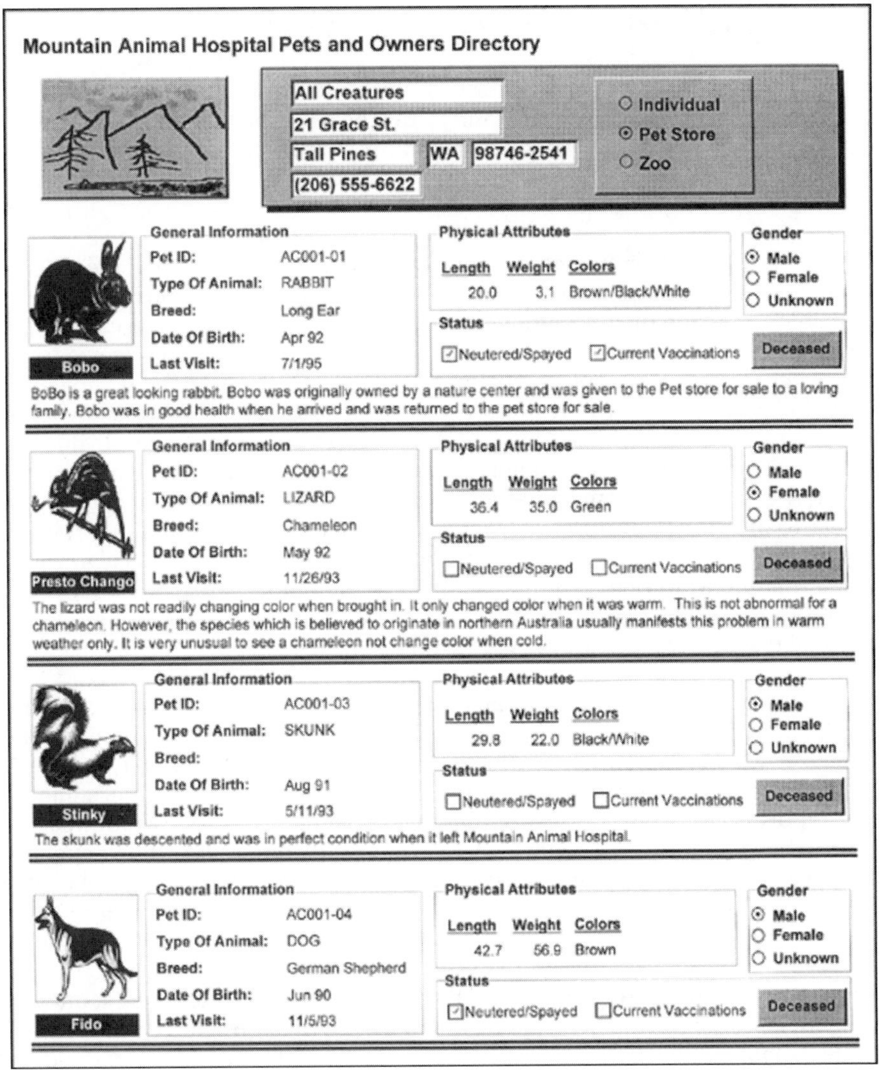

Figure 20-1: An enhanced report

Understanding WYSIWYG Printing

Access has a WYSIWYG (What You See Is What You Get) report writer. As you create controls onscreen, you see instantly how they will look in your report. If you want to see how the data will look, you can take advantage of several types of onscreen preview modes. These modes enable you to see the actual data without involving a hard-copy device.

The Access Report Writer enables you to add color, shading, or reverse video (white letters on a black background) to your report text and controls. You can even color or shade the background of report sections, and you see each effect immediately. Although what you see on the Report Design window seems to be exactly what you'll see when you print, several factors determine just how close what you see is to what you really get. The first problem is with fonts. If you use Microsoft Windows and TrueType fonts, generally about 95 percent of your fonts appear perfectly, both on the Report Design window on-screen and in the hard-copy report. A common problem is that not all letters fit on the report even though they appear to fit in the Report Design window. Another problem is that controls shift slightly from perfect alignment. For example, although the Report Design window shows that the word Deceased fits perfectly in the report, when you view the report in print preview mode or print it to a printer, only the letters Decease are printed. The final d simply vanishes.

Other problems occur when you place controls tightly within a rectangle or group box. Most of the time the print preview modes are perfect for determining what the hard-copy will look like, whereas the Report Design window view may differ slightly. The print preview (or hard copy) should be your only method of determining when your report is complete. Make sure that you're using the correct Windows screen driver when you preview a report; you can get vastly different results depending on the driver. For example, a dot-matrix driver is probably only 100–150 dpi (dots per inch), whereas a laser Printer can be 600 dpi; higher values mean higher resolution (a clearer image).

In this chapter, you modify your report from Chapter 19 to look like the one shown in Figure 20-1. Before you begin, you should start with a design. Figure 20-2 is a sample design for enhancing the report. Lines and rectangles are drawn in the design. Changes to controls and their appearances are noted with instructions and arrows that point to the area to be changed.

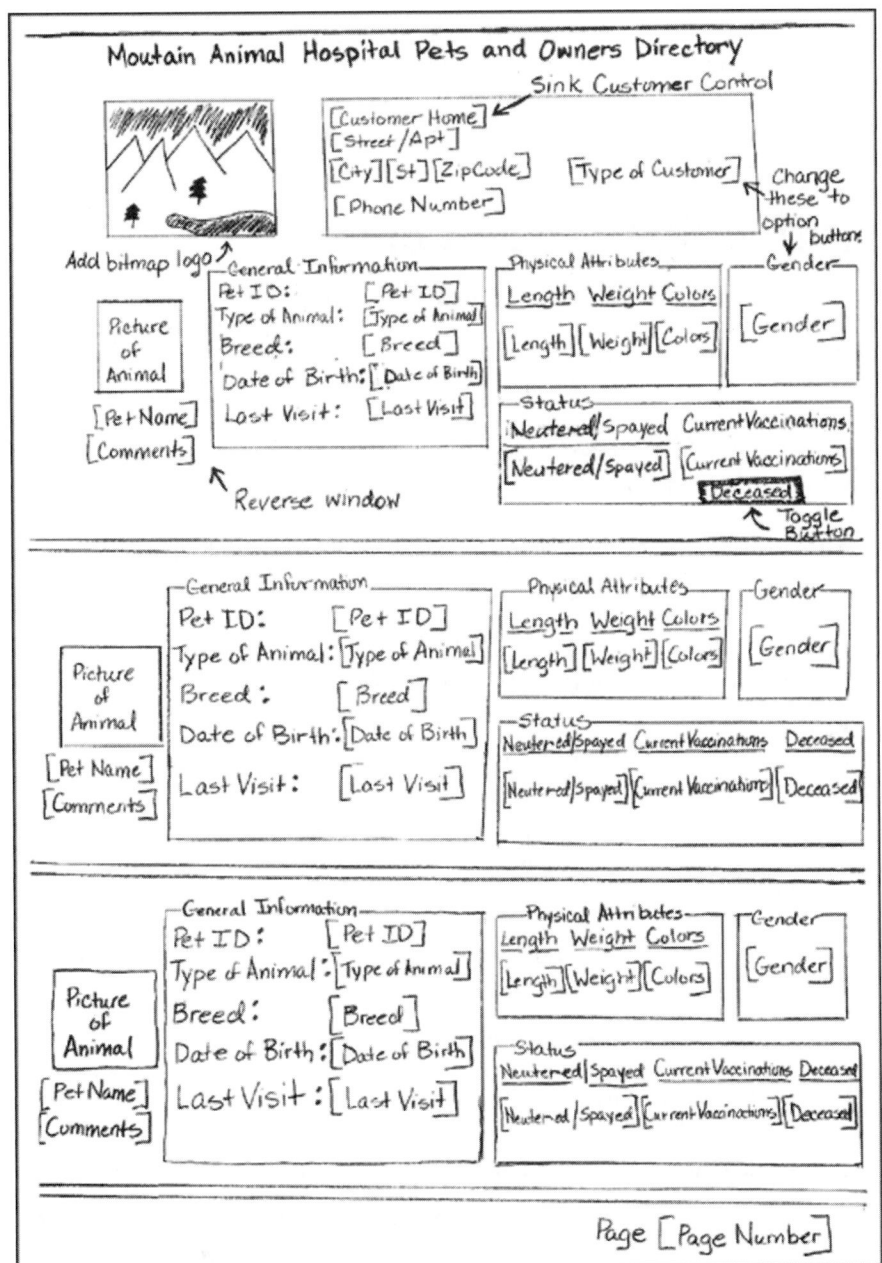

Figure 20-2: A design for report enhancements

If you are following the examples, you should have the Pets and Owners report (created in Chapter 19) open in the Report Design window or the Pets and Owners - Unformatted report design that came in your Mountain Animal Hospital database open.

Enhancing Text-Based Controls

Before you begin using such display items as shading or three-dimensional effects, it's important to get the data right. If your enhancements include control changes, start with these changes.

Enhancing label controls

You can enhance label controls in several ways, such as these:

✦ Change the type style of the text font (Arial, Times New Roman, Wingdings, etc.)

✦ Change the text font size (from 4 to 200 points)

✦ Change the text font style (bold, italic, underline)

✦ Change the text color (using the Fore Color button)

✦ Add a shadow

Changing text fonts and size

Chapter 19 explains how to change the text font type, size, and style. Now you learn to make additional changes as you change the title to match the design shown in Figures 20-1 and 20-2.

These figures show that the text needs to be left justified on the page and made one size smaller.

To change the font placement and size, follow these steps:

1. Select the label control with the text Mountain Animal Hospital Pets and Owners Directory.

2. Drag the label control to the left side of the Report window.

3. Change the control font size to 16 by changing the font size on the formatting toolbar.

Tip   You can select the font in the Properties window for the control but it is easier to use the formatting toolbar.

Using the AutoFormat Button

As in the Form designer, Access has an AutoFormat feature in the Report Design window. The AutoFormat button can assign predefined styles to a report and its controls. To use the AutoFormat functions, click the AutoFormat button on the toolbar when you're in a report design. Access displays the AutoFormat dialog box for reports, as shown in Figure 20-3. Select the desired AutoFormat and click OK to complete the formatting. All your controls (and the overall look of the form) are changed, as shown in the AutoFormat preview.

Tip If you want to format controls the same way, then group them using the Group function (new in Access 2000 and 2002). This can be done the same way it is done in forms. Select the controls that you want to group by holding down the Shift key and clicking the controls that you want to group. In order to group controls you need to click Forma > Group after you select the controls to group. Once grouped, these controls can be formatted at the same time by selecting the group or one at a time by selecting a control inside the group.

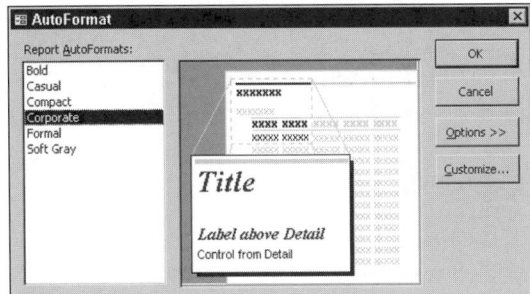

Figure 20-3: The AutoFormat dialog box

Creating a text shadow

Text shadows create a three-dimensional look. They make text seem to float above the page while text shadows stay on the page. You can create text shadows for a report using these techniques:

+ Duplicate the text.
+ Offset the duplicate text from the original text.
+ Change the duplicate text to a different color (usually a lighter shade).
+ Place the duplicate text behind the original text.
+ Change the original text Back Color Transparent button.

Note   Access has a shadow effect on the Special Effects button under the Formatting toolbar. This effect creates a shadow only on boxes or on the text box, not on the text itself. Compare the Mountain Animal Hospital Pets and Owners Directory in Figure 20-4 with that in Figure 20-5.

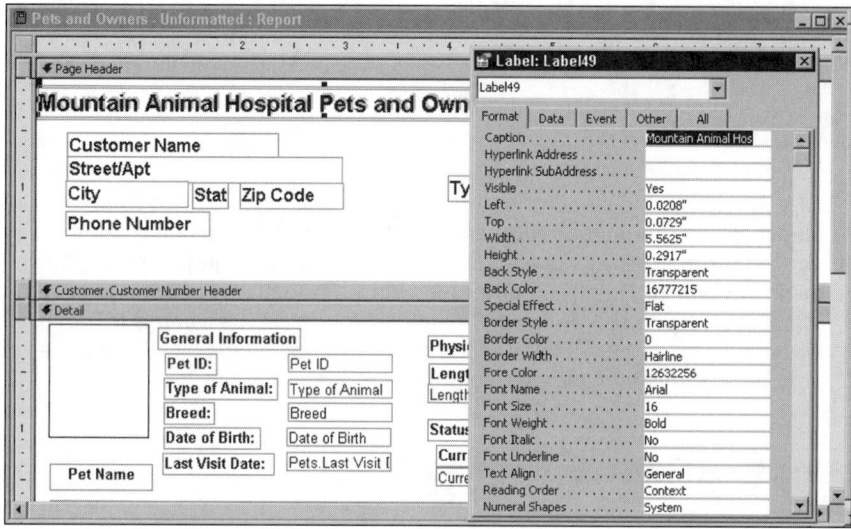

Figure 20-4: Label control properties

To create a shadow for the title's text, follow these steps:

1. Select the label control with the text Mountain Animal Hospital Pets and Owners Directory.

2. Select Edit ⇨ Duplicate.

3. Select light gray from the Foreground Color window to change the duplicate text color.

4. Drag the duplicate text slightly to the right and upward to lessen the offset from the original text below.

5. Select Format ⇨ Send to Back.

6. Select the original copy of the text (the one now in front).

7. Click the Transparent button in the Back Color window.

The text now appears to have a shadow, as shown in Figure 20-4. You may need to adjust the shadow text to make it look perfect. The box around the label control is not visible when the report is printed or in print preview, as shown in Figure 20-5.

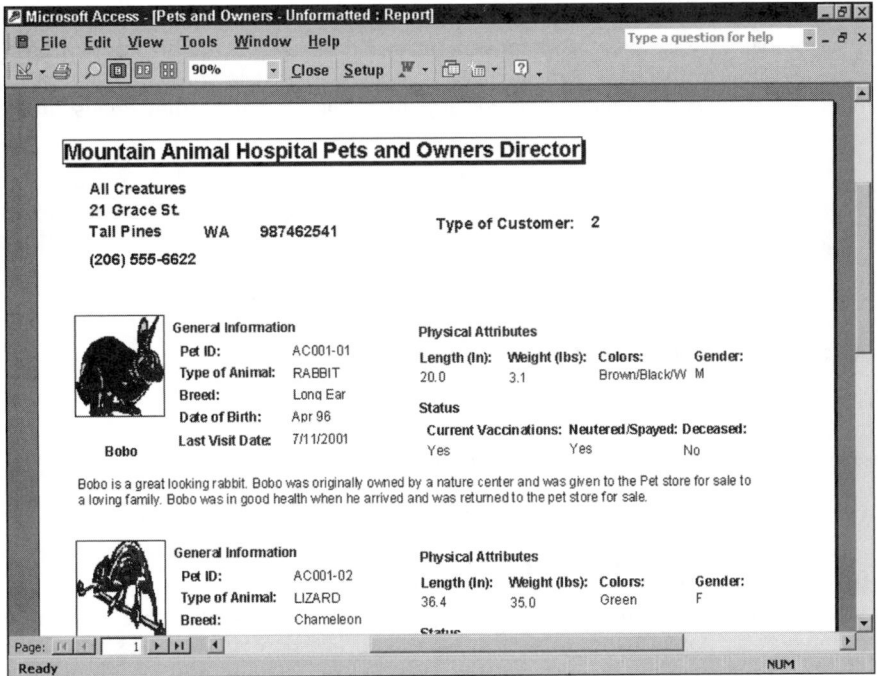

Figure 20-5: Displaying the Print Preview window

Tip

Although the onscreen shadow looks great, it does not print correctly on most monochrome printers. Normally, you get just two lines of black text that look horrible. Unless you have a printer that prints text in shades of gray (using graphics rather than text fonts) or a color printer that prints in gray, avoid using shadowed text on a report. You may also notice in Figure 20-5, the entire word **Directory** is not displayed at the top of the report. Sometimes, you have to go back and make labels wider because they do not print (or print preview) correctly. Usually, it just needs to be a couple pixels wider.

For our purposes, select the shadow box you just created and remove it to continue with the tutorials.

Displaying label or text box control properties

As you use formatting to change values in a label or text box control, you change their properties. Figure 20-4 displays the property sheet for the label control you just created. As you can see in the figure, many properties (described in Chapter 16) can be affected by the formatting windows.

Although you can set many of these controls from the property sheet, it's much easier to drag the control to set the Top, Left, Width, and Height, and to use the Formatting toolbar to set the other properties of the control.

Tip

Access (like other Microsoft Office products) has a Format Painter on the standard toolbar. This excellent and convenient tool enables you to copy styles from one selection to the next. Simply click the item whose style you want to copy, then click the Format Painter button, and then click the item that needs the style change.

A better idea than to shadow the text is to shadow the label box. You can do this easily by deleting the duplicate text label, selecting the original label, and using the Format bar to change the special effect to Shadowed. This technique displays a cleaner look, as shown in Figure 20-5.

Working with multiple-line text box controls

There are two reasons to use a multiple-line text box:

✦ To display a Text data type on multiple lines

✦ To display large amounts of text in a Memo data type

Displaying multiple lines of text using a text box

In the sample report, the Street/Apt text box control in the page header sometimes contains data that takes up more than one line. The way the text box control is sized, you can see only the first line of data. There are generally two ways to see multiple lines of text in a text box control:

✦ Resize the control vertically to allow more lines to be displayed.

✦ Change the Can Grow or Can Shrink properties.

When you resize a control by making it larger vertically, it uses as much space as you created for the field of the record. This leaves excess space for the field if the content's length changes from record to record. For example, most of the values of the Street/Apt text box control use one line; some use two. If you resize the Street/Apt text box control to display two lines, the control displays two lines for every customer. This leaves a blank line between the Street/Apt control and the City control whenever the Street/Apt value uses only one line.

One solution to this problem is to use the Can Grow or Can Shrink properties of the text box control instead of resizing the control. If you change the value of the Can Grow property to Yes, the control grows vertically if there are more lines than can be displayed in the default control. Another solution is to resize the control so that it's larger and then use the Can Shrink property to remove any blank lines if the value of the data does not use the full size of the control.

In addition to setting the Can Grow property in a text box control to Yes, the property can also be set for the detail, group header, group footer or report header or footer sections. This enables the entire section to grow or shrink along with the controls within it.

Displaying memo fields in multiple-line text box controls

The Memo data type fields generally use large amounts of text. You can display these fields on a report by simply placing the text box in the desired section (usually the detail section) and resizing it to the desired width and height.

In a form, you can add scrollbars to display any text that doesn't fit the space allotted. In a report, you don't have that option. So to display text properly, use the Can Grow and Can Shrink properties. In Chapter 19, you create a large text box control to accommodate several lines of memo text, and you set the Can Grow and Can Shrink properties to Yes. Check the Can Grow and Can Shrink properties to verify that they are set to Yes for the Comments text box control and resize the field. To do so, follow these steps:

1. Select the Properties button on the toolbar to display the property sheet.

2. Select the Comments text box control.

3. Change the height of the control to one line to fit the Comments caption.

4. Verify that the Can Grow property is Yes.

5. Verify that the Can Shrink property is Yes.

6. Shrink the detail section height by dragging the page footer border upward until it's just below the Comments control.

To see the effect of the Can Grow and Can Shrink properties, display the report in the Print Preview window. Notice the Comment line and the shadowed line in Figure 20-5, which shows the Print Preview window. Looking at the print preview in zoom mode shows that the spaces between the records are the same, regardless of the size of the Comments field. If no comment text is present, the next record begins immediately below the preceding record's information.

Tip   To enhance a control, use the properties in Access 2002 that enable you to enter margins for all sides of a control (top, bottom, left, and right). You can also add line spacing to a control. To use these properties, display the property sheet for the control and select the format tab. Enter the margins and line spacing in inches.

Adding New Controls

You can change many data types to control types other than text boxes. These data types include Text, Number, and Yes/No. The other control types you can use are

✦ Option buttons

✦ Check boxes

✦ Toggle buttons

Note   Access enables you to change some control types from one type to another type. Generally, text box controls can become combo box or list box controls; check boxes, option buttons, and toggle buttons are interchangeable.

Displaying values with option groups and option buttons

In your design, as shown in Figure 20-2, are two text box controls that should be changed to option buttons within an option group. These text box controls are the Type of Customer field in the page header section and the Gender field in the detail section.

An option group is generally bound to a single field or expression. Each button in the group passes a different value to the option group, which in turn passes the single choice to the bound field or expression. The buttons themselves are not bound to a field — only to the option group box.

Cross-Reference   If you haven't used an option button or option group yet, read Chapter 14 before continuing.

You can use only numeric data values to create an option button within an option group. The Type of Customer field is relatively easy to change to an option group; its values are already numeric, expressed as customer types 1, 2, or 3.

Creating the option group

To create the option group for the Type of Customer control, you must first delete the existing Type of Customer control. Then you can create a new option group and use the Option Group Wizard to create the option buttons.

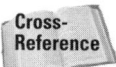

Cross-Reference   Chapter 17 offers a more complete example of creating an option group and option buttons with the Option Group Wizard.

Follow these steps to create an option group using the Option Group Wizard:

1. Delete the existing Type of Customer control.

2. Select the Option Group button from the Toolbox.

3. Drag the Type of Customer field from the field list to the space in the page header section.

   The first screen of the Option Group Wizard should be visible (as shown completed in Figure 20-6). Enter the text label for each option button that will be in your option group, just as you would do in a datasheet. You can press the down-arrow (↓) key to move to the next choice.

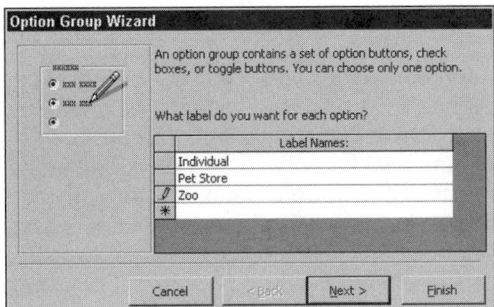

Figure 20-6: Entering the option group choices

4. Enter Individual, Pet Store, and Zoo, pressing the down-arrow (↓) key between choices.

5. Click the Next button to move to the default option Wizard screen.

   The next screen enables you to select the default control for when the option group is selected. Normally, the first option is the default. To make a different button the default, first select the Yes option button and then select the new default value from the combo box that shows your choices. In this example, the first value will be the default automatically.

6. Click the Next button to move to the Assigning Values screen of the Wizard.

   The next Wizard screen displays the actual values you entered, along with a default set of numbers that will be used to store the selected value in the bound option group field. The screen looks like a datasheet with two columns. In this example, this is the Type of Customer field. Your first choice, Individual, is automatically assigned a 1, Pet Store a 2, and Zoo a 3. When Pet Store is selected, a 2 is stored in the Type of Customer field.

   In this example, the default values are acceptable. Sometimes you may want to assign values other than 1, 2, 3, and so on. For example, you might want to use 100, 200, and 500. As long as you use unique numbers, you can assign any values you want.

7. Click the Next button to move to the next Wizard screen.

   In this Wizard screen, you have to decide whether to bind the option group itself to a form field or to leave it unbound. The first choice in the Wizard, Save the value for later use, creates an unbound field. When you are using the option group in a dialog box that uses the selected value to make a decision, you don't want to store the value in a table field. In this example, the second value, Store the value in this field, is selected automatically because you started with the Type of Customer field. If you want to bind the option group value to a different table field, you can select from a list of all form fields. Again, in this example, the default is acceptable.

8. Click the Next button to move to the Wizard screen that sets the option group style.

Again, as shown in Figure 20-7, the defaults are acceptable for this example. Notice that your actual values are used as a sample. In this Wizard screen, the upper half of the Wizard screen enables you to choose which type of buttons you want. The lower half enables you to choose the style for the option group box and the type of group control. The style affects the option group rectangle. If you choose Raised, Sunken, Etched, or Shadowed, that value is applied to the Special Effect property of the option group. Additionally, for Option buttons and Check boxes, if you choose any of the special effects, the property for each option button or check box is set to the special effect.

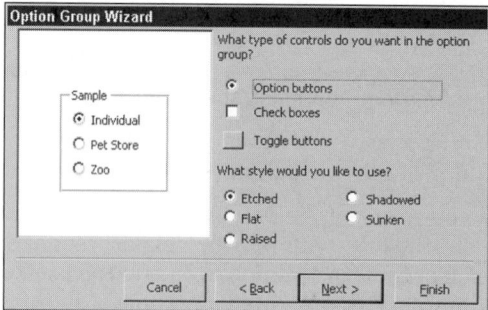

Figure 20-7: Selecting the type and look of your buttons

Note   As you change your selections, the Sample changes as well.

9. Click the Next button to move to the final option group Wizard screen.

   The final screen enables you to give the option group control a label that will appear in the option group border. You can then add the control to your design and optionally display help.

10. Accept Type of Customer as your label for the Option Group.

11. Click the Finish button to complete the Wizard.

   Your Wizard work is now complete, and the controls appear on the design screen. Eight controls have been created: the option group, its label, three option buttons, and their labels. In this example, you don't want the option group label.

12. Select the option group label Type of Customer, and click the Delete key to remove it.

Creating an option group with a calculated control

You also want to display the Gender field as a set of option buttons. There is one problem, however. The Gender field is a text field with the values of M, F, and U. You can create option buttons only with a numeric field. You can do this easily with the

Type of Customer field, which is numeric. How can you solve this problem with the Gender field? The solution is to create a new calculated control that contains an expression. The expression must transform the values M to 1, F to 2, and U to 3. You create this calculation by using the Immediate IF function (IIf), with this expression:

```
=IIf([Gender]="M","1",IIf([Gender]="F","2","3"))
```

The first IIf function checks the value of Gender; if the value is "M," the value of the calculated control is set to 1. If the value is not "M," the second IIf checks for a Gender value of "F." If the value is "F," the calculated control value is set to 2. If the value is not "F," the value of the calculated control is set to 3. To create this new calculated control, follow these steps:

1. Create a new text box control alongside the Status text control, as shown in Figure 20-8.

2. Delete the attached label control.

3. Display the All sheet of the Properties window for the text box control.

4. Change the Control Name property to Gender Number.

5. Type =IIf([Gender]="M","1",IIf([Gender]="F","2","3")) in the Control Source property. (Remember that you can press Shift+F2 to zoom.)

6. Change the Visible property to No.

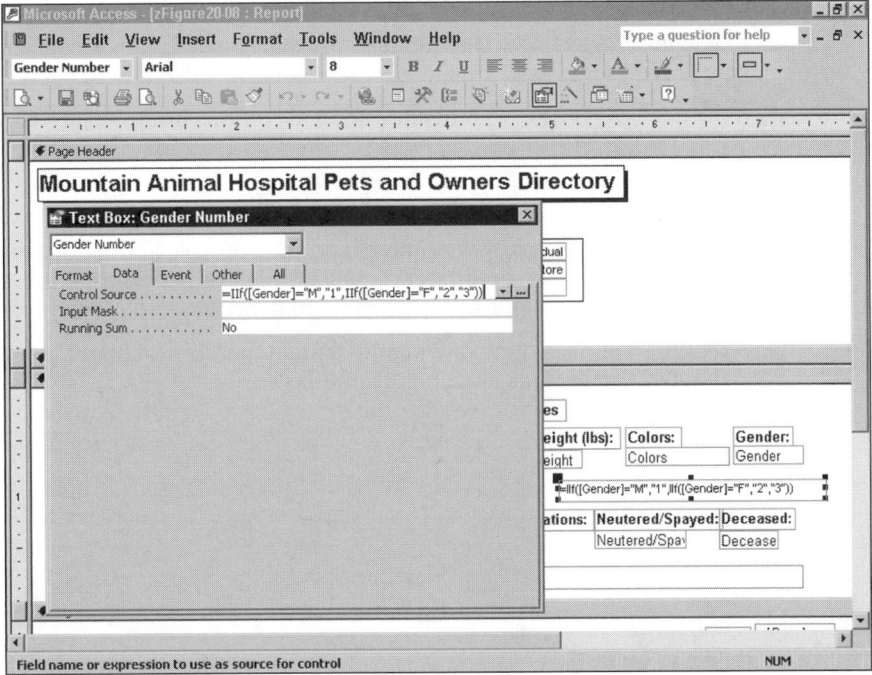

Figure 20-8: Creating a calculated control

Because you changed the Visible property of the calculated control to No, the control is not displayed when you produce the report. After you create the calculated control, you can use it as the control source for an option group. Figure 20-8 shows this new calculated control at the bottom-right of the screen. If you look at the report in print preview, you will see that the control is not visible.

To create the option group for Gender (based on this calculated control), follow these steps:

1. Delete the existing Gender text box and label control in the detail section.

2. Select the Option Group button from the Toolbox.

3. Drag the Option Group rectangle to the space in the detail section. The first screen of the Option Group Wizard should be displayed.

4. Enter Male, Female, and Unknown, pressing the down-arrow (↓) key between choices.

5. Click the Next button three times to move to the Control Source screen.

   In this Wizard screen, you have to decide whether the option group itself will be bound to a form field or unbound. In this example, you will use the first choice in the Wizard, Save the value for later use, which creates an unbound field. You cannot select a calculated field in the Wizard; after completing it, you will change the control source of the option group.

6. Click the Next button to move to the Option Group Style Wizard screen.

   Again, for this example, the defaults are acceptable. Notice that your actual values are used as a sample.

7. Click the Next button to move to the final Option Group Wizard screen.

8. Accept Gender.

9. Click the Finish button to complete the Wizard.

   Your Wizard work is now complete, and the controls appear on the design screen. Currently, as an unbound control, the Control Source property is blank. You must set this to the calculated control Gender Number.

10. Select the option group control and change the Control Source property to =[Gender Number], as shown in Figure 20-9.

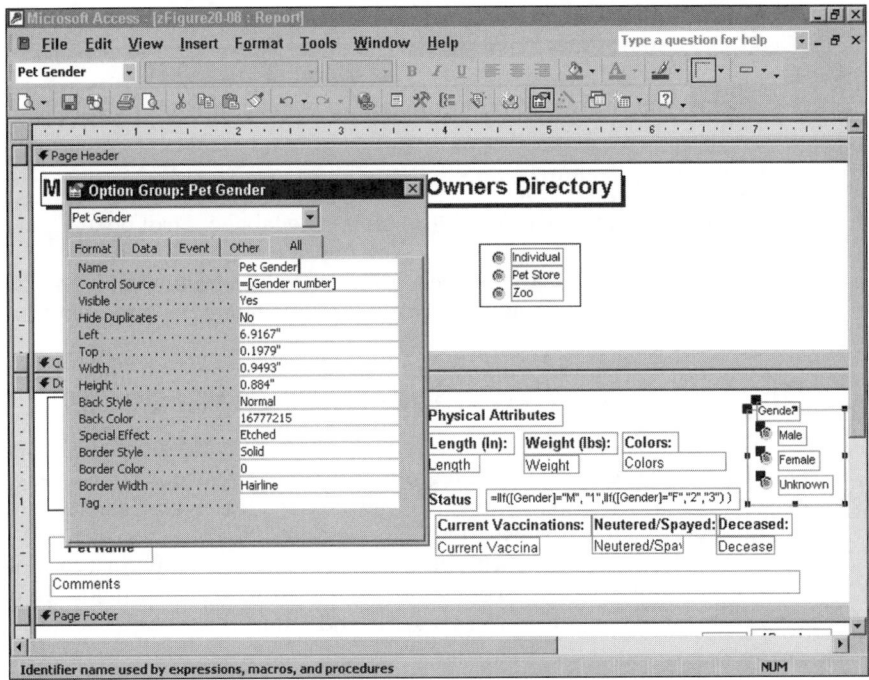

Figure 20-9: Completing an option group for a calculated control

11. Name the control Pet Gender by changing the Name property to Pet Gender.

Caution

You must not name this control Gender. The Pets table already has a field named Gender; if you duplicate the name as a control, you will receive an error.

You may need to change the size of the rectangle to fit within the 8-inch form width. If you have to make it smaller, remember to change the width (which may be larger than 8 inches now).

12. Resize the option group rectangle and reset the width of the form to 8 inches.

The last task is to enhance all the text on the control buttons to 12-point bold. To accomplish this, follow these steps:

1. Select the entire Gender option group box, all the buttons and their attached labels.

2. Click the Bold button on the toolbar.

3. Select Format ⇨ Size ⇨ To Fit to resize the label control boxes.

You may still need to align the labels before your task is complete. The final design for the option buttons is shown in Figure 20-9, including the option button properties.

Displaying Yes/No values with check boxes

You can make Yes/No values more readable by using check boxes. Although you could also use them in an option group, the primary purpose of a check box is to display one of two states for a single value; check boxes are easier to create than option groups. You will now change the Neutered/Spayed and Current Vaccinations fields into check boxes. As with option button controls, you must first delete the existing text box controls to create a check box that uses the fields. To create the check boxes, use Figure 20-10 as a guide and follow these steps:

1. Select the Neutered/Spayed and Current Vaccinations text box controls (and their associated labels) in the detail section.

2. Press Delete to delete both the text box controls and the attached label controls.

3. Select the Check Box button from the Toolbox.

4. Using Figure 20-10 as a guide, drag the Neutered/Spayed and Current Vaccinations fields from the field list to create two new check boxes.

5. Select both check box controls; change the font size to 10.

6. Size the controls to fit; move them as necessary.

The completed check boxes are shown in Figure 20-10.

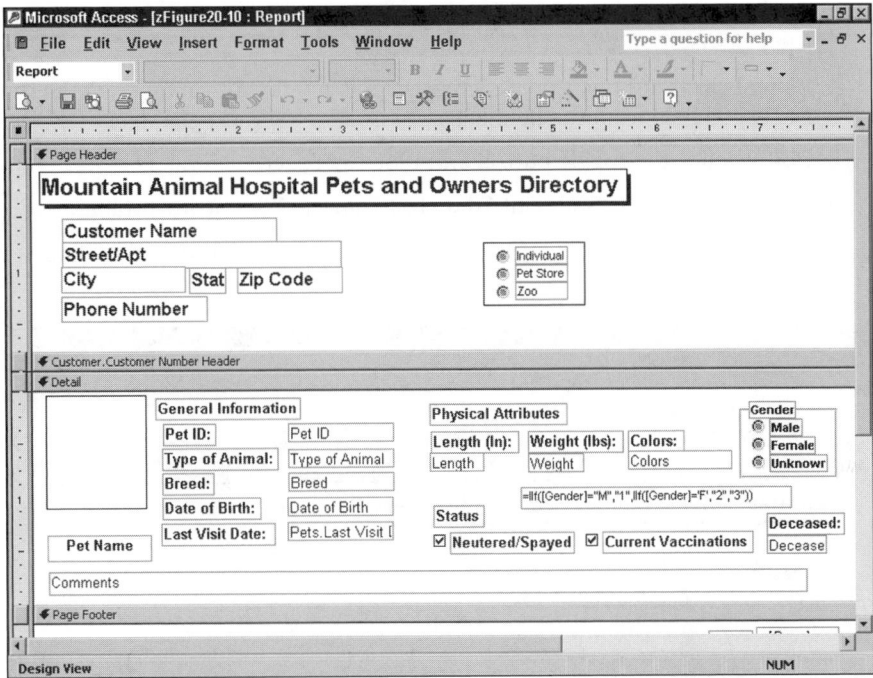

Figure 20-10: The completed check boxes

Displaying values as toggle buttons

You can use toggle buttons as another way to make Yes/No data types easier to read. A toggle button appears to sit above the screen if the value of the Yes/No data type is No. If the value is Yes, the button appears to be depressed. To create a toggle button for the Deceased field, follow these steps:

1. Select the Deceased text box control (and its associated label) in the detail section.

2. Press Delete to delete both the text box control and the attached label control.

3. Select the Toggle Button icon from the Toolbox and the field Deceased from the field list.

4. Using Figure 20-11 as a guide, create a new toggle button by dragging the Deceased field from the field list.

5. Double-click the toggle button and type Deceased.

6. Select Bold and the 10-point Font size from the Formatting toolbar.

7. Select Format ➪ Size ➪ To Fit to fit the button around the caption text.

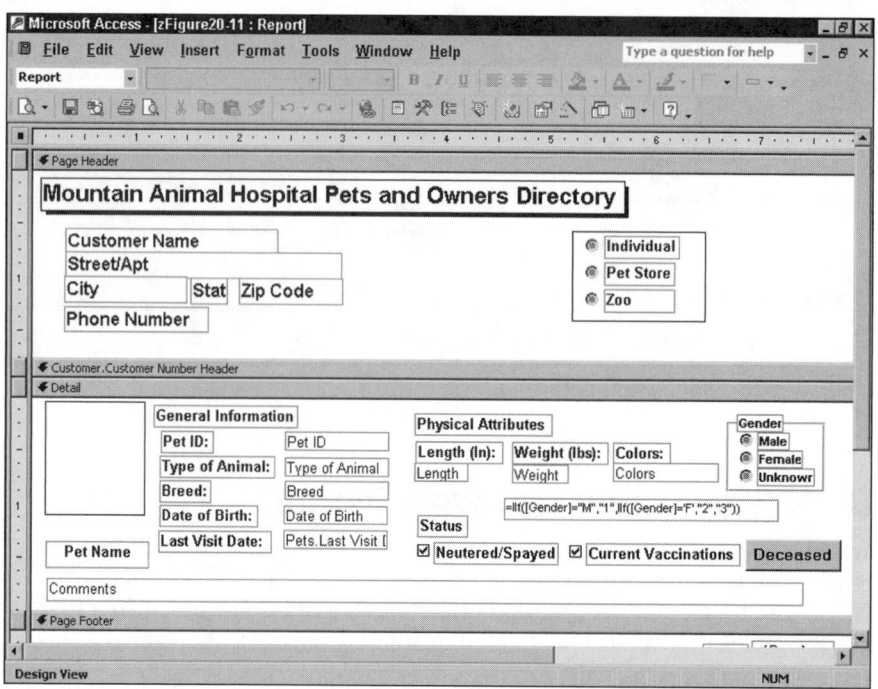

Figure 20-11: Creating a toggle button

Though it looks like a command button, it is actually a toggle button that can be pressed and appear to be sunken and then pressed again and appear to be raised.

Note   You will probably not normally use a toggle button on a report unless you make sure the two different states can be viewed on a printed page or pictures are going to be used to convey a true or false value.

The toggle button is displayed with the caption centered within the control.

Note   A picture rather than text can be displayed on the face of the toggle button by entering the filename of a bitmap image in the Picture property of the toggle button. Use the builder button to display the Insert Picture dialog box, as shown in Figure 20-12.

Remember that Access enables you to change some controls from one type to another; first select the control (right-click to display the shortcut menu), and then select the new control style from the Change To option.

Displaying bound OLE objects in reports

In the report you are creating in this chapter, a picture of each animal is shown in the detail section. Some animals are displayed as they look, but others appear stretched out of proportion. Presto Chango (who is not really a hunchbacked lizard) illustrates this distortion.

Pictures are stored in OLE controls. The two types of OLE controls are listed below:

✦ **Bound object frames.** Pictures are stored in a record

✦ **Image frames.** Pictures are embedded or linked to a report section itself

In this report, there is already a bound object frame. The Picture field is an OLE data type that has bitmaps embedded in each record. The Picture bound object control gets its values from the Picture field in the Pets table.

Displaying an image in a report

You can also add an image object to your report by pasting a bitmap from the Clipboard or by embedding or linking a bitmap file that contains a picture. As you learned in the form chapters, on the disk that accompanies this book is a bitmap called MTN.BMP. In this section, you learn to add this bitmap to the page header section (if you copied it to your Access directory).

Using Figure 20-12 as a guide, move the customer information to the right side of the page header section and then add the bitmap to the left side after creating the image frame. To add an unbound object frame, follow these steps:

1. Select the customer information in the page header section and move it to the right, as shown in Figure 20-12.

2. Click the Image button in the Toolbox.

3. Click the left corner below the title; drag the box so that it's sized as shown in Figure 20-12. The Insert Picture dialog box appears.

   From this dialog box, you can select the picture filename you want to insert into your report.

Tip   If you don't see the preview of the picture as shown in Figure 20-12, select the Views button ➪ Preview from the Insert Picture toolbar.

4. Select MTN.BMP from your Access directory (or wherever you copied the files for the book) and click OK.

5. Display the property sheet.

6. Change the Size Mode property to Stretch.

7. Change the Border property so that the picture does not simply blend into the background (there is too much white in the picture); change the border color to black or make the border three-dimensional (as shown in the next step).

8. Click the Raised button in the Special Effect formatting window.

The image frame is now complete.

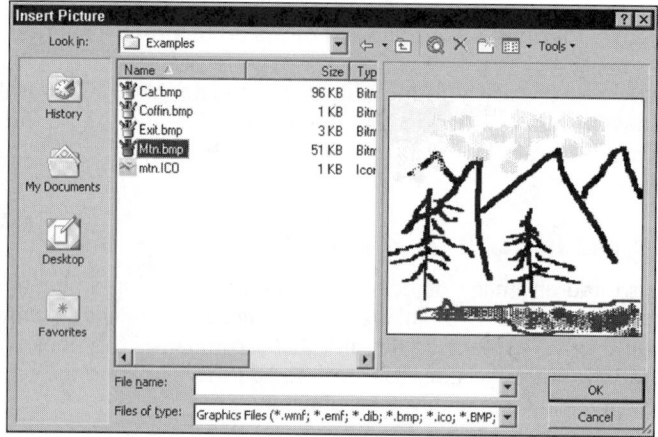

Figure 20-12: Adding a bitmap image to a report

Working with Lines and Rectangles

You can use lines and rectangles (commonly called boxes) to make certain areas of the report stand out or to bring attention to desired areas of the report. In Figure 20-1 are several groups of lines and rectangles that are used to emphasize data in the report. You need several rectangles and two different lines to complete the lines and boxes in this report. Figure 20-13 will be used as a guide for creating emphasis, boxes, and lines.

To create the rectangle for the page header, follow these steps, using Figure 20-13 as a guide:

1. Select the Rectangle button in the Toolbox.
2. Click the upper-left part of the page header section to the right of the picture and just below the title.
3. Drag the rectangle around the entire set of customer text boxes and option buttons.
4. Select Format ⇨ Send to Back to redisplay the text boxes and option buttons.

Note You may notice that when you create the rectangle, it blocks out the controls beneath it. Sending the rectangle to the background makes the controls reappear.

You can also redisplay the controls by changing the Transparent button of the Back Color. This option, however, does not enable you to add other shading effects. For a rectangle, you should always select Send to Back.

The next three rectangles are in the detail section. You can create the rectangles by following the same steps you used to create the rectangle in the page header section. As you create them, you may find yourself rearranging some of the controls to fit better within the rectangles. Also change the label controls for Length, Weight, and Colors, as shown in Figure 20-13.

Several lines are needed for the report. A single line needs to be added to the top of the report above the title, and two lines need to be added below the Comments text box. To add these lines, complete the next set of steps, using Figure 20-13 as a guide (you can also take this opportunity to remove the shadow on the title if you added it earlier):

1. Click the title line (Mountain Animal Hospital Pets and Owners Directory).
2. Turn off the border shadow and make the background transparent using the Format bar.
3. Move the title line down, leaving sufficient room to place a thick line.
4. Click the Line button in the Toolbox.
5. Create a new line above the title in the page header, across the entire width of the report. Be careful not to extend into your printer's non-printing area. The example has a ¼" margin on each side.
6. Select choice 3 from the Border Width window of the Formatting toolbar to make the line thicker.
7. Create a new line below the Comments text box in the detail section.

8. Again, make the line thickness 3 from the Border Width window to make the line thicker.

9. Duplicate the line below the comments and align it with the line above.

Tip   If you hold down the Shift key while creating a line, the line remains perfectly straight, either horizontally or vertically, depending on the initial movement of drawing the line.

Emphasizing Areas of the Report

The report is now almost complete, but several tasks remain. According to the original printout and design shown in Figures 20-1 and 20-2, you still need to shade the rectangle in the page header, add a shadow to the rectangle, sink the Customer text box controls, create an etched effect for the Type of Customer option group box, and change Pet Name to reverse video.

Adding background shading

A background shade can be added to any control. Adding background shading to a rectangle shades any controls contained within the rectangle. You can, however, add background shading to all controls that are selected at one time. To add background shading to the rectangle in the page header section, follow these steps:

1. Select the Rectangle control in the page header section.

2. Select the light gray Back Color.

Sinking controls

Generally, you cannot sink controls in a report; they don't look sunken on a white background. You can, however, use a gray background to enhance the depth of a control; both sunken and raised controls stand out on a gray background. Because you just added a gray background to the rectangle in the page header, you can sink or raise controls within the rectangle. To give the Customer text box controls a sunken appearance, follow these steps:

1. Select each of the Customer text box controls in the page header section.

2. Click the Sunken selection from the Special Effects button.

If you sink or raise a check box, Access uses a different, smaller check box that has the appearance of depth.

Etched controls

Next, give the rectangle inside the large rectangle an etched look. Like sunken controls, etched controls look much better on a gray or dark background. To give the Type of Customer option group control an etched look, follow these steps:

1. Select the Type of Customer option group control.

2. Click the Etched selection from the Special Effects button.

Creating a shadow on a rectangle

To emphasize an area of the report, add a shadow to any control. Most commonly, rectangles and text boxes are the types of controls given this effect. Shadows are created by adding a solid-color rectangle that is slightly offset and behind the original control. If the background is light or white, you need a dark-colored rectangle. If the background is dark or black, you need a light-colored or white rectangle. To create a shadow for the page header rectangle, follow these steps:

1. Select the rectangle in the page header.

2. Click the Special Effects button in the Formatting toolbar.

3. Select Shadow from the window.

Changing text to a reverse video display

Text really stands out when you create white text on a black background. This is called reverse video; it's the opposite of the usual black on white. You can convert text in a label control or text box to reverse video by changing the fill color to black and the text color to white. To change the Pet Name text control to reverse video, follow these steps:

1. Select the Pet Name text control (not the label control).

2. Click on the black Back Color button.

3. Click the white Fore Color button.

Figure 20-13 shows the final report in the Report Design window.

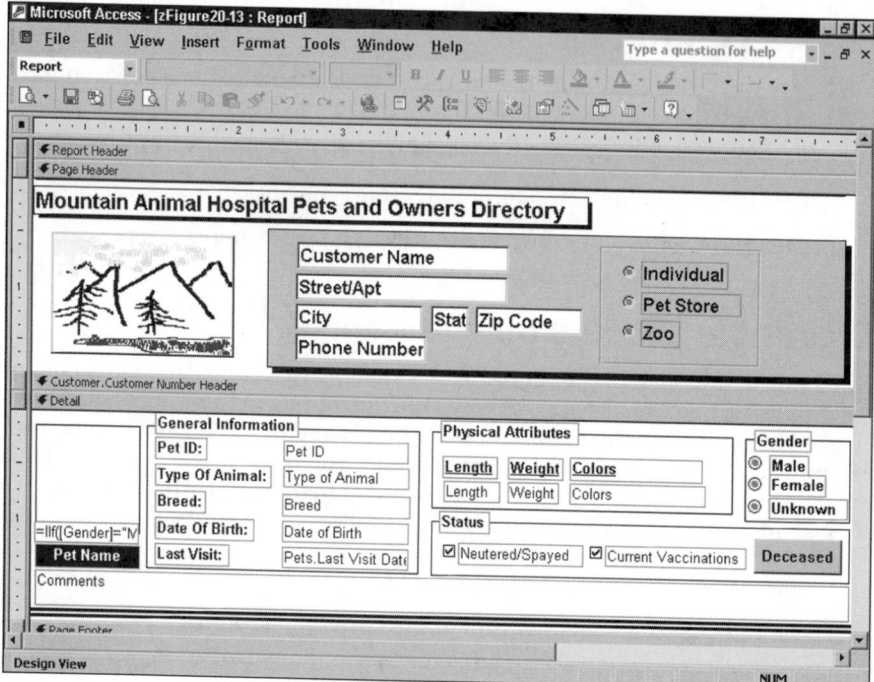

Figure 20-13: The final report in design view

Seeing Your Output in Different Ways

You can see your output from a report in several ways:

✦ Print previewing

✦ Printing to hard copy

✦ Printing to a file

✦ Printing the report definition

Using the Print Preview window

Throughout this chapter, you used the Print Preview window to view your report. Figure 20-5 displays your report in the Print Preview window in a zoomed view. This enables you to see your report with the actual fonts, shading, lines, boxes, and data that will be on the printed report. When the print preview mode is in a zoomed view, you can press the mouse button to change the view to a page preview (where you can see the entire page).

You can use the horizontal and vertical scroll bars to move around the page or move from page to page by using the page controls in the bottom-left corner of the window.

The page preview mode of the Print Preview window displays an entire page of the report, as shown in Figure 20-14. The mouse pointer is shaped like a magnifying glass in Print Preview windows; using this pointer during page preview enables you to select a portion of the page and then zoom in to that portion for a detailed view.

In Figure 20-14 is a representation of the printed page. You use the navigation buttons (located in the lower-left section of the Print Preview window) to move between pages, just as you would use them to move between records in a datasheet.

The first nine buttons displayed on the toolbar provide quick access to printing tasks:

✦ **Design.** Switches between design view, print preview, or layout view

✦ **Print.** Displays the Print dialog box

✦ **Zoom.** Toggles in and out of Page Preview and Zoomed view

✦ **One Page.** Displays a single page in the Print Preview window

✦ **Two Pages.** Displays two pages in the Print Preview window

✦ **Setup.** Displays the Page Setup screen

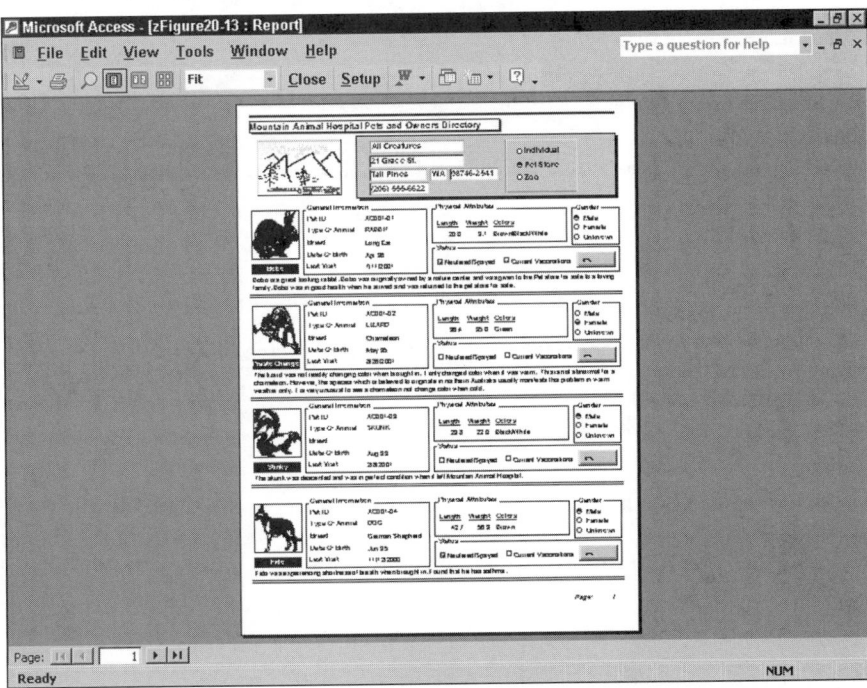

Figure 20-14: Displaying a report in page preview mode in the Print Preview window

✦ **Multiple Pages.** Displays from 1 x 1 to 2 x 3 pages in the Print Preview window

✦ **Zoom Control.** Select Percent of Size to Zoom: Maximum 1000%, 500%, 200%, 150%, 100%, 75%, 50%, 25%, 10%, Fit to Window (you can also type a specific percentage in this control)

✦ **Close Window.** Returns to Design view

You are not limited to a one- or two-page preview. As Figure 20-15 shows, the View ⇨ Pages menu enables you to select 1, 2, 4, 8, or 12 pages to preview. In Figure 20-15, eight pages have been selected and are visible. You can also right-click on the Print Preview page and select pages or the Zoom percentage. When you use the shortcut menus, you can select as many as 20 pages to preview at a time; you can also determine their arrangement in rows and columns (2 x 4, 5 x 4, 3 x 4, and so on).

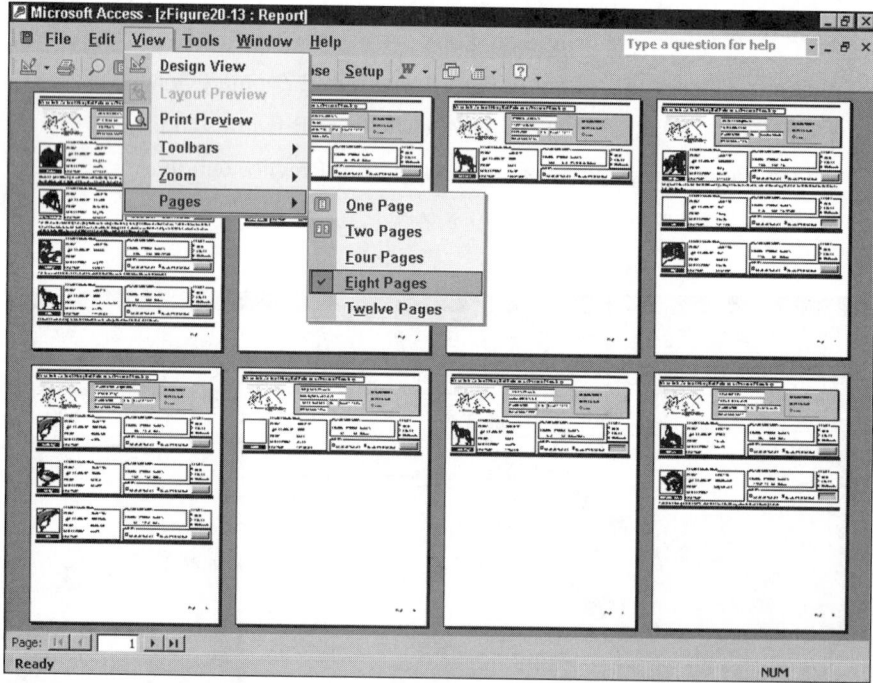

Figure 20-15: Multi-page print preview mode

If you are satisfied with the report after examining the preview, select the Print button on the toolbar and print it. If you are not satisfied with your report, select the Close button to return to the Report Design window and make additional changes.

Using layout previews

Layout preview is different from a print preview. A print preview uses a query's dynaset; layout preview displays sample data (ignoring criteria) or joins in an underlying query.

The purpose of a layout preview is strictly to show you field placement and formatting. Thus, you can create a report design without having to assemble your data properly; in a large query, this can save considerable time. You can see a sample preview by one of two methods: Select View ➪ Layout Preview, or click the Report View button and then select the Layout Preview button (the bottom one) on the Report Design toolbar. You can switch back to the Report Design window by selecting the Close Window button if you entered the Print Preview from the Report Design window. If you entered from the Database window, you are returned there.

Tip   You can also zoom in to a layout page preview on the sample data or print the sample report from the Layout Preview window.

Printing a report

You can print one or more records in your form (exactly as they look onscreen) from several places:

✦ Select File ➪ Print in the Report Design window

✦ Select File ➪ Print in the Preview window

✦ Select File ➪ Print in the Database window with a report highlighted

Caution   If you are in the Print Preview window, the actual data prints. If you are in the Layout Preview window, only sample data prints.

If you select the Print button in the Preview window, all your data starts printing immediately and you cannot control which data is to be printed.

The Print dialog box

After you decide to print your report, the Print dialog box is displayed, as shown in Figure 20-16. The Print dialog box enables you to control several items by providing these choices:

✦ **Name.** Select the printer from a drop-down list.

✦ **Print Range.** Select whether to print the entire report or selected pages.

✦ **Copies.** Select the number of copies to print.

✦ **Collate.** Select whether to collate copies.

✦ **Print to File.** Select this to print to a file rather than to the printer.

The Print dialog box that is displayed is specific to your printer and based on your setup in Microsoft Windows. Although each printer is different, the dialog box is essentially the same. Generally, dot matrix or impact printers have a few more options for controlling quality than do laser printers.

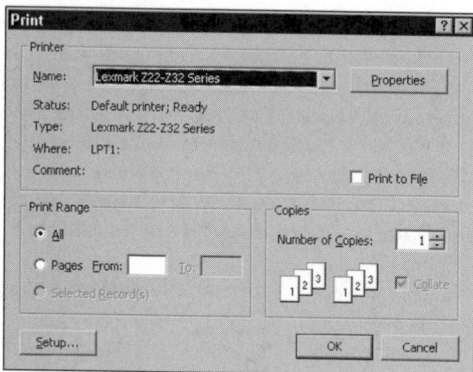

Figure 20-16: The Print dialog box

Assuming that you set up a printer in Windows, you can click OK to print your form. Your form is printed using the font you selected for display (or the nearest printer equivalent). The printout contains any formatting in the form, including lines, boxes, and shading. Colors are converted to shades on a monochrome printer.

If you need to additionally set up your Windows printer options, choose the Properties button in the Print dialog box. This dialog box sets up your printer, not your report. To fine-tune the setup of your report, use the Setup button (which provides more options).

You can display print setup options in other ways as well, including the following:

✦ Select File ➪ Page Setup from the Report Design window.

✦ Select File ➪ Page Setup from the Database window.

New Feature   Access 2002 provides a shortcut to the Page Setup window. The Setup button located on the Print Preview toolbar saves you a step by opening the Page Setup form automatically.

The Page Setup dialog box

The Page Setup dialog box, shown in Figure 20-17, is divided into three tabbed dialog boxes: Margins, Page, and Layout. (You use the Layout tab in Chapter 28 when you work with labels and multicolumn reports.)

✦ **Margins.** Set the page margins; also has option for Print Data Only

✦ **Page.** Select page orientation, paper size and source, and printer device

✦ **Layout.** Select grid settings, item size, and layout items

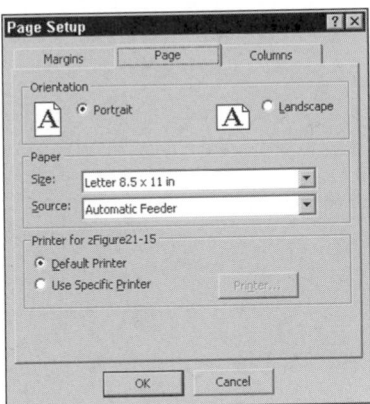

Figure 20-17: The Page tab in the Page Setup dialog box

The Page tab enables you to control the orientation of the report. There are two choices: Portrait and Landscape. Clicking the Portrait button changes the report so that the page is taller than it is wide. Clicking the Landscape button changes the report orientation so that the page is wider than it is tall.

Tip   A good way to remember the difference between landscape and portrait is to think of paintings. Portraits of people are usually taller than they are wide; landscapes of the outdoors are usually wider than tall. When you click either button, the Page icon (the letter A) changes to show your choice graphically.

The Paper section indicates the size of the paper to use, as well as the paper source (for printers that have more than one source available). Clicking Source displays a drop-down list of paper sources available for the selected printer. Depending on the printer selected, you may have one or more paper trays or manual feed available. Click the source to use.

Clicking Size displays a drop-down list box showing all the paper sizes available for the selected printer (and paper source). Click the size to use.

If you click the Print Data Only check box on the Margins tab, Access prints only the data from your report and does not print any graphics. (This feature is handy if you use preprinted forms.) Also, printing complex graphics slows down all but the most capable printers; not printing them saves time.

The Margins section shown in Figure 20-18 displays (and enables you to edit) the left, right, top, and bottom margins. To edit one or more of these settings, click the appropriate text box and type a new number.

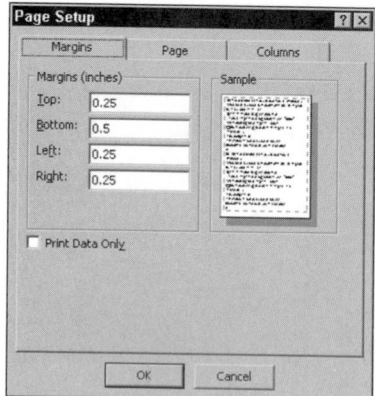

Figure 20-18: The Margins tab in the Page Setup dialog box

 Caution

Page Setup settings are stored with each report. It's therefore possible to use several different printers for various reports as long as you don't use the default Windows printer. This can be a problem, however, because if you exchange files with another user who doesn't have the same printer installed, the other user must modify the Page Setup settings.

Someone may send you a report that you can't view or print because a Windows printer driver you don't have is used. If the report was created with a driver not installed on your system, Access displays a dialog box and enables you to print with your default printer.

✦   ✦   ✦

Creating Calculations and Summaries in Reports

✦ ✦ ✦ ✦

In This Chapter

Designing a report with multiple group totals

Creating several levels of sorting and grouping totals

Entering and using expressions and functions in text boxes

Using concatenation in text expressions

Calculating sums for each group

Calculating running sums

Calculating percentages based on group totals

Creating a report cover page

✦ ✦ ✦ ✦

In the preceding two chapters, you learned to design and build reports from a blank form. You also learned how to create striking and effective output using many of the advanced features in Access. In this chapter, you learn to use expressions to calculate results.

On the CD-ROM

If you don't want to build the reports created in this chapter, they are included on your CD in the Reports object button. The reports are named Monthly Invoice Report—No Cover, Monthly Invoice Report, Monthly Invoice Report—Percentages, and Monthly Invoice Report—Running Sum.

Designing a Multilevel Grouping Report with Totals

In this chapter, you create a report that displays information about visits to the hospital for each customer's pets on specific days. This report displays data in an invoice format that lists the type of visit, treatments given, medication dispensed, and the cost of each of these items. The data is totaled for each line item and summarized for each visit. The report can display multiple pets for the same customer on the same day.

Finally, totals are shown for each visit by a customer, including the total amount spent, any discounts, and tax. Figure 21-1 is a sample printed page of the report. Later in this chapter, you learn to enhance this report by displaying individual line-item percentages and cumulative running totals.

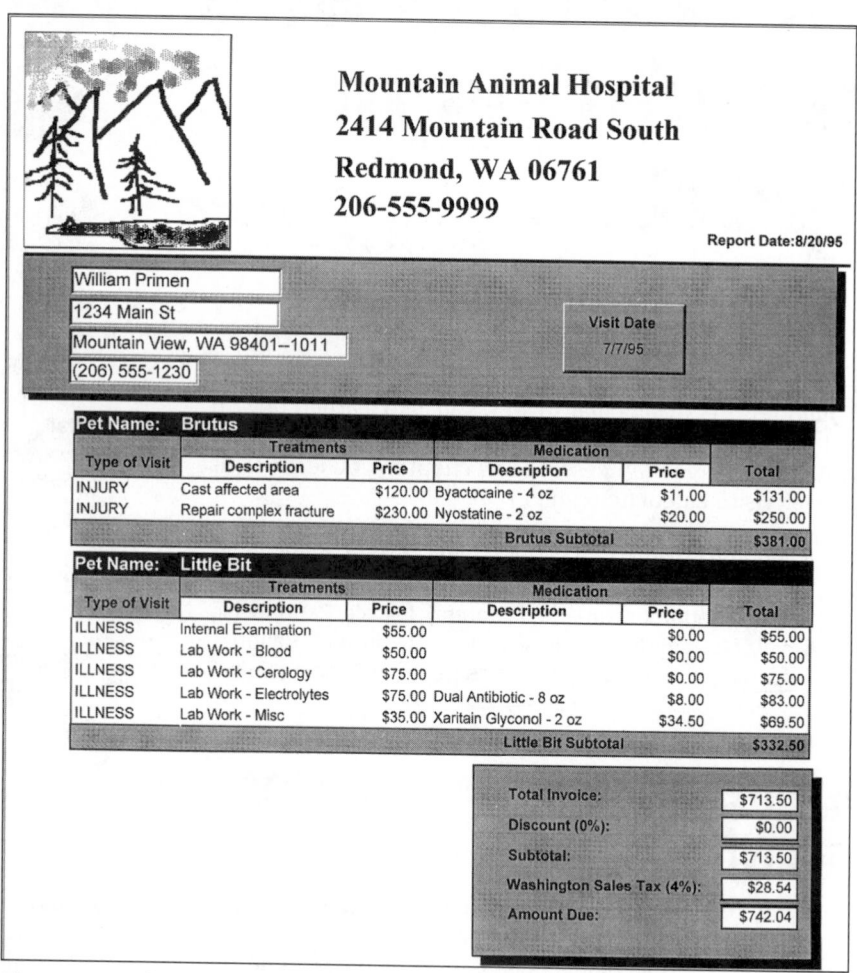

Figure 21-1: The sample Invoice Report page

Designing the Invoice Report

The Invoice Report is an excellent example of the types of tasks necessary to create common types of reports. It uses many of Access's advanced report-writing features — sorting and grouping, group summaries, text expressions, and graphical objects. Invoice Report's design includes

- ✦ The Mountain Animal Hospital name, address, phone number, and logo on the top of every page

- ✦ Owner detail information (customer name, street/apartment, city, state, ZIP Code, and telephone)

- ✦ Visit date

- ✦ Pet name

- ✦ Visit detail information for each pet (including type of visit, treatment, treatment price, medication, medication price, and total cost)

- ✦ A subtotal that summarizes each pet's visit details (total cost subtotal for the pet)

- ✦ A subtotal that summarizes the total cost for each pet on a visit date for a particular owner and then calculates a total that lists and incorporates the owner's discount and proper state sales tax

The report design must also be shaped according to these considerations:

- ✦ You must sort the report by the field's Visit Date, Customer Number, and Pet ID (in that order).

- ✦ No more than one visit date per printed page.

- ✦ No more than one customer per printed page.

- ✦ One or more pets belonging to the same owner can appear on each printed page.

- ✦ If you have more than one pet per invoice, the pets should be listed in Pet ID order.

The design for this report is shown in Figure 21-2. As you can see, each section is labeled, and each control displays either the field name control or the calculated control contents. With the exception of the Mountain Animal Hospital logo (an unbound object frame) and several lines and rectangles, the report consists primarily of text box controls.

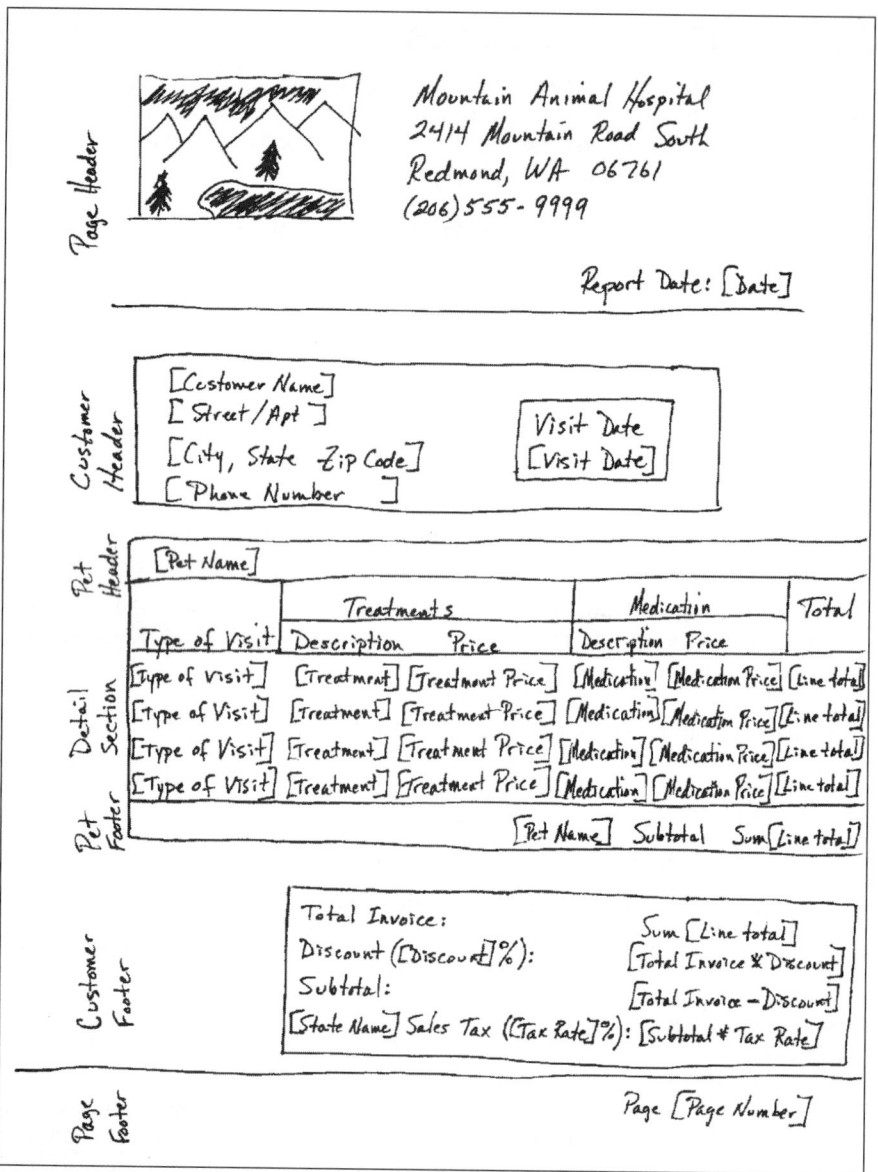

Figure 21-2: A design for the Invoice Report

Designing and creating the query for the report

The Invoice Report uses fields from practically every table in the Mountain Animal Hospital database. Although the design in Figure 21-2 shows the approximate position and use of each control, it is equally important to perform a data design that lists each table field or calculated control. This data design should include the purpose of the field or control, and the table in which the field originates. Using this kind of design plan, you can be sure to build a query that contains all the fields you may need. Table 21-1 lists these controls, the section in the report where they are used, and the originating table. (Important: Do this type of data design before creating the query from which you will build your report.)

Table 21-1
The Data Design for the Invoice Report

Report Section	Control Purpose	Type of Control	Table Field/ Calculation	Table
Page header	Logo	Unbound object frame		
Page header	Name and address	Label controls (4)		
Page header	Report date	Calculated text box	Date Function	
Customer header	Customer name	Bound text box	Customer Name	Customer
Customer header	Street and apt.	Bound text box	Street/Apt	Customer
Customer header	City	Bound text box	City	Customer
Customer header	State	Bound text box	State	Customer
Customer header	ZIP Code	Bound text box	ZIP Code	Customer
Customer header	Phone number	Bound text box	Phone Number	Customer
Customer header	Visit date	Bound text box	Visit Date	Visits
Pet header	Pet name	Bound text box	Pet Name	Pets

Continued

Table 21-1 *(continued)*

Report Section	Control Purpose	Type of Control	Table Field/ Calculation	Table
Pet header	Text labels	Label controls (8)		
Detail	Type of visit	Bound text box	Visit Type	Visit Details
Detail	Treatment	Bound text box	Treatment	Treatments
Detail	Treatment price	Bound text box	Treatment Price	Visit Details
Detail	Medication	Bound text box	Medication Name	Medications
Detail	Medication price	Bound text box	Medication Price	Visit Details
Detail	Line total	Calculated text box	Treatment Price + Medication	
Pet footer	Pet name	Calculated text box	Pet Name + Text (Line Total)	Pets
Customer footer	Text labels	Label controls (3)	Lines 1, 3, 5	
Customer footer	Discount label	Calculated text box	Text + Discount	Customer
Customer footer	State sales tax	Calculated text box	State Name + Tax Rate	States/ Visits
Customer footer	Total invoice	Calculated text box	Sum(Line Total)	
Customer footer	Discount amount	Calculated text box	Total Invoice * Discount	
Customer footer	Subtotal	Calculated text box	Total Invoice – Discount	
Customer footer	Sales tax	Calculated text box	Subtotal * Tax Rate	Visits
Customer footer	Amount due	Calculated text box	Subtotal + Sales Tax	
Page footer	Page number	Calculated text box	Text + Page Number	

After you complete the data design for a report, you can skim the Table column to determine the tables necessary for the report. When you create the query, you may not want to select each field individually. If not, use the asterisk (*) field to select all the fields in each table. This way, if a field changes in the table, the query still works with your report.

Note

Remember that if a table field name changes in your query, you need to change your report design. If you see a dialog box asking for the value of a specific field when you run your report — or the text #Error appears in place of one of your values after you run it — chances are that a table field has changed.

After examining Table 21-1, you may notice that every table in the Mountain Animal Hospital database is needed for the report — with the exception of the Animals lookup table. You may wonder why you need any of the four lookup tables. You use the States, Animals, Treatments, and Medications tables primarily as lookup tables for data validation when adding data to forms, but you can also use them to look up data when printing reports.

In the Invoice Report, the State Name field from the States table is used for looking up the full state name for the sales tax label in the Customer footer. The Tax Rate field can also be found in the States table, but at the time of the visit, the current tax rate is copied to the Visits table for that record. Only the codes are stored in the Visit Details table, so Access looks up the Treatment and Medication Name fields from their respective tables.

These seven tables are all joined together using the Monthly Invoice Report query, as illustrated in Figure 21-3.

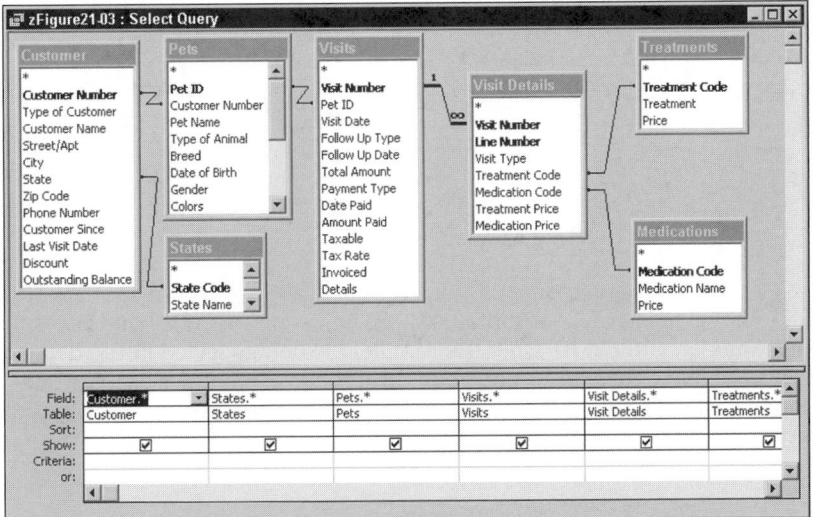

Figure 21-3: The Query Design window for the Monthly Invoice Report query

After your query is completed, you can create your report.

Cross-Reference

Chapter 19 provides a detailed explanation of how to create a new report from a blank form; it also shows you how to set page size and layout properly. If you are unfamiliar with these topics, read Chapter 19 before continuing. This chapter focuses on multiple-level groupings, calculated and summarized fields, and expressions.

Designing test data

One of the biggest mistakes that you can make when designing and creating complex reports is to not check the results that the report displays. Before creating a complete report, you should have a good understanding of your data. To check the results, create a query using the same sorting order that the report uses and then create any detail line calculations. You can then check the query's datasheet results, using them to check the report's results. When you're sure that the report is using the correct data, you can be sure that it will always produce great results. Figure 21-4 is a simple query (the Monthly Invoice Report — Test Data) to use for checking the report that you create in this chapter.

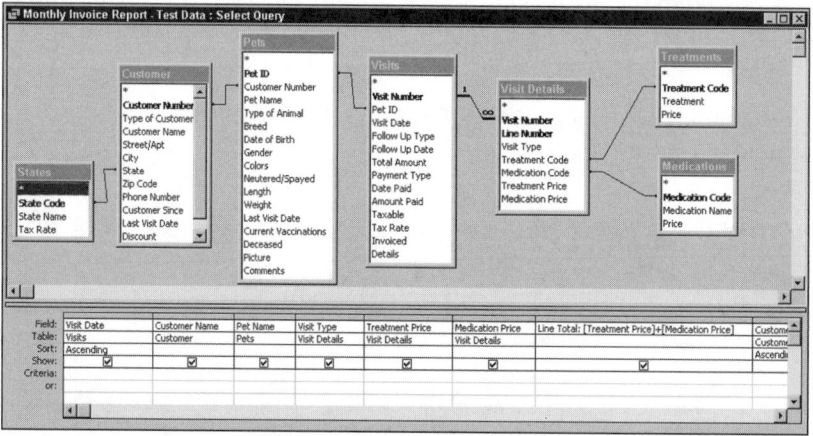

Figure 21-4: A query for checking data results

The query shown in Figure 21-4 contains three fields for sorting: Visit Date, Customer Number, and Pet ID. Only the first field is being viewed in the dynaset; the other two fields have the Show check box turned off. When you save this query and then reopen it, the Customer Number and Pet ID fields are moved to the end of the query grid.

Normally, you can make a copy of the report query, adding the sorting orders and using only the detail fields that you need to check totals. You can then add the numbers manually or convert the query to a Total query to check group totals. Figure 21-5 shows the datasheet that's produced by this query; you can compare the results of each task in the report design to this datasheet.

Visit Date	Customer Name	Pet Name	Visit Type	Treatment Price	Medication Pric	Line Total
11/11/1992	William Primen	Little Bit	ILLNESS	$35.00	$34.50	$69.50
11/11/1992	William Primen	Little Bit	ILLNESS	$50.00	$0.00	$50.00
11/11/1992	William Primen	Little Bit	ILLNESS	$75.00	$8.00	$83.00
11/11/1992	William Primen	Little Bit	ILLNESS	$75.00	$0.00	$75.00
5/22/1996	Animal Kingdom	Tom	PHYSICAL	$20.00	$0.00	$20.00
5/22/1996	Animal Kingdom	Tom	GROOMING	$20.00	$0.00	$20.00
5/22/1996	Animal Kingdom	Tom	PHYSICAL	$50.00	$11.50	$61.50
7/22/1996	Michael Johnson	Rover	PHYSICAL	$50.00	$0.00	$50.00
7/22/1996	Michael Johnson	Rover	PHYSICAL	$20.00	$0.00	$20.00
10/4/1997	Animal Kingdom	Tom	PHYSICAL	$20.00	$6.00	$26.00
10/10/1997	Petra Irish	Jimeny	PHYSICAL	$10.00	$0.00	$10.00
10/10/1997	Petra Irish	Jimeny	PHYSICAL	$20.00	$0.00	$20.00
10/10/1997	Petra Irish	Jimeny	PHYSICAL	$20.00	$0.00	$20.00
11/11/1997	Karen Rhodes	Golden Girl	PHYSICAL	$50.00	$0.00	$50.00
12/4/1997	George Green	Killer	PHYSICAL	$50.00	$0.00	$50.00
1/1/1998	Johnathan Adams	Rising Sun	INJURY	$0.00	$0.00	$0.00
1/22/1998	Wanda Greenfield	Sammie Girl	PHYSICAL	$10.00	$0.00	$10.00
1/22/1998	Wanda Greenfield	Sammie Girl	PHYSICAL	$20.00	$0.00	$20.00
2/22/1998	Anita Zimmerman	Midnight	PHYSICAL	$50.00	$0.00	$50.00
3/19/1998	Karen Rhodes	Golden Girl	GROOMING	$20.00	$0.00	$20.00
3/19/1998	Karen Rhodes	Golden Girl	INJURY	$230.00	$11.50	$241.50
3/19/1998	Karen Rhodes	Golden Girl	INJURY	$57.00	$14.00	$71.00
3/19/1998	Karen Rhodes	Golden Girl	GROOMING	$25.00	$34.50	$59.50

Record: 1 of 145

Figure 21-5: The datasheet showing test data

Creating a Multilevel Grouping Report with Totals

After you've completed the report planning and data testing, it's time to create the new report. Here are the steps to create a new report (and bind it to a query):

1. Press F11 to display the Database window if it isn't already displayed.

2. Click the Reports object button.

3. Click the New toolbar button. The New Report dialog box appears.

4. Select the Monthly Invoice Report query.

5. Select Design View.

6. Click OK.

7. Maximize the Report window.

A blank Report Design window appears showing three sections (Page Header, Detail, and Page Footer). The report is bound to the query Monthly Invoice Report; data from that query is used when you view or print the report. The fields from the query are available for use in the report design and appear in the Field List window.

You must also change the Printer Setup settings and resize the Report Design window area for the report.

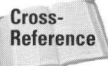 **Cross-Reference** For details about changing Printer Setup settings and resizing the Report Design window area, see Chapter 20.

To specify Page Setup settings, follow these steps:

1. Select File ➪ Page Setup.

2. Select the Margins tab.

3. Click the Left Margin setting and change the setting to 0.250.

4. Click the Right Margin setting and change the setting to 0.250.

5. Click the Top Margin setting and change the setting to 0.250.

6. Click the Bottom Margin setting and change the setting to 0.250.

7. Click OK to close the Page Setup window.

Follow these steps to set the report width:

1. Click the rightmost edge of the report body (where the white area meets the gray).

2. Drag the edge to the 8-inch mark on the ruler.

3. Release the mouse button.

These steps complete the initial setup for the report. Next, you create the report's sorting order.

Creating the sorting orders

In a query, you can specify sorting fields just as you did in the test query that you created earlier. In a report, however, you must also specify the sorting order when you create groups; Access ignores the underlying query sorting. In the underlying query for this report, no sorting is specified because it must be entered here as well.

This report design has three sorting levels: Visit Date, Customer Number, and Pet ID. You need to use all these levels to define group headers, and you need the latter two levels for group footers. Look at the original design in Figure 21-2 — Visit Date is not shown as a group. In the "Creating the Visit Date header" section later in this chapter, you learn why it's necessary for a grouping to use the Visit Date header section.

Before you can add a grouping, you must first define the sort order for the report. You've already learned to do this task by using the Sorting and Grouping box (shown completed in Figure 21-6).

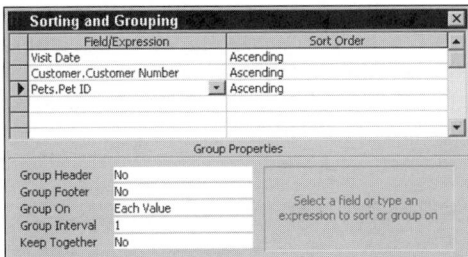

Figure 21-6: Creating the sorting orders

To add the sorting orders as shown in Figure 21-6, follow these steps:

1. Click the Sorting and Grouping button on the toolbar to display the Sorting and Grouping box.

2. Click in the first row of the Field/Expression column of the Sorting and Grouping box. A down-arrow displays.

3. Click the arrow to display a list of fields in the Monthly Invoice Report query.

4. Select the Visit Date field in the field list. Notice that Sort Order defaults to Ascending.

5. Click in the second row of the Field/Expression column.

6. Click the arrow to display a list of fields in the Mountain Invoice Report query.

7. Select the Customer.Customer Number field in the field list. Notice that Sort Order defaults to Ascending.

8. Click in the third row of the Field/Expression column.

9. Click the arrow to display a list of fields in the Mountain Invoice Report query.

10. Select the Pets.Pet ID field in the field list. Notice that Sort Order defaults to Ascending.

Tip   To see more of the Field/Expression column, drag the border between the Field/ Expression and Sort Order columns to the right (as shown in Figure 21-6).

You next learn to create the detail section for this report. Because this chapter focuses on expressions and summaries, be sure that you have read Chapters 19 and 20 and that you understand how to create and enhance the labels and text boxes in a report.

Creating the detail section

The detail section is shown in its entirety in Figure 21-7. This section has been completed and resized. Notice that no space has been allowed above or below any of the controls, which allows multiple detail records to be displayed as one comprehensive section on a report. Because this section must fit snugly between the Pet header and Pet footer, as shown in Figures 21-1 and 21-2, it has been resized to the exact size of the controls.

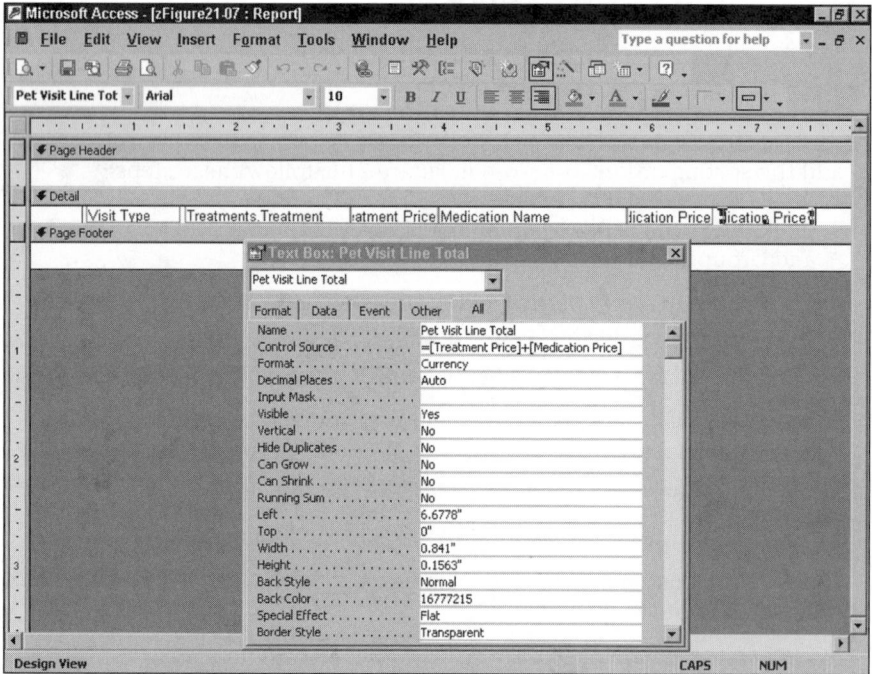

Figure 21-7: The detail section

Creating the detail section controls

The detail section has five unlabeled bound text box controls, two line controls, and one calculated control:

✦ A Vertical line control

✦ Visit Details.Visit Type, bound text box control

✦ Treatments.Treatment, bound text box control

✦ Visit Details.Treatment Price, bound text box control

✦ Medications.Medication Name, bound text box control

✦ Visit Details.Medication Price, bound text box control

✦ Calculated unbound text control (formula is =[Treatment Price]+ [Medication Price])

✦ A Vertical line control

You need to drag each of these bound text box controls from the Report window field list onto the detail section and then properly size the controls. The default text box property Auto Label under the Format menu should be set to No.

The two line controls are vertical lines: One is on the left side of the detail section under the left edge of the Type of Visit text box control, and the other is on the right side of the detail section under the right edge of the calculated control.

The last control is a calculated text box control. This control calculates the total of the Treatment Price and the Medication Price for each detail line. Enter this formula into a new unlabeled text box: =[Treatment Price]+[Medication Price]. A calculated control always starts with an equal sign (=), and each field name must be placed in brackets. Figure 21-7 also shows the property sheet for this calculated text box control, which is named Pet Line Visit Total. The Pet Line Visit Total control is formatted with the Currency format property so that the dollar signs appear. If any of the totals is over $1,000.00, the comma also appears. The Decimal Place property is set to Auto, which is automatically set to 2 for the Currency format.

Creating calculated controls

You can use any valid Access expression in any text control. Expressions can contain operators, constants, functions, field names, and literal values. Some examples of expressions are

✦ **=Date( )** Date function

✦ **=[Customer Subtotal]*[Tax Rate]** A control name multiplied by a field name

✦ **=Now( )+30** A literal value added to the result of a function

The control (Control Source property), which is shown in Figure 21-7, calculates the total for each individual line in the detail section. To create this calculated control, follow these steps:

1. Create a new text control in the detail section, as shown in Figure 21-7.

2. Display the property sheet for the new text box control.

3. Enter =**[Treatment Price]+[Medication Price]** in the Control Source property cell.

4. Set the Format property to Currency.

Naming controls used in calculations

Every time you create a control, Access automatically inserts a name for it into the Control Name property of the control's property sheet. The name is really a description that defines which kind of control it is; for example, text controls show the name Field and label controls show the name Text. A sequential number follows each name. An example of a complete name is "Field13." If the next control that you create is a label, it is named "Text14." These names can be replaced with user-defined names, such as Report Date, Sales Tax, or any other valid Access name, which lets you reference other controls easily (especially controls that contain expressions).

For example, if you have the fields Tax Rate and Subtotal and want to calculate Amount of Tax Due, you enter the expression =**[Tax Rate]*[Subtotal]** and call it "Amount of Tax Due." You can then calculate Total Amount Due by entering the expression =**[Subtotal]+[Amount of Tax Due]**. This expression lets you change an expression in a calculated field without changing all other references to that expression. To change the name of the control for Treatment Price + Medication Price Total, follow these steps:

1. Select the calculated control (=[Treatment Price]+[Medication Price]).

2. Display the property sheet.

3. Select the Name property.

4. Replace the default with Pet Visit Line Total.

Caution   You can't use a calculated control name in a summary calculation. Instead, you must summarize the original calculation. For example, rather than create an expression such as =Sum(Pet Visit Line Total), you must enter the summary expression =Sum([Treatment Price]+[Medication Price]).

Testing the detail section

As you complete each section, compare the results against the test datasheet that you created, as shown in Figure 21-5. The easiest way to view your results is either to select the Print Preview button on the toolbar (to view the report on-screen) or to print the first few pages of the report. Figure 21-8 displays the Print Preview screen. If you compare the results to the test data in Figure 21-5, you see that all the records are correctly displayed. You may notice, however, that the records are not exactly in the right order. This is acceptable as long as groups of the same visit date for the same customer and pet are together. Because the data isn't sorted by the line number in the Visit Details table yet, the final sort is not precise.

Notice that the calculated control correctly calculates the sum of the two numeric price text box controls and displays them in the Currency format.

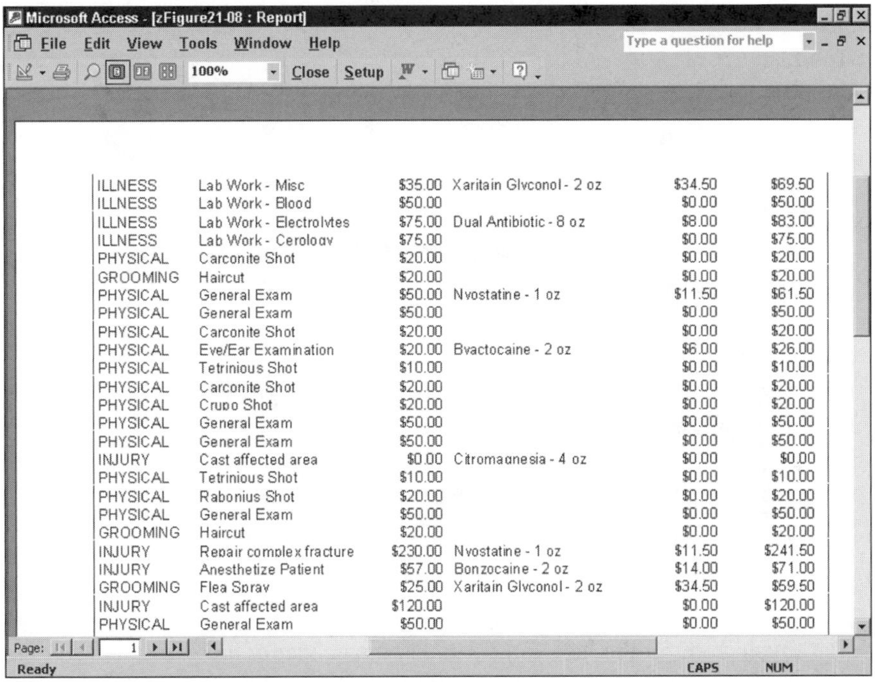

ILLNESS	Lab Work - Misc	$35.00	Xaritain Glvconol - 2 oz	$34.50	$69.50
ILLNESS	Lab Work - Blood	$50.00		$0.00	$50.00
ILLNESS	Lab Work - Electrolytes	$75.00	Dual Antibiotic - 8 oz	$8.00	$83.00
ILLNESS	Lab Work - Cerologv	$75.00		$0.00	$75.00
PHYSICAL	Carconite Shot	$20.00		$0.00	$20.00
GROOMING	Haircut	$20.00		$0.00	$20.00
PHYSICAL	General Exam	$50.00	Nvostatine - 1 oz	$11.50	$61.50
PHYSICAL	General Exam	$50.00		$0.00	$50.00
PHYSICAL	Carconite Shot	$20.00		$0.00	$20.00
PHYSICAL	Eve/Ear Examination	$20.00	Bvactocaine - 2 oz	$6.00	$26.00
PHYSICAL	Tetrinious Shot	$10.00		$0.00	$10.00
PHYSICAL	Carconite Shot	$20.00		$0.00	$20.00
PHYSICAL	Crupo Shot	$20.00		$0.00	$20.00
PHYSICAL	General Exam	$50.00		$0.00	$50.00
PHYSICAL	General Exam	$50.00		$0.00	$50.00
INJURY	Cast affected area	$0.00	Citromagnesia - 4 oz	$0.00	$0.00
PHYSICAL	Tetrinious Shot	$10.00		$0.00	$10.00
PHYSICAL	Rabonius Shot	$20.00		$0.00	$20.00
PHYSICAL	General Exam	$50.00		$0.00	$50.00
GROOMING	Haircut	$20.00		$0.00	$20.00
INJURY	Repair complex fracture	$230.00	Nvostatine - 1 oz	$11.50	$241.50
INJURY	Anesthetize Patient	$57.00	Bonzocaine - 2 oz	$14.00	$71.00
GROOMING	Flea Sprav	$25.00	Xaritain Glvconol - 2 oz	$34.50	$59.50
INJURY	Cast affected area	$120.00		$0.00	$120.00
PHYSICAL	General Exam	$50.00		$0.00	$50.00

Figure 21-8: A print preview of the detail section

Creating the Pet ID header and footer sections

When the detail section is complete, you can move outward to create the inner group headers and footers. The innermost group is the Pet ID group. You need to create both a header and a footer for this section.

To create group headers and footers for the Pet ID sort that you already created, you only have to change the Group Header and Group Footer properties of the Pets.Pet ID Field/Expression to Yes (as shown in Figure 21-9). To make this change, follow these steps:

1. Display the Sorting and Grouping box if it isn't already displayed.
2. Click the Pets.Pet ID row in the window.
3. Click the Group Header property and change it to Yes.
4. Click the Group Footer property and change it to Yes.

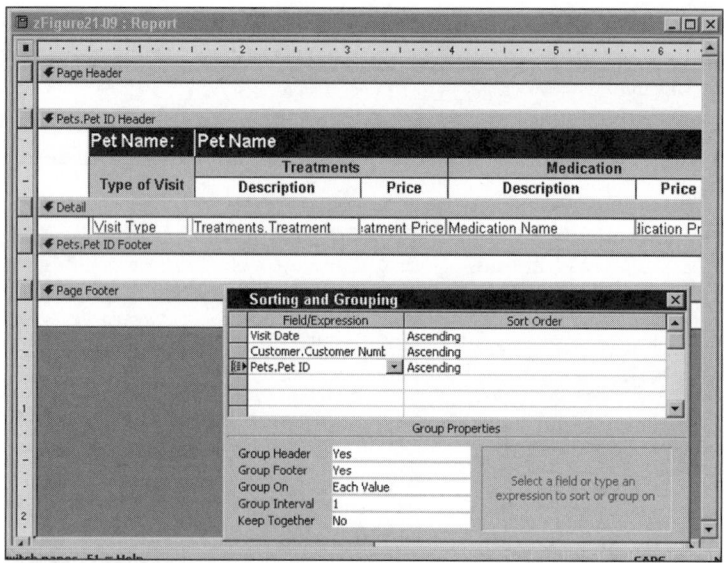

Figure 21-9: The Report Design window for the Pets.Pet ID group header

Note   After a group header or footer is defined, the first column of the Sorting and Grouping box for the field you created in the header or footer displays a grouping icon (the same icon you see when you select the Sorting and Grouping button on the toolbar).

The Pet ID header and footer sections should now be displayed.

Creating the Pet ID header controls

The Pets.Pet ID group header, shown in Figure 21-9, along with the Sorting and Grouping box, creates a group break on Pet ID, which causes each pet's individual visit details to be grouped together. This is the section where the pet's name is displayed, as well as labels that describe the controls that appear in the detail section.

No calculated controls are in this header, nor any lines or rectangles. With the exception of the pet name itself, in fact, all controls are label controls. Each label control is stretched so that the borders make perfect rectangles on the desired areas and the text is centered where appropriate. The Font/Fore Color and Fill/Back Color buttons are then used for coloring the background and the text.

Notice the use of reverse video in the Pet Name label and text control. Also notice that the Type of Visit, Treatments, Medication, and Total label controls display black text on a light gray background. This setup, along with the borders, creates a visually appealing section. There is no room between the bottom of the controls and the bottom of the section. This (along with the lack of space in the detail section) creates the illusion that several sections are really one. You create the label controls Type of Visit and Total which appear to have bottom-aligned text by pressing Ctrl+Enter before you enter the text, forcing the text to the second line.

Creating the Pet ID footer controls

The Pets.Pet ID group footer, shown in Figure 21-10, is where you subtotal all the visit detail information for each pet. Thus, if a pet has more than one treatment or medication per visit, the report summarizes the visit detail line items in this section; a summary displays, even if the pet has only one detail record.

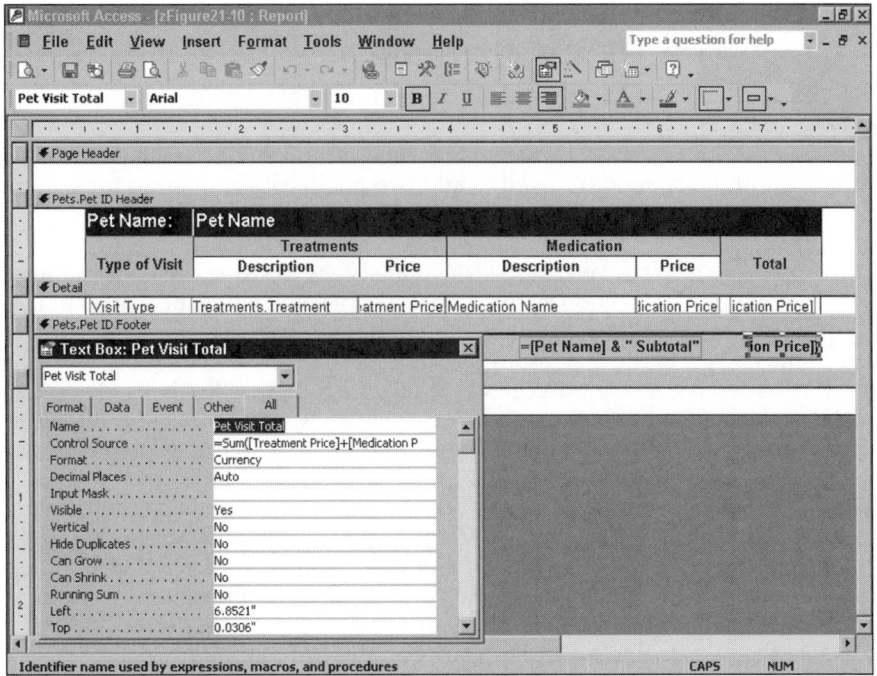

Figure 21-10: Creating a group summary control

The Pets.Pet ID footer section contains three controls:

- ✦ **Rectangle.** Displays the boundaries of the section and is shaded in light gray
- ✦ **Text Box control.** Displays Pet Name and the text Subtotal
- ✦ **Summary text box control.** Displays the total of all Pet Visit line totals for each pet

The rectangle completes the area displayed under the detail section; it serves as a bottom cap on the preceding two sections. Notice that no space has been allowed between the top of the controls and the top of the section. Notice also how the edges line up, setting the entire section (Pet ID header, detail section, Pet ID footer) apart from other areas of the report.

The first control combines the Pet Name field with the text Subtotal. This is done using a process known as *concatenation.*

Using concatenation to join text and fields

Concatenation operators can combine two strings. (A *string* is either a field or an expression.) You can use several different operators for concatenation, including these:

+   Joins two Text data type strings

&   Joins two strings; also converts non-Text data types to Text data

The + operator is standard in many languages, although it can easily be confused with the arithmetic operator used to add two numbers. The + operator requires that both strings being joined are Text data types.

The & operator also converts non-string data types to string data types; therefore, it is used more than the + operator. If, for example, you enter the expression ="Today's Date Is:" & Date(), Access converts the result of the date function into a string and adds it to the text Today's Date Is:. If the date is August 26, 2001, the result returned is a string with the value Today's Date Is:8/26/01. The lack of space between the colon and the 8 is not an error; if you want to add a space between two joined strings, you must add the space by pressing the spacebar on your keyboard.

Access can join any data type to any other data type using this method. If you want to create the control for the Pet Name and the text Subtotal with this method, you enter the expression =**[Pet Name] & " Subtotal"**, which appends the contents of the Pet Name field to the text Subtotal. No conversion occurs because the contents of Pet Name and the literal value Subtotal are both already text. Notice the space between the first double quotation mark and the text Subtotal.

Note If you use the + operator for concatenation, you must convert any non-string data types; an example is using the CStr( ) function to return a date with the Date( ) function to a string data type. If you want to display the system date with some text, you have to create a text control with the following contents:

```
="Today's Date Is: " +cstr(Date())
```

You can insert the contents of a field directly into a text expression by using the ampersand (&) character. The syntax is

```
="Text String "&[Field or Control Name]&" additional text
string"
```

or

```
[Field or Control Name]&" Text String"
```

Use this method to create the control for the Pet Name text box control by following these steps:

1. Create a new text control in the Pets.Pet ID footer section.

2. Enter the expression = **[Pet Name]&" Subtotal"** (as shown in Figure 21-10).

Calculating group summaries

Creating a sum of numeric data within a group is very simple. The following is the general procedure for summarizing group totals for bound text controls:

1. Create a new text control in the group footer (or header).

2. Enter the expression =**Sum([Control Name])** where Control Name is a valid field name in the underlying query or the name of a control in the report.

If, however, the control name is for a calculated control, you have to repeat the control expression. Suppose that in the Pets.Pet ID footer you want to enter the following expression into the text box control to display the total of the detail line:

```
=Sum([Pets Line Visit Total])
```

If you try this, it won't work; that is simply a limitation of Access. To create a sum for the totals in the detail section, you have to enter

```
=Sum([Treatment Price]+[Medication Price])
```

This is how the summary that's shown in Figure 21-10 was created.

Access 2002 knows to total the detail lines for the Pet ID summary because you put the summary control in the Pets.Pet ID section. Each time the value of the Pet ID changes, Access resets the summary control automatically. Later, when you create this same summary control in the Customer ID footer section, Access resets the total only when the value of Customer ID changes.

You can use expressions in a report in two ways. First, you can enter the expression directly in a text control. For example, enter

```
=[Treatment Price]+[Medication Price]
```

Second, you can create the expression in the underlying query, as you see in Table 21-2, where you create a field named Line Total in the query itself. You can then use the calculated field of the query in a text control on the report. The advantage of the first method is that you have the flexibility to create your expressions on the fly as well as the ability to reference other report objects, such as text controls with expressions. The disadvantage is that you can't use summary expressions on calculated controls.

If you add a calculated field to your underlying query, you can then refer to this field in the detail section or in any group section. This is the syntax that you use:

```
=Sum([Calculated Field Name])
```

If you want to create the detail section Line Total and Pet ID Subtotal by using the calculation from the query, first you create the query's calculated field as

```
Line Total: [Treatment Price]+[Medication Price]
```

Then you create the summary control in the report as

```
=Sum([Line Total])
```

Both methods work, and both are acceptable.

Use the Print Preview window to check the progress of your report. Figure 21-11 displays the report created so far; notice how the three sections come together to form one area.

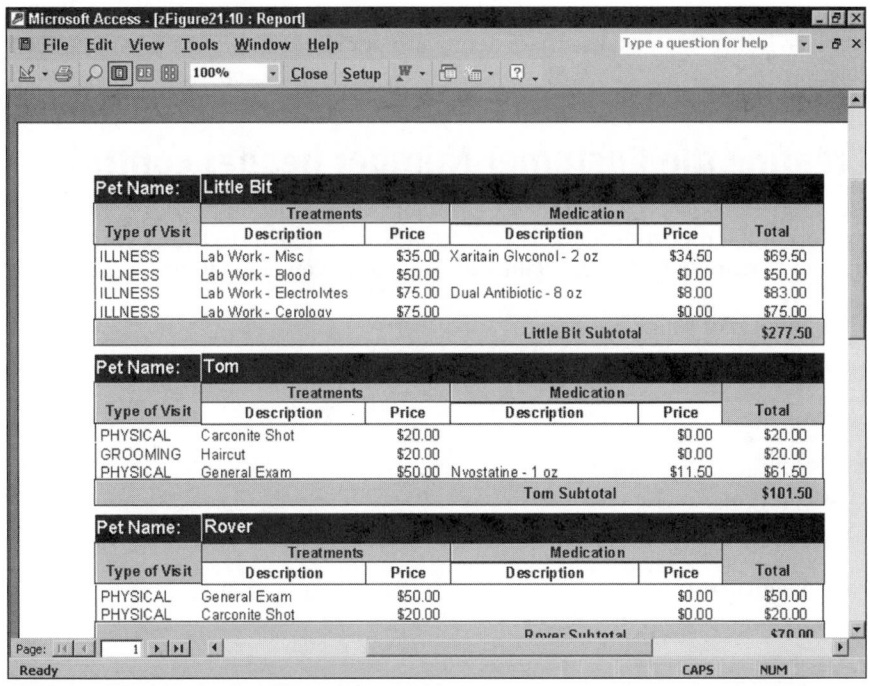

Figure 21-11: The Print Preview window of a report's Pet ID group header, the detail, and the group Pet ID footer sections

Creating the Customer Number header and footer sections

When the Pet ID sections are complete, you can move outward again to create the next outer group header and footer. As you move outward, the next group is Customer Number; you can create a header and footer for this section by following these steps:

1. Display the Sorting and Grouping box, if it isn't already displayed.

2. Click the Customer.Customer Number row in the window.

3. Click the Group Header property and change it to Yes.

4. Click the Group Footer property and change it to Yes.

One task remains: Each new customer for a specific date should be displayed on a separate page. As it currently exists, the report has no specific page breaks. You can create a page break every time the customer number changes by setting the

Force New Page property of the Customer.Customer Number header to Before Section. Doing this ensures that each customer's information is printed on a separate page.

Creating the Customer Number header controls

Figure 21-12 shows the Customer.Customer Number group header completed (at the top of the report design). This section is very similar to the Customer section that you create in Chapters 19 and 20. You use seven fields in this section:

- ✦ Customer Name
- ✦ Street/Apt
- ✦ City
- ✦ State
- ✦ ZIP Code
- ✦ Phone Number
- ✦ Visit Date

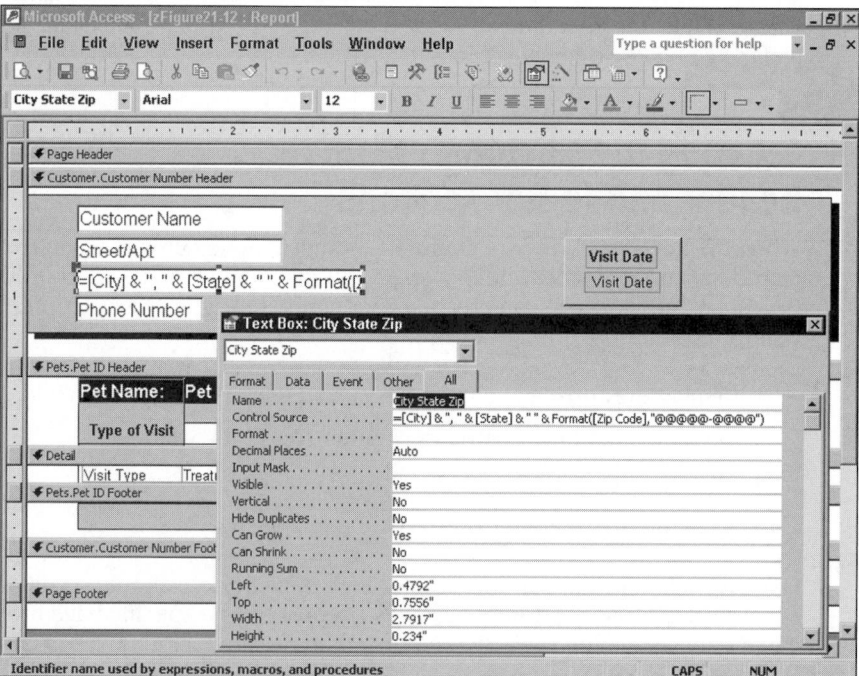

Figure 21-12: The Report Design window for the Customer.Customer Number group header

The first six fields shown in the text box controls on the left side of the rectangle are from the Customer table; the Visit Date control on the right side is from the Visits table. The entire section is surrounded by a gray shaded rectangle and a shadow box.

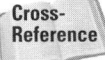

Cross-Reference

Chapter 20 explains how to create this effect.

The Visit Date control has an attached label and is surrounded by a transparent rectangle (which you create by setting the Back Color window's Transparent button). The control uses the etched appearance option; the Customer controls are sunken (a three-dimensional effect created by selecting the Sunken button in the Special Effect window).

One change you can make is to rearrange the display of the City, State, and ZIP Code fields. Rather than display these fields as three separate controls, you can concatenate them to appear together. You can save space by compressing any trailing spaces in the city name, adding a comma after city, and also by compressing the space between State and ZIP Code. You can make these changes by creating a concatenated text box control. Follow these steps:

1. Delete the City, State, and ZIP Code controls in the Customer Number header.

2. Create a new unlabeled text box control.

3. Enter **=[City]&", &[State]& "&[ZIP Code]** in the Control Source property of the text box control.

The only problem with this expression is that the ZIP Code is formatted in the ZIP Code table field, using the @@@@@-@@@@ format to add a hyphen between the first five and last four characters. As currently entered, the control may display the following value when run: Mountain View, WA 984011011. You still need to format the ZIP Code field. Normally, the function Format( ) is used for formatting an expression. In this example, you should write the function as

```
Format([ZIP Code],"@@@@@-@@@@")
```

You can add this function to the concatenation expression, substituting the Format expression in place of the ZIP Code field. To complete this example, change the control to

```
=[City]&", "&[State]&" "&Format([ZIP Code],"@@@@@-@@@@")
```

To check the Customer Number group heading, view the report in the Print Preview window, as shown in Figure 21-13.

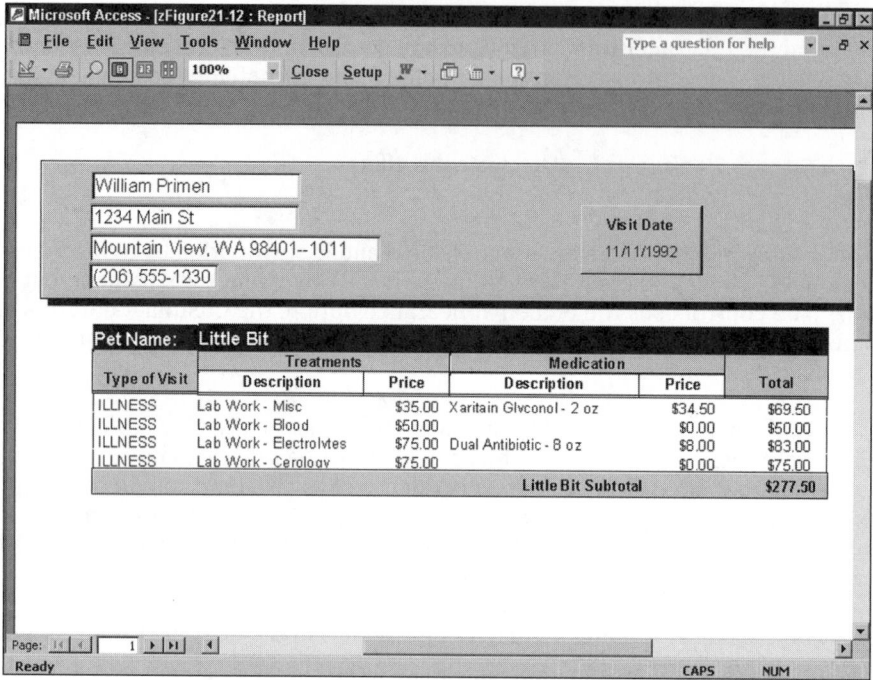

Figure 21-13: Viewing the report in the Print Preview window

Creating the Customer Number footer controls

The Customer.Customer Number footer section contains 10 controls: 5 label controls and 5 text box controls. The text box control expressions (and their associated labels) are listed in Table 21-2.

Table 21-2
Expressions in the Customer Number Footer

Expression Name	Label	Text Box Control
Customer Total	Total Invoice: [Medication Price])	=Sum([Treatment Price]+
Discount Amount	="Discount	=[Customer Total] *[Discount] ("&[Discount]*100&"%):"
Customer Subtotal	Subtotal:	=[Customer Total]–[Discount Amount]
State Sales Tax	=[State Name]& "Sales Tax(" & [Visits.Tax Rate]* 100 & "%):"	=[Customer Subtotal] *[Visits.Tax Rate]
Amount Due	Amount Due:	=[Customer Subtotal]+[State Sales Tax]

Each of the concatenated label controls uses the same standard notation that you learned previously in this chapter; each of the text box controls is a simple expression. Notice that Customer Total uses exactly the same expression as the Pet ID total, except that now it resets the total by Customer Number.

The Customer.Customer Number footer (shown in Figure 21-14) is where you create and summarize the line-item totals for each pet for a particular owner for a particular visit. You also want to display a customer's discount rate, the amount of the discount in dollars, the customer's state, the state sales tax as a percentage, the state sales tax in dollars, and (finally) a total for the amount due. All this information appears in separate boxes with shadows; you create these boxes by using the shadow special effect on the rectangle. The next sections provide the steps for each of the controls.

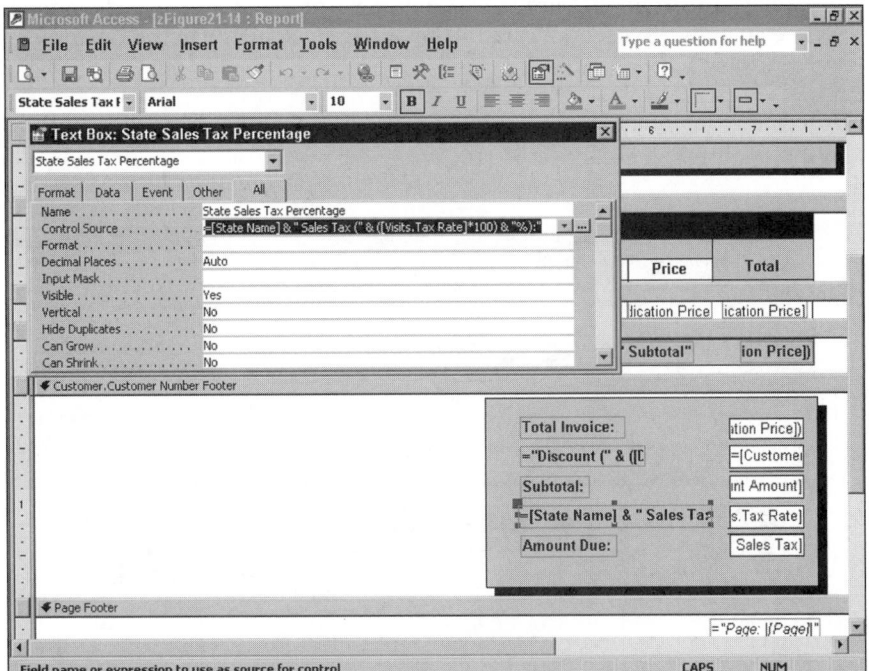

Figure 21-14: The Report Design window for the Customer.Customer Number group footer

To create the label for Total Invoice (and for the text box controls), follow these steps:

1. Create a new label control.

2. Change the Caption property to Total Invoice:.

3. Create a new text box control.

4. Change the Name property to Customer Total.

5. Change the Control Source property to =Sum([Treatment Price]+ [Medication Price]).

Follow these steps to create the Discount Amount label and text box controls:

1. Create a new label control.

2. Change the Control Source property to ="Discount ("&[Discount]*100&"%):", which concatenates the word *Discount* with the customer's discount rate and then multiplies by 100 to give a percentage.

3. Create a new text box control.

4. Change the Name to Discount Amount.

5. Change the Control Source to =[Customer Total]*[Discount], which multiplies the customer's discount rate by the amount calculated in the Customer Total control.

To check the Customer Number group footer, view the report in the Print Preview window, as shown in Figure 21-15.

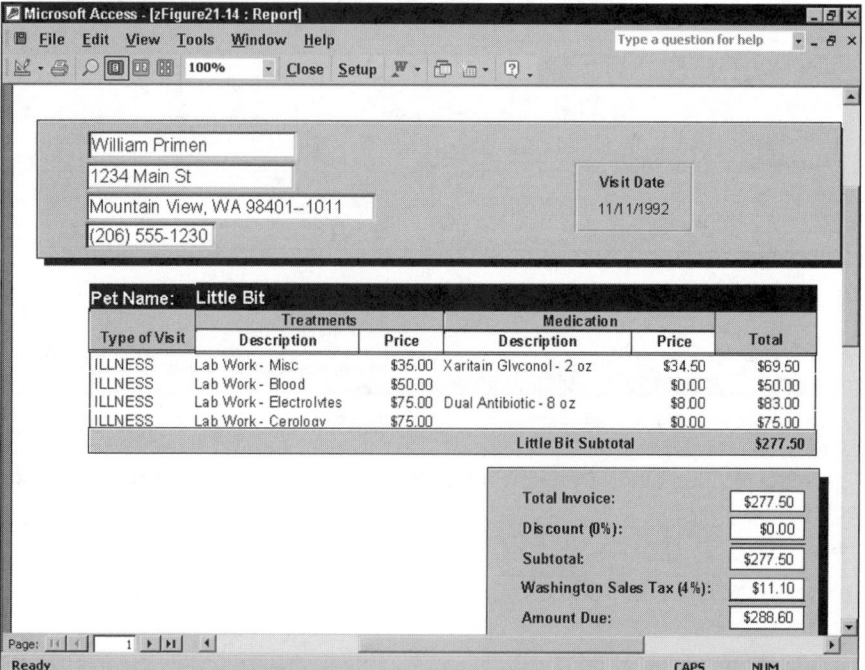

Figure 21-15: Viewing the report in the Print Preview window

To create the Customer Subtotal label and text box controls, follow these steps:

1. Create a new label control.

2. Change the caption to Subtotal:.

3. Create a new text box control.

4. Change the Name to Customer Subtotal.

5. Change the Control Source to =[Customer Total]-[Discount Amount], which subtracts the amount calculated in the Discount Amount control from the sum calculated in the Customer Total control.

Create the State Sales Tax label and text box controls with these steps:

1. Create a new label control.

2. Change the Control Source to =[State Name] & " Sales Tax ("&[Visits.Tax Rate]*100&"%):", which concatenates the customer's state name (full spelling) and the words *Tax Rate* with the customer's tax rate, and then multiplies by 100 to give a percentage.

3. Create a new text box control.

4. Change the Name to State Sales Tax.

5. Change the Control Source to =[Customer Subtotal]*[Visits.Tax Rate], which multiplies the customer's state tax rate by the amount calculated in the Customer Subtotal control.

Next, create the Amount Due label and text box controls:

1. Create a new label control.

2. Change the Caption to Amount Due:.

3. Create a new text box control.

4. Change the Name to Amount Due.

5. Change the Control Source to =[Customer Subtotal]+[State Sales Tax], which adds the customer's calculated state sales tax to the amount calculated in the Customer Subtotal control.

Creating the Visit Date header

You have one more group header to create — Visit Date — but it won't display anything in the section. The section has a height of 0"; essentially, it's closed. The purpose of the Visit Date header is to force a page break whenever the Visit Date changes. Without this section, if you were to have two customer records for the same customer on different dates that appear consecutively in the report's dynaset, the records would appear on the same page. The only forced page break that you've created so far is for Customer Number. By adding one for Visit Date, you complete the report groupings. To create the Visit Date grouping for the header and add the page break, follow these steps:

1. Display the Sorting and Grouping box if it isn't already displayed.

2. Click the Visit Date row Field/Expression column.

3. Click the Group Header property.

4. Click the arrow and select Yes from the drop-down list.

5. Double-click the section to display its property sheet.

6. Change the Height property to 0.

7. Change the Visible property to No.

8. Change the Force New Page property to Before Section.

Creating the page header controls

The page header appears at the top of every page in the Invoice Report. The Sorting and Grouping box do not control the page header and footer controls; View ⇨ Page Header/Footer have to be selected. In this report, the page header has been open all the time. This section contains a small version of the Mountain Animal Hospital logo in the upper-left corner, as well as the name, address, and phone number for the hospital. The section also contains the report date and a horizontal line at the bottom to separate it visually from the rest of the page. By default, the page header and footer are created and displayed automatically when a new report is created. All you have to do is change the height and add the proper controls.

Cross-Reference In Chapter 20, you learn to add the unbound bitmap MTN.BMP to the report. The label controls that display the Mountain Animal Hospital page header are four separate controls. The only control that needs explanation is the Report Date control.

Access offers several built-in functions that let you display and manipulate date and time information. The easiest function to start with is the Date( ) function, which returns the current system date when the report is printed or previewed. To add a text control to the report header that displays the date when the report is printed, follow these steps:

1. Create a new text control in the page header, as shown in Figure 21-16.

2. Display the control's property sheet.

3. In the Control Source property cell, type =**"Report Date: "&Date( )**.

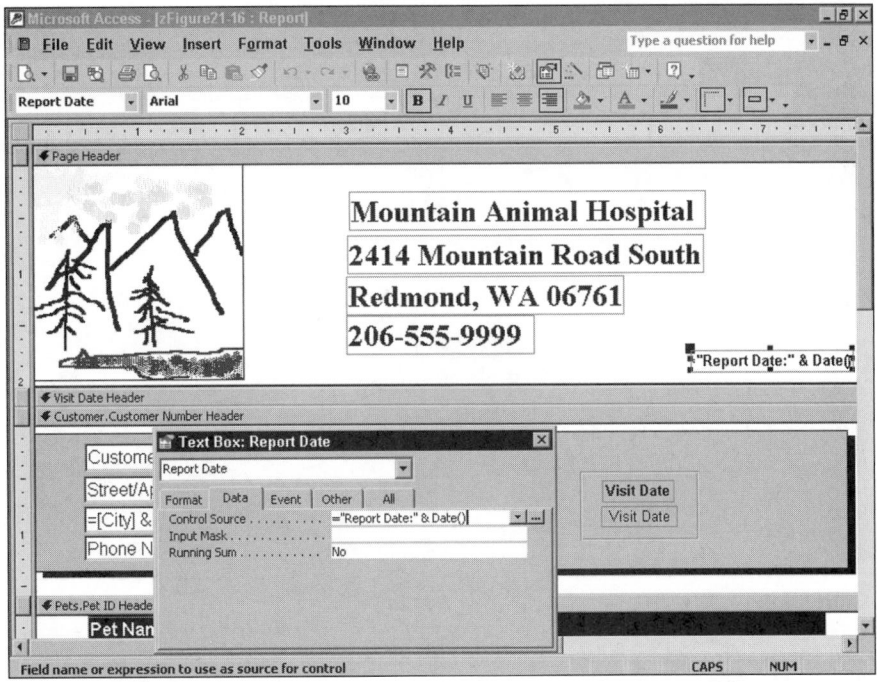

Figure 21-16: The page header

This process concatenates the text Report Date with the current system date.

Another date function that Access offers is DatePart( ), which returns a numeric value for the specified portion of a date. The syntax for the function is

```
DatePart(interval,date,firstweekday,firstweek)
```

where *interval* is a string expression for the interval of time that you want returned and *date* is the date to which you want to apply the function.

Table 21-3 lists some valid intervals and the time periods that they represent.

The date can be a literal date (such as 1-Jan-2001) or a field name that references a field containing a valid date.

Table 21-3 DatePart( ) Intervals	
Interval	*Time Period*
yyyy	Year
q	Quarter
m	Month
y	Day of year
d	Day
w	Weekday
ww	Week
h	Hour
n	Minute
s	Second
Expression	*Result*
=DatePart("yyyy",25-Dec-2001)	2001 (the year)
=DatePart("m",25-Dec-2001)	12 (the month)
=DatePart("d",25-Dec-2001)	25 (the day of the month)
=DatePart("w",25-Dec-2001)	6 (the weekday; Sunday=1, Monday=2 . . .)
=DatePart("q",25-Dec-2001)	4 (the quarter)

Creating the page footer controls

Normally, the page footer is used to place page numbers or to hold page totals. For this report, the footer's only purpose is to display a thick, horizontal line at the bottom of every page, followed by the page number in the bottom-right corner.

To number the pages in your report, Access provides the Page function. You access it by using it in an expression in a text control that returns the current page of the report. As with all expressions, one that has the Page property in it must be preceded by an equal sign (=). To create a footer with a page number, follow these steps:

1. Create a new text control in the lower-right section of the page footer.

2. Display the control's property sheet.

3. In the Control Source property cell, type =**"Page: "&Page**.

4. Select the Italics button on the toolbar.

Although it makes the most sense to put the page number in the page header or page footer, you can place a control with the Page property in any section of your report. You can also use the Page property as part of an expression. For example, the expression =Page*10 displays the result of multiplying the actual page number by 10.

You have now completed the Monthly Invoice Report. Compare your report design with the one shown originally in Figure 21-2, and then compare it with the final output in Figure 21-17. Figure 21-17 shows Page 24 of the report—a good example of displaying all the sections on one page. (Look back at Figure 21-1 to see a hard copy of the report page.)

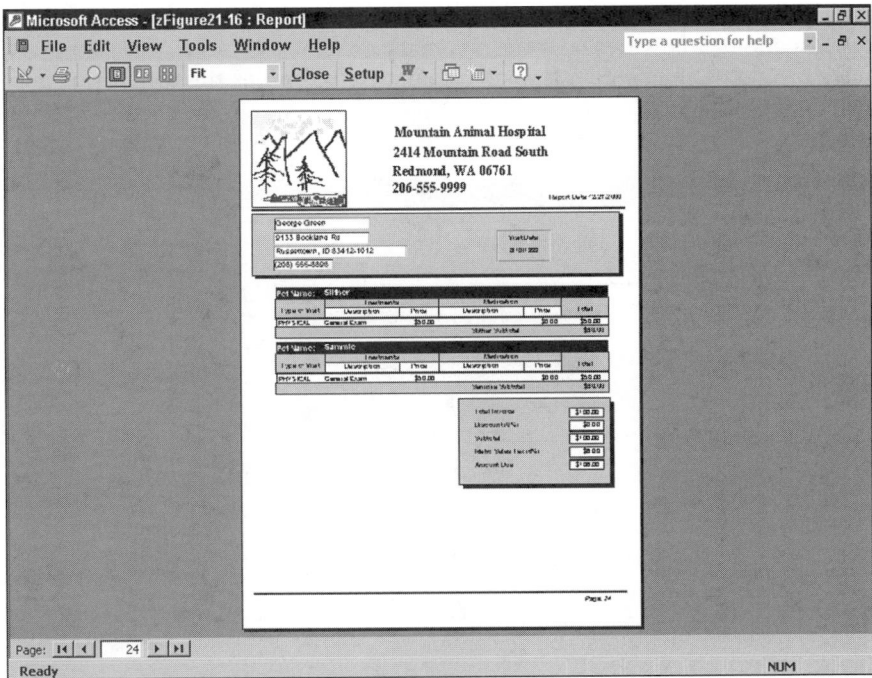

Figure 21-17: The report design output on-screen

Before moving on, you need to create a few more controls. Because Access features a two-pass report writer, you can create controls based on your knowledge of the final report. For example, you can create a control that displays the percentage of one total to a grand total or create a cumulative total to display cumulative totals.

Calculating percentages using totals

To determine what percent each line is of the total cost for a pet's visit, calculate a line percentage. By comparing the line item to the total, you can calculate the percentage of a particular item to the whole. To do this, you need to move all the controls for the Pet ID header and footer and the detail section to the far left side of the report. To create a new control that displays what percentage each pet represents of the whole (Mountain Animal Hospital Charges), follow these steps:

1. Duplicate the Pet Visit Line Total control.

2. Position the duplicate to the right of the original.

3. Change the Control Source to =[Pet Visit Line Total]/[Pet Visit Total].

4. Change the Format property to Percent.

5. Create a new label control with the caption "Percent" above it, as shown in Figure 21-18.

The calculation takes the individual line total control [Pet Visit Line Total] in the detail section and divides it by the summary control [Pet Visit Total] in the page header section. The Percent format automatically handles the conversion and displays a percentage.

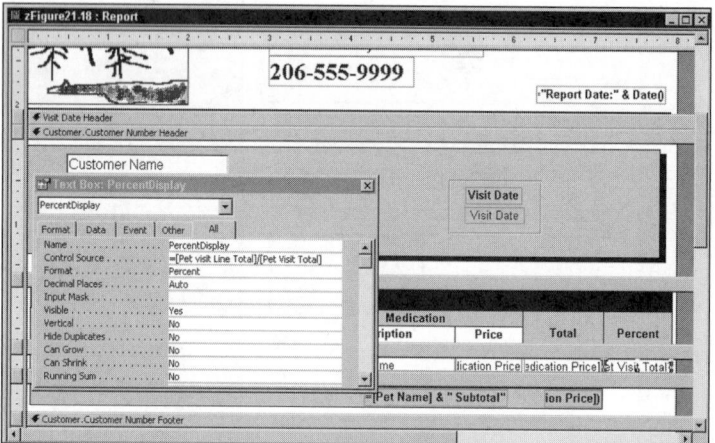

Figure 21-18: Creating a percentage control

Calculating running sums

Access also lets you calculate running sums (also known as *cumulative totals*) easily — simply change the Running Sum property for a control. To create a running total of how much is spent as each pet's charges are totaled, follow these steps:

1. Duplicate the rectangle and its controls in the Pets.Pet ID footer section.

2. Display the new rectangle just below the existing one, as shown in Figure 21-19.

3. Select the label control and change the caption to =[**Customer Name]&"'s Running Total".**

4. Select the new control with this expression: =Sum([Treatment Price]+[Medication Price]).

5. Display the control's property sheet.

6. Change the Name to "Running Total."

7. Click the Running Sum property.

8. Select Over Group from the drop-down list, as shown in Figure 21-19.

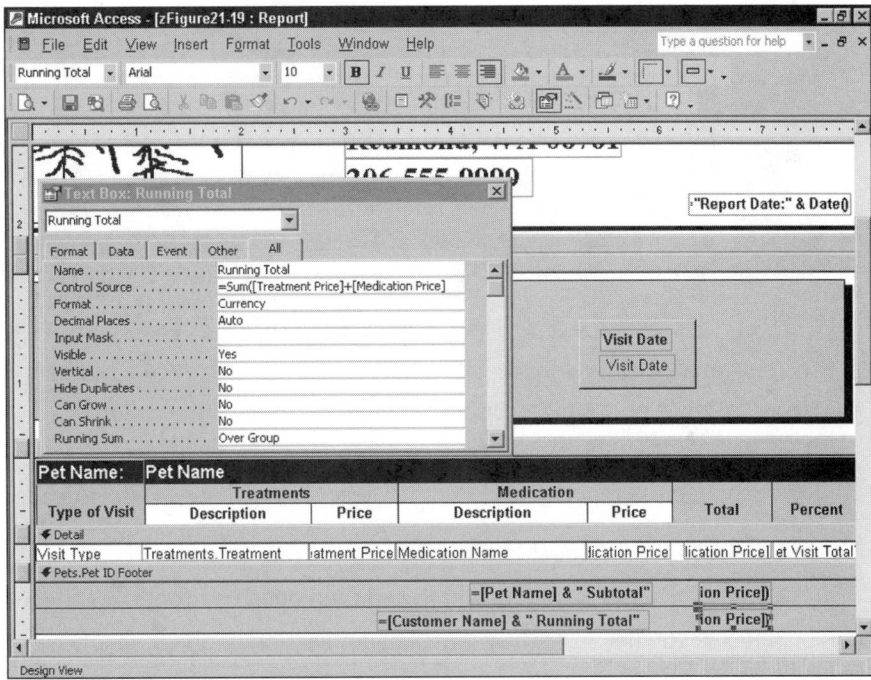

Figure 21-19: Creating a running sum control

Access now adds the current subtotal to all previous subtotals for each owner. You can also create a running sum across all values in a report. This is useful to present an overall summary in the report's footer section.

You can display percentages and the running total with a print preview, as in Figure 21-20.

Creating a title page in a report header

The primary purpose of the report header is to provide a separate title page. The report header must contain Mountain Animal Hospital's logo, name, address, and phone number, as well as a report title. In the sample Monthly Invoice Report file, all of these controls are created for you.

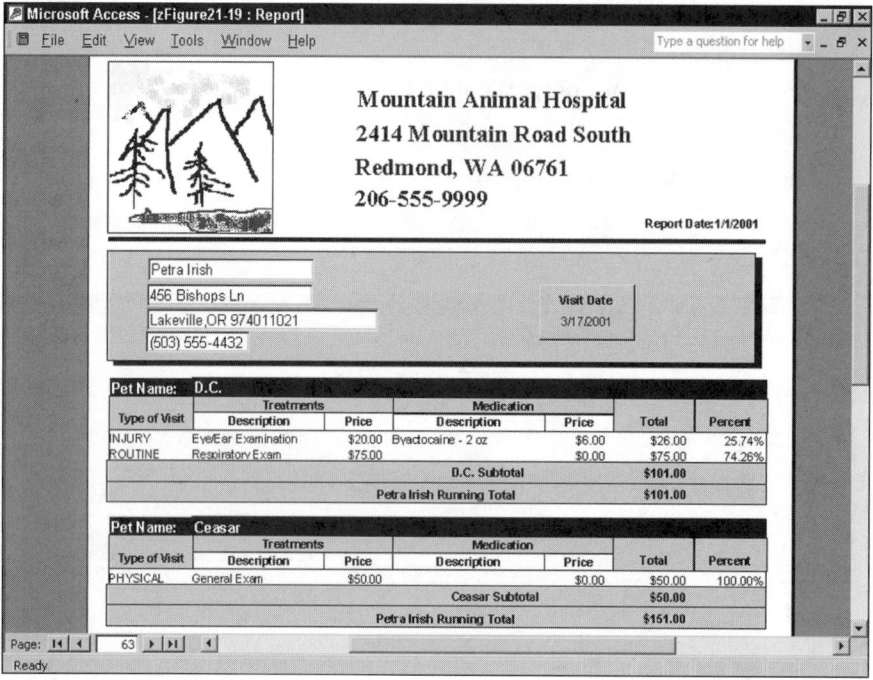

Figure 21-20: A print preview displaying percentages and running totals

If you created the report from scratch, these steps create a report header:

1. Select View ➪ Report Header/Footer.

2. Click the report header section and then open its Properties sheet.

3. Resize the height of the report header section to about 9 inches.

4. Set the Force New Page property of the report header section to After Section so that a page break occurs after the report header.

5. Create label controls for the report title, name, address, and phone.

6. Create an image picture control (using MTN.BMP) and change the Size Mode property to Stretch.

Using the report footer

The report footer isn't actually used in this report; it's displayed because the report header can't be displayed in Design view without it. You normally use the report footer for grand totals that occur once in the report. You can also use it in an accounting-type report or in a letter concerning the totals for an audit trail.

✦   ✦   ✦

Advanced Access Database Topics

♦ ♦ ♦ ♦

In This Part

Chapter 22
Working with
External Data

Chapter 23
Working with
Advanced Select
Queries

Chapter 24
Working with Action
Queries

Chapter 25
Advanced Query
Topics

Chapter 26
Working with
Subforms

Chapter 27
Creating Mail Merge
and Label Reports

♦ ♦ ♦ ♦

Working with External Data

✦ ✦ ✦ ✦

In This Chapter

Linking to external data

Splitting an Access database into programs and data

Working with linked tables

Importing external data

Creating import/export specifications

Exporting to external tables and files

✦ ✦ ✦ ✦

So far, you have worked only with data in Access tables. In this chapter, you explore the use of data from other types of files. You learn to work with data from database, spreadsheet, HTML, and text-based files. After describing the general relationship between Access and external data, this chapter explains the major methods of working with external data: linking and importing/exporting.

Access and External Data

Exchanging information between Access and another program is an essential capability in today's database world. Information is usually stored in a wide variety of application programs and data formats. Access (like many other products) has its own native file format, designed to support referential integrity and provide support for rich data types, such as OLE objects. Most of the time, this format is sufficient; occasionally, however, you need to move data from one Access database file to another, or even to or from a different software program's format.

Types of external data

Access has the capability to use and exchange data among a wide range of applications. For example, you may need to get data from other database files (such as FoxPro, dBASE, or Paradox files) or obtain information from an SQL Server, Oracle, or a text file. Access can move data among several categories of applications:

✦ Other Windows applications

✦ Macintosh applications (Foxbase, FoxPro, Excel)

✦ Spreadsheets

✦ PC database management systems

✦ Server-based database systems (ODBC)

✦ Text and/or other mainframe files

Methods of working with external data

Often you will need to move data from another application or file into your Access database, or vice-versa. You may need to obtain information you already have in an external spreadsheet file. You can reenter all the information by hand — or have it imported into your database. Perhaps you need to put information from your Access tables into Paradox files. Again, you can reenter all the information into Paradox by hand or have the information exported to the Paradox table. Access has tools that enable you to move data from a database table to another table or file. It could be a table in Access, dBASE, or Paradox; it could be a Lotus 1-2-3 spreadsheet file. In fact, Access can exchange data with more than 15 different file types, including the following:

✦ Access database objects (all types, all versions)

✦ dBASE III+, IV, and 5

✦ FoxPro (all types using the ODBC drivers)

✦ Paradox 3.x, 4.x, 5.0, 7, and 8

✦ Text files (ANSI and ASCII; DOS or OS/2; delimited and fixed-length)

✦ Lotus WK1, WK3, and WJ2

✦ Excel 3, 4, 5-7, 97-2002

✦ ODBC (Microsoft SQL Server, Sybase Server, Oracle Server, and other ODBC 1.1-compliant databases)

✦ HTML tables, lists, documents

✦ XML documents

✦ Outlook and Outlook Express

✦ Exchange documents

✦ Microsoft IIS 1 and 2

✦ Microsoft Active Server Pages

✦ Microsoft Word Merge documents

✦ Rich Text Format documents

Access can work with these external data sources in several ways: linking, importing, and exporting. Table 22-1 lists and describes each method.

Table 22-1
Methods of Working with External Data

Method	Description
Link	Creates a link to a table in another Access database or links to the data from a different database format
Import	Copies data from a text file, another Access database, or another application's format into an Access table
Export	Copies data from an Access table to a text file, another Access database, or another application's format

Note   Open Database Connectivity, or ODBC, is a standard method of sharing data between databases and programs. They use the Structured Query Language, or SQL, to manipulate the external data.

Should you link to or import data?

As Table 22-1 shows, you can work with data from other sources in two ways: linking or importing. Both methods enable you to work with the external data. There is a distinct difference between the two methods:

✦ Linking uses the data in its current file format (such as a dBASE or Paradox file).

✦ Importing makes a copy of the external data and brings the copy into the Access table.

Each method has clear advantages and disadvantages.

Note   What is called *linking* in Access 2002 was called *attaching* in Access 2.0 and 1.x.

When to link to external data

Linking in Access enables you to work with the data in another application's format — thus sharing the file with the existing application. If you leave data in another database format, Access can actually make changes to the table while the original application is still using it. This capability is useful when you want to work with data in Access that other programs also need to work with. For example, you might need to obtain updated personnel data from a dBASE file (maintained in an existing networked dBASE application) so that you can print a monthly report in Access. Another example is when you use Access as a front end for your SQL database — you can link to an SQL table and update the data directly to the server, without having to "batch upload" it later.

If you plan on using a table from another Microsoft Access database that is shared on a network, it is a good idea to simply link to it rather than import it. If another application will continue to be used to update and work with data in an external table (like in another format — dBASE or Paradox), it is best to link to it.

You can link to the following types of data in Access 2002: another Access table, Excel spreadsheets, Exchange documents, Outlook documents, Paradox files, Text files, HTML Documents, dBASE files, and ODBC databases.

Caution   Access 2002 has the capability to link to HTML tables and text tables for read-only access. You can use and look at tables in HTML or text format; however, the tables cannot be updated nor records added to them using Access. Also, if you are working with Paradox files and they do not have a primary key field defined (a .PX file associated with the .DB table) you will only be able to read the data — not change it.

The biggest disadvantage of working with linked tables is that you lose the internal capability of Access to enforce referential integrity between tables (unless you are linked to an Access database).

When to import external data

Access cannot link to certain file formats; these include Lotus 1-2-3 spreadsheet files. If you need to work with data from formats that cannot be linked to, you must import it.

Importing in Access enables you to physically bring an external table or data source into a new Access 2002 table. By doing this, Access will automatically convert data from the external format and copy it into Access. You can even import data objects into another Access database (rather than the one currently open) or Access project. If you know that you will use your data in Access only, you should import it. Generally, Access works faster with its own tables.

Of course, importing data means that you have significantly increased the storage space required for that particular data, since it now resides in two different files on the storage device.

Note   Because importing makes another copy of the data, you may want to erase the old file after you import the copy into Access. Sometimes, however, you won't want to erase it. For example, the data may be sales figures from a Lotus spreadsheet still in use. In cases such as this, simply maintain the duplicate data and accept that storing it will require more space.

One of the principal reasons to import data is to customize it to meet your needs. Once a table has been imported, you can modify the structure, data types, and assign table-based rules for the table. You can specify a primary key, change field names (up to 64 characters), and set other field properties.

Working with Other Access Databases

Access can open only one database at a time; therefore, you can't work directly with a table in a different database. Even so, if you need to work with tables or other Access objects (such as forms and queries) from another Access database, you don't have to close the current one. Instead, simply import or link the object in the other database to your current database. You'll be able to view or edit data directly in more than one database table.

Note

When you link to a table in another Access database, you cannot do everything you can do with tables in the primary database from the currently open database. For instance, you cannot define a primary key or enforce referential integrity. However, if all the tables you want to work with are in an external Access database, you can open that database and specify all the table properties you wish to set: defining a primary key, defining relationships between tables, setting referential integrity between tables, changing a data type, specifying default values or validation rules, or even creating new indexes.

With linked tables, on the other hand, you are restricted to setting very limited field properties. For example, you cannot specify a primary key or assign a data entry rule (like only accept a date of birth less than today), which means that you can't enforce integrity against the linked table.

Data in unsupported programs

Although uncommon, there may be times that you need to work with data from a program that is not stored in the supported external database or file format. In cases such as this, the programs usually can export or convert their data in one of the formats recognized by Access. To use the data in these programs, export it to a format recognized by Access and then import it into Access. Most applications can export to dBASE file format. If the dBASE format is not available, most programs, even those on different operating systems, can export data to delimited or fixed-width text files, which you can then import into Access. When exporting to text files you will lose any indexes associated with the tables.

Automating import operations

If you will be importing data from the same source frequently, you can automate the process by creating a macro or a Visual Basic for Applications procedure. This can be very helpful for those times when you have to import data from an external source on a regular schedule or you have complex requirements that must be met for importing the data.

Linking External Data

As the database market continues to grow, the need to obtain information from many different sources will escalate. If you have information captured in an SQL Server table or a Paradox table, you don't want to reenter the information from these tables into Access. Ideally, you want to open the table and use the information in its native format, without having to copy it or write a translation program to access it. For many companies today, this capability of accessing information from one database format while working in another is a primary goal.

Copying or translating data from one application format to another is both time-consuming and costly. The time it takes can mean the difference between success and failure. Therefore, you want a heterogeneous environment between your DBMSs and the data. Access provides this environment through linking tables.

Access can directly link to several database management system (DBMS) tables individually or simultaneously. After an external file is linked, Access builds and stores a link to the table. As pointed out previously, Access can link to other Access database tables; to non-Access database tables such as dBASE, FoxPro, and Paradox; and to non-database tables such as spreadsheets, HTML tables, and text tables. You can also split an Access database into separate databases, for easier use in a multi-user or client-server environment.

On the CD-ROM

The examples in this chapter use the database Access Import-Export.mdb. This database is included on your CD-ROM along with several different types of DBMS files: dBASE, Paradox, Excel spreadsheet, HTML, and text files. If you wish to follow along and perform the steps, you will need to use these files.

Types of database management systems

Access enables you to connect, or link, to several different DBMSs, directly accessing information stored in them. Access supports the following database systems:

- ✦ Other Access database tables
- ✦ dBASE (versions III, IV, and 5)
- ✦ FoxPro (via the FoxPro ODBC driver)
- ✦ Paradox (versions 3.0, 4.x, 5.x, and 7–8)
- ✦ Microsoft SQL Server, Sybase Server, Oracle, or any ODBC-aware database

You can link to any of these table types, individually or mixed together. If you link to an external file, Access displays the filename in the Database Table window (just as it does for other Access tables), but the icon linked with the table will be different. It starts with an arrow pointing from left to right and points to an icon. An arrow pointing to a table icon tells you that it's an Access table, arrow to a dB icon tells you that it's a dBASE table, and so on. Figure 22-1 shows several linked in the list, which are all external tables. These tables are linked to the current database. Notice that all the linked tables have an icon with an arrow. (The icon clues you in to the type of file that is linked.)

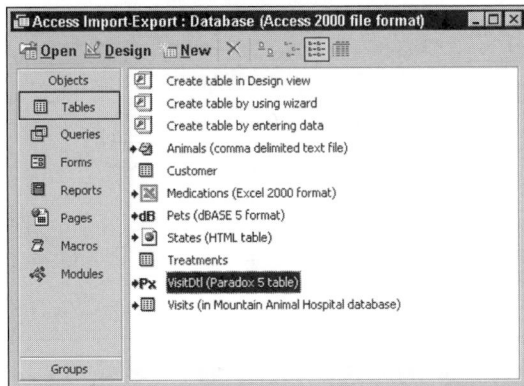

Figure 22-1: Linked tables in an Access database. Notice that each linked table has a graphic right arrow and another symbol for an icon.

In Figure 22-1, the arrows that appear to the left of some of the table names indicate linked tables. In addition to the link arrow indicator, you can tell by their icon which type of file they are linked to. For instance, Excel has the graphic X symbol in a box, Paradox has the Px symbol, dBASE tables have the dB symbol, an HTML table has a page with a picture of the world on it, and a Text file has a Notebook icon.

After you link a table to your Access database, you can use it as you would any other table. You can query against it, link another table to it, and so on. For example, Figure 22-2 shows a query designed using several linked tables: Customer (from current Database), PETS (from dBASE 5 table), Visits (from another Access database), Visits Details (from a Paradox 5 table), Treatments (from current database) and Medications (from an Excel 2000 spreadsheet). Your application does not have to use Access tables at all; you can just as easily link to the Paradox and FoxPro tables.

This query will be built later in this chapter after linking all the tables in the Access Import-Export database. Once created and run, it will display data from all the tables, both internally and externally linked information, the same as any Select query. Figure 22-3 shows the resulting dynaset as viewed in the datasheet.

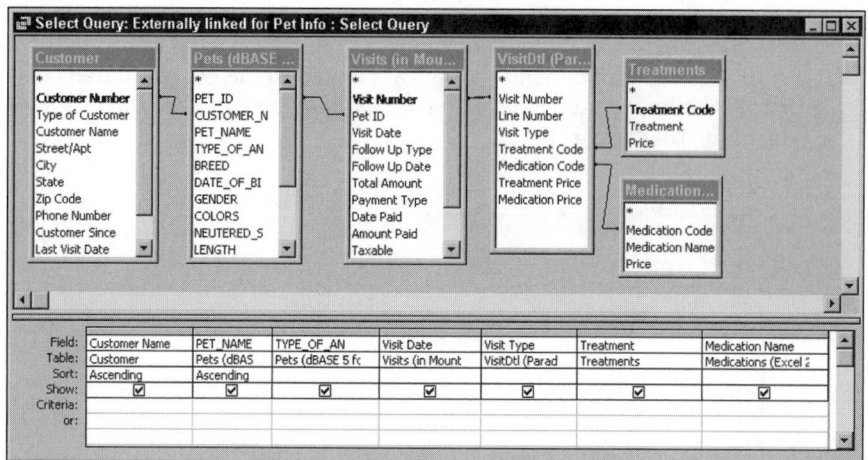

Figure 22-2: A query designed using externally linked tables

Select Query: Externally linked for Pet Info : Select Query

Customer Name	PET_NAME	TYPE_OF_AN	Visit Date	Visit Type	Treatment	Medication Name
Adam Johnson	Fi Fi	DOG	05/09/1999	ILLNESS	Lab Work - Cerology	
Adam Johnson	Fi Fi	DOG	05/09/1999	ILLNESS	General Exam	Zinc Oxide - 4 oz
Adam Johnson	Fi Fi	DOG	05/09/1999	ILLNESS	Lab Work - Misc	
All Creatures	Bobo	RABBIT	07/11/2001	PHYSICAL	General Exam	
All Creatures	Bobo	RABBIT	02/04/1999	GROOMING	Brushing	
All Creatures	Bobo	RABBIT	02/04/1999	GROOMING	Bathing	
All Creatures	Bobo	RABBIT	07/11/2001	PHYSICAL	General Exam	
All Creatures	Bobo	RABBIT	07/11/2001	GROOMING	Haircut	
All Creatures	Bobo	RABBIT	02/04/1999	PHYSICAL	General Exam	
All Creatures	Fido	DOG	11/03/1999	GROOMING	Brushing	
All Creatures	Fido	DOG	11/03/1999	GROOMING	Flea Spray	
All Creatures	Fido	DOG	11/12/2000	INJURY	Anesthetize Patient	Nyostatine - 2 oz
All Creatures	Fido	DOG	11/12/2000	INJURY	Cast affected area	
All Creatures	Presto Chang	LIZARD	02/03/2001	INJURY	Clean Area	Glyconfate - 1 oz
All Creatures	Presto Chang	LIZARD	08/26/2001	PHYSICAL	General Exam	
All Creatures	Presto Chang	LIZARD	11/06/1999	PHYSICAL	Eye/Ear Examination	
All Creatures	Presto Chang	LIZARD	02/03/2001	INJURY	Amputation of limb	Byactocaine - 4 oz
All Creatures	Stinky	SKUNK	02/08/2001	GROOMING	Brushing	
All Creatures	Stinky	SKUNK	02/08/2001	PHYSICAL	General Exam	

Record: 1 of 145

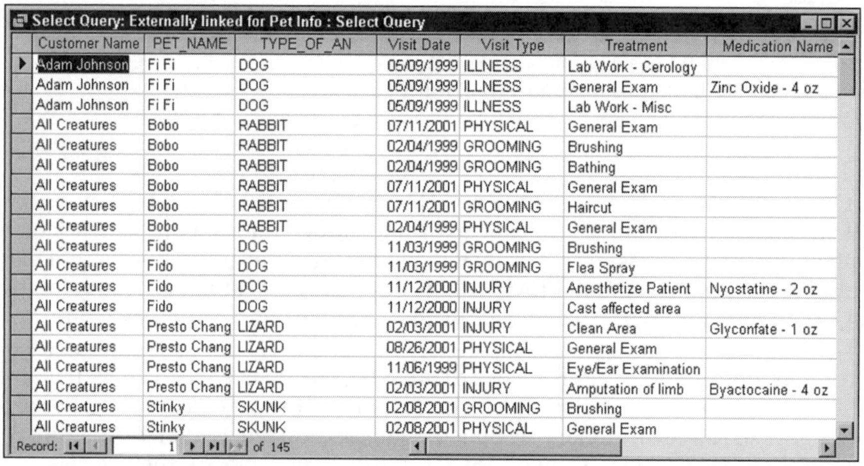

Figure 22-3: The datasheet view of externally linked data

In Figure 22-3 the column heading names come from the field names in the underlying external tables. For instance, the second column, PET_NAME, comes from the underlying field name in the dBASE 5 table Pets. The TYPE_OF_AN field name comes from the same table. You can make the names more understandable by assigning a new name in the QBE pane of the query when you are designing it.

Note

After you link an external table to an Access database, you cannot move the table to another drive or directory. Access does not actually bring the file into the MDB file; it maintains the link via the filename and the drive: path. If you move the external table, you have to update the link using the Linked Table Manager, explained in the "Viewing or changing information for linked tables" section later in this chapter.

Linking to other Access database tables

When you work with an Access database, normally you create every table you want to use in it. If the table exists in another Access database, however, you can link to the table in the other Access database (rather than re-creating it and duplicating its data). You may, for example, want to link to another Access table that is on a network.

After you link to another Access table, you use it just as you use another table in the open database. To link to the Customer table in the Mountain Animal Hospital Access database from the Access Import-Export.mdb database file, follow these steps:

1. Open the Access Import-Export.mdb database.

2. Select File ➪ Get External Data ➪ Link Tables . . . (or right-click anywhere in the Tables container and select Link Tables . . . from the menu. Access opens the Link dialog box, as shown in Figure 22-4.

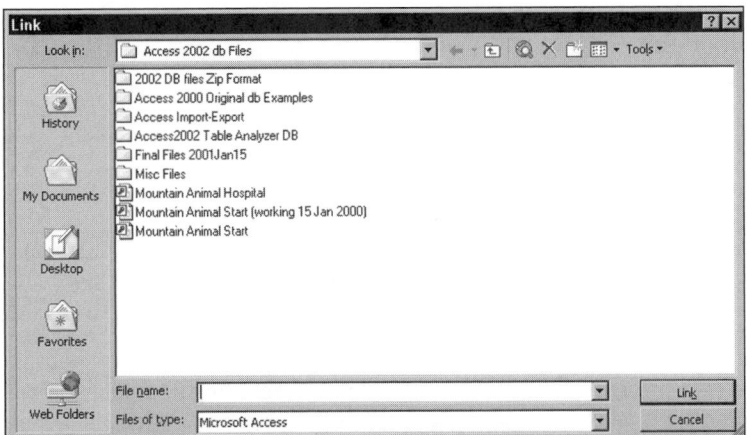

Figure 22-4: The Link dialog box opened for selecting which external table or .MDB to link to. The default file type is Microsoft Access.

Using the Link Tables dialog box, you can select the .MDB file you want to link to. You can also change the type of files displayed in the Link dialog box; it can link to any type of external data. Though the default is to show only Access files (.MDB), you can link to any of the supported file types.

3. Find and select the Mountain Animal Hospital.MDB file in the dialog box. You may have to search for a different drive or directory.

4. Double-click the Mountain Animal Hospital.MDB file (or select it and click the Link button). Access will close the dialog box and display the Link Tables dialog box.

   The Link Tables dialog box enables you to select one or more tables from the database selected (in this case Mountain Animal Hospital).

5. Select Visits and click OK. Double-clicking the table name will not do anything — to select it, you must highlight it and then click OK.

After you link the Visits table from the Mountain Animal Hospital database, Access returns to the Database window and shows you that the table is now linked to your database. Figure 22-5 shows the Visits table linked to the current database. Notice the arrow on the Visits table's icon; it shows that the table has been linked from another source.

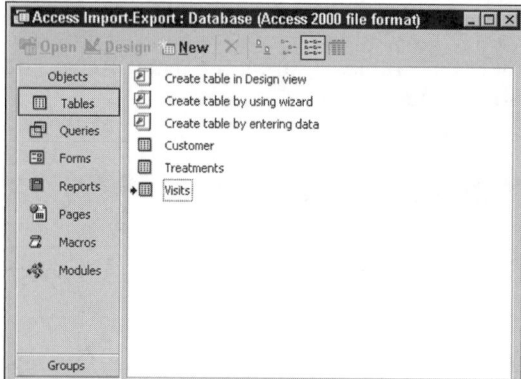

Figure 22-5: The Database window with the Visits table added. Its table icon has a right-pointing arrow to the table.

Tip   You can link more than one table at a time by selecting each table before you click the OK button. You can also use the Select All button to select all the tables.

Linking to dBASE and FoxPro databases (tables)

You can link to DBF files in either dBASE or FoxPro format. As with other Access database tables, after an xBASE (dBASE or FoxPro) file is linked, you can view and edit data in the DBF format.

dBASE and FoxPro save tables in individual files with the extension DBF. In xBASE, these DBF files are called databases. In Access, however, a table is equivalent to an xBASE database. (Access considers a database a complete collection of all tables and other related objects.) To maintain consistency in terminology, this book considers xBASE databases to mean the same thing as dBASE or FoxPro tables.

Access and dBASE/FoxPro indexes

When you link a dBASE or FoxPro file, you can also tell Access to use one or more index files (NDX and MDX for dBASE, and IDX and CDX for FoxPro). The use of these indexes will improve performance of the link between xBASE and Access.

Caution
> Microsoft has created dBASE ISAM drivers for Microsoft Jet 4.0 that do not require the installation of the Borland Database Engine (BDE), as in previous versions of Access, to provide full read/write access to dBASE files. The default ISAM drivers that ship with Microsoft Data Access Component (MDAC) 2.1 and later only enable read-only access to dBASE files unless the BDE is installed. To obtain these ISAM drivers that will give you full read/write access to dBASE files, you must contact Technical Support at Microsoft, and they will send them to you. You can also download the updated version of Microsoft Jet 4.0 from Microsoft's download center http://www.microsoft.com/download/. Once at the site, select Keyword search, enter the words "Jet 4.0" in the keyword entry field, select your operating system, and click the Find It button to find the correct drivers. If you would prefer to use the BDE drivers, you can download them from http://www.borland.com/download/ or http:/www.imprise.com/download/ then choose BDE (Borland Database Engine) to jump to the correct link. If you do not have any version of the BDE on your machine, you will have to download two files — the most current update (which will only update an older version) and an older version, which is found via a hyperlink on the current version page.

If you inform Access of the associated index files, Access will update the indexes every time it changes the DBF file. By linking a DBF file and its associated indexes, Access can link to DBFs in real time in a network environment. Access recognizes and enforces the automatic record-locking feature of dBASE and FoxPro as well as the file and record locks placed with xBASE commands and functions.

Caution
> You should always tell Access about any indexes associated with the database. If you don't, it will not update them; dBASE or FoxPro will have unexpected problems if their associated index files are not updated.

When you tell Access to use one or more associated indexes (NDX, MDX, IDX, or CDX) of a dBASE or FoxPro file, Access maintains information about the fields used in the index tags in a special information file. This file has the same name as the dBASE or FoxPro file with an INF extension.

If you link a dBASE or FoxPro file and associated indexes, Access must have access to the index files in order to link the table. If you delete or move the index files or the Access INF file, you will not be able to open the linked DBF file.

Linking to an xBASE table

Linking to FoxPro tables and dBASE tables works the same. For example, to link the dBASE V table PETS.DBF and its associated memo file (DBT), follow these steps:

1. Open the Access Import-Export database and select File ⇨ Get External Data ⇨ Link Tables.

2. In the Link dialog box, select Files of type: dBASE 5. Access displays the dBASE 5 DBF files only.

3. Double-click Pets.DBF in the Select Index Files list box. (The associated memo file Pets.DBT is linked automatically.)

4. Access activates the Select Index Files box and displays all NDX and MDX files.

5. Select the Pets.MDX and click the Select button.

   Access displays a dialog box that informs you that it has added the index Pets.MDX.

6. Click the OK button to return to the Select Index Files dialog box.

Note   If there are any other indexes to associate with this table, you select them here. If there were no indexes associated with this table you would simply close this dialog box without selecting an index.

7. Click the Close button.

   If there is more than one index selected or a Multiple Index file (MDX) is selected with more than one index associated with the table, Access displays another, smaller, dialog box that is titled "Select Unique Record Identifier." Figure 22-6 shows this dialog box.

8. Select the Pet_ID index as the Unique Record Identifier (primary key) and click the OK button.

   Access then displays a dialog box that informs you that it has successfully linked 'Pets'.

9. Click the OK button to return to the Link dialog box.

   You are returned to this dialog box so that you can continue to select additional tables to link to.

10. Click the Close button to finish linking the Pets dBASE file. Access displays the Database window with the file Pets.dbf linked.

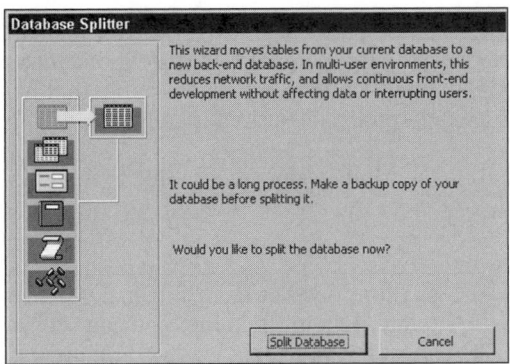

Figure 22-6: The Select Unique Record Identifier dialog box. Here you specify the index name that is the primary key field for the linked table.

Note

You can cancel linking at any time by clicking the Cancel button in the Select File dialog box before you select a table.

When you add index files, Access automatically creates and updates an Access information file. This file contains information about the index and associated dBASE or FoxPro file, has the same name, and ends in the extension INF.

Linking to Paradox tables

You can link to Paradox .DB files in either Paradox 3.x, 4.x, 5.x, 7, or 8 format. After a Paradox file is linked, you can view and edit data just like an Access database table.

Caution

Microsoft has created Paradox ISAM drivers for Microsoft Jet 4.0 that do not require the installation of the Borland Database Engine (BDE) as in previous versions of Access to provide full read/write access to Paradox files. The default ISAM drivers that ship with Microsoft Data Access Component (MDAC) 2.1 and later, only enable read-only access to dBASE files unless the BDE is installed. To obtain these ISAM drivers that will give you full read/write access to Paradox files you must contact Technical Support at Microsoft and they will send them to you. You can also download the updated version of Microsoft Jet 4.0 from Microsoft's download center http://www.microsoft.com/download/. Once at the site, select Keyword search, enter the words "Jet 4.0" in the keyword entry field, select your operating system, and click the Find It button to find the correct drivers. If you would prefer to use the BDE drivers, you can download them from http://www. borland.com/downloads/ or http://www.inprise.com/downloads/, and then click the choice BDE (Borland Database Engine) to jump to the correct link. If you do not have any version of the BDE on your machine, you will have to download two files — the most current update (which will only update an older version) and an older version, which is found via a hyperlink in the current version page.

Access and Paradox index files

If a Paradox table has a primary key defined, it maintains the index information in a file that ends in the extension PX. When you link a Paradox table that has a primary key defined, Access links the associated PX file automatically.

If you link a Paradox table that has a primary key, Access needs the PX file in order to open the table. If you move or delete the PX file, you will not be able to open the linked table.

If you link a Paradox table to Access that does not have a primary key defined, you will not be able to use Access to update data in the table; you can only view it. This is true even if you have the BDE or new ISAM drivers loaded. You must have a primary key field defined in the Paradox table or it is not updateable when linked.

Like dBASE files, Access can link to DBs in real time in a network environment. Access recognizes and enforces the file- and record-locking features of Paradox.

To link to the Paradox 5 table VisitDtl, follow these steps:

1. In the Access Import-Export database, select File ➪ Get External Data ➪ Link Tables.

2. In the Link dialog box, select Files of type: Paradox. Access displays just the Paradox .DB files.

3. Select the VisitDtl Paradox file and click the Link button.

   Access displays a dialog box that says "Successfully linked 'VisitDtl.'"

4. Click OK to return to the Link dialog box.

5. Click Close to return to the database container.

Figure 22-7 shows that the Paradox table VisitDtl has been linked to. Notice that the dBASE Pets table has also been linked to successfully.

The Access 2002 Link Wizard

As in the steps followed previously, when you link to an Excel spreadsheet, HTML table, or text file, Access 2002 automatically runs a Link Wizard to help you. In each case, you are asked whether the first line (record) contains the field names for the fields. If it does, click the check box to turn it on. If the first record does not hold the field names, you are given the option of specifying a name for each field or accepting the default names (field1, field2, field3, and so on).

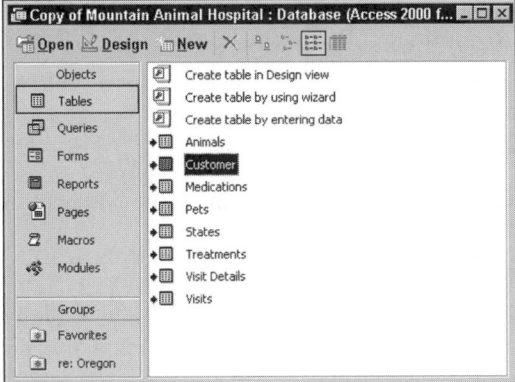

Figure 22-7: The Paradox table is now linked into the database.

Linking to non-database tables

You can also link to non-database tables, such as Excel, HTML, and text tables. When you select one of these types of data sources, Access runs a Link Wizard that prompts you through the process.

If you link to an Excel table, you can update its records from within Access 2002 or any other application that can update Excel spreadsheets.

Follow these steps to link to the Excel Medications spreadsheet:

1. In the Access Import-Export database, select File ➪ Get External Data ➪ Link Tables.

2. In the Link dialog box, select Files of type: Excel. Access displays the Excel files only.

3. Select the Medications file and click the Link button.

   The Link Spreadsheet Wizard is activated, as shown in Figure 22-8. Here you will tell Access how to use the Spreadsheet. The first screen shows the table (Medications) name in the top half and the sample data in the worksheet in the bottom half.

4. Click Next to continue through the Wizard.

   The next screen is displayed and shows a check box (First Row Contains Column Headings). The bottom of the screen has changed showing the field headings above the contents and grayed out.

5. Make sure that the check box is checked and the field headings are correct. Then click the Next button to continue through the Wizard.

Access displays the final screen of the Wizard and prompts for a table name to give the file Medications.xls.

6. Accept the table name Medications and click the Finish button.

Access displays a dialog box that says "Finished linking table 'Medications' to file Medications.xls."

7. Click OK to return to the database container.

Unlike linking to other Access, Paradox, and dBASE tables, Access immediately returns you to the database container, instead of the Link dialog box to link to another table.

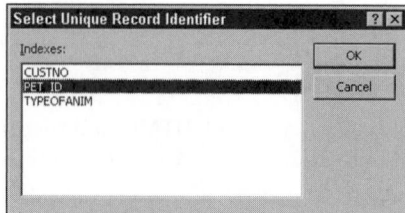

Figure 22-8: The first screen of the Link Spreadsheet Wizard

With the Excel Medications table linked, the database container should display four linked tables — Pets (dBASE 5 type), VisitDtl (Paradox 5 type), Visits (Access 2000 table in the Mountain Animal Hospital database), and the Medications (Excel file).

The other two types of non-database files that you can link to are HTML documents and text files. To link to these, Access also uses a Wizard to help you view and work with the contents. Linking to HTML and text tables will enable you to view and use tables in queries, forms, and reports. However, you cannot change the current record contents or add new records.

Follow these steps to link to the lookup table States, an HTML document:

1. Open the Access Import-Export database and select File ⇨ Get External Data ⇨ Link Tables.

2. In the Link dialog box, select Files of type: HTML. Access displays the HTML files only.

3. Select the States file and click the Link button.

Access starts the Link HTML Wizard and displays the first screen. It has a check box on the top half (First Row Contains Column Headings) and the bottom shows the contents of the HTML file.

4. Make sure that the check box First Row Contains Column Headings is not checked. Then click the Next button.

   Access displays the next screen where you can change the names of the fields and their data type. Figure 22-9 shows this screen. Notice that the bottom half shows the field contents and three column headings — Field1 (partially obscure), Field2, and Field3. It also has an Advance button that enables you to specify more advanced options. The top half has two entry fields — one for the field name, the other for the Type of Data. It also has a check box that will enable you to skip importing the current field in the HTML table.

5. Change the field name for the first column from 'Field1' to State Abbr. The Data type should remain Text.

6. Click in the second column of the lower part of the screen, and the entire column should be highlighted.

   If you accidentally press the Enter key, Access displays the next screen. If this happens, simply click the Back button to return to the current screen.

7. Change the field name for the second column from 'Field2' to State Name. The Data type should remain Text.

8. Click the third column to highlight it.

9. Change the field name for the final column from 'Field3' to Tax Rate. The Data type should remain Double.

10. Click the Next button.

    Access displays the final screen of the Wizard and prompts for a table name to give the file States.html.

11. Accept the table name States and click the Finish button.

    Access displays a dialog box that says "Finished linking table 'States' to file . . . States.html."

12. Click the OK button to return to the database container.

    Unlike linking to other Access tables, Paradox, and dBASE tables, Access immediately returns you to the database container, instead of the Link dialog box to link to another table.

Finally, follow these steps to link to the lookup table Animals, a text file:

1. Open the Access Import-Export database and select File ➪ Get External Data ➪ Link Tables.

2. In the Link dialog box, select Files of type: Text. Access displays just the Text files.

Figure 22-9: The HTML Wizard screen that is used to name the column headings (field names) for the linked table

3. Select the Animals file and click the Link button.

Access starts the Link Text Wizard and displays the first screen. It has two radio buttons in the top half (Delimited and Fixed Width) and the bottom shows the contents of the HTML file.

4. Since this table only has one row, either radio button can be selected. However, to understand what this Wizard can do, select the first choice 'Delimited – Characters such as a comma or tab separate each field' and click the Next button.

Access displays the next screen, which will differ based on the choice you specified for the type of text file — fixed width or delimited. In this case it displays a screen that asks which delimiter the file uses for separating the fields in each row. Since there is only one row, accept the default value of Comma. The center of this screen has a check box that asks if the first row contains the field names.

5. Make sure the 'First Row Contains Field Names' check box is not selected and click the Next button.

Access displays the screen where you can specify the field names for each column.

6. Change the field name for the column from 'Field1' to Animal. The Data type should remain Text.

7. Click the Next button.

Access displays the final screen of the Wizard and prompts for a table name to give the file Animals.txt.

8. Accept the table name Animals and click the Finish button.

Access displays a dialog box that says "Finished linking table 'Animals' to file . . . Animals.txt".

9. Click the OK button to return to the database container.

Unlike linking to other Access tables, Paradox and dBASE tables, Access immediately returns you to the database container, instead of the Link dialog box to link to another table.

At this point all the tables have been linked into the database. The database container should now look like the one in Figure 22-10.

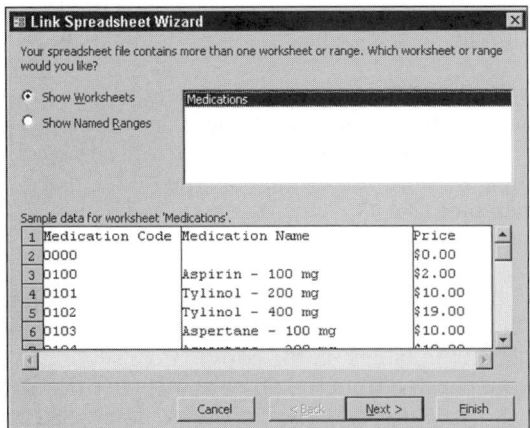

Figure 22-10: All the tables linked into the database system

Splitting an Access database into two linked databases

Generally, you can split an Access application into two databases. One contains only your tables; the other contains all your queries, forms, reports, macros, and modules. This is extremely important when moving an application to a multiuser environment. The database with the queries, forms, reports, macros, and modules is installed on each client machine, while the database containing the source tables is installed on the server. This arrangement has several major benefits:

✦ Everyone on the network shares one common set of data.

✦ Many people can update data at the same time.

✦ When you want to update the forms, reports, macros, or modules, you don't have to interrupt processing or worry about data corruption.

When creating an application for a multi-user environment, you should consider designing the objects that will be in your database, anticipating putting them into two Access databases; it's easier to complete your application later. In General, it may prove more efficient to put all your data (tables) in their own database and all the visual objects and code in another. By separating these objects initially, you will find it easier to build the visual objects and associated code as you create the objects. There are some things you just can't do with a linked table without doing a little extra work; these tasks include finding records and importing data. By using different techniques with linked tables, however, you can do anything you can do with a single database.

If you're starting from scratch, you first create a database with just the tables for your application. You then create another new database and link the tables from the first database to the second, as explained in the section "Linking to other Access database tables" earlier in this chapter.

But if you have already built a system with all your objects (including the tables) in one database file, it's a little more difficult to split your tables. One method is to create a duplicate copy of your database. In one version, you delete all objects, leaving only the tables. In the other version, you delete only the tables. Then you use the database file without the tables as a starting point and then link to all the tables in the table database.

Access 2002 includes a Wizard called the Database Splitter that can do this for you automatically. Using the Mountain Animal Hospital database, for example, you can make a copy of the database, split all the tables (in the copy) into a separate database file. Once the tables are separated from the other objects in the database, you can use the tables just as you did before; and you can always import all the tables back into the original database if you want.

Follow these steps to make a copy of the Mountain Animal Hospital database and split it:

1. Select File ⇨ Open to display the Open database window.

2. Highlight the Mountain Animal Hospital database and press Ctrl-C to make a copy of the file in memory.

3. Press Ctrl-V to paste the Copy of the file in the same directory as the original file. Access will name it 'Copy of Mountain Animal Hospital.'

4. Highlight the new table 'Copy of Mountain Animal Hospital' and open it.

   With the file copied and open you are ready to start.

Note   The Database Splitter is *not* installed if you selected the standard installation option when you installed Office XP. If this is the case, have your Office XP CD handy when you choose the Database Splitter.

5. Start the Database Splitter Wizard by selecting Tools ⇨ Database Utilities ⇨ Database Splitter.

This starts the Wizard to help you split a single database into two files. The first Wizard screen simply confirms that you want to split the database, as shown in Figure 22-11.

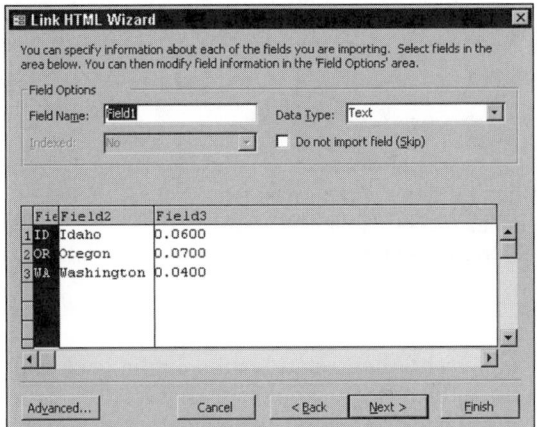

Figure 22-11: The Database Splitter Wizard. This is the first of two screens.

6. Click the Split Database button.

The Wizard opens a Create Back-End Database dialog box and prompts you for the File name of the database to store all the tables in. The default name is Copy of Mountain Animal Hospital_be.mdb ("be" for back-end).

7. Accept the default name of the table for the back-end (same name with "be" added) and press the Split button.

The Wizard creates the new database and moves all the tables to it. Then it automatically creates links to those tables so all the existing objects continue to work — forms, reports, and others. Finally it displays an information dialog box that says, "Database successfully split."

8. Press the OK key in the information dialog box that says "Database successfully split."

Access creates the new database, copies all the tables from the original database to the new database, and then links to them. When the process is done, a message tells you that the database was successfully split. Figure 22-12 shows the original database file (Copy of Mountain Animal Hospital) with all the tables linked to an external source (Copy of Mountain Animal Hospital_be).

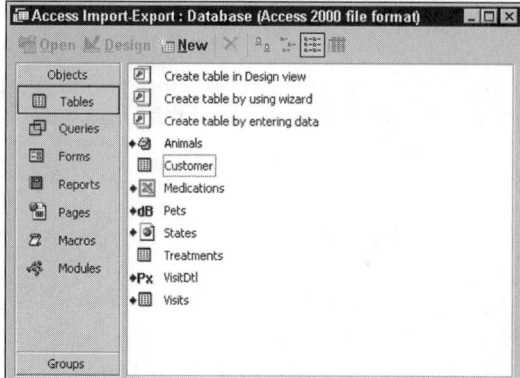

Figure 22-12: The database named Copy of Mountain Animal Hospital with all the tables moved (split off) to another database (Copy of Mountain Animal Hospital_be) and linked to

If you were to examine the tables and their relationships in the back-end database (Copy of Mountain Animal Hospital_be) you would see that all the relationships and referential integrity rules were also copied into the new database automatically.

Working with Linked Tables

After you link to an external table from another database, you can use it just as you would use another Access table. You can use it with forms, reports, and queries. When working with external tables, you can modify many of their features; for example, you can set view properties and relationships, set links between tables in queries, or rename the table.

Setting view properties

Although an external table can be used like another Access table, you cannot change the structure (delete, add, or rearrange fields) of an external table. You can, however, set several table properties for the fields in a linked table:

- ✦ Format
- ✦ Decimal Places
- ✦ Caption
- ✦ Input Mask

✦ Unicode Compressions

✦ IME Sequence Mode

✦ Display Control

Setting relationships

New Feature

Access 2002 enables you to set permanent relations at the table level between non-Access external tables and Access tables through the Relationship builder, although it does not enable you to specify Referential Integrity between these external files and local tables. In previous versions of Access you could set a relationship between an external table and another Access table in a query only, and then use the query in a form, another query, or a report. By contrast, Access 2002 enables you to create forms and reports based on relationships set up in the Relationship builder — building an SQL statement that is stored in the Record Source property of the form or report. Of course you can still build an external query and use that query for your form or report.

Note

If you link to tables from another Access database that already have relationships set between them, they will automatically inherit the relationship properties (referential integrity) set in the other database. These links cannot be deleted or changed.

Figure 22-13 shows the Relationships builder window active with all the tables linked to each other at table level. To create these links, simply activate the Relationships window and build the relations between all the tables of the system. When building them you notice that you can link the tables and Access will recognize the type of link (one-to-many or one-to-one), but you will not be able to Enforce Referential Integrity between tables.

Note

The tables that have been linked in this chapter do not have relationships set. You will need to link your tables using the Relationship builder if you want to permanently link them.

Setting links between external tables

To set a link between an external table and another Access table, you can specify the link at the table level by using the Relationships builder tool or by simply creating a query and use the drag-and-drop method of setting links. After a link is set, you can change the join properties from inner join to external join by double-clicking the link.

Tip

If you set the relationships between the tables at the table level, the query will automatically bring the links in as you add the tables. The default link type is always an inner join. However, you will still have to specify an outer join if you wish to change to that type (left or right).

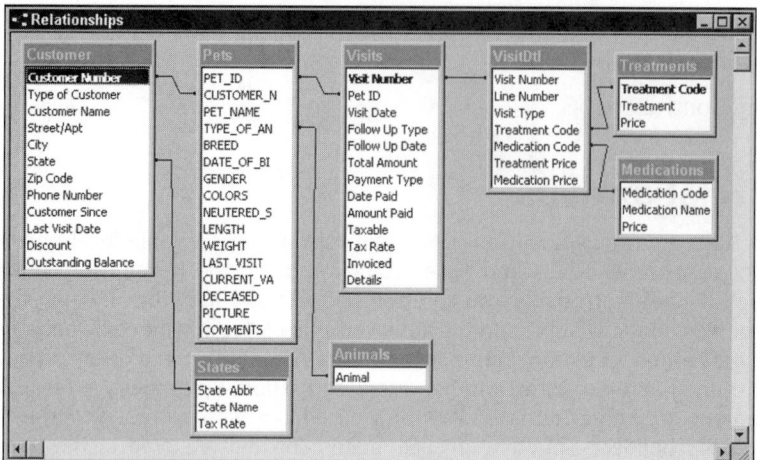

Figure 22-13: The relationships window with all the tables related together. All but two of these tables are external tables that are linked into the database.

Using external tables in queries

When using a query, you can join the external table with another table, internal or external, as long as it is linked in the database. This gives you powerful flexibility when working with queries. Figure 22-14 shows a query using several different database sources:

✦ An Excel spreadsheet (Medications)

✦ An HTML document (table) (States)

✦ Access tables (both internal and linked) (Customer, Visits, and Treatments)

✦ A Paradox table (VisitDtl)

✦ A dBASE IV table (Pets)

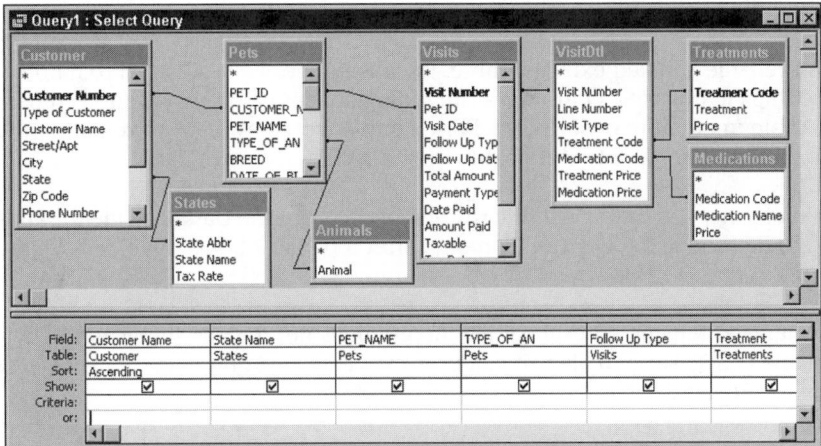

Figure 22-14: A query using several externally linked database tables

Notice that the query in Figure 22-14 has joins between all tables. This query will obtain information from all the tables and display a datasheet similar to the one in Figure 22-15.

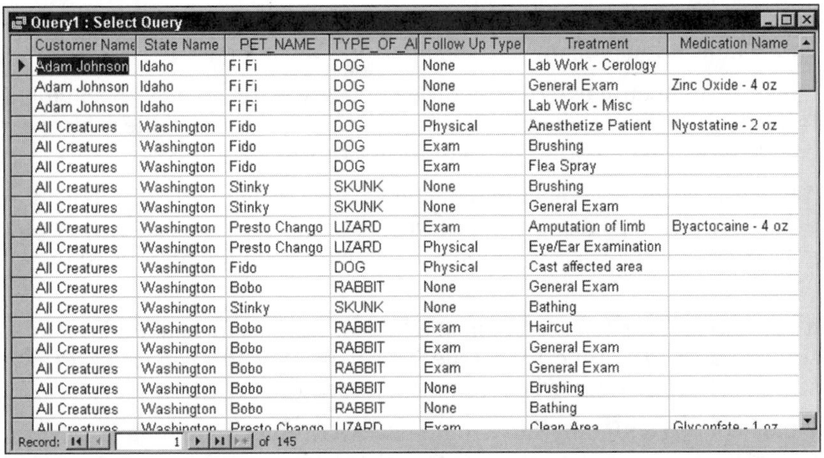

Customer Name	State Name	PET_NAME	TYPE_OF_A	Follow Up Type	Treatment	Medication Name
Adam Johnson	Idaho	Fi Fi	DOG	None	Lab Work - Cerology	
Adam Johnson	Idaho	Fi Fi	DOG	None	General Exam	Zinc Oxide - 4 oz
Adam Johnson	Idaho	Fi Fi	DOG	None	Lab Work - Misc	
All Creatures	Washington	Fido	DOG	Physical	Anesthetize Patient	Nyostatine - 2 oz
All Creatures	Washington	Fido	DOG	Exam	Brushing	
All Creatures	Washington	Fido	DOG	Exam	Flea Spray	
All Creatures	Washington	Stinky	SKUNK	None	Brushing	
All Creatures	Washington	Stinky	SKUNK	None	General Exam	
All Creatures	Washington	Presto Chango	LIZARD	Exam	Amputation of limb	Byactocaine - 4 oz
All Creatures	Washington	Presto Chango	LIZARD	Physical	Eye/Ear Examination	
All Creatures	Washington	Fido	DOG	Physical	Cast affected area	
All Creatures	Washington	Bobo	RABBIT	None	General Exam	
All Creatures	Washington	Stinky	SKUNK	None	Bathing	
All Creatures	Washington	Bobo	RABBIT	Exam	Haircut	
All Creatures	Washington	Bobo	RABBIT	Exam	General Exam	
All Creatures	Washington	Bobo	RABBIT	Exam	General Exam	
All Creatures	Washington	Bobo	RABBIT	None	Brushing	
All Creatures	Washington	Bobo	RABBIT	None	Bathing	
All Creatures	Washington	Presto Chango	LIZARD	Exam	Clean Area	Glyconfate - 1 oz

Record: 14 ◄ 1 ► ►I ►* of 145

Figure 22-15: A datasheet display of the dynaset created by the query in Figure 22-14

Renaming tables

You can rename a linked external table. Because Access enables you to name a table with as many as 64 characters (including spaces), you may want to rename a linked table to be more descriptive. For example, you may want to rename the dBASE table called PETS to Pets Table from dBASE.

To rename a file, you can select Edit ➪ Rename . . . from the Database menu. Another (quicker) method is to click the filename; after a pause, click it again, and enter a new name.

Note   When you rename an external file, Access does not rename the actual DOS filename or SQL Server table name. It uses the new name only in the Table object list of the Access database.

Optimizing linked tables

When working with linked tables, Access has to retrieve records from another file. This process takes time, especially when the table resides on a network or in an SQL database. When working with external data, you can optimize performance by observing these points:

✦ Avoid using functions in query criteria. This is especially true for aggregate functions, such as DTotal or DCount, which retrieve all records from the linked table automatically and then perform the query.

✦ Limit the number of external records to view. Create a query specifying a criterion that limits the number of records from an external table. This query can then be used by other queries, forms, or reports.

✦ Avoid excessive movement in datasheets. View only the data you need to in a datasheet. Avoid paging up and down and jumping to the last or first record in very large tables. (The exception is when you're adding records to the external table.)

✦ If you add records to external linked tables, create a form to add records and set the DataEntry property to True. This makes the form an entry form that starts with a blank record every time it's executed.

✦ When working with tables in a multi-user environment, minimize locking records. This will free up records for other users.

Deleting a linked table reference

Deleting a linked table from the Database window is a simple matter of doing three things:

1. In the Database window, select the linked table you want to delete.

2. Press the Delete key or select Edit ➪ Delete from the Database menu.

3. Click OK in the Access dialog box to delete the file.

Note   Deleting an external table deletes only its name from the database object list. The actual file is not deleted.

Viewing or changing information for linked tables

If you move, rename, or modify tables or indexes associated with a linked table, you can use the Linked Table Manager Wizard to update the links. (Otherwise, Access will not be able to find them.)

To use this tool, select Tools ➪ Database Utilities ➪ Linked Table Manager. Access will display a dialog box similar to the one shown in Figure 22-16. Select the linked table that needs the information changed and click the OK button; Access will verify that the file cannot be found and will display a Select New Location of [table name] dialog box. Using this dialog box you can find the missing file and reassign the information for the external link to Access. If all the files are already linked correctly, clicking the OK button will make Access go out and verify that all the selected tables are linked correctly and display an information box that says "All selected linked tables were successfully refreshed."

Tip   If you check the Always prompt for new location check box it will prompt you for the tables that you select every time you run this Wizard — even if Access knows where the tables are located. It is best to leave this check box off.

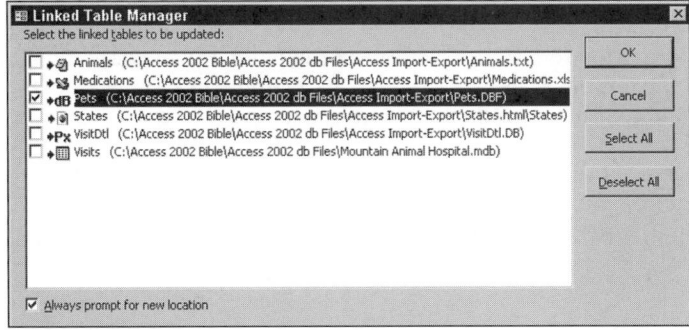

Figure 22-16: The Linked Table Manager enables you to relocate external tables that have been moved.

Note   If the Linked Table Manager Wizard is not present on your computer, Access will automatically prompt for you to enter the "original" Office CD into the CD-ROM to load it. If you did not instruct Office to install the Additional Wizards component during the Setup process it will be loaded at this time.

Importing External Data

When you import a file (unlike when you link tables), you copy the contents from an external file into an Access table. You can import external file information from several different sources:

- ✦ Microsoft Access (other unopened database objects: forms, tables, and so on)
- ✦ Microsoft Excel (all versions)
- ✦ Exchange documents
- ✦ Outlook documents
- ✦ Paradox 3.x, 4.x, 5.0, 7.0, and 8.0
- ✦ FoxPro (all versions using ODBC drivers)
- ✦ dBASE III, IV, and 5
- ✦ SQL databases (Microsoft SQL Server, Sybase Server, and Oracle Server)
- ✦ Delimited text files (fields separated by a delimiter)
- ✦ Fixed-width text files (specific widths for each field)
- ✦ Lotus 1-2-3 DOS and 1-2-3 for Windows (versions WKS, WK1, and WK3)
- ✦ HTML documents
- ✦ XML Documents
- ✦ IDC/HTX (Microsoft Internet Information Server)
- ✦ Any other ODBC Databases

You can import information to either new tables or existing tables, depending on the type of data being imported. All data types can be imported to new tables, but only spreadsheet and text files can be imported to existing tables.

When Access imports data from an external file, it does not erase or destroy the external file. Therefore, you will have two copies of the data: the original file (in the original format) and the new Access table.

Note If the filename of the importing file already exists in an Access table, Access adds a chronological number (1, 2, 3, and so on) to the filename until it has a unique table name. For example, if an importing spreadsheet name is Customer.XLS and there is an Access table named Customer, the imported table name becomes Customer1. If Customer and Customer1 tables already exist, Access creates a table named Customer2.

Importing other Access objects

You can import other Access database tables or any other object in another database. You can therefore import an existing table, query, form, report, macro, or module from another Access database. You can also import custom toolbars and menus.

As an example, use these steps to import the States table from the Mountain Animal Hospital Access database:

1. In the Access Import-Export database, click the Tables button to see the list of tables and then select File ➪ Get External Data ➪ Import. (An Import dialog box appears.)

2. In the Import dialog box, select Files of type: Microsoft Access.

3. Double-click Mountain Animal Hospital.MDB.

   Access closes the Import select database dialog box and opens the Import Objects dialog box, as shown in Figure 22-17. At the bottom of this selection box, you can click the Options>> button; the dialog box expands to offer several additional import options.

4. In the box, select the States table by clicking States and then clicking the OK button.

Access imports the States table into the Access Import-Export database and closes the Import Objects dialog box. You can select more than one item at a time, using the Select All and Deselect All buttons to select or deselect all the objects in a specific category or by control-clicking if you only desire a few.

The Options>> button enables you to further define how to import Access data. You can choose to import relationships, custom toolbars, and import/export specifications from an Access database. You can determine whether the tables you import come in with just the table design, or with the data as well. Finally, the last set of options enables you to decide whether queries you import come in as queries or run as make-table action queries to import a new table.

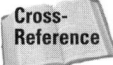

Cross-Reference See Chapter 24 for details about make-table queries.

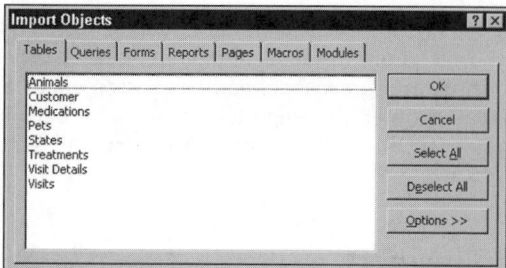

Figure 22-17: The Import Objects dialog box after clicking the Options button. You can expand Import window by clicking on the Options>> button to see additional choices.

The States table appears in the Database window display without a link symbol in the icon. It has also changed names to States1 since there is already a States table in the database container — States, a linked HTML file. Unlike linking the table, you have copied the States table and added it to the current database. Therefore, because it's not linked but instead an actual part of the database, it occupies space like the original Access table does.

Besides adding tables from other Access databases, you can also add other objects (including queries, forms, reports, macros, or modules) by clicking each of the tabs in the Import Objects dialog box. You can select objects from each and then import them all at one time.

Importing non-Access PC-based database tables

When importing data from PC-based databases, you can import two basic categories of database file types:

✦ xBASE (dBASE, FoxPro)

✦ Paradox

Each type of database can be imported directly into an Access table. The native data types are converted to Access data types during the conversion.

You can import any Paradox (3.0 through 7/8), dBASE III, dBASE IV, dBASE V, FoxPro, or Visual FoxPro database table into Access. To import one of these, simply select the correct database type in the Files of type: box during the import process.

After selecting the type of PC-based database, select which file you want to import; Access imports the file for you automatically.

Tip   Many FoxPro tables can be imported like dBASE files, since they have the same xBASE structure. If you need to import a FoxPro table that uses the newer format, you will need to import it using the ODBC drivers method.

If you try to import a Paradox table that is encrypted, Access prompts you for the password after you select the table in the Select File dialog box. Enter the password and click the OK button to import an encrypted Paradox table.

When Access imports xBASE fields, it converts them from their current data type into an Access data type. Table 22-2 lists how the data types are converted.

Table 22-2 Conversion of Data Types from xBASE to Access	
xBASE Data Type	*Access Data Type*
Character	Text
Numeric	Number (property of Double)
Float	Number (property of Double)
Logical	Yes/No
Date	Date/Time
Memo	Memo

When importing any xBASE database file in a multi-user environment, you must have exclusive use of the file. If other people are using it, you will not be able to import it.

As with xBASE tables, when Access imports Paradox fields, the Paradox fields are converted from their current data type into an Access data type. Table 22-3 lists how the data types are converted.

Table 22-3 Conversion of Data Types from Paradox to Access	
Paradox Data Type	*Access Data Type*
Alphanumeric	Text
Number	Number (property of Double)
Short Number	Number (property of Integer)
Currency	Number (property of Double)
Date	Date/Time
Memo	Memo
Blob (Binary)	OLE

Importing spreadsheet data

You can import data from Excel or Lotus 1-2-3 spreadsheets to a new or existing table. The key to importing spreadsheet data is that it must be arranged in tabular (columnar) format. Each cell of data in a spreadsheet column must contain the same type of data. Table 22-4 demonstrates correct and incorrect columnar-format data.

Note   You can import or link all the data from a spreadsheet, or just the data from a named range of cells. Naming a range of cells in your spreadsheet can make importing into Access easier. Often a spreadsheet is formatted into groups of cells. One group of cells may contain a listing of sales by customer, for example. The section below the sales listing may include total sales for all customers, totals by product type, or totals by month purchased. By naming the range for each group of cells, you can limit the import to just one section of the spreadsheet.

Table 22-4 represents cells in a spreadsheet, in the range A1 through F7. Notice that the data in columns A, B, and C and rows 2 through 7 is the same type. Row 1 contains field names. These columns can be imported into an Access table. Column D is empty and cannot be used. Columns E and F do not have the same type of data in each of their cells; they may cause problems when you try to import them into an Access table.

	Table 22-4				
	Spreadsheet Cells with Contents				
A	B	C	D	E	F
1	TYPE	WEIGHT	BDATE	JUNK	GARBAGE
2	DOG	122	12/02/92	123	YES
3	CAT	56	02/04/89	22	134.2
4	BIRD	55	05/30/90	01/01/91	DR SMITH
5	FROG	12	02/22/88	TEST	$345.35
6	FISH	21	01/04/93	═══	══
7	RAT	3	02/28/93	$555.00	⇐═ TOTAL

Figure 22-18 shows an Excel spreadsheet named MORECUST.XLS (actually a spreadsheet with some of the same fields and data as other Mountain Animal Hospital tables).

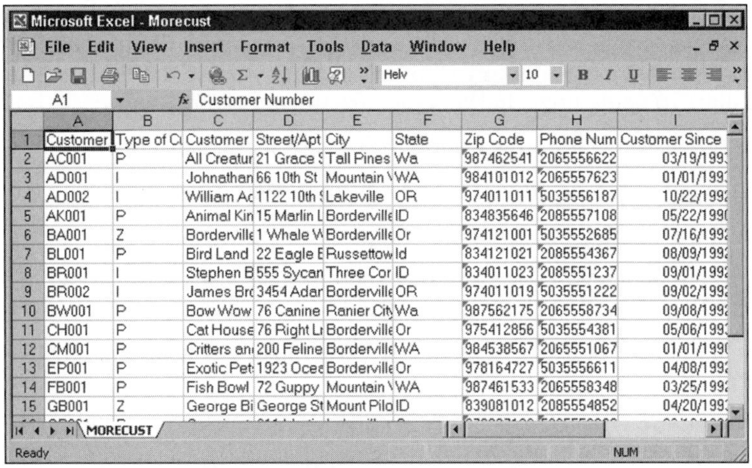

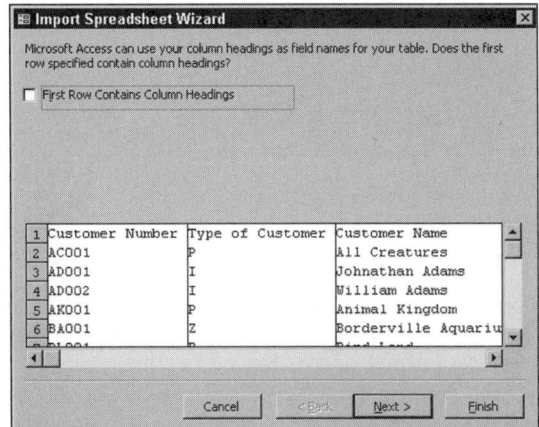

Figure 22-18: An Excel spreadsheet containing columns of information that could be imported easily into an Access table

To import the Excel spreadsheet named MORECUST.XLS, follow these steps:

1. Open the Access Import-Export database and select File ➪ Get External Data ➪ Import.

2. In the Import dialog box, select Files of type: Microsoft Excel.

3. Double-click MORECUST.XLS in the select box.

   Access closes the Import box and displays the first Spreadsheet Import Wizard screen; the screen resembles the one shown in Figure 22-19.

Figure 22-19: The first Import Spreadsheet Wizard screen

This screen displays a sample of the first few rows and columns of the spreadsheet. You can scroll the display to see all the rows and columns if you want. Enter the starting row number to import the data. To use the first row of the spreadsheet to name fields in the table, use the check box.

4. Click the check box First Row Contains Column Headings to turn it on.

The display changes to show the first row and column headings.

5. Click Next> to display the second screen.

This screen enables you to determine where the data will go. You can create a new table (the default radio button) or add to an existing table.

6. Click Next> to accept the default value of creating a new table and display the third screen.

This screen (shown in Figure 22-20) enables you to click each column of the spreadsheet to accept the field name, change it, and decide whether it will be indexed; the Wizard determines the data type automatically. You can also choose to skip each column if you want. You will specify the Primary Key field after this screen.

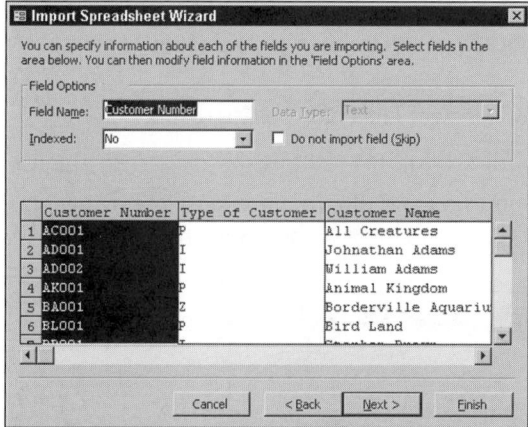

Figure 22-20: Determining the field names and data types

7. Click Next> to display the next Import Spreadsheet Wizard screen.

This screen enables you to choose a field for the primary key. You can let Access create a new AutoNumber field (by choosing Let Access add Primary Key), enter your own (by selecting Choose my own Primary Key and selecting one of the columns), or have no primary key. Figure 22-21 shows these options.

8. Select Choose my own Primary Key and select the Customer Number field.

9. Click Next to display the last Import Spreadsheet Wizard screen.

    The last screen enables you to enter the name for the imported table and (optionally) run the Table Analyzer Wizard.

10. Accept the default Table name of MORECUST and click Finish to import the spreadsheet file. Access 2002 informs you that it imported the file successfully in an information box. Simply click OK to have Access return to the database.

The filename now appears in the Access database window. A standard Access table has been created from the original spreadsheet file.

Figure 22-21: In this screen you determine which field will be used for the primary key — you can select an existing field or have Access create a new one for you.

Importing from word-processing files

Access does not offer a specific way to import data from word-processing files. If you need to import data from a word-processing file into Access, convert the word-processing file to a simple text file first and then import it as a text file. Most word processors have the capability to convert their formatted text-to-text files or ASCII files.

Importing text file data

Mainframe data is ordinarily output to a text file for use in desktop applications. You can import from two different types of text files: delimited and fixed-width. Access uses an import/export specification file as a guide in processing these types of files.

Access 2002 uses one Wizard for both types of text files. The Import Text Wizard assists you in identifying the fields for the import/export specification.

Delimited text files

Delimited text files are sometimes known as *comma-delimited* or *tab-delimited* files; each record is on a separate line in the text file. The fields on the line contain no trailing spaces, normally use commas as field separators, and require certain fields to be enclosed in a delimiter (such as single or double quotation marks). Usually the text fields are also enclosed in quotation marks or some other delimiter, as in these examples:

```
"Irwin","Michael","Michael Irwin Consulting",05/12/72
"Prague","Cary","Cary Prague Books and Software",02/22/86
"Zimmerman-Schneider","Audrie","IBM",01/01/59
```

Notice that the file has three records (rows of text) and four fields. A comma separates each field, and the text fields are delimited with double quotation marks. The starting position of each field, after the first one, is different. Each record has a different length because the field lengths are different.

Note   You can import records from a delimited text file that has fields with no values. To specify a field with no value, place delimiters where the field value would be, and put no value between them (for example, "Irwin","Michael",,05/12/72). Notice that in the preceding example there are two commas after the field content "Michael" and before the field content 05/12/72. The field between these two has no value; it will be imported with no value into an Access file.

Fixed-width text files

Fixed-width text files also place each record on a separate line. However, the fields in each record are of a fixed length. If the field contents are not long enough, trailing spaces are added to the field, as shown in the following example:

```
Irwin      Michael  Michael Irwin Consulting      05/12/82
Prague     Cary     Cary Prague Books and Software 02/22/86
Zimmerman  Audrie   IBM                            01/01/59
```

Notice that the fields are not separated by delimiters. Rather, they start at exactly the same position in each record. Each record has exactly the same length. If a field is not long enough, trailing spaces are added to fill the field.

You can import either a delimited or a fixed-width text file to a new table or existing Access table. If you decide to append the imported file to an existing table, the file's structure must match that of the Access table you're importing to.

Note   If the Access table being imported has a key field, the text file cannot have any duplicate key values or the import will report an error.

Importing delimited text files

To import a delimited text file named MEDLIMIT.TXT, follow these steps:

1. In the Access Import-Export database, select File ➪ Get External Data ➪ Import.

2. In the Import dialog box, select Files of type: Text files.

3. Double-click MEDLIMIT.TXT in the File Name list box.

   Access displays the first screen of the Import Text Wizard dialog box for the table MEDLIMIT.TXT. The dialog box resembles the one shown in Figure 22-22.

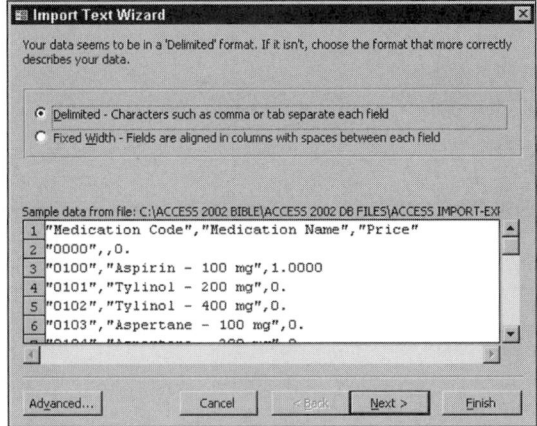

Figure 22-22: The first Import Text Wizard screen

This screen displays the data in the text file and guesses whether the text file is delimited or fixed-width. As you can see, the Wizard has determined correctly that the file is delimited.

Note   Notice, at the bottom of the screen, the button marked Advanced. Click it to further define the import specifications. You will learn more about this option in the section "Importing fixed-width text files" following this section; generally, it's not needed for delimited files. Click the Cancel button to return to the Import Text Wizard.

4. Click the Next> button to display the next Import Text Wizard screen.

   As you can see in Figure 22-23, this screen enables you to determine which type of separator to use in the delimited text file. Generally, this separator is a comma, but you could use a tab, semicolon, space, or other character (such as an asterisk), which you enter in the box next to the Other option button. You can also decide whether to use text from the first row as field names for the imported table. It has correctly assigned the comma as the separator type and the Text Qualifier as quotation marks (").

Note   A *Separator* is as the specific character that was placed between the fields in a delimited text file — often it is a comma or semicolon, although it can be any specific character. There can be a problem with the separator used — for example, in this case, the separator is a comma — if any of the fields have a comma in them. It could case a problem when trying to import the data (last name of IRWIN, Michael versus next name of PRAGUE, Sr., Cary — Cary's record has what appears to be an extra field in the last name — Sr). This can cause all sorts of problems when importing the data. The *Text Qualifier*, for delimited text files refers to the marks that are often placed around text fields versus numeric and date fields. Often they are single quotation or double quotation marks.

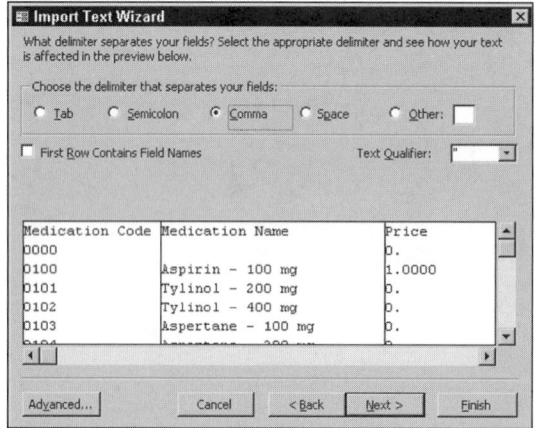

Figure 22-23: The second Import Text Wizard screen

5. Click the First Row Contains Field Names check box to use the first row for field names. Access will redisplay the text file with the first row as the column headers.

6. Click the Next> button to display the next Import Text Wizard screen.

This screen enables you to determine whether you're storing the imported data in a new table or an existing table. If you decide to use an existing table, you have to choose it from a list.

The next few screens are exactly the same as the Spreadsheet Import Wizard screens shown in the "Importing spreadsheet data" section earlier in this chapter.

7. Accept the default value of In a New Table and click the Next> button to display the next Import Text Wizard screen.

   This screen enables you to select each column of the Text Import grid, accept or change the field name, decide whether it will be indexed, and set the data type (which is also automatically determined by the Wizard), or even skip adding the field to the final table. As with the Spreadsheet Import Wizard, you move from field to field by selecting the next field column — once selected you can change its options also. You can choose to skip a column if you want.

8. Click Next> to display the next Import Text Wizard screen.

   This screen enables you to choose a field for the primary key. You can enable Access to create a new AutoNumber field (by choosing Let Access add Primary Key), enter your own (by selecting Choose my own Primary Key and selecting one of the columns), or have no primary key.

9. Click the option button that says Choose my own Primary Key and select the field Medication Code.

10. Click Next> to display the last Import Text Wizard screen.

    The last screen enables you to enter the name for the imported table and (optionally) run the Table Analyzer Wizard.

11. Accept the default name of Medlimit and click Finish to import the delimited text file.

Access creates a new table, using the same name as the text file's name, then it displays an information box informing you that it created the table successfully; clicking the OK button returns you to the database. The filename appears in the Access Database window, where Access has added the table MEDLIMIT.

Importing fixed-width text files

In fixed-width text files, each field in the file has a specific width and position. Files downloaded from mainframes are the most common fixed-width text files. As you import or export this type of file, you must specify an import/export setup specification. You create this setup file by using the Advanced options of the Import Table Wizard.

To import a fixed-width text file, follow these steps:

1. Open the Access Import-Export database and select File ➪ Get External Data ➪ Import.

2. In the Import dialog box, select Files of type: Text files.

3. Double-click PETFIXED.TXT in the File Name list box. Access opens the first screen of the Import Text Options Wizard dialog box for the table PETFIXED.TXT.

This screen displays the data in the text file and guesses whether the type of text file is delimited or fixed width. As you can see, the Wizard has correctly determined that it's a fixed-width file.

4. Click Next> to display the next Import Text Wizard screen.

This screen makes a guess about where columns begin and end in the file, basing the guess on the spaces in the file. Notice that it has missed several fields in the second column (combining them all together).

Figure 22-24 shows that Access has not done a good job in this file. It has recognized the first field correctly, but the second four fields have been lumped together. You'll need to add field break lines in the structure.

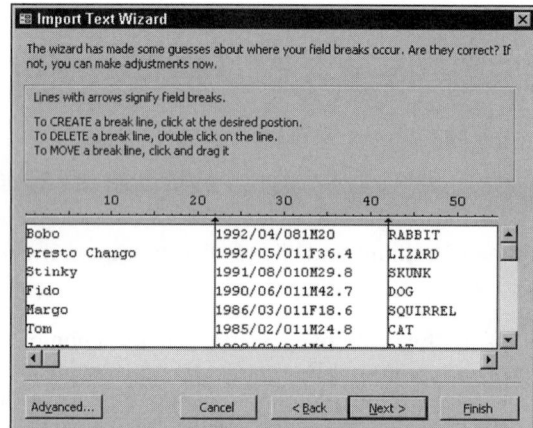

Figure 22-24: The Import Text Wizard's attempt to split the fields. Notice that several fields are merged together in the second column.

As you can see in Figure 22-24, you can drag a field break line, add one, or delete one to tell Access where the fields really are.

5. Move to position 32 (between the 08 and 1 of the first record named Bobo).

6. Once the pointer is in position on the lined bar in the center, create a break line by clicking at that position.

If you make a mistake and put the line in the wrong place, simply highlight the line and either move it by dragging it or double-click it to delete it.

7. Move to position 33 (between the 1 and M) and add another break.

8. Move to position 34 (between the M and 20) and add another break.

After you have accomplished Steps 5 through 8 you should have a break between the end of the Date field, the beginning and end of the Type of Animal field (1, 2, 3), the Gender field (M, F), and the beginning of the Weight field. Figure 22-25 shows the corrected field specifications for the table.

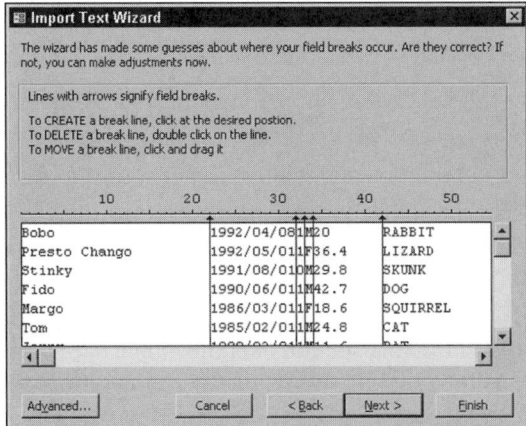

Figure 22-25: The field breaks now set correctly for the fields of the fixed-width table

As you use these tools to define the field widths, you're completing an internal data table known as Import/Export Specifications.

9. Click the Advance button to activate the Import Specification window for the Petfixed table.

Figure 22-26 shows the Import Specification screen after clicking the Advanced button in the Import Text Wizard.

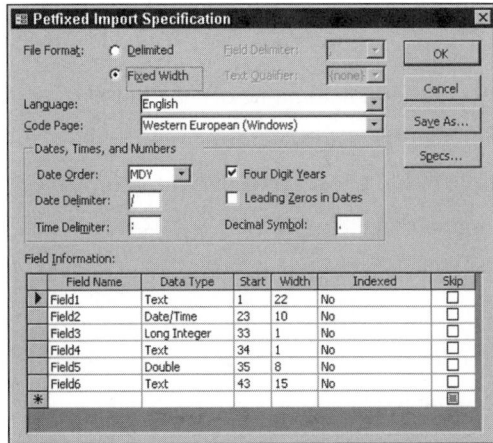

Figure 22-26: The Import Specification screen for fixed-width text files

The section labeled Dates, Times, and Numbers describes how date, time, and numeric information is formatted in the import file.

10. Make sure that the Four Digit Years check box is on.

11. Click the Leading Zeros in Dates check box on.

The month and day in the data being imported includes a leading zero for numbers less than 10.

12. Click in the Date Order combo box and change the order from MDY (month day year) to YMD (year month date).

In this example, the date field is formatted with the year first (four digit), then the month followed by the day.

The bottom half of the Import Specifications dialog box has a section named the Field Information section. This section lists the name, data type, and position of each field in the import table. Although you can manually type the specifications for each field in this file, in this example you can accept the field information that Access has created for you and return to the Import Text Wizard.

13. Click the OK button to return to the Import Text Wizard.

14. After you return to the Wizard, press the Next> button to move to the next screen.

This screen enables you to determine whether the records should be added to a new table or an existing one.

15. Click the Next> button again to move to the next screen.

This screen enables you to specify the field names and any indexes for the fields.

16. With the first column highlighted, enter a field name of Pet Name.

17. Click the second field column named Field2.

18. With the Field2 highlighted, enter a field name of Date of Birth.

19. Click the next field column named Field3.

20. With the Field3 highlighted, enter a field name of Neutered/Spayed.

21. Click the next field column named Field4.

22. With the Field4 highlighted, enter a field name of Gender.

23. Click the next field column named Field5.

24. With the Field5 highlighted, enter a field name of Length.

25. Click the next field column named Field6.

26. With the Field6 highlighted, enter a field name of Pet Type.

27. Click the Next> button to move to the next screen.

This screen enables you to specify a primary key.

28. Click No Primary Key.

29. Click the Next> button.

This step takes you to the last screen where you can name your file.

30. Accept the default name of Petfixed and click the Finished button.

Access again informs you that it has imported the file. Clicking the OK button will close the Wizard and return you to the database.

Using the Import Specification window

In earlier versions of Access, you had to specify the import/export specifications manually, specifying field lengths, delimited or fixed text, type of delimiter, how to export date fields, and so on. Although you can still specify this information by using the Import Specification window, as in Step 9 above, it is easier to use the graphical tools (built into the Import Wizard) of Access 2002.

Although the Import Text Wizard generally does a good job of importing your data correctly, at times you may need to specify field lengths and data types manually. If you use the Import Specification dialog box (shown in Figure 22-26), you can change or set all the options on one screen, which can be helpful.

One advantage of using this screen is the capability to specify the type of file to be imported from or exported to. The Language and Code Page fields determine the type of format. The default language is English. The Code Page combo box displays the code page types that are available for the language you select. Specifically, these choices are available for the English language:

✦ OEM United States

✦ Unicode

✦ Unicode (Big-Endian)

✦ Unicode (UTF-7)

✦ Unicode (UTF-8)

✦ Western European (DOS)

✦ Western European (ISO)

✦ Western European (Windows)

The default value is the Western European (Windows). You may need to set this value if you are running a language that does not use the Roman character set used in English, French, German, etc. You can also specify the Field Delimiter option for delimited text files; the delimiter is used to separate the fields. You do this by using a special character such as a comma or semicolon. Four field-separator choices are available in this combo box:

;	Semicolon
{tab}	Tabulation mark
{space}	Single space
,	Comma

When working with delimited files, you can also specify your own field separator directly in this combo box.

Also, when working with delimited files, you can specify the Text Qualifier. It specifies the type of delimiter to be used when you're working with Text-type fields. Normally, the *text* fields in a delimited file are enclosed by specified delimiters (such as quotation marks). This is useful for specifying Number-type data (such as Social Security numbers) as Text type rather than Number type (it won't be used in a calculation). You have three list box choices:

{none}	No delimiter
"	Double quotation mark
'	Single quotation mark

The default value is a double quotation mark. This list box is actually a combo box; you can enter your own delimiter. If the one you want is not among these three choices, you can specify a different text delimiter by entering a new one directly in the combo box — for example, the caret symbol (^).

Note If you use comma-delimited files, created by other PC-based databases, you should set the text qualifier to the double quotation mark (") and the field delimiter to a comma (,) if that is what they are in the text file being imported or linked.

Caution If you specify your own delimiter, it must be the same on both sides of the text. For example, you can't use both of the curly braces ({ }) as user-specified delimiters; you can specify only one character. If you specify the left curly brace, Access looks for only the left curly brace as a delimiter — on both sides of the text:

{This is Text data enclosed in braces{

Notice that only the left brace is used.

When Access 2002 imports or exports data, it converts dates to a specific format (such as MMDDYY). In the example MMDDYY, Access converts all dates to two digits for each portion of the date (month, day, and year), separating each by a specified delimiter. Thus, January 19, 2002 would be converted to 1/19/02. You can specify how date fields are to be converted, using one of six choices in the Date Order combo box:

✦ DMY

✦ DYM

✦ MDY

✦ MYD

✦ YDM

✦ YMD

These choices specify the order for each portion of a date. The D is the day of the month (1-31), M is the calendar month (1-12), and Y is the year. The default date order is set to the American format of month, day, and year. When you work with European dates, the order must be changed to day, month, and year.

You use the Date Delimiter option to specify the date delimiter. This option tells Access which type of delimiter to use between the parts of date fields. The default is a forward slash (/), but this can be changed to any user-specified delimiter. In Europe, for example, date parts are separated by periods, as in 22.10.01.

Note When you import text files with Date-type data, you must have a separator between the month, day, and year or else Access reports an error if the field is specified as a Date/Time type. When you're exporting date fields, the separator is not needed.

With the Time Delimiter option, you can specify a separator between the segments of time values in a text file. The default value is the colon (:). In the example 12:55, the colon separates the hours from the minutes. To change the separator, simply enter another in the Time Delimiter box.

You use the Four Digit Years check box when you want to specify that the year value in date fields will be formatted with four digits. By checking this box, you can export dates that include the century (such as in 1881 or 2001). The default is to include the century.

The Leading Zeros in Dates option is a check box where you specify that date values include leading zeros. You can specify, for example, that date formats include leading zeros (as in 02/04/00). To specify leading zeros, check this box. The default is without leading zeros (as in 2/4/00).

Importing HTML tables

Access 2002 enables you to import HTML tables as easily as any other database, Excel spreadsheet, or text file. You simply select the HTML file you want to import and use the HTML Import Wizard. It works exactly like the link HTML Wizard described in detail earlier in this chapter.

Modifying imported table elements

After you import a file, you can refine the table in Design view. The following list itemizes and discusses some of the primary changes you may want to make to improve your table:

- ✦ Add field names or descriptions. You may want to change the names of the fields you specified when you imported the file. For example, xBASE databases enable no more than ten characters in their names and no spaces.

- ✦ Change data types. Access may have guessed the wrong data type when it imported several of the fields. You can change these fields to reflect a more descriptive data type (such as Currency rather than Number, or Text rather than Number).

- ✦ Set field properties. You can set field properties to enhance the way your tables work. For example, you may want to specify a format or default value for the table.

- ✦ Set the field size to something more realistic than the 255 bytes (characters) Access allocates for each imported text field. Make the names descriptive enough without the need to make them too long — for example, "Last Name" versus "Last Name of the owner of pets coming from the merge table from Doctor Zervas's old practice." "Last Name" is sufficient to clarify what the contents of the field are.

- ✦ Define a primary key. Access works best with tables that have a primary key. You may want to set a primary key for the imported table.

Troubleshooting import errors

When you import an external file, Access may not be able to import one or more records, in which case it reports an error when it tries to import them. When Access encounters errors, it creates an Access table named Import Errors (with the user's name linked to the table name). The Import Errors table contains one record for each record that causes an error.

After errors have occurred and Access has created the Import Errors table, you can open the table to view the error descriptions.

Import errors for new tables

Access may not be able to import records into a new table for the following reasons:

✦ A row in a text file or spreadsheet may contain more fields than are present in the first row.

✦ Data in the field cannot be stored in the data type Access chose for the field. (Text in a numeric field — best case will import as 0s — or numeric trying to store in a date field.)

✦ On the basis of the first row's contents, Access automatically chose the incorrect data type for a field. The first row is OK, but the remaining rows are blank.

✦ The date order may be incorrect. The dates are in YMD order but the specification calls for MDY order. (When Access tries to import 991201, it will report an error because it should be in the format of 120199.)

Import errors for existing tables

Access may not be able to append records into an existing table for the following reasons:

✦ The data is not consistent between the text file and the existing Access table.

✦ Numeric data being entered is too large for the field size of the Access table.

✦ A row in a text file or spreadsheet may contain more fields than the Access table.

✦ The records being imported have duplicate primary key values.

The Import Errors table

When errors occur, Access creates an Import Errors table you can use to determine which data caused the errors.

Open the Import Errors table and try to determine why Access couldn't import all the records. If the problem is with the external data, edit it. If you're appending records to an existing table, the problem may be with the existing table; it may need modifications (such as changing the data types and rearranging the field locations). After you solve the problem, erase the Import Errors file and import the data again.

Note   Access attempts to import all records that do not cause an error. If you re-import the data, you may need to clean up the external table or the Access table before re-importing. If you don't, you may have duplicate data in your table.

Access attempts to import all records that do not cause an error. If you re-import
the data, you may need to clean up the external table or the Access table before
re-importing. If you don't, you may have duplicate data in your table.

If importing a text file seems to take an unexpectedly long time, it may be because of too many errors. You can cancel importing by pressing Ctrl+Break.

Exporting to External Formats

You can copy data from an Access table or query into a new external file. This process of copying Access tables to an external file is called exporting. You can export tables to several different sources:

✦ Microsoft Access (other unopened databases)

✦ Delimited text files (fields separated by a delimiter)

✦ Fixed-width text files (specific widths for each field)

✦ Microsoft Excel (all versions 3, 4, and 5–7)

✦ Lotus 1-2-3 and 1-2-3 for Windows (versions WK1, WK3, and WJ2)

✦ Paradox 3.x, 4.x, 5.0, and 7–8.

✦ FoxPro 2.x and Visual FoxPro 3.0 (through ODBC)

✦ dBASE III, dBASE IV, and dBASE 5

✦ Microsoft Active Server Pages

✦ Microsoft IIS 1–2

✦ XML document

✦ HTML document (as tables)

✦ Text files

✦ Rich text formats (RTF)

✦ Word Mail Merge (.txt)

✦ ODBC Data Sources SQL databases (Microsoft SQL Server, Sybase Server, and Oracle Server)

When Access exports data from an Access table to an external file, the Access table isn't erased or destroyed. This means that you will have two copies of the data: the original Access file and the external data file.

Exporting objects to other Access databases

You can export objects from the current database to another, unopened Access database. The objects you export can be tables, queries, forms, reports, macros, or modules. To export an object to another Access database, follow these generic steps:

1. Open the database that has the object you want to export and select File ➪ Export from the Database menu.

2. Access opens the standard Save As dialog box — the same one that appears whenever you save an object to another name. The difference is that you can specify a different format (Save as type). When you open the combo box, a list of formats appears. Select the one you want; Access will save the data to that format.

When this process is complete, Access copies to the other database the object you specified and immediately returns you to the Database window in Access.

Note   If you attempt to export an object to another Access database that has an object of the same type and name, Access warns you before copying. You then have the option to cancel or overwrite.

Exporting objects to other external databases or to Excel, HTML, or text files

You can also export objects to databases (such as ODBC, dBASE, Paradox, and FoxPro) and text files (delimited and fixed width). To export any of these objects, simply follow these generic steps:

1. Select File ➪ Export from the Database menu.

2. Select the type of file you want the object to be saved to and specify a name.

3. Click the Save button.

Note   If you save a table to an HTML table, Access 2002 will create the HTML document, and if you check the Save formatted and the Autostart check boxes in the Export to dialog box you can have Access start your browser to show you the form it created. Figure 22-27 shows the Customer's table exported as a formatted HTML table and displayed automatically in the Browser.

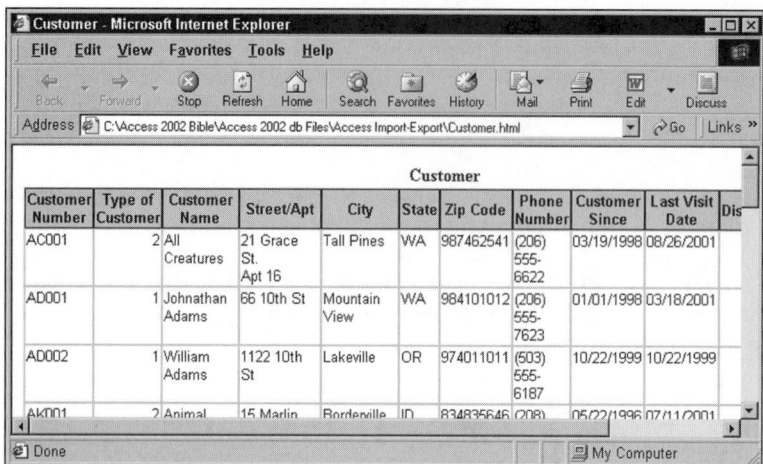

Figure 22-27: Internet Explorer browser displaying the Customer's table exported to an HTML file

✦   ✦   ✦

Working with Advanced Select Queries

♦ ♦ ♦ ♦

In This Chapter

Creating queries that
calculate totals

Performing totals on
groups of records

Using different types
of queries that total

Specifying criteria for
queries that total

Creating crosstab
queries

Specifying criteria for
crosstab queries

Specifying fixed
column headings for
crosstab queries

Creating a parameter
query

Running a parameter
query

Using the Parameter
Query dialog box to
specify the order of
parameters

♦ ♦ ♦ ♦

In this chapter, you work with advanced select queries.
Other parts of this book (especially Chapter 13) explain
relatively simple select queries, in which you select specific
records from one or more tables based on some criteria. This
chapter shows you queries that display totals, create cross-
tabulations, and obtain criteria from the user at run time.

Select queries specify criteria for single or multiple fields
(including calculated fields) using multiple tables. Select
queries may also work with wildcard characters and fields not
having a value (Is Null). Functions in queries can specify
record criteria or create calculated fields. Finally, Access
queries are a great tool for performing ad-hoc what-if
scenarios.

This chapter focuses on three specialized types of advanced
select queries:

+ **Total.** Calculates totals for records

+ **Crosstab.** Summarizes data in an easy-to-read, row-and-
  column format

+ **Parameter.** Obtains criteria by prompting the operator
  of the query

Creating Queries That Calculate Totals

Many times, you want to find information in your tables based on data related to the total of a particular field or fields. For example, you may want to find the total number of animals you've treated or the total amount of money each customer spent on animals last year. Access supplies the tools to accomplish these queries without the need for programming.

Access performs calculation totals by using nine aggregate functions that let you determine a specific value based on the contents of a field. For example, you can determine the average weight of all cats, the maximum and minimum length of all animals you have treated, or the total count of all records in which the type of animal is either a duck or a fish. Performing each of these examples as a query results in a dynaset of answer fields based on the mathematical calculations you requested.

To create a total query, you use a new row in the Query by Example (QBE) pane — the Total: row. The following section describes this handy tool in detail.

Showing and hiding the Total: row in the QBE pane

To create a query that performs a total calculation, create a select query and then activate the Total: row of the QBE pane. You can activate the Total: row by using either of these two selection methods (but first, open a new query using the Pets table):

On the CD-ROM   You can use the Mountain Animal Start Database for the examples in this chapter.

✦ Select View ⇨ Totals from the Design menu.

✦ Select the Totals button (the Greek sigma symbol button (Σ) which is to the right of the midway mark) on the toolbar (seventh from the right side).

Figure 23-1 shows the Total: row after it is added in the QBE pane. The Totals button is selected on the toolbar and the Total: row is placed in the QBE pane between the Table: and Sort: rows.

Note   If the toolbar is not visible, select View ⇨ Toolbars from the Query menu. Then select Query Design and close the dialog box.

If the Table: row is not present on your screen, the Total: row appears below the Field: row and above the Sort: row. You can activate the Table: row by selecting View ⇨ Table Names from the Design menu.

To deactivate the Total row in the QBE pane, simply reselect either activation method (the Design menu or the Totals button). The Totals button is a toggle-type control that alternately turns the Total: row on and off.

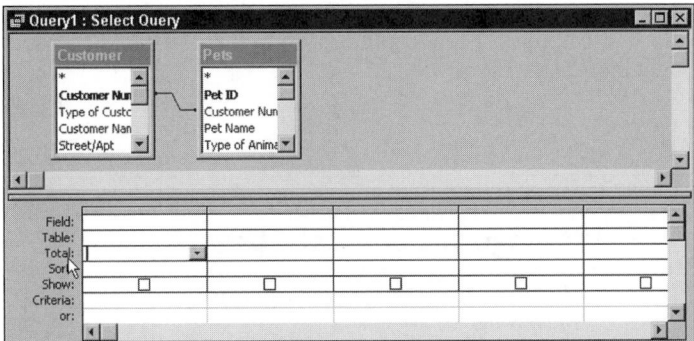

Figure 23-1: The Total row of the QBE pane is active in this figure. Notice the arrow pointing to the Total: row label, just below the Table: row.

The Total: row options

You can perform total calculations on all records or groups of records in one or more tables. To perform a calculation, you must select one of the options from the drop-down list in the Total: row for every field you include in the query, including any hidden fields (with the Show: option turned off). Figure 23-2 shows the drop-down list box active in the Total: row of the field Pet Name.

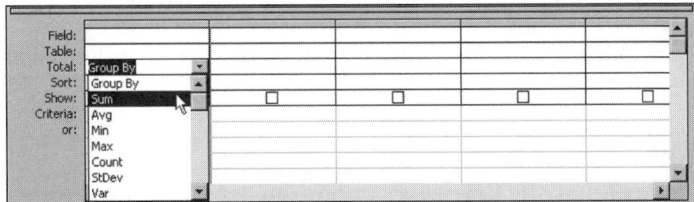

Figure 23-2: The drop-down list box of the Total: row activated. It has 12 choices in it. The Group By option is already selected, but the sum option is highlighted as the cursor moves on it.

Although only 8 options are shown in Figure 23-2, you can choose from 12. You can view the remaining options by using the scroll bar on the right side of the box. The 12 options can be divided into four distinct categories: group by, aggregate, expression, and total field record limit. Table 23-1 lists each category, its number of Total options, and its purpose.

What Is an Aggregate Function?

The word *aggregate* implies gathering together a mass (a group or series) of things and working on this mass as a whole—a single entity. Therefore, an aggregate function is a function that takes a group of records and performs some mathematical function against the entire group. The function can be a simple count or a complex expression you specify, based on a series of mathematical functions.

Table 23-1
Four Categories of Total Options

Category	Number of Options	Purpose of Operator
Group By	1	Groups common records together. Access performs aggregate calculations against the groups.
Aggregate	9	Specifies a mathematical or selection operation to perform against a field.
Expression	1	Groups several total operators together and performs the group totals.
Total Field Record Limit	1	Limits records before record limit performing a total calculation against a field.

The Group By, Expression, and Total Field Record Limit categories have one option each. The Aggregate category has nine options, all of which are used by the other three categories. The following sections provide details about the options available in each category.

Group By category

This category has one option, the Group By option. You use this option to specify that a certain field in the QBE pane will be used as a grouping field. For example, if you select the field Type of Animal, the Group By option tells Access to group all cat records together, all dog records together, and so on. This option is the default for all Total: cells. In other words, when you drag a field to the QBE pane, Access automatically selects this option. Figure 23-2 shows that this is also the first choice in the drop-down list box. These groups of records will be used for performing some aggregate calculation against another field in the query. We discuss this subject in more detail in the section titled "Specifying criteria for a Group By field" later in this chapter.

Expression category

Like the Group By category, the Expression category has only one option: Expression. This is the second-from-last choice in the drop-down list. You use this option to tell Access to create a calculated field by using one or more aggregate calculations in the Field: cell of the QBE pane. For example, you may want to create a query that shows each customer and how much money the customer saved, based on the individual's discount rate. This query requires creating a calculated field that uses a sum aggregate against the Total Amount field in the Visits table, which is then multiplied by the Discount field in the Customer table. We discuss this type of calculation in detail in the section "Creating expressions for totals" later in this chapter.

Total Field Record Limit category

The Total Field Record Limit category is the third category that has a single option: the Where option. This option is the last choice in the drop-down list. When you select this option, you tell Access that you want to specify limiting criteria against an aggregate type field, as opposed to a Group By or an Expression field. The limiting criteria is performed before the aggregate options are executed. For example, you may want to create a query that counts all pets by types of animals that weigh less than 100 pounds. Because the Weight field is not to be used for a grouping (as is Type of Animal) and won't be used to perform an aggregate calculation, you specify the Where option. By specifying the Where option, you are telling Access to use this field only as a limiting criteria field — before it performs the aggregate calculation (counting types of animals). This type of operation is also discussed in detail later in this chapter.

Aggregate category

The Aggregate category, unlike the others, has multiple options that you can choose from (a total of nine options): Sum, Avg, Min, Max, Count, StDev, Var, First, and Last. These options appear as the second through tenth options in the drop-down list. Each option performs an operation on your data (check out Table 23-2 for how you can use each option) and supplies the new data to a cell in the resulting dynaset. Aggregate options are what database designers think of when they hear the words *total query*. Each of the options performs a calculation against a field in the QBE pane of the query and returns a *single answer* in the dynaset.

For example, you may want to determine the maximum (Max) and minimum (Min) weight of each animal in the Type of Animal field in the Pets table. There can only be one maximum weight for all the animals. Several animals may have the same maximum weight, but only one weight is the heaviest. Another example of a total query would be if you wanted the total number (Count) of animals in the Pets table (again, the query returns a single answer). You can use these aggregate options to solve these types of queries.

Whereas the Group By, Expression, and Total Field Record Limit categories of options (which we discuss in previous sections) can be used against any type of Access field (Text, Memo, or Yes/No, for example), some of the aggregate options can be performed against certain field types only. For example, you cannot perform a Sum option against Text type data; nor can you use a Max option against an OLE object.

Table 23-2 lists each option, what it does, and which field types you can use with the option.

Table 23-2 Aggregate Options of the Total: Row		
Option	**Finds**	**Field Type Support**
Count	Number of non-Null values in a field	AutoNumber, Number, Currency, Date/Time, Yes/No, Text, Memo, OLE object
Sum	Total of values in a field	AutoNumber, Number, Currency, Date/Time, Yes/No
Avg	Average of values in a field	AutoNumber, Number, Currency, Date/Time, Yes/No
Max	Highest value in a field	AutoNumber, Number, Currency, Date/Time, Yes/No, Text
Min	Lowest value in a field	AutoNumber, Number, Currency, Date/Time, Yes/No, Text
StDev	Standard deviation of values in a field	AutoNumber, Number, Currency, Date/Time, Yes/No
Var	Population variance of values in a field	AutoNumber, Number, Currency, Date/Time, Yes/No
First	Field value from the first record in a number, table, or query	AutoNumber, Currency, Date/Time, Yes/No, Text, Memo, OLE object
Last	Field value from the last record in a number, table, or query	AutoNumber, Currency, Date/Time, Yes/No, Text, Memo, OLE object

Performing totals on all records

You can use total queries to perform calculations against all records in a table or query. For example, you can find the total number of animals in the Pets table, the average weight, and the maximum weight of the animals. To create this query, follow these steps:

1. Select the Pets table.

2. Click the Totals button on the toolbar to turn it on.

3. Double-click the Pet ID field in the Pets table.

4. Double-click the Weight field in the Pets table.

5. Double-click the Weight field in the Pets table again.

6. In the Total: cell of Pet ID, select Count.

7. In the Total: cell of Weight, select Avg.

8. In the second Total: cell of Weight, select Max.

Your query should look similar to Figure 23-3.

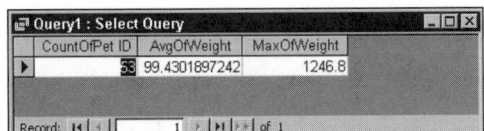

Field:	Pet ID	Weight	Weight		
Table:	Pets	Pets	Pets		
Total:	Count	Avg	Max		
Sort:					
Show:	☑	☑	☑	☐	☐
Criteria:					
or:					

Figure 23-3: A query against all records in the Pets table to show three calculated values — count, average weight, and maximum weight

This query calculates the total number of pet records in the Pets table as well as the average weight of all animals and the heaviest weight of all the animals.

Note   The Count option of the Total: cell can be performed against any field in the table (or query). However, Count eliminates any records that have a Null value in the field you select. Therefore, you may want to select the primary key field on which to perform the Count total because this field cannot have any Null values, thus ensuring an accurate record count.

If you select the Datasheet button on the toolbar, you should see a datasheet similar to Figure 23-4. Notice that the dynaset has only one record. When performing calculations against all records in a table or query, the resulting dynaset will have only one record.

Query1 : Select Query

CountOfPet ID	AvgOfWeight	MaxOfWeight
53	99.4301897242	1246.8

Record: 1 of 1

Figure 23-4: This datasheet of a dynaset was created from a total query against all records in a table. It only has one row, or record, in the dynaset.

Note Access creates default column headings for all total fields in a totals datasheet, such as those shown in Figure 23-4. The heading name is a product of the name of the total option and the field name. Thus, in Figure 23-4 the heading names are CountOfPet ID, AvgOfWeight, and MaxOfWeight. You can change a column heading name to something more appropriate by renaming the field in the QBE pane of the Design window. As with any field that you want to rename, place the insertion point at the beginning of the field cell to be renamed (to the left of the field name) and type the name you want to display followed by a colon.

Performing totals on groups of records

Most of the time, you need to perform totals on a group of records rather than on all records. For example, you may need to calculate the total number of animals you've treated for each type of animal. In other words, you want to create a group for each type of animal (bear, cat, dog, and so on) and then perform the total calculation against each of these groups. In database parlance, this is known as control *break totaling.*

Calculating totals for a single group

When you create your query, you specify which field or fields to use for grouping the totals and which fields to perform the totals against. Using the preceding example, to group the Type of Animal field, you select the Group By option of the Total: cell. Follow these steps to create the query:

1. Open a new query and select the Pets table.

2. Click the Totals button (the Greek sigma symbol button, Σ) on the toolbar to turn it on, if it is off.

3. Double-click the Type of Animal field in the Pets table.

4. Double-click the Pet ID field in the Pets table.

5. In the Total: cell of Type of Animal, make sure that the Group By is selected.

6. In the Total: cell of Pet ID, select Count.

The query in Figure 23-5 groups all like animals together and then performs the count total for each type of animal based on the steps you followed above. Unlike performing totals against all records, this query produces a dynaset of many records — one record for each type of animal. Figure 23-6 demonstrates how the datasheet looks.

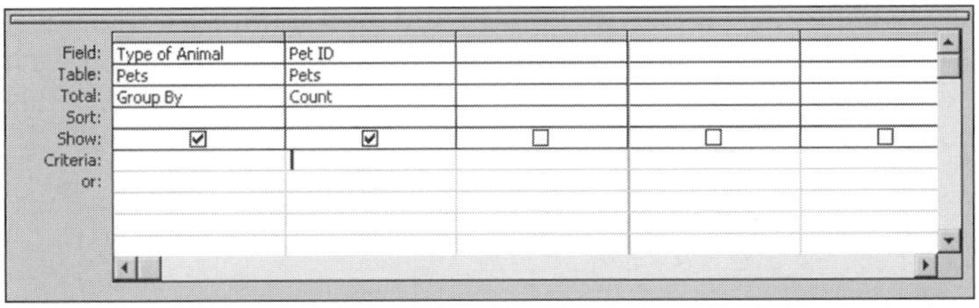

Figure 23-5: Totals against a group of records. First it groups all like pets together; then it counts the number of similar pets.

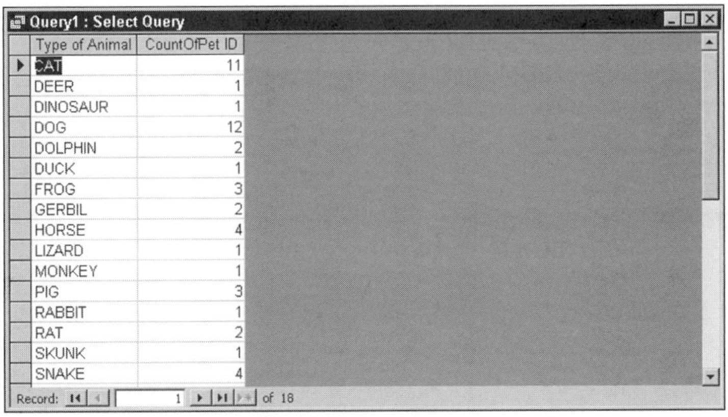

Figure 23-6: Datasheet of totals against the group Type of Animal field and the number of pets for each type

The dynaset in Figure 23-6 has a single record for each type of animal. The count was performed against each type of animal; there are 11 cats, 1 deer, 1 dinosaur, 12 dogs, and so on. The Group By field displays one record for each unique value in that field. The Type of Animal field is specified as the Group By field and displays a single record for each type of animal, showing Cat, Deer, Dog, and so on. Each of these records is shown as a row heading for the datasheet, indicating a unique record for each type of animal specified that begins with the Group By field content (bear, bird, and so on). In this case, each unique record is easy to identify by the single-field row heading under Type of Animal.

Calculating totals for several groups

You can perform group totals against multiple fields and multiple tables as easily as with a single field in a single table. For example, you may want to group by both customer and type of animal to determine the number of animals each customer owns by animal type. To create a total query for this example, you specify Group By in both Total: fields (Customer Name and Type of Animal).

This query, shown in Figure 23-7, uses two tables and also groups by two fields to perform the count total. First, the query groups by Customer Name and then by Type of Animal. When the Datasheet button on the toolbar is selected, a datasheet similar to the one shown in Figure 23-8 appears.

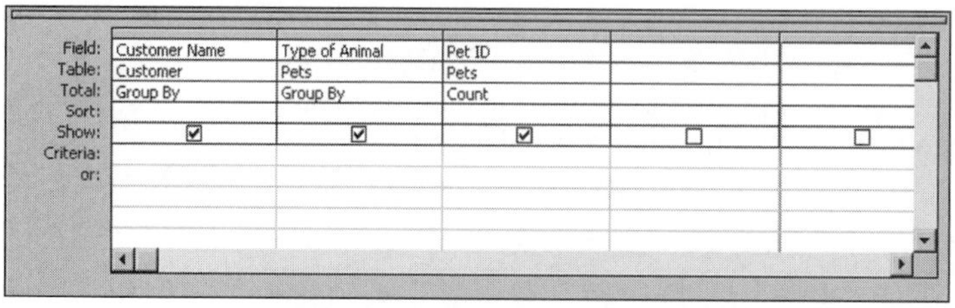

Field:	Customer Name	Type of Animal	Pet ID		
Table:	Customer	Pets	Pets		
Total:	Group By	Group By	Count		
Sort:					
Show:	☑	☑	☑	☐	☐
Criteria:					
or:					

Figure 23-7: A multiple-table, multiple-field Group By total query to show all Customers and how many pets each owns broken down by the type of pet

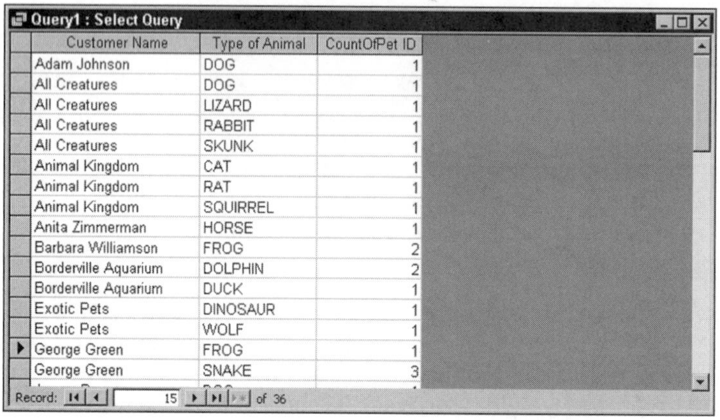

Query1 : Select Query

Customer Name	Type of Animal	CountOfPet ID
Adam Johnson	DOG	1
All Creatures	DOG	1
All Creatures	LIZARD	1
All Creatures	RABBIT	1
All Creatures	SKUNK	1
Animal Kingdom	CAT	1
Animal Kingdom	RAT	1
Animal Kingdom	SQUIRREL	1
Anita Zimmerman	HORSE	1
Barbara Williamson	FROG	2
Borderville Aquarium	DOLPHIN	2
Borderville Aquarium	DUCK	1
Exotic Pets	DINOSAUR	1
Exotic Pets	WOLF	1
George Green	FROG	1
George Green	SNAKE	3

Record: 14 ◀ | 15 | ▶ ▶I ▶* | of 36

Figure 23-8: Datasheet of a multiple-field Group By query

The datasheet in Figure 23-8 shows several records for the customer All Creatures. This customer has one dog, one lizard, one rabbit, and one skunk. Notice that Borderville Aquarium has two dolphins and one duck, and George Green has one frog and three snakes. This datasheet has a unique record based on two Group By fields: Customer Name and Type of Animal (as shown in Figure 23-7). Therefore, the unique row headings for this datasheet are created by ordering (Group By) both fields — first the Customer Name and then the Type of Animal.

Tip   You can think of the Group By fields in a total query as fields that specify the row headings of the datasheet. The Group By option creates the rows of the resulting dynaset in sorted order within each column.

Access groups records based on the order of the Group By fields in the QBE pane (from left to right). Therefore, you should pay attention to the order of the Group By fields. Although the order doesn't change the aggregate totals of the fields, the order of Group By fields does determine how the results are displayed in the datasheet. If you place the Type of Animal field before the Customer Name field, the resulting datasheet shows the records in order by animal first and then customer. Figure 23-9 demonstrates this setup, showing the cat records and their owners (with the total number) and then the deer records and their owners, and so on.

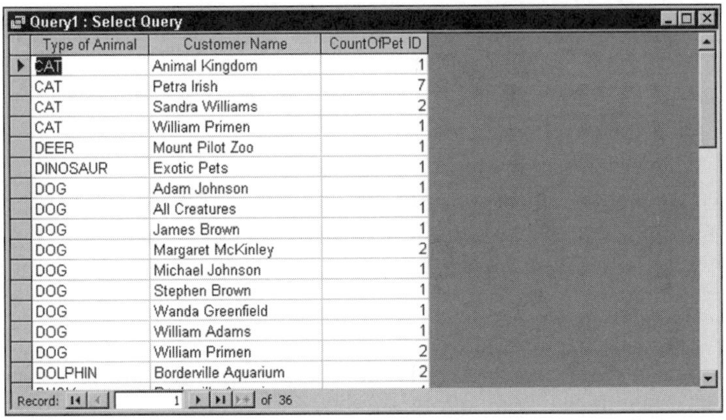
Query1 : Select Query

Type of Animal	Customer Name	CountOfPet ID
CAT	Animal Kingdom	1
CAT	Petra Irish	7
CAT	Sandra Williams	2
CAT	William Primen	1
DEER	Mount Pilot Zoo	1
DINOSAUR	Exotic Pets	1
DOG	Adam Johnson	1
DOG	All Creatures	1
DOG	James Brown	1
DOG	Margaret McKinley	2
DOG	Michael Johnson	1
DOG	Stephen Brown	1
DOG	Wanda Greenfield	1
DOG	William Adams	1
DOG	William Primen	2
DOLPHIN	Borderville Aquarium	2

Record: 1 of 36

Figure 23-9: Changing the order of Group By fields. This datasheet has Type of Animal before Customer Name (versus the opposite in Figure 23-8).

By changing the order of the Group By fields in a totals query, you can look at your data in new and creative ways.

Specifying criteria for a total query

In addition to grouping records for total queries, criteria to limit the records that will be processed or displayed in a total calculation can be specified. When you're specifying record criteria in total queries, several options are available. A criterion against any of these three fields can be created:

- ✦ Group By
- ✦ Aggregate Total
- ✦ Non-Aggregate Total

Using any one, any two, or all three of these criteria types, you can easily limit the scope of your total query to finite criteria.

Specifying criteria for a Group By field

To limit the scope of the records used in a grouping, you can specify criteria in the Group By fields. For example, to calculate the average length and weight of only three animals — duck, frog, and lizard — requires specifying criteria on the Group By field Type of Animal. This type of query looks like Figure 23-10. Notice that the Group By field, Type of Animals, has a criteria of 'In("duck", "frog", "lizard"). The other fields, Pet ID, Length, and Weight specify aggregate totals — count and Avg.

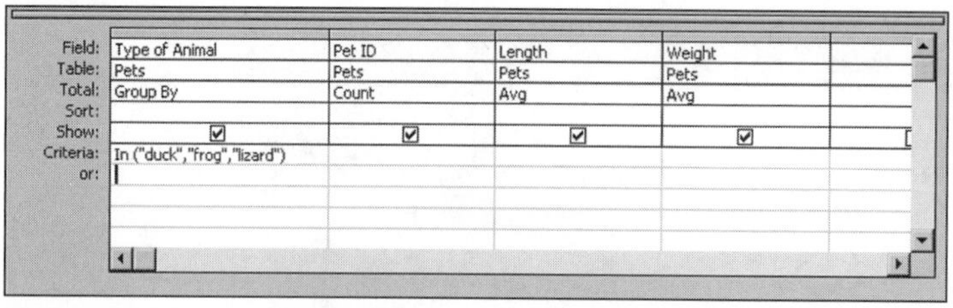

Figure 23-10: Specifying criteria in a Group By field. The Type of Animal uses the In() function to specify three types of Animals to look at.

By specifying criteria in the Type of Animal field, you can ensure that Access performs the aggregate calculations on only those records that meet the Group By criteria. In this example, the count, average length, and average weight will be performed only for animals that are ducks, frogs, and lizards. This query results in a three-record dynaset, with one record each for ducks, frogs, and lizards. Each record shows the total number of pets, the average length of each type, and the average weight of each type.

Specifying criteria for an Aggregate Total field

At times you may want a query to calculate aggregate totals first and then display only those totals from the aggregate calculations that meet a specified criterion. More specifically, you may want to perform aggregate calculations against *all* records and then add to the dynaset only those aggregate totals that meet a certain criterion. In effect, you're saying "I won't know which records I want to see until they're all totaled first. Then I want to see only those records that meet a particular criterion in my dynaset."

For example, you may want a query to find the average length of all animals, grouped by type of animal, where the average length of any animal is greater than 20 inches. This query should look like Figure 23-11. Notice that the criterion >20 is placed in the Aggregate Total field, Length. This query calculates the average length of all animals grouped by type of animal. Then the query determines whether the calculated totals for each record are greater than 20. Records greater than 20 are added to the resulting dynaset, and records less than or equal to 20 are discarded. The criterion is applied after the aggregate calculations are performed.

Field:	Type of Animal		Pet ID		Length				
Table:	Pets		Pets		Pets				
Total:	Group By		Count		Avg				
Sort:									
Show:		☑		☑		☑		☐	
Criteria:					>20				
or:									

Figure 23-11: A query with a criterion set against an Aggregate Total field (Avg of the Length field, greater than 20)

Specifying criteria for a Non-Aggregate Total field

The preceding section showed you how to limit the records after performing the calculations against total fields. You also can specify that you want Access to limit the records based on a total field before performing total calculations. In other words, you can limit the range of records against which the calculation is performed. Doing so creates a criterion similar to the first type of criteria in the preceding example; the field you want to set a criterion against is not a Group By field.

The preceding section shows you how to limit the fields included in the dynaset by using the Group By criteria, which allows you to state specific criteria for which records you want to appear in the resulting dynaset. Suppose, however, that you want to filter the group of records based on criteria that you don't want in the resulting dynaset. Access allows you to do this as well. You can limit the range of records against which the calculation is performed, and you can make this limitation based on criteria that you don't want to appear in the resulting dynaset.

For example, you may want to display the total amount of money charged for each animal during the first half of 1999 (through 30 Jun 1999) starting with February 9. You want to use the Visit Date field to specify criteria, but you don't want to perform any calculations against this field or to use it to group by; you don't even want to show the field in the resulting datasheet.

Figure 23-12 shows how the query should look. Here you used the Where type of Total to limit the scope of records shown. Notice that Access automatically turned off the Show: cell in the Visit Date field; when using a Where clause this field can not be used in the query. If you wanted to also see the Visit Date field, simply add a second Visit Date field to the QBE pane.

Note
In the query you just completed, Access displays only those records for pets that have visited the hospital from February 9 to June 30, 1999, inclusive. All other records are discarded.

Access automatically turns off the Show: cell whenever it encounters a Where option in the Total: cell of a field. Access understands that you are using the field only to specify criteria and that you don't want to see the actual field value displayed for the criteria field. The reason is that Access uses the field to evaluate the

Where criteria before performing the calculation. Therefore, the contents are useful only for the limiting criteria. If you try to turn on the Show: cell, Access displays an error message. If you need to see the field contents in the datasheet, simply add a second copy of the field to the QBE pane. Only the field that has the Where condition in the Total: row is not shown.

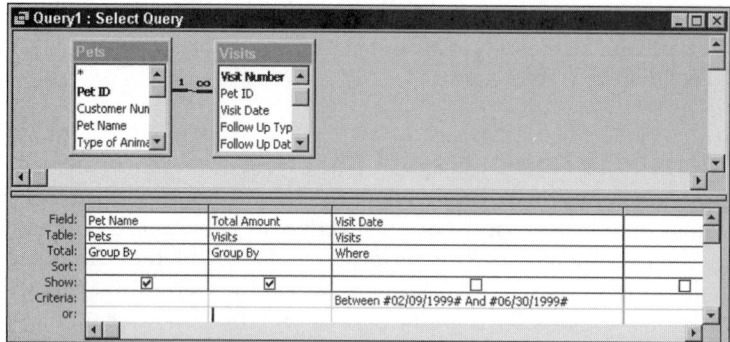

Figure 23-12: Specifying criteria for a Non-Aggregate field. Here you used the 'Where' type of Total to limit the scope of the records shown.

Creating expressions for totals

In addition to choosing one of the Access totals from the drop-down list, you can create your own total expression based on several types of totals, such as using Avg and Sum or multiple Sums together. Or you can base your expression on a calculated field composed of several functions; or on a calculated field that is based on several fields from different tables.

Suppose that you want a query that shows the total amount of money each customer owed before discount. Then you want to see the amount of money these customers saved based on their discount (a calculated field you create named Total Saved). You further want the information to be grouped by customer and sorted by highest amount owed. Finally you want the Total Saved field to display dollar amounts (format like this $111.11). Follow these steps to create this query:

1. Start a new query and select the Customer, Pets, and Visits tables.

2. Click the Totals button (the Σ) on the toolbar to turn it on.

3. Double-click the Customer Name field in the Customer table.

4. Double-click the Total Amount field in the Visits table.

5. In the Total: cell of Customer Name, make sure the Group By is selected.

6. In the Total: cell of Total Amount, select Sum.

7. In the Total Amount column select a Sort: order of Descending.

8. Click on an empty Field: cell in the QBE pane.

9. Type Total Saved:Sum([Visits].[Total Amount]*[Customer].[Discount]) in the cell.

10. In the Total: cell of Total Saved expression, select Expression.

11. Making sure the cursor is still in the Total Saved field, click the Criteria: cell.

12. If the Property sheet is not opened, right mouse click to bring up the right click menu and select Properties.

13. On the General tab, select a Format of Currency (for the Total Saved field).

Your query should be similar to Figure 23-13. Notice that the query uses two fields from different tables to create the Total Saved: calculated field. You had to specify both the table and the field name for each field the Sum function used — [Visits].[Total Amount], and [Customer].[Discount].

Note

You had to use the Pets table, although you did not use any of its fields in the QBE pane for the query. It was necessary to use the Pets table to maintain and build a link between the Customer table and the Visits table. In other words, if you had omitted the Pets table, there would be no way to link the Customer table to the Visits table.

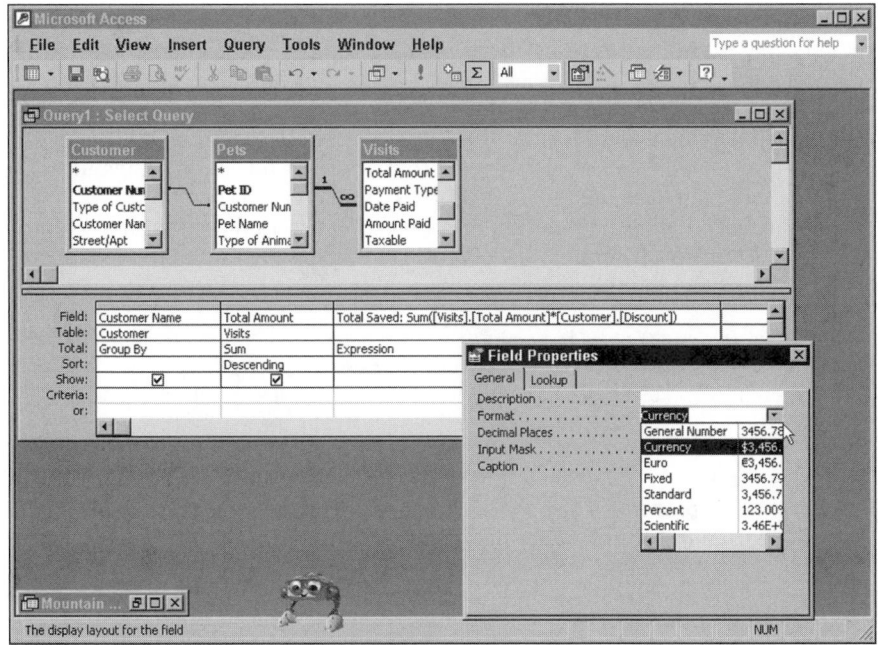

Figure 23-13: A query using an Expression Total:. Notice that the expression is built based on fields from two different tables — Customer and Visits.

If you click the Datasheet button on the toolbar, your dynaset should be similar to Figure 23-14. The Total Saved field is a calculated field that you created using the expression you built and specified as an Expression Total:. Notice that the resulting display shows a currency format for the Total Saved field.

Customer Name	SumOfTotal Amount	Total Saved
Animal Kingdom	$1,448.00	$289.60
George Green	$1,389.50	$0.00
Petra Irish	$1,340.80	$0.00
All Creatures	$1,122.00	$224.40
Johnathan Adams	$936.00	$46.80
William Primen	$843.50	$0.00
Karen Rhodes	$793.00	$0.00
Sandra Williams	$643.00	$0.00
William Price	$385.00	$0.00
Stephen Brown	$316.00	$0.00
Sandra Young	$234.00	$0.00
Adam Johnson	$167.80	$0.00
Tyrone Potter	$106.00	$0.00

Record: I◄ ◄ 1 ► ►I ►* of 20

Figure 23-14: A datasheet created by an Expression total

Note   In the datasheet in Figure 23-14, the calculated field Total Saved shows the information in Currency format, using the Dollar sign and two decimal places. If you did not specify a format for the field in the query design you would see as many as 12 decimal places and no dollar sign. If all you want to do is limit the number of decimal places, while using the thousands comma you can specify a format of Standard.

Although specifying a Field format is relatively easy to do in the QBE pane, it has one drawback — you do not visually see that a format has been assigned to the field. In lieu of using the field format property you can also use the Format() function around the Sum() function making the Calculated field more complex, yet visibly accurate. For example, to do so, add the following line to the existing criteria formula in the calculated field cell:

```
Total Saved:  Format(Sum([Visits].[Total
Amount]*[Customer].[Discount]), "Standard")  or -
Format(Sum([Visits].[Total Amount]*[Customer].[Discount]),
"Currency")
```

Tip   Using the Format function in the calculated field cell takes precedence over the format field property. If you specify a format function in the calculated field cell, it will be used instead of the format property you set in the property list.

At this point you should close the query without saving it because it will not be used again.

Creating Crosstab Queries

Access permits use of a specialized type of total query—the crosstab—to display summarized data in a compact and readable format. A crosstab query summarizes the data in the fields from your tables and presents the resulting dynaset in a row-and-column format.

Understanding the crosstab query

Simply put, a crosstab query is a spreadsheet-like summary of the things specified by the row header and column header that is created from your tables. This query presents summary data in a spreadsheet-like format created from fields that you specify. In this specialized type of total query, the Total: row in the QBE pane is always active. The Total: row cannot be toggled off in a crosstab query!

In addition, the Total: row of the QBE pane is used for specifying a Group By total option for both the row and the column headings. Like other total queries, the Group By option specifies the row headings for the query datasheet and comes from the actual contents of the field. However, unlike other total queries, the crosstab query also obtains its column headings from the value in a field (table or calculated) rather than from the field names themselves.

Note   The fields used as rows and columns must always have Group By in the Total: row. Otherwise, Access reports an error when you attempt to display or run the query.

For example, you may want to create a query that displays the Type of Animal field as the row heading and the owner's state as the column heading, with each cell containing a total for each type of animal in each state. Table 23-3 demonstrates how you want the query to look.

In Table 23-3, the row headings are specified by Type of Animal: Cat, Deer, Dog, and so on. The column headings are specified by the state: ID, OR, and WA. The cell content in the intersection of any row and column is a summary of records that meets both conditions. For example, the Cat row that intersects the OR column shows that the clinic treats seven cats in the state of Oregon. The Dog row that intersects with the WA column shows that the clinic treats five dogs in the state of Washington.

This table shows a simple crosstab query created from the fields Type of Animal and State, with the intersecting cell contents determined by a Count total on any field in the Pets table.

Table 23-3 A Typical Crosstab Query Format			
Type of Animal	*ID*	*OR*	*WA*
Cat	1	7	3
Deer	1	0	0
Dinosaur	0	1	0
Dog	2	4	5
Dolphin	0	2	0

Creating the crosstab query

Now that you have a conceptual understanding of a crosstab query, it is time to create one. To create a crosstab query like the one described in Table 23-3, follow these steps:

1. Start a new query and select the Customer and Pets tables.
2. Double-click the Type of Animal field in the Pets table.
3. Double-click the State field in the Customer table.
4. Double-click the Pet ID field in the Pets table.
5. Select Query ➪ Crosstab in the Query menu or press the Query Type button on the toolbar (this method displays a drop-down list showing the types of queries) and select Crosstab Query.
6. In the Crosstab: cell of Type of Animal, select Row Heading.
7. In the Crosstab: cell of State, select Column Heading.
8. In the Crosstab: cell of Pet ID, select Value.
9. In the Total: cell of Pet ID, select Count.

Your query should look similar to Figure 23-15. Notice that Access inserted a new row named Crosstab: between the Total: and Sort: rows in the QBE pane.

As Figure 23-15 demonstrates, you must specify a minimum of three items for crosstab queries:

✦ The Row Heading field
✦ The Column Heading field
✦ The summary Value field

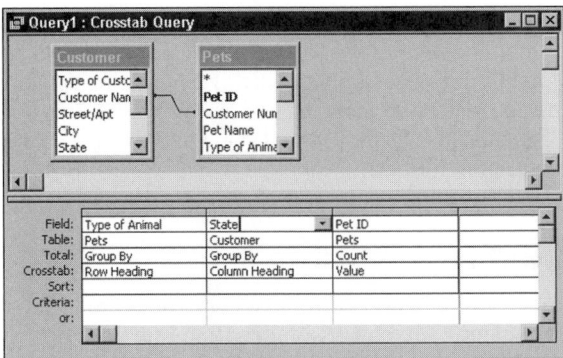

Figure 23-15: Creating a crosstab query of Customer states and type of Animal

These three items are specified in the appropriate Crosstab: cells of the fields. After you specify the contents for the three Crosstab: cells, you specify Group By in the Total: cell of both the Row Heading and the Column Heading fields and an aggregate Total: cell operator (such as Count) for the Value field.

If you have done this procedure correctly, selecting the Datasheet button on the toolbar reveals a datasheet similar to Figure 23-16.

Notice that the dynaset is composed of distinct (non-repeating) rows of animals, three columns (one for each state), and summary cell contents for each animal against each state; that is, the clinic treats no deer in the state of Oregon or Washington, but it does treat one in Idaho. When there are no values found, a null value is used rather than 0.

Type of Animal	ID	OR	WA
CAT	1	7	3
DEER	1		
DINOSAUR		1	
DOG	2	4	5
DOLPHIN		2	
DUCK		1	
FROG	1	2	
GERBIL			2
HORSE	2		2
LIZARD			1
MONKEY	1		
PIG			3
RABBIT			1
RAT	1		1

Record: 1 of 18

Figure 23-16: Datasheet of a crosstab query. Notice that the Headings for both the columns and rows are actual field values from the tables.

Tip   Figure 23-16 shows the default display value for null values — a blank cell. You can force Access to display a zero in these cells by simply entering a Format field property for the Pet ID field (Total Count, Crosstab Value field) by entering the format value of **0;;;0** (a zero, followed by three semicolons and another zero). This format tells Access to display all regular values as their actual value and the null values as a zero (fourth option in the custom format).

Entering multiple-field row headings

When working with crosstab queries, only one summary Value field and one Column Heading field can be specified. You can add more than one Row Heading field, however. By adding multiple Row Heading fields, you can refine the type of data to be presented in the crosstab query.

Suppose that you're interested in seeing the types of animals from the last crosstab query further refined to the level of city. In other words, you want to see how many of each type of animal that you have from each city within each state. To accomplish this task you will need to switch the type of headings being displayed — making the Type of Animal the Column Headings and the State/City fields the Row Heading. Such a query is shown in Figure 23-17. Notice that it has two Crosstab: cells that show Row Heading for the fields State and City. Access groups the Crosstab: rows first by the State and then by the City. Access specifies the group order from left to right. Effectively, you are changing the orientation of the row/column of the previous example.

Field:	State	City	Type of Animal	Pet ID		
Table:	Customer	Customer	Pets	Pets		
Total:	Group By	Group By	Group By	Count		
Crosstab:	Row Heading	Row Heading	Column Heading	Value		
Sort:						
Criteria:						
or:						

Figure 23-17: Crosstab query using two fields for the row heading. The Type of Animals field is now used for the column headings of this crosstab query.

Access presents a datasheet similar to the one shown in Figure 23-18 when the Datasheet button on the toolbar is selected. The row heading depends on both the State and City fields. The dynaset is displayed in order: first by state (ID, OR, WA) and then by city within the state (Borderville, Mount Pilot, Russettown, and so forth).

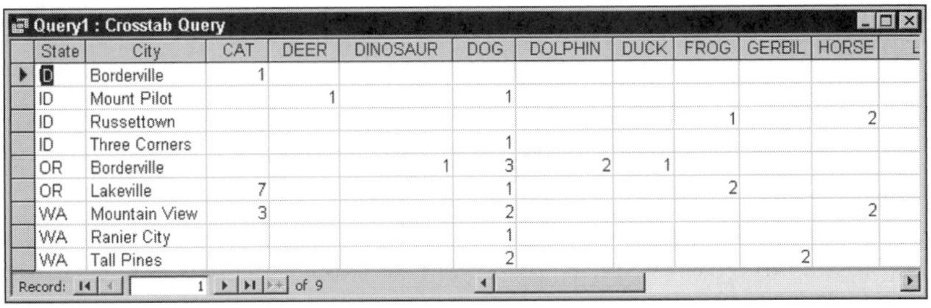

Figure 23-18: Datasheet with multiple-field row headings (State and then City) of a crosstab query

A crosstab query can have several row headings but only one column heading. To achieve the same effect as a several-field column heading and a single-field row heading, simply reverse the heading types. Change the multiple-field column headings to multiple-field row headings and change the single-row heading to a single-column heading.

Tip Although Access limits you to a single field column heading it is possible to create a multi-field column heading, as in a State and City, using a Calculated field. You can create a Calculated field of [State]+' '+[City] to create a Column Heading field and specify the Type of Animal as the Row Heading. The resulting datasheet will display all the combined Values of State and City as individual column heading — ID Borderville, ID Mount Pilot, ID Russettown, ID Three Corners, OR Borderville, and on and on.

Specifying criteria for a crosstab query

When working with crosstab queries, you may want to specify record criteria for the crosstab. Criteria can be specified in a crosstab query against any of these fields:

- ✦ A new field
- ✦ A Row Heading field
- ✦ A Column Heading field

Specifying criteria in a new field

You can add criteria based on a new field that will not be displayed in the crosstab query itself. For example, you may want to create the crosstab query you see in Figure 23-17, in which the two fields, State and City, are used as the row heading. However, you want to see only records in which the type of customer is an individual (or the contents equal the number 1). To specify criteria, follow these additional steps:

1. Start with the crosstab query shown in Figure 23-17.

2. Double-click the Type of Customer field in the Customer table to add it to the QBE pane.

3. Select the Criteria: cell of Type of Customer.

4. Type **1** in the cell.

Note   The Crosstab: cell of the Type of Customer field should be blank. If it is not, select (not shown) to blank the cell.

Your query should resemble the one shown in Figure 23-19. Notice that you added a criterion in a field that will not be displayed in the crosstab query. The Type of Customer field is used as a grouping field and because nothing appears in the Crosstab row, the field value is not displayed.

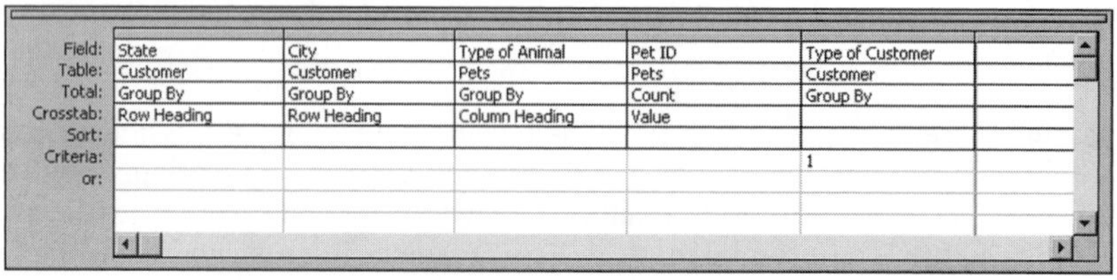

Field:	State	City	Type of Animal	Pet ID	Type of Customer	
Table:	Customer	Customer	Pets	Pets	Customer	
Total:	Group By	Group By	Group By	Count	Group By	
Crosstab:	Row Heading	Row Heading	Column Heading	Value		
Sort:						
Criteria:					1	
or:						

Figure 23-19: Specifying a criterion in a crosstab query on a new field. The Type of Customer has a criterion of '1' and the Crosstab: cell is left blank.

Now that the new criterion is specified, you can click on the Datasheet button of the toolbar to see a datasheet similar to the one portrayed in Figure 23-20.

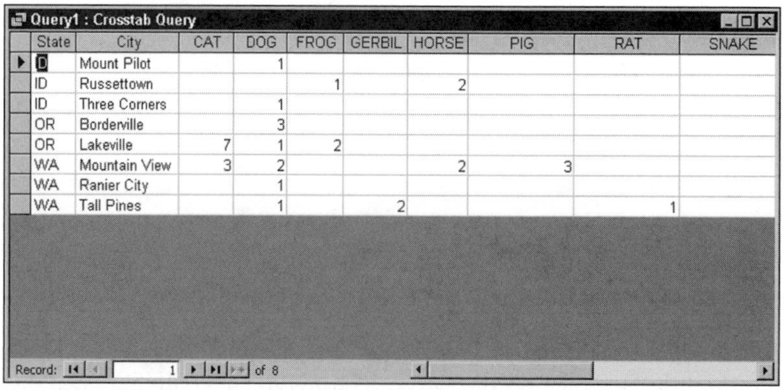

State	City	CAT	DOG	FROG	GERBIL	HORSE	PIG	RAT	SNAKE
ID	Mount Pilot		1						
ID	Russettown			1		2			
ID	Three Corners		1						
OR	Borderville		3						
OR	Lakeville	7	1	2					
WA	Mountain View	3	2			2	3		
WA	Ranier City		1						
WA	Tall Pines		1		2			1	

Record: ⏮ ◄ [1] ► ⏭ ►* of 8

Figure 23-20: The datasheet after specifying a criterion on a new field. It shows a crosstab only for all customers who have a type of '1' (individual).

The datasheet in Figure 23-20 shows only columns and rows in which at least one of the intersecting row cells has a value. First, it only has eight rows, instead of 13 in Figure 23-17 — five were removed since there are no values in the columns of those rows. Second it only has eight columns versus 18 in Figure 23-17 — the columns that have no value in any of the cells have been removed. Several types of animal columns are gone. Deer, Dolphins, Ducks, and others are missing because no individual customers own these types of animals.

Specifying criteria in a Row Heading field

You can also specify criteria for a field being used for a row heading. When you specify a criteria for a row heading, Access excludes any rows that do not meet the specified criteria.

For example, you may want to create a crosstab query for all animals where the state is Idaho (ID). To create this query, start with the crosstab query shown in Figure 23-17. If you created the last query, remove the Type of Customer column from the QBE pane. To create this query, make the QBE pane look like Figure 23-21. When this query is viewed, only records from Idaho are seen.

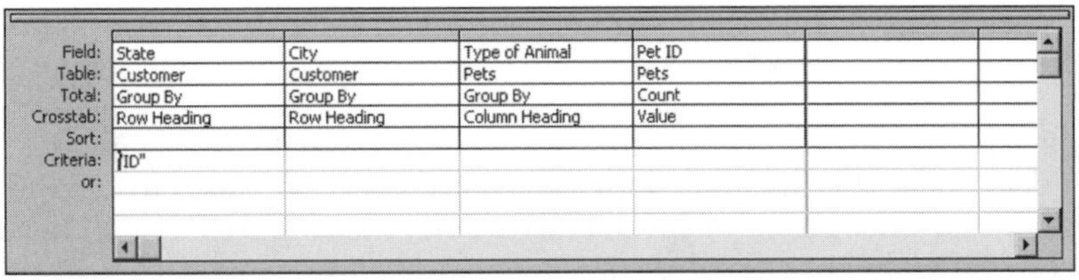

Field:	State	City	Type of Animal	Pet ID		
Table:	Customer	Customer	Pets	Pets		
Total:	Group By	Group By	Group By	Count		
Crosstab:	Row Heading	Row Heading	Column Heading	Value		
Sort:						
Criteria:	"ID"					
or:						

Figure 23-21: Criteria set against a Row Heading field — State for all Idaho customers

You can specify criteria against any field used as a Row Heading field or for multiple Row Heading fields to create a finely focused crosstab query.

Specifying criteria in a Column Heading field

You can also specify criteria for the field you use as the column heading. When you specify the criteria for a column heading, Access excludes any columns that don't meet the specified criteria. For the next example, you want a crosstab query for any animal that is either a cat or a dog. To create this query, again start with the crosstab query shown in Figure 23-17. If you created the last query, remove the criteria for the State field from the QBE pane. The QBE pane should look similar to that in Figure 23-22.

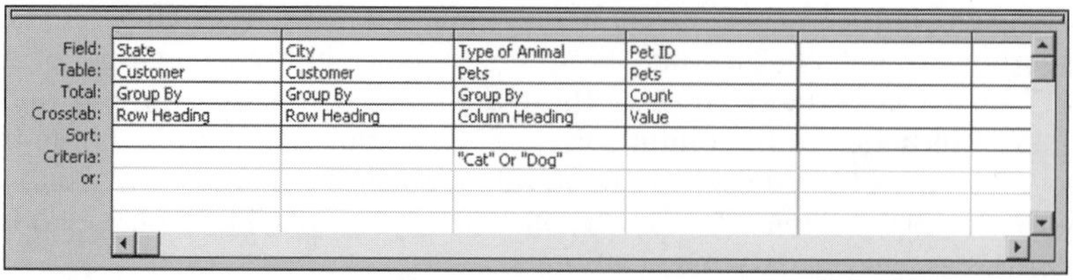

Figure 23-22: A criterion specified against the Column Heading field — Type of Animal. Here you only want to see two columns — Cats and Dogs.

The specified criterion is placed in the Criteria: cell of the Column Heading field Type of Animal. If you now select the Datasheet button on the toolbar, you should see a datasheet that has only two column headings: Cat and Dog. The other headings are eliminated.

Specifying criteria in multiple fields of a crosstab query

Now that you've worked with each type of criterion separately, you may want to specify criteria based on several fields. In the next example, you learn to create a complex crosstab query with multi-field criteria. You want a row heading based on the Type of Animal field, a column heading based on the short Month form ('mmm') value of the Visit Date field, and Value cells based on the Sum of Total Amount.

Finally, you want to limit the months to part of 2000. To create this complex crosstab query, make the QBE pane look like Figure 23-23. You need to use the Pets and Visits tables. Notice that you specified a column heading based on a calculated field. The calculated field Feb2Mar does not have to have a name specified — Expr1 is sufficient.

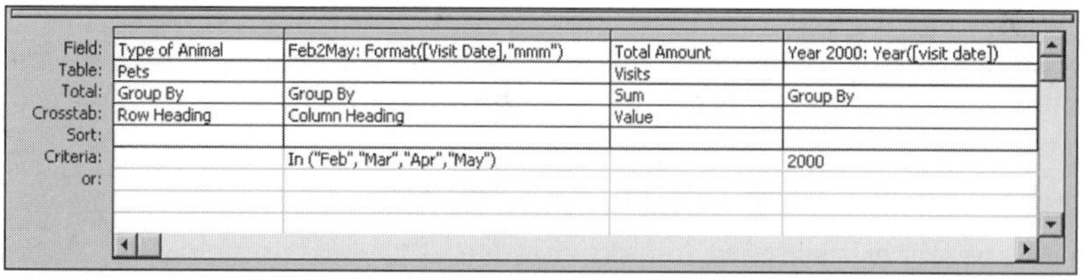

Figure 23-23: A complex crosstab query with two field criteria and a calculated field

This query should display a datasheet in which the columns are Feb, Mar, Apr, and May for the year 2000. When you select the Datasheet button on the toolbar, you see a datasheet similar to Figure 23-24. The datasheet has four columns; the order of the columns is alphabetical (Apr, Feb, Mar, May), not the chronological, by-month order (Feb, Mar, Apr, May) you entered in the Criteria: cell of the field. The next section shows you how to fix the column order so that the months display in chronological order.

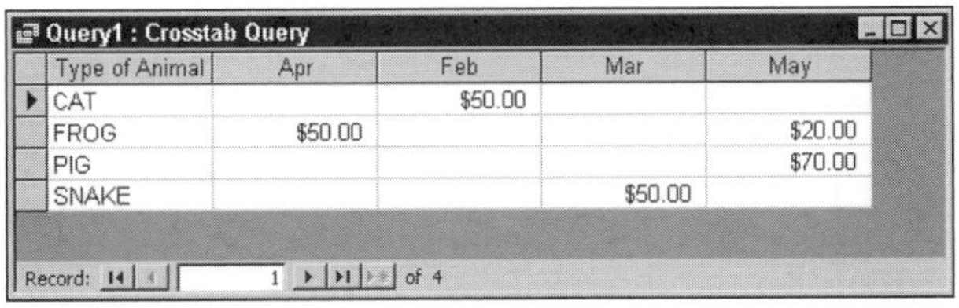

Query1 : Crosstab Query

Type of Animal	Apr	Feb	Mar	May
CAT		$50.00		
FROG	$50.00			$20.00
PIG				$70.00
SNAKE			$50.00	

Record: 1 of 4

Figure 23-24: A datasheet of very complex crosstab criteria

Specifying fixed column headings

At times, you will want more control over the appearance of the column headings. By default, Access sorts column headings alphabetically or numerically. This sort order can be a problem, as in the preceding example and as illustrated in Figure 23-24. Your columns will be more readable if the columns are in chronological Month order rather than alphabetical order. You can use the option Column Headings in the Query Properties box to solve this problem. This option lets you

✦ Specify an exact order for the appearance of the column headings

✦ Specify fixed column headings for reports and forms that use crosstab queries

To specify fixed column headings, follow these steps:

1. Begin with the crosstab query shown in Figure 23-23. Move the pointer to the top half of the query screen and click it once to make sure you are in the top pane.
2. If the Property window is not already open, click the Properties button (a hand holding a piece of paper) on the toolbar or select View ➪ Properties from the Query Design menu.
3. Select the Column Headings text box entry area (third choice).
4. Type Feb, Mar, Apr, May in the box.

The Query Properties dialog box should look like the one shown in Figure 23-25. When you move to another entry area, Access converts your text into “Feb,” “Mar,” “Apr,” and “May” in the Query Properties dialog box.

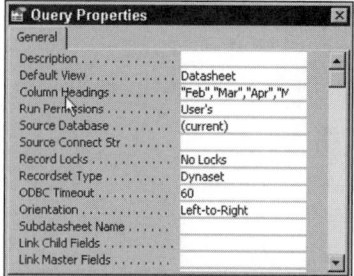

Figure 23-25: The Query Properties dialog box specifying a display order for the Column Headings

If you look at the datasheet, you see that it now looks like Figure 23-26. The order for the column headings is now chronological Month order.

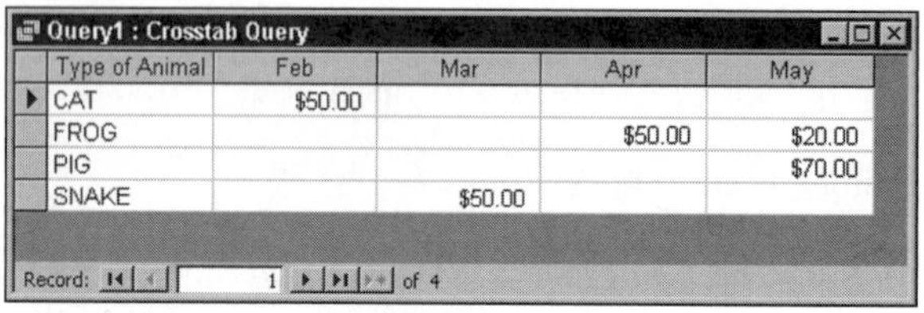

Type of Animal	Feb	Mar	Apr	May
CAT	$50.00			
FROG			$50.00	$20.00
PIG				$70.00
SNAKE		$50.00		

Record: 14 ◄ | 1 | ► ►1 ►* of 4

Figure 23-26: The datasheet with the column order specified in month chronological order

The Crosstab Query Wizard

Access employs several Query Wizards, which are helpful additions to the query design surface. One such Wizard, the Crosstab Query Wizard (see Figure 23-27), is an excellent tool to help you create a simple crosstab query quickly. To see the Crosstab choice simply click on the new button, and the New Query selection window will appear as in Figure 23-27.

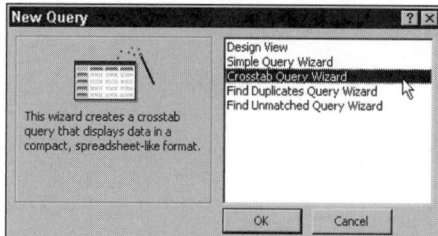

Figure 23-27: Selecting the Access Query Wizard from the New Query dialog box

The Crosstab Query Wizard has some limitations, however:

✦ To use more than one table for the crosstab query, you need to create a separate query that has the tables you need for the crosstab query. For example, you may have a Group By row heading from the Pets table (Type of Animal) and a Group By column heading from the Customer table (State). The Crosstab Query Wizard allows you to select only one table or query for the row and column heading.

The workaround: Create a query of the Customer and Pets tables, selecting the All Fields reference for each, and save this intermediate query. Then use this intermediate query as the record source for the Wizard.

✦ The limiting criteria for the Wizard's query cannot be specified.

The workaround: Make the Wizard do the query and then go in and set the limiting criteria.

✦ You can not use a calculated field for Row or Column headings

The workaround: Add the calculated field to an intermediate query and use the query for the Wizard.

✦ Column headings or column orders cannot be specified.

The workaround: Again, have the Wizard create the query and then modify it.

To use the crosstab query wizard, click the New button in the database window toolbar after pressing the Queries Object button and then select the Crosstab Wizard (third from the top, Figure 23-27) in the dialog box. Click OK and then follow the prompts. Access asks for

✦ The table or query name for the source

✦ The fields for the row headings

✦ The fields for the column headings

✦ The field for the body

✦ The title

After you specify these things, Access creates your crosstab query and then runs it for you.

Creating a Parameter Query

You can automate the process of changing criteria for queries that you run on a regular basis by creating parameter queries.

Understanding the parameter query

As the name parameter suggests, a parameter query is one you create that prompts the user for a quantity or a constant value every time the query is executed. Specifically, a parameter query prompts the user for criteria each time it is run, thereby eliminating the need to open the query in design mode to change the criteria manually.

Parameter queries are also very useful with forms or reports because Access can prompt the user for the criteria when the form or report is opened.

Creating a single-parameter query

You may have queries that require different values for the criteria of a field each time someone runs them. Suppose that you have a query that displays all pets for a specific customer. If you run the query often, you can design a parameter query to prompt the user for a customer number whenever the query runs. To create the query, follow these steps:

1. Starting with a select query, select the Customer and Pets tables.
2. Double-click the Customer Number field in the Customer table.
3. Double-click the Customer Name in the Customer table.
4. Double-click the Pet Name field in the Pets table.
5. Click the Criteria: cell for Customer Number.
6. Type [Enter a Customer Number] in the cell.
7. Deselect the Show: cell of Customer Number if you don't want this field to show in the datasheet. It has been left visible in the upcoming example figure.

That's all there is to creating a single-parameter query. Your query should resemble Figure 23-28.

In the preceding example, you created a parameter query that prompts the user for a customer number by displaying the message Enter a Customer Number each time the query is run. Access will convert the user's entry to an equals criteria for the field Customer Number. If a valid number is entered, Access will find the correct records.

Running a parameter query

To run a parameter query, select either the Run button or the Datasheet button on the toolbar. A parameter dialog box appears on-screen, such as the one shown in Figure 23-29, prompting the user for a value.

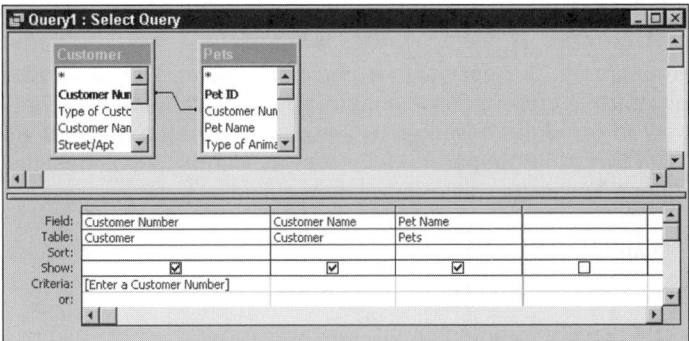

Figure 23-28: A single-parameter query that will prompt the user for the Customer ID to show every time the query is run

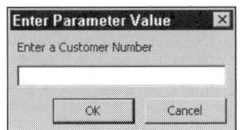

Figure 23-29: The Enter Parameter Value dialog box asking for a Customer ID number

After the user enters a value (for example IR001) and presses Enter, Access runs the query based on the criteria entered. If the criteria are valid, the datasheet shows records that match the criteria; otherwise, the datasheet displays no records. If the user simply presses the Enter key without entering a value, Access runs the query and displays no records — in this case the value becomes null.

If the user types IR001 in the parameter dialog box, Access displays a datasheet similar to Figure 23-30.

Customer	Customer Name	Pet Name
▶ IR001	Petra Irish	D.C.
IR001	Petra Irish	Jimeny
IR001	Petra Irish	Shadow
IR001	Petra Irish	Romeo
IR001	Petra Irish	Ceasar
IR001	Petra Irish	Jameo
IR001	Petra Irish	Tigger

Record: ◄◄ ◄ 1 ► ►► ►* of 7

Figure 23-30: Datasheet of records for Customer number IR001 that the user entered into the parameter dialog box

The records displayed in Figure 23-30 are only those for Petra Irish, whose customer number is IR001.

Creating a multiple-parameter query

You are not limited to creating a query with a single parameter. You can create a query that asks for multiple criteria. For example, you may want a query that displays all pet and visit information based on a type of animal and a range of visit dates. You can design this multiple-parameter query as simply as you designed the single-parameter query. To create this query, follow these steps:

1. Select the Pets and Visits tables.

2. Double-click the Pet Name field in the Pets table.

3. Double-click the Type of Animal field in the Pets table.

4. Double-click the Visit Date field in the Visits table.

5. Click in the Criteria: cell for Type of Animal.

6. Type [Enter an Animal Type] in the cell.

7. Click in the Criteria: cell for Visit Date.

8. Type Between [Start Date] And [End Date] in the cell.

Steps 6 and 8 contain the prompt messages for the prompt criteria. When run, this query will display three parameter query prompts. Your query should resemble that shown in Figure 23-31.

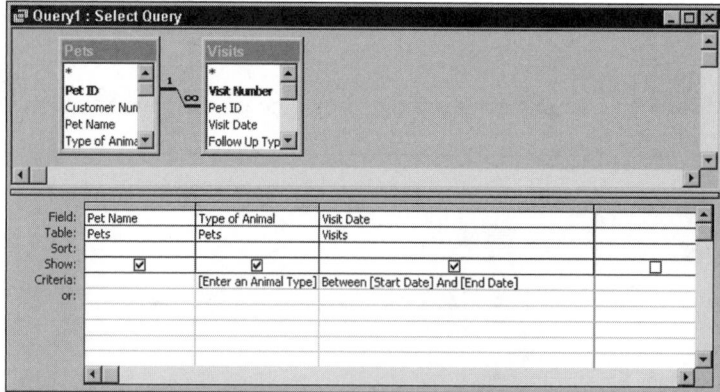

Figure 23-31: A parameter query with three criteria specified within two columns — Type of Animal and Visit Date

When this query runs, Access prompts the user for the three criteria in this order:

✦ Enter an Animal Type

✦ Start Date

✦ End Date

Like the single-parameter example, the user must enter valid criteria. If the user enters valid criteria in all three dialog boxes, Access displays all records meeting the specified criteria. Otherwise, it displays no records.

Specifying parameter order

By default, the Access prompt order of parameters is from left to right, based on the position of the fields and their parameters. However, you can override the prompt order by selecting Query ▷ Parameters and specifying an order.

To specify a prompt order, enter the criteria on the QBE pane just as you have been doing. For example, to specify a prompt order of Start Date, End Date, and Animal Type, follow these steps:

1. Start with the query in Figure 23-31.

2. Select Query ▷ Parameters.

3. Type **[Enter an Animal Type]** in the first cell under the Parameter column.

4. Press Tab to move to the Data Type column.

5. Enter Text or select the Text type from the drop-down list.

6. Press Tab to move to the Parameter column.

7. Type **[Start Date]** in the first cell under the Parameter column.

8. Press Tab to move to the Data Type column.

9. Type **Date/Time** or select the Date/Time type from the drop-down list box.

10. Press Tab to move to the Parameter column.

11. Type **[End Date]** in the first cell under the Parameter column.

12. Press Tab to move to the Data Type column.

13. Type **Date/Time** or select the Date/Time type from the drop-down list.

14. Press Enter or click OK to leave the dialog box.

Your Query Parameters dialog box should look like that shown in Figure 23-32.

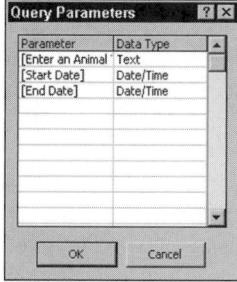

Figure 23-32: The Query Parameters dialog box with parameter values added

Notice that the message prompt in the Parameter column must match exactly the message prompt in each of the Criteria: cells of the QBE pane. If the prompt message does not match, the query will not work correctly. Access will prompt for the values in the QBE pane and for any error values you have typed in the Query Parameters dialog box. It will ignore the error values and only use the actual values from the QBE pane. But this can cause the user a lot of confusion.

✦   ✦   ✦

Working with Action Queries

✦ ✦ ✦ ✦

In This Chapter

Understanding what
action queries are

Learning how action
queries work

Creating an update
action query

Creating new tables
with a make-table
query

Creating an append
query

Creating a delete
query

Using query wizards

Troubleshooting
action queries

✦ ✦ ✦ ✦

In this chapter, you learn about a special type of query, called the action query, which enables you to change the field values in your records. For example, you can change a medications field to increase all prices by 10 percent or delete all information from the records of a deceased animal.

About Action Queries

The term action query defines a query that does something more than simply select a specific group of records and then present it to you in a dynaset. The word "action" suggests performing some operation — doing, influencing, or affecting something. The word is synonymous with operation, performance, and work. This is exactly what an action query does — some specific operation or work.

An action query can be considered a select query that is given a duty to perform against a specified group of records in the dynaset.

Types of action queries

When you create any query, Access creates it as a select query automatically. You can specify a different type (such as action) from the Query Design menu. From this menu, you can choose from several types of action queries. The menu's selections are Make Table, Update, Append, and Delete.

Like select queries, action queries create a dynaset that you can view in a datasheet. To see the dynaset, click the Datasheet button on the toolbar. Unlike select queries, action queries perform an action — specified in the Query by Example (QBE) pane of the query design — when you click the Run button (the button with the exclamation point) on the toolbar.

You can quickly identify action queries in the Database window by the special exclamation point icons that sit beside their names (to the right side). There are four different types of action queries (see Figure 24-1); each has a different icon.

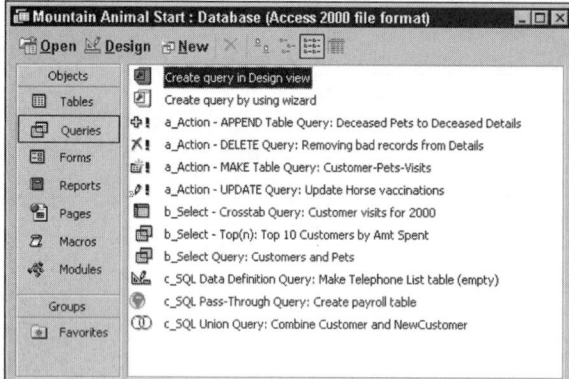

Figure 24-1: The query container of the Database window showing the different types of queries and their icons — including Select, Action, and SQL specific queries

Looking at Figure 24-1, the four types of action queries can be seen toward the top of the container. Notice that each has a unique icon associated with it. All have the Exclamation point as part of the icon — the Append shows a Plus sign and the exclamation point, the Delete has a graphical X and the exclamation point, the Make Table has a new table (starburst over top-right corner) and the exclamation point, and the Update has a pencil writing and the exclamation point.

Uses of action queries

Action queries can accomplish these tasks:

✦ Delete specified records from a table or group of tables

✦ Append records from one table to another

✦ Update information in a group of records

✦ Create a new table from specified records in a query

These examples describe some practical uses for action queries:

✦ You want to create history tables and then copy all inactive records to them. (You consider a record inactive if a customer hasn't brought a pet to the office in more than three years.) You decide to remove the inactive records from your active database tables.

- What to do? Use a make-table query to create the history tables and a delete query to remove the unwanted records.

✦ One of your old clients, whom you haven't seen in more than four years, comes in with a new puppy; you need to bring the old information back into the active file from the backup files.

- What to do? Use an append query to add records from your backup tables to your active tables.

Caution Unlike select queries, which display data in a specific manner, Action Queries perform actions against the data stored in the underlying tables. This action may be copying the information (data) to another table, modifying the contents of records within the current table, or even deleting records in the current table.

Because of the destructive nature of action queries, it is a good idea to observe the following rules: Always back up your table before performing the Action query, and always create and view the action query (use the Datasheet button on the toolbar) before performing it.

The process of action queries

Because action queries are irreversible, follow this four-step process when you're working with them:

1. Create the action query specifying the fields and the criteria.

2. View the records selected in the action query by clicking the Datasheet button on the toolbar.

3. Run the action query by clicking the Run button on the toolbar.

4. Check the changes in the tables by clicking the Datasheet button on the toolbar.

Caution Consider backing up your table before creating and running action queries.

If you follow these steps, you can use action queries relatively safely.

Viewing the results of an action query

Action queries perform a specific task — many times a destructive task. Be very careful when using them. It's important to view the changes that they will make (by clicking the datasheet button) before you run the action query and to verify afterward that they made the changes that you anticipated. Before you learn how to create and run an action query, it's also important to review the process for seeing what your changes will look like before you change a table permanently.

Scoping Criteria

Action queries can use any expression composed of fields, functions, and operators to specify any limiting condition that you need to place on the query. Scoping criteria are one form of record criteria. Normally, the record criteria serve as a filter to tell Access which records to find and/or leave out of the dynaset. Because action queries do not create a dynaset, you use scoping criteria to specify a set of records for Access to operate on.

Viewing a query before using update and delete queries

Before actually performing an action query, you can click the Datasheet View button to see which set of data the action query will work with. Meanwhile, when you're updating or deleting records with an action query, the actions take place on the underlying tables that the query is currently using. To view the results of an update or a delete query, click the Datasheet button to see whether the records will be updated or deleted before committing the action.

Note   If your update query made changes to the fields you used for selecting the records, you may have to look at the underlying table or change to a Select query to see the changes. For example, if you deleted a set of records with an action button, the resulting select dynaset of the same record criteria will show that no records exist — the condition specified has been performed. By removing the delete criteria, you can view the remaining table and verify that all the records specified have been deleted.

Switching to the result table of a make-table or append query

Unlike the update or delete queries, make-table and append queries copy resultant records to another table. After specifying the fields and the criteria in the QBE pane of the Query Design window, the make-table and the append queries copy the specified fields and records to another table. When you run the queries, the results take place in another table, not in the current table.

Pressing the Datasheet button shows you a dynaset of only the criteria and fields that were specified, not the actual table that contains the new or added records. To view the results of a make-table or append query, open the new table and view the contents to verify that the make-table or append query worked correctly. If you won't be using the action query again, do not save it. Delete it.

Reversing action queries

Action queries copy or change data in underlying tables. After an action query is executed, it cannot be reversed. Therefore, when you're working with action queries, create a select query first to make sure that the record criteria and selection are correct for the action query.

Caution Action queries are destructive; before performing one, always make a backup of the underlying tables. You may also consider removing the Action query from your database once the action has been performed if the query will not be used again in the future.

Creating Action Queries

Creating an action query is very similar to creating a select query. You specify the fields for the query and any scoping criteria.

In addition to specifying the fields and criteria, you must tell Access to make this query an action-specific one — Append to, Make new table, Update to, or Delete where.

Creating an update action query to change values

In this section, you learn to handle an event that requires changing many records.

Suppose that the city of Mountain View has passed an ordinance that requires horses within its borders to receive a new type of vaccination starting this year. After all of the horses have been vaccinated, you want to update your records to show that they have been vaccinated. To create this query, you work with the Customer and Pets tables and change the existing status of the Current Vaccinations field in the Pets table from No to Yes wherever the field shows a current vaccination status for Horses from Mountain View.

It's possible to update each record in a table individually by using a form or even creating a select query dynaset to make these changes in the datasheet; however, this process can take a very long time if there are many records to change. The method is not only time-consuming but also inefficient. In addition, this method lends itself to typing errors as you enter new text into fields.

The best way to handle this type of event is to use an update action query to make many changes in just one operation. You save time and eliminate many of those typos that crop up in manually edited records.

To create an update query that performs these tasks, follow a three-step process:

1. Create a select query. View the data you want to update by pressing the Datasheet button.

2. Convert the select query to an update query; then run the update query after you're satisfied that it will affect only the records you want to affect.

3. Check your results.

Creating a select query before an update action

As outlined earlier, the first step in making an update query is to create a select query. In this particular case, the query is for all customers who live in Mountain View and own horses. Perform these steps to create this query:

1. Create a new query using the Customer and Pets tables from the Mountain Animal Start database.

2. Select the City field from the Customer table and Type of Animal and Current Vaccinations fields from the Pets table.

3. Specify a criterion of Mountain View in the City field and Horse in the Type of Animal field.

   The Select Query Design window should now resemble the one in Figure 24-2. Notice that the QBE pane shows all three fields but shows criteria in only the fields City and Type of Animal.

4. Examine the datasheet to make sure that it has only the records you want to change. Return to the design surface when you're finished.

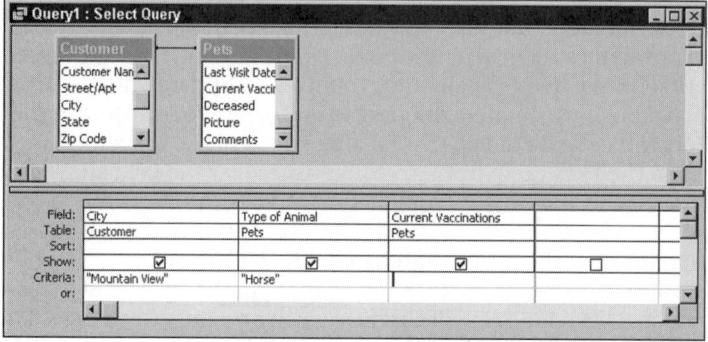

Figure 24-2: Creating a select query to be converted to Update query to change the value of the Current Vaccinations field

The select query datasheet should resemble the one shown in Figure 24-3. Notice that only the records for horses whose owners reside in Mountain View appear in the dynaset. It shows a Yes or No instead of 0 or –1 — this is done by specifying the field property Format as type Yes/No in the field Current Vaccination of the QBE pane. Your example may show zeros instead — to see Yes/No, simply specify a field property of Yes/No as the Format type for the column.

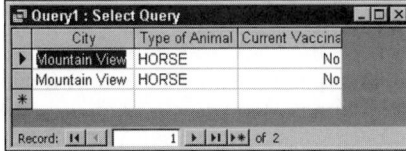

Figure 24-3: Dynaset showing only the records for horses whose owners live in Mountain View

As you see in Figure 24-3, in this case both records show No for the Current Vaccination. (In our example, this is because, prior to the passage of the ordinance of the city — as pointed out early in this section — the animals were not required to have vaccinations in this city. In reality, some animals may have been vaccinated already and may show different results.) You are now ready to convert the select query to an update query.

Converting a select query to an update query

After you create a select query and verify the selection of records, it's time to create the update query. To convert the select query to an update query, follow these steps:

1. Select Update Query from the Query Type button on the toolbar or select Query ➪ Update from the menu.

   Access changes the title of the Query window from Query1: Select Query to Query1: Update Query. Access also adds the Update To: property row to the QBE pane, above the Criteria: row.

2. In the Update To: cell of Current Vaccinations, enter Yes as shown in Figure 24-4.

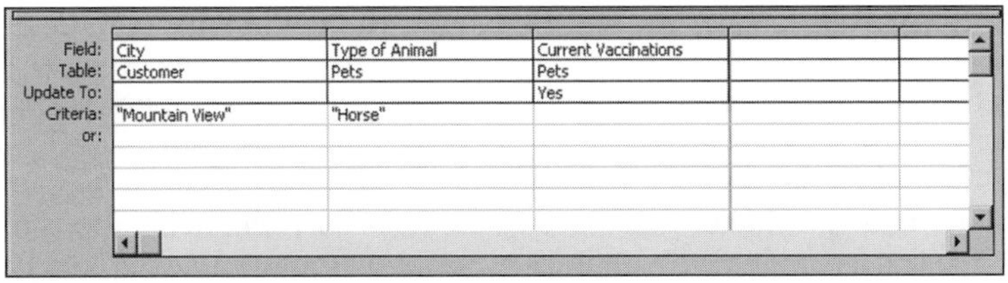

Field:	City	Type of Animal	Current Vaccinations		
Table:	Customer	Pets	Pets		
Update To:			Yes		
Criteria:	"Mountain View"	"Horse"			
or:					

Figure 24-4: The design pane for the update query. Notice that the Current Vaccination Update To: cell has "yes" in it.

3. Click the Run button on the toolbar (or select Query ➪ Run from the menu).

Access displays the dialog box shown in Figure 24-5. This dialog box displays a message: You are about to update x row[s]. Once you click Yes, you can't use the Undo command to reverse the changes. Are you sure you want to update these records? Two command buttons are presented: Yes and No. (If the Help Office Assistant balloon is active, it will display a "memory bubble" type tip or message balloon with the same information and choices.)

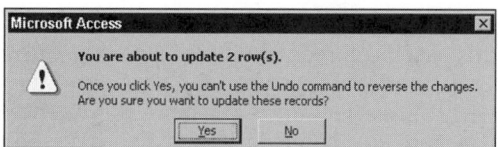

Figure 24-5: The dialog box for updating records warns you that you are about to update x row(s) and that this action is irreversible.

4. Click the Yes button to complete the query and update the records. Selecting No stops the procedure (no records are updated).

Caution   If you're changing tables that are attached to another database, you cannot cancel the query once started.

Note   You can change more than one field at a time by filling in the Update To: cell of any field that you want to change. You can also change the field contents of fields that you used for limiting the records, that is, the criteria.

Checking your results

After completing the update query, check the results by clicking the datasheet button and examining the values in the datasheet. You could have converted back to a Select query to be safe; however, the Update query can be viewed more quickly by clicking the datasheet button — the Update has already been performed at this stage.

The update made permanent changes to the field Current Vaccinations for all horses whose owners live in Mountain View. If you did not back up the Pets table before running the update query, you cannot easily restore the contents to their original Yes or No settings. (You'll need a good memory if your query affects more than a few records!)

Note   If you update a field that was used for a limiting criterion, you must change the criterion in the select query to the new value to verify the changes.

Creating a new table using a make-table query

You can use an action query to create new tables based on scoping criteria. To make a new table, you create a make-table query. Consider the following situation as an example that might give rise to this particular task and for which you would create a make-table query.

Suppose a local pet-food company has approached you for a mailing list of customers who own dogs or cats. This company wants to send these customers a coupon for a free four-pound bag of food for each animal they own. The pet-food company plans to create the mailing labels and send the form letters if you supply a table of customer information, pet names, and type of animal. The company also stipulates that, because this is a trial mailing, only those customers you've seen in the past six months should receive letters.

You have decided to send the company the requested table of information, so now you need to create a new table from the Customer and Pets tables. A make-table query will perform these actions.

Creating the make-table query

You decide to create a make-table query for all customers who own dogs or cats and who have visited you in the past six months. Perform these steps to create this query:

1. Create a new query using the Customer and Pets tables of the Mountain Animal Start database.

2. Select Make Table from the Query Type button on the toolbar.

    Access displays the Make Table dialog box, as shown in Figure 24-6.

Figure 24-6: The Make Table dialog box with a table name entered. Notice that the table can be saved in this database or another.

3. Type **Mailing List for Coupons** in the Table Name: field; press Enter or click OK. Notice that the name of the window changes from Query1: Select Query to Query1: Make Table Query.

4. Select the mailing information fields (Customer Name through ZIP Code) from the Customer table and the fields Pet Name, Type of Animal, and Last Visit Date from the Pets table.

5. Specify the criteria In("CAT","DOG") in the Type of Animal field and > Between Date() – 180 And Date() [for last six months] in the Last Visit Date field.

The Query Design window should resemble the one shown in Figure 24-7. The fields are resized so that they all appear in the QBE pane. Two fields (Type of Animal and Last Visit Date) contain criteria.

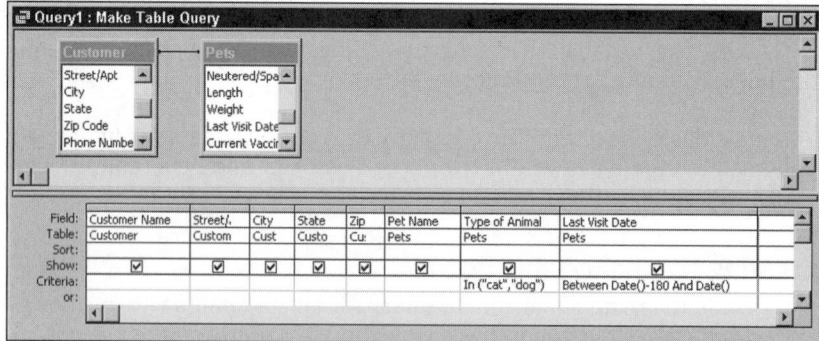

Figure 24-7: The Customer and Pets tables are in the top pane; the fields Customer Name, Street/Apt, City, State, ZIP Code, Pet Name, Type of Animal, and Last Visit Date are in the bottom pane. It has two criteria: Type of Animal must be a cat or dog and the Last Visit Date must have been in the past six months.

6. Click the Datasheet View button on the toolbar to view the dynaset (see Figure 24-8).

7. Make sure that the dynaset has only the records you specified.

8. Click the Design button to switch back to the Query Design view.

9. Deselect the Show: property of the field Last Visit Date.

You do not want to copy this field to the new table Mailing List for Coupons. Only those fields selected with a check mark in the check box of the Show: row are copied to the new table. By deselecting a field with a criteria set, you can base the scoping criteria on fields that will not be copied to the new table.

10. Click the Run button on the toolbar or select Query ➪ Run from the menu.

Access indicates how many records it will copy to the new table (see Figure 24-9).

Customer Name	Street/Apt	City	State	Zip Code	Pet Name	Type of An
All Creatures	21 Grace St.	Tall Pines	WA	987462541	Fido	DOG
Stephen Brown	555 Sycamore /	Three Corners	ID	834011023	Suzie	DOG
James Brown	3454 Adams St	Borderville	OR	974011019	John Boy	DOG
Wanda Greenfie	66 Farmaccess	Tall Pines	WA	984012201	Sammie Girl	DOG
Petra Irish	456 Bishops Ln	Lakeville	OR	974011021	D.C.	CAT
Petra Irish	456 Bishops Ln	Lakeville	OR	974011021	Jimeny	CAT
Petra Irish	456 Bishops Ln	Lakeville	OR	974011021	Shadow	CAT
Petra Irish	456 Bishops Ln	Lakeville	OR	974011021	Romeo	CAT
Petra Irish	456 Bishops Ln	Lakeville	OR	974011021	Ceasar	CAT
Petra Irish	456 Bishops Ln	Lakeville	OR	974011021	Jameo	CAT
Petra Irish	456 Bishops Ln	Lakeville	OR	974011021	Tigger	CAT
Michael Johnso	77 Farmaccess	Ranier City	WA	984012201	Rover	DOG
Adam Johnson	55 Childs Ave	Mount Pilot	ID	834121043	Fi Fi	DOG
Margaret McKin	5512 Green Acr	Borderville	OR	974121001	Rex	DOG
Margaret McKin	5512 Green Acr	Borderville	OR	974121001	Caesar	DOG
William Primen	1234 Main St	Mountain View	WA	984011011	Brutus	DOG
William Primen	1234 Main St	Mountain View	WA	984011011	Cleo	DOG
William Primen	1234 Main St	Mountain View	WA	984011011	Little Bit	CAT
Sandra Williams	2211 Main St	Mountain View	WA	984011021	Flower	CAT

Record: 1 of 19

Figure 24-8: The dynaset of cats and dogs you have seen in the past six months. In this example, the current date is before March 17, 2001. Your results will be different unless you use the same date.

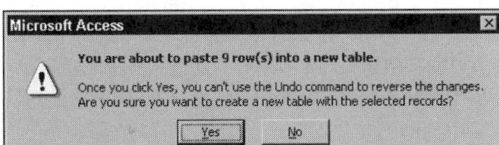

Microsoft Access

You are about to paste 9 row(s) into a new table.

Once you click Yes, you can't use the Undo command to reverse the changes. Are you sure you want to create a new table with the selected records?

Yes   No

Figure 24-9: The dialog box for copying records. If you have the Office Assistant on, it will display the message instead.

11. Click the Yes button to complete the query and make the new table. Selecting No stops the procedure (no records are copied).

When you're creating numerous make-table queries, you need to select Make Table Query from the Query Type button on the toolbar or select Query ⇨ Make Table from the menu; either method renames the make-table query each time. Access assumes that you want to overwrite the existing table if you don't reselect the make-table option. Access warns you about overwriting before performing the new make-table query; as an alternative, you could change the Destination table name on the Property sheet.

Checking your results

After you complete the make-table query, check your results by opening the new table Mailing List for Coupons, which was added to the database container (see Figure 24-10).

Customer Name	Street/Apt	City	State	Zip Code	Pet Name	Type of Animal
All Creatures	21 Grace St.	Tall Pines	WA	987462541	Fido	DOG
Stephen Brown	555 Sycamore /	Three Corners	ID	834011023	Suzie	DOG
James Brown	3454 Adams St	Borderville	OR	974011019	John Boy	DOG
Wanda Greenfie	66 Farmaccess	Tall Pines	WA	984012201	Sammie Girl	DOG
Adam Johnson	55 Childs Ave	Mount Pilot	ID	834121043	Fi Fi	DOG
Margaret McKin	5512 Green Acr	Borderville	OR	974121001	Rex	DOG
Margaret McKin	5512 Green Acr	Borderville	OR	974121001	Caesar	DOG
William Primen	1234 Main St	Mountain View	WA	98401-1011	Cleo	DOG
William Primen	1234 Main St	Mountain View	WA	98401-1011	Little Bit	CAT

Record: 1 of 9

Figure 24-10: The new table Mailing List for Coupons created from a Make Table Query

Note When you create a table from a make-table query, the fields in the new table inherit the data type and field size from the fields in the query's underlying tables; however, no other field or table properties are transferred. If you want to define a primary key or other properties, you need to edit the design of the new table.

Tip You can also use a make-table action query to create a backup of your tables before you create action queries that change the contents of the tables. Backing up a table using a make-table action query does not copy the table's properties or primary key to the new table.

Copying Any Database Object

To copy any database object (table, query, form, or other object) while you're in the Database window, follow these steps:

1. Highlight the object you need to copy.

2. Press Ctrl+C (or select Edit ⇨ Copy) to copy the object to the Clipboard.

3. Press Ctrl+V (or select Edit ⇨ Paste) to paste the object from the Clipboard.

4. Enter the new object name (table, form, and so forth) and click the OK button in the dialog box. If the object is a table, you also can specify Structure with or without the data or append it to an existing table.

Creating a query to append records

As the word append suggests, an append query attaches or adds records to a specified table. An append query adds records *from* the table you're using to another table. The table you want to add records to must already exist. You can append records to a table in the same database or in another Access database.

Append queries are very useful for adding information to another table on the basis of some scoping criteria. Even so, append queries are not always the fastest way of adding records to another database. If you need, for example, to append all fields and all records from one table to a new table, the append query is not the best way to do it. Instead, use the Copy and Paste options on the Edit menu when you're working with the table in a datasheet or form.

Note You can add records to an open table. You don't have to close the table before adding records. However, Access does not automatically refresh the view of the table that has records added to it. To refresh the table, press Shift+F9. This action requires the table so that you can see the appended records.

When you're working with append queries, be aware of these rules:

1. If the table you're appending records to has a primary key field, the records you add cannot have Null values or duplicate primary key values. If they do, Access will not append the records and you will get no warning.

2. If you add records to another database table, you must know the location and name of the database.

3. If you use the asterisk (*) field in a QBE row, you cannot also use individual fields from the same table. Access assumes that you're trying to add field contents twice to the same record and will not append the records.

4. If you append records with an AutoNumber field (an Access-specified primary key), do not include the AutoNumber field if the table you're appending to also has the field and record contents (this causes the problem specified in rule 1). Also, if you're adding to an empty table and you want the new table to have a new AutoNumber number (that is, order number) based on the criteria, do not use the AutoNumber field.

By following these simple rules, your append query will perform as expected and become a very useful tool.

Here's an example that will help illustrate the use of append queries: Every February you archive all records of animals that died during the preceding year. To archive the records, you perform two steps. First, you append them to existing backup files. Second, you delete the records from the active database.

In this case, you want to add records to the backup tables for deceased animals in your active tables. In other words, you will copy records to three tables: Pets, Visits, and Visit Details. You need three backup files to perform this exercise. To create the backup files, perform the following steps:

1. Press F11 or Alt+F1 to display the Database window.

2. Click the Tables object button to display the list of tables.

3. Click the Pets table to highlight it.

4. Press Ctrl+C (or select Edit ➪ Copy) to copy the object Pets table to the Clipboard.

5. Press Ctrl+V (or select Edit ➪ Paste) to display the Paste Table As dialog box.

6. Click Structure Only in the Paste Options section of the dialog box (or press Alt-S to select Structure Only).

7. Click the Table Name: box and type Deceased Pets Backup.

8. Click OK (or press Enter after typing the filename).

9. Open the Pets Backup table (it should be empty); then close the table.

Repeat this process for both the Visits and Visit Details tables, naming them Deceased Visits Backup and Deceased Visit Details Backup, respectively.

To create an append query that copies the deceased animals' records, follow a three-step process:

1. Create a select query to verify that only the records that you want to append are copied.

2. Convert the select query to an append query and run it.

3. Check your results.

Note   When you're using the append query, only fields with names that match in the two tables are copied. For example, you may have a small table with six fields and another with nine. The table with nine fields has only five of the six field names that match fields in the smaller table. If you append records from the smaller table to the larger table, only the five matching fields are appended; the other four fields remain blank.

Creating the select query for an append query

To create a select query for all pets that died last year, along with their visit histories, follow these steps:

1. Create a new query using the Pets, Visits, and Visit Details tables from the Customer Animal Start database.

2. Select the Deceased field from the Pets table.

3. Specify a criterion of Yes in the Deceased field.

You may want to select some additional fields from each table, such as Pet Name, Visit Date, Visit Type, Treatment Code, and so forth. The Select Query Design window should resemble the one shown in Figure 24-11. The only field and criterion that must be in this select query is the first field: Deceased. If you add any other fields, make sure that you remove them before converting this query to an append query.

4. Go to the datasheet and make sure that all the Deceased field contents say Yes (see Figure 24-12).

5. Return to design mode.

6. If you added additional fields to look at, remove all fields from the QBE pane except the Deceased field with the Criteria: of Yes.

With the select query created correctly, you are ready to convert the select query to an append query.

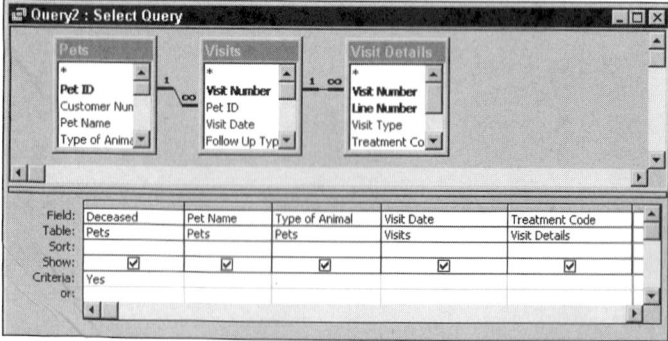

Figure 24-11: The tables Pets, Visits, and Visit Details are in the top pane, and selected fields are in the QBE pane. Only the first field must be there for an append query.

Converting to an append query

After you create the select query and verify that it is correct, you need to create the append query (actually, three different append queries — one each for the tables Visit Details, Visits, and Pets — because append queries work with only one table at a time). For this example, first copy all fields from the Visit Details table. Then copy all the fields from the Visits table. Finally, copy all the fields from the Pets table.

Deceased	Pet Name	Type of Animal	Visit Date	Treatment Code
Yes	Tom	CAT	05/22/1996	0300
Yes	Tom	CAT	05/22/1996	0102
Yes	Tom	CAT	05/22/1996	2002
Yes	Tom	CAT	10/04/1997	0303
Yes	John Boy	DOG	09/02/1998	0300
Yes	John Boy	DOG	11/03/2000	0300
Yes	Romeo	CAT	10/04/1999	0100
Yes	Romeo	CAT	10/04/1999	0101
Yes	Romeo	CAT	10/04/1999	0105
Yes	Romeo	CAT	10/04/1999	0100
Yes	Romeo	CAT	10/04/1999	0101
Yes	Romeo	CAT	10/04/1999	0102
Yes	Romeo	CAT	10/04/1999	0404

Record: 1 of 17

Figure 24-12: A dynaset of records for all deceased animals. This will be converted to an append query.

To convert the select query to an append query and run it, perform the following steps:

1. Make sure that only the Deceased field is present in the QBE pane.

2. Deselect the Show: property of the Deceased field.

3. Select Append from the Query Type button on the toolbar, or select Query ⇨ Append from the Design menu.

   Access displays the Append dialog box, as shown in Figure 24-13.

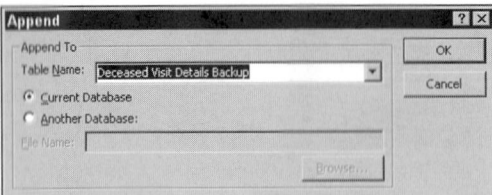

Figure 24-13: The Append dialog box. Use this box to select the table you want to append records into.

4. Type Deceased Visit Details Backup in the Table Name: field or select it from the pull-down menu and either press Enter or click OK.

5. Drag the asterisk (*) field from the Visit Details table to the QBE pane to select all fields.

   The QBE pane should look like Figure 24-14. Access automatically fills in the Append To: field under the All field-selector column.

   At this point you can click the datasheet button to see what records Access will actually append to the new table. After you view the records, you should then return to the design mode to continue with the action query.

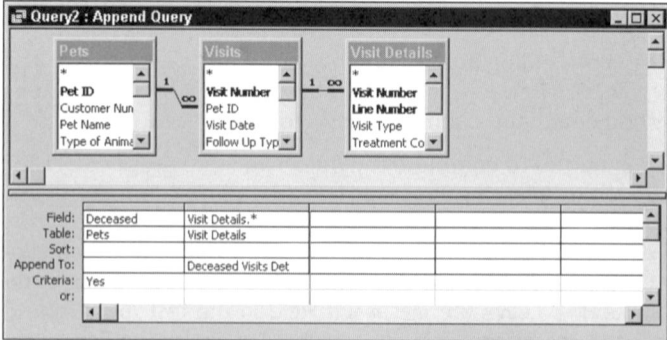

Figure 24-14: The QBE pane for an appended query. Append all deceased records from the Visits Details table into another table.

6. Click the Run button on the toolbar (or select Query ↻ Run from the menu).

Access displays a dialog box that displays the message You are about to append x row[s]. Then it presents two buttons (Yes and No). After you click Yes, the Undo command cannot be used to reverse the changes.

7. Click the Yes button to complete the query and copy (append) the records to the backup table. Selecting No stops the procedure (no records are copied).

Tip

After you have run the Append query, you may want to open the Deceased Visits Details Backup table to verify that it copied the records over — if you are following along with the example tables, it should have 17 records in the table.

After the Visit Details records for deceased animals are backed up, you are ready to append records into the Deceased Visits Backup table and the Deceased Pets Backup table. Before you append fields from these other tables, however, you must remove the previous All selector field [Visit Details.*] from the QBE pane and the Visit Details table from the top pane.

To append the Visits records, follow these steps:

1. Continuing with the same query above, delete the asterisk (*) field for the Visits Details table.

2. Remove the Visit Details table from the query.

3. Select the asterisk (*) field for the Visits table and drag it down to the QBE pane.

4. Reselect Query ↻ Append to activate the Append dialog box.

5. Type, or select, **Deceased Visits Backup** for the name of the table to append to and click the OK button.

6. Click the Run button on the toolbar (or select Query ➯ Run from the menu).

   Access displays a dialog box that displays the message You are about to append x row[s]. Then it presents two buttons (Yes and No). After you click Yes, the Undo command cannot be used to reverse the changes.

7. Click the Yes button to complete the query and copy (append) the records to the backup table. Selecting No stops the procedure (no records are copied).

Tip

To create an Append query for the Pets table, you will need to remove the Visits table from the query (which will also remove the All selector field for the [Visits.*] QBE automatically). Leave the Deceased Field in the first row of the QBE pane with a criteria of Yes. Then select the asterisk (*) field for the Pets table. Reselect Query ➯ Append, and type, or select, **Deceased Pets Backup** for the name of the table to append to. Access will add the field name **Deceased** from the Append To: cell of the Deceased Field cell — remove it from the Append To: cell — making the cell blank. Finally, click Run.

Caution

If you create an append query by using the asterisk (*) field and you also use a field from the same table as the All asterisk field to specify a criterion, you must take the criteria field name out of the Append To: row. If you don't, Access reports an error. Remember that the field for the criterion is already included in the asterisk field.

Checking your results

After you complete the three append table queries, using the Mountain Animal Start database, re-check your results. To do so, go to the Database window and select each of the three tables to be appended to (Deceased Pets Backup — 5 records, Deceased Visits Backup — 8 records, and Deceased Visit Details Backup — 17 records); view the new records.

Creating a query to delete records

Of all the action queries, the delete query is the most dangerous. Unlike the other types of queries you've worked with, delete queries wipe out records from tables permanently and irreversibly.

Like other action queries, delete queries act on a group of records on the basis of scoping criteria.

A delete action query can work with multiple tables to delete records. If you intend to delete related records from multiple tables, however, you must do the following:

✦ Define relationships between the tables in the Relationships Builder.

✦ Check the Enforce Referential Integrity option for the join between tables.

✦ Check the Cascade Delete Related Records option for the join between tables.

Figure 24-15 shows the Edit Relationships dialog box for the join line between the Pets and Visits tables. Notice that the options Enforce Referential Integrity and Cascade Delete Related Records are both selected (as is Cascade update).

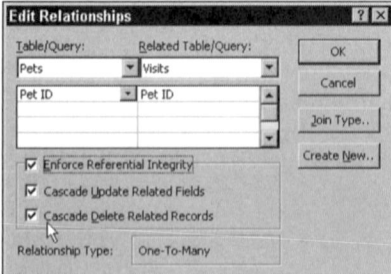

Figure 24-15: The Edit Relationships dialog box, showing that Referential Integrity is being Enforced and the Cascade Delete Related Records is active

When working with one-to-many relationships without defining relationships and putting Cascade Delete on, Access deletes records from only one table at a time. Specifically, Access deletes the many side of the relationship first. Then you must remove the many table from the query and delete the records from the one side of the query.

This method is time-consuming and awkward. Therefore, when you're deleting related records from one-to-many relationship tables, make sure that you define relationships between the tables and check the Cascade Delete box in the Relationships dialog box.

Caution Because of the permanently destructive action of a delete query, always make backup copies of your tables before working with them.

The following example illustrates the use of Access action queries. In this case, you have a large number of records to delete from the Pets, Visits, and Visit Details tables.

You are going to delete all records of deceased animals. Recall that you already copied all deceased pet records to backup tables in the append query section. The tables you're dealing with have these relationships:

✦ One pet has many visits.

✦ One visit has many visit details.

Both of these are one-to-many relationships. As a result, if you don't define permanent relationships between the tables and turn on Cascade Delete, you'll need to create three separate delete queries. (You would need to delete from the Visit Details, Visits, and Pets tables — in that order.)

With relations set and Cascade Delete on, however, you have to delete only the records from the Pets table; Access automatically deletes all related records. Assume for this example that you have already appended the records to another table — or that you have made a new table of the records that you're about to delete, set up permanent relationships among the three tables, and turned on Cascade Delete for both relationships (that is, between Pets and Visits and between Visits and Visit Details).

Creating a cascading delete query

To create a cascading delete query for all pets that died last year, along with their visit histories, perform these steps:

1. Create a new query using the Pets table only from the Mountain Animal Start database.

2. Select Query ➪ Delete from the Design menu.

   The name of the window changes from Query1: Select Query to Query1: Delete Query. A new row is added to the QBE pane – Delete:. This row is immediately above the Criteria field.

3. Select the Deceased field from the Pets table.

   The Delete: cell of the Deceased field will say "Where" in it.

4. Specify the criterion Yes in the Deceased field.

5. Select the all fields selector from the Pets table — asterisks (*) field and drag it to the QBE pane.

   The Delete: cell of the Pets.* field will say "From" in it. The Delete Query Design window is shown in Figure 24-16. Notice that it has the criteria field, Deceased, in the first column with a criteria set of Yes and the Pets.* field in the second column. The Delete: row shows a value of Where under the Deceased column and From under the Pets.* column.

6. Go to the datasheet and verify that only records that say Yes (or display a negative 1) are there.

7. Return to the Design window.

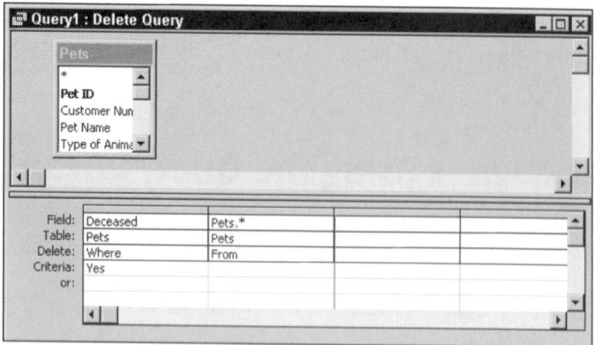

Figure 24-16: The delete query's QBE pane. The Delete: row has been added to the pane and the where and from conditions are automatically set by Access.

8. Click the Run button on the toolbar (or select Query ➪ Run from the menu).

   Access displays a dialog box with the message: You are about to delete x row[s] from the specified table (Pets). After you click Yes, you can't use the Undo command to reverse the changes. Are you sure that you want to delete the selected records? In this case it will report you are about to delete 5 rows from the Pets table. However, Access will also automatically delete the 8 rows from the Visits table and the 17 rows from the Visit Details table. It will not report how many rows will be deleted from the other tables that are linked to the table you selected.

9. Click the Yes button to complete the query.

   The records are removed from all three tables. When you click Yes, Access deletes the records in the Pets table and then automatically deletes the related records in the Visits and Visit Details tables. Selecting No stops the procedure (no records are deleted).

Remember that a delete query permanently and irreversibly removes the records from the table(s). Therefore, it is important that the records to be deleted are backed up before they are deleted.

Checking your results

After completing the delete query, you can check your results by pressing the Datasheet button on the toolbar. If the delete query worked correctly, you will see no records in the datasheet.

You have now deleted all records of deceased animals from the database tables Pets, Visits, and Visit Details.

Tip Delete queries remove entire records, not just the data in specific fields. If you need to delete only values in specific fields, use an update query to change the values to empty values.

Creating other queries using the Query Wizards

In the preceding chapter, you learned to use a Query Wizard to create a crosstab query. Access has two other Wizards that can help maintain your databases:

✦ Find Duplicate Query Wizard, which shows duplicate records in a single table on the basis of a field in the table.

✦ Find Unmatched Query Wizard, which shows all records that do not have a corresponding record in another table (for example, a customer with no pets or a pet with no owner).

The Find Duplicate Query Wizard works on a single table. The Find Unmatched Query Wizard compares records from one table with another.

These Wizards (along with all the others, such as the Crosstab Wizard) are listed when you first start a new query.

Find Duplicate Query Wizard

This Wizard helps you create a query that reports which records in a table are duplicated using a field or fields in the table as a basis. Access asks which fields you want to use for checking duplication and then prompts you to enter some other fields that you may want to see in the query. Finally, Access asks for a title and then it creates and displays the query.

This type of Wizard query can help you find duplicate key violations, a valuable trick when you want to take an existing table and make a unique key field with existing data. If you try to create a unique key field and Access reports an error, you know that you have either Nulls in the field or duplicate records. The query helps find the duplicates.

Find Unmatched Query Wizard

This Wizard helps you create a query that reports any orphan or widow records between two tables.

An orphan is a record in a many-side table that has no corresponding record in the one-side table. For example, you may have a pet in the Pets table that does not have an owner in the Customer table (the pet is an orphan).

A widow is a record in the one side of a one-to-many or one-to-one table that does not have a corresponding record in the other table. For example, you may have a customer who has no animals in the Pets table.

Access asks for the names of the two tables to compare; it also asks for the link field name between the tables. Access prompts you for the fields that you want to see in the first table and for a title. Then it creates the query.

This type of query can help find records that have no corresponding records in other tables. If you create a relationship between tables and try to set referential integrity, but Access reports that it cannot activate the feature, some records are violating integrity. This query helps find them quickly.

For instance, in the Mountain Animal Start database, you were not able to specify Enforce Referential Integrity between the Customer and Pets table when specifying Relationships in the Relationship builder. This is due to the fact that there are *orphan* records in the Pets table. (In addition to an orphan record, there is a widow record — a Customer without pets; however, this will not affect referential integrity.) Using this Wizard you can quickly find and remove these orphan and widow records — thus going back and setting referential integrity between the two tables in the Relationship builder.

To create an unmatched record from Customers to Pets (Customers with no pets) query, in the Mountain Animal Start database, using the Wizard, perform these steps:

1. Select the Query button and press the New button of the Query container of the Database window.

   Access displays the New Query window.

2. Select Find Unmatched Query Wizard from the choices and double-click it or click OK.

   The Find Unmatched Query Wizard first screen appears, as in Figure 24-17.

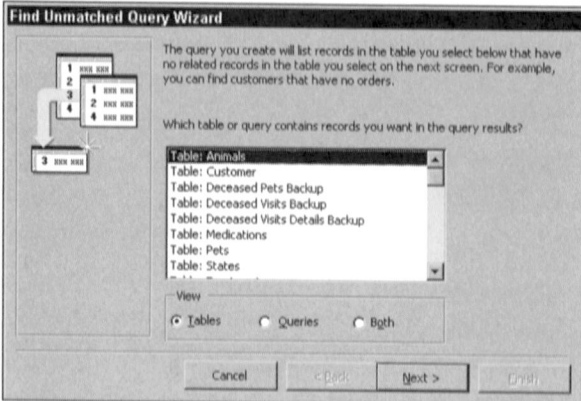

Figure 24-17: The first screen of the Unmatched Query Wizard. Here is where you select the Customer table.

3. Select the Customer table from the first screen of the Wizard by either high-lighting it and pressing the Next button or double-clicking the Customer table name.

Figure 24-18 shows the second screen that the Wizard displays. Here you select the second table to match against.

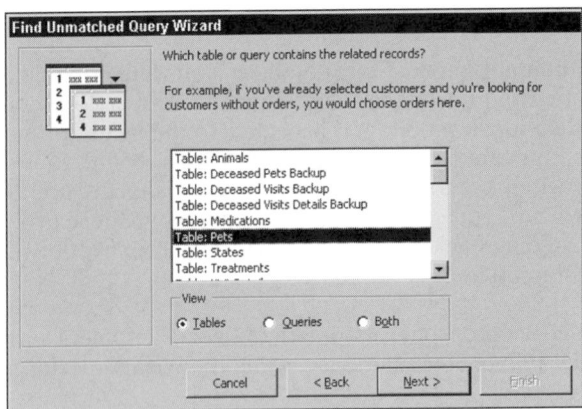

Figure 24-18: This is the second screen, where you select the Pets table.

4. Select the Pets table from the choices and press the Next button.

5. Make sure the Customer number field is highlighted in both tables as in Figure 24-19 and click the Next button.

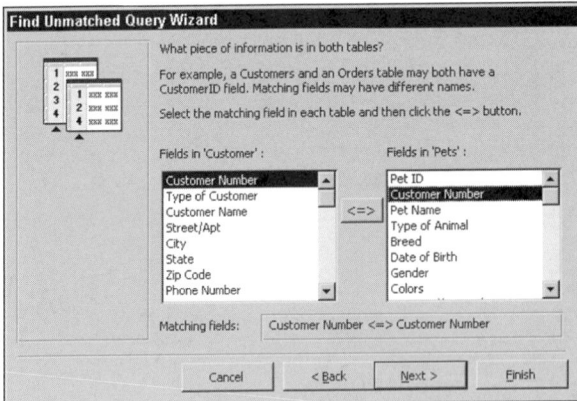

Figure 24-19: This is the third screen, where you verify the common or linked field.

6. Select the fields you wish to see in the query — Customer Number, Customer Name, City, and State. Then press the Next button for the final screen, which is show in Figure 24-20.

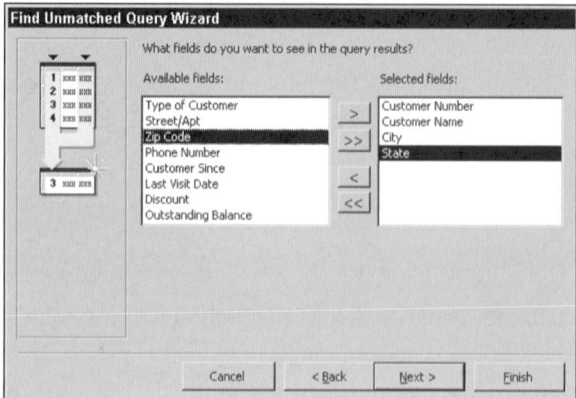

Figure 24-20: This is the fourth screen, where you select fields to see in the query.

7. In the final screen you can specify a new name for the query — simply accept the default name — Customer Without Matching Pets, and click the Finish button.

After the Query is created and you press the Finish button, Access automatically opens the query and shows any records that are widows (Customers with *no* Pets). Figure 24-21 shows one record that was found having no pets — Carla Jones, Customer Number JO003.

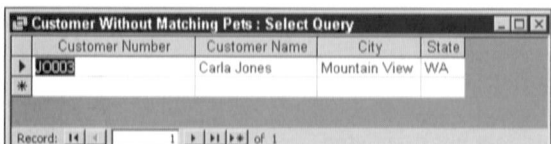

Figure 24-21: The datasheet shows the results of the Find Unmatched Query created with the Wizard.

After you have created the wizard, you can easily delete this single record by selecting it in the datasheet and pressing the delete key. Then answer Yes to "are you sure you want to delete these records?" The unmatched record will be removed from the Customer table.

However, this will not resolve your problem of setting up referential integrity between the Customer and Pets tables. There is actually a pet record that has no owner record associated with it in the Mountain Animal Start database. So you need to remove all orphaned Pets records (Pets records that have no Customer) before setting up Referential integrity between the two tables. To accomplish this, follow these steps:

1. Select the Query button and press the New button of the Query container of the Database window.

2. Select Find Unmatched Query Wizard from the choices.

3. Select the PETS table from the first screen of the Wizard and press the Next button.

4. Select the CUSTOMER table from the choices and press the Next button.

5. Make sure the Customer Number field is highlighted in both tables and press the Next button.

6. Select the fields you wish to see in the query — Pet ID, Customer Number, Pet Name, and Type of Animal. Then press the Next button for the final screen.

7. In the final screen you can specify a new name for the query — simply accept the default name — Pets Without Matching Customer and press the Finish button.

As Figure 24-22 shows, Access displays a single record — a dog named Brownie with a Customer Number of IZ001. This is the bad record that is disallowing setting up of referential integrity between the Customer and Pets table. You can now remove this record and go back and create referential integrity between the two tables in the Relationship builder.

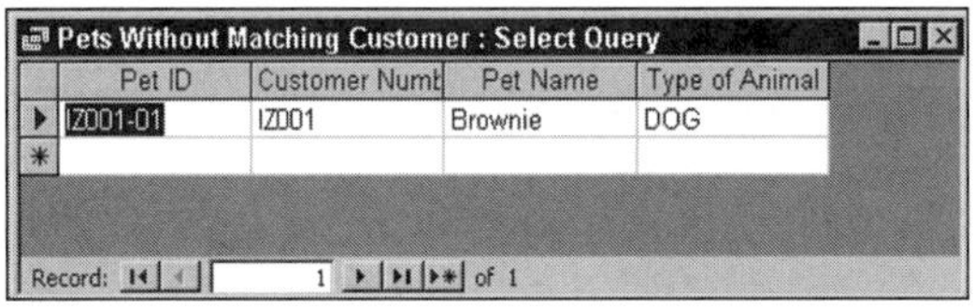

Figure 24-22: A single pet record that has no related Customer record. This orphan record was found by creating a query using the Find Unmatched Query Wizard.

Saving an action query

Saving an action query is just like saving any other query. From design mode, you can save the query and continue working by clicking the Save button on the toolbar (or by selecting File ↪ Save from the Query menu). If this is the first time you're saving the query, Access prompts you for a name in the Save As dialog box.

You can also save the query and exit by either selecting File ➪ Close from the menu or double-clicking the Control menu button (in the top-left corner of the Query window) and answering Yes to this dialog box question: Save changes to the design of '<query name>'? You also can save the query by pressing F12.

Running an action query

After you save an action query, you can run it by double-clicking its name in the Query container (window). Access will warn you that an action query is about to be executed and ask for confirmation before it continues with the query.

Troubleshooting Action Queries

When you're working with action queries, you need to be aware of several potential problems. While you're running the query, any of several messages may appear, including messages that several records were lost because of key violations or that records were locked during the execution of the query. This section discusses some of these problems and how to avoid them.

Data-type errors in appending and updating

If you attempt to enter a value that is not appropriate for the specified field, Access doesn't enter the value; it simply ignores the incorrect values and converts the fields to Null values. When you're working with append queries, Access will append the records, but the fields may be blank!

Key violations in action queries

When you attempt to append records to another database that has a primary key, Access will not append records that contain the same primary key value.

Access does not enable you to update a record and change a primary key value to an existing value. You can change a primary key value to another value under these conditions:

- ✦ The new primary key value does not already exist.
- ✦ The field value you're attempting to change is not related to fields in other tables.

Access does not enable you to delete a field on the one side of a one-to-many relationship without first deleting the records from the many side.

Access does not enable you to append or update a field value that will duplicate a value in a unique index field—one that has the Index property set to Yes (No Duplicates).

Record-locked fields in multi-user environments

Access will not perform an action query on records locked by another user. When you're performing an update or append query, you can choose to continue and change all other values. But remember this: If you enable Access to continue with an action query, you won't be able to determine which records were left unchanged!

Text fields

When appending or updating to a Text field that is smaller than the current field, Access truncates any text data that doesn't fit in the new field. Access does not warn you that it has truncated the information.

✦   ✦   ✦

Advanced Query Topics

In This Chapter

Using calculated fields

Understanding what happens when queries are saved

Hiding fields and columns

Sorting fields and using existing indexes

Setting query design options

Setting query properties

Viewing and using SQL statements

In this chapter, you work with queries in greater detail and complexity than in earlier chapters. So far, you have worked with all types of queries: select, action, crosstab, and parameter. You have not, however, worked with all the options that can be used with these types of queries.

This chapter focuses on a wide range of advanced query topics. You will read several topics that were explained in other chapters; this chapter addresses them in greater detail. A firm understanding of advanced queries can prevent unexpected problems when running the queries and interpreting the results of your queries.

Using Lookup Tables and Joins

A lookup table is used to validate the entry of data or find additional information based on a key value. Such a table uses, by definition, a many-to-one relationship; many records in the primary table can reference information from one record in the lookup table. A lookup table can be permanent or transient:

- ✦ **Permanent.** Created solely for lookup purposes
- ✦ **Transient.** Used as either a lookup table or a primary table

The Mountain Animal Hospital database has four permanent lookup tables: States, Pets, Treatments, and Medications.

Note The examples in this chapter use the Mountain Animal Start database, which has the same exact tables as the Mountain Animal Hospital database.

Using the DLookUp( ) Function for Lookup Tables

Another way to find specific lookup information based on a field is to create a calculated field using the DLookUp( ) function. DLookUp( ) finds information in a table that is not currently open. While it can be easy to program and works well with small amounts of records, if your tables contain more than 5,000 records you should do this with DAO code (see Chapters 31 and 32). This is the general syntax for the DLookUp( ) function:

```
DLookUp("[Field to display]", "[Lookup Table]", "<Criteria for
Search>")
```

"[Field to display]" in quotation marks is the field in the lookup table you want to find.

"[Lookup Table]" in quotation marks is the table containing the field you want to display.

"<Criteria for Search>" in quotation marks signifies criteria used by the lookup function.

Access suggests that Criteria for Search is not necessary, but if you want to use a different criterion for each record, it is essential. When you use DLookUp( ), the format of your criteria is critical. The syntax of Criteria for Search is as follows:

```
"[Field in Lookup Table] = '<Example Data>' "
```

You can replace the equal operator with any valid Access operator.

'<Example Data>' in single quotation marks is usually a literal, such as 'DOG' or 'AC001'. If the data is a field in the current table, you must use the following syntax:

```
"& [Field in This Table] & "
```

Notice that the field is surrounded with double quotation marks (") and ampersands (&).

Although using the DLookUp( ) function to build a calculated field seems complex, it can be a simple way to create a query for use by a form or report. To create a query that finds the medication name and treatment in the Treatments and Medications tables, follow these steps:

1. Select the Visit Details table from the Mountain Animal Start database, in the query design window.

2. Double-click the Visit Type field in the Visit Details table.

3. In an empty field in the QBE pane, type: Treatment Type:DLookUp ("[Treatment]", "[Treatments]","[Treatment Code]="&[Visit Details]. [Treatment Code]&""").

   Note: Before the &[Visit Details] is a single quotation, then a double quotation mark.

   After [Treatment Code]& is a double, then a single, then another double quotation mark.

4. In another empty field in the QBE pane, type Medication Type: DLookUp ("[Medication Name]", "[Medications]","[Medication Code] = '"&[Visit Details]. [Medication Code]&""").

When you enter the field name of the current table in the criteria for the DLookUp( ) function, you must not use spaces. After the equal sign, type the entry in this format:

```
single quote - double quote - ampersand - [field name] -
ampersand - double quote - single quote - double quote
```

No spaces can be entered between the quotation marks (single or double).

Figure 25-3 shows how the query looks after the calculated fields Treatment Type and Medication Type are entered. Notice that you don't see the entire formula you entered.

If you're having problems typing in Steps 3 or 4, press Shift+F2 to activate the Zoom window. After activating the window, the entire contents will be highlighted; press F2 again to deselect the contents and move to the end of them.

If you now select the Datasheet option using the Query View button on the toolbar, you see a datasheet similar to Figure 25-4. Notice that several records have no medication name, because these treatments required no medication. The results should be identical with the method shown in Figure 25-2 (less the Visit Number column).

The Customer table is an example of a transient lookup table. When you're working with a form to add pet personal information (name, type, and so on), the Customer table becomes a lookup table based on the customer number. Although the Customer table is a primary table of the database, in this case it becomes a lookup table for the Pets table.

Working with lookup tables in queries requires an understanding of joins and how they work. For example, you may be interested in displaying visit details along with the specific treatment and medication given for each visit. Treatment and medication information comes from the lookup tables — in this case, Treatments and Medications. To create this query, follow these steps:

1. Select the Visit Details, Treatments, and Medications tables, from the Mountain Animal Start database, and join them if they are not already joined using standard inner joins (the value must be found in both tables from Visit Details to Treatments and Visit Details to Medications).

2. Double-click the Visit Number field in the Visit Details table.

3. Double-click the Visit Type field in the Visit Details table.

4. Double-click the Treatment field of the Treatments table.

5. Double-click the Medication Name field of the Medications table.

Your query should look like Figure 25-1. Notice that Visit Details uses both Treatments and Medications as lookup tables.

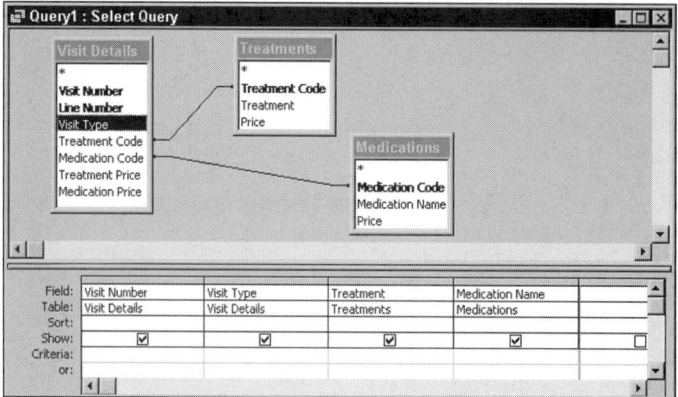

Figure 25-1: Creating a query with two lookup tables. Treatments and Medications are the lookup tables for Visits Details.

After you create the query, select the Datasheet option from the Query View button on the toolbar to display a dynaset similar to the one in Figure 25-2. (Clicking once toggles back and forth between the Design view and the Datasheet. Clicking the drop-down arrow displays all three options: Query View, Datasheet, and SQL.)

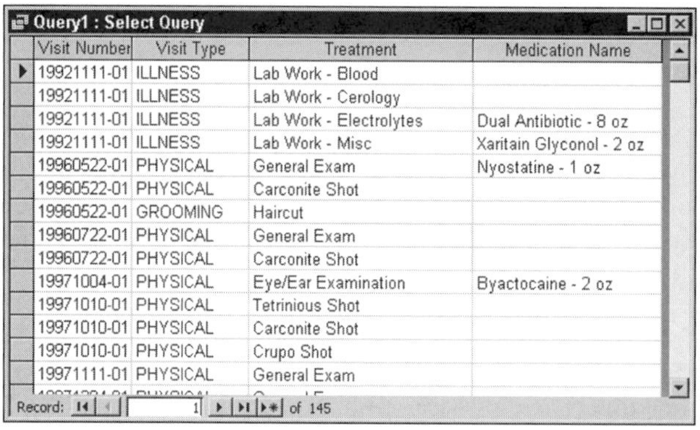

Visit Number	Visit Type	Treatment	Medication Name
► 19921111-01	ILLNESS	Lab Work - Blood	
19921111-01	ILLNESS	Lab Work - Cerology	
19921111-01	ILLNESS	Lab Work - Electrolytes	Dual Antibiotic - 8 oz
19921111-01	ILLNESS	Lab Work - Misc	Xaritain Glyconol - 2 oz
19960522-01	PHYSICAL	General Exam	Nyostatine - 1 oz
19960522-01	PHYSICAL	Carconite Shot	
19960522-01	GROOMING	Haircut	
19960722-01	PHYSICAL	General Exam	
19960722-01	PHYSICAL	Carconite Shot	
19971004-01	PHYSICAL	Eye/Ear Examination	Byactocaine - 2 oz
19971010-01	PHYSICAL	Tetrinious Shot	
19971010-01	PHYSICAL	Carconite Shot	
19971010-01	PHYSICAL	Crupo Shot	
19971111-01	PHYSICAL	General Exam	

Record: ◄ ◄ 1 ► ►I ►* of 145

Figure 25-2: The resulting Datasheet of the query created with two lookup tables

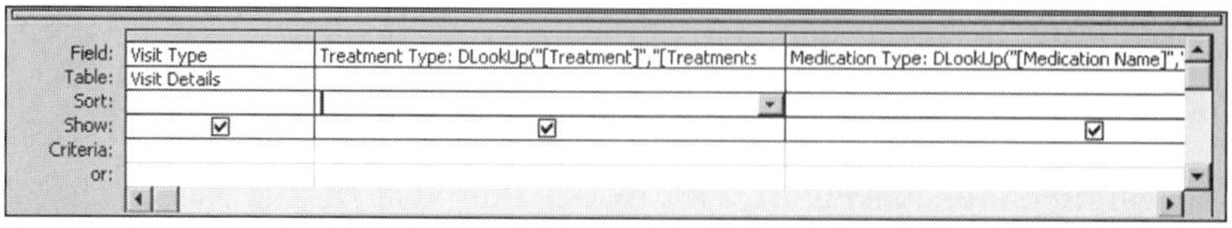

Field:	Visit Type	Treatment Type: DLookUp("[Treatment]","[Treatments	Medication Type: DLookUp("[Medication Name]",
Table:	Visit Details		
Sort:			
Show:	☑	☑	☑
Criteria:			
or:			

Figure 25-3: The QBE pane showing two calculated fields using the DLookUp( ) function

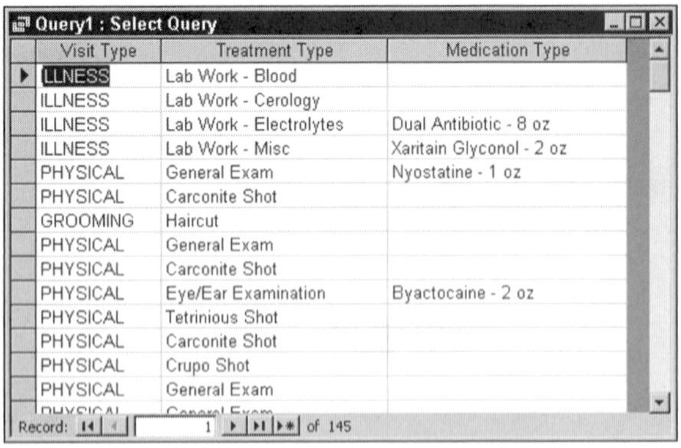

Figure 25-4: The resulting datasheet using the DLookUp function for two fields

Using Calculated Fields

Queries are not limited to actual fields from tables; you can also use calculated fields (created by performing some calculation). A calculated field can be created in many different ways, including the following:

✦ Concatenating two Text type fields using the ampersand (&)

✦ Performing a mathematical calculation on two Number type fields

✦ Using an Access function to create a field based on the function

In the next example, you create a simple calculated field, Total Due, from the Outstanding Balance and Discount fields in the Customer table by following these steps:

1. Create a new query by using the Customer table.

2. Select the Outstanding Balance and Discount fields from the Customer table.

3. Click an empty Field: cell of the QBE pane.

4. Press Shift+F2 to activate the Zoom box (or right-mouse click and select Zoom).

5. Type Total Due: Format([Outstanding Balance]-[Outstanding Balance]* [Discount],"currency").

6. Click the OK button in the Zoom box (or press Enter).

Figure 25-5 shows the expression from Step 5 being built in the Zoom window. Total Due is the calculated field name for the expression. The field name and expression are separated by a colon.

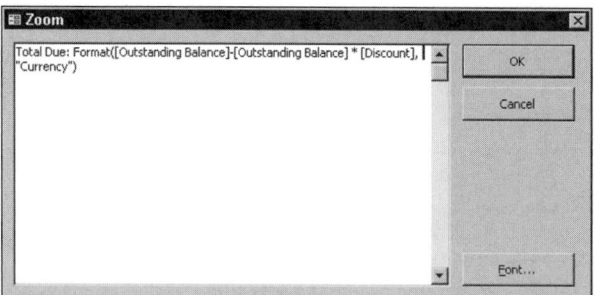

Figure 25-5: Creating a simple calculated field

Access 2002 has an Expression Builder that helps you create any expression, such as a complex calculated field for a query. In the next example, you create a calculated field named Next Visit Date that displays a date six months in the future. You can use this date for a letter you plan to send to all customers; the date is based on the Last Visit Date field of the Pets table. To create this calculated field, follow these steps:

1. Create a new query using the Pets table from the Mountain Animal Start database.

2. Select the Type of Animal and Last Visit Date fields from the Pets table.

3. Click an empty Field: cell in the QBE pane.

4. Activate the Expression Builder by clicking the Build button on the toolbar (fourth from right side, the wand with three stars to the left and three dots across the bottom). Another method is to right-click to display the shortcut menu and select Build, while in an empty Field: cell of the QBE pane.

   Access displays the Expression Builder dialog box, as shown in Figure 25-6.

   In the next several steps you will build the expression DateAdd("m",6,[Pets]![Last Visit Date]) for the calculated field. The DateAdd function adds a specified number of days, weeks, months, quarters, or years to another date. In this example, it is adding six months to the Last Visit Date value.

5. Go to the bottom-left window of the Expression Builder dialog box and expand the Functions tree by double-clicking it.

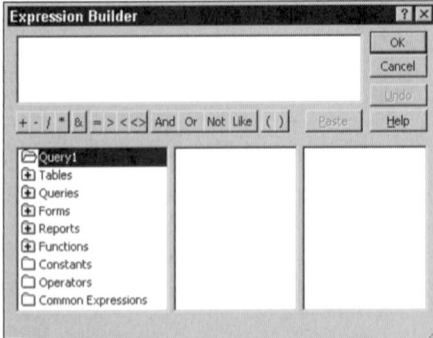

Figure 25-6: The Expression Builder dialog box. This dialog box can be used to create any type of expression you want.

6. Select the Built-in Functions choice (double-click it).

   Access places information in the two panes to the right of the one you're in (see Figure 25-7).

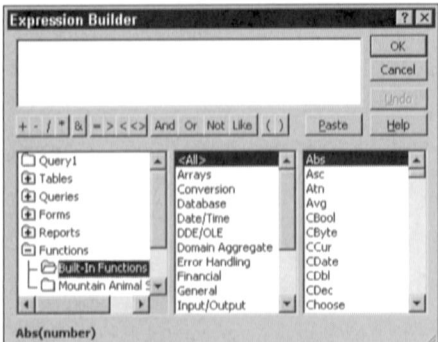

Figure 25-7: Expanding the Built-In Functions choice of the first window opens the other two, displaying a multitude of functions.

7. Go to the third window (which lists all the functions).

   You could have gone to column two first and selected Date/Time function type. This would cause Access to only display date/time functions in the third column. However, this step was skipped because the third column has all functions and you can just as easily find the one needed in this example.

8. Move down through the column and select the DateAdd function (double-click it).

Access places the function in the top-left window, with information about the three necessary parameters.

9. Go to the top-left window and click the parameter <interval>.

10. Once the parameter is highlighted, simply type "m" (quotation mark, m, quotation mark).

11. Click <number> and replace it with 6.

12. Click <date> to highlight it.

The function should look like the one in Figure 25-8.

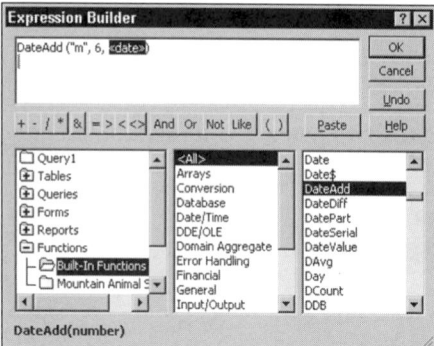

Figure 25-8: The Expression builder being used to create a calculated field. The <date> parameter needs to be replaced with a field name.

13. Go back to the bottom-left window; double-click Tables.

14. Select the Pets table (click it once).

Access moves the parameter <value> into the third, rightmost, column.

15. Select [Last Visit Date] from the middle window on the bottom (double-click it).

Access places the table and field names (separated by an exclamation mark) in the last part of the DateAdd function.

16. Click OK in the Expression Builder.

Access returns you to the QBE pane and places the expression in the cell for you.

17. Access assigns a name for the expression automatically, labeling it Expr1. Should your field now show this name, change it from Expr1 to Next Visit Date by overwriting it.

If you perform these steps correctly and widen the column to display the entire expression, the cell should look like Figure 25-9. The DateAdd( ) function enables you to add six months to the field Last Visit Date in the Pets table. The m signifies that you are working with months rather than days or years.

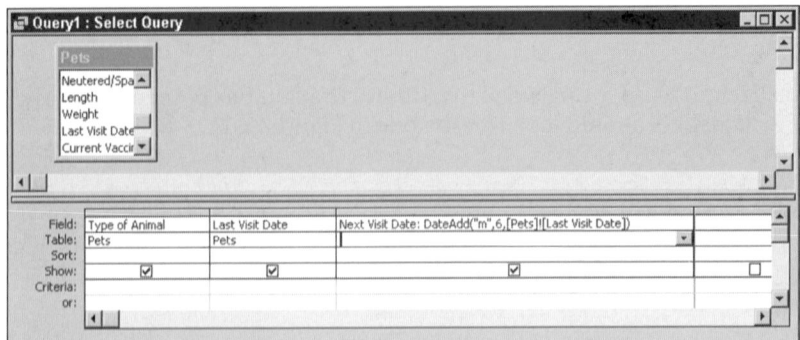

Figure 25-9: A query showing a calculated field build in the Expression builder and named Next Visit Date.

Of course, you could type in the calculated field, but the Expression Builder is a valuable tool when you're creating complex, hard-to-remember expressions.

Finding the Number of Records in a Table or Query

To determine quickly the total number of records in an existing table or query, use the Count(*) function. This is a special parameter of the Count( ) function. For example, to determine the total number of records in the Pets table, follow these steps:

1. Start a new query using the Pets table.

2. Click the first empty Field: cell in the QBE pane.

3. Type Count(*) in the cell.

Access adds the calculated field name Expr1 to the cell in front of the Count( ) function. Your query's QBE pane should now look like Figure 25-10. This query as created is pretty useless, since you can obtain the same information by simply selecting fields and setting no conditions in a query and then looking at the bottom of the datasheet on the navigation line when you view it.

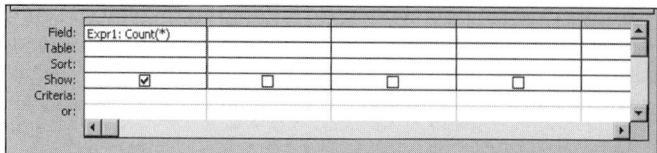

Figure 25-10: The QBE pane of a query using the Count(*) function

The datasheet now has a single cell that shows the number of records for the Pets table. The datasheet should look like the one in Figure 25-11.

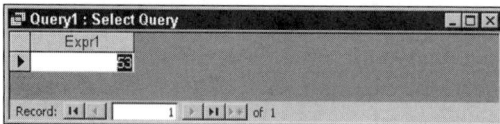

Figure 25-11: The datasheet of a Count(*) function
for the Pets table

If you use this function with the asterisk wildcard (*), this is the only field that can be shown in the datasheet, although you can use additional fields to set a criterion.

The Count(*) function can also be used to determine the total number of records that match a specific criterion. For example, you may want to know how many cats you have in the Pets table. Follow these steps to ascertain the number of cats in the table:

1. Start a new query and select the Pets table.
2. Click the first empty Field: cell in the QBE pane.
3. Type Count(*) in the cell.
4. Double-click the Type of Animal field of the Pets table.
5. Deselect the Show: cell for Type of Animal.
6. Type CAT in the Criteria: cell for Type of Animal.
7. Go back to the first cell Expr1:Count(*).
8. Replace Expr1: with Total Cats:.

Figure 25-12 shows how the query should look. If you select the Datasheet option from the Query View button on the toolbar, Access again displays only one cell in the datasheet; it contains the number of cats in the Pets table. You could have given the Count(*) expression any name such as "Total Number of Cats in Pets Table" instead of using "Total Cats"; you could have left the default expression name of Expr1 if you wished. Renaming the default Expr1 to something more understandable makes the datasheet value more understandable.

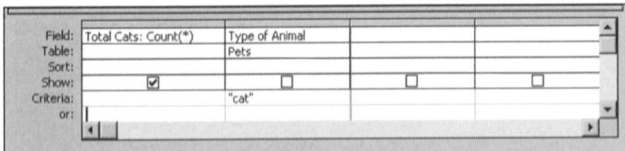

Figure 25-12: The query QBE pane that is used to show the number of cats

Remember that only the field that contains the Count(*) function can be shown in the datasheet. If you try to display any additional fields, Access reports an error.

Finding the Top (n) Records in a Query

Access not only enables you to find the number of records in an existing table or query, but also provides the capability of finding the query's first (n) records (that is, a set number or percentage of its records).

Suppose that you want to identify the top 10 animals that you have treated—in other words, for which animal has which owner paid the most to your business? To determine the top 10 animals and their owners, follow these steps:

1. Create a new query using the Customer, Pets, and Visits tables.

2. Select Customer Name from the Customer Table, Pet Name and Type of Animal from the Pets table, and Total Amount from the Visits table.

3. Click the Totals button (_) on the toolbar.

4. Change Group By (under the Total Amount field) to Sum.

5. Sort the Total Amount field in Descending order.

   The resulting query should look like the one in Figure 25-13.

6. Click the Top Values combo box next to the Total button (_) on the toolbar.

7. Enter 10 in the Top Values property cell.

   If you click the selection arrow of the Top Values combo box, you will see a series of default values — 5, 25, 100, 5%, 25%, and all. You can select one of these or type in your own value as was done here — 10.

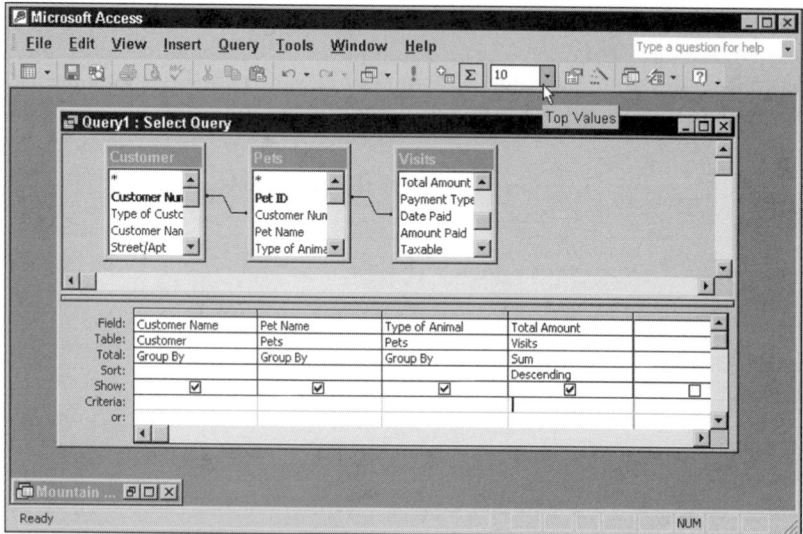

Figure 25-13: A total query with three Group By fields. Notice the arrow is pointing to the Top Values combo box on the toolbar.

You are ready to run your query. When you click the Query View button on the toolbar, you should see the top 10 money-producing records in the dynaset, which should look like Figure 25-14. The three Group By columns sum any data with the Customer Name, Type of Animal, and Pet Name. While the Pet Name is theoretically unique, this technique enables you to display each of the values so that you can see the Customer Name and Type of Animal.

Customer Name	Pet Name	Type of Animal	SumOfTotal Amount
George Green	Adam	FROG	$1,239.50
Animal Kingdom	Margo	SQUIRREL	$1,162.50
Karen Rhodes	Golden Girl	HORSE	$793.00
Johnathan Adams	Patty	PIG	$622.00
All Creatures	Presto Chango	LIZARD	$570.00
Petra Irish	D.C.	CAT	$495.80
William Primen	Brutus	DOG	$431.00
Petra Irish	Tigger	CAT	$410.00
Sandra Williams	Flower	CAT	$360.00
William Primen	Little Bit	CAT	$332.50

Figure 25-14: Datasheet view of the dynaset of the top ten money-producing pets in a query

SQL-Specific Queries

Access has three query types that cannot be created by using the QBE pane; instead, you type the appropriate SQL (Structured Query Language) statement directly in the SQL view window. These SQL-specific queries are as follows:

✦ Union query: Combines fields from more than one table or query into one recordset.

✦ Pass-through query: Enables you to send SQL commands directly to ODBC (Open Database Connectivity) databases using the ODBC database's SQL syntax.

✦ Data definition query: Enables you to create or alter database tables or create indexes in a database, such as Access databases directly.

To create any of these queries, select from the Query ⇨ SQL Specific menu the type you want to create. (No applicable button is available on the toolbar.)

In addition to these three special SQL-specific queries, you can use SQL in a sub-query (inside a standard Access query) to define a field or define criteria for a field.

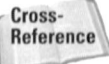

Cross-Reference
The "Understanding SQL" section at the end of this chapter provides a primer on SQL. You may want to read it before diving into the following SQL Queries.

Creating union queries

Union queries enable you to quickly combine fields from several tables or queries into one field. The resultant snapshot (like a dynaset) is not updateable.

For example, suppose a competing veterinarian retires and gives you all the client records from her practice. You decide to create a union query to combine the data from both practices and examine it. You will need to take your original Customer table (with 24 records) and combine it with the records from the New Customer table (9 records). Figure 25-15 shows a union query that returns the customer name, customer number, city, and state in order (by customer number). To create this query, follow these steps:

1. Create a new query using no tables (close the Show Table dialog box without adding tables).

2. Select Query ⇨ SQL Specific ⇨ Union from the Query Design menu bar.

   An SQL window is opened. This window is used to type in the Union Query that you wish to create.

3. Type **SELECT [Customer Name], [Customer Number], [City], [State] FROM Customer** on the first line.

4. Press Enter to move down a line in the SQL window.

5. Type **UNION SELECT [Customer Name], [Customer Number], [City], [State] FROM [New Customer]** on the second line of the SQL window.

The fields being specified for the union *must* be the same as those in the first table.

6. Press Enter to move down to another blank line in the SQL window.

7. Type **ORDER BY [Customer Number];** (ends with semi-colon) on the third line.

Your query should look similar to the one in Figure 25-15. You do not have to have a blank line between each of the parts of the statement as in the one shown in Figure 25-15.

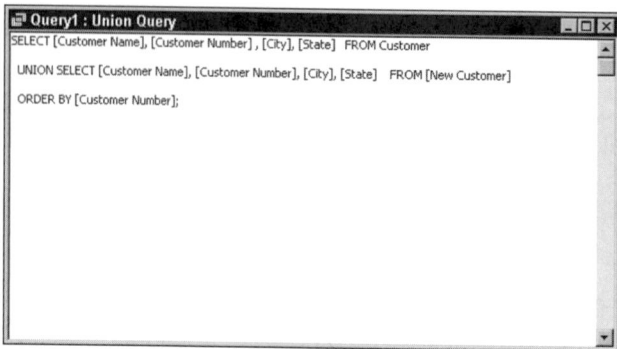

Figure 25-15: An SQL union query that combines the field contents of two different tables to be displayed as a single dynaset

Notice that a union query has two or more SQL SELECT statements. Each SELECT statement requires the same number of fields, in the same order.

If you run this query you will see the information requested in order by Customer Number as shown in Figure 25-16. If you look closely at records 14 and 15 you will see that they both have the same Customer Number — GR001, although they have different names (George Green and George Grunge). There are other records in this datasheet that also have duplicate Customer Numbers.

Note   The dynaset created from a Union query is not updateable.

This union dynaset comprises 32 records (combining 24 from the Customers and 9 from the New Customers tables). One record seems to be missing. It must be a duplicate record.

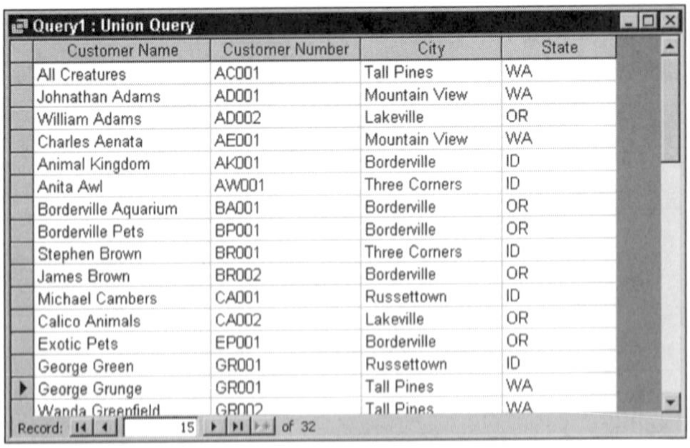

Query1 : Union Query

Customer Name	Customer Number	City	State
All Creatures	AC001	Tall Pines	WA
Johnathan Adams	AD001	Mountain View	WA
William Adams	AD002	Lakeville	OR
Charles Aenata	AE001	Mountain View	WA
Animal Kingdom	AK001	Borderville	ID
Anita Awl	AW001	Three Corners	ID
Borderville Aquarium	BA001	Borderville	OR
Borderville Pets	BP001	Borderville	OR
Stephen Brown	BR001	Three Corners	ID
James Brown	BR002	Borderville	OR
Michael Cambers	CA001	Russettown	ID
Calico Animals	CA002	Lakeville	OR
Exotic Pets	EP001	Borderville	OR
George Green	GR001	Russettown	ID
George Grunge	GR001	Tall Pines	WA
Wanda Greenfield	GR002	Tall Pines	WA

Record: 15 of 32

Figure 25-16: The resulting dynaset of the union query shown in Figure 25-15

When you use Union command in the SQL SELECT statement, it copies only those records that are NOT duplicates when it joins the tables. The contents of all the fields being selected in the SQL Union query determine if duplication exists. If two records have the same contents in all the fields selected, they are considered duplicates and only one record will be displayed. If there are other fields, not used in the Union query, that have different values, they are not used to determine duplicity. If you want to see all records from the Union of two tables, simply use the keyword ALL after the UNION command; that is, UNION ALL SELECT. If you add this to the example above you will see two records for AC001 - All Creatures (one from the Customer table, one from the New Customer table). And a record count of 33.

Creating pass-through queries

A pass-through query sends SQL commands directly to an SQL database server (such as Microsoft SQL Server, Oracle, and so on). Often these database servers are known as the back-end of the system; with Access being the client tool or front end. You send the command by using the syntax required by the particular server. Be sure to consult the documentation for the appropriate SQL database server.

You can use pass-through queries to retrieve records or change data, or to run a server-side stored procedure or trigger. They can even be used to create new tables at the SQL server database level (versus local tables).

After you create a pass-through query, you need to specify information about the database you want to connect to. You can type a connection string in the ODBCConnectStr property of the query property sheet directly or click Build and enter the information about the server you want to connect to. If you do not specify a connection string, you are prompted for the connection information when you run the query.

Figure 25-17 shows a pass-through query for a Microsoft SQL Server that creates a new table named Payroll and defines the fields in the table. A pass-through query is not limited to data definitions (creating a table or index); it can be any valid SQL statement to examine or manipulate the records in a back-end server.

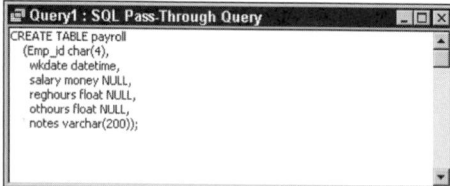

Figure 25-17: A pass-through query for SQL Server that will create a table named payroll in a database that resides on an SQL Server

Caution   Never attempt to convert a pass-through query to another type of query. If you do, Access erases the entire SQL statement you had typed in.

Caution   When working with pass-through queries, you should not perform operations that change the state of the connection. Halting a transaction in the middle, for example, may cause unexpected results.

Creating data definition queries

Of the three SQL-specific queries, the data definition query is the least useful against local tables. Everything that can be done with it also can be done using the design tools in Access. The data definition query is, however, an efficient way to create or change database objects. With a data definition query, any of these SQL statements can be used:

✦ CREATE TABLE

✦ ALTER TABLE

✦ DROP TABLE

✦ CREATE INDEX

✦ DROP INDEX

For example, you could type the following code into the SQL query window (Data Definition Query) to create a local Access table named TelephoneList:

```
CREATE TABLE TelephoneList
( [TeleID] integer, [FullName] text, [Address1] text,
[Address2] text, [Address3] text, [Country] text, [Phone 1]
text, [Phone 2] text, [FaxPhn 1] text, [Notes] memo,
CONSTRAINT [Index1] PRIMARY KEY ([TeleID]) );
```

Once created, this query could be run to create a new table named Telephone List. You could create a second Data-Definition Query to create an index for the table. For instance you could create an index that would be in order by country and full name:

```
CREATE INDEX CountryName ON TelephoneList ([Country],
[FullName]);
```

Note   You can have only one SQL statement in each Data-Definition Query.

Creating SQL subqueries in an Access query

Access 2002 enables you to create an SQL SELECT statement inside another select query or action query. You can use these SQL statements in the Field row to define a new field, or in the Criteria row to define criteria for a field. Using subqueries, you can do the following:

✦ Find values in the primary query that are equal to, greater than, or less than values returned by the subquery using the ANY, IN, or ALL reserved words.

✦ Test for the existence of a result from a subquery using the EXISTS or NOT EXISTS reserved words.

✦ Using the ANY, IN, or ALL reserve words in a subquery, you can compare values in the main query to the results of the subquery (not equal, equal, greater than, or less than).

✦ Create nested subqueries (subqueries within subqueries).

You can place an SQL statement in the Field: cell or in the Criteria: cell of the design grid. You would place it in the Field: cell to create a new field for the query. In contrast, you can use an SQL statement in the Criteria: cell of a field to define the criteria used for limiting the records of the cell.

How Queries Save Field Selections

When you open a query design, you may notice that the design has changed since you last saved the query. When you save a query, Access rearranges (even eliminates) fields on the basis of several rules:

✦ If a field does not have the Show: box checked but has criteria specified, Access moves it to the rightmost columns in the QBE pane.

✦ If a field does not have the Show: box checked, Access eliminates it from the QBE pane column unless it has sorting directives or criteria.

✦ If you create a totaling expression with the Sum operator in a total query, Access changes it to an expression using the Sum function.

Because of these rules, your query may look very different after you save and reopen it. In this section, you learn how this happens (and some ways to prevent it).

Hiding (not showing) fields

Sometimes you won't want certain fields in the QBE pane to show in the actual dynaset of the datasheet. For example, you may want to use a field such as Customer Number to specify a criterion or a sort without showing the actual field.

To hide, or exclude, a field from the dynaset, you simply click off the Show: box under the field you want to hide. Figure 25-18 demonstrates this procedure. Notice that the field Type of Customer is used to specify a criterion of displaying only individuals ("1"). Because you don't want the Type of Customer field in the actual datasheet, you deselect the Show: cell for the Type of Customer field.

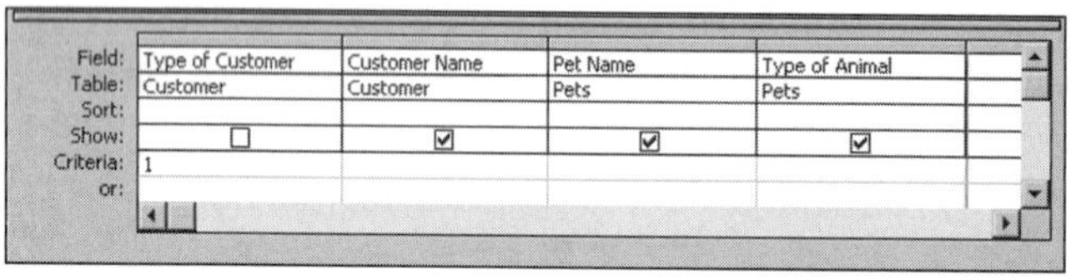

Figure 25-18: The easiest way to hide a field is to uncheck the Show: check box of the field, as in Type of Customer.

Any fields that have the Show: cell turned off (and for which you entered criteria) are placed at the end of the QBE pane when you save the query. Figure 25-19 shows the same query as Figure 25-18 after it is saved and redisplayed on the design screen. Notice that the Type of Customer field has been moved to the end (extreme right) of the QBE pane. The location of a hidden field will not change the dynaset. Because the field is not displayed, its location in the QBE pane is unimportant. You always get the same results, even if you've placed a hidden field in the QBE pane.

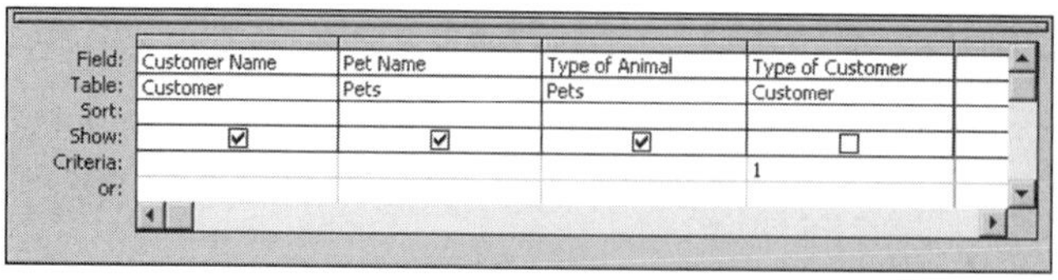

Figure 25-19: A query that has been saved with a hidden field (show unchecked); the field is moved to the end of the query. (Compare Figure 25-18.)

If you hide any fields in the QBE pane that are not used for sorts or criteria, Access eliminates them from the query automatically when you save it. If you want to use these fields and need to show them later, you'll have to add them back to the QBE pane.

Note　If you're creating a query to be used by a form or report, you must show any fields it will use, including any field to which you want to bind a control.

Renaming fields in queries

When working with queries, you can rename a field to describe the field's contents more clearly or accurately. This new name is the one that would be shown in the datasheet of the query. For example, you may want to rename the Customer Name field to Owner Name. Renaming is useful for working with calculated fields or calculating totals; Access automatically assigns nondescript names such as Expr1 or AvgOfWeight, but it's easy to rename fields in Access queries. To change the display name of the Customer Name field, for example, follow these steps:

1. Create a new query and select the Customer table.

2. Double-click the Customer Name field.

3. Place the cursor in front of the first letter of Customer Name in the Field: cell.

4. Type Owner Name: (be sure to include the colon).

Figure 25-20 shows the query field renamed. The field has both the display name, which is Owner Name, and the actual field name, which is Customer Name.

When you view this query, the new Column heading is Owner Name, instead of Customer Name.

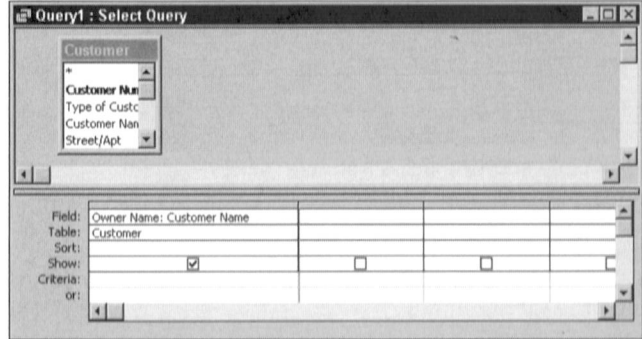

Figure 25-20: A query field with the Customer Name field renamed to Owner Name for display purposes

Tip   When naming a query field, delete any names assigned by Access (to the left of the colon). For example, remove the name Expr1 when you name the calculated field.

If you rename a field, Access uses only the new name for the heading of the query datasheet; it does the same with the control source in any form or report that uses the query. Any new forms or reports you create on the basis of the query will use the new field name. (Access does not change the actual field name in the underlying table.)

When working with renamed fields, you can use an expression name (the new name you specified) in another expression within the same query. For example, you may have a calculated field called First Name that uses several Access functions to separate an individual's first name from the last name. For this calculated field, use the field called Owner Name that you created earlier.

Note   When you work with referenced expression names, you cannot have any criteria specified against the field you're referring to. For example, you cannot have a criterion specified for Owner Name if you refer to Owner Name in the First Name calculation. If you do, Access will not display the contents for the expression field Owner Name in the datasheet.

Hiding and unhiding columns in the QBE pane

Sometimes you may want to hide specific fields in the QBE pane. This is not the same as hiding a field by clicking the Show: box. Hiding a column in the QBE pane is similar to hiding a datasheet column, which is easy: you simply resize a column (from right to left) until it has no visible width. Figure 25-21 shows several fields in the QBE pane; in the next example, you hide one of its columns.

Field:	Customer Name	City	State	Pet Name	Type of Animal
Table:	Customer	Customer	Customer	Pets	Pets
Sort:					
Show:	☑	☑	☑	☑	☑
Criteria:					
or:					

Figure 25-21: A typical QBE pane showing fields from two tables — Customer and Pets

If you create the query shown in Figure 25-21, you can then hide the City column. Follow these steps to hide the City column:

1. Move the mouse pointer to the right side of the City field on the field selector. The double-arrow sizing pointer displays.

2. Click the right side of the City field and drag it toward the Customer Name field until it totally disappears.

Figure 25-22 shows the QBE pane with the City field being hidden. In the picture, the field wasn't completely hidden so that you can see where the column has been moved to (next to Customer Name) and the double-arrow sizing pointer.

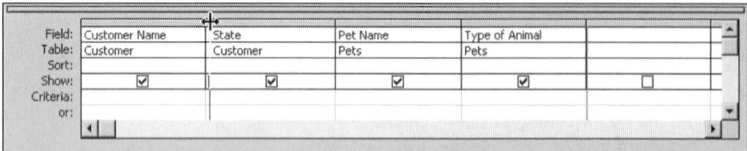

Figure 25-22: The QBE pane with a column being hidden by moving the double-arrow pointer

Note   Although the City field is hidden in the QBE panel of the design surface, it is still shown in the datasheet when you click the Datasheet button. Hiding a field in the query design *only* hides it in the query design.

After you hide a field, you can unhide it by reversing the process. If you want to unhide the City column, follow these steps:

1. Move the mouse pointer to the left side of the field State on the selector bar (the bar with arrows appears). Make sure that you are to the right of the divider between Customer Name and State.

2. Click the left side of State and drag it toward the Pet Name field until you size the column to the correct length.

3. Release the button; the field name City will appear in the column you unhide.

Query Design Options

There are several specifiable default options when working with a query design. These options can be viewed and set by selecting Tools ✑ Options from the main menu and then selecting the Tables/Queries tab. Figure 25-23 shows this Options dialog box.

These five items can be set for queries:

✦ Show Table Names

✦ Output All Fields

✦ Enable AutoJoin

✦ Run Permissions

✦ SQL Server Compatibility Syntax (ANSI 92)

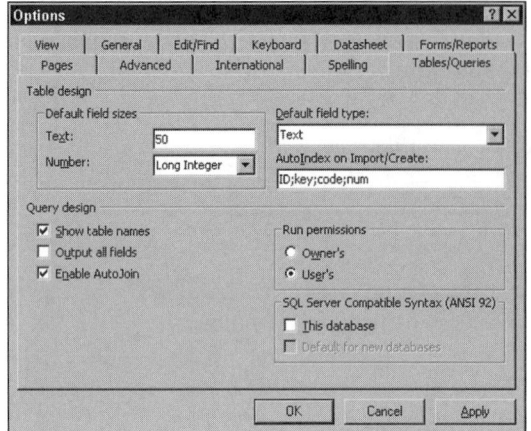

Figure 25-23: The Table/Queries page of the Options dialog box. The lower half concerns the fields for queries.

Generally, the default for Show Table Names is Yes, and the default for Output All fields is No. Run Permissions offers a choice of either the Owner's permission or the User's (the default). Enable AutoJoin controls whether Access will use common field names to perform an automatic join between tables that have no relationships set; the default value is Yes. The final section determines if the current database should use ANSI 92 SQL Server Syntax; the default is No.

Tip   When you set query design options, they specify default actions for new queries only; they do not affect the current query. To show table names in the current query, select View ⇨ Table Names from the main Query menu while designing the query.

Table 25-1 describes each Query design option and its purpose.

Table 25-1
Query Design Options

Option	Purpose
Show Table Names	Shows the Table: row in the QBE pane when set to Yes; hides the Table: row if set to No.
Output All Fields	Shows all fields in the underlying tables or only the fields displayed in the QBE pane.
Enable AutoJoin	Uses common field names to perform an automatic join between tables that have no relationships set to occur; the tables must have a field with the same name and type of data and one of the fields must be a primary key field.
Run Permissions	Restricts use in a multi-user environment; a user restricted from viewing the underlying tables can still view the data from the query. If set to Owner's the user cannot view data returned from the query or run an action query.
SQL Server Compatible	Select This Database to enable ANSI-92 SQL query mode so you can create and run queries using ANSI 92 SQL Syntax. This is compatible with Microsoft SQL Server. Existing queries may not run correctly if you set this option after creating other queries.

Setting Query Properties

While creating a query you can set query properties several ways — click the Properties button on the toolbar, or right-click Properties and choose it from the shortcut menu, or select View ✧ Properties from the main Query menu. Access displays a Query Properties dialog box. Your options depend on the query type and on the table or field with which you're working.

You can use the query-level properties just as you would the properties in forms, reports, and tables. Query-level properties depend on the type of query being created and on the table or field with which you're working. Table 25-2 shows the query-level properties you can set.

Table 25-2
Query-Level Properties

Property	Description	Query	Select	Crosstab	Update	Delete	Make-Table	Append
Description	Text describing table or query	X	X	X	X	X	X	
Output All Fields	Show all fields from the underlying tables in the query	X			X	X	X	
Top Values	Number of highest or lowest values to be returned	X			X	X	X	
Unique Values	Return only unique field values in the dynaset	X				X	X	
Unique Records	Return only unique records for the dynaset	X		X	X		X	
Run Permissions	Establish permissions for specified user	X	X	X	X	X	X	
Source Database	External database name for all tables/queries in the query	X	X	X	X	X	X	
Source Connect Str	Name of application used to connect to external database	X	X	X	X	X	X	
Record Locks	Records locked while query runs (usually action queries)	X	X	X	X	X	X	
ODBC Time-out	Number of seconds before reporting error for opening DB	X	X	X	X	X	X	

Property	Description	Query	Select	Crosstab	Update	Delete	Make-Table	Append
Filter	Filter name loaded automatically with query	X						
Order By	Sort loaded automatically with query	X						
MaxRecords	Max number of records returned by ODBC database	X						
SubDatasheet Name	Identify subquery	X		X		X	X	
Link Child Fields	Field name(s) in subquery	X	X	X		X	X	
Link Master Fields	Field name(s) in main table	X	X	X		X	X	
Subdatasheet Height	Maximum height of subdatasheet	X	X	X		X	X	
Subdatasheet Expanded	Records initially in their expanded state?	X	X	X		X	X	
Column Headings	Fixed column headings		X					
RecordSet Type	Which tables can be edited		X					
Use Transaction	Run action query in transaction?			X	X	X	X	
Fail on Error	Fail operation if errors occur			X	X			
Destination Table	Table name of destination					X	X	
Destination DB	Name of database					X	X	
Dest Connect Str	Database connection string					X	X	

Understanding SQL

When you use the graphical tools of the Query design to create a Query by Example, Access converts what you create into a Structured Query Language (SQL) statement. This SQL statement is what Access actually executes when the query runs.

Many relational databases use SQL as a standardized language to query and update tables. SQL is relatively simple to learn and use. Even so, Access does not require you know it or use it — though Access uses it, you won't ever have to know that it's there.

Viewing SQL statements in queries

If you're familiar with SQL, you can view and/or edit an SQL statement created by Access. If you make changes to an SQL statement, Access reflects them automatically in the QBE pane.

To view an SQL statement that Access creates while building the query, select View ➪ SQL View from the Query menu. Figure 25-24 shows a typical SQL statement that will display the fields Customer Name and State for dogs in Idaho or Oregon.

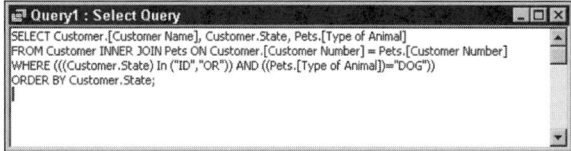

Figure 25-24: An SQL statement in the Access query window

Tip If you want to modify an existing SQL statement or create your own, enter changes directly into the SQL dialog box. To add new lines in the dialog box, press Enter.

SQL statements can be used directly in expressions, macros, forms, and reports, as in the RowSource or RecordSource properties of a form or report. You don't have to "know the language" to use SQL statements directly. You can create the needed statement (for such purposes as selecting specific records) in the Query Design window. Then activate the SQL view window and copy (Ctrl+C) the entire SQL statement you created. Switch to where you want to use the statement and paste it (Ctrl+V) where you need it (for example, the RowSource property of the property sheet).

Note You can create SQL statements in the SQL view window. Whether you write your own statement or edit one, Access updates the Query Design window when you leave the SQL view window. Tables are added to the top portion; fields and criteria are added to the QBE pane.

An SQL primer

Until now, you have created queries using the query designer of Access. You have even been told that you can examine the SQL statement Access builds by selecting View ⇨ SQL View from the menu.

As you already know, one way to learn SQL statements is to build a query graphically and then view the corresponding SQL statement in the SQL view window. Earlier, for example, Figure 25-24 showed this SQL statement:

```
SELECT Customer.[Customer Name], Customer.State, Pets.[Type of
Animal]
FROM Customer INNER JOIN Pets ON Customer.[Customer Number] =
Pets.[Customer Number]
WHERE (((Customer.State) In ("ID","OR"))
AND ((Pets.[Type of Animal])="DOG"))
ORDER BY Customer.State;
```

Four common SQL commands

The statement in Figure 25-24 uses the four most common SQL commands. Table 25-3 shows each command and explains its purpose.

Table 25-3
Four Common SQL Keywords/Commands/Statements

Keyword	Purpose in SQL Statement
SELECT	This command/keyword starts an SQL statement. It is followed by the names of the fields that will be selected from the table or tables (if more than one is specified in the FROM clause/command). This is a required keyword.
FROM	This keyword specifies the name(s) of the table(s) containing the fields specified in the SELECT command. This is a required keyword. If more than one table is used you need to also specify a JOIN type, known as a Table Expression.
WHERE	This command specifies any condition used to filter (limit) the records that will be viewed. This keyword is used only when you want to limit the records to a specific group on the basis of the condition.
ORDER BY	This command specifies the order in which you want the resulting dataset (the selected records that were found and returned) to appear.

Using these four basic keywords, you can build very powerful SQL statements to use in your Access forms and reports.

The SELECT statement

The SELECT statement (or command) is the first word found in two query types; in a select query or make-table query, the SELECT statement specifies the field(s) you want displayed in the Results table.

After specifying the keyword SELECT, you need to specify the fields you want to display (for more than one, use a comma between the fields). The general syntax is

```
SELECT Field_one, Field_two, Field_three ...
```

where Field_one, Field_two, and so on are replaced with the names of the table fields.

Notice that commas separate each field in the list from the others. For instance, if you want to specify customer name and city using fields from the Customer table, you would specify the following:

```
SELECT [Customer Name], City
```

Note   The field name Customer Name needs brackets around it since it has a space in the name (see sidebar).

If you need to view fields from more than one table, then specify the name of the tables in which to find the fields. The SELECT statement would, for example, look like this to select fields from both the Customer and Pets table:

```
SELECT Customer.[Customer Name], Customer.City, Pets.[Type of
Animal], Pets.[Pet Name]
```

When you build a query in Access, it places the table name before the field name automatically. In reality, you need only specify the table name if more than one table in the SQL statement has fields with the same name. For instance, a field named Customer Number appears in both the Customer table and the Pets table. If you want to SELECT a [Customer Number] field in your SQL statement, you must specify which of these to use—the one in Customer or the one in Pets.

The following SQL SELECT Statement illustrates the syntax:

```
SELECT Customer.[Customer Number], [Customer Name], City, [Type
of Animal], [Pet Name]
```

Tip   Although table names are not required for non-duplicate fields in an SQL statement, it's a good idea to use them for clarity.

Using the Brackets Around Field Names

The SELECT statement just described uses brackets around the field name Customer Name. Any field name that has spaces within it requires the use of brackets. The brackets, [ ], let the SQL parser knows you are referring to a specific field. If the field has no spaces, you do not need to use the brackets.

You can use the asterisk wildcard (*) to specify that all fields should be selected. If you're going to select all fields from more than one table, specify the table, a period (.), and then the name of the field—in this case, the asterisk.

Specifying SELECT predicates

When you create an SQL SELECT statement, several predicates can be associated with the SELECT clause:

✦ ALL
✦ DISTINCT
✦ DISTINCTROW
✦ TOP

The predicates are used to restrict the number of records returned. They can work in conjunction with the WHERE clause (actually in SQL terminology the WHERE *condition*) of an SQL statement.

The ALL predicate is the default. It selects all records that meet the WHERE condition specified in the SQL statement. Selecting it is optional (it's the default value).

Use the DISTINCT predicate when you want to omit records that contain duplicate data in the fields specified in the SELECT statement. For instance, if you create a query and want to look at both the Customer Name and the Type of Animal the customer owns, without considering the number of animals of a given type, the SELECT statement would be as follows:

```
SELECT DISTINCT [Customer name], [Type of Animal]
```

If a customer owns two dogs—that is, has two Dog records (one named Bubba and one named Killer) in the Pets table—only one record will appear in the resulting datasheet. The DISTINCT predicate tells Access to show only one record if the values in the selected fields are duplicates (that is, same customer number and same type of animal). Even though two different records are in the Pets table, only one is shown. DISTINCT eliminates duplicates on the basis of the fields selected to view.

The DISTINCTROW predicate is unique to Access. It works much like DISTINCT, with one big difference: It looks for duplicates on the basis of all fields in the table(s), not just the selected fields. For instance, if a customer has two different Dog records in the Pets table and uses the predicate DISTINCTROW (replacing DISTINCT) in the SQL statement just described, both records are displayed. DISTINCTROW looks for duplicates in all the fields of the Customer and Pets tables. If any field is different (in this case, the name of the pet), then both records are displayed in the datasheet.

The TOP predicate is also unique to Access. It enables you to restrict the number of displayed records, basing the restriction on the WHERE condition to the TOP <number> of values. For instance, TOP 10 will display only the first 10 records that match the WHERE condition. You can use TOP to display the top five customers who have spent money on your services. For instance, the following SELECT statement will display the top five records:

```
SELECT TOP 5 [Customer Name]
```

The TOP predicate has an optional keyword, PERCENT, that displays the top number of records on the basis of a percentage rather than a number. To see the top 2 percent of your customers, you would use a SELECT statement like this one:

```
SELECT TOP 2 PERCENT [Customer Name]
```

The FROM clause of an SQL statement

As the name suggests, the FROM clause specifies the tables (or queries) that hold the fields named in the SELECT statement. This clause is required; it tells SQL where to find the records. If you fail to use the FROM portion of the SELECT statement, you will receive an error. Due to the required use of the FROM clause, some people refer to the SELECT statement as the SELECT ... FROM Statement.

When you're working with one table (as in the original example of Figure 25-24), the FROM clause simply specifies the table name:

```
SELECT [Customer Name], City,
FROM Customer
```

When you are working with more than one table, you can supply a Table Expression to the FROM clause to specify which data will be retrieved. The FROM clause is where you set the relationship between two or more tables for the SELECT statement. This link will be used to display the data in the resulting data sheet.

The Table Expression can be one of three types:

✦ INNER JOIN ... ON

✦ RIGHT JOIN ... ON

✦ LEFT JOIN ... ON

Use INNER JOIN ... ON to specify the traditional inner or equi-join of Access. For instance, to join Customers to Pets via the Customer Number field in the FROM clause, the command would be

```
SELECT Customer.[Type of Customer], Pets.[Type of Animal]
FROM Customer INNER JOIN pets ON Customer.[Customer Number] =
Pets.[Customer Number]
```

Notice that the FROM clause specifies the main table to use (Customer). Then the INNER JOIN portion of the FROM clause specifies the second table to use (Pets). Finally, the ON portion of the FROM clause specifies which fields will be used to join the table.

The LEFT JOIN and RIGHT JOIN work exactly the same, except that they specify an outer join instead of an inner join (equi-join).

The WHERE clause of an SQL statement

Use the WHERE clause (or condition) of the SQL statement only when you want to specify a condition. (This clause is optional, unlike SELECT ... and FROM.)

The original SQL statement you started with (for example) specified the following WHERE clause:

```
WHERE ((((Customer.State) In ("ID","OR"))
AND ((Pets.[Type of Animal])="DOG"))
```

The WHERE condition can be any valid expression. It can be a simple, one-condition expression (such as the one just given) or a complex expression based on several criteria.

Note If you use the WHERE condition, it must follow the FROM clause of the SQL statement.

The ORDER BY clause

Use the ORDER BY clause to specify a sort order. It will sort the displayed data by the field(s) you specify after the clause, in ascending or descending order. In the original example, you specified a sort order by Customer Number:

```
ORDER BY Customer.[Customer Name];
```

Specifying the end of an SQL statement

Because an SQL statement can be as long as 64,000 characters, a way is needed to tell the database language that you've finished creating the statement. End an SQL statement with a semicolon (;).

Note   Access is very forgiving about the ending semicolon. If you forget to place one at the end of an SQL statement, Access will assume that it should be there and run the SQL statement as if it were there. On the other hand, if you place a semicolon inside an SQL statement accidentally, Access will report an error and attempt to tell you where it occurred.

Using SELECT, FROM, WHERE, and ORDER BY, you can create some very powerful SQL statements to display and view data from your tables.

For instance, you can build an SQL statement that will do the following:

1. Select the Customer Name and City, Pet Name, and Type of Animal fields.

2. Join FROM the Customer and Pets tables, where the Customer and Pets tables are linked ON the Customer Number.

3. Display only records where the Type of Customer is a pet store (type = 2).

4. Sort the data in order by the Customer Number.

The SQL statement could be

```
SELECT [Customer Name], City, [Pet Name], [Type of Animal]
FROM Customer INNER JOIN Pets ON Customer.[Customer Number] =
Pets.[Customer Number]
WHERE [Type of Customer] = 2
ORDER BY Customer.[Customer number];
```

This is a quick overview of SQL statements and how to create them in Access 2002. Various other clauses (keywords/options) can be used with SQL statements. SQL is relatively easy to understand and work with.

Note   You can find a wealth of information on SQL on the Internet. For example, a more in-depth introduction to Structure Query Language (SQL) can be found by visiting the following site on the internet to review a great paper written by Jim Hoffman of Cincinnati, Ohio: http://w3.one.net/~jhoffman/sqltut.htm.

✦   ✦   ✦

Working with Subforms

◆   ◆   ◆   ◆

In This Chapter

Understanding what
a subform is

Creating a subform
with a Wizard

Creating a subform
by dragging a form
from the Database
window to a form

Adding validation to
a subform

Adding totals to a
subform

◆   ◆   ◆   ◆

Subforms give you great flexibility in displaying and entering data with multiple tables. You can still edit all the
fields without worrying about integrity problems. With a subform, you can even enter data into a one-to-many form
relationship.

What Is a Subform?

A subform is simply a form within a form. It enables you to
use data from more than one table in a form; you can display
data from one table in one format while using a different format for data from the other table. You can, for example, display one customer record on a form while displaying several
pet records on a datasheet subform.

Although you can edit multiple tables in a typical form, using
a subform gives you the flexibility to display data from several
tables or queries at one time.

As you may recall, you can display data on a form in several
ways:

   ◆ **Form.** Display one record on a form

   ◆ **Continuous.** Display multiple records on a form

   ◆ **Datasheet.** Display multiple records using one line per
     record

Including a subform on your form enables you to display your
data in multiple formats, as shown in Figure 26-1. This figure
shows a form for entering visit details. It shows data from a
query that lists information from the Customer, Pets, and
Visits tables at the top, in a Form view. At the bottom is a subform that displays information from the Visit Details table.
Notice that both the form and the subform have record selectors; each acts independently.

The subform contains data from three tables. In addition to its data from Visit Details, the subform shows descriptions of each treatment from the Treatments table, and medication listings from the Medications table. As you'll learn when you create this form later in this chapter, a drop-down list box appears when you select either of these latter fields in the datasheet. Each one is a combo box that enables you to select a description from the Treatments or Medications table; then it will store the appropriate code in the Visit Details table for you.

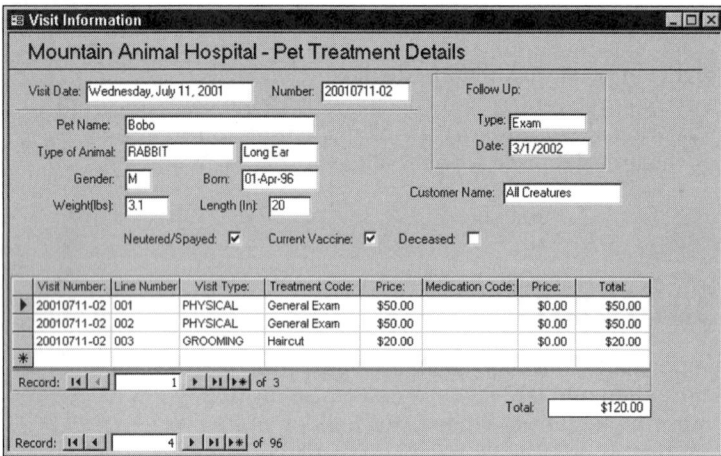

Figure 26-1: The form for adding visit details

When you create a subform, you link the main form to it by a common field of expression. The subform will then display only records that are related to the main form. The greatest advantage of subforms is their capability to show the one-to-many relationship. The main form represents the one part of the relationship; the subform represents the many side.

You can create a subform in several ways:

   ✦ Use the Form Wizard when you create a new form.

   ✦ Use the Subform Wizard in an existing form.

   ✦ Use the Subform button in the toolbox and modify control properties.

   ✦ Drag a form from the Database window to another form.

Creating Subforms with the Form Wizard

The Access Form Wizard can create a form with an embedded subform if you choose more than one table (or use a query with more than one table). If you don't use the Wizard, you have to create both the form and subform separately; then you embed the subform and link it to the main form.

Creating the form and selecting the Form Wizard

The Form Wizard creates both the form and the subform automatically when you specify more than one table in a one-to-many relationship. In this example, you create a form that displays information from the Customer table on the main form; the subform shows information from the Pets table. To create the form, follow these steps:

1. Create a new form by selecting the Forms object button in the Database window and clicking the New toolbar button.

2. Select Form Wizard in the New Form dialog box and select the Customer table from the tables/queries combo box, as shown in Figure 26-2.

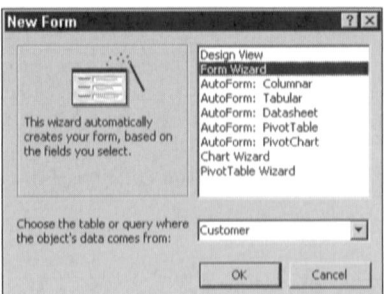

Figure 26-2: Selecting the Form Wizard

After you select the Form Wizard and the table or query to use for the new form, you need to select the fields for the main part of the form.

Choosing the fields for the main form

You then select each of the fields you want on the main form. The Customer table will be used for these fields. Figure 26-3 shows the completed field selection. To select the fields for this example, follow these steps:

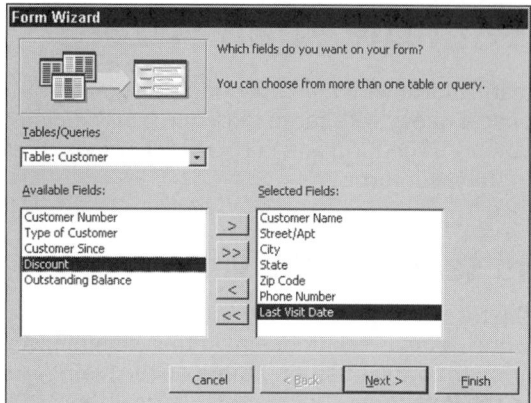

Figure 26-3: Selecting the fields for the main form

1. Select Customer Name and click the > button.

2. Select Street/Apt and click the > button.

3. Select City and click the > button.

4. Select State and click the > button.

5. Select Zip Code and click the > button.

6. Select Phone Number and click the > button.

7. Select Last Visit Date and click the > button.

Tip   You can also double-click any of the fields instead of selecting the field and clicking the > button.

Selecting the table or query that will be the subform

Because a subform uses a data source separate from the form, you have to select the table or query to be used on the subform. You do this from the same wizard screen without pressing the Next button. To select another table/query for the form, select the Pets table from the combo box, as shown in Figure 26-4. This table will be the subform of the primary form.

You will notice after a few seconds that the field list below in the Available Fields list box changes to display fields in the Pets table. The fields already selected from the Customer table in the Selected Fields list box remain.

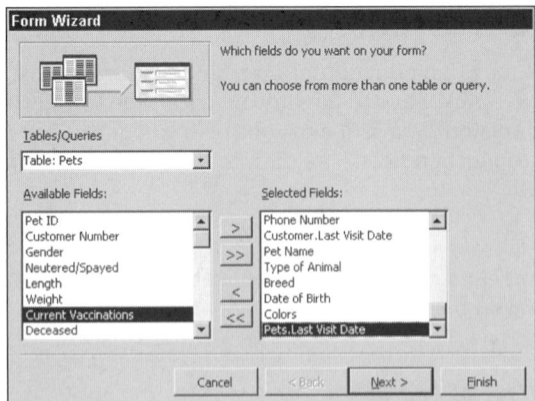

Figure 26-4: Selecting the fields for the subform

Choosing the fields for the subform

Fields for the subform are selected in exactly the same way as fields for the main form. Those you select from the Pets table will be added to the list of fields already selected from the Customer table.

To select the fields for the subform, follow these steps:

1. Select Pet Name and click the > button.

2. Select Type of Animal and click the > button.

3. Select Breed and click the > button.

4. Select Date of Birth and click the > button.

5. Select Colors and click the > button.

6. Select Last Visit Date and click the > button.

7. Click the Next > button to move to the next dialog box.

Note Notice the Pets.Last Visit Date field in the Selected Fields list box. Because both tables have a field named Last Visit Date, a prefix is added from the table that uniquely identifies the field.

After you select the fields for the Pets table, you can move to the next Wizard screen to decide how the linkage between forms will be built and how the data on the form will look.

Selecting the form data layout

The next dialog box is shown as part of a conceptual diagram in Figure 26-5. A multi-table relationship gives you many ways to lay out the data. The top part of the figure shows an automatic decision Access makes on the basis of the one-to-many relationship between Customer and Pets. The data is viewed by Customer, with a subform with the Pets data.

On the left side of the dialog box, you can choose how you want to view your form. Below the field view diagram, you can select whether you want to see your data as a Form with subform(s) or as Linked forms.

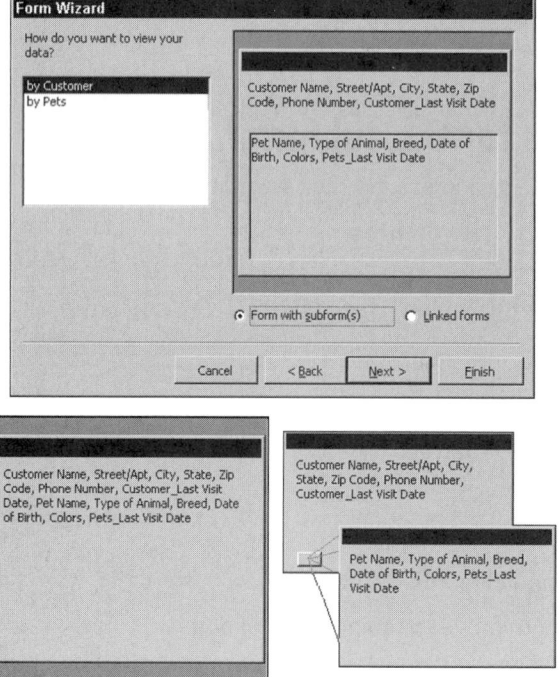

Figure 26-5: Selecting the data layout

In the top part of the figure that shows the entire Form Wizard dialog box, you can see the form with a subform: Customer fields are on the main form, and Pets fields are on the subform. The bottom-left part of the diagram shows conceptually what the data would look like if you viewed the data by Pets instead. The data from both tables would be placed on a single form. The bottom-right part of the figure shows how it would look if you chose to view the data by Customer but chose Linked forms instead. Rather than creating a Customer form with an embedded Pets subform, Access would create a Customer form with a button to display the Pets form.

After you select the type of form you want (the data is viewed by Customer, with a Form with subform(s) with the Pets data), you can click the Next> button to move to the subform layout screen.

Selecting the subform layout

When you create a form with an embedded subform, you must decide which type of layout to use for the subform. The four possibilities are tabular, datasheet, PivotTable, and PivotChart. The datasheet is the easiest, but it may not be the choice you want to accept. Datasheets are rigid by nature; you cannot change certain characteristics (such as adding multi-line column headers or precisely controlling the location of the fields below). You should choose a tabular layout for added flexibility. Whereas a datasheet combines the headers and data into a single control type (the datasheet itself), a tabular form places the column headers in a form header section, placing the field controls in the form's detail section. A tabular format creates a Continuous Form layout and also enables you to add any type of control to the subform where datasheets are limited to text boxes, check boxes, and combo boxes.

Select the Tabular layout, as shown in Figure 26-6.

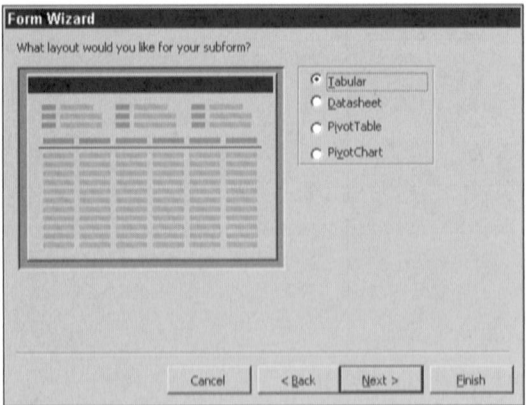

Figure 26-6: Selecting the subform tabular layout

Selecting the form style

As with other Form Wizards, you can determine how the form will look by selecting one of the AutoFormat choices. The style applies to the main form. The subform, displayed as either a separate tabular form or a datasheet, has the same look.

Cross-Reference

Chapter 8 explains in more detail the process of determining a form's look and Form Wizards in general.

You can accept the default Standard style and click the Next > button to move to the final dialog box. This box enables you to select the title for the form and the subform.

Selecting the form title

You can accept the default titles (the table names Access gives the main form and subform), or you can enter a custom title. The text you enter appears in the form header section of the main form. (See Figure 26-7.)

Note

In this example, you might see the names Customer1 and Pets Subform1 if you are using the Mountain Animal Hospital example database, because there are already forms with the names Customer and Pets Subform. The 1's indicate that there are already forms with this name. If you were using a database where there were no Customer or Pets Subforms, the names would not have a 1 appended to them and would look like Figure 26-7. If you see these object names and want to overwrite the objects, you can change the names and continue. The new objects will replace the original objects.

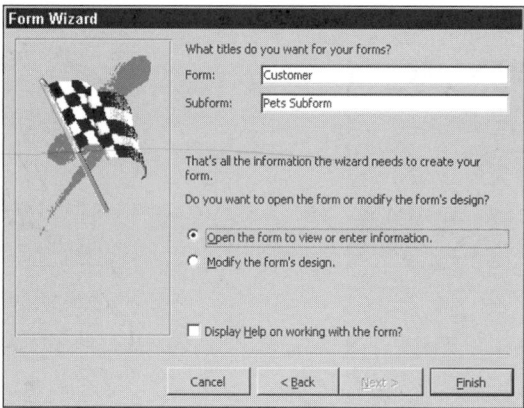

Figure 26-7: Selecting titles for the form and subform

When you accept the names (or enter names of your choice), both the form and subform are saved as forms; they will appear in the Database window when you select Forms. You should try to name your forms and subforms something similar so that you can tell that they go together. After you complete this step, you can view your form or its design.

Displaying the form

After the forms are named, the screen displays either the form or its design, depending on the option button you choose. In this example, you see the form, as shown in Figure 26-8.

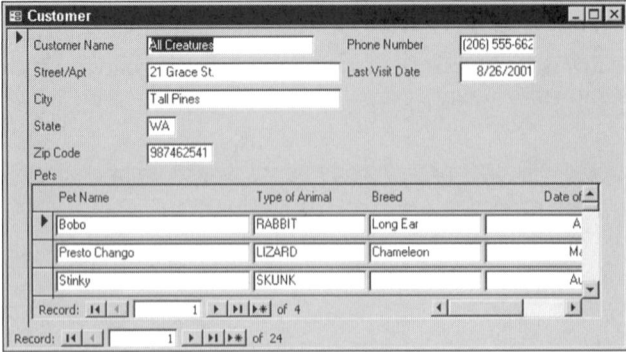

Figure 26-8: The Customer and Pets form

The tabular form layout was chosen for the subform. Whether you create your subform through a Wizard, by dragging one to the form, or by using the toolbox, Access creates a datasheet, tabular (continuous) form, PivotTable, or PivotChart. You can change this by changing the Default View property to Single Form, Continuous Forms (Tabular), Datasheet, PivotTable, or PivotChart.

While you can see the subform design within the rectangle around the subform area, you cannot change the subform design until you click the subform area and double-click it.

As you can see, the subform only shows a portion of the fields. The controls need to be resized. The main form controls also show data that is cut off (controls that are not wide enough to display the data). You can change the main form and subform all you need to. You can move fields around, adjust column widths, change the formatting, modify the distance between rows, and rearrange columns. When you make these changes, you'll see them in effect the next time you view the subform. If you scroll down to the bottom of the subform, you'll notice that the asterisk (*) appears in the record selector column. As with any continuous form or datasheet, you can add new records by using this row.

Both the main form and the subform have record selectors because they are separate forms. As you use the outer record selector on the main form, you move from one customer record to another, and the link automatically changes which pets are displayed. This way, when you look at the record for All Creatures, you see pets for All Creatures. When you switch to Animal Kingdom, its pets are displayed.

When you use the inner record selector of the subform, you can scroll the records within the tabular form, datasheet, PivotTable, or PivotChart. This capability is especially important if more records are on the subform than can be displayed in the subform area. You can use the scrollbar, too.

Displaying the main form design

To understand how the forms are linked from main form to subform, view the main form in Design view, as shown in Figure 26-9.

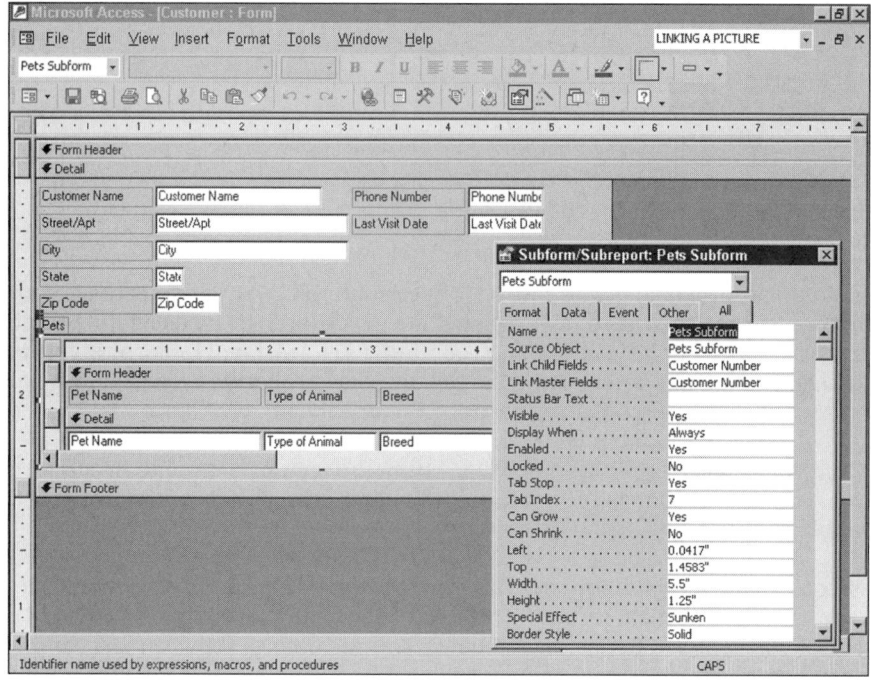

Figure 26-9: The Customer and Pets main form design

The design for the main form shows the fields from the Customer table at the top and the subform control at the bottom. The subform control is similar to other controls (such as the unbound object control). It stores the name of the subform and displays the controls in the subform.

Note   If you are used to using any older version of Microsoft Access, you previously saw only a gray box indicating the subform. You had to double-click the subform control to see the subform form itself.

Caution   If you do not use the wizard to create your forms and subforms, you must always first create the form you intend to use as a subform; the main form will not be usable until the subform form is created.

The Subform control property sheet is also shown. Notice the two properties Link Child Fields and Link Master Fields; these properties determine the link between the main form and the subform. The field name from the main table/query is entered in the Link Master Fields property. The field name from the subform table/query is entered in the Link Child Fields property. When the form is run, the link determines which records from the child form are displayed on the subform.

Tip   In previous versions of Microsoft Access before Access 2000, you could double-click the subform and instantly open the subform form. Access 2002 improves this by letting you work with the subform live in the main form. However, the subform control limits the space in which you have to work. You may find it easier to close the main form containing the subform control and open the subform form itself.

Note   The subform control is used for both subforms and subreports.

Displaying the subform design

To understand how the subform is built, view the subform form in Design view (as shown completed in Figure 26-10). You should close the Customer form and open the Pets Subform form in design view.

A subform is simply another form; it can be run by itself without a main form. You should always test your subform by itself, in fact, before running it as part of another form.

In Figure 26-10, you can see that all the fields are from the Pets table. You can also create a subform design with fields from multiple tables by using a query as the data source.

You might have noticed in the Customer form that the width of the Pets Subform control was 5.5". You need to resize the controls in this form to fit within this 5.5" space including any scroll bars. You also want to move the controls closer to each other to save space. This natural restriction of space in a form is known as real-estate issues and is generally a user interface designer's biggest challenge just as a home builder's challenge is designing a large home to fit on a small lot.

After rearranging the controls to fit in a smaller space, you also have to adjust the form width by selecting the area running vertically along the right edge of the form where the pointer will change to a double-headed horizontal arrow and move the border line to the left until it intersects the top ruler at a position slightly less than 5.5". This way there is room for a scroll bar.

You also may want to center the labels on all of the controls to more evenly distribute them. Figure 26-10 shows a final attempt at this.

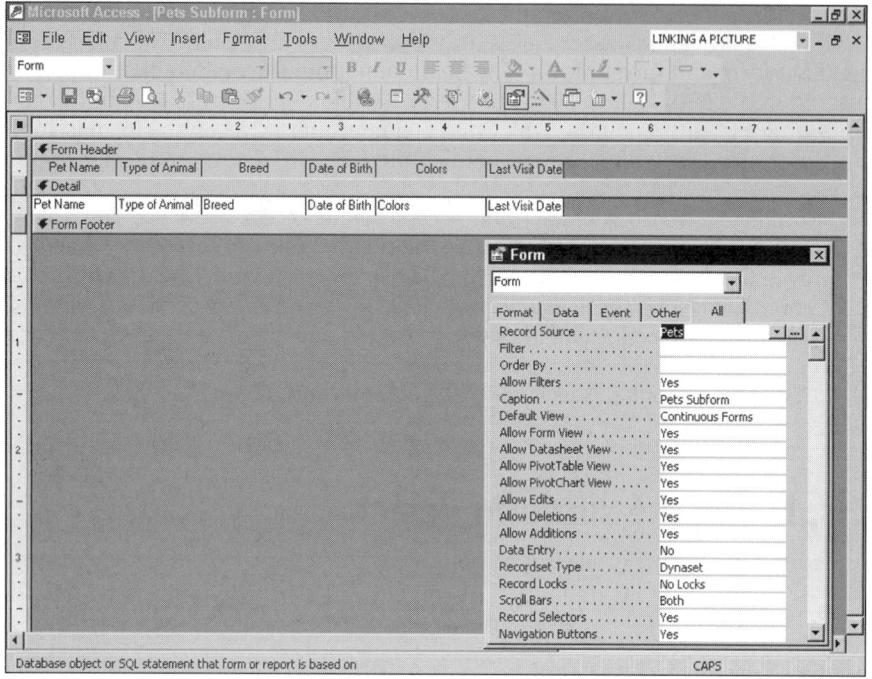

Figure 26-10: The Pets subform design

Notice that in the Form property sheet for the Pets subform, the Default View property is set to Continuous Forms. This will print the data in a tabular view, which gives you complete control over how the data looks and also over validation. For this example, you will change it to Continuous Forms. This means that the subform is displayed as a continuous form displaying multiple records, whether it is run by itself or used in a form. You can change it to a datasheet if you want or create a multiple-line form (which would then display its multiple lines on a subform).

Tip A subform that will be viewed as a datasheet needs only to have its fields added in the order you want them to appear in the datasheet. Remember that you can rearrange the fields in the datasheet.

Tip You can use the form footer of a subform to calculate totals or averages and then use the results on the main form. You learn how to do this later in this chapter.

The Form Wizard is a great place to start when creating a form with a subform. In the next section, however, you learn to create a subform without using a Form Wizard. Then you customize the subform to add combo box selections for some of the fields as well as calculate both row and column totals.

Creating a Simple Subform Without Wizards

As mentioned, there are several ways to create a subform without Wizards. You can drag a form from the Database window to a form, or you can use the Subform tool in the toolbox. The most desirable way is to drag the form from the Database window, because Access will try to create the links for you.

On the CD-ROM

In this section, you create the form shown in Figure 26-11. The entire form is on the CD-ROM that accompanies this book, in the Mountain Animal Hospital database, and is called Adding Visit Details. The completed subform is called Data for Subform Example.

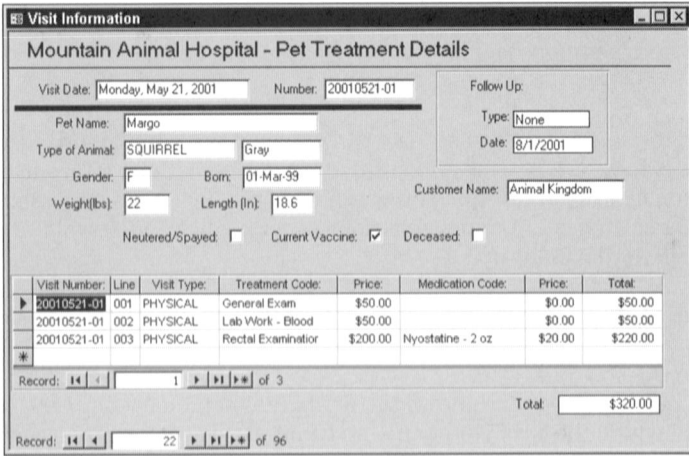

Figure 26-11: The Adding Visit Details form

In this chapter, you'll work with only the Adding Visit Details form as a main form; you create and embed the Data for Subform Example form as a subform. (You may want to copy the Adding Visit Details form from the example disk and then delete the subform and subform totals box. You can use that copy to create the main form for this section of the chapter and save yourself a great deal of work.)

The Adding Visit Details form is divided into several sections. The top half uses the query Pets, Owners, and Visits to display data from the Pets, Customer, and Visits tables. The Adding Visit Details form's only purpose is to enable you to add or review details about an existing visit. The middle of the form contains the subform that displays information about the visit details in a datasheet. Data in this subform comes from the query Data for Subform Example. Finally, there is a total for the data in the subform displayed in a text box control in the main form.

Creating a form for a subform

The first step in creating an embedded subform is to create the form to be used as the subform. Of course, this process begins with a plan and a query. The plan is what you see in Figure 26-11. This datasheet, however, is not just a few fields displayed as a datasheet. The field Visit Type is a combo box that uses a value list; you create that layer in this section. The fields Treatment Code and Medication Code do not display codes at all; instead, they display the treatment description and the medication description. The Price fields come from the Treatments table and Medications table by way of links. Finally, Total is a calculated field.

In this example, you will use a simple datasheet and add data validation to the form used for the datasheet. To create this datasheet, you start by writing the query. Figure 26-12 shows the query used for the subform.

Note This figure is a composite of two screen shots to show all the fields selected in the query.

At the top of the query, you can see the three necessary tables. Notice that the Visit Details table is joined to both the Treatments and Medications tables using a right outer join. You learned about this subject in Chapter 13. This is necessary so that if a Visit Detail record has either no treatment or no medication, it will not appear because of referential integrity.

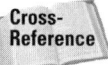

Cross-Reference Chapter 11 discusses the implications of referential integrity on a system using lookup tables.

The bottom pane of the query shows the fields that can be used for the datasheet. These fields include the Visit Number, Line Number, Visit Type, Treatment Code, and Medication Code fields from the Visit Details table. The fields Treatment and Price (from the Treatments table) and the fields Medication Name and Price (from the Medications table) can be used to display the actual data they name rather than the codes. This datasheet can be further enhanced by using combo boxes, as you'll soon see.

The final field in the query, Total: [Treatments].[Price]+[Medications]. [Price], names the field Total and sets the calculation to the total of both Price fields — the one in the Treatments table and the one in the Medications table. This field displays the line totals for each record in the datasheet.

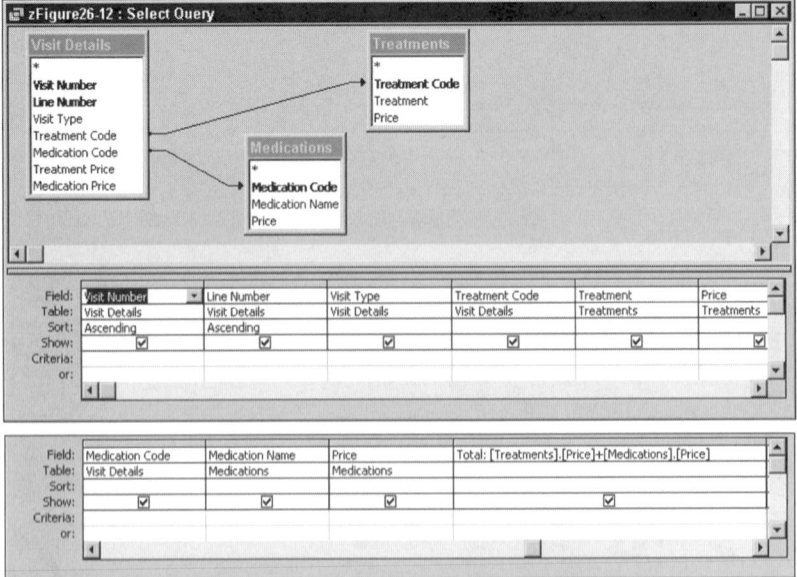

Figure 26-12: A composite figure showing the subform query

Creating a subform datasheet is an iterative process; you have to see how many fields can fit across the screen at one time. If your goal is not to use a horizontal scrollbar, you'll have to use only as many fields as you can fit across the screen.

You can create the basic subform either by using a Form Wizard or by creating a new form and placing all the needed fields in it.

To create the initial subform, follow these steps:

1. Create a new blank form, using the query Data for Subform Example as the Record Source.

2. Open the Field List window and drag all the fields to the form.

3. Change the Default View property to Datasheet, if it is not already, as shown in Figure 26-13.

4. Display the form as a datasheet to check the results.

When you display the datasheet, you see that the fields don't even come close to fitting. There simply isn't enough room to display all of them. There are two solutions: Use a scrollbar or get creative. By now, you have learned enough to get creative!

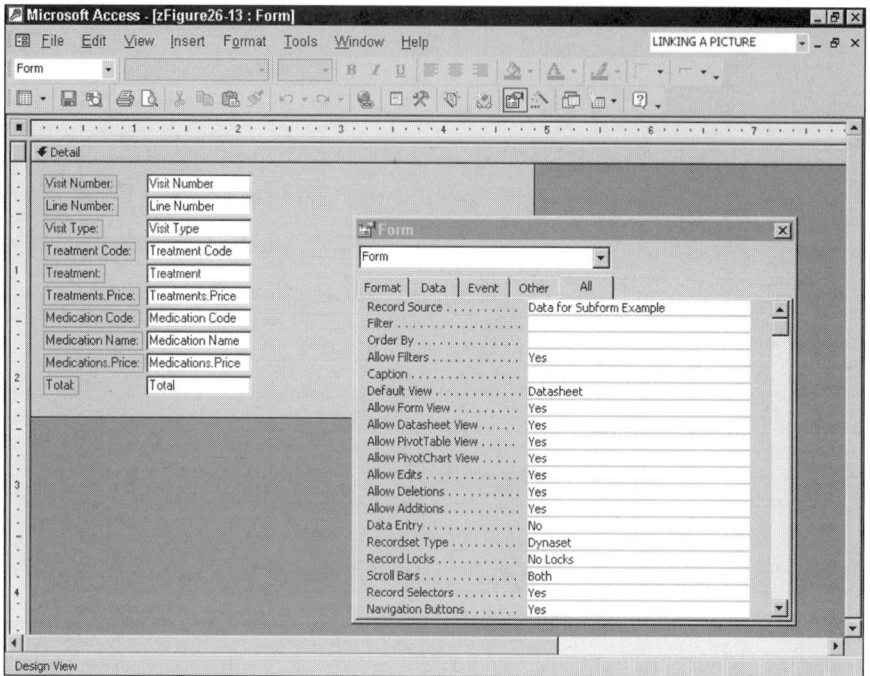

Figure 26-13: Creating the subform

First, which fields are absolutely necessary to the entry of data, and which are strictly lookup fields? The first necessary field is Visit Number — it's used to link to the main form and must be included. Next is Line Number, the second field that makes up the multiple-field key in Visit Details. You must enter a Visit Type for each record, so that field needs to stay. Next come the details themselves. To enter a treatment, you must enter a treatment code and a medication code (if any). The codes themselves are used to look up the description and price. Therefore, you need only Treatment Code and Medication Code. Even so, you also want to display the prices and the line total. So the only fields you can eliminate are Treatment and Medication Name — and even then the datasheet doesn't fit across the page. To make it all fit, follow these steps:

1. Switch to Form Design view.

2. Delete the controls Treatment and Medication Name.

3. Change the labels for Treatments.Price and Medications.Price to simply Price.

4. Switch back to Datasheet view.

5. The fields still don't fit. By changing the column widths, however, you can fix that. Adjust the column widths, as shown in Figure 26-14.

6. Save the form as Data for Subform Example.

This is usually a good starting point. Notice that in Figure 26-14 some extra space shows on the right side. Because this datasheet will be placed in the center of another form, you must take into consideration the space the record selector column and scrollbar of the main form will use. After you view the datasheet in the main form, you can make final adjustments. You may also wonder why so much space was left for the Treatment Code and Medication Code columns. Later, when you change these columns into combo boxes, you'll need this amount of space. (Normally, you might not have realized this yet.)

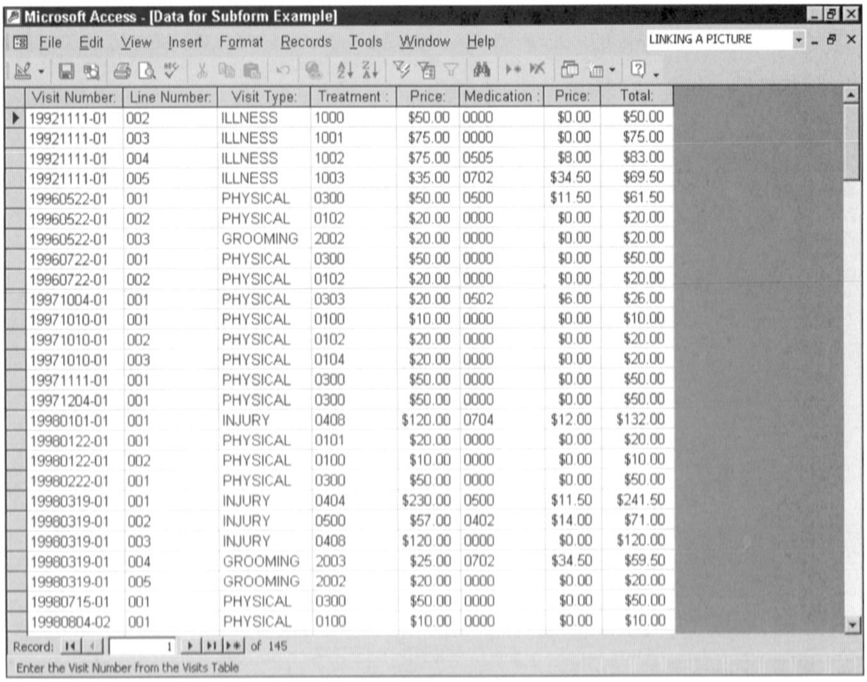

Visit Number:	Line Number:	Visit Type:	Treatment :	Price:	Medication :	Price:	Total:
19921111-01	002	ILLNESS	1000	$50.00	0000	$0.00	$50.00
19921111-01	003	ILLNESS	1001	$75.00	0000	$0.00	$75.00
19921111-01	004	ILLNESS	1002	$75.00	0505	$8.00	$83.00
19921111-01	005	ILLNESS	1003	$35.00	0702	$34.50	$69.50
19960522-01	001	PHYSICAL	0300	$50.00	0500	$11.50	$61.50
19960522-01	002	PHYSICAL	0102	$20.00	0000	$0.00	$20.00
19960522-01	003	GROOMING	2002	$20.00	0000	$0.00	$20.00
19960722-01	001	PHYSICAL	0300	$50.00	0000	$0.00	$50.00
19960722-01	002	PHYSICAL	0102	$20.00	0000	$0.00	$20.00
19971004-01	001	PHYSICAL	0303	$20.00	0502	$6.00	$26.00
19971010-01	001	PHYSICAL	0100	$10.00	0000	$0.00	$10.00
19971010-01	002	PHYSICAL	0102	$20.00	0000	$0.00	$20.00
19971010-01	003	PHYSICAL	0104	$20.00	0000	$0.00	$20.00
19971111-01	001	PHYSICAL	0300	$50.00	0000	$0.00	$50.00
19971204-01	001	PHYSICAL	0300	$50.00	0000	$0.00	$50.00
19980101-01	001	INJURY	0408	$120.00	0704	$12.00	$132.00
19980122-01	001	PHYSICAL	0101	$20.00	0000	$0.00	$20.00
19980122-01	002	PHYSICAL	0100	$10.00	0000	$0.00	$10.00
19980222-01	001	PHYSICAL	0300	$50.00	0000	$0.00	$50.00
19980319-01	001	INJURY	0404	$230.00	0500	$11.50	$241.50
19980319-01	002	INJURY	0500	$57.00	0402	$14.00	$71.00
19980319-01	003	INJURY	0408	$120.00	0000	$0.00	$120.00
19980319-01	004	GROOMING	2003	$25.00	0702	$34.50	$59.50
19980319-01	005	GROOMING	2002	$20.00	0000	$0.00	$20.00
19980715-01	001	PHYSICAL	0300	$50.00	0000	$0.00	$50.00
19980804-02	001	PHYSICAL	0100	$10.00	0000	$0.00	$10.00

Figure 26-14: Adjusting the subform datasheet

Adding the subform to the main form

After the subform is complete, you can add it to the main form. The easiest way is to display the main form in a window and then drag the subform to the main form. This action automatically creates the subform object control and potentially links the two forms.

To add the Data for Subform Example to the Adding Visit Details form you're using as the main form, follow these steps:

1. Display the Adding Visit Details form in a window in Design view so that you can also see the Database window.

2. Display the form objects in the Database window.

3. Click the form name Data for Subform Example and drag it to the Adding Visit Details form, as shown in Figure 26-15.

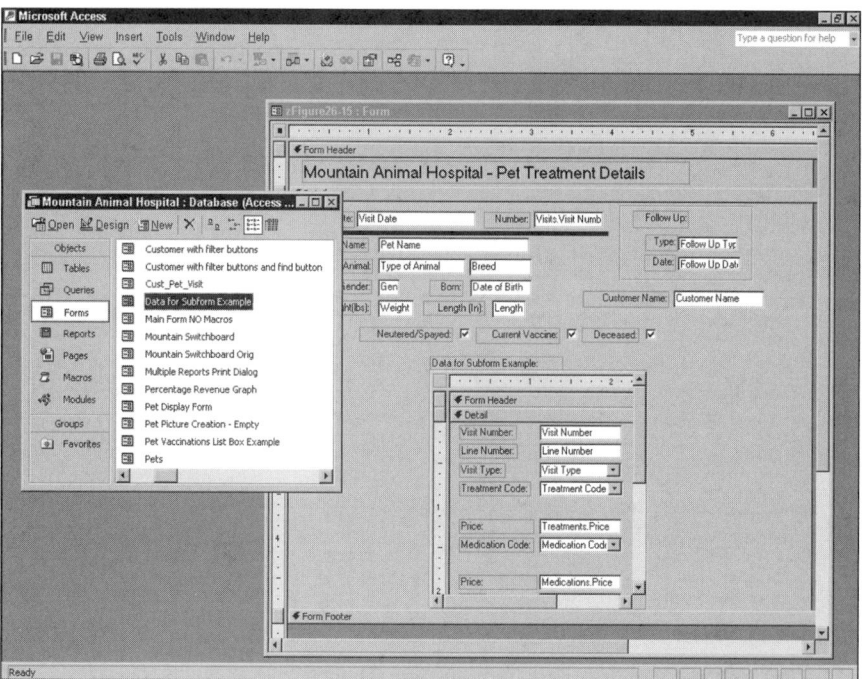

Figure 26-15: The form for Adding Visit Details

4. Maximize the Form window.

The subform is displayed showing the form view. However, you will want to see it in a datasheet. Because the Default View of the Data for Subform form is Datasheet, you will see this when the form is displayed in Form view.

Tip   Sometimes, to resize a control properly, you must display it in form view, note the height or width to change, switch to design view, make your changes, and then start the process over again. You should not feel that this is design by trial and error; it's a perfectly normal development process.

5. Resize the subform so that it fits on-screen below the three check boxes. It should begin around the 2-inch mark and go down to the 3-inch mark. The width should be approximately 6¼ inches.

6. Delete the subform label control.

7. Display the property sheet for the subform control to see if there was an automatic link. If not, you will manually link the fields.

The form should look like Figure 26-16. Notice that the Link Child Fields and Link Master Fields sections are not filled in. This means that the main form (Master) and the subform (Child) are not linked because the primary key for the Visit Details table is a multiple-field key. Access cannot automatically link this type of primary key.

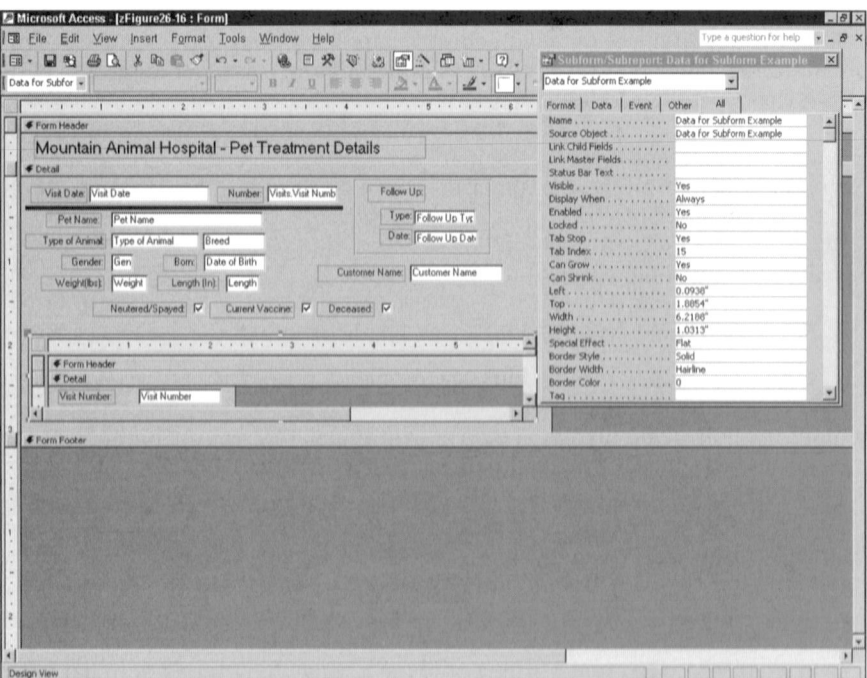

Figure 26-16: The subform in the main form

Linking the form and subform

When you drag a form from the Database window onto another form to create a subform, Access tries automatically to establish a link between the forms. This is also true when you drag a form or report onto a report.

Access establishes a link under these conditions:

✦ Both the main form and subform are based on tables, and a relationship has been defined with the Relationships command.

✦ The main form and the subform contain fields with the same name and data type, and the field on the main form is the primary key of the underlying table.

If Access finds a relationship or a match, these properties show the field names that define the link. You should verify the validity of an automatic link. If the main form is based on a query, or if neither of the conditions just listed is true, Access cannot match the fields automatically to create a link.

The Link Child Fields and Link Master Fields property settings must have the same number of fields and must represent data of the same type. For example, if the Customer table and the Pets table both have Customer ID fields (one each) that contain the same type of data, you enter Customer ID for both properties. The subform automatically displays all the pets found for the customer identified in the main form's Customer ID field.

Although the data must match, the names of the fields can differ. For example, the Customer ID field from the Customer table can be linked to the Customer Number field from the Pets table.

To create the link, follow these steps:

1. Enter Visit Number in the Link Child Fields property.

2. Enter Visit Number in the Link Master Fields property.

Without the link, if you display the form, you see all the records in the Visit Details table in the subform. By linking the forms, you see only the visit details for the specific visit being displayed on the main form.

Display the form, as shown in Figure 26-17. Move between the various records. Notice that the only visit numbers displayed in the datasheet are the same as the visit numbers in the main form. In Figure 26-17, you may notice that the user will have to enter the Treatment Code and Medication Code. In the type of systems that Access enables you to create, you should never have to enter a code that can be looked up automatically. You can change some of the fields in the datasheet to use lookup tables by creating combo boxes in the subform.

Adding lookup tables to the subform fields

You can change the way the data is displayed on a subform of a main form by changing the design of the subform itself. You now make three changes:

✦ Display the Visit Type field as a value list combo box.

✦ Display the Treatment Code as a combo box showing the Treatment Name, letting Access enter the Treatment Code automatically.

✦ Display the Medication Code as a combo box showing the Medication Name, letting Access enter the Medication Code automatically.

Cross-Reference   Combo boxes are discussed in detail in Chapter 17.

By changing a field in a subform to a combo box, when you click the field in the datasheet of the subform, the list will drop down and you can select from the list.

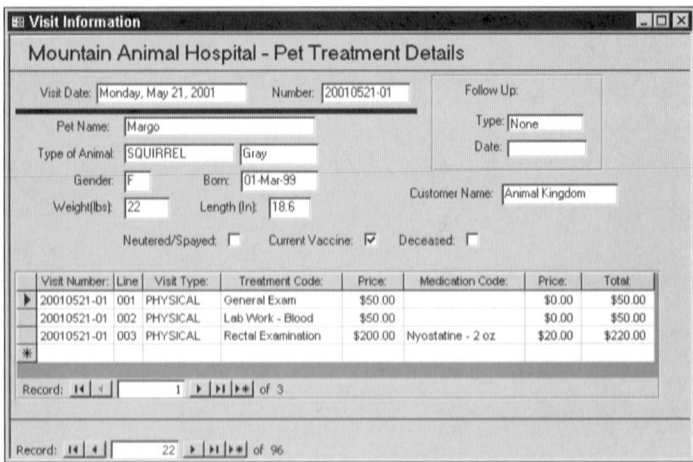

Figure 26-17: Displaying the main form and the subform

The first control you need to change is the Visit Type field. To create a value list combo box without using the Wizard, follow these steps:

1. Display the subform in the Design view.

2. Select the existing Visit Type text box control.

3. From the menu bar, select Format ⇨ Change To ⇨ Combo Box.

4. With the Visit Type combo box selected, display the property sheet.

5. Select Value List for the Row Source Type property.

6. Enter INJURY;PHYSICAL;GROOMING;HOSPITAL in the Row Source property.

7. Set the Column Count property to 1 and the Column Widths to 1".

8. Set the Bound Column property to 1 and the List Rows property to 8.

9. Set the Limit To List property to No to enable an alternative treatment type to be added.

This combo box and property sheet are shown in Figure 26-18.

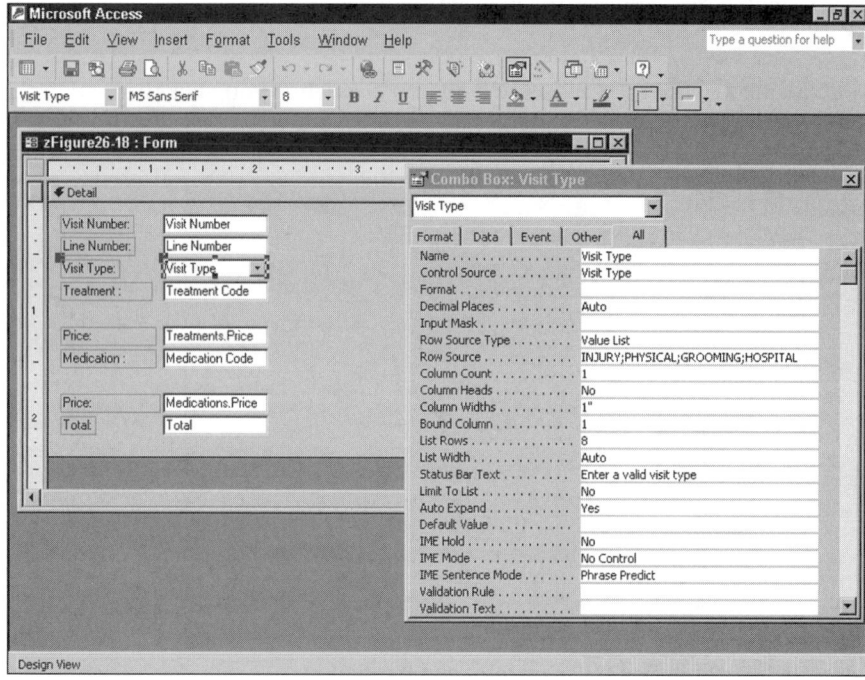

Figure 26-18: Creating a value list combo box for the Visit Type field

> **Note**   You can also display fields in a datasheet as check boxes or as individual option buttons. You cannot display an option button group, a list box, or a toggle button in a datasheet.

When a user clicks the Visit Type field in the datasheet, the combo box appears. When a user selects the arrow, the list box is displayed with the values INJURY; PHYSICAL; GROOMING; or HOSPITAL. Because the Limit To List property is set to No, a user can also add new values to the Visit Details table.

The next two combo boxes are very similar. You want to create two combo boxes. The first one enables you to see the treatment descriptions rather than the treatment codes. When you select a treatment description, the code is entered automatically. The second combo box is the same, except that it uses the Medications table rather than the Treatments table.

To create these combo boxes, you need to create several queries. Figure 26-19 shows the query for the Treatment Code combo box. You have to create this query and name it Treatment Lookup.

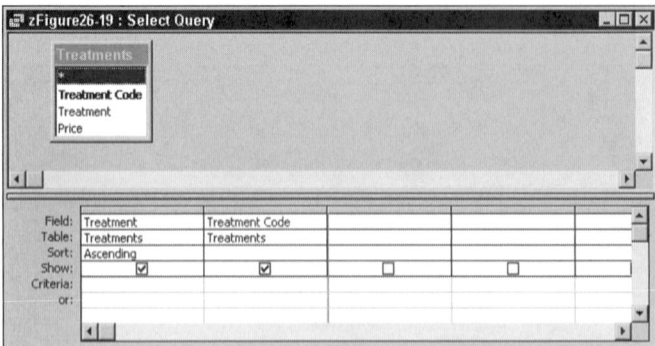

Figure 26-19: The query for the Treatment Code combo box

As you can see, both fields come from the Treatments table. The fields appear in the combo box in order of the value of Treatment. This is the treatment name. This is an alphabetical listing because the field is a Text field data type. Notice that two fields are used in the query. The treatment code will be hidden so that only the treatment name is displayed.

After you create the query, you can create the combo box. To create the combo box for the treatment code, follow these steps:

1. Display the subform in the Design view.

2. Select the existing Treatment Code text box control.

3. From the menu bar, select Format ⇨ Change To ⇨ Combo Box.

4. With the Treatment Code combo box selected, display the property sheet.

5. Select Table/Query for the Row Source Type property.

6. Enter Treatment Lookup in the Row Source property.

7. Set the Column Count property to 2 and the Column Heads property to Yes.

8. Set the Column Widths property to 2";0".

9. Set the Bound Column property to 2 and the List Rows property to 4.

10. Set the List Width property to 2".

11. Set the Limit To List property to Yes so that the user must select from the list.

Figure 26-20 shows this combo box completed. When the form is run and the user selects the Treatment Code field, the list of valid treatment codes is shown. Because the Bound Column is 2 (the hidden Treatment Code column), Access places the value of the Treatment Code in the Treatment Code field in the Visit Details table.

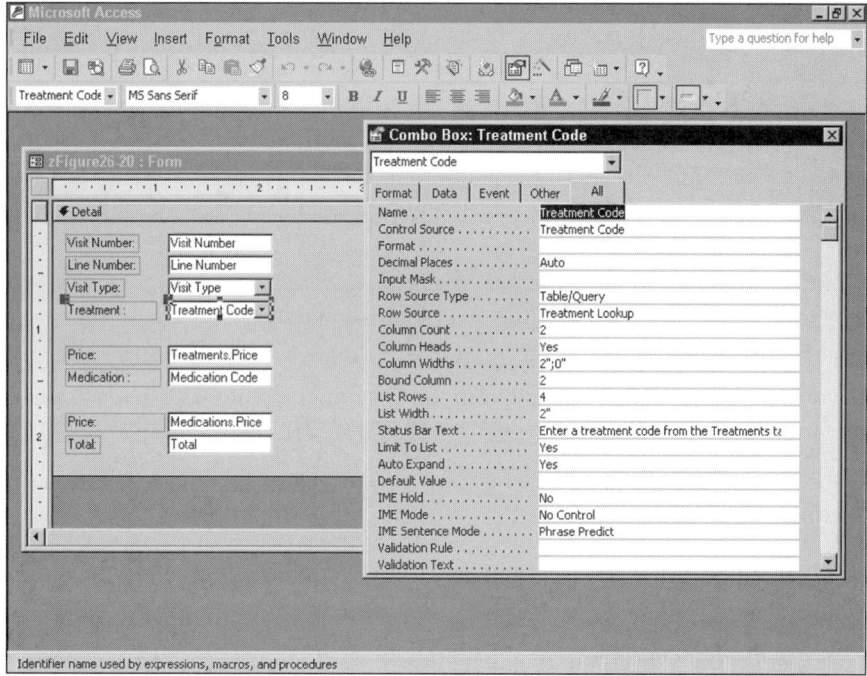

Figure 26-20: Creating a combo box for the Treatment Code

The Medication Code lookup table is virtually identical to the Treatment Code lookup table; only the field name is different. To create this combo box, you also need to create a query. Figure 26-21 shows the query for the Medication Code combo box.

As you can see, all these fields come from the Medications table. They appear in the combo box in order of the value of the Medication Name (an alphabetical listing because the field uses the Text data type). Notice that two fields are used in the query. The Medication Code is hidden; only the Medication name is displayed.

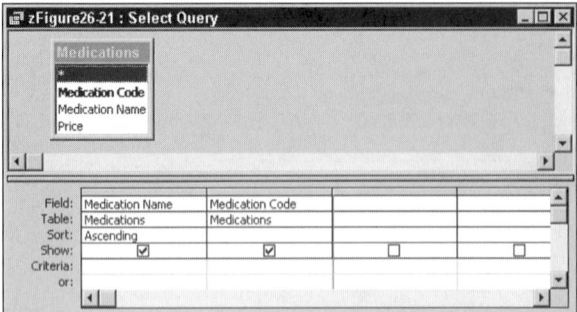

Figure 26-21: The query for the Medication Code combo box

After you create the query, you can create the combo box. To create the combo box for the Medication Code, follow these steps:

1. Display the subform in Design view.

2. Select the existing Medication Code text box control.

3. From the menu bar, select Format ⇨ Change To ⇨ Combo Box.

4. With the Medication Code combo box selected, display the property sheet.

5. Select Table/Query for the Row Source Type property.

6. Enter Medications Lookup in the Row Source property.

7. Set the Column Count property to 2 and the Column Heads property to Yes.

8. Set the Column Widths property to 2";0".

9. Set the Bound Column property to 2 and the List Rows property to 4.

10. Set the List Width property to 2".

11. Set the Limit To List property to Yes so that the user must select from the list.

Figure 26-22 shows this combo box completed. When the form is run and the user selects the Medication Code field, the list of valid medication codes is shown. Because the Bound Column is 2 (the hidden Medication Code column), Access places the value of the Medication Code in the Medication Code field in the Visit Details table.

After you make these changes, you can test your changes. You may want first to display the form as a datasheet in the Form view of the subform. You can also close the form and display the subform in the main form. Close the subform and run the main form named Adding Visit Details.

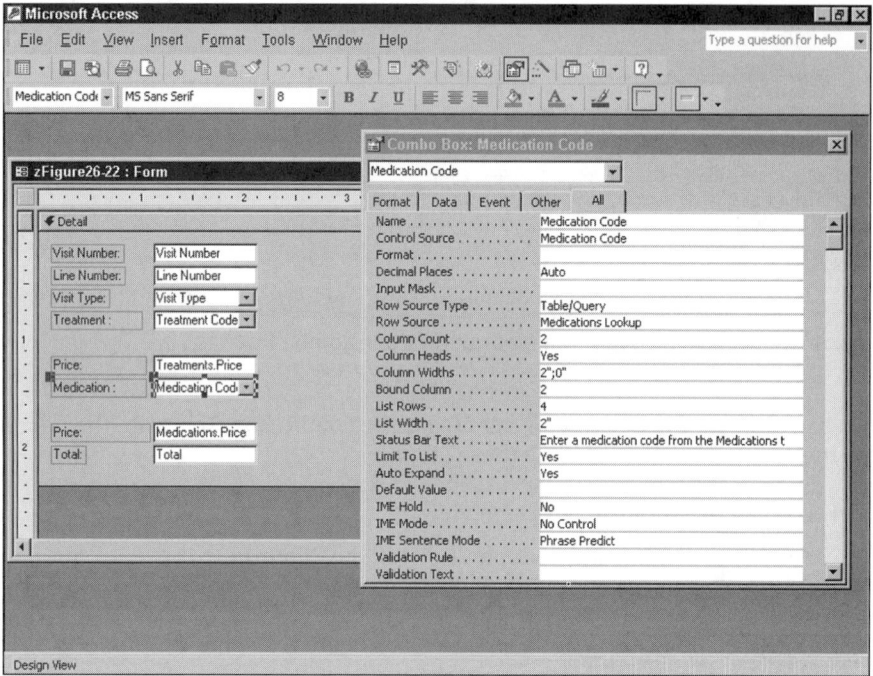

Figure 26-22: Creating a combo box for the Medication Code

First, you can test the combo boxes. Click the Visit Type field. An arrow should appear. When you click the arrow, the list of valid visit types is displayed. You can then select the desired visit type or enter a new one in the combo box. When the combo box is closed, Access enters this data into the Visit Type field of the Visit Details table.

When you select the Treatment Code field and select the arrow, a combo box is also displayed, as shown in Figure 26-23. The combo box displays only three columns because the List Rows property is set to 4 and the Column Heads property is set to Yes.

The treatment description is shown in its entirety, even though the Treatment Code field entry area is smaller. This is controlled by setting the List Width property to 2. If you leave this property set to the default (Auto), your data may be truncated (displayed with too much white space after the values) because the list width will be the size of the actual combo box control on the subform. When you select the desired treatment, Access automatically enters the hidden value of the treatment code in the Treatments table into the Treatment Code field in Visit Details.

The Medication Code field works in exactly the same way. Notice that as you select various treatments, the price is updated automatically in each line to reflect the selection. As either Treatment Price or Medication Price changes, the Total field is also updated.

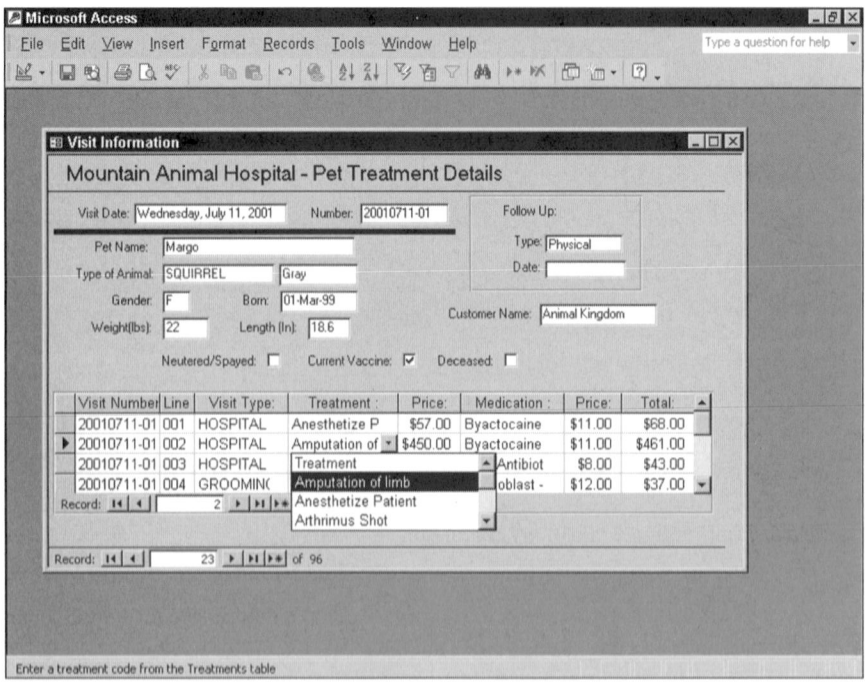

Figure 26-23: Displaying the subform

The last change to make to the form is to create a field to display totals of all the line items in the datasheet.

Creating totals in subforms

To create a total of the line items in the subform, you have to create an additional calculated field on the form you're using as a subform. Figure 26-24 shows a new field being created in the form footer on this form.

Just as you can create summaries in reports, you can create them in forms. Use the form footer; that way, the calculation occurs after all the detail records are processed. When the form is displayed in Single-form view, this total is always equal to the detail record. In Continuous-form or Datasheet view, however, this calculation is the sum of the processed record.

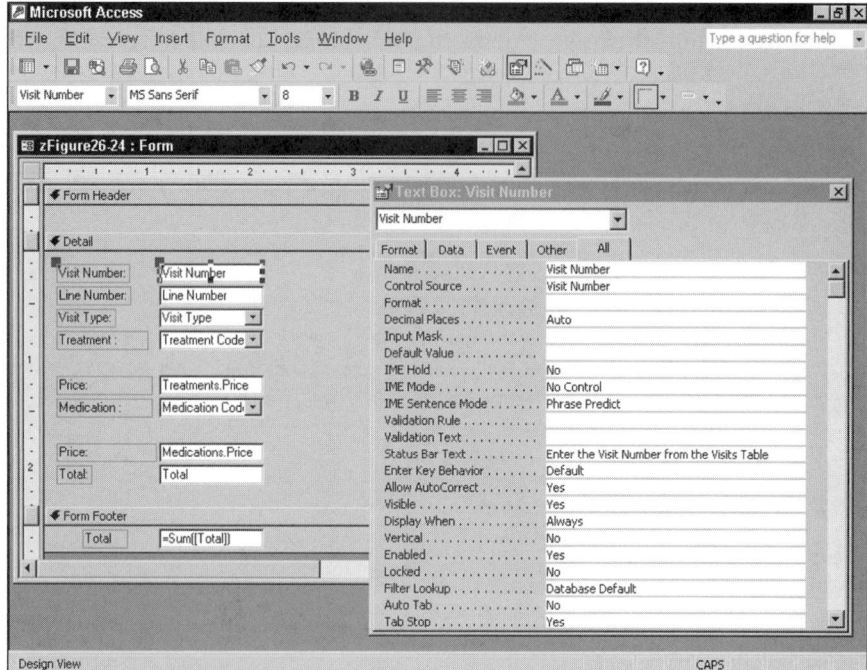

Figure 26-24: Creating a summary calculation

As shown in Figure 26-24, the text box Control Source property is the expression =Sum([Total]). This is the sum of all the values in the Total field. To display the data as a dollar amount, the field's Format property should be set to Currency and the number of decimal places set to 2.

Although the text box control was created in the subform, it's displayed by a text box control (which refers to the subform control) placed in the main form. This control is shown in Figure 26-25.

Because the field is in another form, it must be referred to with the fully qualified terminology:

```
Object type![Form name]![Subform name].Form![Subform field
name]
```

As you can see in the property sheet, the Control Source property is as follows:

```
=[Forms]![Adding Visit Details]![Data for Subform
Example].[Form]![Total Sum]
```

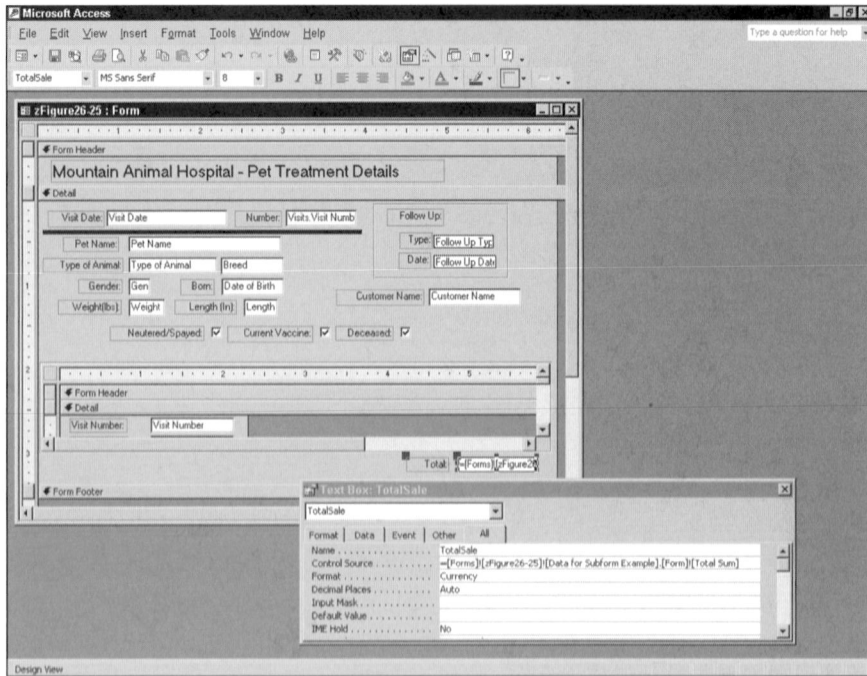

Figure 26-25: Referring to a control in another form

The first part of the reference specifies the name of the form; Form tells Access that it's the name of a form. By using the ! character, you tell Access that the next part is a lower hierarchy. The control name [Total Sum] contains the value to be displayed.

The final form, including the total for the subform, is shown in Figure 26-26.

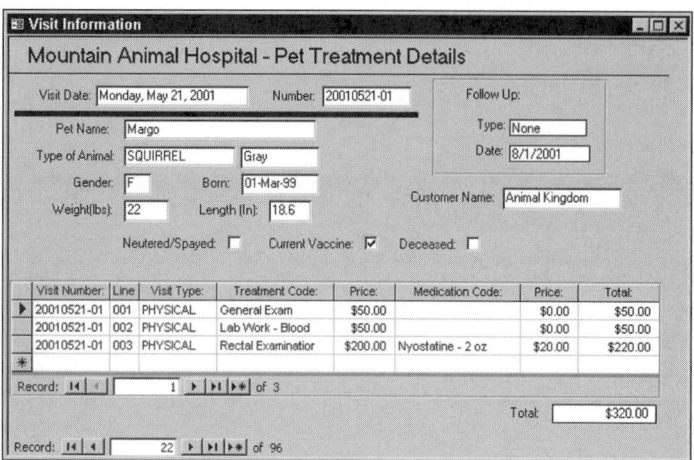

Figure 26-26: Displaying the totals

✦   ✦   ✦

Creating Mail Merge and Label Reports

◆ ◆ ◆ ◆

In This Chapter

Using the Label Wizard

Modifying mailing-label reports

Using the expanded Page Setup dialog box

Understanding snaked column reports

Creating a snaked column report

Creating a mail merge letter in Access

Using the Access to Word Mail Merge Wizard

◆ ◆ ◆ ◆

For correspondence, you often need to create mailing labels and form letters, commonly known as mail merges. The Access Report Writer helps you create these types of reports as well as the reports with multiple columns known as snaked column reports.

Creating Mailing Labels Using the Label Wizard

You create mailing labels in Access by using a report. You can create the basic label by starting from a blank form, or you can use the Label Wizard. This Wizard is much easier to use and saves you a great deal of time and effort.

Access 2002 has no special report for creating mailing labels. Like any other report, the report for a mailing label is made up of controls; the secret to the mailing label is using the margin settings and the Page Setup screen.

In previous chapters, you learned how to use the Page Setup dialog box to change your margins. One of the tabs in the dialog box is Columns. When you select this tab, the Columns dialog box expands to reveal additional choices you use to control the number of labels across the report as well as how the data is placed on the report. You learn how to use this dialog box later in this chapter.

The best way to create mailing labels is to use the Label Wizard. You create a new report to be used for a mailing label just as you create any other report (see Figure 27-1). To create a new report for a mailing label, follow these steps:

1. From the Database window, click the Reports object button.

2. Click the New toolbar button to create a new report.

3. Select Label Wizard.

4. Select Customer from the table/query combo box.

5. Click OK.

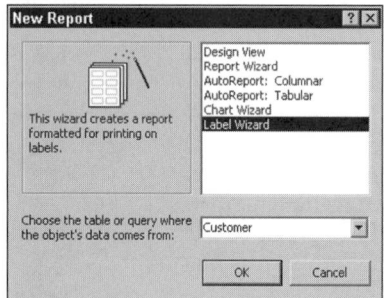

Figure 27-1: Choosing the Label Wizard

The Label Size dialog box will now display.

Selecting the label size

The first Wizard dialog box you see will ask you to select a label size. You can select the type of label stock you want to print to. Nearly a hundred Avery label stock forms are listed. (Avery is the world's largest producer of label paper.)

There are 40 other brands of labels that you can select from, including

AE	Agipa	A-ONE	Boeder	CoStar
Durable	Ero	Formtec	Herlitz	Herma
HP	Inmac	Kokuyo	Leitz	Maco
NCR	Pimaco	RankXerox	Rotary Card	Unistat

To select a different type of label other than Avery, click on the Filter by Manufacturer combo box to display the manufacturers available.

You can find in these lists nearly every type of paper these manufacturers make. You can select from lists of English or metric labels. You can also select sheet feed for laser printers or continuous feed for tractor-fed printers. Select between the two using the option buttons below the label sizes.

If you do not see the Avery labels in the Label Wizard, click the Show custom label sizes check box to turn it off.

The list box shown in Figure 27-2 contains three columns:

✦ **Product number.** The model number on the Manufacturer label box.

✦ **Dimensions.** The height and width of the label in either inches or millimeters.

✦ **Number across.** The number of labels that are physically across the page.

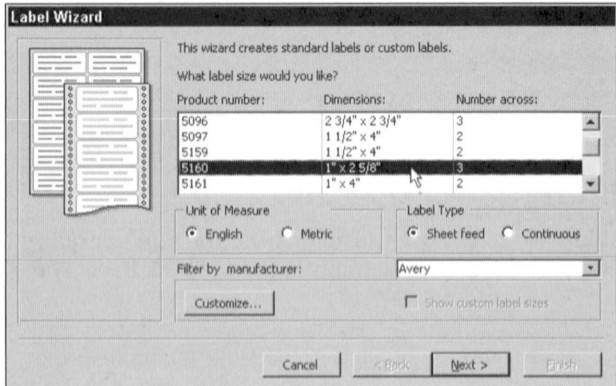

Figure 27-2: Selecting the label size

When you select a label size, you're actually setting the Page Setup parameters, as you learn later in this chapter.

Select Avery number 5160, as shown in Figure 27-2. Notice that there are three labels across and that the size is shown as 1" x 2⅝". You'll see these values again when you examine the Page Setup dialog box. After you select the label size, you can again click on the Next button to go to the next dialog box.

Note   You can also select the Customize button to create your own label specifications if the labels you're using are not standard labels.

Selecting the font and color

The next dialog box (shown in Figure 27-3) displays a set of combo boxes that enable you to select various attributes about the font and color of the text to use for the mailing label. For this example, click on the Italic check box to turn on the italic effect. Notice that the sample text changes to reflect the difference. Accept the remaining default choices of Arial, 8, Light, and black text. Click on the Next button to move to the next dialog box.

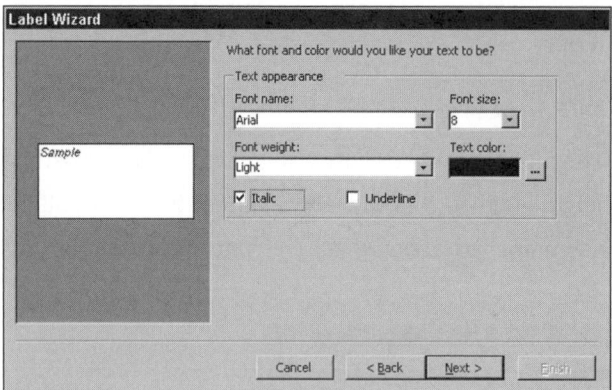

Figure 27-3: Selecting the font type, size, and color

Creating the mailing-label text and fields

The next dialog box enables you to choose the fields from the table or query to appear in the label. You can also add spaces, unbound text, blank lines, and even punctuation.

The dialog box is divided into two areas. The left area, titled Available fields, lists all the fields in the query or table. Figure 27-4, shown completed, displays the fields from the Customer table. The right area, titled Prototype label, shows the fields used for the label and displays a rough idea of how the mailing label will look when it's completed.

Note   The fields or text you use in this dialog box serve only as a starting point for the label. You can make additional changes later in the Report Design window.

You can select a field either by double-clicking the field name in the Available fields area or by selecting the field name and then clicking on the > command button between the two areas. You can remove a field by highlighting it and then pressing Delete on your keyboard. You move to the next line by pressing the Tab key.

You may enter text at any point by simply placing your cursor where you want to insert the text and then typing the text, including spaces and punctuation marks.

If you add a new line to the label and leave it blank, it will appear only as a blank line on the label (provided you have also manually changed the Can Shrink property to No for the unbound text box control you created to display that blank line). The default property for this control is Yes; the blank line is not displayed, and the lines above and below the blank line appear together.

To create the label as shown completed in Figure 27-4, follow these steps:

1. Double-click the Customer Name field in the Available fields list.

2. Press the Tab key to go to the next line.

3. Double-click the Street/Apt field in the Available fields list.

4. Press the Tab key to go to the next line.

5. Double-click the City field in the Available fields list.

6. With your cursor on the space after the City field, type a comma (,) to add a comma to the label.

7. Press the spacebar to add a blank space to the label after the comma.

8. Double-click the State field in the Available fields list.

9. Press the spacebar to add a blank space to the label after the State field.

10. Double-click the Zip Code field in the Available fields list.

11. Click the Next button to go to the next dialog box.

The completed label is displayed in Figure 27-4.

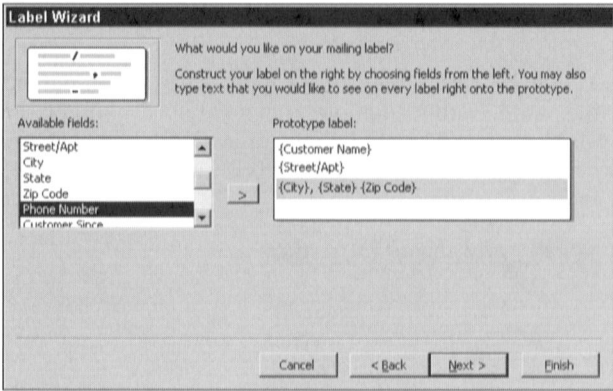

Figure 27-4: The completed label in the Label Wizard

Sorting the mailing labels

The next dialog box will prompt you to select a field on which to sort, as shown in Figure 27-5. Depending on how you have your database set up (and on how you want to organize your information), you may sort it by one or more fields. The dialog box consists of two sections; one lists the available fields, the other, the selected sort fields. To select a field, double-click it (it will appear in the right-side column labeled Sort by:) or use the arrow buttons (> and >>). The single > means that only the highlighted field will be selected; the double > means that every field showing in the column will be selected. In this example, you will select Customer Name as the field to sort by. When you're done, click Next to bring up the final dialog box.

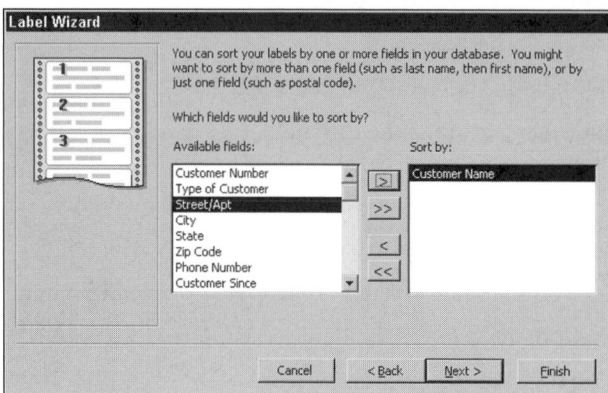

Figure 27-5: The Label Wizard's Sort By dialog box

The order of fields in the Sort by column is their sort order, from the top down. If a database has first and last name, you can select the last name, then the first name.

The last dialog box of the Label Wizard names your report. The default name is Label, followed by the table name. In this example, that's Labels Customer. Make it a meaningful name, such as Customer Mailing Labels. This dialog box is shown in Figure 27-6. (Do not choose Finish; you use this dialog box in the next section.)

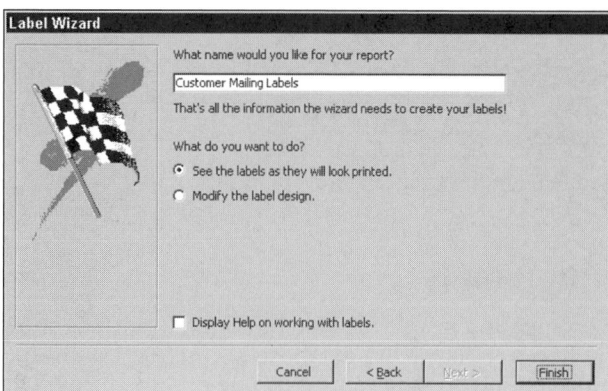

Figure 27-6: The final mailing Label Wizard dialog box

Displaying the labels in the Print Preview window

The final dialog box in the Label Wizard also enables you to decide whether to view the labels in the Print Preview window or to modify the report design in the Report Design window.

Make sure that "See the labels as they will look printed" is selected, and click the Finish button. You are taken directly to the Print Preview window (as shown in Figure 27-7). This is the normal Print Preview window for a report. By using the magnifying glass mouse pointer, you can switch to a page view to see an entire page of labels at one time, or you can zoom in to any quadrant of the report. By using the navigation buttons in the bottom, left corner of the window, you can display other pages of your mailing label report.

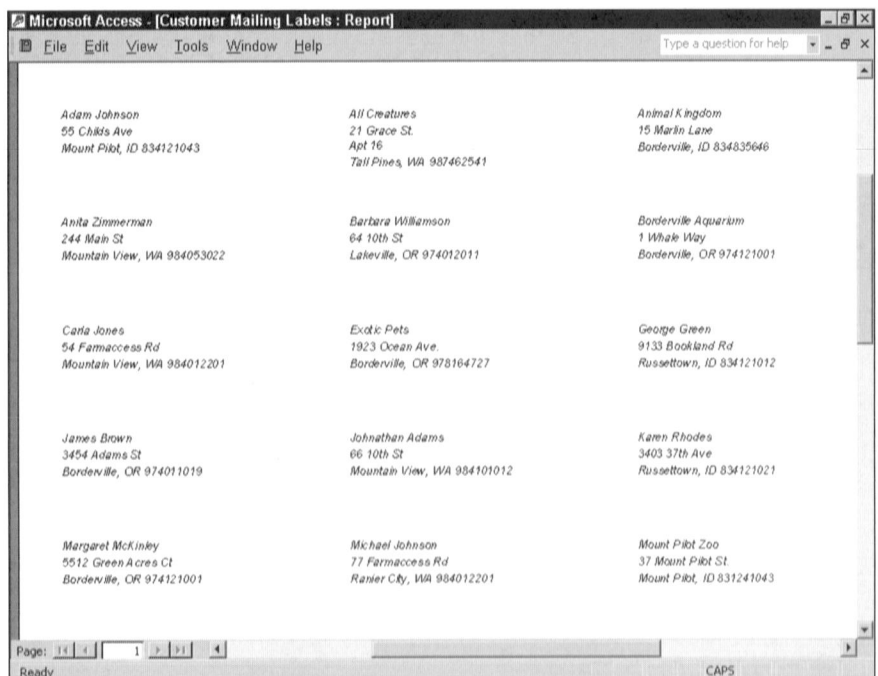

Figure 27-7: Viewing labels in the Print Preview window

Note   Remember that a mailing label is simply a report; it behaves as a report normally behaves.

You can print the labels directly from the Print Preview window, or you can click the first button on the toolbar to display the Report Design window.

Modifying the label design in the Report Design window

When you click the Close Window button, the label design appears in the Report Design window, as in Figure 27-8. Notice that the height of the detail band is 1 inch and the right margin of the report is 2⅜ inches. This gives you the measurement you defined when you chose the label size of 1" x 2⅝". The difference between 2⅜ and 2⅝ is the settings in the page setup box (discussed later in this chapter).

In the report print preview, the first record's ZIP code value is 834121043. The Zip Code field can be formatted using the @@@@@-@@@@ format to separate the first five and last four characters. (@ means accept any character.) This format displays the stored sequence of nine numbers with a hyphen placed where it properly goes. If there are only five numbers, then that is all that is displayed.

You may notice that there is a function named Trim in front of the concatenated string. The Trim function is added by the wizard and removes any unused spaces in the fields. If your City field is 20 characters and contains New York, you don't want 12 blank spaces before the comma and state values. Trim handles that problem. The control source expression below and shown in Figure 27-8 solves for the zip code.

```
=Trim([City] & ", " & [State] & " " & Format([Zip Code],
"@@@@@-@@@@")).
```

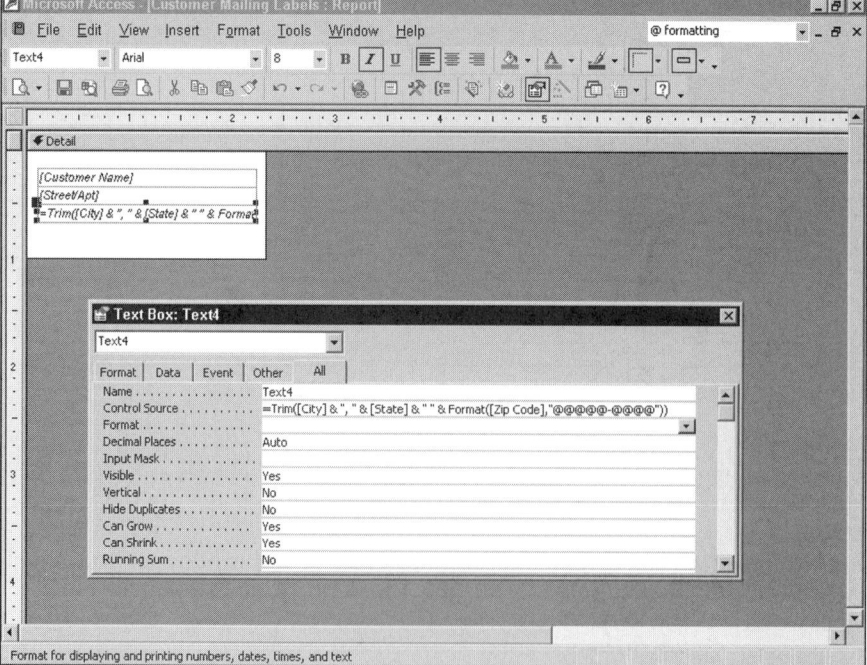

Figure 27-8: The Report Design window

Another change you could make is to the font size. In this example, Arial (the Helvetica TrueType font) with a point size of 8 is used. Suppose that you want to increase the text size to 10 points. You select all the controls and then click the Font Size drop-down list box and change the font size to 10 points. The text inside the controls becomes larger, but the control itself does not change size. As long as the text is not truncated or cut off on the bottom, you can make the font size larger.

You can also change the font style of any text. For example, if you want only the Customer Name text to appear in italics, you will need to select the other two text box controls and deselect the Italics button on the toolbar. Earlier, you specified in the Wizard that all three fields should be italics.

Now that you've changed your text like you want it, it's time to print the labels. Before you do, however, you should examine the Page Setup window.

To display the Page Setup window, select File ➪ Page Setup. The Page Setup window appears. Here, you can select the printer, change the orientation to Portrait or Landscape (have you ever seen landscape label paper?), change the Paper Size or Source settings, and set the margins. The margin setting controls the margins for the entire page. These affect the overall report itself, not just the individual labels.

To view the settings of each label and determine the size and number of labels across the page, select the Columns tab. The window then displays additional options, as shown in Figure 27-9.

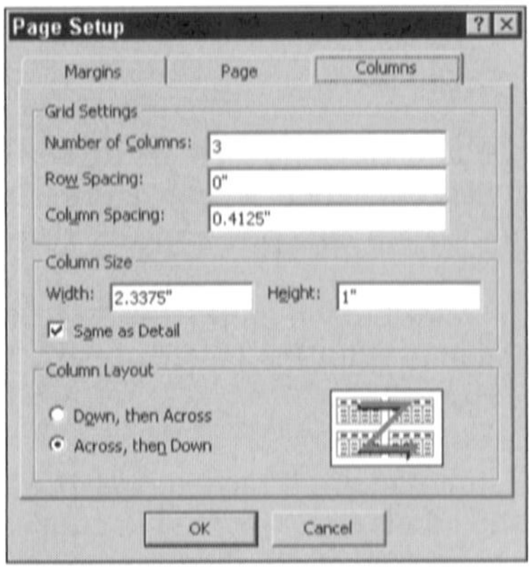

Figure 27-9: The Columns page from the Page Setup window

Figure 27-9 shows the Columns page. You first need to click the Margins tab and make sure the top and bottom margins are set to 0.5" and the left and right margins to 0.3".

Several items appear in the Columns dialog box. The first three items (under the Grid Settings) determine the spacing of the labels on the page:

✦ **Number of Columns.** Number of columns in the output

✦ **Row Spacing.** Space between the rows of output

✦ **Column Spacing.** Amount of space between each column (this property is not available unless you make the Items Across property greater than 1)

The Column Size settings determine the size of the label:

✦ **Width.** Sets the width of each label

✦ **Height.** Sets the height of each label

✦ **Same as Detail.** Sets the Width and Height properties to the same width and height as the detail section of your report

The Column Layout section determines in which direction the records are printed:

✦ **Down, then Across.** Prints consecutive labels in the first column and then starts in the second column when the first column is full

✦ **Across, then Down.** Prints consecutive labels across the page and then moves down a row when there is no more room

After the settings are completed, you can print the labels.

Printing labels

After you create the labels, change any controls, and view the Page Setup settings, you can print the labels. It's a good idea to preview the labels again. Figure 27-10 shows the final labels in the Print Preview window. The ZIP code appears correctly.

You can print the labels by simply selecting the Print button on the toolbar and then clicking OK in the Print dialog box. You can also print the labels directly from the Report Design window by selecting File ➪ Print.

Of course, you must insert your label paper first. If you don't have any #5160 label paper, you can use regular paper. If you want the labels to be printed in consecutive format, like a telephone directory, select Down, then Across in the Columns tab shown in Figure 27-9. In fact, that's another feature of Access reports — the capability to create what is known as a snaked column report.

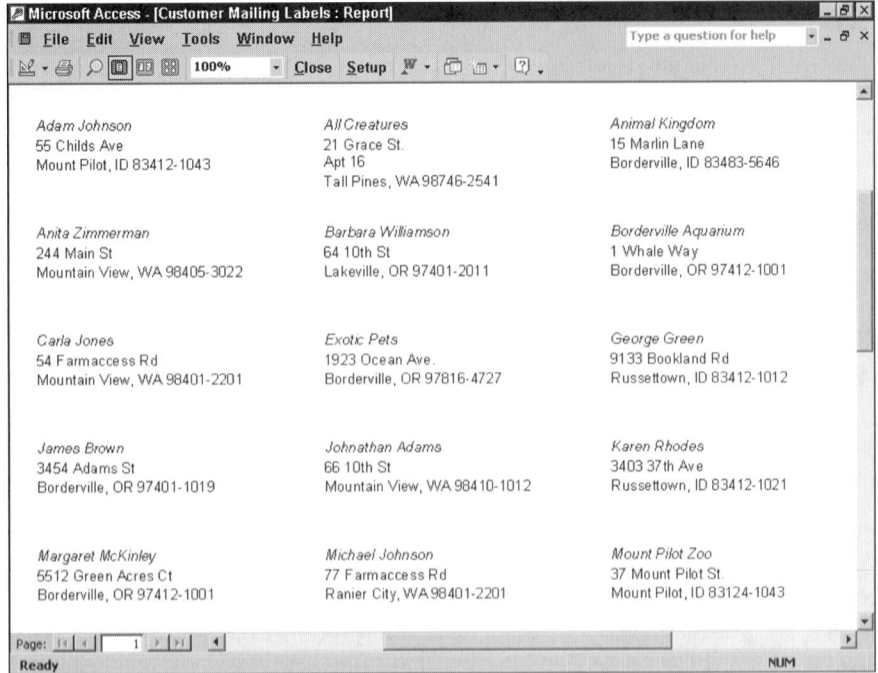

Figure 27-10: The final report print preview

Creating Snaked Column Reports

All the reports discussed in this book so far are either form-based (that is, free-form) or single-column lists. (Single column means that each column for each field appears only once on each page.) Often this is not the best way to present your data. Access gives you another option: snaking columns. This option enables you to define the sections of a report so that they fit in an area that is less than half the width of the printed page. When the data reaches the bottom of the page, another column starts at the top of the page; when there is no more room on the page for another column, a new page starts.

The snaked column technique is commonly used for text in telephone directories or newspapers and other periodicals. An example of a database use is a report that prints several addresses, side by side, for a page of adhesive mailing labels you feed through your laser printer. You just learned how to create labels for mailing. Now you will learn how to apply these same techniques in a report. Snaked column reports have a major difference from mailing labels: They often have group sections, page headers, and footers; mailing labels have only data in the detail section.

The general process for creating a snaked column report is as follows:

✦ Decide how you want your data to be displayed: How many columns do you want? How wide should each column be?

✦ Create a report that has detail and group section controls no wider than the width of one column.

✦ Set the appropriate options in the Page Setup dialog box.

✦ Verify your results by using print preview.

Creating the report

You create a snaked column report in the same way you create any report. You start out with a blank Report Design window. Then you drag field controls to the report design and add label controls, lines, and rectangles. Next, you add any shading or special effects you want. Then you're ready to print your report. The major difference is the placement of controls and the use of the Page Setup window.

Figure 27-11 shows a completed design for the Customers By State (three snaking columns) report. The report displays a label control and the date in the page header, along with some solid black lines to set the title apart from the directory details. The detail section contains information that lists the customer number, customer name, address, and phone number. Then, within this section, you see three information fields about the customer's history with Mountain Animal Hospital. The page footer section contains another solid black line and a page number control.

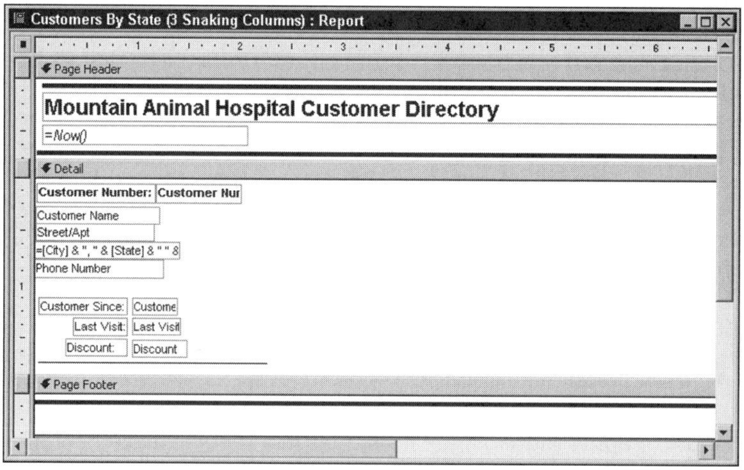

Figure 27-11: Defining a snaked column report design

What's important here is to make sure that the controls in the detail section use no more space for their height or width than you want for each occurrence of the information. Because you're going to be printing or displaying multiple detail records per page in a snaked column fashion, you must note the size. In this example, you can see that the detail section data is about 1¾ inches high and about 2 inches wide. This is the size of the item you will define in the Columns dialog box.

Before continuing, you have to specify a sort order for the report. The report should be placed in order by State and then by Customer Number. You can do this by clicking the Sorting and Grouping button on the toolbar and typing the names of the fields in the dialog box.

Defining the page setup

Earlier in this chapter, in the "Creating Mailing Labels" section, you learned how to use Page Setup settings. Because you created the labels by using the Label Wizard, the values for the Page Setup were automatically adjusted for you. Next, you learn how to enter these values manually. Figure 27-12 shows the Page Setup dialog box and the settings used to produce the Customer Directory report. Again, it doesn't show you the settings for the margins. Before continuing, click on the Margins tab and set the left and right margins to 0.5" (the top and bottom should be 1 inch). Then click on the Columns tab to continue.

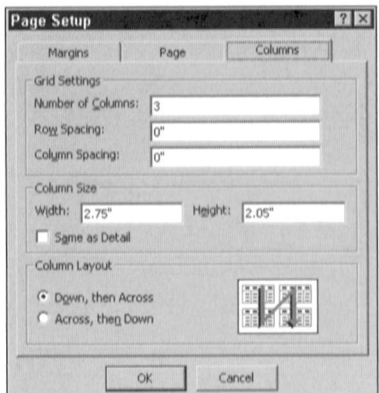

Figure 27-12: Defining the layout setup for a snaked column report

The first group of settings (Grid Settings) to change are the Number of Columns, Row Spacing, and Column Spacing. Notice that the Number of Columns setting is set to 3. This means that you want three customer listings across the page. This and the other two settings actually work together. As you learned in the section about mailing labels, these controls set the spacing between groups of data and how the data is to be shown (the number of columns). The Row Spacing should be set to 0.2" and the Column Spacing set to 0.4". This is one way to set up the multiple columns and allow enough space between both the rows and the columns.

The next grouping is the Column Size settings. In this example, the data is 1¾ inches high and about 2 inches wide in the detail section. You can define Width as 2.75 in and Height as 2.05 in. By adjusting the Grid Settings and Column Sizes, you control how your columned report will look.

Notice that the final grouping, Column Layout section, offers two settings: Down, then Across or Across, then down. The icon under Column Layout shows the columns going up and down. You saw in Figure 27-9 that when the setting is Across, then Down, the icon shows rows of labels going across. In this customer directory, you want to fill an entire column of names first before moving to the right to fill another column. Therefore, you select the Down, then Across setting.

Printing the snaked column report

After the expanded Page Setup dialog box settings are completed, you can print your report. Figure 27-13 shows the top half of the first page of the final snaked column report in the Print Preview window. The data is sorted by state and customer number. Notice that the data snakes down the page. The first record is for Customer Number AK001, in Idaho. Below that is customer BR001. There are four customers in the first column. After the fourth customer, the next customer (Customer Number MP002) is found at the top of the middle column.

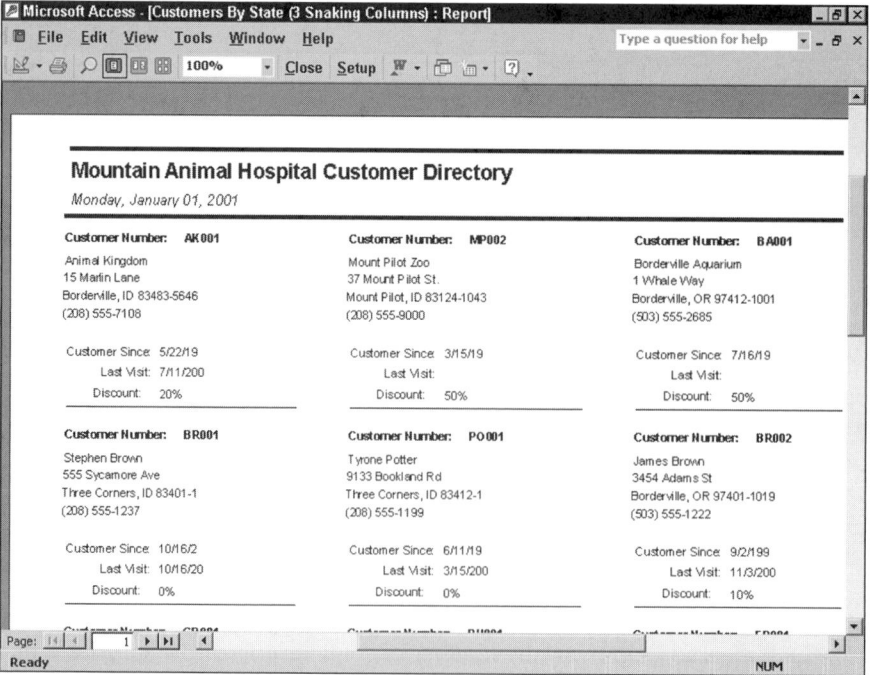

Figure 27-13: A snaked column report

Creating Mail Merge Reports

Now that you have learned how to create snaked column reports and mailing labels (actually, they are the same thing), there is one more type of report to create—the mail merge report (also known as a form letter). A mail merge report is simply a report containing large amounts of text that have embedded database fields. For example, a letter may contain within the body of the text the amount a customer owes and the name of a pet.

The problem is how to control the word wrap. This means that the text may occupy more than one line, depending on the length of the text and the embedded field values. Different records may have different length values in their embedded fields. One record may use two lines in the report, another may use three, and another may require only one.

Access 2002 contains a Report Wizard that exports your data to Microsoft Word and launches the Word Print Merge feature. Why would you want to use a word processor, however, when you're working in a database? What happens if you don't use Word? Most word processors can perform mail merges using database data. Access itself does not have a specific capability to perform mail merging. Even so, as you see in this section, Access can indeed perform mail merge tasks with nearly the same precision as any Windows word processor!

In the first section of this chapter, you created mailing labels that indicated a special offer. You can use these labels to address the envelopes for the mail merge letter you now create. Suppose that you need to send a letter to all your customers who have an outstanding balance. You want to let them know that you expect payment now.

Figure 27-14 shows a letter created with Access. Many of the data fields embedded in this letter come from an Access query. The letter was created entirely with the Access Report Writer, as were its embedded fields.

Mountain Animal Hospital
2414 Mountain Road South
Redmond, WA 06761
(206) 555-9999

January 03, 2001

All Creatures
21 Grace St.
Tall Pines, WA 98746-2541

Dear All Creatures:

It has come to our attention that you have an outstanding balance of $2,000.00. We must have payment within 10 days or we will have to turn this account over to our lawyers. We give great service to your pets. In fact, according to our records, we have helped care for your animals since March 1998.

The entire staff is very fond of your animals. They especially like Bobo, and they would be very upset if your pet was no longer cared for by us. Since your last visit date on August 26, 2001, we have tried to contact you several times without success. Therefore, we are giving you 10 days to pay at least half of the outstanding balance, which comes to $1,000.00.

In advance, thank you, and we look forward to hearing from you and receiving your payment by January 13, 2001.

Sincerely,

Fred G. Rizzley

President
Mountain Animal Hospital

Figure 27-14: A letter created with the Access Report Writer

Assembling data for a mail merge report

You can use data from either a table or a query for a report. A mail merge report is no different from any other report. As long as you specify a table or query as the control source for the report, the report can be created. Figure 27-15 shows a typical query used for the letter.

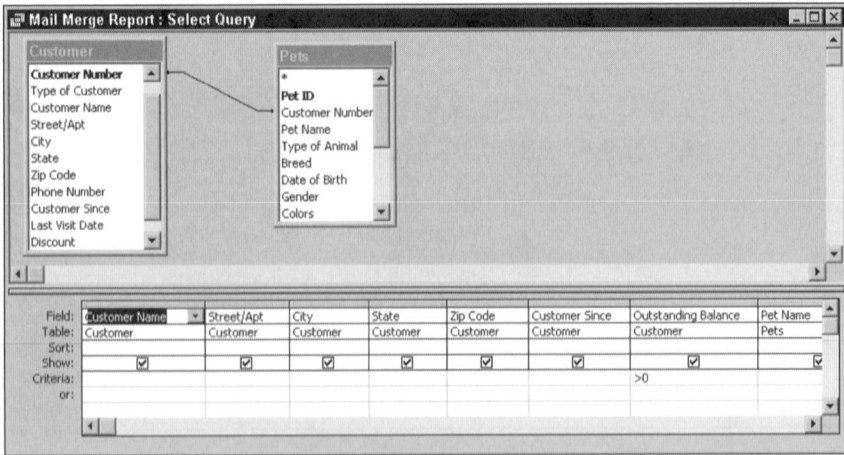

Figure 27-15: A typical query for a mail merge report

Table 27-1 shows the fields or functions embedded in the text blocks used to create the letter. Compare the values in each line of the letter (shown in Figure 27-14) to the fields shown in the table. Later in this chapter, you'll see how each field or function is embedded in the text.

Table 27-1		
Fields Used in the Mail Merge Report		
Field Name	*Table*	*Usage in Report*
Date( )	Function	Page header; displays current date; formatted as mmmm dd, yyyy
Customer Name	Customer	Page header; displays customer name
Street/Apt	Customer	Page header; displays street in the address block
City	Customer	Page header; part of city, state, ZIP code block
State	Customer	Page header; part of city, state, ZIP code block

Continued

Table 27-1 *(continued)*		
Field Name	**Table**	**Usage in Report**
Zip Code	Customer	Page header; part of city, state, ZIP code block; formatted as @@@@@-@@@@
Customer Name	Customer	Detail; part of salutation
Outstanding Balance	Customer	Detail; first line of first paragraph; formatted as $#,##0.00
Customer Since	Customer	Detail; fourth line in first paragraph; formatted as mmmm yyyy
Pet Name	Pets	Detail; first line in second paragraph
Last Visit Date	Customer	Detail; second and third lines in second paragraph; formatted as mmm dd, yyyy
Outstanding	Customer	Detail; fifth line in second paragraph; formatted as $#,##0.00 Balance *.5 Calculation
Date Add( );	Function	Detail; second line in third paragraph; Date Add adds ten days Now( ) Function to system date Now( ); formatted as mmmm dd, yyyy

Creating a mail merge report

After you assemble the data, you can create your report. Creating a mail merge report is much like creating other reports. Frequently a mail merge has only a page header and a detail section. You can use sorting and grouping sections, however, to enhance the mail merge report (although form letters normally are fairly consistent in their content).

Usually the best way to begin is with a blank report. Report Wizards don't really help you create a mail merge report. After you create a blank report, you can begin to add your controls to it.

Creating the page header area

A form letter generally has a top part that includes your company's name, address, and possibly a logo. You can print on preprinted forms that contain this information, or you can scan in the header and embed it in an unbound object frame. Usually, the top part of a form letter also contains the current date along with the name and address of the person or company to whom you're sending the letter.

Figure 27-16 shows the page header section of the mail merge report. In this example, an unbound bitmap picture is inserted that contains the Mountain Animal Hospital logo. The text for the company information is created with individual label controls. As you can see in the top half of the page header section, the current date is also displayed along with a line to separate the top of the header from the body of the letter. You can see the calculated text box control's properties at the bottom of Figure 27-16. The Format( ) and Date( ) functions are used to display the date with the full text for month, followed by the day, a comma, a space, and the four-digit year.

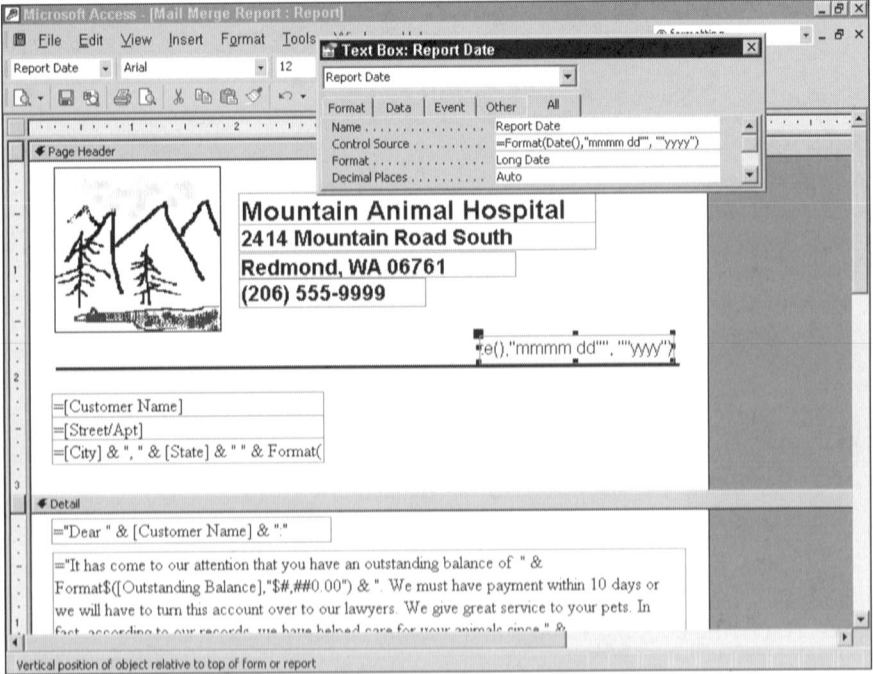

Figure 27-16: The page header section of a mail merge report

The date expression is entered as

```
=Format(Date( ),"mmmm dd, yyyy")
```

and then automatically changed to

```
=Format(Date(),"mmmm dd""."" yyyy")
```

This expression takes the system date of 1/03/2001 and formats the date as January 3, 2001.

The customer name and address fields are also displayed in the page header. The standard concatenated expression is used to display the city, state, and ZIP code fields:

```
=[City] & ", " & [State] & " " & Format([Zip Code],
"@@@@@-@@@@")
```

Working with embedded fields in text

The body of the letter is shown in Figure 27-17. Each paragraph is one large block of text. A standard text box control is used to display each paragraph. The text box control's Can Grow and Can Shrink properties are set to Yes, which allows the text to take up only as much space as needed.

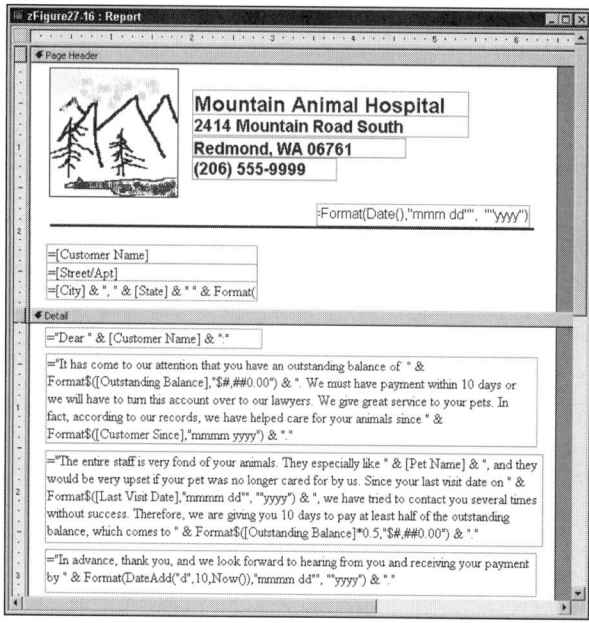

Figure 27-17: The body of the letter in the Report Design window

Embedded in each text block are fields from the query or expressions that use the fields from the query. In the page header section, the & method is used to concatenate the city, state, and ZIP code. Although this method works for single concatenated lines, it does not enable word wrapping, which is critical to creating a mail merge report. If you use this method in large blocks of text, you get only a single, truncated line of text.

Note   As you learned in Chapter 21, the & method of concatenation handles word wrap within the defined width of the text box. When the text reaches the right margin of a text box, it shifts down to the next line. Because the Can Grow property is turned on, the text box can have any number of lines. It's best to convert non-text data to text when you concatenate with the & method. Although this conversion isn't mandatory, the embedded fields are displayed more correctly when they are correctly converted and formatted.

The first text block is a single-line text box control that concatenates the text "Dear" with the field Customer Name. Notice the special symbols within the first text box control. Remember that each text box is made up of smaller groups of text and expressions. By using the & character, you can concatenate them.

The expression ="Dear" & [Customer Name] & ":" begins with an equal sign and a double quote. Because the first item is text, it's surrounded by " characters. [Customer Name] needs to be enclosed in brackets because it's a field name; it should also be surrounded by & characters for concatenation. The colon at the end of the expression appears in the letter; it is text and must be surrounded by double quotes.

The next control produces the first paragraph of the letter. Notice that there are five lines in the text box control but only four lines in the first paragraph of the letter (as shown in Figure 27-14). If you compare the two figures carefully, however, you'll see that the text box for the date is on the fifth line of the paragraph in the text control, whereas it's in the fourth line of the paragraph in the printed letter. This is a good example of word wrap. The lines shrank to fit the data.

The first line of the text control simply displays a text string. Notice that the text string is both enclosed in double quotes and concatenated to the next expression by the & character. The second line begins with an expression:

```
Format$([Outstanding Balance],"$#,##0.00") & "."
```

The expression converts the numeric expression to text and formats the field Outstanding Balance so that it shows a dollar sign, a comma (if the value is 1,000 or more), and two displayed decimal places. Without the format, the field would have simply displayed 381 rather than $381.00 for the first record.

The rest of the second line of the paragraph through the end of the fourth is one long text string. It's simply enclosed in double quotes and concatenated by the & character. The last line of the first paragraph contains an expression that formats and converts a date field. The expression Format$([Customer Since],"mmmm yyyy") formats the date value to display only the full month name and the year. (The date format in the page header demonstrated how to display the full month name, day, and year.)

 Tip   The maximum length of a single concatenated expression in Access is 254 characters between a single set of quotes. To get around this limitation, just end one expression, add an & character, and start another. The limit on the length of an expression in a single text box is 2,048 characters (almost 40 lines)!

The last line of the second paragraph formats a numeric expression, but it also calculates a value within the format function. This is a good example of an expression within a function. The calculation [Outstanding Balance] * .5 is then formatted to display dollar signs, and a comma if the number is 1,000 or more.

The last paragraph contains one text string and one expression. The expression advances the current date Now( ) by 10 days by using the expression DateAdd("d",10,Now()).

The bottom of the letter is produced using the label controls, as shown in Figure 27-17. These label controls display the closing, the signature, and the owner's title. The signature of Fred G. Rizzley is created here by using the Script font. Normally, you would scan in the signature and then use an unbound frame object control to display the bitmap picture that contains the signature.

One thing you must do is set the Force New Page property of the detail section to After Section so that a page break is always inserted after each letter.

Printing the mail merge report

You print a mail merge report in exactly the same way you would print any report. From the Print Preview window, you can simply click the Print button. From the Report Design window, you can select File ➪ Print. The report is printed like any other report.

Using the Access Mail Merge Wizard for Microsoft Word

Another feature in Access 2002 is a Wizard to open Word automatically and start the Print Merge feature. The table or query you specify when you create the new report is used as the data source for Microsoft Word print merge.

To use the Mail Merge Wizard in Access 2002, you must have Microsoft Word.

1. From the Database container window, click either the Tables or Queries object button.

2. Select the table or query you want to merge with Word.

3. Click the OfficeLinks drop-down button on the toolbar.

4. Select Merge It with Microsoft Word to start the Microsoft Word Mail Merge Wizard, as shown in Figure 27-18.

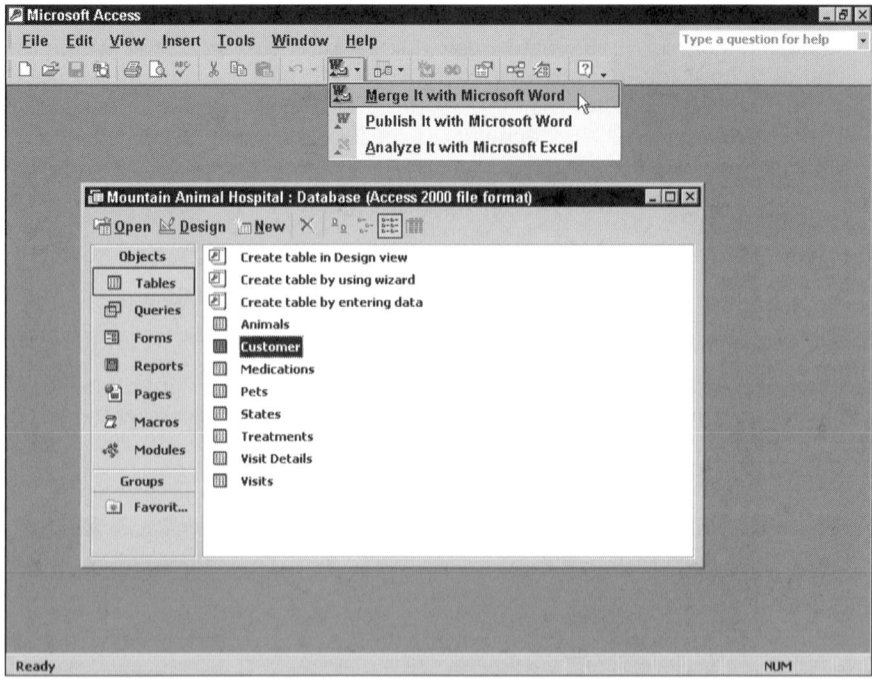

Figure 27-18: Selecting the Microsoft Word Mail Merge Wizard

5. After you select the Microsoft Word Mail Merge Wizard, Access displays the Microsoft Word Mail Merge Wizard screen, as shown in Figure 27-19.

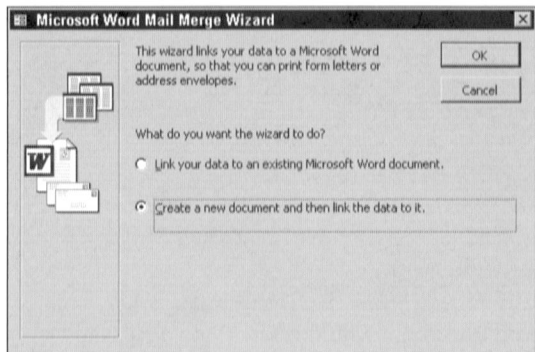

Figure 27-19: The Microsoft Word Mail Merge Wizard dialog

6. This screen enables you to decide whether to link your data to an existing Word document or to create a new document. If you select the option that says to Link your data to an existing Microsoft Word document, Access displays a standard Windows file-selection box that enables you to select an existing document. The document is retrieved, Word is displayed, and the Print Merge feature is active. You can then modify your existing document.

7. In this example, you start with a new document.

8. Select the option Create a new document and then link the data to it.

9. Click OK to launch Word and display the Print Merge toolbar.

Microsoft Word 2002 moves beyond wizards and embraces a new technology known as the task pane. As you can see in Figure 27-20 to the right of the standard Word window, the task pane combines traditional help and task-oriented wizards to attempt to simplify complex processes.

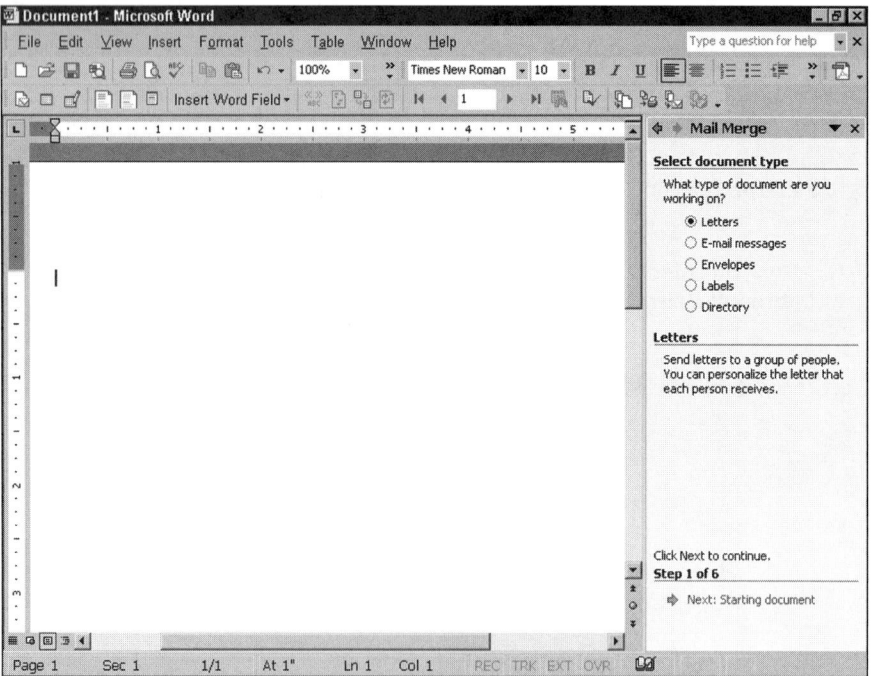

Figure 27-20: A blank Microsoft word document with the Task Pane displayed

Note   If you used Microsoft Access 1.0-2.0, you might remember a technology known as cue cards. Task panes are the next generation of cue cards.

Tip   You can display a task pane in any Office XP application by right-clicking any toolbar and selecting Task Pane.

While you don't need to use the task pane to create a mail-merge document, it is a
good idea to understand how it can help you. As you can see in Figure 27-20, the
first task pane asks you to select whether you want to create a letter, e-mail message, envelope, labels, or telephone-type directory. Based on your choices, different
successive choices are available. For example, if you select Envelope, various envelope options are displayed in the later task panes. For this example, select the
default choice of Letters.

Then click the Next button at the bottom of the pane. You are presented with the
following choices:

> Use the current document.
>
> Start from a template.
>
> Start from existing document.

If you choose to start from an existing document or template you can then select
one to bring to the Word document area. Figure 27-21 shows a document that has
been entered without any mail-merge fields. You generally start with a document
that has already been entered or you can type one in.

Mail merge means that when the document is printed, data values from fields in a
table are merged into the document. In this example, as you can see in Figure 27-21,
place holders in the form of xxx's have been entered will fields will be entered.

If you use the task pane, the next pane enables you to select recipients from an
existing list you have created, a list of Microsoft Outlook contacts, or you can enter
a new list. In this example, the recipients are part of the Customer table and do not
have to be selected separately.

Note   If you choose to select recipients, you can edit the data in your table using a pop-
up dialog and sort the data by any column, eliminate blank records, and even
select specific records.

The next task pane (4 of 6) enables you to add specific types of information to your
letter as shown in Figure 27-21. These special helpers include help for the following
fields:

> Address blocks
>
> Greeting lines
>
> Electronic postage
>
> Postal bar code
>
> and more items that enable you to insert the merge fields.

Figure 27-21 also shows the Insert Merge Field dialog box, showing all of the fields in the Customer table that can be used within the letter.

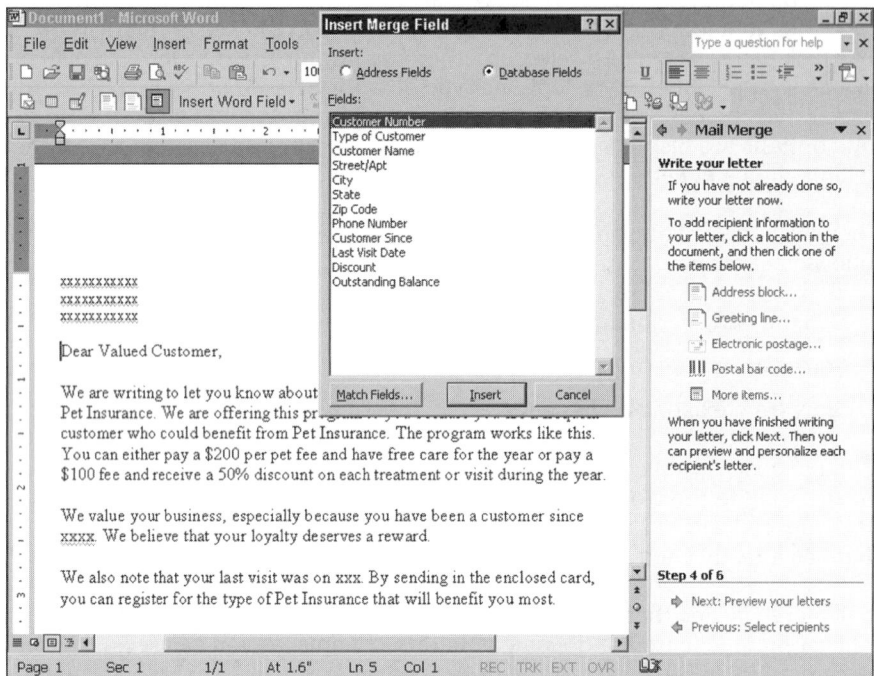

Figure 27-21: A Microsoft Word document ready for table fields to be entered

Once you decide where you want to include fields from your table in your letter, you can position your cursor in your letter and then select the field or fields you want in each position by simply double-clicking on them. Figure 27-22 shows the letter after the fields have been entered.

Tip   You can also display the field list for the merge by pressing the Insert Merge Fields button located next to the Insert Word Field text on the Mail Merge toolbar.

Notice the name and address information at the top of the letter. This is made up of five separate fields. In the second sentence of the second paragraph, a field named Customer Since has been added for the first year the customer came to the veterinarian. In the last paragraph, a field named Last Visit Date was added in the first sentence.

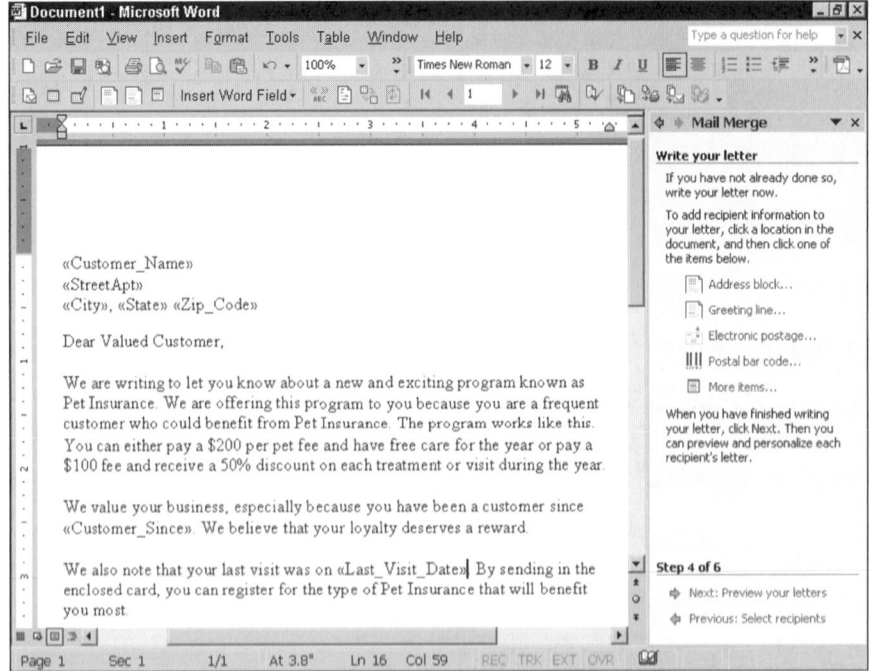

Figure 27-22: The Microsoft Word document with fields entered for the mail merge

The next step automatically merges your date and displays the first record in your letter. As you can see, not only is the name and address of your customer displayed, but the Customer Since value and Last Visit Date value are displayed.

The task pane displays some buttons that enable you to move between records and see how they are displayed as shown in Figure 27-23. The task pane also enables you to exclude specific data records or edit the data while you are looking at the letter.

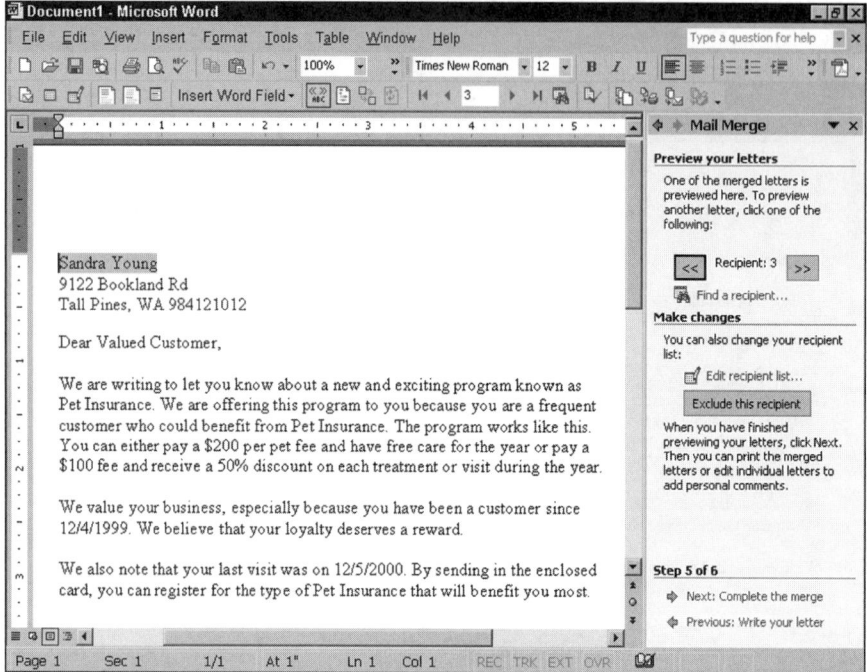

Figure 27-23: The Microsoft Word document displayed in preview mode with the data fields merged

After you are through selecting the data you want, you can move to the last task pane and print all the letters or even edit individual letters before printing them. These are incredibly powerful new features and only available with Microsoft Word 2002. By combining the database power of Access and the word processing and editing features of Word, you have a very powerful environment.

✦   ✦   ✦

Access Application Tools

✦   ✦   ✦   ✦

In This Part

Chapter 28
Working with Macros
and Events

Chapter 29
Using Macros in
Forms and Reports

Chapter 30
Working with Visual
Basic in Access 2002

Chapter 31
Using Visual Basic in
Forms and Reports

Chapter 32
Creating
Switchboards,
Command Bars,
Menus, Toolbars, and
Dialog Boxes

✦   ✦   ✦   ✦

Working with Macros and Events

✦ ✦ ✦ ✦

In This Chapter

Understanding how macros work

Examining the components of the Macro window

Creating and running a macro

Editing, deleting, and renaming macros

Creating a macro that starts automatically

Creating macro groups

Supplying conditions to macros

Troubleshooting macros

Understanding how events work

Learning how events are triggered

✦ ✦ ✦ ✦

When working with a database system, the same tasks may be performed repeatedly. Rather than doing the same steps each time, you can automate the process with macros.

Database management systems continually grow as you add records in a form, perform ad hoc queries, and print new reports. As the system grows, many of the objects are saved for later use — for a weekly report or monthly update query, for example. You tend to create and perform many tasks repetitively. Every time you add customer records, for example, you open the same form. Likewise, you print the same form letter for customers whose pets are overdue for their annual shots.

You can create Access macros to perform these tasks, and run them from various locations within Access. You may also group related macros into a single macro object. After you have created these small programs, you may want certain macros to take effect whenever a user performs some action (such as pressing a button or opening a form). Access uses events to trigger macros automatically.

Understanding Macros

Access macros automate many repetitive tasks without your having to write complex programs or subroutines. In the example of the form letter for customers whose pets are overdue for annual shots (Chapter 27), a macro can perform a query and print the results for all such customers.

What is a macro?

Unlike macros in spreadsheets, Access macros normally are not used to duplicate individual keystrokes or mouse movements. They perform specific, user-specified tasks, such as opening a form or running a report.

Every task you want Access to perform is called an action. Access 2002 provides 55 actions that can be selected and performed in your macros. For example, you may have a macro that performs the actions shown in Figure 28-1:

✦ Place the hourglass on the screen

✦ Automatically open a form

✦ Display a message box that says that the macro is complete

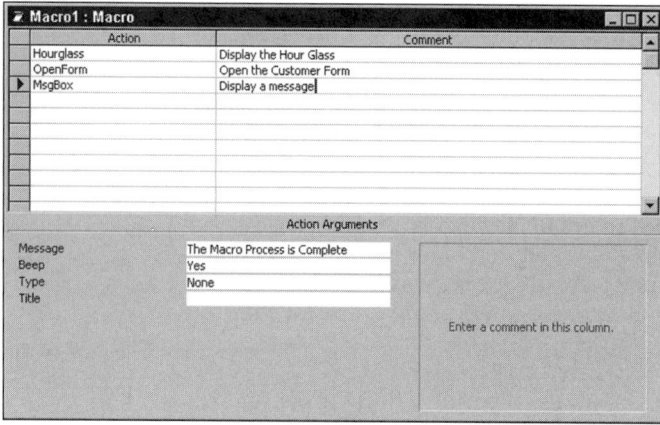

Figure 28-1: A macro designed with three actions (tasks)

Macro actions are created in a Macro Design window. Most macros are normally executed by entering their name in one of the Event property cells of a form or report. However, you can also run a macro directly from inside the macro portion of the database container.

When to use a macro

Macros can be used for any repetitive task that you do in Access, saving time and energy. In addition, because the macro performs the actions the same way each time, macros add accuracy and efficiency to the database. Macros can perform such tasks as

✦ Running queries and reports together

✦ Opening multiple forms and/or reports together

✦ Checking for data accuracy on validation forms

✦ Moving data between tables

✦ Performing actions when you click on a command button

As an example, a macro can find and filter records for a report, which allows you to add a command button to a form that when clicked tells the macro to perform a user-specified search. Macros such as this example can be used throughout the Access database system.

The Macro Window

As with other Access objects, a macro is created in a graphical design window. To open a new Macro window, follow these steps:

1. In an open database, press F11 (or Alt+F1) to select the Database window.

2. Click the Macros object button.

3. Click the New toolbar button in the Database window.

After you complete these steps, Access displays an empty Design window, similar to that in Figure 28-2. Notice the different parts of the window in this figure.

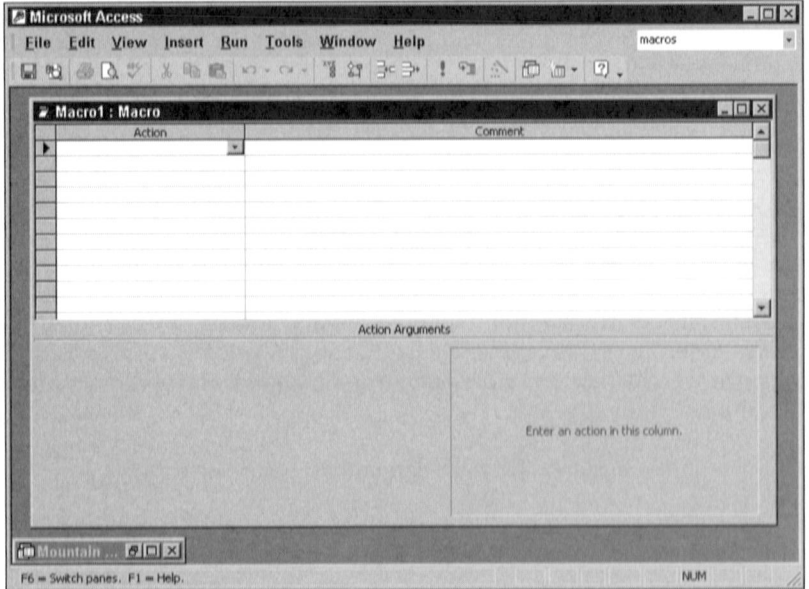

Figure 28-2: An empty Macro Design window

As Figure 28-2 shows, the Macro Design window has four parts, a menu and a toolbar above the Design window and two windowpanes:

✦ Action pane (top portion of the window)

✦ Argument pane (bottom portion of the window)

The Action pane

By default, when you open a new Macro Design window, as in Figure 28-2, Access displays two columns in the Action pane (top pane): Action and Comment. Two more columns, Macro Name and Condition, can be displayed in the Action pane by selecting View ⇨ Macro Names and View ⇨ Conditions, or by clicking on the equivalent icons on the toolbar. The Macro Names button is under the Window menu choice — it is a box with the letters 'XYZ' atop two smaller boxes. The Condition button is also under the Window menu choice — it is a box with a diamond on the left-top corner and a box to its right and below it, with lines going to all three objects.

Tip   If you want to change the default so that all four columns are open, select Tools ⇨ Options, click the View tab, and place a check mark next to both items in the Show in macro design (Names column and Conditions column).

Each macro object that you create can contain more than one macro, with each of the macros containing its own actions. The Macro Names column shows the name of each macro within the macro object. The Conditions column is used to specify a condition that can be used to let you run or skip a macro based on that condition, such as SALEAMT > 200.

Each macro can have one or many actions (individual tasks for Access to perform). You add individual actions in the Action column, and you can add a description of each action in the Comment column. Access ignores the comments when the macro is run.

The Argument pane

The Argument pane (lower portion of the window) is where you supply the specific arguments (properties) needed for the selected action. Most macro actions need additional information to carry out the action, such as which object should be used. For example, Figure 28-3 shows the action arguments for a typical action named OpenForm, which opens a specific form, Customer, and sets a condition of Type of Customer = individual (1).

The OpenForm action has six different arguments that can be specified:

✦ **Form Name.** Specifies the form for Access to open

✦ **View.** Specifies the view mode to activate: Form, Design, Print Preview, Datasheet, PivotTable, or PivotChart

✦ **Filter Name.** Applies the specified filter or query

✦ **Where Condition.** Limits the number of records displayed

✦ **Data Mode.** Specifies a data-entry mode: Add, Edit, or Read Only

✦ **Window Mode.** Specifies a window mode: Normal, Hidden, Icon, or Dialog

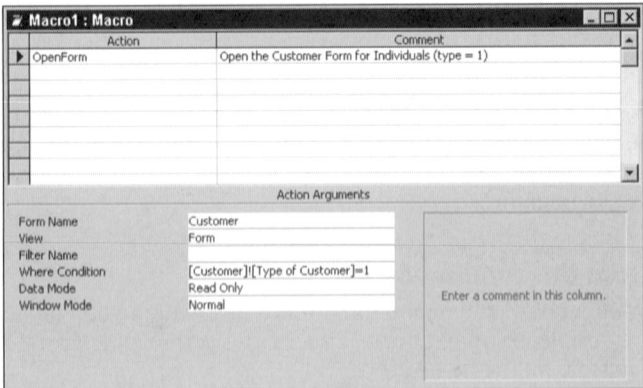

Figure 28-3: Arguments displayed for the OpenForm action. It will open the Customer form and specify a condition of type of customer is individual.

Note   Some actions, such as Beep and Maximize, have no arguments, but most actions require at least one argument.

Creating a Macro

To create a macro, you use both the Action and Argument panes of the Macro window. After you supply actions and associated arguments, you save the macro for later use.

On the CD-ROM   If you have been following along and building all the objects from the earlier chapters you can continue to use the Mountain Animal Start.mdb Database. However, if you have not been creating the tables, queries, forms, and reports in the earlier chapters, you will need to use the Mountain Animal Macros.mdb database. This file is located on the CD-ROM that came with this book. It contains all the objects you will use when creating macros in this chapter and the next.

 **Note**   The examples used in this chapter will not be used in any other chapter. They are here to familiarize you with the process of creating and working with macros in Access. In the next chapter you will build several macros that will offer a viable way to use macros in Access applications.

Entering actions and arguments

Actions are added to a macro in any of several ways:

✦ Enter the action name in the Action column of the Macro window.

✦ Select actions from the drop-down list of actions (in the Action column).

✦ Drag-and-drop an object from the Database window into an action cell.

The last method, drag-and-drop, is useful for common actions associated with the database. For example, you can drag a specific form to an action cell in the macro Action column; Access automatically adds the action OpenForm and its known arguments (such as the form name).

Selecting actions from the combo box list

The easiest way to add an action is by using the combo box, which you can access in any action cell. For example, to open a form, specify the action OpenForm. To create the OpenForm action, follow these steps:

1. Open a new Macro Design window.

2. Click the first empty cell in the Action column.

3. Click the arrow that appears in the action cell.

4. Select the OpenForm action from the combo box.

 Tip   You don't have to add comments to the macro, but it's a good idea to document the reason for each macro action (as well as providing a description of the entire macro).

Specifying arguments for actions

After entering the OpenForm action, you can enter the arguments into the bottom pane. Figure 28-3, which displays the completed arguments, shows that the bottom pane has six action arguments associated with this specific action. The arguments View (Form) and Window Mode (Normal) have default values. Because Access does not know which form you want to open, you must enter at least a form name. To open the form named Customer as a dialog box in read-only mode, enter the three arguments Form Name, Where Condition, and Data Mode, as shown in Figure 28-3.

To add the arguments, follow these steps:

1. Using the macro just created with OpenForm in the action, Click the Form Name cell in the Argument pane (or press F6 to switch to the Argument pane, lower pane).

2. Select the Customer form from the drop-down list (or type the name).

3. Click the Where Condition cell.

4. Type in `[Customer]![Type of Customer] = 1` in the cell or build the condition using the Expression Builder.

5. Click the Data Mode cell.

6. Select the Read Only choice from the drop-down list (or type the choice).

Your macro should now resemble the one in Figure 28-3. Notice that the Form Name is set to Customer, The Condition has been set to select and view ONLY Individual customers (type =1), and the Data Mode is set to Read Only.

Before you can run this or any macro, it must be saved. To close and save this macro, follow these steps:

1. Select File ➪ Close from the Macro Design menu or click the exit button.

   Access opens an information box that asks if you want to save changes to the design of macro 'Macro1'.

2. Press the Yes Button.

   Access opens the save as dialog box with the default name of 'Macro1' in the text box.

3. Type `OpenCustomerRO` in the text box.

4. Either press the Enter key or click the OK button to save the macro.

   Access saves the Macro and returns you to the database container.

A similar macro is used in Chapter 29 to open the Customer form when the Pets form is opened.

Specifying actions by dragging and dropping objects

You can also specify actions by dragging and dropping objects from the Database window. When you add actions in this manner, Access adds the appropriate arguments automatically. To add the same form (Customer) to an empty Macro window, follow these steps:

1. Start with an empty Macro Design window.

2. Select Window ➪ Tile Vertically from the Design menu. Access places the Macro and Database windows side by side.

3. Click on the Forms object button in the Database window. Access displays all the forms, as shown in Figure 28-4.

4. Click and drag the Customer form from the Database window. Access displays a Form icon as it moves into the Macro window.

5. Continue to drag the Form icon, and drop it in any empty action cell of the top Action pane of the Macro window.

Access displays the correct action and arguments automatically, placing the OpenForm action in the Action cell and the Customer name in the Form Name in the Arguments pane.

This macro will NOT be used further in this book, so you do not have to save it. It is used to demonstrate the process of using drag-and-drop to accomplish the same steps taken in the previous example. At this point you should close the macro and NOT save it or simply remove the OpenForm action from the top pane to make the macro blank again.

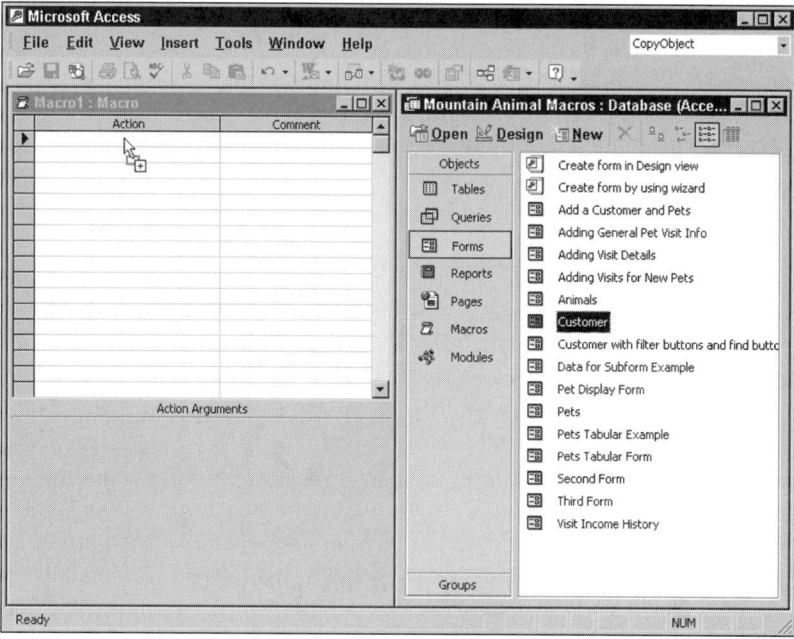

Figure 28-4: The Macro and Database windows are tiled side-by-side. The pointed icon has been changed to a form plus sign as it moves into the Macro Window to be dropped in the Action cell.

Note   After using the drag-and-drop method to select actions, you may need to modify the action arguments to further refine them from their default values. Recall that in the last example the Where Condition and Data Mode were changed for the form.

Adding multiple actions to a macro

A macro can have multiple actions assigned to it, not just a single action. For example, you may want to have Access open two forms, displaying an hourglass while they are opening. Finally, you can have the computer beep for the user after completing the macro. To accomplish these multiple actions, follow these steps:

1. Open a new Macro Design window.
2. Click the first empty cell in the Action column.
3. Select the Hourglass action from the drop-down list or type it.
4. Click in the Comment cell alongside the Hourglass action.
5. Type Display the hourglass while the macro is running.
6. Click the next empty cell in the Action column.
7. Select the OpenForm action from the drop-down list or type the name of the action.
8. Click the argument cell Form Name.
9. Select the Add a Customer and Pets form.
10. Click the Comment cell alongside the OpenForm action.
11. Type Open the Add a Customer and Pets form.
12. Click the next empty cell in the Action column.
13. Select the OpenForm action from the drop-down list or type the action.
14. Click the argument cell Form Name.
15. Select the Adding Visit Details form.
16. Click the Comment cell alongside the OpenForm action.
17. Type Open the Adding Visit Details form.
18. Click the next empty cell in the Action column.
19. Select the Beep action from the drop-down list or type the action.

Your macro design should now look similar to Figure 28-5. This macro opens both forms as it displays the hourglass. After both forms are open, the macro beeps to signal that it is finished.

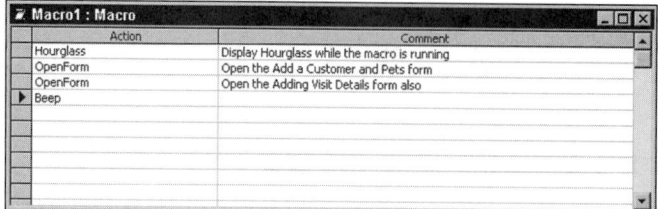

Figure 28-5: Adding multiple actions to a single macro. This one opens two forms and beeps when done.

Tip   When you're adding more than one action, you can specify each action, one after the other, with several rows of spaces between them. These blank rows can contain additional lines of comments for each macro action.

At this point you can see what the macro does by saving and running it. To do this quickly while still in the Macro Design screen, following these steps:

1. Click on the Run button (the red exclamation point on the toolbar) or select Run ➪ Run from the menu.

   Access informs you that you must save the macro before running it.

2. Select the Yes button to save your macro.

   Access opens the Save As dialog box.

3. Type `OpenTwoForms` in the text box and either press the Enter key or click the OK button.

   Access saves the form and runs the macro — showing the hourglass and opening the two forms, finally beeping.

4. Under the forms the macro is still open.

Access opened the forms so quickly that you probably did not see the Hourglass displayed, although it was. Using this method of running a macro you can test to see if it works correctly. However, this is not the normal way that a macro would be executed. Normally you will attach the completed macro to an event property of a form or report. Attaching the macro to an event property is covered later in this chapter.

Note   You should close both forms and leave the macro open for the next section.

Rearranging macro actions

When you work with multiple actions in a macro, you may change your mind about the order of the actions. For example, you may decide that the macro created in Figure 28-5 should have the Beep action come first in the macro. To move the action, follow these steps:

1. Select the Beep action by clicking the row selector to the left of the action name.

2. Click the highlighted row again and drag it to the top row.

Deleting macro actions

If you no longer need an action in a macro, you can delete the action. In the example of the macro shown in Figure 28-5, to delete the action to open the form Adding Visit Details, follow these steps:

1. Select the action OpenForm for Adding Visit Details by clicking the row selector to the left of the action's name.

2. Press Delete or select Edit ⇨ Delete Row from the menu.

> **Tip**
>
> You can also delete a row by using the right-click shortcut menu: Select the row to delete, press the right mouse button, and select Delete Row.

You have already saved two macros above using two different methods. It is important to stress again that before you can run a macro, it must be saved. After you save a macro, it becomes another database object that can be opened and run from the Database window. In general to save a macro, follow these steps:

1. Select File ⇨ Save from the Macro Design menu or click the Save button on the toolbar.

2. If the macro has not been saved, you must enter a name in the Save As dialog box. Press Enter or click OK when you're through.

> **Tip**
>
> The fastest way to save a macro is to press F12 or Alt+F2 and give the macro a name. Another way is to double-click the Macro window's Control menu (top-left corner) and select close the window, or click on the Exit button, and answer the appropriate dialog box questions. You can also save a macro by running it and you will be prompted to save it before it is executed.

Editing existing macros

After a macro is created, it can be edited by following these steps:

1. In the Database window, select the Macros object button.

2. Highlight the macro you want to edit.

3. Click the Design button in the Database window.

With the macro in design mode you can now add additional actions or modify existing actions. Once you edit the macro you will need to save it again.

Copying entire macros

To copy a macro, follow these steps:

1. Click the Macros object button in the Database window.

2. Select the macro to copy.

3. Press Ctrl+C or select Edit ➪ Copy to copy the macro to the Clipboard.

4. Press Ctrl+V or select Edit ➪ Paste to paste the macro from the Clipboard.

5. In the Paste As dialog box, type the macro's new name.

Renaming macros

Sometimes you need to rename a macro because you changed the event property in the form or report property. To rename a macro, follow these steps:

1. Select the Database window by pressing F11 or Alt+F1.

2. Click the Macros object button to display all the macro names.

3. Highlight the macro name to change.

4. Choose Edit ➪ Rename from the Database menu or right-click and choose Rename from the shortcut menu.

5. Enter the new name.

Running Macros

After a macro is created, it can be run from any of these locations within Access:

✦ A Macro window

✦ A Database window

✦ Other object windows

✦ Events such as a form opening or closing

✦ Another macro

Running a macro from the Macro window

A macro can run directly from the Macro Design window by clicking the toolbar's Run button (the exclamation mark) or by choosing Run from the Design menu.

Running a macro from the Database window

A macro can be run from the Database window by following these steps:

1. Click the Macros object button in the Database window.

2. Select the macro to run.

3. Either double-click the macro or choose the Run button.

Running a macro from any window in the database

To run a macro from any window in the database, follow these steps:

1. Select Tools ➪ Macro from the menu.

2. In the Macro dialog box, enter the name or select it from the drop-down list.

3. Click OK or press Enter.

Running a macro from another macro

To run a macro from another macro, follow these steps:

1. Add the action RunMacro to your macro.

2. Enter the name of the macro you want to run in the Macro Name argument.

Running a macro automatically when you open a database

Access can automatically run a macro each time a database is opened; there are two ways to do this. One way is by using a special macro name, AutoExec, that Access recognizes. If Access finds it in a database, it executes this macro automatically each time the database is opened. For example, you may want to open some forms and queries automatically after opening the database.

To run a macro automatically when a database is opened, follow these steps:

1. Create a macro with the actions you want to run when the database is opened.

2. Save the macro and name it AutoExec.

If you close that database and reopen it, Access runs the AutoExec macro automatically.

Tip   If you have a macro named AutoExec but you don't want to run it when you open a database, hold down the Shift key as you select the database in the Open Database dialog box.

The second method makes use of Access 2002's option for setting Startup properties. As shown in Figure 28-6, you can enter the name of a form that you want to start when Access is opened. This form can contain the name of a macro to run when the form is loaded. The Startup properties window is displayed by selecting Tools ➪ Startup from any window. The options that you set in the Startup properties window are in effect for as long as the Access database is open. You can set many options from the Startup properties window; for instance, you can change the title bar of the Access Main window, specify the name of an icon file to use when Access is minimized (and shown in the top-left corner of the Main window), automatically display a form/page, and affect many Access custom menus and toolbars.

Cross-Reference   You can learn more about form events in the "Understanding Events" section later in this chapter, and in Chapter 30.

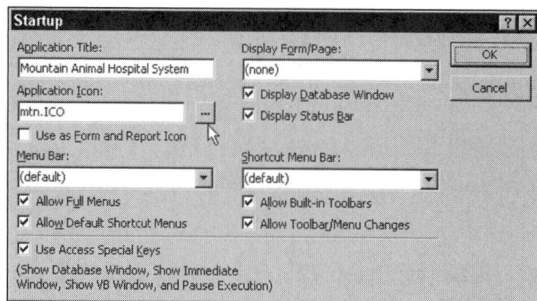

Figure 28-6: Using the Startup properties to give the Application a name and associate an icon with it

Macro Groups

As you create macros, you may want to group a series of related macros into one large macro object. Once a group of macros are created, you can use any macro in the group by referring to the group name and the macro name. This is demonstrated later in this chapter. To do this, you need some way of uniquely identifying the individual macros within the group. Access lets you create a macro group (a macro object that contains two or more macros).

Creating macro groups

Like individual macros, macro groups are database objects. When you look in the macro object list in the Database window, you see only the macro group's name. Inside the group, each macro has a unique name that you assign (along with the actions for each macro).

You may, for example, want to create a macro that is a group of all macros that is capable of opening two different forms (Customer and Pets) and can close all forms. To create this type of macro, follow these steps:

1. In the Database window, select the Macros object button.

2. Click the New toolbar button in the Database window. Access opens the Macro Design window.

3. Select View ⇨ Macro Names or select the Macro Names button on the toolbar. Access adds the Macro Name column to the Action pane.

4. In the Macro Name column, type CustomerOpen.

5. In the Action column, next to the macro CustomerOpen that you just entered, Select OpenForm.

   At this point you could move to the comment cell and enter a comment for this action.

6. In the Bottom pane, click in the Form Name field and type or select Customer.

7. Return to the top pane, skip a row, and in the Macro Name column type PetsOpen.

8. In the Action column, next to the macro CustomerOpen that you just entered, Select OpenForm.

9. In the Bottom pane, click in the Form Name field and type or select Pets.

10. Return to the top pane, skip another row, and in the Macro Name column type CloseAllForms.

11. In the Action column, next to the macro CloseAllForms that you just entered, Select Close

12. In the Bottom pane, click in the Object Type field and type or select Form.

13. Click in the Object Name field and type or select Pets.

14. Return to the top pane, in the Action column, one line immediately below the macro CloseAllForms that you just entered, Select Close.

15. In the Bottom pane, click in the Object Type field and type or select Form.

16. Click in the Object Name field and type or select Customer.

17. Save the macro group, naming it Open and Close Forms.

Figure 28-7 shows how a macro group will look. Notice that there are three separate macros in it: CustomerOpen, PetsOpen, and Close All Forms. The Arguments pane shows only the arguments for the second close of the macro named CloseAllForms.

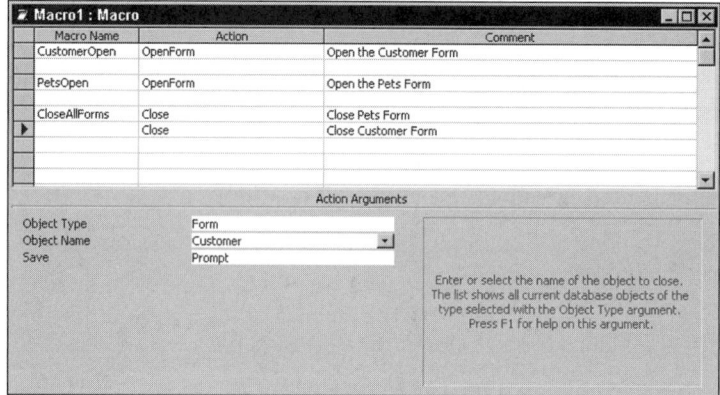

Figure 28-7: A macro group with three different macros

Tip   Although not necessary for macros in the macro group to work properly, it's a good idea to leave a blank line between macros to improve readability and clarity.

Running a macro in a macro group

After you create a macro group, you'll want to run each macro inside the group. To run one, you must specify both the group name and the macro name.

Cross-Reference   In the "Understanding Events" section later in this chapter, you learn to use the events that run macros.

To specify both group and macro names, enter the group name, a period, and then the macro name. If you type Open and Close Forms.PetsOpen, for example, you are specifying the macro PetsOpen in the group macro named Open and Close Forms.

Note   If you run a macro group from the Macro Design window or from the Database window, you cannot specify a macro name inside the macro group. Access will run only the first macro or set of actions specified in the group macro. Access stops executing actions when it reaches a new macro name in the Macro Name column.

To run a macro inside a group macro, using the other windows in the database or another macro, you enter both the macro group name and macro name, placing a period between the two names.

Tip   You also can run a macro by selecting Macro from the Tools menu and typing the group and macro name.

Supplying Conditions for Actions

In some cases, you may want to run some action or actions in a macro only when a certain condition is true. For example, you may want to display a message if no records are available for a report and then stop execution of the macro. In such a case, you can use a condition to control the flow of the macro.

What is a condition?

Simply put, a condition is a logical expression that is either True or False. The macro follows one of two paths, depending on the condition of the expression. If the expression is True, the macro follows the True path; otherwise, it follows the False path. Table 28-1 shows several conditions and the True/False results.

Table 28-1		
Conditions and Their Results		
Condition	*True Result*	*False Result*
Forms!Customer!State="WA"	If the state is Washington	Any state except Washington
IsNull(Gender)	If no gender is specified	Gender is male or female (not Null)
Length <= 10	If length is less than or equal to 10 inches	If length is greater than 10
Reports![Pet Directory] ![Type animal] = "CAT" OR Reports! [Pet Directory]! [Type of Animal] = "DOG"	If type of animal is cat or dog	Any animal other than cat or dog

Activating the Condition column in a macro

As Table 28-1 demonstrates, a condition is an expression that results in a logical answer of Yes or No. The answer must be either True or False. You can specify a condition in a macro by following these steps:

1. Enter the Macro Design window by creating a new macro or editing an existing one.

2. Select View ⬦ Conditions or click on the Conditions button on the toolbar.

    The Condition column is inserted to the left of the Action column. If the Macro Name column is visible, the Condition column is between the Macro Name and the Action columns (see Figure 28-8).

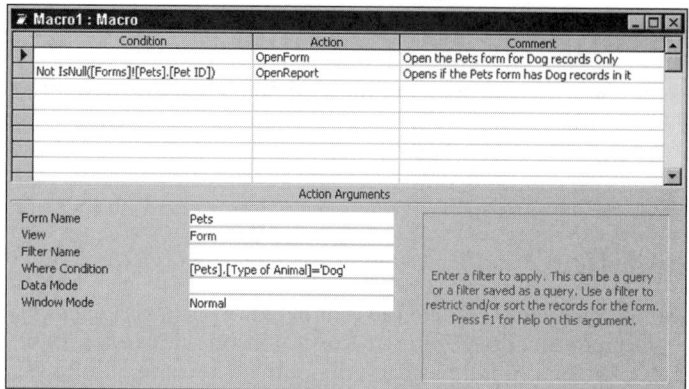

Figure 28-8: The Condition column is added to the Macro Design window. This figure does not show the Macro Name column active.

With the Condition column visible, you can specify conditions for one or many actions within a macro.

Tip In Figure 28-8, you can see that the Condition and Comment columns are wider than the Action column. You can widen or shrink columns by positioning the mouse pointer on the column border and dragging the column line. You can also resize the height between the rows. but that resizes all of the rows.

Specifying a condition for a single action

Besides specifying a condition for a single action, you can specify a condition that is effective for multiple actions. That is, a single condition that causes several actions to occur. In this way, you can also create an If-Then-Else condition.

You may want to specify a condition for a single action. An example is activating the report Pet Directory and displaying only the Dog records. However, this report should be activated only when there are Dog records in the form Pets. If no Dog records are present, you want the macro to skip activation of the report and display a message to the user. To have the macro specify this condition, you simply need to create a condition for the OpenReport action in the query and specify a filter condition for both actions as shown in Figure 28-8. To create this macro, follow these steps:

1. Start with a new macro.

2. In the Macro window, click the Conditions button on the toolbar.

3. In the first action cell of the Action pane, select OpenForm.

4. In the Form Name cell of the Argument pane, select Pets.

5. In the Where Condition cell of the Argument pane, type [Pets].[Type of Animal]='Dog'.

Referring to Control Names in Expressions

When working with macros, you may need to refer to the value of a control in a form or report. To refer to a control in a form or report, use this syntax:

```
Forms!formname!controlname
Reports!reportname!controlname
```

If a space occurs within the name of a form, report, or control, you must enclose the name in brackets. For example, Forms![Add a Customer and Pets]!State refers to the State control (field on a form) on the currently open form called Add a Customer and Pets.

If you run a macro from the same form or report that contains the control, you can shorten this syntax to the control name.

Note: To reference a control name on a form or report, first make sure that the form or report is open.

6. Return to the top and select the second row Action cell of the Action pane, select OpenReport.

7. In the Report Name cell of the Argument pane, select Pet Directory.

8. In the View cell of the Argument pane, select Print Preview.

9. In the Where Condition cell of the Argument pane, type `[Pets].[Type of Animal]='Dog'`

10. Returning to top, Click the Condition cell next to the action OpenReport.

11. Type `Not IsNull(Forms![Pets]![Pet ID])`.

12. Save the macro and name it Dog Form Report.

Your macro should now resemble the one in Figure 28-8. If you save and run this macro, it will open the Pets table (with 12 records in the dynaset) and then, if there are Dog records in it, also open the report Pet Directory in Print Preview mode with only the same 12 Dog records in it.

In this example, the condition specified is True if there are no records (the first Pet ID is Null) in the open form Pets (meaning there are no dog records). If the condition is True (no records), when the macro is run, the action OpenReport is not performed; otherwise, the report is opened in print preview mode.

Note   When you specify conditions in a macro and reference a control name (field name), the source (form or report) of the control name must already be open.

Specifying a condition for multiple actions

If you want Access to perform more than one action, add the other actions below the first one. In the Condition column, place an ellipsis (...) beside each action. Figure 28-9 is a macro in which two actions are performed based on a single condition. Notice that the condition has been changed from Not IsNull to IsNull. Follow these steps to modify the Dog Form Report macro:

1. Open the Dog Form Report macro in Design mode.

2. Select the second row (highlighting it by clicking on the selector cell — it shows an arrow when clicked).

3. Select Insert Rows from the menu or click on the Insert Rows button.

   Access places a blank row between the OpenForm action row and the OpenReport row.

4. Click on the Insert Rows button a second time to add another blank row between the OpenForm and OpenReport.

5. Move to the second row and select MsgBox from the Action cell.

6. Go to the Message property (Arguments pane) and type There are no Dog records found.

7. Move to the Condition cell of the MsgBox action and type IsNull([Forms]![Pets].[Pet ID]).

8. Move to the third row and select StopMacro from the Action cell.

9. Move to the Condition cell of the StopMacro action and type ... (the ellipsis) in the cell.

10. Move to the Condition cell of the OpenReport Action row and remove the condition.

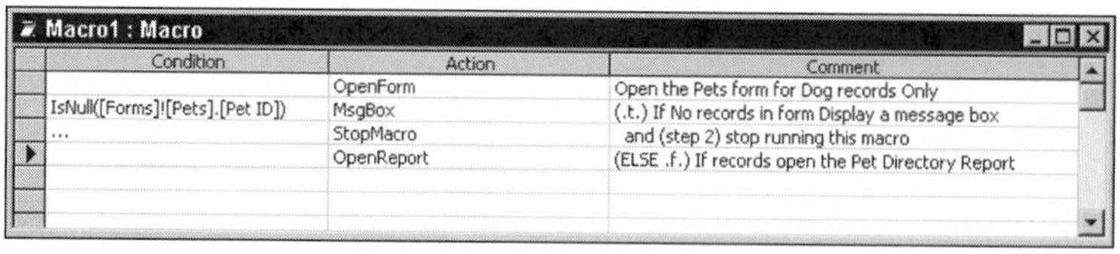

Condition	Action	Comment
	OpenForm	Open the Pets form for Dog records Only
IsNull([Forms]![Pets].[Pet ID])	MsgBox	(.t.) If No records in form Display a message box
	StopMacro	and (step 2) stop running this macro
...	OpenReport	(ELSE .f.) If records open the Pet Directory Report

Figure 28-9: This macro performs two actions based on a single condition if true and one action if false.

In Figure 28-9, the condition IsNull(Forms![Pets]![Pet ID]) performs the two actions MsgBox and StopMacro if the condition is True (no dog records in form Pets). Notice the ellipsis (...) in the cell immediately under the specified condition, which is the Condition cell for the action StopMacro.

When you run the macro, Access evaluates the expression in the Condition cell. If the expression is True, Access performs the action beside the expression and then all the following actions that have an ellipsis in the Condition column. Access continues the True actions until it comes to another condition (using the new condition from that point on).

If the expression is False, Access ignores the action (or actions) and moves to the next action row that does not have an ellipsis (in this case the OpenReport Action row).

Note   If Access reaches a blank cell in the Condition column, it performs the action in that row regardless of the conditional expression. The only way to avoid this is to control the flow of actions by use of a redirection action such as RunMacro or StopMacro. For example, if the second conditional action (StopMacro) is not after the MsgBox action, the OpenReport action is executed regardless of whether the conditional expression is True or False. On the other hand, the MsgBox action takes effect only if the field Pet ID is Null (True).

Controlling the flow of actions

By using conditional expressions, the flow of action in the macro is controlled. The macro in Figure 28-9 uses the action StopMacro to stop execution of the macro if the field is Null, thereby avoiding opening the report Pet Directory if the table is empty.

Several macro actions can be used to change or control the flow of actions based on a condition. The two most common are the actions StopMacro and RunMacro; they also control the flow of actions within a macro.

Troubleshooting Macros

Access has two tools to help troubleshoot macros:

- ✦ Single-step mode
- ✦ The Action Failed dialog box

Single-step mode

If unexpected results occur while running a macro, you can use single-step mode to move through the macro one action at a time, pausing between actions. Single-step mode lets you observe the result of each action and isolate the action or actions that caused the incorrect results.

To use single-step mode, click the Single-Step button on the toolbar. To use this feature on the macro in Figure 28-9, follow these steps:

1. Edit the macro in the macro design window.

2. Click the Single-Step button on the toolbar or select Run ⟡ Single Step.

3. Run the macro as you normally do or by clicking the Run button on the toolbar.

Access displays the Macro Single Step dialog box, showing the macro name, the action name, and the arguments for the action (see Table 28-2). Figure 28-10 is a typical Macro Single Step dialog box.

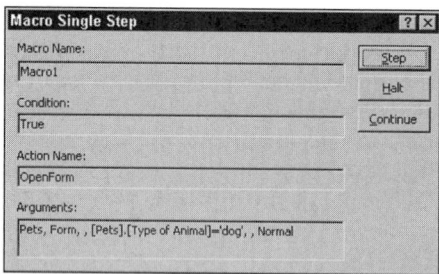

Figure 28-10: The Macro Single Step dialog box for the macro from Figure 28-9

	Table 28-2 Macro Single-Step Button Options	
Button	**Purpose**	
Step	Runs the action in the dialog box. If no error is reported, the next action appears in the dialog box.	
Halt	Stops the execution of the macro and closes the dialog box.	
Continue	Turns off single-step mode and runs the remainder of the macro.	

Once the Single-Step Dialog box is active you can step through the macro, one line at a time, by clicking on the Step button. This button will let you see what is occurring in the macro at each level by looking at the Condition box, Action Name, and Arguments box. If you just want to run the remainder of the query without stepping through it, click on the Continue button.

The Action Failed dialog box

If a macro action causes an error (either during single-step mode or when running normally), Access opens a dialog box that looks exactly like the Macro Single Step dialog box, except that the only available button is the Halt button.

To correct the problem, choose Halt and return to the Macro Design window.

Understanding Events

With the actions stored in macros, you can run the macro either via a menu choice or by naming the macro AutoExec. The AutoExec macro runs automatically each time the database is opened. Access also offers another method to activate a macro: Base it on a user action.

For example, a user can activate a macro by clicking on a command button or by the action of opening a form. To accomplish this, Access takes advantage of something known as an event.

What is an event?

An Access event is the result or consequence of some user action. An Access event can occur when a user moves from one record to another in a form, closes a report, or clicks on a command button on a form.

Your Access applications are event-driven. Objects in Access respond to many types of events. Access responds to events with behaviors that are built in for each object. Access events can be recognized by specific object properties. For example, if a user clicks the mouse button with the pointer in a check box, the property OnMouseDown recognizes that the mouse button was clicked. You can have this property run a macro when the user clicks the mouse button.

Events in Access can be categorized into seven groups:

- ✦ Windows (Form, Report) events: Opening, closing, and resizing
- ✦ Data events: Making current, deleting, or updating
- ✦ Focus events: Activating, entering, and exiting
- ✦ Keyboard events: Pressing or releasing a key
- ✦ Mouse events: Clicking or pressing a mouse button down
- ✦ Print events: Formatting and printing
- ✦ Error and timing events: Happening after an error has occurred or some time has passed

In all, more than 50 events can be checked in forms and reports to specify some action after they take place.

How do events trigger actions?

You can have Access run a macro when a user performs any one of the 53 events that Access recognizes. Access can recognize an event through the use of special properties for forms, controls (fields), and reports.

For example, Figure 28-11 shows the property sheet for a form named Pet Display Form. This form has many properties, which may be used to respond to corresponding events. Forms aren't the only objects to have events; form sections (page header, form header, detail, page footer, form footer) and every control on the form (labels, text boxes, check boxes, and option buttons, for example) have events, too.

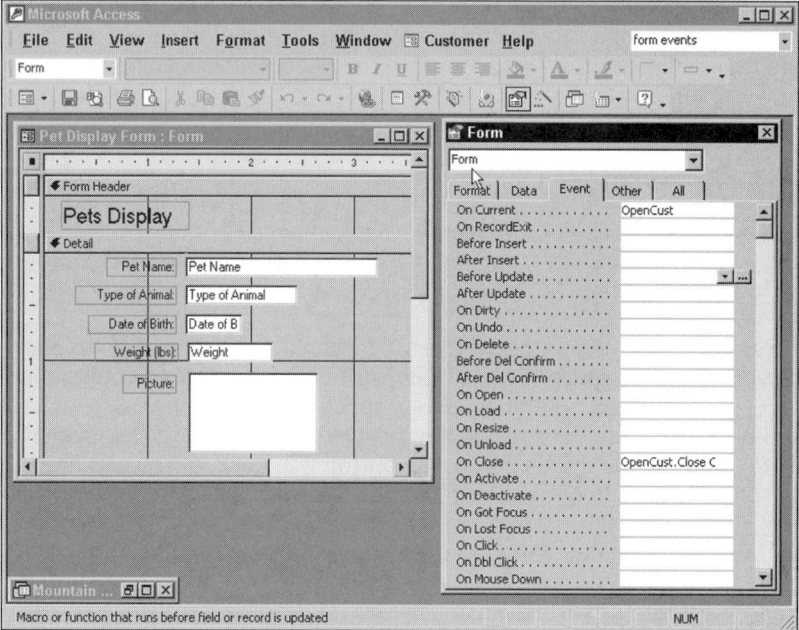

Figure 28-11: The property sheet for a form, showing the OnOpen property entered. This figure shows the form Pets Display Form in Design mode with the property sheet open.

Where to trigger macros

In Access, you can run event-driven macros by using properties in forms and reports. There are no event properties for tables or queries.

Even so, when you work with forms, you can run macros based on Access switchboards (full-screen button-type menus), command buttons, and pull-down menus. These features make event-driven macros powerful and easy to use. In the next several chapters, you learn about many events and the macro actions that events can use.

✦   ✦   ✦

Using Macros in Forms and Reports

In This Chapter

Responding to events in forms and reports

Using macros in forms

Validating data with a macro

Filtering records with a macro

Using macros in reports

Creating accelerator keys (hot keys)

At this point you should know how to create and run macros, and you should know how to start a macro automatically when you open a database. In addition, you should be able to create and specify conditions for macros.

The macros in the previous chapter were used to demonstrate how to build macros. In this chapter you're going to learn how to use macros in real examples by using tables, forms, queries, and reports that you created in previous chapters.

On the CD-ROM

As with the previous chapter, if you have created all the objects in the book up to this point, you can use the Mountain Animal Start.mdb database. If you have not, you may want to use the Mountain Animal Macro.mdb database that is on the CD-ROM.

Types of Macros

Macros are Access objects consisting of one or more actions such as opening a dialog box, running a report, or even finding a record.

Usually, you create macros to perform repetitive tasks or a series of required actions following an initial action. For example, macros can synchronize two forms while a user moves from record to record. They can also validate new data after it is entered by a user.

Before activating a macro, you need to decide where and how you will use it. For example, you may have a macro that opens the Customer form, and you want Access to run the macro every time a user opens the Pets form. In this case, you place the name of the macro in the On Open property of the Pets form. Then, every time a user opens the Pets form, the On Open property will trigger the macro that opens the Customer form.

Or you may want to trigger another macro every time a user presses a keyboard accelerator key (also known as a hot key). For example, if you want an Import dialog box to be activated when a user presses Ctrl+I, you should attach the macro to the key combination Ctrl+I in a hot-key macro file.

Although the second macro performs some tasks or actions, it is different from the first macro. The second macro is activated by a user action (pressing a hot key); the first one is activated when a user performs some specific action recognized by a form property.

Macros can be grouped together based on their usage. The four basic groups are

✦ Form

✦ Report

✦ Import/Export

✦ Accelerator keys

The most common macros are those used in forms and reports. Using macros in these objects enables you to build intelligence into each form and report. Macros are also used for importing or exporting data to and from other data sources. Finally, macros can be activated by the use of hot keys.

A Review of Events and Properties

Simply put, an *event* is some user action. The event can be an action such as opening a form or report, changing data in a record, selecting a button, or closing a form or report. Access recognizes approximately 60 events in forms (52 for the form itself, and more for the controls on the form) and reports (10 for the report and report sections; more for the controls on the report).

To recognize one of these events, Access uses form or report *properties*. Each event has an associated form or report property. For example, the On Open property is associated with the event of opening a form or report.

You trigger a macro by specifying the macro name. The name is specified as a parameter for the event property you want to have the macro run against. For example, if you want to run a macro named OpenPets every time a user opens the Customer form, you place the macro name OpenPets in the parameter field alongside the property On Open in the form named Customer.

Macros for forms

You can create macros that respond to form events. These events are triggered by some user action, such as opening a form or clicking a command button on a form. Access knows when a user triggers an event through its recognition of event-specific form properties. Forms enable you to set properties for field controls. These properties can be quite useful during the design phase of a form, such as when you use a property to set a format or validation rule.

However, macros give you added power by enabling you to specify actions to be performed automatically based on a user-initiated event. The event is recognized by Access by use of event properties such as Before Update, On Delete, or On Enter. Unlike a simple format or field-level validation rule, a macro can perform multiple-step actions based on the user event. For example, after a user presses the Delete key to delete a record but before the deleted record is removed from the table, you can have a macro that automatically runs and asks the user to verify that the record should be deleted. In this case, you use the On Delete property to trigger execution of the macro.

Macros for forms can respond both to form events and control events. Form events take effect at the form level; control events take effect at the individual control level. Form events include deleting a record, opening a form, or updating a record. These events work at the form and record levels. Control events, on the other hand, work at the level of the individual control. These controls are the ones you specify when you create your form and include such items as a field (text box), a toggle button, or an option button — even a command button. Each control has its own event properties that can trigger a macro. These events include selecting a command button, double-clicking a control, and selecting a control.

By specifying a macro at the control level, you can activate a customer form when the user double-clicks a field object or its label object. For example, you may have a form that identifies the customer by name but gives no additional customer information. When the user double-clicks the customer's name, your macro can activate a customer form that shows all the customer information. To accomplish this, you use the field object property On Dbl Click to specify a macro that opens the customer form. Then the macro will run and open the Customer form each time the user double-clicks the Customer field.

Figure 29-1 shows the Cust_Pet_Visit form with a label named Customer Name; note the field containing the name All Creatures. When the user double-clicks either the label (Customer Name) or the name (All Creatures), the Customer form opens. Notice that the name of the form is Cust_Pet_Visit, yet the caption displayed in the title bar shows the text "Customers, Pets, and Visits information." The text on the title bar of the form is actually set by setting the Caption property of the form.

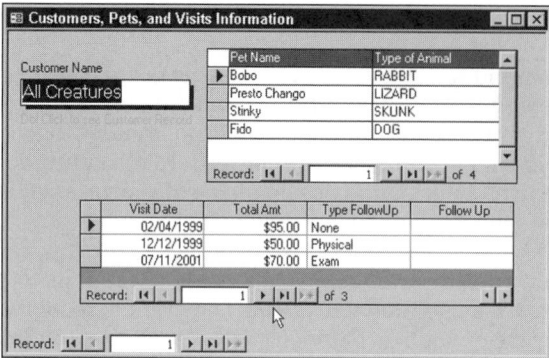

Figure 29-1: A typical form with labels and controls (fields). This form is one of the most complex you could build with one primary table and two subforms with details.

The form in Figure 29-1 does display a light note that says a user can initiate a macro by double-clicking the label or field. The On Dbl Click property is set for the field to automatically execute the macro that opens the Customer form. Figure 29-2 shows that the macro is specified in the On Dbl Click property. The macro group name is Cust_Pet_Visit_Update Form, and the specific macro name in the group is ShowCustomer.

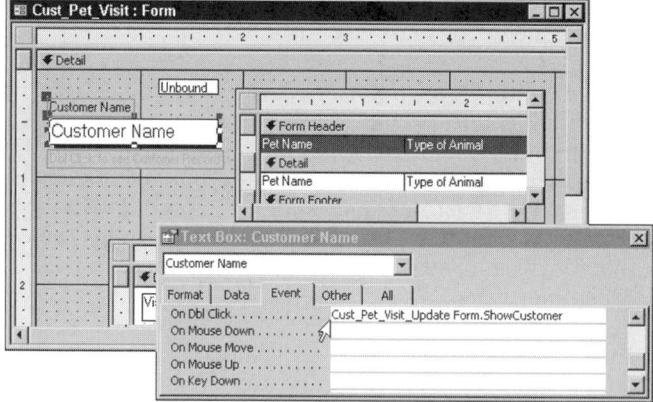

Figure 29-2: Using a form event — On Dbl Click to call a macro that will open the Customer form

Note   By using the properties of text boxes, the event is triggered when it occurs on the text box (field) or its associated label.

Macros for reports

Just as with forms, macros can also enhance the use of reports. You may, for example, want to prompt a user for a range of records to be printed before printing the report. You may want to display a message on the report whenever a certain condition is met. You may even want to underline or highlight a field on the basis of its value, such as when the value is too small or too large. Macros give you this type of refined control in reports.

Macros for reports can respond both to report events and report section events. Report events take effect at the report level; report section events take effect at the section level of the report.

By specifying a macro at the report level, you can perform actions that would affect the entire report — for example turning off a detail section of the report to only display total information.

You could also create a macro for a report that could be attached at report level or to a form that would produce a snapshot file (high-resolution graphical report) of the report to be published on the network.

Macros for importing and exporting

A macro can be created using one of four Transfer actions to import or export objects. Using these macro actions you can import/export databases, spreadsheets, text (including HTML tables), and SQL databases.

These types of macros can be run stand-alone or attached to a form object.

Macros for Keyboard accelerators

A macro can also be associated with a specific key or combination of keys, called a keyboard accelerator. When a macro is assigned to a key combination, a user pressing that key or key combination activates it. For example, you may assign the key combination Ctrl+P to print the current record displayed on-screen. Another example is assigning the key combination Ctrl+N to skip to the next record in the report or form. Creating macros for hotkeys gives you additional capabilities in your forms and reports without requiring you to write complicated programs.

You use most hot-key macros when you work with forms and reports, although hot-key macros can be used in queries or other Access objects.

Form-Level Event Macros

When you work with forms, you can specify macros based on events at the form level, the section level, or the control level. If you attach a macro to a form-level event, whenever the event occurs, the action takes effect against the form as a whole (such as when you change the record pointer or leave the form).

Attaching macros to forms

To have your form respond to an event, you write a macro and attach it to the event property in the form that recognizes the event. Many properties can be used to trigger macros at the form level. Table 29-1 shows each property, the event it recognizes, and how the property works.

Many form-level events can trigger a macro. These events work only at the level of forms or records. They take effect when the pointer is changed from one record to another or when a form is being opened or closed. Control at a level of finer detail (such as the field level) can be obtained by using the control-level events covered later in this chapter.

Table 29-1
The Form-Level Events and Associated Properties

Event Property	When the Macro Is Triggered
On Current	When you move to a different record and make it the current record.
* On Record Exit	Immediately after the data in a record has been updated — can be used to validate data across form/subform combinations. Opposite of On Current event.
Before Insert	After data is first entered into a new record but before the record is actually created.
After Insert	After the new record is added to the table.
Before Update	Before changed data is updated in a record.
After Update	After changed data is updated in a record.
On Dirty	When a record is modified.
* On Undo	When a user has returned a form to clean state — record set back to unmodified state — opposite of On Dirty.
On Delete	When a record is deleted but before the deletion takes place.
Before Del Confirm	Just before Access displays the Confirm Delete dialog box.
After Del Confirm	After the Delete Confirm dialog box closes and confirmation has happened.

Event Property	When the Macro Is Triggered
On Open	When a form is opened, but the first record is not displayed yet.
On Load	When a form is loaded into memory but not yet opened.
On Resize	When the size of a form changes.
On Unload	When a form is closed and the records unload and before the form is removed from the screen.
On Close	When a form is closed and removed from the screen.
On Activate	When an open form receives the focus, becoming the active window.
On Deactivate	When a different window becomes the active window but before it loses focus.
On Got Focus	When a form with no active or enabled controls receives the focus.
On Lost Focus	When a form loses the focus.
On Click	When you press and release (click) the left mouse button on a control in a form.
On Dbl Click	When you press and release (click) the left mouse button twice on a control/label in a form.
On Mouse Down	When you press the mouse button while the pointer is on a form.
On Mouse Move	When you move the mouse pointer over an area of a form.
On Mouse Up	When you release a pressed mouse button while the pointer is on a form.
* On Mouse Wheel	When you spin the mouse wheel.
On Key Down	When you press any key on the keyboard when a form has focus; when you use a SendKeys macro.
On Key Up	When you release a pressed key or immediately after the SendKeys macro.
On Key Press	When you press and release a key on a form that has the focus; when you use the SendKeys macro.
Key Preview	(YES or NO) Evoke keyboard macros for forms before keyboard events for macros.
On Error	When a run-time error is produced.
On Filter	When a filter has been specified but before it is applied.
On Apply Filter	After a filter is applied to a form.
On Timer	When a specified time interval passes.
TimerInterval	Specify the Interval in milliseconds.
* Before Screen Tip	When the screen tip is activated.

Continued

Table 29-1 *(continued)*	
Event Property	*When the Macro Is Triggered*
* On Cmd Enabled	When a command has become enabled in a PivotChart or PivotTable.
* On Cmd Checked	When a command has been checked (checked on the toolbar).
* On Cmd Before Execute	When a command has been executed (after the execution).
* On Data Change	When a new data object is required (for example, filtering on a PivotTable).
* On Data Set Change	When a new data set for the chart changes (for example when filtered).
* On PivotTable Change	Whenever the list field, field set, or total is added or deleted in a PivotTable.
* On Selection Change	When a user makes a new selection — cannot be cancelled.
* On View Change	When a different PivotTable view of the current data is opened.
* On Connect	When a PivotTable connects to the underlying recordset.
* On Disconnect	When a PivotTable disconnects to the underlying recordset.
* Before Query	When a PivotTable is about to get a new data object.
* On Query	When the PivotTable receives new data object.
* After Layout	When the PivotChart has already been laid out but before any rendering is done.
* Before Render	When the PivotChart is about to paint itself on the screen (before drawing begins).
* After Render	When the object has been rendered in the PivotChart.
* After Final Render	When all the chart objects have been rendered.
* Begin Batch Edit	Fires when a user begins editing a batch in ADPs (form in batch edit mode).
* Undo Batch Edit	Fires when a user undoes edits in a batch in ADPs (form in batch edit mode).
* Before Begin Transaction	Before a batch transaction begins in ADPs (form in batch edit mode).
* After Begin Transaction	After a batch transaction begins in ADPs (form in batch edit mode).
* Before Commit Transaction	After you request a commit, but before the commit actually takes place in ADPs (form in batch edit mode).
* After Commit Transaction	After a commit has been completed in ADPs (form in batch edit mode).
* Rollback Transaction	Fires a batch transaction rollback in ADPs (form in batch edit mode).

 **New Feature**   Those Events marked with an asterisk are new to Access 2002.

Opening a form with a macro

Sometimes you may want to open a form with a macro. For example, each time you open the Pets Display form, you may also want to open the Customer form, enabling a user to click either form to see information from both at one time.

To accomplish this, create a macro named OpenCust and attach it to the On Open property of the Pets Display form.

To create the macro, follow these steps:

1. Click the Macros object button in the Database window to select the Macro Object list.

2. Click the New toolbar button to display the Macro Design window.

3. Click the first empty Action cell.

4. Select the OpenForm action from the drop-down menu of the Action cell.

5. Click in the Form Name cell of the Action Arguments (bottom part of window).

6. Select or type Customer.

7. Save the macro by clicking the Save button on the toolbar and naming the macro OpenCust.

Notice that in Figure 29-3 the OpenCust macro has only one action — OpenForm, with the action argument Form Name of Customer.

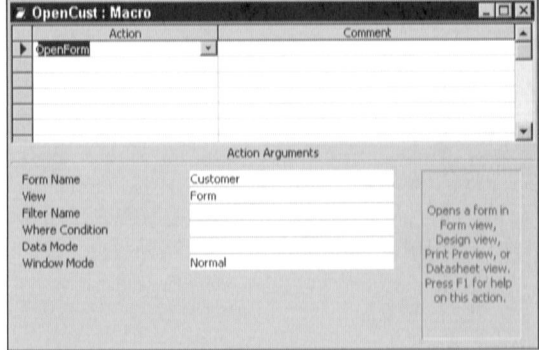

Figure 29-3: A macro to open the Customer form

The macro in Figure 29-3 has only a single action associated with it, which is the OpenForm action. This action has six possible arguments, although you entered only the form name Customer in the example. You accepted the default values of the other arguments. This action opens the specified form (Customer) for you automatically.

With the OpenCust macro created, you need to enter design mode for the Pets Display form to attach the macro OpenCust to the form property On Open.

Attaching a macro to a form

With the OpenForm macro saved, you are now ready to associate, or attach, it with the On Open property of the form Pet Display Form. To attach the OpenCust macro to the form, follow these steps:

1. Click the Forms object button in the Database window to select the Form list.

2. Select the form named **Pet Display Form** and bring it into design mode.

3. Display the property sheet by clicking the Properties button on the toolbar.

   The title of the Property window dialog box should be Form. If it isn't, select the form by clicking the gray box in the top-left corner of the form (where the rulers intersect).

   Another method of selecting is to select form from the drop-down combo box in the Properties dialog box.

4. Select the Event tab from the tabs at the top of the Property window.

5. Move to the On Open property in the Form property window. Select or type the macro name OpenCust in the On Open property cell.

   The property sheet should look similar to the one in Figure 29-4. Notice that the macro name OpenCust is placed in the property area of the On Open property.

6. Save the form and return to the Database window.

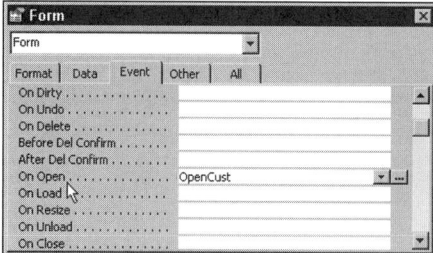

Figure 29-4: Entering a macro in the On Open property of the Pet Display form to open the Customer form automatically

With the OpenCust macro attached to the form Pets Display, you are ready to try running it. Open the Pets Display form. Notice that Access automatically opens the Customer form for you, placing it alongside the Pets Display form. Now you can use either form by clicking it to look at the individual records. Figure 29-5 shows both forms open.

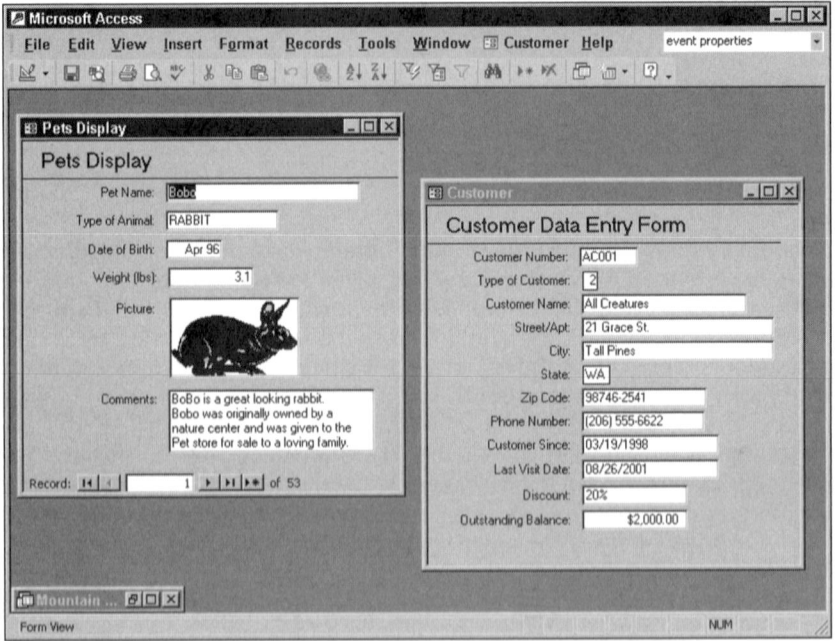

Figure 29-5: Two forms open; one form is opened automatically by a macro attached to the On Open property of the other form

The only problem with these two forms is that they are not related. Each time you change the pet, the customer form does not update — it would be nice if the Customer form showed you the correct owner of the pet.

Of all the form-level events, the most common are On Open and On Current. Although the other events are available for use, these two are used for as much as 80 percent of all form-level macros.

Synchronizing two forms with On Current

The forms in Figure 29-5 are independent of each other. Therefore, when you skip through the Pets Display form, the Customer form is not automatically updated to display the related owner information for the pet. To make these two forms work together, you synchronize them by relating the data between the forms with the On Current property.

You can use the same macro you used before (OpenCust), but now you must specify a Where condition for the OpenForm action. The condition on which to synchronize these two forms occurs when the Customer Number is the same in both forms. To specify the synchronizing condition between these two forms, follow these steps:

1. Open the macro OpenCust in design mode.

2. Click the Where Condition box of the Action Arguments.

3. Type [Customer Number] = Forms![Pet Display Form]![Customer Number].

   You can open the Zoom window to type in the above condition and click OK to save it to the Where Condition cell.

4. Resave the OpenCust macro.

Notice in Step 3 that you typed [Customer Number], which is the control name for the Customer Number field in the Customer form. You typed this name on the left side of the expression without reference to the form name. The left side of the Where expression in an OpenForm action uses the form specified in the Form Name action argument (three lines above). The right side of the expression requires the keyword Forms, the form name, and the control name.

Note   If you specify an unopened form in the Where Condition box, you will get an error message at run time, but not as you create the macro.

Now that you have modified the macro, you need to set the On Current property of the Pets Display form.

To add the OpenCust macro to the form, follow these steps:

1. Open the Pets Display form in design view.

2. Remove the macro from the On Open property of the form.

3. Move to the On Current property of the Property window.

4. Type OpenCust in the On Current parameter box.

5. Save the changes to the form.

Now, when you open the Pets Display form and a pet record is displayed, the Customer form also opens and displays the correct owner for that pet. As you change pets, the Customer form automatically displays the new owner information. These two forms are now synchronized.

Note   Even though the two forms are synchronized on the basis of the On Current property, you must still close both forms separately. Closing one form does not automatically close the other. If you want to close both forms at the same time automatically, you need to specify another macro for the On Close property. This will be done in the next section of this chapter.

To see how these two forms work together, open the Pets Display form, and then with the Pets Display form selected click the Datasheet button on the toolbar to change the Pets form to a datasheet view (or right-click the form and select datasheet view from the pop-up menu). The Customer form should remain as a form (do not change to datasheet view). If you click a different pet record in the Pets datasheet, the Customer form is updated automatically to reflect the new owner. Figure 29-6 demonstrates how this process works.

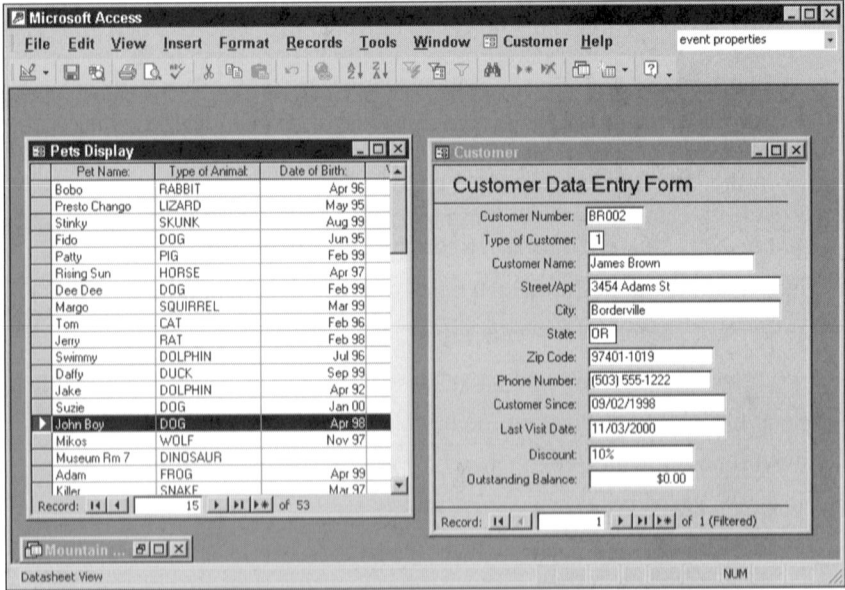

Figure 29-6: Two forms synchronized by running a macro triggered by the On Current event of the pets form

As Figure 29-6 demonstrates, you are not limited to a single-record view when synchronizing forms. The Pets Display form has been set to Datasheet; as you click different records in the datasheet, the Customer form is updated automatically to reflect the new owner.

The On Current property of the Pets form triggers the OpenCust macro every time the record changes. If you click the next navigation button, you see that the Customer form shows only one record—the owner record related to the current individual pet record in the Pets form. Notice that in the bottom of the Customer form in Figure 29-6, the record number shows Record 1 of 1 (Filtered). The Where condition in the macro acts as a filter to the Customer form.

If you know this, you can easily understand the use of the On Current property: It activates a macro that performs actions based on the specific record indicated by the form that is using the On Current property. In this case, the current pet record triggers the macro that finds the correct owner in the Customer form. Every time the pet record changes, the On Current property is activated and the next owner is found.

Running a macro when closing a form

At times, you'll want to perform some action when you close or leave a form. For example, you may want Access to keep an automatic log of the names of everyone using the form. Or, using the two forms from the preceding examples, you may want to close the Customer form automatically every time a user closes the Pets Display form.

To close the Customer form automatically every time the Pets Display form is closed, you need to create a new macro to perform the actions. Then you need to attach the macro to the On Close property of the Pets Display form.

To create a macro that closes a form, follow these steps:

1. Select the OpenCust macro and enter design mode.
2. Activate the Macro Name column by clicking the Macro Name button on the toolbar. This step enables you to create a macro group.
3. Select a blank Macro Name cell below the OpenForm action.
4. In the empty Macro Name cell, type Close Customer.
5. Select the empty Action cell alongside the Close Customer macro name.
6. Select the Close action from the pull-down menu.
7. Select the action argument Object Type.
8. Type (or select) Form.
9. Select the action argument Object Name.
10. Type (or select) the form name Customer. The macro should now look similar to Figure 29-7.
11. Re-save the macro with the new changes.

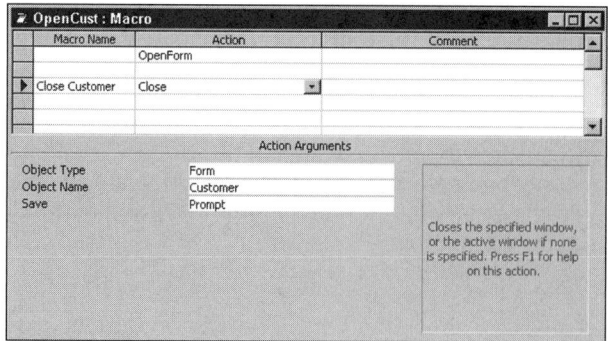

Figure 29-7: Adding a Close action macro to a macro group

Figure 29-7 shows the new macro Close Customer added to the macro OpenCust. Until now, the OpenCust macro has been a single-purpose macro. Adding another macro has made it into a group macro of two macros. The first macro is the default macro, which opens a form, and the second is a macro named Close Customer.

Cross-Reference   Macro groups are covered in Chapter 28.

The Close Customer macro has only one action: Close. This action has two arguments, both of which must be entered. The first argument is the Object Type, which specifies the type of object to close (form or report, for example). The second argument is the Object Name, which specifies by name the object to close (in this case, the form named Customer).

Now that the Close Customer macro is created, attach it to the form named Pets Display by following these steps:

1. Select the Pets Display form and click Design.

2. Activate the property sheet for the form.

3. Select the On Close property in the property sheet.

4. Type OpenCust.Close Customer or select from the pull-down menu in the On Close property parameter box. The property sheet should look like Figure 29-8.

5. Save the form with the new changes.

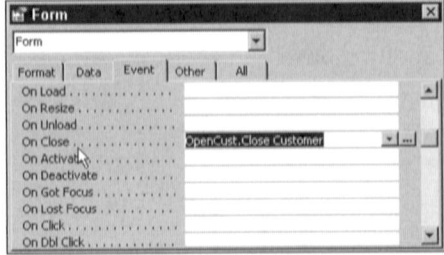

Figure 29-8: The property sheet with the On Close property set

Note   As Figure 29-8 shows, when typing or selecting the macro name in the On Close parameter box, you specify the macro group name. Then you type a period (.) followed by the name of the macro.

Opening the Pets Display form continues to maintain the current owner information in the Customer form because you left the macro with its On Current property set. Now, however, the On Close property is also set. Because you specified On Close with the Pets Display form, the Customer form closes automatically when you close the Pets Display form.

The macro attached to the On Close property simply closes the Customer form. If a user accidentally closes the Customer form and then the Pets Display form, Access does not report an error. Therefore, you don't have to specify an On Close for the Customer form to enable closing only via the Pets Display form. Using this principle, you can have one form that specifies the closing of many forms. If the forms are open, Access closes them; otherwise, Access issues the Close command with no harm done.

Confirming a delete with On Delete

The On Delete property can be used to execute a macro that displays a message and confirms that a user wants to delete a record. For example, to create a macro named ConfirmDelete, follow these steps:

1. Enter the macro design mode, create a new macro, and click the Conditions button on the toolbar to add the Condition column.

2. Select the first Condition cell.

3. Type MsgBox("Do you Want to Delete this Record?", 273, "Delete")<>1.

   The MsgBox() function is explained in detail in the sidebar after the next section.

4. Select the Action cell next to the Condition box.

5. Select or type the CancelEvent action.

6. Select the next Condition cell.

7. Type an ellipsis, which is three periods (...).

8. Select the Action cell next to the Condition box.

9. Select or type the StopMacro action.

10. Select the next Action cell.

11. Select or type the SendKeys action.

12. Select the Keystrokes action argument.

13. Type {Enter}.

14. Save the macro, naming it ConfirmDelete.

The macro should look like the one in Figure 29-9. Notice that this macro also uses the CancelEvent action. The condition for this macro uses the MsgBox() function (for a detailed explanation, see the sidebar "Using the MsgBox() function," later in this chapter).

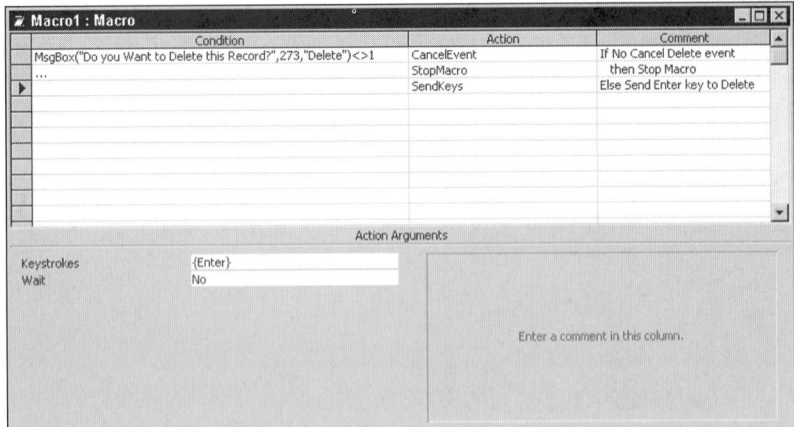

Figure 29-9: A macro to delete a record via a confirmation message

The macro in Figure 29-9 shows the use of another new action: SendKeys. This action enables you to send prearranged keystrokes to Access or another active application. The passed keystrokes are processed just as though you pressed them while working in an application. In this case, Access displays a message box like the one in Figure 29-10. Notice that the message box has two buttons: OK and Cancel. Access displays the box and waits for a keystroke. When a user selects the Cancel button, the macro cancels the delete event and stops the macro.

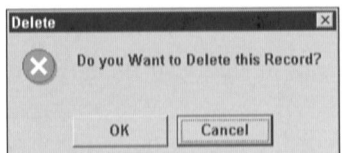

Figure 29-10: A message box for the delete macro

If a user clicks the OK button in the message box, the macro performs the SendKeys action. In this case, the macro sends the Enter keystroke. If the user does not take this action, Access displays its Delete message dialog box, forcing the user to verify again that the record should be deleted. Using SendKeys sends the Enter keystroke to the Access Delete message box, telling it to accept the deletion.

Caution This macro does not bypass referential integrity between tables. If you have referential integrity set (Chapter 6) between the Customer table and the Pets table and have not authorized Cascade Delete through the entire application, the macro fails. To override this, either set up cascade deletes through all the tables or expand the macro to perform a cascade delete by creating an SQL statement and running the SQL statement (use the RunSQL action).

Next, with the delete macro ConfirmDelete completed, attach it to the Pets Display form by placing the macro name in the entry box of the On Delete property of the form. Figure 29-11 shows the property sheet for the Pets Display form with the On Delete property set.

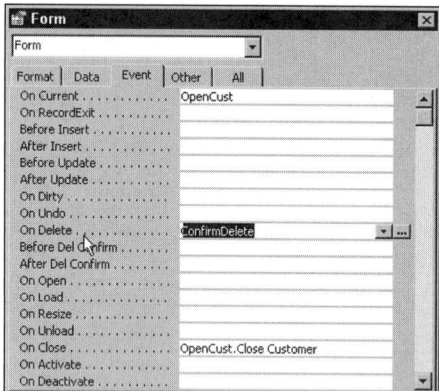

Figure 29-11: Setting an On Delete property of the Pets Display form

To see how this macro and the On Delete property work, follow these steps:

1. Display the first record in the Pets Display form.

2. Select Edit ➪ Delete Record from the main menu.

    Access responds with the message box you saw in Figure 29-10. In this message box, the Cancel button is the default.

3. Click the Cancel button to not delete this record.

Using the MsgBox( ) Function

The MsgBox( ) function is a very powerful function that can be used to display a message in a dialog box, wait for a user response, and then return a value based on the user's choice. The function has three arguments:

```
MsgBox("message" [, type of msg [, box title ] ] )
```

✦ The message here is the string displayed in the dialog box as a message.

✦ The type of msg is the numeric expression controlling the buttons and icons in the dialog box.

✦ The box title is the string displayed on the title bar of the dialog box.

Only the message is required. If you don't specify type of msg or box title, Access displays one button: OK. There is no icon and no title.

Access offers a wide range of type of message numbers. The type of message number specifies three message parts:

✦ Number and type of buttons

✦ Icon style

✦ Default button

The following table describes each:

Number and Button Type

Value	Display Button
0	OK
1	OK, Cancel
2	Abort, Retry, Ignore
3	Yes, No, Cancel
4	Yes, No
5	Retry, Cancel

Icon Style

Value	Display	Icon
0	None	
16	x	Letter X, (Critical) in a circle
32	?	Question mark (Information) in a balloon
48	!	Exclamation sign (Warning) in a triangle
64	i	Letter 'i' (Information) in a balloon

Default Button

Value	Button
0	First
256	Second
512	Third

Continued

Continued

Using the preceding table, specify the second parameter of the MsgBox( ) function by summing the three option values. For example, you can have a message box show three buttons (Yes, No, and Cancel [3]), use the Question mark (?) [32], and make the Cancel button the default [512]. Just add the three values (512+32+3) to get the second parameter number, which is 547.

If you omit type of msg in the function, MsgBox displays a single OK button and makes it the default button with no icon displayed.

Besides displaying the message box with all the options, the MsgBox() function also returns a value that indicates which button the user selects. The number it returns depends on the type of button selected. The following table shows each button and the value that MsgBox() returns:

Button Selected	Value Returned
OK	1
Cancel	2
Abort	3
Retry	4
Ignore	5
Yes	6
No	7

If the dialog box displays a Cancel button, pressing the Esc key is the same as selecting the Cancel button.

Control Event Macros

So far, you have worked with event macros at the form level. You can also trigger macros at the control level, using an event as a basis. When you attach a macro at the control level, the macro takes effect against the control. For example, you can immediately verify complex data validation at the field level (rather than when the record is exited) by using the field's Before Update property rather than the property at the form level.

Attaching macros to controls

To have a control respond to an event, you write a macro and attach the macro to the property in the control that recognizes the event. Several properties can be polled to trigger macros at the control level. Table 29-2 shows each property, the event it recognizes, and how it works.

As Table 29-2 demonstrates, you can use any of the control-level events to trigger a macro. One of these, On Click, works only with command buttons.

Table 29-2
The Control-Level Events and Associated Properties

Event Property	When the Macro Is Triggered
Before Update	Before changed data in the control is updated to the table
After Update	After changed data is updated in the control to the data
On Dirty	When the contents of a form or text of combo box or tab control changes
* On Undo	When the form is returned to a clean state
On Change	When the contents of a text box or combo box's text changes
On Updated	When an OLE object's data has been modified
On Not In List	When a value that isn't in the list is entered into a combo box
On Enter	Before a control receives the focus from another control
On Exit	Just before the control loses focus to another control
On Got Focus	When a non-active or enabled control receives the focus
On Lost Focus	When a control loses the focus
On Click	When the left mouse button is pressed and released (clicked) on a control
On Dbl Click	When the left mouse button is pressed and released (clicked) twice on a control/label
On Mouse Down	When a mouse button is pressed while the pointer is on a control
On Mouse Move	When the mouse pointer is moved over a control
On Mouse Up	When a pressed mouse button is released while the pointer is on a control
On Key Down	When any key on the keyboard is pressed when a control has the focus or when the SendKeys macro is used
On Key Press	When a key is pressed and released on a control that has the focus or when the SendKeys macro is used
On Key Up	When a pressed key is released or immediately after the SendKeys macro is used

 **New Feature** The On Undo event is new to Access 2002.

Forms have several different types of objects on them: labels, text boxes, OLE (Object Linking and Embedding) objects, subforms, command buttons, check boxes, and so on. Each of these has several event properties associated with it. You can attach a macro, an expression, or Visual Basic code to any of them. To see any object's event properties, simply activate the Properties dialog box and select event properties while working with the object.

Working with Macros on Forms

You can group macros for forms into six categories according to their functions:

✦ Validating data

✦ Setting values

✦ Navigating between forms and records

✦ Filtering records

✦ Finding records

✦ Printing records (covered in Chapter 32)

Each category uses specific macro actions to perform its job.

Validating data

You already worked with macros to validate data at both the form level and the control level. When validating data, you can work with several macro actions: MsgBox, CancelEvent, StopMacro, GoToControl, GoToRecord and SetValue.

The most common event properties that trigger validation macros are the On Delete and Before Update properties, although any property can be used.

Displaying a message

To display a message, you use the MsgBox action. This action has four arguments:

✦ **Message.** Specifies the user message in a dialog box

✦ **Beep.** Sounds a computer beep when the dialog box is opened

✦ **Type.** Specifies the type of icon displayed in the dialog box, such as the stop sign, a question mark, and so on

✦ **Title.** Specifies a user-entered title for the box

Canceling events

To cancel an event, use the CancelEvent action. This action has no arguments — it simply cancels the event that triggers the macro to run. For example, if the macro is attached to the Before Update property of a form, the update is canceled.

Stopping a macro

To stop execution of a macro, use the StopMacro action. This action stops execution of the macro immediately and returns the user to the calling form. This action is useful for stopping a macro based on a condition specified in the macro.

Going to a specific control

If you need to return to a specific control (field) in a form, use the GoToControl action. This action has one argument: the control name. If you supply a control name, this action takes you to that control. You normally use this action just before you use the StopMacro action.

Setting values

By setting control, field, and property values with macros, data entry is easier and more accurate. Besides these advantages, several forms, databases, and reports can be linked to make them work together more intelligently.

Setting values with a macro can accomplish these tasks:

- ✦ Hide or display a control on the basis of a value in the form (Visible property).
- ✦ Disable or lock a control on the basis of a value in the form (Enable and Locked properties).
- ✦ Update a field in the form on the basis of the value of another control.
- ✦ Set the value of a control in a form on the basis of the control of another form.

The SetValue action is used to set values with a macro. This action has two arguments:

- ✦ **Item.** The name of the control or property
- ✦ **Expression.** The expression used to set the value

Caution   If you use the SetValue action to change the value of a control (field) being validated, do not attach it to the Before Update property. Access cannot change the value of a control while it is being validated; it can change the value only after it has been saved. Use the After Update property instead.

You cannot use the SetValue macro action on bound or calculated controls on reports; the same is true for calculated controls on forms.

Converting a field to uppercase

If you enable entry of a field in either uppercase or lowercase, you may want to store it in uppercase. To accomplish this, create a macro that uses the SetValue action to set the value of the field for you. In the Item argument box, enter the name of the field to convert to uppercase. In the Expression argument box, enter the function UCase( ) with the name of the field to be converted. The function UCase( ) must already exist. Figure 29-12 shows the arguments for converting the field Customer Name to uppercase.

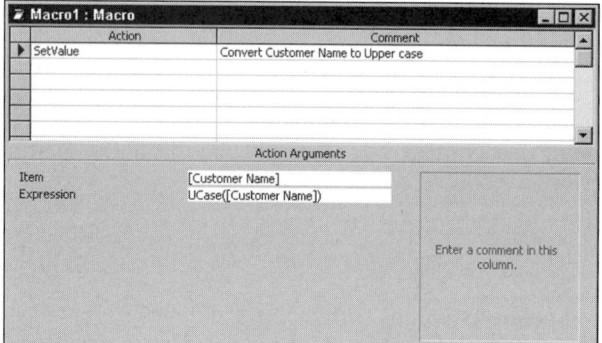

Figure 29-12: Converting a field to uppercase using a macro

After creating the macro, you use it by placing the macro name in the After Update event of the property sheet of the field name Customer Name.

If the user enters a customer name in lowercase or mixed case, Access automatically runs the macro and converts the field to uppercase when the user completes the update.

Assigning values to new records

When you add new records to a form, it is often convenient to have values automatically filled in for fields using values from another open form. SetValue is also used to do this.

For example, after adding a new customer in the Customer form, you may immediately want to add a pet record in another form and have the Customer Number automatically filled in.

To accomplish this, the After Update event on the Customer form can be programmed to add a pet record after the customer record's Pet Name value is changed. A macro opens the Pets Display form in the Add Mode using the OpenForm action. The next macro action, SetValue, automatically sets the value of Customer Number in the Pets Display form to the Customer Number in the Customer form. Figure 29-13 shows the arguments for this macro.

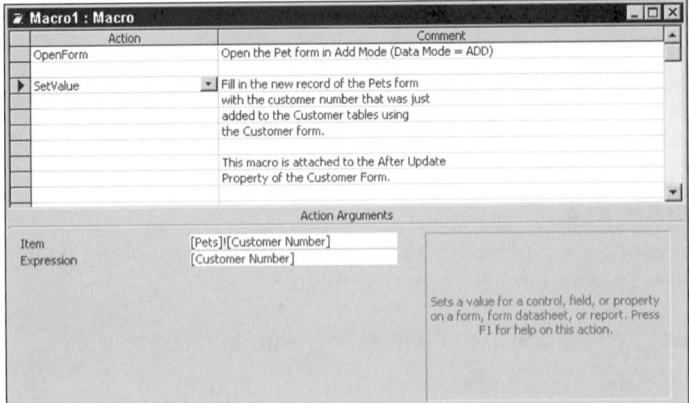

Figure 29-13: Macro arguments to set a field value in another form (Pets) on the basis of a value in the current form (Customer)

Note   The Item argument can also use its full syntax instead of the abbreviation shown in Figure 29-13. The syntax is

```
Forms![Pets]![Customer Number]
```

The Expression argument refers to the Customer Number in the open form, which is the Customer form. When working with the SetValue action in this way, you must specify the entire syntax for the name of the field being replaced in the Item box.

Navigating in forms and records

Whenever you need to move to a specific control (field), record, or page in a form, you use the GoToXXXX actions, where XXXX represents the control, record, or page.

Moving to a specific control

To move to a specific control, use the GoToControl action. This action has one argument, which is Control Name. To move to a specific field, supply the control name in the argument.

Moving to a specific record

To move to a specific record in a table, query, or form, use the GoToRecord action. This action has four arguments:

✦ **Object Type.** Type of object (form, table, or query)

✦ **Object Name.** Name of the object specified in Object Type

✦ **Record.** Specifies which record to go to (preceding, next, new, first, last, and so on)

✦ **Offset.** The number of records to offset from (if 10, go back 10 records)

Using this action, you can move to any record in a form, query, or table.

Moving to a specific page

To move to a specific page and place the focus in the first control of the page, use the GoToPage action. This action has three arguments:

✦ **Page Number.** Specifies the page number you want to move to

✦ **Right.** The upper-left corner of the page (horizontal position)

✦ **Down.** The upper-left corner of the page (vertical position)

This action is useful for working with multiple-page forms.

Filtering records

You can create a macro or series of macros to filter records in a form. For example, you may want to have a Customer form with four buttons to limit the form's records to a single state or to allow all states. (Even though you haven't learned about buttons yet [command buttons are covered in chapter 32], you can learn how they would interact with a group of macros.) The form will look similar to Figure 29-14. Notice that four buttons are in the box named Filter Records. The Washington Button is selected and the bottom of the form informs you that there are 10 records for Washington (filtered).

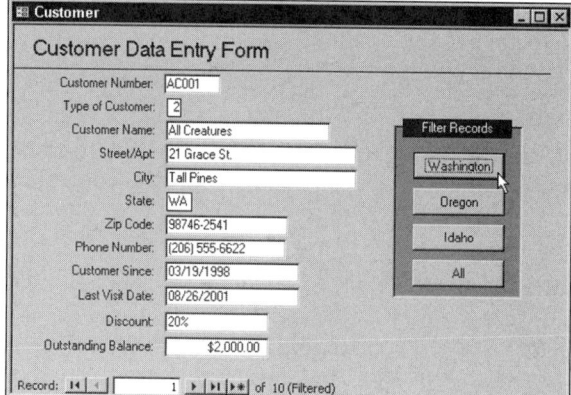

Figure 29-14: A form with buttons used to activate filter macros. The macros are attached to the On Click event property of the Command buttons.

Each button in Figure 29-14 is attached to a different macro. Three of the macros use the ApplyFilter action, and one uses the ShowAllRecords action.

Using the ApplyFilter action

To set a filter condition in a macro, use the ApplyFilter action. This action has two arguments: Filter Name and the Where Condition. You can use either one, but you should use only one unless you pre-define a filter and want to filter the filter. For this example, you use the Where Condition argument. To create a macro named StateFilter.WA, follow these steps:

1. Enter the Macro Design window.

2. Enter the macro name Set WA into the group macro StateFilter.

3. Select or type ApplyFilter for the action.

4. Type [State] = "WA" in the Where Condition argument box.

After you create this macro, create two more macros: one named StateFilter.Set ID, the other named StateFilter.Set OR (macro group named StateFilter). These macros set a condition equal to the individual state. After it is created, you can save it to a macro group name StateFilter.

Using the ShowAllRecords action

When you create filter conditions with macros, you should always create another macro that uses the ShowAllRecords action. This action removes an existing filter set by another macro. This action has no arguments. For the next example, create a macro named StateFilter.Set All with the ShowAllRecords action. When you complete this process, all four macros should look like the ones in Figure 29-15.

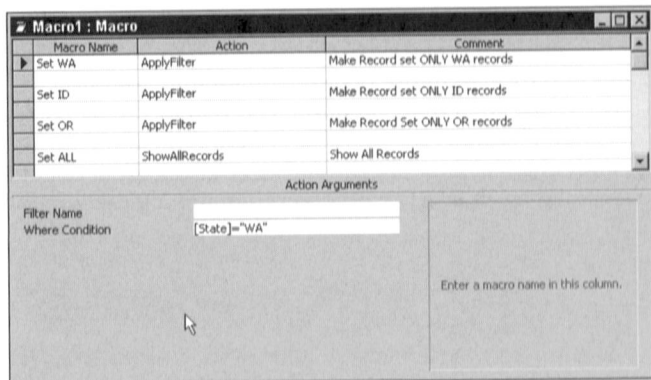

Figure 29-15: A macro group with four filter macros used to limit the records viewed in a form

Running filter macros

To run a filter macro, attach the macro name to the On Click property of the appropriate command button. Then the macro will execute and implement the filter condition every time the button is selected.

To attach the filter macros to the buttons of the form Customer with Buttons, follow these steps:

1. Open the Customer with Buttons form in Design mode.
2. Active the Property dialog box.
3. Select the Washington Button on the right side of the form.
4. Select or type the macro name StateFilter.Set WA in the On Click event property box.
5. Select the Oregon Button on the right side of the form.
6. Select or type the macro name StateFilter.Set OR in the On Click event property box.
7. Select the Idaho Button on the right side of the form.
8. Select or type the macro name StateFilter.Set ID in the On Click event property box.
9. Resave the form.

This form can now be used to view records by state or all records, simply by clicking the appropriate filter button.

Finding records

One of the most powerful ways of using macros is to locate user-specified records. This type of macro uses two macro actions: GoToControl and FindRecord. For example, you can add a search routine to the Customer with Buttons form, as shown in Figure 29-16. To do this, you create an unbound combo box; as you can see in Figure 29-17, it is named CustomerSelect. After creating the unbound combo box, you need to create and attach a macro to the AfterUpdate event of the control to move the record pointer in the table to the first record matching the Customer name selected.

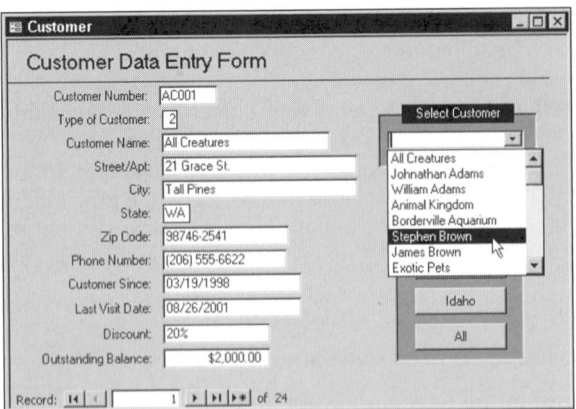

Figure 29-16: The Customer form with a combo box added. It is used to find records based on a Customer name.

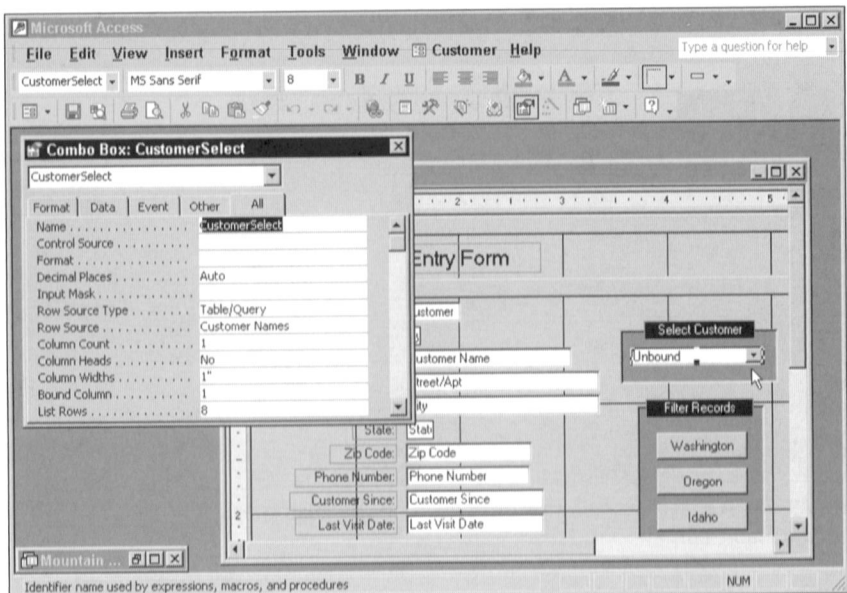

Figure 29-17: The property sheet for the unbound combo box shows the Name given of CustomerSelect. This name will be referred to later in a macro to find customer records.

Your property sheet for the combo box should look similar to Figure 29-17.

After creating the unbound combo box, you can beautify the label and combo box area, as shown in Figure 29-16. These enhancements aren't required.

After the combo box is created and the form saved and closed (you may want to rename it to "Customer with filter and find"), you are ready to create the FindRecord macro to find the customer record by the Customer Name field. Before you can attach the macro, you must first create the macro. Create a new macro by first selecting New from the macro section of the database container. When you are in the macro design screen, you can create the macro by following these steps:

1. Select or type GoToControl in the first empty Action cell.

2. Type [Customer Name] in the Control Name argument cell.

3. Select or type FindRecord in the next empty Action cell.

4. Type =[CustomerSelect] in the Find What argument box.

5. Save the macro, naming it FindRecord.

That's it! Your macro should now resemble the one in Figure 29-18.

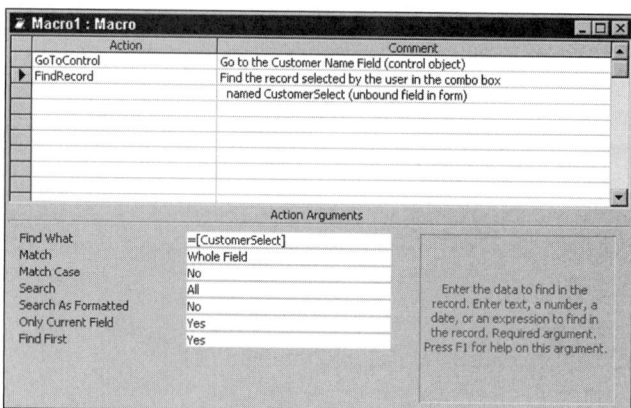

Figure 29-18: A macro to find a record based on the customer's name attached to an unbound field

In the GoToControl argument, you placed the form control name [Customer Name], which is the same as the field name, to limit the scope of the search to the current field (Customer Name). Then, in the FindRecord argument Find What, you placed the control name for the unbound combo box. By placing the unbound combo box in the Find What box, you specify that the macro will find the name via the combo box but update the record on the basis of Customer Name.

Caution   Note that you entered an equal sign before the control name CustomerSelect in the Find What argument box. If you don't enter the equal sign, the macro will not work.

Now that you have created the macro, you're ready to attach it to the After Update property for the unbound combo box. To attach the macro, follow these steps:

1. Open the Customer with Buttons form (that has new command button on it) and activate the Properties dialog box.

2. Move to the After Update property of the CustomerSelect control (unbound combo box).

3. Type FindRecord in the Action Arguments cell (the name of the macro).

4. Save the form.

The form now uses the combo box to find any customer!

Report Event Macros

Just as with forms, reports can also use macros that perform actions based on events you specify. You can work with macros at the report level or the section level. If you attach a macro at the report level, it takes effect when the event occurs against the report as a whole, such as when you open or close the report. If you attach the macro at the section level, it takes effect when the event occurs within a section (such as when you format or print the section).

Several event properties can be used for report-level macros. Table 29-3 shows each property, the event it recognizes, and how it works.

As Table 29-3 illustrates, you can use any of the report-level events to trigger a macro. These events can be used just as you use their counterparts in forms.

Table 29-3
The Report-Level Events and Associated Properties

Event Property	When the Macro Is Triggered
On Open	When a report is opened but before it prints
On Close	When a report is closed and removed from the screen
On Activate	When a report receives the focus and becomes the active window
On Deactivate	When a different window becomes the active window
On No Data	When the report has no data passed to it from the active table or query
On Page	When the report changes pages
On Error	When a run-time error is produced in Access

Opening a report with a macro

You may want to use the On Open property of a report to run a macro that prompts the user to identify the records to print. The macro can use a filter or use the ApplyFilter action to the limit, which records to print in the report.

For example, you may want to activate a form or dialog box that prompts the user to identify a state or to print the report Customer Mailing Labels. To accomplish this task, create a filter macro similar to the one in the section on forms and attach it to the On Open property of the report.

The On No Data event can also be a good property to attach a macro to. This event is used to run a macro or code when there are no records found in the dataset sent to the report.

Deactivating a section of a report with a macro

Another macro that can be useful is one that actually changes the visible property of a control object on a report or even an entire section. For example, the report, Invoice with Detail Section hidden, as shown in Figure 29-19 shows a portion of page 1 of the report.

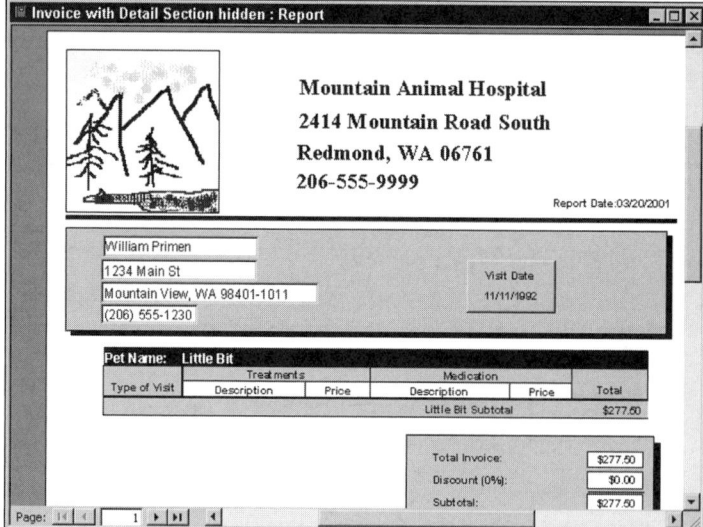

Figure 29-19: A report form with the detail section for the visit information of a pet missing

This report has a macro attached to the On Open even of the form. The macro actually uses the SetValue action to change the visible value of the detail section of the report. To change the visibility of a report section, you must specify which section. To create this macro, follow these steps:

1. Create a new macro.

2. Select the SetValue action.

3. Move to the argument pane and select the Item text box.

4. Click the build button of the Item text box to activate the Expression Builder.

5. Select Reports, All Reports, Invoice with Detail Section Hidden report from the leftmost list box.

6. Move to the second list box (in the middle) and select Detail from the middle list box.

7. Move to the last list box and select Visible in this list box.

   The expression builder should now show the following expressions:

   Reports![Invoice with Detail Section hidden].Section(0).Visible

8. Click the OK button to return to the Item text box.

9. Select the Expression text box.

10. Type No in the text box.

11. Close and Save the macro, naming it **Set Section Off.**

With the macro now created, you can attach it to the On Open property of the report, Invoice with Detail Section hidden. Then when you run the report, you will see that the detail section of the report has been eliminated in the final display or printing of the report.

This macro would probably be better placed in some form that would enable you to turn the section off based on a user request by pressing a command button. That way you can use the same form to show all detail records or to eliminate them.

Creating a Report Snapshot macro

One way a macro can be functional with Reports is by creating one that will create a Report Snapshot. A Report Snapshot (covered in Chapter 20) is a file that is created from the report that is saved using the extension *.snp. It contains a high-fidelity copy of each page of an Access report, preserving the graphics and embedded objects of the report for viewing.

Although not formally a report macro, in the sense of attaching it to a report event, it is a very useful macro that will enable you to create visual report files that can be sent to other users, across a network, or even published on the Internet.

To create a stand-alone macro that will open the report, Monthly Invoice Report – No Cover, in preview mode and copy it to a Snapshot view file that has the user supply the name at the time it is run, follow these steps:

1. Create a new macro.
2. Select the OpenReport action.
3. Move to the Argument pane and select Monthly Invoice Report – No Cover from the Report Name text box.
4. Select Print Preview from the View text box.
5. Move to the top pane and select Output To as the second action in this macro.
6. Move to the Argument pane and type or select Report in the Object Type text box.
7. Select Snapshot Format from the Output Format.
8. Close and Save the macro, naming it **Snapshot OutPut To - .**

The macro should now look similar to the one in Figure 29-20.

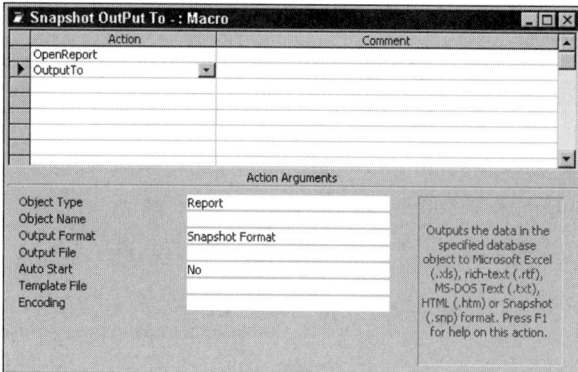

Figure 29-20: A macro to create a Report Snapshot

With the macro complete, you can run it by either attaching it to an event property of a form or by selecting and running it from the macro section of the database container.

For this exercise, highlight the macro, Snapshot OutPut to -, in the macro section of the database container and either click the Run button in the container or double-click the name. When the macro runs, it will display the report in Print Preview mode in one window and activate the Output to dialog box and prompt you for a name to save the snapshot file to. You can give it any name you want and click the OK button. After you have given it a name, Access will take the report and save it in snapshot view. Figure 29-21 shows the snapshot file in the Snapshot viewer of Microsoft Office.

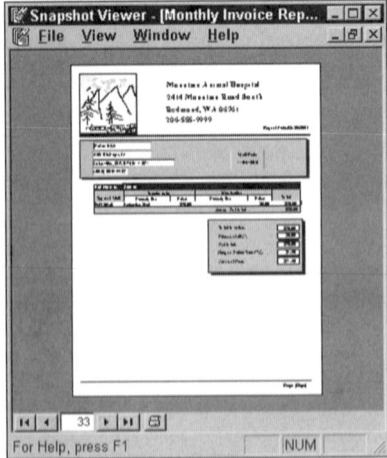

Figure 29-21: A snapshot file of an Access report in the Snapshot viewer

This file can be published to the Web, e-mailed to a person, or simply viewed on your computer inside the Snapshot viewer. You can click it and view it in full-page view and even print it from the Snapshot Viewer.

Report Section Macros

Besides the report-level properties, Access offers three event properties that you can use at the section level for a report macro. Table 29-4 shows each property, the event it recognizes, and how it works.

Table 29-4
The Report Section-Level Events and Associated Properties

Event Property	Event	When the Macro Is Triggered
On Format	Format	When Access knows what data goes in a section (but before laying out the data for printing).
On Print	Print	After Access lays out the data in a section for printing (but before printing the section).
On Retreat	Retreat	After the Format event but before the Print event; occurs when Access has to "back up" past other sections on a page to perform multiple formatting passes. This is in all sections except the Headers and Footers.

Using On Format

You use the On Format property when a user's response can affect page layout or when the macro contains calculations that use data from sections you don't intend to print. The macro will run before Access lays out the section (following your other property settings for the report, such as Keep Together, Visible, or Can Grow).

You can set the On Format and On Print properties for any section of the report. However, the On Retreat is not available for the page header or page footer sections.

For example, you may want to highlight some data on the form, based on a certain condition the macro determines. If the condition is met, the macro uses the SetValue action to change a control's Visible property to Yes.

Using On Print

You use the On Print property when no user's response affects page layout or when the macro depends on what page it finds the records to be printed. For example, you may want to have a total calculation placed in either the header or footer of each page.

Using On Retreat

You use the On Retreat property when the report must return to a previous report section to determine where the controls and sections are and if they will fit in the given space left on a page. For example, you may want to trigger an On Retreat where you have Groups with the KeepTogether property set to Whole Group or

With First Detail. Another example is when you have a subreport or subform that has the Can-Grow and/or Can-Shrink properties set to Yes and you want to make sure it all fits on a single page.

Report Properties

When you work with macros that use the On Print and On Format properties of report sections, you may need to use two special conditional printer properties:

✦ Format Count

✦ Print Count

These two conditional printer properties are used in the Condition Expression column of a macro. Both are read-only properties; Access sets their values. Therefore, you can check these properties, but you cannot change their values. These properties determine when an event occurs twice.

Using Format Count

The Format Count property is used as a macro condition to determine the number of times the On Format property setting is evaluated for the current line on the report.

It is possible for a line to be formatted more than once. For example, when the labels are printed, the last label may not fit on a page; there may be room for only one line of a two-line label. If the label won't fit on the page, Access prints it on the next page. The Format Count for any lines moved from the bottom of the page to the top of the next page is set to 2 because the lines are formatted twice.

If you are accumulating a count of the number of labels being printed, you use the Format Count property in the Condition box of the macro to disregard counting the label a second time.

Using Print Count

Like the Format Count property, the Print Count property is used as a macro condition. This property determines the number of times the On Print setting is evaluated for the current line of the report.

It is possible for part of a record to be printed on one page and the remainder to be printed on the next page. When that occurs, the On Print event occurs twice, so the Print property is incremented to 2. When this occurs, you don't want to have the macro perform its action twice; therefore, you check to see whether the Format Count has changed, and then you stop the macro action.

To understand how this works, suppose that you have a macro that counts the number of records being printed on a page. The record number is placed in the page footer section of each page of the report. If a record is printed across two pages, you want the records counted on only one of the pages.

Working with macros in reports

Like form macros, report macros can be triggered at two levels — report and section. However, unlike form macros, they cannot be triggered at control levels (labels, text boxes, check boxes, etc.) A macro triggered at the report level can prompt a user for a range of records to print before doing anything with the report.

On the other hand, a section-level macro can be used for printing messages on a report when a condition is met. For example, if a customer has not paid on his or her bill in 30 days, the report may print a reminder line that a partial payment is overdue.

Report-level macros can be executed before or after a report is printed or previewed. Section-level macros can be executed before or after a section of the report is printed or previewed. Thus, section-level macros tend to be used for actions that are more refined, such as including conditional lines of text in the report.

Underlining data in a report with a macro

You can use a macro to underline or highlight data dynamically in a report. This is accomplished by hiding or displaying controls and sections.

Suppose that you print the report named "Monthly Invoice Report - No Cover" and you want to underline the Amount Due control if the total amount is more than $500.00. You do this by adding a control to the group footer named Customer.Customer Number Footer and creating a macro that toggles the Visible property for the control. Follow these steps to add a line to the report:

1. Open the report "**Monthly Invoice Report – No Cover**" in design mode.
2. Activate the Property Dialog box and Toolbox.
3. Move to the bottom of the report in the Customer.Customer Number Footer.
4. Select a line from the Toolbox and place below the Amount Due: Label field.
5. Go to the Property box and click the All tab.
6. Type **AmtDueLine** in the Name property.
7. Select **6 pt** in the Border Width property.
8. Save the form.

Now your form should look like the one in Figure 29-19. Figure 29-22 shows a line added below the Amount Due control of the Monthly Invoice Report – No Cover report.

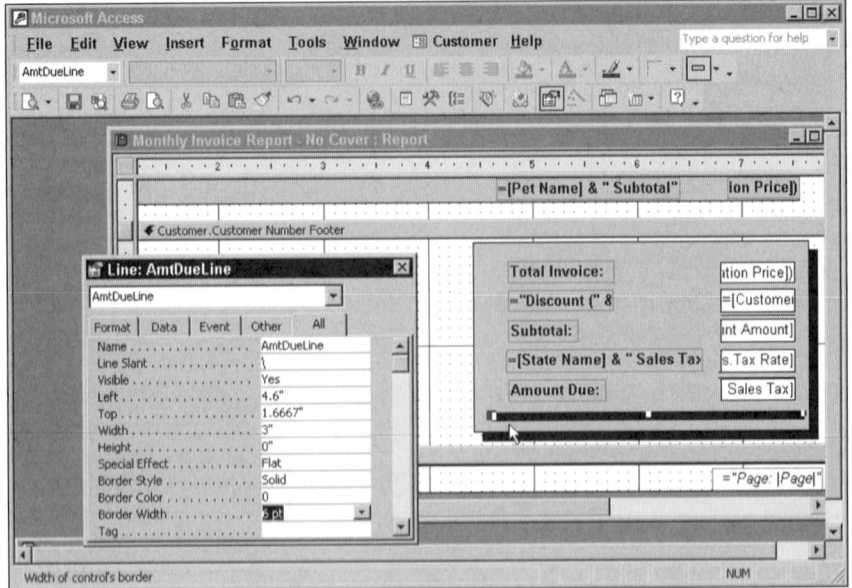

Figure 29-22: A report form with a line added to the Footer section

In Figure 29-22, the Visible property is set to Yes (default value) in the property sheet for the control AmtDueLine. This property will be manipulated by the macro created in the next section.

With the control (line) placed on the report, create a macro that sets the Visible property for this control. This macro requires two conditions—one for [Amount Due]>500 and the other for not being greater than this amount. To create the macro, follow these steps:

1. Create a macro named PrtLine.
2. Activate the Condition column and select an empty cell in the Condition column.
3. Type [Amount Due]>500 in the Condition cell.
4. Select the associated Action cell.
5. Select or type SetValue.

6. Select the Item argument.

7. Type [AmtDueLine].[Visible].

8. Select the Expression argument.

9. Type Yes.

10. Select another empty Condition cell.

11. Type Not [Amount Due]>500.

12. Select the associated Action cell.

13. Select or type SetValue.

14. Select the Item argument.

15. Type [AmtDueLine].Visible.

16. Select the Expression argument.

17. Type No.

18. Save the macro, naming it PrtLine.

The macro should look similar to the one in Figure 29-23. Notice that the macro in this figure has a separate condition to turn the Visible property on (set to Yes) and off.

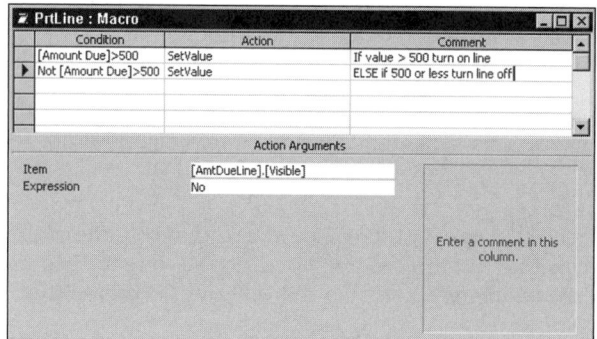

Figure 29-23: A macro to turn the Visible property of the AmtDueLine control on or off

Now that the macro is created, it needs to be attached to the group section named Customer.Customer Number Footer in the Monthly Invoice Report. The macro is attached to the On Format property of the section. Figure 29-24 shows the property sheet with the macro added to the On Format property of the correct footer section.

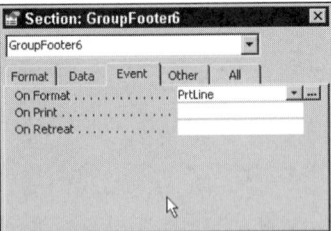

Figure 29-24: A property sheet with a macro name PrtLine set in the On Format property

Hiding data in a report with a macro

Data in a report can be hidden with the same method you just used to display or hide a line — setting the Visible property to Yes or No in a macro. After you set the property to Yes or No in a macro, attach the macro to the On Format property of the section where the data resides.

Filtering records for a report with a macro

Creating a macro and attaching it to the On Open property of the report can filter records for a report. This provides a consistent way of asking for criteria. The On Open property runs the macro no matter how the user opens the report. For example, a user can double-click the report name, choose a command from a custom menu, or select a command button on a form. If the On Open property is used to trigger the macro, you have to run the dialog box against only this single property.

Chapter 32 shows a menu and dialog box that perform this type of filtering.

Macros for Importing and Exporting

You can easily use data from other formats in Access. You can import, export, and attach tables via commands from the File menu in the Database window. However, if you consistently transfer the same data, you may want to automate the process in a macro.

Using command buttons to import or export

If you create a macro to transfer data, you can activate the macro by using a command button and the On Click property of the button.

When you create the macro, Access provides three actions to help you transfer the data. Essentially, these actions save your data in a database, SQL database, spreadsheet, or text type format:

✦ TransferDatabase

✦ TransferSpreadsheet

✦ TransferSQLDatabase

✦ TransferText

By using these actions and their arguments, you can create very powerful (but simple) import/export macros, or more accurately transfer-data macros.

Creating Keyboard Accelerators (Hot Keys)

A macro can be assigned to a specific key or combination of keys, such as Ctrl+D. After a macro is assigned to a key, the key is known as a hot key or keyboard accelerator. By assigning hot keys, you can create one macro to perform an action no matter which form, view, or table you're in. For example, the Ctrl+D key combination can be used to display a form in datasheet view instead of form view.

You can assign macros to any number of hot keys. All hot-key macros are stored in a single group macro that Access uses. That group macro is known as a key assignment macro. When you open a database, Access looks for a macro named AutoKeys. If the macro exists, it runs automatically, assigning macros to hot keys. Figure 29-25 shows two hot-key assignments in an AutoKeys macro — Ctrl+D and Ctrl+R.

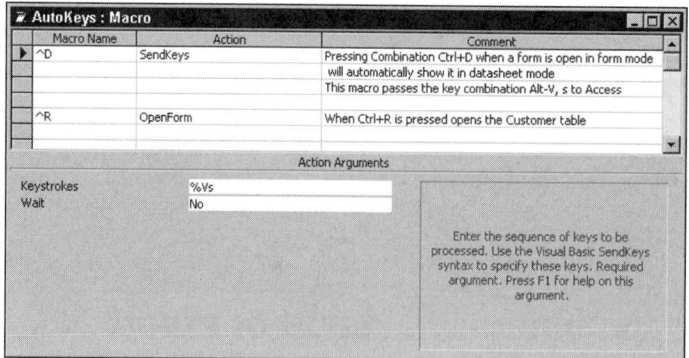

Figure 29-25: A macro that assigns hot keys to the AutoKeys macro

Notice that there are two different types of hot keys assigned to the macros in Figure 29-25. One assigns the keystrokes to print a single record from any open object in Access (Ctrl+D) and uses the SendKeys action. The second macro, assigned to Ctrl+R, uses the OpenForm action.

Creating a hot-key combination

To create a hot-key combination and assign actions to it requires creating a special macro named AutoKeys and using macro names based on the key combination you want to use to specify an action. The macro names can be based on a specific Access syntax called SendKeys syntax; otherwise, they can use the typical macro actions.

Using SendKeys syntax for key assignments

When you enter a key combination in the Macro Name column, you specify the key combination by using a specific syntax known as SendKeys syntax. Table 29-5 shows several key combinations and their corresponding SendKeys syntax. When you assign actions to a key combination, you enter the SendKeys syntax in the Macro Name column.

Using Table 29-5 as a reference, you see that to assign some macro actions to the Tab key, you name a macro {TAB} in the group macro AutoKeys. To find more on SendKeys, you can look up help for SendKeys in the Visual Basic Help (activated by creating a module and calling help).

Table 29-5
SendKeys Syntax

Key Combo	SendKeys Syntax	Key Combo	SendKeys Syntax
Backspace	{BKSP} or {BS}	F2	{F2}
Caps Lock	{CAPSLOCK}	Ctrl+A	^A
Enter	{ENTER} or ~	Ctrl+F10	^{F10}
Insert	{INSERT}	Ctrl+2	^2
Left Arrow	{LEFT}	Shift+F5	+{F5}
Home	{HOME}	Shift+Delete	+{DEL}
PgDn	{PGDN}	Shift+End	+{END}
Escape	{ESC}	Alt+F10	%{F10}
Scroll Lock	{SCROLLLOCK}	Left arrow 10 times	{LEFT 10}
Tab	{TAB}	Shift+BA together	+(BA)

Creating a hot key

To create a hot key, follow these pseudo steps:

1. Create a macro named AutoKeys.

2. Type the key combination in the Macro Name column.

3. Type the set of actions you want to associate with the key combination.

4. Repeat Steps 2 and 3 for each hot key to which you want to assign actions.

5. Save the macro.

Access makes the key assignment immediately. When you press the key combination, Access runs the macro actions. In the preceding steps, you can also make several key assignments, creating a macro for each key combination. Just remember to name the macro group AutoKeys.

✦   ✦   ✦

Working with Visual Basic in Access 2002

✦ ✦ ✦ ✦

In This Chapter

Using the Database
Wizard to create
instant applications

Understanding the
basics of Visual Basic

Creating a new
module

Using the Module
window

Using the Command
Button Wizard to
create Visual Basic
code

Converting macros to
Visual Basic

✦ ✦ ✦ ✦

Chapters 28 and 29 explain how to create macros to auto-mate operations. You can, however, program Access in other ways. Writing Visual Basic modules is the best way to create applications. Adding error routines, setting up repetitive looping, and adding procedures that macros simply can't perform give you more control of application development. In this chapter, you learn how to build an application framework and how to extend the power of an application using Visual Basic.

Instant Applications Using the Access 2002 Database Wizard

It's 3 p.m. on a Friday. A potential new client has just called and said he hears that you do great work. The client wants a custom system to do whatever — and wants to see a prototype of what you can do by Monday morning at 10 a.m. Do you cancel the weekend picnic with the family? Do you reschedule your golf or tennis match and order plenty of Jolt Cola? No. There's a great way to get started: create a prototype using the Access 2002 Database Wizard!

An application prototype presents a preview of how the completed application may function. A prototype consists of the basic framework of the application: the main switchboard, some tables and queries, and a scaled-down version of the application's most significant forms and reports. The prototype provides a visual tool for planning and designing the finished application. The Database Wizard provides a quick and easy way to get your application prototype up and running.

The Database Wizard is similar to Table Wizards. Table Wizards in Access 2002 enable you to choose business and personal table definitions — expenses, contact management, order entry, time and billing, and so on — from a list. Some definitions contain multiple tables, such as Orders and Items. After you select your table(s), Access displays a set of fields and enables you to choose which ones to include. The program then builds the table for you. Optionally, you can also have a simple AutoForm created. Although this feature is a real time-saver, it pales in comparison with the Database Wizard.

Cross-Reference   For a review of using the Table Wizard, see Chapter 5.

The Access 2002 Database Wizard takes the concept of Table Wizards to a new dimension by combining the best features of Access Wizards with the amazing power of an application generator. Application generators have been popular for many years in some products. These tools eliminate the tedious process of building the basic elements of an application from scratch over and over again for each new application you create. They enable you to quickly generate the basic building blocks of your application and establish a consistent look and feel from one application to another.

The Access 2002 Database Wizard doesn't require you to define a table design first; it doesn't make you create a form or report; it simply builds a complete, customizable application, including tables, forms, modules, reports, and a user-modifiable switchboard (the application's main menu). The Wizard doesn't build just one table or form. The Database Wizard builds groups of tables; adds the table relationships; builds forms for each table, including one-to-many forms, where appropriate; and even adds critical reports for the type of application you are building. This process means that the Wizard creates an entire ready-to-run application. As you go through the Wizard process, you determine which fields from each table definition are used; some fields are mandatory, and some are optional. You can always make changes after the application is built.

The order-entry application you build in this chapter creates 10 tables, 14 forms, and 8 reports, including customer reports, sales reports, and even an aged-receivables statement — everything you need to start a basic order-entry system.

Getting started

You start the Database Wizard by choosing New From Template ➪ General Templates in the task pane. Access 2002 displays the New dialog box. Select the Databases tab, as shown in Figure 30-1. Each icon represents a different application the Database Wizard can create. When you create an application, that application is created in its own database container.

The Database Wizard enables you to choose among a wide variety of applications, as follows:

✦ Asset Tracking

✦ Order Entry

✦ Contact Management

✦ Resource Scheduling

✦ Event Management

✦ Service Call Management

✦ Expenses

✦ Time and Billing

✦ Inventory Control

✦ Ledger

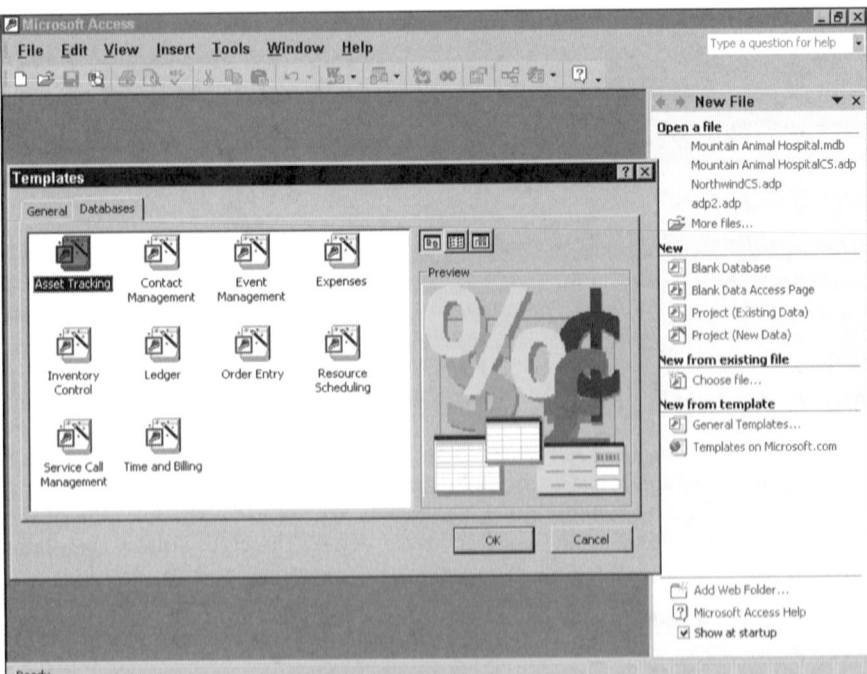

Figure 30-1: Starting the Database Wizard

When you decide which application is closest to the one you want to create, double-click it to start defining your own application. For the example in this chapter, choose the Order Entry application.

When you choose the Order Entry application, the File New Database dialog box appears. Use this dialog box to enter a name for the database. This dialog box is a standard File navigation-type dialog box that enables you to select the drive, directory, and database name. The default name is the name of the application. In this example, the name is Order Entry1.mdb. You can make the name anything you want, and you can change it later by renaming the database with the Windows Explorer. Press the Create button to create the new database.

When the Wizard starts, the dialog box shown in Figure 30-2 appears, showing a pictorial representation of the system. In this example, the dialog box tells you that six basic functions will be created: Customer information, Order information, Order Details, Payment information, Product information, and My Company Information. These functions generally are tables or forms. After you view this introductory dialog box, you can click the standard Next> button to go to the next dialog box.

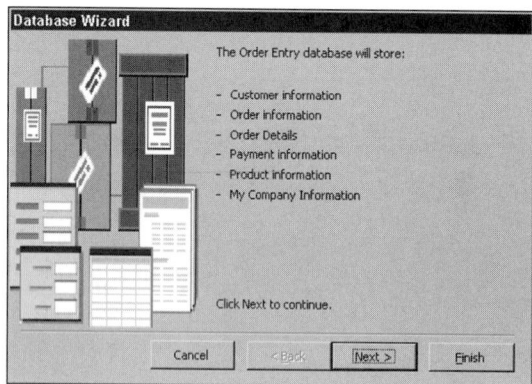

Figure 30-2: Learning what the database will create for you

Working with tables and fields

The next Wizard screen (see Figure 30-3) enables you to work with the tables and fields of the database. Most of the fields and tables are mandatory, but you also can select optional fields for each table. The tables are listed on the left side of the dialog box, and the fields that make up the table are on the right side of the dialog box.

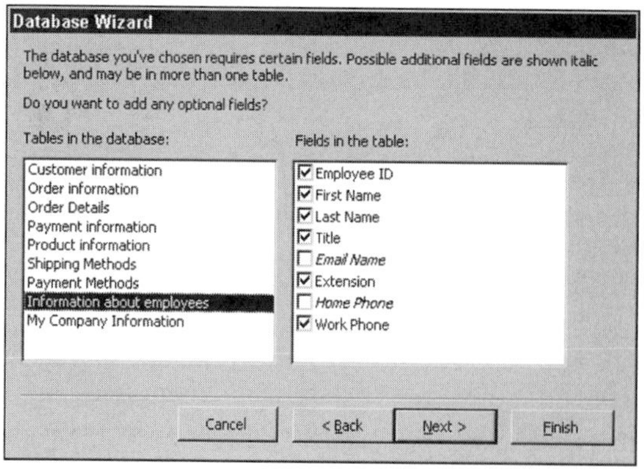

Figure 30-3: Working with tables and fields

As you select each table, the list of fields changes. Fields that are optional appear italicized. When you check the fields, the Wizard includes them in the table design.

Selecting AutoFormat styles

After you make your selections, you can move to the next Wizard screen, which enables you to select the style for your forms. You can choose any of the AutoFormat options shown in Figure 30-4. If you created your own AutoFormats, they are listed here, too.

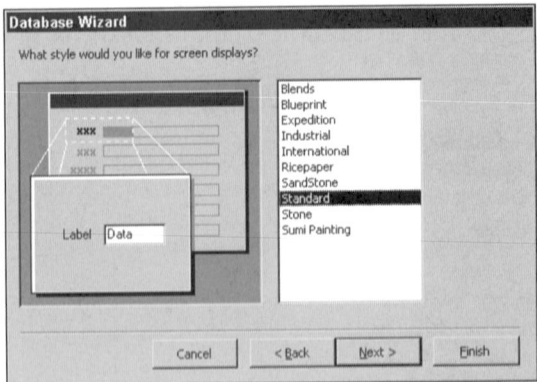

Figure 30-4: Selecting an AutoFormat for the screens

After you select the style of your forms, you can do the same for reports. The next Wizard screen (see Figure 30-5) enables you to select an AutoFormat style for printed reports. You can add your own formats for each of the reports the Wizard creates.

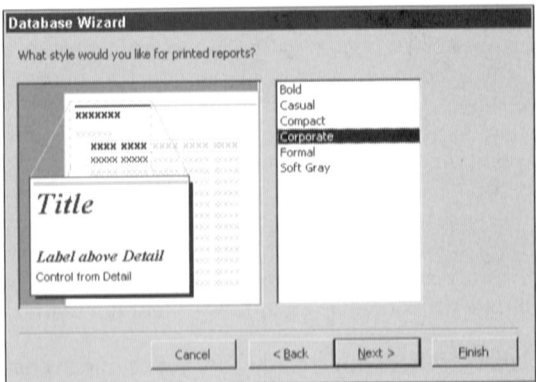

Figure 30-5: Selecting an AutoFormat for a report

Customizing by selection

After you select the style of forms and reports, you see a Wizard screen that enables you to give your application a title and even a bitmap picture, as shown in Figure 30-6.

On the CD-ROM

In Figure 30-6, the standard title of Order Entry has been changed to Mountain Scenes Order Entry, and the client's logo (a small sun rising over a mountain, the same one as Mountain Animal Hospital) has been included. This is found on your CD-ROM and is called MTN.BMP.

You can scan a logo or select any standard Windows image file for inclusion in the application. When you click the Picture button, the Database Wizard displays a dialog box you can search to find the desired picture. The picture appears on all your reports.

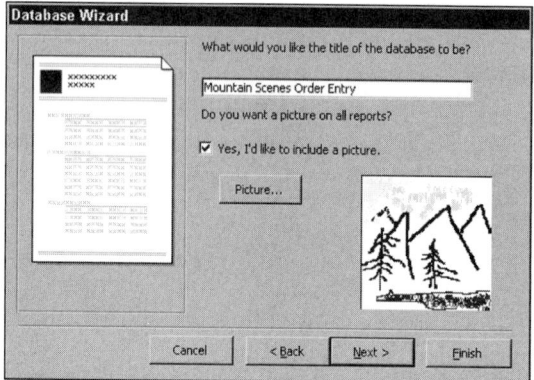

Figure 30-6: Renaming the application and adding a picture

When you complete this Wizard screen and click the Next> button, the last Database Wizard screen appears. This Wizard screen, which displays a checkered flag, asks whether you want to display help on using a database and whether you want to start the application after it is built. Clicking the Finish button clears the screen and builds the application.

As the creation process progresses, you see a dialog box displaying the Wizard's magic wand and two progress meters. The top progress meter displays the overall progress. The bottom progress meter displays the progress Access is making with creating each object — first the tables and then the relationships, queries, forms, switchboards, reports, and even database properties. Below this dialog box, you can see the Database window filling with names as each new object is created.

Note

The first time you use the Database Wizard, you are asked for your company name, address, and related information. To avoid errors in creating the new database, complete all of the requested information. After you complete this screen, use the Close box to create the new application and display its switchboard.

Using the switchboard system

If you elected on the last Wizard screen to start the application, the main switchboard appears (as shown in Figure 30-7), and the Database window is minimized. Otherwise, the Database window is displayed.

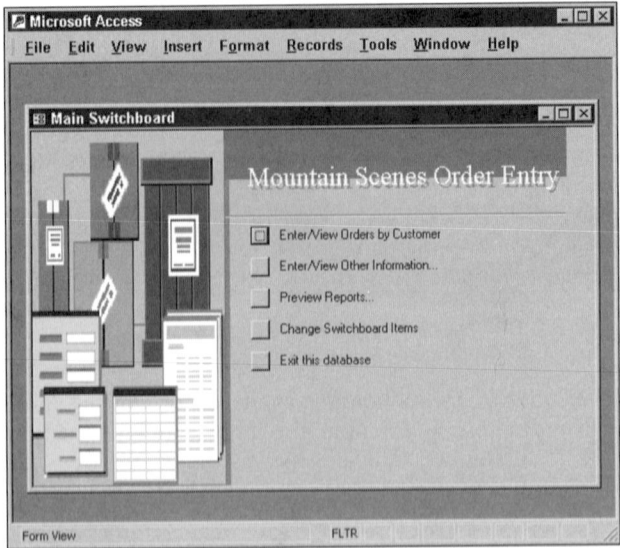

Figure 30-7: The main switchboard

The main switchboard is your gateway to the system's functions. As you see in Figure 30-7, the switchboard displays five main items. The first item — Enter/View Orders by Customer — displays the one-to-many orders form (see Figure 30-8), where you can review or edit all the orders sorted by customer name. The next item — Enter/View Other Information — displays another switchboard screen that enables you to display all the peripheral forms for editing all the support tables. In this example, these tables include Employees, Company Information, Products, Payment methods, and Shipping methods. At the bottom of each screen (other than the main switchboard) is the option Return to Main Switchboard.

In Figure 30-8, you see a form that actually is a summary of a specific customer's orders. At the bottom of the form are several buttons for displaying an order, displaying a payment, or printing an invoice for the customer. If you look at the order form itself, you see that it has several supporting tables, such as products, employees, payment methods, and shipping methods. The form has embedded subforms that enable you to select data from these lookup tables. From the data-entry switchboard screen, you can even set various global company options, such as company name and address, payment terms, and other information used for invoices and other reports.

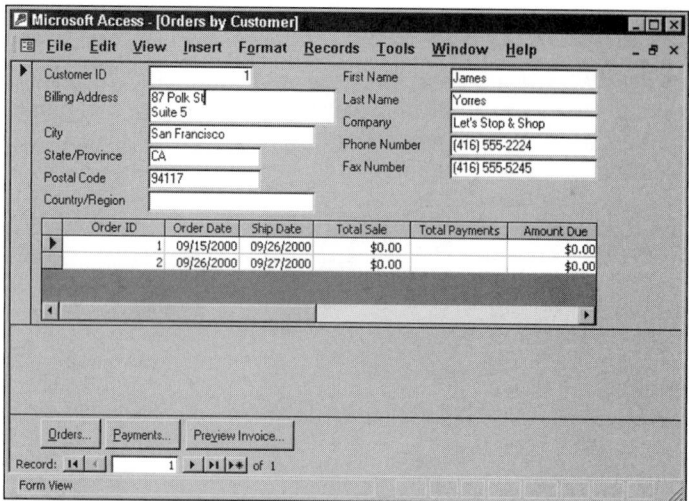

Figure 30-8: A typical one-to-many form

Besides the data-entry switchboard, a switchboard is available for viewing and printing your reports. For the Order Processing example, the reports include Customer Listing; Invoice; Receivables Aging Report; and Sales by Customer, Employee, or Product. The company name and logo (if specified) appear at the top of each report.

Although the forms and reports are simple, they serve as a great starting point for creating more robust applications. Obviously, the Wizard decides the choices of forms and reports, but you can create your own forms and reports and then add them to the Order Entry switchboard. One of the options in the main switchboard enables you to customize the switchboards themselves.

Customizing the switchboards

The Database Wizard contains a series of hierarchical screens (similar to the Menu Builder) that enable you to create and maintain switchboard items. Unfortunately, this technology works only in the Database Wizard. When you eventually become more proficient in building switchboards yourself, you can copy the switchboards and the supporting tables to other applications. However, you must have access to the Access 2002 Wizard libraries because some of the code resides in the common areas.

Figure 30-9 shows one of the screens used to customize the switchboards. This screen shows the switchboard definition for Figure 30-7. To customize a switchboard, you start with the Switchboard Page definitions, which list the switchboard's name. In Figure 30-9, this switchboard is named Main Switchboard. Each page contains the items shown in Figure 30-9, and you can edit each item. When you edit an item, you enter the item name (text) and the command, which is similar to the macro commands but more explanatory. There are only eight commands:

- ✦ GoTo Switchboard
- ✦ Open Form in Add Mode
- ✦ Open Form in Edit Mode
- ✦ Open Report
- ✦ Design Application
- ✦ Exit Application
- ✦ Run Macro
- ✦ Run Code

With these eight commands, you can do almost anything. Based on which of the eight commands you select, the last entry area changes to display the name of the switchboard, form, report, macro, or Visual Basic function.

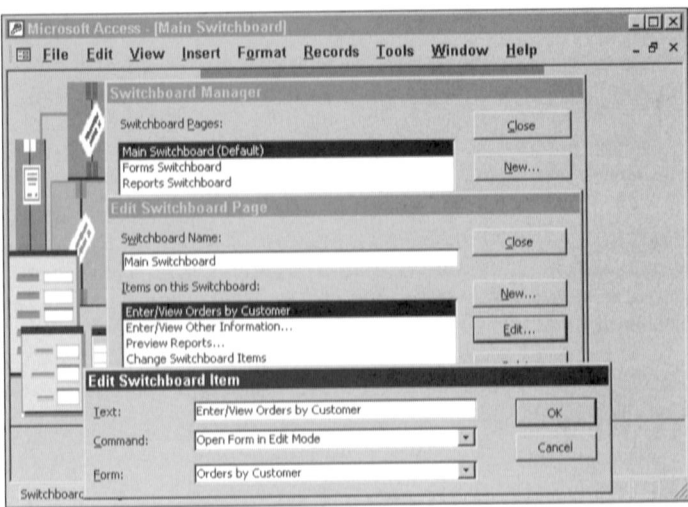

Figure 30-9: Modifying a switchboard

Although the Database Wizard enables you to create instant applications, these applications are very simple — good for only the most basic business or personal applications. As a starting point, though, they are excellent for new users and even for developers who need to prototype a system fast. Because you can customize everything (especially the switchboards), you can develop a custom solution quickly to get started or impress your customers.

Creating Programs in Visual Basic for Applications

Access has an excellent variety of tools that enable you to work with databases and their tables, queries, forms, and reports without ever having to write a single line of code. At some point, you may begin building more sophisticated applications. You may want to make your applications more "bulletproof" by providing more intensive data-entry validation or implementing better error handling.

Some operations cannot be accomplished through the user interface, even with macros. You may find yourself saying, "I wish I had a function that would. . . ." or "There just has to be a function that will let me. . . ." At other times, you find that you are continually putting the same formula or expression in a query or filter. You may find yourself saying, "I'm tired of typing this formula into. . . ." or "Doggone it, I typed the wrong formula in this. . . ."

For situations such as these, you need the horsepower of a high-level programming language. Access provides a programming language called Visual Basic for Applications Edition (VBA), which extends the capabilities of Access, offering power beyond the scope of macros.

Visual Basic has become the common language for all Microsoft applications. Visual Basic is in all Microsoft Office XP applications, including Access, Word, Excel, PowerPoint, and Outlook. It is also in Project. Visual Basic is a modern, structured programming language that offers many of the programming structures programmers are accustomed to: If. . .Then. . .Else, Select Case, and so on. Visual Basic enables a programmer to work with functions and subroutines in an English-like language. The language also is extensible (capable of calling Windows API routines) and can interact through ADO (Active Data Objects) or DAO (Data Access Objects) with any Access or Visual Basic data type.

Getting started with Visual Basic programming in Access requires an understanding of its event-driven environment.

Understanding events and event procedures

In Access, unlike traditional procedural programming environments, the user controls the actions and flow of the application. The user determines what to do and when to do it, such as changing information in a field or clicking a command button. They determine the flow of action and through events, the application determines what action to take or ignore. In contrast, procedural oriented programming languages require that the programmer determine the flow of what actions the user must follow. In fact, the programmer must program for all possibilities of user intervention — keystrokes a user may enter in error and actions to take based on the actions taken by the user.

Using macros and event procedures, you implement the responses to these actions. Access provides event properties for each of the controls you place on the form. When you attach a macro or event procedure to a control's event property, you do not have to worry about the order of actions a user may take on a particular form.

In an event-driven environment such as Access, the objects — forms, reports, and controls — respond to events. Basically, an event procedure is program code that executes when an event occurs. The code is directly attached to the form or report that contains the event being processed. An Exit command button, for example, exits the form when the user clicks that button. Clicking the command button triggers its On Click event. The event procedure is the program code (or macro) that you create and attach to the On Click event. Every time the user clicks the command button, the event procedure runs automatically.

Cross-Reference   For a fuller explanation of macros and events, see Chapters 28 and 29.

There are two types of procedures:

✦ Subs

✦ Functions

Sub and function procedures are grouped and stored in modules. The Modules object button in the Database window stores the common procedures that any of your forms can access. You can store all your procedures in a single module. Realistically, though, you'll probably want to group your procedures into separate modules, categorizing them by the nature of the operations they perform; for example, an Update module might include procedures for adding and deleting records from a table.

Sub procedures

A sub procedure is program code that does not return a value. Because it does not return a value, a sub procedure cannot be used in an expression or be called by assigning it to a variable. A sub procedure typically runs as a separate program called by an event in a form or report.

You can use a sub procedure to perform actions when you don't want to return a value. In fact, because you cannot assign a value to a control's event properties, you can only create sub procedures for an event.

You can call subs and pass a data value known as a parameter. Subs can call other subs. Subs also can call function procedures.

The code statements inside the sub procedure are lines of Visual Basic statements. These statements make up the code you want to run every time the procedure is executed. The following example shows the Exit command button's sub procedure:

```
Sub Button_Click ()
  DoCmd.Close
End Sub
```

The Button_Click () sub procedure is attached to the Exit command button's On Click event. When the user clicks the Exit command button, the command DoCmd Close executes to close the form.

Function procedures

A function procedure returns a value. You can use functions in expressions or assign a function to a variable.

Like sub procedures, function procedures can be called by other functions or by subs. You also can pass parameters to a function.

You assign the return value of a function to the procedure name itself. You then can use the value that is returned as part of a larger expression. The following function procedure calculates the square footage of a room:

```
Function nSquareFeet (dblHeight As Double, dblWidth As Double)
As Double
  nSquareFeet = dblHeight * dblWidth
End Function
```

This function receives two parameters for the height and width of the room. The function returns the results to the procedure that called it by assigning the result of the calculation to the procedure name (nSquareFeet).

To call this function, you could use code like this:

```
dblAnswer = nSquareFeet(xHeight, xWidth)
```

Creating a new module

Using the Module window, you can create and edit Visual Basic code or procedures. A procedure is simply some code, written in a programming language that follows a series of logical steps in performing some action. You could, for example, create a Beep procedure that makes the computer beep as a warning or notification that something has happened in your program. Each procedure is a series of code statements that performs an operation or calculation.

Modules are the containers used to organize your code. You can think of a module as being a library of procedures. You can create many modules for an Access database.

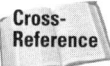
Cross-
Reference
For more information about modules, see Chapter 31.

For this example, you can use the Mountain Animal Modules database, or you can open a new blank database. To create a new module, follow these steps:

1. Click the Module object button in the Database window.

2. Click the New toolbar button.

Access opens Microsoft Visual Basic and creates a new module, named Module1, in a Module window. This new module should look like the one shown in Figure 30-10. In this figure, notice that Access places two lines of text in the first line in the window, beginning with Option Compare Database and then Option Explicit.

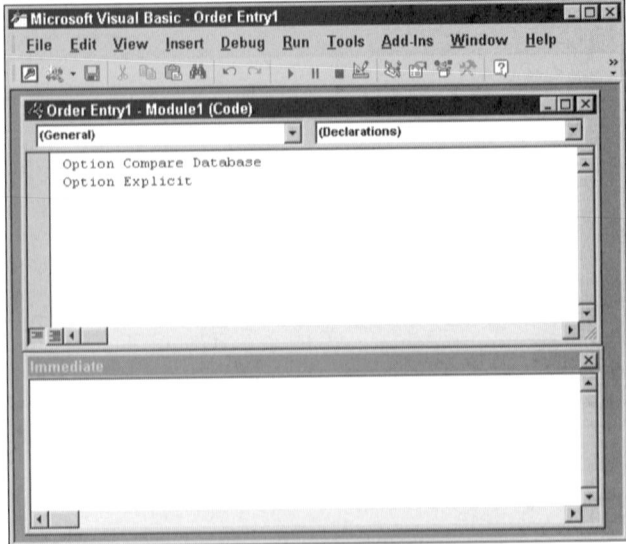

Figure 30-10: The newly opened module window

Note   If the new module you open does not show the first two lines of code you will need to check to see if the Required Variable Declaration has been turned on (recommended) The Option Explicit statement appears if you turn on the option Require Variable Declaration. To check the status of this option, follow these steps:

1. Open an existing module, or create a new one. The Module window displays in Microsoft Visual Basic.

2. Select Tools ⊹ Options . . . from the Module window toolbar. The Options dialog box displays.

3. In the Editor tab, check the box for Require Variable Declaration.

Notice that the Module window in Figure 30-10 displays the tools for the Visual Basic editor. Also notice the two combo boxes just below the toolbar. The right combo box displays Declarations, because you currently are in the declarations part of the module.

Each module includes two or more sections:

✦ A single declarations section

✦ A section for each procedure

The module is a convenient way to place a group of related event procedures in a single collection. Every form or report you create in your database contains a built-in form module or report module. This form or report module is an integral part of each form or report; it is used as a container for the event procedures you create for the form or report. Generally, if only a single form or report object will use the module, it should go behind the form or report. To view the module behind a form, follow these steps:

1. Open the form in Design view.

2. Select View ➪ Code from the Design window menu. The Module window displays the form's module.

   If the module will be needed for several forms or reports, it should be placed in a standard module. Standard modules are stored in the Modules tab of the database container.

The declarations section

You can use the declarations section to declare (define) variables you want to use in procedures. A variable is a temporary storage location for some value and is given a name. You can declare variables that will be used only by the procedures in a module or by all procedures across all modules within a database. Examples of variables include:

✦ IntCounter (an integer variable)

✦ CurMySalary (a currency variable)

✦ TodaysDate (a date variable)

Caution If you have the line of code Option Explicit in your module, which is the default in Access 2002 Visual Basic, you must explicitly declare your variables or you will get an error when you try to use them. This speeds up execution of Visual Basic modules. If you have a small application, you might want to remove the Option Explicit line of code, which will enable you to use variables without first defining their name and data type.

You are not required to declare variables in this section, because variables can also be declared in the individual procedures. In fact, if you remove the Option Explicit line from a procedure or function, you don't have to declare a variable at all. Access enables implicit variable declarations — that is, declarations created on the fly. If you enter a variable name in an expression and the variable hasn't been declared, Access accepts and declares it for you, giving it the data type consistent with its first use.

Working in the Module Window

Whenever you create Visual Basic procedures for your Access applications, you write that code in a Module window. Although the Module window is confusing at first, it is easy to understand and use after you learn how each part is used.

When you enter Design mode of a module — whether it is via a form or report module or the module object (Database window) — the Visual Basic Module window and its associated menu and toolbar open to enable you to create or edit your procedures.

When you open a module from the Modules object button of the Database window, the Module window has the same features as the Module window for a form or report design window. The only difference between the two is that for a form (or report) module, the Object and Procedure combo boxes on the toolbar list the form's objects and events. You can select these objects and events to create or edit event procedures for the form. The object combo box for a module you open from the Database window displays only one choice: General. The Procedure combo box contains only the names of existing procedures.

The Module window has four basic areas: the menu bar, the toolbar, the code window, and the immediate window.

The menu bar of the Module window has ten menus: File, Edit, View, Insert, Debug, Run, Tools, Add-Ins, Window, and Help.

The Module window's toolbar (shown in Figure 30-10) helps you create new modules and their procedures quickly. The toolbar contains buttons for the most common actions you use to create, modify, and debug modules.

The code window — the most important area of the Module window — is where you create and modify the Visual Basic code for your procedures. The code window has the standard Windows features that enable you to resize, minimize, maximize, and move the window. You also can split the window into two areas. At times, you may want to edit two procedures at the same time; perhaps you need to copy part of one procedure to another. To work on two procedures simultaneously, simply choose Window ⇨ Split from the Module window toolbar. You can resize the window by moving the split bar up and down. Now you can work with both procedures at the same time. To switch between windows, press the F6 key or click the other window.

The Immediate window enables you to try a procedure while you are still in the module. See the "Checking your results in the Immediate window" section in this chapter for an example.

Tip   Entering the declaration statement Option Explicit forces you to declare any variables you will use when creating procedures for the module. Although this procedure involves a little more work, it speeds execution of module code by Access. For others who may need to work with your code later on, declaring variables provides assistance in documenting your code.

Creating a new procedure

After you complete any declarations for the module, you are ready to create a procedure. Follow these steps to create a procedure called BeepWarning:

1. Go to any empty line in the Module window.
2. Type Sub BeepWarning to name the module. The module window should look similar to Figure 30-11.
3. Press Enter.

If you enter the name of a function you previously created in this module (or in another module within the database), Access informs you that the function already exists. Access does not enable you to create another procedure with the same name.

Notice that when you pressed Enter, Access did three things automatically:

✦ Placed the procedure named BeepWarning in the Procedure combo box in the toolbar
✦ Placed parentheses at the end of the procedure name
✦ Added the End Sub statement to the procedure

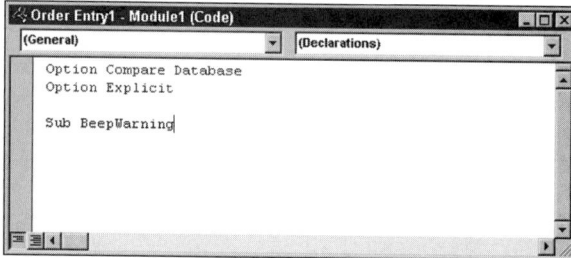

Figure 30-11: Entering a new procedure in the Module window

You are no longer in the declarations section of the module; you are now in an actual procedure.

Now you can enter the lines of code needed for your procedure. Enter the following lines of code into the module:

```
Dim xBeeps, nBeeps As Integer
nBeeps = 5
For xBeeps = 1 To nBeeps
  Beep
Next xBeeps
```

In this example, you are running the program five times. Don't worry about what the procedure does — you learn more about how to program specific tasks in Chapter 31.

Your completed function should look like the one shown in Figure 30-12.

When BeepWarning runs, it beeps for the number of times specified.

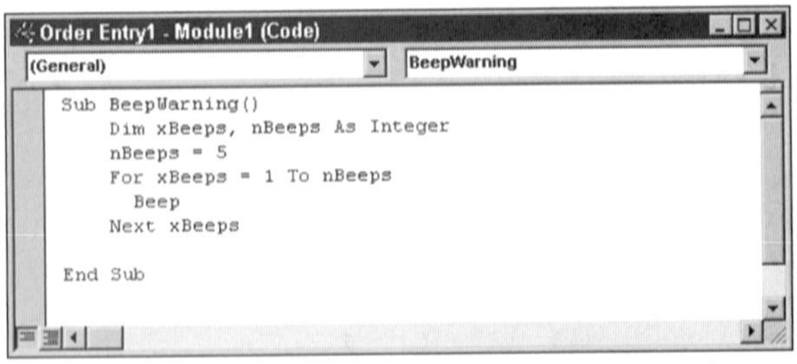

```
Order Entry1 - Module1 (Code)
(General)                          BeepWarning

Sub BeepWarning()
    Dim xBeeps, nBeeps As Integer
    nBeeps = 5
    For xBeeps = 1 To nBeeps
       Beep
    Next xBeeps

End Sub
```

Figure 30-12: The BeepWarning procedure completed

Using the Access 2002 Module Help

Suppose that you know you want to use a specific command but can't remember the syntax (syntax is computer grammar). Access 2002 features two types of module help, Auto List Members and Auto Quick Info, to help you create each line of code.

Auto List Members is automatically displayed when you type the beginning of a command that has objects, properties, and methods following the main object. For example, if you enter DoCmd, a list of the possible commands is displayed, as shown in Figure 30-13. You can scroll through the list box and select the option you want.

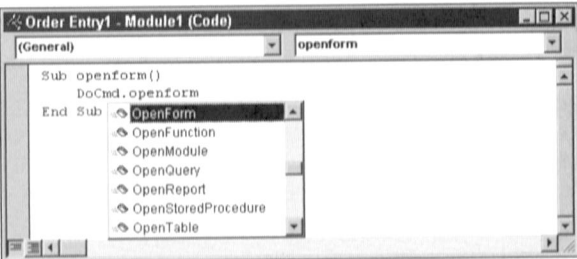

Figure 30-13: Access 2002 Auto List Members help in a module

In this example, the OpenForm command is being chosen. After you choose an option, either more Auto List Members help is displayed or, if the rest of the command options are parameters for the other type of module help, Auto Quick Info is displayed, as shown in Figure 30-14.

Auto Quick Info help guides you through all the options for the specific command. The bold word is the next parameter to be entered. Figure 30-14 shows that there are many parameters in the OpenForm command. When you enter the form name, the next section will become bolded. As you enter each parameter or a comma to skip a parameter, the next section in the help becomes bolded. You can remove the help by pressing Esc.

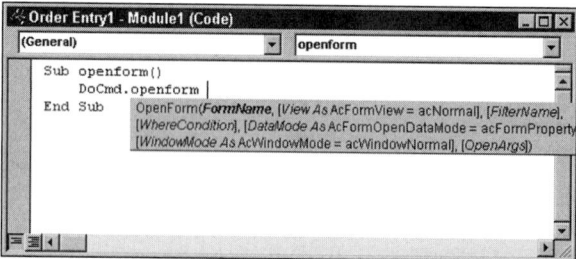

Figure 30-14: Access 2002 Auto Quick Info help in a module

Compiling procedures

After you create all the procedures, you should compile them by choosing Debug ➪ Compile from the module menu. The debug process checks your code for errors (a procedure known as syntax checking) and also converts the programs to a form your computer can understand. If the compile operation is not successful, an error window appears.

Note   Access compiles all uncompiled procedures in the module, not just the current procedure.

Saving a module

When you finish creating your procedures, you should save them by saving the module. As you do any other Access object, you can save the module by choosing File ➪ Save or else they will be saved automatically when you close the window. You should consider saving the module every time you complete a procedure.

Creating procedures in the Form or Report Design window

All forms, reports, and their controls can have event procedures associated with their events. While you are in the design window for the form or report, you can add an event procedure quickly in one of three ways:

✦ Choose Build Event from the shortcut menu (see Figure 30-15).

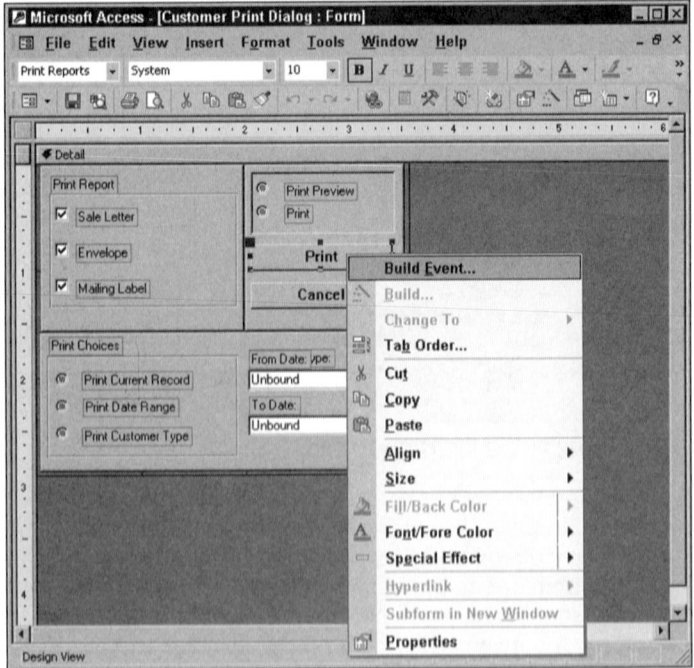

Figure 30-15: Shortcut menu for a control in the form design window

✦ Choose Code Builder in the Choose Builder dialog box when you click the ellipsis button to the right of an event in the Property dialog box.

✦ Enter the text Event Procedure or select it from the top of the event combo box (see Figure 30-16).

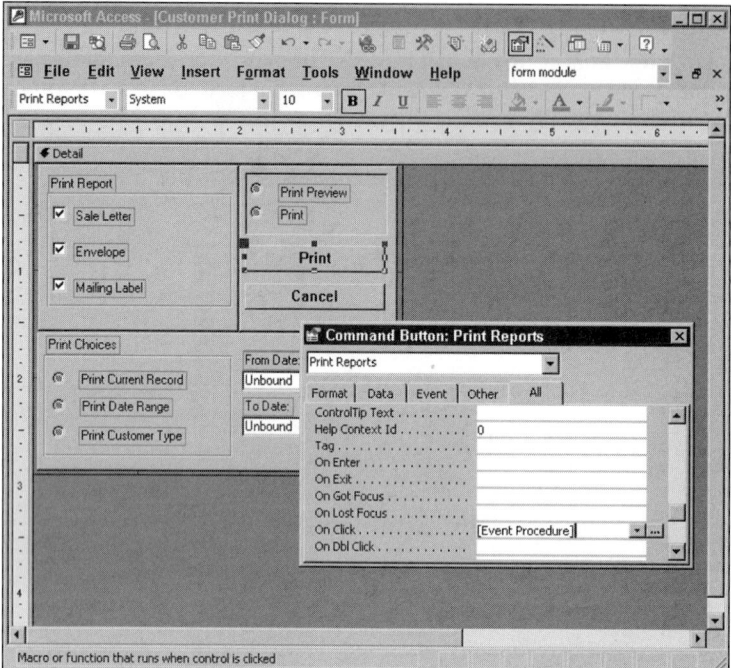

Figure 30-16: Properties dialog box in the Form Design window

Whether you choose the Build Event from the shortcut menu choice or click the ellipsis button in the Property dialog box, the Choose Builder dialog box appears. Choosing the Code Builder item opens the Module window in Visual Basic, as shown in Figure 30-17. In Visual Basic, if you click the View Microsoft Access button, you can toggle back and forth between the Access form designer and the Visual Basic Module window.

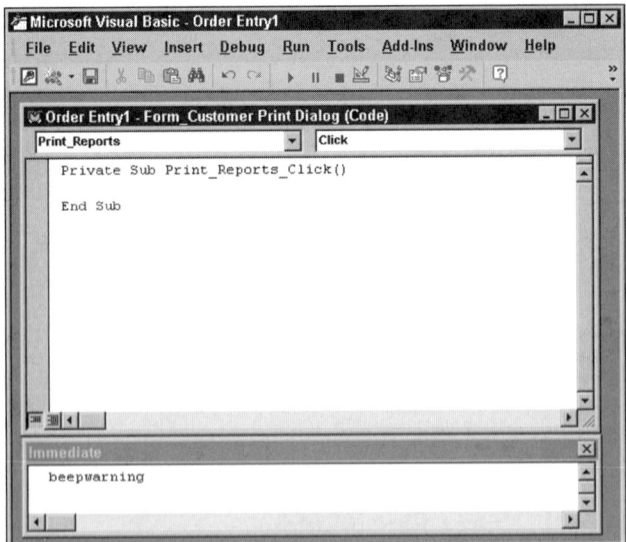

Figure 30-17: A form module open in the Form Designer

Note

If an event procedure is already attached to the control, the text [Event Procedure] is displayed in the event area. Clicking the Builder button instantly displays the procedure for the event in a Visual Basic Module window — hence the name Event Procedure.

Editing an existing procedure

To edit an existing procedure, follow these steps:

1. Click the Modules object button in the Database window.

2. Double-click the module name that contains the procedure. The declaration portion of the module appears.

3. Find the procedure you want and select it from the pull-down menu on the right of the module window.

Tip

After you are in a module, you can select any procedure in another module quickly by pressing F2 or choosing View ⇨ Object Browser. Access displays the Object Browser dialog box, shown in Figure 30-18. Highlight a different module name in the Modules section of the View Procedures dialog box to see the names of all procedures in the new module. When you select a module, you then can select a method and display the function call, as shown in Figure 30-18.

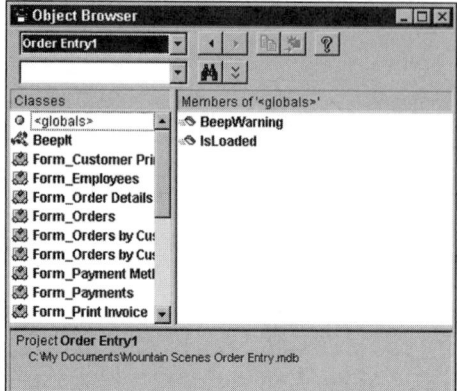

Figure 30-18: Selecting a procedure to edit

Checking your results in the Immediate window

When you write code for a procedure, you may want to try the procedure while you are in the module, or you may need to check the results of an expression. The Immediate window enables you to try your procedures without leaving the module. You can run the module and check variables. You could, for example, type **?** and the name of the variable.

To view the Immediate window, choose View ➪ Immediate Window. Figure 30-19 shows the Immediate window.

After you create a sub-procedure, you can run it to see whether it works as expected. You can test it with supplied arguments.

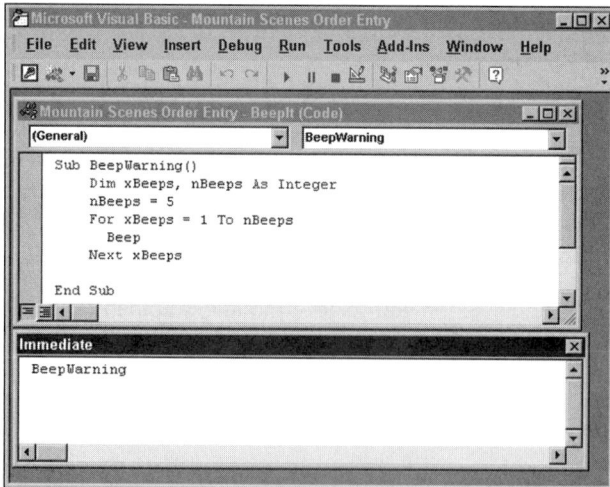

Figure 30-19: The Immediate window

To run the BeepWarning sub procedure, follow these steps:

1. Activate the Immediate pane by selecting it from the View menu, or clicking in it.

2. Type BeepWarning and press Enter. The BeepWarning sub runs.

You may have heard five beeps or (if you have a really fast machine) only a few beeps because the interval between beeps is short.

Figure 30-19, earlier in this section, shows this command.

Migrating from Macros to Visual Basic

Should you now concentrate on using Visual Basic for your applications, or continue to use macros? The answer depends on what you are trying to accomplish. The fact that Access 2002 includes Visual Basic does not mean that Access macros are no longer useful; it simply means that Access developers will want to learn Visual Basic and add it to their arsenal of tools for creating Access applications.

Visual Basic is not always the answer. Some tasks, such as assigning global key assignments, can be accomplished only via macros. You can perform some actions more easily and effectively by using a macro.

A Visual Basic procedure may offer better performance. The opposite also is true: A Visual Basic procedure may run at the same speed as a macro counterpart, or even more slowly. If you code everything in your application using Visual Basic, you may find that the time needed to create an application actually increases.

When to use macros and when to use Visual Basic procedures

In Access, macros often offer an ideal way to take care of many details, such as running reports and forms. Because the arguments for the macro actions are displayed with the macro (in the bottom portion of the Macro window), you can develop applications and assign actions faster. You won't have to remember complex or difficult syntax.

Several actions you can accomplish via Visual Basic are better suited for macros. The following actions tend to be more efficient when they are run from macros:

✦ Using macros against an entire set of records — for example, to manipulate multiple records in a table or across tables (such as updating field values or deleting records)

✦ Opening and closing forms

✦ Running reports

Note   Visual Basic supplies a DoCmd Object you can use to accomplish most macro actions. This object actually runs the macro task. You could, for example, specify DoCmd.Close to run the close macro and close the current active form. Even this method has flaws. DoCmd cannot perform at least eight macro actions: AddMenu, MsgBox, RunApp, RunCode, SendKeys, SetValue, StopAllMacros, and StopMacro. Some of these actions have Visual Basic equivalents.

Although macros sometimes prove to be the solution of choice, Visual Basic is the tool of choice at other times. You probably will want to use Visual Basic rather than macros when you want to perform any of the following tasks:

✦ Create and use your own functions. In addition to using the built-in functions in Access, you can create and work with your own functions by using Visual Basic.

✦ Create your own error routines and messages. You can create error routines that detect an error and decide what action to take. These routines bypass the cryptic Access error messages.

✦ Use OLE and DDE to communicate with other Windows applications or to run system-level actions. You can write code to see whether a file exists before you take some action, or you can communicate with another Windows application (such as a spreadsheet), passing data back and forth.

✦ Use existing functions in external Windows DLLs. Macros don't enable you to call functions in other Windows Dynamic Link Libraries.

✦ Work with records one at a time. If you need to step through records or to move values from a record to variables for manipulation, code is the answer.

✦ Maintain the application. Unlike macros, code can be built into a form or report, making maintaining the code more efficient. Additionally, if you move a form or report from one database to another, the event procedures built into the form or report move with it.

✦ Create or manipulate objects. In most cases, you'll find that it's easiest to create and modify an object in that object's Design view. In some situations, however, you may want to manipulate the definition of an object in code. Using Visual Basic, you can manipulate all the objects in a database, including the database itself.

✦ Pass arguments to your Visual Basic procedures. You can set arguments for macro actions in the bottom part of the Macro window when you create the macro, but you can't change arguments when the macro is running. With Visual Basic, however, you can pass arguments to your code at the time it's run or use variables for arguments — something you can't do with macros. This capability gives you a great deal of flexibility in the way your Visual Basic procedures run.

✦ Display a progress meter on the status bar. If you need to display a progress meter to communicate progress to the user, Visual Basic code is the answer.

Tip

If you create a form or report that will be copied to other databases, create your event procedures for that form or report in Visual Basic instead of using macros. Because macros are stored as separate objects in the database, you have to remember which ones are associated with the form or report you are copying. On the other hand, because Visual Basic code can be attached to the form or report, copying the form automatically copies the Visual Basic event procedures associated with it.

Converting existing macros to Visual Basic

After you become comfortable with writing Visual Basic code, you may want to rewrite some of your application macros as Visual Basic procedures. As you set off on this process, you quickly realize how mentally challenging the effort can be as you review every macro in your various macro libraries. You cannot merely cut the macro from the Macro window and paste it into a Module window. For each condition, action, and action argument for a macro, you must analyze the task it accomplishes and then write the equivalent statements of Visual Basic code in your procedure.

Fortunately, Access provides a feature that converts macros to Visual Basic code automatically. One of the options in the Save As dialog box is Save As Visual Basic Module; you can use this option when a macro file is highlighted in the Macros object window of the Database window. This option enables you to convert an entire macro group to a module in seconds. To start this process, choose File ⇨ Save As, as shown in Figure 30-20.

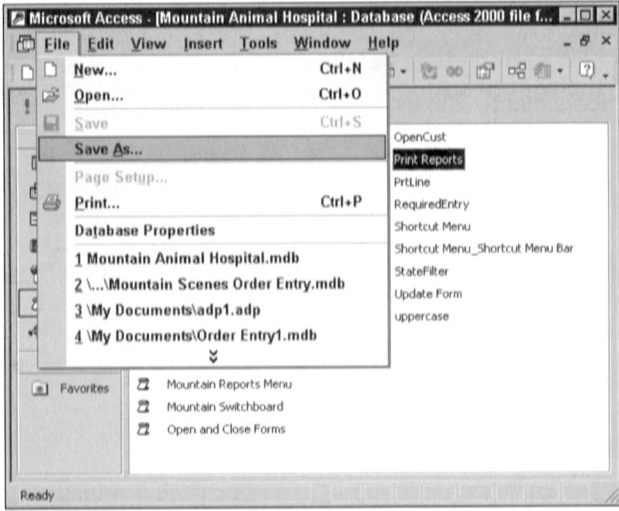

Figure 30-20: Choosing File ⇨ Save As

To try the conversion process, convert the Print Reports macros in the Mountain Animal Hospital database. Figure 30-21 displays the macros for the Print Reports macro group.

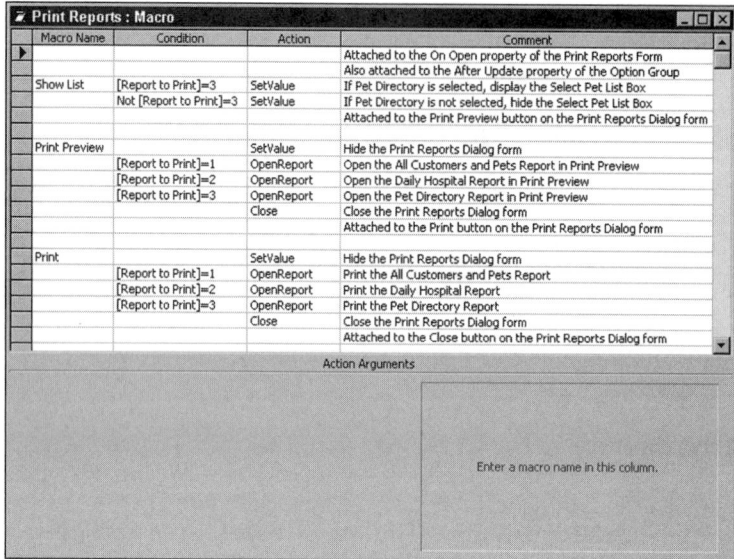

Figure 30-21: The Print Reports macro group

Follow these steps to run the conversion process:

1. Click the Macros object button of the Database window.

2. Select the Print Reports macro library.

3. Choose File ⇨ Save As. The Save As dialog box appears, as shown in Figure 30-22.

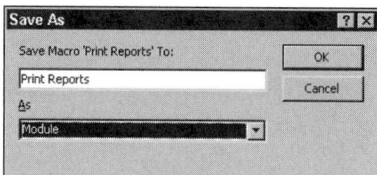

Figure 30-22: The Save As Visual Basic Module dialog box

4. Choose Save as Module and click OK. The Convert Macro dialog box appears, as shown in Figure 30-23.

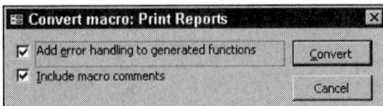

Figure 30-23: The Convert Macro dialog box

5. Select the options that include error handling and comments and click Convert.

   Access briefly displays each new procedure as it is converted. When the conversion process finishes, the Conversion Finished message box appears.

6. Click OK to remove the message box.

7. Access displays the Modules object window of the Database window, as shown in Figure 30-24. Access names the new module Converted Macro - Print Reports.

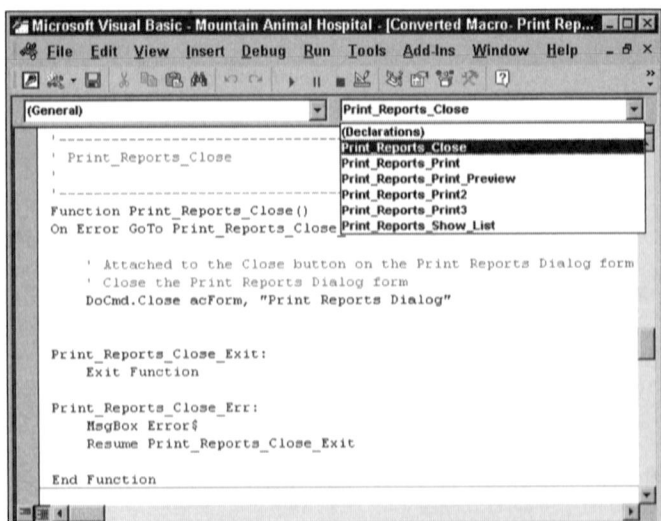

Figure 30-24: The newly converted module

When you open the Module window for the new module, you can view the procedures created from the macros. Figure 30-24 shows the four functions that Access created from the Print Reports macro: Print_Reports_Close, Print_Reports_Print, Print_Reports_Print_Preview, and Print_Reports_Show_List. Figures 30-25 and 30-26 show samples of the new procedures.

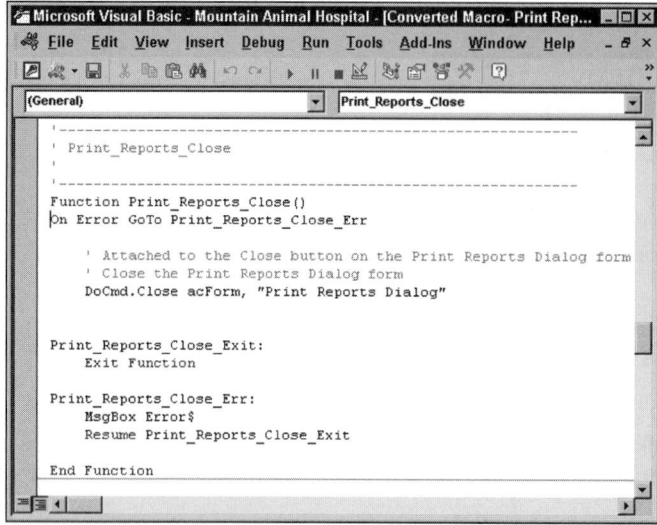

Figure 30-25: The Print_Reports_Close function

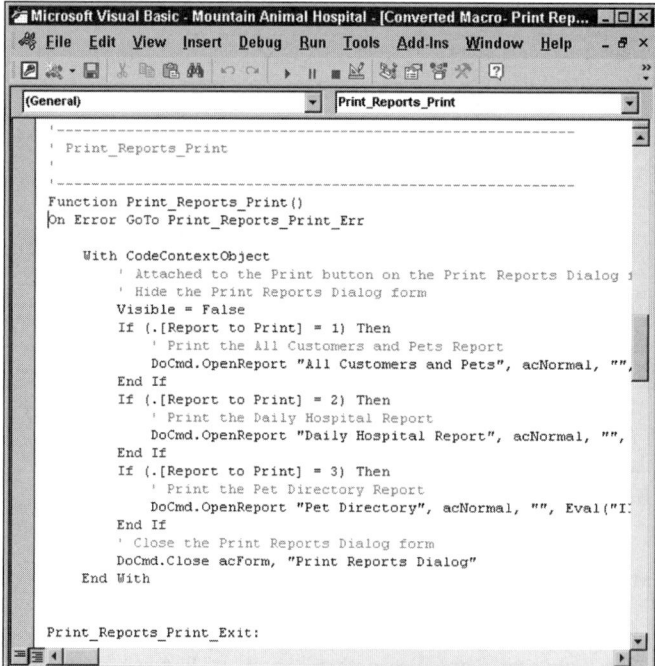

Figure 30-26: The Print_Reports_Print function

At the top of each function, Access inserts four comment lines for the name of the function. The Function statement follows the comment lines. Access names the functions, using the macro library's name as a prefix (Print_Reports); the macro name (if one is supplied) for the suffix; and Close for the Close function.

When you specify that you want Access to include error processing for the conversion, Access automatically inserts the OnError statement as the first command in the procedure. The OnError statement tells Access to branch to other statements that display an appropriate message and then exit the function.

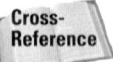

Cross-
Reference   Error processing is covered in more detail in Chapter 31.

The statement beginning with DoCmd is the actual code that Access created from the macro. The DoCmd methods run Access actions from Visual Basic. An action performs important tasks, such as closing windows, opening forms, and setting the value of controls. In the Close macro, for example, Close Print Reports Dialog closes the Print Reports dialog box. Access converts the Close macro action arguments to the properly formatted parameters for the DoCmd methods.

In the Print_Reports_Print function, the group of statements beginning with the With command retrieves the settings of some of the controls in the Print Reports dialog box. The DoCmd action prints various reports based on the value of the settings in the dialog box. Chapter 31 covers conditional structures, such as the If. . .End If statements you see in these functions.

Tip   You also can convert macros that are used in a form by choosing Tools ➪ Macro ➪
         Convert Form's Macros to Visual Basic in Forms Design view.

Using the Command Button Wizard to create Visual Basic code

A good way to learn how to write event procedures is to use the Command Button Wizard. When Access creates a command button with a Wizard, it creates an event procedure and attaches it to the button. You can open the event procedure to see how it works and then modify it to fit your needs.

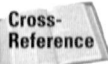

Cross-
Reference   For more information about the Command Button Wizard, see Chapter 32.

The Wizard speeds the process of creating a command button because it does all the basic work for you. When you use the Wizard, Access prompts you for information and creates a command button based on your answers.

You can create more than 30 types of command buttons by using the Command Button Wizard. You can create a command button that finds a record, prints a record, or applies a form filter, for example. You can run this Wizard by creating a new command button on a form. Figure 30-27 shows a command button being created in the Record Operations category, with the Delete Record action.

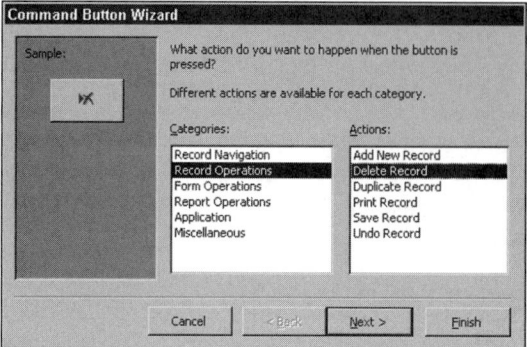

Figure 30-27: The Command Button Wizard

 Note

In the Mountain Animal Hospital database is a form named Button Wizard Visual Basic Samples. This form, shown in Figure 30-28 in Design mode, contains the result of running the Button Wizard with several selections. The Button Wizard Visual Basic Samples form contains a dozen command buttons created with the Command Button Wizard. You can review the procedures for each command button on the form to see how powerful Visual Basic code can be.

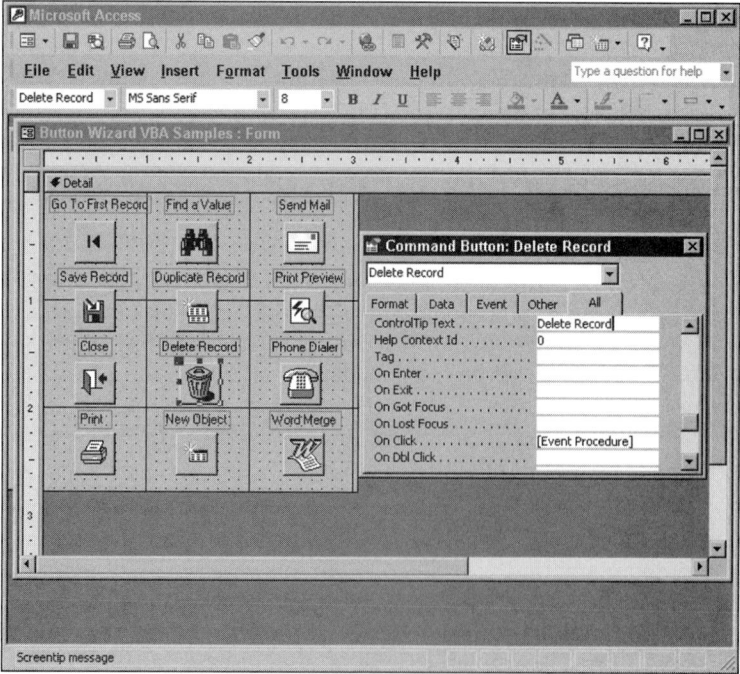

Figure 30-28: Examples of Command Button Wizard buttons

To view the sample code, follow these steps:

1. Display the Button Wizard Visual Basic Samples form in Design view.

2. Display the Property window for the desired button.

3. Click the Builder button (. . .) for the On Click event property to display the command button's Module window, with the procedure.

Figure 30-28 shows the property sheet for the Delete Record command button and Figure 30-29 shows the code for the Delete Record command button.

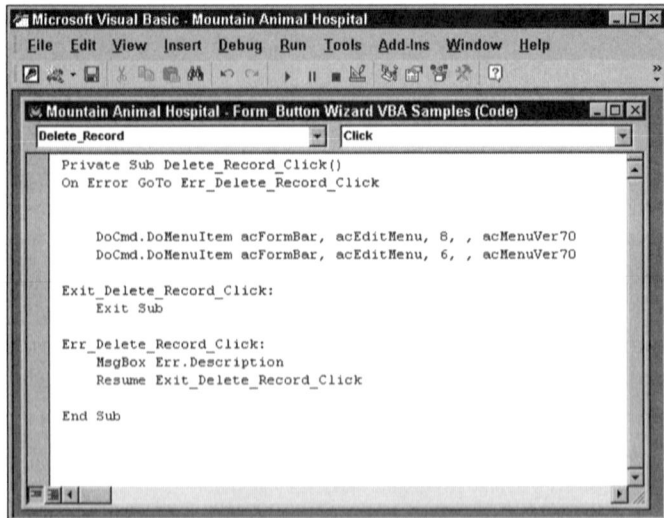

Figure 30-29: The Delete button's On Click procedure

Figure 30-30 shows the code for a Dialer command button. The Phone_Dialer_Click procedure retrieves the text in the current field and then passes the text to a utility that dials the telephone.

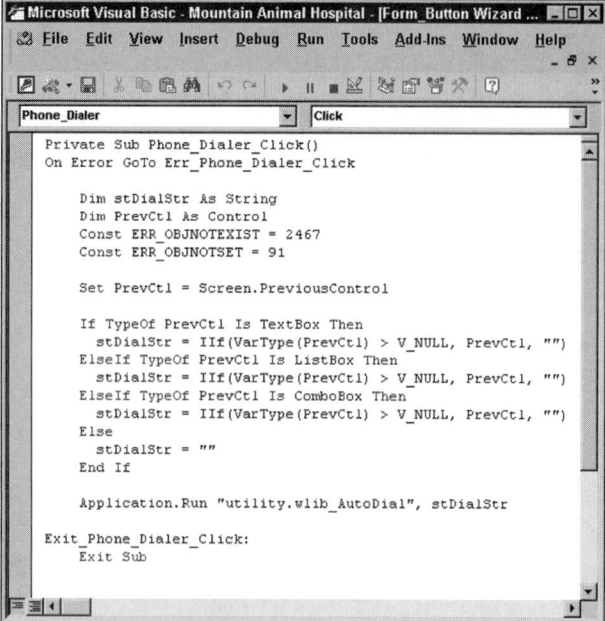

```
Microsoft Visual Basic - Mountain Animal Hospital - [Form_Button Wizard ...  _ □ X
 File   Edit   View   Insert   Debug   Run   Tools   Add-Ins   Window   Help
                                                                       _ ₽ ×
  Phone_Dialer                          Click

   Private Sub Phone_Dialer_Click()
   On Error GoTo Err_Phone_Dialer_Click

       Dim stDialStr As String
       Dim PrevCtl As Control
       Const ERR_OBJNOTEXIST = 2467
       Const ERR_OBJNOTSET = 91

       Set PrevCtl = Screen.PreviousControl

       If TypeOf PrevCtl Is TextBox Then
         stDialStr = IIf(VarType(PrevCtl) > V_NULL, PrevCtl, "")
       ElseIf TypeOf PrevCtl Is ListBox Then
         stDialStr = IIf(VarType(PrevCtl) > V_NULL, PrevCtl, "")
       ElseIf TypeOf PrevCtl Is ComboBox Then
         stDialStr = IIf(VarType(PrevCtl) > V_NULL, PrevCtl, "")
       Else
         stDialStr = ""
       End If

       Application.Run "utility.wlib_AutoDial", stDialStr

   Exit_Phone_Dialer_Click:
       Exit Sub
```

Figure 30-30: The Phone Dialer command button's On Click procedure

✦   ✦   ✦

Using Visual Basic in Forms and Reports

✦ ✦ ✦ ✦

In This Chapter

Understanding modules

Using variables and data types

Working with Visual Basic logical constructs

Handling errors

Filtering data programmatically

Programming list and combo boxes

Updating tables

Using ADO and DAO

✦ ✦ ✦ ✦

T he Visual Basic language offers a full array of powerful commands for manipulating records in a table, controls on a form, or just about anything else. This chapter continues Chapter 30's discussion of working with procedures in forms, reports, and standard modules.

Understanding Modules

Chapter 30 allows you to create a few sample procedures and you become somewhat familiar with the Visual Basic programming environment. But you may still be a little uncomfortable with modules and procedures, as well as unsure when and how to create them.

Modules and their procedures are the principal objects of the Visual Basic programming environment. The programming code that you write is placed in procedures that are contained in a module. The procedures can be independent procedures, unrelated to a specific form or report, or they can be integral parts of specific forms and reports.

Two basic categories of modules can be stored in a database:

> ✦ **Form/Report.** CBF - Code Behind Form/CBR - Code Behind Report
> ✦ **Standard Modules.** Stored in the Module Object

As you create Visual Basic procedures for your Access applications, you use both types of modules.

Form and report modules

All forms and reports, and their controls, can associate event procedures with their events. These event procedures can be macros or Visual Basic code. Every form or report you create in your database contains a form module or report module. This form or report module is an integral part of the form or report and is used as a container for the event procedures you create for the form or report. This method is a convenient way to place all of a form's event procedures in a single collection.

Creating Visual Basic event procedures in a form module can be very powerful and efficient. When an event procedure is attached to a form, it becomes part of the form. When you need to copy the form, the event procedures go with it. If you need to modify one of the form's events, you simply click the ellipsis button for the event, and the form module window for the procedure appears. Figure 31-1 illustrates accessing the event procedure of the First Record button's On Click event shown in the form named Button Wizard Visual Basic Samples. Notice that in the On Click property is the text [Event Procedure]. When you click the Builder button next to [Event Procedure], you will see the module window for that form (and specifically the On Click event for that button control).

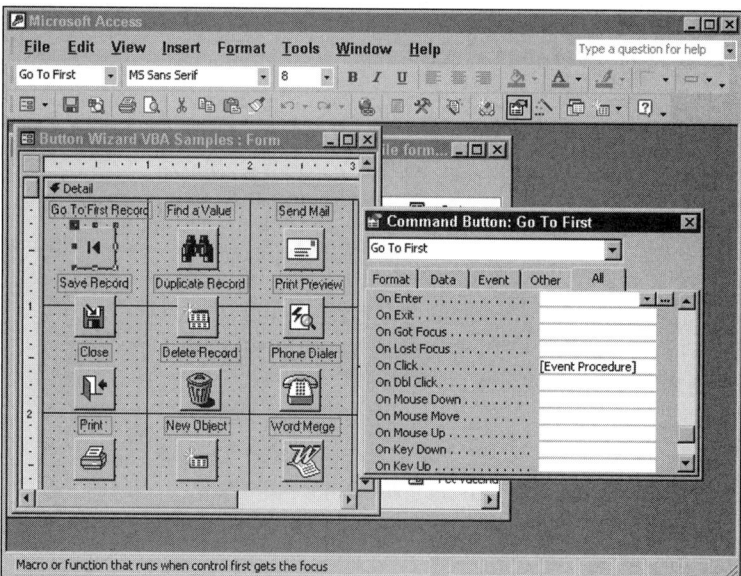

Figure 31-1: Accessing a control's event procedure from the Property Sheet

Cross-Reference   For more about the Button Wizard Visual Basic Samples form, see Chapter 30 (especially Figure 30-28).

Event procedures that work with a single form or report belong in the module of the form or report. A specific form's module should contain only the declarations and event procedures needed for that form and its controls (command buttons, check boxes, text labels, text boxes, combo boxes, and so on). Placing another form's or report's event procedures in this form's module doesn't make sense.

Standard modules

Standard modules are independent from form and report modules. These modules can be used to store code, in the form of procedures, that can be used from anywhere within your application. In early versions of Access (1.0 through 2.0), standard modules were known as global modules.

You can use standard procedures throughout your application for expressions, macros, event procedures, and even other procedures. To use a standard procedure, you simply call it from a control as a function or an event based on an event procedure, depending on the type of procedure that it is. Remember that two basic types of procedures are stored in modules:

✦ Subs, which perform actions without returning a value

✦ Functions, which always return a value

 Tip   Procedures run — modules contain. A procedure is executed; it performs some action. You create the procedures that your application will use. Modules, on the other hand, simply act like containers, grouping procedures and declarations together. A module cannot be run; rather, you run the procedures that are contained in the module. These procedures can respond to events or can be called from expressions, macros, and even other procedures.

You use the Modules container of the database to store your standard procedures. The module container is the section of the database that has an object button labeled Modules.

Although you can place any type of procedure in any module, you should group your procedures into categories. Most modules contain procedures that are related in some way. Figure 31-2 shows a standard module called Calendar. The Calendar module contains some procedures for working with dates, called DayOfWeek and Due28Day.

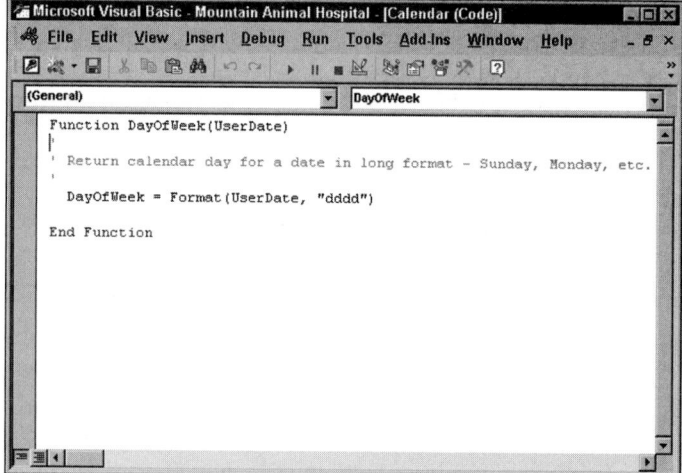

Figure 31-2: A standard module containing date-manipulation procedures

To begin creating more sophisticated procedures with Visual Basic, you need to understand some of Visual Basic's fundamental programming elements. These basic elements include the following:

✦ Variables and how they interact with data

✦ Data types

✦ Programming syntax for logical constructs

Although this book is not a how-to programming book, it attempts to explain the concepts of the Visual Basic environment in Access and how you can use it to manipulate Access objects.

Using Variables

One of the most powerful concepts in programming is the variable. A variable is a temporary storage location for some value and is given a name. You can use a variable to store the result of a calculation, or you can create a variable to make the value of a control available to another procedure.

To refer to the result of an expression, you create a name to store the result. The named result is the variable. To assign an expression's result to a variable, you use the = operator. Following are some examples of calculations that create variables:

```
counter = 1
counter = counter + 1
today = Date()
```

Naming variables

Every programming language has its own rules for naming variables. In Visual Basic, a variable name must meet the following conditions:

✦ Must begin with an alphabetical character

✦ Must not contain an embedded period or type-declaration character

✦ Must have a unique name; the name cannot be used elsewhere in the procedure or in modules that use the variables

✦ Must be no longer than 255 characters

Although you can make up almost any name for a variable, most programmers adopt a standard convention for naming variables. Some common practices include

✦ Using uppercase and lowercase characters, as in TotalCost

✦ Using all lowercase characters, as in counter

✦ Preceding the name with the data type of the value. A variable that stores a number might be called nCounter.

> **Tip**
>
> When creating variables, you can use uppercase, lowercase, or mixed-case characters to specify the variable or call it later. Visual Basic variables are not case-sensitive. This fact means that you can use the TodayIs variable later without having to worry about the case that you used for the name when you created it; TODAYIS, todayis, and tOdAyIs all refer to the same variable. Visual Basic automatically changes any explicitly declared variables to the case that was used in the declaration statement (Dim statement).

When you need to see or use the contents of a variable, you simply use its name. When you specify the variable's name, the computer program goes into memory, finds the variable, and gets its contents for you. This procedure means, of course, that you need to be able to remember the name of the variable.

Visual Basic, like many other programming languages, allows you to create variables on the fly. In the Counter = 1 example, the Counter variable was not declared before the value 1 was assigned to it.

Declaring variables

Declaring a variable before assigning anything to it sets up a location in the computer's memory for storing a value for the variable ahead of time. The amount of storage allocated for the variable depends on the type of data that you plan to store in the variable. More space is allocated for a variable that will hold a currency amount (such as $1,000,000) than for a variable that will never hold a value greater than, say, 255.

Even though Visual Basic does not require you to declare your variables before using them, it does provide various declaration commands. Getting into the habit of declaring your variables is good practice. Declaring a variable ensures that you can assign only a certain type of value to it — always a number or always characters, for example. In addition, you can attain real performance gains by pre-declaring variables. For purposes of maintenance, most programmers like to declare their variables at the top of the procedure, in the declarations section of the module.

Caution   Although Visual Basic does not require initial declaration of variables, you should avoid using undeclared variables. If you do not declare a variable, the code may expect one type of value in the variable when another is actually there. If, in your procedure, you set the variable TodayIs to Monday and later change the value for TodayIs to a number (such as TodayIs = 2), the program generates an error when it runs.

The Dim statement

To declare a variable, you use the Dim statement. When you use the Dim statement, you must supply the variable name that you assign to the variable. The format for the Dim statement is

```
Dim [variable name] [As [type]]
```

Figure 31-3 shows the Dim statement for the variable xBeeps. Notice that the variable name follows the Dim statement. In addition to naming the variable, you can use the optional As clause to specify data type for the variable. The data type is the kind of information that will be stored in the variable: String, Integer, Currency, and so on. The default data type is known as variant. A variant data type can hold any type of data.

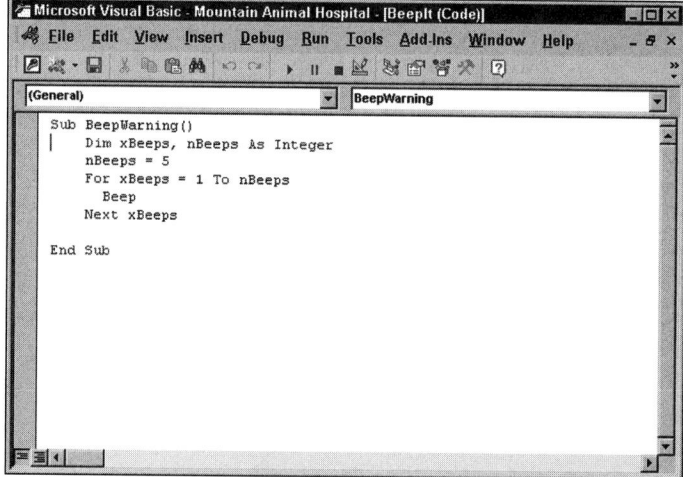

Figure 31-3: Using the Dim statement to declare a variable

When you use the Dim statement to declare a variable in a procedure, you can refer to that variable only within that procedure. Other procedures, even if they are stored in the same module, do not know anything about the variable. This is known as a private variable because it was declared in a procedure and is only known in the procedure where it was declared and used.

Variables can also be declared in the declarations section of a module. Then, all the procedures in the module can access the variable. Procedures outside the module in which you declared the variable, however, cannot read or use the variable.

The Public statement

To make a variable available to all modules in the application, use the Public keyword when you declare the variable. Figure 31-4 illustrates using the Public keyword to declare a variable. Notice that the statement is in the declarations section of the module. Public variables must be declared in the declarations section of the module.

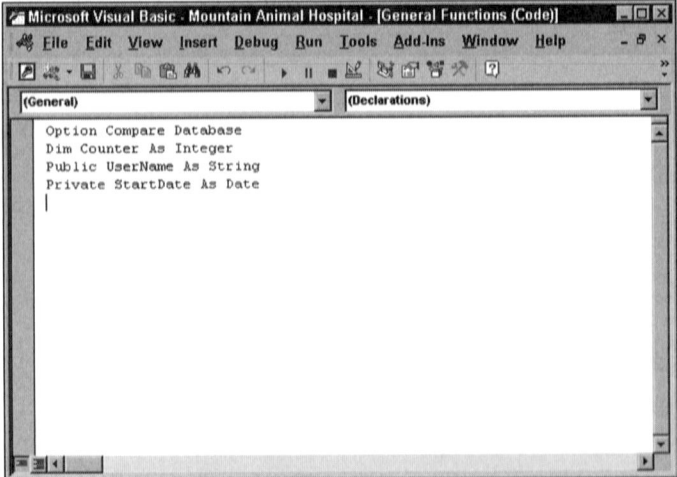

Figure 31-4: Declaring a public variable

Caution   You cannot declare a variable public within a procedure. It must be declared in the declarations section of a module. If you attempt to declare a variable public within a procedure, you receive an error message.

Although you can declare a public variable in any module, it seems logical to declare public variables only within the module that will use them the most. The exceptions to this rule are true global variables that you want to make available to all procedures across modules and that are not specifically related to a single module. You should declare global variables in a single standard module so you can find them easily.

Tip

In a standard, report, or form module, you can refer to a public variable from a different form or report module. To access the value of a public variable from another module, you must qualify the variable reference, using the name of the form or report object. Employee_MainForm.MyVariable, for example, accesses a form named Employee_MainForm and obtains the value of the variable MyVariable.

The Private statement

The declarations section in Figure 31-4 shows the use of the Dim and Private statements to declare variables. Technically, there is no difference between Private and Dim, but using Private at the module level to declare variables that are available to only that module's procedures is a good idea. Declaring private variables does the following things:

✦ Contrasts with Dim, which must be used at the procedure level, distinguishing where the variable is declared and its scope (Module versus Procedure)

✦ Contrasts with Public, the other method of declaring variables in modules, making understanding your code easier

Tip

You can go to the declarations section of a module while you are creating an event procedure in a form by selecting declarations from the Procedure combo box. Another way to move to the declarations section is to select (general) in the Object combo box. Figure 31-5 shows the Module window combo boxes.

When you declare a variable, you use the AS clause to assign a data type to the variable. Data types for variables are similar to data types in a database table definition.

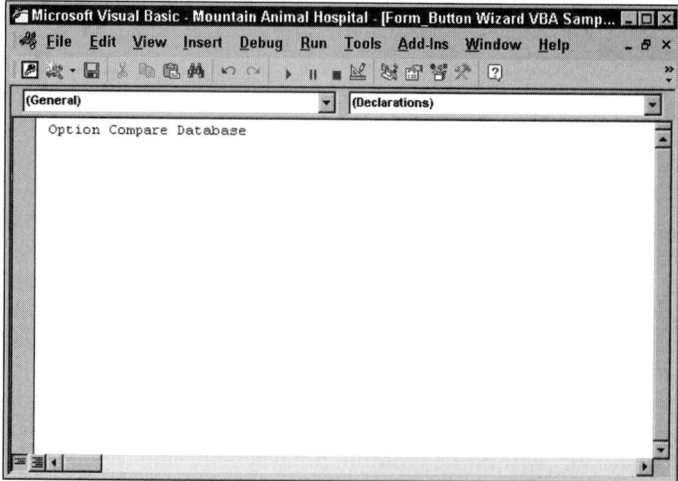

Figure 31-5: Accessing a module's declarations section

Working with Data Types

When you declare a variable, you also can specify the data type for the variable. All variables have a data type. The type of variable determines what kind of information can be stored in the variable.

A string variable — a variable with a data type of string — can hold any values ranging from A–Z, a–z, and 0–1, as well as formatting characters (#, -, !, and so on). Once created, a string variable can be used in many ways: comparing its contents with another string, pulling parts of information out of the string, and so on. If you have a variable defined as a string, however, you cannot use it to do mathematical calculations. Conversely, you cannot assign a number to a variable declared as a string.

Table 31-1 describes the 11 data types that Visual Basic supports.

Table 31-1		
Data Types Used in Visual Basic		
Type	**Range**	**Description**
Boolean	True or false	2 bytes
Byte	0 to 255	1-byte binary data
Currency	–922,337,203,685,477,5808 to 922,337,203,685,477,5807	8-byte number with fixed decimal point
Decimal	+/–79,228,162,514,264,337,593,543,950,335 with no decimal point +/–7.9228162514264337593543950335 with 28 places to the right of the decimal; smallest non-zero number is +/–0.0000000000000000000000000001	14 bytes
Date	01 Jan 100 to 31 Dec 9999	8-byte date/time value
Double	–1.79769313486231E308 to –4.94065645841247E–324	8-byte floating-point number
Integer	–32,768 to 32,767	2-byte integer
Long	–2,147,483,648 to 2,147,483,647	4-byte integer
Object	Any object reference	4 bytes
Single	negative values: –3.402823E38 to –1.401298E–45 positive values: 1.401298E–45 to 3.402823E38	4-byte floating-point number

Continued

Table 31-1 (continued)		
Type	**Range**	**Description**
String (variable-length)	0 to approximately 2,000,000,000	10 bytes plus length of string
String (fixed-length)	1 to approximately 65,400	Length of string
Variant (with numbers)	Any numeric value up to the range of Double	16 bytes
Variant (with characters)	0 to approximately 2,000,000,000	22 bytes plus length of string
User-defined (using Type)	Same as Range of its data type	Number required by elements

Most of the time you use the string, date, integer, and currency or double data types. If a variable always contains whole numbers between –32,768 and 32,768, you can save bytes of memory and gain speed in arithmetic operations if you declare the variable an integer type.

When you want to assign the value of an Access field to a variable, you need to make sure that the type of the variable can hold the data type of the field. Table 31-2 shows the corresponding Visual Basic data types for Access field types.

Table 31-2 Comparative Data Types of Access and Visual Basic	
Access Field Data Type	**Visual Basic Data Type**
AutoNumber (Long Integer)	Long
AutoNumber (Replication ID)	—
Currency	Currency
Computed	—
Date/Time	Date
Memo	String
Number (Byte)	Byte
Number (Integer)	Integer
Number (Long Integer)	Long

Access Field Data Type	Visual Basic Data Type
Number (Single)	Single
Number (Double)	Double
Number (Replication ID)	—
OLE object	String
Text	String
Hyperlink	String
Yes/No	Boolean

Now that you understand variables and their data types, you're ready to learn how to use them in writing procedures.

Understanding Visual Basic Logical Constructs

One of the real powers of a programming language is the capability to have a program make a decision based on some condition. Visual Basic has this capability in two varieties: *conditional processing* and *repetitive looping*.

Conditional processing

Often, a program in Visual Basic performs different tasks based on some value. If the condition is True, the code performs one action. If the condition is False, the code performs a different action. An application's capability to look at a value and, based on that value, decide which code to run is known as conditional processing.

The procedure is similar to walking down a path and coming to a fork in the path; you can go to the left or to the right. If a sign at the fork points left for home and right for work, you can decide which way to go. If you need to go to work, you go to the right; if you need to go home, you go to the left. In the same way, a program looks at the value of some variable and decides which set of code should be processed.

Visual Basic offers two sets of conditional processing statements:

✦ If. . .Then. . .Else. . .End If

✦ Select Case

The If. . .Then. . .Else. . .End If statement

The If. . .Then and If. . .Then. . .Else statements allow you to check a condition and, based on the evaluation, perform a single action. The condition must evaluate to True or False. If the condition is True, the program moves to the next statement in the procedure. If the condition is False, the program skips to the statement following the Else statement, if present, or the End If statement if there is no Else clause.

In Figure 31-6, the Print Reports dialog box displays an option group, called Report to Print, that displays three reports. When you choose the Pet Directory report, a list of pets appears at the bottom of the dialog box. When you choose either of the other two reports, the list of pets disappears. Figure 31-7 shows the dialog box with the All Customers and Pets report option selected and nothing displayed in the now-invisible list box.

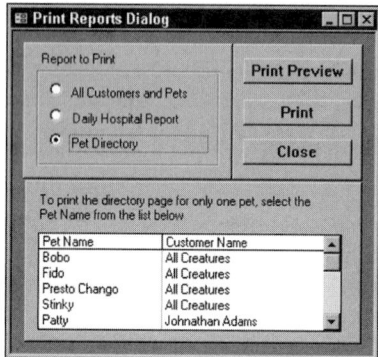

Figure 31-6: Choosing the Pet Directory report in the Print Reports dialog box

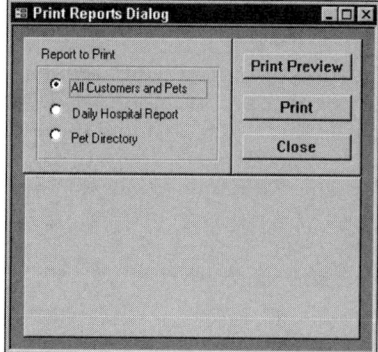

Figure 31-7: Choosing the All Customers and Pets report in the Print Reports dialog box

The "Converting existing macros to Visual Basic" section of Chapter 30 explains how to make the Select Pet list box visible and invisible in the Print Reports dialog box. Figure 31-8 illustrates the Show List macro for the Print Reports dialog box. The two condition statements determine which SetValue action to use to set the Select Pet list box's Visible property to Yes when the Pet Directory option is selected and to No when another report option is selected.

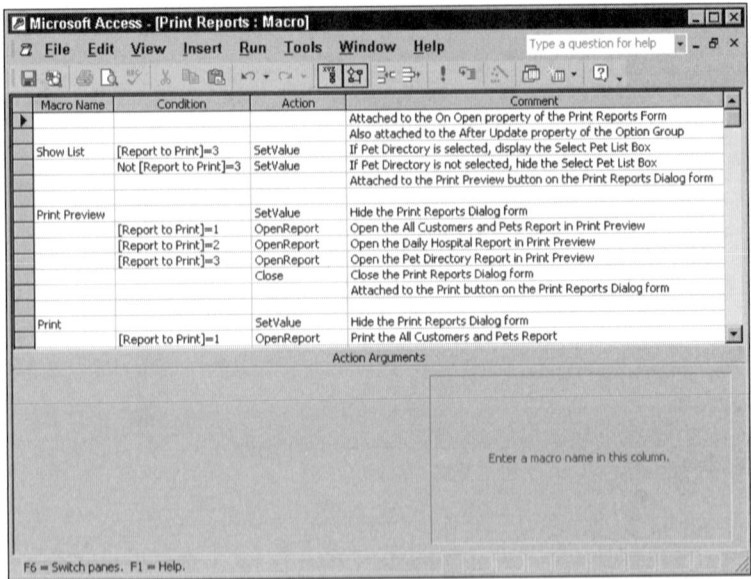

Figure 31-8: Using a macro (Show List) to make a control visible

You can write a procedure to perform the same actions as the Show List macro. Figure 31-9 shows the Print_Reports_Show_List procedure. Notice that the If. . . Then. . .End If construct replaces the Condition statement used in the macro.

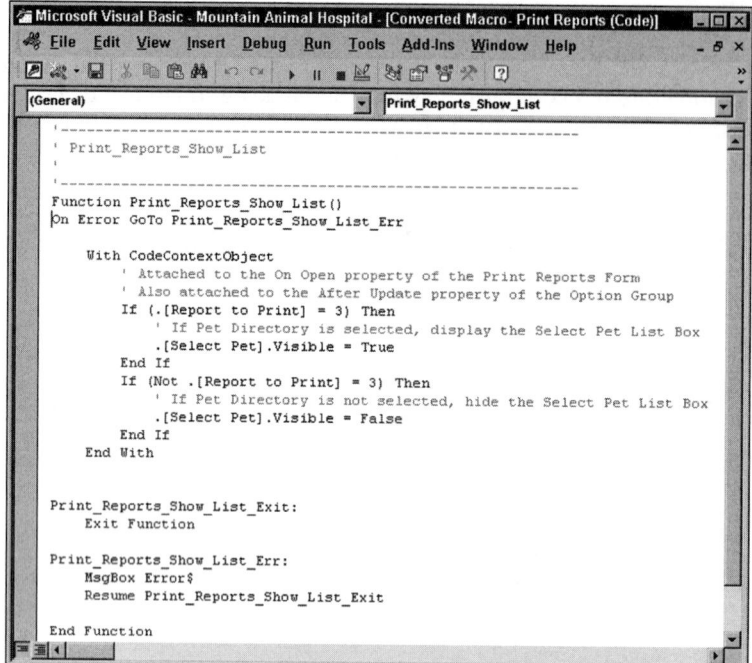

Figure 31-9: Using the If. . .Then. . .End If statement

The Else statement is optional. You can use Else to test for a second condition when the If statement evaluates to False or just to perform an alternate set of actions when the If statement is false. When the If statement is True, the program executes the statements between the If statement and the Else statement. When the If statement evaluates to False, the program skips to the Else statement, if it is present. Then, if the Else statement is True, the program executes the following statement. If the Else statement is False, the program skips to the statement following the End If statement.

Figure 31-10 illustrates the Print_Reports_Show_List procedure with an Else statement.

When you have many conditions to test, the If. . .Then. . .Else statements can get rather complicated. A better approach is to use the Select Case construct.

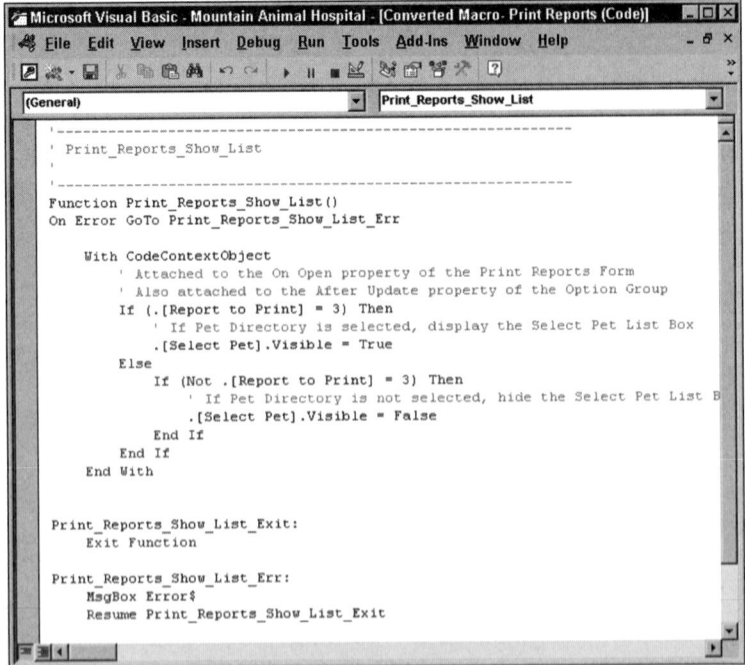

Figure 31-10: Using the Else statement

The Select Case. . .End Select statement

Visual Basic also offers a command for checking more than one condition. You can use the Select Case statement to check for multiple conditions. Following is the general syntax of the statement:

```
Select Case test_expression
    Case expression value1
        code statements here (test expression = value1)
    Case expression value2
        code statements here (test expression = value2) ...
    Case Else
        code statements (test expression = none of the values)
End Select
```

Notice that the syntax is similar to that of the If. . .Then statement. Instead of a condition in the Select Case statement, however, Visual Basic uses a test expression. Then each Case statement inside the Select Case statement tests its value against the test expression's value. When a Case statement matches the test value, the program executes the next line or lines of code until it reaches another Case statement or the End Select statement. Visual Basic executes the code for only one matching Case statement.

Note
If more than one Case statement matches the value of the test expression, only the code for the first match executes. If other matching Case statements appear after the first match, Visual Basic ignores them.

The Print Reports dialog box prints a different report for each of the three Report to Print options. Figure 31-11 shows the Print command button's Print macro. The three condition statements determine which OpenReport action is used to print the appropriate report.

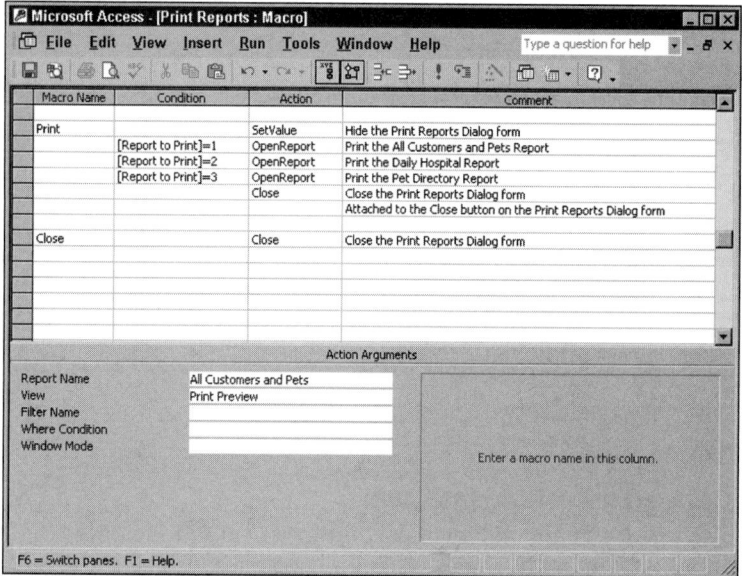

Figure 31-11: Using a macro to print a report

The Print_Reports_Print procedure, illustrated in Figure 31-12, performs the same actions as the Print macro. Notice that the procedure replaces each of the macro's Condition statements with a Case statement.

The Select Case statement looks at the value of the control Report to Print and then checks each Case condition. If the value of Report to Print is 1 (All Customers and Pets), the Case 1 statement evaluates to True, and the All Customers and Pets report prints. If Report to Print is not 1, Visual Basic goes to the next Case statement to see whether Report to Print matches that value. Each Case statement is evaluated until a match occurs or the program reaches the End Select statement.

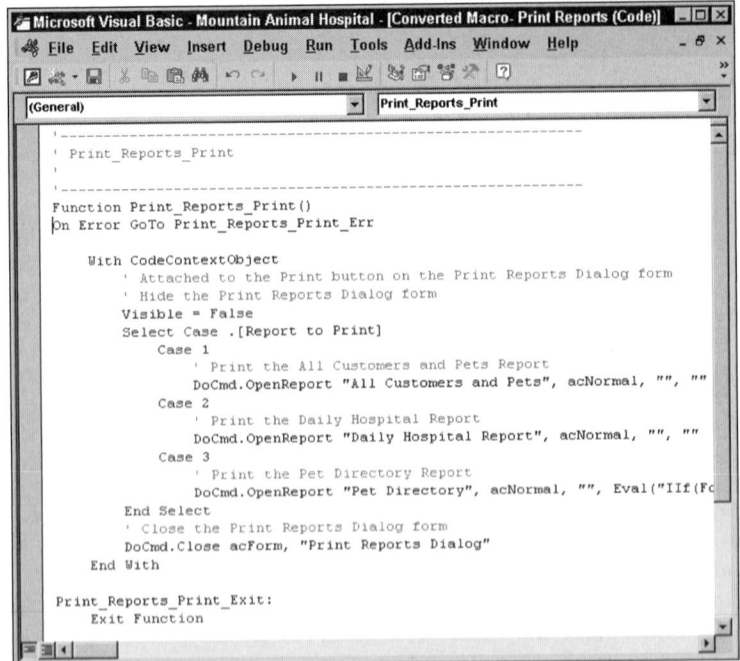

```
Microsoft Visual Basic - Mountain Animal Hospital - [Converted Macro- Print Reports (Code)]   _ □ ×
 File  Edit  View  Insert  Debug  Run  Tools  Add-Ins  Window  Help          _ ⊖ ×

(General)                              ▼   Print_Reports_Print                ▼

'-----------------------------------------------------------
' Print_Reports_Print
'
'-----------------------------------------------------------
Function Print_Reports_Print()
On Error GoTo Print_Reports_Print_Err

    With CodeContextObject
        ' Attached to the Print button on the Print Reports Dialog form
        ' Hide the Print Reports Dialog form
        Visible = False
        Select Case .[Report to Print]
            Case 1
                ' Print the All Customers and Pets Report
                DoCmd.OpenReport "All Customers and Pets", acNormal, "", ""
            Case 2
                ' Print the Daily Hospital Report
                DoCmd.OpenReport "Daily Hospital Report", acNormal, "", ""
            Case 3
                ' Print the Pet Directory Report
                DoCmd.OpenReport "Pet Directory", acNormal, "", Eval("IIf(Fc
        End Select
        ' Close the Print Reports Dialog form
        DoCmd.Close acForm, "Print Reports Dialog"
    End With

Print_Reports_Print_Exit:
    Exit Function
```

Figure 31-12: Using the Select Case statement

The Case Else statement is optional. The Case Else clause always is the last Case statement of Select Case. You use this statement to perform some action when none of the Case values matches the test value of the Select Case statement.

In some procedures, you may want to execute a group of statements more than one time. Visual Basic provides some constructs for repeating a group of statements.

Repetitive looping

Another very powerful process that Visual Basic offers is repetitive looping—the capability to process some series of code over and over. The statement or group of statements is processed continually until some condition is met.

Visual Basic offers two types of repetitive-looping constructs:

✦ Do. . .Loop
✦ For. . .Next

The Do. . .Loop statement

The Do. . .Loop statement is used to repeat a group of statements while a condition is true or until a condition is true. This statement is one of the most common commands that can perform repetitive processes.

Following is the format of the Do. . .Loop statement:

```
DO [While | Until condition]
      code statements [for condition = TRUE]
      [Exit DO]
      code statements [for condition = TRUE]
LOOP [While | Until condition]
```

Notice that the Do. . .Loop statement has several optional clauses. The two While clauses tell the program to execute the code inside Do. . .Loop as long as the test condition is True. When the condition evaluates to False, the program skips to the next statement following the Loop statement. The two Until clauses work in just the opposite way; they execute the code within Do. . .Loop as long as the condition is False. Where you place the While or Until clause determines whether the code inside Do. . .Loop executes at least once. If you place the clause at the beginning of the statement and the condition is met (until) or not met (while), the statement will not execute at all. If you place the clause at the end of the statement, the statement will execute once before evaluating the condition for the first time.

The Exit Do clause is used to terminate Do. . .Loop immediately. The program then skips to the next statement following the Loop statement.

The Print_Reports_Print2 procedure, illustrated in Figure 31-13, prints multiple copies of the report, based on the value of the Number of Copies control on the form. Notice that the procedure declares a Counter variable. The program increments the Counter variable each time the report prints. When Counter is greater than Number of Copies, Do. . .Loop stops printing copies of the report.

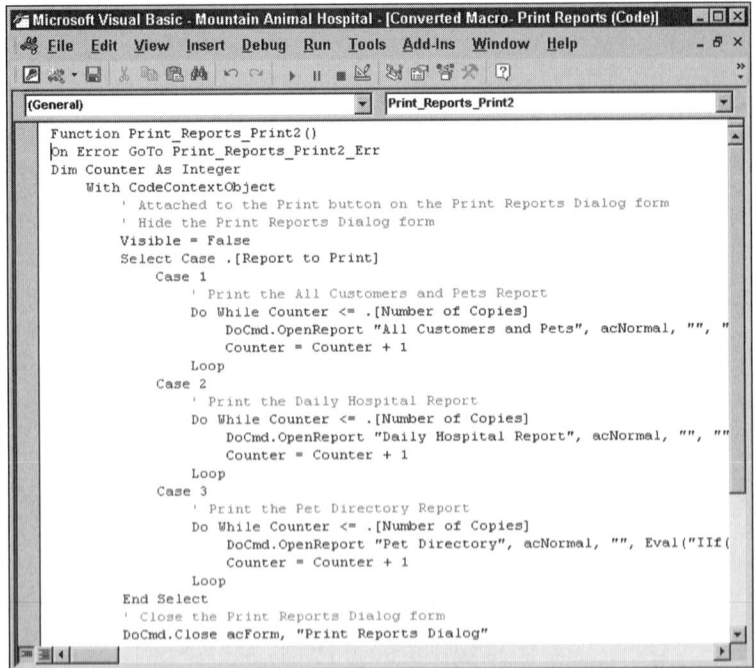

Figure 31-13: Using the Do. . .Loop statement

The While clause causes the Do...Loop to exit when Counter reaches the limit. Using the While or Until clause is equivalent to using the Exit Do statement within the loop. The following is the same Do...Loop example using the Exit Do statement:

```
Do
    Docmd.OpenReport ...
    Counter = Counter + 1
    If Counter > .[Number of Copies] Then
        Exit Do
    End If
Loop
```

The While and Until clauses provide powerful flexibility for processing Do. . .Loop in your code. Table 31-3 describes the various alternatives for using the While and Until clauses and how they affect the processing of code.

Table 31-3
Repetitive Looping Using Do. . .Loop
with the While and Until Clauses

Pseudo Code	Purpose of Do. . .Loop
Do	Code starts here If condition Then Exit Do End If.
Loop	The code always runs. The code has some conditional statement (If. . .Then) that, if True, runs the Exit Do statement. The Exit Do statement allows the user to get out of Do. . .Loop. If that statement were missing, the code inside the loop would run forever.
Do	While condition code starts here for the condition on the Do While line being TRUE.
Loop	The code inside the Do While loop runs only if the condition is True. The code runs down to the Loop statement and then goes back to the top to see whether the condition is still True. If the condition is initially False, Do. . .Loop is skipped; if the condition becomes False, the loop is exited when the code loops back to the Do While line. Exit Do is not needed for this purpose.
Do	Until condition code starts here for the condition on the Do Until line being FALSE.
Loop	This code works the opposite way from Do While. If the condition is False (not True), the code begins and loops until the condition is True; then it leaves the loop. Again, the loop and its code are skipped if the Until condition is True.
Do	Code starts here code starts here for the condition on the Do While line being TRUE.
Loop While	This code always runs at least one time. First, the code is executed condition and reaches the Loop While line. If the condition is True, the code loops back up to process the code again; if not, the code loop ends.
Do	Code starts here for the condition on the Do Until line being FALSE.
Loop Until	This code works similarly to the preceding one. The code always condition runs at least one time. When the code reaches the Loop Until line, it checks to see whether the condition is True. If the condition is True, the code drops out of the loop. If the condition is False, the code loops back up to redo the code.

The For. . .Next statement

For. . .Next is a shortcut method for the Do. . .Loop construct. You can use For. . .Next when you want to repeat a statement for a set number of times. The Step clause followed by an increment lets you process the loop in a non-single step amount. For example, if start number was 10 and end number was 100 and you wanted to increment the counter by 10 each time you would use Step 10. Though the loop would only be executed 10 times the value of the counter would be 10, 20, 30, and so on, instead of 1, 2, 3, and so on.

Following is the general syntax of the For. . .Next statement:

```
For counter variable name  = start number  To end number
[Step increment]
code statements begin here and continue to Next If condition
code
[Exit For]
End If code can continue here after the Exit for
Next [counter]
```

You can code the Print_Reports_Print2 procedure by using the For. . .Next construct. In Figure 31-14, notice that the For. . .Next statements replace the Do While. . .Loop statements of the Print_Reports_Print3 procedure. Notice also that the statement Counter = Counter + 1 is omitted.

At the start of the For. . .Next loop, the program initializes Counter to 1; then it moves on and executes the DoCmd statement. Whenever the program encounters the Next statement, it automatically increments Counter and returns to the For statement. The program compares the value of Counter with the value in the Number of Copies control. If Counter is less than or equal to Number of Copies, the DoCmd executes again; otherwise, the program exits the loop.

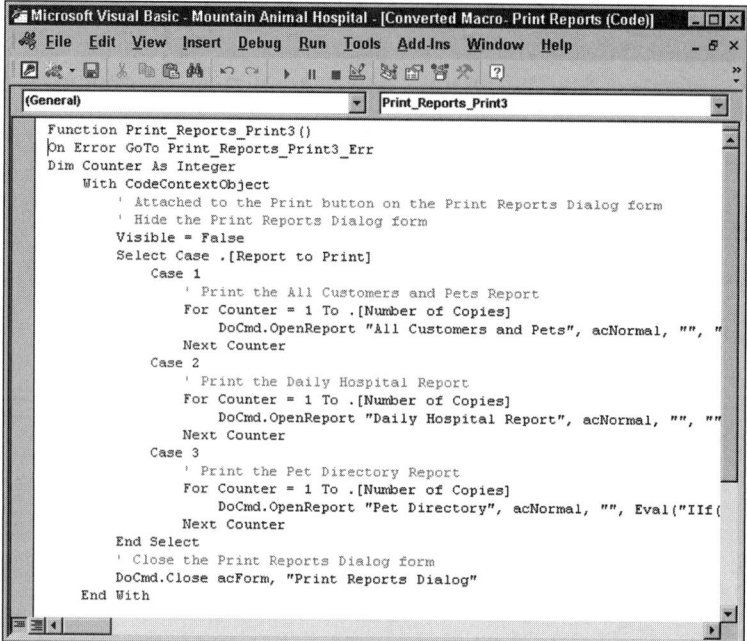

Figure 31-14: Using the For. . .Next loop

Planning for Runtime Errors

Whenever you write your own procedures, it is a good idea to plan for any error conditions that may occur when your procedure runs.

If an error occurs when you run a procedure, Access displays an error message and stops executing the program. When the procedure terminates, your application can end up in a state of flux, depending on the nature of the error.

Cross-Reference   For more information about debugging and compiling procedures, see Chapter 30.

Even though you may have tested and retested the procedures in your application, things still can go wrong. Reports and forms can be deleted, and tables can become corrupted. When you write your procedures, you cannot alleviate situations like these. You can, however, provide a means of recovering from errors gracefully.

Adding error-handling code to a procedure

If any error occurs when you run your procedure, and you did not include an On Error statement, Access displays a message and stops running the procedure. Adding an On Error statement to a procedure allows the procedure to keep running even if an error occurs.

Following is the syntax for the On Error statements:

```
On Error GoTo labelname
On Error Resume Next
```

Using the On Error GoTo statement signals Access that you want it to perform some special instructions if an error occurs anywhere in the procedure. The GoTo label-name clause tells Access where to look for the special instructions. You replace the keyword labelname with a label name. For example, the Print_Reports_Close procedure, illustrated in Figure 31-15, closes the Print Reports dialog box. If the Print Reports dialog box is missing when the procedure runs, an error occurs. The On Error GoTo statement at the top of the procedure provides a way to recover from errors.

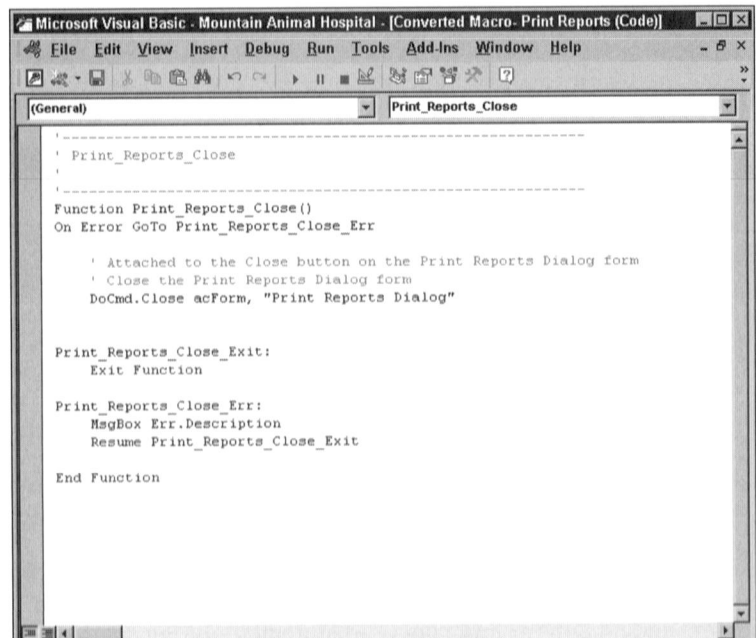

Figure 31-15: The On Error GoTo statement

On Error Resume Next tells Access that you want to ignore the error and go on to the next statement. This can be dangerous if the statement that gets ignored because of an error contained an important instruction, such as to multiply two numbers. With the calculation not performed, all sorts of things can begin to go wrong. You should use On Error Resume Next only in procedures where such mistakes can't happen.

A label name is used to identify a special section of code somewhere in your procedure. A label name can be any combination of characters that start with a letter and end with a colon. In Figure 31-15, the On Error statement for the Print_Reports_Close function points to the line label Print_Reports_Close_Err. At the bottom of the function, you see Print_Reports_Close_Err:. If an error occurs when Print_Reports_Close runs, Access looks for the section of code that starts with Print_Reports_Close_Err: and executes the statements that follow.

The lines of code that follow a label name are called a *subroutine*. A subroutine is like a procedure within a procedure. The commands in a subroutine can be executed multiple times by the sub or function that contains the commands; or they may not execute at all, depending on the purpose of the error-handling routine. An error-handling subroutine, such as Print_Reports_Close_Err, runs only if an error occurs in the Print_Reports_Close function.

You can add subroutines anywhere in your procedure. Usually, you add subroutines to the bottom of your procedure, somewhere after the Exit Sub (or Exit Function) statement and before the End Sub (or End Function). Be careful of where you add subroutines to your procedure, however, because Access runs all the lines of code in your procedure until it reaches an Exit or End statement. Even though you have labeled a section of code, Access skips line labels and runs the subroutine's lines of code as though they are part of the main procedure. In the example in Figure 31-15, the Print_Reports_Close_Err subroutine was added below the Exit Function statement because the subroutine is to run only if an error occurs.

A subroutine can branch to another subroutine within a procedure. Notice that the Print_Reports_Close_Err subroutine calls the Print_Reports_Close_Exit subroutine, using the Resume command. The Print_Reports_Close_Exit subroutine simply exits the function.

The Resume command tells Access to exit the error subroutine and continue running the code in the main procedure. You must tell Access when to end an error-handling subroutine by using a Resume statement or an Exit Sub (or Exit Function) statement. If you do not end your subroutine appropriately, Access assumes that any statements in the rest of the procedure are part of the subroutine and continues running the lines of code in the procedure until it reaches the End statement. If Access encounters an End Sub (or End Function) statement during an error-handling subroutine, an error occurs.

In the Print_Reports_Close function, the Print_ Reports_Close_Exit subroutine contains the Exit Function statement. If no error occurs when the procedure runs, Access automatically runs the Print_Reports_Close_Exit subroutine and exits the function. If an error occurs, Access runs the Print_Reports_Close_Err subroutine and then branches to Print_Reports_Close_Exit.

Including only one Exit statement in your procedure is good programming practice. Instead of branching to another subroutine, you could just as easily have added the statement Exit Function to Print_Reports_Close_Err. By using a subroutine to exit the function, you can exit from anywhere in the procedure without inserting multiple Exit statements.

Displaying meaningful runtime error messages

Even though recovery from most errors that occur in your application is possible, it is important to notify the user any time an error occurs. That way, if what the user sees next on-screen seems to be abnormal, he or she has some idea why. If an error occurs in retrieving data from a table, for example, and the next screen displays empty controls, the error message alerts the user that something has gone wrong with the application.

When you notify the user that an error has occurred, you also should supply an appropriate message that gives the user some idea what the problem is. You can determine the cause of any error condition by using the built-in error-trapping mechanism in Access. Access has a code and message assigned for any possible error situation that could occur. You can retrieve this information to display a meaningful message in a message box.

To retrieve the message for an error, use the Err.Description command. As shown in Figure 31-16, the error subroutine for the Find_Record_Click sub uses the MsgBox command to display a message box whenever an error occurs in the procedure. The Err.Description command tells the message box to retrieve and display the text of the error.

Note　　In early versions of Access, the Error$ statement returned the description for an error code. Visual Basic includes Error$ so that Access 2002 can be compatible with code from earlier versions of Access. Even though Error$ is a valid command, you should use Err.Description in any new procedures that you write.

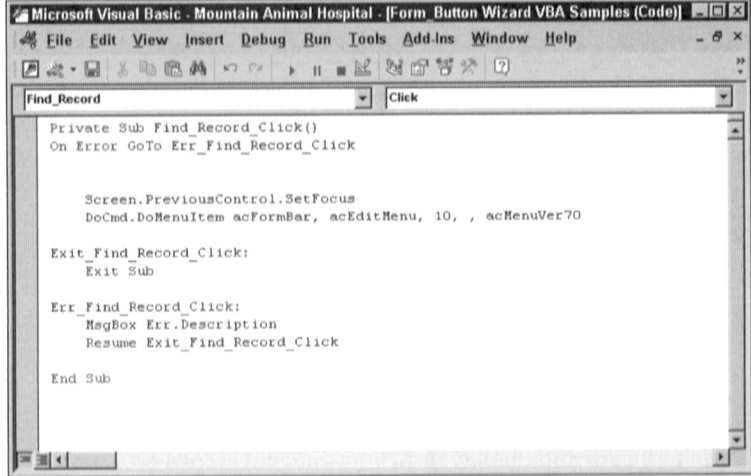

Figure 31-16: Displaying a runtime error message

Trapping for specific error codes

Even though Access supplies a complete set of generic message codes and descriptions, you sometimes want to be even more specific about the error condition. You can test for a specific error code and then display your own message whenever that error occurs. For other errors, you may want to use the generic message descriptions.

In Figure 31-17, the RoundIt_Err subroutine first checks the value of the error code. For Error Code 13, a more meaningful message than the generic message Type mismatch appears. For any error code other than 13, the Err.Description command displays the generic message text.

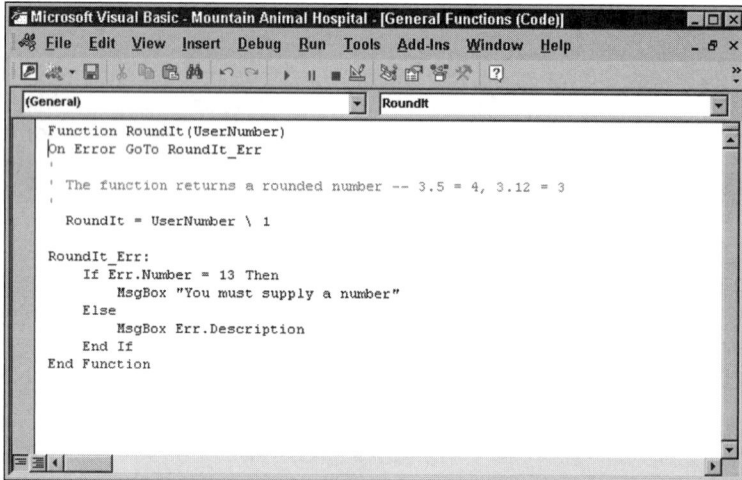

```
Function RoundIt (UserNumber)
On Error GoTo RoundIt_Err
'
' The function returns a rounded number -- 3.5 = 4, 3.12 = 3
'
    RoundIt = UserNumber \ 1

RoundIt_Err:
    If Err.Number = 13 Then
        MsgBox "You must supply a number"
    Else
        MsgBox Err.Description
    End If
End Function
```

Figure 31-17: Trapping a specific error

Filtering Records in Procedures

One of the most common features you will want to provide in your applications is the capability to locate data quickly. Having multiple ways to search for a specific record quickly is important and productive.

You can create intelligent search dialog boxes to locate and display or print records, using different search types. In this section, you learn how you can use Visual Basic code to locate and display or print a specific record or a set of records, using search criteria.

Displaying a dialog box for selecting a record

You can add a Find button to the Customers form to display the Search for Customer dialog box, shown in Figure 31-18. This dialog box provides two ways of searching for a customer. Each method displays a list of customers. The contents of the list box change, depending on the type of search that you select. When you select a customer in the list box (by clicking an entry in the list box and then clicking the OK button, or by double-clicking an entry in the list box), the Search for Customer dialog box closes, and the Customers form displays the selected customer record.

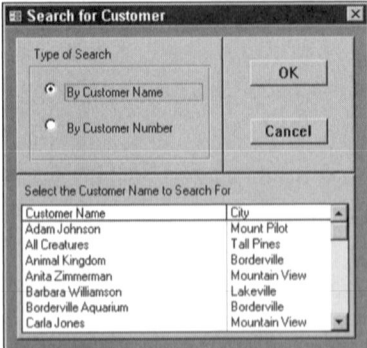

Figure 31-18: Searching for a customer

Refreshing the items for a list box

The Customers form uses an option group that contains two option buttons, a list box, and two command buttons. The secret to changing the contents of the list box is manipulating its Row Source property each time you click an option button. When you click one of the option buttons, a simple procedure updates the contents of the list box at the bottom of the form.

The bottom rectangle of the form is a list box. When you click an option button in the Type of Search option group, the list box displays the customer list, using a different set of fields and in different order.

Figure 31-19 illustrates the Design view for the dialog box, showing the properties for the By Search Type list box. The Row Source property is a select query instead of a table. You can build a select query by using the standard query screen. When you select the Row Source property and click the ellipsis button (. . .), the SQL statement translates back to its query equivalent, and the query design screen appears, as shown in Figure 31-20.

Tip

Notice in Figure 31-19 that the Bound Column property is set to 3 and that the list box displays only two columns. The third column is the Customer Number field. The Customer Number is used in the search procedure. Even though the Customer Number is not visible in the dialog box, you can access its value along with the other visible fields in the selected list box row.

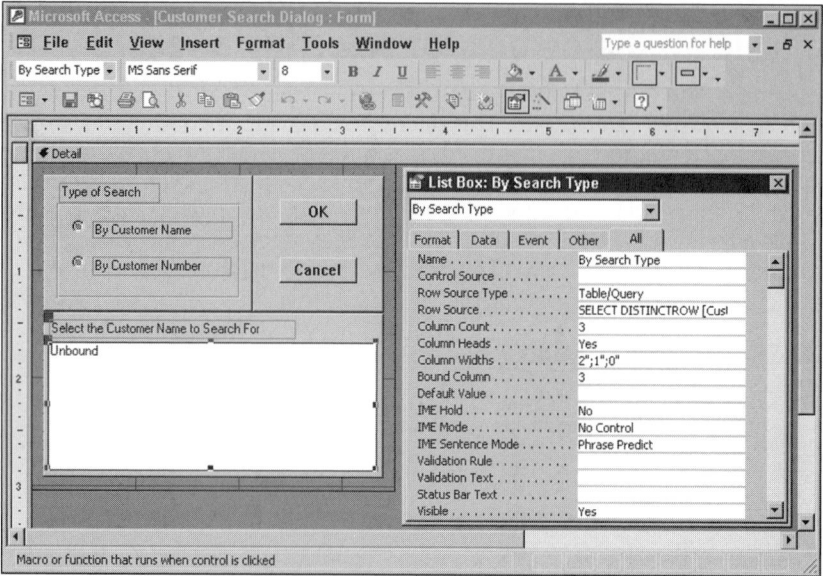

Figure 31-19: Designing a list box for search criteria

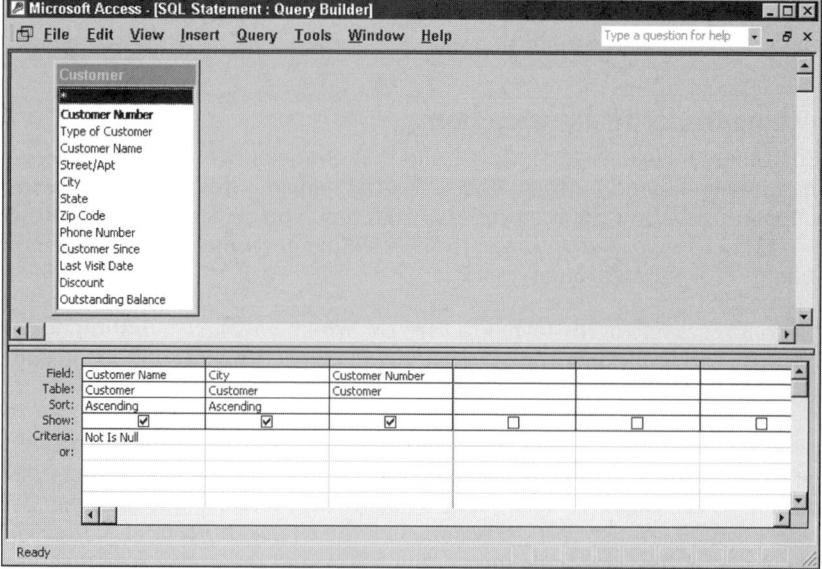

Figure 31-20: Using the Query Builder to generate an SQL statement

If you want to view the SQL statement that Access creates for you, choose View ⇨ SQL View in the Query Builder window. The SQL statement window, shown in Figure 31-21, appears when you choose View ⇨ SQL View.

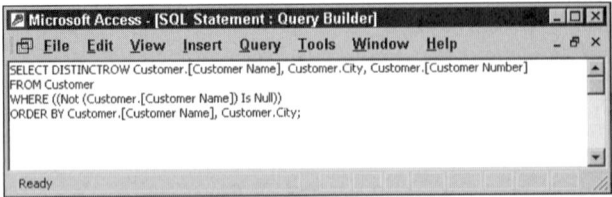

Figure 31-21: Viewing the SQL statement for a query

The Type of Search option group has an associated After Update event procedure that changes the Row Source query each time the option button changes. Figure 31-22 shows the Type_of_Search_AfterUpdate procedure.

The Type_of_Search_AfterUpdate procedure displays the Customer Name and City fields when the By Customer Name option button (Type of Search.Value = 1) is selected. The By Customer Number option (Type of Search.Value = 2) displays the Customer fields Customer Number and Customer Name in the list box, in Customer Number order. The procedure sets the Row Source property to the appropriate select query for each Type of Search option.

Tip

One secret to this method of updating the contents of the list box is to initially set the Row Source property to Null. Because Access reruns the query as you specify each property setting, the Row Source property must be set to Null; otherwise, the query is run as each property is changed. This method speeds the query by preventing Access from unnecessarily retrieving the query results for each property setting in the procedure.

Another way to make the list box display itself faster is to store the queries as actual queries. You can create and name the queries by using the Queries object button of the Database window. Instead of typing the SQL statement in the procedure, you set the Row Source property to the query name. This method runs the query 10 percent to 40 percent faster.

Finding the selected record

The OK command button in the Customer Search dialog box runs a simple Visual Basic program that locates the record that you selected in the list box and displays the record in the associated form. Figure 31-23 shows the OK_Click procedure for the OK button.

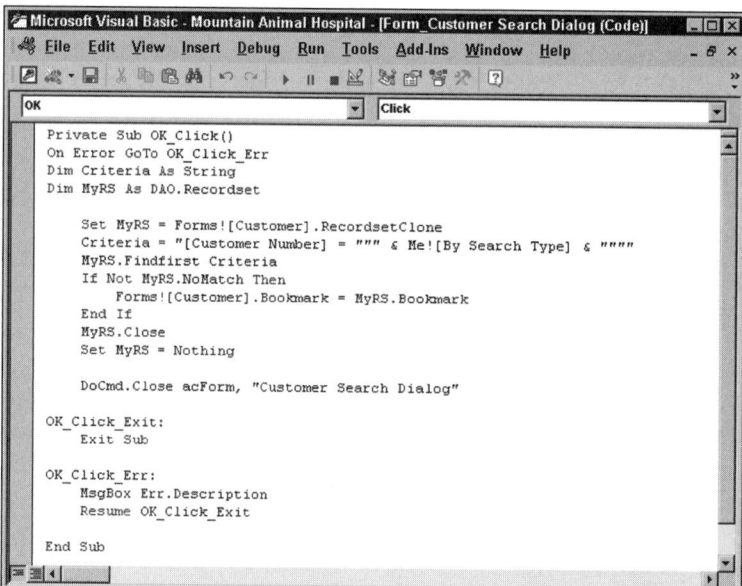

Figure 31-22: Updating the properties of a list box

```
Microsoft Visual Basic - Mountain Animal Hospital - [Form_Customer Search Dialog (Code)]
File  Edit  View  Insert  Debug  Run  Tools  Add-Ins  Window  Help

Type_of_Search                              AfterUpdate

    Private Sub Type_of_Search_AfterUpdate()
        With CodeContextObject
        If .[Type of Search] = 1 Then
            .[By Search Type].RowSource = ""
            .[Search Text].Caption = "Select the Customer Name to Search For
            .[By Search Type].ColumnCount = 3
            .[By Search Type].ColumnWidths = "2 in;1 in;0 in"
            .[By Search Type].BoundColumn = 3
            .[By Search Type].RowSource = "SELECT Customer.[Customer Name],Custom
        ElseIf .[Type of Search] = 2 Then
            .[By Search Type].RowSource = ""
            .[Search Text].Caption = "Select the Customer Number to Search For
            .[By Search Type].ColumnCount = 2
            .[By Search Type].ColumnWidths = "1 in;2 in"
            .[By Search Type].BoundColumn = 1
            .[By Search Type].RowSource = "SELECT [Customer Number],[Customer Nam
        End If
        End With
    End Sub
```

```
Microsoft Visual Basic - Mountain Animal Hospital - [Form_Customer Search Dialog (Code)]
File  Edit  View  Insert  Debug  Run  Tools  Add-Ins  Window  Help

OK                                          Click

    Private Sub OK_Click()
    On Error GoTo OK_Click_Err
    Dim Criteria As String
    Dim MyRS As DAO.Recordset

        Set MyRS = Forms![Customer].RecordsetClone
        Criteria = "[Customer Number] = """ & Me![By Search Type] & """"
        MyRS.Findfirst Criteria
        If Not MyRS.NoMatch Then
            Forms![Customer].Bookmark = MyRS.Bookmark
        End If
        MyRS.Close
        Set MyRS = Nothing

        DoCmd.Close acForm, "Customer Search Dialog"

    OK_Click_Exit:
        Exit Sub

    OK_Click_Err:
        MsgBox Err.Description
        Resume OK_Click_Exit

    End Sub
```

Figure 31-23: Using a Visual Basic program to find a record

The OK_Click procedure uses the FindFirst method to locate a record. The FindFirst method works just like the Find command (Edit menu). The criteria are the same as the fields in the Find dialog box.

The RecordsetClone method makes a copy of the rowsource of the Customer form. The FindFirst method searches the cloned recordset for the first record that meets the specified criteria. If a match is found, then the form's recordpointer jumps to the bookmark that matches the cloned recordset's bookmark value. An object's bookmark property contains a value that uniquely identifies each record for the object.

Note A recordset is the collective name that is given to table, dynaset, or snapshot type recordset object. Simply put, they are a set of records that behave as objects. In this connotation, they are a temporary table object (consisting of a set of records) that exists in memory only. Recordsets can consist of all of the rows from a single database table, or records from a combination of two or more tables that have been joined together. They cannot be stored permanently in the database. When the procedure ends, they are removed from memory.

Note A recordpointer is a placeholder, or marker, that maintains where in the program is currently pointing to in the recordset. In other words, if the program starts processing records in the recordset, the recordpointer tells the program which record is currently being pointed to and should be used next.

Using intelligent search dialog boxes, you can easily provide your user a multitude of ways to search for a record. You can have as many intelligent search dialog boxes in an application as you need, each dialog box working with a different form and a different set of tables and fields.

Selecting a set of records to print

Another useful feature in professional applications is the capability to print reports quickly and easily, without having to sit in front of a computer and select one report after another. You can create an intelligent Print dialog box to print reports, envelopes, and mailing labels for one record or for a set of records.

You can add a Print button to a form to display the Print dialog box, shown in Figure 31-24. This Print dialog box can print up to three reports at the same time and also provides three methods of selecting the records to be printed. Different options for filtering records appear, depending on the type of criteria you select. When you click the OK button, the Print dialog box closes, and the report or reports print for the selected customers.

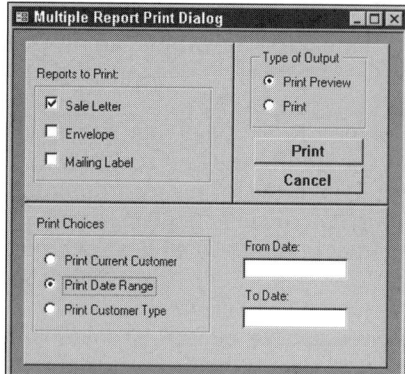

Figure 31-24: Selecting records to print

The Customers form uses a group of check boxes, two option groups, and two command buttons. You use the check boxes — named Sale Letter, Envelope, and Mailing Label — to select the report or reports to be printed. You can select one or more reports to print at the same time. The three reports are called Customer Sale Letter, Customer Envelope, and Customer Mailing Label. You can view the reports from the Database container.

Using Visual Basic to display and hide controls

The Print Choices option group, named Print Criteria, runs a Visual Basic procedure that displays and removes form controls, based on the selected option button. When the dialog box opens, the From Date, To Date, and Customer Type controls are hidden. Figure 31-25 shows the dialog box in Design view. The Customer Type combo box displays beneath the From Date text box.

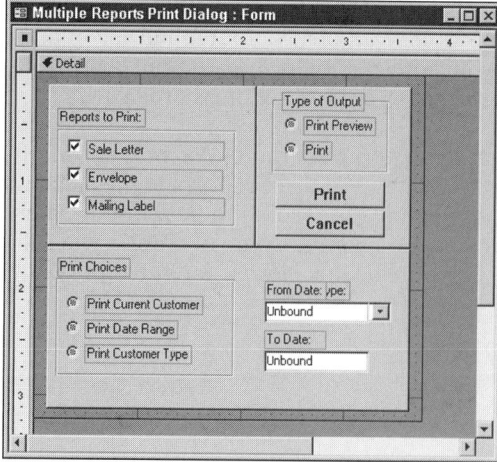

Figure 31-25: Displaying and hiding controls on a form

The Visual Basic procedure for the Print Choices option group is shown in Figure 31-26. When you select the Print Current Record option, the procedure hides the From Date, To Date, and Customer Type controls. The report or reports print only for the current record. When you select the Print Date Range option (Print Criteria = 2), the From Date and To Date text boxes appear. You then specify a beginning date and ending date to print all customers whose Last Visit Date falls between the two dates. When you select the Print Customer Type option (Print Criteria = 3), the Customer Type combo box appears, allowing you to print the selected reports for all customers whose Customer Type matches the type you selected. Notice that the procedure sets the Visible property for the controls to either True or False, which displays or hides them.

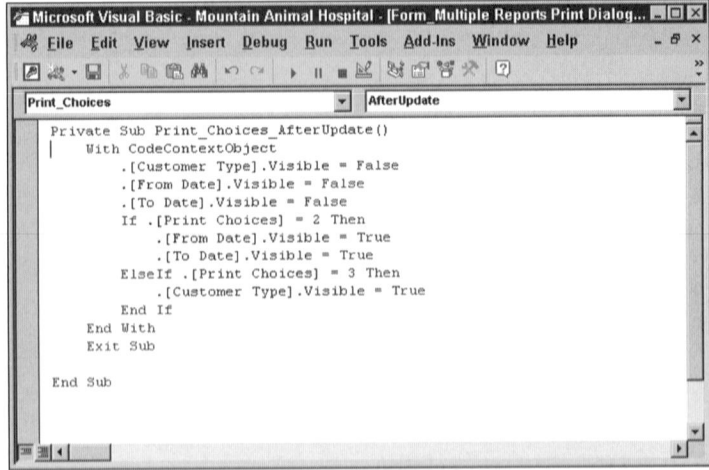

Figure 31-26: Using a procedure to display and hide controls on a form

Printing records by using selection criteria

The Print command button in the dialog box runs the Print_Customers_Click procedure. Listing 31-1 shows the procedure, which is triggered by the command button's On Click event property.

Notice that the Print_Customers_Click procedure uses the Select Case structure to test the value of the Print Criteria option group. Each Case statement includes three sets of If. . .End If statements for testing which of the reports is selected. Separate If. . .End If statements were used instead of a single If. . .Else. . .End If structure, because you can select multiple reports to print.

Listing 31-1: Opening a report using a procedure

```
Private Sub Print_Customers_Click()
    Dim ReportDest As String
    'Hide the Customer Multiple Report Print Dialog
    Me.Visible = False
    ' Destination is Print Preview
    If Me![Type of Output] = 1 Then
        ReportDest = acPreview
    Else        ' Destination is printer
        ReportDest = acNormal
    End If
    ' Determine Print Criteria selected
    Select Case [Print Criteria]
        Case 1    ' Current Customer
            ' Print Sale Letter
            If Me![Sale Letter] = -1 Then
                DoCmd.OpenReport "Customer Sale Letter",
ReportDest, , "[Customer]![Customer
Number]=Forms![Customer]![Customer Number]"
            End If
            ' Print Envelope
            If Me![Envelope] = -1 Then
                DoCmd.OpenReport "Customer Envelope",
ReportDest, , "[Customer]![Customer
Number]=Forms![Customer]![Customer Number]"
            End If
            ' Print Mailing Label
            If Me![Mailing Label] = -1 Then
                DoCmd.OpenReport "Customer Mailing Labels",
ReportDest, , "[Customer]![Customer
Number]=Forms![Customer]![Customer Number]"
            End If
        Case 2      ' Date Range
            If Me![Sale Letter] = -1 Then
                DoCmd.OpenReport "Customer Sale Letter",
ReportDest, , "[Customer]![Last Visit Date] Between me![From
Date] and me![To Date]"
            End If
            ' Print Envelope
            If Me![Envelope] = -1 Then
                DoCmd.OpenReport "Customer Envelope",
ReportDest, , "[Customer]![Last Visit Date] Between me![From
Date] and me![To Date]"
            End If
            ' Print Mailing Label
            If Me![Mailing Label] = -1 Then
                DoCmd.OpenReport "Customer Mailing Labels",
ReportDest, , "[Customer]![Last Visit Date] Between me![From
Date] and me![To Date]"
```

```
                End If
        Case 3       ' Customer Type
            ' Print Sale Letter
            If Me![Sale Letter] = -1 Then
                DoCmd.OpenReport "Customer Sale Letter",
ReportDest, , "[Customer]![Type of Customer]=me![Customer
Type]"
            End If
            ' Print Envelope
            If Me![Envelope] = -1 Then
                DoCmd.OpenReport "Customer Envelope",
ReportDest, , "[Customer]![Type of Customer]=me![Customer
Type]"
            End If
            ' Print Mailing Label
            If Me![Mailing Label] = -1 Then
                DoCmd.OpenReport "Customer Mailing Labels",
ReportDest, , "[Customer]![Type of Customer]=me![Customer
Type]"
            End If
    End Select

End Sub
```

Working with Combo-Box and List-Box Controls

You have seen in previous examples how combo boxes and list boxes provide an effective method of validating data entry in a form. These boxes can display a list of values that the user can choose so that the user does not have to memorize customer numbers, for example, or remember the spelling of a customer's name.

Figure 31-27 shows the Select a Pet combo box for the Add a New Visit Entry form. In the Mountain Animal Hospital database, the name of the form is Adding Visits for New Pets.

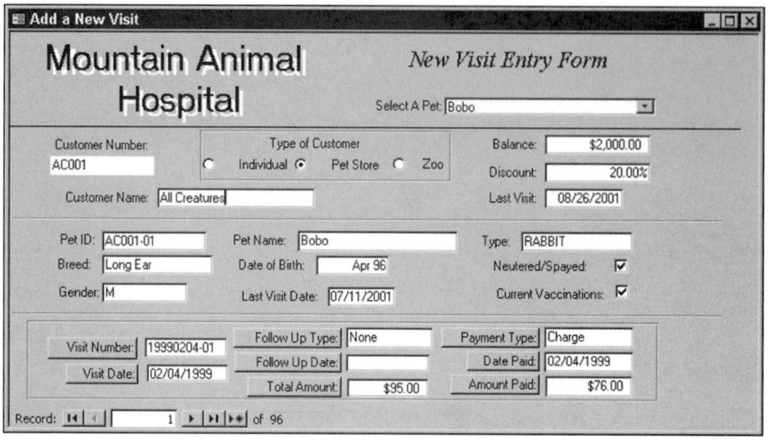

Figure 31-27: Using a combo box to validate data entry

Handling a combo box entry that is not in the list

As an option, you can set up a combo box to accept a value that is not in the list. Suppose that a customer brings in a new pet for a visit. The Select a Pet combo box in the New Visit Entry form displays only pets that have visited Mountain Animal Hospital before. Instead of making the user exit the New Visit Entry form and enter the new-patient pet in the Pets form, you can allow the user to type the name of the pet in the combo box. When the user types in the combo box a value that is not in the list of values, the Pets Data Entry form automatically appears. When the user completes the information for the pet and closes the Pets Data Entry form, the New Visit Entry form appears, and the combo box displays the pet in the list.

Entering in the combo box an item that is not in the list of valid values triggers the NotInList event. Figures 31-28 and 31-29 show the properties for the Select a Pet combo box. By connecting an event procedure to the NotInList event, you can override the normal Not in list error that is built into Access and allow the user to add the new value to the list. Notice that you also must set the LimitToList property to Yes.

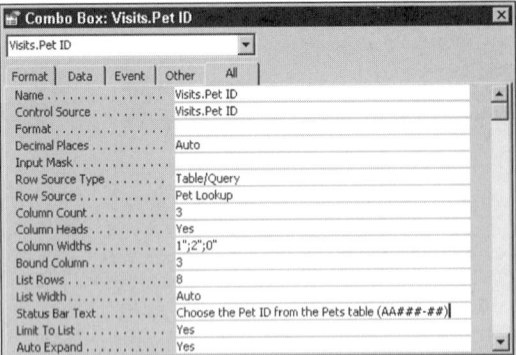

Figure 31-28: Limiting combo box values to items in the list

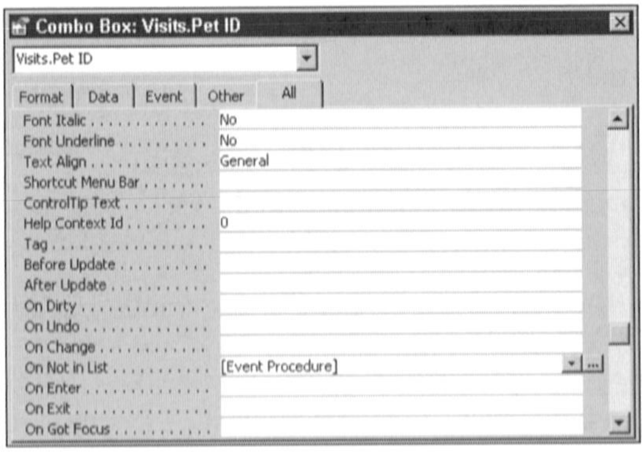

Figure 31-29: Handling combo box values that are not in the list

The LimitToList property determines how Access responds to entries that do not match any of the list items. When you set LimitToList to No, Access accepts anything that the user enters, as long as the entry conforms to the ValidationRule property, if one exists. When you set LimitToList to Yes and the user enters an invalid value, Access checks to see whether an event procedure exists for the NotInList event property. If no procedure is attached, Access displays the standard Item Not In List error message; otherwise, Access does not display the error message and runs the procedure instead. Figure 31-30 shows the NotInList procedure, called Visits_Pet_ID_NotInList, for the Select a Pet combo box.

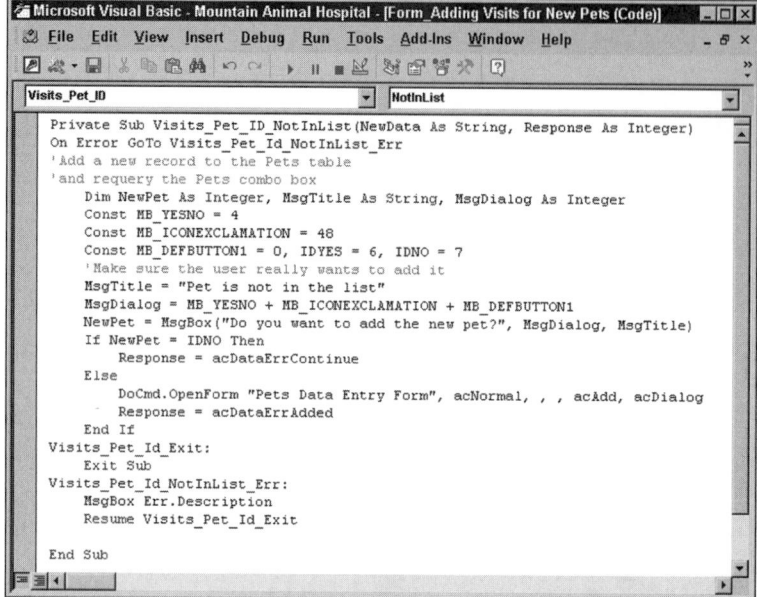

Figure 31-30: A procedure for combo box values that are not in the list

Caution Make sure that you change the Limit To List property in the combo box to No before using the On Not in List event.

The Const declarations at the top of the Visits_Pet_ID_NotInList procedure are called symbolic constants. Constants are variables whose values do not change during execution of the procedure, and symbolic constants are names for certain constants.

Symbolic constants are names for certain values that are available anywhere in your Visual Basic procedures. The actual values may be 0, 1, or 2, but providing a meaningful name makes it easier to understand what your code is doing. Using all-uppercase characters to name symbolic constants helps to differentiate them from variables. Constants that are built into Access are upper- and lowercase and begin with the letters ac.

The constants used in this procedure are used as the arguments for the MsgBox function. Instead of using numbers such as 52 and 0 as the arguments, you can create a meaningful name that makes it easier to understand what your code is doing.

This procedure first displays a confirmation message to make sure that the user really wants to add the new item. If the user chooses No (they do not want to add the item), the procedure ends. The user then must choose a valid item from the list.

Before exiting a NotInList procedure, you must set the Response variable to one of three values. The Response variable tells Access what to do with the invalid item.

The three values for the Response variable are represented by symbolic constants. These symbolic constants are built into Access and are available to any of your Visual Basic programs. Table 31-4 describes the three Response values.

	Table 31-4
	Values for the Response Variable

Value	*Description*
acDataErrDisplay	Displays the standard error message and does not add the item to the list
acDataErrContinue	Does not display the standard error message and does not add the item to the list
acDataErrAdded	Does not display the standard error message and reruns the query for the RecordSource

Tip   If you use acDataErrContinue or acDataErrAdded as Response values, you need to make sure that you display a message to the user at some point in your procedure. Otherwise, the user will not be able to leave the field and will not know why.

If the user does want to add the new item to the combo box, the Visits_Pet_ID_NotInList procedure displays a blank Pets Data Entry form. When the user closes the Pets Data Entry form, Visits_Pet_ID_NotInList sets the value for the Response variable before exiting. Setting Response to acDataErrAdded tells Access to query the list of items for the combo box again. When Access re-queries the Select a Pet combo box list, it retrieves the newly added pet from the Pets table.

Handling MultiSelect list boxes

Sometimes it makes sense for a field to have more than one value at a time. With MultiSelect list boxes, you can provide a list of values for a field and allow the user to select one or more items.

In the Pet Vaccinations List Box Example form, shown in Figure 31-31, you can select one or more vaccination types in the list box on the left. When you click the Add button, the selected items appear in the Current Vaccinations list box on the right. When you select one or more items in this list box and click the Remove button, the selected items disappear from the Current Vaccinations list box.

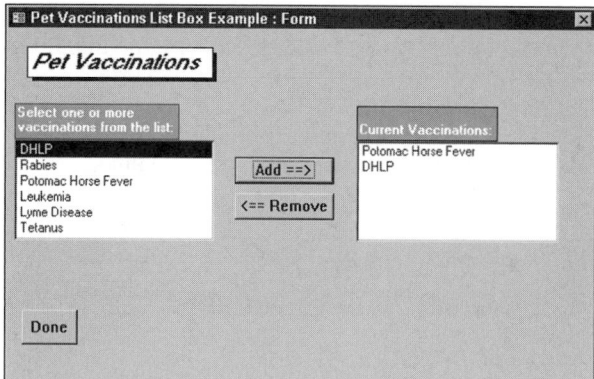

Figure 31-31: Making multiple selections in a list box

You use the MultiSelect property of a list box to specify whether, and how, a user can make multiple selections in a list box. Figure 31-32 shows the properties of the Vaccinations list box for the Pet Vaccinations form. Notice that the MultiSelect property is set to Extended.

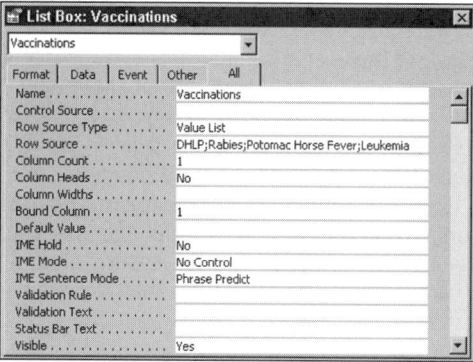

Figure 31-32: Setting the properties for a MultiSelect list box

Setting MultiSelect to Simple or Extended allows the user to select multiple items. If you want to use the normal single-selection list box, set MultiSelect to None. Table 31-5 lists the MultiSelect property settings.

Table 31-5
MultiSelect Property Settings

Setting	Visual Basic	Description
None	0	(Default) Multiple selection isn't allowed.
Extended	1	Shift+click or Shift+arrow key extends the election from the previously selected item to the current item. Ctrl+click selects or deselects an item.
Simple	2	Multiple items are selected or deselected by clicking them with the mouse or pressing the spacebar.

The Add command button in the Pet Vaccinations form runs the Add_Button_Click procedure, shown in Figure 31-33. The procedure is triggered by the command button's On Click event.

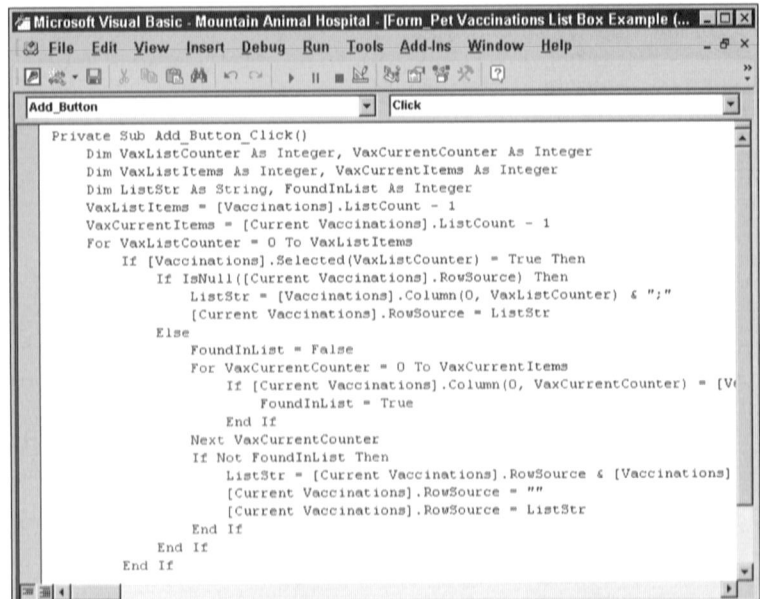

Figure 31-33: Processing the selected items in a MultiSelect list box

The Add_Button_Click procedure checks each item in the Vaccinations list box to see whether the item is selected. The list box's ListCount property tells you how many items are in the list. To refer to an individual item in the list, you refer to its numbered position in the list. The position numbers start at 0, so the first item is 0, the second is 1, and so on. An item is selected when its Selected property is True and unselected when the Selected property is False. To find out whether the first item in the Vaccinations list is selected, for example, you use the following statement:

```
If [Vaccinations].Selected(0) = True Then
```

The parentheses following the Selected property indicate which items in the list you are interrogating.

If a Vaccinations item is selected, the procedure copies it to the Current Vaccinations list box. If the item is already in the Current Vaccinations list box, however, it cannot be copied again. The OK_Button_Click procedure checks each item in the Current Vaccinations list to see whether it matches the selected item in the Vaccinations list. To refer to the items listed in a list box, you use the Column property. When you use the Column property, you supply a column number and a row number. Column numbers and row numbers also start at 0. The Current Vaccinations list box uses only one column (0). To refer to the second item in the Current Vaccinations list, you use the following syntax:

```
[Current Vaccinations].Column(0, 1)
```

If the selected Vaccinations item is in the Current Vaccinations list, the procedure does not add it to the Current Vaccinations list. The procedure loops back to the top and checks the next Vaccinations item.

If the selected Vaccinations item is not in the Current Vaccinations list, the procedure adds the item to the Current Vaccinations list box. To add an item to a list box, you concatenate it to the Row Source property. Because the Row Source property and the list box item are strings, you add them together, using the & operator. To delimit one list-box item from another, you also must add a semicolon (;) to the end of the string.

The Remove button on the Pet Vaccinations form runs the Remove_Button_Click procedure. The procedure is shown in Figure 31-34.

The Remove_Button_Click procedure removes items from the Current Vaccinations list box. Basically, the procedure adds all the unselected items to a string variable, ignoring any selected items; then it assigns the string variable to the RowSource property of the Current Vaccinations list box.

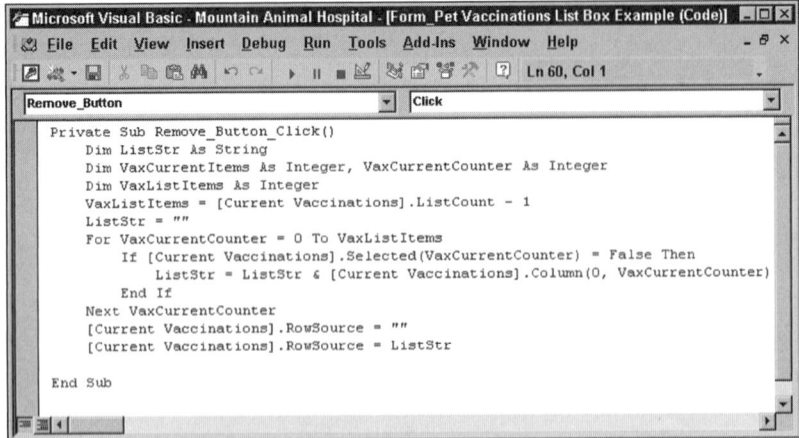

Figure 31-34: Removing items from a list box

Creating Programs to Update a Table

Updating data in a table by using a form is easy; you simply place controls on the form for the fields of the table that you want to update. For example, Figure 31-35 shows the Visit Information form. The name of the form is Adding Visit Details and Updating Customer. The fields that you see on the form update the Pets, Customer, and Visits tables.

Sometimes, however, you want to update a field in a table that you do not want to display on the form. When information is entered in the Visit Information form, for example, the Last Visit Date field in the Customer table should be updated to reflect the most recent date on which the Customer visited the animal hospital. When you enter a new visit, the value for the Last Visit Date field is the value of the Visit Date field on the Visit Information form.

Because the Last Visit Date field can be derived from the Visit Date field, you do not want the user to have to enter it. Theoretically, you could place the Last Visit Date field as a calculated field that is updated after the user enters the Visit Date field. Displaying this field, however, could be confusing and really has nothing to do with the current visit.

The best way to handle updating the Last Visit Date field is to use a Visual Basic procedure, as described in the "Updating a record" section.

You can use Visual Basic procedures to update individual fields in a record, add new records, or delete records.

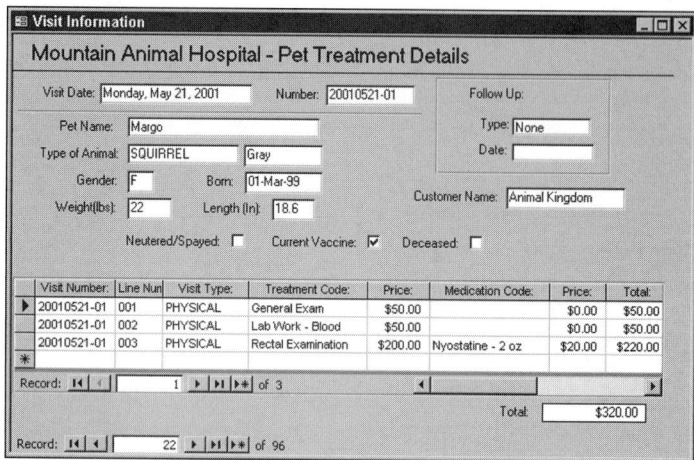

Figure 31-35: Using a form to update data in tables

Updating fields in a record using ADO and DAO

You can update the Last Visit Date field by using a Visual Basic procedure. The AfterUpdate event for the Visit Information form runs a procedure to update the Customer table. The procedure is shown in Figure 31-36.

The Form_AfterUpdate procedure for the Visit Information form updates the Last Visit Date in the Customer table. This procedure uses special programming language to operate directly on a table in the Mountain Animal Hospital database.

The programming language used to access and manipulate the data in a database is called ActiveX Data Objects, or ADO. When you update data by using a form, Access itself uses an entire system of programs, written in ADO, to access and update the database.

ADO is a versatile means of accessing data from various locations. The Mountain Animal Hospital examples you have seen so far show you how you can use Access to update data in a local Access database. That is, all of the tables, queries, forms, and reports are stored in one Access database located either in a folder on your desktop or on a server. But in fact Access, as a client-server development tool, can interact with all kinds of databases. You can develop forms and reports in one Access database that get their data from an entirely separate Access database that may be on your local desktop or on a remote server. You can even link to non-Access databases like Oracle and SQL Server just as easily as linking to an Access database.

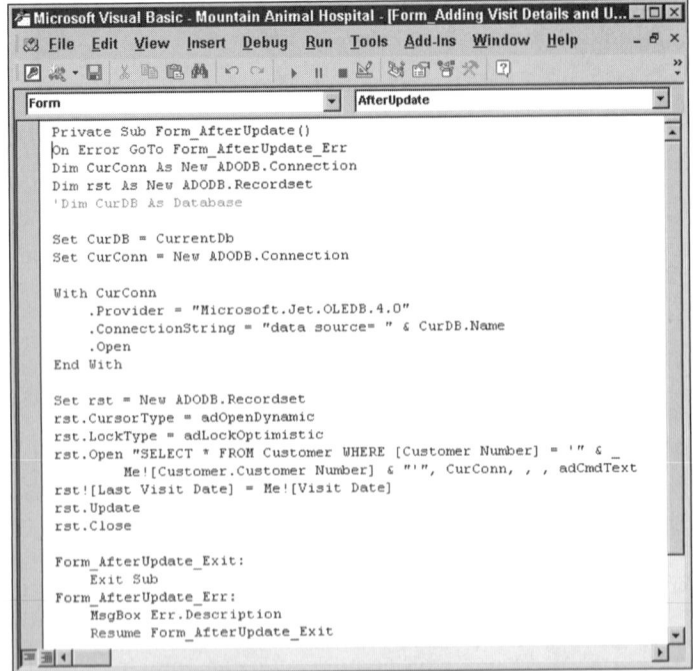

```
Microsoft Visual Basic - Mountain Animal Hospital - [Form_Adding Visit Details and U...  _ □ X
 File   Edit   View   Insert   Debug   Run   Tools   Add-Ins   Window   Help        _ 8 X

Form                          ▼   AfterUpdate                                        ▼

Private Sub Form_AfterUpdate()
On Error GoTo Form_AfterUpdate_Err
Dim CurConn As New ADODB.Connection
Dim rst As New ADODB.Recordset
'Dim CurDB As Database

Set CurDB = CurrentDb
Set CurConn = New ADODB.Connection

With CurConn
    .Provider = "Microsoft.Jet.OLEDB.4.0"
    .ConnectionString = "data source= " & CurDB.Name
    .Open
End With

Set rst = New ADODB.Recordset
rst.CursorType = adOpenDynamic
rst.LockType = adLockOptimistic
rst.Open "SELECT * FROM Customer WHERE [Customer Number] = '" & _
         Me![Customer.Customer Number] & "'", CurConn, , , adCmdText
rst![Last Visit Date] = Me![Visit Date]
rst.Update
rst.Close

Form_AfterUpdate_Exit:
    Exit Sub
Form_AfterUpdate_Err:
    MsgBox Err.Description
    Resume Form_AfterUpdate_Exit
```

Figure 31-36: Using ADO to update a table

As a data access interface, ADO allows you to write programs to manipulate data in local or remote databases. Using ADO, you can perform database functions including querying, updating, data-type conversion, indexing, locking, validation, and transaction management.

Earlier versions of Access included the Data Access Objects, or DAO, data access interface. Improvements in data access technology have taken Access to new levels as a client-server development tool. ADO, a refinement of DAO, represents these improvements and provides a simpler, more powerful array of data access tools. Figure 31-37 shows the same Form_AfterUpdate procedure using DAO code.

Caution

Visual Basic currently supports DAO. However, Microsoft does not plan to provide any future DAO enhancements. All new features will be incorporated only into ADO. You should use ADO for any new development projects.

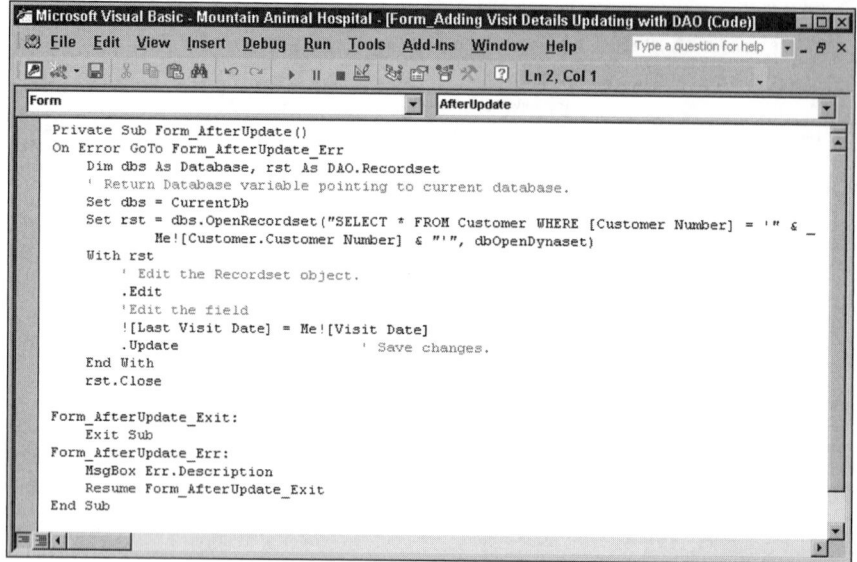

Figure 31-37: Using DAO to update a table

As you can see in the Form_AfterUpdate procedures, you can combine Visual Basic code with methods and functions from ADO and DAO.

Writing an ADO procedure

To use ADO functions and methods, you first declare ADO variables, using the Dim and Set statements. The Dim statements in this example declare ADO variables for the name of the connection (CurConn) and the recordset that the procedure wants to access (rst). A connection is a communication line into the database. A recordset is simply a set of records from a database table or the set of records that result from running a query. The Set statement assigns a value to an ADO variable. The variable CurDB is assigned to the current database — Mountain Animal Hospital, in this example. You use CurrentDb to refer to the currently active database. You use the Open method to establish a link to a database or recordset.

When you use data access objects, you interact with data almost entirely by using Recordset objects. Recordset objects are composed of rows and columns, just like database tables.

Before you can open a connection, you need to define its properties. The Provider and ConnectionString properties describe what kind of database to connect to and the name of the database.

Tip   With DAO, the Provider property was unnecessary. DAO was designed for Access or Jet databases. Since ADO is a generic interface, you must specify the Provider name. For Access 2002 or Jet 4.0 databases, the Provider name is Microsoft. Jet.OLEDB.4.0.

After you have set the connection properties, you can open the connection. The Open method establishes the connection. When the Open method executes, it inherits the properties that have already been set for the connection. You can make a recordset updatable by setting its properties prior to executing the Open method. The CursorType and LockType properties determine how ADO can access and modify the recordset.

Table 31-6 describes the recordset properties you can set.

	Table 31-6 Recordset Properties		
ADO Cursor Type	**ADO Lock Type**	**DAO Type**	**Description**
adOpenForwardOnly	adLockReadOnly	DbOpenSnapshot with dbForwardOnly option	You can only scroll forward through records. This improves performance in situations where you do not need to update, as in finding records and printing reports.
adOpenKeyset	adLockOptimistic	dbOpenDynaset	You can't see records that other users add, although records that other users delete are inaccessible from your recordset. Data changes by other users are automatically applied to the recordset.
adOpenStatic	adLockReadOnly	dbOpenSnapshot	A static copy of a set of records that you can use to find data or generate reports. Additions, changes, or deletions by other users are not visible.

Writing a DAO procedure

The Dim statements in the DAO example declare DAO variables for the name of the database (dbs) and the recordset that the procedure wants to access (rst). The Set statement assigns a value to a DAO variable. The variable dbs is assigned to the current database—Mountain Animal Hospital, in this example. You use the OpenRecordset function to retrieve data from a table or query.

Tip
DAO and ADO share some data types. Since both ADO and DAO have a Recordset type, you must precede the variable name with the appropriate class. When you are referring to a DAO recordset, you use the DAO.Recordset data type. ADO recordsets are referred to as type ADODB.Recordset.

The first argument for the OpenRecordset function is the table name, query name, or an SQL statement. The example in this section uses an SQL statement to retrieve the Customer record for the customer referred to in the Visit Information form.

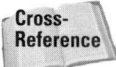

Cross-Reference
To learn about writing SQL statements to retrieve data from a table, see Chapter 26.

You can choose the type of Recordset object that you want to create by using the second argument of the OpenRecordset method. If you don't specify a type, the Microsoft Jet database engine attempts to create a table-type Recordset. The table recordset type usually is the fastest of the three types, because you are opening the table directly and don't require the overhead of filtering records. When the source for the Recordset is a query or SQL statement, as in the example, you cannot use the Table type. The Dynaset type makes the most efficient use of memory, because it loads only the unique key values from the table.

When the Recordset has been opened, you can begin working with the values in its rows and columns. The statements between the With and End With commands apply to the rst object — the Recordset of data from the Customer table.

Before you can modify any of the data in a Recordset, you need to tell Jet ahead of time, using the DAO command Edit. The Edit command copies the current record to a buffer so you can change any of the fields in the record.

Note
With ADO, the Recordset opens in Edit mode automatically. In DAO, you must explicitly issue the Edit method for each record to edit.

Before you enter the Edit command, however, you need to make sure you are in the record you want to edit. When a Recordset opens, the current record is the first record. Because the SQL statement in the example in this section is based on the table's unique key, you know that the first record in the Recordset is the only record.

To update a field in the current record of the Recordset, you simply assign a new value to the name of the field. In this example, you assign the value of the Visit Date field on the Visit Information form to the Last Visit Date field in the Recordset.

After you make the desired changes in the record, use DAO's Update method to save your changes. The Update method copies the data from the buffer to the Recordset, overwriting the original record.

Caution The method of updating is one of the biggest differences between DAO and ADO. In ADO, changes are automatically saved when you move to another record or close the recordset. In DAO, If you edit a record and then perform any operation that moves to another record without first using Update, you lose your changes without warning. In addition, if you close a recordset or end the procedure that declares the recordset or the parent Database object, your edited record is discarded without warning.

To cancel pending changes to a recordset in either ADO or DAO, use the CancelUpdate method. In ADO, you must issue the CancelUpdate method before moving to another record.

The Close statement at the end of the Form_AfterUpdate procedure closes the Recordset. Closing recordsets when you finish using them is good practice.

Updating a total field for a record

In the Pet Treatment Details example, the form's Total field contains the sum of all of the prices of the treatments and medications the pet received for that specific visit. The Total field could be designed as a calculated field that simply grabs the total from the subform's footer. For example, the calculated field's control source could be

```
=[ Data for Subform Example].Form![Total Sum]
```

The Total Sum field in this example is also a calculated field that contains the control source:

```
=Sum([Medication Price]+[Treatment Price])
```

The Total Sum field simply totals up all of the medication and treatment prices displayed in the subform for that visit.

Although using a calculated field to tabulate the visit total is an efficient design method for this example, this calculated value is not stored in the table itself. Any other form or any report that also needs to include the total visit amount must rerun the calculation. Performing the calculation over and over again can be costly in terms of performance. For forms and reports where updates to the visit detail information are not required, such as a Customer Invoice, it would be faster and easier if the visit total was available instantaneously.

You can make a total field available instantly by storing the value in a field in the table. A single form in the application takes care of tabulating the total and updating the value in the table. After the total has been saved in the table, any other form or report can display it simply by including the field in the form's Recordsource.

 **Caution**   In order to take full advantage of the efficiency of storing the calculated total, the form that includes the total amount field must not provide the ability to update the underlying information included in the calculated total. For the Pet Visit Invoice, for example, the invoice might display information about the visit such as Pet Name, Visit Date, or even the detail items like treatment and medication codes. However, if the user has the ability to update any of this information, you must also include the ability to recalculate the total field.

The form Adding Visit Details Updating Total Amount illustrates the features required to store a total field in the form's underlying table. The field Total Amount shows the total for the detail information included in the form's subform. The control source for the Total Amount field, shown in Figure 31-38, is set to the Total Amount field in the Visits table.

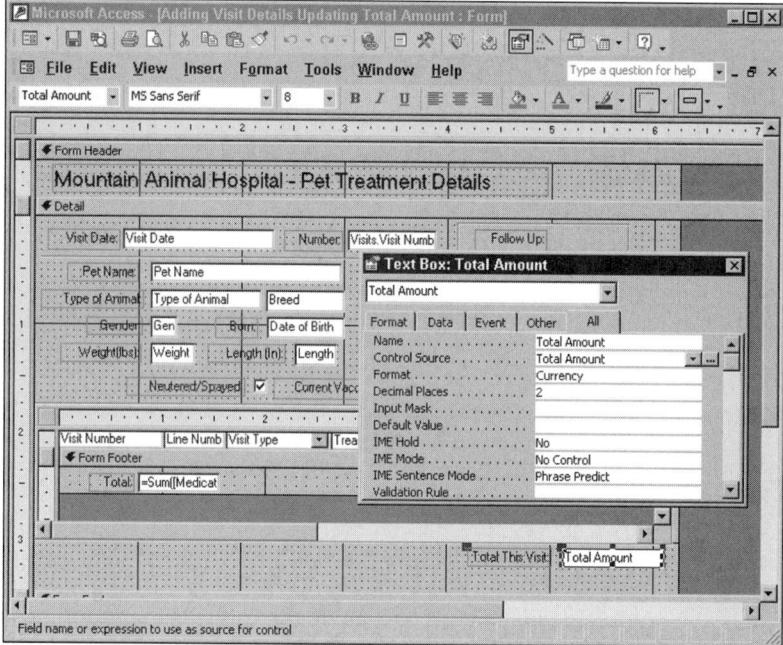

Figure 31-38: Displaying a stored total on a form

The Total Amount field must be recalculated whenever any of the following events occur in the form:

✦ Moving from one visit record to another

✦ Adding a new detail record (treatment or medication)

✦ Deleting a detail record

✦ Updating the price of a treatment or medication

To recalculate the total when any of these events occur, you must create Visual Basic procedures. For tasks like this, you will find ADO and DAO indispensable. The code to recalculate the Total Amount field can be accomplished in a single procedure. Figure 31-39 shows the CalculateTotal procedure.

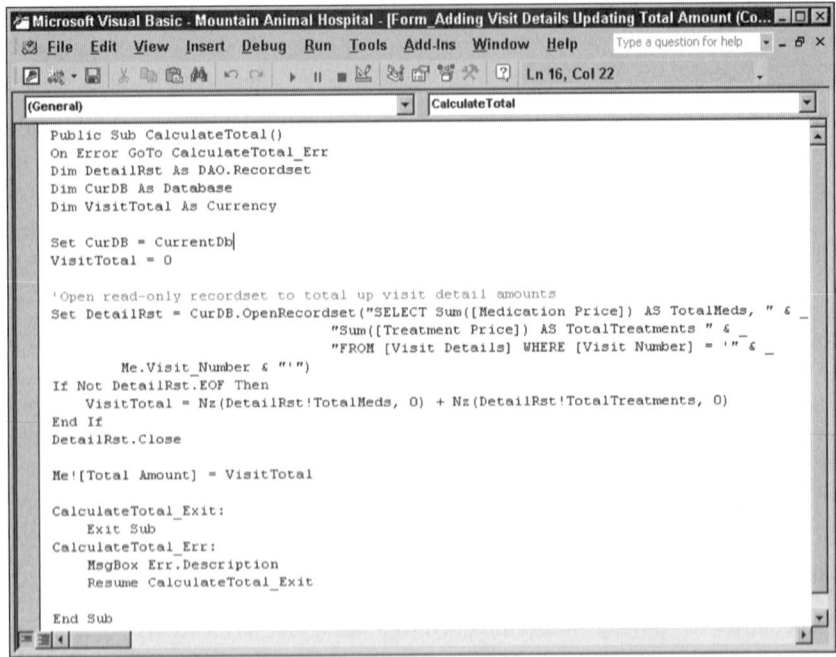

```
Public Sub CalculateTotal()
On Error GoTo CalculateTotal_Err
Dim DetailRst As DAO.Recordset
Dim CurDB As Database
Dim VisitTotal As Currency

Set CurDB = CurrentDb
VisitTotal = 0

'Open read-only recordset to total up visit detail amounts
Set DetailRst = CurDB.OpenRecordset("SELECT Sum([Medication Price]) AS TotalMeds, " & _
                           "Sum([Treatment Price]) AS TotalTreatments " & _
                           "FROM [Visit Details] WHERE [Visit Number] = '" & _
          Me.Visit_Number & "'")
If Not DetailRst.EOF Then
    VisitTotal = Nz(DetailRst!TotalMeds, 0) + Nz(DetailRst!TotalTreatments, 0)
End If
DetailRst.Close

Me![Total Amount] = VisitTotal

CalculateTotal_Exit:
    Exit Sub
CalculateTotal_Err:
    MsgBox Err.Description
    Resume CalculateTotal_Exit

End Sub
```

Figure 31-39: Using DAO to recalculate a total field

The CalculateTotal procedure uses DAO to create a recordset that sums up the medication and treatment prices in the Visit Details table for the current visit. The variable VisitTotal is used to temporarily hold the recordset's sum. At the top of the procedure, VisitTotal is initially set to 0. The DAO code checks to see if the recordset returned a record. If the recordset is at the end of the field (EOF), then the recordset did not find any detail records for the current visit — the VisitTotal variable remains set to 0. If the recordset did return a record, then the VisitTotal variable is set to the recordset's TotalMeds field plus the TotalTreatments field. At the end of the procedure, the form's Total Amount field is set to the value of the VisitTotal variable.

Note   Since the form's Total Amount field is bound to the table's Total Amount field, setting the form's value also updates the value in the table.

To recalculate the Total Amount field when moving from visit record to visit record, you use the form's On Current event. The form's On Current event, shown in Figure 31-40, simply calls the CalculateTotal procedure.

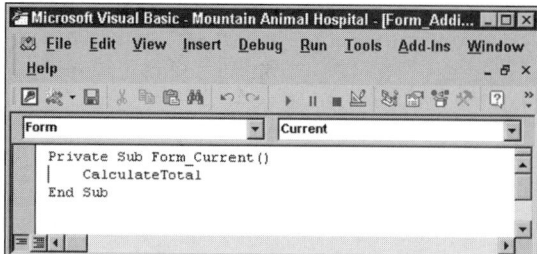

Figure 31-40: Recalculating the total field when moving from record to record

To recalculate the Total Amount when a visit detail record is deleted, you use the After Delete Confirm event in the subform. Add the call to the CalculateTotal procedure in the code window for the After Delete Confirm event the same way it appears for the On Current event.

A single event can handle recalculating the Total Amount when new visit details are added or when visit detail prices are changed. For both of these events, you can use the subform's After Update event. The After Update event occurs when either a new record is entered, or when any value is changed for an existing record. Add the call to the CalculateTotal procedure in the After Update code window the same way it appears for the On Current and After Delete Confirm event procedures.

Adding a new record

You can use ADO and DAO to add a record to a table just as easily as you can update a record. To add a new record to a table, you use the AddNew method. Listing 31-2 shows the ADO procedure for adding a new customer to the Customer table.

Listing 31-2: **Adding a new record to a table using ADO**

```
   Private Sub New_Customer_Click()
On Error GoTo New_Customer_Click_Err
Dim CurConn As New ADODB.Connection
Dim rst As New ADODB.Recordset
Dim curdb As Database

Set curdb = CurrentDb
Set CurConn = New ADODB.Connection

With CurConn
    .Provider = "Microsoft.Jet.OLEDB.4.0"
    .ConnectionString = "data source= " & curdb.Name
    .Open
End With

Set rst = New ADODB.Recordset
```

```
rst.CursorType = adOpenDynamic
rst.LockType = adLockOptimistic
rst.Open "Customer", CurConn, , , adCmdTable
    With rst
        'Add new record to end of Recordset object
        .AddNew
        ![Customer Number] = "CT-001"
        ![Customer Name] = "Charles Townshend"   'Add data
        .Update                               'Save changes
    End With
rst.Close
New_Customer_Click_Exit:
    Exit Sub
New_Customer_Click_Err:
    MsgBox Err.Description
    Resume New_Customer_Click_Err
End Sub
```

Listing 31-3 shows the DAO procedure for adding a new customer to the Customer table.

Listing 31-3: **Adding a new record to a table using DAO**

```
Private Sub New_Customer_Click()
On Error GoTo New_Customer_Click_Err
Dim dbs As Database, rst As DAO.Recordset
'Return Database variable pointing to current database
Set dbs = CurrentDb
Set rst = dbs.OpenRecordset("Customer", dbOpenDynaset)
With rst
    'Add new record to end of Recordset object
    .AddNew
    ![Customer Number] = "CT-001"
    ![Customer Name] = "Charles Townshend"  'Add data
    .Update                               'Save changes
End With
rst.Close
New_Customer_Click_Exit:
    Exit Sub
New_Customer_Click_Err:
    MsgBox Err.Description
    Resume New_Customer_Click_Exit
End Sub
```

As you see in these two examples, using the AddNew method is very similar to using the Edit method. The AddNew method creates a buffer for a new record. After entering the AddNew command, you simply assign values to the fields. When you enter the Update command, the new record buffer is added to the end of the Recordset.

Deleting a record

To remove a record from a table, you use the ADO or DAO method Delete. Listing 31-4 shows the ADO procedure for deleting a record from the Customer table.

Listing 31-5 shows the DAO procedure for deleting a record from the Customer table.

Notice that for both ADO and DAO you need to code only one statement to delete a record. You do not precede the Delete method with Edit or follow it with Update. As soon as the Delete method executes, the record is removed from the Recordset permanently.

Listing 31-4: Deleting a record from a table using ADO

```
Private Sub Delete_Customer_Click()
On Error GoTo Delete_Customer_Click_Err
Dim CurConn As New ADODB.Connection
Dim rst As New ADODB.Recordset
Dim CurDB As Database

Set CurDB = CurrentDb
Set CurConn = New ADODB.Connection

With CurConn
    .Provider = "Microsoft.Jet.OLEDB.4.0"
    .ConnectionString = "data source=" & CurDB.Name
    .Open
End With

Set rst = New ADODB.Recordset
rst.CursorType = adOpenDynamic
rst.LockType = adLockOptimistic
rst.Open "SELECT * FROM Customer WHERE [Customer Number] = '" &
_
        Me![Customer Number] & "'", CurConn, , , adCmdText

With rst
    'Delete the record
    .Delete
End With
rst.Close
Delete_Customer_Click_Exit:
    Exit Sub
Delete_Customer_Click_Err:
    MsgBox Err.Description
    Resume Delete_Customer_Click_Exit
End Sub
```

Listing 31-5: **Deleting a record from a table using ADO**

```
Private Sub Delete_Customer_Click()
On Error GoTo Delete_Customer_Click_Err
Dim dbs As DAO.Database, rst As DAO.Recordset
'Return Database variable pointing to current database
Set dbs = CurrentDb
Set rst = dbs.OpenRecordset("SELECT * FROM Customer WHERE " & _
                            "[Customer Number] = '" &
Me![Customer Number] & "'", _
                                dbOpenDynaset)

With rst
    'Delete the record
    .Delete
End With
rst.Close
Delete_Customer_Click_Exit:
    Exit Sub
Delete_Customer_Click_Err:
    MsgBox Err.Description
    Resume Delete_Customer_Click_Exit
End Sub
```

Using ADO to manipulate data in your database can be very powerful. Listing 31-6 shows a more complex example of the capabilities of ADO. The Clone_Customer_ Click procedure creates a new record from an existing record.

This procedure uses a record from the Customer table as a template to create a new Customer record. The procedure first opens a recordset containing the template customer's information. The template recordset is copied to another new recordset by using the clone method.

The clone method creates an exact copy of the original recordset. Any changes made to one recordset are automatically applied to the other. In other words, if you change the information for the State field in the cloned recordset for Customer Number "AN-001," the State information is automatically changed for Customer Number "AN-001" in the original recordset.

Next, the procedure adds a new record to the cloned recordset. The Customer Number, Customer Name, and Phone Number fields are set to the information for the new customer. The City, State, and Zip Code fields are set to the information for the original template customer.

The Update method saves the information for the new customer. Saving the new customer record in the cloned recordset automatically adds the new record to the original recordset.

Listing 31-6: **Cloning a record**

```
Private Sub Clone_Customer_Click()
On Error GoTo Clone_Customer_Click_Err
Dim CurConn As New ADODB.Connection
Dim rst As New ADODB.Recordset, rstCln As New ADODB.Recordset
Dim CurDB As Database

Set CurDB = CurrentDb
Set CurConn = New ADODB.Connection

With CurConn
    .Provider = "Microsoft.Jet.OLEDB.4.0"
    .ConnectionString = "data source= " & CurDB.Name
    .Open
End With

Set rst = New ADODB.Recordset
rst.CursorType = adOpenKeyset
rst.LockType = adLockOptimistic
rst.Open "SELECT * FROM Customer WHERE [Customer Number] = '" &
_
        Me![Customer Number] & "'", CurConn, , , adCmdText

Set rstCln = rst.Clone

With rstCln
    'Create a new record with new Customer Number, Customer
Name, Phone Number
    '   but copy City, State, Zip from previous recordset
    .AddNew
    ![Customer Number] = "CT-001"
    ![Customer Name] = "Charles Townshend"
    ![Phone Number] = "(860)555-1222"
    ![City] = rst![City]
    ![State] = rst![State]
    ![Zip Code] = rst![Zip Code]
    .Update
End With
rstCln.Close
rst.Close
Clone_Customer_Click_Exit:
    Exit Sub
Clone_Customer_Click_Err:
    MsgBox Err.Description
    Resume Clone_Customer_Click_Exit
End Sub
```

✦   ✦   ✦

Creating Switchboards, Command Bars, Menus, Toolbars, and Dialog Boxes

✦   ✦   ✦   ✦

In This Chapter

Creating a switchboard by using a form and command buttons

Using the Command Button Wizard

Using the Picture Builder

Adding a custom command bar to a form

Creating custom menu bars

Creating custom toolbars

Creating shortcut menus

Creating control tips

Creating a Print dialog box

Using the Access 2002 Tab control

✦   ✦   ✦   ✦

In prior chapters, you learn how to create individual Access objects, such as tables, queries, forms, reports, and macros. You work with each object interactively in Access, selecting the Database window and using the assorted objects.

In this chapter, you tie these objects together into a single database application — without having to write or know how to use a complex database program. Rather, you automate the application through the use of switchboards, dialog boxes, and menus. These objects make your system easier to use, and they hide the Access interface from the final user.

Switchboards and Command Buttons

A *switchboard* is fundamentally a form. The switchboard form is a customized application menu that contains user-defined command buttons. With these command buttons, you can run macros that automatically select actions, such as opening forms or printing reports.

Using a switchboard button, you can replace many interactive user steps with a single button selection (or *click*). For example, if you want to interactively open the Add a Customer and Pets form, you must perform three actions: Switch to the

Database window, select the Forms tab, and open the form. If you use a switchboard button to perform the same task, you simply click the button. Figure 32-1 shows the switchboard window with several buttons. Each command button triggers a macro that performs a series of steps, such as opening the Customer form or running the Hospital Report.

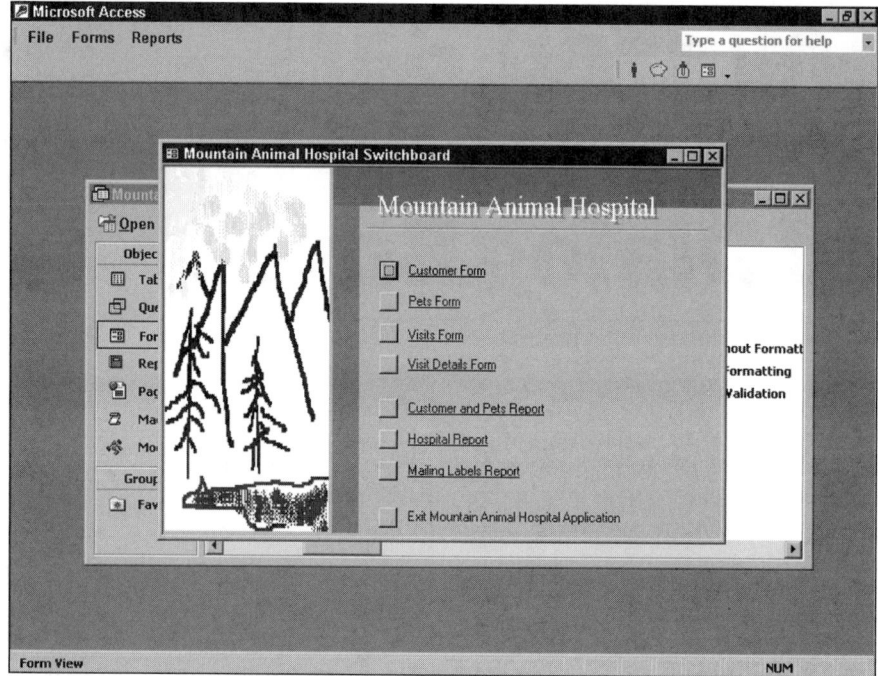

Figure 32-1: A switchboard with several command buttons for forms and reports

By using a switchboard and other objects that we discuss in this chapter, you can tie your database objects together in a single database application. The application has a user interface that you create rather than the Access interactive interface. A primary component of that user-defined interface is the switchboard that you create.

Using a switchboard

A switchboard's primary use is as an application interface menu. The switchboard in Figure 32-1 is the application interface menu for the Mountain Animal Hospital database. As the figure shows, the switchboard contains several command buttons. When the user clicks on any switchboard button, a macro is triggered that performs some action or a series of actions.

Creating the basic form for a switchboard

You create a switchboard by adding command buttons to an existing Access form. The form in Figure 32-1 is a standard Access 2002 display form. Forms can have many uses, including data entry, data display, and switchboards.

Because switchboard forms are used as application menus, they tend to use a limited number of form controls. Typically, you find command buttons, labels, object frames (OLE objects, such as pictures), lines, and rectangles. Normally, switchboards lack the other types of form controls, such as text boxes (bound to fields), list and combo boxes, graphs, subforms, and page breaks.

To create a basic switchboard form, you place labels like titles and group headings on the form. In addition to the labels, you may also want to place lines, rectangles, and pictures on the form to make it aesthetically appealing. You create the basic switchboard form by using the techniques that you learn in the chapters that cover form objects.

Consider, for example, the switchboard in Figure 32-1. Apart from the command buttons, this is a typical Access application form. Its major components are a title, some other text controls, various colored rectangles, a line, and a picture (image control).

Working with command buttons

Command buttons are the type of form control that you use to run macros or VBA routines. Command buttons are the simplest type of form controls, having the single purpose of executing a macro or VBA procedure that can exist behind a form or in a module procedure.

In this example, you create command buttons that run macros. As you learn in previous chapters, macros perform a multitude of tasks in Access, including

- ✦ Opening and displaying other forms
- ✦ Opening a pop-up form or dialog box to collect additional information
- ✦ Opening and printing reports
- ✦ Activating a search or displaying a filter
- ✦ Exiting Access

On the CD-ROM The Mountain Animal Hospital database on your CD-ROM contains a form named *Mountain Switchboard-No Buttons*. You can use that as a starting point to create your switchboard.

Figure 32-2 shows a command button named *Command01* and its property sheet. This property sheet contains the event properties available for a command button.

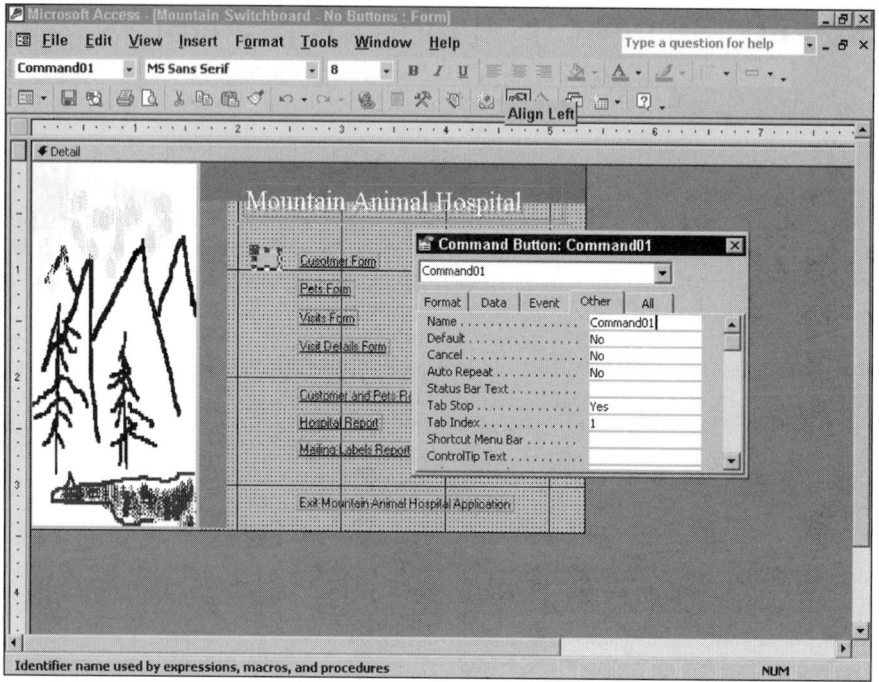

Figure 32-2: A single-button switchboard form with its open property sheet

Each event property can trigger a macro. For example, to trigger a macro named *OpenCust* when the user clicks on the button, place the OpenCust macro in the parameter box for the On Click property. The keyword *On* identifies an event property. The property identifies the user event that must occur to trigger an action.

On Click and On Dbl Click are mutually compatible. If you activate both the On Click property (giving it a macro name) and the On Dbl Click property, Access follows this order of precedence for the mouse clicking and trapping:

1. On Click (single click)
2. On Dbl Click (double-click)
3. On Click (single click)

In other words, Access processes an On Click first and then an On Dbl Click and, finally, an On Click again. Access always processes the On Click if it is defined. To prevent the second On Click macro from running, place a CancelEvent action in the On Dbl Click macro.

In addition, if the macro you call from an On Click opens a dialog box (message box, pop-up form, and so forth), the second click is lost and the On Dbl Click is never reached. If you use On Click and On Dbl Click, the On Click should not open a dialog box if you need to capture the On Dbl Click.

What Is Focus?

To understand the terminology associated with command buttons, you need to know the term *focus*. The two command button properties On Enter and On Exit gain or lose focus. In other words, the focus represents the next item of input from the user. For example, if you tab from one button to another, you lose the focus on the first button as you leave it, and you gain the focus on the second as you enter it. In a form with several command buttons, you can tell which button has focus by the dotted box around the label of the button. Focus does not denote the state of input, such as when you press a button; rather, focus is the object that is currently active and awaiting some user action.

The focus for mouse input always coincides with the button down, or *pointer*, location. Because focus occurs at the moment of clicking a command button, the property On Enter is not triggered. The reason for this is that On Enter occurs just before the focus is gained; that state is not realized when you select a command button by using a mouse. The On Enter state never occurs. Rather, the focus and On Click occur simultaneously, bypassing the On Enter state.

Creating command buttons

A command button's primary purpose is to activate, or run, a macro. Access gives you two ways to create a command button:

✦ Click the Command Button icon in the Form toolbox.

✦ Drag a macro name from the database container to the form.

In this chapter, both these methods are used at least once as you learn to create the eight command buttons that are shown in Figure 32-1 (four buttons to display a form, three to display a report, and one to exit the application). In this first example, you learn to create the first form button using the Command Button Wizard.

When using the Command Button Wizard, in addition to creating a command button, you can also automatically display text or embed a picture on the button. More importantly, you can create VBA modules to perform tasks (even if you don't know a single command in VBA) including

✦ Record Navigation (Next, Previous, First, Last, Find)

✦ Record Operations (Save, Delete, Print, New, Duplicate)

✦ Form Operations (Open, Close, Print, Filter)

✦ Report Operations (Print, Preview, Mail)

✦ Applications (Run Application, Quit, Notepad, Word, Excel)

✦ Miscellaneous (Print Table, Run Query, Run Macro, AutoDialer)

Cross-Reference

In Chapter 33, you learn to create and edit Visual Basic code with the Command Button Wizard.

To create the Customer button using the Command Button Wizard, follow these steps:

1. Open the Mountain Switchboard — No Buttons form in Design mode.
2. Make sure that the Control Wizard icon is toggled on.
3. Click the Command Button icon in the toolbox.
4. Place the mouse pointer on the form in the form design screen in the upper left corner of the light gray rectangle and draw a small rectangle next to the text *Customer Form*.

Note

Command buttons have no control source. If you try to create a button by dragging a field from the Field List, a text box control (not a command button) is created. You must draw the rectangle or drag a macro to create a command button.

The Command Button Wizard displays the dialog box that's shown in Figure 32-3. You can select from several categories of tasks. As you choose each category, the list of actions under the *When button is pressed* header changes. In addition, the sample picture changes as you move from action to action. In Figure 32-3, the specified category is Form Operations and the desired action is Open Form.

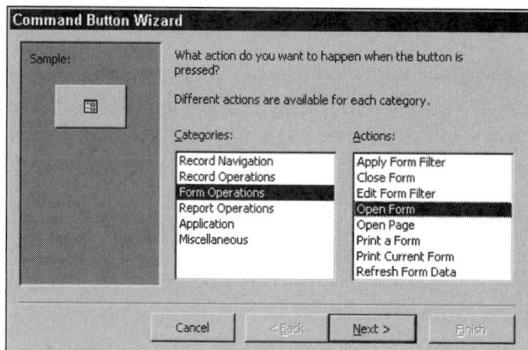

Figure 32-3: The Command Button Wizard's Categories and Actions dialog box

5. Choose the Form Operations category and the Open Form action.
6. Click Next> to move to the next3 screen.

   The Wizard displays a list of the Mountain Animal Hospital database's forms.

7. Select the Customer form and Click Next> to move to the next Wizard screen.

The next screen is a specific dialog box for this button. Because you chose the Open Form action, Access uses built-in logic to ask what you want to do now with this form. As Figure 32-4 shows, Access can automatically write a VBA program behind the button to open the form and show all records; if necessary, it can let you specify fields to search for specific values after you open the form.

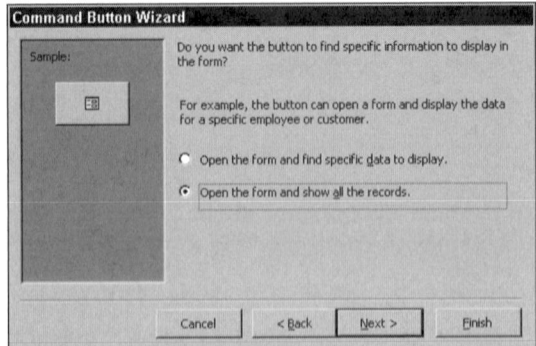

Figure 32-4: The Command Button Wizard open orm with a specific data question

8. Select Open the form and show all the records. Then Click Next> to move on.

The next screen lets you decide what you want to appear on the button. You can display text or a picture on the button. You can resize the button to accommodate any size text. The default is to place a picture on the button. You can choose from the default button for the selected action, or you can click in the Show All Pictures check box to select from over 100 pictures. You also can click on the Browse button to select an icon (.ICO) or bitmap (.BMP) file from your hard drive or CD. For this example, simply display the text *Customer* on the button.

9. Click on the Text option button and erase the Open Form text in the text box.

The sample button displays nothing instead of the picture (see Figure 32-5).

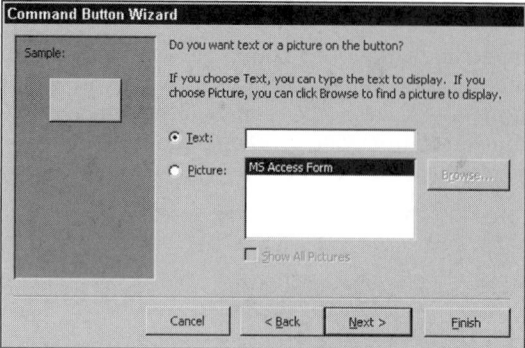

Figure 32-5: Selecting a picture or text for the button

10. Click Next> to move to the final Wizard screen, which lets you enter a name for the button and then display the button on the form.

11. Enter **Customer** as the name of the button and click Finish.

The button appears on the Form Design screen, as shown in Figure 32-6.

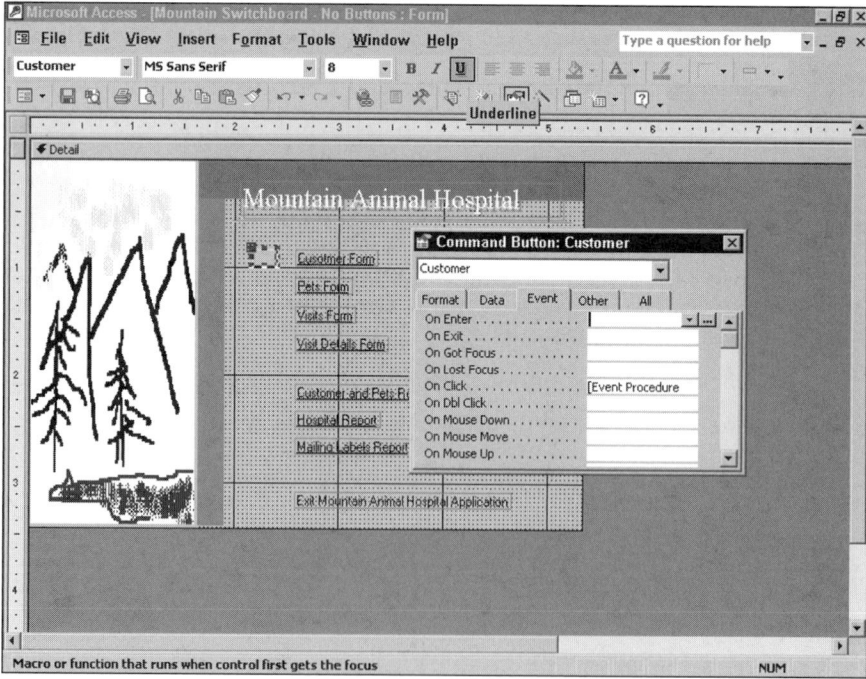

Figure 32-6: Adding a button to the form design

Notice the property sheet displayed in Figure 32-6. The On Click property displays *Event Procedure*, which means that a module is stored *behind* the form. You can see this VBA module library by pressing the Builder button (three dots) next to the [Event Procedure] text. When you click the Customer button, the VBA program runs and the Customer form opens.

 **Note**

A module window appears with the specific VBA program code necessary for opening the Customer form (see Figure 32-7). You don't need to look at this code unless you plan to change the program. This topic is discussed in Chapters 30 and 31.

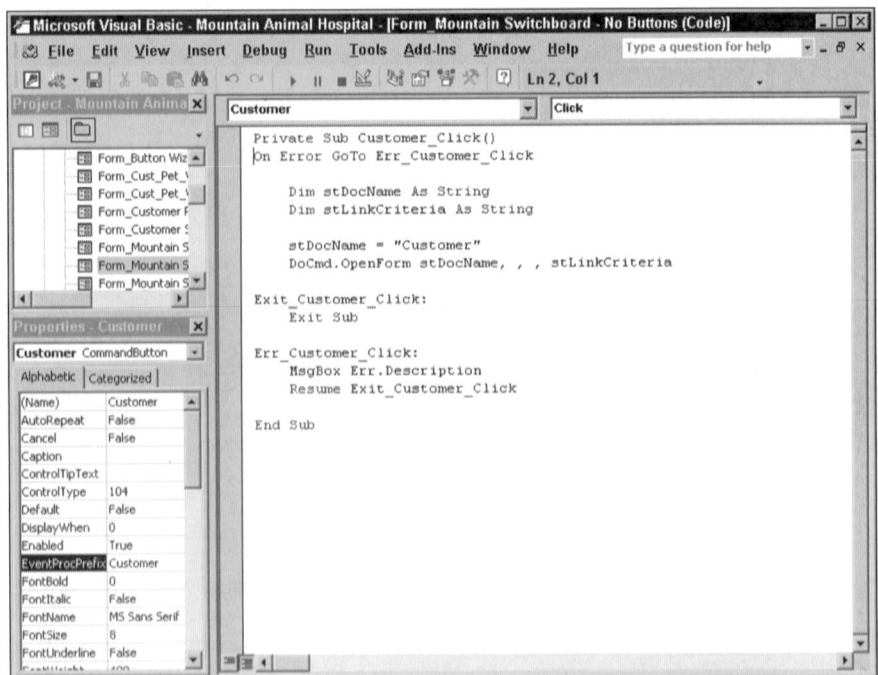

Figure 32-7: The event procedure module for opening the Customer form

You can create a command button and attach a macro very easily — or attach pictures — without using the Wizard. However, if you want to dabble in Visual Basic, the Command Button Wizard is a great place to start.

You may want to create buttons for all the forms and reports. You can use the Command Button Wizard, as shown on the previous page (except for the reports for which you use the Report Operations options). If you are planning on using a macro or want to create an event procedure yourself, click on the first button and choose Edit ✐ Duplicate from the menu bar to duplicate the button. You would then only need to change the text or graphic on each button and change the code or macro behind each button's On Click event.

Note   This only duplicates the button itself, not the code behind the button.

After you duplicate the Customer button for all the other text entries except the last one, your screen should look like the one shown in Figure 32-8.

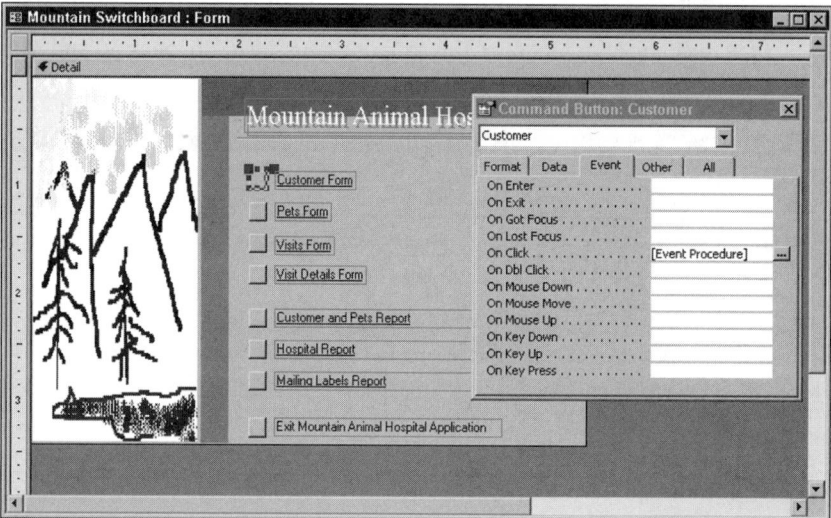

Figure 32-8: All buttons on-screen

Linking a command button to a macro

As soon as you create a command button in the Design window, it becomes active. You can click on it, although it doesn't perform any action unless you created it with the Wizard. Switching to the Form window by clicking on the Form button on the toolbar displays the switchboard. You can use any of the seven buttons that you created in form design mode.

Each time you click on a button, it graphically pushes down, showing that it is selected. Except for the Customer button, however, nothing else occurs; only the button movement happens. By switching back to design mode and clicking on the Design button on the toolbar, you can link a macro to the button.

To link a command button to a macro, enter the macro name into the property cell of one of the command button's event properties. To see the property sheet for a command button, follow these steps:

1. In design mode, click the command button next to the text Pets Form.

2. Click the Properties button on the toolbar or select View ➪ Properties.

A property sheet similar to the one in Figure 32-8 should be visible on your screen. Notice that the event properties begin with the word *On* in the property sheet.

The property most commonly used to link a command button to a macro is On Click. This property runs a macro whenever a user clicks the button. When the button is selected, the On Click property becomes True and the specified macro runs. To associate the Pets macro in the Mountain Switchboard macro group, follow these steps:

1. Click the Pets command button.

2. Click the On Click property cell in the property sheet for the command buttons.

3. Select Mountain Switchboard.Pets from the list of macros in the cell and press Enter.

Make sure that both the macro group name and then the macro name separated by a period display in the On Click property.

Note   When you enter a macro name, the macro doesn't have to exist. You can enter the name of a macro that you want to create later. In this way, you can create the switchboard first and the macros later. If the macro name that you enter in the On Click cell doesn't exist when you open the form and click the button, Access displays an error message.

By using these methods, you can now complete the properties for seven of the form's buttons, assigning a macro for each button on the basis of the On Click property. Table 32-1 shows each button name and the macro that it calls.

Table 32-1
The Seven Form and Report Buttons and Their Macro Names

In Rectangle	Button Function	Macro for On Click
Form	Customer	Event Property (created by Button Wizard)
Form	Pets	Mountain Switchboard.Pets
Form	Visits	Mountain Switchboard.Visits
Form	Visit Details	Mountain Switchboard.Visit Details
Report	Customer and Pets	Mountain Switchboard.Customer and Pets
Report	Hospital Report	Mountain Switchboard.Hospital Report
Report	Customer Labels	Mountain Switchboard.Customer Labels

The macros for the Mountain Switchboard

In this example, each command button opens either a form or a report by using the OpenForm or OpenReport macro actions. The Exit button closes the form with the Quit macro action.

You can create each macro and its actions by following these general steps:

1. Enter a macro name in the Macro Name column.

2. Enter a macro action in the Action column (such as OpenForm, OpenReport, or Close) or select the macro action from the drop-down list box.

3. Enter a macro argument (name of the form or report) for each action.

4. Optionally, enter a remark (as a reminder) in the Comment Column.

Another way to add a macro action and argument is to drag the form or report from the Database window to the macro's Action column. Access automatically adds the correct action in the Action column, which is OpenForm or OpenReport. Access also adds the correct argument in the Name cell of the arguments.

If you want to create the group macro for this chapter, follow Table 32-2. This table shows each macro name, the action for each macro, and the form or report name. (These are shown in Figure 32-9.) The Mountain Switchboard macro should already exist in the Macro Object list of the Database window.

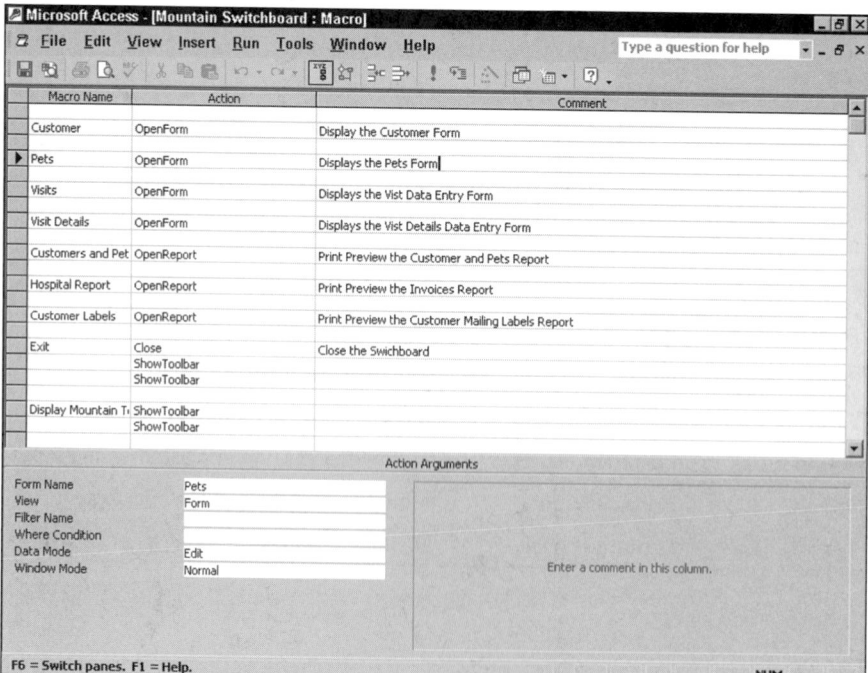

Figure 32-9: The seven macros used for Mountain Switchboard

Table 32-2
Macros Used in the Group Macro

Macro Name	Action	Argument Name (Form, Report, Object)
Customer	OpenForm	Customer
Pets	OpenForm	Pets
Visits	OpenForm	Adding General Pet Visit Info
Visit Details	OpenForm	Adding Visit Details
Customer and Pets	OpenReport	Pets and Owners
Hospital Report	OpenReport	Invoices
Customer Label	OpenReport	Customer By State (three snaking columns)
Exit	Close	Mountain Switchboard

Table 32-2 shows that the Close action closes the Mountain Switchboard form. These macros work with the actual Mountain Switchboard form. You learn to create the Exit command button next.

Dragging a macro to the form to create a button

The Mountain Switchboard form already has an Exit command button. You may want to add a more graphical exit button however. Earlier in this chapter, you learn a way to add a command button in the Form Design window. Another way that you can create a command button is to drag-and-drop a macro name from the macro Database window to a position on the switchboard.

For example, to create an Exit command button for the Mountain Switchboard form by using the drag-and-drop method, follow these steps:

1. Enter the design mode for the Mountain Switchboard form — No Buttons.

2. Delete the current command button next to the text *Exit Mountain Animal Hospital Application* and the text label as well.

3. Activate the Database window by pressing F11 or Alt+F1.

4. In the Database window, click the Macro object button to display all macros.

5. Highlight Mountain Switchboard on the Macro Object list.

6. Click on the Mountain Switchboard macro; drag-and-drop it onto the form below the rectangles.

7. Click on the button name and change it to Exit.

8. Click in the cell of the On Click property of the Exit button.

9. Move to the end of the macro group name and type **.Exit**.

Your screen should now look similar to the screen shown in Figure 32-10. Notice that when you add the macro to the form using the drag-and-drop method, Access automatically creates a command button, names it the same as the macro, and places the macro name (in this case, a group name) in the On Click property of the button.

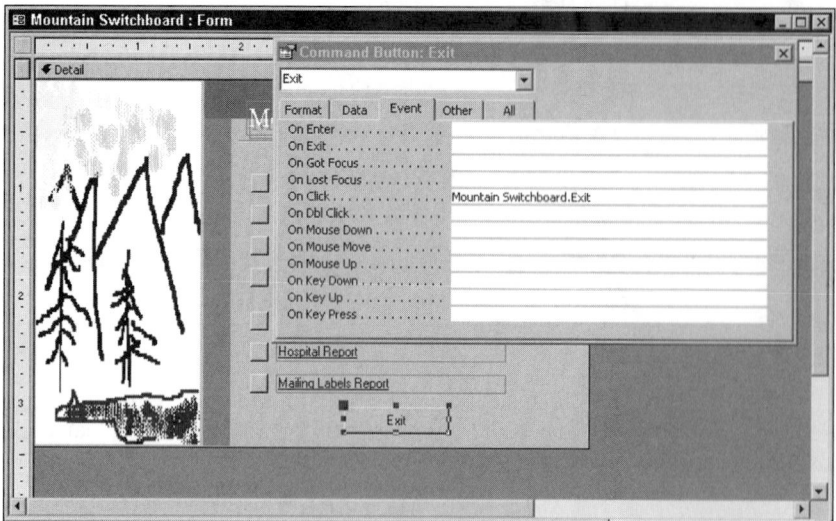

Figure 32-10: The new button that you created by dragging and dropping a macro onto the form

When you add the macro name to the On Click property, you don't have to add the macro group name. Rather, you move to the end and place a period after the group name, and then the macro name. Access automatically brings the group name into the On Click property for you.

Note   If you drag-and-drop a macro that is not a group macro, Access correctly places the macro name in the On Click property and names the button the same as the macro.

Note   If you drag a macro group, as you did in this example, and do not add a macro name to the On Click property, Access runs the first macro in the macro group.

Adding a picture to a command button

The first seven command buttons that you create contain nothing in the Caption property of the button. The last button currently contains the Mountain text in the Caption property of the command button. However, you can have any button display a picture instead. For example, the CD-ROM in the back of the book contains a file named *EXIT.BMP* (as well as a sampler of pictures for command buttons), which is a bitmap of an exit sign. You can have the Exit command button show the picture EXIT.BMP rather than the word *Exit*.

To change a command button to a picture button, use one of these methods:

✦ Type the name of the bitmap (.BMP) containing the picture into the Picture property of the button.

✦ Use the Picture Builder to select from an icon list that comes with Access.

✦ Specify the name of an icon or bitmap file.

To change the Exit command button to the picture button EXIT.BMP, follow these steps:

1. In the Mountain Switchboard form, click on the Exit command button.

2. Display the Property window.

3. Select the Picture property for the Exit button.

4. Click the Builder button (three dots on a little button).

The Picture Builder dialog box appears. No picture appears because the button that you are modifying has none. Because you are adding a picture for an Exit button, you may want to see if Access contains an Exit button. You can scroll down the list of Available Pictures, as shown in Figure 32-11. Access has an Exit picture, but it may not be what you want. You can select any bitmap or icon file on your disk.

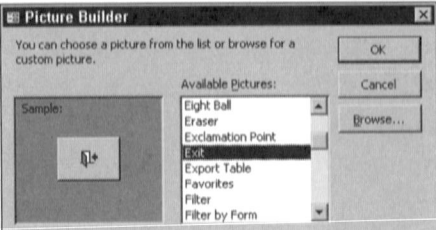

Figure 32-11: The Picture Builder

5. Click the Browse button.

The Select Bitmap dialog box shows a standard Windows directory list. Select the directory that contains your file.

6. Select the directory that contains the EXIT.BMP file, select the file, and click Open (see Figure 32-12). The bitmap appears in the sample area. Although it doesn't fit in the sample, it should fit on the button when it is displayed.

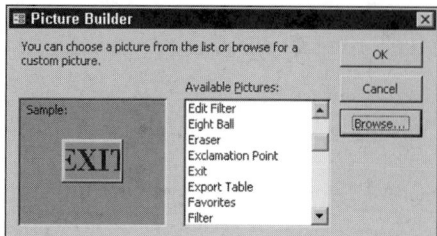

Figure 32-12: Viewing a sample bitmap
in Picture Builder

7. Click OK to accept the bitmap.

Access places the path of the bitmap in the Picture property. After you save
the application, however, the bitmap is no longer required to exist in the path
because it is embedded in the database.

8. Resize the button so that the picture shows only the word *Exit*.

Your form should look like the one shown in Figure 32-13. Notice that Access
added the path and filename of the bitmap to the Picture cell for the Exit button.

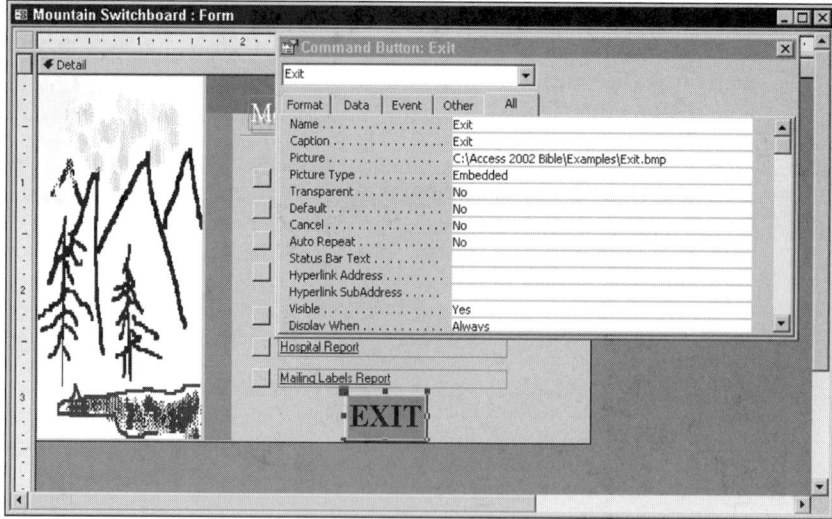

Figure 32-13: The final form with a Picture button added

You also can type the filename directly into the Picture property. If Access can't find the picture file, it displays a dialog box stating that it can't find your file. If you know the drive and directory where the file is located, enter them in the Picture cell with the filename (for example, C:\Access 2002 Bible\Examples\EXIT.BMP).

Database Creations, Inc., offers two libraries of over 1,500 button-size pictures, each like the 100 that come with the Access 2000 Picture Builder. If you want to purchase the Picture Builder Add-On Picture Pack, see the ad at the back of the book.

This action completes the Mountain Switchboard. Save your switchboard. Your next task is to customize the menu bar to correspond to the buttons on the switchboard so you can make your choices from the menu or the buttons.

Creating Custom Menu Bars, Toolbars, and Shortcut Menus

Not only can you create switchboards with Access, you can also create a custom drop-down menu bar that adds functionality to your system. You can add commands to this menu that are appropriate for your application. These commands may be the actions specified in your switchboard command buttons. When you create a custom drop-down menu bar, the new bar replaces the Access menu bar.

Tip   Only a form references the menu bar; you can create a single menu bar and use it for several forms.

Figure 32-14 shows the Mountain Switchboard with a custom drop-down menu bar. Each choice on the bar menu (File, Forms, and Reports) has a drop-down menu.

You can create custom menus in Access 2002 in two ways:

✦ Use the Access 2002 Command Bar Object.

✦ Use macros (this was the only way to create menus in Access 2.0 and Access 95).

Tip   If you previously created menus in Access 2.0 or Access 95, you can convert them to the new menu bar object by selecting the macro to be converted and then by choosing Tools ➪ Macro ➪ Create Menu from Macro. You also can use the other two options, Create Toolbar from Macro and Create Shortcut Menu from Macro, to create these objects.

If you have menus that you previously created in Access 97 or Access 2000, you don't need to convert them. Access 97 or 2000 menus can be used "as is" in Access 2002.

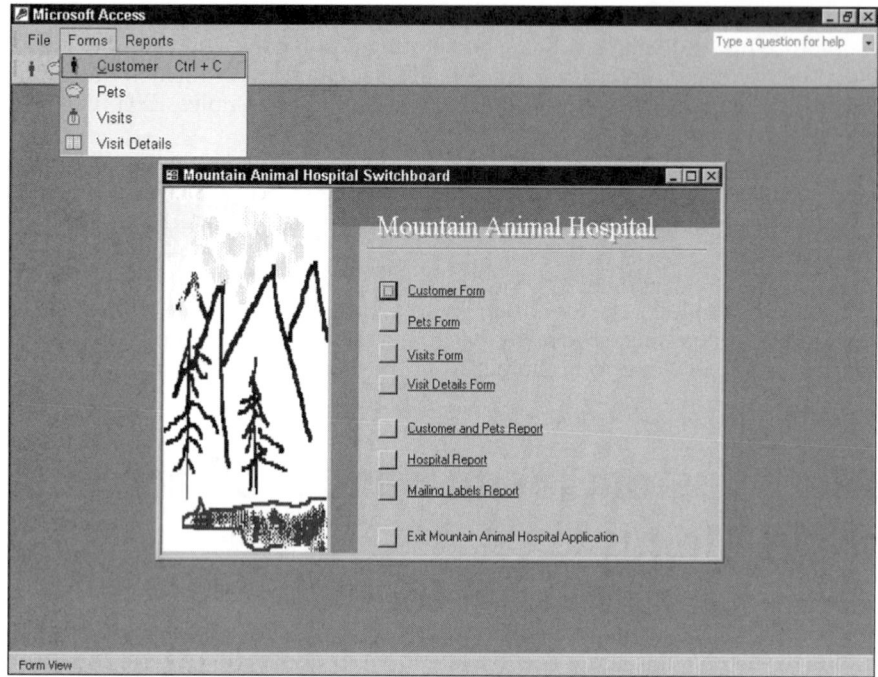

Figure 32-14: The custom drop-down menu bar

Understanding command bars

The Access 2002 Command Bar object lets you create three types of menus:

- ✦ **Menu Bars.** Menus that go along the top of your forms and that can have drop-down menus too

- ✦ **ToolBars.** Groups of icons generally found under the menu bars

- ✦ **Shortcut Menus.** Pop-up menus that display when you right-click on an object

Command Bars enable you to duplicate the Access 2002 user interface, including adding pictures to your menus.

Creating custom menu bars with command bars

You can create the custom menu bar that's shown in Figure 32-14 by first creating the top-level menu consisting of three elements — File, Forms, and Reports. You can create the top-level menu by selecting View ➪ Toolbars ➪ Customize, as shown in Figure 32-15.

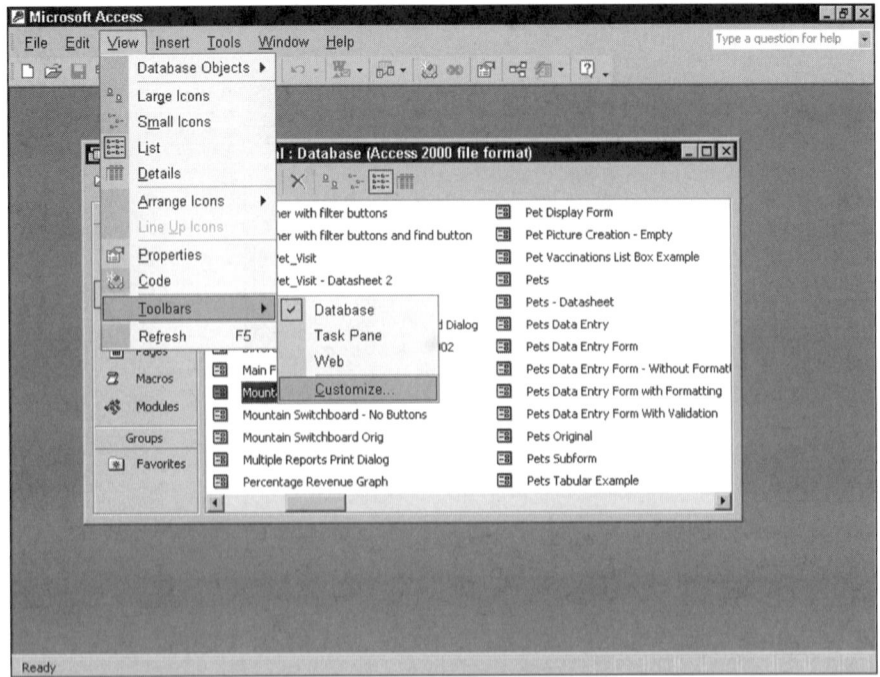

Figure 32-15: Selecting the View ⇨ Toolbars ⇨ Customize menu option

If you've never really looked at an Access 2002 menu bar, Figure 32-15 is a good example because many of the menu bars have pictures in front of the text. Notice the separator lines on the View menu — you learn how to add these lines in this chapter. Also notice the check box on the toolbar's submenus. This option indicates whether the menu bar is displayed. In this example, only the Database menu bar is displayed. The Web menu bar is hidden.

Cross-Reference

You learn about Access 2002 and the Internet in Chapters 35 and 36.

Select Customize and the dialog box that's shown in Figure 32-16 appears. Notice that your Office Assistant, if it's enabled, also displays because this is a difficult feature to understand — Microsoft has decided that you need help.

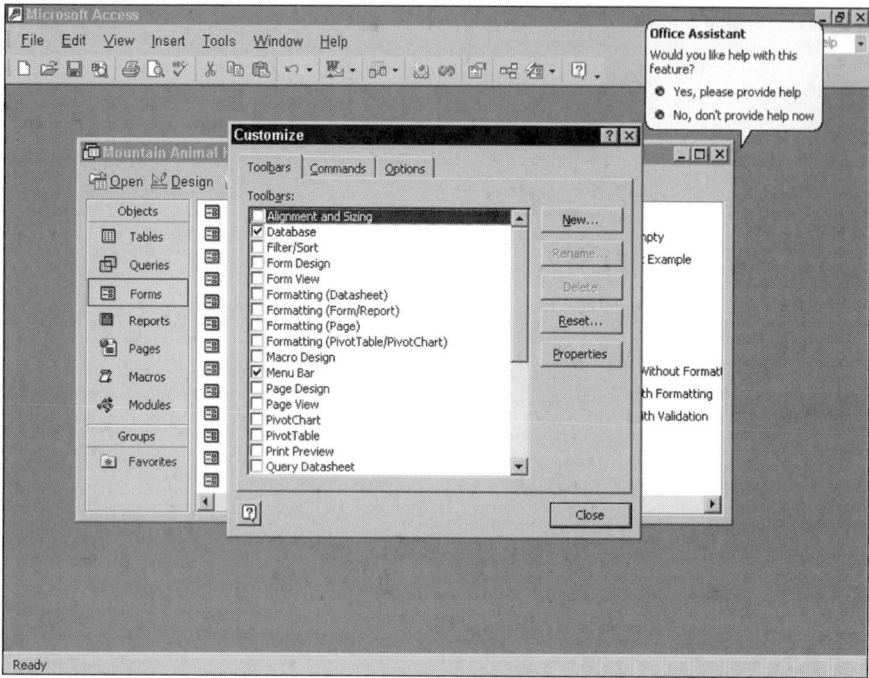

Figure 32-16: The Customize dialog box for toolbars

Changing existing menus and toolbars

From this dialog box, you can also select any of the preexisting menus and toolbars and customize them by adding, removing, or moving menu items. You can also change pictures and the purpose of the menu.

To change the menu items, display the toolbar or menu that you want to change and then directly change it by clicking the menu items that you want to manipulate. If you click and hold the mouse on a menu item, a submenu item, or a toolbar icon, a little gray button appears over the top of the item. You can then move the icon to a different location by dragging it to the new location. To remove the menu item or icon, simply drag it to a place away from the toolbar. To add a new item, select the Commands tab in the Customize dialog box, find the category that contains the item you want, and then drag the item to the toolbar or menu.

You can create a whole new item by selecting All Macros or New Menu and dragging it to the menu or toolbar that you want it to be on. See the next section to learn how to add a new menu.

Creating a new menu bar

To create a new menu bar, select New from the Customize dialog box, as shown in
Figure 32-16. A dialog box appears, asking you to name the custom toolbar. The
default name is Custom 1. Name this new menu bar *Mountain Custom Command Bar*
and click OK.

A small, gray rectangle (the new menu bar) appears in the center of the screen, next
to the Customize dialog. The new command bar name also appears in the list at the
bottom of the Toolbars list, as shown in Figure 32-17.

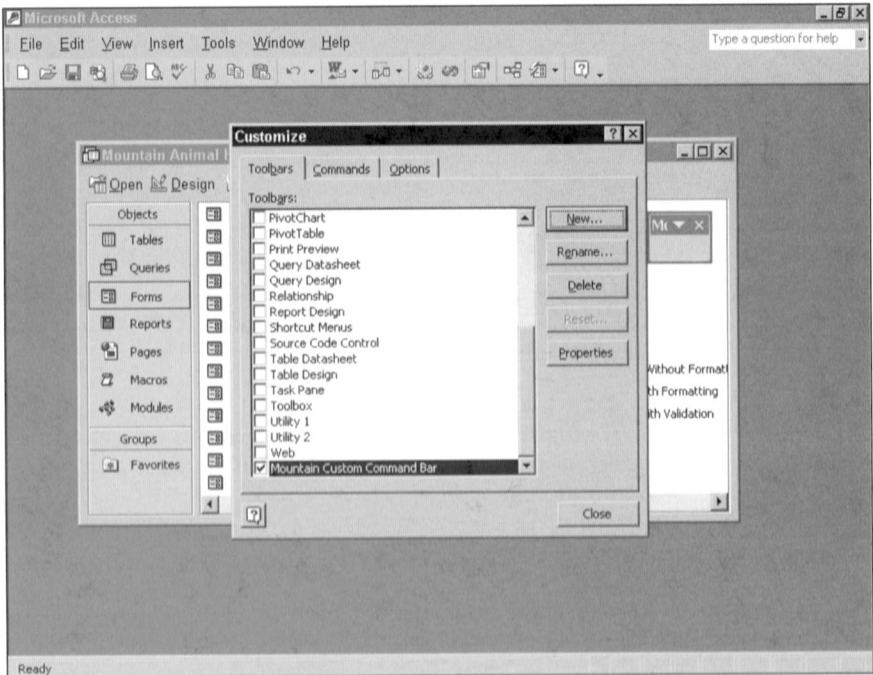

Figure 32-17: A new menu bar

Tip

You can move this menu to the top of the screen by dragging it so that it looks like
a normal menu bar with no items, as shown in Figure 32-18. The Mountain bar is
at the top, above the standard menu bar.

Before you begin to drag commands or text to the command bar, you must decide
what type of command bar it is. Select the menu bar (Mountain Custom Command
Bar) on the Toolbars tab in the Customize dialog box and then click on the
Properties button.

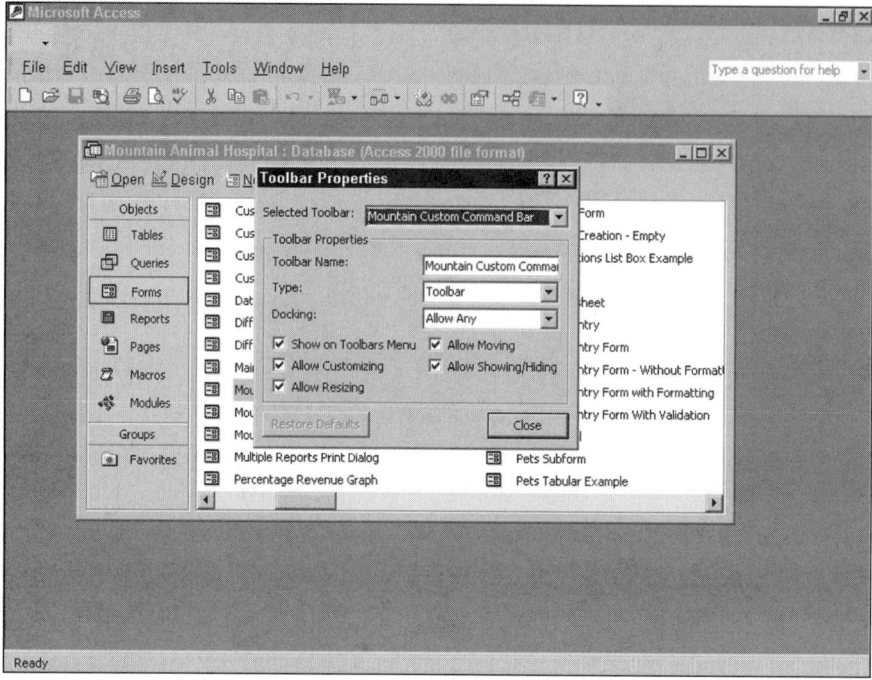

Figure 32-18: The Toolbar Properties dialog box

Figure 32-18 shows the Toolbar Properties dialog box. Here you can select each of the command bars in your system. The important portion of this dialog box is the middle portion. The first option is Type.

You have three Type choices:

✦ **Menu Bar.** Used for drop-down menus of commands containing text and, optionally, pictures

✦ **Toolbar.** Used for button bars of pictures only

✦ **Popup.** Used either for drop-down menu lists or shortcut menus; can contain pictures and text

For this example, you want to create a menu, so choose the Menu Bar option.

The next option, Docking, has four options:

✦ **Allow Any.** Allows docking horizontally or vertically

✦ **Can't Change.** Can't change where the command bar is docked

✦ **No Vertical.** Can dock only horizontally (across the screen)

✦ **No Horizontal.** Can dock only vertically (up and down the screen)

The rest of the options are five check boxes:

✦ **Show on Toolbars Menu.** Displays the selected toolbar on the View ⇨ Toolbars menu list

✦ **Allow Customizing.** Allows the user to change this with the Customize menu

✦ **Allow Resizing.** Allows you to resize a floating toolbar or menu bar

✦ **Allow Moving.** Lets you move the menu or toolbar between floating or docking

✦ **Allow Showing/Hiding.** Lets you show/hide the menu through the View ⇨ Toolbars menu

For this example, you can select all the choices to give the menu maximum flexibility.

Adding a submenu to a custom menu bar

Most menu commands are placed on submenus. It is rare for a top-level menu item to do anything but display a submenu. The submenu contains the actual menu item that — when clicked — runs the desired action, such as opening a form or printing a report.

To create a submenu, you essentially repeat the steps that you use to create the Mountain Custom Command Bar. To create the submenu menu bar, select New from the Customize dialog box, as originally shown in Figure 32-16, drag it to the Mountain Custom Command Bar, and drop it. The New Menu text appears on the menu bar. Click on it again, and a gray rectangle appears, as shown in Figure 32-19. This is the submenu.

Edit the name of the submenu by right-clicking it, and then name it *File* by clicking in the Name area and changing the name from New Menu to File. Repeat these steps for two additional new submenus, and name them *Forms* and *Reports*.

After you have defined your three menus, you can add commands to the submenus. Again, you can drag the menu commands directly to the submenu area.

Dragging the New Menu item to another menu automatically links the main menu and the submenu and makes the original menu choices non-selectable. The main menu (Mountain Custom Command Bar) is now permanently a menu bar. You can still change the defaults for the submenu items as you create them to display text, pictures, or both.

Caution   After you add submenus to a menu bar, you can't change it to a toolbar or pop-up menu.

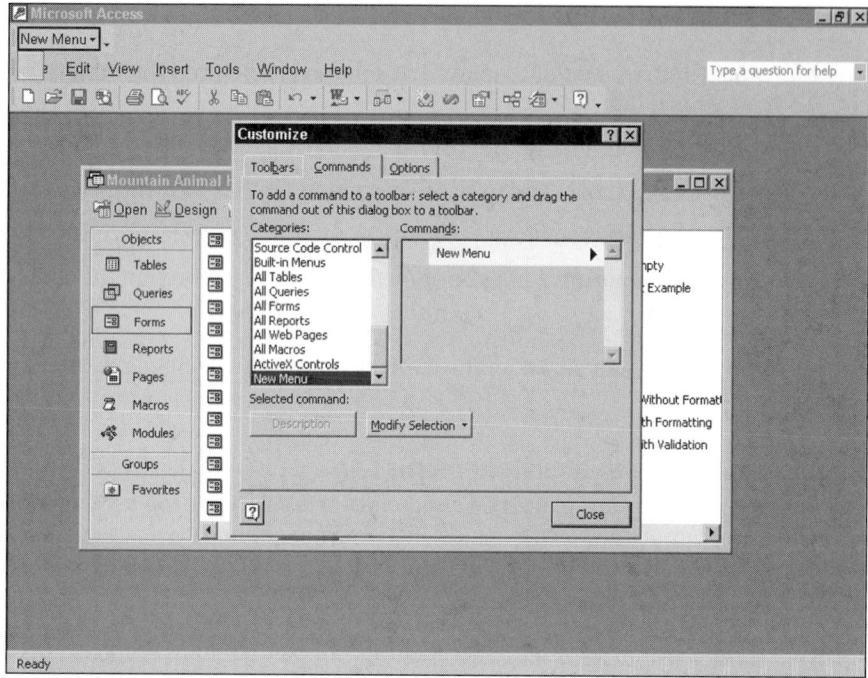

Figure 32-19: Creating a submenu

Adding commands to a menu bar to create a submenu

You can add commands to a custom menu bar by dragging any of the preexisting commands to the menu bar, or you can add any of your tables, queries, forms, reports, or macros to the menu bar. You can add any of these items to pre-existing menus as well.

Using a preexisting command fills in all the options for you. Unless you are planning to use an action found on one of the Access 2002 menus, however, you should create your own menus by first creating a new command bar and making it a menu bar, as discussed in the previous section.

After you have defined the blank submenus on the menu bar, you can drag commands to them. For this example, you may want to add the Forms menu items first. Follow these steps to add an item to display the Customers form when the first item is selected on the Forms menu:

1. Select Commands from the View ➪ Toolbars ➪ Customize dialog box.

2. Select All Forms from the Categories list.

3. Select Customer from the Commands list and drag it to the Forms menu bar. When you drop it, the text Customer appears on the menu bar.

4. Repeat the process for the Pets command, as shown in progress in Figure 32-20.

5. Repeat the process for the Adding General Pet Visit Info form and name it *Visits*.

6. Repeat the process for the Adding Visit Details form and name it *Visit Details*.

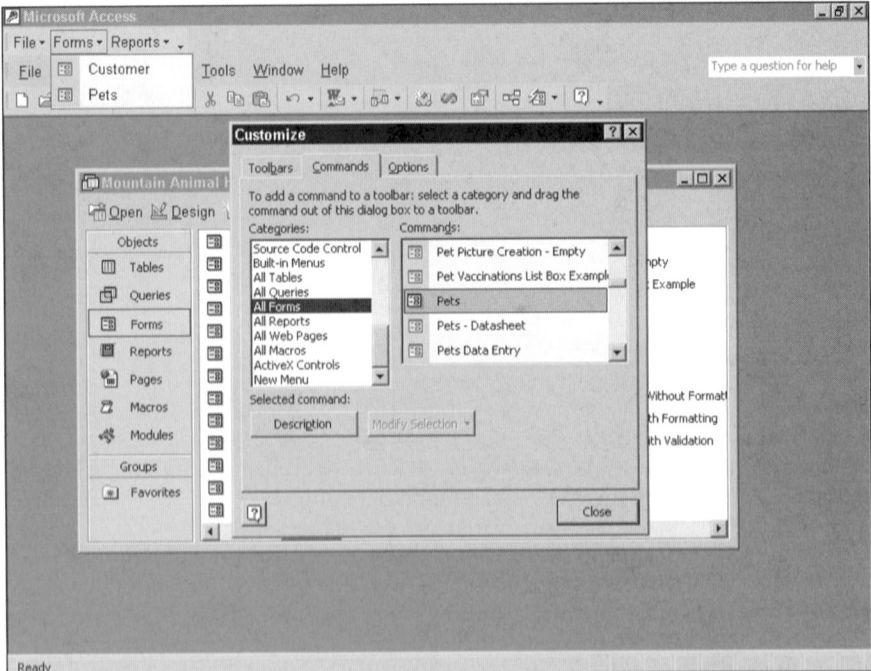

Figure 32-20: Creating a submenu item

Changing the look of the submenu items

When you click on the Forms menu, each of the items has a form icon. If you right-click on any of the submenu items with the View ➪ Toolbars ➪ Customize menu active, you can change the picture, or even change whether a picture is displayed at all. Figure 32-21 shows the Change Button Image selection of the View ➪ Toolbars ➪ Customize menu. Notice that all four button images have been changed; to do this, simply right-click each menu item, select Change Button Image, and then select the desired picture.

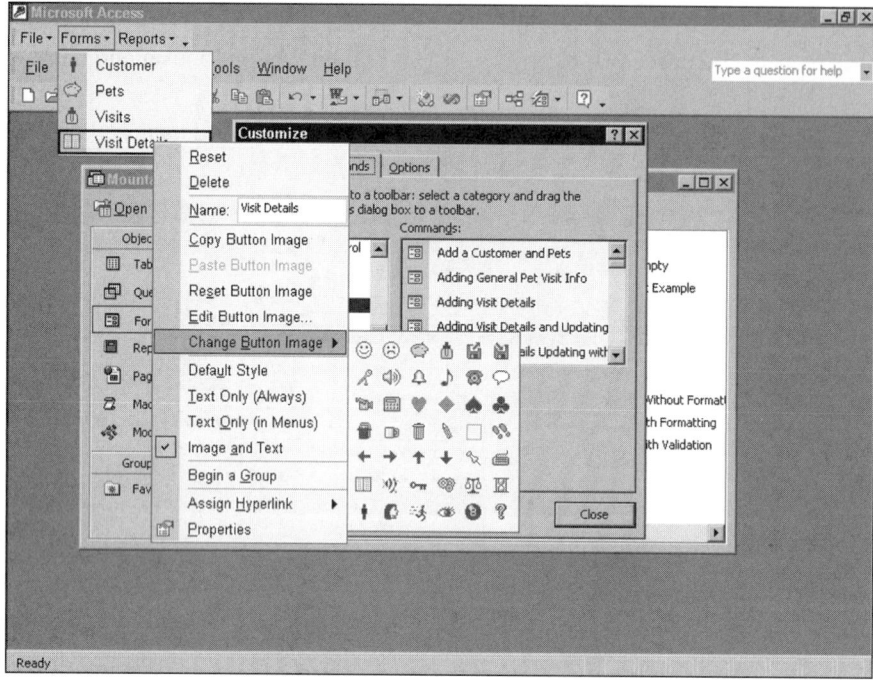

Figure 32-21: Changing the display of a menu bar item

The shortcut menu contains five options for changing pictures on menus or toolbar icons:

✦ **Copy Button Image.** Copies the current button face image to the Clipboard

✦ **Paste Button Image.** Copies the current picture in the Clipboard to the button face

✦ **Reset Button Image.** Changes the button face image to the default image

✦ **Edit Button Image.** Uses the internal image editor to change an image

✦ **Choose Button Image.** Changes the button face image from a list of images stored in Access

You can change the button image in several ways. The easiest method is to select from a set of button images that Access stores internally, as shown in Figure 32-21. When you choose a picture and click OK, the button image changes.

As Figure 32-21 shows, you don't have many pictures to choose from. You can, however, create your own image and copy it to the Clipboard. After you have an image on the Clipboard, you can use the Paste Button Image option of the shortcut menu to add the image to the button. You must size the image to fit the button. You can also use the Edit Button Image to change the image after you've placed it on the button face. You can edit the button face by moving the image around and changing individual pixels of color.

As Figure 32-21 also shows, you can change the caption of the text and the way it's displayed. You have four additional options for displaying the menu or toolbar option:

✦ **Default Style.** Displays image and text for menu bars, pictures for toolbars, and both for pop-ups

✦ **Text Only (Always).** Displays text only for menu bars and pop-ups

✦ **Text Only (in Menus).** Displays text on menu bars and graphics on toolbars and both on pop-ups

✦ **Image and Text.** Displays pictures and text on menu bars and pop-ups

> **Tip**
> To remove the images and display just text, select the Text Only choice for each submenu item.

> **Tip**
> If you check the Begin a Group check box, Access places a horizontal separator line before the menu item.

You can further customize each item for the your specific purpose. You can display the properties for any menu by clicking on the Properties button, shown at the bottom of Figure 32-21. Figure 32-22 shows the properties for the Customer Item that has been enhanced. Here you set the rest of the actions for the menu item.

Each menu item has a list of properties, as shown in Figure 32-22. After the Control Properties window displays, you can change the Selected Control to any of the menu items without returning to the previous menu. Changing the caption changes the text on the menu.

> **Tip**
> To define a hot key for the menu item, you can add an ampersand (&) in front of the hot-key letter.

The caption property has been changed with the addition of an ampersand (&) in front of the letter *C*. This allows you to press the letter *C* after displaying the Forms menu in this example. Any letter can be used as a hot key by placing the ampersand before it. If you set up an AutoKeys macro list, you can also specify the shortcut text, as shown in Figure 32-22. Notice the Ctrl + C next to the Customer menu item as well as in the shortcut text area.

You also can define the screen tip text for the control by entering text in the ScreenTip area.

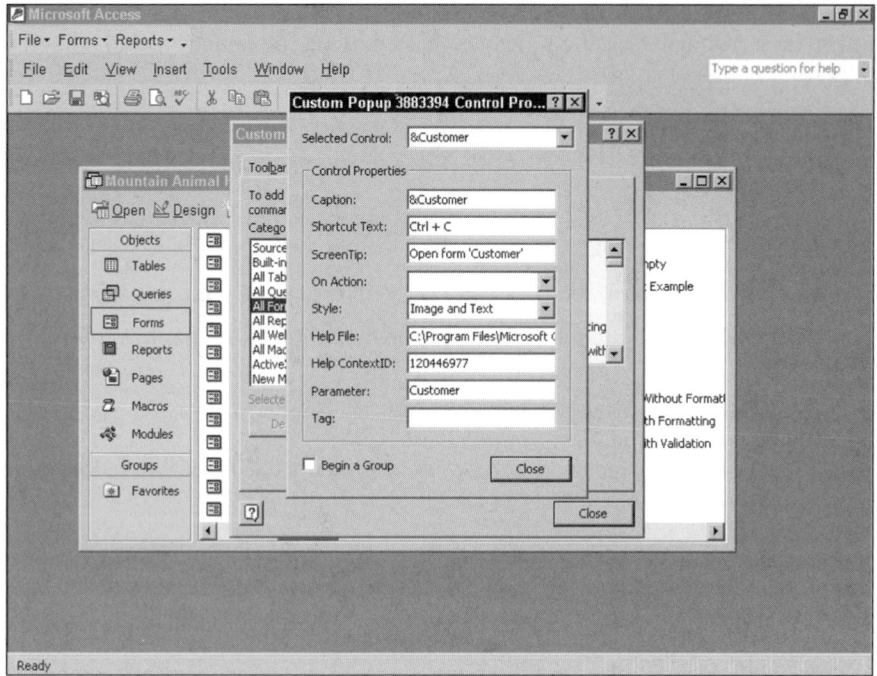

Figure 32-22: Changing the display of a menu bar item

The most important option is normally the On Action item. This option allows you to specify a VBA function or macro that should run when the menu item is selected. In this example, because you drag each form from the forms list to the menu, the action is already known in the Properties sheet for the item. In fact, the name of the form to open is stored in the Parameter option of the window.

The other options let you choose the Help File name and entry point if you click on Help while selecting the menu. The Parameter entry is used to specify optional parameters when calling a VBA function.

You can complete the Reports menu items by dragging the desired reports to the Reports menu item from the All Reports commands. You can add the Exit function to the File menu by dragging the Exit command from the File category.

Attaching the menu bar to a form

After you have completed the Mountain Custom Command Bar menu bar and its submenus, you are ready to attach the menu bar to a form.

To attach a menu bar to a form, open the form in design mode and set the Menu Bar property of the form to the menu bar name. To attach the Mountain Custom Command Bar menu bar to the Mountain Switchboard — No Buttons form, follow these steps:

1. Open the Mountain Switchboard — No Buttons form in design mode.

2. Display the property sheet by clicking on the Properties button on the toolbar if it is not already displayed.

3. Click on the small black box to the left of the ruler (immediately below the toolbar).

    Access displays the title *Form* for the property sheet.

4. Click on the Menu Bar property of the Property window.

5. Select the Mountain Custom Command Bar from the pull-down menu (or type the menu bar name).

By following these steps, you attach the menu bar named Mountain Custom Command Bar with its drop-down menus to the form. You should have a design screen similar to the one shown in Figure 32-23.

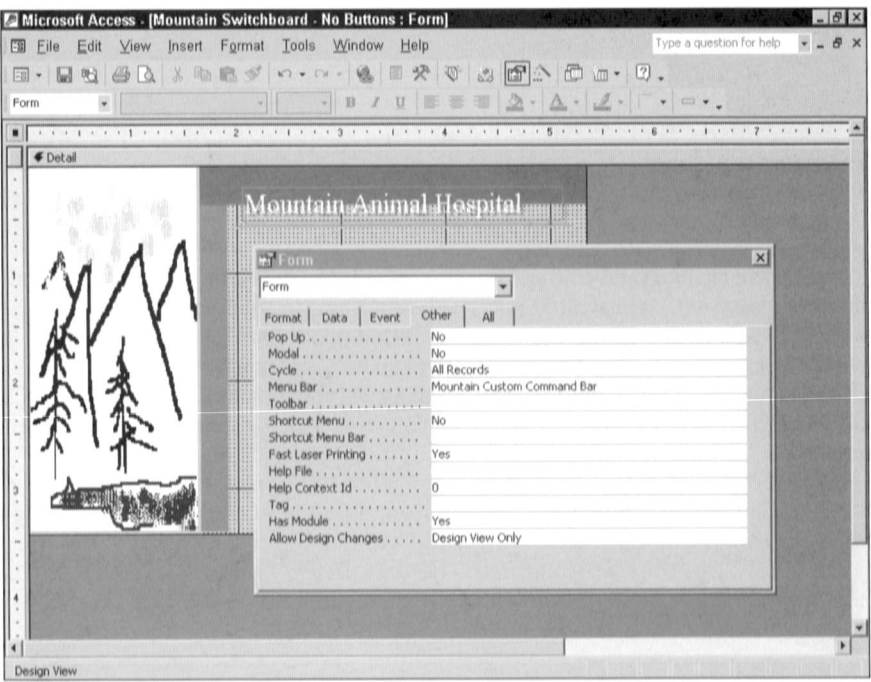

Figure 32-23: Attaching a menu bar to the form using the Menu Bar property

Creating shortcut menus

Access 2002 allows you to create *custom shortcut menus* that open when you right-click them. These menus can replace the standard shortcut menus in Access 2002. Shortcut menus can be defined for the form itself or for any control on the form. Each control can have a different shortcut menu.

A shortcut menu is simply another type of command bar. You can begin a shortcut menu by selecting View ➪ Toolbars ➪ Customize and then choosing the New button from the Toolbars tab of the Customize dialog box. In this example, you can name the new menu *Pets Shortcut*.

After you create the new command bar, you can select it and click on the Properties button in the Customize dialog box. The Toolbar Properties dialog box displays. Change the Type to Popup, as shown in Figure 32-24.

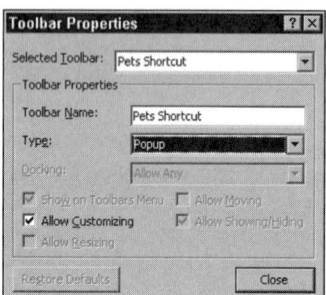

Figure 32-24: Changing a new toolbar to a pop-up shortcut menu

Changing the type of the toolbar from the default Menu Bar to Popup raises a message warning you that you must edit the menu items in the Shortcut Menus Custom section. Shortcut Menus is a standard Access 2002 toolbar, as shown in Figure 32-25. When you click on Shortcut Menus, a list of all menu bars appears on a command bar. By selecting any of these menu items, such as Database, Filter, or Form (which are shown on the left side of the menu bar in Figure 32-25), a submenu displays listing all of the shortcut menus available on the standard Access design screens.

The last item on the command bar is Custom. When you click on this item, a list of all the shortcut (pop-up) menus that you have defined displays. The only shortcut menu defined prior to this point in the book is the Pets Shortcut. Notice the blank menu bar in Figure 32-25, to the left of the Pets Shortcut menu. This is where you drag your selections.

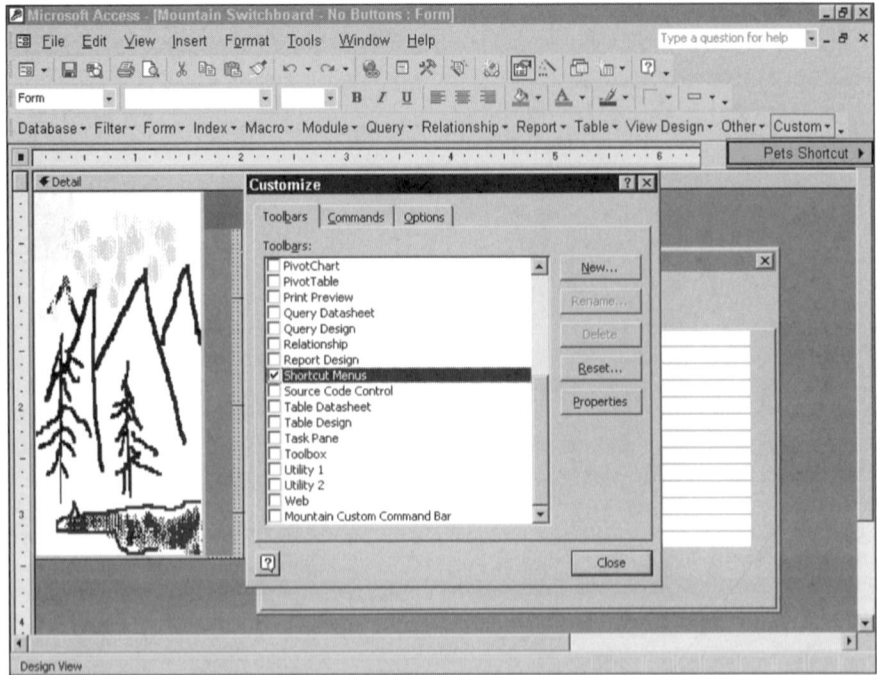

Figure 32-25: Displaying the list of custom shortcut menus

You add menu items to a shortcut menu in exactly the same way that you add any menu item. Although the empty Pets Shortcut menu rectangle displays, as shown in Figure 32-25, click on the Commands tab in the Customize dialog box and then select All Forms in the Categories list. You can then drag any command to the shortcut menu. For this example, add four forms (Pets, Customers, Visits, and Visit Details) by dragging the four forms (Pets, Customers, Adding General Pet Visit Info, and Adding Visit Details) to the menu. Then add three items for the reports — Customer and Pets, Hospital Reports, and Customer Labels — by first selecting All Reports in the Categories list.

As you add each of the forms and reports, it appears on the shortcut menu. Notice that the forms and reports display a different icon next to the menu text. You can display the menu to change the details of each of these menu items by clicking the item and then right-clicking. The shortcut menu in Figure 32-26 has been defined and each of the original form and report names has been changed to the more standard names for the example. Also notice the separator line between the forms and reports. You can create this line by selecting the Begin a Group option while on the Customer and Pets report, as shown in Figure 32-26. If you want to, you can change the pictures for each of the icons next to the menu item by using the button image options.

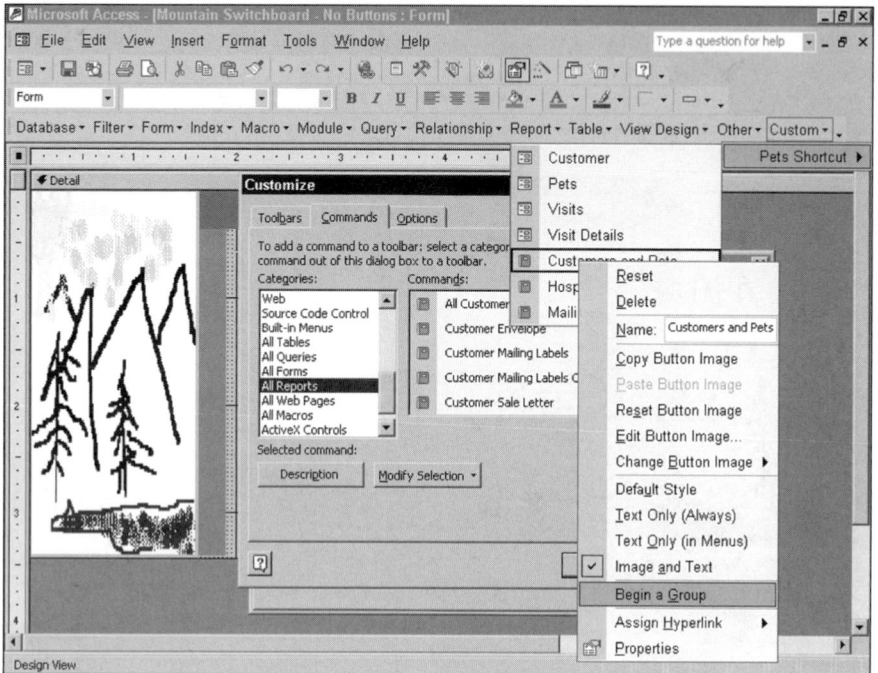

Figure 32-26: Modifying the shortcut menu bar

Tip

By clicking on Properties for any of the menu items, you can set the shortcut keys, ToolTips, actions, and Help file.

After you create the menu definition and save the shortcut menu, you can attach the shortcut menu to either the form or any control on the form. If you attach the shortcut menu to a form, it overrides the standard shortcut menu for the form. If you attach a shortcut menu to a control, it displays only after you right-click the control. Figure 32-27 shows the Pets shortcut menu being attached to the Shortcut Menu Bar property of the Mountain Switchboard — No Buttons.

You may also notice that the Shortcut Menu property is set to Yes. This is for either the default shortcut menus or the shortcut menus that you create. If it is set to No, you don't see any shortcut menus when you right-click.

Figure 32-28 shows the shortcut menu on the Mountain Switchboard — No Buttons form. The menu displays to the right of wherever you clicked the mouse, even if it extends beyond the window. The actions listed in the menu macro run when you select the desired menu item.

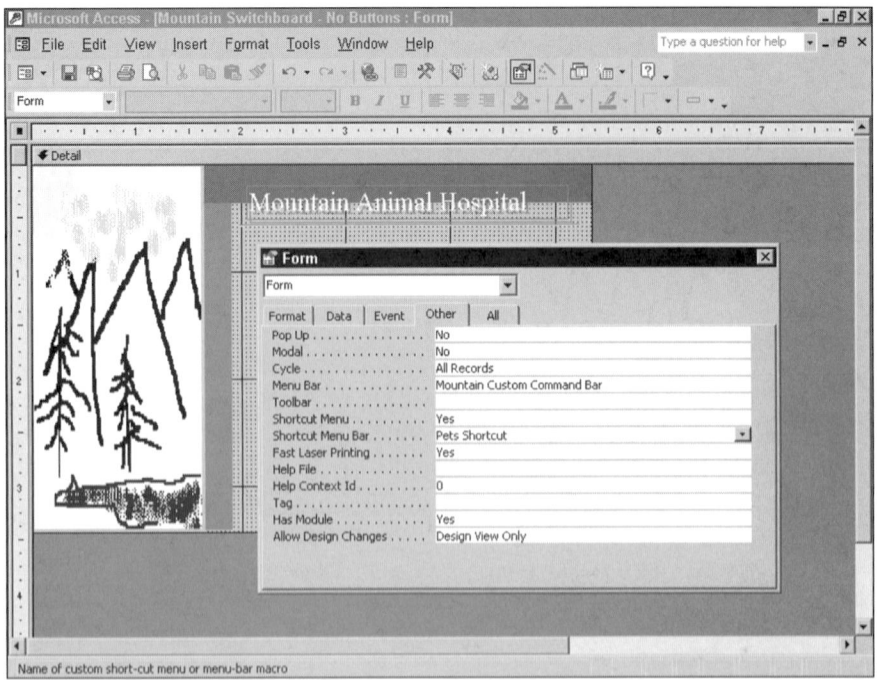

Figure 32-27: Adding the shortcut menu to the form

Note   If you want to delete a shortcut menu, you must first select the shortcut menu by displaying the list of toolbars in the View⟳Toolbars⟳Customize dialog box and then click on the Properties button. The Shortcut menus are visible only by opening the Selected Toolbar combo box. You must change the type from Popup to Menu Bar. After you do this, you can return to the Toolbars tab, where you can now see the shortcut menu, and press the Delete button. Remember that when you change a command bar to a pop-up menu, it is visible only on the shortcut menu's Custom tab or in the Selected Toolbar list in the Toolbar Properties dialog box.

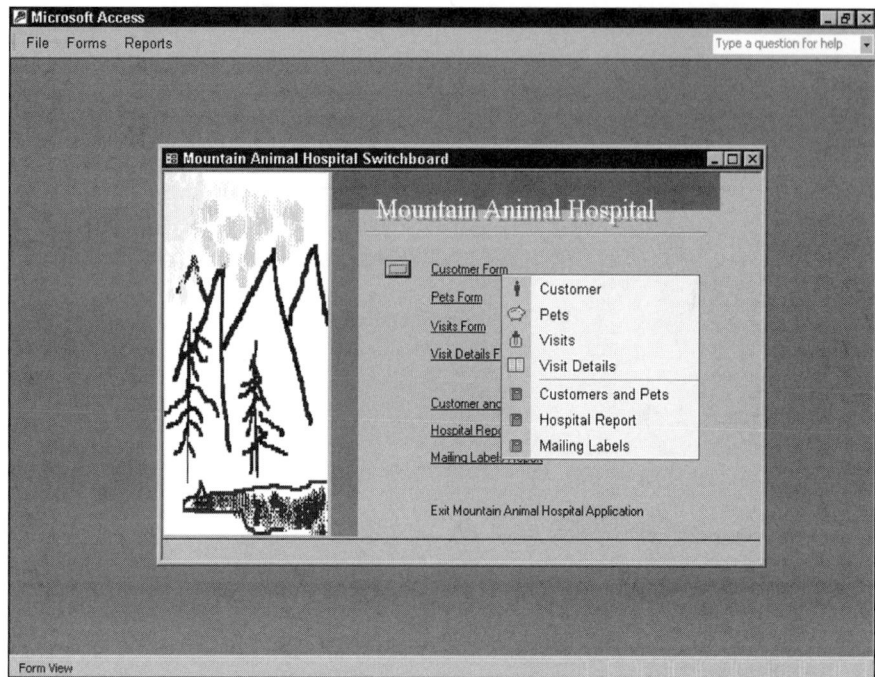

Figure 32-28: Viewing the form with the shortcut menu

Creating and using custom toolbars

Access has always let you define new toolbars for your application and customize existing toolbars. However, Access 2002 also has new features, such as customizing the pictures on the buttons (known as *button faces*). For example, suppose that when you display the Mountain Switchboard, you want a toolbar that lets you open the various forms with one button push. You can create a new toolbar or even add some icons to the standard form toolbar. For this example, you create a new toolbar.

A toolbar is just another type of command bar.

To create a custom toolbar, follow these steps:

1. Select View ➪ Toolbars ➪ Customize.
2. Click the New button from the Toolbars tab in the Customize dialog box.
3. Type **Mountain Toolbar** in the New Toolbar dialog box and click OK.
4. Select Properties.

You can see that the new command bar is created as a toolbar. You can close the Properties window and drag the four forms to the toolbar. You use the same technique to do this as you use when creating menu bars and shortcut menus. When the empty Mountain Toolbar rectangle displays, click the Commands tab in the Customize dialog box and then select All Forms in the Categories list. You can then drag any command to the shortcut menu. For this example, add four forms (Pets, Customers, Visits, and Visit Details) by dragging the four forms (Pets, Customers, Adding General Pet Visit Info, and Adding Visit Details) to the menu and change the button face for each button. After you finish, you can see the completed toolbar, as shown in Figure 32-29. This figure also shows how to change a button image on the last item by first selecting the item and then right-clicking the item. Notice that 'Default Style is chosen to display only the button face.

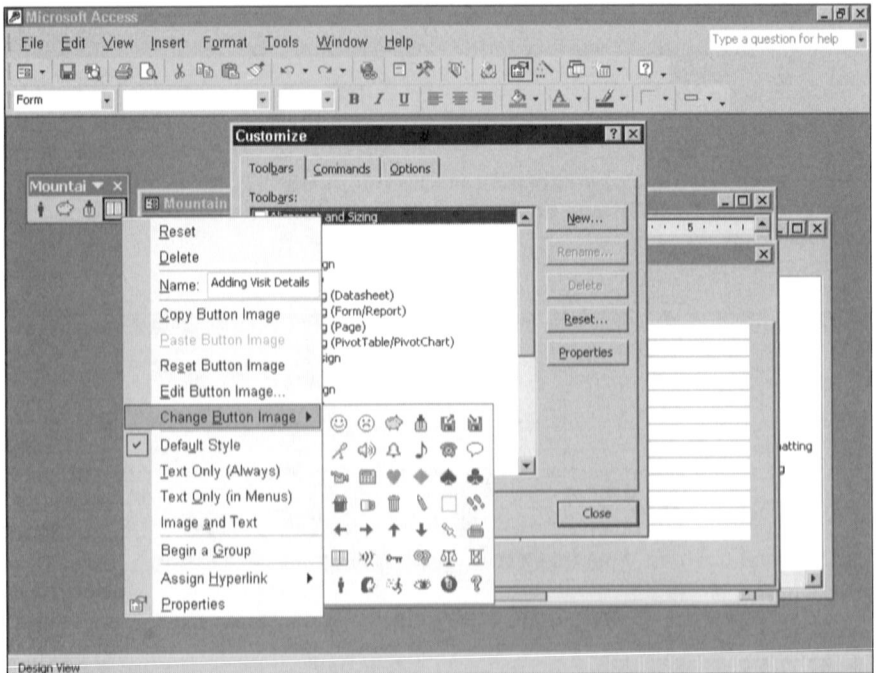

Figure 32-29: Creating a new toolbar

Tip

You can add a space and a separator line between icons by selecting Begin a Group on the icon that you want placed to the left of the line.

Attaching the toolbar to a form

After you complete Mountain Toolbar, you are ready to attach the toolbar to a form.

To attach a toolbar to a form, open the form in design view and set the Toolbar property of the form to the toolbar name. To attach Mountain Toolbar to the Mountain Switchboard — No Buttons form, follow these steps:

1. Open the Mountain Switchboard — No Buttons form in design view.
2. Display the property sheet by clicking the Properties button on the toolbar if it is not already displayed.
3. Click the small blank box to the left of the ruler (immediately below the toolbar).

   Access displays the title *Form* for the property sheet.
4. Click the Toolbar property in the Property window.
5. Select the Mountain Toolbar from the pull-down menu (or type the toolbar name).

By following these steps, you can attach the Mountain Toolbar with its picture buttons to the form. You should end up with a design screen similar to the one shown in Figure 32-30.

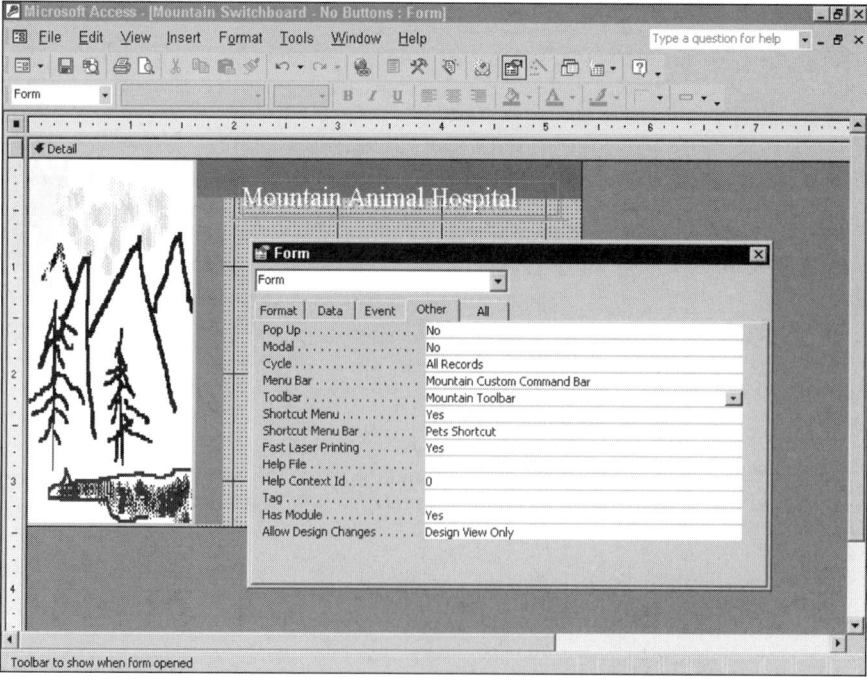

Figure 32-30: Attaching a toolbar to the form using the Toolbar property

When you set a form's menu bar or toolbar to a custom menu bar or toolbar, the menu bar and toolbar display automatically when you open the form. When the focus changes to another form, the custom menu bar and toolbar for the previous form are removed. The menu bar and toolbar are replaced with the newly displayed form's menu bar and toolbar if the form's properties specify them.

After you have made these changes, you can display the Mountain Switchboard — No Buttons, as shown in Figure 32-31. Mountain Toolbar displays on the screen. The tool tip displays when you hold the mouse pointer over one of the toolbar buttons.

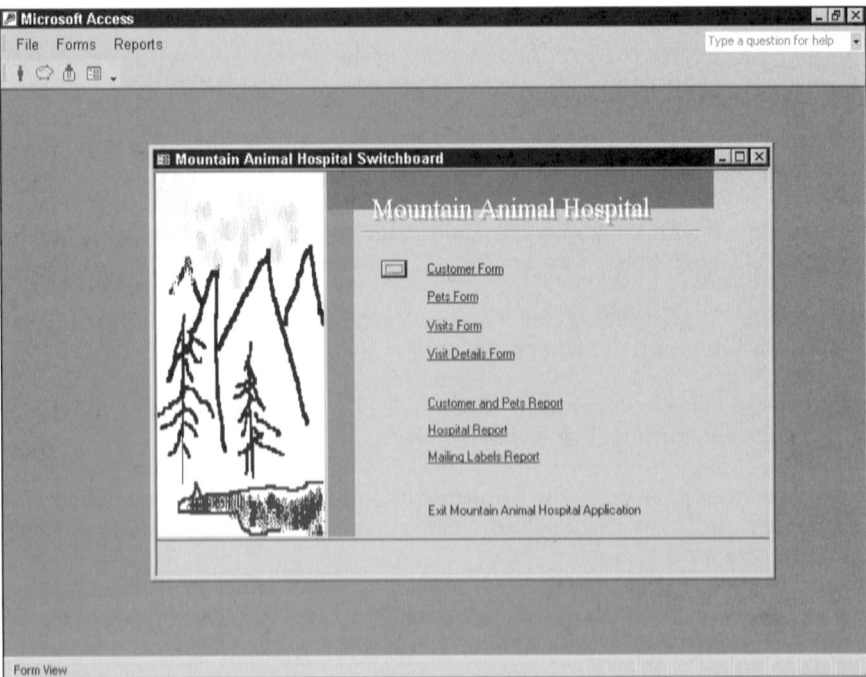

Figure 32-31: Displaying a custom toolbar in a form

Adding control tips to any form control

Although you must add screen tips by using the toolbar customization windows, you can add a tool tip known as a *control tip* to any control. When you place your mouse pointer on a control, textual help resembling a tool tip displays with a yellow background. You can create a control tip by entering text into the ControlTip Text property of any control. Whatever you enter into this property displays when you place the mouse pointer on a control and pause it there for about a second.

Running a macro automatically when you start Access

After you create the switchboard, a menu bar, and the associated submenus and toolbars, you may want Access to open the form automatically each time you open the database. One method to automatically load a form at startup is to write an AutoExec macro. When Access opens a database, it looks for a macro named AutoExec. If the macro exists, Access automatically runs it. To create an AutoExec macro to open the switchboard automatically, follow these steps:

1. Create a new macro (you name it *AutoExec* later).

2. Type **Minimize** (or select the action) in the next empty Action cell.

3. Type **OpenForm** (or select the action) in the next empty Action cell.

4. Type **Mountain Switchboard** (or select the switchboard form name) in the Form Name cell in the Action Arguments pane.

Save the macro with the name *AutoExec*. After you do this, Access runs the macro automatically each time you open the database.

The AutoExec macro shows two actions. The Minimize action minimizes the Database window and the OpenForm action opens the switchboard.

Tip   To bypass an AutoExec macro, simply hold down the Shift key while you select the database name from the Access File menu.

In early versions of Access, the Autoexec method was the only way to launch a form at startup. Access 95 and later versions provide an easier way to automatically launch a form at startup.

Controlling options when starting Access

Rather than run a macro to open a form when Access starts, you can use the Access 2002 startup form to control many options when you start Access, including

✦ Changing the text on the title bar

✦ Specifying an icon to use when Access is minimized

✦ Global custom menu bar

✦ Global custom shortcut menu bar

✦ Display a form on startup (for example, the application's switchboard)

✦ Control the display of default menus, toolbars, the Database window, and the status bar

Figure 32-32 shows the Access 2002 Startup dialog box. You can display this by selecting Tools ⇨ Startup or by right-clicking the border of the Database window and selecting Startup.

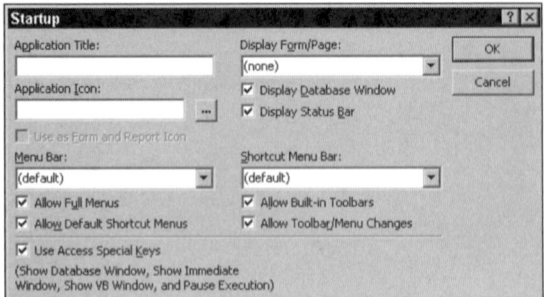

Figure 32-32: The Startup options window

Tip   This tool replaces both the AutoExec macro and items formerly specified in the Access 2.0 INI file.

Creating a Print Report Dialog Box Form and Macros

A dialog box is also a form, but it's different from a switchboard in that the dialog box usually displays information, captures a user entry, or lets the user interact with the system. In this section, you create a complex dialog box that prints reports and labels.

By using a form and some macros, you can create a dialog box that controls printing of your reports. This dialog box can display a list of pets and their owners (see Figure 32-33) so that you can print only a single page of the Pets Directory without having to change the query.

Although this dialog box is more complex than a switchboard, it uses the same types of Access objects, which include the following:

✦ Forms

✦ Form controls and properties

✦ Macros

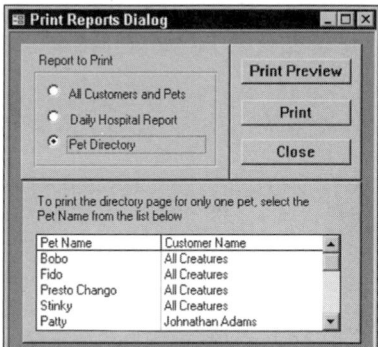

Figure 32-33: A Print Reports dialog box

Creating a form for a macro

The form that you create in this example displays the various controls. The form contains three basic sections.

The upper-left corner of the form contains three option buttons, which are placed within an option group. The option buttons let you select one of the three listed reports. Each of the reports is already created and can be seen in the Database window. If you select All Customers and Pets or the Daily Hospital Report, you can print or preview that report. If you select Pet Directory, as shown in Figure 32-33, you see a list box of pets and their owners. You can then choose a pet name for a printout from the Pet Directory report for only that one pet. If you don't choose a pet name, records for all pets are printed from the Pet Directory report.

The upper-right corner of the form contains three buttons. Each button runs a different macro in the Print Report macro library. The first option button, Print Preview, runs a macro that opens the selected report in a Print Preview window. The second option button, Print, runs a macro that prints the selected report to the default printer. The last button, Close, simply closes the form without printing any reports.

To create a form for your macro, first create a blank form and size it properly by following these steps:

1. Create a new blank form unbound to any table or query.

2. Resize the form to 3½ inches × 3 inches.

3. Change the Back color to dark gray.

Three rectangles are placed on the form to give it a distinctive look. You can create the three rectangles (as shown in Figure 32-33) by following these steps:

1. Click on the Rectangle button in the toolbox.

2. Using Figure 32-33 as a guide, create three separate rectangles.

Each rectangle in this example is shown with the Raised special effect. To create this effect, follow these steps:

1. Select a rectangle.

2. Change the Back color to light gray.

3. Click on the Raised special-effect button in the Special Effect window.

4. Click on the Transparent button in the Border Color window.

5. Repeat Steps 1 through 4 for the second and third rectangles.

6. Finally, to enhance the Raised special effect, drag each rectangle away from the adjacent rectangles so that the darker background of the form shows between the rectangle borders. You may need to resize one of the rectangles to line up the edges.

Creating the option group

After you create the form and the special effects, you can create the necessary controls.

The first set of controls is the option group. In Chapter 18, you learn to use the Option Group Wizard to create option buttons. To create the option group and option buttons, follow the steps given here and use Figure 32-34 as a guide. In this example, the option group buttons are not bound to a field; they are used to select the report to print—not to enter data:

1. Click the Option Group button in the toolbox, making sure that the Control Wizard icon is on.

2. Draw an option-group rectangle within the upper-left rectangle, as shown in Figure 32-34.

3. Enter All Customers and Pets, Daily Hospital Report, and Pet Directory as three separate labels in the first Option Group Wizard.

4. Click the Finish button to exit the Wizard screen.

   Your option buttons and the option group appear in the first rectangle. You may need to move or resize the option group's box to fit properly. You may also need to change the color and caption for the "Report to Print" label for the option group.

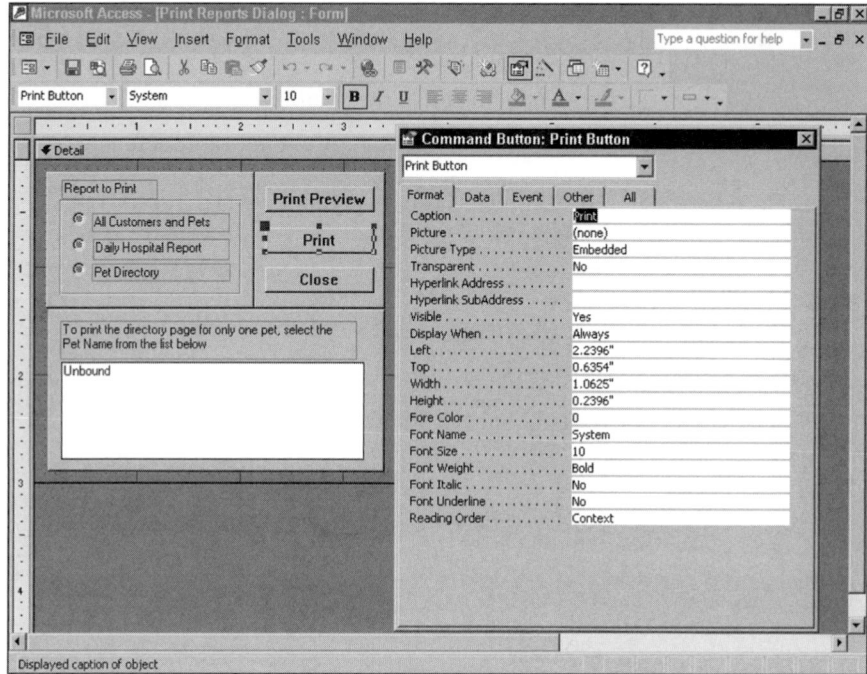

Figure 32-34: The Print dialog box in Design view

Creating command buttons

After you complete the option group and the option buttons, you can create the command buttons. These pushbuttons trigger the actions for your dialog box. Figure 32-33 shows the three buttons:

    ✦ **Print Preview.** Displays the selected report in the Print Preview window

    ✦ **Print.** Prints the selected report to the default print device

    ✦ **Close.** Closes the dialog box

To create each command button, follow the next set of steps. Because each button is the same size, duplicate the second and third buttons from the first:

    1. Turn the Wizard off, then Click the command button in the toolbox.

    2. Create the first command button, as shown in Figure 32-34.

3. Select Edit ➪ Duplicate to duplicate the first command button.

4. Move the button below the first.

5. Select Edit ➪ Duplicate to duplicate the second command button.

6. You may need to move the button into position, as shown in Figure 32-3.

You now need to change the command button captions. The remaining steps show how to make these changes.

7. Select the first command button and change the Caption property to Print Preview.

8. Select the second command button and change the Caption property to Print.

9. Select the third command button and change the Caption property to Close.

Creating a list box on the print report form

The last control that you need in the dialog box is the list box that displays the pet name and customer name when you click the Pet Directory option button. To create the list box, follow these steps, using Figure 32-35 as a guide. In this example, you create the list box without using the wizard:

1. Click on the List Box button in the toolbox. Make sure that the Control Wizard icon is off.

2. Using Figure 32-35 as a guide, create the list box rectangle.

3. Move the label control to a position above the list box if necessary.

4. Resize the label control so that the bottom-right corner is just above the list box, as shown in Figure 32-35.

5. Using the formatting windows, change the Back color of the label to light gray to match the background of the bottom rectangle.

6. Change the Caption property for the list box by clicking the label of the field (the caption in the label itself), typing **To print the directory page for only one pet**, and then selecting the Pet Name from the list below. The text in the label wraps automatically as you type.

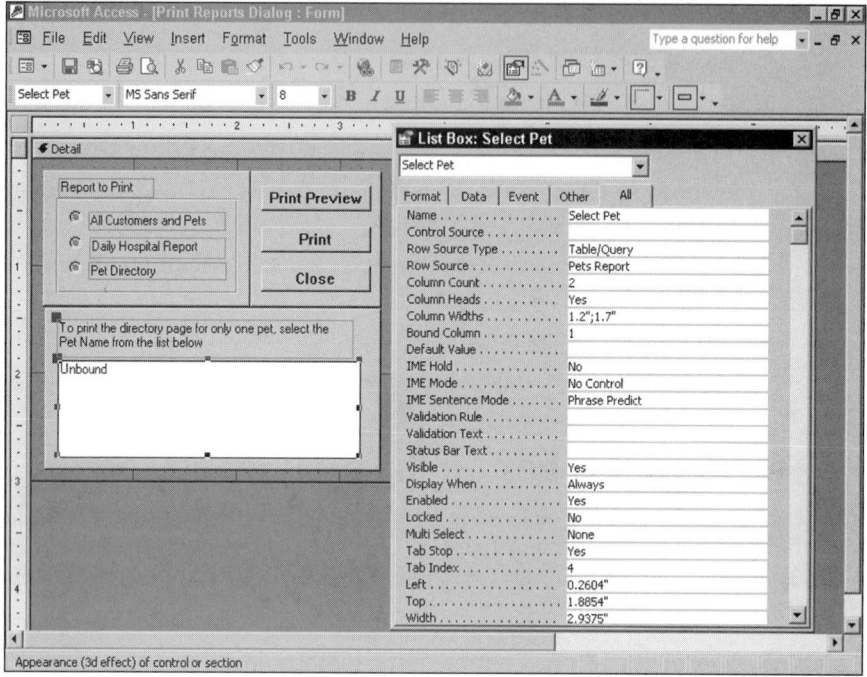

Figure 32-35: The list box definition on the form

After you have created the list box and label, you must define the columns of the list box. To define the columns and data source for the list box, follow these steps, using Figure 32-35 as a guide:

1. With the list box selected, change the Name property to Select Pet.

2. Make sure that the Row Source Type indicates Table/Query.

3. Change the Row Source to Pets Report.

4. Change the Column Count to 2.

Caution   You must create the Pets Report before you try to run this form. The Pets Report is a simple query that you create using an interesting technique (see the sidebar, "The Pets Report query for the Print Reports form list box," for more information).

5. Change Column Heads to Yes.

6. Change the Column Widths to 1.2, 1.7.

7. Make sure that the Bound Column property indicates 1.

Before continuing, you should save the form. Save the file but leave the form on-screen by selecting the menu option File ➪ Save. Name the form *Print Reports Dialog Box*.

When you have completed the form, you are halfway done. Your next task is to create each of the macros that you need and create the macro library. When you complete that task, you can add the macros to the correct event properties in the form.

Creating the print macros

Macros are attached to the events of controls or objects. These events include entering, exiting, updating, or selecting a control. In this example, macros are attached to several controls and objects. Table 32-3 shows the macros that you create for this example and how they run.

Table 32-3			
Macros for the Print Reports Form			
Macro Name	*Attached to Control/Object*	*Attached to Property*	*Description*
Show List	Form	On Open	Displays list box if the third option button is on
Show List	Option group	After Update	Displays list box if the third button is selected
Print Preview	Print Preview	On Click	Displays selected report in print-preview mode when Print Preview button is selected
Print	Print button	On Click	Prints selected report if Print button is selected
Close	Close button	On Click	Closes form if Close button is selected

Creating the Print macro group

In the preceding two chapters, you learn that creating a macro library is the same as creating any macro. You create a macro group by following these steps:

1. From the Form window toolbar, click the New Object icon and select New Macro to create a new macro.

2. Select View ➪ Macro Names or click the Macro Names button on the toolbar to display the Macro Names column.

3. Select View ➪ Conditions or click the Conditions button on the toolbar to display the Condition column.

As you may recall, the Macro Names and Conditions menu options add two columns to the basic Macro window. You use these columns to enter more parameters into the macro. The Macro Name column is used for creating the individual macro entry points in a macro library. The Condition column determines whether the action in the Action column should be run (on the basis of the conditions). To create the macro, follow these steps:

1. In the third row of the Macro Name column, type **Show List**.

2. In the seventh row of the Macro Name column, type **Print Preview**.

3. In the fourteenth row of the Macro Name column, type **Print**.

4. In the twenty-first row of the Macro Name column, type **Close**.

5. Select File ➪ Save As and name the macro *Print Reports*.

You can see these macro names along with their conditions and actions in Figure 32-36.

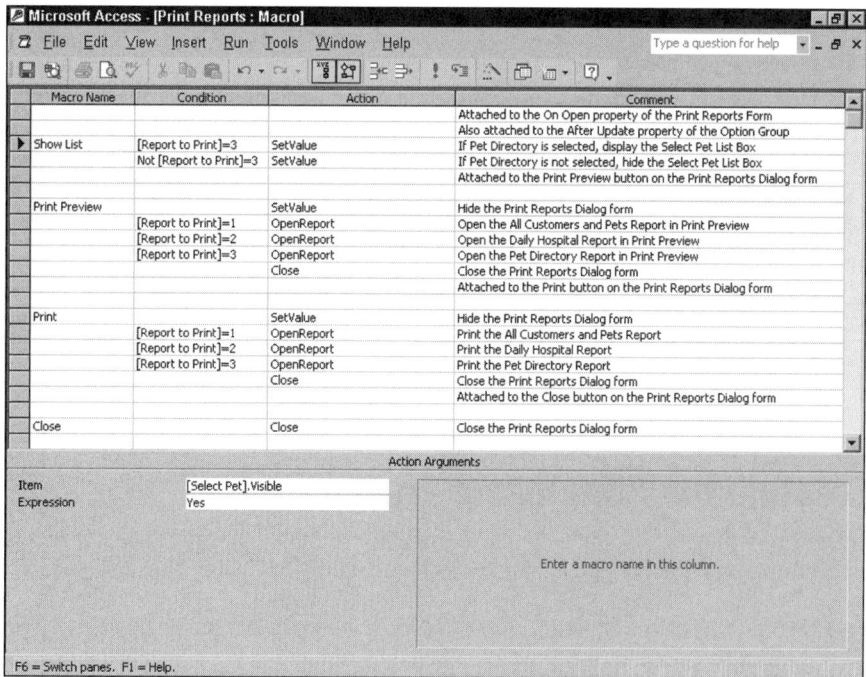

Figure 32-36: Creating the Show List macro and the Print Reports macro group

Creating the Show List macro

The Show List macro either displays or hides the list box that lists the pet names and customer names. This macro uses the SetValue macro command to run from either the form object or the option group control. The SetValue macro command lets you set a property of a control in the form. In this example, the list box is named *Select Pet*. The Visible action argument is set to Yes to display the list box or No to hide the list box.

Two conditions are needed for the Show List macro. The first condition holds if the third option button has been clicked; the second condition holds if the button has not been clicked. The Macro Name column has already been set to Show List.

In the first line of the Show List macro, set the Condition column to [Report to Print]=3 to reflect the third option button being clicked in the option group. This line displays the list box, so the action of the macro is set to SetValue, the Item action argument is set to [Select Pet].Visible, and the Expression action argument is set to Yes. Figure 32-36 displays these settings.

You can also see the second line of the Show List macro and comments in Figure 32-36. Notice in the second line that the Condition column indicates that the third option button in the option group has not been clicked and is therefore set to Not [Report to Print]=3. This line hides the list box, so the action of the macro is SetValue, the Item property is set to [Select Pet].Visible, and the Expression property is set to No. To create the macro, follow these steps:

1. Type the first two lines in the Comment column, as shown at the top of Figure 32-36.

2. Move the cursor to the first line of the Show List macro row.

3. Place the cursor in the Condition column and type **[Report to Print]=3**.

4. Place the cursor in the Action column and either select or type **SetValue**.

5. Press F6 to move to the Item property in the Action Arguments pane and type **[Select Pet].Visible**.

6. Move to the Expression property and type **Yes**.

7. Press F6 to return to the Action column and then move to the Comment column.

8. Enter the comments in the Comment column, as shown in Figure 32-36.

9. Move your cursor to the second line of the Show List macro row.

10. In the Condition column, type **Not [Report to Print]=3**.

11. In the Action column, type (or select) **SetValue**.

12. Press F6 to move to the Item box in the Action Arguments pane and type **[Select Pet].Visible**.

The Pets Report Query for the Print Reports Form Lis

The Pets Report is a simple query that has the Customer and Pets tables related by the Customer Number field. The query has two fields displayed: Pet Name from the Pets table and Customer Name from the Customer table. The data is sorted first by Customer Number and second by Pet Name.

The following figure shows the partial datasheet for this list box. The Pet Name field is in the first column and the Customer Name field is in the second column. The data is sorted first by the customer number and second by the pet name. As you learned previously, to sort data by two fields, you must place the fields in the Query Design window in the order in which you want the two fields sorted.

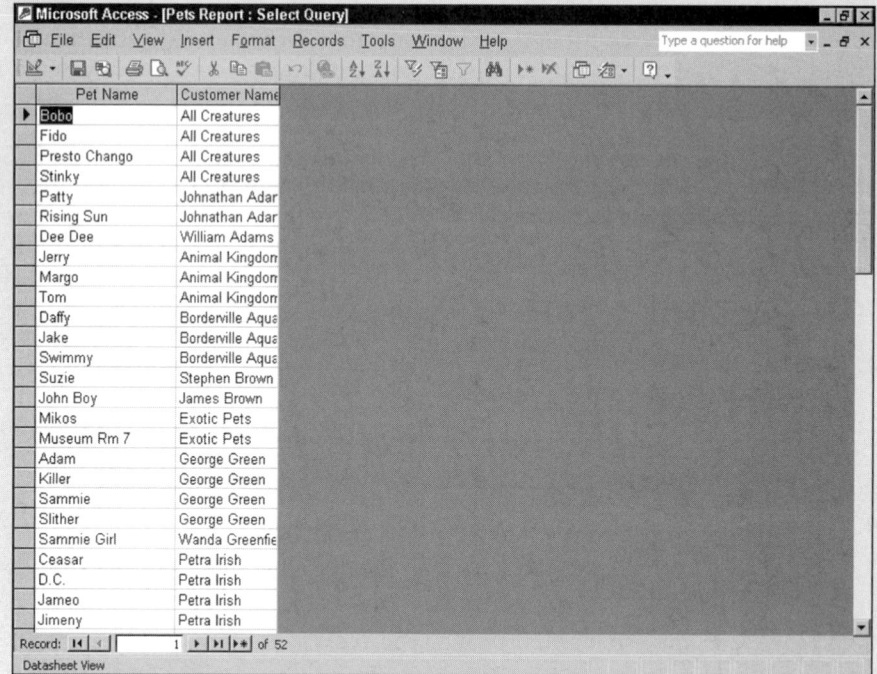

The partial datasheet for the Pets Report query

To sort by the customer number first and then by the pet name, you must place the Customer Number field first in the query but not select it to show. You then place the Customer Name field third in the query and select it. The query places Customer Name first in the datasheet. The following figure shows the query design after it's been saved and reopened. Remember that Access rearranges fields when a field isn't selected to be viewed because the Show check box is unchecked.

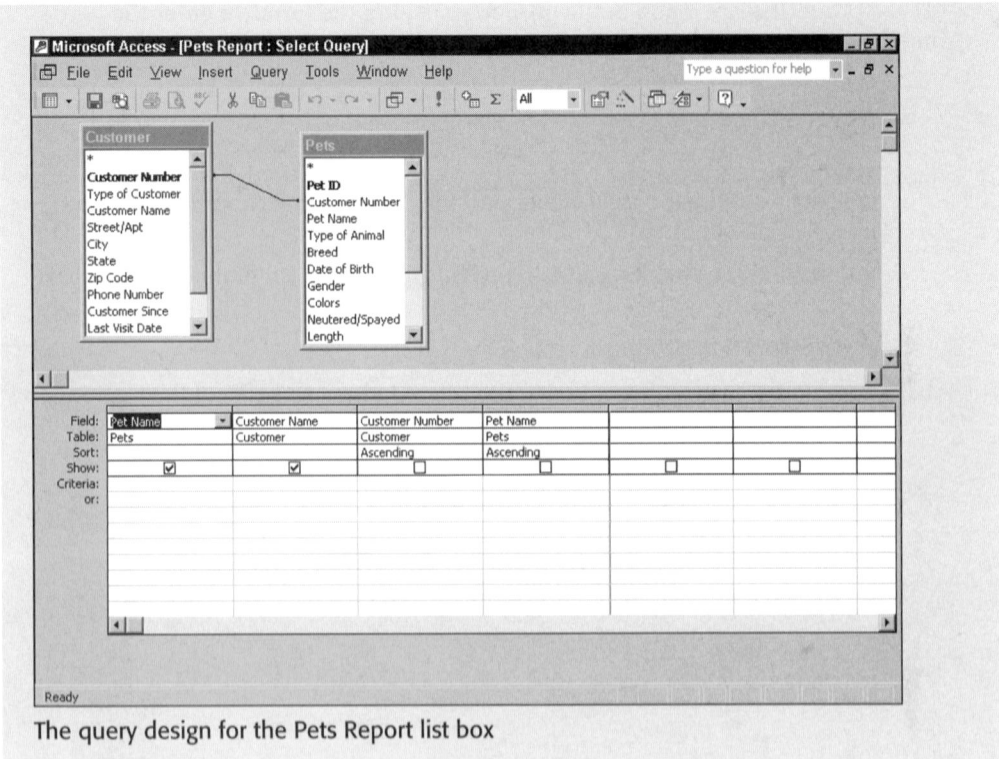

The query design for the Pets Report list box

13. Move to the Expression property and type **No**.

14. Press F6 to return to the Action column and then move to the Comment column.

15. Enter the comments in the Comment column, as shown in Figure 32-36.

After you complete the Show List macro (as explained in the following section), you can enter the calls to the macro in the form events properties. After this task is completed, test the macro. Before continuing, select File ➪ Save to save the Print Reports macro library and leave it open on-screen.

Entering the Show List macro calls

You are now ready to enter the macro calls for the Show List macro. This macro is called from two places:

✦ The On Open property of the form object

✦ The After Update property of the option group control

These properties are found in the property sheet of the form. To enter the two macro calls, follow these steps:

1. With the Print Reports Macro window open, select Window ⇨ Print Reports Dialog: Form.

2. Make sure that the Form's Property window is displayed. If not, click the Properties button on the toolbar and then on the gray square next to the intersection of both form rulers.

3. Enter Print Reports.Show List in the On Open property of the Form property sheet.

4. Click the Option Group control.

5. Enter Print Reports.Show List in the After Update property of the Option Group property sheet, as shown in Figure 32-37.

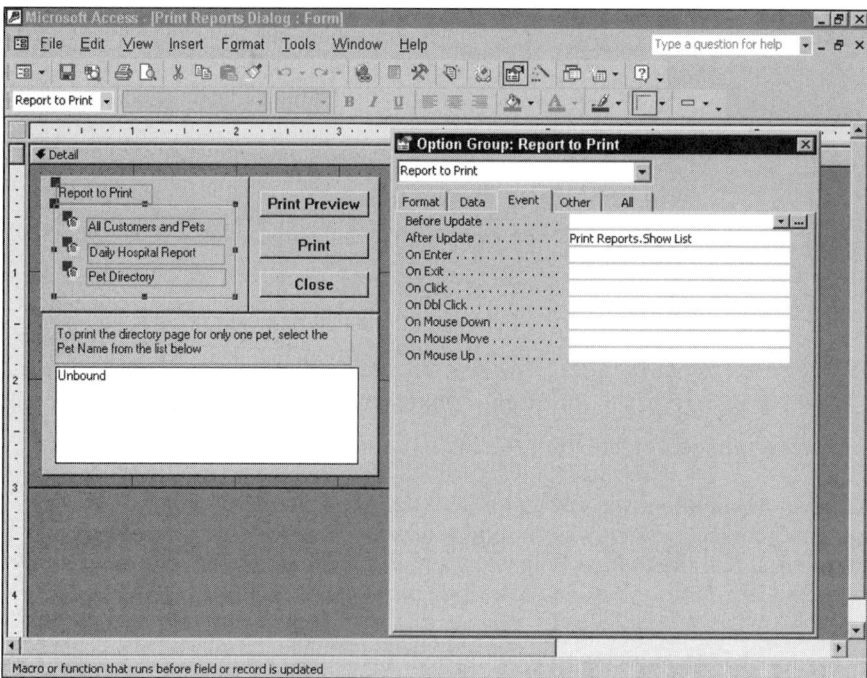

Figure 32-37: Entering the macro call

Test this macro by clicking on the Form View button on the toolbar. As you click on the first and second option buttons, the list box should become invisible. When you select the third option button, the list box should reappear. Return to the Design window before continuing.

Creating the Print Preview macro

The Print Preview macro is the next macro that you need to create. Switch to the Macro window by selecting Window ➪ 3 Print Reports: Macro. This macro is fairly complicated, although it uses only three different macro commands. As you enter the macro commands, you may need to add more lines to the Macro window. Select Insert ➪ Row whenever you need to add a new row to the Macro window.

Note   You must first select a row to add a new row.

Figure 32-38 shows the completed Print Preview, Print, and Close macros in the Macro window. You can enter all the comments and create the first macro row by following these steps:

1. Type all the lines in the Comment column, as shown in Figure 32-38.

2. Move the cursor to the first line of the Print Preview macro row.

3. In the Action column, type (or select) **SetValue**.

4. Press F6 to move to the Item property of the Action Arguments pane and type **Visible**.

5. Move to the Expression box in the Action Arguments pane and type **No**.

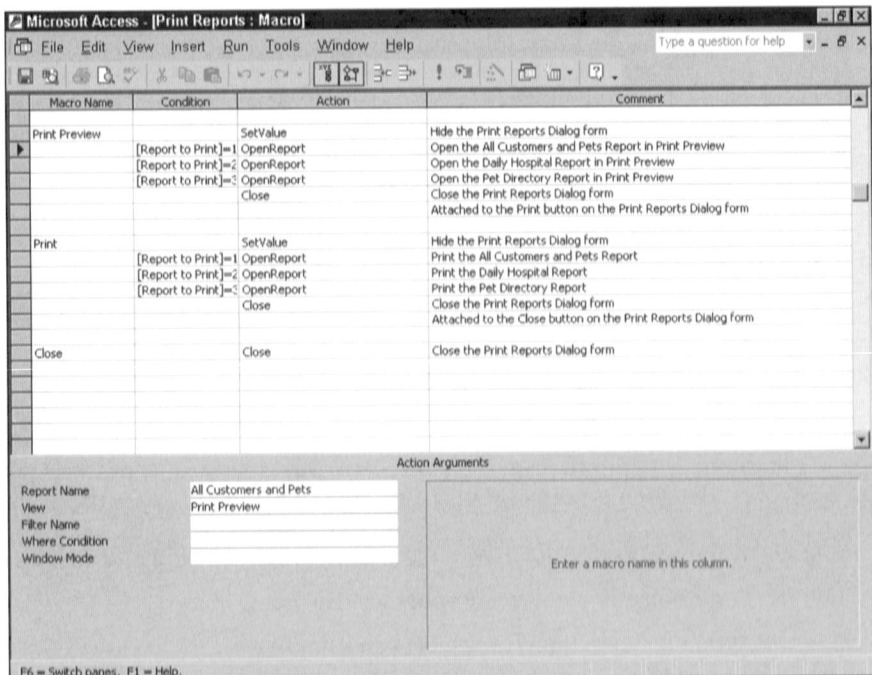

Figure 32-38: Creating the Print Preview macro

Because no control is specified, it defaults to the form itself. This hides the entire Form window when the Print Reports macro is started.

The next three lines of the macro determine the actions that you need to take when the Print Preview button is selected for each of the possible option button choices. The first two choices simply display the selected report in a print preview mode. The third choice displays a report by selecting the pet name chosen from the list box. To create the next row, follow these steps:

1. Move your cursor to the second row of the Print Preview macro.

2. In the Condition column, type **[Report to Print]=1**.

3. In the Action column, type (or select) **OpenReport**.

   The OpenReport macro command opens the report specified in the Action Arguments pane of the Macro window.

4. Press F6 to move to the Report Name box in the Action Arguments pane of the Print Preview macro and type **All Customers and Pets**.

5. Move to the View box in the Action Arguments pane and type **Print Preview**.

6. Press F6 to return to the Action column.

These action arguments specify to open the All Customers and Pets report in a Print Preview window. The second Print row of the Print Preview macro is very similar to the first, except that you must reference the second option button being selected. To create the next row, follow these steps:

1. Move the cursor to the third row of the Print Preview macro.

2. In the Condition column, type **[Report to Print]=2**.

3. In the Action column, type (or select) **OpenReport**.

4. Press F6 to move to the Report Name box in the Action Arguments pane and type **Daily Hospital Report**.

5. Move to the View box in the Action Arguments pane and type **Print Preview**.

6. Press F6 to return to the Action column.

The third OpenReport row contains an extra action argument that the first two rows don't use. The Pet Directory report must use the results of the list box selection to determine whether to print the entire Pets Directory report or to print only the report for the specific pet selected. To create the next row, follow these steps:

1. Move the cursor to the fourth row of the Print Preview macro and insert a row.

2. In the Condition column, type **[Report to Print]=3**.

3. In the Action column, type (or select) **OpenReport**.

4. Press F6 to move to the Report Name box in the Action Arguments pane and type **Pet Directory**.

5. Move to the View box in the Action Arguments pane and type **Print Preview**.

6. Move to the Where Condition box and type the following:

```
=IIF(Forms![Print Reports Dialog]![Select Pet]Is
Null,"","[Pet Name] = Forms![Print Reports Dialog]![Select
Pet]")
```

The Where Condition specifies the condition when the pet name is selected. The condition has two parts: The first part of the IIf (Immediate IF) function handles the condition when no pet name is selected, and it forms the object hierarchy. The hierarchy is

✦ **Object.** Forms

✦ **Form name.** Print Reports Dialog box

✦ **Control name.** Select Pet (the list box)

✦ **Selection.** Is Null

Note   Each of the hierarchy objects is separated by an exclamation mark (!).

If no pet name is selected, then all the pet records are used. The second half of the IIf function is used when a pet name is selected. The second half of the function sets the value of Pet Name to the value chosen in the list box control.

Creating the Print macro

You can create the code for the Print macro by copying each line from the Print Preview macro. Then substitute Print for Print Preview in the View box of the Action Arguments pane for each OpenReport action.

Creating the Close macro

The Close macro simply uses Close for the action. Enter Form for the Object Type and Print Reports Dialog for the Action Arguments object name.

Entering the Print Preview, Print, and Close macro calls

You use the command buttons to trigger an action. Each uses the On Click property. To enter the three macro calls, follow these steps:

1. From the Print Reports Macro window, select Window ⟡ 2 Form: Print Reports Dialog.

2. Make sure that the property sheet is displayed. If not, click the Properties button on the toolbar.

3. Display the Print Preview command button property by clicking the Print Preview button.

4. Enter Print Reports.Print Preview in the On Click property of the button's property sheet, as shown in Figure 32-39.

5. Display the Print command button property sheet by clicking the Print button.

6. Enter Print Reports.Print in the On Click property of the button's property sheet.

7. Display the Close command button property sheet by clicking the Close button.

8. Enter Print Reports.Close into the On Click property of the button's property sheet.

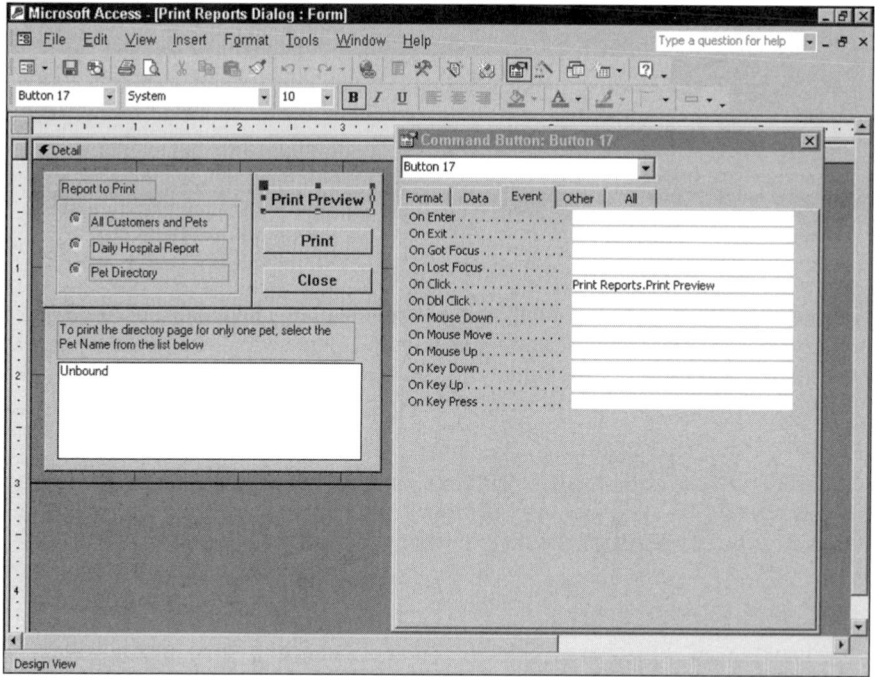

Figure 32-39: Entering the Print Preview macro call into the command button's property sheet

Sizing the dialog box and changing form properties

The last step in creating a dialog box is to change the Form window properties and size and place the window. You need to set several form properties. The properties and their explanations are listed in Table 32-4.

Table 32-4
Properties for a Form Dialog Box

Property	Value	Description
Default View	Single Form	Displays the form as a single form; necessary for forms that take up less than half a page
Views Allowed	Form	User can't switch into datasheet mode
Scroll Bars	Neither	(Scroll bars should be omitted in a dialog box)
Navigation Buttons	No	Record navigation buttons are not displayed
Record Selectors	No	Doesn't display standard record selectors at the bottom left of the form
Auto Resize	Yes	Automatically resizes the form when opened
Auto Center	Yes	Automatically centers the form when opened
Border Style	Dialog	Makes border non-sizable
Pop Up	Yes	Allows the form to be displayed on top of other windows as a pop-up dialog box
Modal	Yes	User must make a choice before leaving the dialog box

Set the Pop Up property to No if the dialog box calls any other windows. If this property is set to Yes, the dialog box is always displayed on top; you can't get to other windows without first closing the dialog box.

Using the Access 2002 Tab Control

Today, most serious Windows applications contain tabbed dialog boxes. Tabbed dialog boxes look very professional. They allow you to have many screens of data in a small area by grouping similar types of data and using tabs to navigate between the areas.

Access 2002 provides a built-in tab control similar to the one that has been in Visual Basic for many years.

Creating a new form with the Access 2002 tab control

The Access 2002 tab control is available on the Form Design toolbar. This control is called a *tab control* because it looks like the tabs on a file folder. Figure 32-40 shows the Access 2002 Form Design window with the toolbar showing the tab control icon and a tab control already under construction on the design screen.

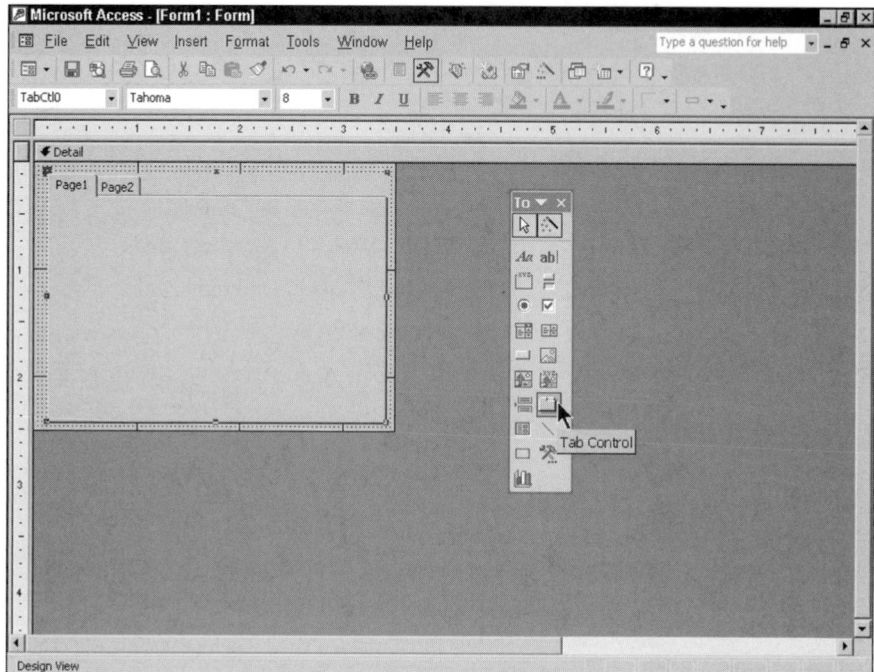

Figure 32-40: Creating an Access 2002 tab control

In this example, you create a Print Reports Dialog form that contains a tabbed dialog box, which shows a larger view of the Pet Directory so that you can see more data.

You create a new tab control the same way you create any Access control. You select the Tab Control button, as shown in Figure 32-40, and then draw a rectangle to indicate the size of the control.

The tab control contains pages. When you first place a new tab control, it initially contains two tab pages. Each tab that you define creates a separate page. As you choose each tab in Design view, you see a different page. You can place other controls on each page of the tab control. The control can have many pages. You can have multiple rows of tabs, each with its own page. You can place new controls onto a page or copy and paste them from other forms or other pages. You can't drag and drop between pages of a tab control, however. To change the active page for the tab control, click the page that you want and it becomes active (even in design mode).

You insert new pages by selecting the Insert ➪ Tab Control Page option or by right-clicking a tab and choosing the Insert command. The new page is inserted before the selected page. You delete pages by selecting a tab and pressing the Delete key, or by choosing the Edit ➪ Delete menu option, or by right-clicking a tab and selecting the Delete command.

Caution This deletes the active page and all the controls on it.

You can size the tab control but not individual pages. Individual pages don't have visual appearance properties — they get these from the tab control. You can click on the border of the tab control to select it. You can click directly on a page to select that page. As with an Access detail section, you can't size the tab control smaller than the control in the rightmost part of the page.

Tip You must move controls before resizing.

Tip For this example, you can copy all the controls from the original Print Report Dialog except the List Box and its caption and paste them on Page 1 of the tab control. Copy and paste the List Box control and its caption to Page 2 of the tab control. Remember that you move between tab pages by clicking on the tab — even in Form Design view. When you are done, your tabbed dialog box should look like the one in Figure 32-41.

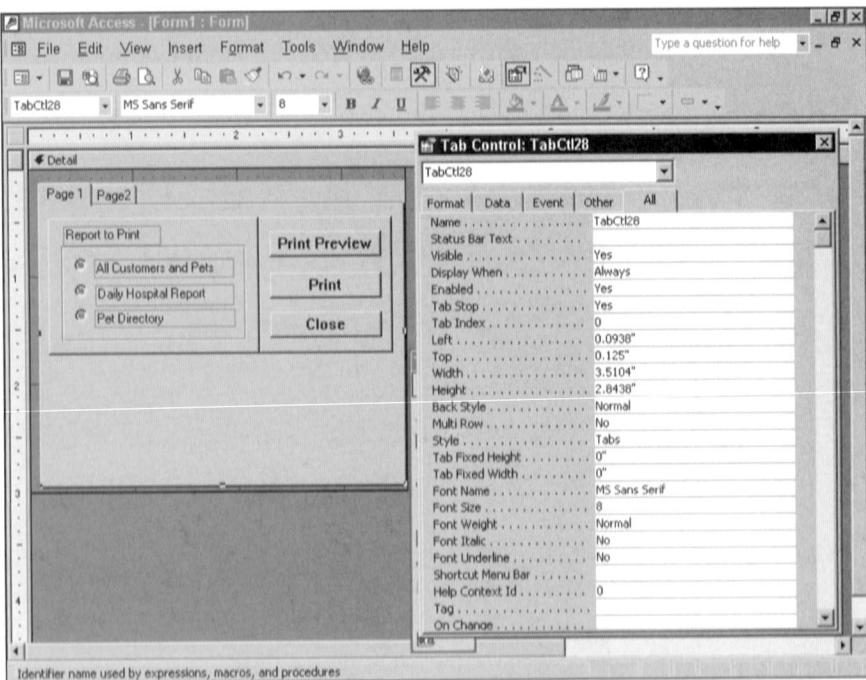

Figure 32-41: Tab control properties

Access 2002 Tab control properties

Like any control, the tab control has a variety of properties. The tab control has a separate set of properties for the tab control as well as for each page of the tab control. Figure 32-41 shows the property window for the tab control. Notice that there is no Control Source property. The tab control is only a container for other controls. The form can be bound to a table or query, and each control placed on a tab page can be bound to a table field, but the tab control and its pages can't be bound by themselves to a data source.

The tab control has many properties found in most controls, such as a Name, Status Bar Text, Visible, Enabled, Tab Stop, and the position and size properties. The tab control also has several unique properties. The Multi Row, Style, Tab Fixed Height, and Fixed Width properties are only found in the tab control.

Working with multiple rows

The first unique property is Multi Row. This is either Yes or No. The default is No. When you change the value to Yes and you have more tabs than can fit in the width of the tab control, the tabs jump to a new row (see Figure 32-42). If you make the tab control wider, the tab may return to a single row. You can create as many rows as you have vertical space. The tab control can be as wide as the form width allows. Figure 32-42 shows one-, two-, and three-row tab controls. The middle tab control has an uneven number of tabs on each row. This is perfectly acceptable; the tabs grow to fill the available space. The tab control at the bottom was sized too small to fit the number of tabs and the Multi Row property was set to No. Navigation buttons appear to fill the space.

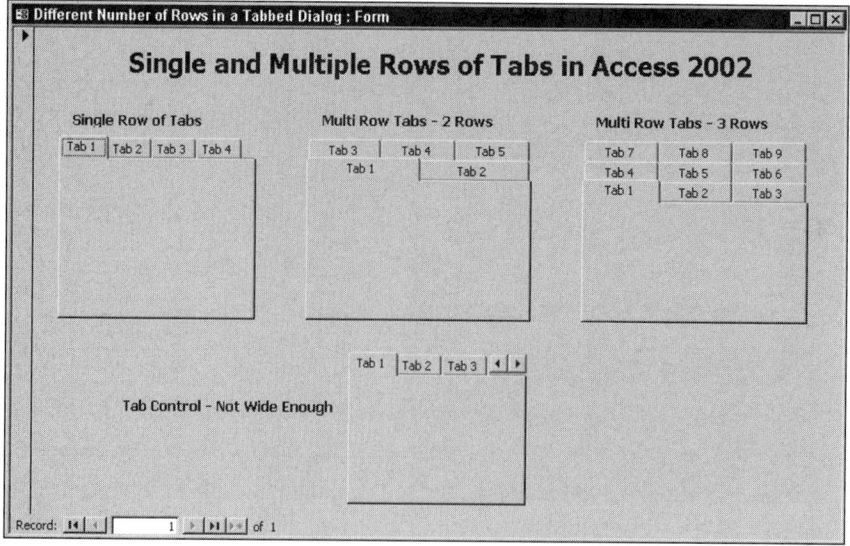

Figure 32-42: Using the Multi Row property

Setting the height and width of the tabs

Two properties affect the size of the tabs in the tab control: Tab Fixed Height and Tab Fixed Width. The default for both of these properties is 0. When the properties are set to 0, each tab is just wide enough and tall enough to accommodate its contents. If the properties are greater than 0, the tab is the exact size specified.

The style of a Tab control

The next unique property is the Style property, which has three settings — Tabs, Buttons, and None — as shown in Figure 32-43. The Tabs setting is the default and creates the standard square tabs. Using the Buttons setting makes the tabs look like raised and sunken command buttons. The effect shown in Figure 32-43 looks more like a toolbar than a set of tabbed folders. You can't see the rectangle, as with the Tabs setting. The third setting, None, removes the tabs from the tab control and leaves an empty gray area. When using this setting, the tab control can act like a multi-page form that you can manage through program code. Using this method provides more control than a standard multi-page form because you don't have to worry about accidentally moving from one page to the next by simply pressing the Page Up or the Page Down keys.

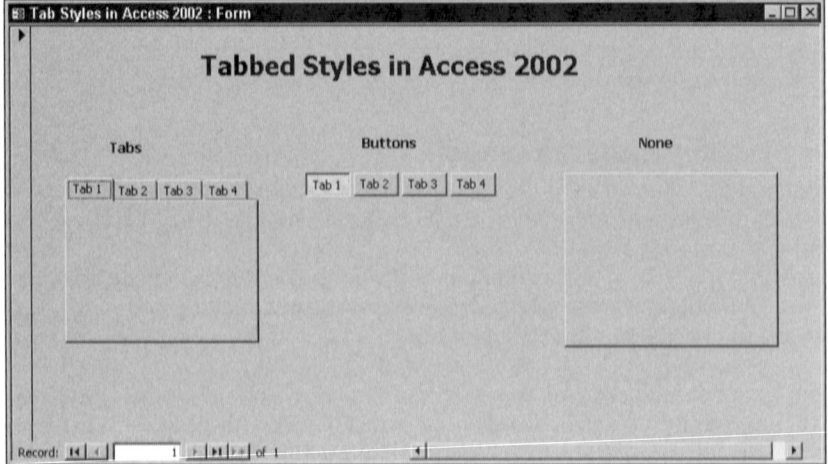

Figure 32-43: Using the Style property

Changing the page order

Another feature of the tab control is the ability to change the order of the pages (tabs) in the same way that you can change the tab order of the controls on the form. Figure 32-44 shows the Page Order dialog box. It lists the text on each tab and lets you use the Move Up and Move Down buttons to rearrange the pages on the tab control.

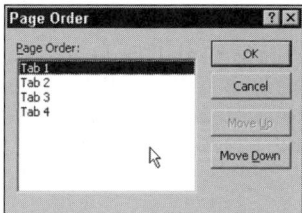

Figure 32-44: Changing the page order

Changing the tab order for controls on a tab page

When you select a form and choose View ⇨ Tab Order, the Tab Order dialog box shows the names of your tab controls. The controls inside the tab control don't show in this dialog box.

To set the tab order for controls within a particular page of a tab control, choose the Tab Order command from the tab control's right-click menu, or select a control on the tab page, and then select View ⇨ Tab Order. You must set the tab order for each page individually.

Tabbing out of the last control inside a tab control page brings you to the next control in the tab order for the form. You can't jump between pages.

Adding pictures to the tab control

You can add a picture to each tab using the page properties for the tab control. You can display the page properties for a particular tab by selecting the tab on the tab control and choosing View ⇨ Properties. To add a picture to the tab, use the Picture property just like you do for a command button, toggle button, image control, or unbound OLE object. When you specify a caption and a picture for a tab, the picture displays to the left of the tab caption.

You can type the full path and name of the bitmap or icon file or use the Access 2002 Picture Builder to select a picture. Figure 32-45 illustrates adding a picture to a tab in the Print Reports Tabbed Dialog form. In the figure, the picture of a printer displays on Page 1.

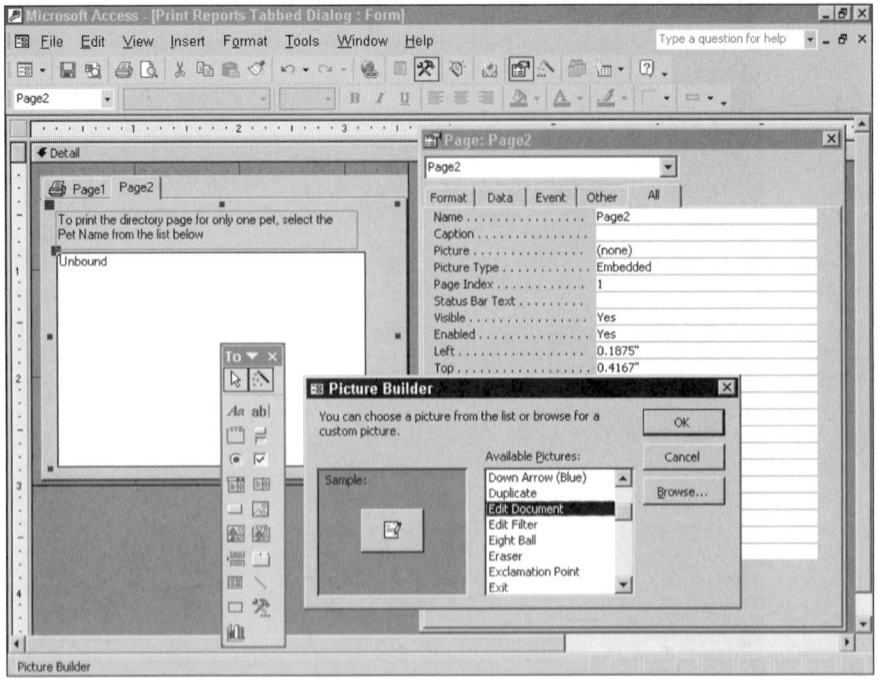

Figure 32-45: Adding a picture to a tab

✦   ✦   ✦

Access and the External World

✦   ✦   ✦   ✦

In This Part

Chapter 33
Moving from Jet to
the SQL Server 2000
Desktop Engine

Chapter 34
Working with Access
Projects

Chapter 35
Using and Creating
Access Objects for
Intranets and the
Internet

Chapter 36
Building Web
Applications, Data
Access Pages, and
XML

✦   ✦   ✦   ✦

Moving from Jet to the SQL Server 2000 Desktop Engine

Understanding the
SQL Server 2000
Desktop Engine

Comparing the SQL
Server 2000 Desktop
Engine to Jet

Working with the
SQL Server 2000
Desktop Engine

Creating tables and
database diagrams
in an Access project

Upsizing from Jet

◆ ◆ ◆ ◆

SQL Server 2000 Desktop Engine is a client/server data engine alternative to the Microsoft Jet database engine. In Access 2000, this was called the *Microsoft Database Engine* (MSDE) and was built on the SQL Server 7 technology. In Access 2002, the SQL Server 2000 Desktop Engine is built on SQL Server 2000 and is compatible with the full Microsoft SQL Server 2000 version, so your client/server application can run on either version. If you anticipate your small workgroup application to eventually accommodate 20 or more users — or even hundreds or thousands of users — you probably want to use SQL Server 2000 Desktop Engine. In this chapter, you learn how to set up SQL Server 2000 Desktop Engine and how you can use it to build powerful client/server database applications.

Understanding SQL Server 2000 Desktop Engine

SQL Server 2000 Desktop Engine is a client/server database engine that is designed to be compatible with the SQL Server database engine. Think of SQL Server 2000 Desktop Engine as a scaled-down version of SQL Server. With some exceptions, it provides all of the power of SQL Server, yet it has been optimized to run on desktop computers running Windows 98, Windows ME (or later), Windows NT 4.0, and Windows 2000 (or later).

Applications developed using SQL Server 2000 Desktop Engine can be run under SQL Server 2000 Standard Edition or SQL Server 2000 Enterprise Edition without modification. This capability is a great advantage to both application developers and their customers.

In the rapidly changing business environments of today, many software development projects begin targeting a handful of users. Within a relatively short span of time, the application needs to be available across the enterprise, consisting of possibly hundreds or thousands of users. In a typical scenario like this, the customer faces expensive development costs and lost time when the application needs to be modified to accommodate the larger environment. Or, in the worst case scenario, the customer may be forced to abandon the smaller application and reengineer it with a client/server toolset. SQL Server 2000 Desktop Engine provides the scalability required by growing business environments.

Developers who don't have access to a network running SQL Server can build client/server applications using SQL Server 2000 Desktop Engine on a personal computer. Some simple changes to the connection information are all that is required when the time comes to connect the application to SQL Server.

Comparing SQL Server 2000 Desktop Engine and Jet

The SQL Server 2000 Desktop Engine is a true client/server database engine. That is, the *interface objects* (forms, reports, and shortcuts to data access pages) are stored locally on the workstation in a Microsoft Access project. The data, however, is stored on a local or network server. Additionally, much of the processing of data (running queries and stored procedures) occurs on the server. This is very different from the Jet database in that regardless of where you have the data, all the records in a table are returned to the local workstation when processing a bound form or report. Client/server architecture minimizes the work of both the client and the server and cuts down on the amount of information traveling over the network.

Microsoft Jet is the default database engine included with Access 2002. SQL Server 2000 Desktop Engine is an alternative database engine to the Microsoft Jet database engine. If you have developed applications in previous versions of Microsoft Access, you should be familiar with Microsoft Jet.

Jet is the file/server data manager behind the Microsoft Access database. A Microsoft Access database can store all of an application's database objects, including the interface objects and the data. Jet moves the data back and forth between tables and forms and reports. Jet is described as a file server database engine because its job is merely to store and retrieve data. There is no distribution of processing between server and workstation as occurs in the client/server architecture.

Although SQL Server 2000 Desktop Engine provides the optimum in power and flexibility, Jet is the appropriate environment for many types of situations. Therefore, it's important to choose the right database engine for the job.

Choosing the right database engine

Designing a database application requires careful consideration of the business environment's current situation, as well as strategic planning for expansion — either in the number of users, or in the volume of data to be stored and retrieved. Delivering an application that's unable to handle the growing needs of the business or, worse, that can't handle even the initial needs of the business environment, can be a real career-buster. Although it's tempting to design every application with a "the sky's the limit" approach so that it can accommodate the full spectrum of business environments, you need to find the right balance between maximum flexibility and simplicity.

When selecting the database engine that is most appropriate for your application, consider these four criteria:

✦ Simplicity

✦ Data integrity

✦ Number of users

✦ Volume of data

In the simplicity category, Jet gets the score. As the default database in Access 2002, creating a Jet database is much easier than creating one for SQL Server 2000 Desktop Engine. It is also the most compatible with previous versions of Access. Although Access provides built-in security administration, Jet databases don't require security (user IDs and passwords). SQL Server 2000 Desktop Engine does require security and uses the Windows NT security model. The memory and hard drive space requirements for Jet databases are low as compared to SQL Server 2000 Desktop Engine.

Tip   You can always upsize a Jet database to SQL Server later on using the Upsizing Wizard. You may need to make some modifications to the application, however.

When considering data integrity, SQL Server 2000 Desktop Engine is the most reliable choice. SQL Server 2000 Desktop Engine includes the same data integrity technology that is provided in SQL Server 2000. All changes that you make to the database are logged to a transaction file. In the event of a database disaster — a hardware failure or power interruption, for example — the database can repair itself using the log file. With Jet, however, this kind of disastrous event can permanently corrupt the database. As anyone who has ever tried to repair an Access database knows, a reliable backup strategy is a must. For some mission-critical applications, though, restoring from yesterday's backup can result in a major business interruption. For those types of applications, SQL Server 2000 Desktop Engine is the best option.

Note   When addressing the limitations of SQL Server 2000 Desktop Engine, remember that it is 100 percent compatible with SQL Server 2000.

Both Jet and SQL Server 2000 Desktop Engine are designed for the single workstation or small workgroup. Generally, SQL Server 2000 Desktop Engine can handle the same number of simultaneous users as Jet. SQL Server 2000 Desktop Engine, however, has a limit of five active simultaneous query batches. That is, the database engine can process up to five queries at one time. SQL Server will queue any subsequent queries until one or more of the previous five query batches completes. Despite this limitation, SQL Server 2000 Desktop Engine, as a client/server database engine, has the performance advantage over Jet even in a small workgroup situation. SQL Server 2000 Desktop Engine processes queries on the server and moves only the resulting data to the client workstation. Jet, on the other hand, must move the data to the client so that the client workstation can process the query.

Both Jet and SQL Server 2000 Desktop Engine have a maximum database size of 2GB. For applications that accumulate a large volume of data over a long period of time, consider including an archive/purge utility in the application. For many business situations, only a relatively small volume of data needs to be active at any point in time.

If you have determined that SQL Server 2000 Desktop Engine is the right database engine to utilize in your database application, you are ready to begin working with this new and powerful feature of Access 2002.

Table 33-1 compares the capabilities of SQL Server and Jet. The table comes from the "Microsoft Access 2000 Data Engine Options" whitepaper and is reprinted with permission from Microsoft.

Table 33-1
Comparison of SQL Server/MSDE and Jet

Requirement	SQL Server	Microsoft Access (Jet) (Use MSDE if These Are Future Requirements)
Scalability	SMP support	No SMP support
	Virtually unlimited number of concurrent users	Maximum of 255 users
	Terabyte levels of data	2 GB of data
	Transaction logging	No transaction logging
Business Critical	7X24 support and QFE	No 7X24 support or QFE
	Point-in-time recovery	Recoverable to last backup
	Guaranteed transaction integrity	No transaction logging
	Built-in fault tolerance	No integrated security with Windows NT
	Security integrated with Windows NT	
Rapid Application	Access is UI for both engines and Prototyping offers WYSIWIG database tools and built-in forms generation	

Installing SQL Server 2000 Desktop Engine

SQL Server 2000 Desktop Engine doesn't install automatically when you install Office 2002. It is provided as a separate installation process included on the Office 2002 CD-ROM.

Hardware requirements

Chances are, if you are successfully running Office 2002 on your personal computer, your hardware meets the minimum requirements for SQL Server 2000 Desktop Engine.

For Windows 2000 computers, SQL Server 2000 Desktop Engine requires 64MB of RAM. For other operation systems, 32MB of RAM is required. SQL Server 2000 Desktop Engine requires approximately 45MB of hard drive space for a typical installation—25MB for program files and 20MB for data files. Optionally, you can store the program files and data files on separate drives. Remember that you need additional space for your database files.

Tip   In reality, you should have a minimum of 128MB on any computer system running Microsoft business software purchased in 2001 or later.

Note   MSDE, Microsoft Data Engine, is the previous version of Microsoft SQL Server 2000 Desktop Engine. MSDE is compatible with SQL Server Version 7. While SQL Server 2000 Desktop Engine provides some additional features, the two desktop versions are very similar. For the purposes of this discussion, any of the concepts that applied to MSDE certainly apply to SQL Server 2000 Desktop Engine.

Software requirements

SQL Server 2000 Desktop Engine requires that Microsoft Windows 98, Windows ME or later, Windows NT 4.0 or later, or Windows 2000 or later be installed on your computer. SQL Server 2000 Desktop Engine does not run on OS/2, Windows 95, or Windows 3.1.

Running the SQL Server 2000 Desktop Engine Installation Program

To install SQL Server 2000 Desktop Engine, insert the Office 2002 CD-ROM into your CD-ROM drive and select Run from the Start menu. In the Run box, type **D:\MSDE2000\Setup.exe** (or use whatever letter corresponds to the drive containing your installation CD-ROM). Click OK to begin the installation.

Caution   If you have installed MSDE, the previous version of SQL Server 2000 Desktop Engine, you should uninstall it before installing SQL Server 2000 Desktop Engine.

Because some Windows programs interfere with the Setup program, the installation program may warn you to shut down any applications that you have currently running. You can simply click on the Continue button to continue the setup, or you can click on the Cancel button to cancel the installation and run the installation later. The installation program installs and configures SQL Server 2000 Desktop Engine automatically. A progress meter displays during the installation and configuration process, as shown in Figure 33-1.

Note   These installation instructions correspond to the installation procedure provided by Microsoft's beta-testing staff at the time this chapter was written. Actual installation instructions may be revised by the time the product is released.

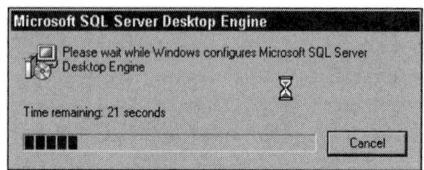

Figure 33-1: The SQL Server 2000 Desktop Engine installation progress meter

When you have installed all of the SQL Server 2000 Desktop Engine files, the progress meter disappears. You should restart the computer to complete the installation.

Customizing the installation of SQL Server 2000 Desktop Engine

The Setup program for SQL Server 2000 Desktop Engine comes with built-in setup parameters. It does not display any screens for customizing the setup for parameters, such as the target directory for the SQL Server 2000 Desktop Engine program files, the target directory for storing the SQL Server data files, or the default SQL Server name. To override these built-in settings, you must run Setup.exe using command-line switches.

These command-line switches customize the installation as shown in Table 33-2:

Table 33-2	
Configuration Options for Installing SQL	
Server 2000 Desktop Engine	
Setting	**Description**
TARGETDIR	The name of the folder to install SQL Server 2000 Desktop Engine. The default value is C:\Program Files\Microsoft SQL Server\.
DATADIR	The name of an optional folder for data files. The default value is the value of TARGETDIR.
COLLATION	The name of a collation sequence.
INSTANCENAME	The name of the SQL Server. The Default value is MSSQLSERVER.

Note You must enter the setting options in uppercase.

The following is an example of entering command-line switches with Setup.exe.

```
Setup.exe \\MySWdisk\SQLSW\ TARGETDIR="C:\Program Files\SQL8\"
DATADIR="C:\Program Files\SQLDATA\"
COLLATION="SQL_Latin1_General_CP1257_CS_AS"
INSTANCENAME=myinstance
```

Starting the SQL Server 2000 Desktop Engine

When you have completed the setup, the SQL Server Service Manager displays on the Windows taskbar. To work with an SQL Server 2000 Desktop Engine database, you must first start the SQL Server Service Manager.

When you install SQL Server 2000 Desktop Engine, SQL Server Service Manager starts automatically. You can run the SQL Server Service Manager any time by choosing it from your Windows taskbar.

The SQL Server Service Manager, shown in Figure 33-2, allows you to choose the type of service that you want to start. The Server box lists the names of the servers that SQL Server Service Manager has found. In this example, the 22HAG server is the name of the desktop where SQL Server 2000 Desktop Engine was installed. The Services box lists the names of the SQL Server services that you can start. The services you can start include

✦ **SQLServer.** Database server for SQL Server

✦ **MSDTC.** Distributed transaction server

✦ **SQL Server Agent.** Runs scheduled administrative tasks

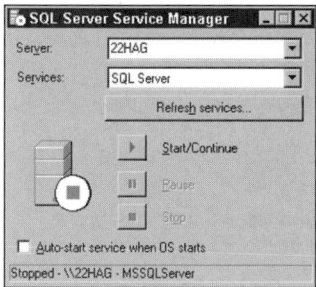

Figure 33-2: Using SQL Server
Service Manager

To start the SQL Server 2000 Desktop Engine, select SQL Server for Services. Then
click Start/Continue.

Tip

Selecting the option "Auto-Start service when OS starts" in the SQL Server Service
Manager automatically starts the service when you boot up Windows.

When SQL Server 2000 Desktop Engine has started, an arrow displays next to the
server in SQL Server Service Manager, as shown in Figure 33-3.

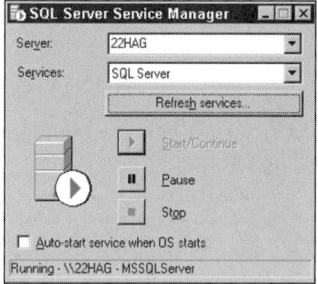

Figure 33-3: Starting SQL Server
2000 Desktop Engine

When SQL Server 2000 Desktop Engine starts, the Pause and Stop buttons in SQL
Server Service Manager are enabled. When you are running SQL Server in a multi-
user environment, you may need to stop the server at some point in order to perform an administrative task. Before stopping the server, select the Pause button to
pause the server. Pausing the server prevents any additional users from logging in

to the server. Then you can alert any currently logged-in users to complete their work and log out of the server. When you are certain that all users have logged out, select the Stop button to stop the server.

Caution Stopping SQL Server prevents anyone from connecting to the database and drops any currently connected users. Disconnecting a user unexpectedly could lead to data loss.

After you have successfully installed SQL Server 2000 Desktop Engine and started the server, it's time to get started building a database.

Creating a SQL Server 2000 Desktop Engine Database

To create an SQL Server 2000 Desktop Engine database, you start by creating a Microsoft Access project. A Microsoft Access project (.adp) is an Access data file that allows you to work directly with SQL Server data. Using a project, you can create and access Microsoft SQL Server 6.5, Microsoft SQL Server 7.0, Microsoft SQL Server 2000, SQL Server 2000 Desktop Engine, or Microsoft Data Engine (MSDE) databases. This section shows how creating a client/server application is very similar to creating a Microsoft Access database. Access projects are explained further in the "Understanding projects" portion of this section.

Note Although SQL Server 2000 Desktop Engine has replaced MSDE, you may have some active MSDE databases that have not been converted to the new version. Access projects allow you to connect to either version.

Creating a project

To begin creating a project, start Microsoft Access. Then select File ⇨ New from the main Access menu, or click on the first icon in the toolbar.

You can also create a new project by clicking on the New Database icon. This is the first icon in the toolbar. It looks like a sheet of paper with the right-top corner bent down.

Caution To create a new project that accesses an SQL database, Microsoft SQL Server Service Manager must be running. Refer to the topic on Starting SQL Server 2000 Desktop Engine to learn how to start the service manager.

The New File task pane appears, as shown in Figure 33-4. The task pane displays four tasks: Open a file, New, New from existing file, and New from template. The New task displays four object types: Blank Database, Blank Data Access Page, Project (Existing Data), and Project (New Data). Select the Project (New Data) object.

Tip   When you first start Access, the New File task pane appears automatically. You can choose the option Project (New Data) on this screen.

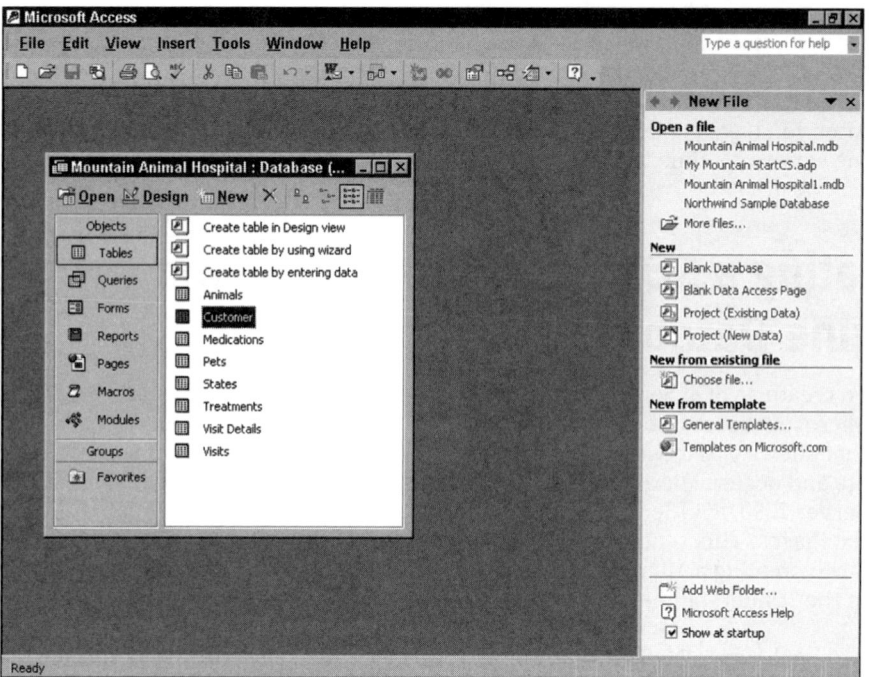

Figure 33-4: The New File task pane

The File New Database dialog box displays, in which you must create a name and location for the database. Figure 33-5 shows the standard Windows file dialog box, which has several information areas to complete. A default name, adp1.adp, displays next to the File name combo box. Adding the .adp file extension is optional; Access adds it automatically during the creation process. Because the database is a standard Windows file, its file name can be any valid Windows long file name. You may also see existing .adp files in the file list area if you previously created any projects. Although the Save in combo box may be set to My Documents, you can change this to any folder name. In this example, the folder name is Microsoft Office 2002.

Type **My Mountain StartCS** in place of adp1.adp as the name for your new database.

Caution   If you enter a file extension other than .adp, Access saves the database file but does not display it in the list of files when you want to open the database later. By default, Access searches for and displays only those files with an .adp file extension.

Figure 33-5: Entering a file name for the new database

If you are following along with the examples in this book, note that we have chosen the name My Mountain StartCS for the name of the database that you create in this chapter. The database in the examples for this section is for our hypothetical business, the Mountain Animal Hospital.

On the CD-ROM The CD-ROM that comes with your book contains the My Mountain StartCS project database file.

After you enter the file name, click the Create button. Access begins creating the new database. To create a new project database, Access needs more information about the connection for your new client/server database. The Microsoft SQL Server Database Wizard screen, shown in Figure 33-6, collects the required connection information.

Figure 33-6: The Microsoft SQL Server Database Wizard

In this wizard, Access needs the name of the server, the logon ID and password of an account with Create Database privileges on the server, and the name of the new SQL Server database. To create the SQL Server database, follow these steps.

1. Type **(local)** as the server name. (In this example, we create an SQL Server 2000 Desktop Engine database on a personal computer.)

2. Type **sa** for the logon ID.

3. Type **My Mountain Start SQL Database** for the database name.

4. Then click Next> to create the new database. Figure 33-7 shows the completed Wizard screen.

Tip   Your machine name can be the server name if the database runs only on your machine. (local) makes the database easier to distribute to other machines.

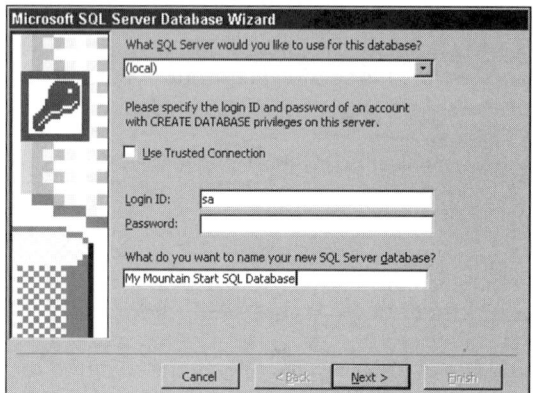

Figure 33-7: Entering the connection information

When a user connects to the SQL Server database through a Microsoft Access project, the connection is enabled through the desktop system's user account. SQL Server verifies that the account name and password were validated when the user logged on to the system and grants access to the database without requiring a separate logon name or password.

There is currently no simple way for a system administrator to create new logon accounts to the locally installed SQL Server database except by using complex SQL commands. Using the default SA account, users can access the SQL Server database through the Access project without any additional security requirements. The administrator of the SQL Server can also add additional security by changing the default SA account password.

The Microsoft SQL Server Database Wizard verifies the entered connection information. When verification is complete, the final Wizard screen displays, as shown in Figure 33-8. Click Finish to create the new database.

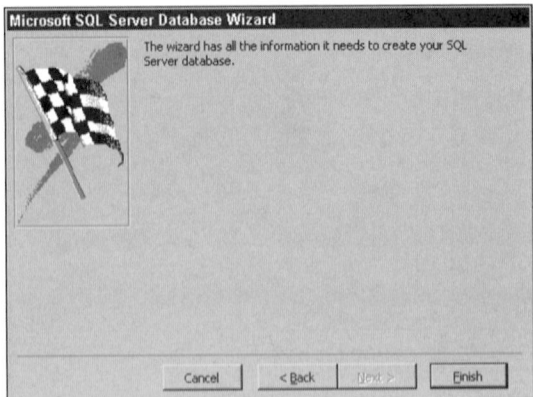

Figure 33-8: The final Microsoft SQL Server Database Wizard screen

The Microsoft SQL Server Database Wizard creates the new database. This process may take a few minutes to complete. After the process is complete, Access displays the Database window for the new empty project database.

Figure 33-9 shows the empty Database window. This window appears similar to the Access database window. If you have ever created an Access database, you are familiar with most of the object buttons in this window.

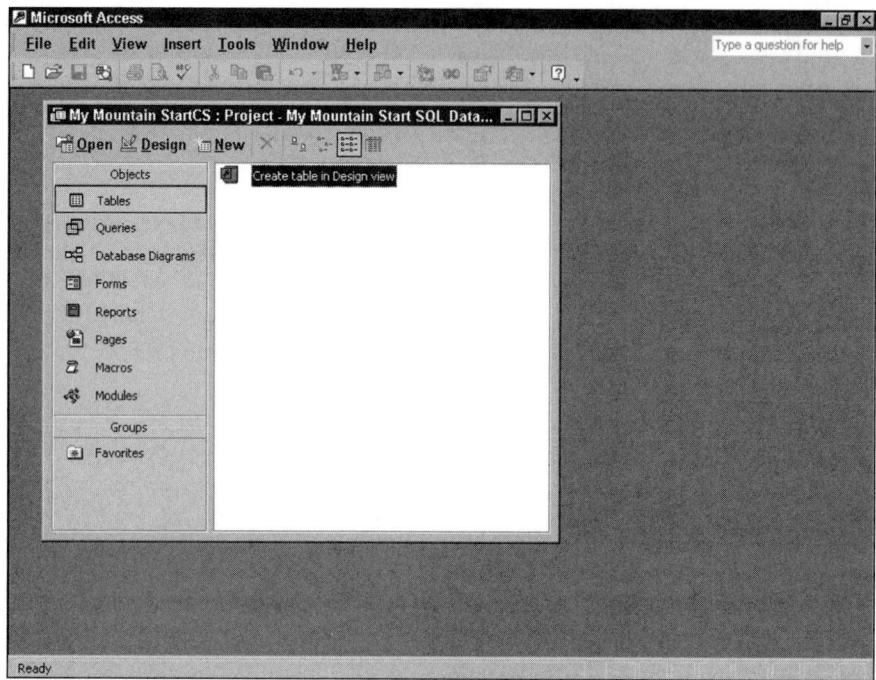

Figure 33-9: The Database window and the empty project

Understanding projects

An Access project file contains only the user-interface objects for an application. It contains only the objects that interact directly with the user — the forms, reports, data access pages, macros, and modules. Creating forms, reports, data access pages, macros, and modules is virtually the same as creating them in an Access database.

The objects that contain data or describe the definitions of the data — the tables, views, stored procedures, and database diagram — are stored in the SQL Server or SQL Server 2000 Desktop Engine database file.

In our example, the Access project file name is My Mountain StartCS.adp. The SQL Server 2000 Desktop Engine database file name is My Mountain Start SQL Database.mdf. The SQL Server 2000 Desktop Engine file is created automatically when you create a new project file.

Even though the data objects are not stored in the Access project file, you can create and work with data objects through an Access project. Although the design tools are different from the tools in Access databases, you should find them just as easy to use.

Table 33-3 compares the objects in a Microsoft Access database to the objects in a Microsoft Access project.

Table 33-3 Comparison of Objects in an Access Database and an Access Project	
Access Database	**Access Project**
Table	Table
Select Query	View
Action Query	Stored Procedure
Parameterized Query	Stored Procedure
Relationship	Database Diagram
Form	Form
Report	Report
Data Access Page	Data Access Page
Macro	Macro
Module	Module

Project objects

The Database window contains a list of the object types available for an Access project. You can select among any of these eight available object types:

✦ Tables

✦ Queries

✦ Database diagrams

✦ Forms

✦ Reports

✦ Pages

✦ Macros

✦ Modules

Click on any one of the objects listed to display a list of existing items for that object type or to create a new item.

Creating a New Table

Creating a table in an Access project is very similar to creating a table in an Access database. Because the topics of creating tables, queries, forms, and reports are covered in detail in other chapters, this section focuses on the design tool methods that differ from Access database design tool methods.

To create a new table, first make sure that the Tables object is selected. Then select the item labeled Create table in Design view. The Table Design window displays.

Working with fields in the Table Design window

Figure 33-10 shows the Table Design window. The table design tool is fairly similar to the Access database table design tool. The Table Design window consists of two areas:

- ✦ The field entry area
- ✦ The field properties area

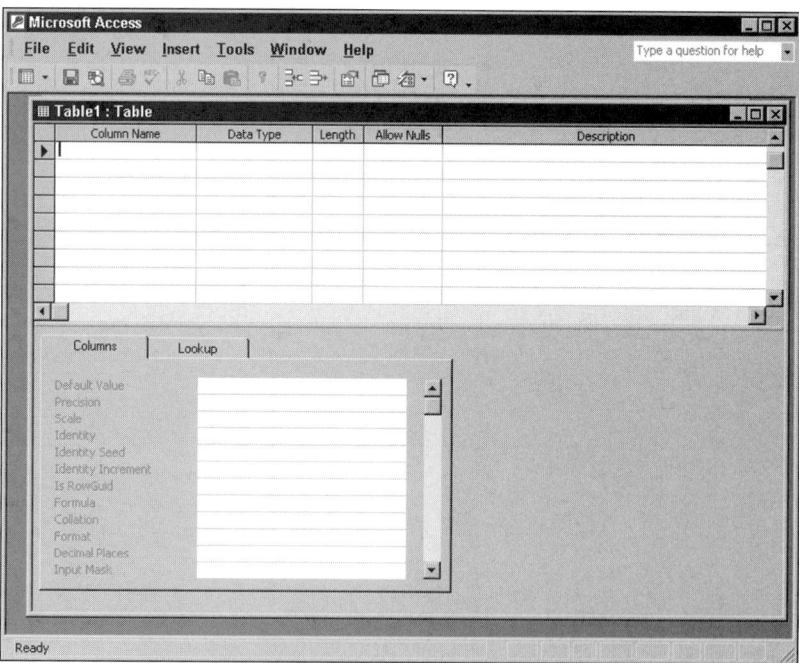

Figure 33-10: The Table Design window

The field entry area is where you enter each field's name and the datatype and length for each field. The properties area is a tabbed dialog box containing the two tabs, Columns and Lookup. The Columns tab contains a list of properties for each field selected in the field entry area. Field properties are a set of characteristics that provide additional control over how the data in a field is stored, entered, or displayed. The Lookup tab allows you to specify the default control type to use for the field when it is placed on a form.

You can create fields by entering a field name and a field data type in each row of the field entry area of the Table Design window. You must enter a data type and length for each field name that you enter. You can further describe each field by completing any of the additional properties available for the data type that you selected.

Table 33-4 describes the data types available for SQL databases and how they compare to Access data types.

<table>
<tr><td colspan="2" align="center">Table 33-4
Comparison of Access and SQL Server Data Types</td></tr>
<tr><td>*Microsoft Access Data Type*</td><td>*SQL Server Data Type*</td></tr>
<tr><td>Yes/No</td><td>Bit</td></tr>
<tr><td>Number</td><td>Tinyint, smallint, int, real, bigint, float, decimal, numeric</td></tr>
<tr><td>Currency</td><td>Money, Smallmoney</td></tr>
<tr><td>Date/Time</td><td>Datetime, Smalldatetime</td></tr>
<tr><td>AutoNumber</td><td>int (with Identity property defined)</td></tr>
<tr><td>Text</td><td>Varchar(n), Nvarchar(n)</td></tr>
<tr><td>Memo</td><td>Text</td></tr>
<tr><td>OLE Object</td><td>Image</td></tr>
<tr><td>ReplicationID (GUID)</td><td>uniqueidentifier (SQL Server 7.0 or later)</td></tr>
<tr><td>Hyperlink</td><td>char, nvarchar (With the Hyperlink property set to Yes)</td></tr>
<tr><td>(no equivalent)</td><td>Nchar</td></tr>
<tr><td>(no equivalent)</td><td>varbinary</td></tr>
<tr><td>(no equivalent)</td><td>smallint</td></tr>
<tr><td>(no equivalent)</td><td>timestamp</td></tr>
<tr><td>(no equivalent)</td><td>Char, nchar</td></tr>
<tr><td>(no equivalent)</td><td>user-defined</td></tr>
<tr><td>(no equivalent)</td><td>sql_variant</td></tr>
</table>

You can also set these properties for each field:

✦ **Default Value.** The default value to set for this column whenever a new row is added to the table.

✦ **Precision.** Maximum number of digits. Default value provided based on data type.

✦ **Scale.** Maximum number of digits to the right of the decimal point. Default is 0.

✦ **Identity.** Autonumbers the records in a table.

✦ **Identity Seed.** The first number to assign to an identify record. Default is 1.

✦ **Identity Increment.** The amount to increment each identity record.

✦ **Is RowGuid.** Shows whether the column is used by SQL Server as a ROWGUID column. You can set this value to Yes only for a column that is an identity column.

✦ **Formula.** Shows the formula for a computed column.

✦ **Collation.** Shows the collating sequence that SQL Server applies by default to the column whenever the column values are used to sort rows of a query result. To use the default collating sequence for the database, choose "<database default>".

✦ **Format.** Shows the display format for the column.

✦ **Decimal Places.** Shows the number of decimal places to be used for displaying values of this column. If you choose Auto, the number of decimal places is determined by the value you choose in Format.

✦ **Input Mask.** Provides a default mask for inputting data into the field.

✦ **Caption.** Shows the text label that appears by default in forms using this column.

✦ **Indexed.** Shows whether an index exists on the column.

✦ **Hyperlink.** Indicates whether the values in this column can be interpreted as hyperlinks.

✦ **IME Mode.** Determines the IME (Input Method Editor) status of the column for entering international data into the values for the column.

✦ **Furigana.** Used with Japanese IME. Indicates a column into which the Furigana equivalent of the text entered by the user is stored. When the user enters a value into this column, that value is stored, and in addition, the Furigana equivalent of the entered text is stored in the column named in this control.

✦ **Postal Address.** Specifies a control or field that displays either an address corresponding to an entered postal code or customer barcode data corresponding to an entered address.

The Table Properties window

Figure 33-11 shows the Table Properties window. The Table Properties window includes five tabs. These five tabs allow you to specify properties for your table.

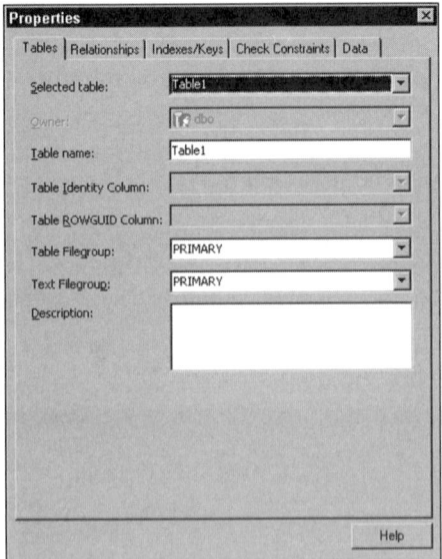

Figure 33-11: Setting the Tables properties

You can set the following properties using the Tables tab:

- ✦ **Selected table.** Shows the name of the table that you have selected. Expand the list to choose a different table whose properties you want to inspect or modify.

- ✦ **Owner.** Shows the name of the table's owner. This property can't be updated. Access sets this property automatically using the logon ID of the user who created the table. The owner name is either a Microsoft SQL Server role or SQL Server user. The drop-down list contains all the users and roles defined in the database. Within the drop-down list, the users and roles have different icons; the role icon shows two faces, the user icon shows only one.

- ✦ **Table name.** Shows the name of the selected table. To rename the table, enter a new name in this box.

- ✦ **Table Identity Column.** Shows the column used by SQL Server as the table's identity column. An *identity column* is a column whose values are auto-incremented. To change the identity column, choose from the drop-down list. Within the drop-down list, you can choose the blank entry to indicate that the table has no identity column.

✦ **Table ROWGUID Column.** Shows the column used by SQL Server as the table's ROWGUID column. The ROWGUID is used for database replication. To change the ROWGUID column, choose from the drop-down list. Within the drop-down list, you can choose the blank entry to indicate that the table has no ROWGUID column.

✦ **Table Filegroup.** Select the name of the file group in which you want to store the selected table data.

✦ **Text Filegroup.** Select the name of the file group in which you want to store the text and images from the selected table.

✦ **Description.** You can enter any text in this field. The text that you enter is implemented as a SQL Server 2000 extended property.

Note   You must have at least one user-defined file group for the Table Filegroup and Text Filegroup settings to be enabled. If you create a database object without specifying its file group, SQL Server assigns it to the default file group. Initially, the default file group is Primary file group.

The Relationships tab, shown in Figure 33-12, shows the relationships properties for the Customer table. You can use this tab to set up relationships between a table and one or more other tables in the database.

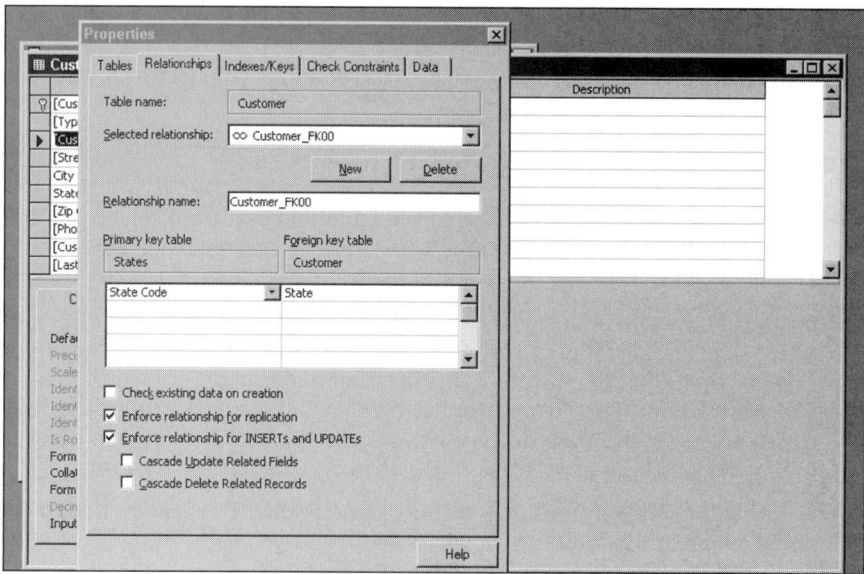

Figure 33-12: Setting the Relationships properties

You can set up a relationship for the table using the following properties:

✦ **Table name.** Shows the name of the table that you have selected.

✦ **Selected relationship.** Shows the name of the selected relationship in your database diagram.

✦ **New.** Choose this button to create a new relationship for the selected database table.

✦ **Delete.** Choose this button to remove the selected relationship from the database.

✦ **Relationship name.** Shows the name of the selected relationship. You can rename the relationship by entering a new name in this box.

✦ **Primary key table.** Shows the name of the primary key table in the relationship, followed by the columns that make up the primary key.

✦ **Foreign key table.** Shows the name of the foreign key table in the relationship, followed by the columns that make up the foreign key.

✦ **Check existing data on creation.** Applies the constraint to data that already exists in the database when the relationship is added to the foreign key table.

✦ **Enforce relationship for replication.** Applies the constraint when the foreign key table is copied to a different database.

✦ **Enforce relationship for INSERTs and UPDATEs.** Applies the constraint to data that is inserted into, deleted, or updated in the foreign key table. Also prevents a row in the primary key table from being deleted when a matching row exists in the foreign key table.

✦ **Cascade Update Related Fields.** Instructs the database to automatically update foreign-key values of this relationship whenever the primary-key value is updated.

✦ **Cascade Delete Related Fields.** Instructs the database to automatically delete rows of the foreign-key table whenever the referred-to row of the primary-key table is deleted.

✦ **Validation Text.** Shows the text that is displayed to the users whenever a row that violates the foreign-key constraint is entered.

Note   When a key icon displays next to the Relationship Name property, this indicates that the selected table acts as the lookup table for the values in the table named as the foreign-key table. An infinity icon indicates that the table contains values that are looked up in the table listed as the primary key. See Chapter 6 for more information about primary and foreign keys.

The Indexes/Keys tab (see Figure 33-13) shows the primary-key columns and other indexes created for the Customers table. You can use the Indexes/Keys tab to specify primary keys, indexes, and unique constraints for the table.

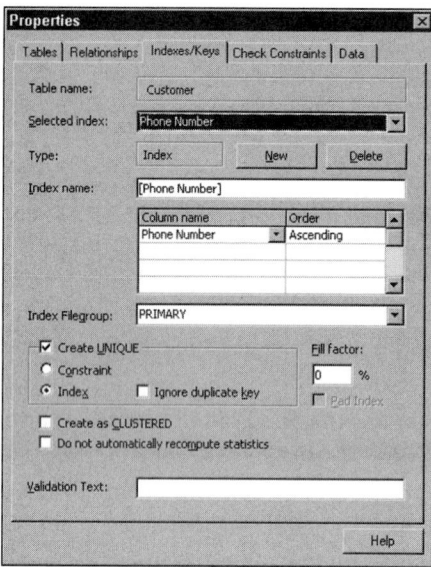

Figure 33-13: Setting the Indexes/Keys properties

Use the following properties to set up an index for the table:

✦ **Table name.** Shows the name of the table that you have selected.

✦ **Selected index.** Shows the name of the first index defined for the table.

✦ **Type.** Shows the index or key object type for the selected table: Index, primary key, or unique constraint.

Note

A constraint is a way to limit the values that a user can enter into a field in a table. A unique constraint ensures that no duplicate values are entered into specified columns that are not a table's primary key. In the Customers table example, the Phone Number column is defined as a unique constraint so a user cannot enter the same phone number for two different customers.

✦ **New.** Choose this button to create a new index, key, or unique constraint for the selected database table.

✦ **Delete.** Choose this button to remove the selected index, key, or constraint from the table.

Note If you try to delete a primary key that participates in relationships, a message appears asking you if you want to delete all the relationships, too. You cannot delete a primary key without first deleting the relationships that it participates in.

✦ **Index name.** Shows the name of the selected index. You can rename the index by entering a new name in this box.

✦ **Column name/Order.** Shows the columns contributing to the index, primary key, or unique constraint, along with whether each column's values are arranged in ascending or descending order within the item. You can add, change, or remove column names in this list. You can also change the ascending/descending setting for each column.

✦ **Index Filegroup.** Select the name of the file group in which you want to store the selected index. Initially, the default file group is the Primary file group.

✦ **Create Unique.** Select this option to create a unique constraint or index for the selected database table. Specify whether you are creating a constraint or index by selecting either the Constraint or Index button. When creating a unique index, you can check the Ignore Duplicate Key option to tell SQL to issue a warning message, ignore the offending incoming row, and try to insert the remaining rows of the bulk insert operation. If you leave it unchecked, the entire bulk insert operation is cancelled if a row violates the unique index.

✦ **Fill factor.** Specifies how full each index page can be. If a fill factor is not specified, the database's default fill factor is used.

✦ **Pad Index.** If you specified a Fill Factor of more than zero percent, and you selected the option to create a unique index, you can tell SQL Server to use the same percentage that you specified in Fill Factor as the space to leave open on each interior node. By default, SQL Server sets a two-row index size.

✦ **Create as CLUSTERED.** Select this option to create a clustered index for the selected database table.

Note In a clustered index, the physical order of the rows in the table is the same as the logical (indexed) order of the index key values. A table can contain only one clustered index. UPDATE and DELETE operations are often accelerated by clustered indexes because these operations require large amounts of data to be read. Creating or modifying a clustered index can be time-consuming, because it is during these operations that the table's rows are reorganized on disk.

✦ **Don't automatically re-compute statistics.** Select this option to tell SQL Server to use previously created statistics. This choice may degrade query performance, but does accelerate the index-building operation.

✦ **Validation Text.** Shows the text that is displayed to the users whenever a row that violates the index, key, or constraint is entered.

When you want to define a non-unique constraint for a table, you can use the Check Constraints tab, shown in Figure 33-14. Constraints are similar to validation rules in an Access database.

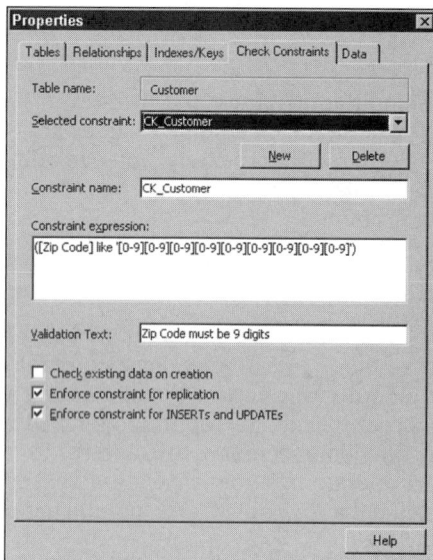

Figure 33-14: Viewing the Check Constraints page

Use the following properties on the Check Constraints tab to set up a new constraint for a table:

✦ **Table name.** Shows the name of the table that you have selected.

✦ **Selected Constraint.** Shows the name of the constraint whose properties you are viewing. To view the properties of a different constraint, select a constraint from the drop-down list.

✦ **New.** Choose this button to create a new constraint for the selected database table.

✦ **Delete.** Choose this button to remove the selected constraint from the database.

✦ **Constraint name.** Shows the name of the constraint whose properties you are viewing. To change the name of the constraint, type the new name here.

✦ **Constraint expression.** Shows the SQL syntax of the selected check constraint. For new constraints, you must enter the SQL syntax before exiting this box. You can also edit existing check constraints.

✦ **Validation Text.** Shows the text that is displayed to the user whenever a row that violates the constraint is entered.

✦ **Check existing data on creation.** When selected, this option ensures that all data that exists in the table before the constraint was created is verified against the constraint.

✦ **Enforce constraint for replication.** Enforces the constraint when the table is replicated into a different database.

✦ **Enforce constraint for INSERTs and UPDATEs.** Enforces the constraint when data is inserted into or updated in the table.

The Data tab allows you to set the sort order and subdatasheet for a table. Figure 33-15 shows the Data tab for the Visit Details table.

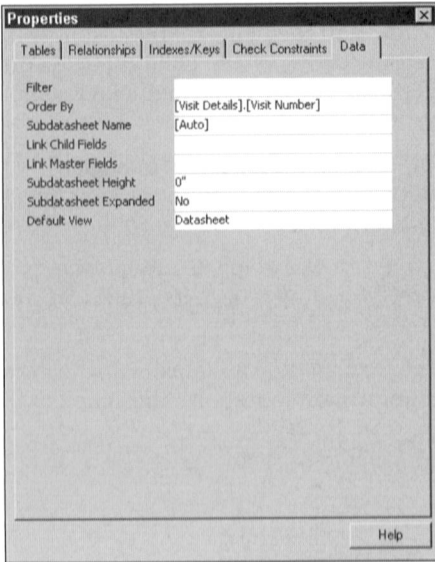

Figure 33-15: Setting the Data properties

To set up a sort order or subdatasheet, use these properties in the Data tab:

✦ **Table name.** Shows the name of the table that you have selected.

✦ **Order By.** This property is a string expression that is the name of the field or fields on which you want to sort records. When you use more than one field name, separate the names with a comma (,).

Caution Setting the Order By property specifies a client-side sorting operation. That is, the data is sorted after the data is returned from the database.

Tip If you want to sort records in descending order, type **DESC** at the end of the string expression.

✦ **Subdatasheet Name.** Specifies or determines the table or query that is bound to the subdatasheet. Choose [Auto] to indicate that Access should use existing relationships in the database to determine which table to bind to the subdatasheet.

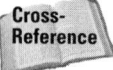

Subdatasheets in a project work just like Access subdatasheets. For more information on working with subdatasheets, see Chapter 6.

✦ **Link Child Fields.** Shows the list of linking fields in the subdatasheet. The fields that you list here should coincide with the fields that you supply in the Link Master Fields control.

✦ **Link Master Fields.** Shows the list of linking fields or controls in the table, view, stored procedure, or in-line function containing the subdatasheet. The fields that you list here should coincide with the fields that you supply in the Link Child Fields control. Each coinciding pair (master, child) of fields don't require the same name, but they must contain the same kind of data and have the same or compatible data types and field sizes.

✦ **Subdatasheet Height.** Shows the default height to display in the subdatasheet. If the subdatasheet contains more rows than the default height accommodates, the subdatasheet appears with a vertical scrollbar.

✦ **Subdatasheet Expanded.** Indicates the saved state of all subdatasheets within the table, view, single-statement stored procedure, or in-line function. Yes means expanded, No means unexpanded.

✦ **Default View.** Shows the view used to display the subdatasheet when the user opens the object or embeds it as a subform or subreport. Your choices are Datasheet, PivotTable, or PivotChart.

Working with Database Diagrams

The Database Diagrams object is similar to Relationships in an Access database. Figure 33-16 shows a database diagram for the My Mountain StartCS project. Although the process of adding tables to the diagram and setting relationships between the tables is similar to how you set relationships in an Access database, database diagrams provide several other powerful features.

When designing a database, you can use the Database Designer to create, edit, or delete tables, columns, keys, indexes, relationships, and constraints. To visualize a database, you can create one or more diagrams illustrating some or all of the tables, columns, keys, and relationships in it.

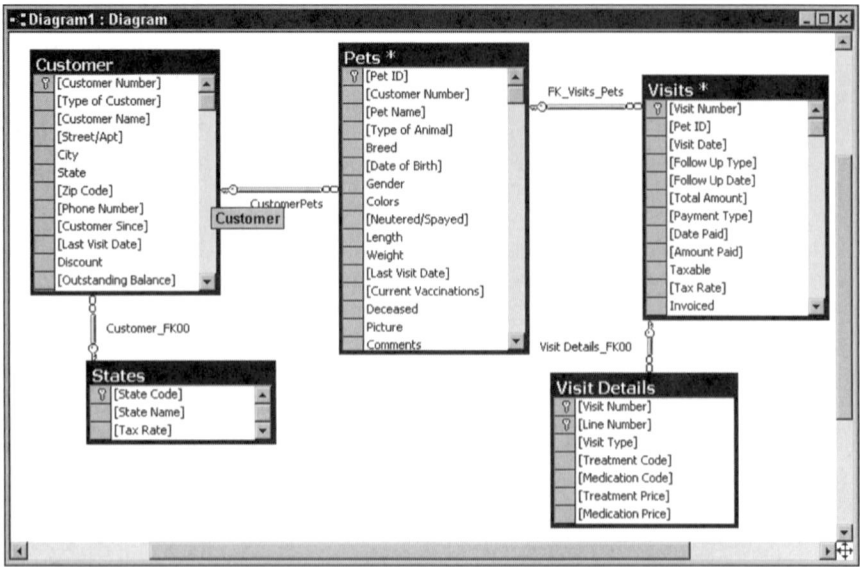

Figure 33-16: Setting relationships in a database diagram

The relationship lines between the tables and their icons make it easy to see how the tables relate to each other. The characteristics of the way the relationship displays in the diagram tell you about how the relationship is set up between the tables.

The endpoints of the line indicate whether the relationship is one-to-one or one-to-many. If a relationship has a key at one endpoint and a figure eight at the other, it is a one-to-many relationship. If a relationship has a key at each endpoint, it is a one-to-one relationship. For a one-to-many relationship, the foreign-key table is the table near the line's figure-eight symbol.

Note   If both endpoints of the line attach to the same table, the relationship is a reflexive relationship.

In the example in Figure 33-16, the CustomerPets relationship defines a one-to-many relationship between the Customer and Pets tables. Each individual row in the Customer table may have one or more related rows in the Pets table. In other words, each customer may own one, two, or maybe even ten pets.

The line itself (not its endpoints) indicates whether the database enforces referential integrity for the relationship when new data is added to the foreign-key table. If the line appears solid, the database enforces referential integrity for the relationship when rows are added or modified in the foreign-key table. If the line appears dotted, the database does not enforce referential integrity for the relationship when rows are added or modified in the foreign-key table.

In the CustomerPets relationship example, the relationship is shown with a solid line. The database enforces referential integrity between the Customer and Pets tables. Enforcing referential integrity means that the foreign-key value in the table on the "many" side must already exist in the primary key table (the "one" side). The CustomerPets relationship ensures that a user can't enter a Customer Number into the Pets table until the Customer Number has been entered into the Customer table.

In addition, you can display labels for each relationship. To display relationship labels, right-click on the database diagram, then select Show Relationship Labels. Default names are assigned to a relationship when the relationship is defined. You can change the default names by assigning a new name in the Properties window for each relationship. To display the Properties window, right-click on a relationship line. Then select Properties. You can change the relationship name by using the Relationships tab of the Properties window, as shown in Figure 33-17.

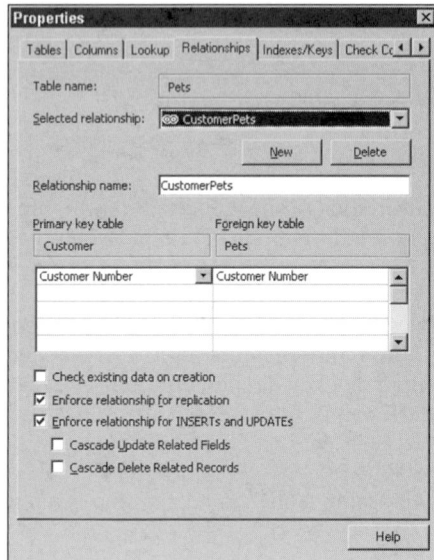

Figure 33-17: Assigning a name to a relationship

For applications that contain dozens of tables, it can be difficult to manage all of the relationships in one diagram. In Access projects, you can create multiple diagrams. You can organize all of your application's relationships into manageable sections that store each section in a separate diagram. In a sales order application, for example, you can have Sales Relationships diagram that includes the Customers, Sales Orders, and Sales Order Line Items tables and Inventory Relationships diagram that includes the Inventory, Inventory Receipts, and Inventory Suppliers tables.

Another powerful feature of Database Diagrams is the capability to create, edit, or delete tables and table-column definitions. You can use Database Diagram as a graphical table designer to modify the columns in a single table, or you can work with the design of multiple tables all at the same time. To modify a table's design, select the table's title bar in the Database Diagram window, then select the Table Modes toolbar button. Then select Column Properties from the Table Modes list, as shown in Figure 33-18.

When you display the column properties for a table, the view of the selected table transforms into a table design view. You can then change any of the properties for a field, or even add or delete fields the same way you work with fields in the Table Design window.

Note   When you make changes to a table in a database diagram, the changes are not actually applied to the database until you save the database diagram. An asterisk (*) displays next to any table name with pending changes to remind you that the changes have not yet been applied.

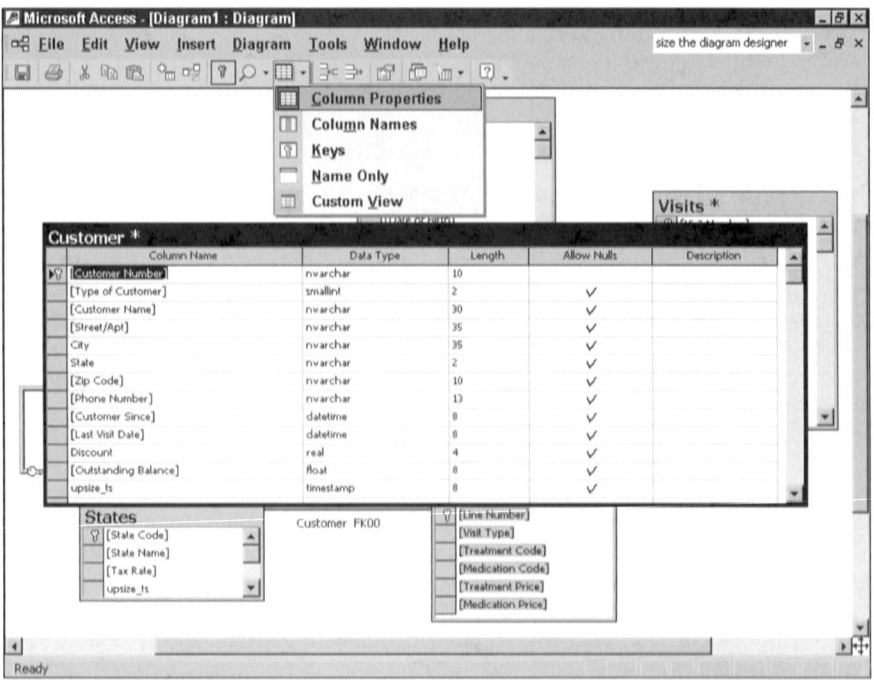

Figure 33-18: Modifying the structure of a table in a Database Diagram

After you save a database diagram, a confirmation message box appears, displaying a listing of the tables to be updated with the changes. An example message box is shown in Figure 33-19. When you modify a table in a database diagram, your modifications are also saved in every other diagram that the table appears in.

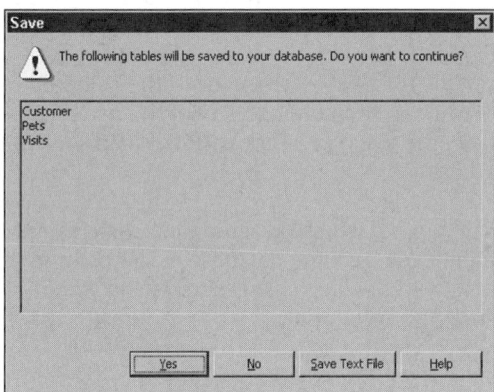

Figure 33-19: Applying database diagram changes to the database

Using the Upsizing Wizard

Many organizations today are becoming more and more dependent on their database applications to manage everyday business operations, and these applications are growing both in volume of data and number of users. Applications that you may have developed using Microsoft Access — even in the past year or two — may be starting to strain the organization's network. At the same time, client/server databases like SQL Server 2000 are becoming more popular, even with smaller businesses, as these databases become easier to install, use, and maintain.

If any of your clients are among the Fortune 500 set, you may be among those who have been recently advised of a new mandate that all applications must conform to client/server technology only — no file-server database management allowed. Your business partner at one of these corporations has probably contacted you in a state of alarm. Having already invested a significant amount of their budget into the Access application that you developed for them, they are naturally concerned that they may have to invest at least the same amount, if not a substantially larger amount, to redesign it to fit the new architecture.

Fortunately, with Access 2002 and its Upsizing Wizard, you can provide a relatively simple and inexpensive solution that retains a significant amount of the original development effort while providing a database that conforms to client/server methodology.

You can convert the tables stored in an existing Microsoft Access database (.mdb) to a client/server database automatically using the Microsoft Access Upsizing Wizard. The Upsizing Wizard takes a Jet database and creates an equivalent SQL Server database with the same table structure, data, and many other attributes of the original database. The Upsizing Wizard re-creates table structures, indexes, validation rules, defaults, autonumbers, and relationships and takes advantage of the latest SQL Server functionality wherever possible.

Before upsizing an application

You should perform these steps prior to converting an application using the Upsizing Wizard:

✦ **Back up your database.** Although the Upsizing Wizard doesn't remove any data or database objects from your Access database, it's a good idea to create a backup copy of your Access database before you upsize it.

✦ **Ensure that you have adequate hard drive space.** At a minimum, you must have enough hard drive space to store the new SQL Server database. Plan to allow at least twice the size of your Access database to allow room for future growth. If you expect to add a lot of data to the database, make the multiple larger.

✦ **Set a default printer.** You must have a default printer assigned, because the Upsizing Wizard creates a report snapshot as it completes the conversion.

✦ **Assign yourself appropriate permissions on the Access database.** You need read/design permission on all database objects to upsize them.

✦ **Start the SQL Server Service Manager.** It must be running for the Upsizing Wizard to create the new SQL Server database.

Starting the Upsizing Wizard

After you have completed the steps to prepare for the conversion, you are ready to upsize your application. First, open the Microsoft Access database that you want to convert. This example upsizes the Mountain Animal Hospital database. Second, select Tools Database Utilities Upsizing Wizard from the Access menu. The first screen of the Upsizing Wizard displays, as shown in Figure 33-20.

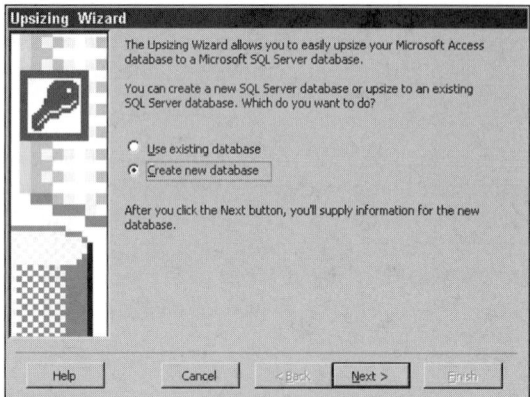

Figure 33-20: The Upsizing Wizard

In the first Upsizing Wizard screen, you can choose to either copy your existing data to an already existing SQL Server database, or to create a new SQL Server database. For this example, choose Create new database. Then click Next>. The second Upsizing Wizard screen displays, as shown in Figure 33-21.

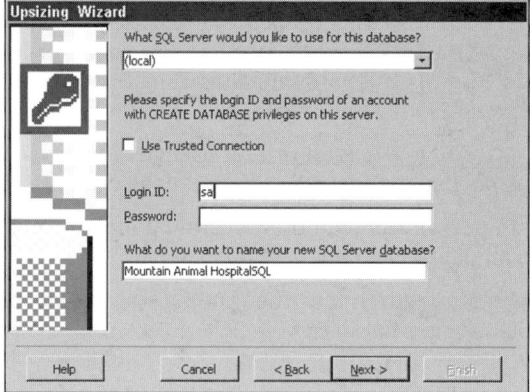

Figure 33-21: Setting up the new SQL Server database

In this Wizard screen, you define the connection information for the new SQL Server database. For this example, type (local) as the name of the SQL Server. Type sa as the login ID. Type Mountain Animal HospitalSQL as the name of the new SQL Server database. Then click Next> to continue.

The next Wizard screen, shown in Figure 33-22, allows you to select the tables to upsize to the new SQL Server database. Click the Next> button to export all of the tables. Then click Next> to continue.

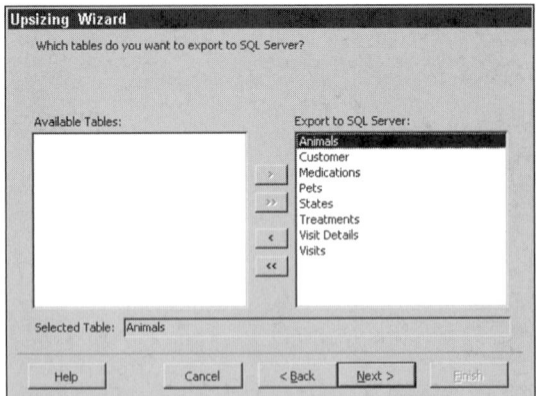

Figure 33-22: Selecting the files to export

In the next screen, which is shown in Figure 33-23, you can take advantage of many of the new database features available in SQL Server, including:

✦ **Indexes.** The Upsizing Wizard converts Microsoft Access primary keys to Microsoft SQL Server non-clustered, unique indexes and marks them as SQL Server primary keys. Other indexes are converted unchanged.

✦ **Validation rules.** The Upsizing Wizard upsizes all table, record, and field validation rules, and field required properties as update and insert triggers.

✦ **Defaults.** The Upsizing Wizard upsizes all default values as ANSI defaults.

✦ **Table relationships.** Choose this option to preserve the relationships that you have defined for your tables. If your Access application uses cascading updates or deletes, also select the Use Triggers option. Use Declared Referential Integrity (DRI) if your application does not make use of cascading updates and deletes.

✦ **Timestamp fields.** Microsoft SQL Server uses a timestamp field to indicate that a record was changed (not *when* it was changed) by creating a unique value field, and then updating this field whenever a record is updated. In general, a timestamp field provides the best performance and reliability. Without a timestamp field, SQL Server must check all the fields in the record to determine whether the record has changed, which slows performance. If you choose Yes, let the Upsizing Wizard decide; timestamp fields are created only for tables that contain floating-point (Single or Double), memo, or OLE object fields.

✦ **Don't upsize any data.** Choose this option if you only want to create the SQL Server database structures using your existing database, but leave the new tables empty.

After you have made all of your selections, click Next> to continue.

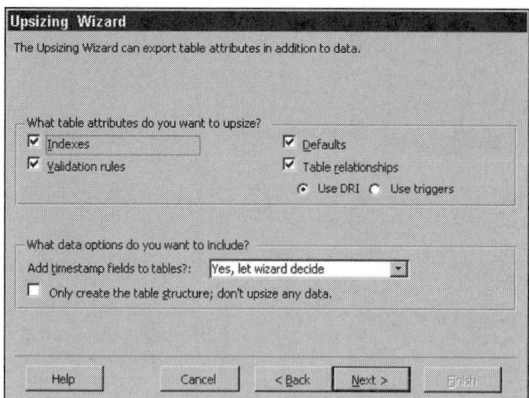

Figure 33-23: Selecting the SQL Server table attributes

Figure 33-24 shows the next Wizard screen. In this screen, you can tell the Upsizing Wizard to change the existing Access application so that it can work with the new SQL Server database. Or, you can tell the Upsizing Wizard to use the existing Access application to create a new Access project.

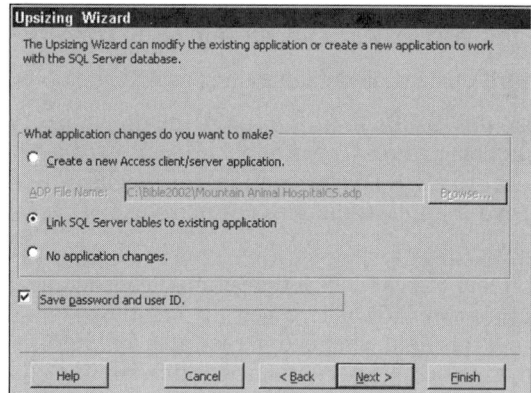

Figure 33-24: Linking the SQL Server tables to an existing application

If you select "Create new Access client/server application," the Upsizing Wizard creates a new Access project. The File Name for the new project (.adp) is the Access application's file name followed by the "CS" suffix. The Upsizing Wizard converts all of the Access application's objects (tables, queries, forms, reports, etc.) into the new Access project.

The "Link SQL Server tables to existing application" tells the Upsizing Wizard to modify your Access database to work with the new SQL Server database. Queries, forms, reports, and data access pages automatically connect to the data in the new Microsoft SQL Server database rather than the data in your Microsoft Access database. The Upsizing Wizard renames the Microsoft Access tables that you upsize with the suffix *local*. For example, if you upsize the Customers table, the table is renamed Customers_local in your Access database. Then, the Upsizing wizard creates a linked SQL Server table named Customers.

Selecting "No application changes" tells the Upsizing Wizard to simply upsize the data to SQL Server. No changes are made to the Access application.

Upsizing the entire Access application to an Access project connected to a SQL Server database converts your application to a true client/server implementation. However, if you have been developing only Access databases until this point, you will find client/server development is very different. The Upsizing Wizard takes you only part of the way. The Upsizing Wizard doesn't make any changes to modules and macros. In Chapter 34, you learn that programming with recordsets in Access projects requires a different command set. You also need to make many changes to your tables and queries to reach full functionality in the new architecture.

For this example, choose the option "Link SQL Server tables to existing application." Although this option continues to use the Jet database engine to retrieve data from the database, it requires the least amount of application modification.

If you leave the "Save password and user ID" option unchecked, users are prompted for the user ID (*SA* in our example) and password (*none* in our example) each time they try to open the SQL Server database.

After you have completed the information for this screen, click Next>.

You have now reached the final Wizard screen, which is shown in Figure 33-25. The Upsizing Wizard now has all of the information that it needs to create the SQL Server database. Click Finish to begin the conversion.

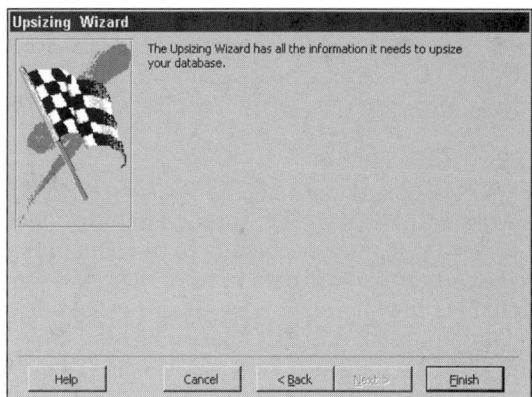

Figure 33-25: The final Upsizing Wizard screen

The conversion process takes several minutes to complete. A message box displays the progress of the conversion, as shown in Figure 33-26.

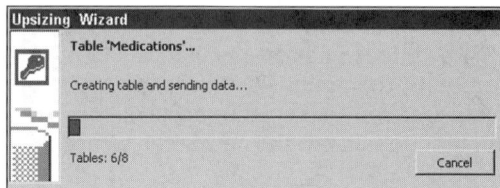

Figure 33-26: Waiting for the Upsizing Wizard to complete the conversion process

Note

If the Upsizing Wizard encounters any referential integrity errors while converting your data to the new SQL Server database, an error message displays. If you encounter an error message, you can click Yes to proceed with the conversion. Any problem data is not converted to the new database. If you don't want to omit the problem data, you must click No to cancel the conversion process.

When the conversion process completes, the Upsizing Wizard automatically displays a report snapshot. An example of the report snapshot is shown in Figure 33-27. The report snapshot includes information about each step of the conversion process for your application. The Upsizing Wizard report contains information about the following:

✦ Database details, including database size

✦ Upsizing parameters, including what table attributes you chose to upsize and how you upsized

✦ Table information, including a comparison of Access and SQL Server values for names, data types, indexes, validation rules, defaults, triggers, and whether or not timestamps were added

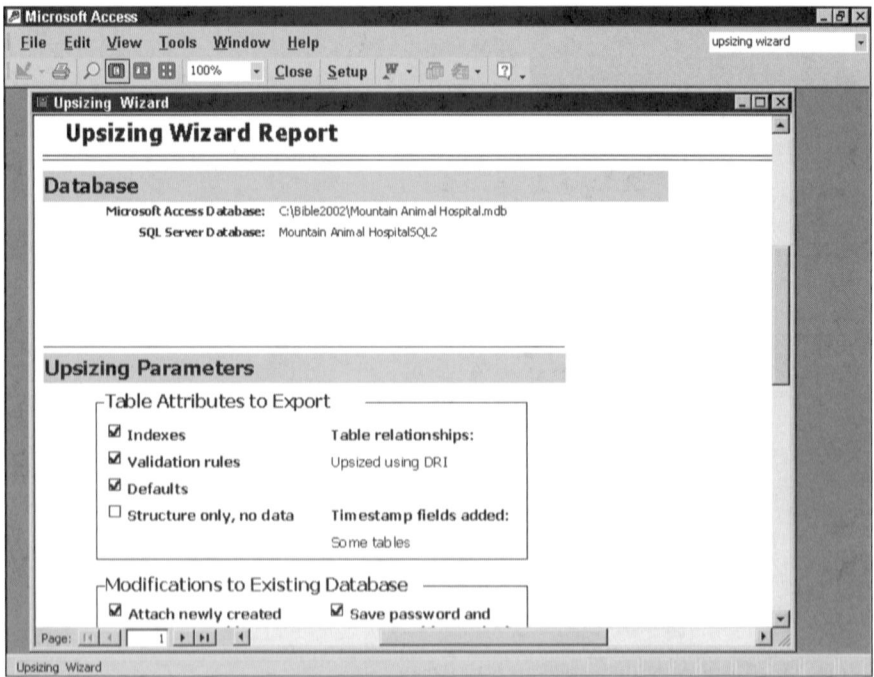

Figure 33-27: The Upsizing Wizard report

✦ Any errors encountered, including database or transaction log full, inadequate permissions, device or database not created, table, default, or validation rule skipped, relationship not enforced, query skipped (because it can't be translated to SQL Server syntax), and control and record source conversion errors in forms and reports

Tip   The report snapshot is stored in the same folder as your application so that you can refer to it later.

After you are finished reviewing the report, close it. When you close the report, the Upsizing Wizard displays the modified Access application. As you can see in Figure 33-28, the tables tab of the Access database container has changed. Each of the original Access tables have been renamed with the suffix _local. An arrow and a world icon precede the SQL Server tables. The arrow indicates that the table is an attached table. The world icon indicates that the table is an ODBC-attached table.

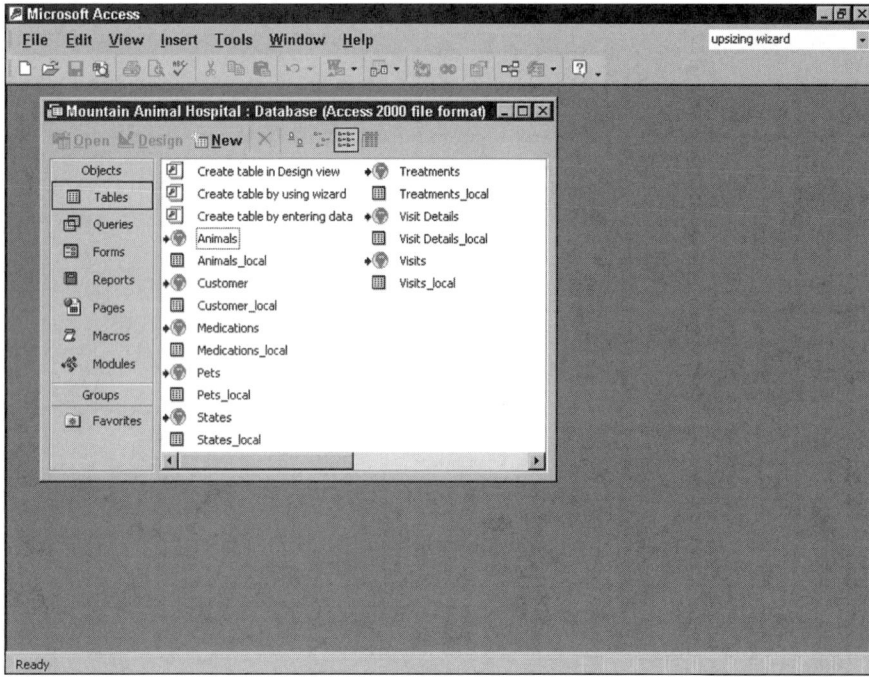

Figure 33-28: Viewing the tables in the upsized database

✦   ✦   ✦

Working with Access Projects

✦   ✦   ✦   ✦

In This Chapter

Upsizing an Access application to client/server

Working with views, stored procedures, and user-defined functions

Using a form to view and update client/server data

✦   ✦   ✦   ✦

The Access 2002 Upsizing Wizard provides a quick and easy way to upsize an Access application's data to SQL Server 2000 Desktop Engine. The simplest and quickest upsizing method simply links the new SQL Server data to the existing Access application. Although this option moves your data to a client/server architecture, it takes you only part of the way. In this chapter, you learn how projects allow you to take full advantage of client/server architecture.

The Upsizing Wizard automatically creates an Access project. A project is an Access file that allows you to work directly with the SQL Server 2000 Desktop Engine database. Even though the data now resides in a client/server database, the linked tables in the existing Access front end (the forms, reports, and data access pages) continue to use the Microsoft Jet database engine to retrieve information from the database.

 **Cross-Reference** For a comparison of Jet and SQL Server 2000 Desktop Engine, see Chapter 33.

Using linked SQL Server tables in an Access front end can be an acceptable solution for most small-workgroup environments. However, for environments with large numbers of users or where large volumes of data are processed, you need a solution that utilizes client/server architecture in both the front-end and back-end databases.

In addition to providing access to SQL Server data, Access projects can also contain *front-end objects,* such as forms, reports, data access pages, macros, and modules. The good news is that if you are moving from an existing Access front end to SQL Server, you don't have to build these objects from scratch. The Access Upsizing Wizard does most of the work for you.

Upsizing to an Access Project

In Chapter 33, you learn how to use the Access Upsizing Wizard to convert Access data to SQL Server 2000 Database Engine. You can use the Access Upsizing Wizard to convert the Access front end, along with its data, to an Access project.

Caution   Back up your database before upsizing.

Starting the Upsizing Wizard

When you are ready to upsize, open the Access application. The following example shows you how to upsize the Mountain Animal Hospital database. Select Tools Database Utilities Upsizing Wizard from the Access menu. The first screen of the Upsizing Wizard displays, as shown in Figure 34-1.

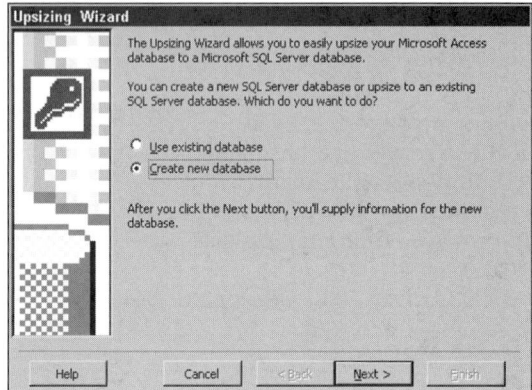

Figure 34-1: The Upsizing Wizard

In the first Upsizing Wizard screen, you can choose to either copy your existing data to an SQL Server database that already exists or to create a new SQL Server database. For this example, choose Create new database. Then click Next>. The second Upsizing Wizard screen displays, as shown in Figure 34-2.

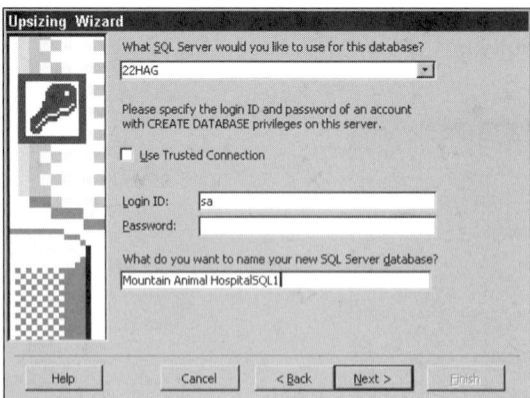

Figure 34-2: Setting up the new SQL Server database

Caution   Be sure to start the SQL Server Service Manager before completing this wizard screen. For a review of starting SQL Server Service Manager, see Chapter 33.

In this wizard screen, you define the connection information for the new SQL Server database. For this example, type **(local)** as the name of the SQL Server. Type **sa** as the login ID. You create the Mountain Animal Hospital SQL in Chapter 33, so for this database, use the name Mountain Animal HospitalSQL1. Then click Next> to continue.

The next wizard screen, shown in Figure 34-3, allows you to select the tables to upsize to the new SQL Server database. Click the >> button to export all of the tables. Then click Next> to continue.

Figure 34-3: Selecting the files to export

In the screen shown in Figure 34-4, you can specify which of the many SQL Server table attributes you want to enable in your new SQL Server database.

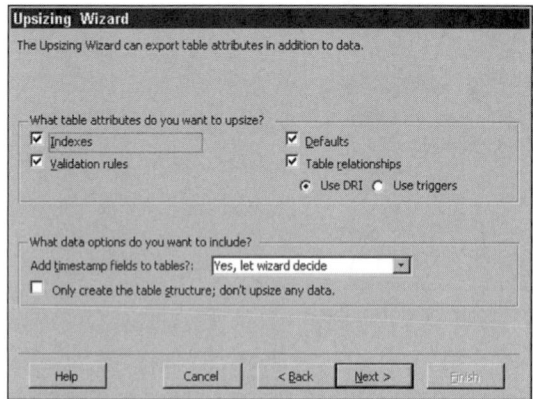

Figure 34-4: Selecting the SQL Server table attributes

 Refer to Chapter 33 for more information on each of these SQL Server features.

When you have made all of your selections, click Next> to continue.

Using the Upsizing Wizard to create a client/server application

Figure 34-5 shows the next wizard screen. Here you can automatically create a Microsoft Access project file to store the application objects for your new client/server application. Choose the option Create a new Access client/server application. The wizard automatically assigns a default name for your new project by adding the suffix "CS" to your Access database file name. Leave the Save password and user ID option unchecked to force the user to enter a logon ID and password whenever the project is opened. After you have completed the information for this screen, click Next>.

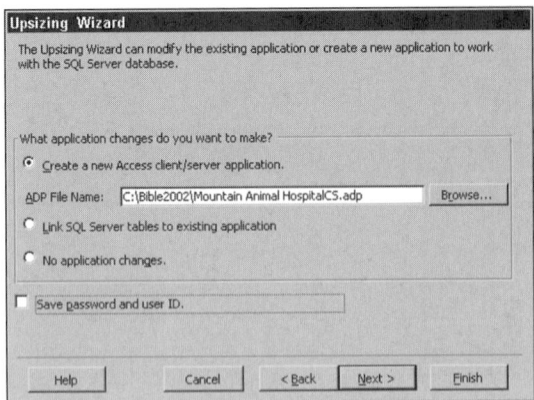

Figure 34-5: Automatically creating an Access project

You have now reached the final wizard screen, which is shown in Figure 34-6. The Upsizing Wizard now has all of the information that it needs to create both the SQL Server database and the Access project. When the conversion process completes, you can specify to either automatically open the new project, or to simply create the new project and leave the existing Access project open. Click Finish to begin the conversion.

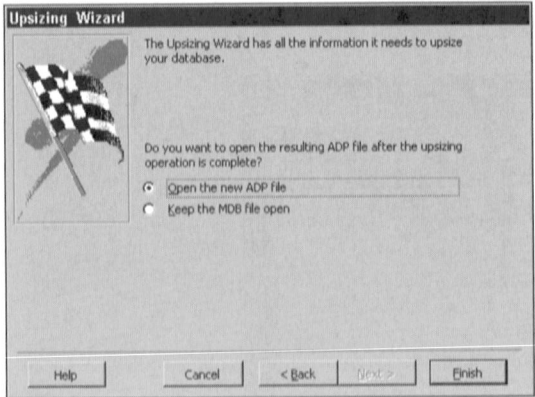

Figure 34-6: The final Upsizing Wizard screen

The conversion process takes several minutes to complete.

When the conversion process completes, the Upsizing Wizard automatically displays a report snapshot. An example of the report snapshot is shown in Figure 34-7. Browse the report snapshot to review the conversion details about each of the objects that the Upsizing Wizard converted.

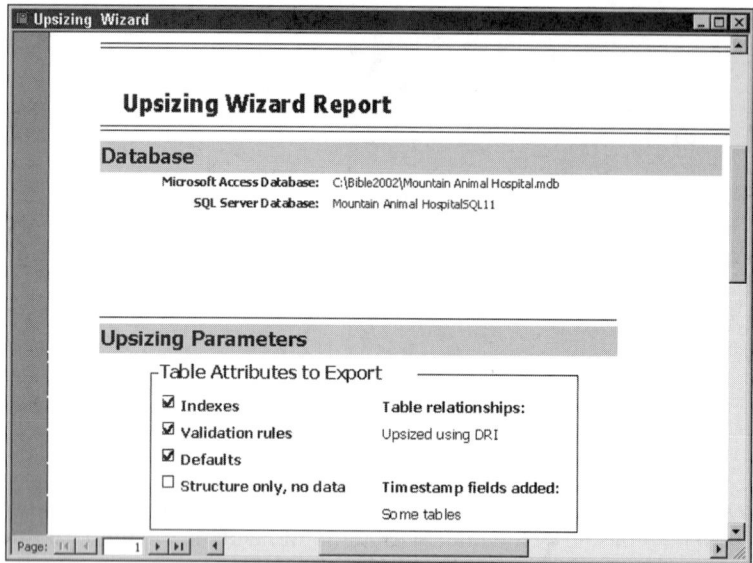

Figure 34-7: The Upsizing Wizard report

After you are finished reviewing the report, close it. When you close the report, the Upsizing Wizard automatically loads the new Access project. Figure 34-8 shows the database container for the Mountain Animal HospitalCS project.

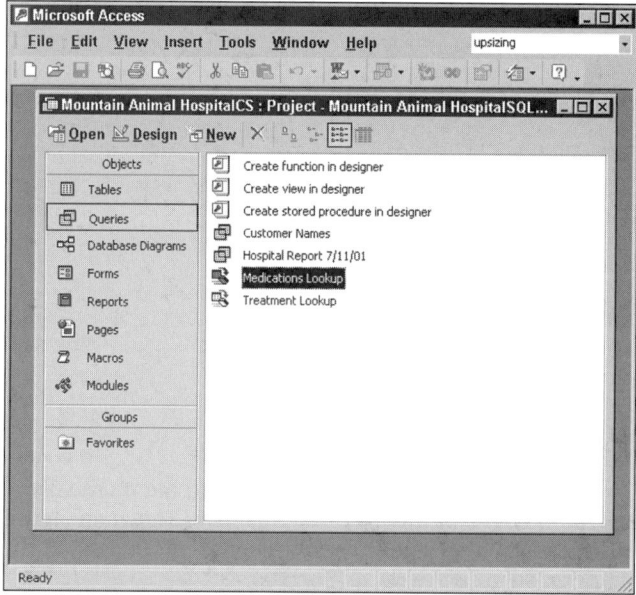

Figure 34-8: The upsized Access project

The Access Upsizing Wizard migrates the native Access objects into their corresponding objects in the new Access project. Although Access projects are organized into the same groupings of objects (tables, queries, forms, reports, etc.) as native Access databases, project objects differ significantly in how they work compared to native Access. The similarities and differences are outlined below.

✦ **Tables:** Individual tables are converted to SQL Server tables. Data types are converted to their corresponding SQL Server data types.

 **Cross-Reference** Refer to Chapter 33 for a listing of SQL Server data types and how they compare to native Access data types.

✦ **Queries:** Converted into views, stored procedures, and functions according to the following rules:

- Select queries that don't have an ORDER BY clause or parameters are converted to views.

- Action queries are converted to stored procedure action queries. Access adds SET NOCOUNT ON after the parameter declaration code to make sure the stored procedure runs.

- Select queries that use either parameters or an ORDER BY clause are converted to user-defined functions. If necessary, the TOP 100 PERCENT clause is added to a query that contains an ORDER BY clause.

- Parameter queries that use named parameters maintain the original text name used in the Access database and are converted either to stored procedures or inline user-defined functions.

✦ **Forms and Reports:** Converted with no changes.

✦ **Data Access Pages:** The Upsizing Wizard changes the OLE DB connection and the data binding information in the Microsoft Office data source control to work with the new SQL Server database and copies the page's corresponding HTML file to the same location as the Access project, renaming the HTML file with a "_CS" suffix. The new pages in the Access project retain the original name, so that hyperlinks between the Access project Pages continue to work.

✦ **Command Bars:** Converted with no changes.

✦ **Macros and Modules:** Converted with no changes.

To take full advantage of SQL Server and an Access project, you need to make some fairly significant changes to your newly converted application. While the Upsizing Wizard tries to make its best guess as to the most efficient conversion approach, you should review the table and query designs and revise them as necessary. Record sources and Control sources for forms and reports are converted without any changes. In an implementation with a large number of users, you don't want to bind forms and reports directly to a table or even a query. Additionally, you need to manually convert code from Data Access Objects (DAO) to ActiveX Data Objects (ADO) in your modules.

Understanding Project Queries

You use queries in an Access project the same way you use them in an Access database — to view, change, add, or delete data.

Projects provide three types of queries for working with data:

✦ Views

✦ Stored procedures

✦ User-defined functions

As Chapter 33 explains, project tables are not stored within the Access project. Neither are views, stored procedures, and user-defined functions. Instead, they are stored in the server database.

Note   Access projects don't store any data or data-definition type objects. Only code-type objects, such as forms, reports, links to data access pages, macros, and modules are stored in the project. All data-related objects are stored directly in the server database.

Creating views

Of the three query types, the view is the type most similar to an Access query. You use a view when you need to retrieve one or more columns from one or more related tables in the database. The View Query Designer works just like the Access Query Designer. If you are comfortable using the Access Query Designer, you find that the Query Designer for a View is just as easy to use.

To create a view, select the Queries object, then select Create view in designer. The Query Designer opens. You can add a table, another view, or a function to the new view by selecting from the list of tables, views, and functions shown in the Show Table window. The Add Table window displays, as shown in Figure 34-9.

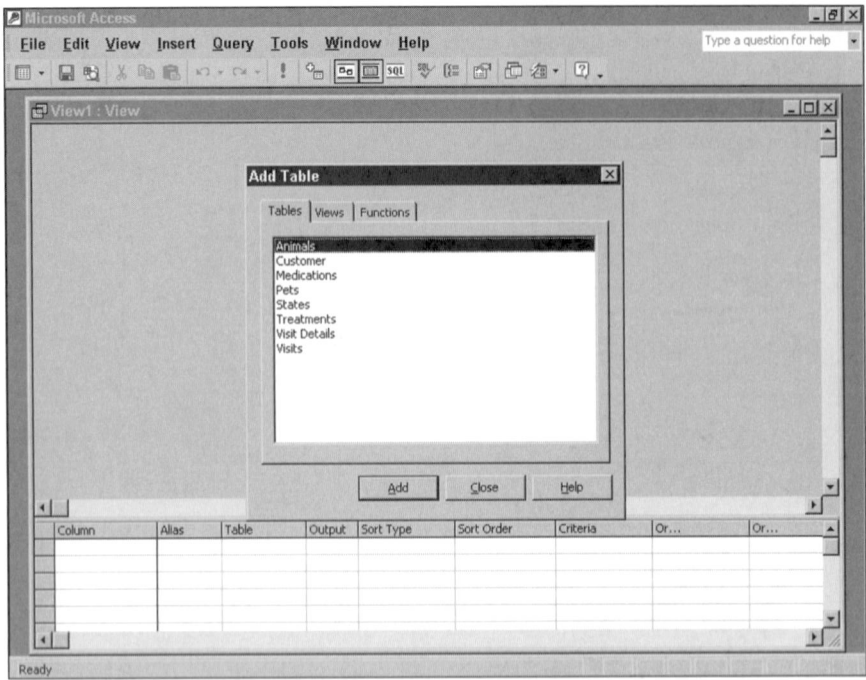

Figure 34-9: The Add Table window in the Query Designer window

You can select columns and enter criteria in the same way that you design queries in an Access database. Figure 34-10 shows the All Pets query in the Query Designer window.

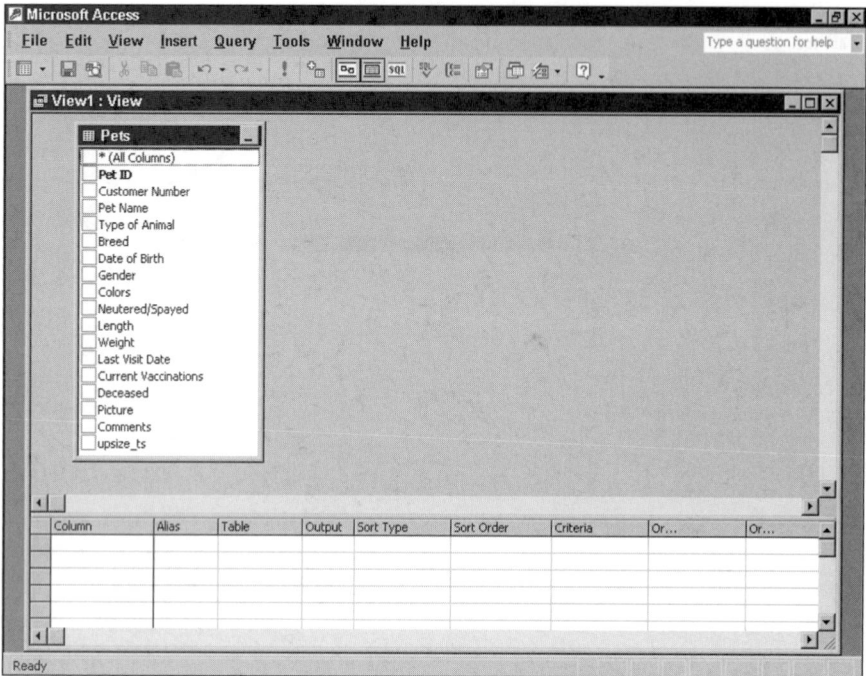

Figure 34-10: The Query Designer window for the All Pets query.

With views, you can retrieve information that is stored in tables or related tables from functions, or even from other views. You can retrieve all the rows and columns from a table, or select individual columns and specify criteria to filter the rows to retrieve. When you select columns and specify criteria, symbols display next to the table's column name to indicate the type of operation to be performed on the field. Figure 34-11 shows that criteria have been specified for the Type of Animal column.

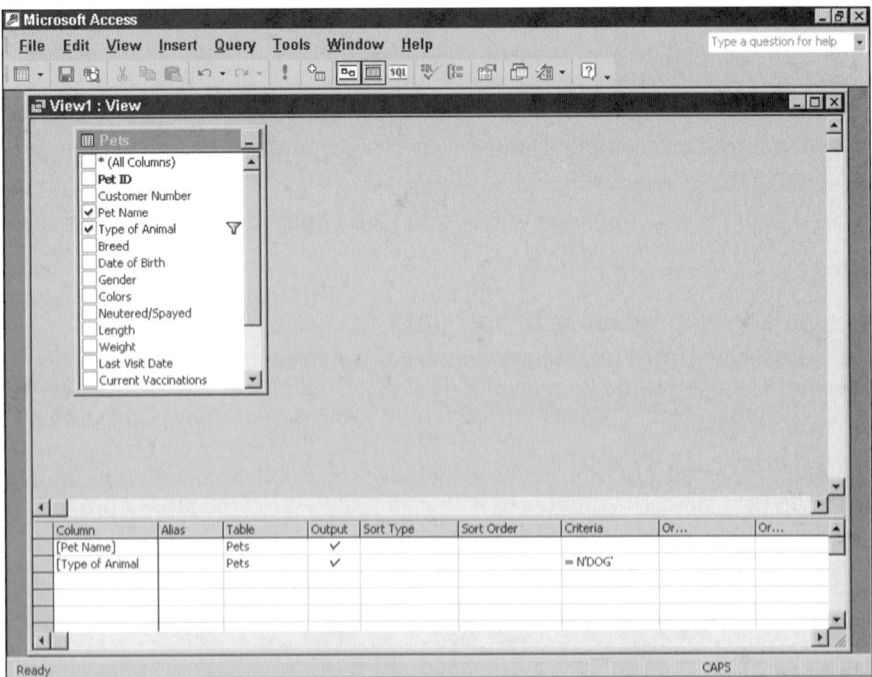

Figure 34-11: Specifying view criteria

Views support only SELECT queries. If you need to use commands, such as UPDATE, INSERT, or APPEND, you must create a stored procedure.

Creating stored procedures

A *stored procedure* is a special type of query that allows you to use commands to manipulate data in the database. Creating a stored procedure is very similar to creating a view or an Access database query.

Stored procedures provide a handy container for storing all of the SQL statements that you use throughout your application. Instead of writing SQL statements in your code, you can store them here and call them from your code in much the same way that you call a function stored in a module. Some of the many benefits of stored procedures are

✦ Can contain multiple SQL statements

✦ Can call another stored procedure name

✦ Can receive parameters and return a value or a result set

✦ Are stored in a compiled state on the server so they execute faster than if they were embedded in your code

✦ Are stored in a common container in your application so that others can maintain them more easily

Using a stored procedure to sort data

To create a new stored procedure, first make sure that the Queries object is selected. Then select the item labeled Create stored procedure in designer. The Design window for the All Pets Sorted stored procedure is shown in Figure 34-12.

The All Pets Sorted stored procedure includes the same table, columns, and criteria as the All Pets view. The difference is that the All Pets Sorted stored procedure specifies a Sort Order for the Pet Name column.

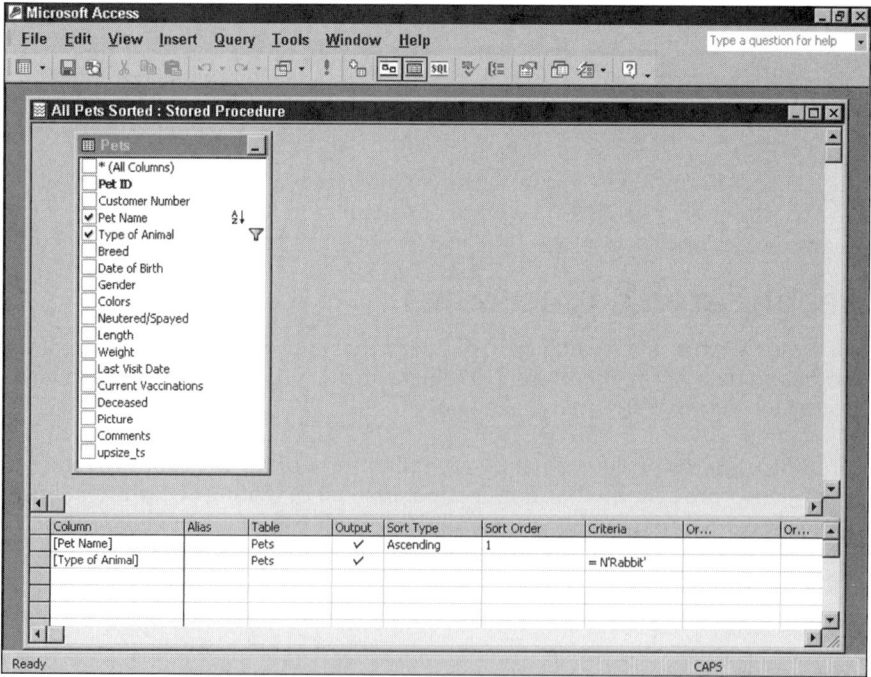

Figure 34-12: Creating a stored procedure

You can specify a Sort Order for a column in a view. However, to sort a view requires the use of the TOP 100 PERCENT clause with the Select statement. When you add a Sort Order to a view, Access automatically adds the TOP 100 PERCENT clause to the Select statement.

Caution   The TOP clause degrades performance because it causes the sorting to be done on the client machine instead of on the server. The TOP clause is not required for sorting Select queries in a stored procedure. The server performs sorting of stored procedure data.

Tip   You can add a view to a stored procedure.

Using parameters with a stored procedure

If you want to run a stored procedure with different criteria values every time you run it, you can add a parameter to the stored procedure's criteria. A *parameter* is a place-holder for the column's criteria. For example, you may want to retrieve all pets that are a certain type of animal. But, you may want to retrieve all rabbit-type pets one time, or all pets that are dogs another time. The All Pets For Type stored procedure uses the Pet_Type parameter, as shown in Figure 34-13.

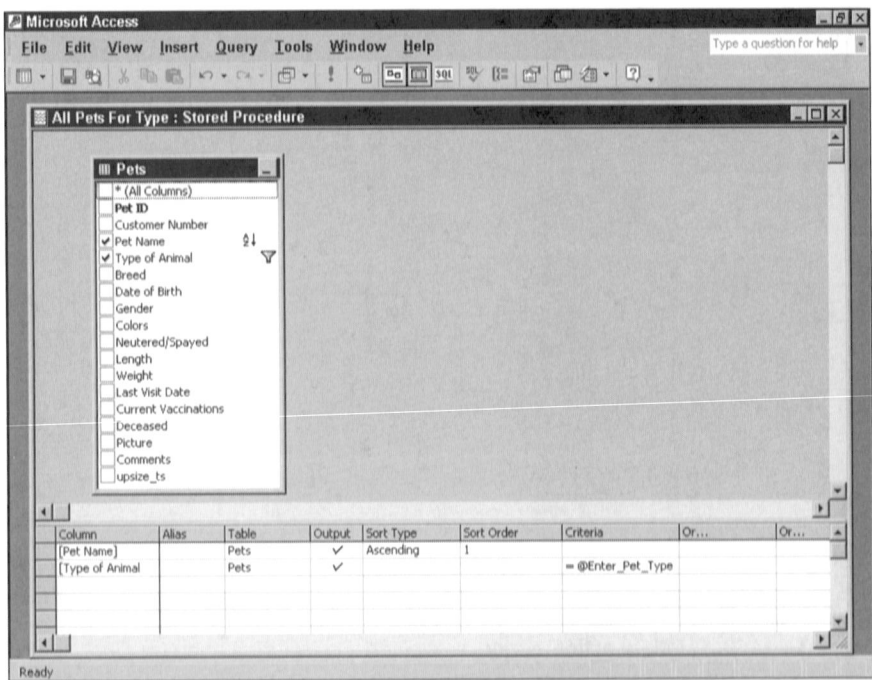

Figure 34-13: Creating a stored procedure with a parameter

Note   You can't specify a parameter in a view.

Using a stored procedure to update data

While views support only Select queries, stored procedures support action queries as well as Select queries. An *action query* is a stored procedure that inserts, modifies, or deletes data by using the SQL INSERT, UPDATE, and DELETE statements. The Update Medication Prices stored procedure, shown in Figure 34-14, is an example of an Update action query.

The Update Medication Prices stored procedure increases each of the values in the Price column in the Medications table by 10 percent. Notice that the Grid pane of the stored procedure contains different columns than the columns shown in the Select query examples. To create an action query using the Query Designer, select the Query menu item. Then choose the type of action query that you want to create: Make-Table, Update, Append, Append Values, or Delete. Figure 34-15 shows the options for the Query menu item.

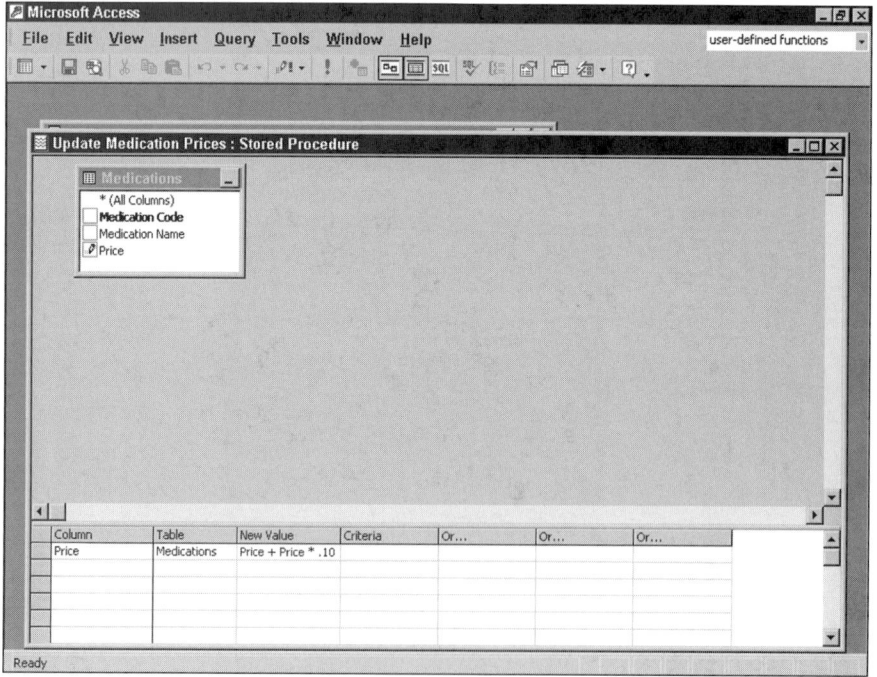

Figure 34-14: An Update action query

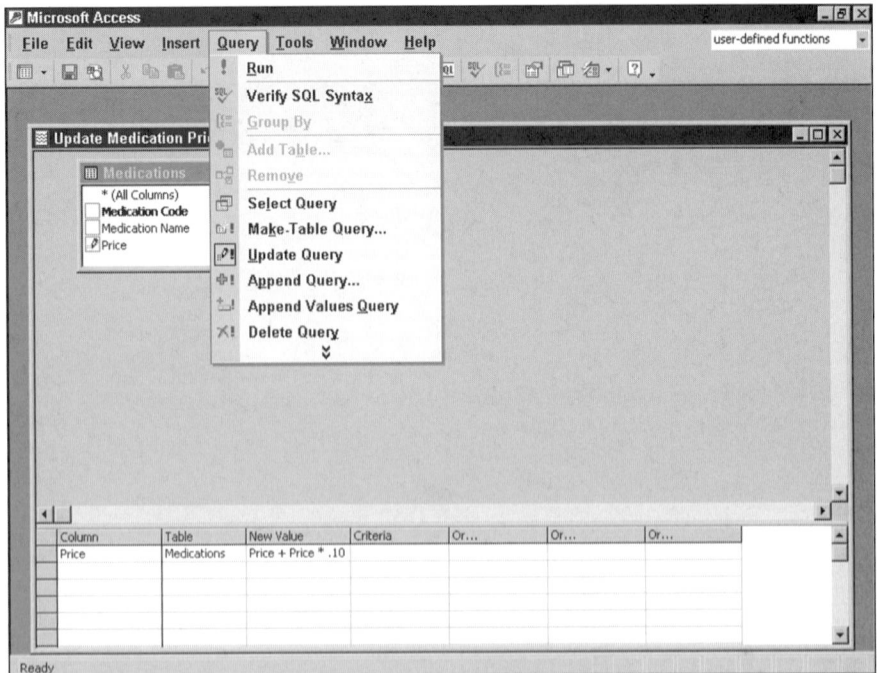

Figure 34-15: Using the Query Designer to create an action query

Creating user-defined functions

User-defined functions combine the best features of views and stored procedures into a single query.

New Feature   You can pass parameters to user-defined functions. They also can include views, stored procedures, or other functions. User-defined functions can't be used to update data in a table.

To create a function, select the Queries object, then select Create function in designer. The Query Designer opens. You can add a table, a view, or another function to the new function by selecting from the list of tables, views, and functions shown in the Show Table window.

The design for the Pets for Type function, shown in Figure 34-16, looks just like the design for the All Pets For Type stored procedure.

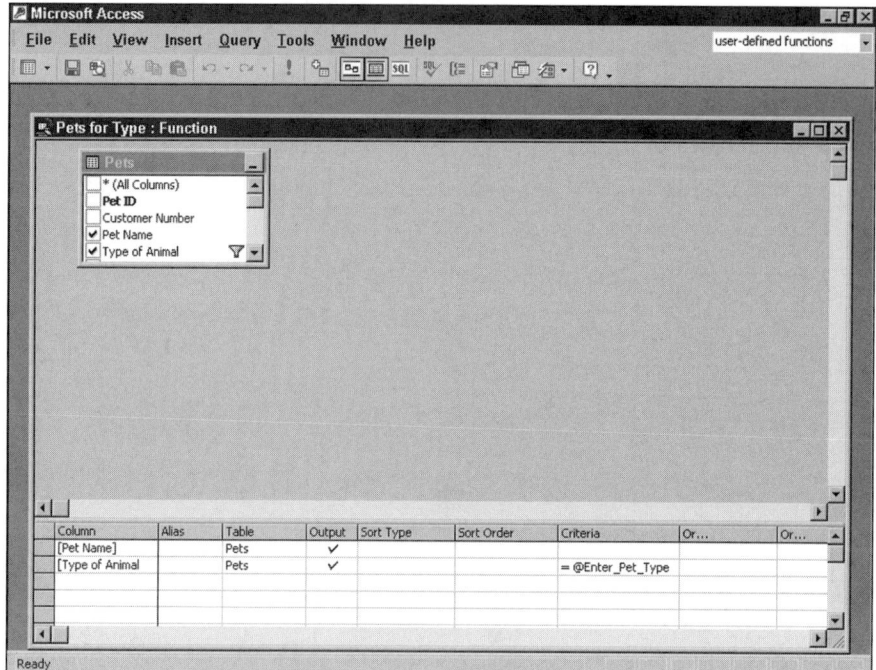

Figure 34-16: Creating a user-defined function

Basically, the user-defined function is a simpler version of the stored procedure. If your query needs to accept one or more parameters and return a single value or a single table, you should use a user-defined function for the query rather than a stored procedure. Stored procedures are geared for performing more complex query operations, such as multiple Select statements, table updates, and returning multiple result sets.

Using Unbound Forms

Access projects allow you to bind a form's Record source directly to a table. A *bound form* is a form that's tied directly to a table or query, providing a constant open connection to all of the data in the table or query. Although this approach is a quick and easy way to present and update data on the form, this is not the most efficient way to work with data in the client/server world.

Bound forms maintain a constant connection between the server and the workstation. The server must maintain a record lock on the data displayed on the form — even if the user is simply viewing it. Open connections and record locks consume server resources. If you are operating in an environment with many users or where users are working with large volumes of data and transactions, you want to use unbound forms.

An *unbound form* is a form that doesn't maintain a constant open connection to a table or query. You retrieve data from a table or query one record at a time. The load on the server is significantly reduced because it doesn't need to maintain open connections or record locks.

Here are some common reasons to implement unbound forms:

✦ Improved performance due to retrieval of a minimal amount of data

✦ Improved control of record-locking conflicts

✦ Bypasses Access automatic record saving, providing ability to confirm saving or canceling record changes

✦ Required for database security considerations

Visual Basic code is used to handle all of the data used in the form. You must write a procedure to handle searching for and displaying the data. You must write other procedures to handle updating the data. The following list covers most of the tasks that a typical unbound form needs to handle:

✦ Retrieving the set of data to be viewed or edited on the form

✦ Loading the data into the form's controls

✦ Searching for another record

✦ Determining when data on the form has changed

✦ Saving changed data

✦ Undoing changes to data

✦ Moving to other records in the set (first, last, next, previous)

✦ Creating a new record

Creating the code for each of these tasks may seem like a lot of work. But if you want to build a true client/server application, this is the best approach.

Working with unbound forms

Creating the Visual Basic functions to display and process data in an unbound form requires the use of the ActiveX Data Objects (ADO) programming model. ADO enables you to write an application to access and manipulate data in a database server through an OLE DB provider. ADO's primary benefits are ease of use, high speed, low memory overhead, and a small hard drive footprint. ADO supports key features for building client/server and Web-based applications.

Cross-Reference

See Chapter 31 to review the basic concepts of the ADO programming model.

For an example of a working unbound form, we use the Customers Unbound form. Figure 34-17 shows the Customers Unbound form in Normal view.

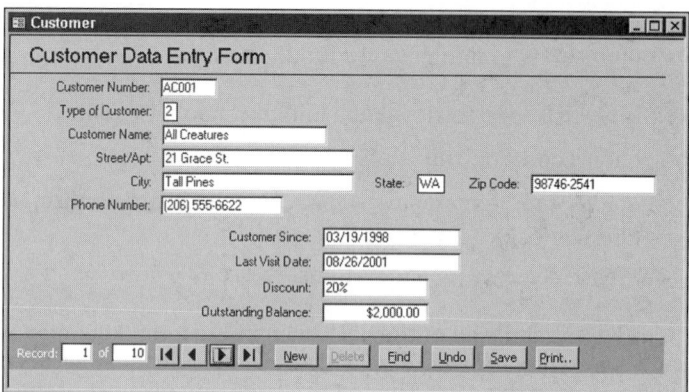

Figure 34-17: Viewing data in an unbound form

The Customers Unbound form demonstrates virtually any function you need to add, edit, delete, and find records. The buttons in the form's footer section perform these functions. The Undo button allows the user to restore the original data for the record after changes have been made but before the Save button is selected. The Print button opens a print dialog that provides several choices for printing the form's data. The Save button allows the user to immediately process changes made to the data.

Note　In bound forms, changes are saved automatically when the user closes the form or moves to another record. Because these automatic update features are disabled when using unbound forms, you must provide a way to actively save the data.

Because the unbound form doesn't have a record source, it doesn't contain any built-in record navigation buttons. The record navigation buttons included on the Customers Unbound form provide the same functionality provided by a bound Access form. The user is also provided with controls to show the current record number as well as the total number of records.

Creating an unbound form

In unbound forms, the form's RecordSource is blank. Additionally, the ControlSource for each of the form's controls is blank. The controls are named using the corresponding column names of the form's table. The Design view of the Customers Unbound form is shown in Figure 34-18.

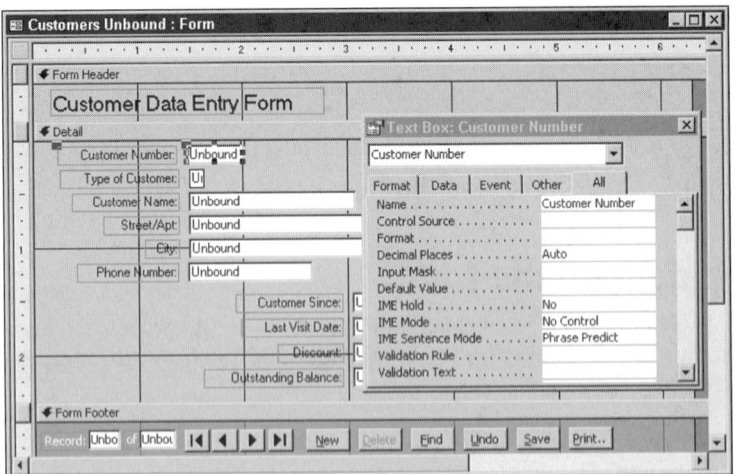

Figure 34-18: Designing an unbound form

Tip

A quick and easy way to set up the controls for an unbound form is to initially bind the form to the table; then, drag the table's fields to the form. This action reduces any errors in naming the fields to match the names of the fields in the table. Before completing the design of the form, remove the ControlSource properties of the fields and the RecordSource property for the form.

On the top right of the Customers Unbound form are four dark gray controls. You use these controls to connect the form to the database. The Visible property of these controls is set to False so that they can't be seen when the user is viewing the form. The names and ControlSource properties for these special fields must be set according to the items listed in Table 34-1.

Table 34-1
Connecting an Unbound Form to a SQL Server Database

Control Name	ControlSource
xProvider	="Provider=SQLOLEDB;"
xDataSource	="Data Source=(local);Database=Mountain Animal HospitalSQL;uid=sa"
xRecordset	="Customer"
xKey	="CustomerNumber"

The bottom right area of the unbound form also contains the following hidden controls:

✦ **FlagEdited.** Checked when a field's data is updated

✦ **FlagFind.** Checked when searched criteria is selected

✦ **UpdateCtr.** Incremented each time the record is changed

Displaying data on the form

The form actually contains only a minimal amount of code. The form's On Load event retrieves the data to display on the form. Figure 34-19 shows the On Load event procedure code.

The On Load event procedure calls the function uf_DisplayRecord. The code for the uf_DisplayRecord function is not stored with the form. In fact, most of the form's code is stored in the Unbound Form Utilities module. By storing these functions in a module, you can use the same functions over and over for any other unbound forms that you want to include in your application. Figure 34-20 shows the Unbound Form Utilities Module Window.

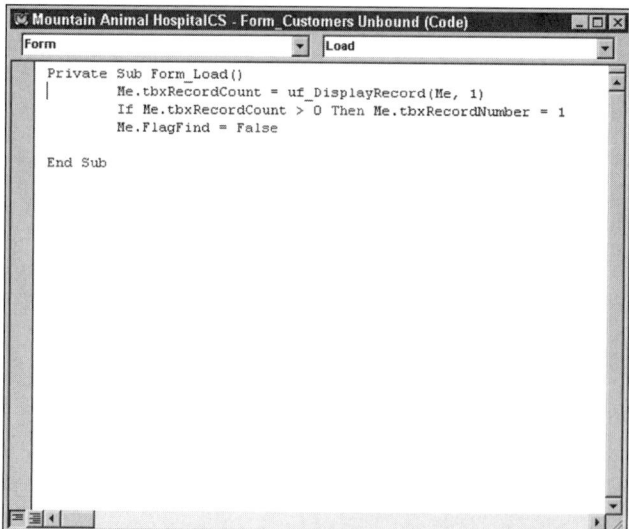

Figure 34-19: The On Load event procedure for an unbound form

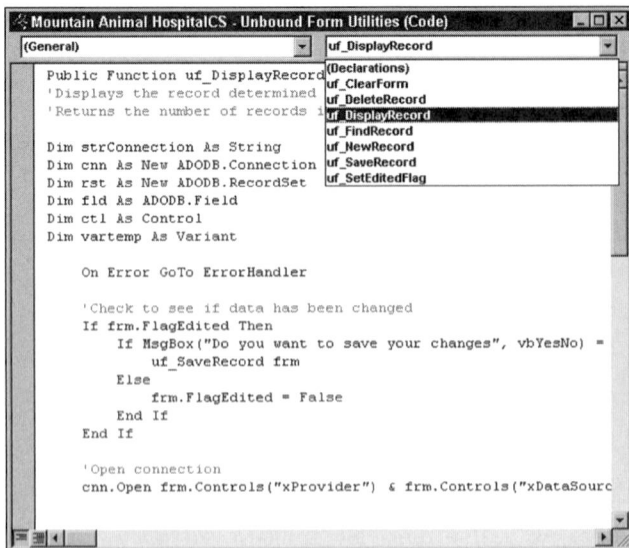

Figure 34-20: The functions of the Unbound Form Utilities module

The first task of the uf_DisplayRecord function is to retrieve the data to display on the form. The following code snippet shows the statements used to retrieve the form's data.

```
'Open connection
    cnn.Open frm.Controls("xProvider") &
frm.Controls("xDataSource")

    'Open recordset
    If Len(frm.Filter) = 0 Then
        rst.Open "Select * From " & frm.Controls("xRecordset")
& " Order by " & frm.Controls("xKey"), cnn, adOpenStatic
    Else
        rst.Open "Select * From " & frm.Controls("xRecordset")
& " WHERE " & frm.Filter & " Order by " & frm.Controls("xKey"),
cnn, adOpenStatic
    End If
```

The uf_DisplayRecord function establishes a connection to the database specified in the form's xProvider and xDataSource fields. Then, it checks the form's filter property. If a filter is not set, the function retrieves all of the rows in the table specified in the form's xRecordset field. If the form's filter is set, the function specifies a WHERE clause to include only some of the rows specified in the form's xRecordset field.

The second task of the uf_DisplayRecord function is to display the first row of retrieved data on the form. The following code snippet shows the statements used to load the data into the form's fields.

```
'Iterate through controls on form that match fields in
recordset
    For Each ctl In frm

        'if error the field is not on the form
        On Error Resume Next
        Err = 0
        vartemp = rst.Fields(ctl.Name).Name
        If Err = 0 Then
            On Error GoTo ErrorHandler
            'if control enables then set default value from tag
            '   and set focus if tab index 0
            If ctl.Enabled Then
                ctl.Value = rst.Fields(ctl.Name).Value
                If ctl.TabIndex = 0 Then ctl.SetFocus
            End If
        End If
    Next
```

Basically, this section of code steps through each of the controls on the form. This is the reason that you name the control to match the name in the database table. The value of the control is set to the value of the column name in the table that matches the control's name. Then, the focus is set to the field that is first in the tab order (TabIndex 0).

Along with the uf_DisplayRecord function, the Unbound Form Functions module contains all of the other functions that make an unbound form work, including

✦ uf_NewRecord — Adds a new record

✦ uf_SaveRecord — Saves the current data on the form to a new or existing record

✦ uf_FindRecord — Finds a set of records meeting a specified criteria

✦ uf_DisplayRecord — Retrieves and displays a selected record

✦ uf_DeleteRecord — Deletes a record

✦ uf_ClearForm — Clears all fields on the form

✦ uf_SetEditedFlag — Is called by a field on the form when the field is updated

On the CD-ROM
You can find both the Customers Unbound form and the Unbound Form Utilities module in the Mountain Animal HospitalCS project file in the Examples folder of this book's CD-ROM.

You should take a few minutes to become familiar with the code for these functions. Each function, except for the uf_SetEditedFlag function, receives the name of the calling form as a parameter.

Updating data

You can use the functions in the Unbound Form Utilities to add new records, delete records, and save edited records. To implement any of these functions in the unbound form, simply create an event procedure for the appropriate button on the form. Then call the function from the button's event procedure.

To add a new record, you create an event procedure for the New button's On Click event. The New button's On Click event calls the uf_NewRecord function. Figure 34-21 shows the On Click event procedure for the Customers Unbound form's New button.

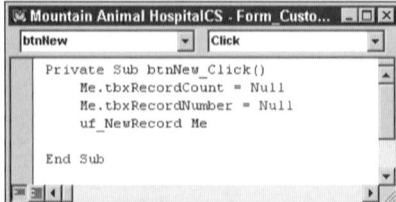

Figure 34-21: Using a button to call an Unbound Form Utilities function

The New button's On Click event procedure first updates the record number and record count fields in the form's navigation button section. These fields should be empty when creating a new record. Then the event procedure calls the uf_NewRecord function passing the name of the form as a parameter.

The uf_NewRecord function sets the form up to enter a new record. The following code snippet shows the statements used to clear the form's fields.

```
'Iterate through controls on form that match fields in recordset
    For Each ctl In frm

            'if error the field is not on the form
            On Error Resume Next
            Err = 0
            vartemp = rst.Fields(ctl.Name).Name
            If Err = 0 Then
                On Error GoTo ErrorHandler
                'if control enables then set default value from tag
                '    and set focus if tab index 0
                If ctl.Enabled Then
                    If IsNull(ctl.Tag) Then
                        ctl.Value = Null
                    Else
                        ctl.Value = ctl.Tag
                    End If
                    If ctl.TabIndex = 0 Then ctl.SetFocus
                End If
            End If
        Next
```

The code in the uf_NewRecord function loops through each field on the form. Each field's value property is set to Null. Then, the focus is set to the first field in the tab order.

Caution   Before clearing the fields on the form, check to see if the user changed any of the data. If the data has changed, prompt the user to save or undo the changes.

You can use the uf_SaveRecord function to save the data on the form. Use the Save button's On Click event to call the uf_SaveRecord function.

The first task of the uf_SaveRecord function is to locate the record in the table. This section of code is illustrated in the following code snippet:

```
'Check to see if data has been changed
    If Not frm.FlagEdited Then
        MsgBox "Nothing to save"
        GoTo Done
    End If

    'Open connection
    cnn.Open frm.Controls("xProvider") &
frm.Controls("xDataSource")

    'Open recordset to determine type of key field and setup
Criteria
    rst.Open "Select * From " & frm.Controls("xRecordset"),
cnn, adOpenStatic
    Select Case rst(frm.Controls("xKey").Value).Type
        Case adChar, adVarWChar, adLongVarWChar
            strCriteria = frm.Controls("xKey") & " = " &
Chr(39) & frm.Controls(frm.Controls("xKey")).Value & Chr(34)
        Case adDate
            strCriteria = frm.Controls("xKey") & " = " & "#" &
frm.Controls(frm.Controls("xKey")).Value & "#"
        Case Else   'assume numeric
            strCriteria = frm.Controls("xKey") & " = " &
str(frm.Controls(frm.Controls("xKey")).Value)
    End Select
    rst.Close

    'Determine if this is a new record or a changed record
    rst.Open "Select * From " & frm.Controls("xRecordset") & "
WHERE " & strCriteria, cnn, adOpenKeyset, adLockOptimistic
```

The function first checks to see if the form has been edited. If not, the function simply exits. Otherwise, it opens a connection to the recordset simply to determine the key field's data type so a criteria string can be created. The criteria string is used to search the recordset for a record with the same key field. This is necessary so the function can determine whether to update an existing record or create a new record.

If it is a new record, the function uses the AddNew method and iterates through the controls on the form that match the fields in the recordset to create a record with the new data. The UpdateCtr field is set to 1 for the new record.

If an existing record has the same key field, then the code must check to make sure that the record has not been changed. The code to perform the check is shown below:

```
'Check to see if this record was already updated by another user
        If rst("UpdateCtr") <> frm.Controls("UpdateCtr").Value Then
            Response = MsgBox("This record was already updated by another user."
& vbCrLf & _
                    "Do you want to overwrite the other user's changes?", _
                    vbInformation + vbYesNo, "Data already changed")
                    If Response = vbNo Then
                        rst.Close
                        Exit Function
                    End If
        End If
```

The UpdateCtr field in the form is compared to the value of the UpdateCtr field in the table. If the two values are different, then the record was updated in between the time that the record was displayed on the form and the time that the user pressed the Save button. A message prompts the user to go ahead and overwrite the record in the table with the user's changes, or to cancel the user's update.

To update the existing record, the values in the form's fields are copied to the recordset's field and the recordset is updated. The code to update the recordset is shown below:

```
    'Iterate through controls on form that match fields in
    recordset
            For Each ctl In frm
                'if error the field is not on the form
                On Error Resume Next
                Err = 0
                vartemp = rst.Fields(ctl.Name).Name
                If Err = 0 Then
                    On Error GoTo ErrorHandler
                    'if control enabled then
                    '    if it is not an auto increment field
                    '        if data is not null or an empty string
                If ctl.Enabled Then
                    If Not
rst.Fields(ctl.Name).Properties("IsAutoIncrement") Then
                        If Not IsNull(ctl.Value) And Not
ctl.Value = "" Then
                                vartemp = ctl.Value
                                rst(ctl.Name).Value = vartemp
                        End If
                    End If
```

```
                End If
            End If
        Next
        'Increment the Update Counter
        rst("UpdateCtr") = rst("UpdateCtr") + 1
        'Update the recordset
        rst.Update
        rst.Close
```

The fields are also checked to see if the field is an "Auto Increment" type and whether it is enabled. If it is an "Auto Increment" type, the field value is not updated. The UpdateCtr is incremented by 1.

A message box displays if the record has been successfully saved, and the FlagEdited field is reset.

Finding a record

You can find records with the function uf_FindRecord. This function can find a record based on criteria entered in any field on the form. The function checks the value of flagFind field on the form. If this flag is true, then the form contains the criteria to do the find. If the flag is false, then the form is cleared so the user can enter the criteria. A message displays, telling the user to enter the criteria and to press the Find button again to retrieve the records.

You can set the default value of this flag to True so that when the form is opened, the user can start entering criteria right away. After the function completes, the resulting criteria is stored in the Form's filter property for later use. The function does a check to see if the current record has been saved before clearing the form out for the criteria.

The heart of the operation of this function is to create a criteria string. Criteria can be specified for any combination of fields on the form. The function creates a criteria string with an "AND" between all of the selected fields. For example, in our sample application you can enter a state, and all records for that state are retrieved. You can search for a customer number or a phone number as well. The code to create the criteria string is shown below:

```
'Iterate through controls on form that match fields in
recordset
        strCriteria = ""
        For Each ctl In frm
          'if error the field is not on the form
          On Error Resume Next
          Err = 0
          vartemp = rst.Fields(ctl.Name).Name
          If Err = 0 Then
            On Error GoTo ErrorHandler
            If ctl.Enabled Then
              If Not IsNull(ctl.Value) And Not ctl.Value = ""
```

```
Then
                    If Len(strCriteria) > 0 Then strCriteria =
strCriteria & " AND "
                  Select Case rst(ctl.Name).Type
                    Case adChar, adVarWChar, adLongVarWChar
                      strCriteria = strCriteria & ctl.Name & " =
" & Chr(39) & ctl.Value & Chr(39)
                      Case adDate
                        strCriteria = strCriteria & ctl.Name & " =
" & "#" & ctl.Value & "#"
                      Case Else   'assume numeric
                        strCriteria = strCriteria & ctl.Name & " =
" & str(ctl.Value)
                    End Select
                  End If
                End If
              End If
          Next
          rst.Close
```

The trick to making the criteria string is to find the fields on the form that the user
has filled in and then look up the type of field in the recordset to determine how to
format the criteria string. For text fields we need to enclose the search value in single quotes, and for dates the search value needs to be enclosed with "#". For numbers, no delimiter is needed.

When all of the controls have been checked, the recordset is opened with the criteria. The code below shows how the criteria string is used to retrieve the data:

```
'Open recordset with criteria
        If Len(strCriteria) > 0 Then strCriteria = " WHERE " &
strCriteria
        rst.Open "Select * From " & frm.Controls("xRecordset")
& strCriteria & " ORDER by " & frm.Controls("xKey"), cnn,
adOpenStatic, adLockBatchOptimistic
        If rst.RecordCount = 0 Then
          MsgBox ("No records found")
          uf_FindRecord = 0
        Else
          uf_FindRecord = rst.RecordCount
          frm.Filter = Mid(strCriteria, 8)   'store the
criteria for later
          frm.FlagFind = False
          frm.FlagEdited = False
          'Display first record
          uf_DisplayRecord frm, 1
        End If
```

If the record count is not zero, the criteria string is stored in the form's filter property and the first record is displayed on the form. The uf_FindRecord function calls
the uf_DisplayRecord function to display the filtered data on the form.

Unbound forms can improve performance when you are developing an application for a client/server database. However, while bound forms in Access provide built-in processing for retrieving and updating data, you need to duplicate this functionality yourself using Visual Basic code and ADO. Hopefully, the Unbound Form Utilities module and Customers Unbound form included with this book can get you well on your way.

✦   ✦   ✦

Using and Creating Access Objects for Intranets and the Internet

✦ ✦ ✦ ✦

In This Chapter

Understanding the Internet, the World Wide Web, and HTML

Displaying the Web toolbar within Access 2002

Exporting Access 2002 objects to HTML

Understanding static and dynamic HTML

Importing HTML data to Access tables

Creating a Hyperlink data type

Adding hyperlinks to forms and reports

✦ ✦ ✦ ✦

T he Internet, and particularly the World Wide Web, has become an important part of all businesses today. Whether you simply use the Internet to search for information or whether you're part of a vast corporate intranet, you need to be able to use Microsoft Access to store and disseminate the data that is moved across the network wire.

Access 2002 contains many features that allow you to store data found on the Internet in your database container in standard Access tables. You can also create a table, form, or report in Access and save it as an HTML-based table, which you can then use on any Web site. In addition, Access 2002 offers a feature known as *data access pages*; these are a special type of Web page. They allow you to view and work with data by using Microsoft's Internet Explorer browser (version 5.x or better), which gives you access to dynamic (live) and static (non-updated) information across an intranet or the Internet. You can store this data in a Microsoft Access database or a Microsoft SQL Server database.

What Are Intranets?

An *intranet* is simply the use of Internet technologies within an organization (or company). Intranets help in cutting costs and offer fast and easy accessibility to day-to-day information. It offers some features that are often lacking in Internet technology—speed, security, and control. It is a network (or networks) that works on a local or wide area network that uses TCP/IP, HTTP, and other Internet protocols and looks like a private version of the Internet. You can use an intranet in much the same way that you use the World Wide Web to store information on home pages and Web sites. One of the leading methods of creating World Wide Web pages is to use HyperText Markup Language (HTML) language. This is the de facto language of the Web. Web browsers (such as Amaya, Internet Explorer, Netscape, Opera, and others) read and interpret this HTML code to display the text and graphics on the screen.

Cross-Reference

This chapter will use the Mountain Animal Data Access Pages database found on the CD-ROM.

On the CD-ROM

This chapter and the next one use the Mountain Animal Data Access Pages.mdb table, which is located on the CD-ROM. If you haven't already installed it on your hard drive, you need to do so now to follow along with the examples.

What Is HTML?

If you're unfamiliar with HTML, you should make this topic your next learning experience. Web pages are formatted by using a special language called HyperText Markup Language (HTML). With HTML, you can create a Web page containing text, pictures, or links to other Web pages. Each Web page is identified by its address, which is called a *Uniform Resource Locator* (URL); for example, http://www.databasecreations.com or http://www.ItInAsia.com. Using Access 2000's Internet tools, you can translate Access 2002 objects and data into HTML-compatible format.

Using the Web Toolbar with Access 2002

Figure 35-1 shows the Access 2002 database container with the Web toolbar, which you can turn on by right-clicking the toolbar and selecting Web or by selecting View ⇨ Toolbars ⇨ Web from any menu. After the Web toolbar displayed, you can use it to access Web sites on the Internet or on your local intranet. When you use the Web toolbar, you launch the default Web browser on your system.

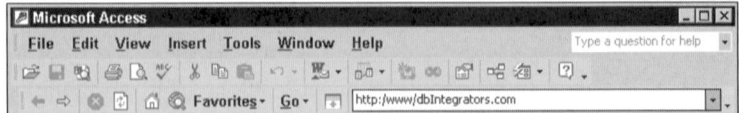

Figure 35-1: The Web toolbar on the Access database container screen

Note
You can also activate/deactivate the Web toolbar at any time by right-clicking any active toolbar and selecting the Web toolbar from the pop-up menu. To take advantage of the Internet features of the Web toolbar in Access 2002, you need the Microsoft Internet Explorer 5.x Web browser (or better), a modem, and an Internet connection or other network connection to access the Internet. After it's been activated, the Web toolbar is available at all times. It is normally the last toolbar displayed in the toolbar area of Access 2002. Like other toolbars it can also be undocked, as shown in Figure 35-2. After it's been undocked, you can place it anywhere along the bottom, right, or left side of the Access window, or simply let it float on the Windows surface, as shown in Figure 35-2.

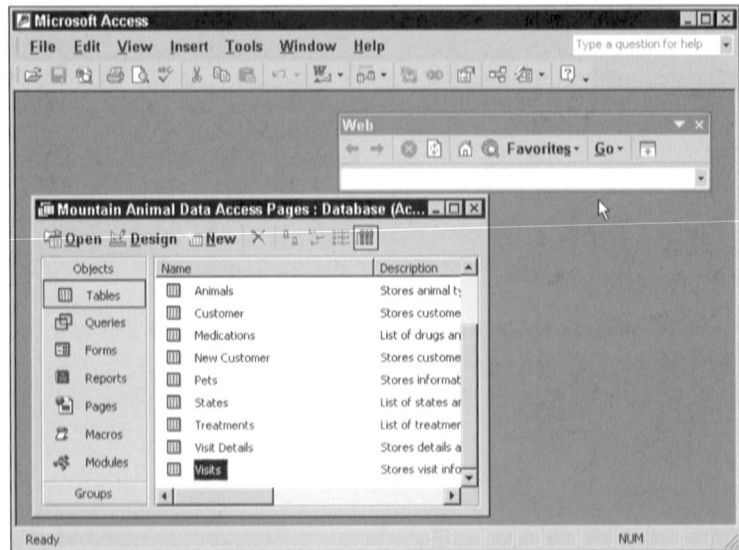

Figure 35-2: The Web toolbar undocked from the toolbar area of Access 2002

After the Web toolbar is active, it is available from any View mode of Access. This includes Datasheet, View, and Design. You can use it to quickly activate your Web browser (IE 5.0 or better) and perform local (intranet) and remote (Internet) Web operations. Figure 35-3 shows Internet Explorer 5.5 active in Access 2002 with a Home Page displayed. To start IE 5.5 simply click the home page button on the Web toolbar.

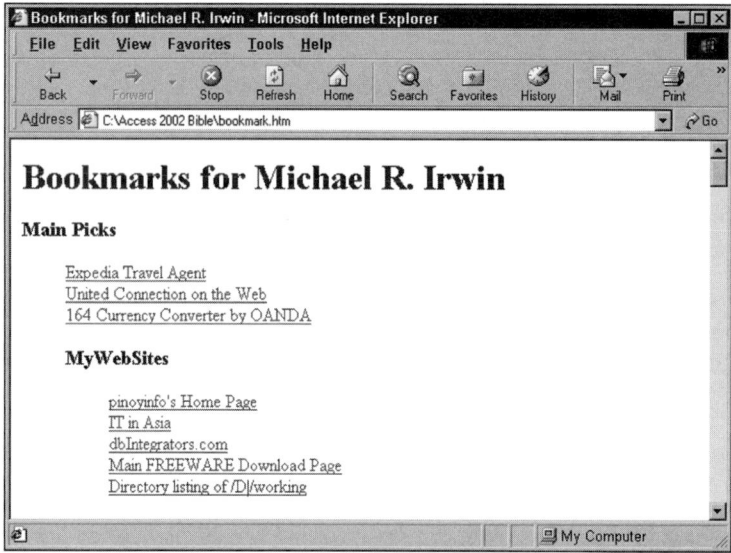

Figure 35-3: Internet Explorer 5.5 running inside Access 2002

It may appear that you are running IE 5.5 independently, but you are actually running the Web browser inside Access 2002. If you click the Back button or press Alt + Right Arrow (⇨), you are returned to the Access database that you were previously working with (in the Access 2002 window).

Tip   You can use the Back and Forward buttons to move back and forth through the browser pages of IE 5.5 and the Access database that you are working with.

The Web toolbar

The Web toolbar contains several buttons specific to working with the Web, as shown in Figure 35-4.

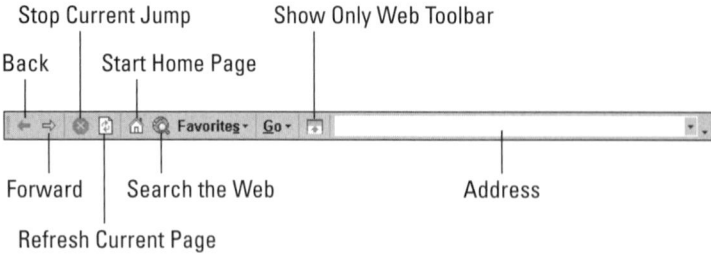

Figure 35-4: Buttons on the Web toolbar

The Favorites and Go buttons are actually pull-down menus of additional actions that are Web-oriented. The Favorites choice displays a series of choices specific to your environment. The Go menu has several choices that you may use:

✦ **Open Hyperlink.** Open an Internet address

✦ **Back.** Go back to the page that called the current page

✦ **Forward.** Go forward to previously viewed page

✦ **Start Page.** Go to the start page (you specify it below)

✦ **Search the Web.** Go to the search page (you specify it below)

✦ **Set Start Page.** Specify a new default start page

✦ **Set Search Page.** Specify a new default search page

✦ **Current open.** Go back to the currently open database

Several of these choices are also available via the buttons on the Web toolbar. The two that you may want to use from the Go menu are Set Start Page and Set Search Page because they are not accessible via the toolbar buttons.

You can set the default home page by using the Set Start Page option from the Go menu on the Web toolbar. In Figure 35-1, you see that the initial URL is http:// www.dbIntegrators.com,; this is the home page for dbIntegrators, LTD.

Tip   When specifying a home page, you are not limited to specifying a Web-based address (such as http://www.dbIntegrators.com). You can also specify a local file, such as your bookmark, or favorites file that the browser uses.

Because this book is about Access 2002 and not specifically about the Internet, we assume that you own a browser and have some experience visiting Web sites on the World Wide Web. This chapter uses Microsoft's Internet Explorer 5.5 for discussion.

Types of Web Pages That Access Can Create

Microsoft Access can create many different types of Web pages. It can create Data Access Pages, up-to-date, read-only data pages, or (static) snapshots of data from a table, query, form, or report.

If you need to manipulate the data from your databases directly in a Web page, you need to create data access pages. If you simply want to have up-to-date, read-only data displayed, you can create Active Server Pages (ASP) or IDC/HTX files used by Microsoft Internet Information Server. If you only want to display a snapshot of information from a specific point and time, you can create plan static HTML documents.

To make sure that your Web pages appear consistent, you can also use an HTML template file that you create.

Data access pages

Data access pages, or DAPs, were first introduced in Access 2000. In the simplest sense, data access pages are a combination of forms and reports for the Web.

Note   DAPs are HTML pages that are attached directly to data in the database and can be used to display static or dynamic information. They can be attached to a single table or several tables via a query. They can be used like Access forms, except that data access pages are designed to run in the Internet Explorer 5.x Web browser. They are HTML pages that can be deployed to the Internet, an intranet, or used within Access 2002.

Access 97 didn't use or create data access pages; however, you had the ability to create a form or report and publish it to an HTML document viewable on the Web. These HTML documents, or pages, were static — the data was fixed, not updatable. Access 2002 still lets you create static data pages from your tables, queries, forms, and reports (discussed later in this chapter), but data access pages remove the interim step of exporting an object to an HTML page, because they are HTML documents from the start. As pointed out at the beginning of this section, data access pages were first introduced in Access 2000.

You can view active and dynamic data, update data, and print data access pages. You can apply filters, sort, or manipulate objects within the HTML document (like Pivot Tables, Charts, and Spreadsheets) in real-time.

New Feature   Access 2002 extends the functionality of data access pages in several areas, including deployment, ability to directly create a data access page from other objects (tables, queries, forms, and reports), and more flexibility in designing and browsing DAPs. It also include more robust support for Extensible Markup Language (XML) — including it in your DAPs. This functionality is a result of the technologies that are built into Internet Explorer (version 5.5 is recommended) and the Office Web Components.

Unlike Access forms and reports, data access pages are stored in the Windows file system as HTML pages, rather than in the Access database or project.

After you create them, you can use data access pages directly in an Access program or within the Web browser. These files are specifically designed for Internet Explorer 5.0 (or greater) and make use of dynamic HTML and XML technology.

Note　At the time of this writing, data access pages (DAPs) work only with Microsoft's Internet Explorer 5.0 (or greater). To take advantage of many of the new features of DAPs in Access 2002, you need to use IE 5.5 (or greater). Many of the features of DAPs also rely upon the Office XP Microsoft Web Components (MSOWC). Both of these applications need to be installed on your computer to take full advantage of the power of DAPs.

Caution　Microsoft Internet Explorer 5.5 doesn't come with Office XP or Access 2002. The Microsoft Web Components does come with Office XP. If you are going to create your DAPs for distribution to users that don't have Office XP or Internet Explorer 5.5 on their computers, they need to download both Internet Explorer 5.5 (IE 5.5) and the new Microsoft Office Web Components from Microsoft's Web site. These files are very large and will take time to download; however, it is a one-time download. Even though a person can download the Web Components from Microsoft's site, you can't distribute your copy of the Web Components with your application.

Data access pages are more than simple forms for the Internet. They offer a totally new way for the user to interact with live data. Using the browser, you can display summarized data, such as Sales By Product or Sales By Month. With a mouse click, you can also display the detail information for each summarized item; for example, individual sales by invoice. The tools to summarize, expand, sort, and filter the data are available in the browser itself. These pages let you work with dynamic information; that is, your browser can access live data from within your databases in an interactive fashion.

New Feature　To build a data access page, users work with the new Data Access Page designer; Access 2002 can open any existing HTML file in this feature. After you open a page in Access, you can add data-bound fields to the page easily and quickly. To build a data access page, users work with the new Data Access Page designer.

Working with dynamic and static views of Web-based data

When working with data in Web-based files, you can access the data statically (data that never changes) or dynamically (data that can change). If the data doesn't change, the HTML file can display the information statically. Data access pages are not necessary to create stagnant data. However, if the data that is to be displayed in the HTML page changes often, you want to display the data dynamically, using a data access page.

Typically, an HTML page, created via the data access page, gets its data from an Access database or an Access project connected to a SQL Server database (version 6.5 or greater).

How Web applications use static HTML pages

Web applications — specifically browsers — use static HTML pages to display data that was originally in a database table or series of tables. It is static; after you create the HTML page, the data in the page doesn't change. The data is a physical part of the page; it is actually embedded in the page.

Access 2002 lets you create a static Web page from any table or query by exporting the datasheet results to an HTML page.

To create a static Web page from any table or query, simply select the table or query object that you want to export from within the correct database container (table or query object type). After you highlight the table or query object, select File ⇨ Export from the menu. An alternate method is to right-click the object (table or query name) and select Export from the pop-up menu. This activates an Export As dialog box that allows you to specify a name for the new file and how you want to save it. Follow these steps to export the Customer table of the Mountain Animal Data Access Pages database to a static HTML page:

1. Select the Customer table in the Mountain Animal Data Access Pages database (only highlight it; you don't need to open it).

2. Select File ⇨ Export from the menu, or right-click and select Export from the pop-up menu; Access displays the Export Table dialog box (and displays the Customer table name in the title bar).

3. Select "HTML documents" from the Save as type text box.

4. Type **CustomerTable** in the File name text box.

5. Click Export to save the Customer table to the file named *CustomerTable.html*.

Figure 35-5 shows the exporting of the Customer table to an HTML page. It shows the active Export [table or query name] As dialog box.

As Figure 35-5 shows, you can specify a specific format for the HTML page to be created. To specify a specific format, simply click the Save formatted check box, and when you click the Save button you are given another dialog box, the HTML Output options, as shown in Figure 35-6. You can specify a specific HTML template format file by typing in a name or by clicking the browse button and selecting from existing HTML templates.

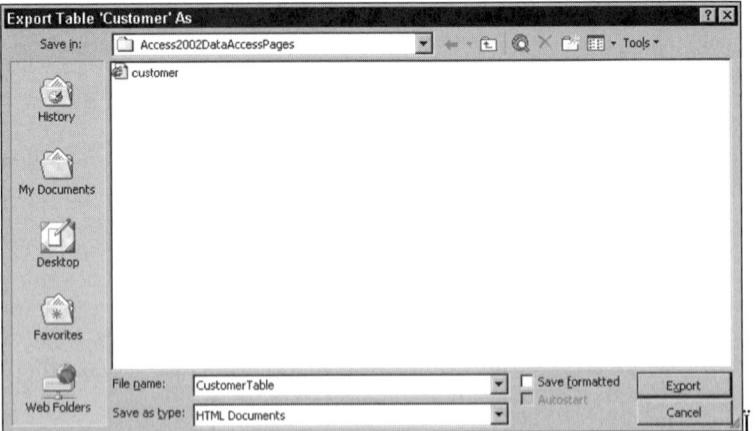

Figure 35-5: Exporting the Customer table to an HTML page

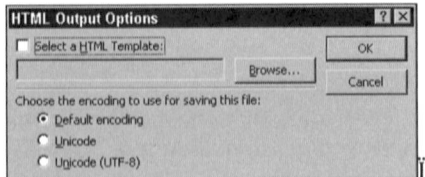

Figure 35-6: Specifying an HTML template format file for saving a table in HTML format

What Are HTML Template Files?

An *HTML template file* is a file that you create in HTML and that is used by Access to enhance the appearance and navigation of your HTML-generated files. You can use it to include a company logo in the header section, a background image in the body section, and your own navigation buttons in the footer section of an HTML report.

The template is a text file that includes HTML tags and tokens that are unique to Access 2002. The tokens are used to tell Access where to insert output and other information in the generated HTML files.

If you specify an HTML template file in the dialog box, Access 2002 merges the HTML template file with the .html, .asp, and .htx output files, replacing the tokens with the appropriate items.

For a more detailed explanation of HTML Template Files see the "HTML template files" section later in this chapter.

How Web applications use dynamic HTML pages

In contrast to static pages, dynamic HTML pages support viewing and working with live, up-to-date data. A Web application can display and work with live data from databases in several ways. Traditionally, this was accomplished using server-side technology. Methods such as CGI (Common Gateway Interface) and Microsoft's ASP (Active Server Pages) do the job. These are programming methodologies that allow you to write code and store it at the server level where the database application resides. Then, when the user wants to look at live data, the user sends a CGI script or ASP query to the database sitting on the Web server. The server takes this request and processes it, returning the requested data to the end user.

Previously, the data being sent back was up-to-date, but not live, and it was stored in an HTML file that your browser displayed. This changed with Access 2000 and is enhanced in Access 2002, which uses ASP technology tied together with Microsoft's implementation of the Extensible Markup Language (XML).

Working with dynamic HTML

You use dynamic HTML when you need to access data that changes frequently and you or your users need to enter and retrieve live data from an Access database using a Web form.

Access 2002 lets you create dynamic HTML pages, or data access pages, from within Access and display them in Access 2002 or Microsoft's Internet Explorer 5.0 or greater. Figure 35-7 shows a data access page in Access. This page displays information about Customers and their Pets.

What Is XML?

XML, or eXtensible Markup Language, is a standard language for describing how data, which is displayed on the Web in browsers, is delivered across the Web. It works in conjunction with Hypertext Markup Language (HTML), which is the language that is used to create and display Web pages. HTML is an excellent tool for displaying text and image information in Web browsers, but is very limited in the way it can handle data and data structures. This job is delegated to XML, which defines the data and how it should be structured, separating the data from the presentation.

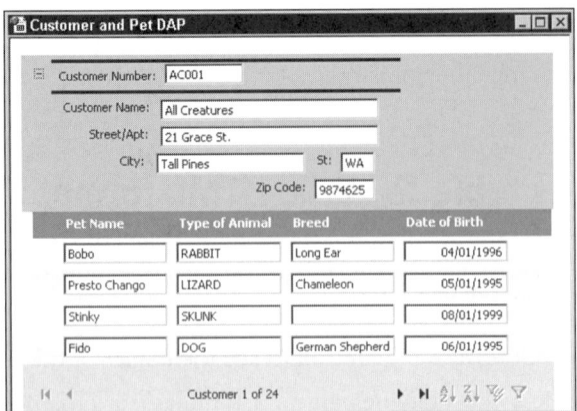

Figure 35-7: A Data Access Page in Access 2002 showing a Customer and the customer's pets

You can create these pages to display and work with your data in either datasheet or form mode.

After you create them, you can add new records, modify existing information stored in the tables, or simply view records in the Access tables from the Web. You can even move between records in the table or from within the browser by using HTML based controls located on the dynamic HTML Web form.

Note   Access 2000 used ActiveX controls for both the navigation bar and the expand/ collapse controls. Access 2002 uses HTML table tags for these controls, thus improving performance of DAPs, and removes the ActiveX controls from the Office Web Components DLL file. Finally, the Navigation control now uses styles and images, letting you customize the images and formatting of the Control.

Exporting Tables, Queries, Forms, and Reports to Web Pages

You may often want to output information from an Access table, query, form, or report to a Web page. Using the File Export option, you can export individual tables, forms, reports, and datasheets to static HTML format. Access 2002 creates one Web page for each report page, datasheet, and form that you export. Exporting objects to HTML format is useful for creating a simple Web application, verifying the format and appearance of an object's output, or adding files to existing Web applications.

When you export an object, you can also specify an HTML template file along with your output files. The HTML template contains HTML tags and special tokens unique to Access 2002 that enhance the appearance, consistency, and navigation of your Web pages.

Exporting an Access table to static HTML format

If you want to export a table to static HTML format, you simply click the table name in the database container and select File ➪ Export. For example, to export the Customer table to an HTML page, follow these steps:

1. In the Database window, click the Table button to see the names of the tables.

2. Select the Customer table by clicking the name. It isn't necessary to open the table.

3. Select Export on the File menu. Access opens the Export dialog box, as shown in Figure 35-8.

4. In the Export dialog box, select the Save as type: text box and click on HTML documents, as shown in Figure 35-8.

5. In the File name: text box, enter the file name Customers, as shown in Figure 35-8.

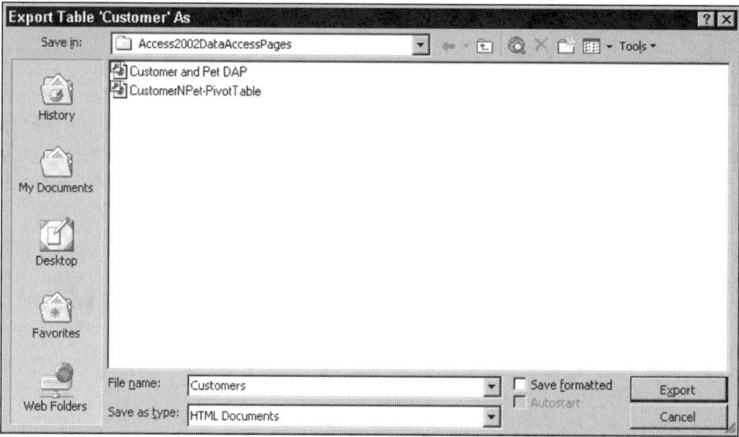

Figure 35-8: The Export dialog box in Access with the type HTML selected

6. Click the Export button.

Note Figure 35-8 shows a check box between the File name: and the Export button. If you select Save Formatted, the HTML Output Options dialog box displays. You can specify an HTML template to use.

The resulting HTML page is based on the entire table. Values from most fields (except OLE objects and hyperlink fields) are output as strings. Fields with a Hyperlink data type are output as HTML links using <A HREF> tags. All unformatted data types, except Text and Memo, are saved with right alignment as the default. Text and Memo fields are saved with left alignment by default. OLE objects are simply ignored and not included in the resulting HTML page.

Figure 35-9 shows the resulting HTML page that you can create by following the above steps. Notice that it doesn't include many items you may expect. For example, it doesn't include column headings for each of the columns. Also, the widths of several of the columns (for example, Customer name and Street/Apt) appear randomly selected. Also, the discount field has been converted from a percentage using the percent sign to a decimal value (20% is now 0.20) and the formatting that should be on the Customer Since field has been removed (03 1998 vs. 03/19/1998).

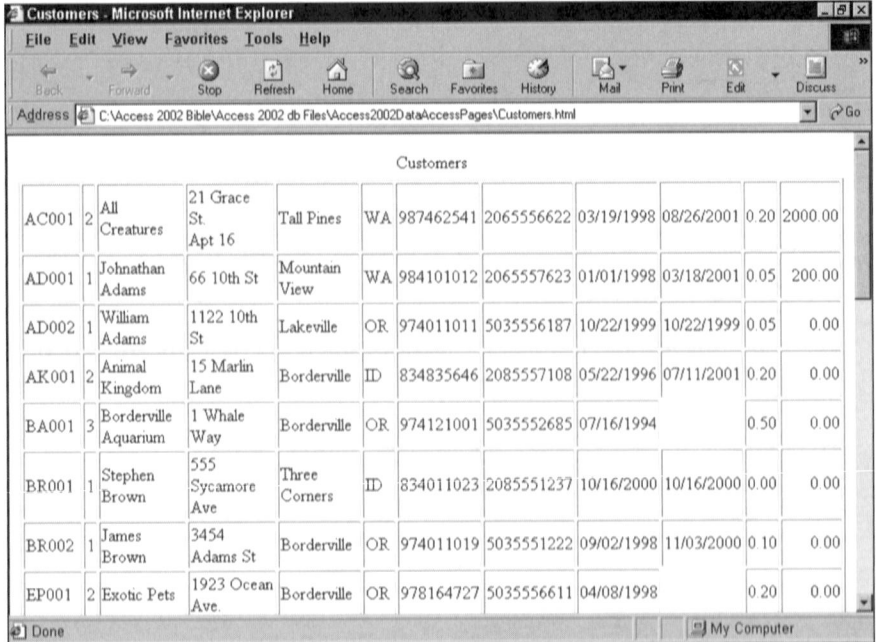

Figure 35-9: The HTML page created by Exporting the Customer table; shown in IE 5.5

Caution When Exporting a table to a HTML file, Access 2002 doesn't save the heading column names, nor does it save data in the same format as it appears in the datasheet—unless you use an HTML template to export the file. It doesn't support the Format or Input Mask Properties of the table.

Tip If you want Access to automatically display the HTML page after generating it, select AutoStart in the Export dialog box and it displays immediately after you create it in Internet Explorer.

Although the layout of the HTML page doesn't simulate the formatting, headers, or even page orientation and margins that are set for the datasheet of the table, you can correct this by using an HTML template file that is covered later in this section.

After you have created your HTML pages, you can publish them to your Web site.

Exporting an Access query datasheet to static HTML format

In the previous section, you export an Access table to an HTML page. Actually, you export the datasheet contents of the table to static HTML format. In addition to tables, you can also export datasheets from queries and forms.

In general, to export a datasheet from a query, simply select the query name instead of the table and follow the steps for exporting a table. If the query is a standard query, the process works exactly like exporting a table.

If you don't specify an HTML format file, the resulting HTML page doesn't show any formatting or input masks. However, it does support the Sort orders and the non-display of any fields that have their Show check box unchecked. Figure 35-10 shows a parameter query in Design mode with two fields specified for a Sort—State, then City. By exporting this query to an HTML document, the HTML page sorts the items in the correct order.

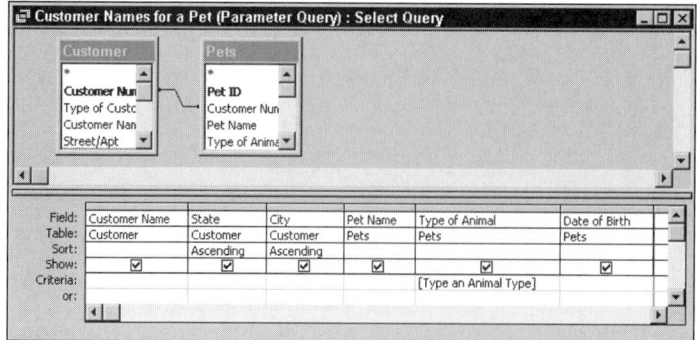

Figure 35-10: A parameter query with two fields specified for sort order

Note This query also has a user parameter specified in the criteria Cell of the Type of Animal (this is used in the example below).

Caution A large datasheet produced from a query may take a long time to output and to display through a Web browser. Consider reducing the size of the datasheet, dividing the datasheet into smaller datasheets by using criteria, such as a date field, or using a report or form to view the data.

One important issue to keep in mind when exporting a query to HTML page is working with *parameter queries* — queries that work interactively with the user at runtime. The resulting HTML document is created *after* the parameter query is run to obtain the parameter from the user. For example, follow these steps to create an HTML document from the Parameter query Customer Names for a Pet (Parameter Query) in the database:

1. In the Database window, click on the Query button to see the names of the query.

2. Select the Customer Names for a Pet (Parameter Query) query.

3. Select File ⇨ Export from the menu. Access displays the Export From As dialog box.

4. In the Save as type box of the Export From As dialog box, select HTML documents. Access automatically assigns the default name of the HTML page as the same name of the query.

5. In the File name text box, change the name of the HTML document to save to "Customer Names for all Cats."

6. Click the Export button. Access responds by displaying the Enter Parameter Value dialog box, as shown in Figure 35-11.

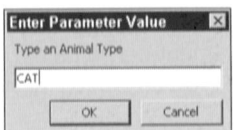

Figure 35-11: The Enter Parameter Value dialog box.

7. Type **CAT** in the Enter Parameter Value dialog box, as shown in Figure 35-11.

8. Click the OK button.

Access creates the new HTML document. If you then open the new HTML file "Customer Names for all Cats," it should look similar to the one shown in Figure 35-12.

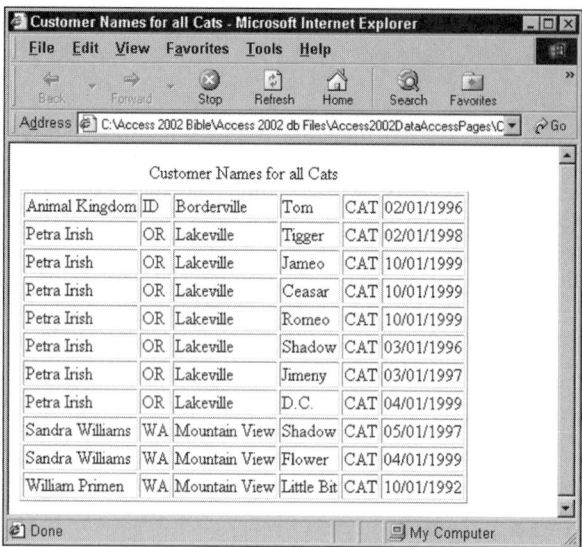

Figure 35-12: The resulting HTML page created from a parameter query

If you compare this HTML page to the structure of the query in Figure 35-10, you can see that it is indeed in sort order by State and City as in the query.

After you create your HTML pages, you can publish them to your Web site.

Exporting an Access form datasheet to static HTML format

In the previous sections you learn how to export an Access table and parameter query to an HTML page. Actually, you export the datasheet contents of them to a static HTML format. In addition to tables and queries, you can also export the datasheet of forms.

Note   Exporting a form to an HTML document doesn't export the form's structure; rather it simply exports the field contents of the form, based on the underlying table or query of the form and the tab order. To see what is actually exported, you can click on the datasheet button on the toolbar when the form is open.

To better understand what actually occurs, consider the Owners & their Animals form (actual name—"Add a Customer and Pets" in the Mountain Animal Data Access Pages.mdb), as shown in Figure 35-13.

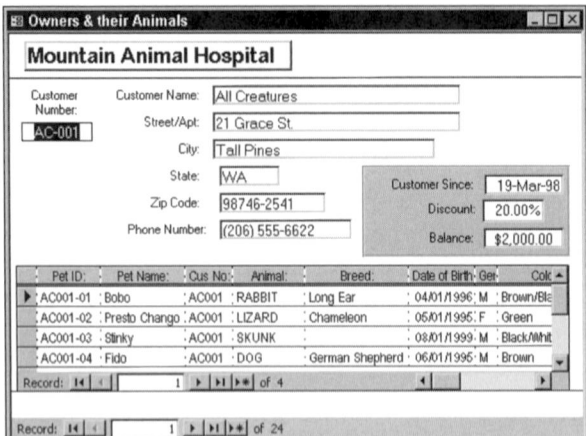

Figure 35-13: The Owners & their Animals form

Examining Figure 35-13 you can see that the form displays the Customer information in the upper portion of the form, one record at a time, while displaying the associated pets records in a datasheet-like subform in the bottom half of the form. Actually this form is a FORM that has a subform included within it.

To understand how Access exports the contents of this form to a HTML document, follow these steps:

1. In the Database window, click the Form button to see the names of the forms.

2. Open the "Add a Customer and Pets" form. Access opens the form, and you can see the same form as shown in Figure 35-13.

3. Either select View ⇨ Datasheet View from the menu or select Datasheet view from the View button on the toolbar.

4. After the datasheet displays, you can scroll from left to right to see the fields being displayed in the datasheet of the form. Access shows 10 fields total, starting with Customer, Customer Name, and ending with Customer Since, Discount, Balance. Figure 35-14 shows the right-most columns of the Datasheet view of the form.

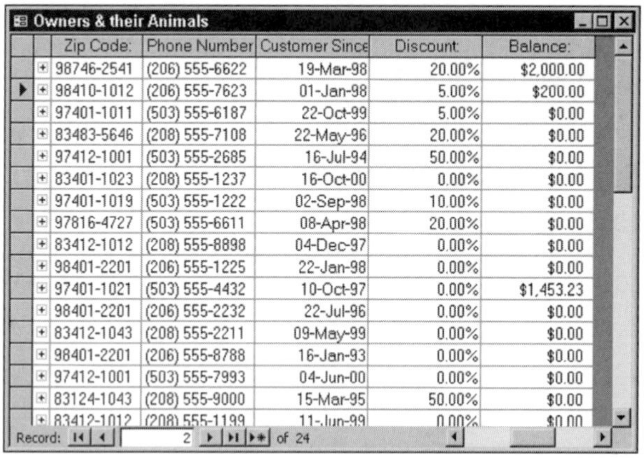

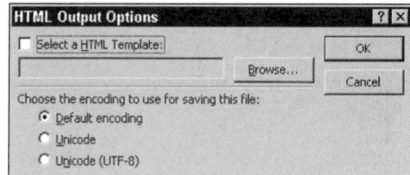

Figure 35-14: Datasheet of the form opened in
Figure 35-13, showing the right-most fields

5. Select File ➭ Export from the menu. Access displays the Export From As dialog box.

6. In the Save as type box of the Export From As dialog box, select HTML documents. Access automatically assigns the default name of the HTML page as the same name of the form. Keep this name for the example.

7. The Save formatted check box is checked and grayed out for the form. You can't change this check box.

8. Click the Export All or Export button, whichever is displayed. Access responds by activating an HTML Output Options dialog box, as shown in Figure 35-15. You use this box to select an HTML template to use for the exporting of the datasheet.

Figure 35-15: The HTML Output
Options dialog box

9. If the check box for "Select a HTML Template" is checked, you need to uncheck it at this time; otherwise skip this step.

10. Click the OK button to start exporting the datasheet of the form.

Unlike exporting a table or query, forms require use of an HTML template file. If you don't specify one, Access automatically uses an internal default value for a format.

Figure 35-16 shows part of the resulting HTML page displayed in Internet Explorer 5.5.

Add a Customer and Pets - Microsoft Internet Explorer

File   Edit   View   Favorites   Tools   Help

Back Forward Stop Refresh Home Search Favorites History Mail Print Edit

Address C:\Access 2002 Bible\Access 2002 db Files\Access2002DataAccessPages\Add a Customer and Pets.html Go

Add a Customer and Pets

Customer Number	Customer Name	Street/Apt	City	State	Zip Code	Phone Number	Customer Since	Discount	Outstanding Balance
AC-001	All Creatures	21 Grace St. Apt 16	Tall Pines	WA	98746-2541	(206) 555-6622	19-Mar-98	20.00%	$2,000.00
AD-001	Johnathan Adams	66 10th St	Mountain View	WA	98410-1012	(206) 555-7623	01-Jan-98	5.00%	$200.00
AD-002	William Adams	1122 10th St	Lakeville	OR	97401-1011	(503) 555-6187	22-Oct-99	5.00%	$0.00
AK-001	Animal Kingdom	15 Marlin Lane	Borderville	ID	83483-5646	(208) 555-7108	22-May-96	20.00%	$0.00
BA-001	Borderville Aquarium	1 Whale Way	Borderville	OR	97412-1001	(503) 555-2685	16-Jul-94	50.00%	$0.00
BR-001	Stephen Brown	555 Sycamore Ave	Three Corners	ID	83401-1023	(208) 555-1237	16-Oct-00	0.00%	$0.00
BR-002	James Brown	3454 Adams St	Borderville	OR	97401-1010	(503) 555-1222	02-Sep-98	10.00%	$0.00

Done   My Computer

Figure 35-16: The HTML page created from the Owners & their Animals form

As Figure 35-16 shows, this HTML page has some basic formatting added. It has the header row with field names above each column. The formatting specified for any fields is shown as formatted in the form (Customer Since, Discount, and Outstanding Balance). Comparing this form to the datasheet of Figure 35-14 you can see that it is a better match than the HTML pages for the tables and queries created earlier.

Note   You can view the HTML source code of any HTML document being viewed in Internet Explorer by selecting View ⟡ Source from the file menu while the HTML document is active.

Tip   If you want Access to automatically display the HTML page after generating it, select AutoStart in the Export dialog box, and it displays immediately after it is created in Internet Explorer.

Caution   If you examine the resulting HTML document created in figure 35-16 and look at the datasheet of figure 35-14 you will see that the field title in figure 35-14 shows Balance as the title, while the HTML document in Figure 35-16 shows Outstanding Balance. Access, in forms, automatically shows the associated label contents for fields when displayed in datasheet mode, vs an HTML document which uses the actual field name.

Comparing the HTML page in Figure 35-16 to the actual form in Figure 35-13, you can see that none of the Pets fields are added to the HTML page — only the Customer fields. When converting a form to an HTML document, only the principal form objects are converted; in this case the Customer information. The Pets fields are actually in a separate form, named "AddCustPetAnimals."

When converting forms, the values from most fields (except OLE objects and hyperlink fields) are output as strings. They are transferred to the HTML document, as shown in Figure 35-16. If you have an OLE object, it is simply ignored when outputting to the HTML page. The hyperlinks are copied over and stored in the HTML document as hyperlinks, using the <A href=...> tag.

After you create your HTML pages, you can publish them to your Web site.

Changing Page Setup properties for datasheets

When exporting a form, table, or query, objects are formatted similarly to the way they appear in the datasheet, including defined Format or Input Mask properties if you specify an HTML template. However, the column widths are automatically fitted to the display page properties of the datasheet (normally 8 inches wide). To change these settings, display the datasheet of the form and use the Page Setup command on the File menu before you export it.

Exporting a datasheet to dynamic HTML format

You can create dynamic HTML documents for datasheets that reside in Microsoft IIS 1-2 (IDC/HTX format) or Microsoft Active Server Pages (ASP format). These pages are created at run-time when the user requests the information — thus, they are dynamic.

When you export a datasheet to either of these formats, the generated HTML document queries the database for current data and sends that information back to the requesting browser.

You can also save forms as ASP files that emulate most of the functionality of the original form and display the data from your database on the Web server.

The process of exporting a dynamic HTML format is essentially the same as exporting a static format except that you choose the Microsoft IIS 1-2 or Microsoft Active Server Pages choice instead of the HTML Documents choice.

 Note   Exporting to an Active Server or IIS 1-2 document is not the same as a data access page. These options create both an HTML document and an appropriate related file for access by the corresponding server (an IIS or an ASP server).

In general, to export a datasheet to dynamic HTML format, follow these steps:

   1. In the Database window, click the name of the table, query, or form that you want to export, and then click Export on the File menu.

2. In the Export dialog box, in the Save as type box, click Microsoft IIS 1-2 or Microsoft Active Server Pages, depending on which dynamic HTML format you want to use.

3. If you want to save to a different drive or directory, click the down arrow at the right of the Save in combo box and select the drive or folder to export to.

4. In the File name box, enter the file name.

5. Click Export.

6. Enter the appropriate information in the HTX/IDC Output Options or Microsoft Active Server Pages Output Options dialog box, as shown in Figures 35-17 and 35-18.

7. For either Output Options box, enter the location of the HTML Template (or let it use the default value) in the HTML Template text box.

8. In the Data Source Name text box, enter the name of the ODBC data source that you connect to when the server-generated HTML files are processed on the Web server.

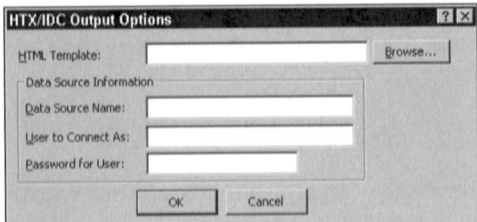

Figure 35-17: The HTX/IDC Output Options dialog box for exporting to a dynamic datasheet

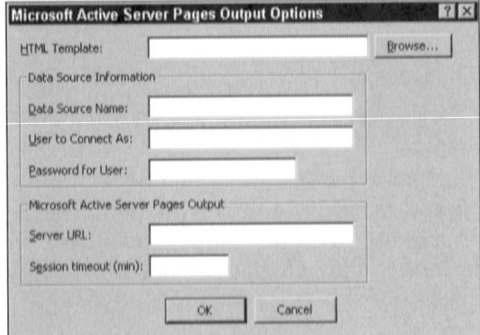

Figure 35-18: The Microsoft Active Server Pages Output Options dialog box for exporting to a dynamic datasheet

Caution   CautionYou must specify the machine or file data source name that you use on the World Wide Web server and—if required—a username and password to open the database. If you are exporting to ASP file format, you must enter the full destination URL for the ASP file's directory (folder). For example, if you are storing the ASP files in the \SalesApp folder on the \\Pubweb server, type `http://pubweb//salesapp/`.

After you finish, you are ready to publish your dynamic HTML document(s) to the Web.

Exporting a form to dynamic HTML format

You can design an Access 2002 form for use in a World Wide Web application and then save it to dynamic HTML format, as ASP files. Several types of forms can be outputted—view forms (to display records), switchboard forms (to act as the home page or to navigate to related pages, such as all reports), and data-entry forms (to add, update, and delete records). Most of the controls on your forms are saved as ActiveX controls that perform the same or similar functions as on the original forms.

Caution   If you have any Visual Basic code behind your forms or controls, none of it is saved or run when you create or activate the ASP file.

In general, to export a form in dynamic HTML format, follow these steps:

1. In the Database window, click the name of the form that you want to export, and then click Export on the File menu.

2. In the Export dialog box, in the Save as type box, click Microsoft IIS 1-2 (*.htx; *.idc) or Microsoft ActiveX Server (*.asp), depending on which dynamic HTML format you want to use.

3. Change the drive or folder to Export to (if you want to) by clicking the Save in: combo box.

4. In the File name box, enter the file name.

5. Click Save.

You must specify the machine or file data source name that you use on the Web server, and—if required—a username and password to open the database. If you are exporting to ASP file format, you must enter the full destination URL for the ASP file's directory (folder). For example, if you are storing the ASP files in the \SalesApp folder on the \\Pubweb server, type `http://pubweb//salesapp/`.

Access 2002 outputs a continuous form as a single form. Access outputs most controls as ActiveX controls but ignores any Visual Basic code behind them. The output files simulate as closely as possible the appearance of the form by creating the appropriate HTML tags to retain attributes, such as color, font, and alignment. However, all data types are output unformatted, and all Format and InputMask properties are ignored.

If a form is in Datasheet view or its Default View property is set to Datasheet when you export to ASP file format, then Access outputs the form as a datasheet. If the form is in Form or Design view, or its Default View property is set to Single Form or Continuous Forms, then Access outputs the form as a form.

After you finish, you are ready to publish your dynamic HTML document(s) to the Web.

Processing an IDC/HTX file on the Web server

After you output a table, query, or form to an IDC/HTX file, Access creates two files — an HTML extension file (*.htx) and an Internet Database Connector file (*.idc). The .idc file contains a query in the form of an SQL statement. For example, exporting the "Pets, Owners & Visits" query produced the .idc file, as shown in Figure 35-19.

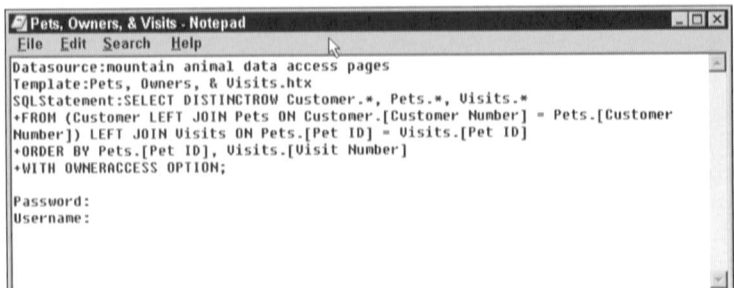

Figure 35-19: The SQL statement created for an .idc file that was exported to Microsoft IIS 2 format

The .htx file is an HTML file that contains the formatting information and placeholders for where to insert the values returned from the query in the .idc file. Figure 35-20 shows the related .htx file for the "Pets, Owners & Visits" query.

Figure 35-20 shows the left-most portion of the Preview view of the .htx file created. It is displayed in Microsoft's FrontPage.

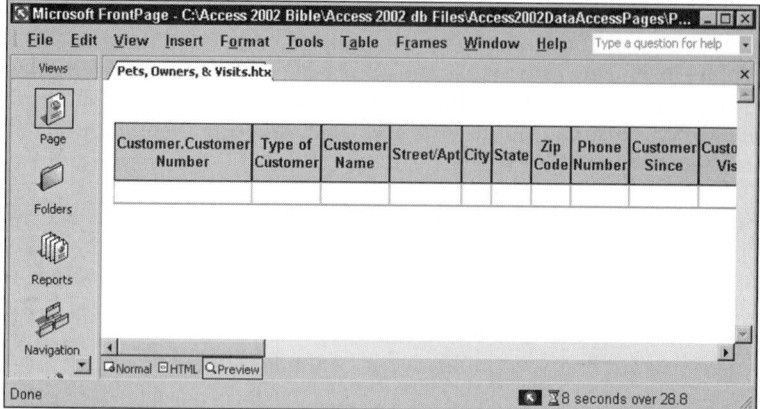

Figure 35-20: A portion of the associated .htx file that was exported to Microsoft IIS 2 format

After you publish the IDC/HTX files to a Web server, IIS can open the database (via an ODBC driver and the .idc file connection information), run the query in the .idc file, obtain the data, merge the results with the .htx file, and publish one .html file, sending it dynamically to the Web browser that requested the information.

Processing ASP files on the Web server

When you export a table, query, or form as an ASP file, Access creates a Microsoft Active Server Page (*.asp) file. Active Server is an integral part of Microsoft Internet Information Server 3.x or later.

The .asp file contains the HTML tags combined with one or more queries in the form of SQL statements, Visual Basic Scripting code (VBScript), and template directives. The .asp file also contains the ODBC connection information to connect to the source database — either an Access or SQL Server database. It includes the data source name and user name/password (can be prompted at run-time).

After you publish an .asp file to a Web server, IIS can do the following: Run the VBScript code located in the .asp file, call ActiveX controls, open the database, run the queries in the .asp file, obtain the results, merge them with the HTML tags, and send the resulting page back to the Web browser that requested the information.

Exporting a report to static HTML format

Reports can also be exported to HTML format. However, reports are always output to a static file format type.

When exporting a datasheet from a table, query, or form, Access creates a single HTML page. Every record that is in the datasheet is placed into the single HTML document. If you have a few thousand records, all of them are submitted to the same page. If the HTML document is too large, it takes a very long time to load in the browser. This is why you should limit the amount of information being exported from a datasheet to an HTML document.

In contrast, exporting Access reports is a bit smarter. When you export a report object, each page of the report is sent to its own HTML document. In other words, if a report has two pages, two HTML documents are created. The second and subsequent pages maintain the same name as the first, simply appending a chronological numeric value (2, 3, 4, etc.) after the primary HTML document name.

To export the "Daily Hospital Report" in the Mountain Animal Data Access Pages database, follow these steps:

1. In the Database window, click the Report button to show the names of the reports.

2. Select the "Daily Hospital Report."

3. Click Export on the File menu (or right-click and select Export).

4. In the Export dialog box, in the Save as type box, click HTML Documents. Access supplies the default name of Daily Hospital Report in the File name text box.

5. In the File name box, change the filename to Daily Hospital Report for 11 Jul 2001.

6. The Save formatted check box is checked and grayed out for the form. You can't change this check box.

7. Click the Export button. Access responds by activating an HTML Output Options dialog box. This box is used to select an HTML template to use for the exporting of the datasheet.

8. If the check box for "Select an HTML template" is checked, you need to uncheck it at this time; otherwise skip this step.

9. Click the OK button to start exporting the report to an HTML document.

Note   In the HTML Output Options dialog box, you can specify an HTML template to use. If you don't specify an HTML template file containing navigation tokens, Microsoft Access 2002 provides a default navigation scheme. The default scheme for Reports includes adding page number and several text navigation links (first, previous, next, and last) at the bottom of each page.

Tip   If you want Access to automatically display the first HTML page of the Report after generating it, select AutoStart in the Export dialog box, and it is displayed immediately after it is created in Internet Explorer.

Figure 35-21 shows the resulting HTML report created by exporting the Access report.

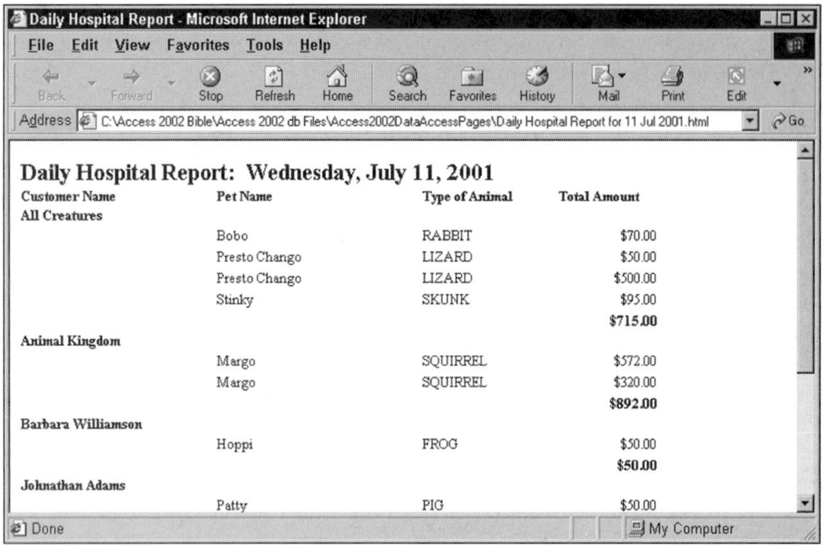

Figure 35-21: The top half of the first page of an HTML document that was created by exporting an Access report

If you move to the bottom of the HTML document in Figure 35-21, you can see several navigation controls similar to the ones shown in Figure 35-22.

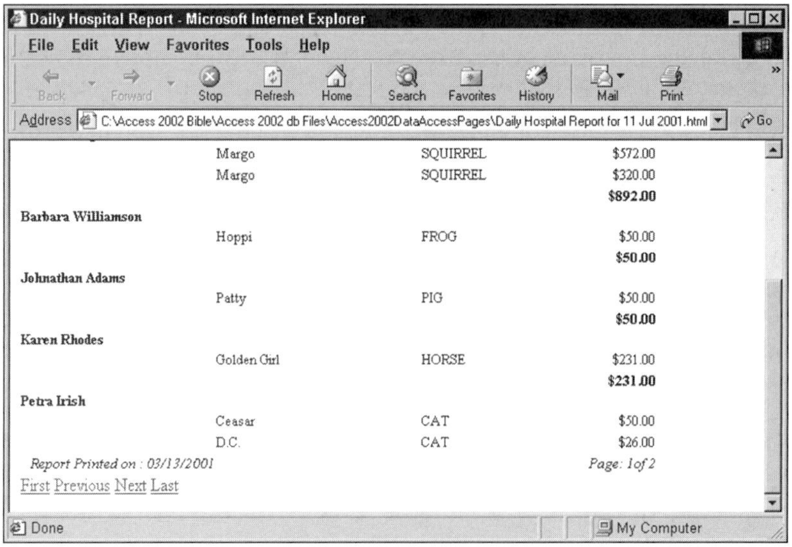

Figure 35-22: The bottom half of the first page of the HTML document that was created by exporting an Access report

Looking closely at the bottom of the page, in Figure 35-22, you see several things automatically added to the report. First is the date it was printed on. To the right of that is the Page counter (1 of 2) and at the very bottom-left corner are four navigation text hyperlinks — First, Previous, Next, and Last. If you click on the Next text, you are taken to the second page of the report.

The HTML file is based on the recordset behind the report, including any current Order By or Filter property settings. If the datasheet contains a parameter query, Access 2002 first prompts you for the parameter values and then exports the results that match the query. Most controls and features of a report, including subreports, are supported except forlines, rectangles, OLE objects, and subforms. However, you can use an HTML template file to include report header and footer images in your output files.

 **Note** If the Access report contains more than one page, Access exports a different HTML document for each page.

The output files simulate as closely as possible the appearance of the report by creating the appropriate HTML tags to retain attributes, such as color, font, and alignment. Fields with a hyperlink data type are output as HTML links using <A HREF> tags. Access outputs a report, unlike a datasheet, as multiple HTML files, one file per printed page. The counting systems for multi-page reports follows the pattern of the file name with no number for the first page, then the file name with an incrementing number for every page after that — Pet Directory.htm, Pet Directory 2.htm, Pet Directory3.htm, and so on. If you create an HTML document for the Pets Directory report, Access will create 53 different pages for the report. The layout of the HTML pages simulates the page orientation and margins set for the report. To change these settings, display the report in Print or Layout Preview, and then use the File menu's Page Setup command before you export it.

You can't output a report to dynamic HTML format.

HTML template files

When Exporting datasheets, forms, and reports to HTML documents, IIS 1 or 2 documents, and ASP documents, you can specify one or more HTML template files, which you can use to enhance the functionality of those pages. Typically, you want to enhance the navigational functionality of datasheets, add graphics or other appearance features, and maintain consistency between your HTML documents. HTML template files let you add these types of enhancements to your static HTML pages or dynamic server-generated HTML files.

For example, you may want to add a company logo in the header of a report or at the top of all HTML static pages; or place navigational controls on your pages.

An HTML template file is a text file that you create by using HTML tags and tokens that are unique to Access. These tokens are used to input specific information into the final HTML document that is created when you export a table, query, form, or report.

Access recognizes eight specific template tokens:

✦ <!—AccessTemplate_Title—>, which is used to place the name of the object in the Browser title bar

✦ <!—AcessTemplate_Body—>, which is used to designate where the output of the object is to be placed in the <body> of the HTML document

✦ <!—AccessTemplate_FirstPage—>, which is used to create an HTML anchor tag (<a href= ...>) in the document to point to the first page of a multi-page document

✦ <!—AccessTemplate_NextPage—>, which is used to create an HTML anchor tag (<a href= ...>) in the document to point to the next page, after the current page, of a multi-page document

✦ <!—AccessTemplate_PreviousPage—>, which is used to create an HTML anchor tag (<a href= ...>) in the document to point to the previous page, after the current page, of a multi-page document.

✦ <!—AccessTemplate_LastPage—>, which is used to create an HTML anchor tag (<a href= ...>) in the document to point to the last page of a multi-page document.

✦ <!—AccessTemplate_PageNumber—>, which is used to display the current page number of the document.

Each of these tokens can be placed in an HTML document that can be used as a template to tell Access 2002 how to format or display the object being exported to HTML code. It lets you enhance the appearance and navigation of your static HTML documents. For instance, you can add images, backgrounds, specify foreground and background colors, and so on to the document.

Figure 35-23 shows a simple HTML template file named "MyTemplate01.htm."

As Figure 35-23 shows, several HTML Access tokens are placed in the HTML code of the template. It uses the token <!—AccessTemplate_Title—> to display the title of the table in the browser when the HTML document is created. It also uses two of the navigational tokens – <!—AccessTemplate_FirstPage—> and <!—AccessTemplate_LastPage—> to place links for multi-page documents.

After you create the template file, you can use it by specifying it in the HTML Output Options dialog box that appears when you specify Save Formatted in the Export dialog box. Figure 35-24 shows the top part of an HTML document that is running in Internet Explorer 5.x and that was exported from a query created on the Customer table. It used the HTML template file MyTemplate01.htm to create the HTML document.

Notice that the exported HTML code shows a graphic and two navigational links (TopPage and LastPage). It also shows the name of the query object (Customer List) that was used for the HTML export and column headings, and some basic color was added to the page.

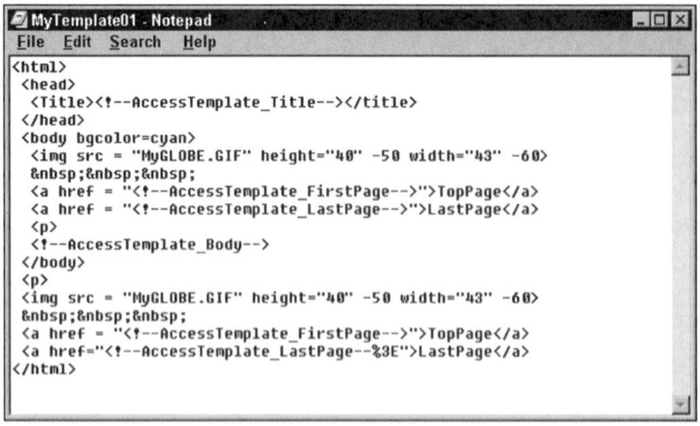

Figure 35-23: An HTML template file

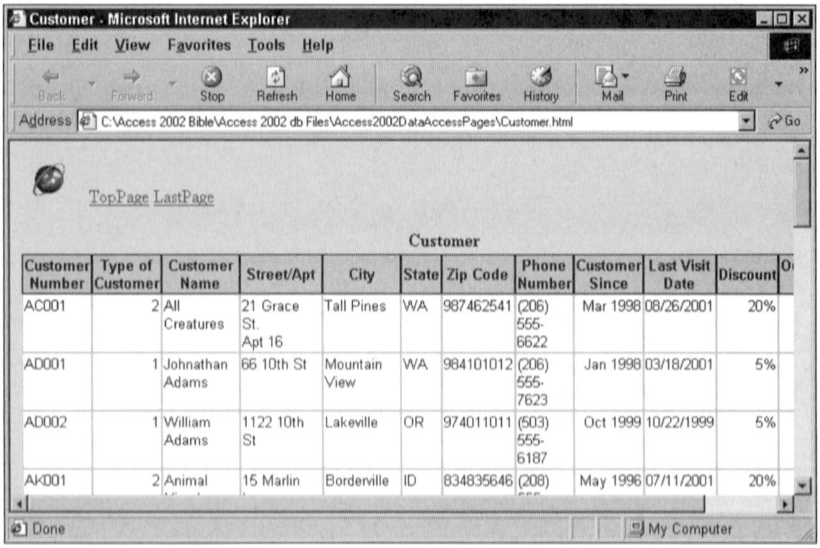

Figure 35-24: The top part of an HTML document in IE that was created using the HTML template file

This is the same Customer table that you exported earlier in this chapter, shown in Figure 35-9. Notice that by using an HTML template file, the Column headers were automatically added (although you did not specify them in the HTML template), the formats for the fields Customer Since and Discount are displayed correctly, and color and navigation links have been added.

Importing and Linking (Read-Only) HTML Tables and Lists

In addition to exporting an HTML table, query, or form datasheet, you can import or link to an HTML table directly. This process uses the standard Import or Linked Table Wizard shown and used in Chapter 22.

Importing an HTML table

When importing, you can only import HTML tables into Access tables — not into queries or forms. For instance, to import the file New Customer.html, follow these steps:

1. Switch to the Database window for the database to show all tables in the database.

2. Select File ➪ Get External Data ➪ Import from the file menu.

3. Select file type HTML Documents (*.html;*.htm).

4. Select the file name New Customer.html, as shown in Figure 35-25.

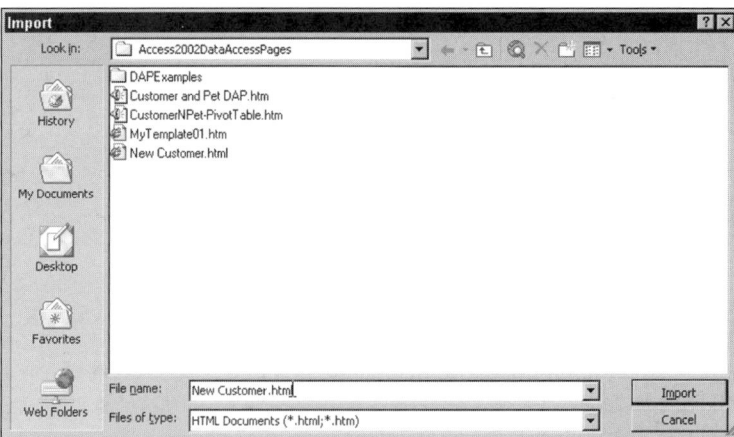

Figure 35-25: The Import dialog box — selecting the New Customer HTML page

5. Click the Import button. Access starts the Import HTML Wizard.

6. Click the First Row Contains Column Headings check box.

7. Review the data and column headings to make sure the table imports correctly and Press the Next button. The next screen asks if you want to import to a New table (default) or to an existing table.

8. Click the Next button to accept the default values. The next screen lets you move through the fields and specify indexing or to Skip the field.

9. Select and Index value of Yes (No Duplicates) for the Customer Number field, as shown in Figure 35-26.

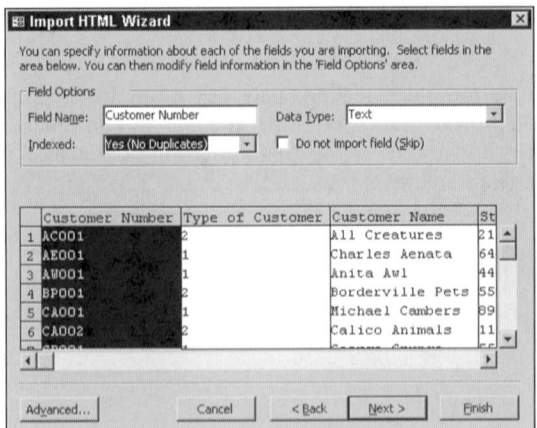

Figure 35-26: The Import HTML Wizard specifying an index field for the Customer Number field

10. Click the Next button. Access moves to the Choose a primary key page. The default value is let Access add a primary key. It adds a new field to the left of the structure labeled ID.

11. Click Choose my own primary key radio button. Access removes the ID field and selects the Customer Number field in the text box.

12. Click the Next button. Access then moves to the last page of the Wizard.

13. Type the name *New Customers* in the Import to Table text box.

14. Click the Finish button. Access imports the file and reports that it did so successfully by displaying a message box.

15. Click OK to return to Database container and see that the New Customers table has been imported.

If your HTML file contains more than one table or list, repeat the steps for each table or list that you want to import or link.

A table that is embedded within a table cell in an HTML file is treated as a separate table when you import or link. A list embedded in a table cell is treated as the contents of a cell, and each item in the list is delimited with the carriage return/ line feed characters.

If the data being imported contains a URL link or file hyperlink, Access converts HTML links to a Hyperlink data-type column, but only if all values in a table column or list contain hyperlink addresses defined by an <A HREF> tag. You can change the data type when using the Import HTML Wizard or the Link HTML Wizard. Access ignores GIF and JPEG images embedded in the HTML tables or lists. For data that spans rows or columns, Access 2002 duplicates the data in each cell. On the other hand, Microsoft Excel 2000 stores the data in the first or upper-left cell and then leaves other cells blank.

Caution
Before continuing on to the next section, you will need to delete the New Customer table that you just created. If you don't delete it and do the linking to an HTML table (same HTML document – New Customer.html) you will be prompted to overwrite existing table to link to it.

Linking to an HTML table

When you link to an HTML table, it is read-only. You are unable to make changes to the table.

For instance, to link to the file Customer.html, follow these steps:

1. Switch to the Database window for the database to show all tables in the database.
2. Select File ⇨ Get External Data ⇨ Link Tables from the file menu.
3. Select file type HTML Documents (*.html;*.htm).
4. Select the file name New Customer.html and either double-click or click the Link button after selecting it. Access starts the LINK HTML Wizard.
5. Check the First Row Contains Column Headings on.
6. Click the Next button. Access takes you to the screen that allows you to skip any fields in the structure.
7. Click the Next button. Access takes you to the last page, which asks if you want to change the name of the Linked file.
8. Click the Finish button to accept the name given. Access displays a message box informing you that it linked to the table correctly.
9. Click OK to be returned to the database container.

The HTML table is now linked in the table section of the database container.

Using Hyperlinks to Connect Your Application to the Internet

Microsoft Access 2002 includes hyperlinks that help you connect your application to the Internet or to an intranet. A hyperlink can jump to a location on the Internet or on an intranet, to an object in your database or in another database, or to a document on your computer or on another computer connected by a network. Normally, you embed a hyperlink in a form. However, by storing hyperlinks in a table, you can programmatically move to Internet URLs or Office objects, such as a Word document by using a bookmark, an Excel spreadsheet using a sheet or range, a PowerPoint presentation using a slide, or an Access object, such as a table, form, or report.

Using the Hyperlink data type

Microsoft Access provides a Hyperlink data type that can contain a hyperlink address. You can define a table field with this data type in order to store hyperlinks as data in a table. Imagine, for a moment, the future where all customershave e-mail addresses — or even their own Web sites. You want to include a customer's e-mail address or Web site in a linkable file much like an automatic phone dialer code is commonly added to a customer's phone number today.

Figure 35-27 shows the Hyperlink data type being defined in the Customer table.

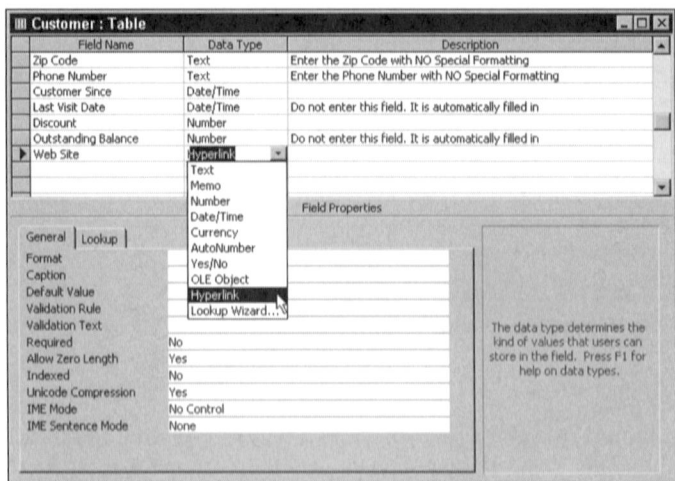

Figure 35-27: Creating a hyperlink in a table design

Using the Hyperlink data type lets you input text or combinations of text and numbers stored as text and used as a hyperlink address. A hyperlink address can have as many as three parts:

- ✦ **Displaytext.** The text that appears in a field or control
- ✦ **Address.** The path to a file (UNC path) or Web page (URL)
- ✦ **Subaddress.** A location within the file or page

The easiest way to insert a hyperlink address in a field or control is to click on Hyperlink menu choice on the Insert menu. The Insert Hyperlink dialog box appears, as shown in Figure 35-28.

The dialog box gives you many options. You can specify an existing file or Web page, an Object in the database, Create a new page, or an e-mail address.

The dialog box in Figure 35-28 shows adding an existing Web page (on the World Wide Web) as a URL for dbIntegrators.com. You see it in the Address text box just above the OK button.

The Hyperlink data type can contain as many as 2,048 characters.

When you click on a hyperlink field, Access jumps to an object, document, Web page, or other destination.

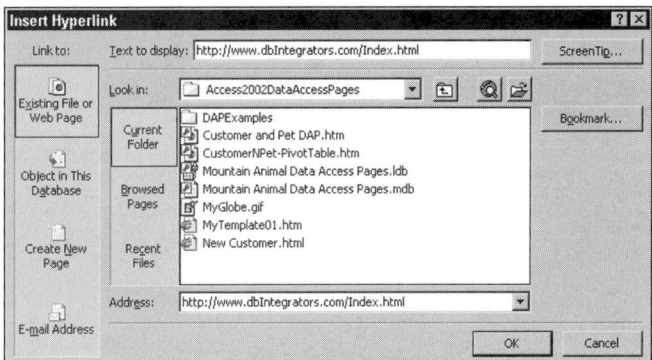

Figure 32-28: Inserting a hyperlink in a table using the Insert Hyperlink dialog box

Hyperlinks are not limited to Web pages. You can specify a hyperlink to forms, reports, or other objects in the database. You can even create a link to an Excel spreadsheet or Word document. For that matter, you can link to any file on your network or across your in-house intranet or the Internet.

Adding a hyperlink to a form, report, or datasheet

You can use hyperlinks in forms, reports, and datasheets to jump to objects in the same or another Access database; to documents created with Microsoft Word, Microsoft Excel, and Microsoft PowerPoint; and to documents on the global Internet or on a local intranet. You can also add hyperlinks to reports. Although hyperlinks in a report won't work when viewed in Access, the hyperlinks do work when you output the report to Word or Excel, or to HTML.

You can store hyperlinks in fields in tables, just as you store phone numbers and fax numbers. For example, the Suppliers table in the Northwind sample database stores hyperlinks to home pages for some of the suppliers.

You can also create a label or picture on a form or report or a command button on a form that you can click to follow a hyperlink path. For example, you can modify the labels in the Mountain Animal Hospital switchboard to use the hyperlink address and sub-address properties.

Figure 35-29 shows the Add a Customer and Pets form open in the form designer and specifying a hyperlink on a label.

If you are going to specify a link to an object in the current database, leave the Hyperlink Address field blank and fill in the Hyperlink SubAddress with the object type and the object name.

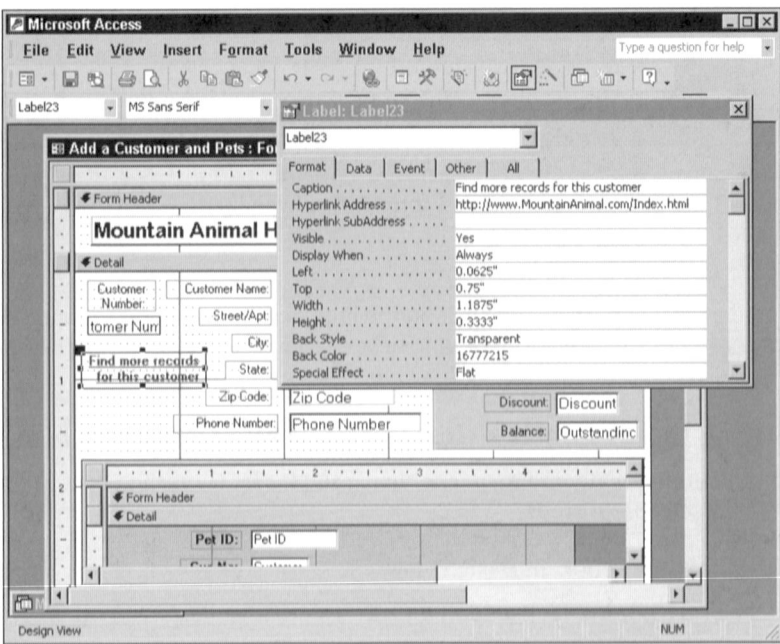

Figure 35-29: Specifying a hyperlink address the form for the label

Follow these steps to add a hyperlink to the Add a Customer and Pets form:

1. Open the Add a Customer and Pets form in Design view.

2. Add a Label like the one shown in Figure 35-29, under the Customer Number field and type **Find more records for this customer**.

3. With the new Label selected, open the Property dialog box.

4. In the text box for the Hyperlink Address, add a valid link (the one shown in Figure 35-29 is not a valid link).

5. Save the form.

After you save the form, you can view it, and it should resemble the one shown in Figure 35-30.

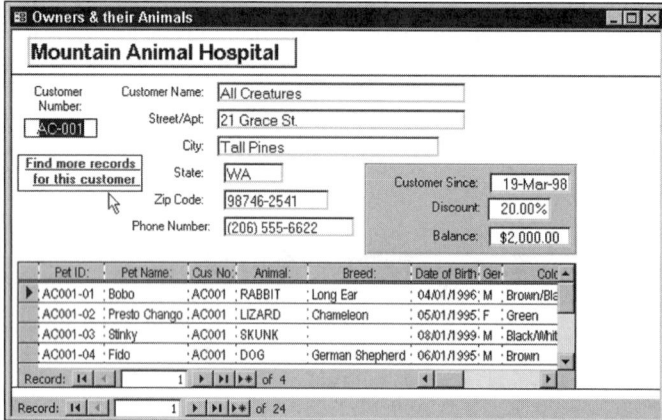

Figure 35-30: The Add Customer and Pets form with a hyperlink created on the form

If you entered a valid hyperlink and click on the link, Access takes you to that location on the Web, or opens the new form, or whichever action is associated with the link.

Creating a label using the Insert Hyperlink button

If you want to automatically create a label using the Insert Hyperlink button on a form, follow these general steps:

1. Open a form or a report in Design view.

2. Click Insert Hyperlink on the toolbar.

3. In the Insert Hyperlink dialog box, specify a UNC path or a URL in the Link to File or Web Page dialog box. If you are unsure of the file name, click the File button to navigate to a file on your hard drive, on a local area network, or on an FTP server that you've registered. For a Web page name, click the Web page button to navigate to the Web page that you want to use.

To jump to a location in a file, enter a location. For example, type a bookmark name for a Microsoft Word document or a slide number for a PowerPoint presentation.

To jump to an Access object, enter the object type and object name (for example, Form Customer), or click the Browse button. The Browse button displays a list of the objects in the current database. Select the object that you want to open.

4. Click OK in the Insert Hyperlink dialog box.

Access adds a label to the form or report. To test the link, right-click the label, point to Hyperlink on the shortcut menu, and click Open.

When you create a label this way, Access sets the Hyperlink Address property of the label to the value that you specified in the Link to File or URL box, and the Hyperlink SubAddress property to the value (if any) that you specified in the Named Location in File box. Access 2002 uses the Caption property for the display text that you see in the label itself. You can change any of these properties to modify the hyperlink.

You can also add hyperlinks to a picture (Image Control) or command button control in the same way.

Browsing Web Pages with the Web Browser Control

The Microsoft Web Browser control is a form control, which you can activate and add to your forms. It lets you browse the World Wide Web; view Web pages; access other documents on your computer, the network, or the Internet; and download data from the Internet, all through a single form in your application.

The Microsoft Web Browser control is an ActiveX control that enables you to view Web pages and other documents on the Internet or an intranet from within an Access 2002 form. The Web Browser control is provided by Microsoft Internet Explorer 5.0 or greater (IE 5.x), which is not included with Microsoft Office 2002. If you don't have IE 5.0 or 5.5, you can download Microsoft Internet Explorer from the Microsoft corporate Web site (http://www.microsoft.com/) free of charge. You can obtain further documentation about the Web Browser control at the URL http://www.microsoft.com/intdev/sdk/docs/iexplore/.

The Web Browser control is automatically registered with the operating system when you install Internet Explorer, so you can use it from Access 2002 without first registering it. To add the Web Browser control to a form, click ActiveX Control on the Insert menu, and then click on Microsoft Web Browser Control in the list of ActiveX controls, as shown in Figure 35-31.

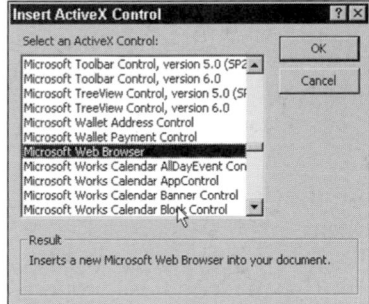

Figure 35-31: Selecting the Microsoft Web Browser ActiveX control from the Insert ActiveX Control dialog box in the Form Design surface

After you've added the Web Browser control to a form, you can use the control's Navigate method to open a Web page within the Web browser window. For example, if you've added a Web Browser control named *WebBrowser1* (which was named automatically by Access) to a form, you can create this Load event procedure for the form's On Load event property:

```
Private Sub Form_Load
   Me!WebBrowser1.Navigate "http://www. ITinAsia"
End Sub
```

This procedure displays the Start page for a Web site called *ITinASIA*. Any time the form opens, the Web page information automatically appears in the WebBrowser ActiveX control area of the form. You can resize this area as you desire.

The sample database has a form named "Customer WebBrowserControl" that uses this ActiveX control. If you aren't connected to the Internet at the time you run the form, IE 5.x loads and reports "Action cancelled ... IE unable to link to the Web page you requested...."

This chapter is just the start of how you can use Access with the Web. The Internet is a continuously evolving technology. The ability to access it and program your Microsoft Access 2002 environment to take advantage of Internet technology has become very important today.

✦   ✦   ✦

Building Web Applications, Data Access Pages, and XML

♦   ♦   ♦   ♦

In This Chapter

Working with data access pages

Creating data access pages using the Wizard

Creating and working with grouped pages

Exporting Access objects to a data access page

Importing an existing data access page

Understanding and working with XML

Exporting an Access object to an XML document

Importing an existing XML document into Access

♦   ♦   ♦   ♦

Using Access 2002, you can create many different types of Web pages. In Chapter 35, you work with Access to create static and dynamic Web pages based on the different objects of Access—tables, queries, forms, and reports. You learn how to create snapshots of your data by creating HTML documents and even up-to-date, read-only data, created at the server side, by creating Active Server Pages (ASP). This chapter demonstrates the power of data access pages in Access 2002.

Data access pages (DAPs) were first introduced in Access 2000. They are a special type of Web page connected directly to the data in your database. This data can be stored in a Microsoft Access database (*.mdb) or a Microsoft SQL Server database (accessed via an Access Data Project database—*.adp).

Working with the Data Access Pages

You can use data access pages like any another Access object — select them from the Pages Object container and use them. Unlike other Access objects, however, you can also use them independently of Access with Microsoft's Web browser.

It's easy to create a new data access page. You can build one from scratch, using the Page Designer, or use a wizard to create a new page.

 **New Feature** Access 2002 has added new functionality to data access pages, the Data Access Page Wizard, and the design tools.

What is a data access page?

In its simplest form, a data access page (DAP) is a Web page that is connected directly to the data in your database. The page allows you to display and sometimes edit the data in the underlying database.

The most exciting part about DAPs is the ability to drill down into grouped data. This ability lets you use DAPs to explore and analyze information stored in the underlying tables. The user can view summary information or drill into the data to learn more about the detail records associated with the summary information.

Figure 36-1 shows a data access page created to display Customer and Pet information. Currently it shows only the customer information, and if you click on the next button of the navigation bar, it moves to the next Customer and shows that customer's information. The pet information is not visible at this time.

To show the pet information, you simply click on the Expand/Collapse control button in the form (to the left of the Customer Number; the mouse pointer in Figure 36-1 is pointing to it). Notice that the Expand/Collapse button (a small box with a visible plus or minus sign) next to the Customer Number is displaying a plus sign. By clicking this object, the information being displayed expands, as shown in Figure 36-2, displaying the pet information for that customer. This process is known as *drilling down* into the data.

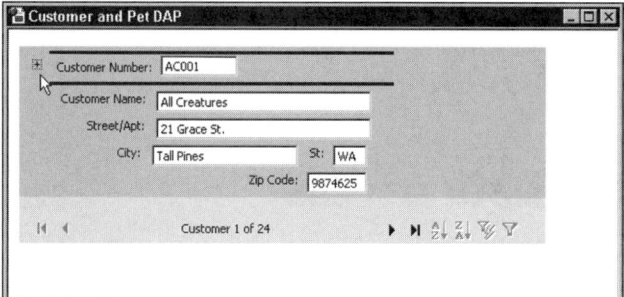

Figure 36-1: A data access page for Customers and Pets in Access 2002 with the Expand/Collapse control closed (+)

Microsoft's Internet Explorer and data access pages

The DAP shown in Figure 36-1 is running in Access 2002. However, you can also run the same data access page in Microsoft's Internet Explorer 5.x. Figure 36-2 shows the same form displayed in IE5.5, with the pet detail area shown by expanding the Customer Expand/Collapse control.

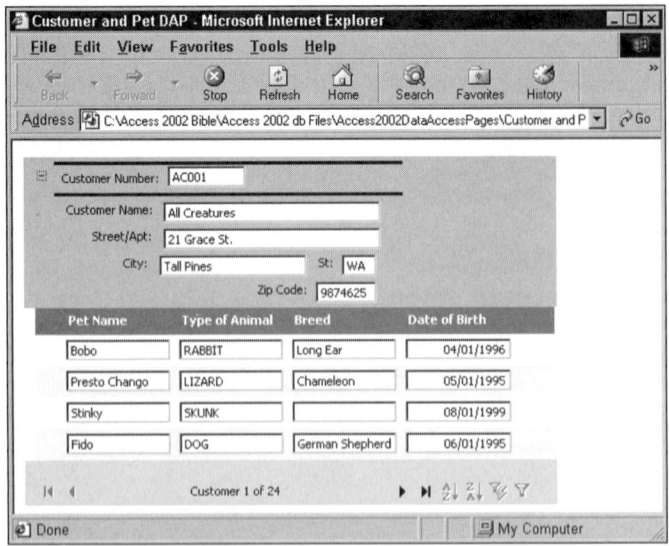

Figure 36-2: The same data access page for Customers and Pets in IE5.5 and the Expand/Collapse control open (-)

To display data access pages, the user needs to have both IE5.x and the Microsoft Office XP Web Components (MSOWC) files installed on their machine. Internally, Access 2002 uses Internet Explorer and MSOWC (Office XP version) to actually display and work with the information in the data access page.

New Feature In Access 2000, each person wanting to use data access pages was required to purchase a separate copy of Microsoft Office for their computer to obtain the MSOWC files, which IE 5.0 needed to access and display DAPs. In Access 2002, this is no longer a requirement. The users must still have IE 5.x and MSOWC, but they can obtain them from Microsoft's Web site.

Tip You can go to Microsoft's Web site at `http://www.microsoft.com` and download the MSOWC (for Office XP) and IE5.5 from the site. You can find these files by searching the support section of Microsoft's site. Downloading these files takes an inordinate amount of time if you are downloading at 56K or slower. You can also contact Customer Support by telephone to have a copy sent for a small shipping charge.

The records in the page shown in Figures 36-1 and 36-2 can be viewed, updated, edited, deleted, filtered — even grouped or sorted. This is live data from an Access database — the Customer and Pets tables.

When Access 2002 creates a new data access page, it actually utilizes Microsoft Internet Explorer 5.x technology (in edit mode) as the actual design environment to create the page within Access.

The Page container of a database

Figure 36-3 shows the database container, Mountain Animal Data Access Pages.mdb with the Pages object button selected and the container active. Inside the Pages container are three choices — two let you create a new data access page (you can create a data access page in Design View by using the wizard), and one lets you edit an existing page (you can edit a Web page that already exists).

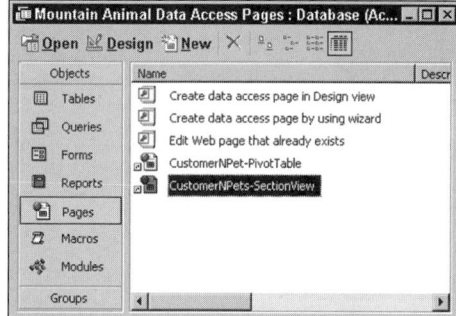

Figure 36-3: The Pages container of a database

When you create a data access page within Access, you are actually creating two separate parts:

✦ The Data Access Page object, which is stored in the Pages container and maintains a link to the underlying HTML file

✦ The HTML document, which contains the HTML and XML code for the page

The HTML document, or file, is stored independently of the DAP object in the database. This allows the browser (IE 5.x or later) to use this file independently of Access. It also makes it easy for you to deploy the HTML documents for use in your intranet or across the Internet.

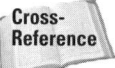

Cross-Reference

The separation of the object and document can cause deployment problems that are covered later in this chapter.

Creating a data access page is very similar to creating a form or report in Access. You use the Data Access Page design mode, or the wizard, to create the page. After it's completed, the page becomes a fully functional HTML document.

When you create your pages, you need to decide if you are creating a page using a single table/query or multiple tables. If you use multiple tables, you create what is known as *grouped pages*.

Creating a single table data access page

You can create a single table data access page by using the wizard or building it yourself in Design view.

Cross-Reference You can also convert an existing table, query, form, or report to a data access page directly. This is covered later in this chapter.

Using the Page Wizard to create a single table data access page

The easiest way to create a single table data access page is to let the Data Access Page Wizard help you. For instance, to create a new data access page for the Customers table, follow these steps:

1. Select the Pages object button from the Objects Bar of the Mountain Animal Data Access Pages.mdb database.

2. Double-click Create data access page by using a Wizard.

3. Select the Customer table from the Tables/Queries drop-down combo box.

   Figure 36-4 shows the first page of the Page Wizard with the Customer table selected.

4. Select Type of Customer, Customer Name, City, State, Zip Code, and Phone Number from the Available fields list box. You can select them by highlighting each field and pressing the right arrow button (>) or by double-clicking the field name.

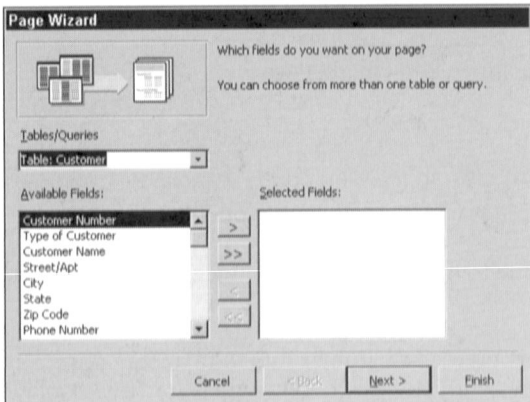

Figure 36-4: The first page of the Page Wizard

5. Click Next> to move to the next page.

   Access displays the grouping levels page of the wizard.

6. Select Type of Customer for a grouping level by double-clicking the field name. Figure 36-5 shows the grouping level set.

7. Click Next> to move to the next page.

Access displays the sort order page of the wizard.

8. Specify Customer name for the sort order on this page.

9. Click Next> to move to the next, and final, page.

10. Specify "Customer Info" as the title for the new page.

11. While still on this page, choose the Open the page radio button.

12. Click the Finish button and be patient. The wizard performs many steps to create the new data access page.

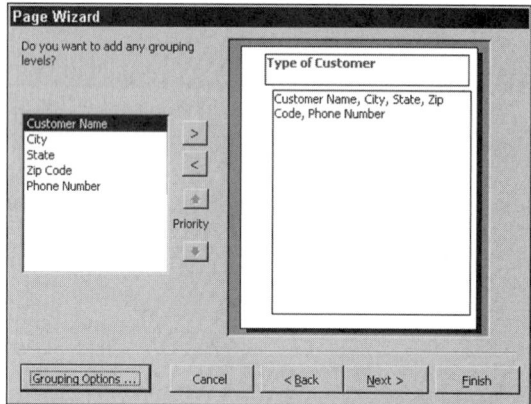

Figure 36-5: The grouping level set in the Page Wizard

Access 2002 creates the new Web document, giving it a title name of "Customer Info" (on the title bar when the HTML document is open).

Access has not saved the file to the hard drive yet; Access has only created and opened it as a virtual file.

Figure 36-6 shows the newly created Customer Info data access page running in Access. As this Figure shows, only the Customer Type is initially displayed on the form. When the page is initially created (using the wizard), the expand button (plus [+] sign) displays next to Group of Customer-Type of Customer. When you click the plus (+) sign, it is replaced by the collapse button (minus [–] sign), and the detail information for each customer displays below the Type of Customer heading.

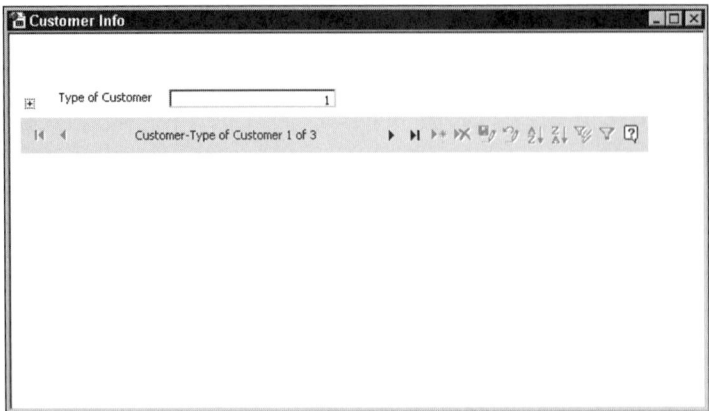

Figure 36-6: The new Customer Info data access page running in Access 2002

The form in Figure 36-6 also has a navigation bar, known as a *record management control* in Access 2000, along the bottom of the page. It shows three records that can be viewed, based on "Customer-Type of Customer." If you click the expand button alongside of the Customer type, you see a second navigation bar (above the first one) also displayed—this one for all the records that match that customer type. These are used to perform several functions, including

- ✦ Moving between records in the page
- ✦ Adding new records to the underlying table(s)
- ✦ Deleting records
- ✦ Sorting records by a specific field
- ✦ Setting filter conditions for viewing records

In addition to these navigational controls, the page also has an expand control next to the Type of Customer text (top-left corner). It is the small box that displays either a plus (+) sign or a negative (–) sign. It is used to expand and close a level of information in the page. In this case, it is used to display individual customer information (level 2) when the negative sign is showing (as in Figure 36-7), or only the Customer type information when the positive sign is showing (as in Figure 36-6). When you run the form, clicking the expand control toggles between expanded (+) and closed (–) modes.

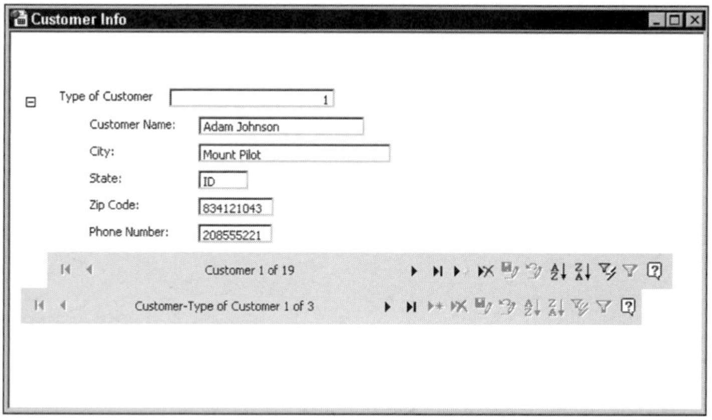

Figure 36-7: The new Customer Info data access page expanded to show both levels of the page

You can change the default action of this expand control before saving your new data access page by making a change to the page in the Design view window. Follow these steps to change the default behavior of the expand control:

1. Click the View button (first button on the toolbar — currently showing the Design view button graphic) or select View ➪ Design View from the menu.

2. Open the Properties dialog box by either selecting View ➪ Properties from the menu or by clicking the Property button on the toolbar.

3. With the property sheet open, right-click the gray Header: Customer-Type of Customer band, as shown in Figure 36-8 (or anywhere in the page — on or below the Header band).

   If you click in a different area, your menu looks slightly different from the one in Figure 36-8.

4. Select Group Level Properties from the menu.

   Access changes the property sheet focus to the properties of the Group level object, as shown in Figure 36-9.

5. Change the ExpandedByDefault property to True, as shown in Figure 36-9.

6. Save your work, by selecting File ➪ Save (or press Ctrl+S, or close the window and answer Yes to the Save Changes dialog box).

   Access opens the Save As Data Access Page dialog box. This is where you save the DAP as an actual HTML document (*.html or *.htm).

7. You can accept the default name of the Customer Info.html and click the Save button.

   Access saves the page as an HTML document and displays a warning dialog box that tells you that the Connection string to this page specifies an absolute page. It lets you know that this page may not work on a network, unless the connection string of the page is changed to a network path (using Universal Naming Convention — UNC). This problem is covered later in this chapter in the section "Making your DAPs available to the Web."

8. Click OK.

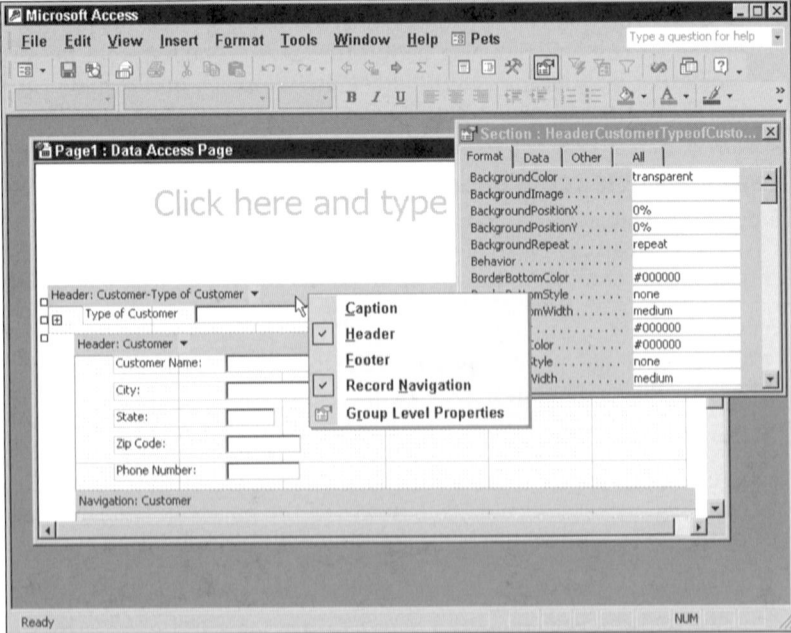

Figure 36-8: Activating the right-click menu. Notice that the Property sheet shows the Section: HeaderCustomerTypeofCustomer object active

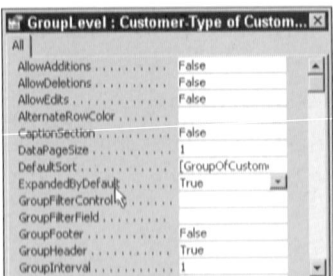

Figure 36-9: Changing the ExpandedByDefault property of the Group Level object

The HTML file is not stored in the database container. Rather, it is stored in the Windows file system in a subdirectory. Microsoft's Internet Explorer 5.x can be used to display and work with these files. Access stores only a page object that points to the HTML file in the Pages container of the database window — not the actual file.

If you saved your page in Step 6 by pressing Ctrl+S or selecting File ➪ Save from the menu, close the page to return to the Pages container of the database.

Note   In Access 2000, you had the option of accomplishing this same process by clicking on the Sorting and Grouping button (the seventh button from the right side of toolbar) or by selecting View ➪ Sorting and Grouping on the menu. This method has been removed from Access 2002.

Creating a single table data access page using Page Design View

Although the easiest way to create a single table data access page is to use the Data Access Page Wizard, it's also good to know how to build a page using the Design View tools. For example, follow these steps to create a new data access page for the Pets table:

1. Select the Page object type from the Object Bar of the Mountain Animal Data Access Pages database.

2. Double-click Create data access page in Design View.

   Access 2002 warns you that the page you are about to create can't be opened in Design view of Access 2000. However, the page can be used in Access 2000, if you have installed the Microsoft Office XP Web Components.

3. Click OK.

   Access 2002 takes you to the page's Design view. If the Property sheet is open, close it at this time.

4. Click in the area "Click here and type title text" (labeled in light gray), and then type **Pets Information**.

5. Click in the area labeled "Drag fields from the Field List and drop them on the page" to select it. Notice that the area has been selected.

   Access 2002 highlights the unbound section of the page.

6. With the Unbound section selected in the Design View, select View ➪ Field List from the menu (or click the Field List button) if the field list is not already open.

   Access opens the Field List, as shown in Figure 36-10.

7. The Tables folder should already be expanded — if it isn't, click it to show all the table names in the list.

8. Click the Pets table to show all the fields from this table.

9. Select the Customer Number, Pet Name, Type of Animal, Breed, Date of Birth, and Last Visit Date fields and drag them to the section on the page labeled "Drag fields from the Field List."

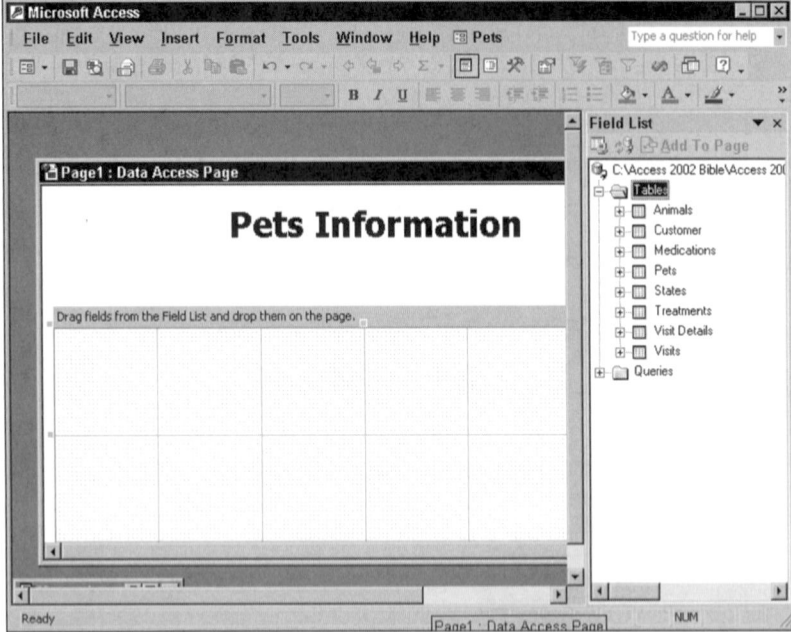

Figure 36-10: The Page Design view with Field List open

Access opens a Layout Wizard as shown in Figure 36-11. This wizard lets you select the method that Access should use to lay out the fields you have selected from the Pets table.

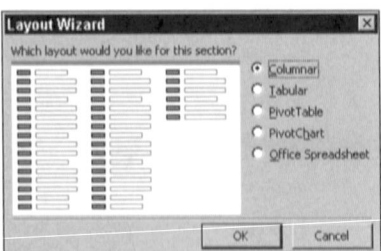

Figure 36-11: The Layout Wizard activated

10. Select the default value (Columnar) and click OK.

Access creates simple bound span (Input Box) and a label for each field. It also changed the section heading by renaming it to "Header: Pets," and added a Navigation: Pets section below the Header section for the Pets table and placed the Record management toolbar and its control objects in it.

11. Save your work and name it *Pets Info.html*.

After you save your data, you can use it in Access 2002 or IE 5.x or later. This page can only be edited in Access 2002. It can be used and displayed in Access 2002 if the user has installed both IE 5.x and the Office XP Web Components DLL on his or her computer.

New Feature

Notice that all of the fields in Figure 36-12 are selected. Access 2002, using Internet Explorer 5.5, lets you select more than one object at a time in the Page Design view. If your computer doesn't have IE5.5, you are only capable of selecting one object at a time with IE 5.0.

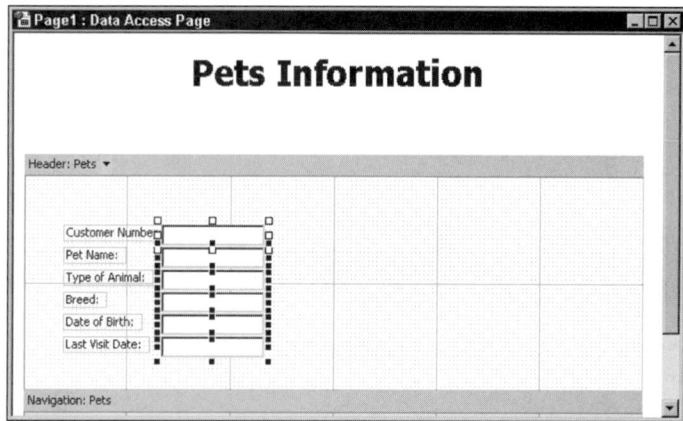

Figure 36-12: The resulting layout of control objects created by the Layout Wizard

Figure 36-13 shows the finished Pets Info page that you just created. Notice that this page doesn't have an Expand/Collapse button. This page could have had additional control objects to make it more functional.

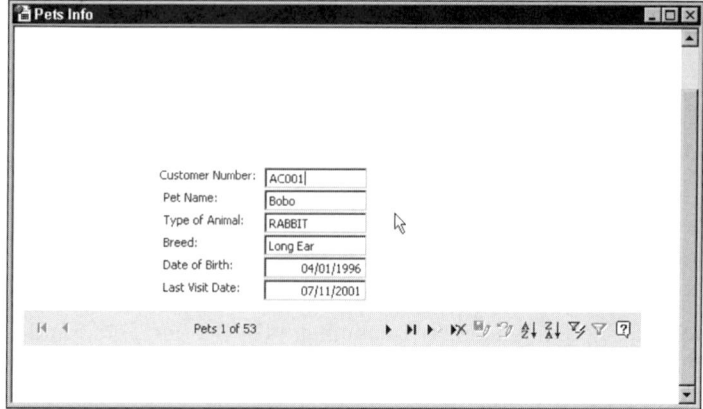

Figure 36-13: The Pets Web page running in Access 2002

Editing a single table Web page that already exists

You can bring any preexisting HTML document into Access by selecting the third choice in the Pages object container—Edit Web page that already exists.

When you select this option, a Locate Web Page dialog box displays so that you can select and open the Web page (*.htm, *.html) file that you want to link to in Access 2002.

For example, to open and link to the Visits Info.htm document, follow these steps:

1. In the Pages container, double-click Edit Web page that already exists.

   Access opens the Locate Web Page dialog box.

2. Select Visits Info.htm from the dialog box and click the Open button.

   Access opens the HTML document in Page Design View and opens the Field list to the Visits table, as shown in Figure 36-14.

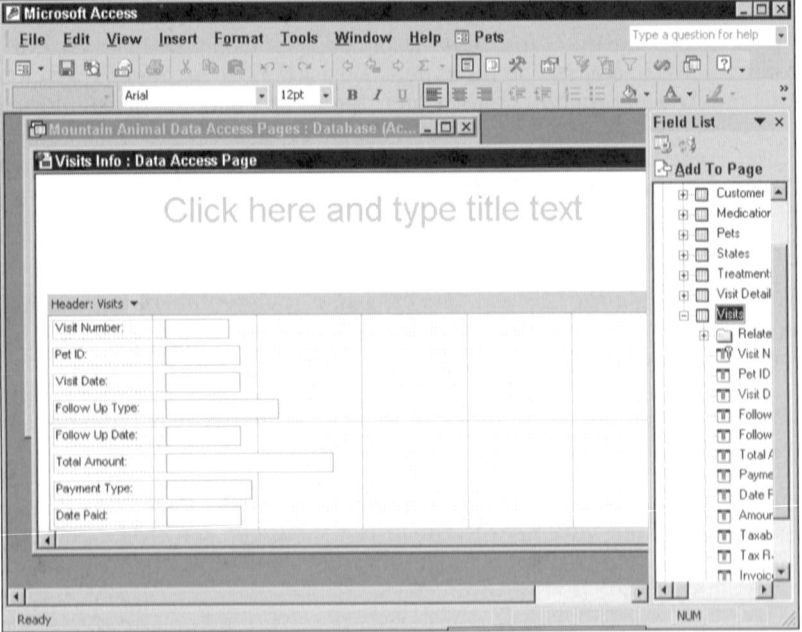

Figure 36-14: The Visits Info.htm document in the Page Design view of Access 2002

3. Make any changes you want to the Visits Info document.

4. Close your page.

Access activates a dialog box, asking you if you want to save changes made to the Visits Info data access page.

5. Select the Yes button to save your work and return to the database.

Notice that when editing an existing Web page, Access 2002 automatically uses the same name as the Web page and displays a link in the Pages container with the same name as the underlying HTML document.

Note

If the existing HTML document that you are editing doesn't contain any Extended Markup Language (*.xml) code, then the data access page displays static data only. If it contains Microsoft's Internet Explorer 5.x–understandable XML code, then it creates a table that displays dynamic Web pages.

Working with multiple tables and grouped pages

Up to this point you have worked with single tables — Customer, Pets, or the Visits table in the Visits Info document.

You have even worked with a simple grouped page in the Customer Info document of Figures 36-6 and 36-7. You created this page by using the Page Wizard. The grouped page was based on the type of Customer in the top-most group and specific customer information in the inner group (detailed customer information).

Although this is one way you can use grouped pages, most of the time you work with multiple related tables, placing each in its own grouping.

Understanding grouped pages

Usually, grouped pages are data access pages that contain data from more than one database object. Most of the time the database objects are tables, but they can also be multiple queries or a combination of tables and queries.

You group a page based on one or more fields from the selected database objects. Each page can contain multiple levels of groups.

You can create grouped data access pages by using the Page Wizard or in the Page Design view. When working with the Design view, you can create new groups by promoting fields or entire objects to a new group, or by dragging fields from other objects into a group section.

After a group is created it can also be demoted.

When creating a grouped page, use the *UniqueTable* property to allow updates to the data in the various groups. Sometimes this property is automatically set.

Creating a grouped data access page using the Page Wizard

By using the Page Wizard, you can create a grouped page for multiple tables. You can create a page using the wizard by selecting a single query with all the appropriate fields in it or by selecting multiple tables when you work with the wizard.

When creating a grouped page with the Page Wizard, the resulting page is based on one recordset and one or more grouping definitions behind the page. The recordset contains information from all tables used and the grouping definition for the fields used in the group. The Page Wizard doesn't prompt you for the Unique Table for the group field, making the page un-updateable. You can manually set the Unique Table property to the appropriate table in the group properties if necessary.

Using a query to create a group data page with the Page Wizard

You can create a grouped page for customers and their pets with visit information (type of medicine and treatment) by using the Customer, Pet, & Visit query. In this case, you may want to show several fields from the related tables, and you need to group the information by the Customer.State field and then create a second grouping by Customer.Type of Customer. The remaining fields remain in the third group.

To create this type of DAP, follow these steps:

1. With the Mountain Animal Data Access pages database open and the Pages object button selected, double click the Create data access page by using wizard choice in the container.

   Access starts the Page Wizard.

2. Select the Query: Customer, Pets, & Visits from the Tables/Query drop-down box on the first page.

3. After you select the query, press or click the ⟡ button to select and move all fields to the Selected fields list box.

4. Click the Next > button to move to the next screen.

5. Select State as a grouping level by highlighting it and pressing the > button. After you select State, select Type of Customer to create a second grouping level.

   At this point, the wizard screen should look similar to the screen shown in Figure 36-15.

6. Click the Next > button.

   Access moves to the sort order screen.

7. Select the Customer Name field in the first combo box to sort by name first.

8. Select the Type of Animal field in the second combo box to then sort by Type of Animal.

9. Click the Next > button.

   Access displays the last screen of the Page Wizard.

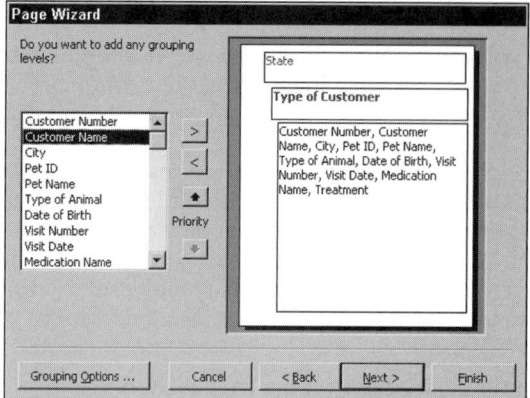

Figure 36-15: Page Wizard with two group
levels set

10. Click the Open the page radio button.

11. Click the Finish button to complete the data access page.

Access creates the DAP with three grouping levels and opens it. If you click on the
Expand/Collapse button for the State field group and then open the Type of
Customer group by clicking on its Expand/Collapse button, your grouped page
should look similar to the one shown in Figure 36-16.

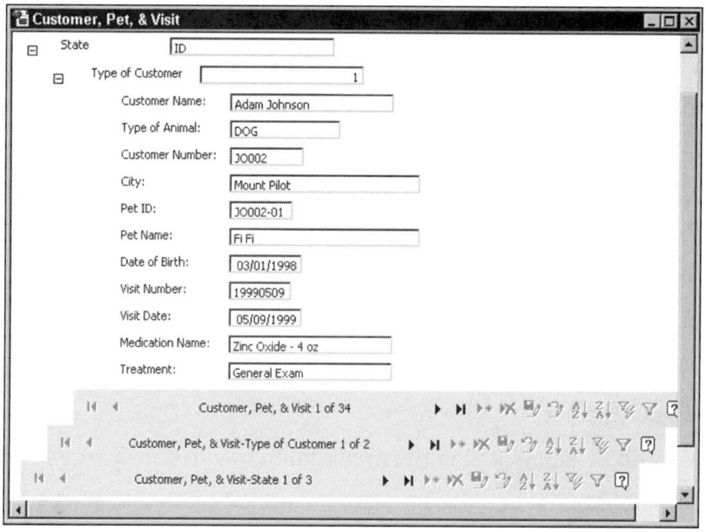

Figure 36-16: A grouped data access page with three levels
of grouping

As Figure 36-16 shows, this page contains three levels of group data. Each level has its own navigation controls. If you click the Next button of either top-level group, the Type of Customer or State, the groups below collapse automatically. The default action for the Expand/Collapse control button is to collapse automatically. You can change this default action by setting a value of True for the ExpandByDefault property of each Group level.

Note   At this point, the DAP isn't saved to an HTML file. You should save your work by clicking the Save button and saving the HTML file.

The resulting group page is one recordset, and one grouping definition is set behind the page. This DAP is not updateable as created. You can tell this by looking at the New, Delete, Save, and Undo buttons of the navigation bar for each group. You can change the UniqueTable property manually to make the innermost group updateable for a specific table.

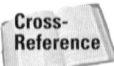

Cross-Reference   You change the UniqueTable property in the next section when you create a multi-grouping page based on two tables.

At this point, you can take the page into the Design view and make any changes to it, such as leaving groups expanded by default, or changing background colors for the individual groups, or even moving fields around. Figure 36-17 shows the same data access page after being redesigned.

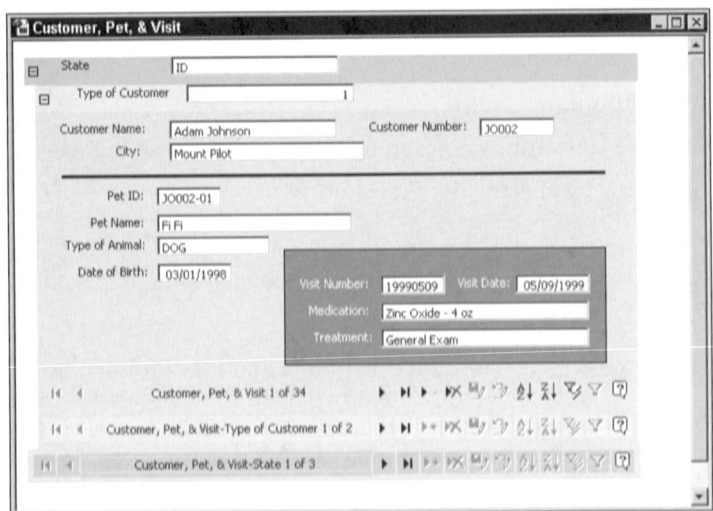

Figure 36-17: The same three group data access page with modification made to the page and the Pets fields of the innermost group updateable

Creating a group data page in the wizard using two tables

You can create a grouped page for customers and their pets by using the two tables — Customer and Pets. In this case, you may want to show several fields from the related tables, and you need to group the information by the Pets.Type of Animal field. The remaining fields remain in the second group.

To create this type of DAP, follow these steps:

1. With the Mountain Animal Data Access pages database open and the Pages object button selected, double-click the Create data access page by using wizard choice in the container.

   Access starts the Page Wizard.

2. Select the Table: Customer from the Tables/Query drop-down box on the first page.

3. Move the Customer Number, Customer Name, City, and State fields to the Selected Fields list box.

4. Select the Table: Pets from the Tables/Query drop-down box on the first page.

5. Move the Pet ID, Pet Name, Type of Animal, and Date of Birth fields to the Selected Fields list box.

6. Click the Next > button to move to the next screen.

   The Grouping levels screen of the Page Wizard is shown.

7. Select the Customer Name field as a grouping level field by highlighting it and pressing the Next > button.

8. Click the Finish button.

   Access creates the DAP with two grouping levels and opens it in Design View.

9. Switch to Page View by clicking the View button.

After you are in View mode, you can expand the Expand/Collapse button for the Customer Name field group to see all the fields in the page. It should look similar to the one shown in Figure 36-18.

You now have a data access page based on Customers and Pets grouped by Customer Name. Notice that you can't update any data in the non-header group (Customer Number field through Date of Birth field) as shown in Figure 36-18. This inability to update data is visibly apparent by the disabled New, Delete, Save, and Undo buttons on the Navigation bar.

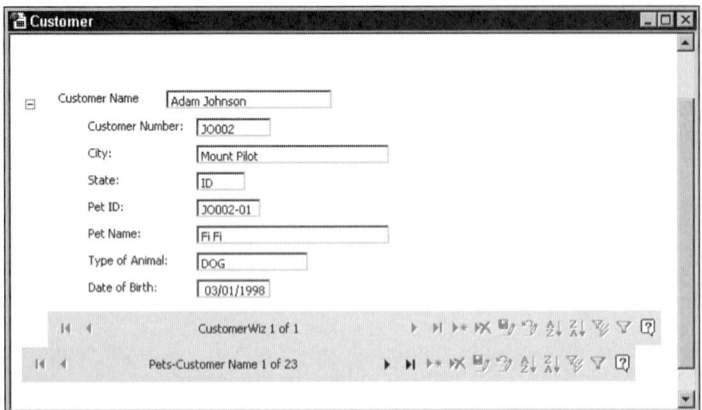

Figure 36-18: Two non-updateable tables, one grouping, and a data access page of customer and pet information

To allow updates to the data in the Pets fields of the group you must set the UniqueTable property of the Section to the Pets table. To set the UniqueTable to Pets, follow these steps:

1. Switch to Design View by clicking the View button.

2. View the Sections Properties for the Header: CustomerWiz section. A quick way to open the Properties dialog box with this section active is to double-click the Header section.

3. In the Properties box for the Section HeaderCustomerWiz, select the Data tab.

4. Select Pets from the UniqueTable property combo box, as shown in Figure 36-19.

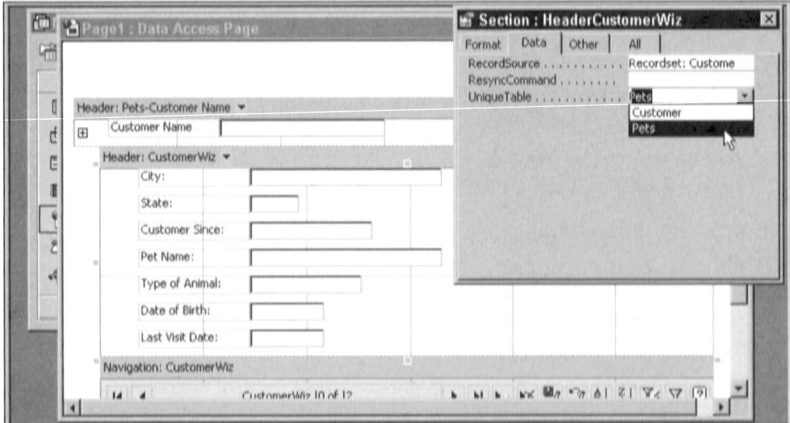

Figure 36-19: Selecting the Pets table for the UniqueTable property of the data access page

Looking at Figure 36-19, you can see that the Group section with the Customer Name is on the extreme left-most side of the Design view and the Group section with Customer and Pet information is indented about ½ inch to the right of the first group. Access automatically indents groups as it creates them.

5. Switch to Page View.

While in Page View, locate and expand the customer Exotic Pets. Notice that you can now update data from the Pets table (Pet ID, Pet Name, Type of Animal, and Date of Birth). The ability to update is shown by the enabled New, Delete, Save, and Undo buttons on the navigation bar.

Note   You can select the Customer table instead of the Pets table — allowing you to edit all the Customer fields except the last name field in the top-most Group Heading. Only the table specified in the UniqueTable property can be updated.

If you wish, you can abandon or save this page to any file name you wish. It will not be used any more in this chapter.

Working with grouped data access pages in Design view

You can also create a grouped data access page in Design view.

New Feature   Access 2002 has added several enhancements to creating grouped pages. These features include Lightweight Headers, automatic indenting, drop zones (used to easily create a new grouping), and selecting multiple objects in Design view (with IE 5.5 installed). These are covered in this section and the next.

Creating a Grouped Data Access Page manually

To manually create a grouped page of Customers and Pets with three groups, follow these steps:

1. From the Pages object in the Database Window, click the New button.

2. In the New Data Access Page dialog box, accept the default of Design View and click OK.

   If you haven't turned off the warning dialog box, Access displays a message telling you that the page created can't be changed in Access 2000. However, if you have loaded Microsoft Office XP Web Components, you are capable of viewing and working with it in Access 2000.

3. If the field list is not open, open it by clicking the Field List button.

4. From the field list expand the Customer table.

5. Select the Customer Number, Customer Name, City, and State fields and drag them to the design grid on the new data access page.

   Access displays the Layout Wizard and asks how you want the fields displayed in the section.

6. Select the default value of Columnar for the layout type and click OK.

Access puts the four fields on the page and names the section *Header: Customer*, as seen in the center left of Figure 36-20. Notice that the labels and text boxes are a set size and the text boxes hide the full text of some of the labels.

7. Drag the Type of Customer field to the page. As it moves into the page, a *new* section appears called "Create New Section Above Customer." Drop the Type of Customer field in this new Section. It receives a bright highlighted border as you move the Type of Customer field into it.

Figure 36-20 shows the new section header appearing where you drop the Type of Customer Field. This is called a *drop zone*. After you drop the field, Access automatically creates a new group based on the Type of Customer.

8. Now you can remove the section at the top that says "Click here and type title text." To remove it, click anywhere on the grayed text.

9. Press the delete key three times to remove this section.

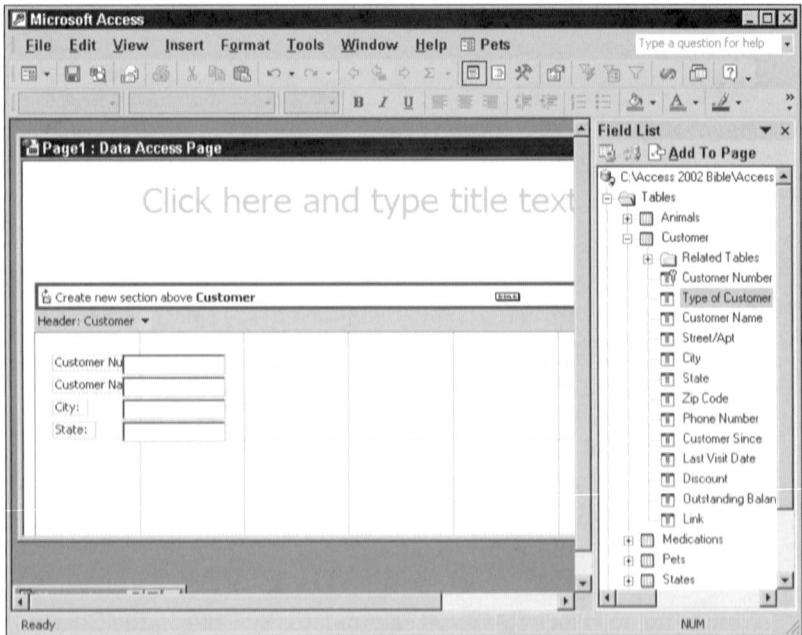

Figure 36-20: The new section header "Create new section above **Customer**" is visible as the Type of Customer field is dragged onto the work surface of the page.

10. Go to the section with the customer fields (Header: Customer) and rearrange the fields by moving them up and then resize the labels to make them fully readable. Then re-size the section so that only a little white space remains after the last field. Figure 36-21 shows how the screen may look after it is fixed.

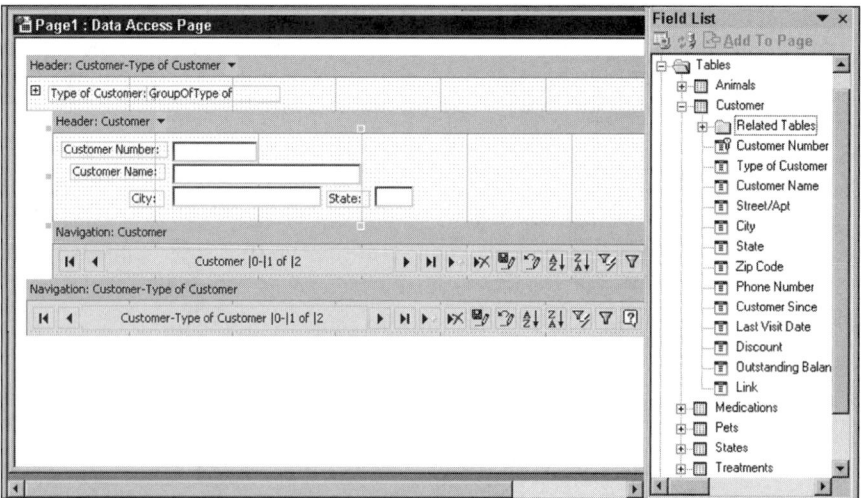

Figure 36-21: The new section header for Type of Customer is visible, and the section labeled Header: Customer, has been re-sized and the fields moved around.

Notice in Figure 36-21 that the groups are automatically indented by Access when it creates them.

11. Click the View button (datasheet icon on left) to see how the page looks so far.

Viewing the data access page, all three Types of Customer records are visible with an Expand/Collapse button to the left of them. When creating a grouping page in this manner, the default value for the DataPageSize property is 10. This means that the grouping shows 10 records at a time.

If you click on the Expand/Collapse button of the first Type of Customer you see that it displays the first 10 (of 19) records for the next group as well. These can be changed later. Figure 36-22 shows the first several records where the Type of Customer is 1.

Notice that in Figure 36-22 you can update the fields in the Customer table section (not the Type of Customer, but all the other fields). Access automatically updates the Section Header: Customer's UniqueTable property with the Customer table name. To verify this, while in Design View, double-click on the Header: Customer table section to activate the property sheet and display all the properties for Section: HeaderCustomer. Then select the Data tab, and the value Customer is placed in the UniqueTable text box.

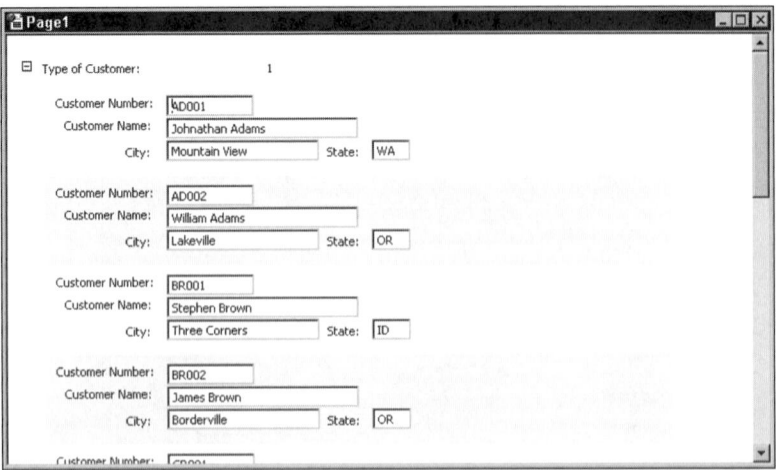

Figure 36-22: The new page with the first Type of Customer section expanded and showing several Customer records for the Type of Customer being 1

12. Return to Design View by clicking the View button again if you haven't returned.

Now you can add the Pets table below the customer group. If the Property sheet is active, close it.

13. Returning to the Field List, expand the Related Tables option under the Customer table. Then expand the Pets table under this option.

14. Select and drag the fields Pet ID, Pet Name, Type of Animal, and Date of Birth on the new drop zone that appears at the bottom of the Header: Customer section (right above the Navigation bar for the Customer section). Figure 36-23 shows the new drop zone named "Create New Section Below Customer." When this new drop zone becomes visible, drop the fields on the left-most side of the new section.

Access displays the Layout Wizard and asks how you want the fields displayed in the section.

15. Select the Tabular radio button and click OK.

Access creates a Caption section and a Header section, putting the titles for each field in the Caption section and the four fields in tabular fashion under the field titles. The field names and titles section may need to be resized at this point.

16. Switch to Page view to examine the data access page.

If you expand both the Type of Customer (1) and then the Customer Number (AD001), your screen should look similar to the one shown in Figure 36-24.

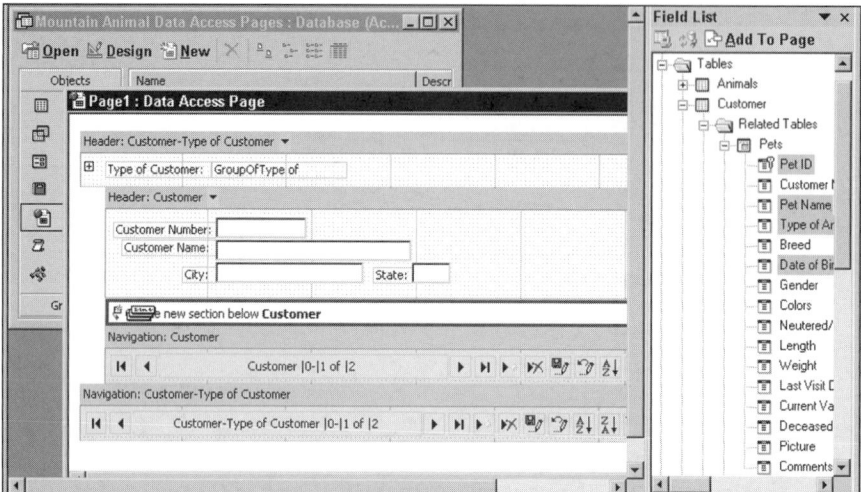

Figure 36-23: Another new drop zone below the Customer Section. This is where you drop the Pets table fields. Notice that the multi-field pointer is on the left-most side of the drop zone.

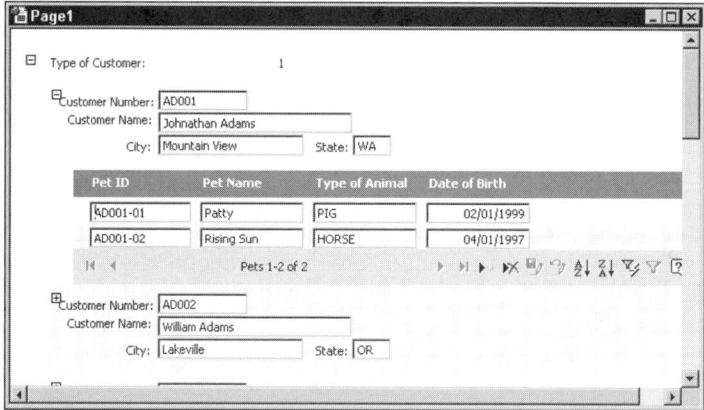

Figure 36-24: A data access page with three groups shown. The first two groups have been expanded.

As Figure 36-24 shows, each group level is indented approximately ½ inch from its higher group. Access 2002 does this automatically when you create the page.

Notice that the fields in the Pets table area (Pet ID, Pet Name, Type of Animal, and Date of Birth) are also updateable by default. This also indicates that the UniqueTable property for this section has been set to the Pets table automatically.

Design Features Enabled by Internet Explorer 5.5

If you have installed Internet Explorer 5.5 in Access 2002, several new features have been added to the design surface of data access pages. The most important one is the ability to select multiple objects while in Design view. Access 2000 DAPs didn't allow you to select multiple controls to move, size, or apply common property settings. In Access 2002, you can select multiple controls and move them or resize them simultaneously. You can even activate the Property sheet, and if you select multiple controls, a Multiple Selection section appears, allowing you to change many format, data, and other properties universally to all the controls selected.

In addition, IE 5.5 has eliminated the alignment and sizing toolbar controls and has added them to the Format menu of the Page Design. If you use IE 5.0, in Access 2002, the alignment and sizing work the same as in Access 2000—using the alignment and sizing toolbar to align or size individually selected controls.

Before continuing, you should save this data access page and name it *Customer and Pets Grouped*.

Creating a grouped page by promoting a field

You can also create a grouped page by promoting a field in an existing group. For instance, you can create a simple data access page of Customers and promote the Type of Customer field in the group to a group above it. To accomplish this, follow these steps:

1. Click Create data access page in Design View in the Pages container of the database window.

2. If the Field List is not active, activate it, and if the properties dialog box is active, turn it off.

3. Expand the Customer Table.

4. Select the Customer Number, Type of Customer, Customer Name, City, and State fields and drag them to the design grid on the new data access page.

   Access creates a Group titled Header: Customer and opens the Layout Wizard.

5. Accept the default value Columnar and click OK.

6. You may rearrange the fields to make the page more pleasing.

7. Select and right-click the Type of Customer field in the Header: Customer group.

   Access opens a right-click menu.

8. Click the menu choice Promote, as shown in Figure 36-25.

   Access moves the field and adds a new group level.

9. Save this page and name it *Customer with Pets Pivot Table*.

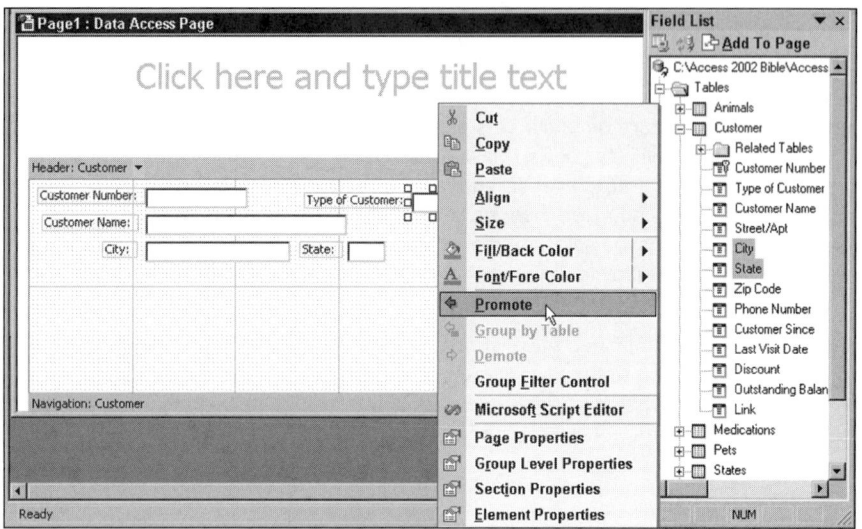

Figure 36-25: The right mouse menu that's used to promote a field to a higher group level

Access promotes the field Type of Customer to its own group above the remaining Customer fields. After it's saved, you can look at the data access page to verify that it promoted the group Type of Customer correctly. It shows all three Type of Customer records with an Expand/Collapse button along each one. Clicking this button shows you the Customer records for each type.

Note   This data access page is used in the next section.

Creating a multi-table page with a pivot table

When working with multiple tables in data access pages, you are not limited to putting fields from a linked table in their own grouping as you did above with the Pets table in Figure 36-24. You can create a simpler page that displays the Pets table in a pivot table.

Pivot tables were first introduced in Access 2000 and offer the ability to place an entire table or select fields from a table in a pivot table that is similar in appearance to a datasheet. This pivot table doesn't have to exist in its own group; rather, it can exist in the current group. For example, to add the Pets table to the Customer and Pets Pivot Table page that you just created in the previous section, follow these steps:

1. Open the Customer and Pets Pivot Table page in Design view, if it isn't already open.

2. If the field list is not active, open it.

3. Expand the Customer table icon and click the Related Tables icon to expand it; finally, expand the Pets table icon.

4. Select the Pet ID, Pet Name, Type of Animal, and Date of Birth fields of the Pets table and drag them to the Group Header: Customer section of the page (below the current fields) and drop them.

   Access displays the Layout Wizard and asks how you want the fields displayed in the section.

5. Choose the PivotTable radio button and click OK.

   Access drops the PivotTable in the group below the Customer fields and automatically adds the link field — Customer Number, naming it *Customer Number1*.

6. Click in the PivotTable on the CustomerNumber1 field and press Delete to remove it from the PivotTable.

7. Resize the pivot table to fit in the space, while showing all the fields.

   The page design should now look similar to the one shown in Figure 36-26.

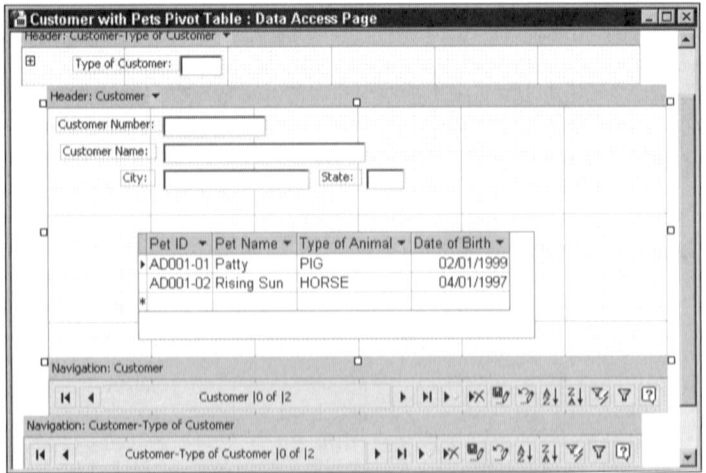

Figure 36-26: A pivot table that has been added to an existing group

8. Switch to Page view to examine the data access page.

9. While in Page view, click the Expand button of the Type of Customer to see the Customer fields and Pet fields (which are in the pivot table).

   The page should now look similar to the one shown in Figure 36-27. Notice that both the Customer fields in the group and the Pet fields in the pivot table are all editable.

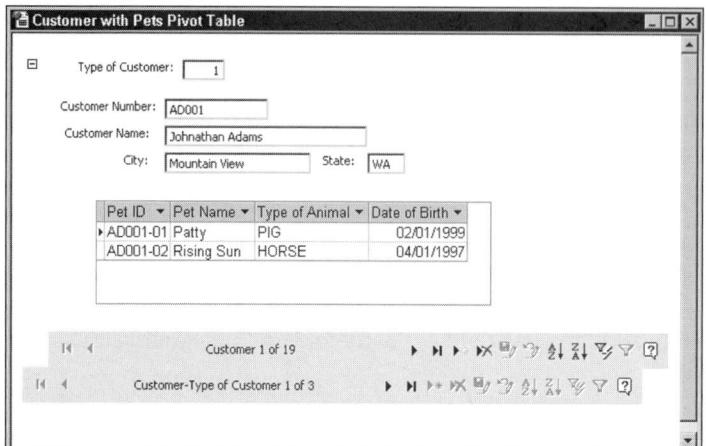

Figure 36-27: A Page view with the pivot table that has been added to an existing group

10. Save your form to Customer and Pets Grouped.

Changing some key properties on data access pages

While creating the data access page Customer and Pets Grouped, Access 2002 automatically assigns values to several properties. This section discusses those properties and how to change them.

Working with group level properties

After you start working with more than one table, you probably put fields in different groups, as in the section "Working with Multiple Tables and Grouped Pages" Earlier in this chapter. You may be interested in changing two properties—DataPageSize and ExpandedByDefault. The DataPageSize property value is set to 10 in many instances. This means that you automatically see up to 10 records for each group of records. The ExpandedByDefault property value is set to False in most instances. You may want to set it to True in some groups so that you automatically see the next level without having to expand the control.

To change these properties, you need to activate the Property sheet and show all the properties related to that group. The property sheet in the Page Design view is different than the one in the forms or Reports Design view,it is lacking the drop-down list field (in forms and reports) that lets you select any control object on the page.

New Feature   In Access 2000 you could change the properties by clicking on the sorting and grouping button or select View⇨Sorting and Grouping in the Page Design View. After selected you would then select the group whose properties you want to change. These choices have been eliminated from Access 2002. In lieu of this method, Access 2002 has added what are called *Lightweight Headers*. These lightweight headers are designed to work with the changes that have been made to Office XP visuals — they are like a menu of choices for each header section. The properties of each section are more discoverable. To get to the properties of any section you can right-click on the header or click on the drop-down arrow in the header as shown in Figure 36-28.

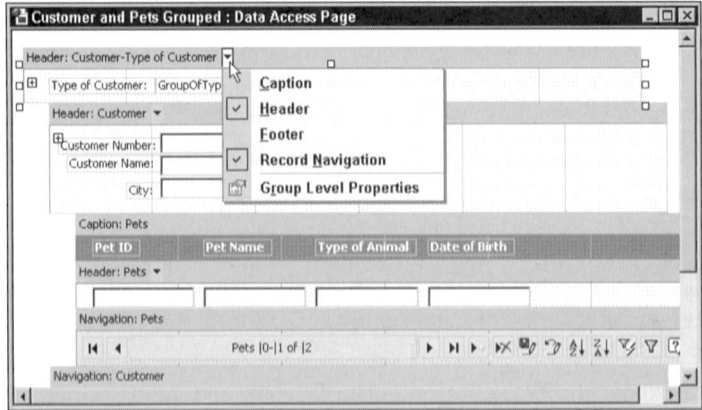

Figure 36-28: A new lightweight header in Page Design view

As Figure 36-28 shows, the lightweight header has five choices — four are toggle switch types (caption, header, footer, and record navigation), and the fifth is the Show the Group Level Properties.

Figure 36-28 also shows that both the Header section and the Record Navigation section are active (check marked on). If you click-off the Record Navigation section the corresponding Navigation control section is removed from the data access page.

Turning on the Caption section creates a new area for the group titled Caption, as in the Caption area for Pets in Figure 36-25, shown earlier in the chapter.

Turning on the Footer section also creates a new area for the group just above the Navigation section, titled Footer.

Caution   If you uncheck the Header section to deactivate it, Access removes the entire section and all corresponding sections for that group — Caption, Footer, and Record Navigator.

Using the lightweight header menu you can access the properties of the Group Level. For instance, you may want to access the Group Level properties for the Type of Customer Group to change the ExpandedByDefault value to True and the DataPageSize property to 1. To accomplish this, follow these steps:

1. Open the Customers and Pets Grouped data access page in Design View.

2. Click the down arrow of the Type of Customer Header bar to activate the Lightweight Headers (or right-click it).

3. Select Group Level Properties from the menu.

   Access opens the property sheet (if it is closed) and displays all the properties for the Group Level Customer-Type of Customer.

4. Select the DataPageSize property in the property box and set to 1.

5. Select the ExpandedByDefault property and select True.

6. Switch to page Page view to examine the data access page.

   While in Page view you can see that the Type of Customer group is automatically expanded showing the next group level (Customer information) — this is because the ExpandedByDefault has been set to True.

7. Click on the Expand/Collapse button of the Type of Customer to close the Customer records.

   Access is only showing one Type of Customer group — this is because the DataPageSize has been reset to 1.

8. Switch to Page view to examine the data access page.

9. Click the down arrow of the Customer Header bar to activate the Lightweight Headers (or right-click it).

10. Select Group Level Properties from the menu for this heading.

11. Select the DataPageSize property in the property box and set to 1.

12. Select the ExpandedByDefault property and also select True.

13. Switch to Page view to examine the data access page with both Expand/Collapse controls set to True.

    While in Page view you can see that the Type of Customer group and the Customer group are automatically expanded showing the next group level (Pet information) — this is because the ExpandedByDefault has been set to True for both. The data access page should look similar to the one in Figure 36-29.

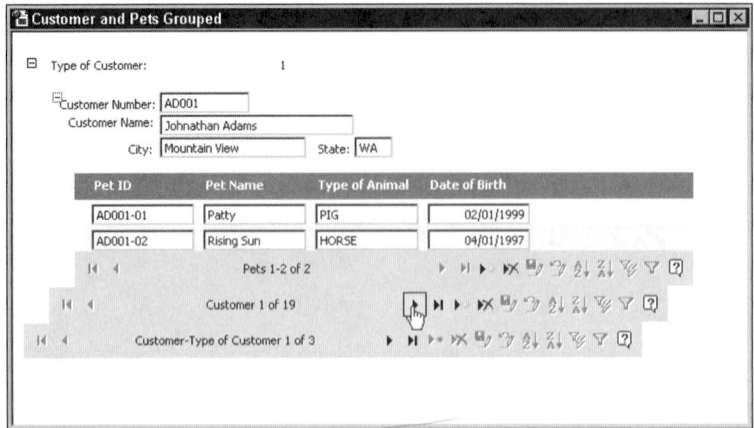

Figure 36-29: A three-group page in Page View with the ExpandByDefault and DataPageSize set

14. Save your page.

Another Group level property, the *RecordSelector*, lets you display a record selector when you have more than one record present on the page — when the DataPageSize property is set to a number greater than 1. The default value for this property is False. For example, you may want to display a record selector for the Pets table group in the same page you just worked with. To put a Record Selector alongside each record in the Pets Group, follow these steps:

1. Open the Customers and Pets Grouped data access page in Design mode.

2. Click the down arrow of the Pets Header bar to activate the lightweight headers (or right click it).

3. Select Group Level Properties from the menu.

   Access opens the property sheet (if it is closed) and displays all the properties for the Group Level Pets.

4. Select the RecordSelector property in the property box and set to True. (It should be the last property of the GroupLevel: Pets.)

5. Switch to page view to examine the data access page with a record selector alongside of each Pets record in the Pets Group Section.

   The new data access page should now look similar to the one shown in Figure 36-30.

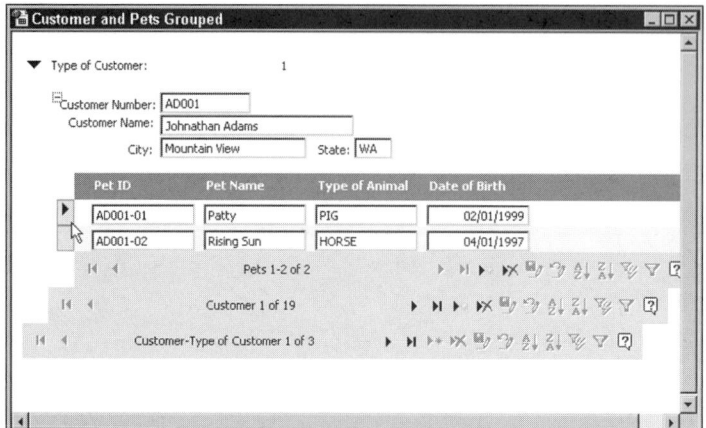

Figure 36-30: A three-group page in Page View with the ExpandByDefault and DataPageSize set

6. Save your page.

The DAP in Figure 36-30 shows record selectors alongside each record of the Pets table (in this case two records). The mouse pointer is pointing to the first record selector. The user can quickly move to any record in the set by clicking the selector.

Changing the absolute path property of a page

If you have not turned the warning off, every time you save a data access page, Access pops up a warning box like the one shown in Figure 36-31.

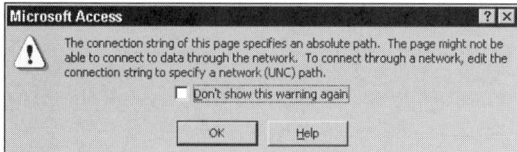

Figure 36-31: The Warning box that appears when saving a DAP

As you can see in Figure 36-31, Access informs you that the connection string for the page is an absolute page (hard-coded to a specific drive and directory). When using this on a network, or when you copy the database and files you need to let Access know where the database is moved. In a network environment, you need to change the connection string to specify a network path, called a Universal Naming Convention (UNC) path.

To change the absolute path for the data source of a data access page you need to change the ConnectionString property of the page. To change the path for the Customer with Pets Pivot Table page, follow these steps:

1. Open the Customer with Pets Pivot Table page in Design view.

2. If the property sheet is not open, open it.

3. Click one time on the title bar of the Page window or in the white area above the top group.

   The Property sheet informs you that it is displaying the properties for the Page by the title, which has changed to Page: Customer with Pets Pivot Table.

4. In the Data tab section; move the cursor to the ConnectionString property text box (second one from the top).

5. While the cursor is in the ConnectionString text box, press the Shift-F2 key combination to activate the Zoom window.

   The Zoom window appears with the entire connect string highlighted.

6. In the Zoom window, move the cursor to the right side of the first line where it says "Data Source=", positioning it just after the equals sign.

7. Select and remove the drive and path information all the way up to the name of the database (Mountain Animal Data Access Pages.mdb) as shown in Figure 36-32. After the physical path is highlighted simply press Delete to remove it.

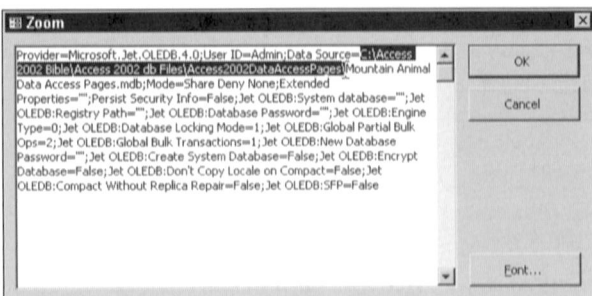

Figure 36-32: The Zoom window with the cursor moved to the insertion point to correct the data source of this database and the physical path highlighted to be removed

8. Click OK to save the changes and return to the property sheet.

9. Save your page.

With the absolute page reference gone you can now use this database on a network drive and simply refer to the database as you do for other files in the network.

There is one other side issue — moving the database. If you move the database and the underlying HTML file you also need to change the hard-coded path of where to find the HTML file from the page object in the Access Pages container. Follow these steps to remove the hard-coded path from the properties of the page object:

1. Select the Pages button of the database and then select (highlight) the Customer with Pets Pivot Table object name.

2. Select View ➪ Properties from the menu or right-click and select Properties from the right-mouse button menu.

   Access opens the Objects Property sheet for the page object Customer with Pets Pivot Table. It should look similar to the one shown in Figure 36-33.

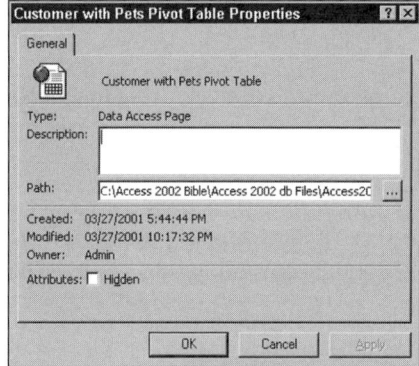

Figure 36-33: The Object property sheet for objects in a database

3. Click in the Path: text box.

4. Remove the path reference to the HTML file name, leaving only the HTML file name in the Path text box.

5. After you have removed the drive and path name, click on the Apply Button to store the file name without a path.

6. Click OK to save the newly set properties.

With the path removed from the page object reference, the database and its associated HTML files can be moved to any drive or directory and will run as expected.

Changing properties of the Expand/Collapse control

New Feature

In Access 2000 the Expand/Collapse control was an ActiveX control. It has been changed to HTML code using graphic files in Access 2002. It has several new properties that you can work with to change the physical appearance of the control.

Under the Format tab of the Control object (Expand/Collapse) property sheet, you can change the *Cursor* property to 16 different values — the default is a pointing hand. This property controls what is displayed when the user moves the cursor over the control. Also of interest is the *Display* property which has seven different values — the default is inline. If you change this property, it controls how the control displays; for instance, if you select block, the control is displayed in an outlined solid block.

Under the Other tab, the *Src* property can be set to change the appearance, or picture, as displayed by the Expand/Collapse control. You have six choices — the default is a Black Plus/Minus sign. You can select a black arrow to have it show a right-pointing arrow when collapsed and a down-pointing arrow when expanded.

Changing properties of the Navigation control

 New Feature In Access 2000 the Navigation control was also an ActiveX control, and you were limited to the functionality of the ActiveX control. In Access 2002, the Navigation control is an HTML table with styles and images associated with all the buttons. This feature lets you customize the images and formatting of the buttons. Also, by using HTML code instead of an ActiveX control, it loads faster and requires fewer resources to operate.

Figure 36-34 shows the Navigation control bar for data access pages.

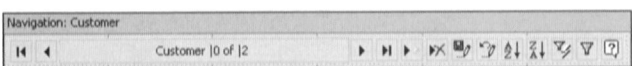

Figure 36-34: The Navigation control for DAPs

The look of the Control and all the buttons on the control are built based on HTML styles. These styles are implemented as classes in the page's <STYLE> tag. Because they are based on styles, you can easily change the look of the Navigation control.

Removing buttons from the navigation bar

Using HTML code makes it a simple matter to remove buttons on the navigation control. For instance, to remove the new, delete, save, undo, filters, sort, and help buttons from the Customer — Type of Customer Navigation bar of the Customer and Pets Grouped page, follow these steps:

1. Open the Customer and Pets Group page in Design view.

2. Move to the bottom of the page in Design view to show the Navigation bar for Customer-Type of Customer.

3. If you have IE 5.5 loaded on your machine, select all the buttons from the New button through the Help button as shown in Figure 36-35. If you don't have IE 5.5 on your machine, you must select each one independently (repeating Steps 3 and 4 until they are all gone).

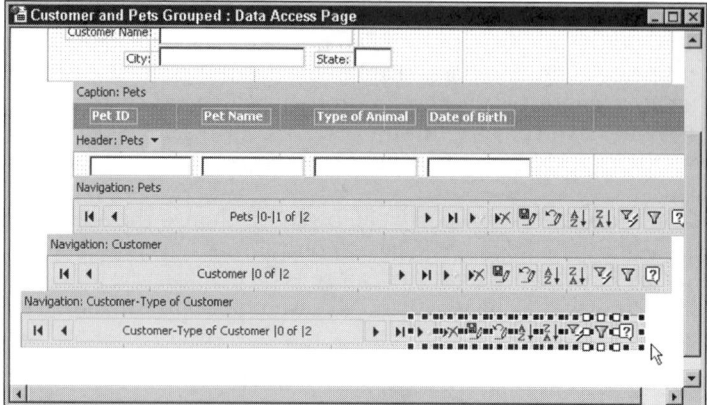

Figure 36-35: Multiple selection of Navigation bar buttons to delete them

4. Press Delete to remove all the buttons at one time. If you don't have IE 5.5 on your machine you must repeat Steps 3 and 4 until all the buttons are removed. At this point, the Navigation bar should look similar to the one shown in Figure 36-36.

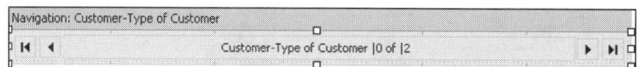

Figure 36-36: The Navigation bar with several buttons deleted

5. With the buttons removed, you can now resize the Navigation bar by selecting the right side and moving it inward (toward the left) until it is resized to what you like.

6. Save your work.

Changing images on a button of the navigation bar

To change the image of any control on the Navigation bar you simply follow these general steps:

1. With the data access page in Design view, click After on the Navigation control.

2. Click the image that you want to change.

3. View the property sheet and select the Other tab.

4. Replace the **Src** property with the path to the new image. It can be a file path or HTTP address.

Specifying default settings for new DAPs

When you add a Caption section to a header, the default background color of the Caption is set to blue as in the Caption section of the Pets table shown in Figure 36-28 earlier in the chapter. This enables the user to visually see a contrast between the sections.

When you right-click to add multiple fields to the header section after adding a Caption, the labels are automatically added to the Caption section (that is, if the control wizards are enabled and you choose Tabular from the Layout Wizard, as you did previously in the chapter with the Pets table in the Customer and Pets Grouped page).

If you add a footer section to a header, the footer section puts a 1-point blue line across the top border.

When you create a new section, Access automatically indents the section a specific amount.

If you have multiple records displayed in a group — such as when the DataPageSize property is set to a number greater than 1, the alternating rows display a different color — for contrast.

All of these actions are controlled by the New default page format properties of Access 2002. Figure 36-37 shows the new options that you can set for data access pages. To access these options, simply select Tools ⸦ Options from the menu and select the Pages tab.

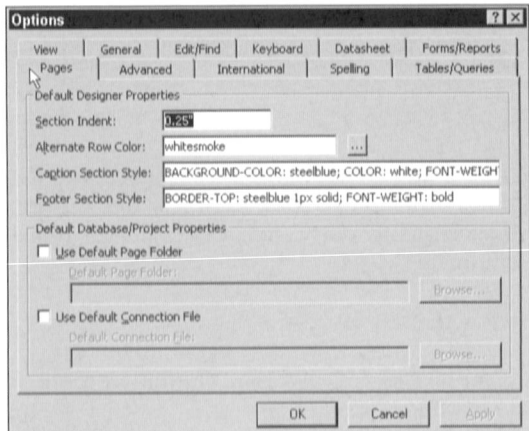

Figure 36-37: The default page format properties of Access 2002

As Figure 36-37 shows, you can change the default values of four properties — Section Indent, Alternate Row Color, Caption Section Style, and Footer Section Style.

Working with the Data Outline in page design

Access 2002 has added a new data outline graphical tool for data access pages. The Data Outline displays a tree-like view of the data model of a data access page. Figure 36-38 shows the Data Outline window open with the data model of the Customer and Pets Grouped data access page.

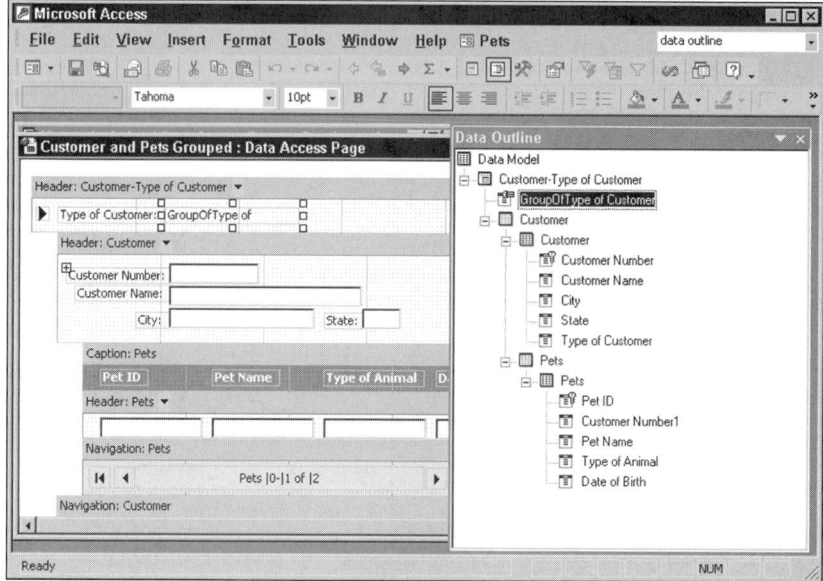

Figure 36-38: The data outline of a data access page

As Figure 36-38 shows, the Data Outline window displays a tree view of the data model of the data access page. It shows the record sources, fields, and any calculated controls on the page. As you click on any object in the data model, it is automatically selected in the Design window.

You can use the data outline to review the structure of a page.

To activate the Data Outline tool, simply select View ➪ Data Outline from the Pages Design view menu or click the Data Outline button.

Saving other Access objects as data access pages

You can convert any table, query, view, form, and report to a data access page. To do this, you simply need to select an object and save it as a data access page. The type of page that is created depends on the type of object being saved.

When you save an object to a data access page, Access uses XML transform internally to create the data access page. This Transform, actually a Style sheet (named ReportML2DAP.xsl) containing XML code, is used to convert the objects into a data access page. However, this is not visible to the user.

To save any of these objects as a data access page, you simply follow these general steps:

1. Select the object you want to create a data access page from in the database.

2. After you select it, choose File ➪ Save As (or right-click and select Save As . . .) from the menu.

   Access opens the Save As dialog box and puts a default name of "Copy of [Object Name]" in the text box, as shown in Figure 36-39.

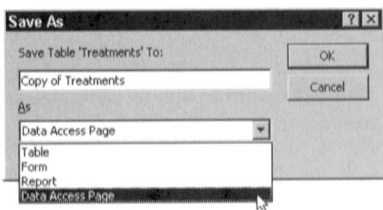

Figure 36-39: The Save As dialog box used to save any object to a data access page

3. Either accept the default Save to file name or enter a new name to save the data access page to.

4. Select Data Access Page in the As: drop-down list box.

5. Click OK.

   Access opens the New Data Access Page dialog box and puts the default name in the text box.

6. Click OK to save the new Web page.

That is all there is to creating a DAP from any database object.

You need to be aware of some other issues when saving certain types of Access objects to a data access page. These issues are covered in the next three sections.

Converting a table, query or view to a data access page

When saving a table, query, or view to a data access page, the new page contains all the fields from the table in a tabular layout. The fields are outlined, record selectors enabled, and the page size set to display 10 records at a time.

The resulting DAP appears similar to a table datasheet. Figure 36-40 shows a data access page created from the Treatments table.

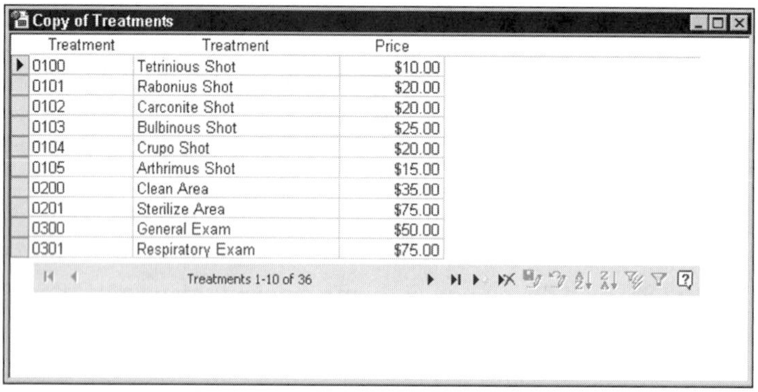

Treatment	Treatment	Price
▶ 0100	Tetrinious Shot	$10.00
0101	Rabonius Shot	$20.00
0102	Carconite Shot	$20.00
0103	Bulbinous Shot	$25.00
0104	Crupo Shot	$20.00
0105	Arthrimus Shot	$15.00
0200	Clean Area	$35.00
0201	Sterilize Area	$75.00
0300	General Exam	$50.00
0301	Respiratory Exam	$75.00

Copy of Treatments — Treatments 1-10 of 36

Figure 36-40: A data access page created from a table

The data access page created in Figure 36-40 is updateable as you can see from the active New and Delete buttons on the Navigation bar.

Caution If the Default view of your object is set to PivotTable or PivotChart view, the page created contains the PivotTable or PivotChart representation of the object instead.

Converting a form to a data access page

When saving a form to a data access page, the new page contains *most* of the fields from the underlying table or query.

When converting a form to a DAP the following objects are either ignored or changed, as follows:

✦ Any bound or unbound object frames are not supported and will not be converted — they are simply ignored.

✦ Toggle buttons and tab controls are not supported and will not be converted — they are simply ignored.

✦ Any diagonal lines will be converted to horizontal lines on the new data access page.

✦ Any subform in a form will not be converted to a data access page.

✦ Any value lists used as row sources will be placed as an unbound list type when converted.

✦ If a list box or combo box uses multiple columns as their data source and display, only the first visible column of the original control will be converted.

✦ Controls placed in the header section will be placed in unbound controls in the caption section of the outermost group level (top level).

✦ Controls placed in the footer section will be placed in unbound controls in the navigation section of the outermost group level (top level).

✦ Pictures in a form are converted to bitmaps and placed in a folder below the current location that is named "Images." These are not pictures in bound object frames — only those that are image types in forms.

✦ Expressions that refer to the properties of a form or subform are ignored.

✦ Any code that would not run in a data access page is imported into the page as a comment block at the end of the document. Any code behind the form or control events is not converted to a data access page.

✦ Hyperlinks associated with a label or command button control are not converted over to the data access page. They will not be active when the form is converted to a page.

✦ If the form contains ActiveX controls, only those controls that support the IpersistPropertyBag interface are implemented in the page.

Creating a DAP from a form with the default view of Single Form

Most forms have the Default View property set to Single Form. If you create a page from a form that has this value, the new data access page looks similar to the form you are creating it from. The fields and text are placed in the same relative position on the new Web document as they were in the form.

For example, follow these steps to create a data access page from the Pets table:

1. Open the form Pets from the Form container of the Mountain Animal Hospital Data Access Pages database.

    The Pets form should look similar to the one shown in Figure 36-41.

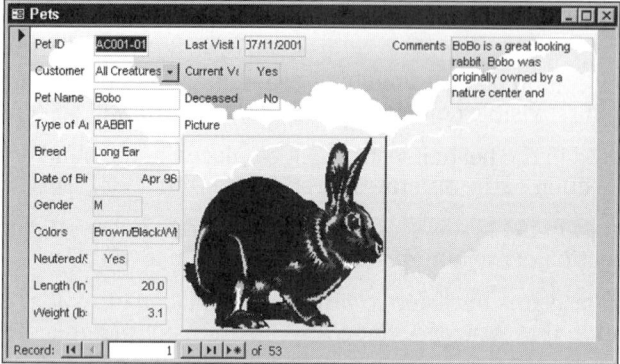

Figure 36-41: The Pets form with a background picture and a bound object (picture of a rabbit)

2. With the form still open, select File ⇨ Save As . . . from the menu.

Access opens the Save As dialog box and puts a default name of "Pets" in the text box.

3. Accept the default "Pets" name and select Data Access Page in the As: drop-down list box.

4. Click OK.

Access opens the New Data Access Page dialog box and puts the default name in the text box.

5. Click OK to save the new Web page.

Access creates the new Pets data access form and then opens it for you to examine. It should look similar to the one shown in Figure 36-42.

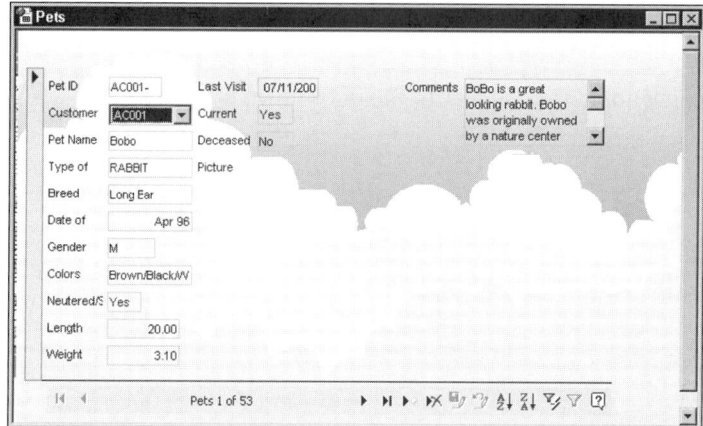

Figure 36-42: A new data access page created from the Pets form

Notice that the new page has the same background picture as the one in the Pets form in Figure 36-41; however, it is missing the picture of the rabbit. Because the rabbit picture is stored in a database and is in a bound object control in the form, it is simply ignored. The other fields are on the page in the same relative positioning as the original Pets form. It even has a Navigation control and a record selected added to the data access page.

If you look in the subdirectory where this data access page was saved you can see that Access also created a directory named Images and placed a new Pets.bmp file in it. The Pets.bmp file is the background graphic that was used by the Pets form and is used by the Pets.html file to display the background.

Creating a DAP from a form with the default view of datasheet

If the form you are converting has the Default View property set to Datasheet, the resulting Datasheet is also a datasheet-like view. The data access page is very similar to the ones you created by saving a table or query.

For example, if you save the "AddCustPetAnimals" form to a data access page, the new page looks like the one in Figure 36-43. Because the form's Default View is set to Datasheet, the page created is also similar to a datasheet.

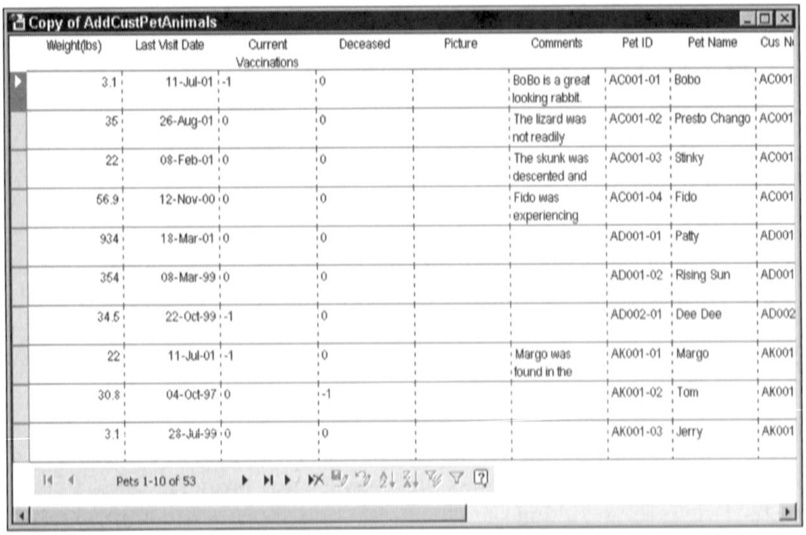

Weight(lbs)	Last Visit Date	Current Vaccinations	Deceased	Picture	Comments	Pet ID	Pet Name	Cus N
3.1	11-Jul-01	-1	0		BoBo is a great looking rabbit.	AC001-01	Bobo	AC001
35	26-Aug-01	0	0		The lizard was not readily	AC001-02	Presto Chango	AC001
22	08-Feb-01	0	0		The skunk was descented and	AC001-03	Stinky	AC001
56.9	12-Nov-00	0	0		Fido was experiencing	AC001-04	Fido	AC001
934	18-Mar-01	0	0			AD001-01	Patty	AD001
354	08-Mar-99	0	0			AD001-02	Rising Sun	AD001
34.5	22-Oct-99	-1	0			AD002-01	Dee Dee	AD002
22	11-Jul-01	-1	0		Margo was found in the	AK001-01	Margo	AK001
30.8	04-Oct-97	0	-1			AK001-02	Tom	AK001
3.1	28-Jul-99	0	0			AK001-03	Jerry	AK001

Figure 36-43: A new data access page created from the AddCusstPetAnimals form

Creating a DAP from a form with the default view of continuous forms

If the form that you are converting has a default the Default View property set to Continuous Forms, the resulting Datasheet has the page size property set to All and the navigation control is present but not used for First Record, Previous, Next, or

Last. However, the Navigation control is still present if the record selector is on in the form. If present, the buttons available are Add, Delete, Sort, Filter and Help. For example, if you save the form Treatments to a data access page, they both look similar to those shown in Figure 36-44.

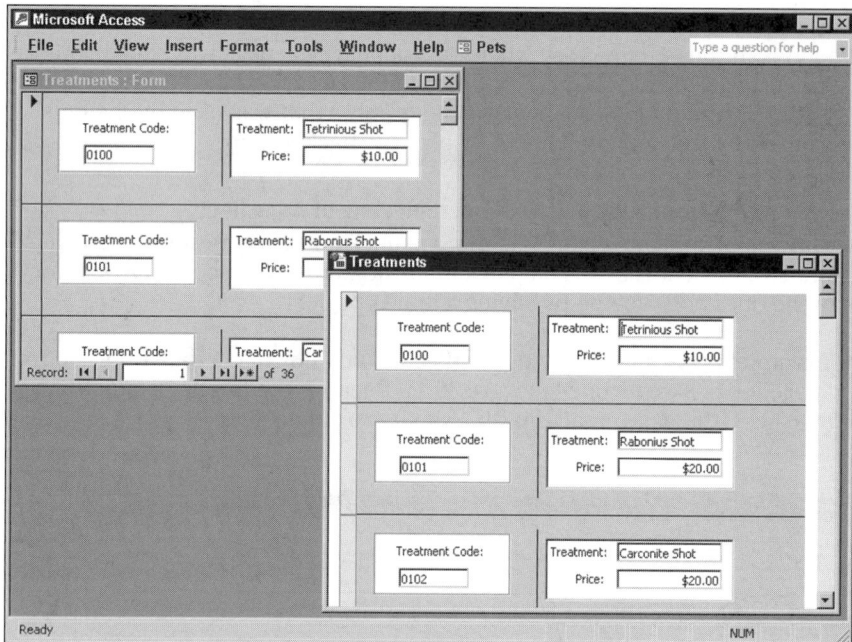

Figure 36-44: A continuous form, Treatments, saved as a page

As Figure 36-44 shows, the Form (top left corner) has the navigational bar visible with the ability to step through the individual form pages. In contrast, the data access page (bottom right corner) created from this form, shows all 36 forms continuous and at the bottom (not visible in the figure) the navigation bar has several buttons deactivated.

Creating a DAP from a form with the default view of PivotTable or PivotChart

If the form that you are converting has the Default View property set to PivotTable or PivotChart view, the resulting Datasheet uses the appropriate ActiveX control to represent the component.

Creating a DAP from a form with a subform

If the form that you are converting has a subform in it, such as the Add a Customer and Pets form shown in Figure 36-45, the subform is not converted.

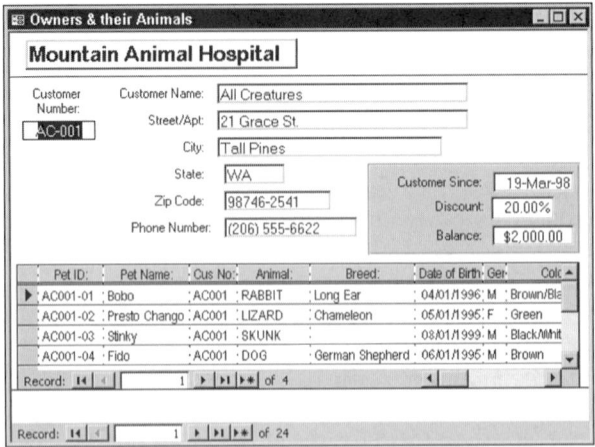

Figure 36-45: A form with a subform to be saved as a data access page

When you convert this form to a data access page, the resulting page looks like the one in Figure 36-46. Notice that none of the Pets information from the subform was brought over to the page from the original form in Figure 36-45.

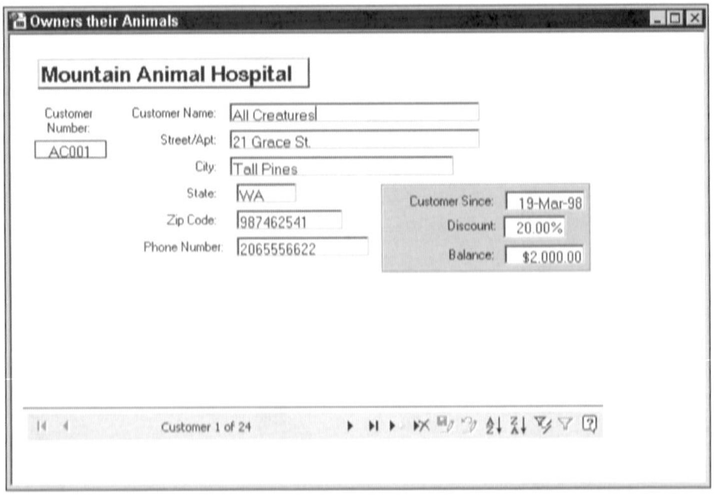

Figure 36-46: A page converted from a form with a subform

Converting a report to a data access page

Reports in Access databases (both *.mdb and *.adp) can be saved as data access pages. The same objects that are ignored or changed in forms are ignored or changed in data access pages.

 **Cross-Reference** See the section titled "Converting a form to a data access page," earlier in this chapter.

Unlike forms, a report is not interactive, data in reports is saved as text boxes in data access pages with a style and appearance similar to what appears on the report.

Because reports only have two views, they are a bit simpler to work with as compared to forms. However, reports support subreports, groupings, multiple columns, multiple headers and footers, ActiveX controls, and many summary functions. Understanding how a report is converted to a DAP is important.

Creating a DAP from a report with multiple columns

When you convert a report that contains multiple columns to a data access page, the resulting page is a single column wide. Figure 36-47 shows the Customers By State (three snaking columns) report on the left side and the resulting data access page on the right side of the screen. Notice that the report has three columns and the resulting data access page only has one.

 Tip To create this report for yourself, simply select the "Customers By State (three snaking columns)" report and save it as a data access page.

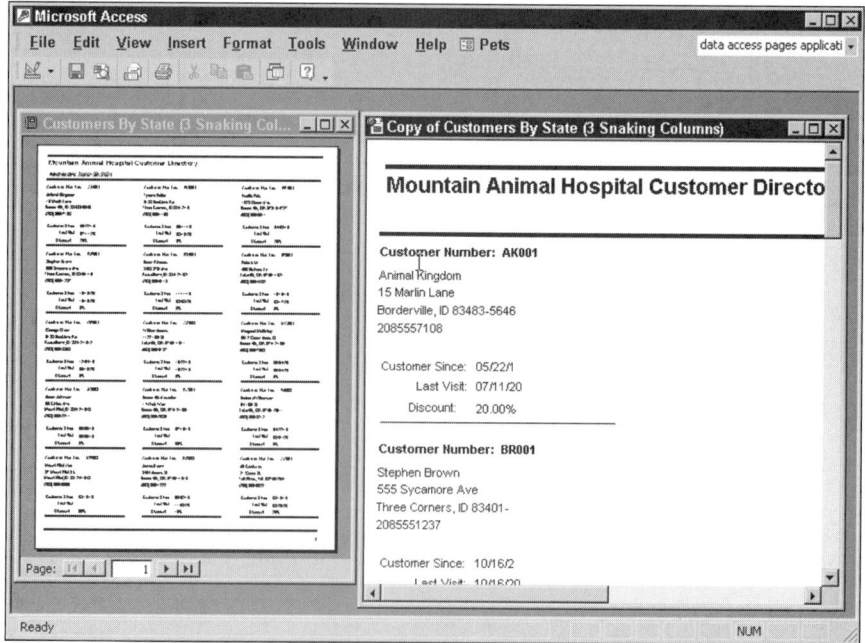

Figure 36-47: A multi-column report and the resulting single column data access page

Creating a DAP from a report with groupings

A report can have up to 10 levels of groupings in Access. When you convert a report that contains groupings to a data access page, each level of groupings is applied to a different level in the data access page. Figure 36-48 shows the Daily Hospital Report, which has three group levels and the resulting data access page, also with three group levels.

Note   To create this report for yourself, simply select the "Daily Hospital Report" report and save it as a data access page.

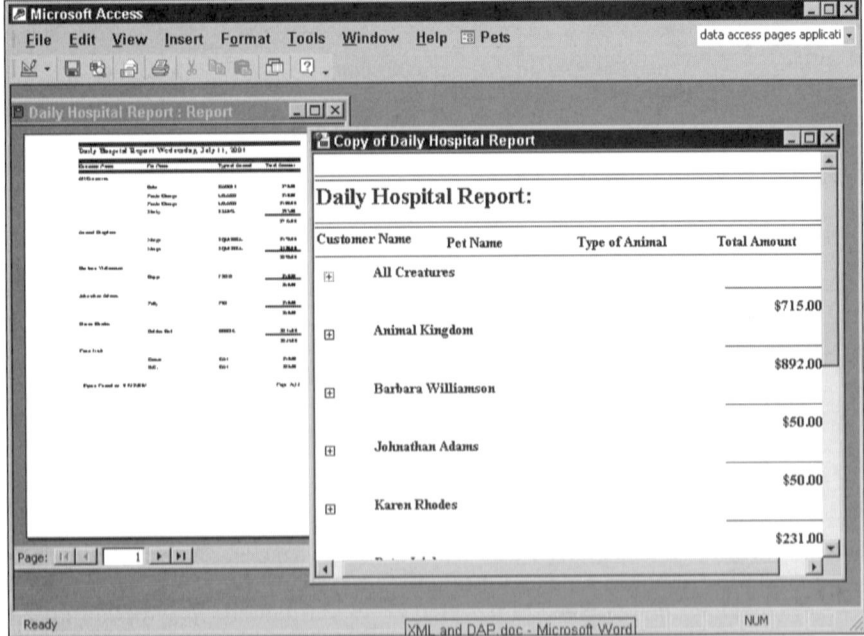

Figure 36-48: A report with grouping and the resulting data access page

Looking at the page created from the Report Daily Hospital Report, you notice that it does not display the same as the report. It has added an Expand/Collapse control to the innermost level with the pet information. It also has also added navigation bars for the second and third (inner most) levels (not shown in Figure 36-48 — you can expand the levels to see them). This makes the data access page more functional. It has also eliminated the page footer formulas for the date the report was printed on and the page numbers, as well as the formula for the final Grand Total. You can go in to Design view and modify the page to correct these problems.

You can get unexpected results when converting multiple grouped reports to data access pages. For instance, if you convert the "All Customers and Pets" report, Access creates a data access page, but not what you expected.

Figure 36-49 shows the Design mode of the Report. It has four headers (groupings): the Report Header, with no content; the Page Header, with the customer information; a Customer.Customer Number Header, with a hidden customer number; and finally the detail section, with the pet information.

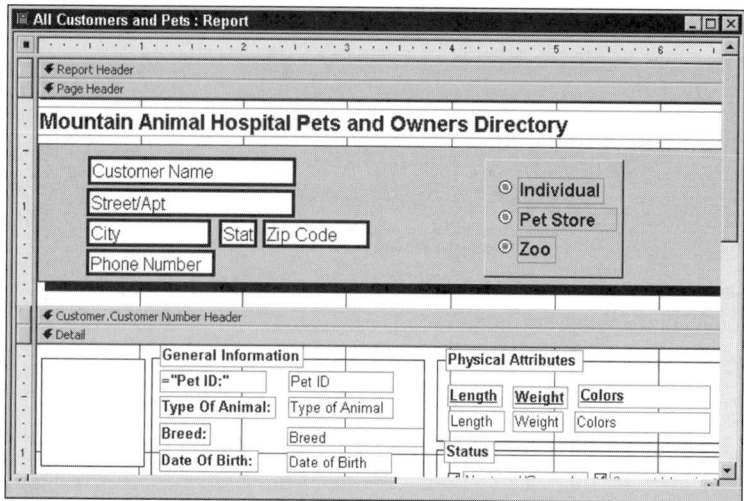

Figure 36-49: A report with four groupings

The resulting data access page has only two groupings and mistakenly places the Customer fields in the Caption section of the top-most group level. Figure 36-50 shows the page in Design view. Notice that none of the fields are linked to the text boxes in the Caption section of the Header Group Level 0.

Creating a DAP from a report with subreports

Like forms with subforms, if you convert a report with a subreport to a data access page, the subreport is not included in the page.

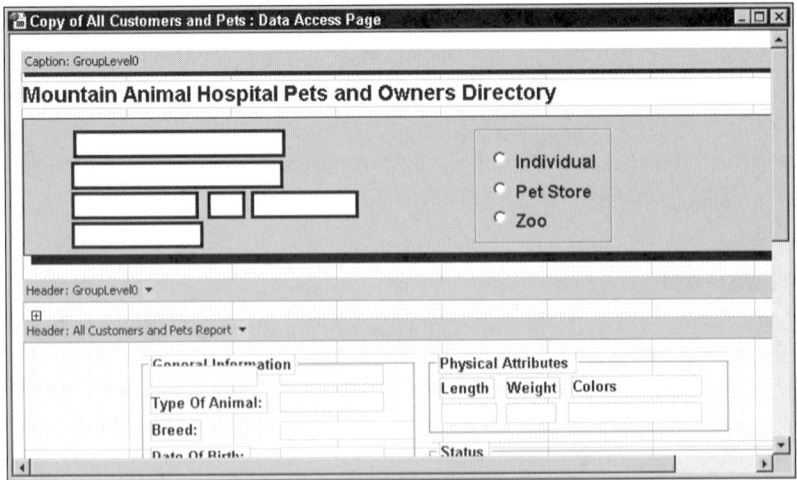

Figure 36-50: The converted data access page from the four-group report — with only two groupings

XML Data and Access

Access 2002 has added a lot more support for Extensible Markup Language (XML) data in data access pages. In version 2000, support for XML was limited to internal usage. You can now include XML in one of three ways:* Link the page to an XML data file by taking the page offline in Internet Explorer 5.x.

✦ Set Data Access Page properties inside Access to allow the page to bind to an external XML data file.

✦ Embed the XML data directly inside the page by setting page properties.

Using XML in Access 2002, data from almost any external application can be transformed for use by Access.

Using Access 2002, you can import and export XML data.

Import XML data into Access (Jet, SQL Server or SQL Server 2000 Desktop Engine — formally known as MSDE) if it was a previously generated XSD file from Access 2002. This gives you the data typing, relationships, keys, and indices.

Export Access objects (tables, queries, views, datasheets, forms, or reports) to XML data (as an XML file) and associated schema (as an XSD file). It can export to Jet, SQL Server, or SQL Server 2000 Desktop Engine databases. You can also export reports as XML/XSD with presentation, which creates the data, and XSL that formats the data, and an ASP or HTML wrapper to view the data/report in a browser capable of using XML. You can take the exported report and bind it to an SQLS2000 database and view live Access reports in the browser.

Using Extensible Stylesheet Language Transformation (XSLT) files you can even convert data into an Access data format.

Understanding XML

Recall that a data access page is a special type of Web page designed to view and work with your data that is stored in an Access database, project, or SQL Server database. These pages can also include data from other sources, including XML data files.

XML is the standards-based language protocol for describing and delivering data across the Web to a browser, just as HTML code is the standard language for creating and displaying Web pages with graphics and text in them.

HTML describes how a Web page should look; in contrast, XML defines the data and describes how the data should be structured. XML separates the data from the presentation so that the same XML data can be presented in multiple ways by using different presentation methods. XML, like HTML, uses tags and attributes. However, XML uses these tags only to delimit pieces of data, leaving the interpretation of the data up to the application that receives and reads it.

By using XML, it is possible to use and move data across the Internet or intranet between dissimilar applications and systems. The XML protocol specifies the guidelines, rules, and formal conventions to be used for designing data formats and structures. By following these recommendations, the data files produced can be easily created and read by different computer systems. XML data structures are self-describing; thus any platform that can interpret XML can use and display the data they contain.

What are XML schemas?

When working with XML you need to describe the structure of the data in a format that Web browsers and other XML-enabled programs can recognize. The *XML schema* (*.xsd) is used to create that description. The XML schema file is a formal specification of the rules for an XML document, specifying a series of element names, as well as which elements are permissible in the document and in which combinations. It is a part of the XML standard, known as the XML Schema standard.

By using a schema, you can verify that any XML document that is used to import data into or export data from Access to another format contains the defined structure and specific data requirements needed by Access. After you create a schema it can be given to your customers or other users to let them use it to structure any data they provide to you.

Using XSL to display XML data

XML uses syntax that describes the data in an XML document without describing how the data should be displayed. Extensible Stylesheet Language (XSL) is what is used to actually tell the XML-enabled program how to display the XML data. Using XSL, you can direct which data should be selected and displayed, and the order of displaying. It uses a combination of XML-like and HTML tags to create a template for creating the output.

When Access creates a data access page using the Save As option, it uses an XML schema file internally and a XSL file named ReportML2DAP.xsl to write the data access page telling the page how to display the data. The contents of that file look like Figure 36-51.

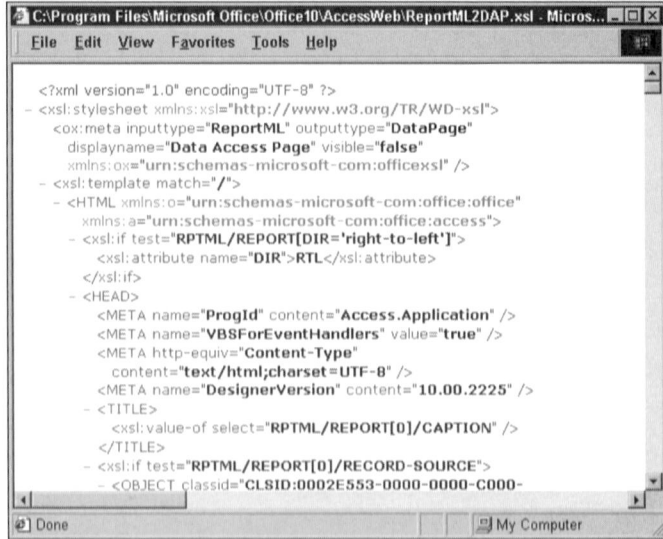

Figure 36-51: The top-most part of the ReportML2DAP.xsl file

If you open the file in Figure 36-51 and scroll through it, you see many new tags that are XML specific. After you became familiar with XML, schema and XSL files, you can modify this one to add additional functionality to the capabilities of exporting an Access object to a data access page.

Tip   XSL files do not have to be linked to XML documents for IE 5.x to display the document correctly.

Exporting to XML

Exporting database data to an XML file is a great way to move and store your information in a format that can be used across the Web. In Access 2002 you can export any of the following:

✦ Just the data from a table, query, datasheet, form, or report in a XML file.

✦ Just the schema (data structure=) of a table, query, datasheet, form, or report to an XML schema file (with the extension of XSD).

✦ Both the data and schema into both XML and XSD files.

✦ Save the structure of a table, query, datasheet, form. or report into a file that describes the presentation (*.xsl) of the structure and data.

Access will create a custom display format (*.xsl) file and can create a Web document to run in either the browser (an HTML document) or Server (an ASP formatted file).

After an XML file is created, it can be bound to an HTTP query request, an SQL Server database, or SQL Server 2000 Desktop Edition to work with live Access reports in a browser.

Exporting a table or query to XML

To export a table or query to an XML document, follow these general steps:

1. Select the table or query object name in the database container.

2. Select File ⇨ Export from the menu (or right-click and select Export . . . from the menu).

Access opens the Export Table dialog box.

3. Select XML documents in the Save as type drop-down list box.

4. Enter a new filename to save the XML document to.

5. Click the Export button.

Access opens the Export XML dialog box as seen in Figure 36-52. It has already selected to export the data and schema.

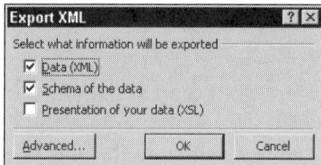

Figure 36-52: The Export XML dialog box

6. If you want to export only the data or only the schema, de-select the item that you don't want to export.

7. If you want to also have Access create an XSL file and an HTML document so that you can view the data, select the check box Presentation of your data (XSL).

8. Click OK.

Access automatically creates all specified files — XML, XSD (and if requested) XSL, and HTML.

Figure 36-53 shows the contents of the XML file created by exporting the Customer table.

Figure 36-53: The Customer.xml file viewed in IE 5.5

Exporting a form or report to XML

To export a form or report to an XML document, follow these general steps:

1. Select the table or query object name in the database container.

2. Select File ➪ Export . . . from the menu (or right-click and select Export . . . from the menu.

Access opens the Export Table dialog box.

3. Select XML documents in the Save as type drop-down list box.

4. Enter a new filename to save the XML document to.

5. Click the Export button.

Access opens the Export XML dialog box. It only has Data (XML) choice checked and a grayed out check box for Presentation of your data (XSL).

Access automatically creates both an XSL and HTML file for the form or report.

6. If you only want to export the data or want to also export the schema, make the correct adjustments.

7. Click OK.

Access creates the XML document, an XSL file, and a corresponding HTML document that can be opened in IE 5.x to look at the data and new page. Figure 36-54 shows the Customer HTML created from the XML, XDS, and XSL documents being viewed in IE5.5.

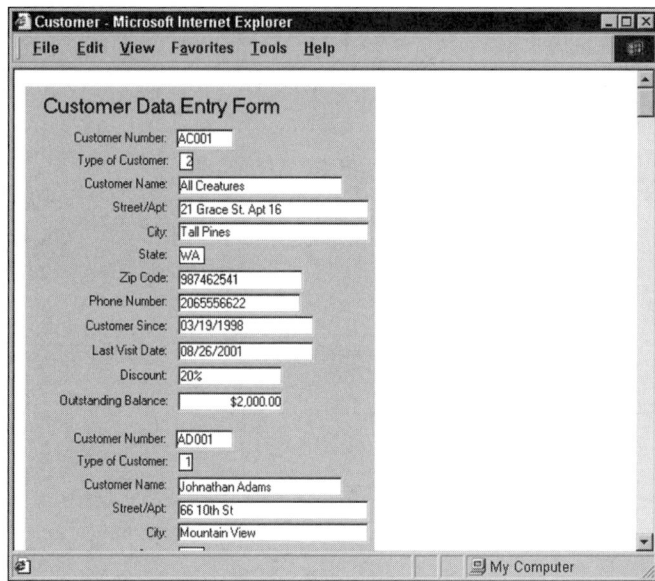

Figure 36-54: The Customer HTML document

Importing XML data

You can also import existing XML documents into Access 2002. They will be imported into an Access table. The actual data is stored in the XML file, and the schema information (structure, keys, and indices) is stored in the XSD file.

 **Caution**   Access 2002 only imports XML documents made by Access 2002.

To import the XML file named Mike's Customer, follow these steps:

1. While the database Access 2002 Data Access Pages is open, select File ⇨ Get External Data ⇨ Import from the menu.

   Access opens the Import dialog box.

2. Select XML Documents (*.xml; *.xsd) from the Files of type drop-down list box.

   Access shows all XML and XSD files.

3. Select Mike's Customer.xml and press the Import button.

   Access displays the Import XML dialog box and shows the Mike's Customer table name. Figure 36-55 shows the dialog box. If you only want to import the structure, you can click the Options button and select structure only.

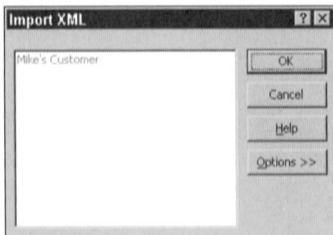

Figure 36-55: The Import XML dialog box

4. Click OK.

   Access imports the table Mike's Customer and displays an information box that tells you that it imported the file.

5. Click OK.

The new table, Mike's Customer, has been added to the database.

When Importing XML files, you can import the XML file or the XSD file. If you want to import the key or indices information (primary keys and secondary) you select the XSD file instead of the XML file.

Tip   If there is only an XSD file (no associated XML document), you can import the structure and key information, but there will be no data in the new database structure. The data is stored in the XML file.

✦   ✦   ✦

Advanced Topics in Access 2002

◆ ◆ ◆ ◆

In This Part

Chapter 37
Optimizing
Performance

Chapter 38
Securing an Access
Application

Chapter 39
Creating Help
Systems in Access
2002

Chapter 40
Using the Microsoft
Office XP Developer

Chapter 41
Integrating with
Microsoft Office XP

Chapter 42
Exploring Replication

Chapter 43
Exploring Add-Ins
and Libraries

◆ ◆ ◆ ◆

Optimizing Performance

✦ ✦ ✦ ✦

In This Chapter

Tuning your computer for maximum performance

Increasing performance dramatically by keeping your code in a compiled state

Using the Access 2002 large database file format

Using MDE databases for better performance

Adjusting the Jet registry settings

Getting the most from your tables

Tuning your queries for maximum speed

Getting the most out of your forms and reports

Increasing performance by optimizing your VBA code

Increasing the perceived speed of your application

Working with large databases

✦ ✦ ✦ ✦

This final part of the book contains advanced level material that is intended to enable you to master some diverse and important topics. The examples in each of the chapters are self-contained and use the Mountain Animal Hospital database, along with some other database files. As you become a more experienced developer, you will find these topics more and more useful. Because each of the remaining chapters deals with separate topics, you can study them in any order you prefer.

When Microsoft introduced 32-bit Access, a number of new performance concerns came part and parcel with the new features and functions. Microsoft has made a conscious effort to improve the performance of Access 2002 with improvements in compilation techniques and features such as light forms. The end result is that Microsoft has helped to ease your burden, but in no way has it completely taken it from you.

Tip   The published minimum RAM requirement for a computer to run Access 2002 on Windows 95/98 is 64MB — with an emphasis on *minimum.* On a Windows 2000 machine, the published minimum is also 64MB of RAM. If you're going to do serious development with Access 2002, you should have at least 64MB of RAM or, preferably, 128MB or more. With today's computers and memory prices, this amount of memory is a valuable investment. In fact, simply adding more memory (32MB to 128MB) will increase speed much more than changing your processor (Pentium II to Pentium III or 4) or speed, due to the fact that Access 2002 must use the hard drive as a virtual memory area if it doesn't have enough memory. Hard drives are slow and big hard drives are even slower — regardless of the processor speed.

Understanding Module Load on Demand

One of the great features of Visual Basic for Applications (the core language that replaced Access Basic in earlier versions of Microsoft Access) is the *load on demand* functionality of VBA. Using load on demand, Access loads code modules only as they are needed or referenced. In previous versions of Access, load on demand of modules wasn't fully realized because loading a module loaded the entire module's potential call tree. With Access 2002, the load on demand feature truly does help reduce the amount of RAM needed and helps your program run faster.

Tip   Because Access doesn't unload code after it has been loaded into memory, you should periodically close your application while you develop. When developing, you have a tendency to open and work with many different procedures in many different modules. These modules stay in memory until you close Access.

Organizing your modules

You should be aware that when any procedure or variable is referenced in your application, the entire module that contains the procedure or variable is loaded into memory. To minimize the number of modules loaded into memory, you need to organize your procedures and variables into logical modules. For example, it's a good idea to place all Global variables in the same module. If only one Global variable is declared in a module, the entire module is loaded into memory. By the same token, you should put only procedures that are always used by your application (such as start-up procedures) into the module containing the Global variables.

Access 2002 prunes the call tree

The *call tree* for a procedure is any additional functions or procedures that the current procedure (or function) has referenced within it, as well as those referenced by the newly loaded functions and procedures, and so forth. Because a procedure may reference numerous additional functions/procedures (stored in different modules) based on the action taken by the procedure, this loading of all potentially called functions/procedures takes a lot of time and memory.

Remember that when a procedure or function is called, the entire module in which that function is stored is placed in memory.

Therefore, a potential call tree consists of all the procedures that *could* be called by the current procedure that you are calling. In addition, all the procedures that could be called from *those* procedures and so forth are also part of the potential call tree. For example:

1. If you call Procedure A, the entire module containing Procedure A is loaded.

2. Modules containing variable declarations used by Procedure A are loaded.

3. Procedure A has lines of code that call Procedures B and C — the modules containing Procedure B and Procedure C are loaded. (Even if the call statements are in conditional loops and are never executed, they are still loaded because *potentially* they could be called.)

4. Any procedures that could be called by Procedure B and Procedure C are loaded, as well as the entire modules containing those potential procedures.

5. And so on and so on and. . . .

Fortunately for all Access developers, this complete loading of a potential call tree has been addressed in Access 2002. Access 2002 automatically compiles modules on demand, rather than the entire potential call tree. However, you can turn this feature off, thus making Access 2002 compile all modules at one time. Do this in the Visual Basic for Applications program rather than in Access. Access 2002 links directly to VBA's development environment for working with Visual Basic code. To check the status of the Compile on Demand option, follow these steps:

1. Select the Modules object type from the Object Bar of the database.

2. Click the NEW object button to activate the Visual Basic Development Environment.

3. Select Tools ⇨ Options. The Options dialog box appears.

4. Select the General tab.

5. Verify that the Compile on Demand check box, located on the bottom right side of the dialog box, is checked. If it's not, select it. Figure 37-1 shows the dialog box with the option selected.

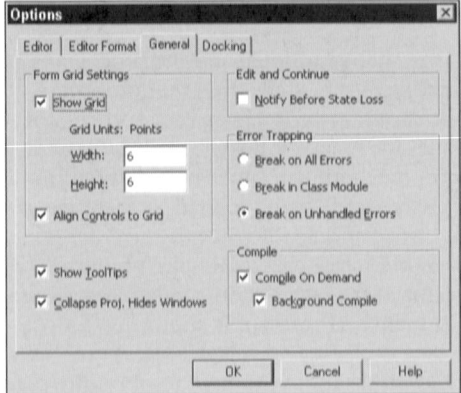

Figure 37-1: For maximum performance, leave the Compile on Demand check box selected.

6. Click OK.

7. Select File ➪ Close and Return to Microsoft Access (Alt + Q) or click the Access button (first button on toolbar) if you want to return to Access and leave the VBA window open.

Tip   Unless you have a specific reason to do so, never deselect the Compile on Demand option. When you deselect this option, you can conceivably cause *all* of the modules in a database to load and compile, simply by calling just one procedure.

With the Compile on Demand option selected, Access 2002 won't load the entire call tree of a module, but will load a portion of the call tree of the executed procedure. For example, if you call procedure A in module A, any modules that contain procedures referenced in procedure A are loaded and compiled. However, Access 2002 doesn't take into consideration procedures that may be called from other procedures in module A, and it doesn't look at the potential call tree of the modules loaded because one of their procedures is referenced in procedure A. Because Access 2002 only loads modules one-deep from the executed procedure's immediate call tree — and *not* the module's call tree — your applications should load and execute many times faster than they did in previous versions.

Even though Access 2002 has made a significant improvement in the way modules are loaded and compiled, you can still do a number of things to reduce the number of modules loaded and compiled. For example, you should never place infrequently called procedures in a module with procedures that are called often. At times, this may make your modules less logical and harder to conceptualize. For example, you may have a dozen functions that perform various manipulations to contact information in your application. Ordinarily, you may make one module called "mdlContacts" and place all the contact-related procedures and variables into this one module. Because Access loads the entire module when one procedure or variable in it is called, you may want to separate the contact-related procedures into separate modules (one for procedures that are commonly used and one for procedures that are rarely used).

Tip   You need to be aware at all times that all modules having procedures referenced in a procedure of a different module are loaded when that procedure is called. In your application, if any of your common procedures reference a procedure that isn't commonly used, you will want to place the uncommon procedure in the same module with the common procedures to prevent a different module (containing the uncommon procedures) from being loaded and compiled. You may even decide to use more than two modules if you have very large amounts of code in multiple procedures that are rarely called. Although breaking related procedures into separate modules may make your code a little harder to understand, it can greatly improve the performance of your application.

To fully take advantage of Compile on Demand, you have to carefully plan your procedure placement. Third-party tools, such as *Total Access Analyzer* from FMS, print a complete module reference report. This can be invaluable for visualizing where all of the potential calls for various procedures are located.

Using the Access 2002 Database File Format

Access 2002 supports several file formats including Access 2002, 2000, and 97. The new Access 2002 file format exists (according to Microsoft literature) to ensure upward compatibility to future versions of Microsoft Access. Some Microsoft literature has claimed that the Access 2002 file format enhanced performance for large database files. We have been unable to verify this on large data databases or large program files, but we do know that Access 2002 is significantly faster than Access 2000 given the proper amount of memory.

You can open and even run Access 97 database files, but you can't make any design changes. You can open Access 2000 database files and make any desired changes to them. However, if you use features specific to Access 2002, a user using Access 2000 won't be able to use those features and may have problems with compiling or running the application.

If you create a new database in Access 2002, the default new database file format is the Access 2000 file format. You can convert an Access 97 or Access 2000 database file to an Access 2002 database file format by using the Tools ➪ Database Utilities ➪ Convert Database ➪ To Access 2002 File Format.

 **Tip**   You can change the default file format for new files by using the Tools ➪ Options ➪ Advanced selection and selecting Access 2002 from the combo box provided.

The Access 2002 file format should be used in an Access 2002-only environment where all users are using Access 2002. Besides complete compatibility with all Access 2002 features, you may experience some performance advantages when using the Access 2002 file format with larger databases. However, in a mixed environment of Access 2000 and Access 2002 users, you should stay with the Access 2000 file format for compatibility with Access 2000 users. An Access 2002 program can attach to Access 97 data files, but if you are trying to accommodate Access 97 users, you should simply stay with Access 97.

Distributing .MDE Files

One way to ensure that your application's code is always compiled is to distribute your database as an .MDE file. When you save your database as an .MDE file, Access compiles all code modules (including form modules), removes all editable source code, and compacts the database. The new .MDE file contains no source code but continues to work because it does contain a compiled copy of all of your code. Not only is this a great way to secure your source code, it also allows you to distribute databases that are smaller (because they contain no source code) and always keep their modules in a compiled state. Because the code is always in a compiled state, less memory is used by the application, and you suffer no performance penalty for code being compiled at run time.

In addition to not being able to view existing code because it is all compiled, the following restrictions apply:

✦ You can't view, modify, or create forms, reports, or modules in Design view.

✦ You can't add, delete, or change references to object libraries or databases.

✦ You can't change your database's VBA project name by using the Options dialog box.

✦ You can't import or export forms, reports, or modules. Note, however, that tables, queries, and macros can be imported from or exported to non-MDE databases.

Tip

If you want to create a demo of your application — and if you don't want the users to be able to see your code or form and report designs — you should create an .MDE file. Because the designs of your forms, reports, and all code modules are simply not present (they are stored in a compiled version only), you don't have to worry about someone stealing your work. An .MDE file is also good for distributing your work in environments where you don't want the user to change your designs.

Because of these restrictions, it may not be possible to distribute your application as an .MDE file. For example, if your application creates forms at run time, you would not be able to distribute the database as an .MDE file.

Caution

You have no way to convert an .MDE file into a normal database file. Therefore, always save and keep a copy of the original database! When you need to make changes to the application, you must open the normal database and then create a new .MDE file before distribution. If you delete your original database, you will be unable to access any of your objects in Design view.

Note

Some prerequisites must be met before a database can be saved as an .MDE file. First, if security is in use, the user creating the .MDE file must have all applicable rights to the database. In addition, if the database is replicated, you must remove all replication system tables and properties before saving the .MDE file. Finally, you must save all databases or add-ins in the chain of references as .MDE files or your database will be unable to use them.

To create an .MDE file:

1. Close the database if it's currently open. If you don't close the current database, Access will attempt to close it for you, prompting you to save changes where applicable. When working with a shared database, all users must close the database; Access needs exclusive rights to work with the database.

2. Select Tools ➪ Database Utilities and then click Make MDE File (see Figure 37-2).

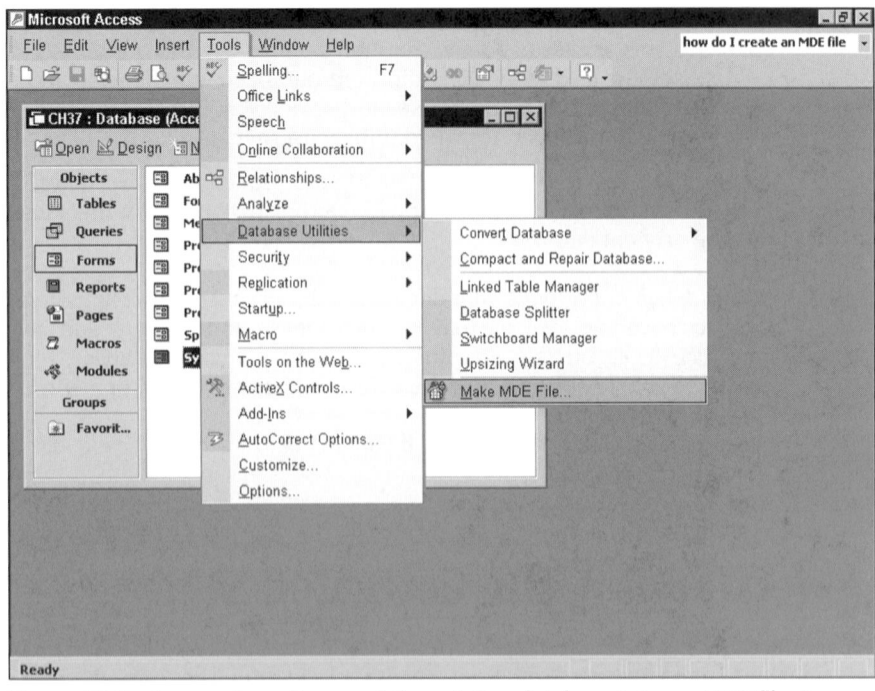

Figure 37-2: Access doesn't convert the existing database into an .MDE file; it creates a new .MDE file for the database.

3. In the Database To Save As MDE dialog box, specify the database that you want to save as an .MDE file, and click Make MDE (see Figure 37-3).

Figure 37-3: If you had a database open at the time you selected Make MDE File, you won't see this form.

If you had a database open when you selected Make MDE File, this step is skipped and Access assumes that you want to use the previously opened database. If you want to use a different database, you need to stop creating the .MDE file, close the database, and select Make MDE File again. At that time, you will be asked for the database to save as an .MDE file.

4. In the Database to Save as MDE dialog box, specify a name, drive, and folder for the database. Don't attempt to save the .MDE file with the same filename as the original database.

Caution Don't delete or overwrite your original database! As stated previously, you have no way to convert an .MDE file to a normal database, and you can't edit any objects in an .MDE file. If you delete or otherwise lose your original database, you will never again be able to access any of the objects in the design environment.

Caution You can only create an .MDE file if you first convert the database into the Access 2002 database format.

Understanding the Compiled State

Understanding how Access performs Compile on Demand is critical to achieving maximum performance from your Access application. However, it is also paramount that you understand what compilation is and what it means for an application to be in a compiled state. Access has two types of code — code that you write and code that Access can understand and execute. Before a procedure of VBA code that you have written can be executed, the code must be run through a compiler to generate code in a form that Access can understand — compiled code. Access lacks a true compiler and instead uses partially compiled code and an interpreter. A true compiler converts source code to machine-level instructions, which are executed by your computer's CPU. Access converts your source code to an intermediate state that it can rapidly interpret and execute. The code in the converted form is known as *compiled code*, or as being in a *compiled state*.

If a procedure is called that isn't in a compiled state, the procedure must first be compiled and then the compiled code is passed to the interpreter for execution. In reality, as previously stated, this doesn't happen at the procedure level, but at the module level; when you call a procedure, the module containing the procedure and all modules that have procedures referenced in the called procedure are loaded and compiled. You can manually compile your code, or you can let Access compile it for you on the fly. It takes time to compile the code, however, so the performance of your application will suffer if you let Access compile it on the fly.

In addition to the time required for Access to compile your code at run time, uncompiled programs use considerably more memory than compiled code. When your application is completely compiled, only the compiled code is loaded into memory when a procedure is called. If you run an application that is in a decompiled state, Access loads the decompiled code and generates the compiled code as needed (explained previously). Access does not unload the decompiled code as it compiles, so you are left with two versions of the same code in memory.

There is one drawback to compiled applications: They use more hard drive space than their decompiled versions. This is because both the compiled and decompiled versions of the code are stored on the hard drive.

Hard drive space shouldn't often become a problem, but if you have an application with an enormous amount of code, you can save hard drive space by keeping it in a decompiled state. Remember that a trade-off is made between hard drive space used and the performance of your database. Most often, when given the choice, a user would rather give up a few megabytes of hard drive space in exchange for faster applications.

Tip You may use this space-saving technique to your advantage if you need to distribute a large application and your recipients have a full development version of Access. By distributing the uncompiled versions, you will need much less hard drive space to distribute the application, and the end users can compile it again at their location. If you are going to do this, you should put the entire application into a decompiled state. The topic of fully decompiling an application is discussed later in this chapter.

Putting your applications code into a compiled state

You have only one way to put your entire application into a compiled state: Use the Compile [mdb name] menu item from the Debug menu on the Modules toolbar in the Visual Basic for Applications development window (see Figure 37-4). To access the Debug menu, you must have a module open. Generally, you should always use the Compile [mdb name] command to ensure that all of the code is saved in a compiled state. Complex applications can take a long time to compile, and, in general, you should only perform a Compile [mdb name] before you distribute your application or before performing benchmark tests.

Note When you use the Compile option in the Debug menu you actually see the name of your project. This is the name that you used to save your database file the first time that it was created or saved. If you later rename the database file, the project name doesn't change. You can change it by using the Tools menu in the module window and selecting the current project name with the word *Properties* beside it.

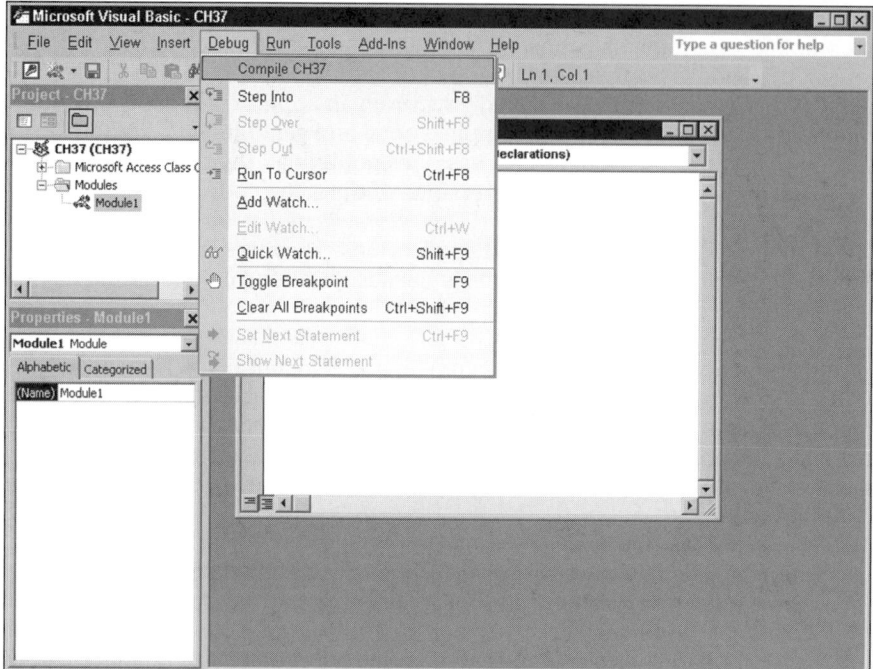

Figure 37-4: Compile [mdb name] (in this example, Ch37) is the only way to fully compile your application.

Access 2002 has an option for compiling code to the Visual Basic for Applications program—Background Compile. Figure 37-1 shows this option under Compile on Demand; the default value for this option is True (selected). This option tells Access to compile code in background rather than to compile it all at one time.

Tip   It is especially important to close your application after performing a Compile [mdb name]. To compile all of your modules, Access needs to load every single one of them into memory. All of this code stays in memory until you close down Access.

Losing the compiled state

One of the greatest roadblocks to increasing the performance of Access applications was the fact that an application could be uncompiled very easily. When the Access application was in an uncompiled state, Access had to constantly compile code as it was called. In fact, losing the compiled state was so easy to do in previous versions of Access that it would often happen without developers even realizing that they had done it.

In Access 2002, only portions of code affected by certain changes are put into an uncompiled state—not the entire application. By itself, this is a tremendous improvement over previous versions of Access.

The following actions will cause portions of your code to be uncompiled:

✦ Modifying a form, report, control, or module. (If you don't save the modified object, your application is preserved in its previous state.)

✦ Adding a new form, report, control, or module (includes adding new code behind a form).

✦ Deleting or renaming a form, report, control, or module.

✦ Adding or removing a reference to an object library or database by using the References command on the Tools menu.

Okay, so you think that you have a handle on code that loses its compiled state? Well, here are a couple of "gotchas" that you need to consider:

✦ If you modify objects like reports or forms at run time through VBA code, portions of your application are put into an uncompiled state when the objects are modified. (Wizards often do this.)

✦ If your application creates objects like reports or forms on the fly, then portions of your application are put into an uncompiled state when the objects are created. (Wizards often do this as well.)

Another serious flaw of Access was that an application's entire compiled state was tied to the filename of the database. This feature meant that your entire application would lose its compiled state, and all code would have to be compiled at the time that it was called if you renamed your database, compacted your database into a database of a different name, or copied your database to a database with a different name.

Fortunately, Access 97 fixed this serious problem, and it doesn't even exist in Access 2002. The compiled state of an application is still tied to its name, but now it is tied to its project name rather than to its filename.

Caution   When you change a project name (but not the filename), the entire application loses its compiled state. Because of this, you should change the project name only if absolutely necessary, and you should perform a Compile [mdb name] immediately after changing the project name.

Distributing applications in a compiled or uncompiled state

When distributing your Access application, you need to take into consideration a couple of issues concerning compilation.

Distributing source code for your application

First and foremost, if you distribute source code and allow your users access to modify or add objects, you must make them completely aware of the compilation issues. If your users don't fully comprehend what is happening with your application's compiled state, then you can be sure that you will receive phone calls about how your program seems to be getting slower the more that users make changes to objects.

Putting an application in an uncompiled state

If your application is the type that will be constantly changing its compiled state (due to creating forms and reports dynamically), or if end users will be making modifications to the application's objects often, or if distributed file size is an issue, then you may want to consider distributing the database in a fully uncompiled state.

To put your entire application into an uncompiled state:

1. Create a new database.
2. Import all of your application objects into the new database.
3. Compact the new database.

Cross-Reference   Later in this chapter, you will also learn how to manually decompile the project. This has more benefits than simply letting the project become partially or completely uncompiled.

Organizing commonly used code that is never modified into a library

After your application is finished and ready for distribution, you may want to consider placing all commonly used code that will never be modified by an end user into a library database. A *library database* is an external database that your application database can reference and access. You will incur slight overhead by calling code from the library rather than by accessing it directly in the parent application, but the benefit is that the library code will never be put into a decompiled state— even if your application creates or modifies objects on the fly or if your users add new or modify existing objects. This technique can greatly increase an application's performance and keep the performance relatively consistent over time.

The first step for referencing procedures in an external database is to create the external database with all its modules, just as you would do in an ordinary Access database.

Caution   Any procedures that you declare as "Private" are not made available to the calling application, so plan carefully what you want and don't want to expose to other databases.

After you have created the database and its modules, you must create a reference to that database in your application database (which is the database that your users will run). To create a reference, first open any module in your application database in Design view. When you have a module in Design view, a new command — References — is available from the Tools menu (see Figure 37-5). Select Tools ⇨ References to access the References dialog box (see Figure 37-6).

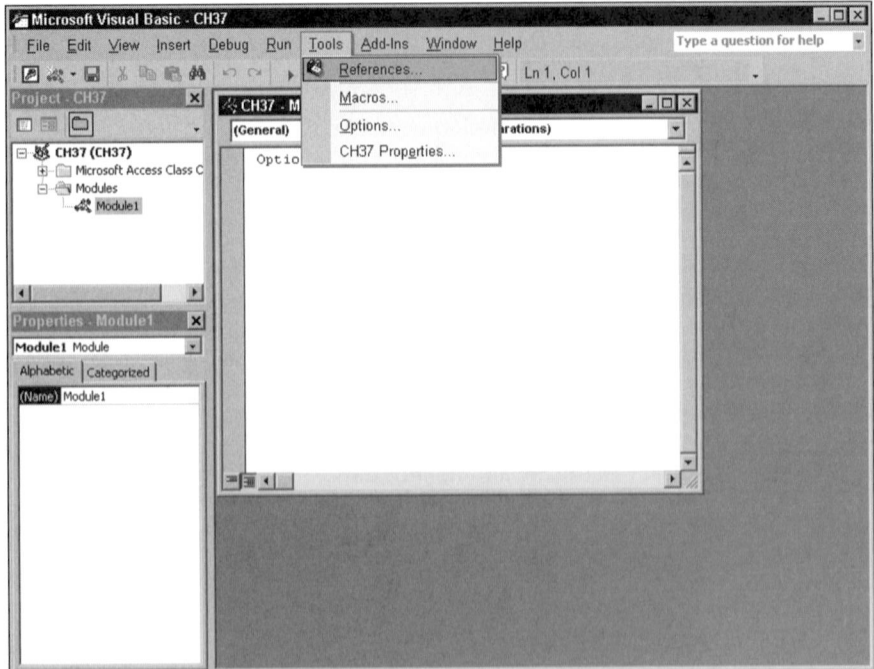

Figure 37-5: The References option only appears on the Tools menu when you have a module open and selected in Design view.

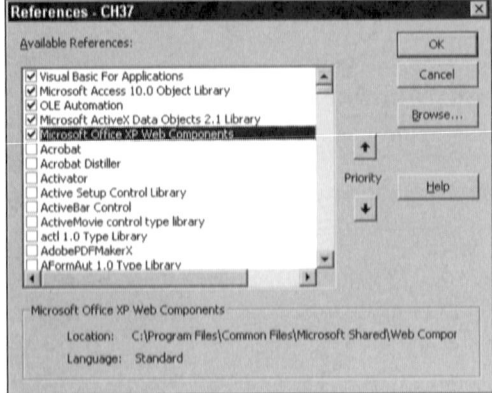

Figure 37-6: The References dialog box is where you resolve references to OLE automation servers and Access library databases.

In the References dialog box, you specify all the references that your application needs for using OLE automation or for using other Access databases as library databases. When making a reference to another Access database, as opposed to an OLE server created with another development tool like Visual Basic, you will probably need to browse for the database. Use the Browse dialog box as if you were going to open the external database. After you have selected the external Access database, it shows up in the References dialog box with a check mark to indicate that it is referenced.

To remove a reference, access the References dialog box again and deselect the referenced item by clicking its check box. After you have made all the references that you need to make, click OK.

After a database is referenced, you can call the procedures in the referenced database as if they existed in your application database. No matter what happens in your application database to cause code to decompile, the referenced database always stays in a compiled state unless it is opened and modified directly by using Access.

To reference an external Access database to call its procedures, follow these steps:

1. Create the library database and its modules.

2. Open the database in which you want to use the external procedures.

3. Open any module in Design view.

4. Select Tools ⇨ References.

5. Select the OLE server that you want to register. If it is an Access database, then you will probably have to use the Browse feature to locate the database.

Tip　If your application uses *add-in databases* (a special type of library database), then you should open the add-in database for read-only access. Opening add-ins for read-only access increases performance because Jet doesn't have to maintain locking information for the add-in database in an .LDB file.

Creating a library reference for distributed applications

If you are distributing your application, references stay intact only if the calling database and the library database are in the same or relative path. For example, if the main database is in C:\myapp on your machine, and if the library database is in C:\myapp\library, then the reference remains intact if the library database is located in the same relative path, such as in C:\newdir for the main database and C:\newdir\library for the library database. If the relative path won't remain consistent upon distribution, then your application's users must add the reference manually or you must create the reference by using VBA code.

The following procedure creates a reference to the file whose name is passed to it. For this function to work, the full filename with path must be passed:

```
bResult = CreateReference("c:\My Documents\MyLib.mdb").
```

The function is:

```
Public Function CreateReference(szFileName As String) As
Boolean
    On Error GoTo CreateReferenceError
    Dim ref As Reference
Set ref = References.AddFromFile(szFileName)
    CreateReference = True
Exit Function
CreateReferenceError:
    MsgBox Err & ": " & Err.Description
    CreateReference = False
    Exit Function
End Function
```

Tip
You can verify that a reference is set by using the `ReferenceFromFile` function. To verify a reference, pass the function, the full path and the filename, like this:

```
bResult =
ReferenceFromFile("C:\Windows\System\mscal.ocx").
```

The function returns True if the reference is valid, False if it isn't.

With the References collection, the primary concern of using and distributing libraries — losing references upon distribution — is now gone. However, library databases still have one major drawback: Access doesn't support circular references. This means that the code in your library databases can't reference variables or call procedures that exist in your parent database.

Whether you distribute your application as one database or as a primary database that uses library databases, if your applications are static (meaning that they don't allow modification of objects by end users or wizards, and don't perform object modifications on themselves), then you should always distribute the databases in a fully compiled state so that your users experience the highest level of performance possible.

Improving Absolute Speed

When discussing an application's performance, the word *performance* is usually synonymous with speed. You will find two types of speed in software development — absolute and perceived. *Absolute speed* refers to the actual speed at which your application performs a function, such as how long it takes to run a certain query. *Perceived speed* is the phenomenon of an end user actually perceiving one application to be faster than another application, even though it may indeed be slower. This phenomenon of perceived speed is often a direct result of visual feedback provided to the user while the application is performing a task. Absolute speed items can be measured in units of time; perceived speed can't be measured in this manner.

Of course, some of the most important items for increasing actual speed are the following:

✦ Keeping your application in a compiled state

✦ Organizing your procedures into "smart" modules

✦ Opening databases exclusively

✦ Compacting your databases regularly

You should always open a database exclusively in a single-user environment. If your application is a stand-alone application (meaning that nothing is shared over a network), then opening the database in exclusive mode can really boost performance. If your application is run on a network and shared by multiple users, then you won't be able to open the database exclusively. (Actually, the first user can open it exclusively, but if they do, no other user can access the database until the first user closes it.) The preferred method for running an application in a network environment is to run Access and the main code .MDB file locally, and then link to a shared database containing the data on the server. If your application is used in this manner, you can open and run the code database exclusively, but you can't use exclusive links to the shared data.

To open a database exclusively in Access 2002, select the pull-down Open button and select Open Exclusive in the Open Database dialog box (see Figure 37-7).

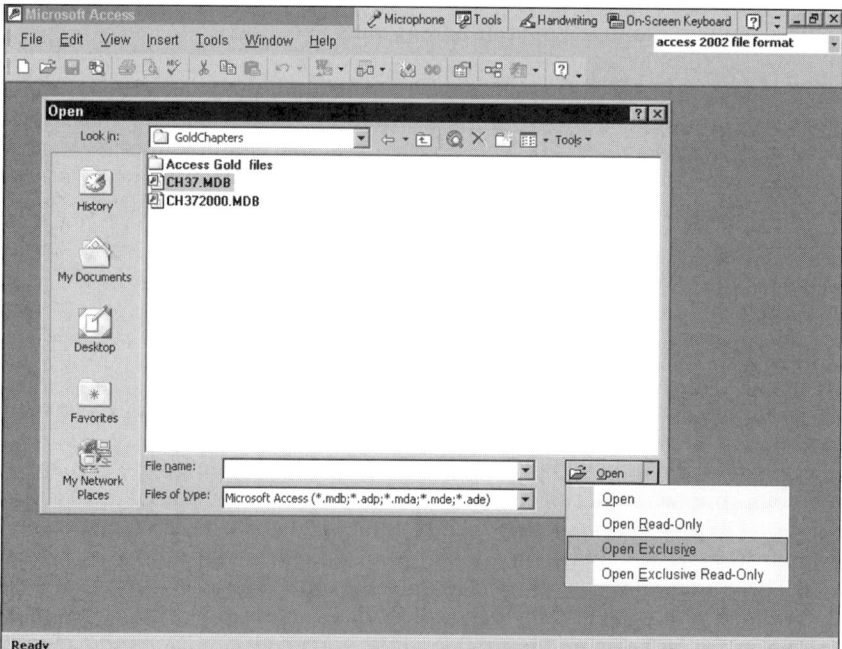

Figure 37-7: Selecting the Open Exclusive button on the pull-down Open button to open a database in a single-user environment to increase the performance of the database.

Tip You can set the default open mode for a database on the Advanced tab of the Options dialog box to Exclusive. The default open mode is Shared.

Another often-overlooked way of maximizing your database's performance is to compact your database regularly. When records are deleted from a database, the hard drive space that held the deleted data is not recovered until a compact is performed. In addition, a database becomes fragmented as data is modified in the database. Compacting a database defragments the database and recovers used hard drive space.

All of the preceding methods are excellent (and necessary) ways to help keep your applications running at their optimum performance level, but these are not the only tasks that you can perform in order to increase the absolute speed of your application. Almost every area of development, from forms to modules, can be optimized to give your application maximum absolute speed.

If you use Jet as your data access engine, an Access application can only run so fast. With Jet, each time you open a table, run a query, or perform an operation on data, all the data referenced by the process or query must be moved from the data database (assuming that you have split your program and data database files) to the computer that's running the program. This means that you may be moving a lot of data across your network. This is simply not fast. An Access project that's using the Microsoft Desktop Engine (SQL Server 2000) can use stored procedures to minimize network traffic and can drastically speed up applications with large data databases. If you are working with large amounts of data, you should strongly consider writing the application using SQL Server as your back-end database file.

Tuning your system

One important aspect of performance has nothing to do with the actual application design; that is, the computer on which the application is running. Even though it's impossible to account for all the various configurations your clients may have, you can do some things for your computer and recommend that end users do for theirs:

✦ Equip the computer with as much RAM as possible. This step often becomes an issue of dollars. However, RAM prices continue to decrease, and adding to a computer's RAM is one of the most effective methods that you can employ to increase the speed of Access.

✦ Make the WinCacheSize parameter for SmartDrive as small as possible, and disable SmartDrive completely on computers with small amounts of memory. You need to determine the size to set this at, based on your system and its memory configuration. Please consult your Windows manuals for more information on SmartDrive.

✦ Don't use wallpaper. Removing a standard Windows wallpaper background can free up anywhere from 25K to 250K of RAM, and removing complicated bitmaps or high-color bitmaps can free up even more space.

✦ Close all applications that aren't being used. Windows makes it very handy to keep as many applications loaded as you want — in the odd chance that you may need to use one of them. Although Windows 98, Windows ME, and Windows 2000 are pretty good at handling memory for multiple open applications, each running application still uses RAM. On machines with little RAM, unnecessary open applications can significantly degrade performance.

✦ Make sure that your Windows swap file is on a fast drive with plenty of free space. If possible, you should also set the minimum hard drive space available for virtual memory to at least 25MB of RAM and make it a permanent swap file.

✦ Defragment your hard drive often. Defragmenting a hard drive allows data to be retrieved from the drive in larger sections, thus causing fewer direct reads and less repositioning of the read heads.

Getting the most from your tables

In addition to reviewing all of the technical issues discussed in the preceding sections, it is advantageous to get back to the basics when designing your applications. Tools like Access enable novices to create relational databases quickly and easily, but they don't teach good database design techniques in the process. An exception to this statement is the Table Analyzer Wizard. Even though the Table Analyzer Wizard offers suggestions that are often helpful in learning good design technique, its recommendations should *never* be taken as gospel. The Table Analyzer has proven to be wrong on many occasions.

Entire volumes of text have been devoted to the subject of database theory. Teaching database theory is certainly beyond the scope of this chapter (or even this book). However, you should be familiar with many basics of good database design.

Creating efficient indexes

Indexes help Access find and sort records faster and more efficiently. Think of these indexes as if they were book indexes. To find data, Access looks up the location of the data in the index and then retrieves the data from its location. You can create indexes based on a single field or based on multiple fields. Multiple-field indexes enable you to distinguish between records in which the first field may have the same value. If they are defined properly, multiple-field indexes can be used by Microsoft's Rushmore query optimization, which is the technology that Jet uses to optimize the speed at which queries execute, based on the search and sort fields of the queries and indexes of the tables included in the queries, in order to greatly speed queries.

Deciding which fields to index

People new to database development typically make two mistakes: First, not using indexes and, second, using too many indexes (usually putting them on every field in a table). Both of these mistakes are serious — sometimes a table with indexes on every field may give *slower* performance than a table with no indexes. Why? When a record is saved, Access must also save an index entry for each defined index. This can take time and use a considerable amount of hard drive space. The time used is usually unnoticed in the case of a few indexes, but many indexes can require a huge amount of time for record saves and updates. In addition, indexes can slow some action queries (such as append queries) when the indexes for many fields need to be updated while performing the query's operations. Figure 37-8 shows the index property sheet for a sample Customer table.

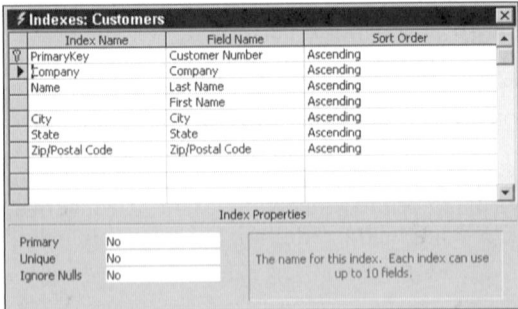

Figure 37-8: Note that common search fields like City and State are indexed.

When you create a primary key for a table, the field (or fields) used to define the key is automatically indexed, and you can index any field unless the field's data type is Memo or OLE Object. You should consider indexing a field if all of the following factors apply:

- ✦ The field's data type is Text, Number, Currency, or Date/Time.
- ✦ You anticipate searching for values stored in the field.
- ✦ You anticipate sorting records based on the values in the field.
- ✦ You will join the field to fields in other tables in queries.
- ✦ You anticipate storing many different values in the field. (If many of the values in the field are the same, the index may not significantly speed up searches or sorting.)

When defining an index, you have the option of creating an ascending (the default) or a descending index.

Tip

Jet can use a descending index when optimizing queries only when the equal sign (=) operator is used. If you use an operator other than the equal sign, such as <, >, <=, or >=, Jet can't use the descending index. If you plan on using operators other than an equal sign on an index, you should define the index as an ascending index.

Using multiple-field indexes

If you often search or sort by two or more fields at the same time, you can create an index for that combination of fields. For example, if you often set criteria for LastName and FirstName fields in the same query, it makes sense to create a multiple-field index on both fields.

When you sort a table by a multiple-field index, Access first sorts by the first field defined for the index. If the first field contains records with duplicate values, Access then sorts by the second field defined for the index, and so on. This creates a drill-down effect. For a multiple-field index to work, a search criterion *must* be defined for the first field in the index, but not for additional fields in the index. In the preceding example, if you wanted to search for someone with the first name *Robert*, but you didn't specify a last name to use in the search, the second field in the index wouldn't be used. If you need to perform searches on the second field in a multiple-field index, but are not always specifying criteria for the first field in the index, then you should create an index for the second field in addition to the multiple-field index.

Continuing with the LastName, FirstName index, if you wanted to search for the first name *John*, the multiple-field index wouldn't be used because you would be attempting to search only on the second field in the index.

Getting the most from your queries

The performance problems of many Access applications result from the design of their queries. Database applications are all about looking at and working with data, and queries are the heart of determining what data to look at or work with. Queries are used to bind forms and reports, fill list boxes and combo boxes, make new tables, and many other functions within an Access application. Because they are so widely used, it is extremely important to optimize your queries. A query that is properly designed can provide results minutes to hours faster than a poorly designed query that returns the same result set. Consider the following:

✦ When designing queries and tables, you should create indexes for all fields that are used in sorts, joins, and criteria fields. Indexes enable Jet to quickly sort and search through your database.

Tip

Sorting and searching is much faster if the indexes are unique rather than nonunique. Also, if you are using conditions in your queries, you will find that queries can run faster if the index is based on ascending order (as opposed to reverse, z to a, or descending order).

✦ When possible, use a primary key in place of a regular index when creating joins. Primary keys don't allow nulls and give the Rushmore query optimizer more ways to use the joins.

✦ Limit the columns of data returned in a select query to only those you need. If you don't need the information from a field, don't return it in the query. Queries run much faster when they must return less information.

If you need to use a field for a query condition *and* if it isn't necessary to display the field in the results table, deselect the view check box to suppress displaying the field and its contents.

✦ When you need to return a count of the records returned by an SQL statement, use Count(*) instead of Count([FieldName]) because Count(*) is considerably faster. Count(*) counts records that contain null fields; Count([FieldName]) checks for nulls and disqualifies them from being counted. If you specify a field name instead of using the asterisk, Count doesn't count records that have a null in the specified field.

You may also replace `FieldName` with an expression, but this slows down the function even further.

✦ Avoid using calculated fields in nested queries. A calculated field in a subordinate query considerably slows down the top-level query. You should use only calculated fields in top-level queries, and even then, only when necessary.

✦ When you need to group records by the values of a field used in a join, specify the Group By for the field that is in the same table that you are totaling. You can drag the joined field from either table, but using Group By on the field from the table that you are totaling yields faster results.

✦ Domain Aggregate functions, such as DLookup or DCount, that are used as expressions in queries slow down the queries considerably. Instead, you should add the table to the query or use a subquery to return the information that you need.

✦ As with VBA code modules, queries are compiled. To compile a query, Jet's Rushmore query optimizer evaluates the query to determine the fastest way to execute the query. If a query is saved in a compiled state, it runs at its fastest speed the first time that you execute it. If it isn't compiled, it takes longer the first time that it executes because it must be compiled, but it then runs faster in succeeding executions. To compile a query, run the query by opening it in Datasheet view and then close the query without saving it. If you make changes to the query definition, run the query again after saving your changes and then close it without saving it.

✦ If you really want to squeeze the most out of your queries, you should experiment by creating your queries in different ways (such as specifying different types of joins). You will be surprised at the varying results.

Getting the most from your forms and reports

Forms and reports can slow an application by taking a long time to load or process information. You can perform a number of tasks in order to increase the performance of forms and reports.

Minimizing form and report complexity and size

One of the key elements to achieving better performance from your forms and reports is reducing their complexity and size. To reduce a form's or report's complexity and size:

✦ Minimize the number of objects on a form or report. The fewer objects used, the less resources needed to display and process the form or report.

✦ Reduce the use of subforms. When a subform is loaded, two forms are in memory—the parent form and the subform. Use a list box or a combo box in place of a subform whenever possible.

✦ Use labels instead of text boxes for hidden fields because text boxes use more resources than labels. Hidden fields are often used as an alternative to creating variables to store information.

Tip
You can't write a value directly to a label like you can to a text box, but you can write to the label's caption property like this: `Label1.Caption = "MyValue"`.

✦ Move some code from a form's module into a standard module. This enables the form to load faster because the code doesn't need to be loaded into memory. If the procedures that you move to a normal module are referenced by any procedures executed upon loading a form (such as in the form load event), then moving the procedures won't help because they are loaded anyway as part of the potential call tree of the executed procedure.

✦ Don't overlap controls on a form or report.

✦ Place related groups of controls on form pages. If only one page is shown at a time, Access doesn't need to generate all of the controls at the same time.

✦ Use a query that returns a limited result set for a form's or report's `RecordSource` rather than using a table or underlying query that uses tables. The less data returned for the `RecordSource`, the faster the form or report loads. In addition, return only those fields actually used by the form or report. Don't use a query that gathers fields that won't be displayed on the form or report (except for a conditional check).

Using bitmaps on forms and reports

Bitmaps on forms and reports make an application look attractive and can also help convey the purpose of the form or report (as in a wizard). However, graphics are always resource-intensive, so you should use the fewest number of graphic objects on your forms and reports as possible. This helps to minimize form and report load time, increase print speed, and reduce the resources used by your application.

Often you will display pictures that a user never changes and that are not bound to a database. Examples of such pictures include your company logo on a switchboard or static images in a wizard. When you want to display an image like these, you have two choices:

✦ Use an Unbound Object Frame

✦ Use an Image control

If the image will never change and if you don't need to activate it in Form Design view, use an Image control. Image controls use fewer resources and display faster. If you need the image to be a linked or embedded OLE object that you can edit, use an Unbound Object Frame. You can convert OLE images in Unbound Object Frames.

Tip If you have an image in an Unbound Object Frame that you no longer need to edit, you can convert the Unbound Object Frame to an Image control by selecting Change To Image from the Format menu.

Tip When you have forms that contain unbound OLE objects, you should close the forms when they are not in use in order to free up resources. Also avoid using bitmaps with many colors — they take considerably more resources and are slower to paint than a bitmap of the same size with fewer colors.

If you want to display an Unbound OLE object but don't want the user to be able to activate it, set its Enabled property to False.

Speeding up list boxes and combo boxes

It's important to pay attention to the optimization of list boxes and combo boxes when optimizing your application. You can take a number of steps to make your combo boxes and list boxes run faster.

✦ When using multipage forms that have list boxes or combo boxes on more than one page, don't set the RowSource of the list boxes or combo boxes until the actual page containing the control is displayed.

✦ Index the first field displayed in a list box or combo box. This enables Access to find entries that match text entered by the user much faster.

✦ Although it's not always practical, try to refrain from hiding a combo box's bound column. Hiding the bound column causes the control's searching features to slow down considerably.

✦ If you don't need the search capabilities of AutoExpand, set the AutoExpand property of a combo box to No. Access is then relieved of the task of constantly searching the list for entries matching text entered in the text portion of the combo box.

✦ When possible, make the first nonhidden column in a combo or list box a text data type, and not a numeric one. To find a match in the list of a combo box or list box, Access must convert a numeric value to text in order to do the character-by-character match. If the data type is text, Access can skip the conversion step.

✦ Often overlooked is the performance gain achieved by using saved queries for RecordSource and RowSource properties of list boxes and combo boxes. A saved query gives much better performance than an SQL SELECT statement because an SQL query is optimized by Rushmore on the fly.

Tip   You will find one problem with combo boxes present in Access 2002, which poses a performance concern. Because Access 2002 supports hyperlinks, Access has to perform some additional work when first painting a combo box; it needs to determine the data type of the combo box.

The result is that the combo box takes a little longer to paint — up to a couple of seconds on some computers. If your combo box is a bound combo box, this isn't a problem because Access gets the data type from the `ControlSource`'s data type. In addition, if you save a `RowSource` for the combo box when you save the form, Access determines the data type from the `RowSource` and doesn't need to determine the data type at run time. The only time that this paint delay is an issue is when you have an unbound combo box that has its `RowSource` set programmatically. When this is the case, the combo box will take slightly longer to paint the first time it is displayed.

Getting the most from your modules

Perhaps the area where you'll be able to use smart optimization techniques most frequently is in your modules. For example, in code behind forms, you should use the Me keyword when referencing controls. This approach takes advantage of the capabilities of Access 2002; using Me is faster than creating a form variable and referencing the form in the variable. Other optimization techniques are simply smart coding practices that have been around for many years. You should try to use the optimum coding technique at all times. When in doubt, try different methods to accomplish a task and see which one is fastest.

Tip   Consider reducing the number of modules and procedures in your application by consolidating them whenever possible. A small memory overhead is incurred for each module and procedure that you use, so consolidating them may free up some memory.

Using appropriate data types

You should always explicitly declare variables using the Dim function rather than arbitrarily assigning values to variables that haven't been dimmed. To make sure that all variables in your application are explicitly declared before they are used in a procedure, while in Visual Basic for Application's design surface, select Tools ⇨

Options, choose the Editor tab, and then set the Require Variable Declarations
option on the tab (second from the top in the Code settings section).

Use integers and long integers rather than singles and doubles when possible.
Integers and long integers use less memory, and they take less time to process than
singles and doubles. Table 37-1 shows the relative speed of the different data types
available in Access.

Table 37-1	
Data Types and Their Mathematical Processing Speed	
Data Type	*Relative Processing Speed*
Integer/Long	Fastest
Single/Double	Next to Fastest
Currency	Next to Slowest
Variant	Slowest

In addition to using integers and long integers whenever possible, you should also
use integer math rather than precision math when applicable. For example, to
divide one long integer by another long integer, you can use the following
statement:

```
x = Long1 / Long2
```

This statement is a standard math function that uses floating-point math. You can
perform the same function by using integer math (notice that the mathematical sign
is the regular slash versus the backward slash) with the following statement:

```
x = Long1 \ Long2
```

Of course, integer math isn't always applicable. It is, however, commonly applied
when returning a percentage. For example, you can return a percentage with the following precision math formula:

```
x = Total / Value
```

However, you can perform the same function using integer math by first multiplying
the Total by 100 and then using integer math like this:

```
x = (Total * 100) \ Value
```

You should also use string functions ($) where applicable. When you are manipulat-
ing variables that are of type String, use the string functions (for example, `Str$()`
as opposed to their variant counterparts (`Str()`). If you are working with variants,

use the non-$ functions. Using string functions when working with strings is faster because Access doesn't need to perform type conversions on the variables.

When you need to return a substring by using `Mid$()`, you can omit the third parameter to have the entire length of the string returned. For example, to return a substring that starts at the second character of a string and returns all remaining characters, use a statement like this:

```
szReturn = Mid$(szMyString, 2)
```

When using arrays, use dynamic arrays with the `Erase` and `ReDim` statements to reclaim memory. By dynamically adjusting the size of the arrays, you can ensure that only the amount of memory needed for the array is allocated.

Tip   In addition to using optimized variables, consider using constants when applicable. Constants can make your code much easier to read and won't slow your application if you compile your code before executing it.

Writing faster routines

You can make your procedures faster by optimizing the routines that they contain in a number of ways. If you keep performance issues in mind as you develop, you will be able to find and take advantage of situations like the ones discussed here.

Some Access functions perform similar processes but vary greatly in the time that they take to execute. You probably use one or more of these regularly, and knowing the most efficient way to perform these routines can greatly affect your application's speed:

✦ For/Next statements are normally faster than Select Case statements. They tend to process less logic.

✦ The `IIF()` function is much slower than a standard set of If/Then/Else statements.

✦ The With and For Each functions accelerate manipulating multiple objects and/or their properties.

✦ Change a variable with Not instead of using an If . . . Then statement. (For example, use x = Not(y) instead of If y = true then x = false.)

✦ Instead of comparing a variable to the value True, use the value of the variable. (For example, instead of saying If X = True then . . ., say If X then . . .)

✦ Use the Requery method instead of the Requery action. The method is significantly faster than the action.

✦ When using OLE automation, resolve references when your application is compiled rather than resolving them at run time by using the `GetObject` or `CreateObject` functions.

Using control variables

When referencing controls on a form in code, there are some very slow ways and some very fast ways to use references to form objects. The slowest possible way is to reference each control explicitly. This requires Access to sequentially search for the form name, starting with the first form name in the database and continuing until it finds the form name in the forms list (msysObjects table). If the form name starts with a z, this can take a long time if the database contains many forms. For example:

```
Forms![Check Writer]![Bank Account Number] = something
Forms![Check Writer]![Bank Account Name] = something
Forms![Check Writer]![Payee] = something
```

If the code is in a class module behind the Check Writer form, you can use the Me reference. The Me reference refers to the open object (forms or reports) and substitutes for Forms![formname]. This is a much faster method because it can go right to the form name. For example:

```
Me!Bank Account Number] = something
Me![Bank Account Name] = something
Me![Check Writer]![Payee] = something
```

If your code is not stored behind the form but is in a module procedure, you can use a control variable like the following:

```
Dim frm as Form
set frm = Forms![Check Writer]
frm![Bank Account Number] = something
frm![Bank Account Name] = something
frm!Check Writer]![Payee] = something
```

This way, the form name is looked up only once. An even faster way is to use the With construct. For example:

```
With Forms![Check Writer]
   ![Bank Account Number] = something
   ![Bank Account Name] = something
   !Check Writer]![Payee] = something
End With
```

You can then reference the variable rather than reference the actual control. Of course, if you don't need to set values in the control but rather use values from a control, you should simply create a variable to contain the value rather than the reference to the control.

Using field variables

The preceding technique also applies to manipulating field data when working with a Recordset in VBA code. For example, you may ordinarily have a loop that does something like this:

```
...
Do Until tbl.EOF
MyTotal = MyTotal + tbl![OrderTotal]
Loop
```

If this routine loops through many records, you should use the following code snippet instead:

```
Dim MyField as Field
...
Set MyField = tbl![OrderTotal]
Do Until tbl.EOF
MyTotal = MyTotal +MyField
Loop
```

The preceding code executes much faster than code that explicitly references the field in every iteration of the loop.

Increasing the speed of finding data in code

Use the FindRecord and FindNext methods on indexed fields. These methods are much more efficient when used on a field that is indexed. Also, take advantage of bookmarks when you can. Returning to a bookmark is much faster than performing a Find method to locate the data.

The procedure shown in Listing 37-1 is an example of using a bookmark. Bookmark variables must always be dimmed as variants, and you can create multiple bookmarks by dimming multiple variant variables. The following code opens the tblCustomers table, moves to the first record in the database, sets the bookmark for the current (first) record, moves to the last record, and finally repositions back to the bookmarked record. For each step, the debug.print command is used to show the relative position in the database as evidence that the current record changes from record to record.

Listing 37-1: **Using a Bookmark to Mark a Record**

```
Public Sub BookmarkExample()
Dim rs As Recordset, bk As Variant
Set rs =
Workspaces(0).Databases(0).OpenRecordset("tblCustomers", _
dbOpenTable)
    ' Move to the first record in the database
      rs.MoveFirst
        ' Print the position in the database
      Debug.Print rs.PercentPosition
    ' Set the bookmark to the current record
      bk = rs.Bookmark
    ' Move to the last record in the database
      rs.MoveLast
```

```
     ' Print the position in the database
     Debug.Print rs.PercentPosition
  ' Move to the bookmarked record
     rs.Bookmark = bk
     ' Print the position in the database
     Debug.Print rs.PercentPosition
rs.Close
Set rs = Nothing
End Sub
```

Eliminating dead code and unused variables

Before distributing your application, remove any *dead code* — code that is not used at all — from your application. You will often find entire procedures, or even modules, that once served a purpose but are no longer called. In addition, it isn't uncommon to leave variable declarations in code after all code that actually uses the variables has been removed. By eliminating dead code and unused variables, you reduce the amount of memory your application uses and the amount of time required to compile code at run time.

> **Tip** Although it isn't easy and often impractical, removing large numbers of comments from your code can decrease the amount of memory used by your application.

Other things that you can do to increase the speed of your modules include opening any add-ins that your application uses for read-only access and replacing procedure calls within loops with in-line code. Also, don't forget one of the most important items: Deliver your applications with the modules compiled.

Increasing network performance

The single most important action that you can take to make sure that your networkable applications run at their peak performance is to run Access and the application database on the workstation and link to the shared network database. Running Access over the network is much slower than running it locally.

Improving Perceived Speed

Perceived speed is how fast your application appears to run to the end user. Many techniques can increase the perceived speed of your applications. Perceived speed usually involves supplying visual feedback to the user while the computer is busy performing some operation, such as constantly updating a percent meter when Access is busy processing data.

Using a splash screen

Most professional Windows programs employ a splash screen, as shown in Figure 37-9. Most people think that the splash screen is simply to show the product's name and copyright information as well as the registered user's information, but this isn't entirely correct. The splash screen greatly contributes to the perceived speed of an application. It shows the user that something is *happening*, and it gives users something to look at (and hence occupy their time) for a few seconds while the rest of the application loads.

Note In large applications, you may even display a series of splash screens with different information, such as helpful hints, instructions on how to use the product, or even advertisements. These are known as *billboards*.

Figure 37-9: A splash screen to display product and version information.

To create a splash screen, create a basic form with appropriate data, such as your application information, logo, and registration information. Then set this form as the Display Form in the Start Up dialog box. Setting the form as the Display Form ensures that the splash screen is the first form to be loaded. You then want to call any initialization procedures from the On Open event of the splash form. A good splash screen should automatically disappear after a few seconds. To make this happen, use the timer event. Chap 37.MDB contains a simple splash screen to help get you started.

You need to remember a few issues when using splash forms:

✦ Never use custom controls in a startup form. Custom controls take time to load and consume resources.

✦ Minimize code in startup forms. Use only code that is absolutely necessary to display your startup form and use a light form if possible.

✦ The startup form should call only initialization procedures. Be careful about call trees; you don't want your startup form triggering the loading of many modules in your application.

Loading and keeping forms hidden

If you have forms that are displayed often, consider hiding them rather than closing them. To hide a form, set its Visible property to False. When you need to display the form again, set its Visible property back to True. Forms that remain loaded consume memory, but they display more quickly than forms that must be loaded each time they are viewed. In addition, if you are *morphing* a form or report (changing the way it looks by changing form and control properties), keep the form hidden until all changes are made so that the user doesn't have to watch the changes take place.

Using the hourglass

When your application needs to perform a task that may take a while, use the hourglass. The hourglass mouse pointer shows the user that the computer is not locked up but is merely busy. To turn on the hourglass cursor, use the Hourglass method like this:

```
DoCmd.Hourglass True
```

To turn the hourglass back to the default cursor, use the method like this:

```
DoCmd.Hourglass False
```

Using the built-in progress meter

In addition to using the hourglass, you should consider using the progress meter when performing looping routines in a procedure. The progress meter gives constant visual feedback that your application is busy, and it shows the user in no uncertain terms where it is in the current process.

Tip   Chap37.MDB includes two types of progress meters. Using the standard Microsoft Access progress meter that is displayed in the status bar creates the first type that is discussed in this chapter. The other meter is a pop-up form that uses a colored rectangle to show the progress of an activity.

The sample database file Ch37.mdb contains a number of progress meter samples. Each uses the progress meter a little differently but all run the same example. The example creates 50,000 records in a table named *SampleData*. Each of the examples uses a simple form with several text box controls and a button to start the process. The basic progress meter form in Design view is shown in the following figure. Each of the examples contain code to display either the built-in Access progress meter or one within the pop-up form. Each contains a button to start the process, as well as two text boxes to display the start time and end time of the process.

The following code demonstrates how to use the built-in progress meter in a loop to show the meter starting at 0 percent and expanding to 100 percent, 1 percent at a time. The first example is named *ProgressMeterUsingBuiltInAccessMeter*. This example doesn't actually use the text box in the sample progress meter form, but rather uses the progress meter built into Microsoft Access that displays as a series of little squares at the bottom left corner of the screen in the status bar.

Caution   If you don't display the status bar, you won't see the built-in progress meter when it runs.

The code to initialize, update, and remove the meter is shown in Figure 37-10.

The first step for using the percent meter is initializing the meter. You initialize the meter by calling the `SysCmd` function like this:

```
ReturnValue = SysCmd(acSysCmdInitMeter, "Creating Records",
counter)
```

The `acSysCmdInitMeter` in this line is an Access constant that tells the function that you are initializing the meter. The second parameter is the text that you want to appear to the left of the meter. Finally, the last value is the maximum value of the meter (in this case, 100 percent). You can set this value to anything that you want. For example, if you were iterating through a loop of 50,000 records, you may set this value to 50,000. Then you can pass the record count at any given time to the `SysCmd` function; Access decides what percentage the meter shows as filled.

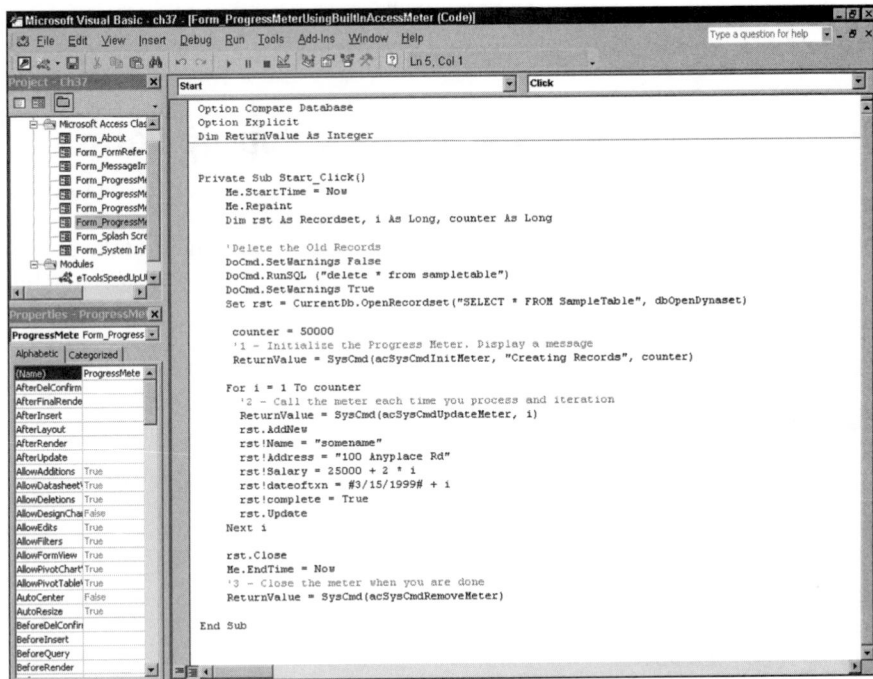

Figure 37-10: Code to run the built-in progress meter

After the meter has been initialized, you can pass a value to it to update the meter. To update the meter, you call the `SysCmd` function again and pass it the `acSysCmdUpdateMeter` constant and the new update meter value. Remember, the value that you pass to the function is not necessarily the percent displayed by the meter. It can be the number of records processed or any number that when divided by the initial counter provides a percentage from 1 to 100. For example, if 50,000 records are being processed and the number 12,500 is passed to the meter, it will display 25 percent.

```
ReturnValue = SysCmd(acSysCmdUpdateMeter, i)
```

After all the records are processed, you will want to remove the meter from the status bar. To do this, use the following command. (There are no parameters to pass when you remove the meter.)

```
ReturnValue = SysCmd(acSysCmdRemoveMeter)
```

The progress meter displayed in the status bar is shown in Figure 37-11.

```
Creating Records  ██████████
```

Figure 37-11: The progress meter displayed in the status bar.

Creating a Progress Meter with a Pop-up Form

To run the sample Progress Meter that uses the pop-up form, open the form ProgressMeterCallingEveryRecord and press the Search button. The progress meter form appears and the bar grows from 0 to 100 percent. This should take about 30 seconds on a high-end Pentium machine, but a little longer on a slower machine.

The Progress Meter form in progress is shown in Figure 37-12.

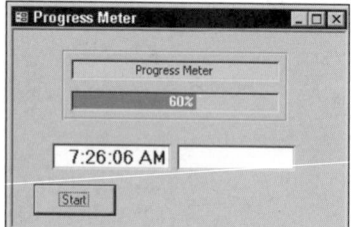

Figure 37-12: A graphical progress meter.

This progress meter has some advantages over the standard Microsoft Access progress meter. The progress meter that comes with Access uses the status bar to display the meter and isn't always as visible as you may want it to be. The pop-up progress meter pops up in the middle of the screen and is immediately visible to the user. The meter that comes with Access, however, usually displays faster because it requires less overhead to run, although with longer tasks the difference may not be noticeable. The speed of the pop-up meter can be controlled by updating the meter every x percent. Therefore, if the form meter is set for fast execution, it displays with comparable speed to that of the built-in meter.

The progress meter form is created from a few simple controls, as shown in Figure 37-9. It contains a rectangle control, two label controls, and option group controls. In Figure 37-12, you can see that the rectangle is shown 60 percent completed. In reality, the width of the rectangle is manipulated by the program that is used to display the meter's progress. The width is reset to 0 when the progress meter starts, and it is slowly built back to its original length.

The code for the progress meter is also simple and shown in its entirety, including the three-line function that is called in Figure 37-13.

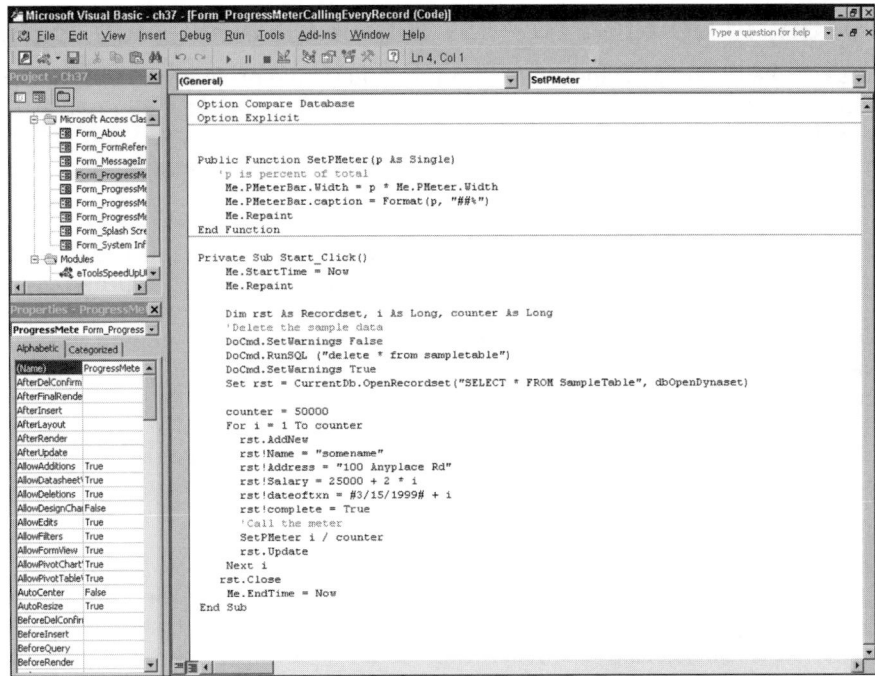

Figure 37-13: The Progress Meter form call to the pop-up progress meter.

The code that calls the meter is one simple line buried in the middle of the iteration loop. It calls the display function by passing it the iteration number and total number of iterations expected. In this example, I is the record number being processed and counter is the expected 50,000 records.

```
SetPMeter i / counter
```

The function SetPMeter only consists of three lines: One to display the rectangle and manipulate its width, one to display the caption on the bar as it grows inside the rectangle in the form, and one to repaint the screen each time so that the bar is animated.

```
Public Function SetPMeter(p As Single)
    'p is percent of total
    Me.PMeterBar.Width = p * Me.PMeter.Width
    Me.PMeterBar.caption = Format(p, "##%")
    Me.Repaint
End Function
```

Speeding up the Progress Meter display

This routine is called whenever you want to update the progress meter. You can decide when to do this. Generally, you should call the progress meter only when it is likely to be updated. If you know that you have 1000 records, you may call the meter every 10 records; if you have 10,000 records, you may call the meter every 100 records.

Although this code is simple, it is not the best. In fact, because this code calls the progress meter for every record, it is much slower than the built-in progress meter. Although the built-in progress meter processes this code in about 10 seconds, on our Pentium III laptop with 128MB of memory, it takes over a minute to run this routine. A better approach is to only call the progress meter once in a while. The following code can replace the call in the code previously discussed.

```
If (i / counter) * 100 = Int((i / counter) * 100) Then
    SetPMeter i / counter
End If
```

The If statement checks to see if the calculation of the completion percentage is an integer (whole number). This calls the progress meter function (SetPMeter) that moves the progress meter rectangle. You may wonder why the If statement is faster because it is run 50,000 times. The reality is that the If statement takes very few resources to process, but a function that changes the width of a rectangle or control, writes to the screen, and then repaints the screen uses a lot of resources — as evidenced by the time to process falling by 90 percent.

Follow these steps to integrate the Progress Meter into your application:

1. Import the Form ProgressMeter into your application.

2. Change the code behind the form to interact with your application.

Working with Large Program Databases in Access 2002

When someone mentions large databases in Microsoft Access, they are generally thinking about a database with tables that contain hundreds of thousands of data records. Though this can be considered to be a large database, another definition is a database that contains hundreds of objects — tables, queries, forms, reports, and thousands of lines of VBA program code. Although you can sometimes solve data performance problems by changing the back end from Jet to SQL Server, you will probably have to deal with much more complex problems if you create applications with many queries, forms, reports, and lots of VBA module code.

If your database has hundreds of objects, especially forms and reports, you may have run into problems that cause your database to exhibit strange behavior. These include:

✦ Not staying compiled or not compiling at all

✦ Growing and growing and growing in size, even after compiling and compacting

✦ Running slower and slower

✦ Displaying the wrong record in linked subforms

✦ Displaying compile errors when you know that the code is correct

✦ Corrupting constantly

Compacting your database doesn't always work as advertised. Compiling and Saving All Modules becomes a long wait with a seemingly perpetual hourglass. After you compact and open the database, it is uncompiled again. If you work with large databases, chances are good that these are well-known experiences. If you have one of these out-of-control databases, this section will show you how to solve these problems and get you up and running fast again.

How databases grow in size

Many things can cause a database to grow. Each time that you add an object to an Access 2002 database (.MDB) file, it gets larger. And why shouldn't it? You are certainly using more space to define the properties and methods of the object. Reports and forms take the most space because the number of properties associated with each form or report and each control on a form or report uses space. Table attachments (links) and queries take up very little space, but VBA code grows proportionally to the number of lines in both modules and code behind forms and reports. If you store data in your program database, this also takes up space proportionally to the number of records in the table. Many other reasons cause a database to grow.

When you first create a database using the Access 2000 or Access 2002 database file formats, it uses about 60KB, depending on your hard drive type, size, and Access format (Access 2002 databases are larger than Access 2000 database files). As you add objects, the database will start to grow. Adding a very simple form takes about 6K, whereas a simple report uses about 25K of hard drive space. Each time that you add another new form or report, more space is used. Each time that you add a new control and define some properties, even more space is used. When you define any event in a form or report that contains even a single line of VBA code, more overhead is used, because the form or report is no longer a lightweight object but one that is VBA-aware. This requires more space and resources than a lightweight form or report containing no VBA code. If you embed images into your forms and reports, then these also will use space. Embedding bound OLE aware data, such as pictures, sound, video, or Word or Excel documents, use more space than unbound objects or images.

Each time that you make a change to any object — even a simple one — a duplicate copy of the object is created until you compact the database. Within even a few hours of work, Access 2002 databases can begin to grow larger and larger. If the database contains thousands of lines of VBA code, the database can grow to two or three times its original size very quickly, especially when compiled and before it is compacted.

Simply compiling and compacting may not be enough

As you add, delete, and modify objects, Access doesn't always clean up after itself. You have probably learned that after you make changes to your objects, especially VBA code, you should open any module and select Debug ⇨ Compile and Save All Modules. After you do this, you should close the module and select the database container and select Tools ⇨ Database Utilities ⇨ Compact Database. This action compacts the database to the same name and reopens the database running any startup commands or Autoexec macros that you may have. For the less aggressive, you may want to close the database first and compact the database to a different name, thus effectively creating a compacted backup. You can then use the new database or delete the old and rename the new database to the original name.

Compiling and Compacting may not be enough to solve some of the problems mentioned at the beginning of the section. We worked with a large database that was originally converted from Access 2.0; we noticed it started at 15MB. After hundreds of minor changes, it was growing at of rate of 50K each time that we compiled and compacted it — even if we added no new objects, properties, methods, or VBA code. Out of necessity, this author has experimented with a variety of techniques to understand this phenomenon and solve our problems. More importantly, strange things started happening.

Even though we noticed that the database was growing larger, it took several compiles and compacts to get it to compile, and frequently after we compacted the database it was no longer compiled. It also ran slower the first time we opened it. When the database displayed compile errors on perfectly written code, we knew that it was time to try new techniques.

Rebooting gives you a clean memory map

We have always noticed that strange behavior in any program gets better when you reboot your system. Access is particularly bad at *memory leaks*, especially if you're going in and out of form, report, and module design. If you don't want to reboot, at least close your database and exit Access before beginning the examination of your problem.

Repair does nothing if the database is not corrupt

We started by trying to repair the database. Though it was not corrupt, we thought maybe that would help. Although the repair utility ran fine and automatically compacted the database, it did nothing else, and the database was still growing.

You can fix a single corrupt form by removing the record source

Sometimes, you may have a single form that doesn't run properly. To fix this, try opening the form in Design view and remove any record source. Then, close and save the form. Reopen the form in Design view and reenter the original (or a new) record source. This may fix your problem. When the record source of an Access form or report is changed, it forces various internal code behind the form to be rebuilt. Sometimes, this simple process works.

Create a new database and import all of the objects

It's important to have your database as clean as possible. Although we're not sure if gremlins crawl into some obscure portion of the database file, we are sure that you can't import or export them. A technique that usually proves to be successful is to simply create a new database and then import all of the objects from the original database. Access 2002 makes it easy to import all of your objects by using the Select All button found in the Import Objects dialog box. You can get to this dialog box by first going to the database container of the new empty database file that you create and then selecting File ⇨ Get External Data ⇨ Import, selecting the original program database, and then pressing the Import button. You can then import all of your objects.

If you have any custom menus and toolbars, or if you have defined any Import/Export specifications, then you should remember to use the Options button and check off those options as shown in Figure 37-14. The default for these options is False. If you have created any startup properties in the database, you will have to create them again because they are not importable.

 **Caution**   If you use externally referenced libraries or add-ins, then you must manually reference these libraries in the new database. You can display a module and use the Tools ⇨ References menu to do this.

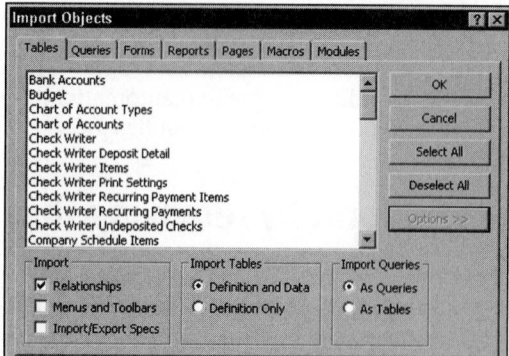

Figure 37-14: Importing Database Objects with the Options button pressed.

After working for some time in our large database, even creating a new database and importing all of the objects failed to help the database stay compiled or become smaller.

The undocumented decompile option in Access 2002

The undocumented startup command-line option is called "/decompile." You may have seen many of the command-line options, such as /nostartup, /cmd, and /compact. This option starts Access 2002 in a special way, and, when a database is opened, saves all VBA modules as text. This works with module objects and all the code behind forms and reports.

To do this, go to the Windows Start menu Run command and type **msaccess /decompile** as shown in Figure 37-15. Hold down the Shift key before you launch Microsoft Access. This prevents any startup forms or autoexec macro processes from running. You don't want the database to run code that forces even a single module to be compiled. This prevents the decompile process from actually doing any good.

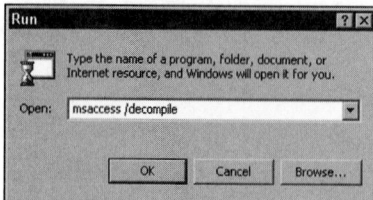

Figure 37-15: Starting Access 2002 with the decompile command-line option.

Access appears to start as usual. It takes about three minutes to open a database and decompile all of the objects in a 20MB database. At this point, the real question was if the database would get sufficiently smaller, run faster, and stay compiled after it was compiled and compacted.

After the database window is displayed, close Access. Don't just close the database window — actually exit Microsoft Access.

After you exit Access, you can restart Access normally. You can then open your database, open any module, and select Debug ⇨ Compile projectname where projectname is simply the name of your project (original database file name). After the database compiles, you should close the module, return to the database container, and select Tools ⇨ Database Utilities ⇨ Compact and Repair Database. You will find that Access runs these procedures much faster than usual.

Caution   Make sure that you immediately exit Access 2002 after it finishes decompiling and then start Access again before running Compile projectname or Compact and Repair Database.

Using our test database, we then went to Windows Explorer and checked the size of the database. It had shrunk from 22MB to 15MB, a reduction of over 30 percent, and it has stayed compiled every time we compact it. The first time we ran the application, it seemed to run faster than ever. We aren't sure why it works faster or differently than manually opening and saving each VBA module as text — it simply does. Even more strangely, the database no longer seems to be growing each time we make a minor change, recompile, and compact the database. Although the decompile option may be a small miracle, it's always a good idea to follow the six steps to success before releasing any application to the ultimate users.

Summary — six steps to large database success

If you're ready to release your application for a real test by the users, you should follow the steps below to ensure a clean-running system:

1. Reboot your computer to clean up memory.

2. Create a new Access database and import all the objects. Then close Access.

3. Restart Access by using the /decompile option while holding down the Shift key. Close Access after the database window is displayed.

4. Restart Access normally while holding down the Shift key.

5. Compile the database.

6. Compact and repair the database.

By releasing a clean, fully compiled and compacted system, you will have fewer problems, your application will run faster, and you will have less technical or maintenance problems.

An interface for detecting an uncompiled database and automatically recompiling

It's very important that you make sure that a database is always in a compiled state. If you release your application as a modifiable .MDB file, your customers may make simple or even complex changes to your application and then complain because their system is running slowly. Although some of your customers may be serious developers, our experience is that many customers who make changes to Access databases don't know about compilation or compacting.

To see if your database is compiled, you can open the Visual Basic window for any module, display the Debug window, and type **? IsCompiled()**, as shown in Figure 37-16. If the database is compiled, it will display True. If it is in a decompiled state, it will display False, as shown in Figure 37-16.

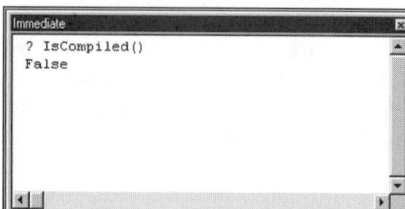

Figure 37-16: Checking to see if an Access 20002 program is compiled.

To solve this problem, you can create an interface that automatically detects if the database is not in a compiled state and then gives the user the option of compiling the application. This is run each time the database is opened. The user still has to compact the database, but the hard part is compiling. Figure 37-17 shows the message that is automatically displayed if the database is uncompiled. The code is shown in the following example.

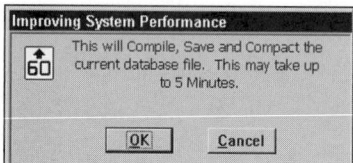

Figure 37-17: A dialog box to help the user compile your application.

One line of code can be added anywhere in your program to detect an uncompiled application and start the process.

```
If IsCompiled() = False Then DoCmd.OpenForm
"MessageImprovingPerformance"
```

The code uses the Access 2002 built-in function IsCompiled to determine the compiled state of the application. If the application isn't compiled, the form is displayed, as shown in Figure 37-17. The user has two choices. If they are still testing, they may not want to compile yet. If they want to compile, they simply have to press the Yes button.

The compile and compact code is shown in Figure 37-18. The application is compiled first and then compacted. If the database is already compiled, the compile function is skipped and the database is only compacted. You can simply insert this module and the message box into any application and call the form.

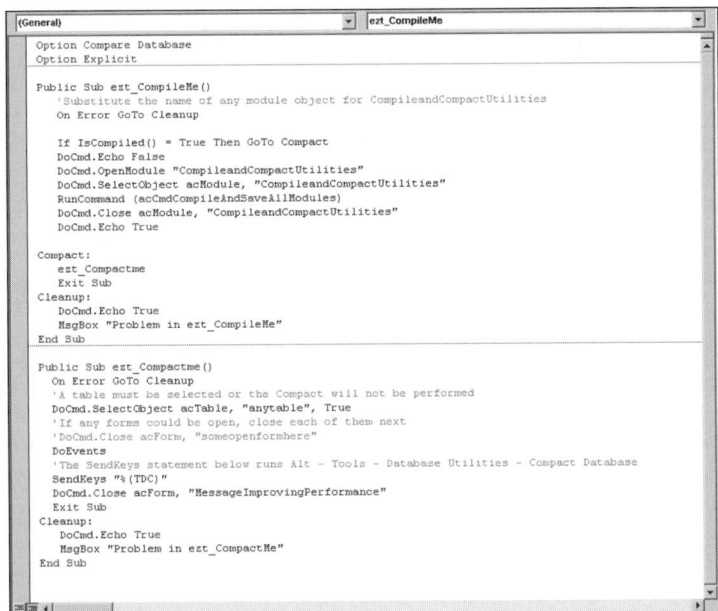

Figure 37-18: A module to automatically compile and compact your database.

Making small changes to large databases – one word – *export*

One final tip for working with large databases: Always work with a copy of the program file and export the changed objects. When you are making lots of changes to a few objects to try a new technique or to get a stubborn algorithm to work, you are constantly opening and closing objects. This tends to negatively affect large databases. Work with a copy of the database, and then when you have the changes just the way you want, you can export the changed objects from the test database to the production database. Any object that you export with the same name as the production database will be exported with a 1 at the end of the name. You can then open the production database, delete the original objects, and rename the changed objects that have a 1 on the end of their name. New objects are obviously exported with their name intact.

Anything that you can do to make fewer changes to a large database, the better off you are. By following the tips and techniques in this section, you will have fewer problems and you will be more productive.

Through judicious use of the techniques discussed in this chapter, you will be able to increase the performance of your Access application to the highest level possible.

✦   ✦   ✦

Securing an Access Application

Although security options can be maintained in Access, Access manipulates security at the Jet engine level. The Jet security model has changed very little since Access 95; in fact, Access 2002 ships with the same version of Jet as Access 2000. Jet's security is still a workgroup-based security model; all users in a workgroup are bound to the same security rules. The rules enforced for individual users may vary from user to user, based on the permissions assigned to each user.

Understanding Jet Security

Jet security is defined at the object level for individuals or groups of users. This type of security is often referred to as *user-level security* and is very similar to the security mechanisms seen on mainframe and server systems. The security model of Jet/Access is rather complex, but it isn't too difficult to understand when broken down into its core components, which are:

- ✦ Workgroups
- ✦ Groups
- ✦ Users
- ✦ Object owners
- ✦ Object permissions

In This Chapter

Understanding Jet security

Deciding on a security level to implement

Creating a database password

Using the /runtime option

Using a database's startup options

Distributing an application as an .MDE file

Manipulating users and groups

Securing objects by using permissions

Using the Access Security Wizard

Encrypting a database

Manipulating security by using DAO code

✦ ✦ ✦ ✦

The two main reasons for employing user-level security are:

✦ To protect sensitive data in the database

✦ To prevent users from accidentally breaking an application by changing the objects (tables, queries, etc.) of the application

By using passwords and permissions, you can allow or restrict access of individuals or groups of individuals to the objects (forms, tables, and so on) in your database. This information, known as a *workgroup,* is stored in a workgroup information file.

Understanding workgroup files

Jet stores security information for databases in workgroup information files, usually the default file is named "SYSTEM.MDW." This *workgroup information file* is a special Access database that contains a collection of user names and passwords, user group definitions, object owner assignments, and object permissions. The SYSTEM.MDW file is often located, by default, in the C:\WINDOWS\Application Data\Microsoft\Access subdirectory. When Access opens a database, it reads the workgroup information file associated with the database. Access reads the file to determine who is allowed — and at what level — access to the objects in the database and what permissions they have to those objects.

> **Note**   If you are upgrading from a previous version, the SYSTEM.MDW file may be located in the C:\WINDOWS\Program Files\Common Files\SYSTEM subdirectory.

You can use the same workgroup file for multiple databases. After you enable security for a database, however, users must use the workgroup information file containing the security information. If users use a workgroup other than the one used to define security, however, they are limited to logging into the database as the Admin user — with whatever permissions the database administrator left for the Admin user.

> **Tip**   When securing a database, one of the first things that you need to do is to remove all permissions for the Admin user. Removing these permissions prevents other users from opening the database as the Admin user by using another Access workgroup file and obtaining the rights of the Admin user. Users can still open the database as the Admin user by using a different workgroup, but they won't have any object permissions. This measure is discussed later in this chapter in the section "Working with workgroups."

Understanding permissions

The permissions in Jet security are defined at the object level; each object, such as a form or report, has a specific set of permissions. The system administrator defines what permissions each user or group of users has for each object. Users may belong to multiple groups, and they always inherit the highest permission setting of any of the groups to which they belong.

For example, every table object has a set of permissions associated with it: Read Design, Modify Design, Read Data, Update Data, Insert Data, Delete Data, and Administrator. (See Table 38-1 later in this chapter for a complete list of permissions and their meanings.) The database administrator has the ability to assign or remove any or all of these permissions for each user or group of users in the workgroup. Because the permissions are set at the object level, the administrator may give a user the ability to read data from Table A, read data from and write data to Table B, but prevent the user from even looking at Table C. In addition, this complexity allows for unique security situations, such as having numerous users sharing data on a network, each with a different set of rights for the database objects. All security maintenance functions are performed from the Tools ⇨ Security menu item (see Figure 38-1).

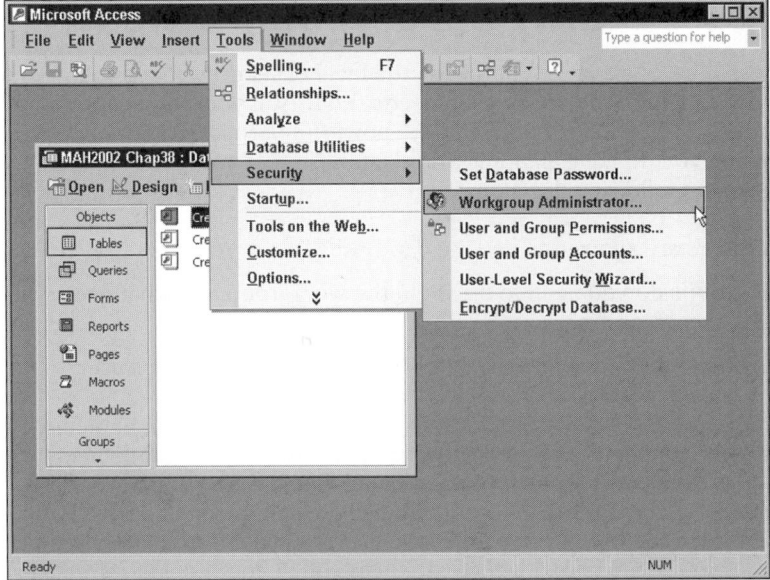

Figure 38-1: All Jet security functions are performed from the Tools ⇨ Security menu.

Understanding security limitations

You need to be aware of the fact that you can't depend on the Jet security model to be foolproof. For example, security holes have been previously discovered and exposed in Access 2.0 and Access 95; in effect, *un*-protecting every database distributed under the assumption that the code and objects were protected. The amount of resources involved in developing an application is often huge, and protecting that investment is essential. The most that you can do for protection is to fully and properly implement the Jet 4.0 security model and use legally binding licensing agreements for all of your distributed applications. Unfortunately, the future security of your databases is at the mercy of software hackers. As of the printing of this book, no *published* holes exist in the Jet 4.0 security model, but, as proven in the past, you aren't guaranteed that this condition won't change.

Tip

We recommend that you use Microsoft Access security to lock up your tables and prevent access to the design of your forms, reports, queries, and modules. However, if you want to control data at the form level — for example, suppose that you want to hide controls or control access to specific form-level controls or data — then you have to write your own security commands. You can also use the operating system (Windows) to prevent access to the directories.

Choosing a Security Level to Implement

As an Access developer, you must decide the level of security required for your application — not every database even needs security. If your application is used solely in-house, then you may not need the powerful permission protection of Jet's security. When you do have an application database that you want to secure, you need to make the following decisions:

- ✦ What users are allowed to use the database?

- ✦ What groups do you need to create in the workgroup and what users will belong to each group?

- ✦ What object permissions need to be limited for each group or user?

After you have made these determinations, you are ready to begin implementing security in your application. Access includes a tool to help you implement security — the User-Level Security Wizard (available from the Tools ➪ Security menu choice). This chapter teaches you how you can implement security by using Access's interface; each security element is discussed in detail. Understanding the workings of the security model will greatly help you in your quest for total security. (The wizard is discussed later in this chapter.)

On the CD-ROM

This chapter uses two databases: MAH2002 Chap38.mdb and MAH2002 SecureWizard.mdb for the examples. Later in this chapter, you will see how the second database is created from the first database. You should move the MAH2002 Chap38.mdb database from the CD, included with this book, into a subdirectory on your hard drive.

Creating a Database Password

You can use Jet security at its most basic level simply by controlling who can open the database. You control database access by creating a password for the databases that you want to protect. When you set a database password for a database, users are prompted to enter the password each time they attempt to access the database. If they don't know the database password, they are not allowed access to the database. When using this form of security, you are not controlling specific permissions for specific users, you are merely controlling who can and can't access the secured database.

To create a database password, follow these steps:

1. In Access, open the MAH2002 Chap38.mdb database exclusively.

Note   You *must* open the database exclusively in order to set the database password. To open the database exclusively, select the Open Exclusive button from the Open pull-down menu in the lower-right corner of the Open dialog box, as shown in Figure 38-2.

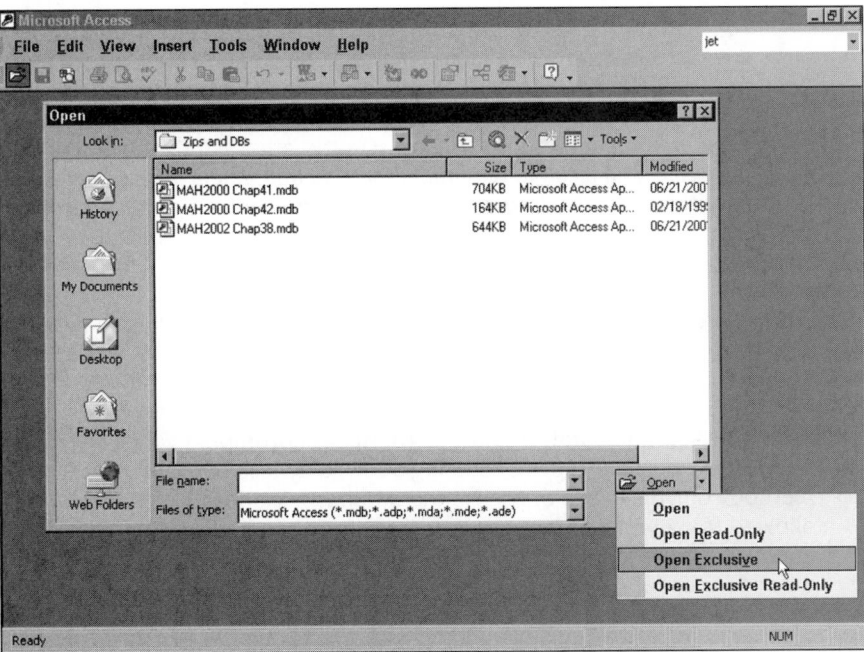

Figure 38-2: Opening a database in exclusive mode.

2. Select Tools ➪ Security ➪ Set Database Password (refer to Figure 38-1).

3. In the Password field, type the password that you want to use to secure the database (see Figure 38-3). Access does *not* display the password; rather, it shows an asterisk (*) for each letter.

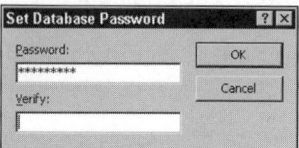

Figure 38-3: Creating a database password is the simplest way to secure your database.

4. In the Verify field, type the password again. This security measure ensures that you don't mistype the password (because you can't see the characters that you type) and mistakenly prevent everyone, including you, from accessing the database.

Tip

For maximum security, when entering a password you should follow standard password naming conventions. That is, you should make it a combination of letters and numbers that won't represent any easily known or deduced combination. People often use a birthday, their name, their address number, or the name of a child or someone that they know. On the other hand, you shouldn't make the password so difficult to remember that you and others accessing the database will have to write it down to use it. A written password is a useless password.

5. Click OK to save the password.

Caution

You can't synchronize replicated databases that have database passwords. If you plan on using Jet's replication features and you need database security, you must use user-level security.

After you save the database password, Access prompts every user of the database to enter the password prior to being allowed access to the database. Although this method controls *who* can access the database, it doesn't control *what* users are allowed to do with the objects and data after they have opened the database. To control objects, you need to fully implement Jet's user-level security, which is discussed in the following section.

Tip

After you have assigned a password to the database, you may want to protect your database further by encrypting it. Encrypting a database makes it unreadable by other programs, such as word processors. Encrypting is discussed in detail later in this chapter.

Note After a database has been protected using a database-level password, you must supply the password before you link to a table in the database. This password is stored in the information that is used to define the link to the table.

To remove a database password, follow these steps:

1. In Access, open the database that you want to unsecure. You must open the database exclusively to be able to unset the database password.

2. Select Tools ⇨ Security ⇨ Unset Database Password. This menu item was previously labeled Set Database Password but was changed when the database password was set.

3. In the password field, type the password of the database (see Figure 38-4).

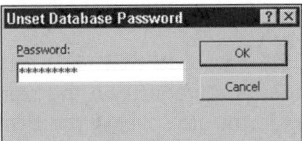

Figure 38-4: You can remove a database password by retyping the password in the Unset Database Password dialog box.

4. Click OK to unset the password.

If you remove a database password from an Access database, users are no longer required to enter a password to access the database unless you have enabled user-level security.

Note Any user who knows the database password has the ability to change or remove the database password. You can prevent this situation by removing the Administer permissions from the database for all users except the database administrator. This is discussed in more detail later in this chapter.

Caution Microsoft Access stores the database password in an unencrypted form. If you have sensitive data, this can compromise the security of the password-protected database. In situations where the data security is critical, you should consider using defined user-level security to control access to sensitive data. User-level security is covered in depth later in this chapter.

Using the /runtime Option

If you're not concerned with protecting your application but simply want to prevent users from mistakenly breaking your application by modifying or deleting objects, you can force your application to be run in Access's *runtime mode*. When a database is opened in Access' runtime mode, all the interface elements that allow changes to objects are hidden from the user. In fact, while in runtime mode, it is impossible for a user to access the Database window. When using the runtime option, you must ensure that your application has a startup form that gives users access to whatever objects that you want them to be able to access. Normally this is the main menu of your application, or main switchboard.

Note You must purchase and install the Microsoft Office XP Developer Edition tools (ODE) to use the /runtime switch. This version of Office includes a runtime version of the program that allows you to distribute a royalty-free licensed copy of your Access 2002 applications to users, whether they have Access on their machine or not.

Tip To assign a form as a startup form, open the database that you want to use, choose Tool ➪ Startup and select the form that you want to be the startup form from the Display Form drop-down list. Startup forms are covered more in-depth in the following section.

Setting Passwords by Using VBA

You also can set database passwords by using VBA code. The following code changes the database password of the currently opened database:

```
Public Sub ChangeDatabasePassword()
  On Error GoTo ChangeDatabasePasswordErr
  Dim szOldPassword As String, szNewPassword As String
  Dim db As Database
  Set db = CurrentDb
  szOldPassword = ""
  szNewPassword = "shazam"
  db.NewPassword szOldPassword, szNewPassword
  Exit Sub
ChangeDatabasePasswordErr:
    MsgBox Err & ":  " & Err.Description
    Exit Sub
  End Sub
```

If no database password is set, you pass a zero-length string ("") as the old password parameter. If a database password is assigned and you want to remove the password, pass the database password as the old password parameter and pass a zero-length string ("") as the new password.

To create a shortcut to start your application in Access's runtime mode, follow these steps, using the MAH2002 Chap38.mdb database:

1. Go to the subdirectory that contains Microsoft Access (MSACCESS.exe).

Note On our computers, the MSACCESS.EXE file is located in the "C:\Program Files\ Microsoft Office\Office 10\" subdirectory.

2. Highlight the Microsoft Access program and select File ➪ Create Shortcut or right-click on the program file and select Create Shortcut from the menu-on-demand.

Windows creates a Shortcut in the same directory, naming it "Shortcut to Msaccess.exe."

3. Right-click the newly created shortcut, then select Properties from the menu, and then click the Shortcut tab when the Properties dialog box opens.

4. In the Target: field, append the following items to the path of MSACCESS.EXE (program): A space, the full path name and filename of the database to open in runtime mode, another space, and then /runtime.

For example, the following command line starts Access and opens the MAH2002 Chap38.mdb database in runtime mode on our computers:

"C:\Program Files\Microsoft Office\Office 10\MSAccess.exe" "C:\Access 2002 Bible\MAH 2002 Gold\MAH2002 Chap38.mdb" /runtime

Note The path to MSAcess.exe should have already been in the Target: field. Note that Windows automatically places the path and filename for MSAccess.exe in quotation marks for Windows 95 and later versions. The /runtime switch should not be enclosed in quotes. If you enclose the /runtime switch in quotes, an error occurs when you attempt to execute the shortcut.

5. After you have specified the path and filename, placing the /runtime switch at the end of the Target: field, you can optionally remove the path name in the Start in: field.

Figure 38-5 shows how the Shortcut properties should look at this point.

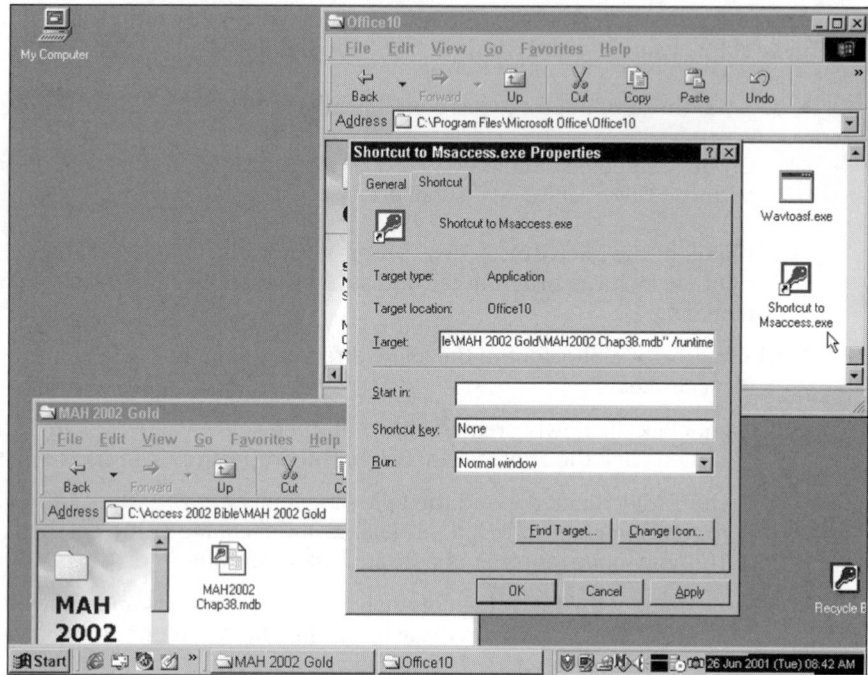

Figure 38-5: Modifying the Target: and Start in: fields of the shortcut by using the /runtime switch of Access 2002.

6. After the fields have been fixed, click the Apply button to make the changes and save the shortcut.

7. Finally, you can rename the shortcut icon to any name that you want and move it from the current directory to another directory, or even the desktop. After you have created the shortcut, you can distribute or re-create the same shortcut for each user installation.

Tip   If your database has a password associated with it, the user will still be prompted to enter the password prior to opening the database.

Using a Database's Startup Options

A slightly more secure alternative to using the /runtime option is to set a database's startup options. Although this provides greater security than the /runtime option, it isn't a complete solution for situations where tight security is paramount. Figure 38-6 shows the Startup options dialog box with the Advanced options displayed. To access the Startup options dialog box, select Tools ➪ Startup.

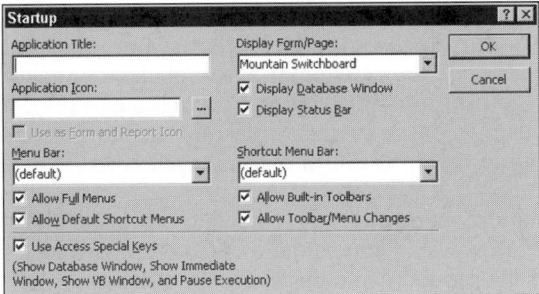

Figure 38-6: Using the Startup options dialog box gives you more security control than by using the /runtime option.

By making the appropriate specifications in the Startup options dialog box, you can do the following:

✦ Assign a title to the application.

✦ Assign an Application Icon to the application.

✦ Assign a form or data access page to immediately run when the database is open.

✦ Prevent the Database window (container) from being displayed.

✦ Prevent the status bar from being displayed.

✦ Designate a menu bar to be used on startup of your application.

✦ Designate a shortcut menu to be used on startup of your application.

✦ Prevent Access's built-in menus (full menus) from being displayed.

✦ Prevent Access's built-in shortcut menus from being displayed.

✦ Prevent Access's built-in toolbars from being displayed.

✦ Prevent users from modifying toolbars (toolbar/menu changes).

✦ Prevent users from using Access's special keys to display the Database window, display the debug window, or pause execution.

To designate the Mountain Switchboard form as the default form to open whenever the MAH2002 Chap38.mdb database is open, follow these steps:

1. With the MAH2002 Chap38.mdb database open, select Tools ⇨ Startup to open the Startup dialog box.

2. Click in the Display Form/Page: field and select the Mountain Switchboard form from the pull-down list (see Figure 38-6).

3. Click OK.

After you have assigned a form to automatically open, you can also specify that the Database window or status bar not be displayed to give even greater security to your application. By selecting these two items, when the user clicks the Close button on the form, the database window (container) won't be available to the user outside of your application. By using a database password and the Startup options, you can assign minimum security to the database and your application.

Caution   The user can bypass the Startup options by simply holding down the Shift key while opening the database. However, if you assign a database password, users will still be required to enter the password in order to use the database.

Distributing a Database as an .MDE File

One way to ensure the security of your application's code, forms, and reports is to distribute your database as an .MDE file, as discussed in the prior chapter. When you save your database as an .MDE file, Access compiles all code modules (including form modules), removes all editable source code, and compacts the database. The new .MDE file contains no source code but continues to work because it contains a compiled copy of all of your code. Not only is this a great way to secure your source code, it also enables you to distribute databases that are smaller (because they contain no source code) and always keep their modules in a compiled state.

In addition to not being able to view your source code, end users can't do the following to an .MDE file database:

✦ View, modify, or create forms, reports, or modules in Design view.

✦ Add, delete, or change references to object libraries or databases.

✦ Change your database's VBA project name by using the Options dialog box.

✦ Import or export forms, reports, or modules. Note, however, that tables, queries, and macros can be imported from or exported to database types other than .MDE databases.

Because of these benefits/restrictions, it may not be possible to distribute your application as an .MDE file. For example, if your application creates forms at runtime, you won't be able to distribute the database as an .MDE file.

Caution   .MDE files can't be converted into a normal database file, so always save and keep a copy of the original database. When you need to make changes to the application, you must open the normal database and then create a new .MDE file before distribution. If you delete your original database, you will be unable to access any of your objects in Design view.

Note   Your database has to meet some requirements before it can be saved as an .MDE file. First, if security is in use, the user creating the .MDE file must have all applicable rights to the database. Second, if the database is replicated, you must remove all replication system tables and properties before saving the .MDE file; you can't create an .MDE file from a replicated database, but you can replicate an .MDE database. Finally, you must save all databases or add-ins in the chain of references as .MDE files, or your database will be unable to use them.

Note   If you have a database open when you select Make MDE File, this step is skipped and Access assumes that you want to use the database that's open. If you want to use a different database, you need to cancel creating the .MDE file, close the database, and select Make MDE File again. Then you are asked for the database to save as an .MDE file.

To create an .MDE file, follow these steps:

1. Close the database if it is currently opened. If you don't close the current database, Access attempts to close it for you, prompting you to save changes where applicable. When working with a shared database, all users must close the database; Access needs exclusive rights to work with the database.

2. Select Tools ➪ Database Utilities and then click Make MDE File ... (see Figure 38-7).

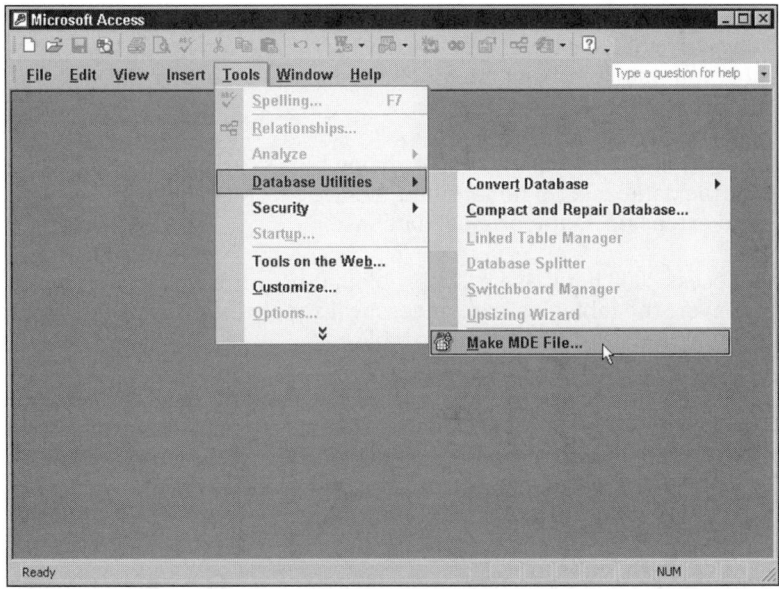

Figure 38-7: Access doesn't convert the existing database into an .MDE file; rather, it creates a new .MDE file for the database.

3. In the Database to Save as MDE dialog box (shown in Figure 38-8), specify the database that you want to save as an .MDE file, and click Make MDE.

Figure 38-8: When your security is active at the Jet level, Jet forces all users to enter a valid user name and password to use the secured database.

Access closes the current dialog box and opens a new dialog box titled "Save As MDE."

Tip   If you attempt to convert an Access 97 or 2000 version database, Access 2002 warns you that you must first convert the database to the newest version of Access (2002).

Caution   If you do not close the current database, Access will skip this step and assume that you want to convert the currently open database to an .MDE file.

4. In the Database to Save as MDE dialog box, specify a name, drive, and folder for the database. Do not attempt to save the .MDE file with the same filename and extension as the original database.

If your Access 2002 database has a problem during the conversion process, Access won't convert the table. Instead, Access will simply inform you that it was unable to create an .MDE database from the database.

Caution   Don't delete or overwrite your original database. As stated previously, MDE files can't be converted to a normal database, and you can't edit any objects in an .MDE file. If you delete or otherwise lose your original database, you will never again be able to access any of the objects in the design environment.

Using the Jet User-Level Security Model

Most often when security is required, setting a database password and runtime options is simply not enough.

When you need more security, you can use Access user profiles that are implemented by the user-level/object permissions security of Jet 4.0. The Jet Database Engine offers additional levels of customization and security for your application. When using Jet level security, you need to complete the following series of functions:

1. Select or create a workgroup database.

2. Define the workgroup database's security groups.

3. Create the users of the workgroup database.

4. Define permissions for each user and security group.

5. Enable security by setting an Admin user password.

Enabling security

Jet database security is always on. Whenever a new workgroup database is created, an Admin user is automatically created within the workgroup. This Admin user has no password assigned to it. When the Admin password is blank, Access assumes that any user attempting to open the database is the Admin user, and that this user is automatically logged in to the database as the Admin user. To force Access/Jet to ask for a valid user name and password to log in to the database (see Figure 38-8), you simply need to create a password for the Admin user (creating passwords are discussed later in this section). To "turn security off," simply clear the Admin user's password. The security permissions that you have designed are still in effect, but Access doesn't ask for a user name and password — it logs on all users as the Admin user with whatever permissions were assigned to the Admin user. Be careful about clearing the Admin user's password when you have modified the permissions of your users.

Tip　If you have cleared the Admin password only to find that some or all of the Admin user's permissions have been revoked, and you need access to the restricted objects or you need to log on as a different user, open the database and create a password for the Admin user, then exit and restart Access 2002 (not the database). When you restart Access, you are prompted to enter a user name and password. Any changes that you make to security won't take effect until you restart Access.

Working with workgroups

A *workgroup* is a collection of users, user groups, and object permissions. You can use a single workgroup file for all of your databases, or you may use different workgroups for different databases. The method that you use depends on the level of security that you need. If you give Administrative rights to users of some databases — but not to users of other databases — then you need to distribute separate workgroup files with each database. Access always uses a workgroup file when you open it. By default, this workgroup file is the SYSTEM.MDW workgroup file. This file comes with Access 2002.

What Is Jet and a User Profile?

When you create a Microsoft Access database (.mdb or .mde), Access uses an internal program to create and work with the database and its objects. Microsoft calls this internal program the *Jet Database Engine*. Its purpose is to retrieve and store data in user and system databases. Some people refer to the Jet engine as a *data manager* that the database system is built upon. Jet only works with Access databases — it doesn't work with other ODBC databases, such as SQL Server, Oracle, and others. Jet is available in three versions — 2.*x*, 3.*x*, and 4.0. The current version of Jet is 4.0 (in Access 2000 and 2002). When you installed Access, the installation program created several registry settings for the Jet engine. You can use the Registry Editor to examine and even change these settings for Access. However, we highly recommend that you do not change the setting in the Microsoft Windows registry.

Using Jet, you can build an Access user profile that is composed of a special set of Window's registry keys, which will override the standard Access and Jet database engine settings.

Creating a new workgroup

You can create new workgroups or join existing workgroups by using the Workgroup Administrator program that comes with Access 2002 (see Figure 38-9). In prior versions of Access (2000 and earlier), you accomplished this by using a separate program named WRKGADM.EXE. In Access 2002, you can access this program from the Tools ➪ Security menu.

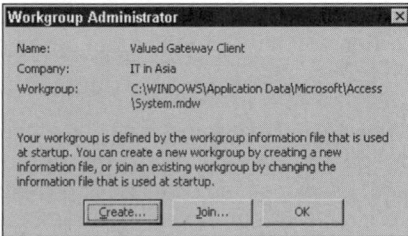

Figure 38-9: Use the Workgroup Administrator program to create new workgroups and to join existing workgroups.

Note   You should completely close down Access when creating new or joining existing workgroups. When you use the Workgroup Administrator to join a workgroup, that workgroup is not actually used until the next time you start Access.

To create a new workgroup file, follow these steps:

1. Start Access (with or without a database), select Tools ⇨ Security, and then click Workgroup Administrator.

2. Click the Create button in the Workgroup Administrator dialog box to display the Workgroup Owner Information dialog box.

3. The workgroup that you create is identified by three components: Name, Organization, and Workgroup ID (see Figure 38-10).

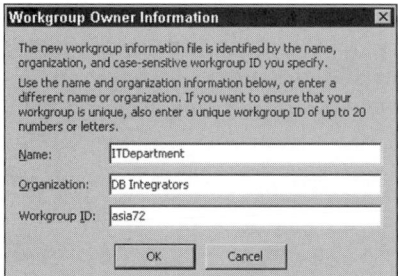

Figure 38-10: Workgroups are identified by these three key pieces of information. A workgroup can't be re-created without all three of these items.

Caution

In order to re-create the workgroup file in the event that it becomes corrupt or deleted, you need all three pieces of information. For this reason, to ensure that no other user can create your workgroup and access your secured database, you should supply a unique, random string for the Workgroup ID. Someone may possibly guess the name and organization used in your workgroup file if he or she knows who you are, but to guess all three items—especially if you create a random, unique ID—is almost impossible.

4. When you are satisfied with your entries, click OK to display the Workgroup Information File dialog box.

5. Enter the name to save the new workgroup file as is, and click OK to save the workgroup (see Figure 38-11). If you choose the existing file, SYSTEM.MDW, you will receive a confirmation box requesting that you confirm replacing the existing file.

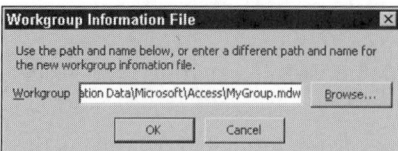

Figure 38-11: After defining your workgroup file, you need to give it a name in order to save it.

6. The Workgroup Administrator displays a confirmation dialog box (see Figure 38-12) containing the information that you entered for the new workgroup and explains the importance of writing down and storing the information. If you are satisfied with your entries, click OK to save your workgroup. If you want to change anything, click the Change button and you are returned to Step 3.

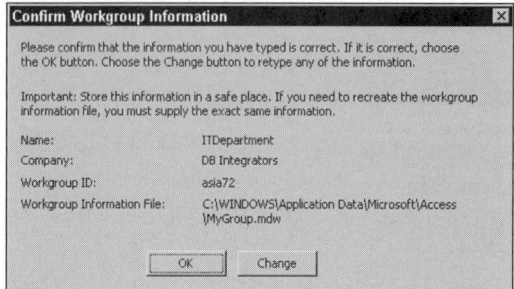

Figure 38-12: Follow the instructions given by this dialog box and write down this information. You may need it if you ever have to re-create the workgroup file.

An information box informs you that you have created the workgroup information file correctly.

Tip

In order to ensure that you can recover from the loss of your workgroup file, you should immediately make a copy of the workgroup file. In addition, you should write down the three pieces of information that you used to create the workgroup file, exactly as they were entered, in the event that you have to re-create the workgroup file from scratch. Store both the backup file copy and the written information in a secure place.

Joining an existing workgroup

When you create a new workgroup, Access automatically joins the new workgroup. If you don't want to use the new workgroup right away, or if at any time you need to use a workgroup other than the current workgroup, you need to join the desired workgroup by using the Workgroup Administrator.

To join an existing workgroup, follow these steps:

1. Activate the Workgroup Administrator program from the Tools ➪ Security menu.

2. The Workgroup Administrator dialog box displays the currently joined workgroup (refer back to Figure 38-9). Click the Join button to select a workgroup file. If you aren't sure of the filename, click the Browse button to display a File dialog box in which to locate the workgroup file.

3. A prompt appears, enabling you to confirm or cancel the joining of the selected workgroup. Click OK and then click Exit to close the Workgroup Administrator program.

Working with users

Every time a user opens an Access (Jet) database, Jet must identify the user opening the database. When security is "off" (in reality, security is never off; rather, "off" means security is at the default minimum—see the following section on enabling security), Jet always assumes that the Admin user is opening the database. When a new workgroup is created, Access automatically creates a default user with the Admin name; the Admin user is given full permissions to all objects in the database. Obviously, when you secure a database, you don't want everyone to be able to open the database with full permissions on all objects, so you must create additional users in the workgroup.

Adding and deleting user accounts

You add, delete, and edit user information with the User and Group Accounts dialog box (see Figure 38-13), which you access through the Tools ➪ Security ➪ User and Group Accounts ... menu item. The Users page (Users tab active) of the User and Group Accounts dialog box consists of two sections. You use the first section to maintain user names and passwords, and you use the second section to assign users to security groups. Assigning users to groups is discussed in detail later in this chapter.

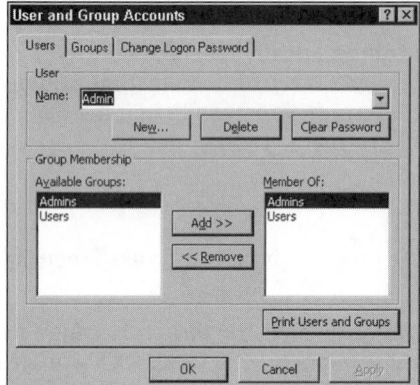

Figure 38-13: Users are maintained in the User and Group Accounts tabbed dialog box.

To fully secure your database with users and groups, you should generally follow these steps:

1. Create a new user.
2. Add the new user to the Admins group.
3. Remove the Admin user from the Admins group.
4. Assign all object ownerships to the new user.

When you create a user, you supply the user name and a personal identifier. Jet then combines these two items and processes them in a special algorithm, producing a unique security ID (SID). It is this SID that Jet uses to recognize users. In order to re-create a user in the workgroup, you need to know the user name and the personal ID (PID) that was used to create the user. Consequently, you should always write down and store all names and PIDs of users that you create in a safe place.

To create a new user in a workgroup, follow these steps:

1. Open the database MAH2002 Chap38.mdb to secure in Access.
2. Select Tools ⇨ Security ⇨ User and Group Accounts to display the User and Group Accounts dialog box.
3. Click the New button in the User section to display the New User/Group dialog box (see Figure 38-14).

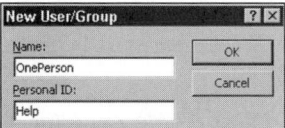

Figure 38-14: Jet employs the user name and personal identifier to create a unique SID for the user.

> **4.** Enter the name **Michaell** for the user and a unique personal ID of **MRI0204**. (You can enter any appropriate information into these two fields, if you don't want to use these example names.) Write this information down and store it in a safe place; you will need it to re-create the user in the workgroup.
>
> **5.** Click OK to save the new user.

After you have created the new user, Michaell, you can assign Group Memberships and/or a password for the user. Notice that Michaell is automatically a member of the Users group. Any new member that is automatically added to the Users group must at least belong to this Group. You can make Michaell a member of the Admins group by simply clicking the Add button in the Group Membership section.

Caution   To fully secure your database, you must remove all permissions for the Admin user, found under the Tools ➪ Security ➪ User and Group Permissions menu. (Working with Admin permissions is covered later in this chapter.) All Admin users share the same SID in all workgroups, on all machines. If you don't remove the permissions for the Admin user, an unauthorized user using a different workgroup can open the database as the Admin user with all permissions of the Admin user. The Admin user can't be deleted, so the Admin user account needs to be adjusted accordingly.

If you want to delete the user Michaell that you just created, follow these steps:

> **1.** Select Tools ➪ Security ➪ User and Group Accounts to display the User and Group Accounts dialog box.
>
> **2.** From the User Name drop-down list, select the User Michaell to delete.
>
> **3.** Click the Delete button to delete the selected user.

Creating and changing user passwords

Any member of the Admins group can remove a password from any user account, but no user can change or create a password for any other user; each user has the ability to change or create only his or her own password, regardless of security permissions.

Caution   If a password has been assigned to any user, then Access will start by first pre-senting the Logon Dialog box (refer back to Figure 38-8).

If no passwords are assigned to any of the users, however, Access 2002 will auto-matically start with the Admin user.

This means that any other users that you create in Security will *not* be able to assign themselves a password without first logging in via the Logon Dialog box (it won't appear). To correct this, you will need to create a password for the Admin user, and then quit Access and restart, logging in as the user whose password you want to change.

To create or change the Admin password, follow these steps:

1. Open the database MAH2002 Chap38.

2. Select Tools ➪ Security ➪ User and Group Accounts.

Caution   Make sure that the user name selected is Admin (not Michaell that you created earlier).

3. Click the Change Logon Password tab (see Figure 38-15).

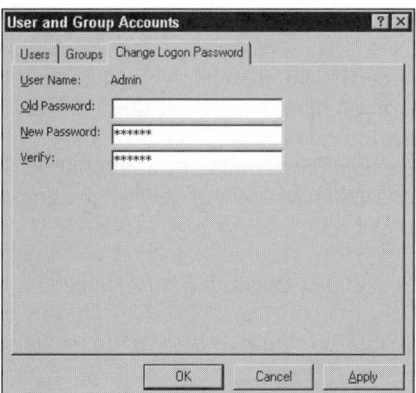

Figure 38-15: The Change Logon Password page of the User and Group Accounts dialog box. Notice that the name is "Admin" and can't be changed.

4. Because no password has been assigned to Admin, leave the Old Password field blank.

Tip If you are logging on for the Admin after you have assigned a password, or if a password exists for the user that you logged on as, enter it in the Old Password field. If no password is assigned to the user, leave the Old Password field blank.

5. Move to the New Password field and enter the new password **HelpMe** (or any other password that you want to assign—remember that Access's security is case-sensitive) in the New Password field. Access *won't* show you the word that you are typing; rather, it shows an asterisk for each character that you type.

6. Move to the Verify field and enter the new password **HelpMe** again. (Again, remember that Access's security is case-sensitive.) Each character is replaced with an asterisk.

7. Click the Apply button to save the new password for the Admin user.

8. Click OK to close the User and Group Accounts dialog box.

Tip After you have created a password for the user, as shown in Figure 28-15, you will have to quit Access 2002 and restart for the changes to take effect. Simply closing the database and opening it again won't activate the security changes (such as assigning a password to Admin) that you made.

Initially, the Admin user must have a password assigned to make sure that Access displays the Logon screen when it starts.

Users can't create or change passwords for users other than themselves, regardless of their permission settings.

Any user who has Admins rights can clear the password of another user so that second user can log in if he or she has forgotten his or her password.

To change another person's password, you will have to start Access and open the database by logging on to the database as the user whose password you want to change.

Working with groups

In addition to users, workgroups contain groups. *Groups* are collections of users; any user may belong to one or more groups. By creating a Group you can easily set up object permissions for sets of users—enabling you to define the permissions once, versus having to assign them separately for each user. When you want a user to have the security permissions of a particular group, you simply add the user to the desired group.

For example, you may have a number of users in a credit department and in a sales department. If you want to allow all of these users to look at a customer's credit history but restrict the sales staff to viewing only basic customer information, you have the following options:

✦ Allow all users in the credit department to log on as one user, and allow all users in the sales department to log on as a different user. You can then restrict the object permissions for each of these two users.

✦ Create an individual user account for each user in each department and assign object permissions for each user.

✦ Create an individual user account for each user in each department, and create a group account for each department. You can then make the permissions assignments for each of the two groups and place each user into his or her respective group to inherit the group's permissions.

The first method is straightforward and simple but presents many problems. If a user transfers from one department to another, he or she has user names and passwords for both departments and may be able to retrieve data that he or she is no longer authorized to view. In addition, if an employee leaves, the user name and password need to be changed, and each user of the workgroup has to be made aware of the change. In a multiuser environment, creating a unique user account for each user and then grouping them accordingly is a much better solution.

Although the second method — that of creating a unique user account and assigning specific permissions to each user — would work, it is an administrator's nightmare. If policy dictates that one of the departments needs to have permissions added or revoked, the change has to be made to each user's account for that department. With the third option, the change can be made to the department group once, and all users inherit the new permission settings.

Adding and deleting groups

Just as Access creates an Admin user in all new workgroups, it also creates two groups: Users and Admins. Every user account in the system belongs to the Users group; you can't remove a user from the Users group. The Admins group is the all-powerful, "Head Boss" group. Users of the Admins group have the ability to add and delete user and group accounts, as well as to assign and remove permissions for any object for any user or group in the workgroup. In addition, a member of the Admins group has the ability to remove other user accounts from the Admins group. For this reason, you need to carefully consider which users you allow to be members of the Admins group. The Admins group and the Users group are permanent groups; they can never be deleted.

Tip   Access doesn't enable you to remove all users from the Admins group; one user must belong to the Admins group at all times (the default is the Admin user). If you were allowed to remove all users from the Admins group, you could set up security so tight that you would never be able to bypass it yourself! In general, when securing a database, you should only place one or two users in the Admins group.

Note Unlike the Admin user's SID, which is identical in every Access workgroup, the Admins group's Security IDs (SIDs) are not identical from workgroup to workgroup, so unauthorized users using a workgroup other than the one that you used to define security can't access your database as a member of the Admins group. The Users group's SIDs are the same throughout all workgroups, however, so you need to remove all permissions for the Users group. If you don't remove permissions from the Users group, any user with any workgroup can open your database with the Users group's permissions.

To create a new group named *Sales,* follow these steps:

1. Open Access and then open the MAH2002 Chap38.mdb database and log in as Admin. Then select Tools ➪ Security ➪ User and Group Accounts to display the User and Group Accounts dialog box.

2. Click the Groups tab.

3. Click the New button to display the New User/Group dialog box (see Figure 38-16).

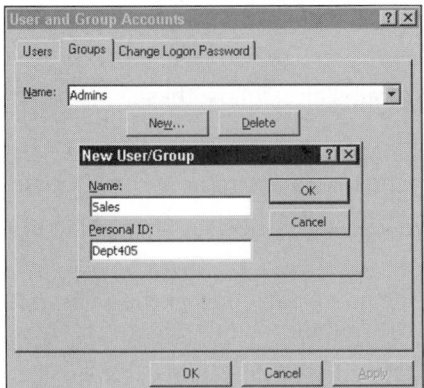

Figure 38-16: Jet uses the group name and personal identifier to create a unique SID for the security group, just as it does for user accounts.

4. Just as you do to create users, enter the group name **Sales** and a personal ID of **Dept405**. (If you aren't following along with this example, you can enter your group name and personal ID.) Also, just as before, write down this information and put it in a safe place because you will need it to re-create the group at a later time.

5. Click OK to save the new group.

6. After this is complete, you can click OK in the Accounts dialog box to save your work.

If, at a later time, you want to delete the same Sales group that you just created, follow these steps:

1. Select Tools ⇨ Security ⇨ User and Group Accounts ... to display the User and Group Accounts dialog box.

2. Click the Groups tab (refer to Figure 38-16).

3. From the drop-down list, select the Sales group to delete.

4. Click the Delete button to delete the selected group.

Assigning and removing group members

Assigning users to and removing users from groups is a simple process. All assignments and removals are performed under the Users tab of the User and Group Accounts dialog box. You may place any user in any group, and users may belong to more than one group. As previously stated, you can't remove a user from the Users group, nor can you remove all users from the Admins group; you must always have at least one user in the Admins group.

To add the user MichaelI to the new group Sales, follow these steps:

1. With the database MAH2002 Chap38.mdb open, select Tools ⇨ Security ⇨ User and Group Accounts to display the User and Group Accounts dialog box.

2. From the User Name drop-down list, select the user MichaelI to modify his group assignments.

3. To assign the user MichaelI to the group Sales, select the Sales group in the Available Groups list and click the Add button (see Figure 38-17).

The selected group, Sales, is then added to the Member Of list.

4. Click OK to save the new group assignments.

To remove the new group Sales from the user MichaelI, follow these steps:

1. With the database MAH2002 Chap38.mdb open, select Tools ⇨ Security ⇨ User and Group Accounts to display the User and Group Accounts dialog box, if it isn't already open.

2. Select the group Sales in the Member Of list and click the Remove button. The selected group is then removed from the Member Of list.

3. Click OK to save the new group assignments.

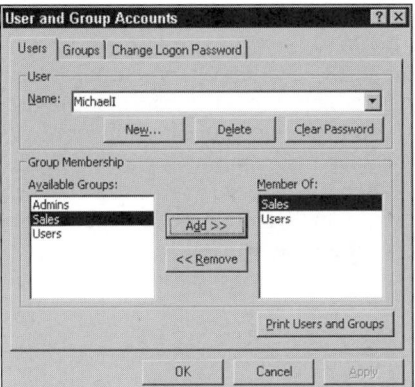

Figure 38-17: Assigning users to groups makes controlling object permissions much easier for the system administrator.

Because Jet uses the same SIDs for all Admin user accounts throughout all workgroups, you always need to remove the Admin user from the Admins group when securing a database. Figure 38-17 shows that the user MichaelI has been added to the Sales group. Notice that MichaelI is a member of two groups — Users and Sales. He was either not assigned or has been removed from the Admins group. Before leaving this section, assign MichaelI to the Admins group, so you can use this example later in this chapter. The only remaining task is to verify that the Users group doesn't contain any permissions that you don't want unauthorized users to have, and that no explicit permissions are assigned to the Sales user account (see the next section, "Securing objects by using permissions").

Securing objects by using permissions

After you have defined your users and groups, you must decide on the specific object permissions that a user or group is to have. Permissions control who can view data, update data, add data, and work with objects in Design view. Permissions are the heart of the Jet security system and can only be set by a member of the Admins group, by the owner of the object (see the next section), or by any user who has Administrator permission on the object in question.

Setting an objects owner

Every object in the database can have an owner. The *owner* is a user account in the workgroup that is designated to always have Administrator rights to the object, regardless of the group to which they belong or of the permissions explicitly applied to them for the object. You can designate one user to be the owner of all the objects in a database, or you may assign different owners to different objects.

Access queries require special consideration when assigning owners to objects. When creating a query, you can set the Run Permissions property of the query to either User's or Owner's (see Figure 38-18). By default, when passwords are activated, this permission is set to User's, which limits the users of the query to seeing only the data that their security permissions permit. If you want to enable users to view or modify data that they don't have permissions for, you can set the Run Permissions property to Owner's. When the query is run with the Owner's permissions (WITH OWNERACCESS OPTION in an SQL statement), users inherit the permissions of the owner of the query when they run the query. These permissions are applicable only to the query, and not to the entire database.

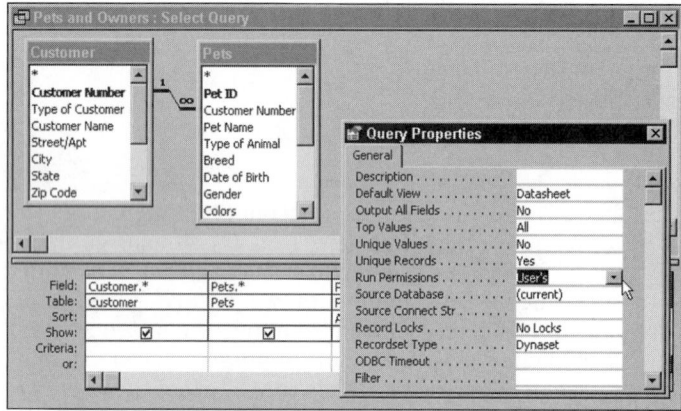

Figure 38-18: Judicious use of OwnerAccess queries enables you to temporarily grant object permissions to users who don't currently have those permissions.

 Tip   When a query's Run Permissions property is set to Owner's, only the owner can make changes to the query. If this restriction poses a problem, you may want to set the owner of the query to a group rather than to a user account. Note that only the owner of an OwnerAccess query can change the query's owner.

 **Note**   If you haven't assigned passwords to Admin or other users, the user is automatically assumed to be Admin and the query's Run Permissions property is set to Owner's.

To change the owner of any object in the database, follow these steps:

1. Select Tools ➪ Security ➪ User and Group Permissions (the third choice in the Security menu) to display the User and Group Permissions dialog box.

2. Click the Change Owner tab (see Figure 38-19).

3. Select the object (or objects) whose ownership you want to transfer. You can select the type of objects to display by changing the Object Type field.

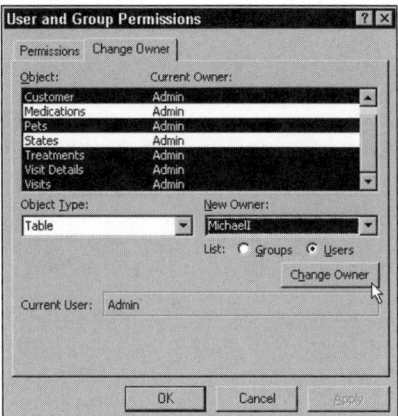

Figure 38-19: Controlling an object's owners is an important step in securing a database. This figure demonstrates changing the selected table objects ownership from the Admin user to the new Group Sales.

4. Select the user or group that you want to make the owner of the selected object. To select a group name, first select the group List radio button.

5. Click the Change Owner button to change the object's owner to the selected user or group.

Note   Not only do each of the objects in a database have an owner, the database also has an owner. You can view the owner of the database by selecting Database from the Object Type drop-down list. You can't change an object's owner by using Access's interface. The only way to change a database's owner is to log on as the user that you want to make the owner of the database, create a new database, and then import the original database into the new database by using the Import Database add-in. When you import a database, the current user is assigned as the new owner of the database and all of the database objects; this is essentially what the Security Wizard (discussed later in this chapter) does for you.

Setting object permissions

Object permissions are the heart of Jet security. One or more object permissions at a time can be set for users and groups. When assigning permissions, you must keep in mind that some permissions automatically imply other permissions. For example, if you assign a user Read Data permission for a table, the Read Design permission is also granted because a table's design must be available to access the data. A more complex example is assigning permission for Insert Data — this automatically grants permission for Read Data and Read Design.

An object's permission assignments are persistent until one of the following conditions occurs:

✦ A member of the Admins group changes the object's permissions.

✦ The object is saved with a new name by using the Save As command from the File menu.

✦ The object is cut and pasted in the Database window.

✦ The object is imported or exported.

If any of the preceding actions occur, all permissions for the manipulated object are lost, and you have to reassign them. This loss of permissions occurs because you are actually creating a new object when you perform any of the actions (versus editing and saving the same object), and new objects are assigned the default permissions that are defined for the object's type.

It's important that you understand the two types of permissions:

✦ Explicit permissions are permissions that are granted directly to a user. When you explicitly assign a permission to a user, no other user's permissions are affected.

✦ Implicit permissions are permissions that are granted to a group. All users belonging to a group implicitly have the permissions of that group.

Note   Because permissions can be assigned implicitly, and because some permissions grant other permissions (as mentioned in the previous discussion of the Insert Data, Read Data, and Read Design permission relationship), users may be able to grant themselves permissions that they don't currently have. Because of this possibility, you must plan carefully when assigning permissions to groups of users and to individual users.

To assign or revoke a user's permissions for an object, follow these steps:

1. Select Tools ➪ Security ➪ User and Group Permissions ... to display the User and Group Permissions dialog box. Make sure that the Permissions tab is active (the first tab).

2. Select the type of object whose permissions you want to change from the Object Type drop-down list (located on the right side and center of the dialog box).

3. Select the user or group account for which you want to modify the permissions (from the User/Group Name list box). To see a list of all Groups, click the List: radio button under the Name section.

4. Select the object (or objects) for which you want to modify the permissions (from the Object Name list box).

5. Select or deselect the permissions check boxes for the object(s) (in the Permissions grouping section of the dialog box — bottom half).

6. Click Apply to commit the permission assignments.

Remember that Admin user SIDs are identical throughout all workgroups, so after you assign Administer permissions to a specific user, you need to remove all permissions for the Admin user in order to secure your database. Figure 38-20 shows the Admin user's permissions being revoked for all tables in the database. Note how all check boxes have been cleared, thus preventing an Admin user from doing anything with the table object. Each Object Type needs to be selected and the process repeated until the Admin user has no permissions for any object.

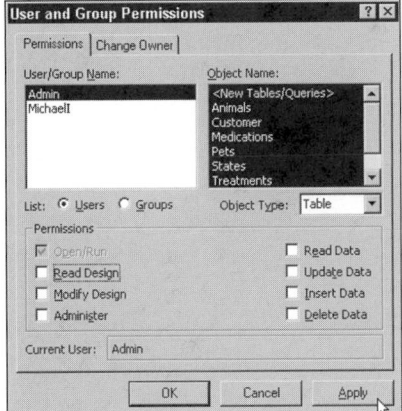

Figure 38-20: Removing all permissions for the Admin user is critical to securing your database.

Setting default object permissions

You can create default permission assignments for each type of object in a database. These default permissions are assigned when a new object is created, imported, or cut and pasted within the database container. You set the default permissions just as you set them for any other object's permissions. You must select the user or group to assign default permissions to, but you don't select a specific object. When you select the Object Type from the drop-down list, the first item in the Object Name list is <New OBJECT>, where OBJECT is replaced with the actual object type selected, such as <New Forms> or <New Tables/Queries>. When you assign permissions for users and groups to these <New> items, the permissions are used as defaults for all new objects of that type.

Tip   When removing default permissions for table objects, if you have created make table queries, you must ensure that any users running the make table query have the ability to create new tables. If you remove a user's permission to create new tables, that user won't be able to execute a make table query.

Setting database permissions

Each database has permissions, just as the objects in the database do. Selecting Database from the Object Type drop-down list will display the database permissions that can be modified (see Figure 38-21). The database permissions enable you to control who has administrative rights to the entire database, who can open the database exclusively (locking out other users), and who can open or run the database.

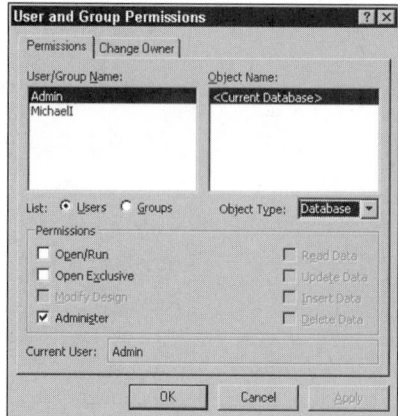

Figure 38-21: You can assign permissions for the entire database, not just for individual objects.

Securing your database for distribution: A basic approach

If you are securing a database for distribution, then setting up detailed security for multiple users for all objects in your database may not be important to you. Often, the only concern with shipping a secured database is protecting your development investment by securing the design of your objects and code. If you need this protection, you can distribute your application as an .MDE file (see the section "Distributing a Database as an .MDE File"), or you can follow these steps:

1. Create a workgroup to distribute with your database.

2. Remove the Admin user from the Admins group.

3. Remove all permissions for the Users group.

4. Remove any and all design permissions for the Admin user for all objects in the database.

5. Don't supply a password for the Admin user.

By not supplying a password for the Admin user, you are telling Access to log on all users as the Admin user. Because the Admin user has no rights to the design of any objects, users can't access your objects or code in Design view.

If you use this method to secure the design of your objects, and you need to modify objects using DAO that the Admin user doesn't have rights for (such as QueryDefs, TableDefs, or reading data from a secured table), then you need to create a temporary workspace as a user with administrative rights for the object.

For example, if you have a table called "tblRegistration" in which you keep registration and licensing information that you don't want the Admin user to be able to update, you can remove the Update Data permissions for the table. However, if you attempt to update the table using DAO, you receive an error because the logged-in user — the Admin user — doesn't have sufficient rights to manipulate the table. You can avoid this error by using a temporary workspace. Creating a temporary workspace is essentially the action of logging into the database as a user in Visual Basic; the login is valid for the scope of the workspace object that you dimension. The following is sample code that creates a temporary workspace and edits the data (changes the Reg Name field to a value of Sue Johnson) in tblRegistration. This example assumes that a valid user by the name of "Richard Irwin" exists in the current workgroup and has the password "Railroad":

```
Dim TempWorkspace As Workspace, MyDB As Database, tbl As Table
Set TempWorkspace = DBEngine.CreateWorkspace("TempWs", _
"Richard Irwin", "Railroad")
 DBEngine.Workspaces.Append TempWorkspace
    Set MyDB = TempWorkspace.OpenDatabase(CurrentDB().Name)
    Set tbl = MyDB.OpenTable("tblUsers")
tbl.Edit
  tbl![Reg Name] = "Sue Johnson"
  tbl.Update
```

The `CreateWorkspace` method of the `DBEngine` object accepts three parameters:

✦ **A name to call the temporary workspace.** In the preceding code sample, the name assigned to the workspace is "TempWs," but you can choose any name.

✦ **The user name to use for logging in.** The preceding example creates a temporary workspace for the user Richard Irwin.

✦ **The user's password.** In the preceding example, Richard Irwin's password is "Railroad."

Tip   Because you must supply the user's password when creating a temporary workspace, and because the user has additional rights (or you wouldn't be following this procedure), it is absolutely critical that you secure the View Design permissions for all modules or forms that use the preceding code. If you don't secure objects that contain the code to create the temporary workspace, users can get the user name and password from your code and log in to the database as that user.

Table 38-1 summarizes permissions that you can assign.

Table 38-1 Summary of Assignable Permissions		
Permission	**Permits a User To**	**Applies To**
Open/Run	Open a database, form, or report, or run a macro.	Databases, forms, reports, and macros
Open Exclusive	Open a database with exclusive access.	Databases only
Read Design	View objects in Design view.	Tables, queries, forms, macros, and modules
Modify Design	View and change the design of objects, or delete them.	Tables, queries, forms, macros, and modules
Administer	For databases, set database password, replicate a database, and change start-up properties. For database objects, have full access to objects and data, including the ability to assign permissions.	Databases, tables, queries, forms, reports, macros, and modules
Read Data	View data.	Tables and queries
Update Data	View and modify but not insert or delete data.	Tables and queries
Insert Data	View and insert but not modify or delete data.	Tables and queries
Delete Data	View and delete but not modify or insert data.	Tables and queries

Using the Access Security Wizard

Access includes a tool to help you secure your databases—the Security Wizard. The Security Wizard enables you to select the objects to secure, and then it creates a new database containing secured versions of the selected objects. The Security Wizard assigns the currently logged-in user as the owner of the objects in the new database and removes all permissions from the Users group for those objects. Finally, the Security Wizard encrypts the new database. The original database is not modified in any way. Only members of the Admins group and the user who ran the Security Wizard have access to the secured objects in the new database.

Tip When you use the Security Wizard, make sure that you are logged in as the user that you want to become the new database's owner. You must already belong to the Admins group and you can't log in as Admin. If you log in as the user Admin, Access will report an error when you attempt to run the Security Wizard. This error tells you that you can't be logged in as the Admin user if the database has been previously secured. If this happens, simply log in as another user that belongs to the Admins group.

To run the Security Wizard, select Tools ⇨ Security ⇨ User-Level Security Wizard when you have logged into the database that you want to work with.

Follow these steps to create and open the MAH2002 SecureWizard database—assuming that user Michaell still has been added to the Admins group—and activate the Security Wizard:

1. While in Windows and outside of Access, go to the subdirectory that holds the MAH2002 Chap38.mdb. Copy this file and name the new copy *MAH2002 SecureWizard.mdb*.

2. Start Access and open the MAH2002 SecureWizard database.

   Access prompts you for a user and password. The database has inherited all the security of the original file when it was created in Windows.

3. Enter **Michaell** in the Name field and click OK. The user Michaell has no password assigned to it.

   Access opens the MAH2002 SecureWizard database.

4. Select Tools ⇨ Security ⇨ User-Level Security Wizard from the menu to start the wizard.

The wizard first informs you that you will need to use either the existing workgroup information file (to modify it) or create a new one for the current open database (see Figure 38-22). Select Create a new workgroup information file and press the Next button.

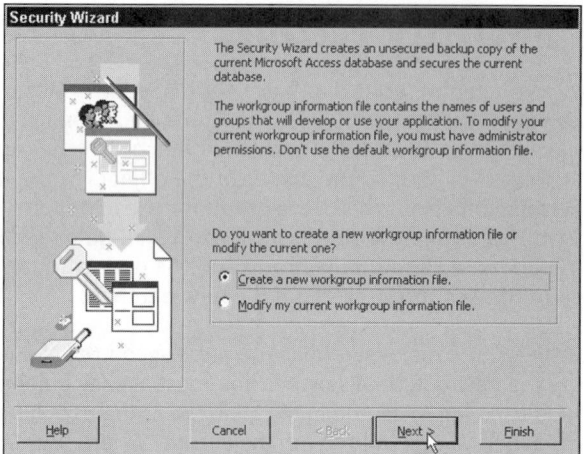

Figure 38-22: The Security Wizard helps jump-start your security implementation.

Tip

If you select Create a new workgroup information file, you are taken to a page that asks you for the filename of the file, a Workgroup ID number (WID—this must be remembered to re-create it later), and, optionally, your name and company. Figure 38-23 shows the Security Wizard screen that enables you to create a new workgroup information file.

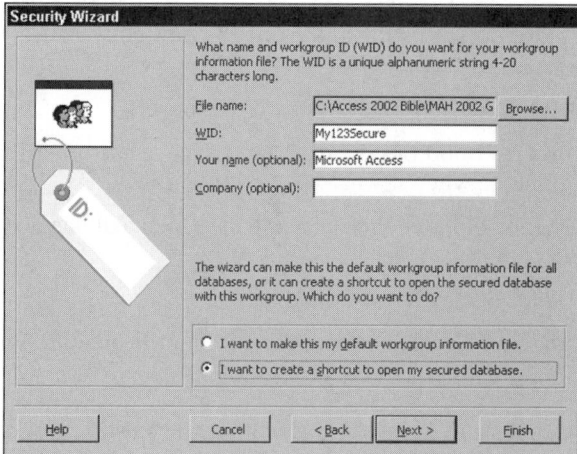

Figure 38-23: Assigning a unique WID and name to new workgroup information file.

When the new workgroup information file screen appears, it automatically assigns a random 20-character string of numbers and letters to the WID (Workgroup ID) field. You can change this WID to any value, as shown in Figure 38-23.

As Figure 38-23 shows, you can choose to make this the new default workgroup file for all databases (not recommended), or have Access 2002 create a shortcut to use this file only for this database (default). Selecting the default and assigning a short-cut associates this file with only one database. Click the Next button to go to the next screen of the wizard.

The next screen of the wizard lets you decide what objects you want to secure. By default, the wizard secures all existing database objects. If you deselect an object type (such as Tables or Forms), none of the objects of that type are exported to the secured database. Figure 38-24 shows this page of the wizard. If you don't want to restrict security permissions for a set of objects but still want those objects included in the new, secured database, then you need to select the objects in the wizard and then modify the user and group permissions for those objects in the new, secured database. When you are satisfied with your object selections, click the Next button to continue.

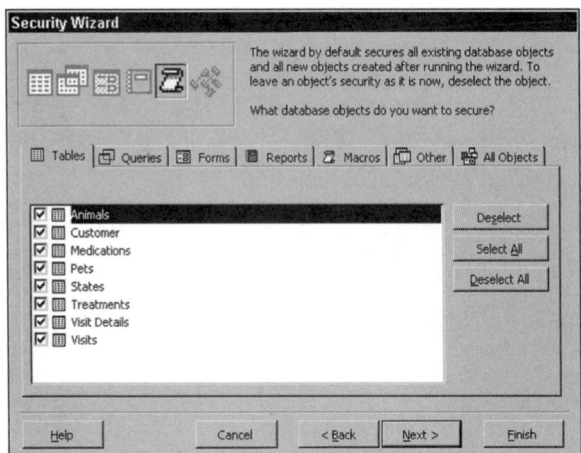

Figure 38-24: The Security Wizard helps jump-start your security implementation by asking which objects you want to protect.

At this point, the wizard asks you for a password that you want to assign for all of your Visual Basic for Applications (VBA) modules that are contained in your database — if they are protected with a password. This screen won't appear if you haven't previously assigned passwords to your VBA modules. If it does appear, you can assign a password and click the Next button to continue.

The next screen of the wizard asks you to input an optional security group account for a series of group actions. These include:

- ✦ Backup Operators — Can open the database exclusively for backing up and compacting.

- ✦ Full Data Users — Can edit data, but not alter design.

- ✦ Full Permissions — Has full permissions for all database objects, but can't assign permissions.

- ✦ New Data Users — Can read and insert data only (no edits or deletions).

- ✦ Project Designers — Can edit data and objects, and alter tables or relationships.

- ✦ Read-Only Users — Can read data only.

- ✦ Update Data Users — Can read and update, but can't insert or delete data or alter design of objects.

Figure 38-25 shows this page with all groups checked (the default is off). After you have selected all groups, click the Next button to continue.

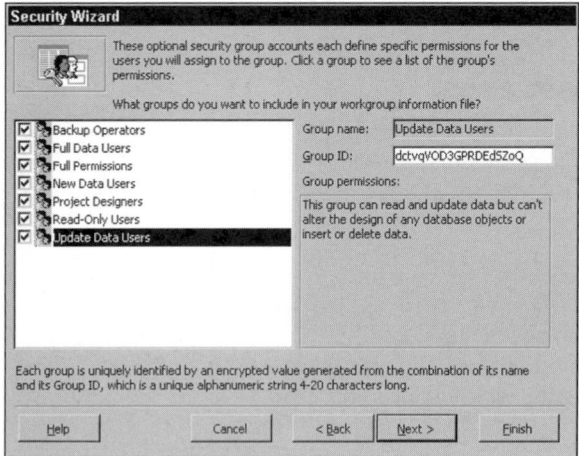

Figure 38-25: Additional optional security groups created for the database.

Notice that the next page of the wizard lets you choose to grant permissions to the Users group (the default is no permissions). By selecting yes, you are able to assign rights to all object types in the database. Figure 38-26 shows this page active with the Yes option selected. The default choice is No, the Users group should not have any permissions. Click the Next button to continue through the wizard.

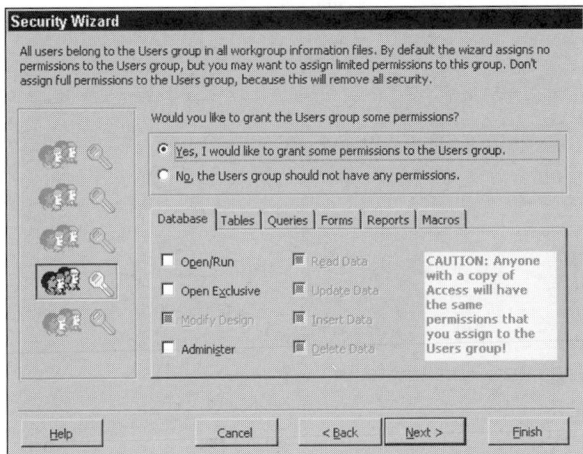

Figure 38-26: The ability to assign permissions to the Users group.

Caution   If you decide to grant some permissions to the Users group, you should be aware that anyone with a copy of Access will have the same permissions that you assign to this group. Essentially, you are opening the database to a security breach if you assign rights to this group.

Figure 38-27 shows the next page of the wizard. This page lets you add users to the workgroup information file. To add a user, you have to put their name and password in the correct fields and click the Add this user to the list button.

As Figure 38-27 shows, you can also remove users from the list by simply selecting their name from the list box on the left side and pressing the Delete user from the list button. Click the Next button to continue through the wizard.

The wizard then takes you to a page that enables you to assign users to groups in your workgroup information file. If you added optional groups from the earlier page (as shown in Figure 38-25), you can now assign each user in your group to these groups by turning the check box on. To select a user to assign rights to, simply select the user from the combo box and then assign that user to groups by using the check boxes. The default value for all users except the person creating the wizard is belonging to new groups. Figure 38-28 shows this page with all check boxes selected. Click the Next button to go to the next screen.

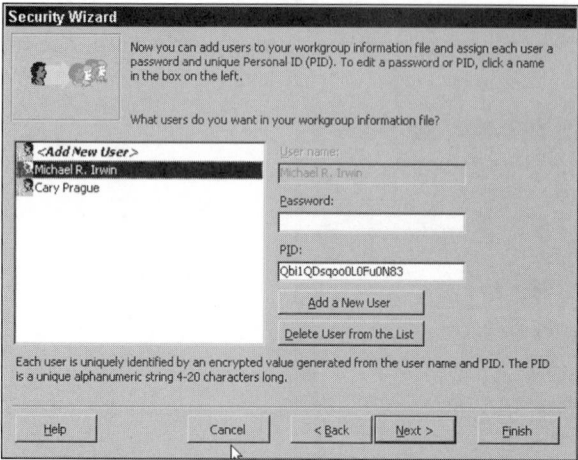

Figure 38-27: Adding users and passwords to the database information file.

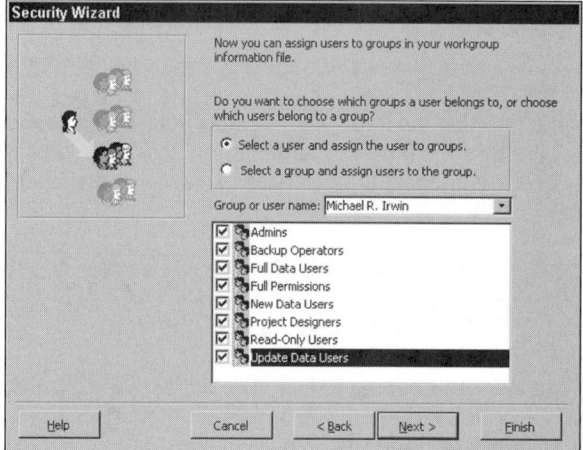

Figure 38-28: Adding users to groups for group rights.

This is the last page of the wizard. After going through the previous pages, the Security Wizard finally asks you to provide a name for the old (now unsecure) database (see Figure 38-29). The default name is the same name as the current database with the extension .bak. Click the Finish button to end the Wizard.

Technically, the Security Wizard doesn't make any modifications to the current database; rather, it makes a backup copy by using the name that you specify and creates an *entirely new* database with secured objects. However, the new database is given the name of the original database. When you distribute your secured application, make sure to distribute the database that the Security Wizard created for you.

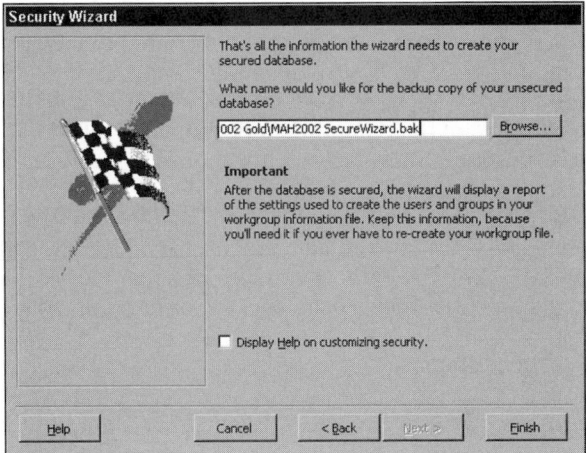

Figure 38-29: In the Final dialog box, the Security Wizard asks you to assign a name to the old database.

Tip   After the database is secured, a report is generated containing all of the settings used to create the users and groups in the workgroup information file. You should keep this information. Should you ever need to re-create the workgroup file, you will require this information.

Caution   If you click the Finish button and Access finds any problems, it won't create the security database or the backup that you requested. Usually you will get this error when you have created the database and logged on as a user that secured the table and then re-logged in as another user to secure it. This wizard works best with databases that have not had any security set up.

Generally, making a copy of the original database and working with the secured database is a good idea. If you make changes to the original database, you will need to run the Security Wizard again to create a secured version of the database. In addition, making a copy of the original database and then removing it from development helps prevent accidentally distributing the unsecured database. After entering the new database name, click Save to save the secured database.

After supplying a name for the backup unsecured database (the original), the Security Wizard creates the database with the secured objects and gives you a summary of every action made by the wizard.

Encrypting a Database

When security is of utmost importance, one final step that you need to take is to *encrypt* the database. Although it takes a great deal of skill (far more than the average computer user — or developer — possesses), using tools to view the actual database structure on the hard drive of the computer is possible. A skilled hacker may use this information to reconstruct SIDs and gain full access to your secured database.

Encrypting a database makes using such tools to gain any useful information about the database virtually impossible. Only the database owner or a member of the Admins group (or a really good computer hacker) can encrypt or decrypt a database.

To encrypt a database, follow these steps:

1. With no database open, select Tools ➪ Security ➪ Encrypt/Decrypt Database (see Figure 38-30).

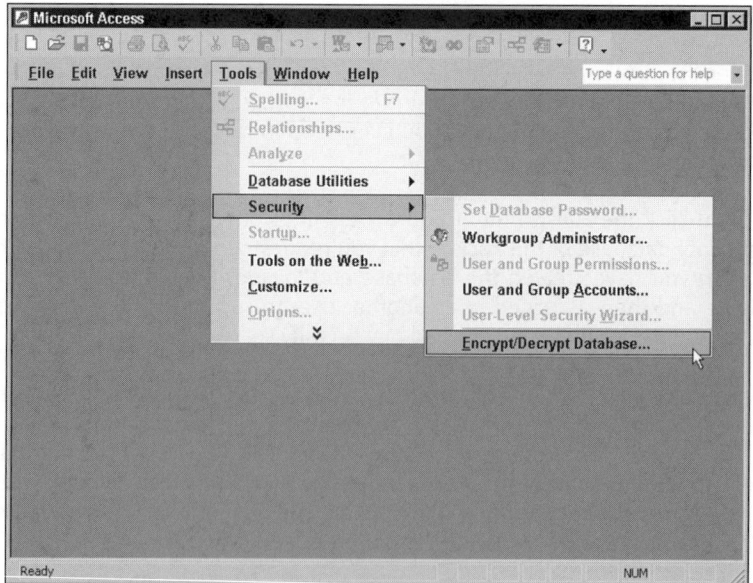

Figure 38-30: Encrypting a database helps ensure its security from highly skilled hackers.

2. Select the database to encrypt from the Encrypt/Decrypt dialog box.

3. Provide a name for the new encrypted database.

Access doesn't modify the original database when it encrypts it. Rather, Access creates a clone of the database and encrypts the clone. Just like when using the Security Wizard, you should make a backup copy of the original database and store it somewhere safe to prevent accidentally distributing the unencrypted database. Remember that in a world of rapidly changing data, your backup will rapidly become out of date.

In addition to encrypting a database by using Access's interface, it's possible to encrypt a database by using VBA code. The following code example can be used to encrypt a database:

```
Public Sub EncryptDatabase()
On Error GoTo EncryptDatabaseErr
Dim szDBName As String, szEncryptedDBname As String
szDBName = _
"c:\Access2002Bible\MAH 2002 Gold\MAH2002 Chap38.mdb"
szEncryptedDBname = _
"c:\ Access2002Bible\MAH 2002 Gold\encrypted.mdb"
DBEngine.CompactDatabase szDBName, szEncryptedDBname,
dbLangGeneral, _ dbEncrypt
Exit Sub
EncryptDatabaseErr:
    MsgBox Err & ":  " & Err.Description
    Exit Sub
End Sub
```

As stated previously, few people have the ability or drive to hack a database in the way that encryption prevents, but encryption is a necessary step for securing highly sensitive databases. If you choose to encrypt a database, you have to accept the following drawbacks:

✦ Encrypted databases don't compress from their original size when used with compression programs, such as PKZIP or the ODE Setup Wizard; encryption modifies the way that the data is stored on the hard drive and renders the compression algorithms useless.

✦ Encrypted databases suffer some performance degradation (up to 15 percent). Depending on the size of your database and the speed of your computer, this loss may not be noticeable.

Note Encrypting a database should be performed as an *additional* step to securing a database by using users, groups, and permissions. Simply encrypting a database does nothing to secure the database from users using Access. Encryption is an addition, not a complete solution, to securing a database.

Decrypting a Database

Access 2002 lets you decrypt a previously encrypted database. To decrypt a database, follow these steps (which are similar to the encrypting process):

1. With no database open, select Tools ➪ Security ➪ Encrypt/Decrypt Database.
2. Select the database to decrypt from the Encrypt/Decrypt dialog box.
3. Provide a name for the new decrypted database.

That is all there is to reversing an encryption.

Manipulating Security Objects Using DAO

An example used in the section on securing your database for distribution earlier in this chapter demonstrates how to create temporary workspaces to gain the permissions of users other than the user that you are logged in as. In addition, it's possible to create users and groups, remove or change passwords, change ownership of objects, and assign permissions for objects — all by using DAO in VBA code.

Creating a user account by using DAO

DAO includes a number of security objects that you can manipulate. First and foremost are the User and Group objects. By using these objects, you can create or delete users, as well as change or remove user passwords. You create Users and Groups by defining the user or group and then appending it to the User or Group collection. The following code creates a new user account by using DAO:

```
Public Sub CreateUser()
Dim usrNew As User, szUserName As String, szPID As String
Dim szPassword As String
szUserName = "Arni Lim"
szPID = "MYPID105"
szPassword = "TheDoc"
  ' Create a new user account.
Set usrNew = DBEngine.Workspaces(0).CreateUser(szUserName, _
szPID, szPassword)
  ' Save the new user account by appending it to Users
collection.
DBEngine.Workspaces(0).Users.Append usrNew
End Sub
```

Changing a user's password by using DAO

The password parameter of the `CreateUser` method is an optional parameter. By using the password property of the user object, the password can also be set as follows:

```
usrNew.PassWord = "TheDoc"
```

This property must be set after the `CreateUser` method and prior to the `Append` method. To change the password of an existing user account, you need to use the `NewPassword` method of the `Users` object, as shown in the following procedure:

```
Public Sub ChangePassword()
On Error GoTo ChangePasswordErr
Dim szUserName As String, szOldPassword As String,
szNewPassword As _ String
szUserName = "Arni Lim"
szOldPassword = "TheDoc"
szNewPassword = "Surgery"
Workspaces(0).Users(szUserName).NewPassword szOldPassword, _
szNewPassword
Exit Sub
ChangePasswordErr:
    MsgBox Err & ":   " & Err.Description
    Exit Sub
End Sub
```

The `NewPassword` method accepts three arguments:

- ✦ The name of the user whose password is to be changed
- ✦ The existing password for the user
- ✦ The new password to assign to the user

If you create procedures that add or change passwords in code, you must protect or delete the code prior to distributing the application in order to prevent a user from obtaining other users' passwords.

Creating a group account using DAO

Creating a group account is much like creating a user account. The difference is that the `Group` object and collection are used in place of the `User` object and collection. The following code creates a new group account:

```
Public Sub CreateGroup()
On Error GoTo CreateGroupErr
Dim grpSales As Group, szGroupName As String, szPID As String
```

```
szGroupName = "Sales"
szPID = "GroupPID0456"
 ' Create the new Group object.
 Set grpSales = DBEngine.Workspaces(0).CreateGroup(szGroupName,
_ szPID)
' Create the new group by appending it to Groups collection.
 Workspaces(0).Groups.Append grpSales
Exit Sub
CreateGroupErr:
    MsgBox Err & ":  " & Err.Description
    Exit Sub
End Sub
```

Changing an object's owner by using DAO

Ownership entitles users to certain irrevocable rights to objects in the database.
You should take great care in protecting the ownership of the objects in your
database. If you need to change an ownership through VBA code, you use the
Owner property of a Document object, as follows:

```
Public Sub ChangeOwner()
On Error GoTo ChangeOwnerErr
Dim db As Database, ctrTemp As Container, docModule As Document
Dim szNewOwner As String
szNewOwner = "Tabatha Thrush"
 ' Return Database variable that points to current database.
 Set db = CurrentDb
' Return Container variable that points to Modules container.
 Set ctrTemp = db.Containers!Forms
' Return Document object that points to mdlUtilities module.
 Set docModule = ctrTemp.Documents!frmSwitchBoard
' Change the owner by setting the Owner property of the
Document _ object
docModule.Owner = szNewOwner
Exit Sub
ChangeOwnerErr:
    MsgBox Err & ":  " & Err.Description
    Exit Sub
End Sub
```

Assigning object permissions by using DAO

Permissions are manipulated by using the UserName and Permissions properties
of a document or container object. For example, the function in the following code
assigns full permissions on all modules for the user Laura Thrush:

```
Sub SetPermissions()
' This procedure is to demonstrate changing user permissions
' programmatically.
On Error GoTo SetPermissionsErr
Dim db As Database, ctr As Container, szUserName As String
szUserName = "Tabatha Thrush"
Set db = CurrentDb()
' Set the container to the table objects
 Set ctr = db.Containers!Modules
 ' Set UserName property to valid existing user account.
 ctr.UserName = szUserName
 ' Set permissions for all table objects
 ctr.Permissions = dbSecFullAccess
Exit Sub
SetPermissionsErr:
    MsgBox Err & ":  " & Err.Description
    Exit Sub
End Sub
```

Tables 38-2, 38-3, and 38-4 show all available permission constants. If you want to set multiple permissions, add the properties together as follows:

```
ctr.Permissions = dbSecDelete + dbSecReadSec
```

Table 38-2
General DAO Permissions Constants

Constant	Description
DbSecNoAccess	No access to the object
DbSecFullAccess	Full access to the object
DbSecDelete	Can delete the object
DbSecReadSec	Can read the object's security-related information
DbSecWriteSec	Can alter access permissions
DbSecWriteOwner	Can change the Owner property setting

The possible settings or return values for the Tables Container object or any Document object in a Documents collection are shown in Table 38-3.

Table 38-3
Constants Applicable Only to Tables, Containers, and Their Documents

Constant	Description
DbSecCreate	Can create new documents (valid only with a Container object)
DbSecReadDef	Can read the table definition, including column and index information
DbSecWriteDef	Can modify or delete the table definition, including column and index information
DbSecRetrieveData	Can retrieve data from the Document object
DbSecInsertData	Can add records
DbSecReplaceData	Can modify records
DbSecDeleteData	Can delete records

The possible settings or return values for the Databases Container object or any Document object in a Documents collection are shown in Table 38-4.

Table 38-4
Constants Applicable Only to Databases, Containers, and Their Documents

Constant	Description
DbSecDBAdmin	Gives the user permission to make a database replicable and to change the database password
DbSecDBCreate	Can create new databases (valid only on the Databases Container object in the system database [SYSTEM.MDW])
DbSecDBExclusive	Exclusive access
DbSecDBOpen	Can open the database

With a full understanding of the Jet security model and how to manage it, you can create databases that protect your development investment and your users' data.

✦   ✦   ✦

Creating Help Systems in Access 2002

✦   ✦   ✦   ✦

In This Chapter

Understanding the
Windows Help
structure

Creating a Windows
Help program by
using Help Workshop

Integrating graphics
and sound in a Help
system

Compiling a Help
system

Integrating a Help
system with your
Access application

Third-party Help tools

✦   ✦   ✦   ✦

One item of an application that is often overlooked entirely is the inclusion of a comprehensive Help system. Creating a complete and useful Help system is a skill unto itself, and programmers often don't take the time to learn how to do it right. Understanding what makes a good Help system and how to create one can be a powerful tool in your development arsenal.

Understanding the Windows Help Structure

Great Help systems are more than just online documentation. A Help system needs to explain the how-to of your application in bits and pieces, and the user needs to be able to access a specific bit or piece of information related to the task at hand with minimum effort. In addition, these bits and pieces — called *topics* — need to be linked in a comprehensive web enabling a user to easily travel from one related topic to another. Each topic can be linked to a form or control's `HelpContextId` property (see Figure 39-1) to provide instant access to the topic when the user presses F1 while the control or form has the focus.

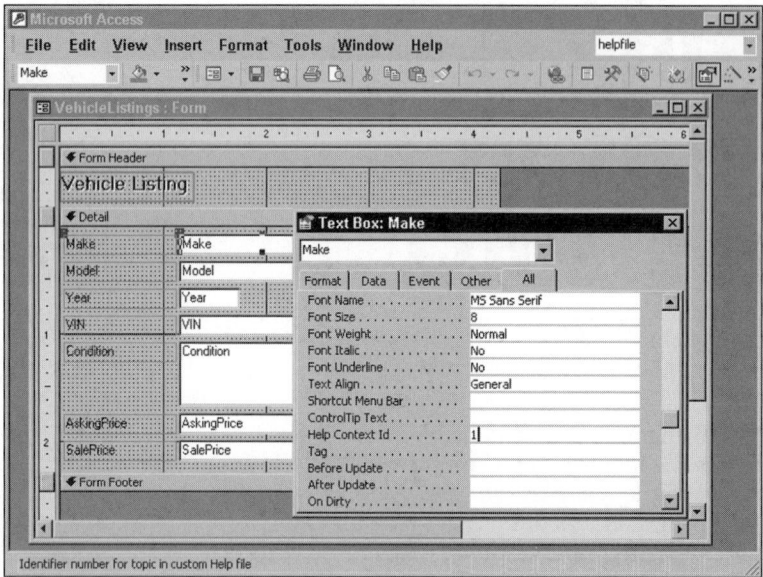

Figure 39-1: You can link Help topics to the form or control they relate to by using the `HelpContextId` property.

Help systems may consist of simple linked text topics, or they may contain graphics and multimedia to help educate the user. A good application of graphics in a Help system is the use of *hotspot graphics* to help explain an application's toolbars. Hotspot graphics, or *hypergraphics*, are graphic pictures that have links assigned to various regions of the graphic. These regions are often invisible; the user knows when the cursor is over a hotspot because the pointer turns into a pointing hand. When the user clicks the hotspot, the topic linked to the hotspot displays. When creating a hypergraphic of a toolbar, you can link a related topic to each tool button in the toolbar graphic. Then users can simply click the button that they want help on to display the appropriate Help topic, just as they would click the button on the toolbar.

The Help interface consists of numerous components, and understanding these components is key to mastering the task of designing great Help files, as well as getting the most out of using a Help file.

The Help Viewer

The Help Viewer is the application that displays the Help system. The Help Viewer contains three panes (see Figure 39-2):

✦ The Topic pane displays on the right side of the Help Viewer. This is where the topic information displays.

✦ The Navigation pane displays on the left side of the Help Viewer. You can customize this pane to display a table of contents, an index, a list of favorite Help topics, or a full-text search tab.

✦ The toolbar, which displays at the top of the viewer, allows users to display or hide the Navigation pane, or move forward to the next topic or back to the previous topic. Stop, Refresh, Locate, and Home buttons are also available.

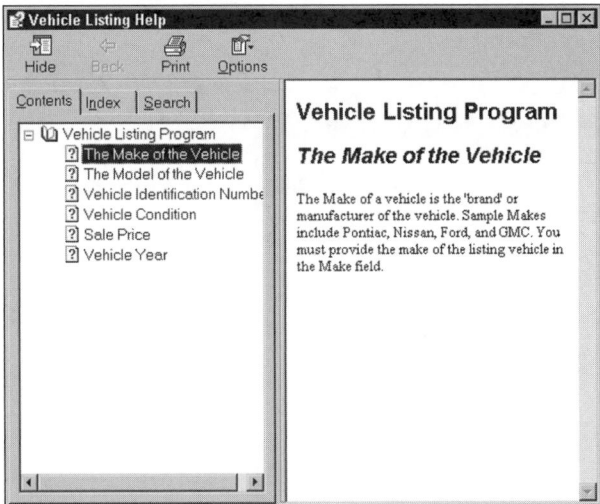

Figure 39-2: The Help Viewer displays the Help system.

You can customize the appearance of the Help Viewer to include or exclude the Index or Search tabs in the Navigation pane. However, every Help system must have a Contents tab. A Contents tab lists the topics that are available when a user clicks Help Topics in your application's Help menu, when a user clicks the Contents tab of any Help topic, or when he or she double-clicks your Help file in Windows Explorer. The Contents feature of a Help system is similar to the table of contents in a book.

The Contents tab

The Contents tab displays the Contents items in a collapsible outline format. Contents items that can be expanded are shown with a closed book icon. To expand a Contents item, select an item, and then select the Open button—or simply double-click the Contents item. When you expand a Contents item, the closed book icon changes to an open book icon, and the individual topics that can be viewed display. Each topic is preceded by a document icon. When users locate the items that they want help with, they can double-click the Help topic, or select it and click the Display button to view the Help topic. To view a specific Help Topic, select the Help Topic item, and then select the Display button — or just double-click the item. The Help Topic displays in the Help Topics dialog box.

The Topic pane

Help topics are the core element of a Help system. Each topic covered in your Help System should be contained in its own Help topic. Help topics are displayed in the Help Topics dialog boxes (see Figure 39-3). A Help Topics dialog box contains information specific to the topic, such as pertinent text, graphics, animation, or sound, and it may contain links to other topics.

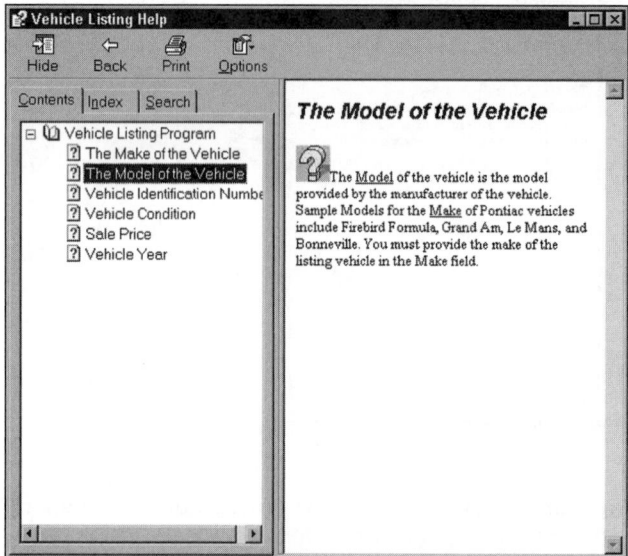

Figure 39-3: The Help Topics pane is where users of your Help system get the topical information that they need.

Office XP Developer includes Microsoft HTML Help Workshop. Microsoft HTML Help 1.3 is the next-generation online help authoring system based on Microsoft WinHelp 4.0. If you've used WinHelp or Help Workshop before, you will be familiar with many of the features of HTML Help and HTML Help Workshop.

Like WinHelp, HTML Help uses a project file to combine topic, contents, index, image, and other source files into one compiled Help file. HTML Help also provides you with HTML Help Workshop, an authoring tool that makes it easy to view, manage, and edit your files in an enhanced user interface. Unlike WinHelp, HTML Help has no practical help system limits. Help file size, topic size, contents entry limits, and keyword limits have all been (essentially) eliminated.

If you want even more control over how HTML Help is displayed and integrated into your solution, you can work directly with HTML Help Application Programming Interface (API) calls from your Visual Basic for Applications (VBA) code.

Tip
Implementing a Help button in Access requires that you use an API call to the HTML Help or WinHelp engine to display the Help topic.

Other help tools that are included in Microsoft XP Developer:

✦ The Answer Wizard Software Development Kit (SDK) — lets you add your own Help topics to the ones provided by the Microsoft Office Assistant.

✦ The HTML Help ActiveX control — for creating Help pages on the Web.

These new tools greatly enhance the usability of the Help interface for the end user of your application.

Creating a Windows Help System

Creating Help systems for Windows involves the following:

✦ Write your Help topic files in HTML. You can use Microsoft Word or any authoring tool to create HTML files, as long as you create standard version 3.2 HTML source code.

✦ Create a Help project file (.hhp) to manage the interface objects that make up your help system — topics, graphics, contents (.hhc), index (.hhk), and other source files — and to define the overall style of these objects.

✦ Create window definitions to define the style of window for displaying the help information.

✦ Create a table of contents file for easy navigation to Help topics.

✦ Create an index file for indexing Help topics.

✦ Compile your Help file. (This is optional if you are using the HTML Help ActiveX control.)

✦ Test the Help system.

Tip
You don't need to include all of your Help topics in one Help file. The Help engine has the capability to use one index and one table of contents for multiple Help files, which is very useful when you have an application that consists of modular components. If the Help engine doesn't locate a referenced Help file on the end user's computer, that Help file's topics won't show up in the table of contents.

Creating Help topics

The most fundamental element in a Help file is the Help topic. The documents that you write are created by using a special formatting language known as *Hypertext Markup Language* (HTML). HTML topic files have an .htm or .html file name extension.

Although each Help topic or Web page that you write appears to be a document with text, graphics, or animated images on it, .htm files are actually text documents that have special HTML formatting codes. These codes, called *tags*, tell a browser how to display each page. Only the text that appears in a topic or Web page is actually in the .htm file. Any graphics, sounds, animated images, or other elements that appear are separate files that your HTML file points to. The browser copies or downloads the graphics, sounds, or other elements when it sees the tags telling it to do so.

Before you begin typing the descriptive text for your topics, you should define a list of all the topics that you want to include in your Help system. After you have created this list, organize it as best as possible (see Figure 39-4). This organization, in effect, creates a level 1 outline for your topics. After you have organized the topics, simply type the descriptive text below each topic. Creating your topics this way simplifies the effort in designing your topic structure.

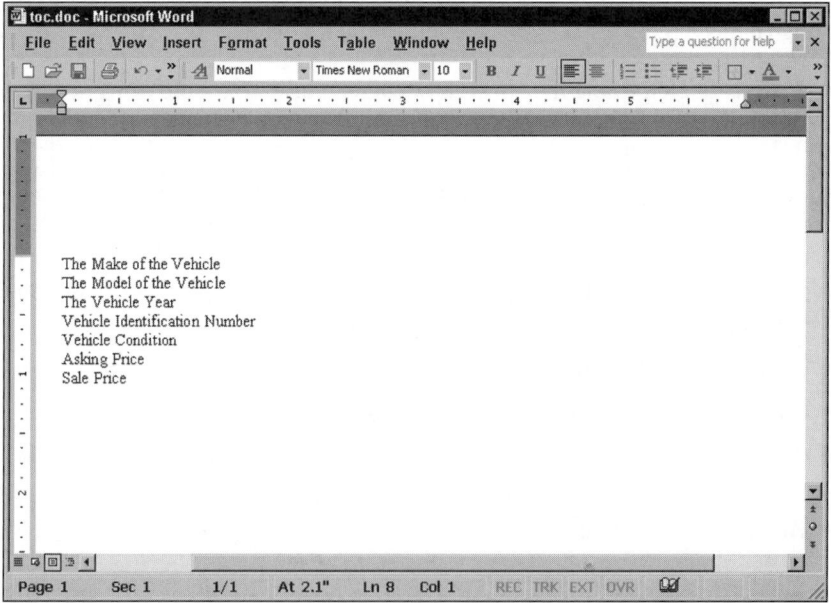

Figure 39-4: Organizing your topic list before you begin writing simplifies the design process.

The easiest way to write your Help system is to create a new HTML file for each Help topic. HTML Help is designed to work with multiple files, each containing a single topic. For larger Help systems, however, you may find it easier to develop one HTML file that contains all of the topics. By using the HTML Help Workshop, you can split the large file into individual HTML files later.

To create an HTML topic file, follow these steps:

1. Create a new document in Microsoft Word (or another product that supports HTML files).

2. Enter the text to be displayed for each topic.

3. Identify separate topic sections with a hard page break. You can create a hard page break in Microsoft Word by selecting Insert ➪ Break and then selecting Page Break.

4. Save the file as a Web page.

Tip   You can create a document template to use when creating your HTML files. A *template* is a file that contains all of the font, style, heading, and design elements that you use most frequently. You can distribute the template to all of the authors who will be creating the Help content files.

Creating a Help project file

After you have written all of the Help content files that you will use in your Help system, you can create an HTML Help Workshop project file. A Help project (.hhp) file contains information about the location of your HTML topic files, contents (.hhc) files, index (.hhk) files, image (.png, .jpg, .gif) files, and other files. Project files also contain Help window definitions and other options that customize the way that a Help system functions.

To create a Help project file, follow these steps:

1. Open the HTML Help Workshop.

2. Select File ➪ New Project. The New Project Wizard opens.

3. Follow the instructions on the proceeding wizard pages to begin creating the new project.

4. On the Existing Files page of the wizard, as shown in Figure 39-5, select the HTML files option to import your existing Help files into the project. The HTML Files Page displays.

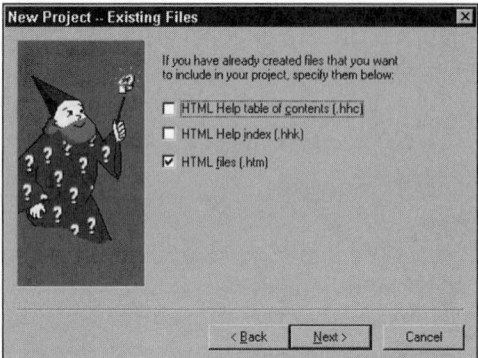

Figure 39-5: Using the New Project Wizard to import HTML files into a new project.

5. On the HTML Files page, shown in Figure 39-6, use the Add button to select the files to import. After you have selected all of the HTML files to include, select the Next button.

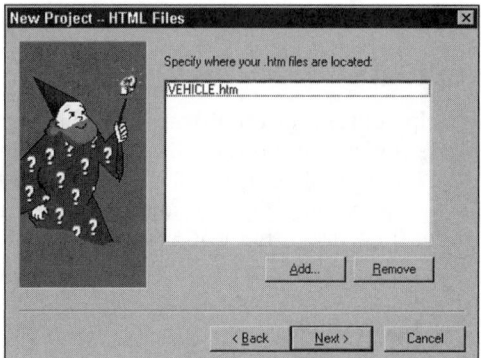

Figure 39-6: Selecting the HTML files to import into a new project.

6. When the Finish page displays, select the Finish button to create the new project. The new project displays, as shown in Figure 39-7.

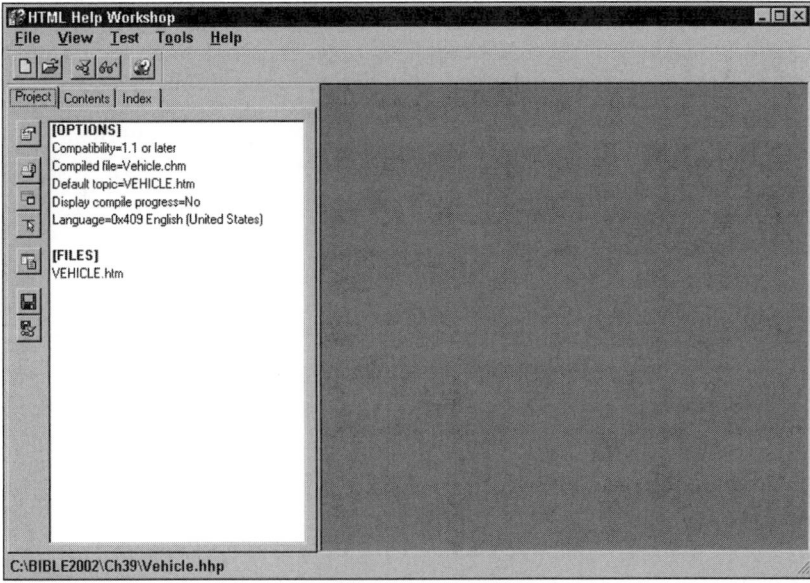

Figure 39-7: A new HTML Help Workshop project.

When you create a new project, contents, or index file, the minimum necessary settings are added automatically. The project file is divided into sections; for example, [FILES] and [OPTIONS] are included in every Help project file. You can edit these sections by double-clicking the section title.

Adding graphics to a topic

Although most of your Help topics will consist primarily of text, it is often beneficial to include graphics in your Help topics. For example, if you use lots of buttons with images on them (such as toolbar images), you can display the picture with its Topic text to help the user associate the image with its function.

You can include the following types of graphics in your Help topics — .gif, .jpg, and .png. To insert a graphic in an HTML file using Microsoft Word, follow these steps:

1. Place the cursor where you want the graphic to appear in the topic.

2. Select Insert ⇨ Picture ⇨ From file from the menu.

3. Select the image file to insert.

Setting the Help project options

Your first task when creating a new Help project is to define the Options for the project. Click the Change Project Options button on the HTML Help Workshop main screen to access the project Options dialog box (see Figure 39-8).

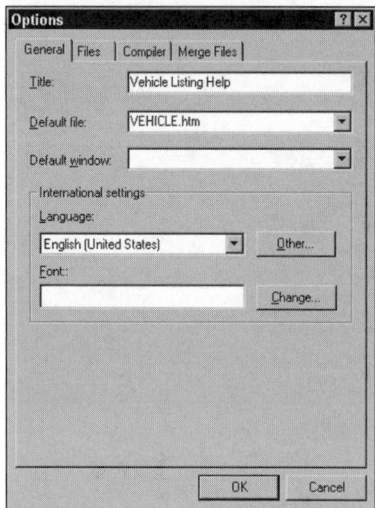

Figure 39-8: The Options dialog box is where you define parameters for your Help project, such as the title for the Help system.

Setting the General tab options

The two main tabs that you need to be concerned with initially are the General and the Files tabs. The General tab is the tab displayed when you first click the Options button. On the General tab, you can modify these settings:

✦ **Title.** This is the text string that appears in the title bar of your Help system. The words *Windows Help* are used if you leave this field blank and if the contents (.htm) file doesn't have a title specified. You should always provide a title specific to your Help program.

✦ **Default File.** This is the first HTML file to open in the Help system.

Setting the Files tab options

Clicking the Files tab on the HTML Help Workshop Options dialog box displays the page that you use to enter information about files associated with the current project (see Figure 39-9). The information that you supply on this tab is discussed in the following section, item by item. However, you need to be aware that you must specify the Contents file to use on this tab, or your Help system won't have Contents. Although you may not have created the Contents file yet, you may still specify the name of the Contents file that you plan to create (with full path), or you may create the Contents file first and then reopen the project and supply the name.

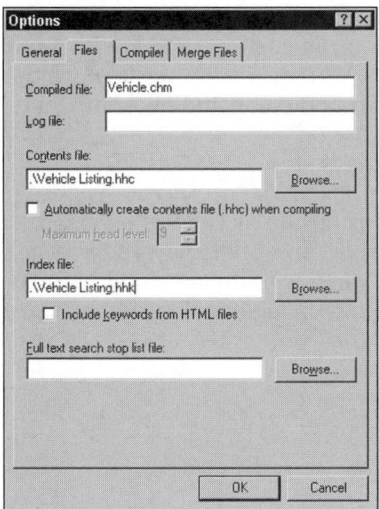

Figure 39-9: To include Contents in your Help file, you must specify the Contents file name here.

The information that you supply on the Files tab consists of the following:

✦ **Compiled file.** This is where you specify the name for your project when it compiles. You can name the file anything that you want, as long as it has the extension .chp. Prefixing the file name with a .\ causes the Help file to be created in the same directory as the HTML Help Workshop.

✦ **Log file.** You can create a text log file when your Help project is compiled by specifying a valid file name here. This log file contains the information printed to the screen during compilation. For small projects, you may not need a log file, so you can leave this box blank. For larger projects, however, you may want to create a log file so you can review errors that you encounter when compiling the project.

✦ **Contents file.** You should always include a Contents for your Help project. Creating a Help Contents is discussed later in this chapter, but this is where you specify the full name and the path of the Contents file.

✦ **Index file.** You should also include an Index for your Help project. Creating a Help Index is discussed later in this chapter, but this is where you specify the full name and the path of the Index file. The specified Help Index must exist when you compile the Help file.

Defining windows

The Help Viewer is the three-paned window in which topics automatically appear. You never have to create a Help Viewer, but you can customize it. You can make changes to just one of the panes or all of them. Window definitions change the size of the Help Viewer window, its position, background color, and other attributes.

To specify the Help Viewer definition, follow these steps:

1. Select the Add/Modify Window Definitions button on the Project page. When you add the first window definition, a prompt displays, as shown in Figure 39-10, requesting the type of new window to define. Enter **Main** as the new type, then click OK. The Window Types dialog box displays, as shown in Figure 39-11.

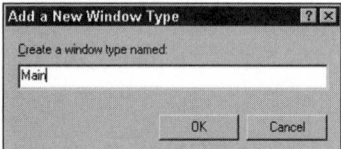

Figure 39-10: Adding the first window type to the Help project.

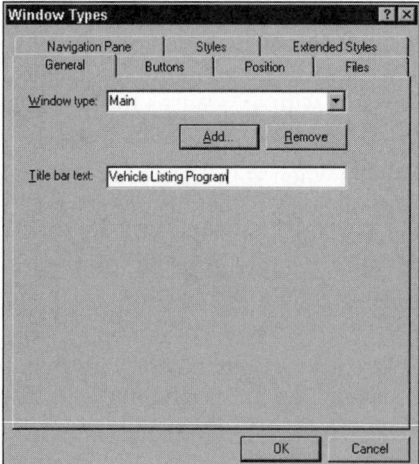

Figure 39-11: Defining the Main window type for the Help Viewer.

2. In the General tab, the Window Type field shows Main as the type that you specified in Step 1. In the Title bar text field, enter an appropriate title for the Main window.

3. In the Navigation Pane tab, select the check box labeled "Window with navigation pane, topic pane, and button."

4. Make sure that the Search Tab option and the Auto sync option are selected, as shown in Figure 39-12.

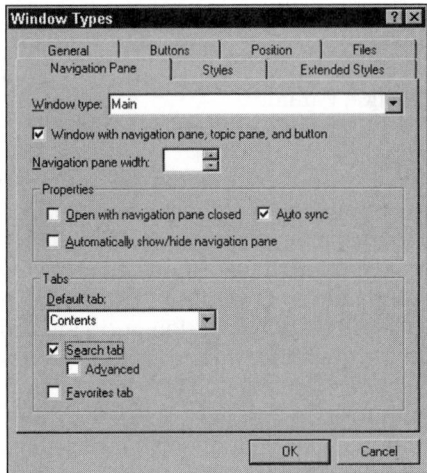

Figure 39-12: Selecting the display options for the window definition.

5. Click OK to save the window definition.

The HTML Help Workshop cross-checks the options that you selected for the new window definition with the Project Options. If the window definition contains any inconsistencies, the Resolve Window Definition Wizard displays, as shown in Figure 39-13.

The first screen in the Resolve Window Definition Wizard displays the name of the window definition that contains the inconsistencies. Click the Next button to continue.

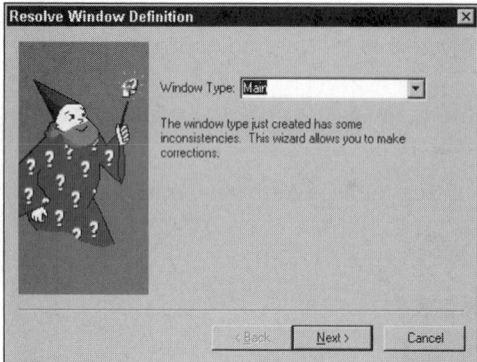

Figure 39-13: The Resolve Window Definition Wizard.

The second wizard screen, shown in Figure 39-14, compares the options that you set for the window definition and the options that you have set in Project Options. In this example, the wizard shows that the Search tab option was selected in the Navigation Pane for the Main window definition. It also shows that the Compile full-text Information option was not selected in Project Options. The wizard recommends that you implement the Compile full-text Information option in order to complement the Search tab definition for the Main window. If you agree with the wizard's recommendation, you can click the Compile full-text Information option in the wizard screen, then click the Next button to continue. The wizard then sets the option in Project Options so that additional new window definitions will include the full-text search feature.

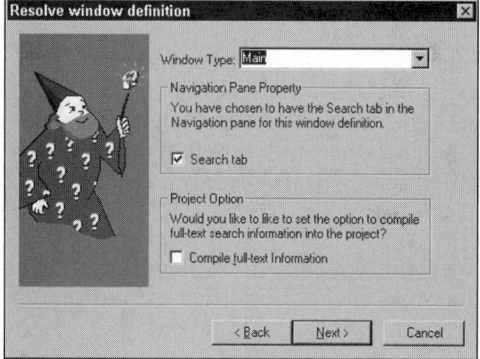

Figure 39-14: Resolving Search option inconsistencies.

Adding topic files to a project file

When you create a new project, you can automatically load existing files. If you create additional HTML files later, you can always add these to your project. You must supply at least one topic file in order to compile a Help project into a Help file. To add or remove topic files in a Help project, use the Add/Remove Topic Files button on the HTML Help Workshop main screen (see Figure 39-15).

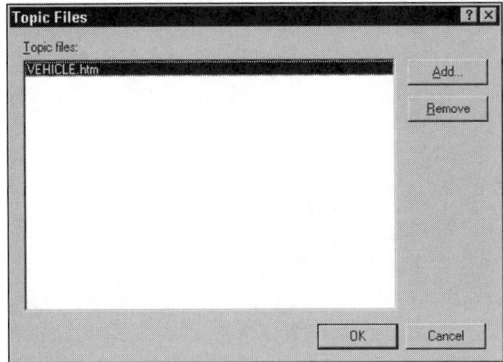

Figure 39-15: Use the Topic Files dialog box to add or remove topic files in your Help project.

To add topic files to your Help project, first select the Add/Remove Topic Files button to display the Topic Files dialog box. Then follow these steps:

1. Click the Add button.

2. Select the topic file that you want to add to the Help project.

3. Click the Open button to add the topic file to the project file. Files that you add to the project appear in the Help project definition script (see Figure 39-16).

To remove a topic file from your Help project, select the Add/Remove Topic Files button to display the Topic Files dialog box, and then follow these steps:

1. Select the file name that you want to remove from the Help project.

2. Click the Remove button.

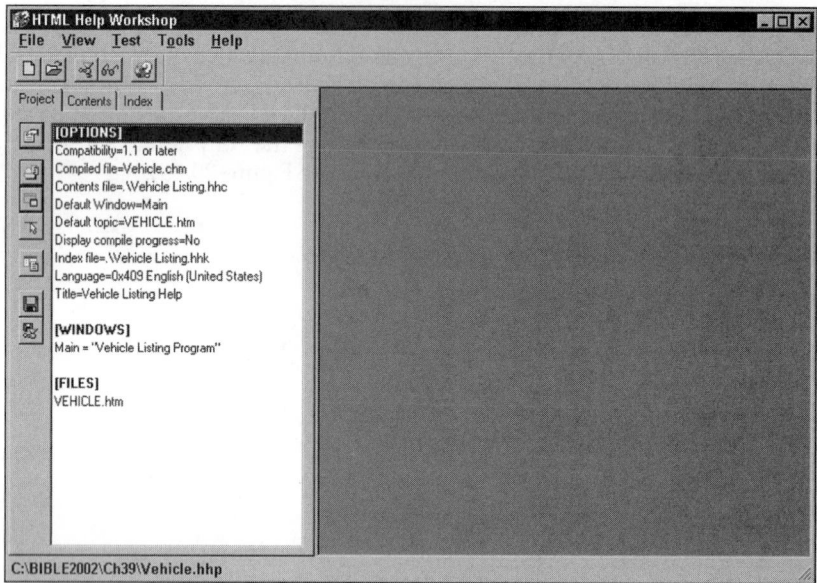

Figure 39-16: As you add files and change options, the text script that defines your Help project changes.

Saving and compiling the project

In order to ensure that you are shipping a Help system without errors or broken links, you need to test your help. In HTML Help Workshop, the Help project file compiles all of the necessary files into a compiled Help (.chm) file. When you compile a Help project, all of the included topic files, bitmap files, and Contents files are placed into one Help file with the .CHM extension.

The compiled Help file can then be placed on your hard drive, a 3.5-inch disk, a compact disc, a server location, an Internet location, or an intranet location.

During compilation, HTML Help Workshop uses the Help project (.hhp) file to determine how HTML topic files, Contents (.hhc) files, index (.hhk) files, image (.jpg, .gif, .png) files, and any other elements that you have added to the project file will look in the single, compressed Help file. If any errors are found during the compilation, compiler messages are generated that point out the problems to the author.

HTML Help Workshop performs these tasks during the compilation process:

✦ Reports missing topics or other errors in Contents and index files

✦ Reports broken links in topic, index, and Contents files

✦ Removes unnecessary white space or comments

To save and compile the project, select the Save all files and compile button on the Project page. As the project compiles, a progress report displays in the right pane of the HTML Help Workshop (see Figure 39-17).

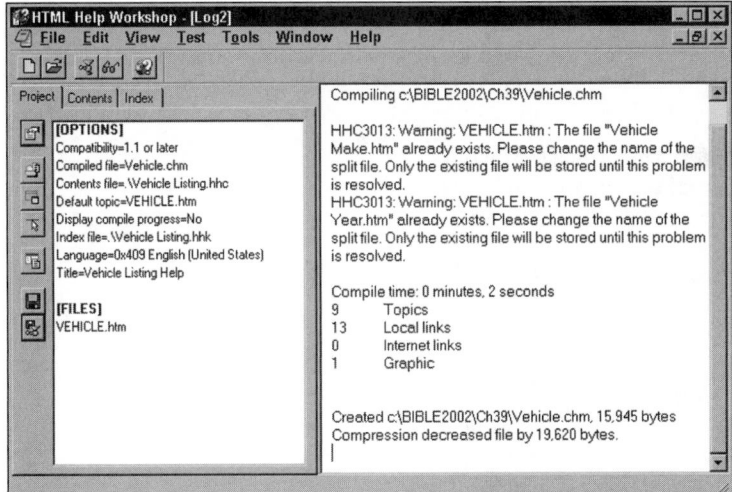

Figure 39-17: The right pane of the HTML Help Workshop displays the results of compilation.

Creating a Table of Contents

When you have finished adding all of the topic files that your Help project will use, you need to create a Contents file for your Help system. It is critical that you create a clear, concise, and comprehensive Contents file to make it easy for users to locate the topics that they need in order to get their job done.

Creating a new Help Contents file

Contents files are ASCII files saved with the .hhc extension. Contents files consist of specifications of three items:

✦ Headings

✦ Topics

✦ Commands

To create a new Contents file by using the HTML Help Workshop, follow these steps:

1. Select the Change Project Options button.

2. Select the Files tab.

3. Specify a file name for the new Contents file.

4. Select the "Automatically create contents file (.hhc) when compiling" check box, as shown in Figure 39-18. In the "Maximum head level" field, click the maximum heading level for which you want entries generated in your Contents file. For example, if you click 3 for the maximum head level, entries are generated with <H1>, <H2>, and <H3> heading tags.

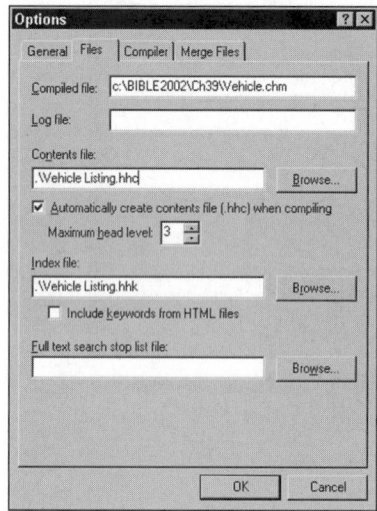

Figure 39-18: Automatically creating a Contents file.

5. Save and compile the project. The new Contents items display on the Contents page, as shown in Figure 39-19.

Caution If you make changes to a Contents file that has been automatically generated, you will lose them if you compile the project again. To prevent this, make sure that the "Automatically create contents file when compiling" check box is cleared before you recompile.

Help Contents are just like tables of contents in books: They are essentially outlines. Headings appear with book pictures in the Help Contents. If the user clicks the book or the heading text, the Contents expands to show all items under the heading. When the HTML Help Workshop automatically creates the Contents file, it looks for text formatted as headings within the HTML files that you have included in the project. The hierarchy of the HTML file's styles becomes the hierarchy of the Contents items. For example, you have formatted your HTML file title as Heading 1, and you have formatted each topic under the title as Heading 2. When the HTML Help Workshop creates the Contents, it uses the Heading 1 items as Contents Headings, and the Heading 2 items as Page items under each respective heading.

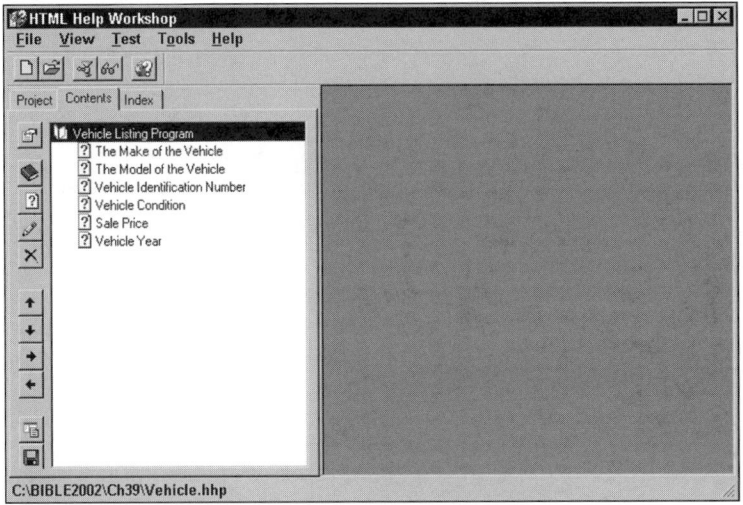

Figure 39-19: The Help system's Table of Contents.

Modifying the Contents items

You can add new Contents headings and pages to the ones that were automatically generated. To add another heading entry to the Contents, follow these instructions:

1. Position the cursor in the Contents page on the item below which is the intended location for the new heading.

2. Select the Insert a heading button to add the heading above the selected item in the Contents page. The Table of Contents Entry dialog box displays (see Figure 39-20).

3. Enter a title for the new heading.

4. Select the Add button. The Path or URL dialog box displays, as shown in Figure 39-21.

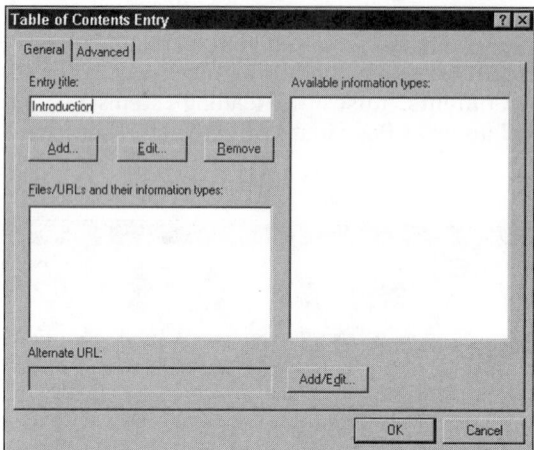

Figure 39-20: Defining a new Table of Contents heading.

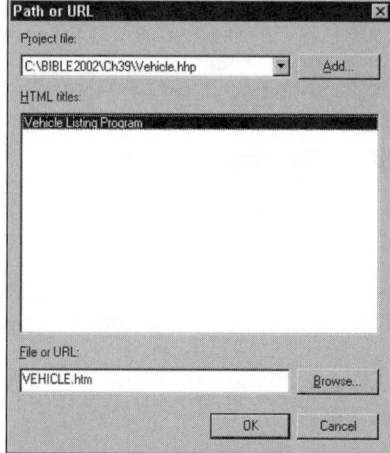

Figure 39-21: Selecting the HTML file for a new heading.

5. Select the HTML file to use for the new heading, then click OK. The file name displays in the Table of Contents Entry dialog box.

6. Click OK to create the heading.

Creating a Help index

Put yourself in the user's seat for a little while and ask yourself this question: If I needed to find this information, what keywords would I expect to find it under? In general, you should specify any and all keywords that a user may use to search for each topic.

Adding keywords to an index

Topic keywords are words that are listed in the index of a Help system. These keywords are used to quickly locate Topics; searching by keywords is faster than performing a full-text search. In addition, you can create keywords that don't even appear in the text of a topic, thereby allowing for many different ways to locate a topic of interest.

Consider using the following types of keywords:

✦ Nontechnical terms that are likely to occur to a beginning user

✦ Technical terms that are likely to occur to an advanced user

✦ Common synonyms for technical terms

✦ Words that describe the topic in a general manner

✦ Words that describe specific subjects within the topic

✦ Inverted forms of keyword phrases, such as "combining Help files" and "Help files, combining"

To add a keyword to the Index, follow these steps:

1. Select the Insert a Keyword button on the Index page. The Index Entry dialog box displays, as shown in Figure 39-22.

2. Enter the keyword to include in the Keyword field, and then select the Add button. The Path or URL dialog box displays, as shown in Figure 39-23.

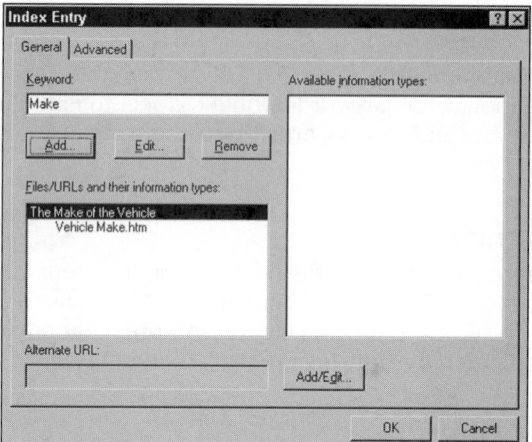

Figure 39-22: Adding a keyword to the Index.

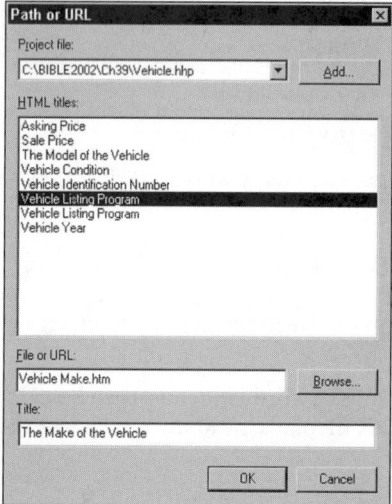

Figure 39-23: Selecting the HTML
file source for the keyword.

3. Select the HTML file or files containing the information for the keyword. Then
click OK. The Index Entry dialog box displays the selected file name.

4. Click OK to save the new keyword.

5. Compile and save the project. Then select View Compiled File. The keyword
displays in the Index page of the Help system, as shown in Figure 39-24.

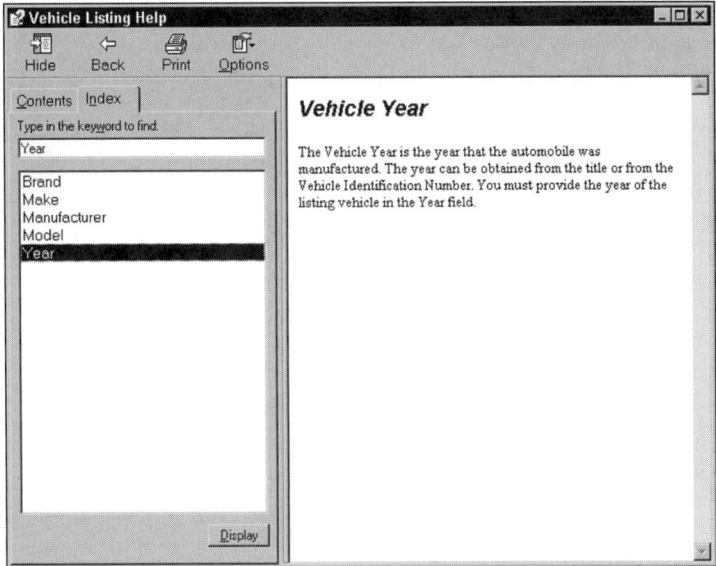

Figure 39-24: Using the Index to locate help by a keyword.

Implementing a full-text search

Index keywords allow you to connect Help files to predefined search words. Users often want to locate information on a topic that doesn't appear in the predefined keyword list. A powerful feature of any Help system is the capability to perform full-text searches. The Search tab of the Help system allows the user to search by using any word or combination of words or letters.

Ordinarily, when a user runs your Help system and clicks the Search tab for the first time, the Find Setup Wizard appears. The wizard helps users set up a full-text search index on their computers. A full-text search index lists all of the unique words in the Help file.

You can create the full-text index for your users and ship it with your Help files. The disadvantage to this technique is that it can greatly add to the disk space needed to distribute your Help file. You can define your full-text search file by using the "Compile full-text search information" check box located on the Compiler tab in the Help project Options dialog box (see Figure 39-25).

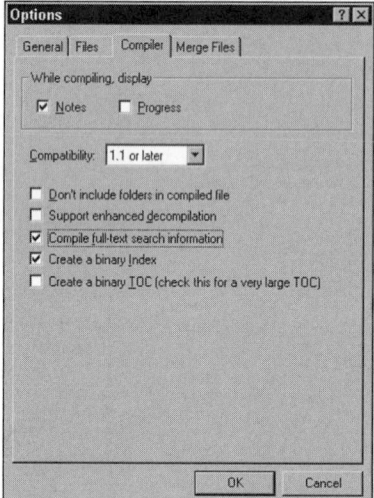

Figure 39-25: Use the Help project Options dialog box to define full-text search files.

When you compile your project with the "Compile full-text search information" option turned on, a full-text search (.fts) file is created for your Help system. You need to distribute this file with your Help file.

Caution   When using HTML Help Workshop, the number of topic files that you can view and add is limited to 5,000. Projects with more than 5,000 files will compile correctly, and links from entries in the index and Contents files will work, but you will need to use a text editor to view, add, or edit them.

Running your compiled Help file

To run your compiled Help file, click the View compiled file button on the toolbar (the button with the eyeglasses on it). When you click this button, HTML Help Workshop displays the View compiled file dialog box (see Figure 39-26). In this dialog box, you tell HTML Help Workshop which Help file to run.

Caution   Remember to save and compile your Help system whenever you make any changes.

After you have selected the compiled Help file name, select the View button to run the Help file. The Help system displays (as shown in Figure 39-27).

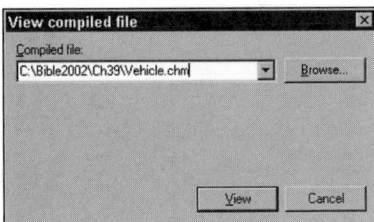

Figure 39-26: It's very important to thoroughly test your Help file before distributing it to users.

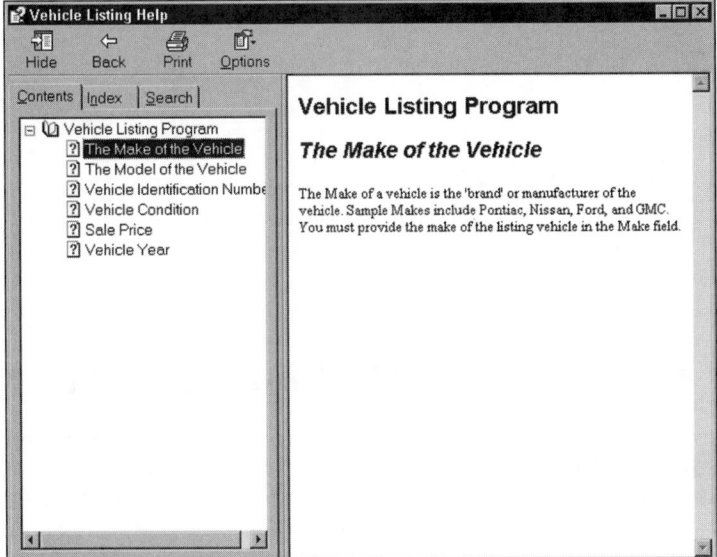

Figure 39-27: A finished Help file showing the Contents tab.

You can now test the contents and topic jumps in the Help file. If you click the Index tab of the Help file's main window, you see a searchable list of all the keyword index entries that you created for the topics (as shown in Figure 39-28).

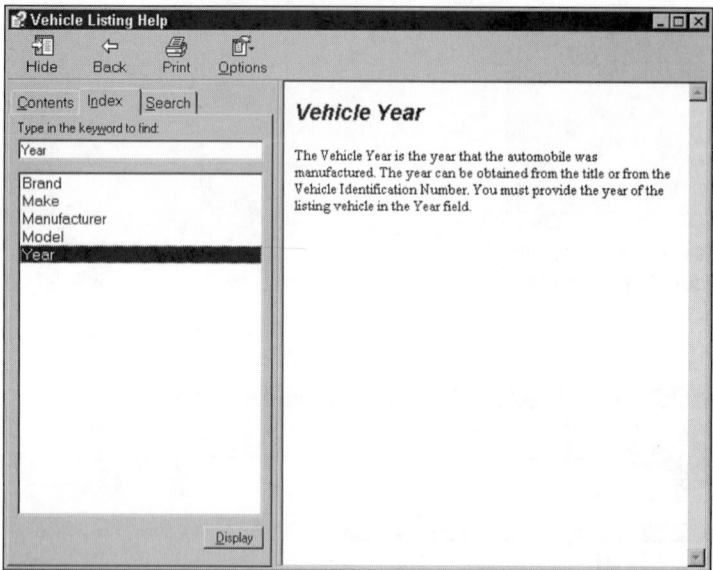

Figure 39-28: The keywords that you created for topics appear in the index for the Help file.

Integrating a Help File with Your Application

After you have created and compiled a working Help file, it's time to integrate it with your Access application. You can tie controls, forms, command buttons, and menu items to specific Help topics by using the techniques described in the following section.

Displaying form-level help

The most common way to link an application to a Help file is to link forms or specific controls to topics in the Help file. You accomplish this task in two stages: First by specifying the Help file to use, and then by setting the Help Context ID property on the forms and controls. See Figure 39-29 for an example of setting the properties for the form.

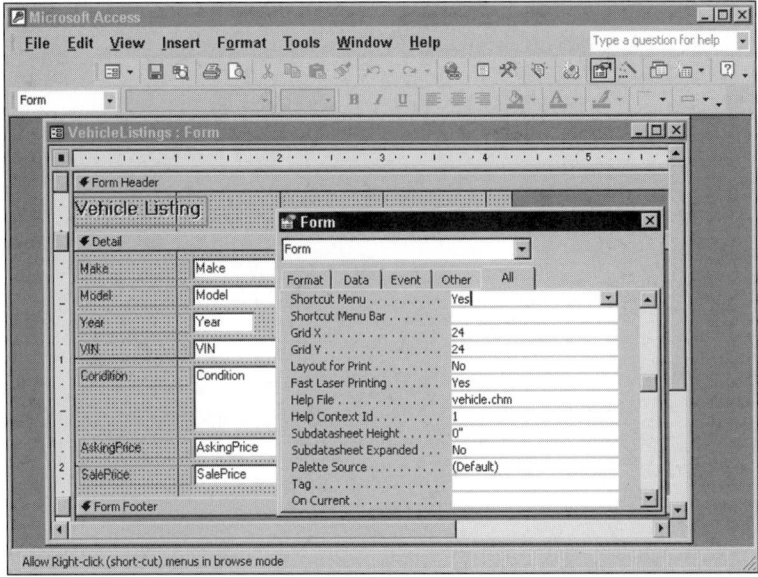

Figure 39-29: Setting up Help for a form.

You must specify the Help file name on each form in your application to prevent Access Help from displaying. If you are distributing your application with the Office XP Developer tools, and you don't supply a Help file name, an error occurs when the user attempts to access help. If the Help file is located in a different folder than the running Access application, the Help File property on the form must include the full path to the Help file.

After you have set the Help File property on each form, you need to set the Help Context ID for the form. This should be the ID of a topic that talks about the form in general.

Displaying control-level help

After you have set the form's Help Context ID, you can set the Help Context IDs of all controls. Specify a unique number for each control that will display a different topic than the topic to which the form is linked. If you don't want a control to display a unique topic, leave its Help Context ID as 0. When the control's Help Context ID is 0, the form's topic displays when the user presses F1 while the control has the focus; otherwise, the topic whose ID matches the Help Context ID of the control with the focus is displayed when the user presses F1. See Figure 39-30 for an example of setting up Help for a control.

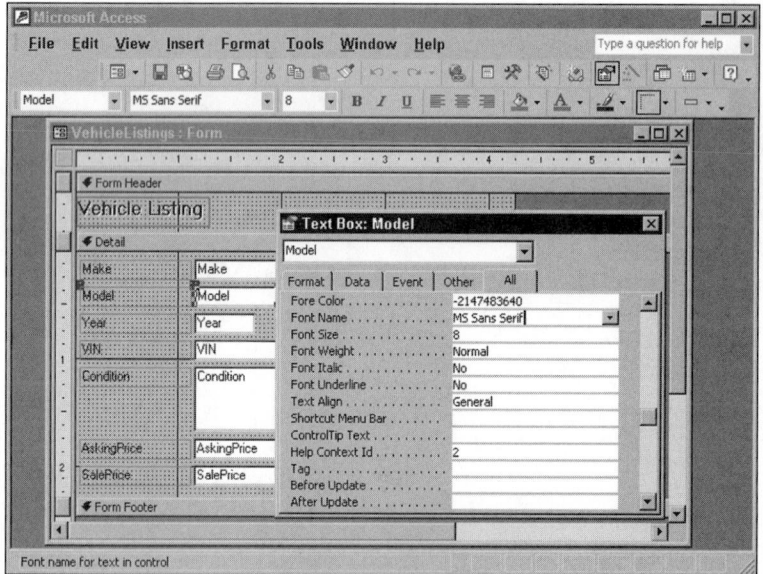

Figure 39-30: Setting up Help for a form control.

Make sure that you set Help Context IDs for the labels as well as the controls. Some users click the text box to get help, while others click the label for the control. This way, the Help topic will display regardless of where the user attempts to locate help.

Tip   If the user presses F1 in a control that has its Help Context ID set to 0, and the form's Help Context ID is also set to 0, Access Help displays. If your application is distributed with the Office XP Developer Tools, Access's Help won't display and an error will occur. For this reason, you should always link each form's Help Context ID to a valid topic.

Mapping a Help Context ID to a Help topic

After you have established Help Context IDs for your forms and controls, you need to map each Help Context ID to its corresponding topic in the Help file. The HTML Help Workshop provides a tool for assigning a unique number to each of your Help file's topics.

The HTMLHelp API, included in HTML Help Workshop, provides information to applications about the Help file. This information enables an application to display a Help window.

Before you can use the HTMLHelp API to map your Help Context IDs, you must first create a header file. The header file establishes a link between the Help Context ID that you set in the application to a symbolic ID that can be used by the HTMLHelp API.

To create the header file, follow these steps:

1. Open Notepad (or your favorite text editor).

2. Create an entry for each symbolic ID, followed by its corresponding numeric ID, by using the following format:

   ```
   #define IDH_symbolicID 1000
   ```

3. You can name the symbolic ID anything that you want. You should name it something that indicates the name of the topic that it refers to — VehMake, for example. The number 1000 in the previous line of code refers to the Help Context ID in your application. See Figure 39-31 for an example header file.

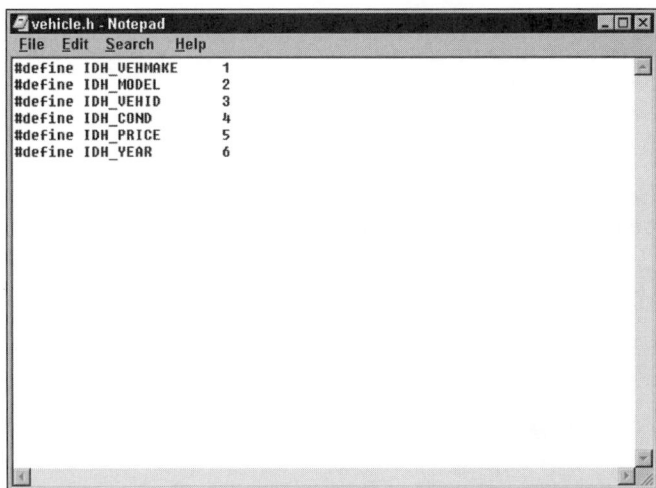

Figure 39-31: Creating a header file.

4. Save the file with a .h extension.

Tip   If you use an IDH prefix with the symbolic ID, as shown in the preceding example, HTML Help Workshop will automatically check that the topics mapped in your project file actually exist in your compiled Help (.chm) file, and that your context-sensitive Help topics are all mapped in your project file.

After you have created the header file, you can set up the HTMLHelp API to use the header file. To set up the HTMLHelp API, follow these steps:

1. Click the HTMLHelp API information button in the HTML Help Workshop. The HTMLHelp API dialog box displays, as shown in Figure 39-32.

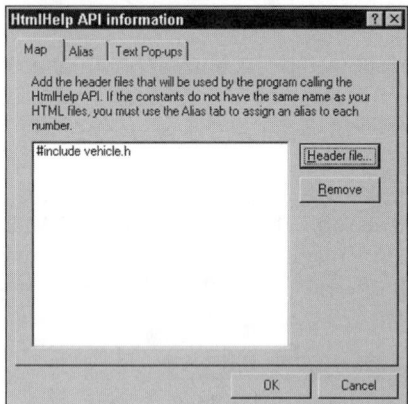

Figure 39-32: Setting up the HTMLHelp API information.

2. Click the Header file button in the Map page of the HTMLHelp API dialog box. The Include File dialog box displays.

3. Enter the name of the header file that you created. Then click OK. The header file name displays in the Map page.

4. Select the Alias page of the HtmlHelp API dialog box (see Figure 39-33).

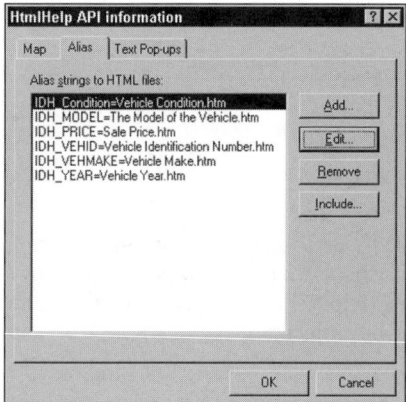

Figure 39-33: Mapping the symbolic IDs to Topics.

5. Select the Add button on the Alias page. The Alias dialog displays, as shown in Figure 39-34.

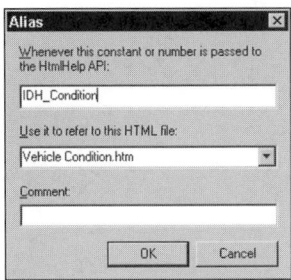

Figure 39-34: Adding an HtmlHelp API map definition.

6. Enter the first symbolic ID that you created in the header file.

7. Select the HTML file that contains the Topic that the symbolic ID refers to. Then click OK.

8. Repeat the Alias definitions for each of the symbolic IDs that you created in the header file.

9. After you have created all of the Alias definitions, click OK to save the HTMLHelp API information.

10. Save and compile the project.

The Map page of the HTMLHelp API allows you to include the header file information in your project. The Alias definitions establish the link between the symbolic IDs and the individual Help topics in the Help system.

Testing the HTMLHelp API

After you have defined the HTMLHelp API information, you can use the HTML Help Workshop to test the API connections. To test each API connection, follow these steps:

1. Select the Test HTMLHelp API button in the HTML Help Workshop. The Test HTMLHelp API dialog box displays, as shown in Figure 39-35.

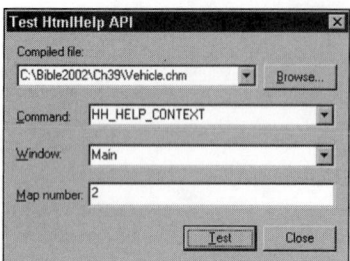

Figure 39-35: Testing the HTMLHelp API definitions.

2. In the Compiled file box, make sure that the correct file displays. If not, select the current project to test. In the command field, select HH_HELP_CONTEXT. In the Map Number field, enter the Help Context ID that you want to test.

3. Select the Test button. The Help Viewer displays the Topic that you entered in the test dialog box.

If you encounter problems when testing the HTMLHelp API information, use the following checklist to locate and solve the problem:

✦ Have you included the numeric ID in the header file?

✦ Have you included the proper header file in the HTMLHelp API dialog box?

✦ Does each symbolic ID that you included in the header file match the alias?

✦ Is the alias mapped to the proper HTML file?

✦ Have you saved and recompiled the project?

Testing Help in Access

After you have created the connections between your Access application and your Help system, you should be able to request help directly from a form in your Access application. To try out your new Access Help system, run the Access form. Then press F1 on any field for which you have set a Help Context ID. The field's Help Topic displays in the Help Viewer, as shown in Figure 39-36.

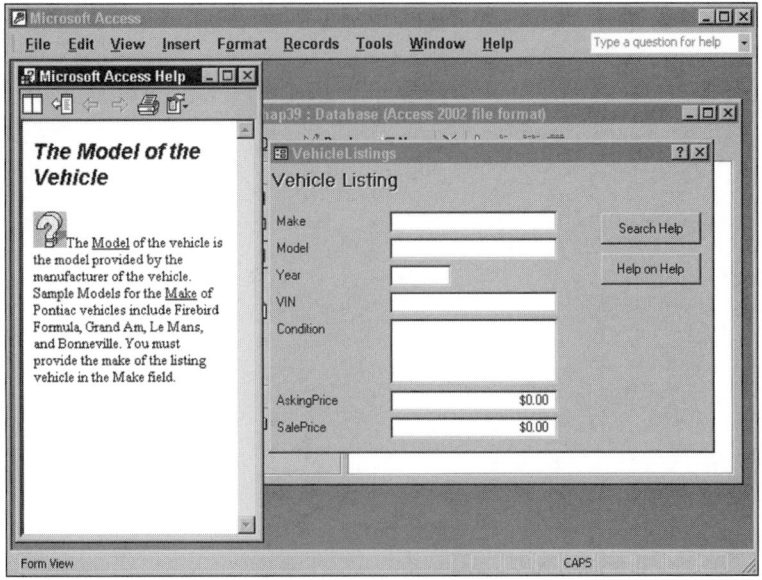

Figure 39-36: Displaying Help in an Access form.

What's this? Help

Clicking the What's This button on the title bar of a form causes the question mark mouse pointer to appear. With the question mark pointer, you can click any control to access its custom Help topic as specified by the control's Help Context ID property. If the control doesn't have a custom Help topic, the form's custom Help topic is displayed. If neither the form nor the control has a custom Help topic, Microsoft Access Help is displayed.

Third-Party Help Tools

A number of tools on the market are designed specifically for creating Help files. Two of the most popular are Doc-2-Help and RoboHelp. These tools will save you days or weeks of work when creating large Help files. The only reason not to invest in one of these tools is cost; they can be rather expensive. If you need to create large, in-depth Help files, however, you should invest in a Help authoring tool.

By supplying complete, accurate Help that is fully linked with your application, you will be providing a professional program that lowers the amount of support required for the application and greatly increases the application's usability.

✦   ✦   ✦

Using the Microsoft Office XP Developer

✦ ✦ ✦ ✦

In This Chapter

Defining the startup parameters of the application

Testing the application

Polishing the application

Creating comprehensive and intuitive menus and toolbars

Bulletproofing the application

Separating the code objects from the tables in the application

Documenting the application

Creating a Help system for the application

Implementing a security structure for the application

Using productivity tools

Packaging and deploying the application

✦ ✦ ✦ ✦

You are indeed lucky if you have the luxury of developing only single-user, in-house applications and never have to worry about distributing an application within a company or across the country. Most developers, in fact, have to worry about application distribution sooner or later. You don't even have to develop commercial software to be concerned with distribution; when you develop an application to be run on a dozen workstations in one organization, for example, you need to distribute your application.

This chapter covers all the preceding points to some degree. However, because some of the listed items, such as splitting tables and creating Help systems, are covered in detail in other chapters, this chapter focuses primarily on using the Packaging Wizard in Microsoft Office XP Developer.

Preparing Your Application for Distribution

You need to be concerned with many issues when preparing an Access application for distribution. Distributing your application properly not only makes installing and using the application easier for the end user but also makes updating and maintaining the application easier for you. In addition, you can decrease the support required for your application by including comprehensive online help.

Defining the startup parameters of the application

An Access database has a number of startup parameters that can greatly simplify the process of preparing your database for distribution (see Figure 40-1). You can access the startup parameters for a database by selecting Tools ⇨ Startup or by right-clicking the database window and selecting Startup. You can still use an Autoexec macro to execute initialization code, but the Startup parameters dialog box enables you to set up certain aspects of your application, thus reducing the amount of startup code that you have to write. It is extremely important to correctly structure the startup parameters before distributing your Access application.

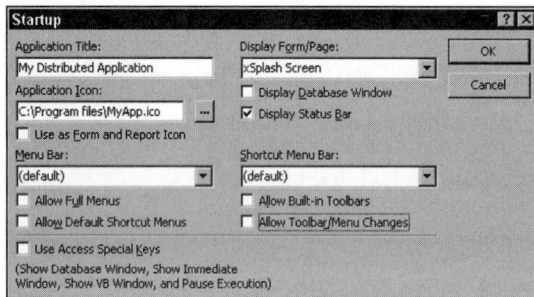

Figure 40-1: The Startup parameters dialog box enables you to take control of your application from the moment a user starts it.

Application Title

The text that you provide in the Application Title box displays on the main Access title bar. You should always specify an application title for your distributed applications. If you don't, Microsoft Access appears on the title bar of your application.

Application icon

The icon that you specify in the Startup dialog box is displayed on the title bar of your application and in the task switcher (Alt+Tab) of Windows. Checking the box "Use asForm and ReportIcon" also displays this icon when a form or report is minimized. If you don't specify your own icon, Access displays the default Access icon; therefore, you should always provide an application-specific icon for your application. You can create small bitmaps in Windows Paint and use available conversion tools to convert a .BMP file to an .ICO file format. You can also create icons or choose from tools such as IconMaker or the Command Bar Image Editor, which are available on many Internet sites or from www.databasecreations.com.

Menu Bar

The Menu Bar box is used to specify a custom menu bar as the default menu bar. If you don't supply a custom menu bar, Access uses its own default menu bar, which may be inappropriate for your application.

Allow Full Menus

This setting determines whether Access displays its menus with all options available to the user or if it disables items that can be used to create or modify objects. If you supply custom menus for all of your forms and reports and set the Menu Bar property to a custom menu bar, this setting has no effect.

Tip

If you supply your own menu bars or use Access's menu bars but don't allow full menus, you must deselect Allow Built-in Toolbars or supply your own custom toolbars for each form. If you don't, the built-in toolbars may give users access to some features that you don't want to make available.

Allow Default Shortcut Menus

The Allow Default Shortcut Menus setting determines whether Access displays its own default shortcut menus when a user clicks an object.

Display Form

The form that you select in this field displays automatically when your application is run. When the form loads, the `Form Load` event fires if it contains any code, thus eliminating the need to use an Autoexec macro. You should consider using a splash screen (which is discussed later in this chapter) as your startup Display Form.

Display Database Window

With most distributed applications, you may never want your users to have direct access to any of your forms or other database objects. Deselecting this option hides the Database window from the user at startup. But unless you also deselect the Use Access Special Keys option (which is discussed later in this chapter), users can press F11 or select Window ⇨ Unhide to unhide the Database window.

Display Status Bar

You can deselect the Display Status Bar option to completely remove the status bar from the screen. However, the status bar is an incredibly informative and easy-to-use tool; it automatically displays the various key-states, as well as the status bar text for the active control. Instead of hiding the status bar, you should make full use of it and only disable it if you have a very good reason to do so.

Shortcut Menu Bar

This setting is similar to the Menu Bar option (which was discussed previously), only it enables you to specify a menu bar to use as the default shortcut menu bar when a user right-clicks an object. Using custom shortcut menus that have functionality specific to your application is always preferable.

Allow Built-in Toolbars

Deselecting this option prevents Access from displaying any of its built-in toolbars. In general, you should always deselect this option and provide your own custom toolbars that you can display by using the Toolbar property for the form.

Allow Toolbar/Menu Changes

Deselecting this option prevents users from modifying either Access's built-in toolbars or your own toolbars, whichever you choose to use. Again, you almost always want to deselect this item to prevent your users from gaining access to features that you don't want them to have.

Use Access Special Keys

If you select this option, users of your application can use keys that are specific to the Access environment in order to circumvent some security measures, such as unhiding the Database window. If you deselect this option, the following keys are disabled:

- **F11 and Alt+F1** — Use these keys to show the database window (if hidden) and bring it to the front.

- **Ctrl+G** — Use this key to display the Immediate window.

- **Ctrl+Break** — In Access projects, use this key to stop Access from retrieving records from the server database.

- **Ctrl+F11** — Use this key to toggle between using a custom menu bar for a form and using a built-in menu bar.

- **Alt+F11** — Use this key to start the Microsoft Visual Basic Editor.

You should always deselect this option when distributing the application.

Using the Startup options saves you many lines of code that you would ordinarily need in order to perform the same functions and enables you to control your application's interface from the moment the user starts it. Always verify the Startup options before distributing your application.

Testing the application before distribution

After you finish adding features and have everything in place within your application, you need to take some time to thoroughly test the application. Testing may seem obvious, but this step is apparently overlooked by many developers, evidenced by the amount of buggy software appearing on the shelves of your local software stores. If you don't believe this to be true, check out the software support forums on the Internet; almost every major commercial software application has some patch available or known bugs that need to be addressed.

Distributing an application that is 100 percent bug-free is almost impossible. The nature of the beast in software development is that if you write a program, someone can — and will — find a way to break it. Specific individuals even seem to have a black cloud above their heads and can usually break an application (in other words, hit a critical bug) within minutes of using it. If you know of such people, hire them! They can be a great asset to you when testing your application.

While working through the debugging process of an application, categorize your bugs into one of three categories:

✦ **Category 1: Major ship-sinking bug.** These bugs are absolutely unacceptable; for example, numbers in an accounting application that don't add up the way they should or a routine that consistently causes the application to terminate unexpectedly. If you ship an application with known Category 1 bugs, prepare yourself for a lynch party from your customers!

✦ **Category 2: Major bug that has a workaround.** Category 2 bugs are fairly major bugs, but they don't stop users from performing their tasks. For example, a toolbar button that doesn't call a procedure correctly is a bug. If the toolbar button is the only way to run the procedure, this bug is a Category 1 bug. If, however, a corresponding menu item calls the procedure correctly, the bug is a Category 2 bug. Shipping an application with a Category 2 bug is sometimes necessary. Although shipping a bug is officially a no-no, deadlines sometimes dictate that exceptions need to be made. Category 2 bugs will annoy your users but shouldn't send them into fits.

If you ship an application with known Category 2 bugs, document them! Some developers have a don't-say-anything-and-act-surprised attitude regarding Category 2 bugs. This attitude can frustrate users and waste considerable amounts of their time by forcing them to discover not only the problem, but also the solution. For example, if you were to ship an application with the Category 2 bug just described, you should include a statement in your application's README file that reads something like this:

The foobar button on the XYZ form does not correctly call procedure suchandsuch. Please use the corresponding menu item suchandsuch found on the Tools menu. A patch will be made available as soon as possible.

✦ **Category 3: Small bugs and minor nits.** Category 3 bugs are small issues that in no way affect the workings of your application. They may be misspellings of captions or incorrect colors of text boxes. Category 3 bugs should be fixed whenever possible but should never take precedence over Category 1 bugs. They should take precedence over Category 2 bugs, but only when they are so extreme that the application looks completely unacceptable.

By categorizing your bugs and approaching them systematically, you can create a program that looks and behaves the way its users think it should. Sometimes you may feel like you will never finish your Category 1 list, but you will. You will surely be smiling the day you check your bug sheet and realize that you're down to a few Category 2s and a dozen or so Category 3s! Although you may be tempted to skip this beta testing phase of development, don't. You will only pay for it in the long run.

Tip   Not all Access features are available when an application is run within the Access runtime environment (which is discussed with the Setup Wizard later in this chapter). You can operate in the runtime environment and use the full version of Access to test for problems with your code and with the runtime environment by using the /Runtime command-line option when starting your Access application. Click Run on the Windows Start menu or create a shortcut. The following command line example starts Access and opens the Invoices database in the runtime environment:

```
C:\OFFICEXP\ACCESS\MSACCESS.EXE /RUNTIME
C:\MYAPPS\INVOICES.MDB
```

You should always test and debug your application in the runtime environment if you plan to distribute the application with the Office XP Developer Packaging Wizard.

Polishing your application

When your application has been thoroughly tested and appears ready for distribution, spend some time polishing your application. Polishing your application consists of

✦ Giving your application a consistent look and feel

✦ Adding common, professional components

✦ Adding clear and concise pictures to buttons

✦ Using common, understandable field labels and button captions

Giving your application a consistent look and feel

First and foremost, you should decide on some design standards and apply them to your application. This is incredibly important if you want your application to look professionally produced. Figure 40-2 shows a form with samples of different styles of controls.

Your design decisions may include the following:

✦ Will text boxes be sunken, flat with a border, flat without a border, chiseled, or raised?

✦ What backcolor will the text boxes be?

✦ What color will the forms be?

✦ Will you use chiseled borders to separate related items or opt for a sunken or raised border?

✦ What size will buttons on forms be?

✦ For forms that have similar buttons, such as Close and Help, in what order will the buttons appear?

✦ Which accelerator keys will you use on commonly used buttons, such as Close and Help?

Making your application look and work in a consistent manner is the single most important way to make it appear professional. For ideas on design standards to implement in your applications, spend some time working with some of your favorite programs and see what standards they use. In the area of look and feel, copying from another developer is generally not considered plagiarism but is rather often looked upon as a compliment. Copying does *not* extend, however, to making use of another application's icons or directly copying the look and feel of a competitor's product; this is very bad practice. For an example of a good look-and-feel environment, see the Microsoft Office Compatible program.

An application may be certified Office Compatible by meeting certain user-interface requirements as laid out by Microsoft. An Office-compatible application uses the same menu structures as all the Office applications, such as Word, Access, Excel, and so on. In addition, toolbars are also similar and, where applicable, have the same button image that Microsoft uses. Making an application look like an Office application saves the developer time by giving clear and concise guidelines for interface features, and helps end users by lowering the learning curve of the application.

Although you may not want to have your application independently tested and certified Office Compatible, you may want to check out the specifications and use some of the ideas presented to help you get started designing your own consistent application interfaces.

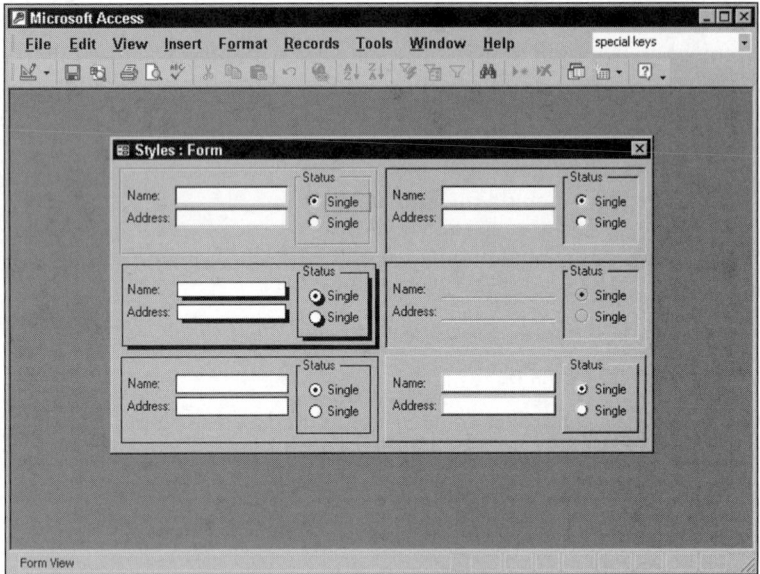

Figure 40-2: You can decide on any interface style that you like for your application. However, after you decide on a style, use it consistently.

Adding common professional components

Most commercial/professional applications have some similar components. The most common components are the splash screen, about box, and switchboard. Be aware that the splash screen (see Figure 40-3 for a good example) not only aids in increasing perceived speed of an application but also gives the application a polished, professional appearance from the moment a user runs the program. Figure 40-4 shows the implementation of Database Creation's splash screen.

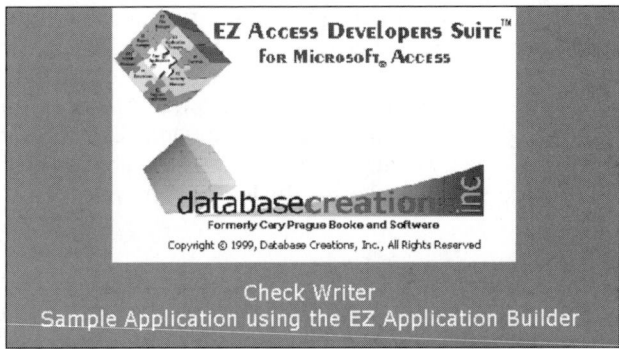

Figure 40-3: A splash screen not only increases perceived speed of your application but also gives your application a professional appearance.

On the CD-ROM

Figure 40-4 shows the design window for a splash screen template that you can use when building your own applications. This form is included in the Ch40Gold.mdb database, located on the CD-ROM that comes with this book. Import this form into your application and use it as a template for creating your own splash screen.

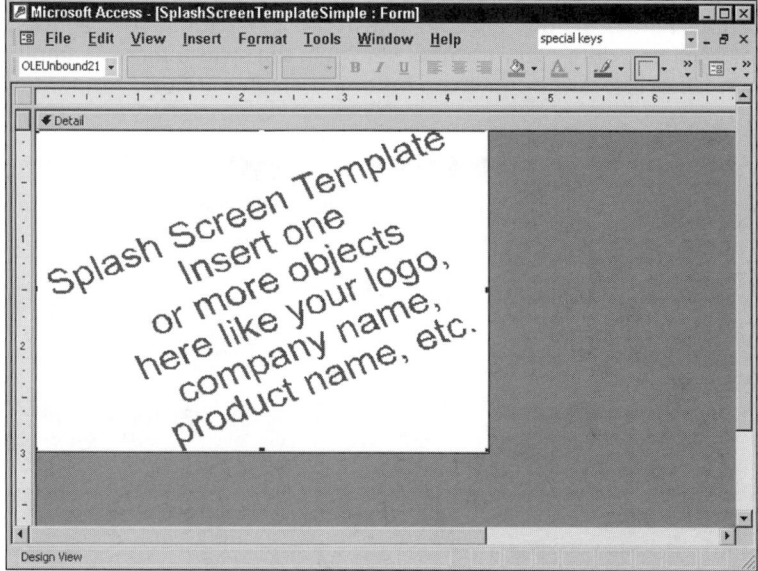

Figure 40-4: Use this form as a template to create your own splash screens for your applications.

Your splash screen should contain the following items:

✦ The application's title

✦ The application's version number

✦ Your company information

✦ A copyright notice

In addition, you may want to include the licensee information and/or a picture on the splash screen. If you use a picture on your splash screen, make it relevant to your application's function. For example, some coins and an image of a check could be used for a check-writing application. If you like, you can also use clipart for your splash screen; just be sure that the picture is clear and concise and doesn't interfere with the text information presented on your splash screen.

To implement the splash screen, have your application load the splash form before it does anything else (consider making your splash screen the Startup Display Form). When your application finishes all of its initialization procedures, close the form. Make the splash form a light form and be sure to convert any bitmaps that you place on your splash screen to pictures in order to decrease the splash form's load time.

The second component that you should implement is an application switchboard. The switchboard is essentially a steering wheel for users to find their way throughout the functions and forms that are available in the application. You can use the switchboard itself as a data-entry form, as shown in the switchboard example in Figure 40-5. You can also use a command button to display another form.

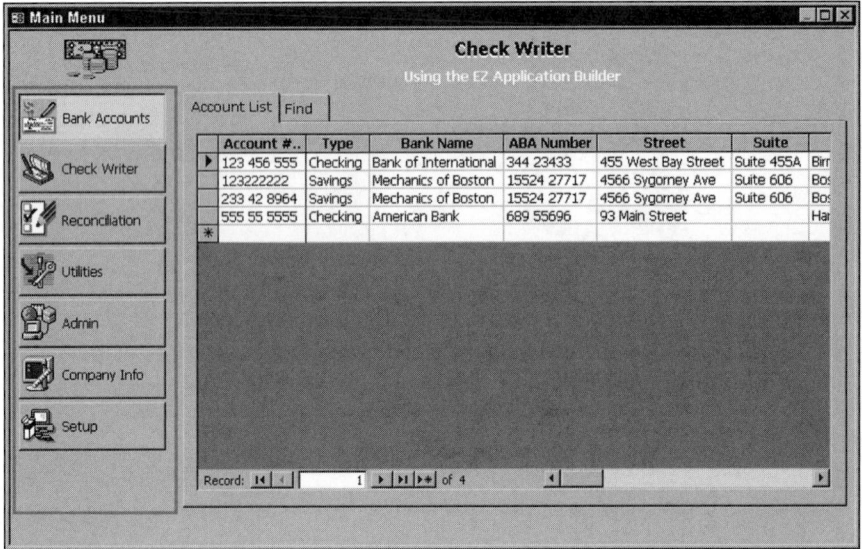

Figure 40-5: The switchboard provides a handy way to navigate throughout the application.

Make sure that the switchboard redisplays whenever the user closes a form. The switchboard provides a familiar place where users can be assured that they won't get lost in the application.

The third component that you should implement is an about box (see Figure 40-6). The about box should contain your company and copyright information, as well as the application name and current version. Including your application's licensee information (if you keep such information) in the about box is also a good idea. The about box serves as legal notice of your ownership and makes your application easier to support by giving your users easy access to the version information. Some advanced about boxes call other forms that display system information (Figure 40-6 has an additional button—System Info). You can make the about box as fancy as you want, but usually a simple one works just fine.

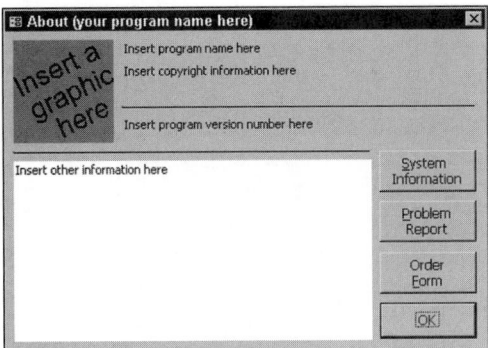

Figure 40-6: The implementation of an about box is a polishing technique that also provides useful information to the user and protects your legal interests.

Most users love pictures, and most developers love to use pictures on buttons. Studies have shown that clear and concise pictures are more intuitive and are more easily recognized than textual captions. Most developers, however, are not graphic artists and usually slap together buttons made from any clipart images that are handy. These ugly buttons make an application look clumsy and unprofessional. In addition, pictures that don't clearly show the function of the button make the application harder to use.

Select or create pictures that end users will easily recognize. Avoid abstract pictures or pictures that require specific knowledge to understand them, such as wiring symbology. If your budget permits, consider hiring a professional design firm to create your button pictures. A number of professional image galleries and tools to create and edit buttons are available.

Tip
A great third-party library of pictures that are specifically designed for Microsoft Access is the Picture Builder Add-On Picture Pack (3000 .BMP pictures specifically sized for buttons). After you've chosen your pictures, use the Command Bar Image Editor to edit and resize pictures. Both are available from Database Creations (www.databasecreations.com).

Picture buttons that are well thought out can really make your application look outstanding, as well as easier to use.

On the CD-ROM
The form shown in Figure 40-7 is a template about box that can be found in the database Ch40Gold.mdb on the CD-ROM that accompanies this book. Import this form into your application and customize it to fit your needs. The about box should be a *modal form* (in other words, it should keep the focus until the form is closed) and should not have minimize or maximize buttons available to the user.

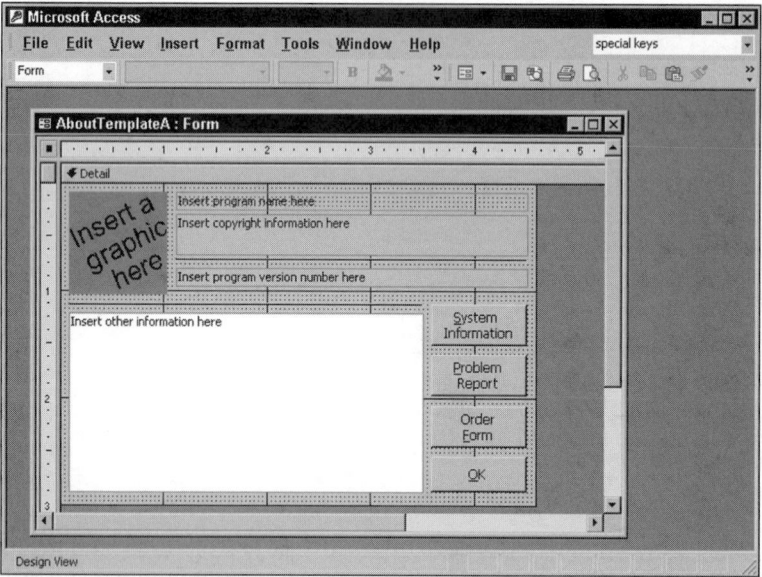

Figure 40-7: You can import and customize this about box template form to meet your needs.

The about box should be accessible from a Help menu on all menu bars. The submenu title should be About My Application. Of course, substitute *Your program name here* with your application's actual name.

The splash screen, about box, and switchboard may seem like trivial features, but they can greatly enhance your application's appeal. They take little time to implement and should be included in all of your distributed applications.

Creating comprehensive and intuitive menus and toolbars

Before you even consider distributing an application, you need to make the application as intuitive as possible. Menus and toolbars are absolutely vital for usability with any Windows application.

Bulletproofing an application

Bulletproofing an application is the process of making the application idiot-proof. It involves trapping errors that can be caused by users, such as invalid data entry, attempting to run a function when the application is not ready to run the function, and allowing users to click a Calculate button before all necessary data has been entered. Bulletproofing your application is an additional stage that should be completed parallel with debugging and should be performed again after the application is working and debugged.

Using error trapping on all Visual Basic procedures

An error-handling routine gives you a chance to display a friendlier message to the user other than some unintuitive default message box, such as the one shown in Figure 40-8.

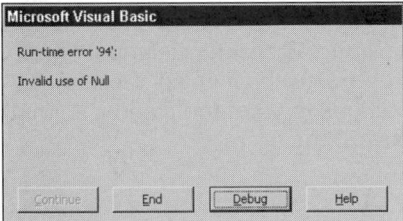

Figure 40-8: An error message resulting from a procedure with no error-handling routine.

One of the most important elements of bulletproofing an application is making sure that the application never *crashes*—that is, never ceases operation completely and unexpectedly. Although Access provides built-in error processing for most data-entry errors (for example, characters entered into a currency field), automatic processing doesn't exist for Visual Basic code errors. You should include error-handling routines in every Visual Basic procedure, even if you use just `On Error Resume Next`.

When running an application distributed with the Office XP Developer Packaging Wizard, any untrapped error encountered in your code causes the program to terminate completely. Your users can't recover from such a crash, and serious data loss may occur. Your users have to restart the application after such an application error.

Separating the code objects from the tables in the application

You should separate your code objects (forms, reports, queries, modules, and macros) from your table objects. Many benefits are gained from distributing these objects in separate .MDB files:

✦ Network users benefit from speed increases by running the code .MDB (the database containing the queries, forms, macros, reports, and modules) locally and accessing only the shared data on the network.

✦ Updates can easily be distributed to users.

✦ Data can be backed up more efficiently because only one file is needed, and disk space and time aren't used to continuously back up the code objects.

All professionally distributed applications — especially those intended for network use — should have separate code and data database (.MDB) files.

Documenting the application

Most developers don't like to write documentation; it's simply no fun and can be quite frustrating and time-consuming. Taking the time and effort now to prepare thorough documentation, however, can save hours of technical support time down the road. Even if you don't plan to distribute a full user's manual, take time to document how to perform the most common functions in your application. If you have created shortcuts, make sure to share them with the users.

Creating a help system

Although documentation is extremely important for getting users started on your application, a Help system that is well-written, thorough, and context-sensitive is just as important. A Help system puts pertinent information at users' disposal with just a click of the mouse or a push of a button.

Implementing a security structure

The final item that you need to consider before distributing your application is the level at which you want to secure your application. You can secure specific individual objects or you can secure your entire application. If it's important to you to secure design permissions for all of your objects in order to protect your source code, then you need to be aware that you can't rely solely on Microsoft's word that the security in Access works. Microsoft touted the security model of Access 2.0 as being the most secure available. It was discovered, however, that an average Access developer can unsecure an Access 2.0 database in about five minutes, with only minimum coding! Although no method for unsecuring a secured Access 97, Access 2000, or Access 2002 application has yet been discovered, a method may be uncovered in the future. You must understand and accept this risk when you distribute a secured Access application.

Using Visual Basic Productivity Tools to Streamline the Development Environment

Office XP Developer provides several tools that can help you create efficient and bombproof Visual Basic programs. These tools can be integrated into the Visual Basic development environment, thus enabling you to develop better code in less time.

What is Office XP Developer?

Office XP Developer replaces the Office Developer Edition Tools, or ODE Tools, that were available with earlier versions of Office. Office XP Developer is the edition of Office geared for Office XP developers building professional applications. When you purchase Office XP Developer, you get Microsoft Office XP Professional Edition, along with a rich set of productivity tools.

The new Office XP Developer features include the following:

✦ **FrontPage Version 2002** makes it easier than ever to create and manage Web sites.

✦ **Visual Basic for Applications (VBA)** is the version of Visual Basic designed for building custom Office XP applications.

✦ **COM Add-in Designer** allows developers to create and debug stand-alone Visual Basic COM add-ins (DLL's) without having to leave the Visual Basic development environment.

✦ **Dashboard Project** makes it easy to build *Digital Dashboards* — an easy-to-use desktop view of important Web-based information and tools.

✦ **Workflow Designer for SQL Server** allows you to build Web-based business solutions that utilize SQL Server data.

✦ **Workflow Designer for Exchange 2000 Server** automates creating business processes to take advantage of all of the features in Exchange Server.

✦ **SQL Server 2000 for Office XP Developer** allows developers to create database applications that can be deployed in standard SQL Server 2000 database implementations.

✦ **Exchange 2000 Server Developer Edition** helps developers test collaborative applications before deployment.

✦ **Visual SourceSafe and Visual SourceSafe Integration** provides check in/check out, versioning, history, and other important source code management functions for use in the Visual Basic for Applications environment.

✦ **Visual Basic Error Handler** automates creating standardized error-handling code with input dialog boxes that capture basic information and insert standardized error-handling code by using a customizable template.

✦ **Visual Basic Code Commenter** creates well-commented code by automatically adding comments and headers to procedures by using customizable templates.

✦ **Code Librarian** provides a centralized repository for prewritten code that can be reused across development teams.

✦ **Code Librarian Viewer** takes advantage of archived code in a Code Librarian database — even if you don't have Code Librarian.

✦ **Royalty-Free Access Runtime** provides developers with the license agreement to distribute Access 2002 applications and Access Data Projects.

✦ **Visual Basic Multi-Code Import/Export** enables you to easily copy Office objects from one project to another.

✦ **Visual Basic String Editor** makes it easier to create strings to embed long scripts or complicated SQL statements into Visual Basic code.

✦ **Microsoft Replication Manager** enables you to view, manage, and synchronize Microsoft Jet databases over a network or over the Internet.

✦ **Visual Basic Packaging Wizard** helps you create installation packages for your Office XP and Visual Basic applications and install them on your users' computers.

✦ **Developer Documentation** printed edition gives you all the important Office XP information at your fingertips.

Installing the Visual Basic productivity tools

The Office XP Developer Visual Basic productivity tools are offered as wizards and add-ins. Wizards and add-ins are extensions that you can add to your Visual Basic development environment to simplify the many tasks involved in developing an application. Because these wizards and add-ins are available only through the Office Developer, they are not installed through the normal Access and Visual Basic installation process. You must install them by using the Add-In Manager.

To install an add-in, follow these steps:

1. Select Add-Ins ⇨ Add-In Manager from the menu. The Add-In Manager dialog box displays, as shown in Figure 40-9.

2. Highlight an add-in from the list and click the desired behaviors in Load Behavior. To unload an add-in or prevent it from loading, clear all Load Behavior boxes.

3. After you finish making your selections, click OK. The Add-Ins menu displays the tools that you selected to load, as shown in Figure 40-10.

Depending on your Load Behavior selections, Visual Basic connects the selected add-ins and disconnects the cleared add-ins. Visual Basic saves your add-in selections between editing sessions.

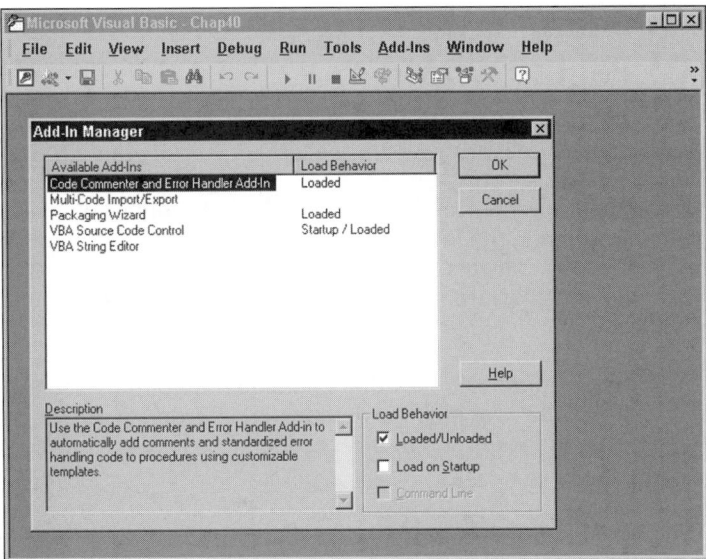

Figure 40-9: Using the Visual Basic Add-In Manager to install an add-in.

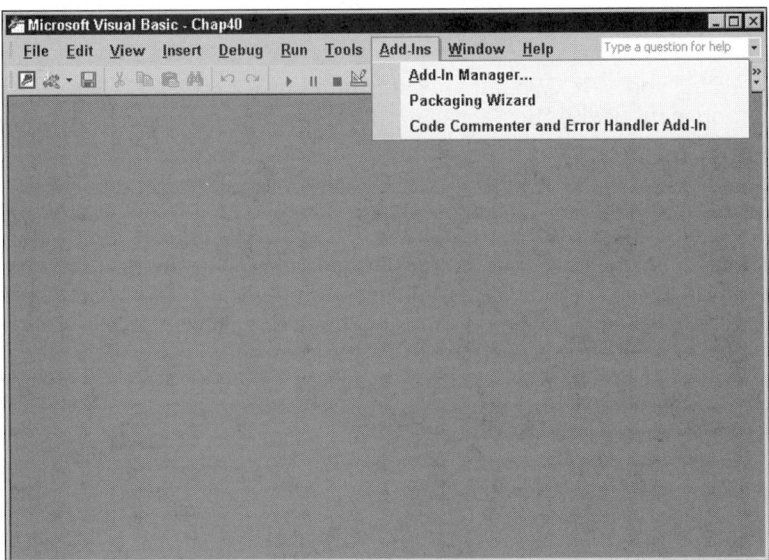

Figure 40-10: The Add-ins menu displays the tools that are loaded.

Creating distribution disks using the Office XP Developer Packaging Wizard

After you finish your application, you need to find a way to distribute it to your customers. Distribution includes delivering all files necessary to run your application on some form of media, such as floppy disk or CD-ROM, or via electronic distribution channels, such as the Internet. The media should include some sort of setup program that automates copying the files to the user's computer, sets up any shortcut items, registers necessary controls, and sets values in the system registry. The Office XP Developer Packaging Wizard guides you through the process of building the distribution program.

A *package* consists of one or more .cab files that contain your compressed project files and any other files that the user must have to install in order to run your application. These files may include setup programs, secondary .cab files, or other required files.

You can freely distribute any redistributable application or component that you create with Microsoft Office XP Developer. However, you should note that because Microsoft FrontPage and Microsoft Outlook only support projects that are based on user profiles, the Packaging Wizard can't package applications by using these products. In addition, the Packaging Wizard can't package workflow applications for Microsoft Exchange Server or Digital Dashboard projects. You can, however, easily package and deploy an Access application.

You may be asking yourself, "What if my users don't own Access?" When you distribute your application with the Packaging Wizard, end users can run your application by using the Access runtime environment without needing to purchase a full version of Access. The Packaging Wizard makes it easy to package and distribute all the necessary runtime files. This is (mostly) transparent to users; they don't realize that Access is running in the background. Certain design interfaces are hidden from users to prevent them from creating Access applications with the runtime executable. Purchasing Office XP Developer gives you the licensing rights to distribute your application with the runtime environment to an unlimited number of users — with no royalty fees! So, even if you plan to create your setup program with a third-party tool, you need to purchase at least one copy of Office XP Developer to obtain the legal rights to distribute your application with the runtime files.

Tip   Note that the runtime version of Access can't be used to open .adp or .ade files; however, you can use the Packaging Wizard to create a setup program to distribute .adp or .ade files to users who already have the full version of Access installed.

When you distribute your application using the Packaging Wizard, you can configure your custom setup program to do the following:

✦ Copy your application's files to specified locations on a user's hard drive.

✦ Create Windows shortcuts that start your application or program files.

✦ Add Windows Registry keys and entries for your application.

✦ Group files, shortcuts, and registry keys and entries into components that users can select to install or uninstall.

✦ Install other Access files, such as drivers for accessing various data sources and any .OCX custom controls that are used by your application.

✦ Run an application or open a file after the setup program is finished installing your application.

Restrictions of the Packaging Wizard

The Access runtime environment is an excellent (and currently the only) way to distribute your applications to users who don't own a licensed copy of Microsoft Access. As previously stated, the Access runtime is almost transparent to the user. Unfortunately, some limitations do exist with the release version of the Office XP Developer. Some of these issues affect the behavior of your application, and some are problems inherent in the Packaging Wizard itself. You need to be aware of the limitations, and you probably want to make your end users aware of some of them as well.

Some key points and pitfalls to be aware of when designing your setup routine include the following:

✦ Runtime applications that don't include custom help files generate errors when referring to the Access Help file. As stated previously, you should always attempt to distribute applications with Help systems. Even a rudimentary Help system is better than no online help at all.

Tip

If you elect against shipping a Help file with your application, you can prevent Access from generating an error by not providing a Help menu item on any of your custom menus and by creating an Autokeys Macro that traps the F1 key. The F1 key doesn't have to do anything in the macro. By simply including it in the Autokeys macro causes the macro to trap the F1 key when it is pressed. This prevents it from being passed to the Access runtime, thus calling up the Help file.

✦ Attempting to close a runtime application with the `CloseCurrentDatabase` method generates an error. The runtime version of Access doesn't run without an application loaded and therefore generates the error if you attempt to close the current database. To terminate your application, use the `Quit` method of the `DoCmd` object.

✦ Uninstalling Microsoft Access 2002 breaks applications installed with a custom setup program. Unfortunately, the uninstall program in Access doesn't know when a runtime Access application is installed on the computer, and it changes registry settings that are crucial to running your runtime Access application.

✦ The Packaging Wizard doesn't support Administrative (setup /a) and Run From Network Server installations. Performing a network installation places all the setup files onto a server drive so that all workstations on the network can run the setup program from the server rather than from floppy disk. If you distribute your application to run in a network environment, instruct your users to copy all files from each disk in the distribution set to the same directory on the network and then run the setup program in this directory from each workstation.

✦ Reinstalling your application with the custom setup program fails if the user has performed a Maintenance Removal of Workgroup Administrator. A user can do this by rerunning the setup program and deselecting the Workgroup Administrator component (which is discussed later in this chapter). If a user removes the Workgroup Administrator component and attempts to reinstall your Access runtime application, the installation fails. Attempting to run the setup program again after the failure results in a successful installation.

Tip   You can prevent end users from removing the Workgroup Administrator component by setting the component to Hidden on the Components page of the Setup Wizard. This setting is discussed later in this chapter.

✦ Very large components (+100MB) show negative numbers in your custom setup program. This bug doesn't affect the installation or workings of your setup routine, but it may confuse end users. Most developers almost never have components this large. If you experience this problem, however, consider breaking the offending component into smaller components.

✦ Removing the component in single-component setup doesn't remove the entire application, and no workaround exists for this. If users want to remove the application completely, they must use the Remove All button.

The Packaging Wizard is unable to use exclusively locked files. If you try to add a file in the wizard that is exclusively locked by another user or another application, the wizard responds with an application-defined or object-defined error. When users trigger this error, Access cancels the creation of your custom setup program disk images. When creating disk images with the Packaging Wizard, you should close all possible applications in order to avoid potential lock conflicts.

Using the Packaging Wizard to create distribution disks

The Packaging Wizard makes it easy for you to create the necessary .cab files and setup programs for your application. Like other wizards, the Packaging Wizard prompts you for information so that it can create the exact configuration that you want.

Setting up the Packaging Wizard
1. Open the project that you want to package or deploy using the wizard.

Note If you are working in a project group or have multiple projects loaded, make sure that the project that you want to package or deploy is the current project before you start the wizard.

2. Use the Add-In Manager to load the Packaging Wizard, if necessary: Select Add-In Manager from the Add-Ins menu, select Packaging Wizard from the list, and then click OK.

Creating a package

After you have loaded the Packaging Wizard add-in into your project workspace, you are ready to begin the process of creating a setup routine for your application.

1. Select Packaging Wizard from the Add-Ins menu to launch the wizard. The first screen of the Packaging Wizard displays, as shown in Figure 40-11.

Figure 40-11: The first page of the Packaging Wizard describes the packaging process.

2. Click Next to begin setting up the package. The Identify Application Package page displays, as shown in Figure 40-12.

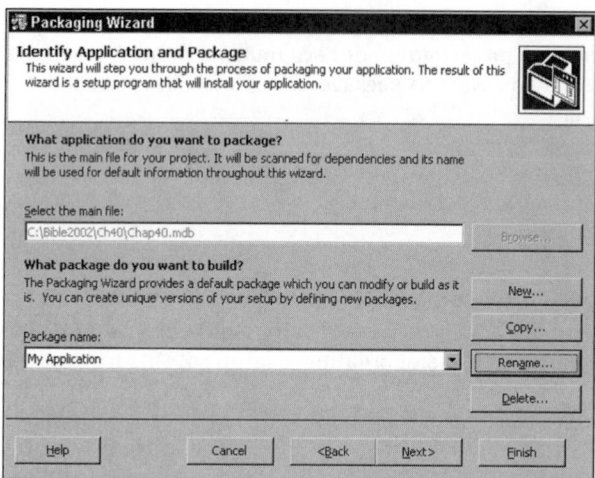

Figure 40-12: The Identify Application Package page of the Packaging Wizard identifies the application to package.

The Identify Application Package allows you to identify the application that you want to package. The Select Main file field on the screen identifies the full path name of the application file for the package. The main file is the file that will be scanned for dependencies in order to determine additional files that should be included in the package. Figure 40-12 demonstrates how you can launch the Packaging Wizard from an application that you want to package. The Packaging Wizard has completed the Select Main file field with the location and filename of the example application—
C:\Bible2002\Ch40\Chap40.mdb.

Note   A dependency (.dep) file contains information about the runtime requirements of an application or component—for example, which files are needed, how they are to be registered, and where on the user's machine they should be installed.

The Package name field defaults to the title "Package for <file Name>"—which is "Package for Chap40" in this example. The list for this field includes all the defined packages for this application. Each package stores information about how to create the setup program for the application. A single main application file can have numerous packages associated with it. The Package name is used as the name of the section header in the packaging definition script file, which is stored as a .pks file in the same folder as the application.

The Identify Application Package page includes the following buttons that you can use to modify the package name:

- **New:** Displays a New Package dialog box, so you can create a new package and give it a name.

- **Copy:** Displays a Copy Package dialog box that makes it possible for you to enter a name and create a copy of your package definition. The copy of the package is based on the original package. When you make changes in the wizard, the changes are saved to the new copy.

- **Rename:** Displays a Rename Package dialog box that makes it possible for you to rename a package.

- **Delete:** Displays a Packaging Wizard dialog box that asks if you are sure you want to permanently delete the packaging definition.

 **Tip** You should assign your package a descriptive name that will be easy to recognize later in the process.

3. Select the Rename button to enter a name for the package and then click Next. The Application Information page displays, as shown in Figure 40-13.

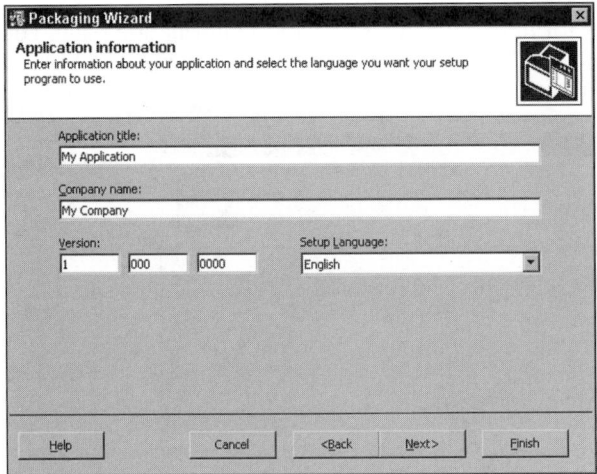

Figure 40-13: The Application Information page of the Packaging Wizard registers the version information for the package.

The Application Information page allows you to register information about the particular application that you want to package, including:

- **Application title:** This defaults to the name that you selected for the package name, but you can change the application name to anything you desire.

- **Company name:** Use this field to specify the name of the company who owns the software. This may be your own organization or your employer's organization if you have developed the application for distribution to many companies. If you custom-developed the application for a specific organization, then you would enter the organization's name here.

- **Version:** This number defaults to 1.000.0000, which is appropriate for the first release of the application. If you are creating a package for a subsequent release, however, you should change the version number accordingly.

Tip

Any time you create a package, you should be sure that the version number for your package has been set accordingly. This is especially important if you are distributing a new version of an existing application: Without the appropriate change in version numbers, the end user's computer may determine that critical files don't need to be updated.

- **Setup Language:** Select this option from the drop-down box. The Packaging Wizard assembles the necessary files to run the setup program for the selected language.

Note

The Access Runtime language files are specified in a later Packaging Wizard page.

4. Complete the information for the Application Information page. Then click Next. The Dependencies page displays, as shown in Figure 40-14.

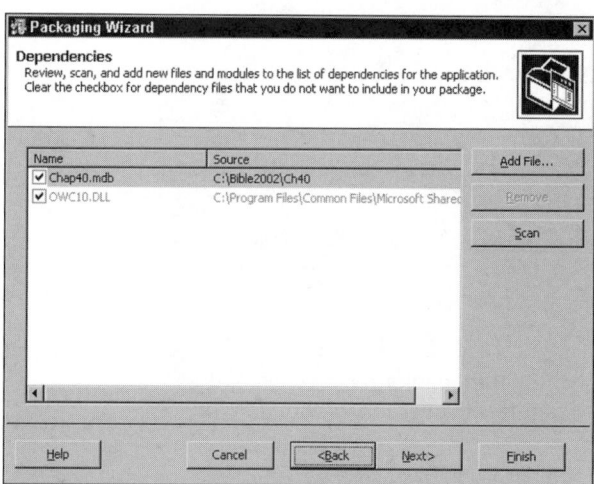

Figure 40-14: The Dependencies page of the Packaging Wizard enables you to verify the files to be included in the setup routine.

The Dependencies page displays a list of the files that will be included in the package and enables you to add additional files to the package or remove unwanted files. You can clear the check box for any file that you don't want to include, or highlight the file name and select the Remove button. Use the Add button to select an additional file name to include in the package. The Scan button analyzes the selected files for dependencies and adds any found dependencies to the list; this button is only enabled when the selected file is a type that can be scanned.

The Packaging Wizard can scan the following types of files:

Application	File extension
Excel	.xls, .xlt, .xlw
Word	.doc, .dot
PPT	.ppt, .pps
VBA	.vba
Access	.mdb, .adp, .mde, .ade. mda, .mdw

5. When you have selected all of the dependency files, click Next. The Modify Installation Locations page displays, as shown in Figure 40-15.

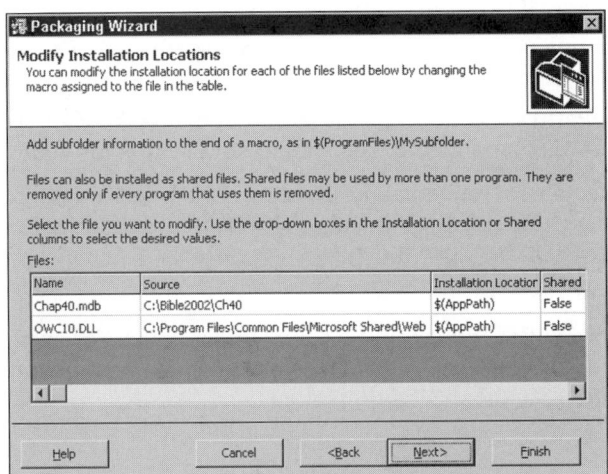

Figure 40-15: Specifying where to install the application's files.

Use the Modify Installation Locations page to change the intended location for your project files that will be installed on the user's computer. You can choose from a series of predefined folder variables that indicate installation locations on the user's machine.

- **$(AppPath)** — This folder is designated by the user running your custom setup program. Think of AppPath as a variable that's used to specify the user-selected folder. Your main application database should always be placed in the AppPath folder. In addition, you should always place your Help files with the application files, so the Help files should also have AppPath specified as their destination folder.

- **$(WinPath)** — This is the Windows folder on the user's machine. Again, think of WinPath as a variable. At runtime, the Setup Wizard determines in what folder Windows resides and places all files that have WinPath as their destination folder in that Windows folder. You should generally avoid placing a file in the Windows folder unless that file is an update to a file that already resides in the Windows folder.

- **$(WinSysPath)** — This folder is the System folder found below the Windows folder. WinSysPath is similar to WinPath in that the Setup Wizard resolves at runtime where the Windows System folder resides and places the appropriate files there. You should place .DLL and .OCX files in the system folder because these files are common components. Avoid placing application-specific files in the System folder.

- **$(ProgramFiles)** — This folder is the folder where application files are usually installed (that is, C:\Program Files).

- **$(CommonFiles)** — Where shared files are usually installed (for example, C:\Program Files\Common Files).

- **$(MSDAOPath)** — Location that is stored in the registry for Data Access Objects (DAO) components. You should not use this for your files.

Although this fact is not immediately apparent, you aren't limited to placing your files in these folders only. You may also specify a subfolder below your AppPath folder. To do this, use the following syntax:

```
$(AppPath)\subfolder
```

Replace the word `subfolder` with the actual folder name. For example, if you want to create a folder called `DATA` under your main application folder, specify the following folder as the destination folder:

```
$(AppPath)\DATA
```

The Setup Wizard determines the AppPath folder name at runtime by letting the user specify the folder. It then creates the folder if it doesn't currently exist and creates any subfolders specified in the `Destination Folder` property of included files.

Tip

If you include a large number of files and offer many components for installation, consider grouping the files or components into subfolders. Grouping makes future updates much easier and makes your application component architecture easier to understand when troubleshooting — if you need to replace a file for component A, for example, you know in which subfolder to look. Keeping only the main application files in the application folder is best whenever possible.

6. After you have selected all of the installation locations, click Next. The Access Runtime page displays, as shown in Figure 40-16.

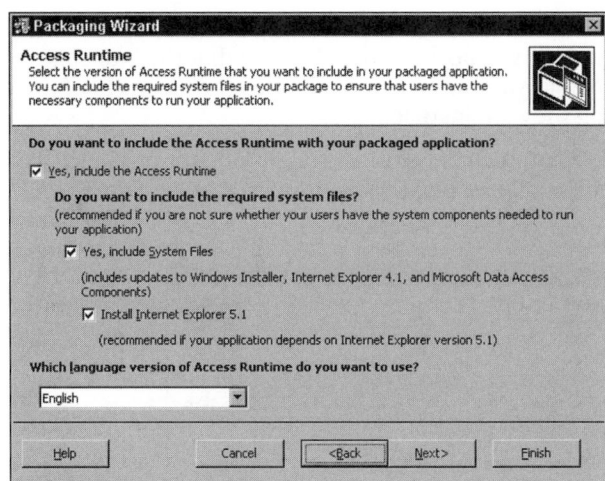

Figure 40-16: Including the Access Runtime files in your installation package.

The Packaging Wizard gives you the option of including the Access Runtime files in your package so that you can distribute Access applications to users who don't have the full version of Access installed on their computers.

To include the Access Runtime files, check the box labeled *Yes, include the Access runtime*. The Access Runtime Wizard page provides the following options for determining which runtime files to include in your package:

Installation selection	Result
System files option unchecked or Internet Explorer 5.1 option unchecked	Access Runtime won't work unless the target computer has Microsoft Windows 2000-level system components.
Yes, include System Files option checked	Will work on all computers with Windows 98 and later. Installs Internet Explorer 4.1.
Install Internet Explorer 5.1	Includes the setup components for Internet Explorer 5.1 and upgrades the user's computer to make sure that applications dependent upon functionality of this version will work correctly.

You can clear the System files and Internet Explorer 5.1 options if you are sure that users have the required files to run your application. Deselecting these options results in a much smaller application setup package.

Caution   The Access Runtime won't work correctly if the user's computer doesn't contain the proper system files.

The last option on the Access Runtime Wizard page is to select the Access Runtime language. It is important to make sure that the language of the system files provided in your application matches the language of the operating system on which they are installed.

7. After you have selected all of the Access Runtime options, click Next. The Access Runtime Properties page displays, as shown in Figure 40-17.

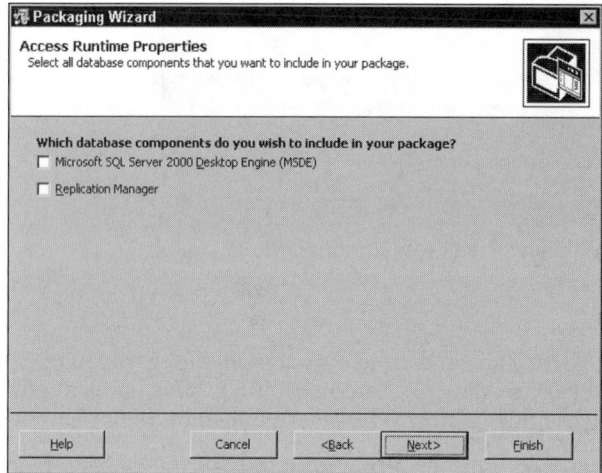

Figure 40-17: Determining the database components to include for an Access Runtime package.

If your application gets its data from the Microsoft SQL Server 2000 Desktop Engine or if the application uses replication, then you need to include some additional files in the package. By selecting either or both of the options on the Access Runtime Properties page, the wizard automatically includes the additional necessary files.

Caution   By selecting the desktop engine box, you significantly increase the size of the package, because all of the desktop engine files are included in the package and are installed on the user's computer during setup.

8. After you have completed the selections on the Access Runtime Properties page, click Next. The Start Menu Shortcuts page displays, as shown in Figure 40-18.

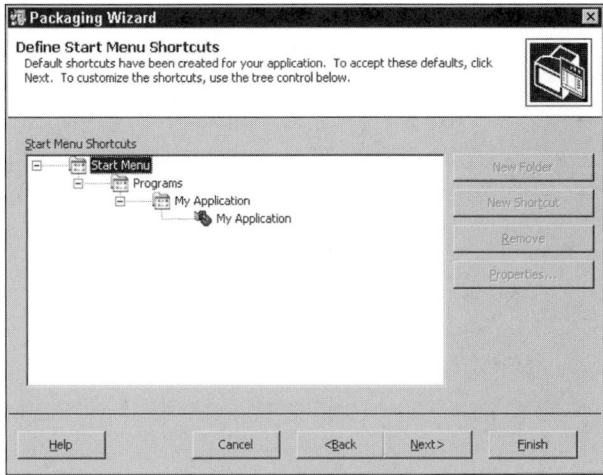

Figure 40-18: Specifying where to place the Start menu icon.

In the Start Menu Shortcuts page, you specify the Start menu groups and group items that should be created on the user's computer during installation of your solution. You can create groups and items for your solution in one of two locations: On the main level of the Start menu, or within the Programs subdirectory of the Start menu.

In addition to creating new Start menu groups and items, you can edit the properties for an existing item, or you can remove groups and items.

9. Make your Start Menu Shortcuts selections, and then click Next. The Run on Complete page displays, as shown in Figure 40-19.

The Run on Complete page allows you to specify an application to run when the setup program completes. To run an application, check the box labeled *Run This Command When Installation Is Finished.* When this box is selected, the combo box displays the list of files that have been added to the project. You can select one of these files, and add further command-line information to these file names as necessary.

 **Tip**

You can specify the Access database filename in the Run on Complete page to automatically launch the Access application when setup completes.

10. After completing the Run on Complete page, click Next. The Build the Application page displays, as shown in Figure 40-20.

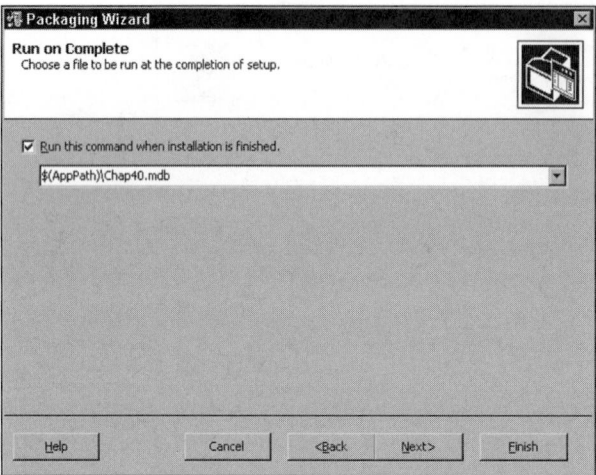

Figure 40-19: Running an application when the setup program completes.

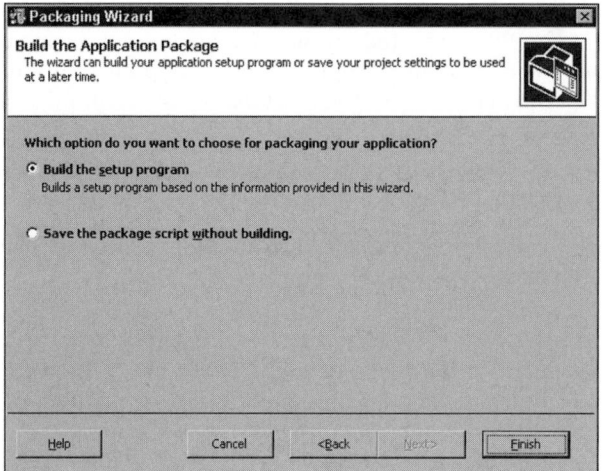

Figure 40-20: Getting ready to build the application setup program.

When the Build the Application page displays, the Packaging Wizard is now ready to use the information that you have specified to build the setup program. On this page, you can choose to build the setup program now or save the package information and build the setup program at a later time.

Note   Both options will save the package information.

11. Select the *Build the setup program* option and click Finish if you are ready to begin building the setup program. The Browse for folder dialog box displays, as shown in Figure 40-21.

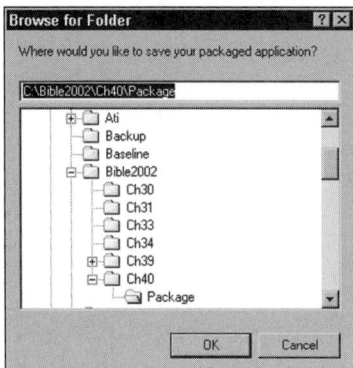

Browse for Folder   [? ×]

Where would you like to save your packaged application?

C:\Bible2002\Ch40\Package

- Ati
  - Backup
  - Baseline
- Bible2002
  - Ch30
  - Ch31
  - Ch33
  - Ch34
  - Ch39
  - Ch40
    - Package

[OK]   [Cancel]

Figure 40-21: Saving the package information.

The Browse for folder dialog box allows you to specify the folder where you want to save the package information script. If you make any changes to the application at a later time, you can tell the Packaging Wizard to reuse the settings that you have already provided for this setup program. The Packaging Wizard saves the settings that you chose as a script. Scripts serve three purposes:

- A script enables you to package the project again later by using the same settings.

- A script provides a way of identifying a package for deployment purposes. When you begin the deployment portion of the wizard, the first step asks you to select a package to deploy. Packages are referred to by the script name that they were given in the packaging process.

- A script allows you to package your project in silent mode. When you run the wizard in silent mode, you must give the wizard the name of a script that it should use.

Note The Browse for folder dialog box allows you to select a folder *only*. The file name for the script is the Package name that you specified in Step 3 of the wizard process.

12. Click OK to begin building the package. The Packaging Wizard creates the setup files. After the Packaging Wizard has finished creating the files, the Package Complete page displays, as shown in Figure 40-22.

The Package Complete page confirms that the setup package was created and indicates the directory where it is located.

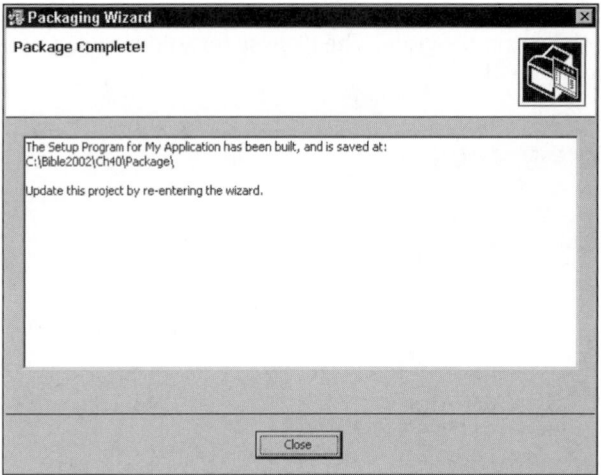

Figure 40-22: Displaying the results of the Packaging Wizard.

13. After you have finished reviewing the confirmation information, click Close. When you close the Package Complete page, the Packaging Wizard closes and the Microsoft Visual Basic window displays.

After the Packaging Wizard finishes creating your package, you can find the setup program in the folder that you selected in the last step of the wizard. You can then test your setup program.

Testing the setup program

Whenever you create a new setup program or make changes to an old one, you should take the time to run the setup program before releasing it to your users. By running the Packaging Wizard using your saved scripts, it is quick and easy to make any last-minute adjustments.

To run the setup program, locate the Setup.exe file in the folder that you indicated to use in the Packaging Wizard. When you run Setup.exe, a professional welcome screen displays, as shown in Figure 40-23.

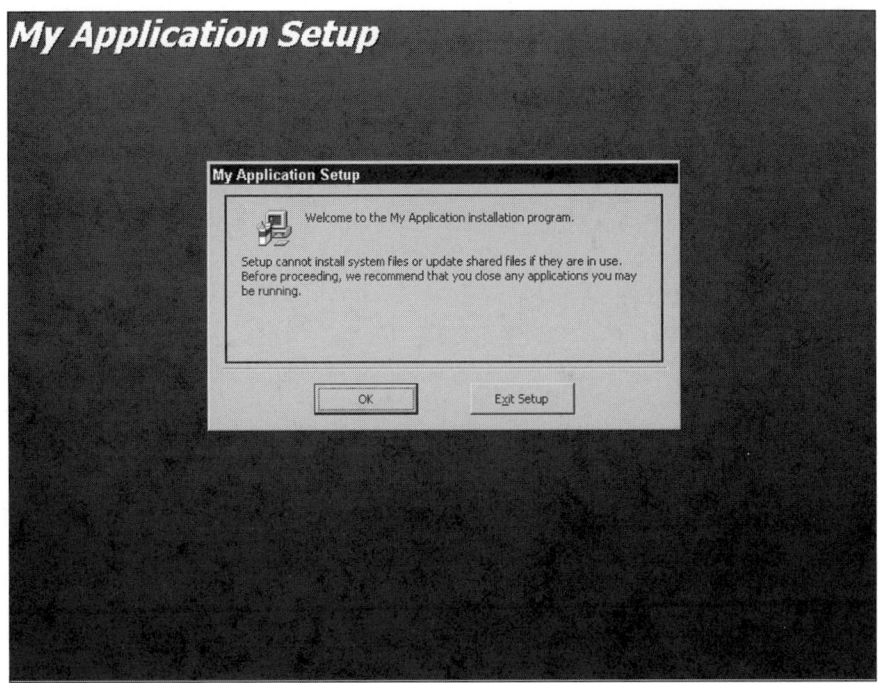

Figure 40-23: The setup program starts with a welcome and a warning about shared files.

After the user clicks OK to continue with the installation, the Application Setup page displays, as shown in Figure 40-24.

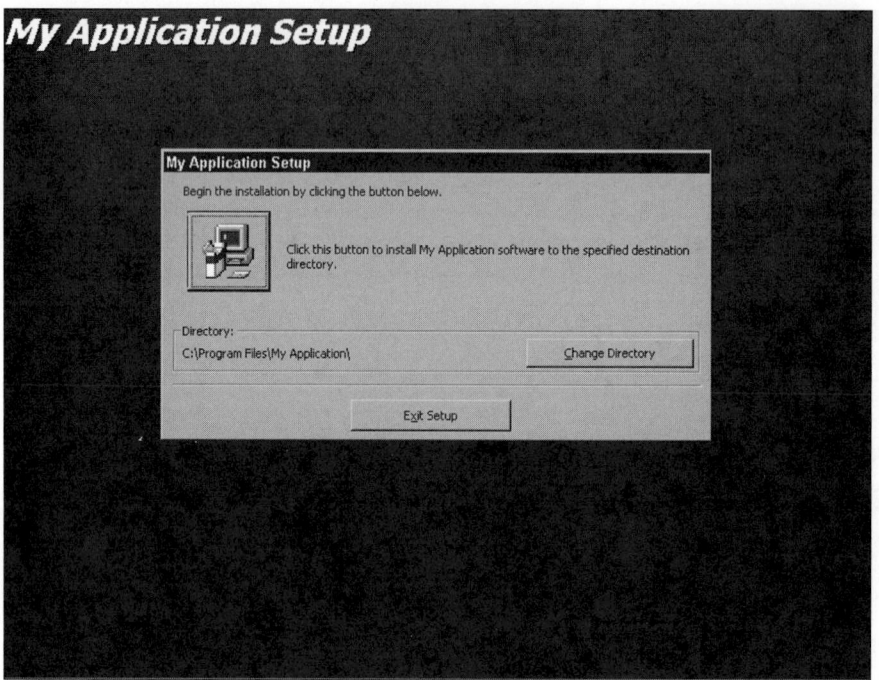

Figure 40-24: The setup suggests the installation folder that you specified in the wizard.

On this page, the user can accept the recommended installation folder that you designated in the Packaging Wizard, or they can select Change Directory to choose another folder.

After the user selects the large button at the top of the Application Setup page, the setup program copies the installation files to the selected folder.

After all the files have been copied, the user can select a Program Group for the application's icon, as shown in Figure 40-25.

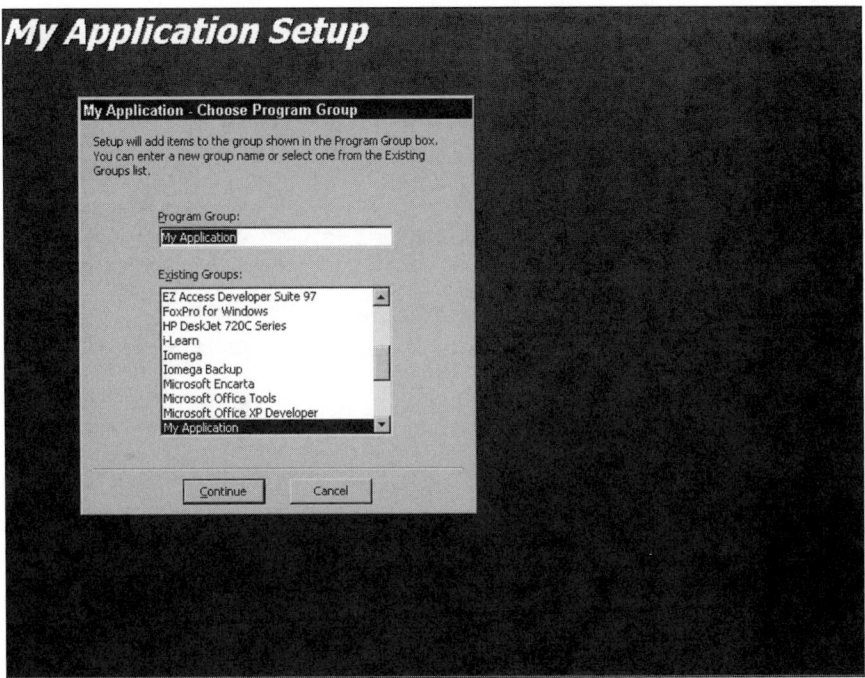

Figure 40-25: Choosing a Program Group for the new application.

The setup program confirms that the installation has been successfully completed, as shown in Figure 40-26.

The Packaging Wizard makes it easy to create a setup routine for any Access application. It virtually eliminates the guesswork involved in identifying all the files that an application needs in order to run correctly. Additionally, it automatically builds a professional installation interface that adds that final finishing touch to a well-built application.

Although deciding what to distribute to your users and how to distribute it requires some time and considerable thought, taking this time and energy to learn the Packaging Wizard enables you to create perfect installations every time!

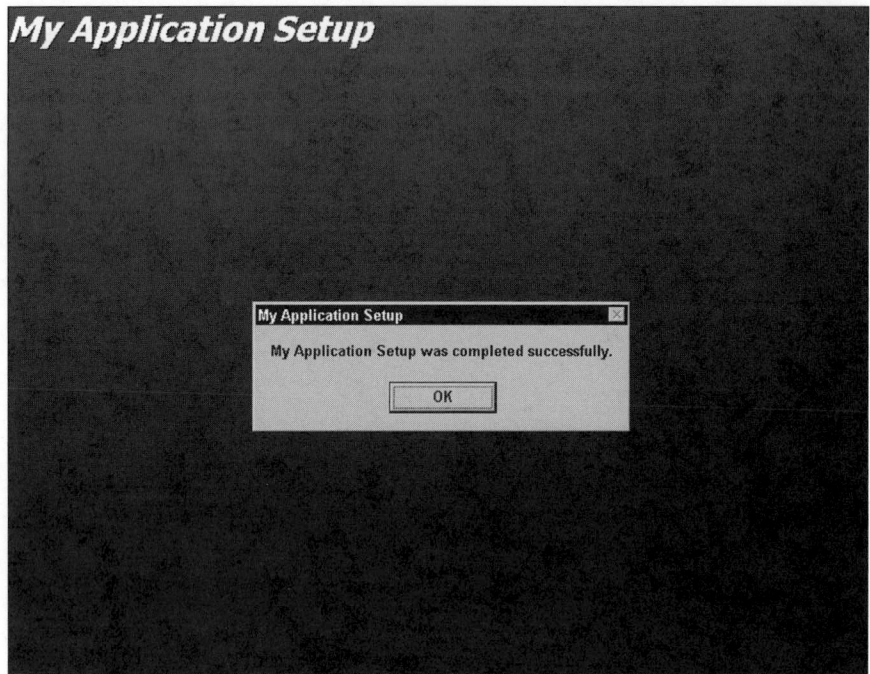

Figure 40-26: After the setup program completes, it informs the user that it completed successfully.

This chapter explored many different steps that are required to produce a top-notch distributed Access application. For each step, you can take dozens and dozens of shortcuts, but *don't*. It isn't uncommon for a company to devote an entire week or longer just to prepare an application for distribution (not writing core code). When you take your time and do these things right, it really shows, and your users will have a smooth-running, intuitive, dependable application that makes their tasks just a little bit easier.

✦   ✦   ✦

Integrating with Microsoft Office XP

In This Chapter

Using Automation to integrate with Office

Creating Automation references

Creating an instance of an Automation object

Getting an existing object instance

Working with Automation objects

Closing an instance of an Automation object

Using Microsoft Word 2002 to create an Automation example

Using Office's Macro Recorder

Programming the Office Assistant

As companies standardize their computer practices and software selections, it is becoming more and more important to develop *total* solutions: In other words, solutions that integrate the many procedures of an organization. Usually, various procedures are accomplished by using different software packages, such as Word for letter writing, Exchange and Outlook for mailing and faxing, and Excel for financial functions. If the organization for which you are developing has standardized on the Microsoft Office suite, you can leverage your knowledge of Visual Basic for Applications to program for all of these products.

Note *Automation,* formerly called *OLE Automation,* is a means by which an application can expose objects, each with its own methods and properties, that other applications can create instances of and control through code. Not all commercial applications support Automation, but more and more applications are adopting Automation to replace the outdated DDE interface. Consult with a specific application's vendor to find out if it supports or plans to support Automation in the program.

Using Automation to Integrate with Office

The Microsoft Office XP applications (the 2002 versions of such products as Word and Excel) mentioned in the previous section all support Automation. Using Automation, you can create objects in your code that represent other applications. By manipulating these objects (setting properties and calling methods), you can control the referenced applications as though you were programming directly in them, thus allowing you to create seamless integrated applications by using Automation.

Creating Automation references

Applications that support Automation provide information about their objects in an *object library.* The object library contains information about an application's properties, methods, and *classes.* An application's class is its internal structure for objects; each class creates a specific type of object — a form, a report, and so on. To reference an application's objects, Visual Basic must determine which specific type of object is being referenced by an object's variable in your code. The process of determining the type of an object variable is called *binding.* You can use two methods for binding an object — *early binding* and *late binding.*

Early binding an object

Using the References dialog box in the Visual Basic for Applications window of Access, you can explicitly reference an object library. When you explicitly reference an object library, you are performing early binding. Automation code executes more quickly when you use early binding.

Note   To access the References dialog box of VBA, you need to activate the Visual Basic window by either creating a new module or displaying the design of an existing module.

To create a reference, first create a new module or open any existing module in your application database in the Visual Basic for Applications Design screen. After you have a module in Design view, a new command, References, is available from the Tools menu (see Figure 41-1). Select Tools ⇨ References to access the References dialog box (see Figure 42-2).

In the References dialog box, you specify all the references that your application needs for using Automation or for using other Access databases as library databases. To select or deselect a reference, click its check box.

Caution   For this chapter, you will need to make sure that several reference libraries are active. You may not initially have the following four references available (checked):

```
Microsoft DAO 3.6 Object Library
Microsoft ActiveX Data Objects Recordset 2.6 Library
Microsoft Word 10.0 Object Library
Microsoft Office 10.0 Object Library
```

If these libraries aren't active (or, visible at the top of the list), find them in the selection list box by scrolling to them, and then check them on.

After you reference an application for Automation, you can explicitly dimension any object variable in that reference library. The New object coding help feature displays the available objects as you type, as shown in Figure 41-3. In addition, after you have selected the primary object and have entered a period (.), the help feature of Access 2002 enables you to select from the available class objects (see Figure 41-4).

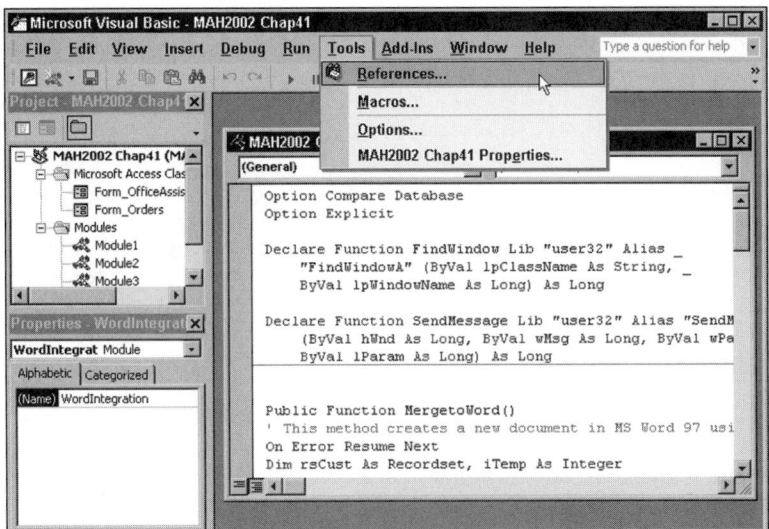

Figure 41-1: The Tools ⇨ References menu item is only available after you have a module in Design or New view in Access. This menu item activates the VBA window.

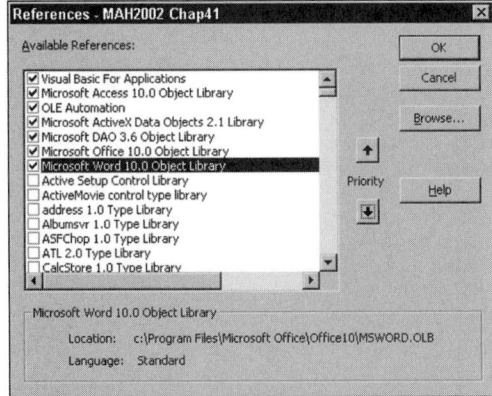

Figure 41-2: Early binding by setting references is the most efficient way to perform Automation.

Late binding an object

If you don't explicitly reference an object library by using the References dialog box, you can set an object's reference in code by first declaring a variable as an object and then using the Set command to create the object reference. This process is known as *late binding*.

To create an object to reference Microsoft Word 2002, for example, you can use the following code:

```
Dim WordObj As Object
Set WordObj = New Word.Application
```

The Set command is discussed in the next section.

Tip   If you create an object for an application that is not referenced, no drop-down help box, such as the ones shown in Figures 41-3 and 41-4, will display.

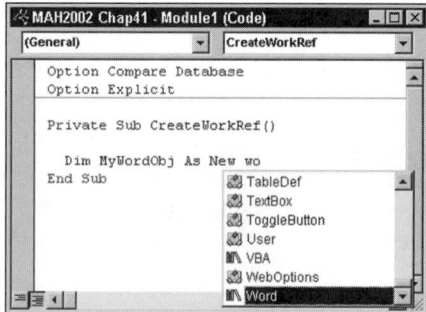

Figure 41-3: When an Automation Server is referenced, its objects are immediately known by Visual Basic.

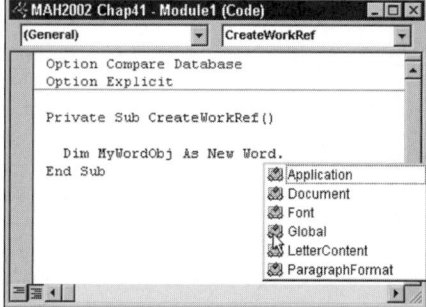

Figure 41-4: The new drop-down syntax help of Visual Basic makes using referenced Automation Servers easy.

Figure 41-3 shows the automatic drop-down box that appears immediately after you type the word *new* in the Dim statement. At this point, you can select one of the application object name types displayed (such as *word*) or enter a new application object name type that you define. Figure 41-4 shows the new drop-down box that appears when you type a period (.) after the object type *word*. This box helps you by displaying all known object types that can be associated with the particular primary object name. In this case, clicking the Application object type adds this to the *word.* portion of the object, thus *word.application.*

Creating an instance of an Automation object

To perform an Automation operation, the operating system needs to start the application — if it isn't already started — and obtain a reference, or *handle*, to it. This reference will be used to access the application. Most applications that support Automation, called *Automation Servers,* expose an Application object. The Application object exists at the top of the object application's hierarchy and often contains many objects, as well.

Using the New keyword to create a new instance

The simplest (and most efficient) method to create any Automation object is to early bind the specific Automation Server reference library to the module by activating it using the Tools ➪ References menu. After you bind it, you can then create a new instance of the object by using the New keyword in Visual Basic. In the examples shown in Figure 41-3 and Figure 41-4, the variable MyWordObj is set to a new instance of Word's Application object. If you had not bound the Microsoft Word 10.0 Object Library you will need to do so or you will receive an error.

Caution   If you don't create a reference to the Automation Server by using the References dialog box, Visual Basic doesn't recognize the object type and generates an error on compile.

Every time you create an instance of an Automation Server by using the New keyword, a new instance of the application is started. If you don't want to start a new instance of the application, use the GetObject function, which is discussed later in this chapter. Not all Automation Servers support the New keyword. Consult the specific Automation Server's documentation to determine whether it supports the New keyword. If the New keyword is not supported, you need to use the CreateObject function, which is discussed in the following section, to create an instance of the Automation Server.

Using the CreateObject function to create a new instance

In addition to creating an instance of an object library by using the New keyword, you can create an instance of an object library by using the CreateObject function. You use the CreateObject function to create instances of object libraries that do not support the New keyword. To use the CreateObject function, first declare a variable of the type equal to the type of object that you want to create. Then use the Set statement in conjunction with the CreateObject function to set the variable to a new instance of the object library.

For example, Microsoft Binder doesn't support the New keyword, but it does provide an object library, so you can reference it by using the References dialog box.

To early bind the object library of Binder, use the `CreateObject` function, as shown in the following code:

```
Dim BinderObj As OfficeBinder.Binder
Set BinderObj = CreateObject("Office.Binder")
```

Note   In the preceding example, the object library name for Binder is `OfficeBinder.Binder`, and the class instance is `"Office.Binder."` You can view the names of object libraries and their available classes by using the Object Browser.

You can create an object instance with the `CreateObject` function, which is late bound, by not declaring the object variable as a specific type. For example, the following code creates an instance of the Binder object by using late binding:

```
Dim BinderObj As Object
Set BinderObj = CreateObject("Office.Binder")
```

Note   If you have different versions of the same Automation Server on your computer, you can specify the version to use by adding it to the end of the class information. For example, the following code uses Office XP as the Automation Server:

```
Dim BinderObj As Object
Set BinderObj = CreateObject("Word.Application.10")
```

Tip   Word 97 was the first true Automation Server, and like its predecessor, Word 2002 doesn't require you to specify a version when creating instances of Word 2002 object libraries; Word 2002 is always used, regardless of the other versions of Word on the computer. In fact, you get an error if you try to specify a version number. Therefore, you can use the following syntax instead:

```
Set BinderObj = CreateObject("Word.Application.10")
```

Getting an existing object instance

As stated previously in this chapter, using the `New` keyword or the `CreateObject` function creates a new instance of the Automation Server. If you don't want a new instance of the server created each time you create an object, use the `GetObject` function. The format of the `GetObject` function is as follows:

```
Set objectvariable = GetObject([pathname][, class])
```

The `pathname` parameter is optional. To use this parameter, you specify a full path and file name to an existing file for use with the Automation Server.

Note   The specified document is then opened in the server application. Even if you omit the parameter, you must still include the comma (,).

The *class* parameter is the same parameter that's used with the `CreateObject` function. See Table 41-1 for a list of some class arguments used in Microsoft Office.

Table 41-1		
Class Arguments for Common Office Components		
Component	*Class Argument*	*Object Returned*
Access	`Access.Application`	Microsoft Access Application object
Excel	`Excel.Application`	Microsoft Excel Application object
	`Excel.Sheet`	Microsoft Excel Workbook object
	`Excel.Chart`	Microsoft Excel Chart object
Word	`Word.Application`	Microsoft Word Application object
	`Word.Document`	Microsoft Word Document object

For example, to work with an existing instance of Microsoft Word, but not a specific Word document, you can use the following code:

```
Dim WordObj as Word.Application
Set WordObj = GetObject(, "Word.Application")
```

To get an instance of an existing Word document called `MyDoc.Doc`, on your C: drive, you can use the following code:

```
Dim WordObj as Word.Application
Set WordObj = GetObject("c:\MyDoc.Doc", "Word.Application")
```

Of course, this code is always placed in a new function or sub that you declare in your module.

Working with Automation objects

After you have a valid instance of an Automation Server, you manipulate the object as though you were writing code within the application itself, using the exposed objects and their properties and methods.

For example, when developing directly in Word, you can use the following code to change the directory that Word uses when opening an existing file:

```
ChangeFileOpenDirectory "D:\My Documents\"
```

Note   Consult the development help for the Automation Server for specific information on the objects, properties, and methods available.

Just as in Access, Word is implicitly using its `Application` object; the command `ChangeFileOpenDirectory` is really a method of the `Application` object. Using the following code, you create an instance of Word's `Application` object and call the method of the object:

```
Dim WordObj As New Word.Application
WordObj.ChangeFileOpenDirectory "D:\My Documents\"
```

Tip   When using Automation, you should avoid setting properties or calling methods that cause the Automation Server to ask for input from the user via a dialog box. When a dialog box is displayed, the Automation code stops executing until the dialog box is closed. If the server application is minimized or behind other windows, the user may not even be aware that he or she needs to provide input, and therefore may assume that the application is locked up.

Closing an instance of an Automation object

Automation objects are closed when the Automation object variable goes out of scope. Such a closing, however, doesn't necessarily free up all resources that are used by the object, so you should explicitly close the instance of the Automation object. You can close an Automation object by doing either of the following:

✦ Using the `Close` or `Quit` method of the object (consult the specific Automation Server's documentation for information on which method it supports).

✦ Setting the object variable to nothing, as follows:

```
Set WordObj = Nothing.
```

The best way to close an instance of an Automation object is to combine the two techniques, like this:

```
WordObj.Quit
Set WordObj = Nothing
```

An Automation example using Word 2002

Perhaps the most common Office application that is used for Automation from a database application like Access is Word. Using Automation with Word, you can create letters that are tailored with information from databases. The following section demonstrates an example of merging information from an Access database to a letter in Word by using Automation and Word's Bookmarks. Ordinarily, you create a merge document in Word and bring field contents in from the records of an Access database. This method relies on using Word's MergeField, which is replaced by the contents of the Database field. It normally requires that you perform this action in Word — thus limiting the scope and capability of the function. For example, you will merge all records from the table that is being used rather than a single record.

The following example uses the Orders form, which calls a module named *WordIntegation.* The WordIntegration module contains a function named *MergetoWord()* that uses the Word Thanks.dot template file.

On the CD-ROM This chapter uses the database MAH2002 Chap41.mdb. You should move the MAH2002 Chap41.mdb database from the CD, included with this book, into a subdirectory on your hard drive. The CD-Rom also includes a word template file named *Thanks.dot,* which needs to be moved to the same directory.

Note When you attempt to run this example, you must make sure that the path for the template in the Visual Basic code is the actual path in which the Thanks.dot template file resides. This path may vary from computer to computer.

The items that are discussed in this Word Automation example include the following:

✦ Creating an instance of a Word object

✦ Making the instance of Word visible

✦ Creating a new document based on an existing template

✦ Using bookmarks to insert data

✦ Activating the instance of Word

✦ Moving the cursor in Word

✦ Closing the instance of the Word object without closing Word

This example prints a thank-you letter for an order based on bookmarks in the thank-you letter template. Figure 41-5 shows the data for customers; Figure 41-6 shows the data entry form for orders; Figure 41-7 shows the Thanks.dot template; and Figure 41-8 shows a completed merge letter.

The bookmarks in Figure 41-7 are shown as grayed large Ibeams (text insert). The bookmarks are normally not visible , but you can make them visible by selecting Tools ⇨ Options and then turning on the Show bookmarks option. The names won't be visible — only the bookmark holders (locations). The names and arrows in Figure 41-7 were placed using text boxes to show where the bookmark names are assigned.

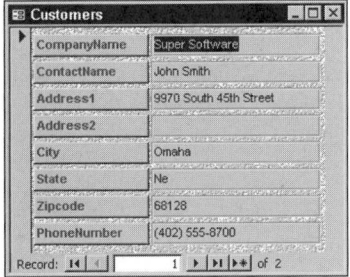

Figure 41-5: Customer data used in the following Automation example is entered on the Customers form.

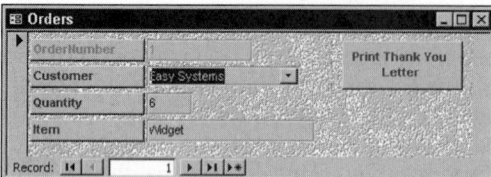

Figure 41-6: Each customer can have an unlimited number of orders. Thank-you letters are printed from the Orders form.

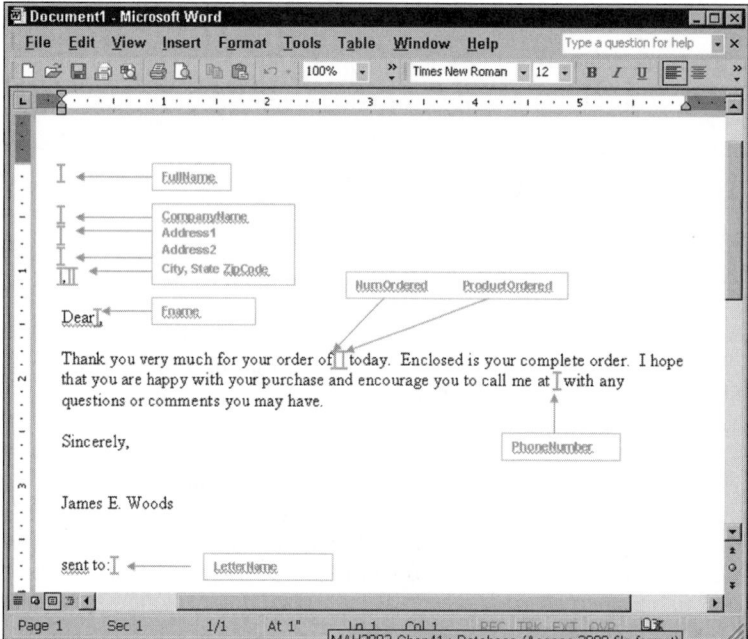

Figure 41-7: The Thanks.dot template contains bookmarks where the merged data is to be inserted.

Caution   If you click the Print Thank You Letter button in Access while Word is open with an existing document — which lacks the bookmark names specified in the code — the fields will simply be added to the text inside Word 2002 at the point where the cursor is currently sitting.

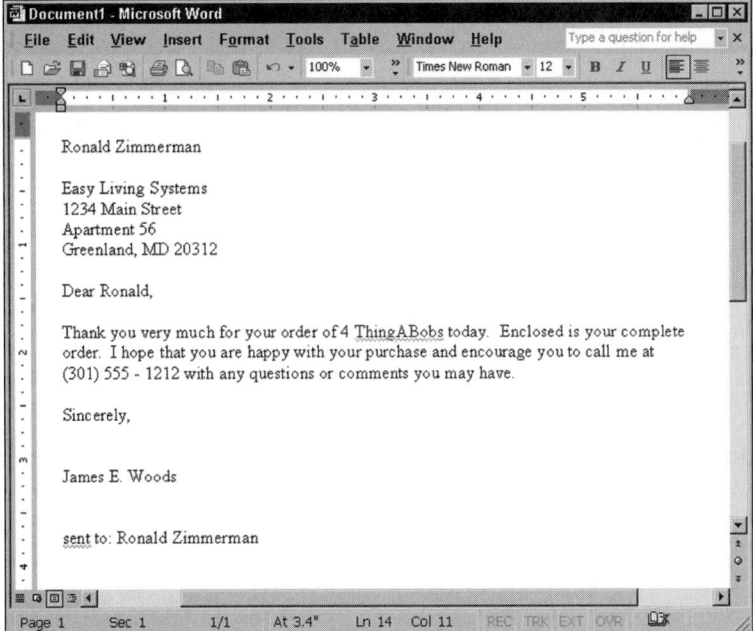

Figure 41-8: After a successful merge, all the bookmarks have been replaced with their respective data.

When the user clicks the Print Thank You Letter button on the Orders form, Word 2002 generates a thank-you letter with all the pertinent information. Listing 41-1 shows the `MergetoWord` function in its entirety. The following listing shows you in-depth how it works.

Listing 41-1: **The MergetoWord Function**

```
Public Function MergetoWord()
' This method creates a new document in MS Word 2002
' using Automation.
On Error Resume Next
Dim rsCust As Recordset, iTemp As Integer
Dim WordObj As Word.Application
Set rsCust =
DBEngine(0).Databases(0).OpenRecordset("Customers", _
dbOpenTable)
rsCust.Index = "PrimaryKey"
rsCust.Seek "=", Forms!Orders![CustomerNumber]
    If rsCust.NoMatch Then
        MsgBox "Invalid customer", vbOKOnly
        Exit Function
    End If
```

Continued

Listing 41-1: *(continued)*

```
DoCmd.Hourglass True
Set WordObj = GetObject(, "Word.Application")
If Err.Number <> 0 Then
    Set WordObj = CreateObject("Word.Application")
End If
WordObj.Visible = True
WordObj.Documents.Add

' WARNING:
' Specify the correct drive and path to the
' file named thanks.dot in the line below.

  Template:="D:\office2002\Templates\thanks.dot",

' The above path and drive must be fixed

NewTemplate:=False
WordObj.Selection.Goto what:=wdGoToBookmark, Name:="FullName"
    WordObj.Selection.TypeText rsCust![ContactName]
WordObj.Selection.Goto what:=wdGoToBookmark,
Name:="CompanyName"
    WordObj.Selection.TypeText rsCust![CompanyName]
WordObj.Selection.Goto what:=wdGoToBookmark, Name:="Address1"
    WordObj.Selection.TypeText rsCust![Address1]
WordObj.Selection.Goto what:=wdGoToBookmark, Name:="Address2"
    If IsNull(rsCust![Address2]) Then
        WordObj.Selection.TypeText ""
    Else
        WordObj.Selection.TypeText rsCust![Address2]
    End If
WordObj.Selection.Goto what:=wdGoToBookmark, Name:="City"
    WordObj.Selection.TypeText rsCust![City]
WordObj.Selection.Goto what:=wdGoToBookmark, Name:="State"
    WordObj.Selection.TypeText rsCust![State]
WordObj.Selection.Goto what:=wdGoToBookmark, Name:="Zipcode"
    WordObj.Selection.TypeText rsCust![Zipcode]
WordObj.Selection.Goto what:=wdGoToBookmark,
Name:="PhoneNumber"
    WordObj.Selection.TypeText rsCust![PhoneNumber]
WordObj.Selection.Goto what:=wdGoToBookmark, Name:="NumOrdered"
    WordObj.Selection.TypeText Forms!Orders![Quantity]
WordObj.Selection.Goto what:=wdGoToBookmark,
Name:="ProductOrdered"
    If Forms!Orders![Quantity] > 1 Then
        WordObj.Selection.TypeText Forms!Orders![Item] & "s"
    Else
        WordObj.Selection.TypeText Forms!Orders![Item]
    End If
WordObj.Selection.Goto what:=wdGoToBookmark, Name:="FName"
    iTemp = InStr(rsCust![ContactName], " ")
```

```
    If iTemp > 0 Then
        WordObj.Selection.TypeText Left$(rsCust![ContactName],
iTemp _ - 1)
    End If
WordObj.Selection.Goto what:=wdGoToBookmark, Name:="LetterName"
    WordObj.Selection.TypeText rsCust![ContactName]
DoEvents
WordObj.Activate
WordObj.Selection.MoveUp wdLine, 6
' Set the Word Object to nothing to free resources
Set WordObj = Nothing
DoCmd.Hourglass False
Exit Function
TemplateError:
    Set WordObj = Nothing
    Exit Function
End Function
```

Creating an instance of a Word object

The first step in using Automation is to create an instance of an object. The sample creates an object instance with the following code:

```
On Error Resume Next
...
Set WordObj = GetObject(, "Word.Application")
If Err.Number <> 0 Then
    Set WordObj = CreateObject("Word.Application")
End If
```

Obviously, you don't want a new instance of Word created every time a thank-you letter is generated, so some special coding is required. This code snippet first attempts to create an instance by using an active instance (a running copy) of Word 2002. If Word is not a running application, an error is generated. Because this function has `On Error Resume Next` for error trapping, the code doesn't fail, but instead proceeds to the next statement. If an error is detected (the `Err.Number` is not equal to 0), an instance is created by using `CreateObject`.

Making the instance of Word visible

When you first create a new instance of Word 2002, it runs invisibly. This approach enables your application to exploit features of Word without the user even realizing that Word is running. In this case, however, it is desirable to let the user edit the merged letter, so Word needs to be made visible by setting the object's `Visible` property to True by using this line of code:

```
WordObj.Visible = True
```

Caution   If you don't set the object instance's `Visible` property to True, you may create hidden copies of Word that use system resources and never shut down. A hidden copy of Word doesn't show up in the Task tray or in the Task Switcher.

Creating a new document based on an existing template

After Word is running, a blank document needs to be created. The following code creates a new document by using the Thanks.dot template:

```
WordObj.Documents.Add
Template:="D:\office2002\Templates\thanks.dot", _
NewTemplate:=False
```

Note   The path must be corrected in order to point to the Thanks.dot template on your computer.

The Thanks.dot template contains bookmarks (as shown in Figure 41-7) that tell this function where to insert data. You create bookmarks in Word 2002 by highlighting the text that you want to make a bookmark, then selecting Insert ➪ Bookmark, and then entering the bookmark name and clicking Add.

Using bookmarks to insert data

Using Automation, you can locate bookmarks in a Word document and replace them with the text of your choosing. To locate a bookmark, use the `Goto` method of the `Selection` object. After you have located the bookmark, the text comprising the bookmark is selected. By inserting text (which you can do by using Automation or simply by typing directly into the document), you replace the bookmark text. To insert text, use the `TypeText` method of the `Selection` object, as shown here:

```
WordObj.Selection.Goto what:=wdGoToBookmark, Name:="FullName"
WordObj.Selection.TypeText rsCust![ContactName]
```

Note   You can't pass a null to the `TypeText` method. If the value may possibly be `Null`, you need to check ahead and make allowances. The preceding sample code checks the Address2 field for a `Null` value and acts accordingly. If you don't pass text to replace the bookmark—even just a zero length string (" ")—the Bookmark text remains in the document.

Activating the instance of Word

To enable the user to enter data in the new document, you must make Word the active application. If you don't make Word the active application, the user has to switch to Word from Access. You make Word the active application by using the `Activate` method of the Word object, as follows:

```
WordObj.Activate
```

Tip Depending on the processing that is occurring at the time, Access may take the focus back from Word. You can help to eliminate this annoyance by preceding the Activate method with a DoEvents statement. Note, however, that this doesn't always work.

Moving the cursor in Word

You can move the cursor in Word by using the MoveUp method of the Selection object. The following example moves the cursor up six lines in the document. The cursor is at the location of the last bookmark when this code is executed:

```
WordObj.Selection.MoveUp wdLine, 6
```

Closing the instance of the Word object

To free up resources that are taken by an instance of an Automation object, you should always close the instance. In this example, the following code is used to close the object instance:

```
Set WordObj = Nothing
```

This code closes the object instance, but not the instance of Word as a running application. In this example, the user needs access to the new document, so closing Word would defeat the purpose of this function. You can, however, automatically print the document and then close Word. If you do this, you may even choose to not make Word visible during this process. To close Word, use the Quit method of the Application object, as follows:

```
WordObj.Quit
```

Inserting pictures by using bookmarks

It is possible to perform other unique operations by using bookmarks. Basically, anything that you can do within Word, you can do by using Automation. The following code locates a bookmark that marks where a picture is to be placed, and then inserts a .PCX file from disk. You can use the following code to insert scanned signatures into letters:

```
WordObj.Selection.Goto what:=wdGoToBookmark, Name:="Picture"
WordObj.ChangeFileOpenDirectory "D:\GRAPHICS\"
WordObj. ActiveDocument.Shapes.AddPicture
Anchor:=Selection.Range, _ FileName:= _
        "D:\GRAPHICS\PICTURE.BMP", LinkToFile:=False,
SaveWithDocument _
        :=True
```

Using Office's Macro Recorder

Using Automation is not a difficult process when you understand the fundamentals. Often, the toughest part of using Automation is knowing the proper objects, properties, and methods to use. Although the development help system of the Automation Server is a requirement for fully understanding the language, the easiest way to quickly create Automation for Office applications like Word is the Macro Recorder.

Most 2002 versions of Office applications have a Macro Recorder located on the Tools menu (see Figure 41-9). When activated, the Macro Recorder records all events, such as menu selections and button clicks, and creates Visual Basic code from them.

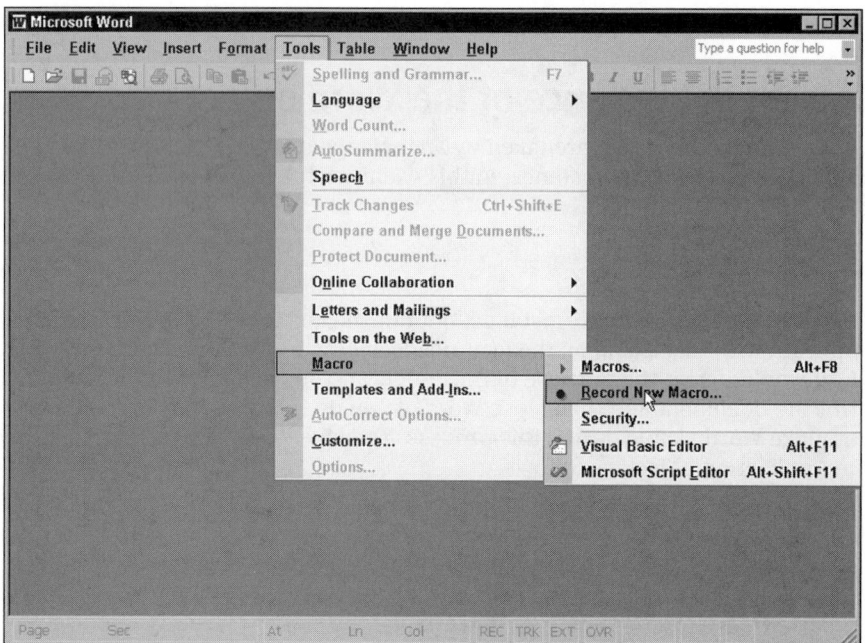

Figure 41-9: The Macro Recorder in Word is a powerful tool to help you create Automation code.

After selecting Tools ➪ Macro ➪ Record New Macro, you must give your new macro a name (see Figure 41-10). In addition to a name, you can assign the macro to a toolbar or keyboard combination and select the template in which to store the macro. If you are creating the macro simply to create the Visual Basic code, the only thing that you need to be concerned with is the macro name.

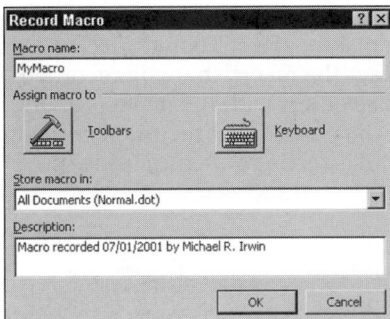

Figure 41-10: Enter a macro name and click OK to begin recording the macro. In this example, the macro is named "MyMacro."

After entering a macro name and clicking OK, the Macro Recorder begins recording events, displays a Stop Recording window, and the arrow changes to an open pointer attached to a cassette, as shown in Figure 41-11. You can stop recording events by clicking the Stop button (the button with a square on it). To pause recording events, click the other button, which is the Pause button.

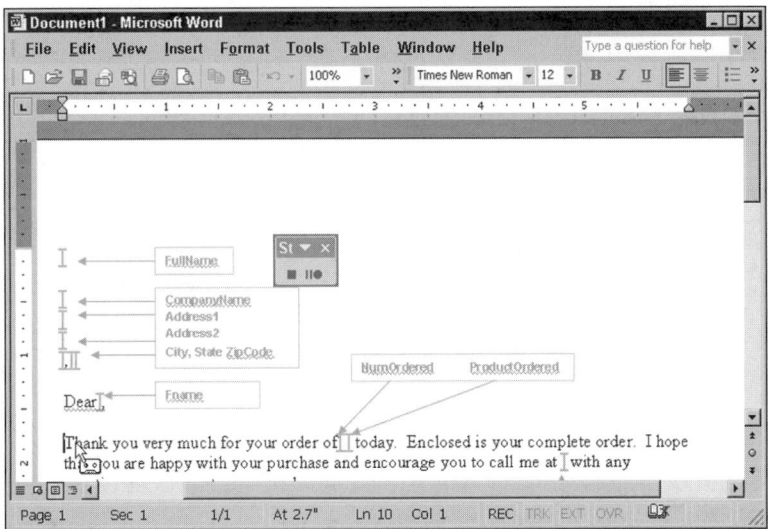

Figure 41-11: The Macro Recorder records all events until you click the Stop button.

After you have finished recording a macro, you can view the Visual Basic code created from your events. To view the code of a macro, select Tools ➪ Macro ➪ Macros to display a list of all saved macros. Then select the macro that you recorded and click the Edit button to display the Visual Basic editor with the macro's code. Figure 41-12 shows the Visual Basic editor with a macro that recorded creating a new document using the Normal template, and inserting a picture using the Insert ➪ Picture ➪ From File menu item.

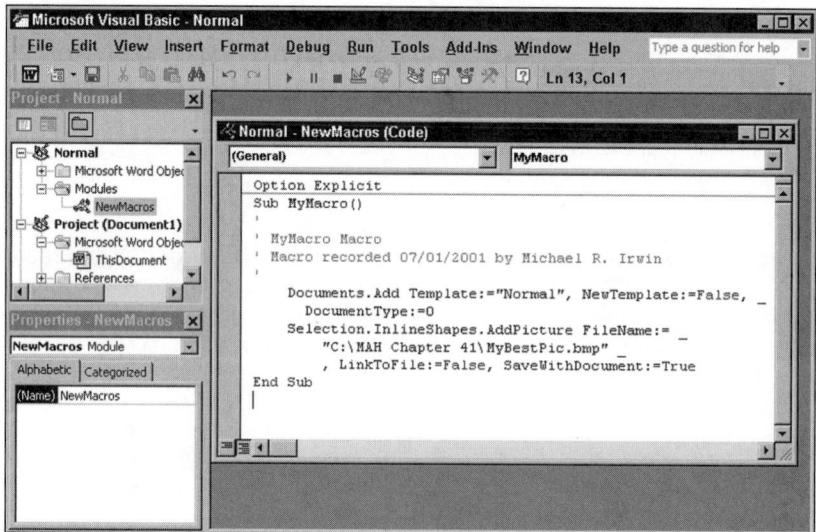

Figure 41-12: The Macro Recorder records all events until you click the Stop button.

In the application for which a macro is created, the Application object is used explicitly. When you use the code for Automation, you must create an Application object accordingly. For example, the preceding macro uses the following code to create a new document:

```
Documents.Add Template:=" Normal.dot", NewTemplate:= False,
DocumentType:=0
```

This code implicitly uses the Application object. To use this code for Automation, copy the code from the Visual Basic editor, paste it into your procedure, and create an object that you use explicitly, as follows:

```
Dim WordObj as New Word.Application
WordObj.Documents.Add Template:=" Normal.dot", NewTemplate:=
False, DocumentType:=0
```

The Macro Recorder enables you to effortlessly create long and complete Automation code without ever needing to read the Automation Server's documentation.

Programming the Office Assistant

Perhaps the most fun Automation Server yet is the Office Assistant. That's right, the Office Assistant is a fully programmable Automation Server! Using the techniques described in this chapter, you can completely control the Office Assistant. Included in the database for this chapter on the companion CD-ROM is an Office Assistant Automation Example form with all the code necessary to control the Office Assistant (see Figure 41-13).

Note The Clippit Office Assistant is checking something in Figure 41-13. The form shown in Figure 41-13 is in the MAH2002 Chap41 database and is named *OfficeAssistant.*

To program the Office Assistant using Automation, you must first ensure that the Office Assistant is installed, and then you must create a reference to the Microsoft Office 10.0 Object Library (see Figure 41-14). To reference the library, you must be in the VBA window and select Tools ➪ References. The fastest way to activate VBA is to design or create a new module from Access.

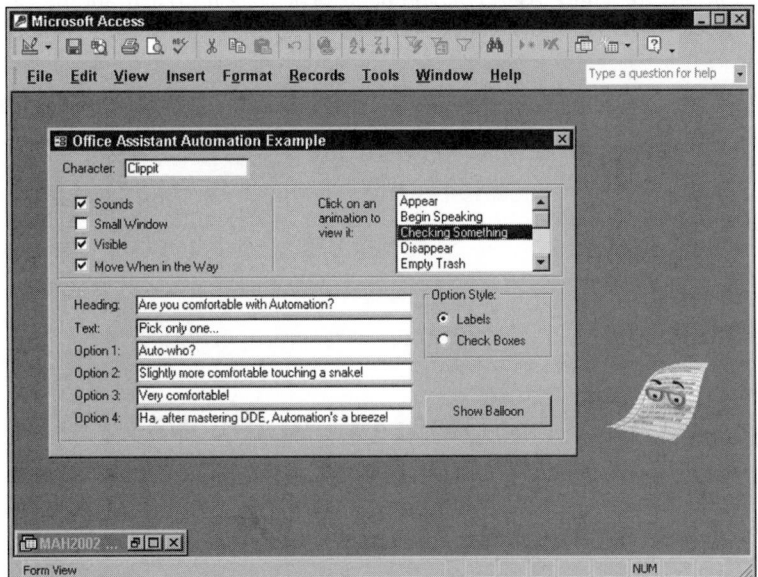

Figure 41-13: The Office Assistant Automation Example form contains all the code that you need to control the Office Assistant.

Note The Office Assistant program, shown in Figure 41-13, shows a check box for Small Window. Note that this will only work in Access 97. The Office Assistant in Office XP is not displayed in a window as in previous versions of Office. Therefore, activating this check box has no effect in Office 2000 or XP.

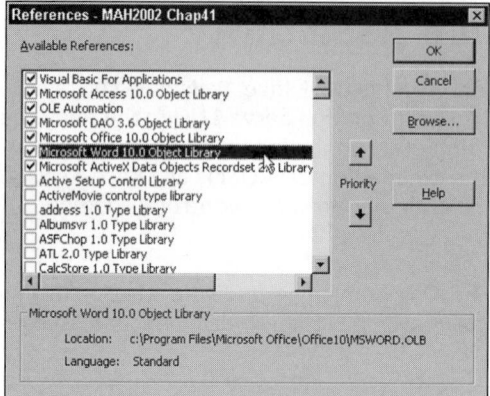

Figure 41-14: Programming the Office Assistant requires that the Office Assistant be installed and referenced in the database.

Tip   If you have installed the Office Assistant and the Office Assistant form, and you *still* can't access the Office Assistant, you need to activate it. To activate the Office Assistant, select Help ⇨ Show Office Assistant. From this point on, it will work correctly.

Hiding and showing the Office Assistant

You can completely hide the Office Assistant at any time by setting its Visible property to False, as follows:

```
Assistant.Visible = False
```

To show the Office Assistant, simply set the Visible property to True.

Keeping the Office Assistant out of the way

You can give the Office Assistant some smarts by instructing it to stay out of the way of other windows. To do this, use the following code to set the Assistant's MoveWhenInTheWay property:

```
Assistant.MoveWhenInTheWay = True
```

When you set the MoveWhenInTheWay property to True, the Assistant recognizes when it is in the way of other windows — as they appear — and it attempts to move itself to a less obtrusive location. If you set the MoveWhenInTheWay property to False, the Office Assistant never moves itself.

Enabling and disabling the Assistant's sounds

You can programmatically enable and disable the Assistant's sounds by setting the Assistant's Sounds property. For example, to enable the Assistant's sounds, set the property to True, as follows:

```
Assistant.Sounds = True
```

To disable all the Assistant's sounds, set the property to False.

Displaying an Assistant animation

Of course, the coolest thing about the Office Assistant is its animation. To display an animation, you simply set the Animation property to the appropriate animation number. For example, to display the Empty Trash animation, as shown in Figure 41-15, you set the Animation property to 116, as follows:

```
Assistant.Animation = 116
```

Note

The sample database on the companion CD-ROM contains a table of all the animations and their respective reference numbers.

You can choose from a number of different Assistants, ranging from a bouncing paper clip to a talking computer. Not every Office Assistant has an animation associated with each entry in the Animations table.

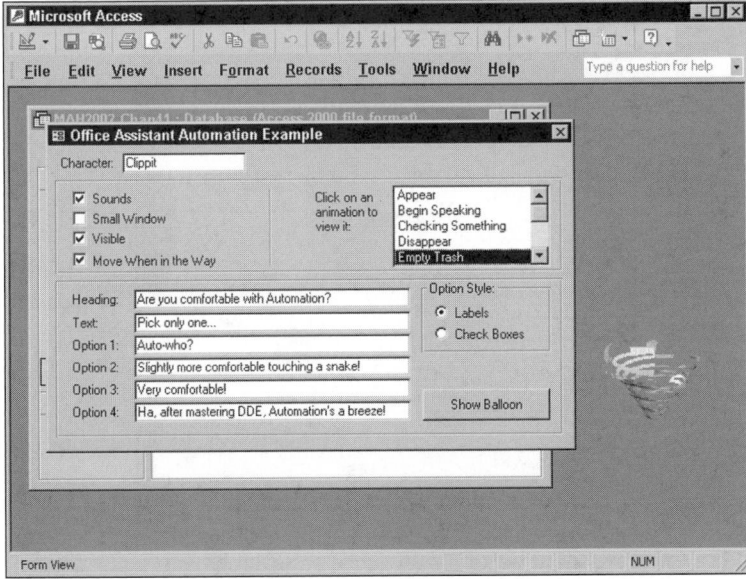

Figure 41-15: Displaying Office Assistant animation is as simple as setting a property.

Displaying information and getting user input by using balloons

The Office Assistant isn't just a passive object taking up space on the desktop. You can also use the Assistant to display dialog boxes and to get user input (see Figure 41-16). These Assistant dialog boxes are called *balloons,* and you create them by using the `NewBalloon` method of the `Assistant` object.

Creating a new balloon

To create a balloon, first dimension a variable as a `Balloon` object. Then set the variable to a new balloon object by using the `NewBalloon` method of the `Assistant` object, as follows:

```
Dim objBalloon As Balloon
Set objBalloon = Assistant.NewBalloon
```

Specifying a balloon's heading and text

You then specify the heading and body text by using the `Heading` and `Text` properties of the new balloon object, as in the following example:

```
objBalloon.Heading = "This is heading text!"
objBalloon.Text = "This is body text."
```

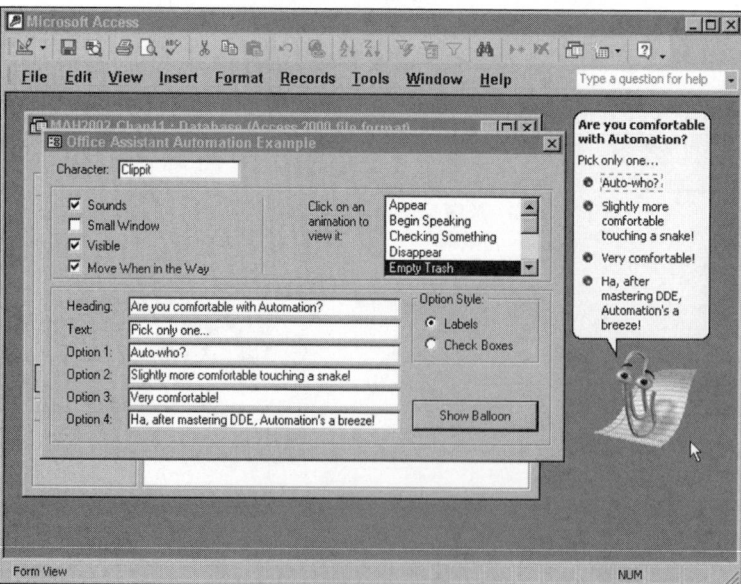

Figure 41-16: The Office Assistant becomes an active assistant when you use balloons.

Specifying a balloon's buttons

Specifying the buttons to be displayed is similar to specifying buttons for dialog boxes — you use a constant. Buttons are defined by setting the `Buttons` property, as follows:

```
objBalloon.Button = buttonconstant
```

The following are valid constants to use in place of `buttonconstant`:

✦ msoButtonSetAbortRetryIgnore

✦ msoButtonSetBackClose

✦ msoButtonSetBackNextClose

✦ msoButtonSetBackNextSnooze

✦ msoButtonSetCancelmsoButtonSetNextClose

✦ msoButtonSetNonemsoButtonSetOK

✦ msoButtonSetOkCancel

✦ msoButtonSetRetryCancel

✦ msoButtonSetSearchClose

✦ msoButtonSetTipsOptionsClose

✦ msoButtonSetYesAllNoCancel

✦ msoButtonSetYesNoCancel

✦ msoButtonSetYesNo

Creating balloon labels and check boxes

You can give the user selections from which to choose by defining a labels or check boxes item. Labels are used in Figures 41-15 and 41-16. Labels are similar to option buttons in that the user can select only one of a given set of labels. Instead of labels, you can allow a user to select a number of items by making them check boxes (see Figure 41-17).

For each label or check box item in a balloon, you set a labels() or check boxes() array item in code, as in the following:

```
objBalloon.Labels(1).Text = "Text for label 1"
objBalloon.Labels(2).Text = "Text for label 2"
...
or
objBalloon.checkboxes(1).Text = "Text for checkbox 1"
objBalloon.checkboxes(2).Text = "Text for checkbox 2"
...
```

Note   A balloon can have up to five labels and five check boxes.

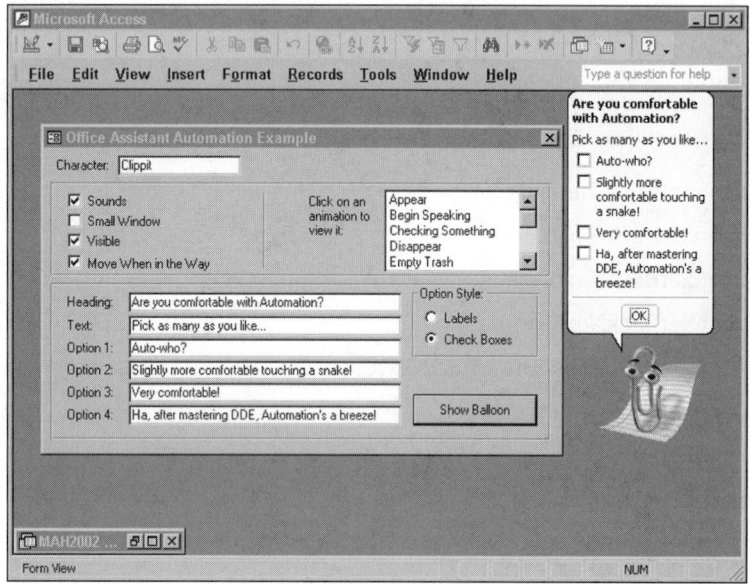

Figure 41-17: You can let a user select a number of items by using the check boxes item.

Displaying a balloon

After the balloon is completely defined, you display the balloon by using the Show method of the Balloon object, as follows:

```
intRetval = objBalloon.Show
```

Note that the Show method returns a value. If the balloon contains labels, the return value is the index of the selected label. To find out which check boxes are selected, you must look through the check boxes items for the balloon, as follows:

```
Dim iCount as integer
For iCount = 1 To objBalloon.Checkboxes.Count
If objBalloon.Checkboxes(iCount).Checked = True Then
MsgBox "Checkbox #" & iCount & " is selected!", vbOKOnly
End If
Next iCount
```

Figure 41-18 shows the result of determining the selected item and creating a new balloon object to tell the user what it was.

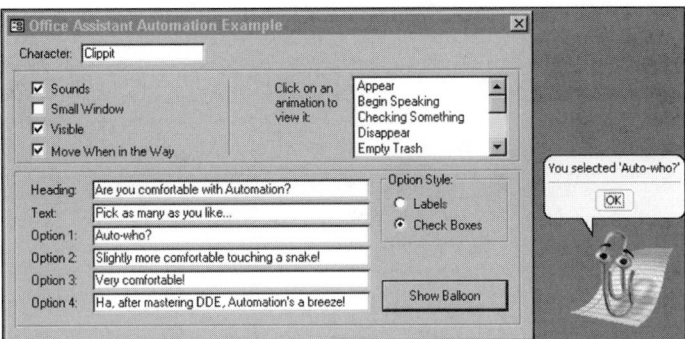

Figure 41-18: To display a new balloon, create a new balloon object.

Using the techniques discussed in this chapter, you can leverage your Visual Basic knowledge and create intelligent and powerful integrated applications.

✦   ✦   ✦

Exploring Replication

◆ ◆ ◆ ◆

In This Chapter

Touring the
replication
components

Creating replicas of
your databases

Synchronizing your
replicas

Resolving conflicts

Creating a new
Design Master

◆ ◆ ◆ ◆

The *replication* feature of Microsoft Jet 4.*x* provides a method for distributing your database, including all of its objects, to other users. The users of a replicated database may have read-only or read-write access, depending on the permissions that you assign to the replica.

If a replicated database has been created as read-write, then the changes made to it can be synchronized with the changes that are made to other replicas. This enables a database to be distributed to other machines and kept up-to-date with other distributed databases. Database changes can be synchronized directly between two replicas or, if direct connection is not possible, the changes can be stored for later update by the target Synchronizer. This feature goes well beyond making a simple copy of the database, because changes to a copy are not easily synchronized back into the master database.

You can use replication to distribute your application code, tables, queries, forms, and reports. You can distribute your application's tables separately from the rest of your database objects — even if your master database contains all objects in a single database. Beginning with Access 97, you have the capability to create and synchronize partial replicas, which provide a means of distributing only the data that's required by a receiving site.

You can also use replication to provide a database or a part of a database to a portable computer, to other machines on the network, or to stand-alone machines. Even though other network-attached machines can be set up to access the same database, instances will occur where you may want to have some of these machines access a replica of the database in order to improve performance.

You should always precede the use of replication with solid planning. Replication isn't free. Several points within the scheme of replication require serious consideration before you decide to adopt this feature. This chapter addresses those considerations and looks at the components of replication and their management.

The Components of Replication

When you create a replica of your database, the database changes in several ways to support the synchronization of changes between the replica that you create and the master database. Understanding these changes is your first task in deciding whether or not to use replication.

At the time you create a replica, Access needs to add several fields and objects to your database in order to track and synchronize updates. These additions increase the size of the database, which is described later in this chapter.

The original database that you are replicating becomes the *Design Master*. If you make any changes to the design of the database—in other words, any changes to the design of any *object* in the database—those changes should be made to the Design Master and then propagated to the replicas.

A replica of the Design Master can receive data changes, including additions, modifications, and deletions, but a replica doesn't support any changes to the design of any of its replicated objects. However, changes to the design of *local objects*, or those objects that are created at the replica, are supported.

You can create multiple replicas from either the Design Master or from any replica that's created from the Design Master. All replicas related to the same Design Master are part of a group called the *Replica Set*.

Nonreplicable database

Your database requires the addition of several system tables, fields, and properties before it can be replicated. Without this additional information in your database, Access can't keep track of changes and therefore can't replicate these changes.

If your database has a password attached to it, you need to remove that password before making the database replicable. A password on the database prevents the synchronization of replicas among the replica set.

On the CD-ROM   This chapter uses the CstPtLit.mdb database. You should move the CsstPtLit.mdb database from the CD included with this book into a subdirectory on your hard drive. This database will be used to create a second database used in this chapter.

Making a database replicable

When you make a database replicable, you are creating a *Design Master* database. For example, to make the CstPtLit.mdb database a Design Master, follow these steps:

1. **Open the CstPtLit database.** If you are in a multi-user environment, make sure that all other users have closed the database. If the database is protected by a password, remove the password before creating a Design Master.

2. **Select Tools ⇨ Replication ⇨ Create Replica from the file menu.** Access 2002 displays a dialog box, which states, "This database must be closed before you can create a replica," and another message informing you that it will convert the database to a Design Master.

3. **Click the Yes button of the dialog box.** Access responds with another dialog box, suggesting that it should make a backup of your database for you and will give the backup an extension of .BAK. You may also see a conversion dialog box.

4. **Click the Yes button of this dialog box.** Access responds with the Save file dialog box, titled "Location of New Replica."

5. **Accept the default name of file "Replica of cstptlit.mdb" by clicking OK.** If you want to select a different name for the new file, you can do it here. However, Access still converts the original table, as well as the new name that you enter (thus it automatically creates a replica of the table at the same time). If you want to prevent people from deleting records in replica databases, check the Prevent deletes check box. You can also specify a Priority for the replica (number) by clicking on the Priority button and then clicking OK when you are finished.

6. **If you selected an existing filename, Access informs you that the file already exists and asks if you want to replace it.** Answer Yes if you didn't accept the default name.

7. **Access converts the table and displays another dialog box, stating that it completed the job.** Click OK.

Caution

If you enter the original name of "CstPtLit.mdb" in the File Name field, Access responds with a verification dialog box and then refuses to allow you to convert the file, because the original and the destination are the same file. This means that you need to create a file under a different name, resulting in Access 2002 creating two tables that are converted (the original and the backup).

After the job is completed, Access will have converted the table and created a second copy (or replica table) of the Design Master (the original).

 **Tip**   You can convert the original table *without* creating a second copy (replica) of a Design Master by simply clicking the Cancel button in Step 5. Access immediately converts the table and skips to Step 7.

After your database is converted, all the objects in it will have a small yellow circle with two arrows attached to the icons, as shown in Figure 42-1.

Figure 42-1: The CstPtLit database converted to a Design Master.

Notice that the icon for all the tables in Figure 42-1 has been changed to include a small circle with two arrows pointing opposite to the right side of the icon.

Design Master

After your database has been made replicable, it is known in the newly created replica set as the Design Master database.

The Design Master and all replicas created from it contain internal IDs that are unique within the replica set. This set ID enables the replica set members to update each other but also prevents them from updating members of other replica sets, even if those sets were created from the same nonreplicable database.

Any changes in the design of replicated objects must be made at the Design Master. These changes are replicated to all the replicas in the set at the time of the next synchronization.

When the Design Master is created, many new object tables are added to your tables container to support the replication of changes.

Note These objects are *not* initially visible to you in the table design surface or from the Property dialog box of any of the objects. However, you can view these system objects by selecting Tools ➪ Options and clicking the System objects box. The System objects are grayed out but visible in the tables container of the database.

The table object MSysAccessObjects has several fields added in order to track changes to tables — s_Generation, s_GUID, and s_Lineage.

The field s_Generation is added to track the number of changes that occur in a row. This field is incremented each time its containing row is updated, and is used during synchronization to satisfy conflicts among other members of the replica set undergoing updates to the same row.

An s_GUID field is added to give each row in a table a unique identifier. This field is an AutoNumber data type with a Replication ID field size — a 16-byte randomly generated field.

The s_GUID field is a Globally Unique ID that is generated by the operating system using time and machine information. A row existing at the time of replication is given an s_GUID that appears in all members of the replica set. New rows that are added to a table in a replica set member are given an ID that is randomly generated. Although unlikely, rows that are added to the same table in different replicas may possibly end up having the same s_GUID value. If this occurs, the synchronization process treats the rows as one row instead of two different rows and selects one of the rows to keep in the replicas, whereas the other row is written to a *conflict table* for your review.

The s_Lineage field is added to hold information regarding the history of changes that have been made to the row. This field plays a role in determining which changes to apply when multiple updates to the same record have been detected during synchronization.

Memo and OLE objects are each given an additional field, which is Gen_fieldname. This field tracks changes to these objects separate from the rest of the row. If a row's changes don't include its memo or OLE object fields, those objects are not updated, which reduces the amount of traffic between the source and the target of a synchronization process.

The conversion and synchronization processes add new system tables to your database, as described in Table 42-1.

Table 42-1
System Tables Added by the Creation and Synchronization of a Replica Set

Table Name	Description
MsysAccessObjects	Used to track changes to records in the tables of the Master set.
MSysACEs	Used internally by Access to determine inheritance ability for all objects in the Master set.
MSysConflicts	Holds conflict information that occurs during the synchronization process.
MSysErrors	Holds the errors that occurred during the synchronization process. The table is not displayed unless errors have occurred.
MSysExchangeLog	Holds information about exchanges between replicas in the set.
MSysGenHistory	Holds information about the generations of the containing replica.
MSysIMEXColumns	Holds information about the Input Method Editor mode column of MS Windows in the Eastern Asian versions only.
MSysIMEXSpecs	Holds information about the Input Method Editor mode Specifications of MS Windows in the Eastern Asian versions only.
MsysObjects	Holds information about all the objects in the Master database, including last update.
MSysOthersHistory	Holds information about the generations of other replicas that the containing database has synchronized with.
MsysQueries	Holds information about all the queries in the Master database.
MsysRelationsips	Holds information about the relationships between tables.
MSysRepInfo	Holds information about the replica set.
MSysReplicas	Holds information about each replica in the replica set.
MsysRepLock	Holds information about any locks in the replica set.
MSysSchChange	Holds Design Master schema (design) changes to be replicated.
MSysSchedule	Holds synchronization schedule and details.
MSysSideTables	Holds the GUIDs of tables involved in conflicts and the names of their associated conflict tables holding the conflict records. Created at time of first conflict.
MSysTableGuids	Holds information about tables and their GUIDs used in synchronization.
MSysTombstone	Holds information about deletions to be replicated.
MSysTranspAddress	Holds information about replica set Transporters.

When errors are detected during synchronization, they are recorded in the MSysErrors system table. When conflicts are detected, the conflicting records are added to the table indicated in the MSysConflicts and MsysSideTables. Conflict tables have names like *tablename Conflict*, where *tablename* is the name of the table in which the conflict was detected.

New properties are added to your database to give each replica set member a unique ID and to indicate whether the member is replicable or not. DesignMasterID is the GUID of the Design Master database, and ReplicaID is the ID of a replica database. A `True` value in the Replicable property indicates that the database is replicable.

Tip

If you have objects that you don't want to replicate, you can create a `KeepLocal` property and set it to `True` prior to creating the replica set.

Any object with a `KeepLocal` property set that is set to `True` doesn't appear in the replicas. If you later want to replicate these objects, add a `Replicable` property to the object and set it to `True`. When you next synchronize the database with other members, the object is replicated into the target replica. This also applies to objects that are created after a database becomes replicable, but only objects from the Design Master. Objects that are created within replicas can't be replicated to other members.

Caution

If any of your tables have AutoNumber fields whose new values are assigned incrementally, these fields will be assigned randomly during the conversion to the Design Master. If the AutoNumber field is a key field, keys are assigned randomly instead of sequentially in order to prevent the same key from being added in multiple replicas. Even though random values are assigned, the same value may possibly be generated in different replicas and may cause a data error when the replicas are synchronized. To eliminate this risk, use the s_GUID field as the key or a value that you can guarantee will be unique among all replicas in the set.

The addition of new fields and tables to your database increases the size of the database and raises some issues that you need to be aware of (see Table 42-2).

Table 42-2
New Field Overhead

Field Name	Description
s_Generation	Long integer used to track changes to a record since the last synchronization
s_GUID	16-byte globally unique identifier
s_Lineage	OLE object used to track the versions and replicas updating a record
Gen_xxx	Long integer for each Memo or OLE field used to track changes to these fields in a record

The addition of three fields, plus an additional field for each OLE Object and Memo field in the table, reduces the number of fields that your application can use due to the limit of 255 fields per table. Likewise, the additional data that is added to support replication can put the record size over the limit of 2,048 bytes and, depending on update activity, can put the database over the total size limit of 1GB. Additionally, disk management needs to be addressed to ensure that sufficient space is available — not only to add records but also to accommodate the replication support data.

After you convert a nonreplicable database to a Design Master, you may then create as many replicas as you need.

Caution   You should never allow users to access the Design Master database. Keep this database protected so that no one can change it and cause those changes to be replicated to other replicas. Likewise, you shouldn't allow the original nonreplicated database to be accessed so that new Design Masters and replica sets can be created. Too many replicas and multiple replica sets of the same database may cause confusion and possibly an environment that is out of synchronization.

You can create replicas from the Design Master or from another replica in the set. Before creating a new replica, however, you need to compress the database and synchronize all members of the set. Doing this ensures that the replica is created quickly and is up to date.

The replicas of a set can be synchronized only with the other members of the same set, including the Design Master. An error occurs if you attempt to synchronize a replica of one set with a replica of a different set.

If objects are created within a replica, they are marked as local and can't be made replicable. If these objects are required to be replicated to other members, you need to either create them in the Design Master or import them from their source database and set their `Replicable` property to `True`.

Creating a Replica

You have five options for creating a replica set for your database, as follows:

✦ **Replication commands in Access** — Access provides a Replication command on the Tools menu. From this menu, you can create the Design Master, the first replica, and additional replicas, and you can synchronize and resolve conflicts — even recover the replica's Design Master if necessary.

✦ **Briefcase replication** — Dragging an Access .MDB file and dropping it on the Windows Briefcase creates a Design Master and a replica, assuming that Access is installed on the machine. You can also use the Briefcase to synchronize the replica with the Design Master. This is perhaps the easiest way to implement replication and is a convenient way to keep a database file up to date.

✦ **Replication in an Access project** — The Microsoft Access project file contains several wizards that you can use to create a publication and subscription.

✦ **Replication programmatically** — In Access 97 and earlier versions, you could only program using Data Access Objects (DAO). DAO provides replication methods that enable you to create and maintain either full or partial replicas from code. You can use DAO methods in Access 2002, but you can also use the newer and more efficient Jet and Replication Objects (JRO) to write procedures to automatically synchronize a user's replica with the rest of the set when the user initially opens the database. To replicate a database programmatically, the database must be closed.

✦ **Microsoft Replication Manager** — The Microsoft Office XP Developer Edition contains a Replication Manager utility. This utility provides access to all the replication functions — with the exception of creating a partial replica, which must be done in code — and offers a facility for scheduling the synchronization of replicas.

Access replication

To convert your database to a Design Master and create the first replica from within Access, select Tools ➪ Replication ➪ Create Replica. This is the same process described earlier in the chapter.

Use the following steps to create a replica of a Design Master table:

1. Open the Design Master table CstPtLit.

2. Select Tools ➪ Replication ➪ Create Replica from the menu. Access opens the Location of New Replica dialog box.

3. Select a name for the replica (the default name is "replica# of [database name]" — where # is a number and [database name] is the current Design Master database name). For this example, type **My Replica of Customer Pets Lite**, as shown in Figure 42-2, and click OK.

4. Access displays a new dialog box informing you that the new replica won't appear in the potential synchronization partners until the database is closed and reopened. The dialog box then asks whether Access should close and reopen the database now. Click Yes in this dialog box.

   The Design Master database closes and then reopens, and then you are returned to the CstPtLit database window.

Note that after you open a Design Master table, the Access title bar identifies your opened database as the Design Master. Click the Tables object button in the database window and select Show System Objects from the Tools ➪ Options menu to see the new tables added to your database during conversion. Figure 42-3 shows the system tables after converting the CstPtLit database.

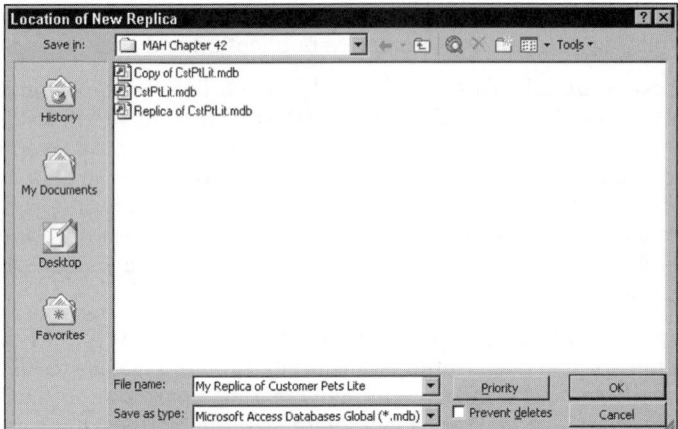

Figure 42-2: Saving a new replica of the table CstPtLit.

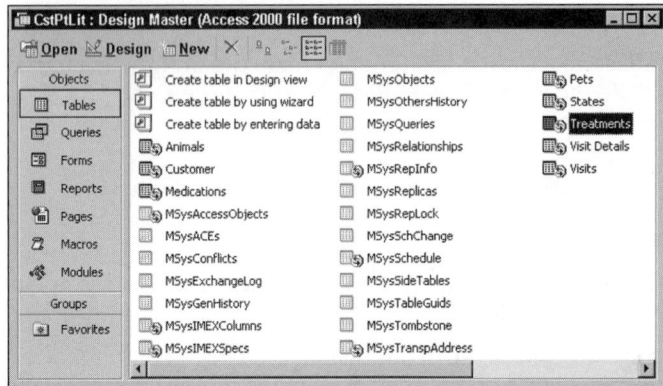

Figure 42-3: The system objects created for the Design Master CstPtLit database.

Notice that the system objects that are used by the Design Master are now visible in Figure 42-3, and notice that they all begin with "MSys." All of the system tables can be quickly identified by the fact that they all begin with "MSys" and the fact that their icons are grayed out. Notice also that only some of the system tables have a replication icon (the icon with a circle and two opposite pointing arrows) attached to them.

If you open the database My Replica of Customer Pets Lite at this point, you will see that the title bar identifies your open database as a *Replica* (see Figure 42-4).

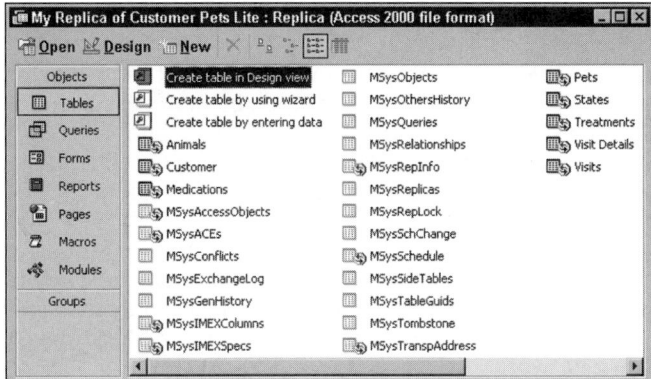

Figure 42-4: An open replica database (notice the name *Replica* at the end of the table).

Briefcase replication

If you installed the Briefcase Replication component when you installed Access, you can use the Windows 95/98/ME/XP Briefcase to convert your database to a replicable form and to synchronize that database with the briefcase replica.

When you install the Briefcase Replication component, it registers a reconciler ClassID with the Briefcase, which is to be launched whenever an .MDB file is dropped onto the Briefcase. The reconciler handles the database conversions and the synchronization of the briefcase replica with its associated replica whenever the user requests an update from the Briefcase menu.

You can establish a Briefcase icon on your Windows desktop by right-clicking the mouse and selecting New Briefcase from the shortcut menu.

Convert your database by dragging it from the Explorer window and dropping it on the Briefcase icon. The reconciler converts your database to the Design Master, leaving it in the source directory and creating a replica in the Briefcase. During this process, you are prompted to make two decisions: Do you want to create a backup of the nonreplicable database before conversion, and which of the two databases should be the Design Master — the original in the source directory or the one in the Briefcase?

For example, you can send the Briefcase to the floppy disk drive, load it onto another computer, and update the replica. When you return the Briefcase to the desktop, you'll want to synchronize the replica updates in the Briefcase with the other replica in the source directory. Briefcase synchronization is covered in more detail later in this chapter.

Replication in an Access project

A Microsoft Access project (*.adp) file contains several wizards that will help you create the publication and subscription. The publication in an Access project is one or more published tables or stored procedure articles. When a database receives tables and data replication from a publisher database it is considered a publication. Access projects support push, pull, and bidirectional synchronization.

When replicating an Access project, you replicate the data only. The forms, reports, and other objects that are contained in the project are left untouched. The project can't contain a Microsoft Access database replica. The replica is only managed by the Jet Engine, and the Access project is managed by SQL Server (desktop version locally or full version on a network).

Replication programmatically using JRO

Using Jet and Replication Objects (JRO) you can programmatically control the exchange of data and design information among members of the replica set in Access database (*.mdb files only). Remember that to replicate a database programmatically, the database must be closed. JRO can only be used with Access 2000 and 2002 databases. For programmatic control of replication in Access 97, you must use DAO. You can also use DAO to programmatically control Access 2000 and 2002 database synchronization. Access 2002 comes with several new properties and methods for you to use when working with replication databases. For example, the following five methods are used when working with replication code:

- ✦ MakeReplicable
- ✦ CreateReplica
- ✦ GetObjectReplicability
- ✦ SetObjectReplicability
- ✦ Synchronize

By using these five methods, you can control the properties of a replica database or even create a replica database. You can manipulate up to nine properties when working with replication in JRO.

Replication using DAO

DAO provides methods that you can use to support either full or partial replication from code. Using these methods, you can convert a database to a Design Master, create additional replicas, synchronize replica members, and resolve conflicts.

Note   MAH2002 Chap42.mdb on the CD-ROM contains a replication lab form (frmReplicationLab) that illustrates the use of the replication methods, as shown in Figure 42-5.

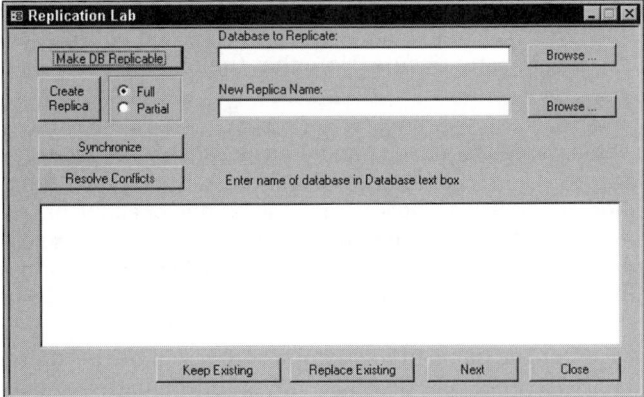

Figure 42-5: The Replication Lab form in MAH2002 Chap42.MDB.

To convert a database to a replicable form, type a database name into the Database text box or click the Browse button to select one.

Click the Make DB Replicable button to create and set the Replicable property on the selected database. This is done in the MakeDesignMaster procedure, as shown in Listing 42-1.

Listing 42-1: **Function to Create and Set the Replicable Property**

```
Public Function MakeDesignMaster(sDatabase As String)
On Error GoTo MDSErrHandler

Dim dbDatabase As Database
Dim dbProperty As Property

Set dbDatabase =
DBEngine.Workspaces(0).OpenDatabase(sDatabase, _    True)
Set dbProperty = dbDatabase.CreateProperty("Replicable", _
dbText)
dbProperty.Value = "T"
dbDatabase.Properties.Append dbProperty
dbDatabase.Close
MakeDesignMaster = True
Exit Function
MDSErrHandler:
MsgBox Err.Description, vbCritical + vbOKOnly, "Conversion _
Error"
MakeDesignMaster = False
Exit Function
End Function
```

The `MakeDesignMaster` procedure creates the Replicable property and assigns the string value "T" to it. When the database is closed at the end of this procedure, the conversion to the Design Master occurs. Note that the database was opened exclusively.

Note   Prior to converting a database, you should ensure that it has been reviewed to remove unwanted data. The existence of unnecessary data only lengthens the conversion process and makes replicas carry the burden of additional records that will never be used. Getting rid of these records prior to conversion is best, because then the system doesn't need to replicate the removal of these records across all replica set members some time after conversion.

To create a replica, enter the name of the database that will be the source of the replica in the Database to Replicate text box, and enter the path and name of the resulting replica in the New Replica Name text box. The database that is entered into the Database text box is expected to be either the name of the Design Master or the name of another existing replica.

Click either the Full or Partial option button and then click the Create Replica button to create the replica database. Selecting the Full option executes the `CreateReplica` procedure, as shown in Listing 42-2. The Partial option procedure is shown in Listing 42-3.

Listing 42-2: **Function to Create a Full Replica of a Database**

```
Public Function CreateReplica(sDatabase As String, sReplicaName
As _ String)
 On Error GoTo CRErrHandler
 Dim dbDatabase As Database
 Dim sDescription As String

 Set dbDatabase =
DBEngine.Workspaces(0).OpenDatabase(sDatabase)
 sDescription = "Replica of " & sDatabase
 dbDatabase.MakeReplica sReplicaName, sDescription
 dbDatabase.Close
 CreateReplica = True
 Exit Function
CRErrHandler:
 MsgBox Err.Description, vbCritical + vbOKOnly, "Create Error"
 CreateReplica = False
 Exit Function
 End Function
```

The `CreateReplica` procedure assigns a description to the replica and then uses the `MakeReplica` method of the database object assigned by the `OpenDatabase` method on the database that you entered in the Database text box.

If you want the replica to be read-only, you can create a `dbRepMake ReadOnly` constant, which can be passed as the third parameter to the `MakeReplica` method. You may want to add this as an option on the form.

When you designate a table as replicable and create a full replica of the database containing that table, all records in the table are replicated to the replica member. You may not need all records for a particular replica user. If this is the case, you can create a partial replica by using the code in Listing 42-3.

Listing 42-3: **Function to Create a Partial Replica of a Database**

```
Public Function CreatePartial(sDatabase As String, sReplicaName
As _ String)
    Dim db As Database, dbReplica As Database
    Dim td As TableDef
    Dim frmFilter As Form

    Set db = OpenDatabase(sDatabase)

    ' Create a replica to hold the partial data
    db.MakeReplica sReplicaName, _
        "Partial Replica of " & sReplicaName, dbRepMakePartial
    db.Close

    ' Set the ReplicaFilter property

    Set dbReplica = OpenDatabase(sReplicaName, True)

    ' Show modal dialog to collect table filter
    DoCmd.OpenForm ("CollectPartialFilter")
    Set frmFilter = Forms("CollectPartialFilter")
    Set td = dbReplica.TableDefs(frmFilter.sFilterTable)
    td.ReplicaFilter = frmFilter.sFilter
    dbReplica.Close

    ' Set the PartialReplica property on relationships here

    ' Create the partial replica
    Set dbReplica = OpenDatabase(sReplicaName, True)
    dbReplica.PopulatePartial sDatabase
    dbReplica.Close
    Exit Function
End Function
```

`CreatePartial` first creates a replica database to hold the partial replica. You do this by using the `MakeReplica` method of the source database.

The next step is to set the filter in the replica database. You accomplish this task by first collecting two items from the user—the table to set a filter on and the filter specification. The lab example allows only one table and filter to be specified. The specifications collected from the `CollectPartialFilter` form are used to set the `ReplicaFilter` property of a table in the replica database.

After the `ReplicaFilter` is set, you can set relationships to pull records that are related to the filtered records. You do this by setting the `PartialReplica` property on all relations to participate in the partial population. The lab does not show the code to carry out this task.

The last step in creating a partial replica is to populate the replica with data according to the filter specification. The `PopulatePartial` method is used on the replica database to cause the `ReplicaFilter` on each table object to be applied to the database that is specified in the `PopulateReplica` method. This action pulls records from tables containing a `ReplicaFilter` property and related records in a `PartialReplica` property. No other data is pulled into the partial replica. To remove a `ReplicaFilter` from a table, set the property to `False`.

Replication Manager 4.0 utility

The Replication Manager utility that is available in the Microsoft Office Developer Edition enables you to manage replica sets from the point of creating the set or additional replica members to the point of synchronizing the set through a scheduled or manual synchronization. There is no facility for resolving conflicts, but you can determine which replicas experienced conflicts or errors and launch Access from within the Manager to resolve them.

Note   The file name of the replication manager is "replman.exe" and if installed with default directories, can be found in the C:\program files\common files\Microsoft shared\replication manager 4.0\ directory.

Tip   The first time that you run the Replication Manager, it activates a wizard that will assist you in setting up the Manager. With this wizard, you can set up your manager to automatically start when Windows starts and to specify the databases it should automatically replicate.

Figure 42-6 shows the Replication Manager Synchronizer window displaying one Synchronizer. The CstPtLit replica set is opened and is managed by the local Synchronizer, which is named "Michael Irwin's Synchronizer." This Synchronizer has three members that it is managing (you can't currently see the names of the databases that are being managed). One of these replicas is the Design Master, as indicated by the Design Master icon. Synchronizer also manages the two replica set members.

In Figure 42-6, note a status message at the bottom of the Manager window indicating that the Synchronizer is idle. We discuss how the Synchronizer is scheduled later in this chapter.

Figure 42-6: The Replication Manager utility window displaying one of its managed replica members.

A Synchronizer, MSTRAN40.EXE, is responsible for monitoring and synchronizing the replicas within one or more replica sets. You can assign as many replicas as necessary to a Synchronizer. When a replica set is opened, the number of replica members in that set managed by a Synchronizer is shown in parentheses below the Synchronizer icon, as shown in Figure 42-6.

When you initially start the Replication Manager, it asks you to configure the Manager. This configuration designates various options that the utility will use in managing replicas, such as the name of a shared network folder that will be used to cache transactions if a remote replica set member can't be accessed during synchronization and the path to the log file the Transporter will use to log its activity.

After the configuration is complete, the Synchronizer for the machine can be started and the Replication Manager can do its work. If the Synchronizer can't be started, then you can't synchronize replicas with the utility; however, you can still synchronize by using one of the other methods discussed in this chapter.

Replicas may be located in any folder on the local machine and assigned to the local machine's Synchronizer, or they may be located in folders of other machines on the network and assigned to other Synchronizers, as is the case in Figure 42-6. The key to keeping these replicas in sync with each other is the knowledge that the Synchronizers have regarding the member locations.

Note When using the Replication Manager to manage your replica sets, don't move replicas or create replicas outside of the Manager. Instead, use the Manager to create replicas and move them to other folders on the network to ensure integrity of the set.

To start managing or to stop managing replicas, use the Managed Replicas choice on the Files menu or click the Managed Replicas button of the Replication Manager, as shown in Figure 42-7. The replicas that are selected in the Managed Replicas dialog box will be managed by the machine's Synchronizer automatically.

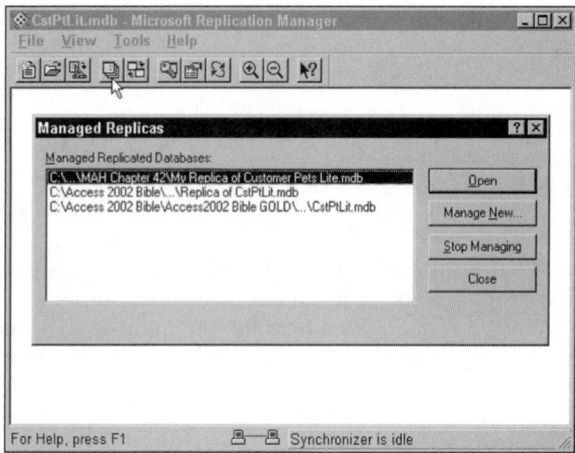

Figure 42-7: The Managed Replicas dialog box of the Replication Manager.

The Synchronizer attempts to synchronize all managed members of a set by directly accessing the members itself and applying the necessary changes. If a replica in the set can't be accessed for any reason, the Synchronizer can't synchronize the replica with the other members of the set. If the Synchronizer runs into problems when it starts and attempts to manage all sets in the manager, it will display a message box, similar to the one shown in Figure 42-8.

If the Synchronizer does run into problems during synchronization, it logs the problems, along with other messages regarding the status of the synchronization in a Synchronizer Log file. This file and the path to it are specified in the Configure Replication Manager Wizard. You should choose a file location on the Synchronizer machine so that the log can be written — even if network connections are down.

You can enter a name for the Synchronizer in the last dialog box of the wizard, which appears under the Synchronizer icon in the Replication Manager Synchronizer window. The machine name is a good choice for the Synchronizer name, although for this example, we used the name "Michael R. Irwin's Synchronization."

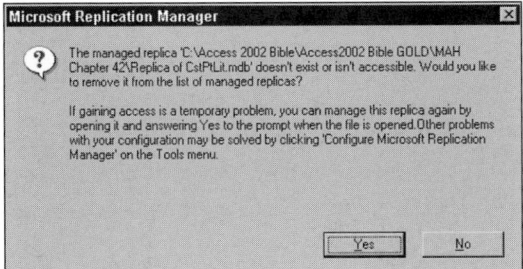

Figure 42-8: The message box that displays if the Replication Manager starts and can't find one of the tables that need to be synchronized.

After the configuration is completed, you are ready to start using the Manager to convert your databases and create and synchronize your replicas.

 **Note**   The Replication Manager does *not* require you to use its facilities for converting your database or creating new replicas. You may use any method presented in this chapter to create the replicas. After they are created, assign the replicas to a Synchronizer in the utility.

Using the Replication Manager to convert a database

To convert a database with the Replication Manager's utility, select Convert Database to Design Master from the Tools menu. After selecting the name of the database to convert to a Design Master, the Convert Database to Design Master Wizard appears.

The first page of the Convert Database to Design Master Wizard is an information screen, stating that it's about to gather the necessary information to convert the selected database to a Design Master database. To move to the next screen, simply press the Next button. You can also stop running the wizard by pressing the Cancel button, or simply select Finish and allow the wizard to use all the default values to create a Design Master.

The next screen that appears is a dialog box. Here you are prompted to choose between making a backup of the selected database or not. If you haven't yet done so, have the wizard create a backup. The next dialog box asks you to enter a description for the entire replica set, as shown in Figure 42-9. This description appears in the title bar of the Replication Manager window whenever you select a member of the replica set. Click Next to continue.

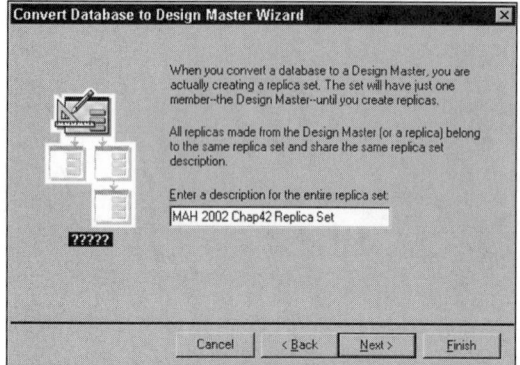

Figure 42-9: The second dialog box (third screen) of the Convert Database to Design Master Wizard is used to specify a description for the replica set.

The next dialog box of the wizard, shown in Figure 42-10, enables you to select the database objects that you want replicated. You can choose to replicate all objects in the database or select specific objects. Consider the target users of the replicas and the objects that they will need. Also consider the time required to synchronize replicas in making your choice of objects. Click Next to continue.

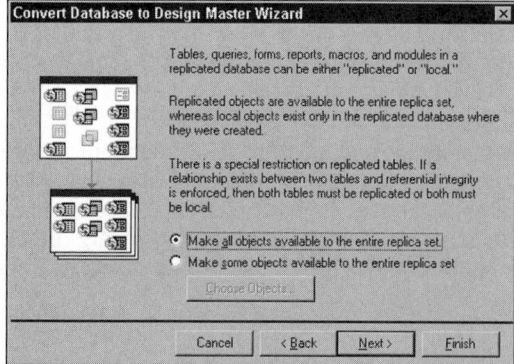

Figure 42-10: The third dialog box of the Convert Database to Design Master Wizard enables you to select database objects to replicate.

Tip   If the data in your database supports partitioning, you can create separate partitions (tables) of the main database and then replicate those partitions to their target users. For example, if your database supports an organization that is broken down into regions, you may have data that can only be accessed by users in a particular region and no one else. By creating a database that maintains only that subset of data, you can reduce the size of the replica and the time required to synchronize it. These partitions should be synchronized only with the main database tables to support global reporting and queries, so that none of the replica data overlaps. Opportunities for other types of partitioning may also exist, so give some thought to your target group and the data that you need to support their requirements before you begin replicating databases. As an alternative to this approach, you can create partial replicas in DAO code.

In the next step of the Convert Database to Design Master Wizard, you are asked to choose between read-only and read-write replicas, as shown in Figure 42-11. Select the appropriate option for your intended usage of the replicas. Click Next to move to the next screen.

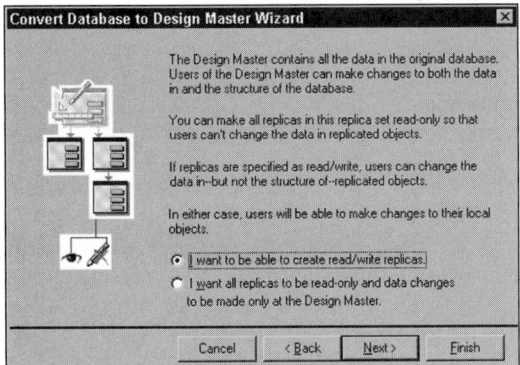

Figure 42-11: Replicas may be designated as read-only or read-write.

The next screen gives you a choice of managing the Design Master with the local Synchronizer or deferring assignment to a Synchronizer until later, as shown in Figure 42-12. Click Next to move to the next screen.

The last screen is an information screen where you must click Finish to continue. When you click Finish, the conversion process starts and then opens the Design Master. After a Design Master has been created, an information box displays, informing you that it is created. Click OK to return to the Replication Manager.

Note Unlike the Access method and the Briefcase method, the Replication Manager doesn't automatically create a first replica member when it converts your database. The outcome of this process is the Design Master only.

Creating replicas of the converted database

To create replicas of your converted database, select New Replica from the File menu, which opens the New Replica Wizard. After you view the first screen and click Next, the New Replica Wizard asks you to select the Design Master as the source of the new replica or another member replica and a Destination name for the new replica. Click Next to move to the next screen.

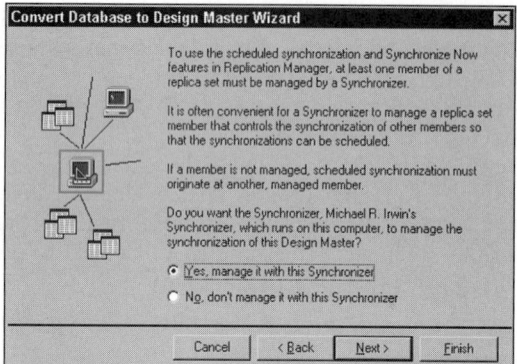

Figure 42-12: The Convert Database to Design Master Wizard gives you the opportunity to synchronize the Design Master with the local Synchronizer or to defer the assignment to a later time.

The next wizard screen prompts you to choose between read-only and read-write attributes for the new replica, as shown in Figure 42-13. Click Next to move to the next screen.

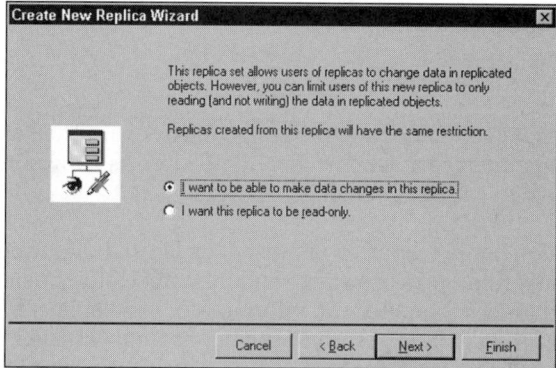

Figure 42-13: A screen of the New Replica Wizard that you use to designate the new replica as read-only or read-write.

Next, the wizard asks you to choose the local Synchronizer or defer Synchronizer assignment for the new replica member, as shown in Figure 42-14. At least one member of the replica set needs to be assigned to a Synchronizer. If you have already assigned the Design Master to a Synchronizer, then you can defer assignment for this replica. Click Next to move to the last screen, where you must press Finish to continue.

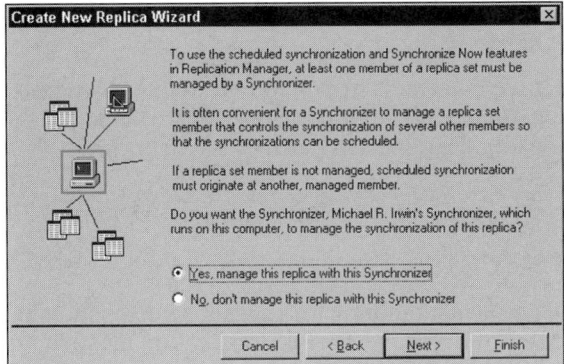

Figure 42-14: Assign the local Synchronizer to manage the new replica or defer assignment.

Finally, the wizard creates the replica and an information box informs you that it has completed. Click OK to end the process. After you have finished using the wizard to create the new replica, an additional count is added to the Synchronization window if you requested it to manage the replicas. If you didn't request it to manage the replicas, they are placed in the Replication Manager window as an unmanaged replica icon. Figure 42-15 shows an unmanaged replica added to the system.

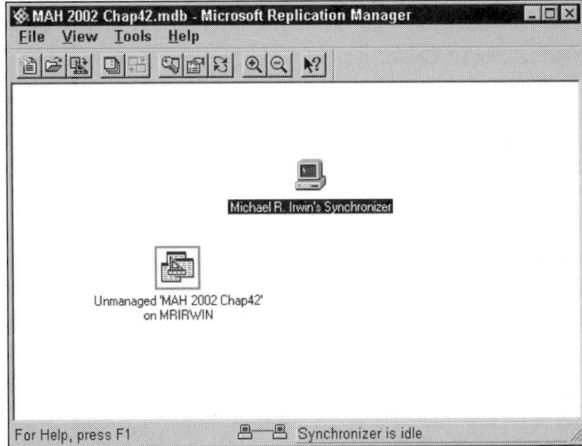

Figure 42-15: An unmanaged replica added to the system.

To view the objects contained in a replica, select the replica member in the Synchronization window and double-click or right-click the mouse to view properties. On the Open Database tab, click the Modify Object Status button. The Modify Object Status dialog box displays the objects that are contained in the replica set and their status.

Synchronizing Replicas

All the replication facilities that have been discussed in this chapter — Access, Briefcase, DAO, and Replication Manager — offer the capability to synchronize members of the replica set. The following section discusses synchronization in each of these four facilities.

Synchronizing with Access

You can synchronize your open replica member with another selected member of the set by choosing Synchronize Now from the Tools ➪ Replication menu in Access.

From the Synchronize Database dialog box, select another replica member to synchronize with from the drop-down list box, or click Browse to specify a member not yet in the list, as shown in Figure 42-16.

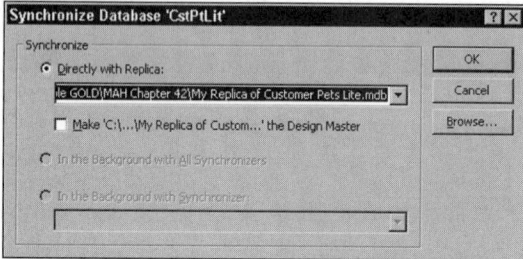

Figure 42-16: The Synchronize Database dialog box asks you to choose a target replica member to synchronize with the current database.

Tip   Replica set member names reside in the MSysReplicas table within each member database. A replica member becomes known to another replica member if one is created from the other or synchronized with the other. If a replica named "Replica xxx1" creates a member replica named "Replica xxx2," then Replica xxx2 is immediately known to Replica xxx1 but is not known to Replica xxx or any other member until Replica xxx2 and Replica xxx are synchronized with each other. At that time, the existence of Replica xxx2 is entered into the MSysReplicas table of Replica xxx and vice versa.

Tip   You can remove a replica from a set by deleting the physical .MDB file. This action, however, doesn't remove the replica entry from the MSysReplicas table in remaining replica member databases, and the Synchronize Database dialog box continues to list the removed replica member in its drop-down list as a candidate for synchronization. To remove a replica from a set and from the candidate list in the Synchronize dialog box, attempt to synchronize the current open replica with the deleted replica. Access will detect the missing database and remove the member from the replica set by removing the entry from the MSysReplicas table.

After deleting the file and removing it from the replica set, open the Replication Manager and the managed replica set member or choose Refresh Synchronization Window from the Tools menu. You will no longer see the deleted replica member in the window. Attempting to remove a deleted replica from a managed set with the Replication Manager utility will only report a problem in its synchronization history details; it doesn't have the same effect as the synchronization from within Access.

Synchronizing from the Briefcase

Select the Details view from the Briefcase View menu to display the replica status information. To start the synchronization process, choose Update All or Update Selection from the Briefcase menu. For the .MDB replica in the Briefcase, a dialog box is presented that depicts the Briefcase replica and its target, as well as the source from which the Briefcase replica was created. Click the Update button to start synchronization.

When the synchronization process ends, the status of the replica in the Briefcase changes to "Up-to-date." Open the target database to verify that the briefcase database changes have been updated or to deal with the conflicts that may have been recorded. Be sure to check the Briefcase database to see if *bidirectional synchronization* (changes passed between Briefcase and target and vice versa) has been performed.

If you subsequently make a design change to the Design Master, you can again select Update from the Briefcase menu to synchronize the design change with the replica.

Synchronizing with DAO

Note On the Replication Lab form (frmReplicationLab) in MAH2002 Chpt42.MDB, which is included on the CD-ROM with this book, enter the names of the replicas in the Database and Replica Name text boxes and click the Synchronize button.

The SyncDBs procedure (which is shown in Listing 42-4) called from the Synchronize button's click event uses the Synchronize method of the database object. The sSyncWithDB string passed into the procedure is the name from the Replica Name text box, and it designates the other member with which the database object is to synchronize.

You may specify the direction of synchronization between the database object (dbDatabase) and the replica (sSyncWithDB) with the second parameter of the Synchronize method.

Use the dbRepImpExpChanges constant to replicate the changes in the dbDatabase database into the sSyncWithDB database.

Use `dbRepImportChanges` to replicate the changes in the `sSyncWithDB` database into the `dbDatabase` database.

The `dbRepImpExpChanges` constant used in the `SyncDBs` procedure yields a bidi-rectional exchange of changes between the two databases.

Listing 42-4: Function to Synchronize Two Replicas Using the Synchronize Method

```
Public Function SyncDBs(sDatabase As String, sSyncWithDB As
String, _
   RepType As Integer)
   On Error GoTo SDBErrHandler
   Dim dbDatabase As Database
   If RepType = 0 Then

      ' Full replica
      Set dbDatabase = _
DBEngine.Workspaces(0).OpenDatabase(sDatabase)
      dbDatabase.Synchronize sSyncWithDB, dbRepImpExpChanges
   Else

      ' Partial replica
      Set dbDatabase = _
DBEngine.Workspaces(0).OpenDatabase(sSyncWithDB)
      dbDatabase.PopulatePartial sDatabase
   End If
   dbDatabase.Close
   SyncDBs = True
   Exit Function
SDBErrHandler:
   MsgBox Err.Description, vbCritical + vbOKOnly,
"Synchronization _
      Error"
   SyncDBs = False
   Exit Function
End Function
```

Note that in Listing 42-4 the use of the `PopulatePartial` method to synchronize the changes contained in a partial replica is indicated in the Replica Name text box with the database indicated in the Database Name text box. You can use this method if you select the Partial option.

`PopulatePartial` synchronizes the changes in the partial replica member with the full database, clears the partial replica, and then repopulates it using the currently specified ReplicaFilter contained in the replica database. This portion of the `PopulatePartial` method is the same behavior that you use to create the partial replica, as discussed previously in this chapter.

Using `PopulatePartial` instead of `Synchronize` ensures that the partial is up to date with the full replica and that no orphaned records are left in the partial replica. Orphaned records can be created whenever a change in the partial replica data causes a record to no longer have the characteristics specified in the ReplicaFilter. Suppose, for example, that your ReplicaFilter asks for all customers in Arizona at the time the partial replica was created. If the replica is updated to change a customer's state to New York, that customer no longer meets the Filter specifications. At synchronize time, `PopulatePartial` will pass the change to the full database and then receive new customers according to the current ReplicaFilter. If the ReplicaFilter still specifies Arizona customers, the customer that was changed to New York won't be pulled into the replica. Had the synchronization process merely exchanged changes, the New York customer would never be updated and therefore would be orphaned from the Arizona customers.

Synchronizing with Replication Manager

Using the Replication Manager, you have two options for synchronizing replicas. You can synchronize on demand or through a synchronization schedule, which you can customize to run on any 15-minute interval within a 24-hour clock.

To synchronize on demand, choose Tools ➪ Synchronize Now. This displays the Synchronize Now dialog box, as shown in Figure 42-17.

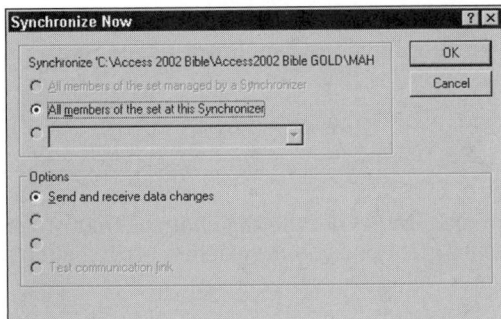

Figure 42-17: The Synchronize Now dialog box in Replication Manager enables you to specify the members to synchronize.

In the Synchronize Now dialog box, you specify the members to synchronize with the selected replica icon. You can synchronize with all other members managed by a Synchronizer, with all members of the set at the local Synchronizer, or with a specific member.

If you select the "All members of the set managed by a Synchronizer" option, you can select the exchange options in the Options frame. Only a bidirectional exchange is possible with the "All members of the set at this Synchronizer" option.

To set up a schedule for synchronizing members of replica sets that are managed by the local Synchronizer, right-click a replica icon and select Edit Locally Managed Replica Schedule from the pop-up menu (see Figure 42-18).

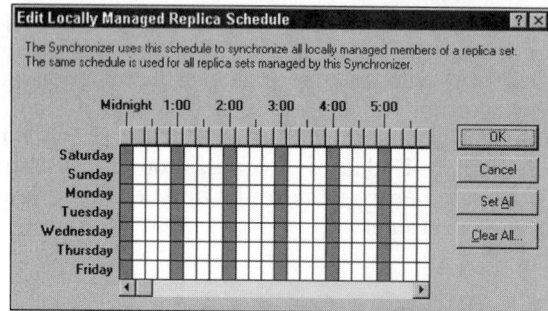

Figure 42-18: The Edit Locally Managed Replica Schedule can be set to automatically synchronize replica members at the local Synchronizer.

Click the cells representing the time of day that you want to schedule a synchronization. Click the button at the top of the schedule grid to select all cells for the indicated time and have synchronization run at that time on every day of the week.

It isn't necessary to have Replication Manager running for the synchronization schedule to take effect, but you do need to have the Synchronizer running.

Resolving Conflicts

When you synchronize replicas, you may detect conflicting changes that prevent one of the change records from being applied, or you may detect errors, such as referential integrity errors or key errors.

Conflicts arise when the same record, which is identified by the GUID, is updated at two replica members in the set. The synchronization process selects one of the records to be applied to the two members being synchronized and writes the other record as a conflict record into a side table created in the database that owns the conflict.

In the case of a conflict, Jet selects the record to apply to the table based on the version number in the record's s_Lineage field. This version number is updated each time the record is changed in each replica, and Jet selects the record that has the highest version number, which is the record changed the most. If the version numbers are identical, then Jet must select one of the records to apply and write the other to the conflict side table.

Errors can result whenever an update or design change from the Design Master violates a Jet- or Access-enforced rule, such as a unique key error or referential integrity error. The error is written into the MSysErrors table of the replica member where the error occurred. Before the members can be considered safely in sync, you must research and resolve all errors among the replicas and resynchronize the set to the point of no errors or conflicts.

Although you can use Replication Manager to determine the outcome of a synchronization, you can't resolve the conflicts or errors within the utility. You can use Access or code your own DAO procedures to handle the resolution of problems.

To view the synchronization results of a replica, right-click a replica icon and select View Local Synchronization History from the pop-up menu.

Resolving conflicts in Access

When you open a database after synchronization, a message box displays, informing you of any synchronization problems that occurred. You have the option to resolve the problems in this message box, or you can resolve the problems at a later time by choosing Resolve Conflicts from the Tools menu. Access displays a dialog box showing you the tables that have problems and the types of problems experienced. Figure 42-19 shows a message that appears when a conflict occurs.

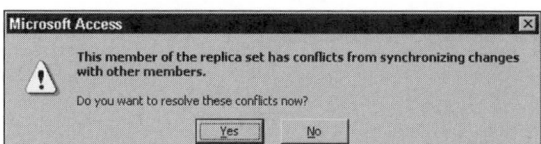

Figure 42-19: A conflict between two databases.

When you resolve conflicts, a dialog box displays, showing the existing record and the conflict record, as shown in Figure 42-20. You are shown a list of tables with conflicts and the number of conflicts in each table. Figure 42-20 shows one conflict (as designated by the number 1 in parentheses) in the Customers table.

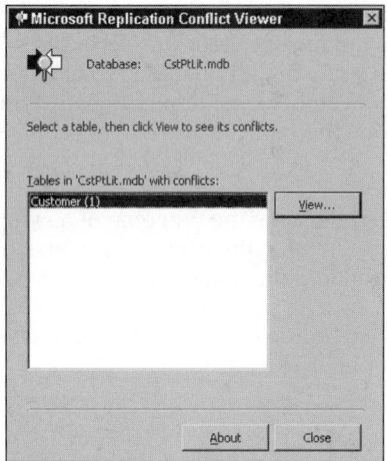

Figure 42-20: The Replication Conflict Viewer dialog box shows one conflict in the Customers table.

If you click the View button, you will see a dialog box similar to the one shown in Figure 42-21. In this case, the Customer Name has a conflict.

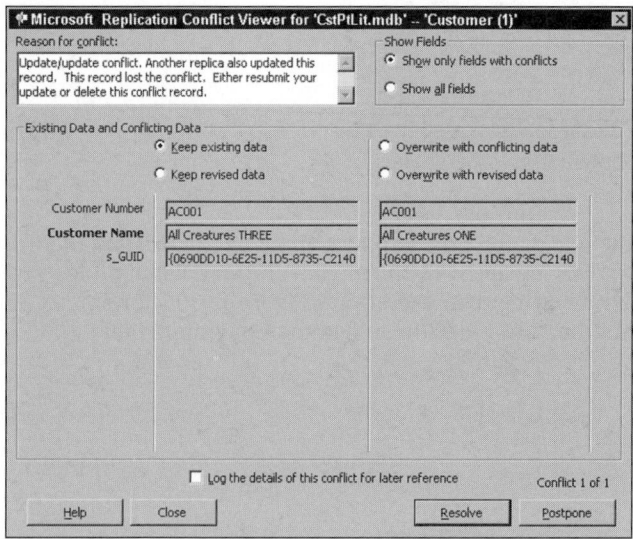

Figure 42-21: The Replication Conflicts Viewer dialog box asks you either to choose to keep the existing record or to overwrite the existing record with the conflict record.

You are asked to choose between keeping the existing data, keeping revised data, overwriting data with the conflict record, or overwriting data with the revised data. After you have made your choice, you can process it by clicking the Resolve button. Selecting any of the four choices deletes the entry from the conflict side table and either moves to the next conflict record or informs you that all conflicts have been processed.

The Data Errors dialog box shows you the error details, such as duplicate values in a key field resulting from the same key being added to a table in the replicas. This error can arise if the key fields are not AutoNumber fields. The action that you take depends on the type of error reported and may involve some extensive research with the replica users to determine how to resolve the error.

After resolving the reported problems, you should resynchronize the set to ensure that all problems have been resolved before releasing the databases into the production environment.

Resolving conflicts with DAO

If conflicts or errors result from the synchronization process, you can resolve them with your own procedures.

The Replication Lab form presents a method to resolve conflicts that is similar to the method used when you chose Resolve Conflicts from the Access Replication menu, but this method only illustrates the handling of conflicts. You can add procedures to handle errors by processing the MSysErrors table.

Processing the MSysErrors table enables you to find the tables that experienced conflicts and step through each conflict. The Replication Lab method asks you to choose either to keep the existing record (the one that was chosen by the synchronization process) or to overwrite it with the conflict record (the one that lost the battle to become a row in the table).

On the Replication Lab form, enter the name of the database for which you want to resolve conflicts in the Database text box and click the Resolve Conflicts button. The click event procedure for the Resolve Conflicts button calls the `ProcessConflicts` function to manage the display of conflicts.

The `ProcessConflicts` function shown in Listing 42-5 sets up the Recordsets that are needed to inspect the conflicts in all tables having conflicts. You can determine these tables by inspecting the table property `ConflictTable`, which returns the name of the side table holding the conflict records. Because this method would require visiting each TableDef in the database, the Replication Lab uses a more direct route to the conflicts by reading MSysSideTables. This system table records the names of the side tables holding the conflict records along with the GUID of the base table in which those conflicts occurred. To determine the name of the base table, another system table is used — MSysTableGuids — which holds the GUIDs and names of all tables in the database.

Listing 42-5: ProcessConflicts Manages the Collection and Display of Database Conflicts

```
Public Function ProcessConflicts(sDatabase As String)

On Error GoTo PCErrHandler

Set dbDatabase =
DBEngine.Workspaces(0).OpenDatabase(sDatabase, _
True)
' Process Conflicts
On Error Resume Next
sSQLStmt = "SELECT [SideTable],[TableName] FROM _
MSysSideTables,MSysTableGuids WHERE MSysSideTables![TableGuid]
= _
MSysTableGuids![s_GUID]"
Set rsSideTables = dbDatabase.OpenRecordset(sSQLStmt, _
dbOpenSnapshot)
    If Err = 0 Then
      If NextSideTable() = False Then
          rsSideTables.Close
            MsgBox "All conflicts have been processed"
      Else
          rc = NextConflict()
        End If
    End If
' Put Your Process Errors Code Here

ProcessConflicts = True
Exit Function

PCErrHandler:
ProcessConflicts = False
Exit Function
End Function
```

Replication Lab steps through each conflict record in the current side table, presents each conflict record along with the existing record in the base table, and asks you to choose between those records. The base table record is selected using the conflict record's GUID field. This process is found in the NextConflict procedure, as shown in Listing 42-6.

Listing 42-6: **Routine to Display the Existing Records and Associated Conflict Records**

```
Public Function NextConflict()
If Not rsConflicts.EOF Then
    Me!OLEControl10.ListItems.Clear
    rsBaseTable.Index = "s_GUID"
    rsBaseTable.Seek "=", rsConflicts![s_GUID]
    If rsBaseTable.NoMatch Then
'Record updated in Source not present in Target
    Else
'Record found is in conflict with the conflict table record
'Add existing record to view
        Set liItem = OLEControl10.ListItems.Add(, "K" & _
CStr(rsBaseTable.Name), CStr(rsBaseTable.Name))
        For i = 1 To rsBaseTable.Fields.Count
          liItem.SubItems(i) = rsBaseTable.Fields(i -1)   .Value
        Next i
      ' Add conflict record to view
        Set liItem = OLEControl10.ListItems.Add(, "K" & _
CStr(rsConflicts.Name), _
CStr(rsConflicts.Name))
        For i = 1 To rsConflicts.Fields.Count
          liItem.SubItems(i) = rsConflicts.Fields(i - 1).Value
        Next i
    End If
    rsConflicts.MoveNext
    NextConflict = True
Else
    NextConflict = False
End If
Exit Function
End Function
```

After all conflicts for a table are resolved, the next side-table is selected. The resolution process repeats until all side-tables have been inspected. The NextSideTable procedure in Listing 42-7 implements this process.

Listing 42-7: **Function to Open a Conflict Table and Its Corresponding Base Table**

```
Public Function NextSideTable()
 If Not rsSideTables.EOF Then
 ' Open the Conflict Table
    Set rsConflicts = _
```

Continued

Listing 42-7: *(continued)*

```
dbDatabase.OpenRecordset(rsSideTables![SideTable],
dbOpenDynaset)
 ' Open the Base Table where conflict occurred
    Set rsBaseTable = _
dbDatabase.OpenRecordset(rsSideTables![TableName],
dbOpenTable)
    Me!OLEControl10.ColumnHeaders.Clear
    Set colHeader = Me!OLEControl10.ColumnHeaders.Add(,
"Table", _
"Table", 2000)
    For i = 0 To rsBaseTable.Fields.Count - 1
       Set colHeader = Me!OLEControl10.ColumnHeaders.Add(, _
(rsBaseTable.Fields(i).Name), _
(rsBaseTable.Fields(i).Name), 2000)
    Next i
 ' 2002 if you want to create the new format
 ' Get the next sidetable holding conflicts
    rsSideTables.MoveNext
    NextSideTable = True
Else
    NextSideTable = False
End If
Exit Function
End Function
```

If you click the Replace Existing button, the existing record in the base table is replaced with the conflict record in the side table. This process is found in the `ReplaceExistingRec` procedure, as shown in Listing 42-8.

Listing 42-8: Function Used to Replace a Base Table Record with a Conflict Record

```
Public Function ReplaceExistingRec()
 'Replace existing base table record with conflict record
 On Error Resume Next
 rsConflicts.MovePrevious
 rsBaseTable.Edit
 For i = 0 To rsConflicts.Fields.Count - 1
    rsBaseTable.Fields(i).Value = rsConflicts.Fields(i).Value
 Next i
 rsBaseTable.Update
 rsConflicts.MoveNext
 Exit Function
 End Function
```

After the conflict is resolved, the conflict record is removed from the side table. When the side table is empty, the table is deleted from the database. This process is implemented in the RemoveConflict procedure, as shown in Listing 42-9. This same function is also called when you elect to keep the existing record.

Listing 42-9: Function to Remove a Conflict Record from a Side Table

```
Public Function RemoveConflict()
  ' This procedure deletes the current conflict record. When the
  _
  conflict
  ' table is empty, the table itself is deleted.
  On Error Resume Next
  rsConflicts.MovePrevious
  rsConflicts.Delete
  rsConflicts.MoveNext
  If rsConflicts.EOF Then
      rsConflicts.Close
      rsSideTables.MovePrevious
      dbDatabase.TableDefs.Delete rsSideTables![SideTable]
      rsSideTables.MoveNext
  End If
  Exit Function
  End Function
```

Building a New Design Master

If the Design Master becomes corrupted or lost, you can designate one of the other replicas as the new Design Master.

With one of the replica databases open in Access, choose Recover Design Master from the Tools ➪ Replication menu. A message box appears, as shown in Figure 42-22, informing you of the current Design Master name and asking you to verify that it has been lost or corrupted. Click Yes to continue.

Access next tells you to synchronize the current database with all other replica members before designating it as the new Design Master. If you have already done this, click Yes.

Access designates the current replica as the Design Master, which enables you to make design changes to the database and replicate those changes to other members in the set.

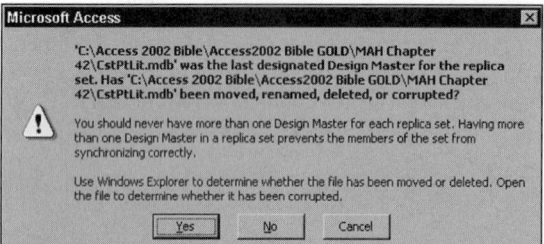

Figure 42-22: Creating a new Design Master.

To designate the current database as the Design Master, Access changed the `DesignMasterID` property of the database to the ID of the replica. This can be accomplished in your own DAO procedures by assigning the current database `ReplicaID` value to the `DesignMasterID` property.

After changing a replica to the Design Master, you need to synchronize the replica with all other members of the set to update their DesignMasterIDs to point to the new Design Master.

✦   ✦   ✦

Exploring Add-Ins and Libraries

Access 2002 *add-ins* are databases that contain procedures and associated objects, which you can add to Access by using the Add-In Manager. With add-ins, you can enhance the functionality of Access or a custom application that has been developed for the Access environment. Access has three types of add-ins — menu add-ins, builder add-ins, and wizard add-ins. This chapter provides an overview of the various add-ins that are prepackaged with Access and presents a hands-on look at building a custom add-in wizard that creates a table, form, and report.

Understanding Types of Add-Ins

Some add-ins are context-specific and are launched when the user attempts to perform some action in a particular context. Examples of context-specific add-ins include the Access Form Wizards, which are invoked when a user builds a new Autoform, and Control Wizards, which are invoked when a user inserts a new control on a form with the Control Wizards enabled. Context-specific add-ins are usually represented as wizard add-ins or builder add-ins.

Add-ins that are not context-specific are generally classified as menu add-ins. They appear on the submenu when you choose Tools ⇨ Add-Ins. In Access 2002, many of the add-ins are found in submenus under the Tools menu. For example, the User-Level Security Wizard can be found under the Security menu of the Tools menu.

You can see the built-in menu add-ins and wizards that are installed by Access 2002 by inspecting the system registry. Using the Registry Editor, expand the tree HKEY_LOCAL_MACHINE\Software\Microsoft\Office\10.0\Access. In this subtree, you see the subkeys labeled Menu Add-Ins and Wizards. Expand these subkeys to see the various built-in add-ins in Access 2002.

In This Chapter

Understanding the types of add-ins

Understanding libraries and how to use them

An overview of built-in add-ins in Access 2002

How to develop and install your own add-ins

Exploring the Add-In Manager

Later in this chapter, you'll explore a custom menu add-in and discover how to register this add-in in the registry. For now, expand the Wizards subkey, the Control Wizards subkey, and the CommandButton subkey. Click once on the subkey labeled MSCommandButtonWizard to see the values registered for this add-in. Note the Library value; this is the database location of the database housing this add-in, the Command Button Wizard. Also note the Function value, which specifies the function in the add-in that Access will call when a user invokes the add-in. You'll become more familiar with these entries when you explore the custom add-in. Figure 43-1 shows this value.

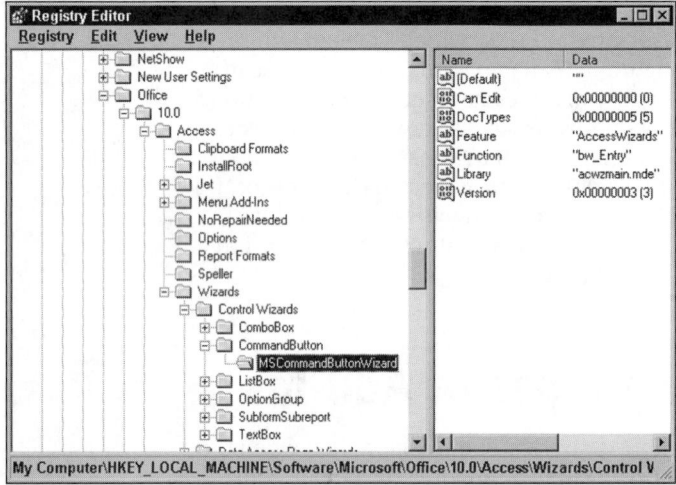

Figure 43-1: Viewing the values registered for a wizard of Access 2002 using the RegEdit program

A *wizard* is an add-in that helps you create objects, such as tables, queries, reports, and forms. Some wizards create entire applications or sets of routines that you can integrate into your database. Access 2002 has several built-in wizards, as you can see in the Registry, that you should find helpful. You'll find many more wizards available from third-party vendors. Wizards are either sold directly for an end-user's use — perhaps to produce a query or report — or are sold to enhance the productivity of Access application developers. As previously mentioned, you also can build your own wizards.

Another type of add-in is a *builder*. Builders are tools that help simplify a task, such as building a formula for a control on a form or report, or setting a control property. Builders are usually simpler than wizards in terms of the user interface and the resulting output of the add-in. Access 2002 installs Property builders and an Expression builder, which you will use quite often as you build your applications.

The third type of add-in is the *menu* add-in. This type of add-in is not associated with any particular context in using Access. You install it, and it becomes a choice found on the Tools ➪ Add-Ins menu (although you can place the add-in on other menus). An example of a menu add-in is one that you can create and add to Access.

Although not actually another type of add-in, you can find several tools under the appropriate section of the Tools menu. For example, you can find the Switchboard Manager under the Database Utilities menu of the Tools menu. And even though this is an add-in, you can no longer find it under the Add-In section of the Tools menu. In Access 97 and earlier versions, it was located under the Add-In menu.

Understanding Libraries

Add-ins are located in a standard Access database and usually have either an .MDA or an .MDE extension. These databases are built with the sole purpose of housing one or more add-in procedures and associated database objects, such as forms, queries, and tables. These types of databases are known as *add-in databases,* but are sometimes referred to as *libraries.*

Although add-ins can be considered library databases, the term *library* is generally reserved for databases that hold Visual Basic routines, which provide utility across several Access applications. Using libraries will enable you to provide procedures that are customized for your business and are available to all Access applications developed for the business. Additionally, a library database provides a central common source for convenient maintenance of the procedures.

Referencing library databases

Library databases are to be used by Access 2002 databases, and must be in Access 2002 format. Library databases also require that a reference be made to them from the calling database. Circular references are not allowed, meaning that you can't establish a reference from YourAccountingLib.MDA to YourMathLib.MDA and have YourMathLib.MDA reference YourAccountingLib.MDA. A library can reference another library, but not each other at the same time.

To establish a reference by using Access menus from YourApp.MDB to YourLib.MDA, for example, follow these steps:

1. Open a module window in YourApp.MDB.
2. Choose Tools ➪ References and then click the Browse button in the References dialog box.
3. In the Files of Type dialog box, select Databases (*.mdb, *.mda, *.mde).
4. Locate your library database (YourLib.MDA in this example).
5. Click OK.

Tip   You should see your library database name in the list of available references in the References dialog box. If your library contains a procedure with a name that is also found in another referenced library, a call to this procedure will invoke the first library in the references list to contain the procedure name. If your code is not being called, you can move your library higher on the list of referenced libraries or rename the procedure so that conflicts do not occur. You should take care in naming library procedures to reduce the risk of collisions with other libraries. Use a naming convention that has a good chance of being unique.

If you want to establish a reference at runtime in Visual Basic code, use one of the `Create reference` methods of the `References` collection.

Tip   Your application database can now call routines in the referenced database. The procedures that are called in your library must be Public procedures and must be resident in standard modules within the library database. Although your library procedures can use Private procedures in the library, the referencing database can't use those Private procedures. Additionally, you can't call functions that are contained in class modules within the library database. To use your library class methods, call public functions that are contained in standard modules that use the library class modules. Your library routines can be set up to return a calculated result and open Access objects that are stored in the library database. You can even use a library database to store custom toolbars.

The .MDE file type, which will be discussed later in this chapter, enables you to save your database as a compressed file with your source code removed. If you choose to save your library database as an .MDE file, and if your database references other databases, those referenced databases must also be in .MDE format before your save operation can be successful.

Calling functions in Dynamic Link Libraries

As you gain experience developing Access applications and libraries, sooner or later you'll find that you need a function that resides in a Windows Dynamic Link Library (DLL) or some third-party DLL. It is quite common today to find Access applications containing calls to the Windows Application Programming Interface (API) to take advantage of the power provided by the API.

To use functions contained in DLLs, you need to declare the functions to VBA. You use the `Declare` statement for this purpose. `Declare` informs VBA of the name of the DLL that contains the function being declared, as well as the arguments and argument types that the function expects. This information enables VBA to check your function call at compile time for proper argument types. The following `Declare` statement is specified in the CH43.MDA General Declarations section of the `General Functions` module to declare the common dialog `GetOpenFileName` function for opening a file (this code is included on the CD-ROM accompanying this book):

```
Declare Function GetOpenFileName Lib "comdlg32.dll" Alias _
"GetOpenFileNameA"  _

(pOpenfilename As OPENFILENAME) As Long
```

In the preceding `Declare` statement, `GetOpenFileName` is the name of the function that is being declared and is specified as residing in the DLL named by the `Lib` argument, comdlg32.dll.

The `Alias` argument specifies that `GetOpenFileNameA` is the actual name of the function in the comdlg32.dll. The program will use `GetOpenFileName`, but the actual function called will be `GetOpenFileNameA`.

The parentheses contain the arguments expected by the `GetOpenFileNameA` function. In this case, the function expects an OPENFILENAME structure to be passed into it. You need to declare this structure before the reference to it in the `Declare` statement.

The final `As Long` indicates to Visual Basic that `GetOpenFileNameA` returns a value of type `Long`. Alternatively, you can specify this return type as follows:

```
Declare Function GetOpenFileName& Lib "comdlg32.dll" Alias _
"GetOpenFileNameA" (pOpenfilename As OPENFILENAME)
```

Note the use of the & symbol at the end of the function name to designate the return type.

You can specify the arguments as `Optional`, `ByVal`, `ByRef`, or `ParamArray` to indicate the means of passing the arguments to the function, and each variable specified can also designate a type. Note that the variables specified in the `Declare` statement need not match those used in the actual call to the function, but the variables used in the call must match the type specified by position.

If you use `Optional` to specify an argument that may be passed to the function or omitted, you must designate the type of the argument as `Variant` and specify all remaining arguments as `Optional` also.

`ByVal` causes the variable's value to be passed to the function instead of to the variable's address. If an argument is designated as `ByVal`, the function can't modify the argument variable (with the exception of `String` arguments, which are covered later in this section).

`ByRef` causes the variable's address to be passed to the function. Argument variables passed in this manner can be modified by the called function. This is the manner in which you pass a variable to receive a return value other than that passed by the function's As `Type` specifier. In other words, some functions pass back a value indicating the success of the function execution in the function's As Type return value but also return other values into variables passed `ByRef`. If you don't specify an argument-passing method, the `ByRef` method is assumed.

The `ParamArray` specification can only be used as the last argument specifier and implies an `Optional` array of `Variant` elements. You may pass any number of arguments in place of this argument specification.

If a function doesn't require any arguments, you need only specify the parentheses with nothing inside of them.

Indicate the type of the argument after the argument name by using `As Type`, where `Type` can be any of the valid Visual Basic types, a user-defined structure as used in the `GetOpenFileName` function, an object type, or the generic type `Object`. If you use ByVal in front of a `String` type, Visual Basic passes a `C-Type` string; that is, a reference to a null-terminated string. This type of argument can be modified by the calling function.

Take a look at the `OpenFileDlg` function in the Ch43.MDA General Functions module. The function first sets up a string variable with the filters that will appear in the File of Type drop-down list in the `OpenFile` dialog box. These are the file types that will be listed in the directories chosen by the user of the File Open dialog box.

Next, various string variables are initialized, which will be assigned to members of the OPENFILENAME structure passed to the `GetOpenFileName` function. The `DlgTitle` string variable, for example, will be assigned to the `lpstrTitle` member of OPENFILENAME to display a custom title in the `FileOpen` dialog box when it appears.

After the initializations, the members of the variable `pOpenfilename` declared as an OPENFILENAME structure are given values before the actual call to the `GetOpenFileName` function. Note that some of the structure variables are assigned a value that is returned from another function, the `lstrcpy` function.

The `lstrcpy` function is another Windows API function found in kernel32.dll, as declared in the `Declare Function` statement in the General Declarations. This function copies the second argument string to the first argument string and returns the address (pointer) of the first argument string as a `Long`. This address is assigned to various member variables of the OPENFILENAME structure, which require an address value. Note that all these member variables begin with the letters *lp*, which stand for *long pointer*. This naming scheme is generally followed throughout the Win32 API.

Tip   Not all structure members with names beginning with the letters *lp* are assigned the return value of `lstrcpy`. Some are assigned a value of zero. A zero value in variables that store long pointers is interpreted as a null pointer. If you are working with API calls that require input address values or pointers and if they will accept null-valued pointers, you can assign zero and the function should be able to accept it.

After you have set up the OPENFILENAME structure for the call, the actual call to `GetOpenFileName` is made to open the `FileOpen` dialog box. The address of the file name chosen by the end user is returned in the `lpstrFile` member of OPENFILENAME. Again, `lstrcpy` assigns the file name to a string variable within the function. Because the `lpstrFile` points to a null-terminated string, one ending in `Chr$(0)`, the function strips the null character at the end of the file name by using the `InStr` and `Left$` functions of VBA. The resulting string is passed back to the caller of `OpenFileDlg`. This file name contains the full path of the file.

Win32 API calls and calls to other DLLs can be very valuable in your Access applications. Of course, you have to know the API functions and their syntax before using them successfully in your application, and some are easier to use than others. If you do decide to use a Win32 API call, you can pick up its declaration statement, structure declarations, and constant declarations from the Win32API.txt file that ships with the Office XP Developer. This is very handy documentation for understanding how to declare and call the available functions.

An Overview of a Few Access 2002 Add-Ins

This section presents an overview of some of Access's built-in add-ins. To give you a feel for the power of these tools, the following add-ins are explored in this section: The Switchboard Manager add-in, the Form Wizard, and the Command Button Control Wizard.

Using the Switchboard Manager

Switchboards are forms in an application that present a road map of the application components or subsystems. Using a switchboard, the end user can easily choose the part of the application that he or she wants to use, usually by clicking a button on the form. The switchboard is a main form presented to the user when the application starts up, or it can be a form buried in the application to help the end user through a series of tasks by acting as a checklist.

You can use the Switchboard Manager to build one or more switchboards for your application or to edit an existing switchboard built previously with the Manager. Use the following steps to create a new switchboard:

1. Click Tools ➪ Database Utilities and then select the Switchboard Manager.

2. If the Switchboard Manager doesn't find its Switchboard Items table resident in your database, it displays a dialog box that asks if you want to build a new switchboard. Click Yes.

3. In the Switchboard Manager dialog box, the default switchboard, which is referred to as a *page*, is highlighted (see Figure 43-2). Click the Edit button to add items to this switchboard.

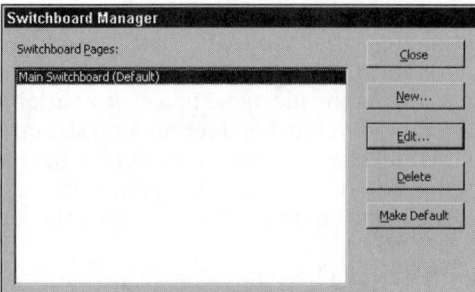

Figure 43-2: The Switchboard Manager dialog box

4. In the Edit Switchboard Page dialog box, you can type a name for the switchboard in the Switchboard Name box to change the default name, or you can use the default name *Main Switchboard* (see Figure 43-3). Click the New button to add a new item to this switchboard. The Edit Switchboard Item dialog box appears.

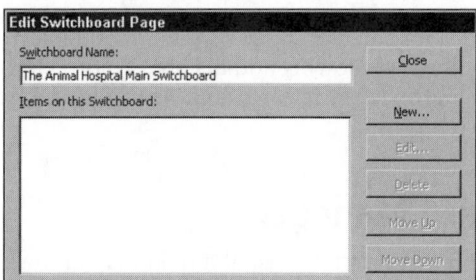

Figure 43-3: The Edit Switchboard Page dialog box

5. The Edit Switchboard Item dialog box presents three choices for the switchboard item (see Figure 43-4). In the Text box, enter a name for the item. This name appears on a switchboard button. In the Command combo box, select the command that you want to activate when the user clicks this button.

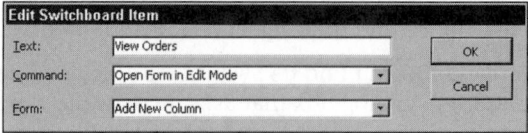

Figure 43-4: The Edit Switchboard Item dialog box

What you enter in the Form box, which is the third entry, varies with the selection in the Command combo box. If you select the command Go To Switchboard, for example, the third entry needs to specify the name of the switchboard to activate. If you specify a command of Run Code, the third entry needs to be the name of the function to run. Some command selections, such as Design Application, don't need a third entry.

6. After entering your choices for this switchboard item, click OK. Repeat adding new items until you have completed your switchboard entries for this switchboard.

7. In the Edit Switchboard Page dialog box, you can edit an item by clicking the Edit button, delete an item by clicking the Delete button, or reposition an item by clicking the Move Up or Move Down buttons.

8. When you have completed your switchboard, click the Close button.

After you have completed these steps, you will notice that the Switchboard Manager has created a Switchboard Items table in your database and a form with the name that you selected in the Edit Switchboard Page dialog box. Open the form to see the result of your work. Try out the choices to ensure that they do what you intended; if they don't, you can reopen the Switchboard Manager to edit your choices. Figure 43-5 shows a single action switchboard.

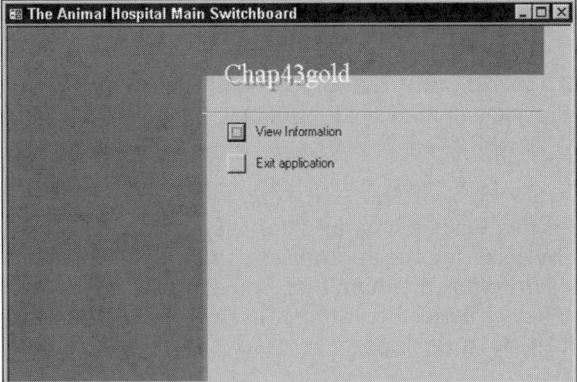

Figure 43-5: A very simple switchboard with two menu choices

Note If you use the Switchboard Manager to create a switchboard form, you should also use the Manager to edit the form. This practice keeps the Manager's table of switchboard items in sync with the form and makes it easier to manage your switchboards.

Using the Form Wizard

The Form Wizard is one of seven wizards that you can choose from when you elect to build a new form. This wizard is an example of an add-in that creates a form object and controls based on selected fields from the table or query that you name in the New Form dialog box before launching the wizard.

The first page of the Form Wizard asks you to select the fields that you want on the form (see Figure 43-6). You can choose to add all fields from the Available Fields list by clicking the >> button, or you can choose specific fields and click the > button for each field to move it to the Selected Fields list box.

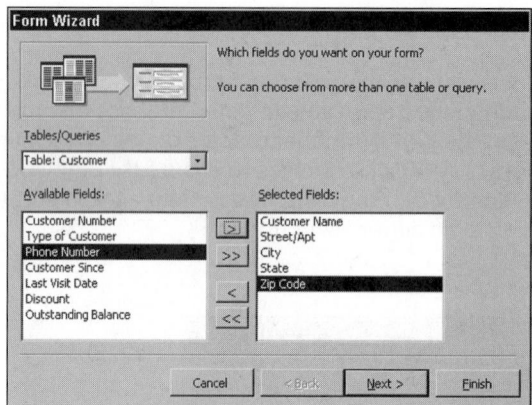

Figure 43-6: The first page of the Form Wizard that ships with Access

If you have relationships established in your database, you can choose fields from multiple tables simply by selecting the appropriate query using multiple tables from the Tables/Queries drop-down combo box. You can also select fields from numerous tables. If you select tables that are not in the relationships, the wizard asks if you want to edit the relationships.

Note If you do elect to edit the relationships, you will need to restart the Form Wizard in order to build your form.

The next page displayed by the wizard depends on the selections that you made on the first page. If you selected fields from only one table or query, the second page that displays asks you what layout you want for the form (see Figure 43-7). You can choose from the options shown in Table 43-1.

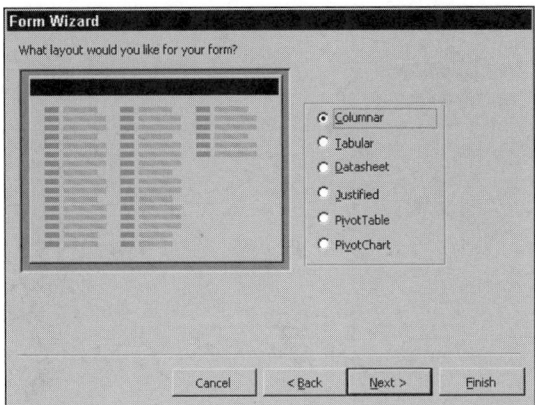

Figure 43-7: The Layout page of the Form Wizard

Table 43-1
Form Wizard Layout Types

Layout Type	Description
Columnar	The selected fields are laid out in a column down the form; one record is displayed at a time.
Tabular	The selected fields are laid out across the form; multiple records are displayed.
Datasheet	The selected fields are laid out in datasheet format across the form width; multiple records are displayed.
Justified	The selected fields are laid out in tabular fashion across the form, but the fields are joined or justified on multiple lines and only one record is displayed at a time.
PivotTable	The form opens in PivotTable view. You can view detail or summarized data by arranging fields in the filter, row, column, and detail areas.
PivotChart	The form opens in PivotChart view. You can display data visually by selecting a chart type and you can view data by arranging fields in the filter, series, category, and data areas.

If you selected fields from multiple tables/queries on the first page of the wizard, the second page asks you for the type of view that you want for each field source (see Figure 43-8). If a table selected in the list box is a one-sided table in the defined relationships (a parent table), you can select the Form with subform(s) option or the Linked forms option for a view. Selecting a many-sided table (a child table) in the list box enables you to choose the Single form option as a view.

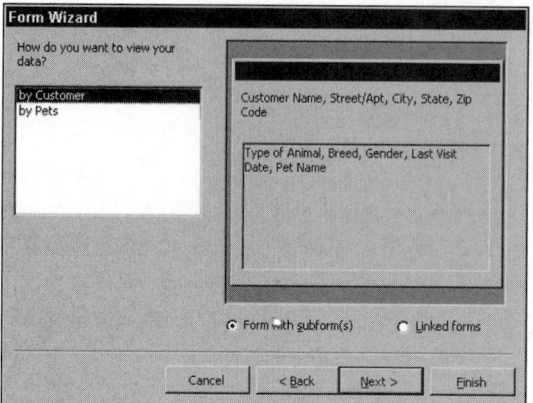

Figure 43-8: The View Selection page of the Form Wizard prompts you for a view type when you have selected fields from multiple related tables/queries.

For a parent table, choosing the Form with subform(s) option creates a parent form containing the fields that you selected from the one side of the related tables, and a subform for the fields that you selected from the many sides of the related tables. Selecting the Linked forms option as a view type creates a parent form for the one-sided fields and a separate child form for the many-sided fields that are linked by a command button on the parent form.

Choosing the Form with subform(s) option causes the next page of the wizard to prompt you for a layout of the subform. You can choose between the Tabular or Datasheet options.

After selecting the fields, the optional view, and the layout, the wizard asks you to select a style for the form and controls (see Figure 43-9). You have ten choices for styles. Selecting the styles from the list displays a preview in the left pane of the page.

The last page of the wizard asks you for a title for your form (see Figure 43-10). If you have linked forms, you can enter a title for each form. The last choice that you have before creating the form is to open the form and view the data that the form is based on or open the form in Design view to make changes. Click the Finish button after making these choices to start the build process.

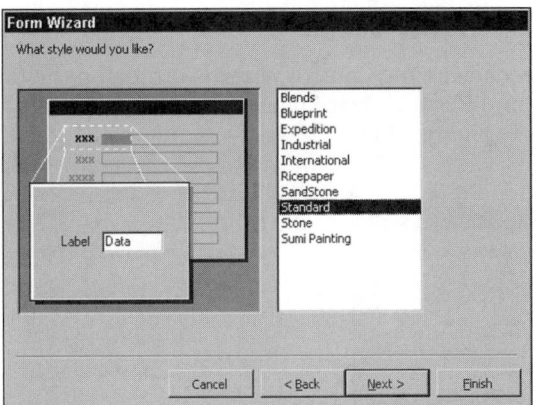

Figure 43-9: The Form Wizard page for selecting the form style applied to the form and controls

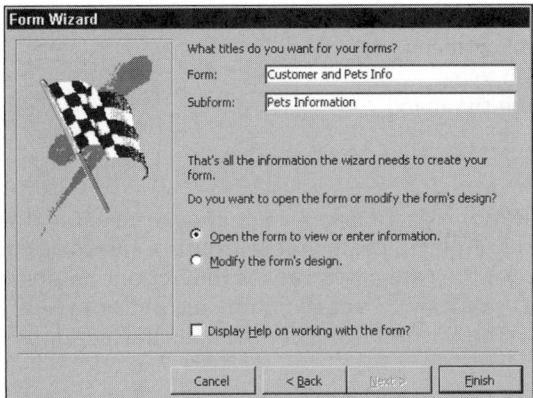

Figure 43-10: The last page of the Form Wizard prompts for a title and for the way that you want the new form to open

The Form Wizard does a good job with the information that it collects, but like many of the wizards, you will most likely use this wizard as a starting point and make your own design changes to achieve the desired result.

Using the Command Button Wizard

If you enable Control Wizards by clicking the Control Wizards button on the toolbox in form design mode, the Command Button Wizard launches when you insert a command button onto a form (see Figure 43-11).

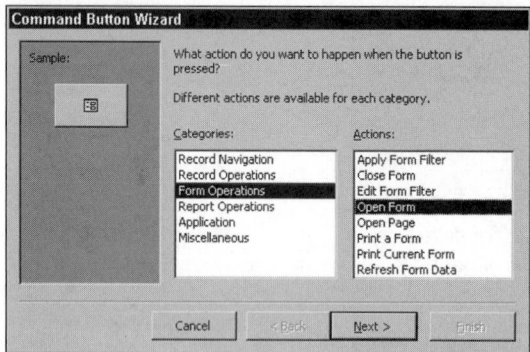

Figure 43-11: The first page of the Command Button Wizard asks you for an action to be associated with the click event of the command button.

The first page of the Command Button Wizard asks you to choose an action to run when a user clicks the command button. You can choose from six categories in the Categories list box. Selecting one of the categories causes the Actions list to be filled with actions in the selected category. Select an action and click the Next button at the bottom of the wizard form. The following are the available action categories:

- ✦ **Record Navigation:** Includes the actions Find Next, Find Record, Go to First Record, and others.

- ✦ **Record Operations:** Includes the actions Add New Record, Delete Record, and others.

- ✦ **Form Operations:** Includes the actions Edit Form Filter, Open Form, Print a Form, and others.

- ✦ **Report Operations:** Includes the actions Preview Report, Print Report, Send Report to File, and others.

- ✦ **Application:** Includes the actions Quit Application, Run Application, Run MS Excel, and others.

- ✦ **Miscellaneous:** Includes the actions Print Table, Run Macro, Run Query, and others.

Subsequent pages of the wizard depend on the selected action. For example, if you choose the Open Form action from the Form Operations category, the next page prompts you for a form name to be associated with the Open command. If you choose Run Query from the Miscellaneous category, the wizard prompts you for the query name to run.

Eventually, you get to choose between having text or a picture on the button (see Figure 43-12). If you choose Text, you can enter the text to be displayed on the button face. If you choose Picture, you can select a picture from the list or click the Browse button to find a picture file to be loaded and displayed on the button face.

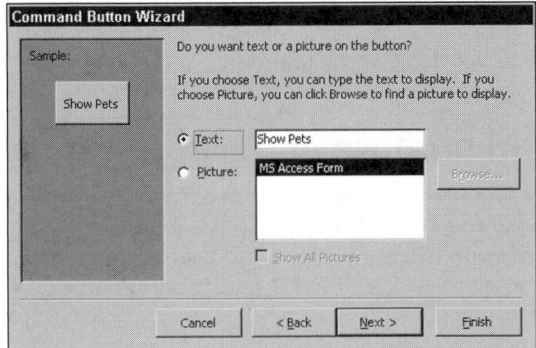

Figure 43-12: The Command Button Wizard dialog box, where you specify your choice of having text or a picture displayed on the button face

The final page of the wizard asks for the name that you want to give to the command button. After entering the name, click the Finish button to set the chosen properties. Canceling from this page only cancels the wizard; it does not cancel the insertion of the command button onto the form. To use the wizard again for this button, delete the button and reinsert a new one onto the form.

The Command Button Wizard is a good example of a property wizard that can help you set up your applications quickly. It also gives you an indication of what you can do with add-in technology.

Creating Your Own Add-Ins

This section presents an overview of the steps for creating and installing an add-in. The CD-ROM at the back of this book contains the file CH43Gold.MDA as a sample add-in, which creates a table, form, and report object based on the selections that you make in the wizard.

The following are the basic steps that you take in developing an add-in:

1. Consider the purpose of the add-in and what type of add-in best fits this purpose.

2. Design the add-in user interface and the flow of control for the add-in.

3. Code the add-in by using code-behind-forms and modules.

4. Test your add-in.

5. Implement your add-in.

    This step includes the preparation of the add-in for use with the Add-In Manager.

The following sections discuss each of these steps in order.

Considering the add-in purpose and type

The first task in developing your add-in is to decide what task the add-in will accomplish. What is the purpose of the add-in? Will it help the end user create some object, such as a report or form? Will it guide the end user through a series of steps toward the completion of some task? Will it aid in setting some property value or in selecting a value for a control?

Thinking about the purpose of the add-in and how it will be used helps you to determine how to design the add-in and how it should be invoked.

If your add-in will create an Access object, such as a form or report, you may want to consider a form or report wizard invoked from the New button on the Form or Report tab of the database window. For this type of add-in, you need to query the end user for information about controls, such as their names and types, about data sources for the form, and about the look and feel of the form layout — just as the built-in Form Wizard does.

If you need to provide an aid for creating a property value, or if you need help deciding on a value for a field based on the answers to a set of questions and values in the database, then you may want to consider using a builder as an add-in launched in the context of a control on a form, or in design mode for a form or report.

When your analysis determines that the add-in is not associated with any particular object or control context and should be generally available to the end user of Access or your application, you can choose to implement a menu add-in that end users can choose whenever they need the tool.

Designing the add-in user interface and flow of control

In designing the add-in user interface and the flow of control within the add-in, you need to consider how the user will interact with the add-in in order to enter information in a logical manner as well as the dependencies among the information collected.

In this phase of the design process, you decide where to place prompts for information, which prompts to group together on a form, and in which order to present the prompts. As in the Form Wizard discussed previously in this chapter, the second page to appear in the wizard is dependent on the user's selection(s) on the first page. When the user selects fields from only one data source, the wizard displays the page prompting for the layout to apply to the form. When the user selects fields from multiple data sources, the wizard displays a prompt for the type of view to use. This dependent action by a wizard may also be necessary in your add-in.

Diagramming flow of control

You may find it helpful to design your add-in flow of control on paper first. Start by drawing boxes to represent pages of dialog to present to the user. Connect those boxes by a line denoting direct passage of control from one page to the next, or by a diamond shape denoting one or more decisions. A diamond may be connected to any number of other boxes. The line connections indicate the path the flow will take based on the outcome of a decision point.

The decisions that you specify can range from very simple to very complex and may include decisions that are based on the outcome of edits on the entered data. If you need to perform edits on the entered data on a page-by-page basis, a decision point in the flow of control may direct the flow back to the same page if the edits fail (see Figure 43-13).

As you draw the boxes, label them with their names and purposes. After you are satisfied with the flow and the decisions controlling that flow, you can go back to the diagram and start designing the user interface for each page.

> **Note** You may find that some add-ins need to present a means for the user to jump from one part of the add-in to another—possibly to skip a section that isn't necessary for the task that the end user wants to perform. In this case, you may provide a set of buttons on the add-in form to enable the end user to jump to the page of interest, or, if many choices are available, a drop-down list of pages from which the end user can choose. On your design diagram, you can designate the direct jump entry points by an arrow or other symbol at the page where the end user may jump to or enter.

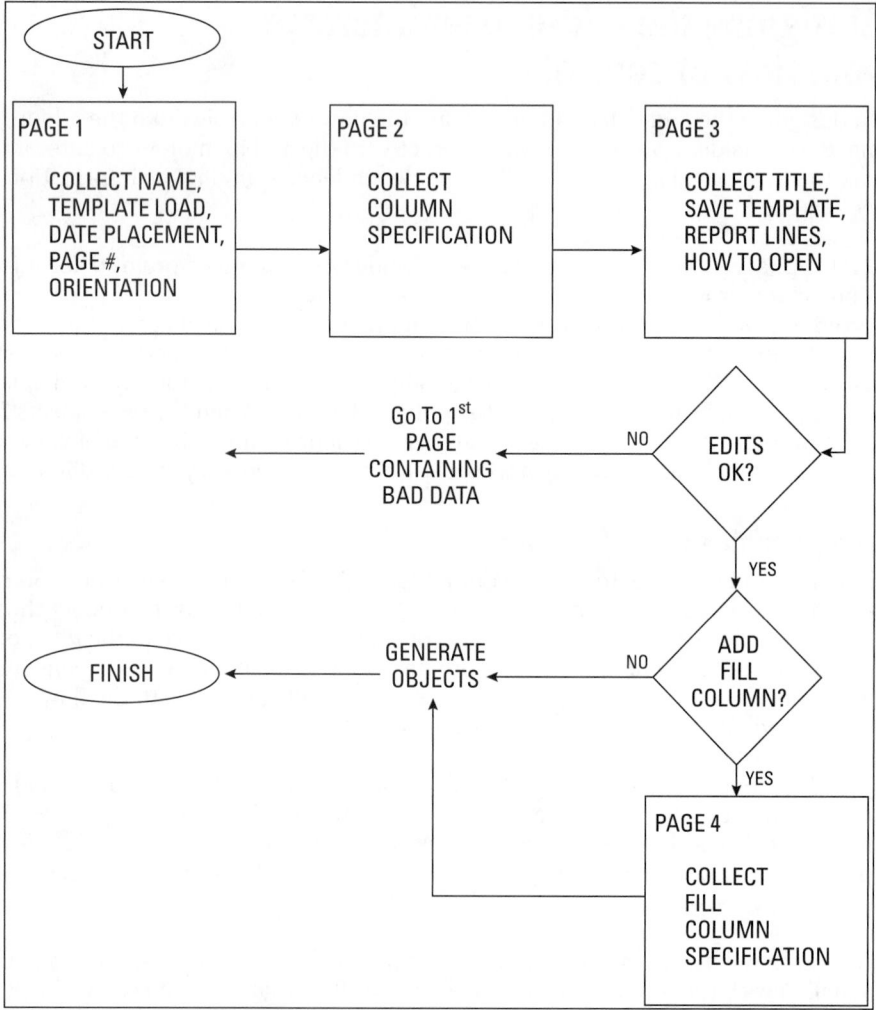

Figure 43-13: An example of a flow of control design for an add-in showing dialog pages and decision points

Designing the interface

You may again want to do the preliminary design for each page by drawing a layout of controls on paper, labeled by the page name to correspond to the flow diagram, or you may want to design a prototype directly in Access form design mode to help you achieve the desired look.

In designing your interface, try to keep it simple and consistent with the interface found in other Access add-ins. Don't try to cram too much into one dialog page. Keep the interface logical and collect information in a manner consistent with the way a typical end user would assume in entering the data. Be forgiving — if the end user makes a mistake, don't blow out of the add-in, making them reenter all the work that they did up to that point. Instead, provide a message indicating the problem and give them a chance to fix it.

> **Tip**
>
> We find it helpful in the design of our add-ins to put navigation buttons in a form footer and to develop the pages of the interface as multiple pages of the same form. We usually provide a means for the end user to save and reload information entered into the wizard. This is especially useful when the add-in collects information that can be used in subsequent uses of the add-in. In a Form Wizard, for example, the end user may enter information to create a particular form and then want to go back later and create basically the same form but with some different choices. End users are very appreciative if they can simply load the add-in choices that they made for the previous form and then make the changes that they want for the new form.

Coding your add-in

When coding your add-in, you need to be aware of which objects you are referring to — those in the database that called the add-in, or those in the database containing the add-in.

> **Note**
>
> An example of the two reference requirements is found in the sample add-in from CH43Gold.MDA on the CD-ROM. This add-in needs to refer to local tables in the add-in database for saving user entries that will be used in building the form and report. It doesn't make sense to create this table in the end user's database, because it is needed by the add-in only for creating the output objects. The output objects, table, form, and report, however, must be stored in the end-user database. You need a way to point your add-in to either the add-in database or the end-user database.

The `CodeDb` function returns a `Database` object that refers to the database in which the code is running. Because your add-in code is running to make the reference to the `CodeDb` function, the database returned is your add-in database. The `Name` property of this `Database` object is the full path and name of the add-in database. This is useful if you need to know where your add-in database resides on the user's hard drive.

The `Generate_Table` function in the CH43Gold.MDA sample wizard needs a database object for the user database that is calling the wizard and a database object for the wizard database. The function starts out by setting two database objects using the familiar `CurrentDb` to refer to the user database and the `CodeDb` function to refer to the wizard database. The syntax is as follows:

```
Dim dbDatabase As Database, userdb As Database
...
Set dbDatabase = CodeDb()
Set userdb = CurrentDb
```

Access 2002 provides several functions that you will find useful in coding your add-in. Table 43-2 shows these functions and their purposes.

Table 43-2	
Add-In Functions for Creating Forms, Reports, and Controls	
Function Name	*Purpose*
`CreateForm`	Creates a form in the user database and returns a `Form` object.
`CreateReport`	Creates a report in the user database and returns a `Report` object.
`CreateControl`	Creates a control on a form and returns a `Control` object. The form on which the control is placed must be open in design mode.
`CreateReportControl`	Creates a control on a report and returns a `Control` object. The report on which the control is placed must be open in design mode.
`CreateGroupLevel`	Creates a group on a report. The report must be open in design mode.

You may specify a template in both the `CreateForm` and `CreateReport` functions. The template is typically used to provide a new form or report with a standard set of properties and controls. This reduces the amount of work that the add-in must perform in order to create the final result. If the `Create` functions don't specify a template, the one designated in the Forms/Reports tab of the Options dialog box is used as a template.

The sample wizard uses these functions to create the data entry form and the report, both of which are based on the table created in the user database. Refer to the functions `Generate_Form`, `Generate_Controls`, and `Generate_Report` to see these functions in action.

In addition to using DAO methods and the preceding functions for creating and manipulating database objects, you may find that you need to generate code to provide some special processing in the resulting objects. In the sample wizard, the `Generate_Code` function creates a series of statements that make up the `Print` event of the Detail section of the newly created report. This code draws lines around the report columns if the user specified this option in the wizard dialog box. The next section explores the powerful module-editing capabilities that you have available to your add-in.

You can run a preliminary test of your add-in by running the entry point function that's called by Access when the user invokes your add-in. Any objects generated by the add-in will end up in the add-in database because the user database and add-in (CodeDb) database are the same database. Using this testing technique, you can at least test the flow of control and generation of objects — but you must wait until after installation into a user environment to complete these tests.

Coding on the run

Your wizard or add-in may need to build or edit modules at runtime. You may need to add code to a form module or, as the sample wizard does, add code to a report module. Or maybe you want to build some functions in a stand-alone module based on information entered by the user. Access provides many module-editing methods to help you build your modules at runtime. This section explains the methods associated with Module objects.

An Access application contains a Modules collection of all open standard and class modules. Each Module object in the Modules collection can be accessed in any of the standard syntax for referencing collection members. Forms and reports have Module properties that return a Module object that refers to their respective code modules. This property is used in the following discussion of the InsertText method. Within a Modules collection, an open form can also be referenced by using the following syntax:

```
Modules!Form_formname
```

Using InsertText

One method that you can use to add code to a module at runtime is the InsertText method. The syntax is as follows:

```
Module object.InsertText string
```

The object to which the InsertText method applies is a form, report, standard module, or class module in your application database. This method inserts the text at the end of the designated module. You have no control over where to insert the code lines with this method.

The following example adds a command button and inserts a Click Event Sub procedure called New_Customer_Click into the Account form:

```
Dim sProcText As String
Dim cmdButton As Control
sProcText = "Private Sub New_Customer_Click()" & vbCrLf
sProcText = sProcText & "MsgBox ""A New Customer Added""" &
vbCrLf
sProcText = sProcText & "End Sub" & vbCrLf
DoCmd.OpenForm "Account", acDesign
Set cmdButton = CreateControl("Account", acCommandButton,
acDetail, _ "", "", (3.25 * 1440), (0.9583 * 1440), (1.0417 *
1440), (0.25 * 1440))
cmdButton.Name = "New_Customer"
```

```
cmdButton.OnClick = "[Event Procedure]"
cmdButton.Caption = "New Customer"
Forms![Account].Module.InsertText sProcText
DoCmd.Close acForm, "Account", acSaveYes
DoCmd.OpenForm "Account"
```

sProcText holds the text to be inserted into the module. vbCrLf is a constant defined by Visual Basic representing a carriage-return line-feed pair that forces line ends within the string.

> **Note**   This example only inserts a subprocedure that does nothing but present a message box when called, but you can code any set of valid statements to build a complete, meaningful procedure for your application. InsertText fails unless you insert at least one statement — even if it's no more than a comment — within the procedure being inserted.

The DoCmd object's OpenForm method opens the form in design mode before adding the new procedure. The InsertText statement requires that the form be opened in design mode.

After opening the form in design mode, the CreateControl function adds a command button that is used to add a new customer. CreateControl returns a Control object, which is assigned to an Object variable called cmdButton.

The cmdButton control sets the name of the command button and its caption and designates that the OnClick event references an event procedure.

The InsertText method is then executed to insert the click event procedure into the form's module. The click event procedure receives the same name as the command button.

After the command button is on the form and tied to an event procedure, you can close the form by using the Close method of the DoCmd object. You can specify an acSaveYes argument to save the form changes without prompting the user.

The Accounts form is then reopened to display the form with the new button. Click the New Customer button to display the message inserted into the event procedure.

Using AddFromFile

Another method that is available to you for adding code to a module is the AddFromFile method, which adds lines from a text file into a module object. The syntax is as follows:

```
Module object.AddFromFile filename
```

Unlike the `InsertText` method—which inserts lines at the end of the module—the lines of the text file are inserted immediately after the declarations section and before the first procedure in the module designated by the module object. As in all module-editing methods, the module object must be open in design mode to enable editing.

The `AddFromString` method works exactly like the `AddFromFile` method, but specifies a string as the source of the text lines instead of a file name.

Using CreateEventProc

The sample add-in discussed throughout this chapter needs to add an `OnPrint` event procedure to the report module that is generated by the wizard. This procedure creates borders around the printed text whenever the `OnPrint` event occurs. As you can see in the add-in, the entire procedure is built using the `InsertText` method. The `CreateEventProc` method is another way to add event procedures to form or report modules. Its syntax is as follows:

Form/Report Module object.CreateEventProc(name of event, name of _ object)

`CreateEventProc` adds a code stub to the specified form or report module for the specified event (first argument) that is associated with the specified object (second argument). A *code stub* consists of the statements that designate the beginning and ending of a procedure. After you have created the code stub for the new procedure, you can add the code that you want to execute for the event. In order to tell Access where to add the new lines of code, however, you need to know the line number of the new procedure in the module. Fortunately, the `CreateEventProc` returns the line number of the first line of the new procedure.

Note Lines in a module are numbered beginning with one. To determine the number of lines in a module, use the `CountOfLines` property.

Using InsertLines, ReplaceLine, and DeleteLines

To insert a line of code into the event procedure created with `CreateEventProc`, you can use the `InsertLines` method with the line number returned from the `CreateEventProc`. When you use the `InsertLines` method, any existing code at the line specified by the *line* argument moves down. The syntax is as follows:

```
Module object.InsertLines starting line, string to insert
```

Tip To add multiple lines, include the intrinsic constant `vbCrLf` at the desired line breaks within the string that make up the *string* argument. This constant forces a carriage return and line feed.

To replace a line, use the `ReplaceLine` method, which replaces the specified line number with the string argument. Its syntax is as follows:

```
Module object.ReplaceLine starting line, string to add
```

You may decide to store a module in your add-in database that contains a set of procedures, which you can use as templates in creating the code that your add-in will insert into the target database. It's likely that these template procedures will contain more code than is necessary for a given target module, and you'll need a way to delete certain lines from the templates as you build the target code. The module's `DeleteLines` method will come in handy for this purpose. The following is the syntax:

```
Module object.DeleteLines starting line, line count
```

`DeleteLines` deletes the number of lines specified by the line count argument, starting at the line specified by the starting line argument. Note that there is no designation of the procedure name in this method. The method works entirely by line numbers. If you know the name of the routine that you want to delete, or maybe an offset from the first line of the routine, how do you get the line number so you can start deleting? The `Find` method can come to the rescue. Use the following syntax:

```
Module object.Find(text to find, starting line, starting
column, _ ending line, ending column, _
optional wholeword, optional matchcase, optional pattern)
```

Tip

The `text to find` argument specifies the text to search for. When you have a module being used to hold template procedures in an add-in, as discussed previously, you can add comment lines or labels to the procedures or parts of procedures that designate the sections that you want to work with. To get the starting position of these procedures or sections, specify the label or keyword in the comment as the `text to find` in the `Find` method and nothing in the starting line argument. The `Find` method returns the line number of the text that you are searching for, and you can add one to get the line after it.

If you know the approximate line number of the text to find in the module, you can set the `starting line` argument to that line number and `Find` will start its search at that line number. Whether the `starting line` argument is preset or not, the `Find` method returns the line number of the location of the search text in the module. The `starting column` can be preset to the column of the starting line in which you want to start the search. `Find` sets the column number of the search text in this argument when it returns with a found condition.

`Ending line` and `ending column` work in a manner similar to `starting line` and `starting column`. You can specify the line that you want the search to stop on in `ending line`, and you can specify the column that you want the search to stop on in `ending column`. On return, `Find` sets the `ending line` argument to the line number that the search text ends on and `ending column` to the column of the line at which the search text ends. The last three arguments are optional. `Wholeword` tells `Find` to search for whole words only. If you specify `port` as a `text to find` argument and set the `wholeword` argument to `True`, `Find` searches for `port` as a whole word. Setting `wholeword` to `False`, or not specifying it at all causes `Find` to stop searching on any word containing `port`, such as sup*port* or r*eport*.

Setting the matchcase argument to True causes Find to match the case of the text to find, and a setting of False disregards case.

You can use wildcard characters, such as * and ?, in the text to find argument to do a pattern-matching search. To initiate pattern matching, set the pattern argument to True.

Tip

You can use Find to search through all occurrences of a text string by issuing the Find method with an empty starting line argument or an argument of 0. If the Find method returns True, the text was found and the starting line argument is set to the line number where the text was found. Issuing the Find method again with this line number preserved in the starting line argument and starting column set to a value at least one greater than the value returned by Find causes the method to find the next occurrence of the text string. Continue with this technique until Find returns False.

Using ProcBodyLine and ProcStartLine

The ProcBodyLine property also returns the starting line number of a given procedure name. The syntax is as follows:

```
Module object.ProcBodyLine(name of proc, kind of proc)
```

Use one of the following predefined constants in the kind of proc argument:

Constant	Procedure Type
vbext_pk_Get	Property Get
vbext_pk_Let	Property Let
vbext_pk_Set	Property Set
vbext_pk_Proc	Sub or Function

ProcBodyLine returns the line number of the Proc statement. If you want the line number of the start of the procedure, which may include comments and compiler constants placed before the procedure statement, use the ProcStartLine property with the same arguments used in the ProcBodyLine.

If you need to retrieve one or more lines from a module, use the Lines property with the first argument set to the starting line number that you want to retrieve and the second argument set to the number of lines to retrieve. Use this syntax:

```
Module object.Lines(starting line, number of lines)
```

Use any of the methods previously discussed to get the starting line number and then the Lines property to retrieve the number of lines that you need in a string variable. You can then edit the string with standard VBA string editing functions and place the lines back into the module or into another module.

Finding the number of lines in a module

Two properties are available to find the number of lines within a module. The ProcCountLines property returns the number of lines in a given procedure, including any comments and compiler constants immediately above the procedure statement. The following is the syntax:

```
Module object.ProcCountLines(name of proc, kind of proc)
```

The kind of proc argument is specified in the same way as for ProcBodyLine, as discussed previously.

The CountOfDeclarationLines property is the second property that returns a line count. This property returns the number of lines in the declaration section of the specified module. The syntax is as follows:

```
Module object.CountOfDeclarationLines
```

Tip

You can use the CountOfDeclarationLines property to find the end of the module's Declaration section.

Compiling modules

After completing your module editing, you can force a compile of the modules by using the RunCommand method of the DoCmd or Application object. For example, to compile and save all modules, execute the following RunCommand before closing the edited modules:

```
DoCmd.RunCommand acCmdCompileAndSaveAllModules
```

When your add-in has finished its work, you should refresh the user's database window to display any new objects that your add-in has added to their database. To do this, execute the RefreshDatabaseWindow method. This is a method of the application object, and there are no arguments to provide.

Preparing your add-in for installation

Now that you have designed, coded, and tested your add-in, you can prepare it for distribution. This section deals with two topics:

✦ Preparing your add-in database so that the Add-In Manager can install it

✦ Saving your add-in as an .MDE file to protect your work and make a smaller file for distribution

To prepare your add-in database for installation, you must first provide the Add-In Manager with some information. The Add-In Manager needs to know what kind of add-in that you want to install and what information that you want to provide to the end user who will perform the installation.

Using the USysRegInfo table

The Add-In Manager uses the USysRegInfo table and several database properties when installing your add-in. The USysRegInfo table is not automatically provided. You can build the USysRegInfo from scratch or import it from any of the add-ins that ship with Access 2002. The layout of the USysRegInfo table is shown in Table 43-3.

Note   The USysRegInfo table is a system table and is usually hidden. To view system tables, click Options on the Tools menu, click the View tab, and then select the System objects check box.

Table 43-3
Definition of the USysRegInfo Table

Field Name	Field Type	Field Size
SubKey	Text	255
Type	Number	Long Integer
ValName	Text	255
Value	Text	255

The records that you insert into the USysRegInfo table depend on the type of add-in that you have built. The first record in this table creates a key in the registry to register your add-in.

The SubKey field of the first record is the key name and must be the same value on all records in the USysRegInfo table describing a given add-in. The SubKey starts with the root of the registry tree under which you want to install your add-in. Set this value to HKEY_LOCAL_MACHINE, or if you are using a profile, set it to HKEY_CURRENT_ACCESS_PROFILE. The next part of the SubKey entry depends on the type of add-in that you are installing. If you are installing a builder, Control Wizard, or ActiveX Control Wizard, the next part of the SubKey must specify Wizards as the subkey under the root that you previously chose, followed by the type of wizard, the subtype of wizard, and the name of the wizard, as shown in the following:

```
HKEY_LOCAL_MACHINE\Wizards\type wizard\subtype wizard\wizard
name
```

For a Control Wizard, set the type of wizard part of the string to Control Wizards and the subtype of wizard to the name of the control that the wizard is associated with. Here is a list of valid control names:

- ✦ BoundObjectFrame
- ✦ CheckBox
- ✦ ComboBox
- ✦ CommandButton
- ✦ Image
- ✦ Label
- ✦ Line
- ✦ ListBox
- ✦ OptionButton
- ✦ OptionGroup
- ✦ PageBreak
- ✦ Rectangle
- ✦ SubformSubreport
- ✦ TextBox
- ✦ ToggleButton
- ✦ UnboundObjectFrame

If you are installing a builder, set the type of wizard to Property Wizards and the subtype of wizard to the name of the property to associate the builder with. You can refer to the Properties dialog box for an object in design mode to find the property name. Enter that name without spaces as the subtype of wizard.

For ActiveX Control Wizards, the type of wizard is ActiveX Control Wizards and the subtype of wizard is the value of the ActiveX control's Class property. To find the class name, select the ActiveX control in design mode and view its Properties dialog box.

The SubKey format is a little different for wizards that create Access objects, such as tables, forms, and reports. With these wizards, the SubKey specifies a type of wizard and wizard name but no subtype of wizard. The format of the SubKey is as follows:

```
HKEY_LOCAL_MACHINE\Wizards\type of wizard\name of wizard
```

The type of wizard may be one of the following values:

✦ Form Wizards

✦ Query Wizards

✦ Report Wizards

✦ Table Wizards

Menu add-ins have a SubKey format that registers your add-in under a Menu Add-Ins subkey rather than a Wizards subkey in the registry. The format of the SubKey is the following:

```
HKEY_LOCAL_MACHINE\Menu Add-Ins\name of add-in
```

The name of the wizard for Access Object Wizards appears in the New Object dialog box, and for a menu add-in, the name of the add-in appears in the Add-Ins submenu. For many of these menu add-ins, you will see an underlined letter in the add-in name. This is an access key for the add-in that enables the end user to access the menu add-in via the keyboard: Pressing Alt and then the underlined key launches the add-in. For example, to launch the Switchboard Manager add-in via the keyboard, hold down the Alt key and press *T* for *Tools*, *I* for Add-*I*ns, and *W* for *Sw*itchboard Manager. To set an access key for your menu add-in, type **&** before the letter that you want for an access key.

The Type field of the first record must be zero to denote that the subkey is to be added to the Registry, and the ValName and Value fields must be blank.

After the first record has been defined, subsequent records define values that are entered into the add-in entry in the registry. All records must have the same SubKey value as the first record to identify them as belonging to that add-in.

The Type field on records that follow the first record denote the type of value to be entered into the registry. These types can be the following:

Type Field Value	Type of Registry Value
1	REG_SZ (String)
4	DWORD (REG_DWORD in the Windows NT registry)

ValName specifies the name of the value to be entered, and Value contains the value itself. The number of values to add to the USysRegInfo table depends on the type of add-in being added. Table 43-4 lists the values that you need to add for the various add-in types. (Remember that all SubKeys are the same as the first record in USysRegInfo for the add-in being defined.)

Table 43-4
Values to Add to the USysRegInfo Table for Add-Ins

Type Field	ValName Field	Value Field
Add-in Type: Control, ActiveX, or Builder Wizards		
4	Can Edit	1 = Wizard can modify control or property; 0 = Wizard can't modify.
1	Description	Text displayed in the Choose Builder dialog box when more than one add-in has been defined for the same control or property.
1	Function	Indicates the name of the function that starts the add-in.
1	Library	Specifies the path and name of the add-in database.
Add-in Type: Access Object Wizards		
1	Bitmap	Specifies the path and name of the bitmap that is displayed for the wizard in the New Object dialog box.
4	Datasource Required	1 = User must specify a table or query name as the source of data for the object to be created by the wizard; 0 = datasource not required; this value is only necessary for Form and Report Wizards.
1	Description	Text displayed in the New Object dialog box.
1	Function	Indicates name of the function that starts the add-in.
4	Index	Specifies the order of the Description text displayed in the New Object dialog box; 0 = The first entry in the dialog box.
1	Library	Specifies the path and name of the add-in database.
Add-in Type: Menu Add-In		
1	Expression	Specifies the name of the function that starts the add-in preceded by an equal sign.
1	Library	Specifies the path and name of the add-in database.

On the
CD-ROM

The CH43Gold.MDA sample add-in on the CD-ROM is an Object Wizard that creates a table, form, and report. The USysRegInfo records for this add-in are shown in Table 43-5.

Table 43-5
USysRegInfo Records Defining the
CH43Gold.MDA Sample Add-In

Subkey	Type	ValName	Value
HKEY_CURRENT_ACCESS_ PROFILE\ Menu Add-Ins\ Bible Sample Wizard	0		
HKEY_CURRENT_ACCESS_ PROFILE\ Menu Add-Ins\ Bible Sample Wizard	1	Expression	=StartWiz()
HKEY_CURRENT_ACCESS_ PROFILE\ Menu Add-Ins\ Bible Sample Wizard	1	Library	ch43Gold.mda

Setting database properties

Your second task in preparing your add-in for installation is to set some database properties. The information that you provide in these properties appears in the Add-In Manager dialog box to identify your add-in and your company. To set these properties, follow these steps:

1. Open the Database Properties dialog box by selecting Database Properties from the File menu or by right-clicking the database container window and selecting Properties.

2. Click the Summary tab in the Database Properties dialog box.

3. Enter a title for your add-in, your company name, and comments. The title appears in the Available Add-Ins list in the Add-In Manager dialog box and in the Add-Ins menu after the end user adds your add-in. The company name appears below the Available Add-Ins list box, and the comments appear directly below your company name.

4. Click OK to close the Database Properties dialog box.

After you have prepared your add-in for installation by the Add-In Manager, you can create an installation disk set. Before you build your installation disk set, however, you may want to save your add-in in .MDE format to reduce the file size and at the same time protect your secrets by removing source code.

Exploring .MDE files

Saving your database as an .MDE file causes Access to compile your database, save it, remove source code, and compact the database. These actions result in a smaller, more efficient database due to source code removal and optimizations.

In the .MDE file format, your database code and objects can't be viewed or modified by others, nor can they import the database forms, reports, and modules to another database. They can, however, import tables, queries, and macros from your database. Aside from these exceptions, though, your design is essentially locked up.

Caution   The .MDE format does come with one drawback: Because your source code is removed from the file, you have nothing to edit should your procedures use the module-editing features of VBA, as discussed previously in this chapter. If your add-in needs to use module editing to add or change add-in code on the fly, you can't use the .MDE format. If your add-in uses these VBA features to modify objects generated into the user database, however, an .MDE format is okay to use. This is generally what you will be doing in an add-in anyway.

If your database references other databases, such as a library database or another add-in database, those databases must also be in .MDE format. You can't access .MDA formatted files from an .MDE file. If you try to create an MDE file from an .MDB or an .MDA that references another Access database or add-in, Access displays an error message and doesn't let you complete the operation. If your .MDE contains references to other databases, make sure you have first saved the other databases as .MDE files. You must begin converting the databases to .MDE files in the order they are referenced. After you convert each database, be sure to update the reference in the calling database to point to the new .MDE file.

Building an .MDE file

To build the .MDE file, follow these steps:

1. Ensure that the database is closed by all possible users.

2. Choose Database Utilities from the Tools menu and click Make MDE File.

3. Enter the name of the database that you want to save in the Database To Save As MDE dialog box and click Make MDE.

4. Enter a database name and choose the .MDE file location in the Save MDE As dialog box.

Caution   The action of creating an MDE file is a one-way street. After the file is created, it's only good for execution. If you need to modify the design or convert to a future version of Access, you will need the original database in non-MDE format. Be sure to save your original database in a safe place.

If you don't use the .MDE format to distribute your database, be sure to compact the database before building your distribution disk set.

Using the Add-In Manager

With your USysRegInfo table and database properties set up, you are now ready to use the Add-In Manager to install your add-in. Note that the Add-In Manager can also be used to uninstall your add-in if necessary (but who would want to?).

Choose Add-Ins from the Tools menu and then click Add-In Manager. The Available Add-Ins list in the Add-In Manager dialog box lists add-ins that are currently installed (those with an *X* next to them) and files in the Office directory with an .MDA or .MDE extension.

You can install one of the add-ins in the list by choosing it and clicking Install, or you can add a new add-in by clicking Add New. After installing the add-ins that you want, click the Close button to exit the Add-In Manager dialog box.

The Add-In Manager accesses your USysRegInfo table and enters the keys and values that you specified into the system registry. You can use the Registry Editor to view your add-in entries.

With your add-in installed by the Add-In Manager, you can now run a complete test of the add-in to determine proper installation and functionality before distribution to your end users.

With the information provided in this chapter and the sample add-in in CH43Gold.MDA, you'll be able to develop your own add-ins and libraries, which will substantially enhance the features of your Access 2002 applications and ease the difficulty of your maintenance tasks.

✦   ✦   ✦

Access 2002 Specifications

This appendix shows the limits of Microsoft Access databases, tables, queries, forms, reports, and macros.

Microsoft Access Database Specifications

Databases

Attribute	Maximum
MDB file size	2GB (minus space needed for system objects)(Because your database can include attached tables in multiple files, its total size is limited only by available storage capacity.)
Number of objects in a database	32,768
Number of Modules	1,000
Number of characters in object names	64
Number of characters in a password	14
Number of characters in a user name or group name	20
Number of concurrent users	255

Tables

Attribute	Maximum
Number of characters in a table name	64
Number of characters in a field name	64
Number of fields in a record or table	255
Number of open tables	2,048 including tables opened by Microsoft Access internally
Table size	2GB (minus space needed for system objects)
Number of characters in a Text field	255
Number of characters in a Memo field	65,535 when entering data through the user interface; 1GB when entering data programmatically
Size of OLE object field	1GB
Number of indexes in a record or table	32
Number of fields in an index	10

Attribute	Maximum
Number of characters in a validation message	255
Number of characters in a validation rule	2,048
Number of characters in a table or field description	255
Number of characters in a record	2,000 (excludes Memo and OLE Object fields)
Number of characters in a field property setting	255

Queries

Attribute	Maximum
Number of tables in a query	32
Number of enforced relationships	32 per table minus indexes that are on the table for the fields or combinations of fields that are not involved in the relationship
Number of fields in a recordset	255
Dynaset size	1GB
Sort limit	255 characters in one or more fields
Number of sorted fields in a query	10
Number of levels of nested queries	50
Number of characters in a cell of the design grid	1,024
Number of ANDs in a WHERE or HAVING clause	99
Number of characters in a SQL statement	64,000 (approximately)

Forms and Reports

Attribute	Maximum
Number of characters in a label	2,048
Number of characters in a text box	65,535
Form or report width	22 inches (55.87 cm)

Continued

Forms and Reports *(continued)*

Attribute	Maximum
Section height	22 inches (55.87 cm)
Height of all sections plus section headers in design view	200 inches (508 cm)
Number of levels of nested forms or reports	7 (form-subform-subform)
Number of fields/expressions you can sort or group on (reports only)	10
Number of headers and footers in a report	1 report header/footer; 1 page header/footer; 10 group headers/footers
Number of printed pages in a report	65,536
Number of characters in an SQL statement that is the Recordsource or Rowsource property of a form, Report or control (both .mdb and .adp)	32,750
Number of controls or sections you can add over the lifetime of the form or report	754

Macros

Attribute	Maximum
Number of actions in a macro	999
Number of characters in a condition	255
Number of characters in a comment	255
Number of characters in an action argument	255

Access Projects Specifications

Access Project

Attribute	Maximum
Number of objects in a Microsoft Access project (.adp)	32,768
Modules (including forms and report modules)	1,000

Attribute	Maximum
Number of characters in an object name	64
Number of columns in a table	250 (MS SQL Server 6.5) 1,024 (MS SQL Server 7.0 and 2000)

Forms and Reports

Attribute	Maximum
Number of characters in a label	2,048
Number of characters in a text box	65,535
Form or report width	22 inches (55.87 cm)
Section height	22 inches (55.87 cm)
Height of all sections plus section headers in design view	200 inches (508 cm)
Number of levels of nested forms or reports	7 (form-subform-subform)
Number of fields/expressions you can sort or group on	10 (reports only)
Number of headers and footers in a report	1 report header/footer; 1 page header/footer; 10 group headers/footers
Number of printed pages in a report	65,536
Number of characters in an SQL statement that is The Recordsource or Rowsource property of a form, Report or control (both .mdb and .adp)	32 ,750
Number of controls or sections you can add over the lifetime of the form or report	754

Macros

Attribute	Maximum
Number of actions in a macro	999
Number of characters in a condition	255
Number of characters in a comment	255
Number of characters in an action argument	255

Microsoft SQL Server database

Maximum capacity specifications can be found in the SQL Server documentation.

Sharing a Database

To share an Access database that is on another computer, you must have one of the following on the other computer: a local installation of Access, a network installation of Access (licensed on a per-user basis), or a run-time application.

Microsoft Office XP Developer includes a royalty free license that allows you to install your run-time application on each computer.

To share a database, follow these steps:

1. Set up a shared folder on the computer that holds the database.
2. Copy the database to the shared folder.
3. Open the shared database from the local machine and verify that it is set to shared mode.
4. Once open, Select Tools ⇨ Options.
5. Select Advanced ⇨ Default open Mode ⇨ Shared.

✦   ✦   ✦

Mountain Animal Hospital Tables

he Mountain Animal Hospital Database file is made up of eight tables. There are four main tables and four lookup tables.

The main tables are

- ✦ Customer
- ✦ Pets
- ✦ Visits
- ✦ Visit Details

The lookup tables are

- ✦ States
- ✦ Animals
- ✦ Treatments
- ✦ Medications

This appendix displays a database diagram of all eight tables and the relations between them. Figures of each of the tables are shown in the Table Design window.

In addition to the Mountain Animal Hospital Database, there are several other databases that are used by the different chapters of this book. These include

- ✦ **Mountain Animal Start.mdb.** This database is used by many chapters to build the new objects. This database contains

  - All eight of the tables mentioned above
  - New Customer table (identical in structure to Customer)
  - Make Customer-Pets-Visits query

- ✦ **Access Import-Export.mdb.** This database is used by the import-export chapter to link and import existing databases from other formats and export to other databases. It is in its own directory under the main example directory. The database contains

  - Customer table
  - Treatments table
  - States table

This directory also contains these files:

  - Text files: Animals.txt; Medlimit.txt
  - Excel files: Medications.xls; Morecust.xls
  - dBASE files: Pets.dbf; Visitdtl.dbf
  - dBASE memo files: Pets.dbt; Visitdtl.dbt
  - dBASE III index file: Visitdtl.ndx
  - dBASE IV index file: Pets.mdx
  - HTML document: States.htm
  - Paradox file: VisitDtl.db

- ✦ **Mountain Animal Macros.mdb.** This database is used by the macro chapters to build the macros used in the book. It is in its own directory under the main example directory. The database contains

  - The primary eight tables in the Mountain Animal Hospital database
  - Queries: Adding General Pet Visit Info; Monthly Invoice Report
  - Forms: Customer; Customer with Buttons; Cust_Pet_Visit; Cust_Pet_Visit – Datasheet 2; Cust_Pet_Visit – Datasheet 3; Pet Display Form
  - Report: Invoice with Detail Section hidden; Monthly Invoice Report – No Cover
  - Macro: Cust_Pet_Visit_Update Form

- ✦ **Table Analyzer DB.mdb:** This database is used by the Access table analyzer to demonstrate how the table analyzer works. This database contains one table, Customer-Pet-Visit.

✦ **Mountain Animal HospitalSQL1.mdf.** This database is used by the SQL Server chapter to build the new objects.

✦ **Mountain Animal HospitalCS.adp.** This database is used by the Access Projects chapter to build the new objects.

✦ **Mountain Animal Data Access Pages.mdb.** This database is used by the Access Data Access Pages chapters to build the new objects and work with Data Access Pages. This database contains

- The primary eight tables in the Mountain Animal Hospital database

- Forms: Add a Customer and Pets (the primary table) and AddCustPetAnimals (its subform); Customer WebBrowserControl

- Reports: All Customer and Pets; Daily Hospital Report; Pet Directory

- Queries: All Customers and Pets Report (used by report); Pets, Owners, & Visits (used by form); Customer — Pet — Visit for HTML file; Customer Names for a Pet (Parameter Query); Daily Hospital Report (used by a report)

- External files: MyGlobe.gif; MyTemplate01.html; New Customer.html

Table Structures

Figure B-1 diagrams the Mountain Animal Hospital database in Access.

Figures B-2 through B-9 show the structures of the eight primary tables in the Mountain Animal Hospital and the Mountain Animal Start databases.

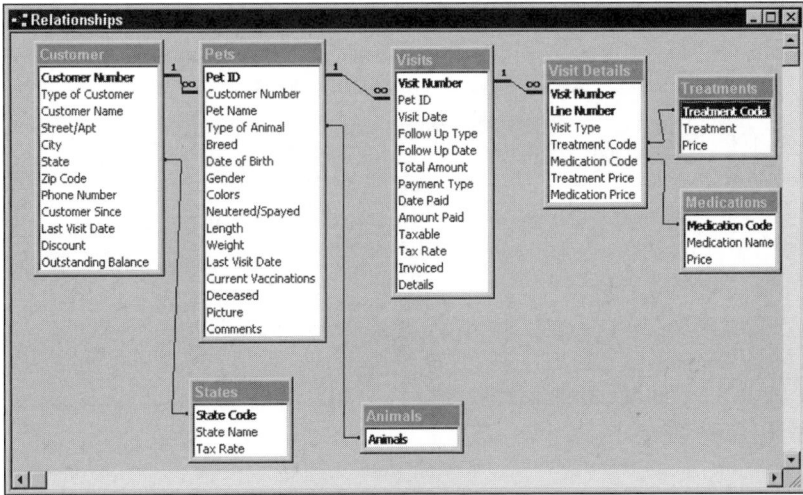

Figure B-1: The database diagram

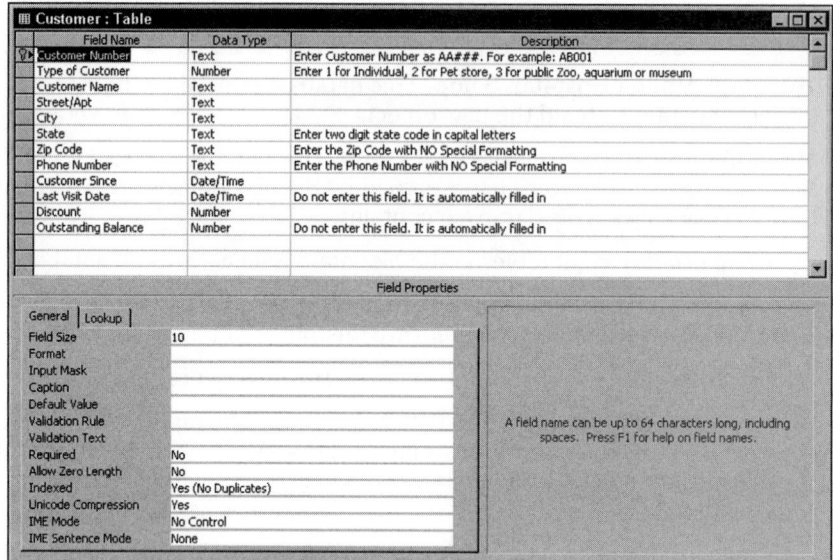

Figure B-2: The Customer table

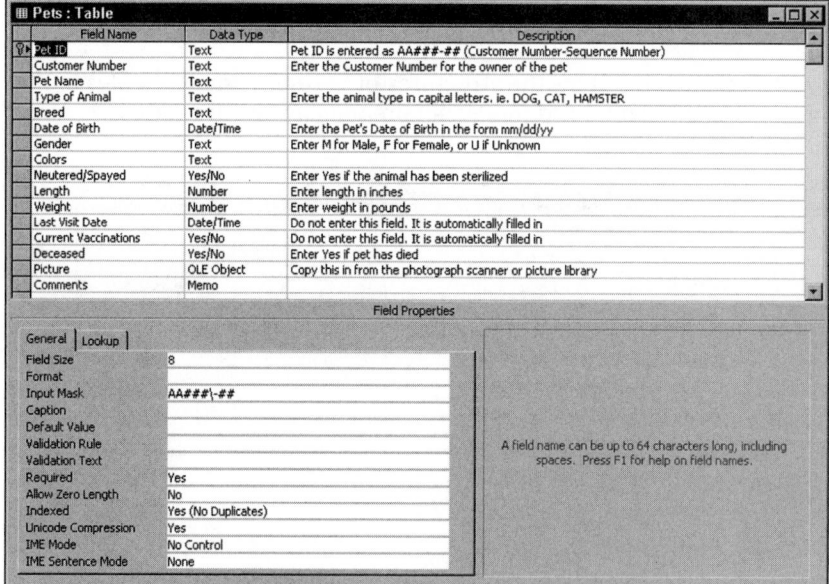

Figure B-3: The Pets table

Visits : Table

Field Name	Data Type	Description
Visit Number	Text	Enter the Visit Number as Year, Juilan day-sequence number (YYYYMMDD-##)
Pet ID	Text	Enter the Pet ID from the Pets table (AA###-##)
Visit Date	Date/Time	Enter the date of the visit. The default is the current date.
Follow Up Type	Text	Enter a valid Follow Up Type
Follow Up Date	Date/Time	Enter the next Follow Up Date
Total Amount	Currency	Do not enter this field. It is calculated by the invoice form
Payment Type	Text	Enter a valid payment type- Cash, Check, Charge, Account, Gratis
Date Paid	Date/Time	Enter the date the invoice is paid
Amount Paid	Currency	Enter the amount that was paid
Taxable	Yes/No	Enter the taxable status as Yes or No
Tax Rate	Number	Do not enter the tax rate. It is copied from the States table
Invoiced	Yes/No	Do not enter this field. It is No until the invoice is mailed and then it is Yes
Details	Memo	Enter any comments about the overall visit

Field Properties

General | Lookup

Field Size	11
Format	
Input Mask	
Caption	
Default Value	
Validation Rule	
Validation Text	
Required	No
Allow Zero Length	No
Indexed	Yes (No Duplicates)
Unicode Compression	Yes
IME Mode	No Control
IME Sentence Mode	None

A field name can be up to 64 characters long, including spaces. Press F1 for help on field names.

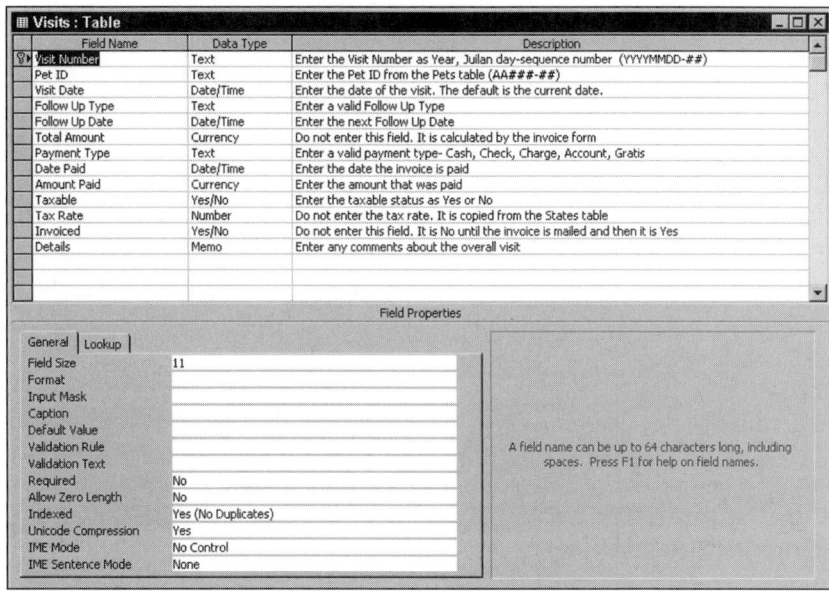

Figure B-4: The Visits table

Visit Details : Table

Field Name	Data Type	Description
Visit Number	Text	Enter the Visit Number from the Visits Table
Line Number	Text	Enter the invoice line number as a three digit number with leading zeros
Visit Type	Text	Enter a valid visit type
Treatment Code	Text	Enter a treatment code from the Treatments table
Medication Code	Text	Enter a medication code from the Medications table
Treatment Price	Currency	Do not enter this amount. It is copied from the Treatments table
Medication Price	Currency	Do not enter this amount. It is copied from the Medications table

Field Properties

General | Lookup

Field Size	11
Format	
Input Mask	
Caption	
Default Value	
Validation Rule	
Validation Text	
Required	No
Allow Zero Length	No
Indexed	Yes (Duplicates OK)
Unicode Compression	Yes
IME Mode	No Control
IME Sentence Mode	None

A field name can be up to 64 characters long, including spaces. Press F1 for help on field names.

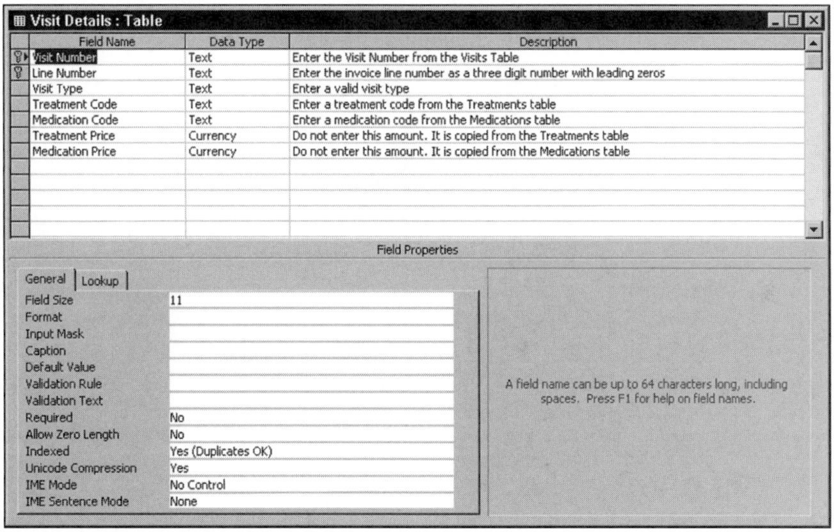

Figure B-5: The Visit Details table

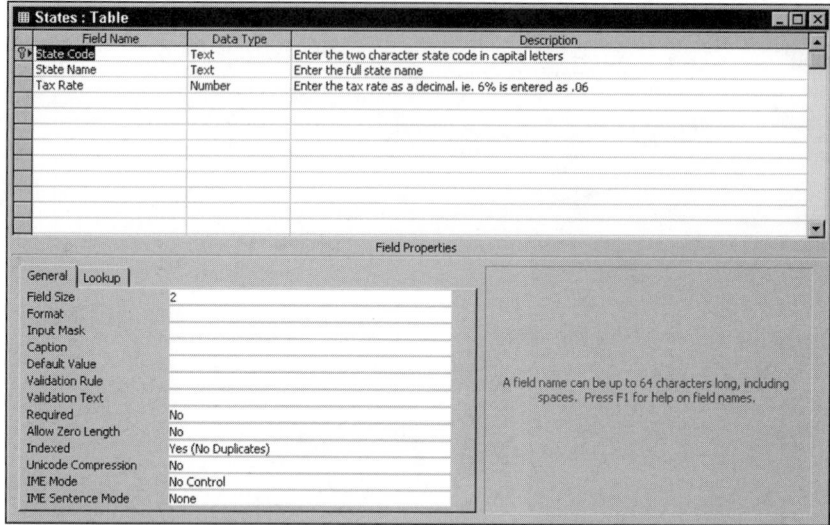

Figure B-6: The States table

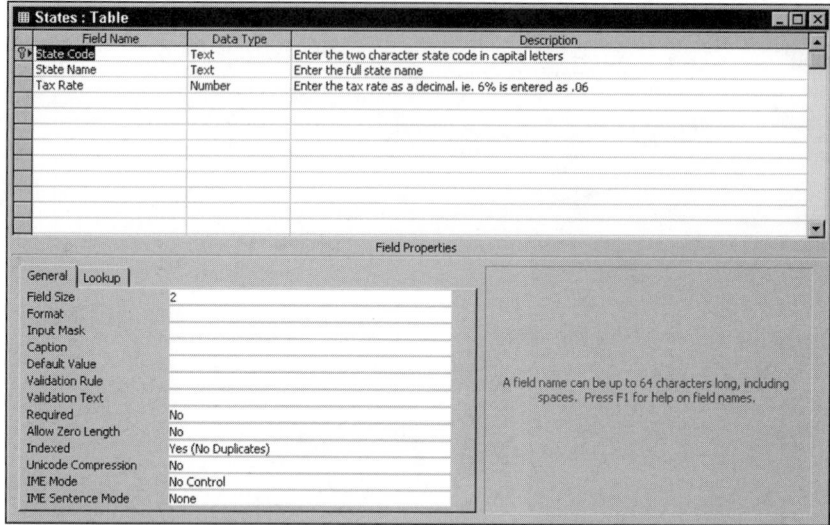

Figure B-7: The Animals table

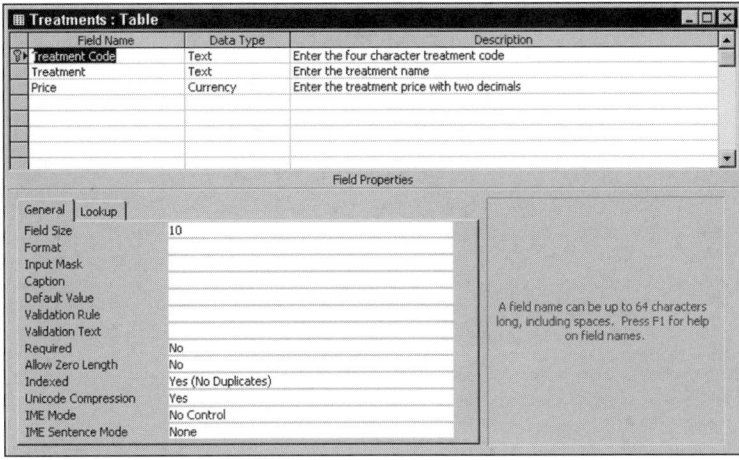

Figure B-8: The Treatments table

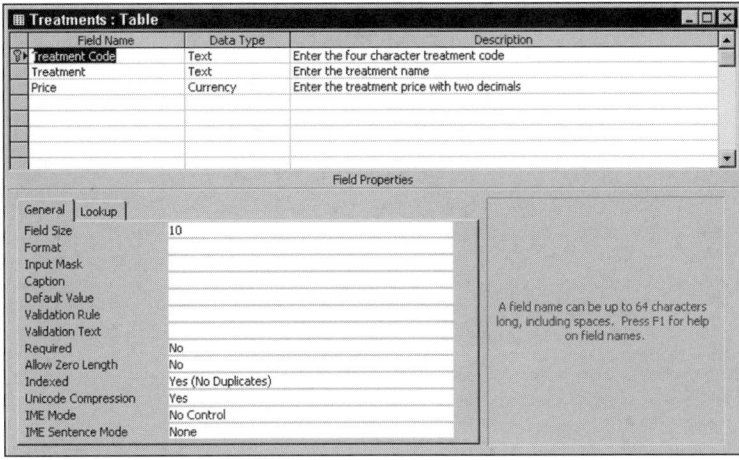

Figure B-9: The Medications table

✦　　✦　　✦

What's On the CD-ROMs

Two CDs are included in the Access 2002 Bible Gold Edition. Each contains examples, demos, trial versions, and free commercial software add-ons for Microsoft Access developers.

CD 1

CD 1 contains all of the example files created or referenced in this book. The CD will automatically load and display a standard installation dialog on your computer. You can use the installation wizard to install the example files and other files or you can run the individual executable files.

There are seven main directories on the CD. Some are divided into subdirectories. Most of the directories or subdirectories contain the executable installation files with an .EXE file extension. You can display the directories and files using Windows Explorer, then double click on any .EXE file to launch the install program for the files you want to copy to your hard drive. Each installation file will ask you where you want to put the file and some will set up a Start menu shortcut for you. You will find the installation wizard easier to use.

The seven main folders include

- ✦ **Acrobat Reader from Adobe** - The freeware version of a reader to view Acrobat .PDF files

- ✦ **Demos** - Demos of Database Creations, Inc. products for Access

- ✦ **eBook** - Text of the Access 2002 Bible Gold Edition in Adobe Acrobat (.pdf) format

- ✦ **Example Files** - Installs all of the database and other files used in the examples in the book

- ✦ **Free Access Software** - Real working software - not demos - from Database Creations, Inc.

✦ **Product Catalog** - Catalogs and brochures of products developed by Database Creations, Inc. and others

✦ **WinZip** - A shareware version of utility to compress data up to 90%. Great for sending files across email

Run the main SETUP.EXE file on the CD-ROM to install the example files used in this book to your hard drive. You need approximately 17MB of disk space to install all the example files and up to 200MB to install all the demos and free software.

Installing the Files on Your Computer

The best way to select and install the various files on your computer is to run the Setup.exe file in the root directory of each CD. This launches the installation wizard and guides you to install the example files and demonstration databases.

Each directory on the CD also contains a standard setup file than can be selected and run to start the install. Other applications, such as product demos and free software, have been separated by directory so you can install only the files you want and given them more readable names. Each directory (with the exception of the *Product Catalogs* directory) contains these .EXE files

All the example .mdb files are Access 2002 or 2000 files. They do not work in Access 97, 95, 2.0, 1.1, or 1.0.

Using the Access 2002 Bible Example Files

When you double-click the file named **SETUP.EXE** in the CD root, you are prompted to install the example files. Once installed, you can open a file by going to the folder you installed the example files to and double-clicking on the file you want to open. If you get an error message opening an Access database, you either have multiple versions of Access on your computer and Access 2002 is not the default or you have never told Windows to associate an .MDB files with the program msaccess.exe (Microsoft Access). Follow the instruction in the next section of this appendix to associate all .MDB files with Access 2002.

Associating an .MDB file with Microsoft Access

To change which program starts when you open a file:

1. In My Computer or Windows Explorer, click the View menu, then click Options.

2. Click the File Types tab.

3. In the list of file types, click the one you want to change (Microsoft Access Databases).

   The settings for that file type are shown in the File Type Details box.

4. Click Edit.

5. In the Actions box, click Open.

6. Click Edit, then specify the program (msaccess.exe) you want to use to open files that have this extension.

Make sure you choose the Access 2002 msaccess.exe if you have other versions of Access on your computer.

Example Files on the Access 2002 Bible CD

Once you install the example files, start Access 2002, then open the .mdb file as you are instructed in the book. The instructions below describe the files in each directory. Don't be afraid to simply install the files on your hard disk and open them. You can delete them later or reinstall them.

Access 2002 Bible Example Files

The root directory of CD 1 contains the file named setup.exe. This file is used to install the Access 2002 Bible example files. Once installed, the example files are installed under your C:\Program Files folder in a directory named Access 2002 Bible Examples. When it is properly expanded, the folder will contain six subfolders each with examples used in different parts of the book.

Acrobat Reader from Adobe

This freeware version of a reader from Adobe lets you view and print files stored in Adobe Acrobat .PDF file formats. In the **Product Catalogs** directory of the CD, you find several catalogs with .PDF file extensions. To view these .PDF files, you must install the Adobe Acrobat reader. Double-click the reader.exe installation file and follow the instructions. To run the installation for Adobe Acrobat, run the file reader.exe found on the CD. Once you have installed the Adobe Acrobat reader, you can display a .pdf file by displaying the file in Windows Explorer and double-clicking the .pdf file name.

eBook

The Access 2002 Bible Gold Edition is on the CD in an electronic (eBook) format. This is a viewable and searchable format. This file is in the eBook directory on the CD and is named eBook.pdf. You can launch the Adobe Acrobat reader, then open the Book.pdf file. You can also copy the .pdf file from the CD to your hard drive.

Demos

This section includes demos from the companies listed below. Just go to the desired directory and double click on the .EXE file. The instructions will take you through installing the demos. Some installations also create product descriptions in Word 2002/2000 format on your hard drive.

Yes! I Can Run My Business Accounting

Yes! I Can Run My Business is the most popular accounting software available for Access users today. The product is fully customizable and includes all source code.

It includes all typical accounting functions, including sales, customers, A/R, purchases, suppliers, A/P, inventory, banking, general ledger, fixed assets, and features multi-company accounting for any size business. Priced under $1,000 for a multi-user LAN version, it is one of the best values for small businesses. You can install the Yes! I Can Run My Business demo by running: Demos\Yes! I Can Run My Business Accounting\yesdemo2k.exe You can also view a product brochure on our accounting software. This brochure is available in electronic format as an Adobe Acrobat .PDF file located in: Demos\Yes! I Can Run My Business Accounting\Yes! I Can Brochure.pdf

POSitively Business

Positively Business is an add-on module for Yes! I Can Run My Business. It adds point of sale functionality and includes all source code. The product includes a mouse-less point of sale interface, security, administrative and setup options, cashiers, cash counter, sales analyzer, barcoding and much more. The software works with standard point of sale hardware including cash drawers, light poles, hand-held scanners, receipt printers and credit card scanning keyboards. Pricing is currently $595 for one register. Call Database Creations or visit www.positivelybusiness.com to learn more. You can install the POSitively Business demo by running: Demos\POSitively Business\posdem2k.exe

EZ Access Developer Tools Suite

The EZ Access Developer Tools is specifically designed for Access 2002, 2000 and Access 97 developers to create great Access applications. The suite consists of eight separate products:

- ✦ EZ Report Manager
- ✦ EZ Search Manager
- ✦ EZ Support Manager
- ✦ EZ Extensions
- ✦ EZ Security Manager
- ✦ EZ File Manager
- ✦ EZ Application Manager
- ✦ EZ Controls

Each can be integrated into your application to provide new functions in a fraction of the time you need to create them yourself. These products will save you hundreds of hours of development time. Think of them as over 100 pre-designed, pre-programmed interfaces you can legally steal and use with your applications!

Read each of the embedded reviewers guides in the demo for a complete overview of each product. Currently, you can purchase the entire EZ Access Developer Tools Suite for $395. View additional information on this product at www.databasecreations.com. You can install the EZ Access Developer Tools Suite demo by running: Demos\EZ Access Tools Suite\EZ Tools Demo.EXE

appBuilder

appBuilder allows Access developers to create an application shell when building custom applications for Access 2002, Access 2000 or Access 97. There are two ways to use the appBuilder. Start with our application shell and add your objects (tables, queries, reports, forms, etc.) or use the Application Generator Wizard to choose, configure and automatically add the components to your Access application. The Wizard guides you through the process of selecting over 40 different features and lets you add your own text and graphics. Then add your tables, queries, forms and reports to the application switchboard you have selected. We include a second wizard to help you build flexible menu systems for your application.

With the appBuilder you receive:

- ✦ appBuilder with 40 components from the EZ Access Developer Tools Suite
- ✦ Application Generator Wizard
- ✦ Menu Editor Wizard
- ✦ On-line Help
- ✦ *Free* Check Writer Application with Source Code
- ✦ Five additional Switchboards not found in the Suite
- ✦ Source code
- ✦ Use Royalty Free in your applications

Purchase the appBuilder for only $495 or, for $595, purchase both the appBuilder and EZ Access Developer Tools Suite. You can install the appBuilder demo by running: Demos\appBuilder\appBuilder Demo 2000.exe

Access Project Security Manager

If you use Access 2002 or Access 2000 Projects with the new MSDE or SQL Server 7, there is no security provided for forms or reports. You only have the limited data security provided by MSDE and SQL Server 7 and no user security. With the Access Project Security Manager, you can easily add your own security. This avoids having to create separate application front ends for each group of users. You can install the Access Project Security Manager demo by running: Demos\Access Project Security Manager\APSM Demo.exe

Inventory Manager 4 with Barcode Modules

The Inventory Manager is an open source code, fully customizable stand-alone inventory management program for Access 2002, 2000, or 97. This product allows you to enter inventory items, enter suppliers and warehouses, and includes a simple chart of accounts and general ledger. Use the Inventory Manager stand-alone or with your existing purchasing or sales applications. The demo also includes a demo version of the optional barcode modules, which allow you to print barcodes and adjust inventory quantities in stock or transfer goods between warehouses. Purchase Inventory Manager 4 for $595 for a multi-user version or for $995 with the bar code modules. You can install the Inventory Manager with Barcode Modules demo by running: Demos\Inventory Manager with Barcoding\invdemo2k.exe You can also view a product brochure located in: Demos\Inventory Manager with Barcoding\invmgr4.pdf

PenSoft Payroll

PenSoft Payroll from PenSoft Corp. is a stand-alone payroll package for small to medium businesses. It interfaces with Yes! I Can Run My Business for complete employee, hour, tax, deduction, and benefit processing. The software contains all tax tables for the United States, its Territories, and Canada. The program supports English and French. You can install the PenSoft Payroll trial version by running: Demos\PenSoft Payroll\p01-demo.exe

appWatcher

The appWatcher is a simple version control add-in for Access. appWatcher watches for and logs changes made to objects in Access databases. The software is a useful tool for developers to record design changes when many developers are modifying the same database or to track changes end users make to an application. You can install the appWatcher demo by running: Demos\appWatcher\watcherdemo2000.exe

Report Manager Professional

The Report Manager Professional is a tool for managing and printing reports you create in Access. All source code is included and you can use the interfaces royalty-free in your applications. You can install the Report Manager Professional demo by running: Demos\Report Manager Pro\rptmgrprodemo.exe

Search Manager Professional

The Search Manager Professional is a collection of powerful search interfaces and search engines for Access applications. All source code is included and you can use the interfaces and search engines royalty free in your applications. You can install the Search Manager Professional demo by running: Demos\Search Manager Pro\searchprodemo.exe

Surgical Strike

Surgical Strike is a product for Access developers that lets you precisely update Access 2002, Access 2000, or Access 97 program or data files. The software creates a small patch file containing updates to be applied to existing databases, either local or remote. Developers provide their users with the patch file for quick and efficient updates without giving users a complete new version of the application. You can install the Surgical Strike demo by running: Demos\Surgical Strike\ssdemo2k.exe

You can also view a product brochure on Surgical Strike. This brochure is available in electronic format as an Adobe Acrobat .PDF file located in: Demos\Surgical Strike\Surgical Strike Brochure.pdf

Free Access Software

The subdirectories under the Free Access Software contain completely usable, unlocked, and unprotected versions of some award winning products. To install each product, go to the subdirectory and double click on the .EXE file. This will install the .MDB file to your hard drive and also install complete documentation that you can view and print using Word 2002 or Word 2000. The files with the word *Sampler* in them are abbreviated versions of the commercially available products. The entire user guide has been provided for these products in Word format. These include:

Business Forms Library Sampler

The Access Business Forms Library Sampler is a sample of the Business Forms Library, a collection of 35 forms and reports. The entire library contains tables, forms, reports, and macros for each of the forms and reports. You can integrate them into your own applications thereby saving you hundreds of hours of work.

Check Writer for Microsoft Access

This is a fully functional copy of our Check Writer software for Access. Write and print checks, create deposits, perform reconciliations and view your check register. All source code is included so you can modify for your needs.

Cool Combo Box Techniques

This is a demonstration database of 25 of the coolest combo and list box techniques. Full documentation is included in the CD directory. This is from a highly acclaimed paper given by Cary Prague at the Microsoft Access conferences.

EZ File Manager Sampler

The EZ File Manager is one of eight products in the new EZ Access Developers Suite. The complete File Utilities tool which helps you compile, compact, repair, and backup attached data databases is included, along with the entire documentation set from the EZ Access File Manager, to give you a complete overview of the product. Install the sampler, then copy the form and module to your own application to add file management capabilities to your application.

EZ Search Manager Sampler

The EZ Search Manager is one of eight products in the new EZ Access Developers Suite. The complete SmartSearch tool is included along with the entire documentation set from the EZ Access Search Manager to give you a complete overview of the product. Install the sampler, then copy the forms to your own application to add an incredibly flexible search interface to your application.

Picture Builder Button Sampler

These bitmaps can be used on Access toolbars or in Access switchboards buttons . To use these button faces, copy the files to your hard disk or use the bitmaps as is.

Product Catalog

For readers wishing to increase their productivity, we include the latest catalogs from Database Creations, Inc., the world's largest Microsoft Access and Office Mail Order Company. Cary Prague, one of the authors of Access 2002 Bible, owns this company. You can also view product updates, more information, and new products, at the Database Creations Website, www.databasecreations.com, or call Database Creations at (860) 644-5891 to receive new printed catalogs and product descriptions. You may also send an email to info@databasecreations.com for information. The files are in these directories:

General Product Catalog	`Product Catalog\2000 Database Creations Catalog.pdf`
EZ Suite Developer Tools Catalog	`Product Catalog\ezproductslck.pdf`
Inventory Manager Brochure	`Product Catalog\Invmgr4.pdf`
Point of Sale Accounting Brochure	`Product Catalog\posbrolck.pdf`
Business! Accounting Sales Sheet	`Product Catalog\sellsheet.pdf`

WinZip

This directory contains WinZip 8.0, a shareware program for compressing data files.

CD 2

Many other vendors provide add-on products for Access developers, power-users, and end-users. These include add-on libraries, converters, tools, developer utilities, search and replace, fonts, help tools, install scripts, and more.

The file Setup.exe will launch an installation wizard to install each of the following demos from various vendors. Because most of the demos require the installation of ActiveX controls or DLLs and you must reboot your computer, only one installation is allowed at a time. You can also launch each installation program directly from the CD. The list below includes the directory and file name at the end of each paragraph.

Most are sold by Cary Prague through his company Database Creations, Inc. (www.databasecreations.com) for 10 to 20 percent off regular prices when you mention the Access 2002 Bible when ordering by phone or from the online store.

✦ FMS Inc. - `www.fmsinc.com` - (703) 356-4700

- Total Access Analyzer 2000 `\fms\taa9demo.exe`

  Demo version. Analyzes database objects to provide documentation, cross-reference, application and flow diagrams, and reports.

- Total Access Components 2000 `\fms\tac9demo.exe`

Demo version. ActiveX controls add features and effects while speeding programming.

- Total Visual CodeTools 2000 `\fms\tct2ktrl.exe`

Demo version. Enterprise-enabled coding tools standardize existing code at the procedure, module, or project level. Also includes a set of coding tools to handle the more mundane tasks of working with VB and VBA.

- Total Access Memo 2000 `\fms:\tam2ktr.exe`

Demo version. Add rich text formatting to Access.

- Total Access Statistics 2000 `\fms\tast2kdemo.exe`

Demo version. Add advanced data analysis to your applications, royalty-free.

- Total Visual Agent 2000 `\fms\tvag9trl.exe`

Demo version. Automate and schedule upkeep for Access/Jet databases.

- Total Visual SourceBook 2000 `\fms\tvsbdemo.exe`

Demo version. Ready-to-run code covers every major area of software development from ADO to XML.

✦ Black Moshannon Systems - `www.speedferret.com` - (814) 345-5657

- SPEEDFerret `\SpeedFerret\setup.exe`

Demo version. Best search and replace utility for code, tables, forms, and reports.

✦ dbi technologies - `www.dbi-corp.com` - (204) 985-5770

- Solutions::Explorer `\dbi_tech\solxdemo.exe`

Demo version. ActiveX controls allow you to add data-mining, explorer system, or help type capabilities to your Windows applications.

- Solutions::PIM Professional

Demo version. Tools for developing creative calendaring, scheduling and personal information management.

- Solutions::Schedule `\dbi_tech\sschd3ac.exe`

Demo version. Adds resource scheduling management capabilities to your Windows applications or ActiveX web pages.

✦ Pendragon Software - `www.pendragonsoftware.com` - (847) 816-9660

- Pendragon Forms `\Pendragon\forms312keval.exe`

Evaluation version. Creates and synchronizes Access-based forms for PalmOS devices.

✦ Powerlan USA - `www.powerlan-usa.com` - (603) 880 9118

- Office Converter `\OfficeConvert\OfficeConverter_v7122.exe`

Demo version. Converts Access, Word, and Excel files to Office 2000 or Office 97. Audits changes, repairs many undocumented problems.

- ✦ InnerMedia - `www.innermedia.com` - (603) 465-3216

  - • DynaZip AX   `\Dynazip\dzaxe.exe`

    Evaluation version. ActiveX controls add data backup and restore capabilities.

- ✦ eHelp Corporation - www.ehelp.com - (800) 478-1062

  - • RoboHelp Office `\RoboHelp\setup.exe`

    Trial version. The easiest way to add help systems to an Access application.

- ✦ Wise Solutions, Inc. Software - www.wise.com

  - • Wise Installer `\Wise Install\wiseeval.exe`

    Evaluation version. Scripting utility outperforms Microsoft Office Developer Edition tools.

Reporting Problems

If you think you have found an example that doesn't work or you have a suggestion, please let us know by email or by visiting the official website for this book at www.databasecreations.com/bible2002. We get back to our readers who ask questions about the book. While we answer questions about the material in the Access 2002 Bible by email, we are unable to take phone calls from readers other than in the normal course of our consulting and mail order business. We will not answer questions concerning problems you are having with your application without charge. We are happy to offer all Access Bible purchasers a reduced consulting rate.

All of the products mentioned in this book are available from:

Database Creations, Inc.
475 Buckland Rd.
S. Windsor, CT 06074 USA
(860) 644-5891 (US and Internationally)
(860) 648-0710 (24hr Fax)
Web: www.databasecreations.com
Company E-Mail: info@databasecreations.com

✦   ✦   ✦

Index

SYMBOLS AND NUMERICS

! (exclamation mark)
  identifier operator, 339–341
  input mask character, 153
  Not word identifier, 377–378
  object hierarchy separator, 1101
" " (double quotation marks)
  expression text delimiters, 338, 339
  format delimiters, 148
  input mask space delimiters, 155
  path/filename delimiters, 1327
  text field delimiters, 726, 734
"& (double quotation mark, ampersand)
  field delimiter, 802
(pound sign)
  date delimiter, 156, 293, 338, 339
  input mask character, 153
  Uniform Resource Locator (URL)
    sub-address prefix, 139
  wildcard character, 227, 325, 326, 377
& (ampersand)
  concatenation operator, 319, 323–324,
    672–673
  format symbol, 147
  input mask character, 153
  menu hot-key letter prefix, 1075
&" (ampersand, double quotation mark)
  field delimiter, 802
' ' (single quotation marks) text field
  delimiters, 728, 734, 802
( ) (parentheses)
  function parameter delimiters, 333
  procedure name delimiters, 976
* (asterisk)
  all-field reference tag, 281–282,
    353–354, 790
  multiplication operator, 318–319, 393–394
  wildcard character, 226–227, 326, 377
+ (plus sign)
  addition operator, 319
  concatenation operator, 319, 672–673
  subdatasheet indicator, 69, 205–206
, (comma)
  class parameter prefix, 1442
  delimited text file separator, 726, 728, 734
  input mask character, 153

– (minus sign)
  input mask character, 153
  subtraction operator, 319
. (period)
  identifier operator, 339, 341
  input mask character, 153
  macro group/name separator, 908
  table/field name separator, 373
... (ellipsis) macro action suffix, 912–913
/ (slash)
  date delimiter, 735
  division operator, 319
  input mask character, 153
: (colon)
  calculated field operator, 806
  field display name operator, 286
  input mask character, 153
  time delimiter, 735
; (semicolon)
  Command function prefix, 47
  delimited text file separator, 734
  input mask character, 152, 153
  list box item separator, 1034
  Structured Query Language (SQL)
    statement delimiter, 831–832
< > (less-than sign, greater-than sign)
    not-equal operator, 322, 380–381
< (less-than sign)
  comparison operator, 293
  format symbol, 147
  input mask character, 153
  less-than operator, 322
<= (less-than sign, equal sign) less-than-or-
    equal-to operator, 322–323
= (equal sign)
  calculated control prefix, 667
  equal operator, 322, 381
  format symbol, 147
  greater-than operator, 323
  input mask character, 153
>= (greater-than sign, equal sign) greater-
    than-or-equal-to operator, 323
? (question mark)
  input mask character, 153
  wildcard character, 227, 326, 377
@ (at sign) format symbol, 147

[ ] (square brackets)
  expression control name delimiters, 338
  field name delimiters, 373, 375, 667, 829
  wildcard character delimiters, 325, 377
\ (backslash)
  input mask character, 153
  integer division operator, 320
^ (caret) exponentiation operator, 321
_ (underscore) input mask character, 152
{ (left curly brace) text file delimiter, 734
∞ (infinity symbol) relationship
      character, 166
3-D View dialog box, 552–553
7-Step Design Method, 89–90

A

accelerator keys, 918, 921, 958–960, 1075,
      1080
Access Delete message box, 933
Access Project Security Manager (on the CD),
      1553
Access window, 54–58
Acrobat Reader (on the CD), 1549–1550
Action Failed dialog box, 914
Activation Wizard, 35
Active Server Pages (ASP), 1188, 1198–1202
ActiveX Control dialog box, 1216
ActiveX Control Wizards, 1525–1526
ActiveX controls
  Active Server Pages (ASP), in, 1200, 1201
  built-in, 566
  Calendars, 566–569
  inserting, 467
  Microsoft Web Browser control, 1215–1216
  types, 566
ActiveX controls demos (on the CD), 566
ActiveX Data Objects (ADO)
  connection, establishing, 1038–1039
  fields, updating using, 1036–1039, 1043
  in forms, unbound, 1167–1168
  procedures, working with, 1036–1039
  records, adding using, 1044–1045
  records, cloning using, 1047–1048
  records, deleting using, 1048–1047
  recordsets, 1038, 1039, 1040
  updating, 1041
  uses of, 1036–1037
  variables, declaring, 1038
Add-In Manager, 1416–1417, 1524–1525, 1529,
      1531
Adding Visit Details form (on the CD), 845
Add-Ins ⇨ Add-In Manager, 1416

add-ins, custom
  creating, 1513–1514, 1517–1524
  database properties, 1529
  Dynamic Link Libraries (DLLs), calling
        functions in, 1502–1505
  flow of control, 1515–1516
  installation, 1524–1531
  libraries, 1501–1502
  purpose, 1514
  Registry subkeys, 1499–1500, 1525,
        1526–1527, 1529
  user interface, 1515, 1516–1517
addition operator, 319
.ade files, 1418
adLock properties, 1039
Admins group, 1342–1343
ADO. See ActiveX Data Objects (ADO)
adOpen properties, 1039
.adp files, 122, 123, 1122, 1418
Advanced ⇨ Default open Mode ⇨ Shared,
      1538
Advanced Search dialog box, 215–216
After event properties, 924, 1044
After Update event property
  controls, 937
  forms, 922, 940, 944, 1097–1098
  macros, calling from, 1097–1098
  procedures using, 1021, 1036, 1044
Alias dialog box, 1397
all-field reference tag, 281–282, 790
Allow properties, 145, 435, 437, 441, 443
ALTER TABLE statements, 816
And operator, 326–327, 386–387, 389–393
Animation property, 1457
Answer Wizard Software Development Kit
      (SDK), 52, 1371
APIs. See Application Programming Interfaces
      (APIs)
appBuilder utility (on the CD), 1552–1553
Append dialog box, 788
application distribution
  components, avoiding large, 1420
  database components, specifying, 1428
  databases, securing for, 1330–1332,
        1350–1352
  dependencies, scanning for, 1425
  described, 1401
  disks, creating, 1418–1419
  files included in, 1424–1425
  installation, running application on
        completion, 1429
  Internet Explorer 5.1, including, 1427

library databases, performance
    optimization using, 1286–1289
licensing, 1321–1322, 1416, 1418
locations for installation, specifying,
    1425–1426, 1431
lock conflicts, 1420
.MDE files, distributing databases as,
    1279–1282, 1330–1332
media choices, 1418
network environments, for, 1420
packages, 1418
packages, application identification for,
    1421–1422
packages, copying definition, 1423
packages, creating, 1431
packages, deleting, 1423
packages, including runtime files, 1427
packages, naming/renaming, 1422, 1423
procedures, referencing in external
    databases, 1286–1288
replication considerations, 1428
script involvement, 1431
setup program, creating, 1431
setup program customization, 1418–1419
setup program, testing, 1432–1436
source code, distributing uncompiled,
    1286
SQL Server 2000 Desktop Engine
    considerations, 1428
Start menu items, specifying, 1429
startup parameters, 1402–1404
system files considerations, 1427–1428
application generators, 962
Application objects, 1441, 1443–1444
Application Programming Interfaces (APIs),
    5–6, 1371, 1394–1395, 1396–1398
Application Title box, 1402
applications, runtime
    about boxes, 1410–1411, 1412
    Access features unavailable in runtime
        environment, 1406
    button images, 1411
    classes, 1438
    closing, 1419
    compilation, 978, 1277–1278, 1279,
        1282–1289, 1316–1317
    compilation, checking for, 1316–1317
    decompilation, 1314–1315
    documentation, 1414
    error trapping, 1413
    icons, custom, 1402
    interface style, 1407–1408

licensing, 1321–1322, 1416, 1418
look and feel consistency, 1407–1408
prototyping using Database Wizard,
    961–969
removing, 1420
runtime files, including in, 1427
security, 1326–1328, 1414
shortcuts for starting, 1327–1328
source code, protecting, 1414
splitting into multiple linked databases,
    709–712
startup options, 1402–1404
templates, 962–963
testing, 1405–1406
titles, 1402, 1423
uninstalling Access 2002, effect on, 1419
version information display, 1409, 1410,
    1424
Workgroup Administrator component
    removal, reinstallation failure from,
    1420
ApplyFilter macro action, 943
appWatcher utility (on the CD), 1554
arithmetic. See mathematical operations
ASP. See Active Server Pages (ASP)
Assistant objects, 1458
Auto List Members help, 977
Auto properties, 438, 464, 515, 1103
Auto Quick Info help, 977–978
AutoCorrect feature, 556
AutoExec macros, 48, 905–906, 1086, 1087,
    1402
AutoForm, 218, 564–565
AutoFormats
    controls, using with, 489–491, 629
    creating, 491
    customizing, 491
    Database Wizard, using with, 965
    Format Painter tool, 491, 632
    forms, using with, 489–491, 839, 965
    reports, using with, 629, 965
AutoJoin, 822, 823
AutoKeys macro, 958, 1075
Automation
    binding, 1438–1441, 1442
    cursor movement, 1451
    dialog box considerations, 1444
    directories, changing, 1443
    document creation based on templates,
        1450
    error handling, 1449
    images, inserting in documents using, 1451

Continued

Automation (*continued*)
   Macro Recorder, using, 1452–1454
   Null values, testing for, 1450
   object instances, activating, 1450–1451
   object instances, closing, 1444, 1451
   object instances, creating, 1441–1442, 1443, 1449
   object instances, getting, 1442–1443
   object instances, making visible, 1449–1450, 1456
   object libraries, referencing, 1455
   object variables, determining type, 1438
   Office Assistant control, 1455–1461
   references, creating, 1438–1441, 1455
   servers, 1287–1288, 1440, 1441–1442, 1455
   Word, working with in, 1440, 1441–1443, 1444–1454
AutoNumber data type
   appending records having, 785
   editing, 230
   grouping options in reports, 615
   introduced, 108
   record identification, role in, 138, 158, 168
   replication, during, 1469
   replication ID data type relation to, 147
   storage size, 137
   type of data stored, 137, 138
   Visual Basic, 1002
AutoReport, 218, 302, 312–313
AutoStart, 1192, 1197, 1203
Avg function, 334

B

Back Color property, 481
Back Style property, 481
backgrounds
   color, controls, 474, 476, 481
   color, data access pages (DAPs), 1233, 1253
   color, graphs, 545
   color, label controls, 481, 1091
   color, table cells, 239
   images, 439, 487–489
   shading, 646
Balloon objects, 1458–1461
BCNF. *See* Boyce-Codd normal form (BCNF)
Beep macro action, 901–902
Before properties, 922, 923, 924, 937, 939
Between . . . And operator, 329, 387–388
bigint SQL Server data type, 1129

billboards, 1304
Binder, 1441–1442
Bit SQL Server data type, 1129
Blends format, 489, 490
BMP files, 520
Boolean data type, 1001
Boolean (logical) operators, 326–328, 371–374, 383–385, 386–387, 389–393
Border properties, 438, 481, 484, 1103
Border Width window, 60–61, 486
borders
   color, 61, 474, 481
   controls, 474, 481
   datasheets, 239
   dialog boxes, 1103
   forms, 438, 455
   graphs, 545, 554
   images, 484
   style, 239, 474
   width, 61, 474, 481
Bottom Margin property, 482
Bound Column property, 511, 517, 855, 1019, 1092
Boyce-Codd normal form (BCNF), 104–106
Briefcase replication/synchronization, 59, 1470, 1473, 1487
Browse for folder dialog box, 1431
Business Forms Library Sampler (on the CD), 1555
Button Wizard Visual Basic Samples (on the CD), 990
Buttons property, 1459
byte data type, 1001

C

.cab files, 1418
Calendar ActiveX controls, 566–569
Calendar Object ⇨ Properties, 568
Calendar Properties dialog box, 568–569
call tree, 1276–1278
Can Grow property, 480, 610, 632–633, 882
Can Shrink property, 480, 610, 632–633, 866
CancelEvent macro action, 932, 939, 1052
Caption property, 145, 434–435, 1091, 1130, 1215
captions
   command button captions, 1091
   field captions, 145, 155
   forms, in, 145, 155, 434–435, 437, 447

hyperlinks, 1215
label controls as, 401
list boxes, 1091
menu bar captions, 1075
SQL Server field captions, 1130
toggle buttons, on, 642
Cartesian product, 358, 359, 367
cascade changes options, 181, 182, 183–184,
    356, 790–791
case conversion using macros, 940
case sensitivity, 227, 377, 997, 1341
Case statements, 1007–1009
Categories and Actions dialog box, 1054
CBF. See Code Behind Form (CBF)
CBR. See Code Behind Report (CBR)
CD-ROM, running Access features from, 24
CD-ROM with this book
    about box template, 1411
    Access Import-Export.mdb, 696
    Access Project Security Manager, 1553
    Acrobat Reader, 1549–1550
    ActiveX controls demos, 566
    Adding Visit Details form, 845
    appBuilder utility, 1552–1553
    appWatcher utility, 1554
    Business Forms Library Sampler, 1555
    Button Wizard Visual Basic Samples, 990
    CheckWriter for Microsoft Access, 1555
    COFFIN.BMP, 504–505
    Cool Combo Box Techniques, 1555
    CstPtLit.mdb, 1464
    Customers Unbound form, 1172
    EXIT.BMP, 1062–1063
    EZ Access Developer Tools, 1551–1552
    EZ File Manager Sampler, 1555
    EZ Search Manager Sampler, 1556
    hands-on tour, 32
    installation, 1548
    Inventory Manager, 1553
    Mountain Animal Data Access Pages
        database, 1180
    Mountain Animal Hospital database, 58,
        64, 125, 493, 1539–1545
    Mountain Animal HospitalCS project, 1172
    Mountain Animal Macro.mdb, 64, 897, 917
    Mountain Switchboard-No Buttons form,
        1051
    MTN.BMP, 525, 643, 966
    My Mountain StartCS project, 1123
    Office Assistant animations list, 1457
    PenSoft Payroll, 1554
    Picture Builder Button Sampler, 1556
    POSitively Business, 1551
    product catalogs, 1549
    Report Manager Professional, 1554
    Search Manager Professional, 1554
    setup, 64
    splash screen template, 1409
    Surgical Strike, 1554–1555
    Table Analyzer DB, 187
    Thanks.dot, 1445
    TomCat.XLS, 532
    Unbound Form Utilities module, 1172
    updates, downloading, 64
    WinZip, 1556
    Yes! I Can Run My Business, 1550–1551
CDX files, 701
Cells Effects dialog box, 238–239
CGI. See Common Gateway Interface (CGI)
ChangeFileOpenDirectory command, 1443
char SQL Server data type, 1129
character coding in import operations,
    733–734
Chart ➪ 3-D View, 552
Chart ➪ Chart Options, 551
Chart ➪ Chart Type, 548–549
chart fonts dialog box, 545–546
Chart Options dialog box, 552
Chart window, 543–544
Chart Wizard, 302, 534–541
charts. See graphs
check box controls
    creating, 409, 412, 502–503
    datasheets, in, 854
    described, 397, 402–403
    forms, in, 112
    label placement, 401
    sizing, 412
    values returned, 382, 403, 502
    visual display, 403
Check Box tool, 502
CheckWriter for Microsoft Access
    (on the CD), 1555
.CHM files, 1382
Choose Builder dialog box, 979
.chp files, 1377
client/server environment, 15–17. See also
    projects, Access; SQL Server 2000
    Desktop Engine

Close button property, 57, 438
Close macro action, 931, 1101
Close procedure statements, 1041
/Cmd command, 47
Codd, E. F., 103–104
Code Behind Form (CBF), 993
Code Behind Report (CBR), 993
Code Builder, 979, 980
Code Librarian, 1415
CodeDb function, 1517
COLLATION collation sequence, 1119
Collation property, 1130
Column Count property, 511, 517, 855
Column Headings property, 825
Column Heads property, 517, 855, 858
Column property, 1034
Column Width dialog box, 237
Column Widths property, 511, 512, 517, 855
columns
    adding, 234
    bound, 511, 517, 855, 1019, 1092
    combo boxes, 505, 517, 858
    database diagrams, working with in, 1141
    deleting, 234
    described, 84
    dragging, 235–236
    fields, dragging to, 76
    fields, relation to, 65, 84
    freezing, 241
    headers, 59, 132–133, 234–235, 748
    headers, displaying in controls, 406, 505
    headers, fixed, 825
    hiding/unhiding, 237, 241, 512
    identity, 1131
    list box column properties, 509–510,
        511–512, 1034, 1092
    mailing labels, in, 872, 875–876
    moving, 235–236
    navigating, 66–69
    reports, 296–297, 302, 873–876, 1262
    ROWGUID, 1130, 1132
    selecting, 284
    snaked, 296, 873–876
    sorting, 59
    SQL Server column properties, 1130, 1131,
        1132, 1141
    width, changing in datasheet view, 59,
        236–237, 285
    width, setting using Column Widths
        property, 511, 512, 517, 855
COM Add-in Designer, 1415

combo box controls
    closed, 505
    columns, 505, 517, 858
    creating, 409, 513–517
    data entry, using for, 505–506, 512–517,
        1028–1031
    described, 72, 397
    fields, inserting in, 513
    labels, 401, 514
    list boxes compared, 407, 505
    Lookup fields as, 158
    multiple-column, 515–517
    open, 505
    queries, creating from, 515–517, 855, 857
    row properties, 515, 858
    single-column, 513–515
    spacing, 506
    speed, optimizing for, 1297–1298
    subforms, in, 853–858
    text boxes, changing from, 512–514
    value list, limiting input to, 515
    Visual Basic, using, 1027–1031
Combo Box tool, 513
Combo Box Wizard, 512–515
Command Bar Image Editor, 1402, 1411
command bars, 1066
command button controls
    click events, 1052, 1059
    control source, 1054
    creating, 989–992, 1053–1058, 1090–1091,
        1512–1513
    data import/export buttons, 957–958
    Delete Record command buttons, 989–991
    dialog boxes, in, 1090–1091
    duplicating, 1057–1058
    event procedures attached to, 989, 1173
    Exit command buttons, 971–972
    forms, opening using, 1054–1056
    hyperlinks, attaching to, 1213, 1215
    images, displaying on, 1055–1056,
        1062–1065, 1411, 1513
    introduced, 397
    label placement guidelines, 401
    macros, attaching to, 1051–1052,
        1058–1062
    naming, 1056
    Phone Dialer command buttons, 991–992
    property sheet, displaying, 1058–1059
    sizing, 1055
    switchboard command buttons, 1049–1050
    text, displaying on, 1055–1056, 1513

Command Button Wizard, 989–992, 1053–1056, 1512–1513
command-line startup parameters, 46–47, 1406
Commit On Close property, 442
Common Gateway Interface (CGI), 1188
/Compact command, 47
comparison operators. *See* relational operators
compilation. *See compilation under specific topics*
Computed data type, 1002
concatenation
    addition operator, using, 319
    calculated fields, using with, 324
    data types, joining using, 324, 672–673
    field contents, inserting in text using, 324, 673, 677, 882–883
    mail merge reports, in, 882–883
    maximum length, 883
    operators, 319, 323–324, 672–673, 882–883
    spaces, adding, 324
Confirm Workshop Information dialog box, 1336
ConflictTable property, 1493
connection
    ActiveX Data Objects (ADO) connection properties, 1038–1039
    data access pages (DAPs) connection string, 1224–1225, 1248
    SQL Server 2000 Desktop Engine connection setup, 1123–1124, 1144
    upsizing, entering connection information in, 1144, 1153
ConnectionString property, 1249
constants, 337, 1030. *See also* variables
Control Box property, 438
control breaks, 611
Control menu button, 57
Control Source property, 528, 667–668, 680, 681, 1169
control tips, 1085. *See also* screen tips; tooltips
Control Wizard, 398, 1525–1526
controls. *See also* option groups; *specific controls*
    3-D effects, 474–476, 477, 481
    alignment, 417–419, 460, 464
    AutoFormat, using, 489–491, 629
    borders, 474, 481
    bound controls, 399–400, 431, 444–446

calculated controls, 399–400, 636–640, 667–668, 673
chiseled effects, 476
color, 474, 476, 481
column header display, 406, 505
compound controls, 450, 464, 599
control tips, setting, 1085
copying, 421
creating, 408–413
data-validation, 397
deleting, 420–421, 459–460, 598–599
described, 396
design standards, 400–408
etched effects, 476, 647
events, 916, 919, 937
expressions, referencing control names in, 911
fields, adding, 409–411
fields, relation to, 589–590
flat, 475
font, 400, 448, 481, 628
forms, adding bound controls to, 444–446
forms, in unbound, 1169
forms, referencing in different, 860–861
grouping, 419–420
handles, 413, 415
Help, control-level, 1367–1368, 1393–1394
hiding/showing using Visual Basic, 1024–1025
hyperlinks in, 1212
image controls, 483–484, 520
images in, 397, 504–505, 1108–1109
introduced, 62
iteration through, 1172, 1175
line controls, 397, 485–486, 667
locking, 939
Lookup Wizard, changing value display using, 461
macros, attaching to, 919, 936–938
macros, disabling using, 939
macros, displaying using, 939
macros, hiding/showing using, 939, 1005
macros, locking using, 939
macros, referencing in, 911
macros, setting values using, 939
macros, underlining using, 954–957
macros, using to go to specific, 939, 941
Memo fields, in, 453–455, 633
moving, 413, 414, 415–417, 450–451, 599–604
names, 340, 431, 639, 668

Continued

controls *(continued)*
    names, default, 413, 668
    object frame controls, bound, 397, 409,
        455–457, 592, 608
    object frame controls, unbound, 397
    Object Linking and Embedding (OLE)
        objects in, 397, 409
    option button controls, 397, 401, 402–404,
        412, 496–501
    page breaks, 397, 619
    properties, 340
    properties, changing, 432–433
    properties, default, 433–434
    properties, displaying, 429–431,
        479–483, 843
    properties, inheritance, 432
    raised effects, 475, 1089
    rectangles, in, 397, 405–406, 474–476,
        485–486
    report detail controls, 601–602
    report footer controls, 671–674, 678–681,
        684–685
    report header controls, 600–601, 670–671,
        676–678, 682–684
    resizing, 843, 850
    reverse video display, 479
    running sum controls, 686–688
    selecting/deselecting, 413–415, 451–452,
        600
    shadow effects, 476, 477–479, 486
    shortcut menus, attaching to, 1078, 1080
    sizing, 411, 413, 415, 416, 419
    styles, 1510
    subform/subreport controls, 397, 839, 841,
        843, 850
    summary controls, 671–672, 673–675
    sunken effects, 475–476, 646
    tab controls, 397, 407–408, 1103–1109,
        1256
    tab order, setting, 452–453
    text conventions, 400, 401
    text, modifying, 447–448, 595
    type, changing, 410, 452
    types, 396–397
    unbound, 399–400, 412–413, 431
    value display, changing using Lookup
        Wizard, 461
    variables, referencing as, 1301
    variables, unbound controls as, 399
    visibility properties, 480, 1005
    Wizards for creating, 398
ControlSource property, 1298

ControlTip Text property, 1085
Conversion Finished message box, 987
/Convert command, 47
Convert Database to Design Master Wizard,
    1481–1483
Convert Macro dialog box, 986–987
Cool Combo Box Techniques (on the CD),
    1555
Copy Package dialog box, 1423
copy-protection scheme, 28, 35
counters, 381–382, 1013
CountOfDeclarationLines property, 1524
CREATE INDEX statements, 816
CREATE TABLE statements, 816
CreateControl function, 1518
CreateForm function, 1518
CreateGroupLevel function, 1518
CreateObject function, 1300, 1441–1442
CreateReport function, 1518
CreateReportControl function, 1518
Crosstab Query Wizard, 766–767
CS project name suffix, 1147
CStr function, 673
cue cards, 886
Currency data type
    case attributes, 227
    conversion to/from other types, 143–144
    decimal places, 145, 154–155
    default value, 155
    formats, 148–149, 756
    grouping options, 615
    introduced, 108
    monetary calculations, in, 138
    storage size, 137
    type of data stored, 137
    validation, automatic, 221
    Visual Basic, 1001, 1002
Cursor property, 1251
Customer Information Screen, 37
Customers Unbound form (on the CD), 1172
Customize dialog box, 1068
Customize Toolbars dialog box, 535
Cycle property, 443

D

DAO. *See* Data Access Objects (DAO)
Dashboard Project, 1415
Data Access Objects (DAO)
    data types, 1040
    fields, updating using, 1039–1041, 1043
    group accounts, creating using, 1363–1364
    object ownership, changing using, 1364

object permissions, assigning using,
 1364–1366
recordsets, 1040
replication using, 1471, 1474–1478
synchronization using, 1487–1489,
 1493–1497
upsizing, 1157
user account creation using, 1362
user passwords, changing using, 1363
Visual Basic Application edition (VBA),
 working with in, 1037–1041, 1043,
 1044–1045, 1362–1366
Data Access Page designer, 1185
data access pages (DAPs)
absolute pages, 1224–1225, 1248
ActiveX controls, 1189
alignment, 1241
browser support, 4, 1185
Caption section, 1239, 1245, 1253
color, 1233, 1253
connection string, 1224–1225, 1248
controls, changes in form conversion to,
 1256–1257
creating by field promotion, 1241–1242
creating using Page Design View,
 1226–1227, 1230, 1236–1239
creating using Page Wizard, 1221–1222,
 1231–1236
creating using Templates dialog box,
 121, 122
data model, displaying, 1254
described, 122, 1184, 1218
drilling down, 1218
drop zones, 1237, 1239–1240
editing, 1220, 1228, 1229–1230
Expand/Collapse controls, 1189,
 1218–1219, 1223–1224, 1233,
 1250–1251
expressions ignored in form conversion
 to, 1257
fields, adding, 1221, 1226–1227, 1231, 1234,
 1236
footer section, 1245, 1253
form conversion to, 1256–1261
group levels, 1221, 1222, 1224, 1231–1232,
 1244–1246
grouped, 1220
grouped, creating, 1230–1232, 1234,
 1236–1239, 1241–1244
grouped, demoting, 1230
grouped, displaying properties of,
 1244–1245
grouped, expanded by default, 1224, 1225,
 1244
grouped, indentation, 1236
grouped, page size setting, 1238
grouped, record selector display in,
 1247–1248
grouped, updating, 1230–1231
grouping definitions, 1231, 1233
headers, 1237, 1239, 1245
hyperlink changes in conversion to, 1257
HyperText Markup Language (HTML)
 document component, 1220, 1224,
 1226, 1229
image changes in conversion to, 1257,
 1259
indentation, 1236, 1253
interactive nature of, 1185
Internet Explorer support of, 4, 1185,
 1218–1219, 1241
labels, 1237, 1253
layout, 1227, 1233, 1237–1238
Multiple Selection section, 1241
navigation controls, 1223, 1233, 1251–1252
object/document separation, 1220
objects, selecting multiple, 1241
Office XP Microsoft Web Components
 (MSOWC), use of, 1185, 1219
page size settings, 1238
Pages container, Data Access Page object
 stored in, 1220
path, 1224–1225, 1248–1250
pivot tables, with, 1242–1244
projects, in, 1157
query conversion to, 1255–1256
Record Navigation section, 1245
record selectors, 1247–1248
records, adding, 1223
records, deleting, 1223
records, filtering, 1223
records per page setting, 1238, 1244
report conversion to, 1261–1265
saving, 1224, 1226, 1227
saving Access objects as, 1255–1265
section headers, 1237
sections, activating/deactivating,
 1245–1246
sections, removing, 1237, 1246
sections, sizing, 1237–1238
sections, unbound, 1226
settings, default, 1253–1254
software requirements, 1218–1219
sorting, 1223, 1231

Continued

data access pages (DAPs) *(continued)*
  table conversion to, 1255–1256
  table pages, multiple, 1220
  table pages, single, 1221–1230
  tables, adding, 1221, 1239
  text boxes, 1237
  tree view, displaying, 1254
  updates, allowing/disallowing, 1230, 1231,
      1233, 1235–1236
  upsizing, 1157
  view conversion to, 1255–1256
Data Entry property, 442
data-entry rules, 109, 145, 146, 152–154
Data Errors dialog box, 1493
data, exporting
  Active Server Pages (ASP), to, 1198–1201
  command buttons for, 957–958
  data types supported, 691–692
  data types unsupported, converting, 695
  dBASE, to, 739
  described, 693
  Excel, to, 739–740
  Extensible Markup Language (XML), to,
      1265–1266, 1267–1270
  FoxPro, to, 739
  HyperText Markup Language (HTML),
      form datasheets to, 1194–1198,
      1200–1201
  HyperText Markup Language (HTML),
      page setup properties when
      exporting to, 1198
  HyperText Markup Language (HTML),
      query datasheets to, 1192–1194
  HyperText Markup Language (HTML),
      report datasheets to, 1202–1205
  HyperText Markup Language (HTML)
      tables, to, 739–740, 1186, 1190–1192
  macros, using, 921, 957–958
  Microsoft IIS 1-2, to, 1198–1200
  name conflicts, 739
  objects, from large databases, 1317–1318
  objects to external databases, 739–740
  overview of Access features, 9–10
  Paradox, to, 739
  Save As options, 739
  text files, to, 739–740
  Web pages, to dynamic, 1198–1201
  Web pages, to static, 1186–1187,
      1190–1198, 1202–1205
data, importing
  Access objects, external, 719–720,
      1313–1314, 1416
  automating, 695

canceling import operations, 737
character coding, 733–734
cleanup, 736–737
command buttons for, 957–958
data type conversion, 721, 736
data types supported, 691–692, 718
date formatting, 731–732, 735
delimiter characters, 726, 728, 734
described, 693
Errors table, 736–737
Excel spreadsheets, 722–725
Extensible Markup Language (XML) data,
    1265, 1270–1271
field properties, modifying in, 736
language settings, 733–734
linking versus, 693–695
lists, HyperText Markup Language
    (HTML), 1208–1210
Lotus spreadsheets, 718, 722
macros, using, 695, 921, 957–958
numeric information, formatting, 731
overview of Access features, 9–10
primary keys, in, 724, 736
storage space issues, 694
tables, 719, 720–721, 736, 1208–1210
text files, delimited, 726, 727–729, 734
text files, fixed-width, 726, 729–733
Text Qualifier, 728, 734
time formatting, 731, 735
troubleshooting, 736–737
uses, appropriate, 694–695
word-processing files, from, 725
data, linking. *See also* Object Linking and
    Embedding (OLE)
applications, splitting into linked
    databases, 709–712
bound objects, 531–533
data types supported, 691–692
data types unsupported, converting, 695
database management systems (DBMS),
    external, 696–699
described, 693
embedding versus, 521–522
Excel objects, 532–533, 705–706
functions in query criteria, 716
graphs, in, 539–540, 542
importing versus, 693–695
indexes, external, 701–703, 704
introduced, 5
optimization, 716
overview of Access features, 9–10
path issues, 698–699
primary key in, 694–695, 703, 704

referential integrity, effect on, 694
table relationship inheritance, 713
table relationships, setting, 713
table view properties, setting, 712–713
tables, between external, 713–714
tables, dBASE, 700–703
tables, deleting link, 717
tables, external Access, 695, 699–700
tables, FoxPro, 700–703
tables, HyperText Markup Language (HTML), 694, 706–707, 1210
tables, moving linked, 717
tables, Paradox, 703–705
tables, performance optimization, 716
tables, renaming linked, 716
tables, text, 707–709
tables, xBASE, 700–703
uses, appropriate, 693–694
Data Outline tool, 1254
data types. *See also specific types*
    action queries, errors in, 799
    ActiveX Data Objects (ADO) types, 1040
    assignment to fields, 136–139
    changing, 143–144, 333, 672, 721, 736
    concatenation, joining using, 324, 672–673
    Data Access Objects (DAO) types, 1040
    listed, 108
    make-table queries, inheritance in, 784
    Paradox, conversion from, 721
    replication ID, 147
    speed considerations, 1298–1300
    SQL Server types, 1129
    storage sizes, 136–137
    validation, automatic, 220–221
    variable names, preceding with, 997
    variables, assignment to, 974, 998, 1000–1003
    variables, default, 998
    Visual Basic types, 1001–1003
    xBASE, conversion from, 721
database design. *See* design
Database Designer, 1138
database diagrams, 350–351, 1127, 1138–1142
Database Documenter, 161
database engines, choosing, 1114, 1115–1116. *See also* Jet; SQL Server; SQL Server 2000 Desktop Engine
database file
    creating, 120
    extensions, 39, 46, 58, 124

naming, 123
opening, 120
database management systems (DBMS), 3, 4, 7–8, 696–699
Database Properties dialog box, 1529
Database Splitter wizard, 124, 710–711
Database to Save as MDE dialog box, 1332
Database window
    described, 57–60
    forms, creating using Objects bar, 426
    forms, displaying in, 72–74
    macros, dragging and dropping from, 899–900
    macros, running from, 905
    startup options, 1403
Database Wizard, 121, 961–969
databases. *See also* synchronization
    add-in databases, 1288, 1529
    compacting, 47, 1291, 1312
    compilation, checking for, 1316–1317
    compilation/decompilation, 1314–1317
    creating blank, 120, 122, 123–125
    creating from existing database, 121
    creating from templates, 121–123
    creating SQL Server databases, 1121–1126
    described, 58, 82–83
    distribution, securing for, 1330–1332, 1350–1352
    encrypting/decrypting, 1324, 1360–1362
    exclusive access, 46, 1290, 1323
    filename extensions, 39, 46, 58, 124
    hyperlinks to, 1212
    library databases, 1286, 1288–1289, 1501–1502
    macros, running on opening, 905–906
    .MDE files, distributing as, 1279–1282, 1330–1332
    naming, 123
    opening at startup, 46–47
    opening previous version databases, 40–42, 47
    opening, running Visual Basic (VBA) procedures at, 47
    opening using File menu, 64, 120
    opening using Windows Explorer, 45
    ownership, 41, 1353
    passwording, 46, 1323–1325
    permissions, 1350–1352
    projects compared, 1127
    publication, 1474
    read-only, 46
    repair, 47, 1115, 1313

Continued

databases *(continued)*
    Security Wizard, secure copies using, 1322,
        1353–1360
    sharing, 46, 1538
    size, maximum, 1116
    size, reducing by decompiling, 1314–1315
    size, working with large, 1310–1318
    specifications, 1534
    splitting, 709–712
    startup, opening at, 46–47
    tables, maintaining in separate, 124,
        709–712, 1413–1414
    tables versus, 67
    user profile options, 46
    username/password options, 46,
        1323–1325
    values, passing to at startup, 47
Databases Container objects, 1366
DATADIR folder, 1119
DataPageSize property, 1238, 1244, 1246–1247
Datasheet Formatting dialog, 239
Datasheet View, 65–69, 265–266, 275, 277,
    435–437
Datasheet window, 213–218
datasheets
    actions possible from, 68
    Active Server Pages (ASP), exporting to,
        1200–1201
    borders, 239
    check boxes in, 854
    column width, changing, 59, 236–237
    columns, adding, 234
    columns, deleting, 234
    columns, freezing, 241
    columns, hiding/unhiding, 237, 241
    columns, moving, 235–236
    data entry, 218–228
    described, 84–85, 87, 211–212
    displaying, 66–69, 214–215
    dynasets display, 282–283
    Excel compared, 133, 211
    field display width, 236–237
    field values, changing, 228–230
    fields, moving, 235–236
    forms versus, 73, 252
    graph data, editing in, 543–544
    hyperlinks in, 216, 1212–1214
    layout, saving, 241
    list box controls in, 854
    navigating, 65–69, 214
    opening, 218
    option buttons in, 854

    printing, 246
    record pointer, 218–219
    record selector column, 67
    records, adding, 217, 219–220, 230,
        232–233
    records, deleting, 217, 229, 233–234
    records, display options, 235–242
    records, navigation, 224–228
    records, saving, 48, 215, 220, 242
    searching in Datasheet view, 215–216, 217
    sorting, 242
    subdatasheets, 160, 205–209, 440, 825,
        1137–1138
    subforms, datasheet, 839, 844
    toggle buttons in, 854
    VCR buttons, 67
date data type, 1001
Date function, 334, 672–673, 682
date operations
    current date, returning, 334
    delimiting date data, 293, 735
    difference between dates, returning, 334
    expressions, in, 339
    fields, inserting dates in, 228
    format, 149–150, 731–732, 735
    forms, inserting dates in, 264
    functions related to, 334
    future dates, calculating, 806–809
    importing text files, format in, 731–732,
        735
    intervals, returning, 334
    intervals, specifying, 683–684, 1025
    leading zeros, 735
    mail merge reports, in, 881
    portions of dates, returning, 683–684
    queries, in, 292–293, 753, 764, 782, 806–808
    range validation, 156
    reports, displaying dates in, 667, 672–673,
        682–684
    returning dates, 333, 334, 672–673
    strings, converting dates to, 672
    validation rules, 156
DateAdd function, 809
DateDiff function, 334, 399
DatePart function, 683
Date/Time data type
    case attributes, 227
    conversion to/from other types, 143–144
    data entry, 221–222
    formats, 149–150
    graphs, in, 538
    grouping options in reports, 614–615

importing, 735
introduced, 108
range validation, in, 156
storage size, 137
type of data stored, 137, 138
validation, automatic, 221
Visual Basic equivalent, 1002
Datetime SQL Server data type, 1129
DAvg function, 336
Day property, 567
DayLength property, 567
DB files, 694
db properties, 1039
dBASE, 18, 700–703, 739
DBEngine objects, 1351
dbIntegrators, LTD., 1183
DBMS. See database management systems
    (DBMS)
DBT files, 702
DCount function, 336, 809–811
DDB function, 335
DDE. See Dynamic Data Exchange (DDE)
Debug ➪ Compile, 978, 1312
decimal data type, 1001, 1129
Decimal Places property, 145, 480, 1130
Declare statements, 1502–1503
Declared Referential Integrity (DRI), 1145
/decompile command, 1314–1315
Default Value property, 145, 1130
Default View property, 435, 437, 1103, 1201,
    1257–1260
Delete queries, 184
Delete Record command buttons, 989–991
Delete Record dialog box, 233
Delete Table dialog box, 163
.dep files, 1422
dependency files, 1422
Description property, 824
design
    changing, 141–144
    code objects, separating from tables, 124,
        709–712, 1413–1414
    conceptual phase, 91
    controls, 400–408
    data redundancy, avoiding, 104, 105, 107
    data separation into fields, 97–103
    data separation into tables, 85–86, 100–106
    database, splitting into linked databases,
        709–712
    data-entry rules, 109
    data-entry screens, 111–112
    fields, 93–103, 108–111
    forms, 111–115, 260–262

menus, 115–116
multi-user environment, 709–710, 823
needs analysis, 90–92
objects, 89
prototyping, 92–93, 961–969
reports, 93–100, 298–301, 583–584, 624,
    657–658
scalability, 104
Seven-Step Design Method, 89–90
switchboards, 115–116, 967–969
tables, 85–86, 100–108, 130, 141–144, 161
test data, 111, 662–663, 668–669
total solutions approach, 1437
user interviews, 91–92
Design View
    fields in, 71–72
    forms, 73–74, 255, 262, 426–427, 472–474
    introduced, 70–72
    Lookup tab, 71
    macros, 895–897
    queries, 75–77, 274, 275–278, 283
    reports, 303, 310–311, 572
    tables, 70–72, 134
DesignMasterID property, 1498
Desktop shortcut icons, 44–45, 906, 1328
Dest Connect Str property, 825
Destination DB property, 825
Destination Folder property, 1426
Destination Table property, 825
Details view, 59
Dialer command buttons, 991–992
dialog boxes
    auto resize, 1103
    Automation considerations, 1444
    borders, 1103
    buttons, 935–936
    centering automatically, 1103
    command buttons in, 1090–1091
    form dialog boxes, 1087, 1103
    icon style in, 935
    list boxes in, 1091–1093
    navigation buttons, 1103
    option groups in, 499, 1089–1090
    pop-up dialog boxes, 1103
    printing, for, 1023–1025, 1087–1088
    record selectors display, 1103
    search dialog boxes, 1019–1023
    sizing, 1102
    tabbed, 407–408, 1103–1109
    user choice, forcing before exit, 1103
    values returned, 936
dictionary, 555, 556
Dim statements, 998–999, 1038

Display Control property, 72, 157
Display property, 1251
Display When property, 480
distribution. *See* application distribution
Dividing Lines property, 438, 487
division operator, 319
DLLs, calling functions in. *See* Dynamic Link Libraries (DLLs), calling functions in
DLookUp function, 802–803
Do. . .Loop statements, 1010–1012
Doc-2-Help, 1399
Document objects, 1365
DoEvents statements, 1451
domain functions, 335–336
double data type, 1001
DRI. *See* Declared Referential Integrity (DRI)
drilling down, 69, 1218
DROP INDEX statements, 816
DROP TABLE statements, 816
drop zones, 1237
Dynamic Data Exchange (DDE), 14
Dynamic Link Libraries (DLLs), calling functions in, 1502–1505
dynasets. *See* queries, dynasets

E

Edit ⇨ Calendar Object ⇨ Properties, 568
Edit ⇨ Can't Undo, 230
Edit ⇨ Clear Grid, 281
Edit ⇨ Cut, 420
Edit ⇨ Delete, 163, 233, 420
Edit ⇨ Delete Column, 234
Edit ⇨ Delete Record, 233, 934
Edit ⇨ Delete Row, 141
Edit ⇨ Duplicate, 477
Edit ⇨ Find, 225, 231
Edit ⇨ GoTo, 225
Edit ⇨ GoTo ⇨ New, 233
Edit ⇨ Paste, 231
Edit ⇨ Paste Special, 533
Edit ⇨ Primary Key, 159
Edit Relationships dialog box, 180, 181–184
Edit ⇨ Rename, 162
Edit ⇨ Replace, 231
Edit ⇨ Save As Picture, 483
Edit Switchboard Item dialog box, 1506
Edit Switchboard Page dialog box, 1506, 1507
Edit ⇨ Undo, 231
Edit ⇨ Undo Cell Edit, 292
Edit ⇨ Undo Current Field/Record, 231
Edit ⇨ Undo Move, 416
Edit ⇨ Undo Saved Record, 231
Edit ⇨ Undo Sizing, 416

Edit ⇨ Undo Typing, 230
Else statements, 1006–1007
Enabled property, 1106
Encrypt/Decrypt dialog box, 1360–1361
encryption, 1324, 1325, 1360–1361
End Sub statements, 976
engines, database. *See* database engines, choosing
Enter Parameter Value dialog box, 769, 1193
entity integrity, 158, 168
equal to operator, 293, 322, 381
Erase statements, 1300
Err.Description command, 1017, 1018
error messages, 493, 494, 495, 1017, 1031
Error\$ statements, 1017
errors
    Automation, handling in, 1449
    codes, retrieving, 1018
    events, 915, 923
    macros, stopping on, 914
    query failure on, 825
    query timeout on, 824
    trapping, 1017–1018, 1413
    Visual Basic error-handling, 1014–1018
    Visual Basic, processing during macro conversion, 987, 989
events. *See also specific event properties*
    batch edit events, 924
    canceling, 939
    control events, 916, 919, 937
    data events, 915
    described, 915, 918
    environment, event-driven, 19
    error events, 915, 923
    filter events, 923
    flow control function of, 970–971
    focus events, 915, 923, 937, 1053
    form events, 916, 919, 922–924
    graph events, 924
    keyboard events, 915, 923, 937
    macros, canceling using, 939
    macros, triggering on, 915–916, 919–920, 922–924, 1052
    mouse events, 915, 919–920, 923, 937
    PivotChart events, 924
    PivotTable events, 924
    print events, 915
    procedures, event, 971, 981, 989, 994–995
    properties, 919
    record events, 922
    report events, 947, 952
    screen tip events, 923
    subform events, 922

time events, 915, 923
transaction events, 924
windows events, 915, 923
Excel
    Access, compared to, 20–21
    Application object, 1443
    class arguments, 1443
    copying ranges, 532
    datasheets compared, 133, 211
    exporting data to, 739–740
    hyperlinks to Excel spreadsheets, 1212
    importing spreadsheets from, 722–725
    linking Excel objects, 532–533, 705–706
    PivotTables, 557–564
    versions supported, 692
Excel Pivot Table form, 255
Exchange 2000 Server Developer Edition,
        1415
Exchange documents, 692, 718
/Excl command, 46
exclusive access, 46, 1290, 1323
Exit command, 1076
Exit Function statements, 1016
Exit Sub statements, 1016
exiting Access, 48–49
Expand/Collapse controls, 1189, 1218–1219,
        1223–1224, 1233, 1250–1251
ExpandedByDefault property, 1224, 1225,
        1233, 1244, 1246–1247
exponentiation operator, 321
Export As dialog box, 1186
Export dialog box, 1190
Export From As dialog box, 1193
Export Table dialog box, 1186, 1268
Export XML dialog box, 1268
exporting data. See data, exporting
Expression Builder, 433, 806–808
Expression property, 1095
expressions
    calculated controls, in, 399–400, 636–640,
        667–668
    control names, referencing in, 911
    creating, 338–339, 433, 493–496, 806–808
    data access pages (DAPs), ignored in form
        conversion to, 1257
    data-validation expressions, 493–496
    dates in, 339
    delimiters automatically inserted, 338
    described, 336
    fields in, 339–341
    functions in, 337
    identifier operators, 339–341
    literal values in, 337

mail merge reports, in, 883
object names in, 337, 338
operators in, 337
page-number, 595–596, 684–685
property values, returning specified, 341
in queries, total, 744, 745, 754–756
reports, in, 595–596, 667–668, 673–675
syntax checking features, 336
text controls, in, 595–596
text elements in, 339
times in, 339
usability hierarchy, in, 5–6
variables, assigning results to, 996
words, reserved, 339–340
extend mode, 284
Extensible Markup Language (XML)
    Access support of, 1184, 1265
    data access pages (DAPs), use in, 1230,
        1255, 1265, 1267
    described, 1188, 1266
    exporting to, 1265–1266, 1267–1270
    Extensible Stylesheet Language (XSL)
        display of, 1267
    HyperText Markup Language (HTML)
        compared, 1266
    importing XML data, 1265, 1270–1271
    schemas, 1266
    templates, 1267
Extensible Stylesheet Language
        Transformation (XSLT), 1266
Extensible Stylesheet Language (XSL), 1267
external data. See data, exporting; data,
        importing; Object Linking and
        Embedding (OLE)
EZ Access Developer Tools (on the CD),
        1551–1552
EZ File Manager Sampler (on the CD), 1555
EZ Search Manager Sampler (on the CD), 1556

F
Fail on Error property, 825
Fast Laser Printing property, 443
fault tolerance, 1116
Fetch Defaults property, 442
Field Size property, 145
fields. See also fields under specific topics
    ActiveX Data Objects (ADO), updating
        using, 1036–1039, 1043
    calculated fields, appropriate use, 100
    calculated fields, creating, 806–808
    calculated fields, formatting, 756
    calculated fields in forms, 460–462

Continued

fields *(continued)*
    calculated fields in queries, 393–394, 674, 761, 805–809, 1295
    calculated fields in reports, 298, 324
    calculated fields, mathematical operators in, 318–319
    calculated fields, non-editable, 230
    calculated fields, total, 1041–1044
    calculated fields, updating using procedures, 1041–1044
    calculated fields using DLookUp function, 802
    columns, dragging to, 76
    columns, relation to, 65, 84
    combining using union queries, 813–815
    combo box controls, inserting in, 513
    controls, adding to, 409–411
    controls, relation to, 589–590
    creating, 135–139
    Data Access Objects (DAO), updating using, 1039–1041, 1043
    data access pages (DAPs), adding to, 1221, 1226–1227, 1231, 1234, 1236
    data access pages (DAPs), creating by promoting, 1241–1242
    decimal places, specifying, 145, 146
    default value, 145, 155
    deleting, 141–142, 192
    description, entering, 139
    design, 93–103, 108–111
    Design View, in, 71–72
    disabled fields, 230
    Display Control value, 72
    display width, 236–237
    dragging, 62, 76, 192–193, 445–446
    expressions, in, 339–341
    filtering by field value, 217, 243–245
    flagging, 1172
    form fields, adding, 255–257, 444–446, 457–459, 835–836, 1508
    form fields, clearing using functions, 1172, 1173–1174
    form fields, editibility settings, 442
    form fields, selecting, 264
    form fields, updating using macros, 939
    graphs, adding to, 538–539
    hyperlinks in, 1212, 1213
    HyperText Markup Language (HTML) field name display, 1197
    import operations, modifying in, 736
    Input Method Editor (IME) modes, 146, 1130

key fields, table linking via, 102, 107, 167
link fields, 173
link fields, automatic update, 356
link fields, form/subform, 834, 843, 851–852
location, changing, 142
locked fields, 230, 462
locked records, in, 230
lookup fields, 107, 158, 199–205, 409
mail merge reports, embedding in, 882–884, 887–888
mailing labels, adding to, 866–867
mandatory, 145
moving, 142
name changes, 136, 141, 142, 234–235, 661
name changes by queries, 819–820
name, display, 286
naming, 108, 136, 373
null values, 84, 145, 388–389
order, changing, 193, 235–236, 284–285
pivot tables, selecting for, 559–560
selection boxes, 255–256, 303
size, default, 145
size inheritance in make-table queries, 784
size, setting, 131, 138, 142–143, 145, 146–147
Structured Query Language (SQL) statements, selecting for, 814, 815, 817, 827, 828–831
subforms, selecting for, 836–837
tables, adding to, 71, 131, 140–141
tables, moving between, 192–193
tables, relation to, 212
text, joining with, 672–673
timestamp fields, 1129, 1145
uneditable fields, 230
values, 85
values, changing in datasheets, 228–230
values, default, 145, 155
values, displaying in related tables, 199–205
values, displaying using Lookup Wizard, 199–205
values, eliminating duplicates in SQL statements, 829–830
values, locating, 225–228
values, returning, 746
values, returning number of non-Null, 746, 747
values, returning totals, 746, 754–755
variable length, 138
variables, referencing as, 1301–1302

File ⇨ Close, 72, 294
File ⇨ Create Shortcut, 1327
File ⇨ Exit, 48
File ⇨ Export, 312, 738
file format, Access 2002
    assessment of, 1279
    converting to, 25, 39–42
    saving in previous versions, 124
File ⇨ Get External Data ⇨ Import, 719, 1313
File ⇨ Get External Data ⇨ Link Tables, 699,
    1210
File ⇨ New, 120
File New Database dialog box, 123, 1122
File ⇨ New Project, 1373
File ⇨ Open, 64
File ⇨ Page Setup, 587
File ⇨ Print, 245
File ⇨ Print Preview, 246
Files of Type dialog box, 1501
Fill/Back Color window, 61
Filter by Form feature, 217, 244–245
Filter property, 441, 825
filtering
    data access pages (DAPs), in, 1223
    default, 160
    events, filter, 923
    field value, by, 217, 243–245
    Form, by, 217, 244–245
    forms, allowing/disallowing in, 441
    forms, applying to, 441, 923, 929, 942–944
    macros, using, 929, 942–944, 948, 957
    pivot tables, in, 562–563
    procedures, in, 1018–1027
    queries, in, 290–291, 825
    replica databases, 1478
    reports, in, 948, 957
    Selection, by, 243–244
    Structured Query Language (SQL)
        statements, specifying in, 827
Find and Replace dialog box, 226–227,
    231–232
Find Duplicate Query Wizard, 794
Find Unmatched Query Wizard, 794–798
FirstDay property, 567
Fix function, 335
FlagEdited controls, 1170
FlagFind controls, 1170
flat files, 186, 190–191
float SQL Server data type, 1129
focus
    events, 915, 923, 937, 1053
    forms, keeping until closed, 442, 1103,
        1411

font
    color, 61, 474, 481, 545–546
    controls, 400, 448, 481, 628
    default, 239
    display fonts, changing, 239–241
    exotic fonts, 448
    graphs, in, 545–546, 549
    italic, 481
    label controls, 481, 482, 628
    mailing labels, 865–866, 871
    Microsoft Office fonts, 400
    name, 481
    printer, specifying for, 440
    printing considerations, 626
    sizing, 240, 481, 545–546
    style, changing, 239, 308, 545–546, 628
    text box controls, 481, 482
    TrueType, 626
    underlined, 448, 482
    weight, 481
    Zoom box font options, 223–224
Font combo box, 240
Font properties, 481, 482
Font/Fore Color window, 60–61, 474
For. . .Next statements, 1013–1014
Force New Page property, 618
Fore Color property, 481
foreign keys, 167, 173–174, 199
Form Design window, 60–61, 979–981
form letters. *See* mail merge reports
Form Toolbox, 74, 398, 410, 412–413
Form view, 266, 435, 437
Form window, 259–260, 262–263
Form Wizards, 254–260, 835–844, 1508–1511
Format ⇨ Align, 417
Format ⇨ Align ⇨ Bottom, 603
Format ⇨ AutoFormat, 489
Format Axis dialog box, 549–550
Format ⇨ Change To, 410
Format ⇨ Change To ⇨ Combo Box, 516, 857
Format ⇨ Change To ⇨ Text Box, 452
Format ⇨ Change To ⇨ Toggle Button, 504
Format ⇨ Column Width, 237
Format Count property, 953–954
Format Data Series dialog box, 550–551
Format ⇨ Datasheet, 238
Format ⇨ Font, 239
Format ⇨ Freeze Columns, 241
Format function, 333, 677, 756
Format Gridlines dialog box, 551
Format ⇨ Group, 419
Format ⇨ Hide Columns, 241
Format ⇨ Horizontal Spacing, 419

Format Painter, 491, 632
format properties of data entered, changing
    case conversion, 147, 148, 221, 940
    color, 148
    currency data, 148–149
    dates, 149–150
    hyperlinks, 151
    macros, using, 940
    numeric data, 148–149
    phone numbers, inserting dashes, 147–148
    times, 149–150
    Yes/No data, 150–151
Format property, 145, 147, 480, 686, 1192
Format ➪ Row Height, 237
Format ➪ Send to Back, 478, 485–486
Format ➪ Size ➪ To Fit, 449
Format ➪ Snap to Grid, 418
Format ➪ Text Box, 547
Format ➪ Unfreeze All Columns, 241
Format ➪ UnGroup, 420
Format ➪ Unhide Columns, 237, 241
Format ➪ Vertical Spacing, 419
Format ➪ Vertical Spacing ➪ Make Equal, 460
Formatting toolbar, 448, 472–474
forms
    Active Server Pages (ASP), saving as,
        1198–1201
    AutoFormat, using, 489–491, 839, 965
    back-version compatibility, 40
    borders, 438, 455
    bound, 1166
    bound fields, adding, 444–446
    centering, 438
    class module, 443
    Close buttons, 438
    closing, 266, 907–908, 928
    closing, running macros on, 930–932
    Code Behind Form (CBF), 993
    columnar, 250, 255, 1509
    command buttons, opening using,
        1054–1056
    control boxes, 438
    corrupt, repairing by removing record
        source, 1313
    creating unbound forms, 1168–1170
    creating using AutoForm, 252–253
    creating using Database window Objects
        bar, 426
    creating using Form Wizards, 254–260,
        1508–1511
    data access pages (DAPs), conversion to,
        1256–1261

data, assembling for, 424–426
data-entry forms, 88, 111–115, 249–253,
    423–429, 1410
data-entry screen design, 111–112
data-entry techniques, 264, 265
Database window, displaying in, 72–74
datasheet forms, 250, 255, 1509
datasheet view, 265–266, 435, 437
datasheets versus, 73, 252
dates, inserting, 264
deletions, allowing, 441
described, 73
design, 111–115
design, displaying, 842–844
design edits, 260–262, 443
Design View, 73–74, 255, 262, 426–427,
    472–474
dialog boxes as, 1087, 1103
display forms, 88
display options, 434–436, 437
dividing lines, 438, 487
edits, allowing, 441
event procedures attached to, 979–981,
    994–995, 1170–1172
Excel Pivot Table form, 255
Extensible Markup Language (XML),
    exporting to, 1269–1270
Field List window, working with, 398,
    409–410, 444
field name changes, 235
fields, adding, 255–257, 444–446, 457–459,
    835–836, 1508
fields, calculated, 460–462
fields, clearing using functions, 1172,
    1173–1174
fields, editibility settings, 442
fields, selecting entire, 264
fields, updating using macros, 939
focus, keeping until closed, 442, 1103, 1411
footers, 467–469
Form view, allowing, 435, 437
format of data entered, changing, 145,
    147–152
forms, specifying in, 441
functions, using to check for updates, 1174
functions, using to clear fields, 1172,
    1173–1174
graphs in, 250, 255, 535–542
headers, 447, 467–469, 487
help, custom, 443, 1367–1368, 1392–1393
hiding, 1305
hyperlinks in, 1211, 1212–1214

hyperlinks to, 1212
HyperText Markup Language (HTML),
    exporting form datasheets to,
    1194–1198, 1200–1201
images in, 260–261, 439–440, 483–484,
    487–489, 1296–1297
insertion point, moving, 264
justified, 1509
labels, 112
layout, 112, 257–258
line breaks, 264
locking, 462
macros, attaching to, 922, 926–927
memo fields, 265
menu bar, using for multiple, 1065
menus, attaching to, 443, 1076–1077, 1079,
    1080
message display, 938
Microsoft Forms collection, 566
Microsoft Web Browser control in,
    1215–1216
Min Max buttons, 438
modal forms, 442, 1103
modules behind, 974, 994–995
moveability options, 441
multiple-page, 428, 463–467
navigating, 262–263, 939, 941–942
navigation buttons, 438, 1168
Object Linking and Embedding (OLE)
    objects in, 264–265, 455–457
one-to-many forms, 964–968
opening from menu bar items, 1076
opening using command buttons,
    1054–1056
opening using macros, 896–897, 902,
    925–926, 1060
opening using Visual Basic, 978
option groups, 397, 404–405, 497–501
order by option, 441
page breaks, 465–467
pivot chart forms, 255, 435, 839, 1509
pivot table forms, 250, 255, 435, 437, 1509
pop-up forms, 442, 1308–1309
printing, 266–267, 440, 443, 469–470
project objects, form, 1127, 1157
properties, 434–443
queries, based on, 88, 254, 424–427
read-only, 441
Record Selector bar options, 436, 437
records, allowing addition, 441
records, deletion in, 264, 441
records, displaying saved, 442
records, editibility settings, 442

records, locking options, 442
records, navigation in, 263
records, saving in, 264, 266
records, specifying source, 441
reports, converting to, 470
reports versus, 298
saving, 266
screen tips, 438
shortcut menus, activating, 443
sizing, 427–429, 438, 439
specifications, 1535–1536, 1537
speed, optimizing for, 1296–1298
startup forms, 47–48, 438, 455, 906,
    1086–1087
status bars, 496
style, 258, 966, 1510
subdatasheets, 440
subforms, combo boxes in, 853–858
subforms, creating by dragging to another
    form, 834, 845, 849–851
subforms, creating using Form Wizard,
    835–844, 1510
subforms, creating using Subform tool,
    834, 845
subforms, creating using Subform Wizard,
    834
subforms, datasheet, 839, 844
subforms, Default View property, 841
subforms, described, 114, 250, 833–834
subforms design, displaying, 843–844
subforms, field selection for, 836–837
subforms, form creation for, 846–849
subforms ignored in conversion to data
    access pages (DAPs), 1256
subforms, layout, 839, 843
subforms, linking by primary keys, 851,
    852
subforms, linking to main form, 834, 843,
    851–852
subforms, PivotChart, 839
subforms, PivotTable, 839
subforms, queries used in, 836, 846–847
subforms, record selectors in, 841
subforms, referential integrity in, 846
subforms, sizing, 843, 851
subforms, style, 839–840
subforms, table relationships layout,
    838–839
subforms, table selection for, 836
subforms, tabular, 839
subforms, text boxes in, 839, 860
subforms, titles, 840
subforms, totals of line items, 859–862

Continued

forms *(continued)*
    subforms using lookup tables, 852–859
    summaries, 859–860
    switchboards as data-entry forms, 1410
    switchboards, creating from, 1051
    synchronizing, 927–929
    tabbing options, 112, 443
    table data source, specifying, 254
    tables, editibility settings, 442
    tables, updating from, 1035, 1036
    tables, working with multiple, 457–463
    tabular forms, 250, 255, 839, 1509
    time, inserting, 264
    titles, 259, 840, 1510
    toolbars, attaching to, 443, 1084–1085
    type, assigning, 255
    types, 250
    unbound, 1166–1167
    unbound, ActiveX Data Objects (ADO)
        programming for, 1167–1168
    unbound, connecting to SQL Server
        database, 1169–1170
    unbound, creating, 1168–1170
    unbound, data display in, 1170–1172
    unbound, data update using, 1173–1176
    unbound, finding records from, 1176–1178
    unbound, record management from, 1168
    unbound, uses of, 1167
    unbound, Visual Basic programming for,
        1167
    undoing changes, 264
    updateability, changing, 462–463
    updates, checking for, 1174
    usability hierarchy, in, 5–6
    validation, form-level, 495, 938–939
    values, inserting, 264
    values, setting using macros, 939–941
    view defaults in conversion to data access
        pages (DAPs), 1257–1260
    view options, 434–436, 437, 441
    What You See Is What You Get
        (WYSIWYG), 10–11
    What's This Button property, 438
    width options, 439
    windows, disabling other, 442
    workspace, 427–429
    World Wide Web, interacting with, 4
    Yes/No options, 403, 501–505
Forms macro condition, 909
Formula property, 1130
FoxPro, 18, 700–703, 739

FROM statements, 827, 830–831
FrontPage Version 2002, 1415
.fts files, 1390
functions. *See also* expressions; Visual Basic
        Application edition (VBA); *specific*
        functions
    aggregate, 744
    Application Programming Interfaces (APIs)
        calls to, 6
    built-in, 15, 807–808
    call tree, 1276–1278
    conversion, 333
    Date/Time, 334
    declaring, 1502
    described, 331
    domain, 335–336
    expressions, in, 337
    fields, clearing using, 1172, 1173–1174
    financial, 334–335
    form fields, clearing using, 1172,
        1173–1174
    forms, using to check for updates, 1174
    mathematical, 335
    modules, storing in, 1170
    parameter format, 333
    parameters, passing to, 972, 1165
    procedures, function, 972
    queries, in, 375, 1158, 1165–1166
    random numbers, returning, 333
    record changes, using to check for, 1175
    searching using, 1172, 1176–1178
    string manipulation, 335
    tasks accomplished by, 331–332
    types, 333
    usability hierarchy, in, 5–6
    user-defined functions (UDFs), 331,
        1165–1166
    variable values, passing to, 1503
Furigana property, 1130

G

Gen_ fields, 1467, 1469
Generate_ functions, 1518
GetObject function, 1300, 1441, 1442–1443
GetOpenFileName function, 1502–1503,
        1504–1505
global modules, 995
GoTo macro actions, 68, 225, 939, 941–942,
        946
Graph window, 543–544
graphics. *See* images

graphs
    alignment, 545, 546
    auto scaling, 553
    axis defaults, 538
    axis height, 554
    axis labels, 549–550
    axis length, 554
    axis orientation, 553
    bar, 548
    borders, 545, 554
    bubble, 548
    colors, 545, 550–551
    column, 548
    cone, 548
    creating, 534–535
    cylinder, 548
    data series, 537, 539, 550–551
    datasheet operations, 543–544
    date/time fields in, 538
    displaying, 541– 542
    doughnut, 548
    editing, 543–545
    elevation, 552
    fields, adding to, 538–539
    fields, linking, 539–540, 542
    font, 545–546, 549
    forms, in, 250, 255, 535–542
    frame, 542, 554
    group options, 539, 540
    legends, 539, 540, 541
    line, 548
    numeric fields in, 538, 539
    orientation, 545, 546
    overview of Access features, 13–14
    patterns, 550–551
    perspective, 553
    pie, 548
    previewing, 538
    printing considerations, 550
    properties, displaying, 543–544
    pyramid, 548
    radar, 548
    recalculating, 541
    reports, in, 302, 534
    rotation, 553
    scaling, 553
    shading, 545
    sizing, 542, 553
    stock, 548
    Structured Query Language (SQL)
        statements in, 542
    summarization, 538–539
    surface, 548
    text, attached, 544–547
    text, free-form, 547
    three dimensional, 548, 552–554
    title, 540, 541
    two dimensional, 548
    type, changing, 548–549
    type, choosing, 537
    XY (scatter), 548
greater-than operator, 293, 323, 381
greater-than-or-equal-to operator, 323
grid, working with
    cell gridlines, 238–239, 246
    clearing grid, 281, 283
    control layout, 398, 417–418
    displaying, 418
    fineness, adjusting, 418
    forms, 398, 417–418, 440
    graphs, 551–552
    mailing labels, 875–876
    Snap to option, 418
Grid X / Y properties, 418, 440
GridCellEffect property, 567
Group Footer property, 614, 669–670
Group function, 629
Group Header property, 614, 669–670
Group objects, 1362–1363
Group On property, 614
Grouping Options dialog box, 304–305
groups. See workgroups

H
.h files, 1395
hardware requirements, 24, 1117, 1143, 1276
Has Module property, 443
Heading property, 1458
Height property, 481
Help ⇨ About, 27
Help combo box, 128
Help File property, 443
Help files, assigning to menus, 1076, 1080
Help ⇨ Microsoft Access Help, 52
Help options
    Menu bar Help, 51–52
    Microsoft Web site, 53–54
    Office Assistant, 8, 49–51
    sample databases, 54
    Screen Tips, 9, 53, 57, 128
    Standard Windows Help, 52
Help ⇨ Show Office Assistant, 1456

Help systems, custom
  application development, place in, 1414
  buttons, Help, 1371
  compilation, 1371, 1382–1383
  compilation, contents file generation
       during, 1384
  compilation, full-text information option,
       1380, 1390
  compilation log file, 1377
  compilation, specifying compiled file
       name, 1377
  contents file, 1371, 1377, 1383–1386
  control-level help, 1367–1368, 1393–1394
  developer tools, 1370–1371, 1399
  F1 key, mapping to, 1367, 1393–1394
  F1 key, preventing from being passed to
       Access runtime, 1419
  file structure, 1371
  form-level help, 443, 1367–1368, 1392–1393
  HyperText Markup Language (HTML) files,
       working with, 1372–1374, 1376
  images, 1368, 1375
  indexes, 1371, 1378, 1387–1388, 1392
  page breaks, 1373
  projects, creating, 1373–1375
  projects, defining parameters, 1376–1378
  projects, editing, 1375
  projects, naming, 1377
  projects, saving, 1382–1383
  projects, sections, 1375
  projects, topic addition to, 1381–1382
  projects, topic removal from, 1381
  running Help files, 1390–1392
  runtime environment limitations, 1419
  Search tab definition, 1380, 1389–1390
  table of contents, 1369–1370
  testing, 1371, 1391, 1397–1399
  title bar text, 1376
  topics, 1367
  topics, adding graphics to, 1375
  topics, adding to projects, 1381–1382
  topics, creating, 1372–1373
  topics, display in Help Topics dialog
       boxes, 1370–1371
  topics, Help Context ID mapping to,
       1394–1397
  topics, importing, 1373–1374
  topics, linking, 1367–1368
  topics, maximum number, 1390
  topics, removing from projects, 1381
  topics, sections, 1373
  Viewer, customizing, 1378

  Web-based, 1371
  What's This? help, 53, 128, 1399
  window definitions, 1378–1380
  Windows Help components used,
       1367–1371
Help Topics dialog box, 1370–1371
Help Viewer, 1368–1369, 1378
Help ⇨ What's This?, 53, 128, 1399
HelpContextId property, 443, 1367–1368,
       1392–1397
.hhc files, 1383
.hhk files, 1371
.hhp files, 1371
Hoffman, Jim, 832
hot keys, 918, 921, 958–960, 1075, 1080
.htm files, 1372
HTML Help Workshop, 1370
HTML Output Options dialog box, 1196, 1203
HTMLHelp API, 1394–1395, 1396–1398
.htx files, 1201–1202
HTX/IDC Output Options dialog box, 1199
Hyperlink data type
  address portion, 1211
  conversion to/from other types, 143–144
  displaytext portion, 1211
  formats, 151
  HyperText Markup Language (HTML),
       exporting to, 1191
  length, maximum, 1212
  parts, 139, 151, 1211
  storage size, 137
  Subaddress portion, 1211
  type of data stored, 137, 139
  Visual Basic equivalent, 1003
Hyperlink property, 1130
hyperlinks
  address portion, 139, 151, 1211
  captions, 1215
  command buttons, attaching to, 1213, 1215
  controls, in, 482, 1212, 1213
  data access pages (DAPs), changes in
       conversion to, 1257
  databases, to, 1212
  datasheets, in, 216, 1212–1214
  Excel spreadsheets, to, 1212
  fields, in, 1212, 1213
  files, to locations in, 1214–1215
  format, 151
  forms, in, 1211, 1212–1214
  forms, to, 1212
  HyperText Markup Language (HTML)
       tables, in imported, 1210

images, attaching to, 1213, 1215
PowerPoint presentations, to, 1214
reports, in, 1212–1214
reports, to, 1212
SQL Server field property, 1130
tables, in, 1211, 1213
Web pages, to, 1212
Word documents, to, 1212, 1214
HyperText Markup Language (HTML).
    See also Web pages
alignment, 1191
anchors, 1206
Browser title bar, displaying text in, 1206
datasheets, page setup properties when
    exporting to, 1198
described, 1180
Extensible Markup Language (XML)
    compared, 1266
field name display, 1197
form datasheets, exporting to, 1194–1198,
    1200–1201
Help topics, writing in, 1372–1374
images, 1375
lists, importing from, 1208–1210
report datasheets, exporting to, 1202–1205
sorting, 1192
static pages, 1185–1187, 1190–1198,
    1202–1205
tables, exporting to, 739–740, 1186,
    1190–1192
tables, importing from, 736, 1208–1210
tables, linking, 694, 706–707, 1210
template files, 1186–1187, 1192, 1203,
    1205–1207, 1373
viewing code, 1197

I

.ICO files, 1055, 1402
IconMaker, 1402
icons
    Access icon, specifying at startup, 1086
    Access, shipped with, 1063
    application icons, 1402
    creating, 1402
    Desktop shortcut, 44–45, 906, 1328
    dialog boxes, icon style in, 935
    menus, on, 1073–1075, 1079
    toolbar icons, 1074, 1082
.idc files, 1201–1202
identifier operators, 339–341
Identity Increment property, 1130
Identity property, 1130

Identity Seed property, 1130
IDX files, 701
If. . .Then. . .Else. . .End If statements,
    1004–1007
If-Then-Else macro condition, 910
IIF (Immediate IF) function. *See* Immediate IF
    (IIF) function
Image SQL Server data type, 1129
images
    alignment, 439–440, 488, 527
    Automation, inserting in documents using,
        1451
    background images, 439, 487–489
    bitmaps, 1296–1297
    borders, 484
    command buttons, on, 1055–1056,
        1062–1065, 1411, 1513
    controls, in, 397, 504–505, 642–643,
        1108–1109
    data access pages (DAPs), changes in
        conversion to, 1257, 1259
    Database Wizard, inserting using, 966
    embedding, 524–527, 528–530
    formats supported, 484
    forms, in, 260–261, 439–440, 483–484,
        487–489, 1296–1297
    Help systems, 1368, 1375
    hyperlinks, attaching to, 1213, 1215
    HyperText Markup Language (HTML) files,
        in, 1375
    icons shipped with Access, 1063
    mail merge reports, in, 880
    menu icons, 1073–1075, 1079
    Navigation bar buttons, on, 1252
    Object Linking and Embedding (OLE),
        using, 524–527, 528–530, 643
    preview, 484
    reports, in, 643–644, 966
    sizing, 260–261, 483, 484, 488, 526–527
    sources, 1065, 1411
    tiling, 440, 488, 527
    toolbar icons, 1074, 1082
IME. *See* Input Method Editor (IME) mode
IME Mode property, 146, 1130
IME Sentence Mode property, 146
Immediate IF (IIF) function, 329, 461, 637,
    1101
Import dialog box, 1208
Import Errors table, 736–737
Import HTML Wizard, 1208–1209
Import Objects dialog box, 719, 720
Import Specification window, 731, 733–735

Import Spreadsheet Wizard, 723–725
Import Table Wizard, 729
Import Text Wizard, 727–733
Import XML dialog box, 1271
importing data. *See* data, importing
In operator, 329, 385–386
Include File dialog box, 1396
Index Entry dialog box, 1387–1388
Indexed property, 146, 1130
indexes
    clustered, 1135
    creating using data definition queries, 813,
        816–817
    described, 173
    displaying, 172
    field indexed value, 71
    fields, adding, 146
    fields, choosing, 1293
    Help system indexes, 1371, 1378,
        1387–1388, 1392
    Jet, descending indexes in, 1294
    linking external database indexes,
        701–703, 704
    multiple-field, 1292–1294
    primary key relation to, 160, 171
    properties, displaying, 160
    queries, updating from, 356
    speed advantages, 146, 158, 171, 173,
        1292–1294
    SQL Server, 1130, 1134
    Structured Query Language (SQL)
        statements affecting, 813, 816–817
Indexes window, 160
INF files, 701
INI files, 46
Input Mask property, 145, 192, 1130
Input Mask Wizard, 154
input masks, 145, 152–154, 494, 1130
Input Method Editor (IME) mode, 146, 1130
Insert ➪ ActiveX Control, 567
Insert ➪ Bookmark, 1450
Insert ➪ Column, 234
Insert ➪ Form, 252, 254
Insert Hyperlink dialog box, 1212
Insert Merge Field dialog box, 888
Insert ➪ New Record, 232
Insert ➪ Object, 265
Insert Picture dialog box, 484, 524–525
Insert ➪ Picture ➪ From File, 1375, 1454
Insert Picture ➪ Views ➪ Preview, 484
Insert ➪ Report, 302, 312
Insert ➪ Row, 141

Insert ➪ Tab Control Page, 1104
Insert ➪ Table, 130
installation of Access
    activation, 35–39
    complete, 28
    custom, 29
    location, changing default, 29
    name entry, 27
    Office components, previous versions, 33
    partial, 24, 30–31
    Product Key, 27
    registration, 28, 35–39
    server installation, 32, 1420
    troubleshooting, 42
    upgrading from earlier versions, 25, 28–29
INSTANCENAME SQL Server name, 1119
Int function, 335
int SQL Server data type, 1129
integer data type, 1001, 1002
integer division operator, 320
Internet Database Connector (.idc) files,
    1201–1202
Internet Explorer
    Access 2002, running inside, 1182
    application distribution, including in, 1427
    data access pages (DAPs) support, 4, 1185,
        1218–1219, 1241
    downloading, 1215
    home page, default, 1183
    Web toolbar features, 1181–1182
Internet extensions, 4
Internet features overview, 14–15
intranets, 1180
Inventory Manager (on the CD), 1553
invoice reports, 297, 656–659, 661, 679–680
IpersistPropertyBag interface, 1257
Is Hyperlink property, 482
Is Not Null operator, 388
Is Null operator, 388
Is operator, 329–330
Is RowGuid property, 1130
ISAM drivers, 701, 703
IsCompiled function, 1316–1317
IsNull macro condition, 909, 912

J
Jet
    backup recoverability, 1116
    Data Access Objects (DAO) recordset
        handling, 1040
    data integrity, 1115, 1116
    databases size, maximum, 1116

default database engine, 1114
fault tolerance, 1116
indexes, descending, 1294
queries, maximum simultaneous, 1116
scalability, 1116
security, 1115, 1319–1322, 1332
simplicity, 1115
SQL Server 2000 Desktop Engine
 compared, 1114
SQL Server as alternative to, 1113
SQL Server table access using, 1147, 1151
transaction logging issues, 1116
users, concurrent, 1115–1116
versions, 1334
Jet and Replication Objects (JRO), 1471, 1474
Join Properties dialog box, 363
joins. *See* table relationships, joins
junction tables, 176–177

K

Kanji Conversion Mode property, 146
KeepLocal property, 1469
kernel32.dll, 1504
Key Preview event property, 923
KEY symbol, 71
keyboard events, 915, 923, 937
Keyboard Language property, 482
keys
 changing, 194–196
 data, duplicate, 196–197
 described, 167
 foreign, 167, 173–174, 199, 1133, 1134–1135
 secondary, 142
 Table Analyzer operations on, 194–197
keys, primary
 advantages of using, 158–159, 170–171
 AutoNumber field assignment, 158, 168
 creating, 159–160, 172–173
 deleting, 142
 determining, 158–161
 display, 167
 import operations, in, 724, 736
 indexes, relation to, 160, 171
 introduced, 71
 length, optimal, 171
 linking operations, in, 694–695, 703, 704
 multiple in same table, 167
 normalization, involvement in, 105–106
 queries, in, 356, 785, 799–800
 sort order considerations, 171
 SQL Server, 1133, 1134–1135
 subform linking by, 851, 852

Table Analyzer operations on, 194–197
table relationships involving, 167
uniqueness, 158, 168
keystrokes, passing to another application,
 933

L

Label Align property, 464
label controls
 3-D effects, 481
 alignment in, 482
 attaching, 411, 421
 borders, 481
 capitalization norms, 401
 color, 481, 1091
 creating Insert Hyperlink button,
  1214–1215
 date display properties, 480
 defaults, changing, 464
 deleting, 420–421, 459–460, 598–599
 described, 397
 font, 481, 482, 628
 hyperlinks in, 482, 1213
 keyboard language, 482
 line breaks, 447, 594
 line spacing, 482
 margins, 482, 609
 moving, 414, 416, 450–451, 599–604
 number display properties, 480, 482
 placement, 401, 481
 properties, displaying, 479–483, 607–608,
  631–632
 reading order, 482
 selecting, 414, 600
 sizing, 411, 449–450, 597
 text boxes, attached to, 411, 421, 595
 text effects, 477–479
 text, modifying, 447–448
 unattached, 447, 593–594
 uses, 397, 401
 visibility properties, 480
Label Wizard, 297, 302, 863–869
labels, mailing. *See* mailing labels
Layout for Print property, 440
layout preview, 572, 651
Layout Wizard, 1227–1228, 1236
Lcase function, 335
Left Margin property, 482
Left property, 481
Len function, 335
Length macro condition, 909
less-than operator, 293, 322, 381

less-than-or-equal-to operator, 322–323
licensing, 26–28, 1321–1322, 1416, 1418
Like operator, 323, 325, 370, 377–380
LimitToList event property, 515, 855,
        1028–1029, 1030
line controls, 397, 485–486, 667
Line Spacing property, 482
Line Width window, 61
line wrap, 402, 877, 882
Line/Border Color window, 61
Line/Border Width window, 474
Link Child Fields property, 208, 542, 825, 843,
        851–852
Link dialog box, 699
Link HTML Wizard, 706–708, 1210
Link Master Fields property, 208, 542, 825,
        843, 851–852
Link Spreadsheet Wizard, 705
Link Text Wizard, 708–709
Link Wizard, 704
Linked Table Manager Wizard, 717–718
linking. See data, linking; Object Linking and
        Embedding (OLE)
list box controls
    captions, 1091
    column header display, 406, 505
    column properties, 509–510, 511–512,
        1034, 1092
    columns, hiding, 512
    combo boxes compared, 407, 505
    creating, 409, 506–508, 510–511
    data entry, using for, 505–512, 1031–1035
    data source, specifying, 506–507, 509–510
    data validation role, 505–512, 1031–1035
    datasheets, in, 854
    described, 397, 406
    dialog boxes, in, 1091–1093
    field list data source, 509–510
    items, adding to, 506–507, 509–510
    items, referencing, 1034
    items, removing, 1031, 1034–1035
    items, returning number of, 1034
    label placement, 401
    macros, hiding/unhiding using, 1095, 1097
    multiple-column, 510–511
    multi-selection, 406, 512, 1031–1035
    position numbers, 1034
    procedures, refreshing using, 1019–1021,
        1022
    query data source, 509–510
    refreshing, 1019–1021, 1022
    row properties, 508–509, 1019
    single-column, 506–508

    sizing, 406, 1091
    spacing, 506
    speed, optimizing for, 1297–1298
    table data source, 509–510
    value list data source, 509–510
    Visual Basic Application edition (VBA),
        512
List Box Wizard, 506–508
List Rows property, 515, 858
List Width property, 855
ListCount property, 1034
Locate Web Page dialog box, 1229
Location of New Replica dialog box, 1471
Locked property, 462
logical operators. See Boolean (logical)
        operators
Logon Dialog box, 1333, 1340
long data type, 1001
Look In combo box, 225
Lookup Wizard, 137, 139, 199–205, 461
lookups. See fields, lookup fields; tables,
        lookup tables
looping, 1009–1014, 1301–1302
Lotus spreadsheets, 692, 694, 718, 722
lpstrFile function, 1505
lstrcpy function, 1504–1505

M

Macro Builder, 433
Macro Design window, 894, 895–897, 909–910
Macro dialog box, 905
Macro Recorder, 1452–1454
Macro Single Step dialog box, 914
Macro Window, 895–897, 904
macros
    aborting execution, 912, 939
    accelerator keys, attaching to, 918, 921,
        958–960
    actions, 894, 896, 898–903, 913–914, 1094
    arguments, 896–899
    AutoExec macros, 48, 905–906, 1086, 1087,
        1402
    back-version compatibility, 40
    beeping when done, 901–902
    calls, 1097–1098, 1101–1102
    case conversion using, 940
    command buttons, attaching to,
        1051–1052, 1058–1062
    commenting, 898
    conditions, 896, 899, 909–913, 1094
    confirm delete macros, 919, 922, 932–934
    control names, referencing, 911
    controls, attaching to, 919, 936–938

controls, disabling using, 939
controls, displaying using, 939
controls, hiding/showing using, 939, 1005
controls, locking using, 939
controls, referencing in, 911
controls, setting values using, 939
controls, underlining using, 954–957
controls, using to go to specific, 939, 941
copying, 904
creating, 897–904, 907
Database window, dragging and dropping from, 899–900
described, 16, 893–894
Design View, 895–897
documenting, 898
editing, 903
errors, stopping on, 914
events, canceling using, 939
events, triggering on, 915–916, 919–920, 922–924, 1052
execution, aborting, 912, 939
export operations, using for, 921, 957–958
field name changes, 235
filter macros, 929, 942–944, 948, 957
flow, controlling, 913
format properties of data entered, changing using, 940
forms, attaching to, 922, 926–927
forms closing, running at, 930–932
forms, closing using, 907–908, 1088
forms, navigating using, 939, 941–942
forms, opening using, 896–897, 902, 925–926, 1060
forms, setting values in using, 939–941
forms, synchronizing using, 927–929
forms, updating fields in using, 939
forms, validation macros in, 938–939
grouping multiple in same macro object, 896, 906–908, 931, 1093–1094
hourglass display while running, 901
import operations using, 695, 921, 957–958
keystrokes, passing to Access, 933
keystrokes, passing to another application, 933
list boxes, hiding/unhiding using, 1095, 1097
menu bar items, assigning to, 1076
message boxes, 912
name, 896, 899
name, changing, 904
Names column, 896, 1094

object hierarchy, 1101
pivot table connection/disconnection, triggering on, 924
print macros, 1008
Print Preview, 1099–1101
records, assigning values to using, 940–941
records, finding using, 944–947
records, navigation using, 939, 941–942
redirection, 913
reports, adding conditional text using, 954
reports, hiding data in using, 957
reports, highlighting data in using, 954–957
reports, opening using, 910–911, 948, 1060, 1088
reports, printing using, 1088, 1093–1102
reports, section data layout using, 952–953
reports, section formatting using, 952–953
reports, section-level activation/deactivation, 948–949, 951–953, 954
reports, snapshots using, 949–951
rows, inserting, 1099, 1100
running at Access startup, 47–48, 906, 1086
running at database opening, 905–906
running before report layout, 952, 953
running before report printing, 952, 953–954
running from another macro, 905
running from any window, 905
running from calls, 1097–1098, 1101–1102
running from Database window, 905
running from Macro Design screen, 902
running from Macro window, 904
running in macro groups, 908
running on form closing, 930–932
running on return to previous report section, 952–953
saving, 899, 902, 903
search routines, 944–947
single-step mode, 913–914
specifications, 1536, 1537
spreadsheet macros compared, 894
SQL Server, 1127
tasks possible using, 894–895
testing, 902, 1098
troubleshooting, 913–914
types, 917–918
usability hierarchy, in, 5–6
validation macros, 938–939
Visual Basic, converting to, 985–989
Visual Basic versus, 983–985

mail merge reports
  concatenation operations, 882–883
  creating, 880
  dates, 881
  described, 877
  expressions in, 883
  fields, embedding, 882–884, 887–888
  images in, 880
  Mail Merge Wizard, using, 884–890
  Microsoft Word, using with, 884–890
  page header, 880–881
  printing, 884, 890
  queries, assembling data using, 879
  recipient information, 879–880, 887–888
  text boxes, 882–883
  word wrap, 877, 882
Mail Merge Wizard, 884–890
mailing labels
  blank lines, 866
  brand, selecting, 864, 865
  color, 865–866
  column settings, 872, 875–876
  creating using Label Wizard, 863–868
  fields, adding to, 866–867
  font, 865–866, 871
  margins, 871, 875
  naming, 868
  number of labels across page, 865
  page orientation, 871
  paper size settings, 871
  paper source settings, 871
  printer feed options, 864
  printer, selecting, 871
  printing, 869, 872–873
  punctuation, 866
  reports, as, 297–298, 863
  sizing, 864–865
  sorting, 867–868
  spacing, 866, 870, 872, 875–876
  ZIP Code format, 870
Make Table dialog box, 781
margins
  label controls, 482, 609
  mailing labels, 871, 875
  Page Setup dialog box option, 654
  reports, 588, 617, 654, 664
  text box controls, 482, 609
mathematical operations. See also queries,
      total queries
  addition, 319
  averages, 334
  count, returning, 336

decimal places, 145, 146, 154–155
depreciation return, 335
division, 319
exponentiation, 321
integer-related, 146, 320, 335, 1002
large numbers, 146
mean, 336
modulo, 321
monetary functions, 334–335
multiplication, 318–319, 393–394
net present value, 334
operators, 318–321
operators, precedence, 331, 332
percentages, 306, 686
queries, in, 381–382, 387, 393–394
random numbers, returning, 333
round numbers, 320
square root, 335
Structured Query Language (SQL)
      functions, 224
subtraction, 319
sums, 319, 334, 580, 667–668, 673
sums, running, 580, 686–688
validation rules, 155
Visual Basic, in, 319
MaxRecords property, 825
MDA files, 46, 1501
MDAC. See Microsoft Data Access
      Component (MDAC)
.MDB files, 39–40, 58, 83, 1283–1284, 1330
.MDE files, 39–40, 1279–1282, 1330–1332, 1501,
      1529–1530
MDX files. See Multiple Index (MDX) files
Memo data type
  conversion from Text type, 144
  data entry, 223–224, 265
  formats, 147–148
  introduced, 108
  queries, in, 376–377
  size, maximum, 136, 138
  type of data stored, 136
  Visual Basic equivalent, 1002
Menu bar Help, 51–52
Menu Bar property, 443, 1077
menu bars. See also switchboards; toolbars
  accelerator keys, setting, 1075
  Access menu bar, 57, 1065, 1067
  commands, adding, 1065, 1068, 1072–1073
  conversion from previous versions, 1065
  creating, 1065, 1066–1068, 1069–1071
  customizing by user, allowing/
      disallowing, 1071

default, specifying, 1403
described, 1066
design, 115–116
docking options, 1070
forms, attaching to, 443, 1076–1077
forms, using single bar for multiple, 1065
Help Files, setting, 1076
hiding/unhiding, 1067, 1071
icons, 1073–1075
items, adding, 1068, 1071
items, creating, 1068
items, moving, 1068, 1070
items, removing, 1068
macros, assigning to menu items, 1076
moving, 1069
moving, allowing/disallowing, 1071
naming, 1069, 1071
option groups, 1075
pop-up menus, changing to, 1071
properties, displaying, 1075
reports, assigning to menu items, 1076
resizing, allowing, 1071
screen tips, assigning, 1075
separators, 1067, 1075
startup, specifying at, 1086
submenus, adding, 1071–1073
submenus, adding commands to,
        1072–1073
submenus, changing icons, 1073–1075
text, customizing, 1075
toolbars, changing to, 1071
Toolbars Menu, displaying on, 1071
Visual Basic functions, assigning to menu
        items, 1076
menus, pop-up, 442, 1070, 1071, 1078, 1103
menus, shortcut
    accelerator keys, setting, 1080
    controls, attaching to, 1078, 1080
    creating, 1078–1082
    deleting, 1081
    described, 1066
    forms, attaching to, 443, 1079, 1080
    Help files, setting, 1080
    icons, 1079
    items, adding, 1068, 1079
    items, creating, 1068
    items, moving, 1068, 1070
    items, removing, 1068
    naming, 1078
    option groups, 1079
    reports, assigning to, 1079
    screen tips, assigning, 1080

separators, 1079
startup, allowing/disallowing at, 1403
startup, specifying at, 1086
merge reports. *See* mail merge reports
MergetoWord function, 1444–1449
"Microsoft Access 2000 Data Engine Options"
        whitepaper, 1116
Microsoft Active Server Pages Output
        Options dialog box, 1199
Microsoft Binder, 1441–1442
Microsoft Data Access Component (MDAC),
        701, 703
Microsoft Database Engine (MSDE), 15, 1113,
        1118, 1121
Microsoft Distributed Transaction
        Coordinator (MSDTC), 1120
Microsoft Forms collection, 566
Microsoft Graph, 112, 534, 542
Microsoft HTML Help 1.3, 1370–1371
Microsoft IIS 1-2. *See* Microsoft Internet
        Information Server IDC/HTX
Microsoft Internet Information Server
        IDC/HTX, 718, 1184, 1198–1202
Microsoft Office. *See also* Excel; Word
    AutoCorrect feature, 556
    Developers Edition, 566
    drag and drop integration, 557
    fonts, 400
    hardware requirements, 24
    Privacy Policy, 36–37
    Product Key number, 27
    software requirements, 24
    spell checking, 554–556
    voice recognition features, 24
Microsoft Office XP. *See also* Office XP
        Microsoft Web Components
        (MSOWC)
    activation, 35–39
    Automation support, 1437
    class arguments, 1443
    installation, 25–35
    license agreement, 26–28
    Macro Recorder, 1452–1454
    referencing Office applications, 1438–1441
    registration, 28, 35–39
    software protection, 28
Microsoft Office XP Developer, 1401,
        1415–1416
Microsoft SQL Server Database Wizard,
        1123–1125
Microsoft Web Browser control, 1215–1216

Microsoft Word Mail Merge Wizard dialog
    box, 885
Min Max Buttons property, 438
Minimize button, 57
Modal property, 442, 1103
Modify Object Status dialog box, 1485
Module Builder, 433
Module objects, 1519
Module window, 972, 973, 975–977
modules. *See also* procedures; Visual Basic
    Application edition (VBA)
    back-version compatibility, 40
    compiling, 1524
    container function of, 995
    creating, 972–974
    creating at runtime, 1519–1524
    declarations section, 973–974, 999, 1000
    editing at runtime, 1519–1524
    field name changes, 235
    form modules, 974, 994–995
    functions, storing in, 1170
    global, 995
    introduced, 972
    load on demand, 1276–1278
    memory, optimizing for, 1276
    Option Compare Database declaration, 973
    Option Explicit declaration, 973, 974, 975
    procedure sections, 974
    procedures, grouping in, 971, 995, 1278
    procedures, relation to, 993, 995
    report modules, 974, 994–995
    saving, 978
    speed, optimizing for, 1298–1303
    SQL Server, 1127
    standard, 974, 995–996
    testing, 982–983
    upsizing, 1147, 1157
    variables, declaring in, 973, 999
    variables, referencing in other modules,
        1000
    VBA module library, 1057
    viewing, 974
modulo operator, 321
Money SQL Server data type, 1129
Month property, 567
MonthLength property, 567
Mountain Animal Data Access Pages database
    (on the CD), 1180
Mountain Animal Hospital database (on the
    CD), 58, 64, 125, 493, 1539–1545
Mountain Animal HospitalCS project
    (on the CD), 1172

Mountain Switchboard-No Buttons form
    (on the CD), 1051
Moveable property, 441
MoveWhenInTheWay property, 1456
MSACCESS.EXE, 44
MSDAOPath folder, 1426
MSDE. *See* Microsoft Database Engine (MSDE)
MSDTC. *See* Microsoft Distributed
    Transaction Coordinator (MSDTC)
MsgBox function, 934–936, 1030
MsgBox macro action, 912, 938
MSOWC. *See* Office XP Microsoft Web
    Components (MSOWC)
MSSQLSERVER SQL Server instance name,
    1119
MSTRAN40.EXE, 1478
Msys tables, 1467–1468, 1472, 1486, 1491,
    1493
Multi Row property, 1106
Multiple Index (MDX) files, 701, 702
multiplication operator, 318–319, 394
MultiSelect property, 406, 512, 1032–1033
My Mountain StartCS project
    (on the CD), 1123

N

Navigation Buttons property, 438, 1103
Nchar SQL Server data type, 1129
NDX files, 701, 702
New Data Access Page dialog box, 1255
New File dialog box, 63, 120–121
New File task pane, 1121–1122
New Form dialog box, 254, 558–559, 835
New keyword, 1441
New Object button, 130
New Object shortcuts, 56
New Package dialog box, 1422
New Project Wizard, 1373–1375
New Query dialog box, 274, 766
New Replica Wizard, 1483–1485
New Report dialog box, 302, 586
New Table dialog box, 130–132
New Toolbar dialog box, 1082, 1083
normalization, 86, 104–106, 186–187
Normalized Data Structure: A Brief Tutorial
    (Codd), 103
Northwind Sample Database, 31–32, 54
/Nostartup command, 47
Not Like operator, 323, 325
Not operator, 328
not-equal operator, 322
NotInList event property, 1028, 1029

Now function, 334, 399
NPV function, 334
Number data type
  case attributes, 227
  conversion to/from other types, 143–144
  data entry, 222
  decimal places, 145, 154–155
  default value, 155
  formats, predefined, 148
  grouping options in reports, 615
  introduced, 108
  storage size, 137
  type of data stored, 137, 138
  validation, 221, 222
  Visual Basic equivalents, 1002–1003
Number of Columns property, 511
Numeral Shapes property, 482
Numeric property, 145
numeric SQL Server data type, 1129
Nvarchar SQL Server data type, 1129

O

object data type, 1001
object design windows, 60–62
Object Linking and Embedding (OLE). *See
     also* data, exporting; data, importing;
     data, linking; OLE Object data type
  controls, OLE objects in, 397, 409
  data types supported, 691–692
  editing OLE objects, 522, 530–531
  embedding bound objects, 528–530
  embedding, creating objects while, 530
  embedding graphs, 535–542
  embedding images, 524–527, 528–530, 643
  embedding unbound objects, 523–527,
    1297
  embedding versus linking, 521–522
  file path considerations, 521
  file size considerations, 521
  forms, in, 264–265, 455–457
  introduced, 4
  linking bound objects, 531–533
  linking Excel objects, 532–533, 705–706
  linking in graphs, 539–540, 542
  linking versus embedding, 521–522
  object frame controls, 397, 409, 455–457,
    592, 608
  object frame labels, 528
  overview of Access features, 14
  queries, in, 382
  reports, OLE objects in, 643
  sizing, 526–527

sorting OLE data, 289
sound objects, editing, 530
storage size limitation, 137
types of objects supported, 222–223
video objects, editing, 530
objects
  application objects, 1441
  Automation objects, 1441
  binding, 1438–1441, 1442
  bound, 520–521
  class arguments, 1443
  classes, relation to, 1438
  copying, 784
  descriptions, entering, 60
  design, 89
  documenting, 61
  front-end, 1151
  importing, 719–720, 1313–1314, 1416
  introduced, 83
  libraries, 1313, 1438, 1455
  ownership, 41, 1345–1347, 1353, 1364
  recordsets as, 1023
  referencing, 1438
  types, 87–89, 520
  unbound, 520–521
  usability hierarchy, in, 5–6
Objects Property sheet, 1250
OCX controls. *See* ActiveX controls
ODBC. *See* Open Database Connectivity
    (ODBC) databases
ODBC Time Out property, 824
ODBCConnectStr property, 815
Office Assistant, 8, 49–51, 1455–1461
Office XP. *See* Microsoft Office XP
Office XP Developer. *See* Microsoft Office XP
    Developer
Office XP Microsoft Web Components
    (MSOWC), 1185, 1219. *See also*
    Microsoft Office XP
OLE. *See* Object Linking and Embedding
    (OLE)
OLE Automation. *See* Automation
OLE Class property, 542
OLE Object data type
  data entry, 222–223
  introduced, 108
  size, 137
  type of data stored, 137, 138
  Visual Basic equivalent, 1003
OLEBoundxx: object frame label, 528
On Activate event property, 923, 947
On Apply Filter event property, 923

On Click event property
    command buttons, using with, 1052, 1059
    controls, 937
    focus, relation to, 1053
    forms, 923, 994
    macros, calling from, 1101–1102
    On Dbl Click mutually compatible with,
        1052
On Close event property, 923, 928, 930,
        931–932, 947
On Cmd Before Execute event properties, 924
On Connect event property, 924
On Current event property, 922, 927–929
On Data event properties, 924
On Dbl Click event property, 919–920, 923,
        937, 1052
On Deactivate event property, 923, 947
On Delete event property, 919, 922, 932–934
On Dirty event property, 922, 937
On Disconnect event property, 924
On Enter event property, 937, 1053
On Error
    event property, 923, 947
    Visual Basic statements, 1014–1015, 1449
On Exit event property, 937, 1053
On Filter event property, 923
On Format event property, 952
On Got Focus event property, 923, 937
On Key event properties, 923, 937
On Load event property, 923, 1170, 1216
On Lost Focus event property, 923, 937
On Mouse event properties, 923, 937
On No Data event property, 947, 948
On Not In List event property, 937, 1030
On Open event property
    forms, 916, 918, 923, 926–927, 1097–1098
    macros, calling from, 1097–1098
    reports, 947, 948, 949
    Visual Basic (VBA) procedures,
        running at, 47
On Page event property, 947
On PivotTable Change event property, 924
On Print event property, 952, 953–954
On Query event property, 924
On Record Exit event property, 922
On Resize event property, 923
On Retreat event property, 952–953
On Selection Change event property, 924, 937
On Timer event property, 923
On Undo event property, 922, 937
On Unload event property, 923
On Updated event property, 937

On View Change event property, 924
OnError statements, 989
Open Database Connectivity (ODBC)
        databases, 692, 693, 718, 813,
        815–816
Open Database dialog box, 1290
Open dialog box, 65
OpenFileDlg function, 1504, 1505
OpenForm
    macro action, 896–897, 898–900, 925–926,
        1060
    Visual Basic command, 978
OpenRecordset function, 1039–1040
OpenReport macro action, 910–911, 950,
        1060, 1100
operating system requirements, 24, 1117
operators. *See also specific operators*
    Boolean (logical) operators, 326–328,
        371–374, 383–385, 386–387, 389–393
    concatenation operators, 319, 323–324,
        672–673, 882–883
    described, 317
    expressions, in, 337
    identifier operators, 339–341
    mathematical operators, 318–321
    precedence, 330–331, 332
    queries, in, 293, 370–374
    relational operators, 293, 321–326, 370–371
    string operators, 323–326
    types, 317
    wildcards, using with, 326
option button controls
    creating, 412
    datasheets, in, 854
    described, 397, 496–497
    display-only, 497
    option groups, in, 497–501
    placement, 401
    sizing when creating, 412
    state display, 403
    values returned by, 403
Option Compare Database module
        declaration statement, 973
Option Explicit module declaration
        statement, 973, 974, 975
Option Group Wizard, 497–500, 634–636
option groups
    boxes, enclosing in, 497–498, 636
    buttons in, 404, 497, 499–500, 634
    calculated controls in, 636–640
    choice, default, 498, 635
    controls, selecting in, 404

creating manually, 501
creating using wizard, 497–501, 634–640,
    1089–1090
described, 397
dialog boxes, in, 499, 1089–1090
forms, in, 397, 404–405, 497–501
menus, in, 1075, 1079
reports, in, 634–640
style, 635–636
text labels, 498, 634, 636
types, 404–405
unbound, 499, 635
values, default, 498–499, 635
Or operator, 327–328, 383–385, 389–393
Oracle Server, 692, 718
Order By property, 825
ORDER BY SQL statements, 827, 831, 1157
Orientation property, 441
Outlook/Outlook Express, 692, 718
Output All Fields property, 824

P

Packaging Wizard, 1416, 1418–1421
page breaks, 397, 465–467, 613, 617–620, 1373
Page Design View, 1226–1227, 1230, 1236–1239
Page function, 595–596, 684–685
Page Order dialog box, 1107
Page property, 684–685
Page Setup dialog box, 587–588, 652–654, 871
Page Wizard, 1221–1222
Pages objects container, 126, 1217, 1220
Paradox, 18, 703–705, 721, 739
parameters
    function parameter format, 333
    functions, passing to, 972, 1165
    introduced, 332
    procedures, using with stored, 1163
    views, in, 1164
passwords
    Admin user, 1333, 1340, 1351
    case sensitivity, 1341
    changing, 1339–1341, 1363
    creating, 1339–1341
    database passwords, 46, 1323–1325
    encryption, 1325
    removing, 1339
    replication, removing before, 1464
    SQL Server 2000 Desktop Engine,
        1124, 1147
    startup options, 46
    Visual Basic for Applications (VBA)
        modules, assigning to using Security
        Wizard, 1355–1356

Visual Basic for Applications (VBA),
        setting using, 1326
    workspaces, temporary, 1352
Paste Special dialog box, 532–533
Paste Table As dialog box, 163–164, 786
PenSoft Payroll (on the CD), 1554
permissions
    Admin user, removing from when securing
        database, 1320, 1325, 1339, 1349
    Administer, 1352
    assigning, 1348–1349
    database permissions, 1350–1352
    default, assigning, 1349–1350
    default, removing, 1350
    Delete Data, 1352
    described, 1320–1321
    explicit, 1348
    implicit, 1348
    Insert Data, 1352
    listed, 1352
    Modify Design, 1352
    object level, set at, 1321
    object permissions, 1347–1348
    object permissions, assigning, 1348–1349
    object permissions, assigning default,
        1349–1350
    object permissions, assigning using Data
        Access Objects (DAO), 1364–1366
    object permissions, removing, 1348–1349,
        1350
    Open Exclusive, 1352
    Open/Run, 1352
    persistence, 1348
    queries, assigning temporarily using, 1346
    Read Data, 1347, 1352
    Read Design, 1347, 1352
    removing, 1348–1349, 1350
    Security Wizard, assignment using,
        1356–1357
    Update Data, 1352
    upsizing, needed for, 1143
Permissions property, 1364
Phone Dialer command buttons, 991–992
Picture Alignment property, 439–440
Picture Builder, 504–505, 1063
Picture Builder Add-On Picture Pack, 1065,
    1411
Picture Builder Button Sampler
    (on the CD), 1556
Picture property, 439, 525, 1065
Picture Size Mode property, 439, 488
Picture Tiling property, 440, 527
Picture Type property, 439, 525

pictures. *See* images
pivot charts
    creating, 564–566
    forms, 255, 435, 839, 1509
    view, allowing, 437
pivot tables
    columns, converting to rows, 563
    creating, 557–560
    crosstab queries compared, 557
    data access pages (DAPs) with, 1242–1244
    data list, displaying, 560–562
    data source, selecting, 559–560
    described, 557
    Excel, 557–564
    filters, 562–563
    forms, 250, 255, 435, 437, 1509
    macros, triggering on pivot table
        events, 924
    rows, converting to columns, 563
    subforms, 839
PivotTable menu, 563–564
PivotTable Wizard, 557
.pks files, 1422
Pop Up property, 442, 1103
population variance, 746
popup menus, 442, 1070, 1071, 1078, 1103
POSitively Business (on the CD), 1551
Postal Address property, 1130
PowerPoint presentations, hyperlinks to,
    1214
Precision property, 1130
Print dialog box, 245, 651–652
printers
    default, 589, 1143
    font, specifying for, 440
    mailing labels feed options, 864
    mailing labels, selecting for, 871
    reports, setup for, 440, 587–589, 651–654
printing
    datasheets, 246
    dialog boxes for, 1023–1025, 1087–1088
    font considerations, 626
    font, specifying, 440
    forms, 266–267, 440, 443, 469–470
    graphs, 550
    macros, print, 1008, 1088, 1093–1102
    mail merge reports, 884, 890
    mailing labels, 869, 872–873
    paper size, 653
    paper source, 653
    preview, 246–247, 1099–1101
    query dynasets, 293

    records, 245–247, 1023–1027
    reports, 311, 589, 651–654, 876
    reverse video issues, 479
    shadow effects, 479, 631
    table design, 161
    table relationships reports, 186
    zoom control, 247
Private statements, 1000
ProcBodyLine property, 1523
ProcCountLines property, 1524
procedures. *See also* modules; Visual Basic
        Application edition (VBA)
    ActiveX Data Objects (ADO), working
            with, 1036–1039
    buttons, attached to, 989, 1173
    call tree, 1276–1278
    calling, 972, 1502
    code, entering in Module window, 975
    command buttons, event procedures
            attached to, 989, 1173
    command completion feature, 977
    compiling, 978, 1277–1278, 1279,
            1282–1289, 1316–1317
    creating in Form Design window, 979–981
    creating in Module window, 976–977
    creating in Report Design window, 979–981
    creating stored procedures, 1161–1163
    creating using Command Button Wizard,
            989–992
    Data Access Objects (DAO), working with,
            1038–1041, 1043, 1044–1045
    database opening, running at, 47
    debug process, 978
    editing, 981–982
    error-handling, 1014–1018
    errors, execution redirection on,
            1015, 1016
    errors, ignoring, 1015
    errors, subroutine execution on,
            1015, 1016
    event procedures, 971, 981, 989, 994–995
    Exit statements, 1016
    fields, updating using, 1035, 1036–1044
    filtering records, 1018–1027
    forms, attached to, 979–981, 994–995,
            1170–1172
    function procedures, 972
    list boxes, refreshing using, 1019–1021,
            1022
    module procedure sections, 974
    modules, grouping in, 971, 995, 1278
    modules, relation to, 993, 995

NotInList procedures, 1028–1031
private, 1286, 1502
queries using stored procedures, 1161–1165
records, adding using, 1035, 1044–1048
records, deleting using, 1035, 1048–1047
recordsets, cloning, 1023
referencing in external databases, 1286–1288
reports, opening using, 1026–1027
selecting, 981–982
stored, 1161–1165
sub procedures, 971–972
subroutines, 1016
syntax checking, 978
tables, updating using, 1035–1036
testing, 982–983
variables, declaring, 974, 998–1000
Visual Basic role in, 971
ProcessConflicts function, 1493
ProcStartLine property, 1523
Product Key, 27
/Profile command, 46
ProgramFiles folder, 1426
programming by exception, 19–20
Programs ➪ Microsoft Access, 43
progress meters, 1305–1310
Project Options dialog box, 1376
projects, Access. *See also* upsizing
creating, 122–123, 1121–1126
data access pages in, 1157
databases compared, 1127
field entry, 1128–1130
file extensions, 1122
forms as project objects, 1127, 1157
introduced, 1121
name, changing, 1285
name, default, 1122
object types stored in, 1126, 1127, 1158
queries, 1127, 1157, 1158–1166
replication, 1471, 1474
reports as project objects, 1127, 1157
specifications, 1536–1537
synchronization, 1474
tables as project objects, 1127, 1157
tables, creating in, 1128
tables, properties in, 1131–1138
tables, stored in server database, 1126
unbound forms in, 1166–1167
unbound forms in, ActiveX Data Objects (ADO) programming, 1167–1168
unbound forms in, connecting to SQL Server database, 1169–1170
unbound forms in, creating, 1168–1170
unbound forms in, data display, 1170–1172
unbound forms in, data update using, 1173–1176
unbound forms in, finding records from, 1176–1178
unbound forms in, record management from, 1168
unbound forms in, uses of, 1167
unbound forms in, Visual Basic programming, 1167
projects, Help. *See* Help systems, custom
Properties window, 60–61
property sheets
command buttons, 1058–1059
controls, 430–431, 479–480, 843
described, 62, 429–431
forms, 262
lookup, 157–158
option group controls, 500–501
Property windows. *See* Property sheets
Provider property, 1038
Public statements, 999–1000
purge utility, 1116
/Pwd command, 46
PX files, 694

Q
QBE. *See* Query by Example (QBE)
QFE. *See* quick fix engineering (QFE)
queries
action queries, 271, 773
action queries, append, 773, 785–790, 799, 800
action queries, backing up before, 775
action queries, checking results, 775–776, 780, 784, 790, 793
action queries, converting select queries to, 779–780
action queries, creating, 777–778, 781–783, 785–789, 790–793, 813–817
action queries, data-type errors in, 799
action queries, delete, 184, 773, 776, 790–794
action queries in projects, 1157
action queries, key violations in, 799–800
action queries, locked record issues, 800
action queries, make-table, 719, 773, 776, 781–784
action queries, reversing, 776–777

Continued

queries *(continued)*
    action queries, running, 799
    action queries, safety tips, 775, 777
    action queries, saving, 798–799
    action queries, scoping criteria, 776
    action queries, select queries versus, 775
    action queries, steps in working with, 775
    action queries, tasks accomplished by, 774–775
    action queries, troubleshooting, 799–800
    action queries, types, 773–774
    action queries, update, 773, 777–780, 799, 800, 1164–1165
    action queries, using stored procedures with, 1164–1165
    Active Server Pages (ASP), saving as, 1198–1199
    ANSI-92 SQL query mode, enabling, 823
    averages, returning, 746, 752
    back-version compatibility, 40
    Between . . . And operators in, 387–388
    Boolean (logical) operators in, 371–374, 383–385, 386–387, 389–393
    capabilities of, 272–273
    Cartesian product, based on, 358, 359, 367
    Cascade Delete Related Records option, 790–791
    case sensitivity, 377
    changing data in, 283
    closing, 78
    column headings, fixed, 825
    column width, changing, 285
    combo box creation from, 515–517, 855, 857
    compiling, 1295
    counters, working with, 381–382
    creating, 74–78, 274–278
    crosstab queries, 272, 757–758
    crosstab queries, Column Heading field, 757, 758, 761, 763–764, 765–766
    crosstab queries, creating, 758–760, 766–767
    crosstab queries, Group By options, 757, 759
    crosstab queries, null values display, 760
    crosstab queries, pivot tables compared, 557
    crosstab queries, Row Heading field, 757, 758, 760–761, 763
    crosstab queries, sort order, 76, 288–290, 765–766

crosstab queries, specifying criteria against Column Heading fields, 763–764
crosstab queries, specifying criteria against multiple fields, 764–765
crosstab queries, specifying criteria against new fields, 761–763
crosstab queries, specifying criteria against Row Heading fields, 763
crosstab queries, summary Value field, 758
currency data, working with, 381–382
data access pages (DAPs), conversion to, 1255–1256
data access pages (DAPs), creating from, 1231–1232
data definition queries, 813, 816–817
data type inheritance in make-table queries, 784
database connection string property, 825
database diagrams, creating, 350–351
database name property, 825
databases, external, 697–698, 714–715, 716, 824
Datasheet View, 275, 277, 283
date operations, 292–293, 753, 764, 782, 806–808
definition, saving, 78
described, 74–75, 87–88, 269–271
design, changing default options, 821–823
Design View, 75–77, 274, 275–278, 283
dynasets, datasheet display, 282–283
dynasets, dynamic nature of, 273
dynasets, hiding fields in, 818–819
dynasets, introduced, 77–78
dynasets, printing, 293
dynasets, tables based on, 273
dynasets, tables versus, 273
dynasets, union, 814–815
exiting, 294
Extensible Markup Language (XML), exporting to, 1268–1269
fail on error, 825
field highest value, returning, 746, 824
Field List Window, working with, 76, 346–347, 348, 349–350
field lowest value, returning, 746, 824
field name changes, 235, 661
field non-Null values, returning number of, 746, 747
field values from first record, returning, 746

field values from last record, returning, 746
field values, returning unique, 824
field values showing all, 824
field values totals, returning, 746, 754–755
fields, adding, 76, 278–282, 286, 351–354
fields, automatic updates, 356–357
fields, calculated, 393–394, 674, 761, 805–809, 1295
fields, changing display name, 286
fields, combining into one recordset, 813–815
fields, displaying, 287–288
fields, group by, 744
fields, hiding, 818–821
fields, limiting by multiple criteria in multiple, 389–393
fields, limiting by multiple criteria in single, 383–389
fields, limiting by single criterion in single, 375–382
fields, rearrangement upon saving, 817–818
fields, referencing, 375
fields, removing, 286
fields, renaming in, 819–820
fields, reordering, 284–285
fields, selecting, 283–284, 353–354
fields, updating, 356–357
filtering, 290–291, 825
Find Unmatched queries, 182
flexibility, 272
forms based on, 88, 254, 424–427
functions in, 375, 1158, 1165–1166
HyperText Markup Language (HTML), exporting query datasheets to, 1192–1194
In operators, using, 385–386
indexes, creating using data definition queries, 813, 816–817
indexes, updating, 356
Internet Database Connector (.idc) files, on, 1202
keys, primary, 356, 785, 799–800
Like operators in, 377–380
lookup tables, using, 803–805
mail merge reports, for, 879
mathematical operations, 381–382, 387, 393–394
null values, searching for, 388–389
numeric data, working with, 381–382, 387, 393–394

Object Linking and Embedding (OLE) objects, working with, 382
OwnerAccess queries, 1346
parameter queries, 767–772, 1157, 1193, 1205
pass-through queries, 813, 815–816
permissions, temporary assignment using, 1346
pivot table analysis, 558
population variance, returning, 746
procedures, stored, 1161–1165
project queries, 1127, 1157, 1158–1166
properties, query-level, 823–825
ranges, specifying, 386–387
record selection criteria, 290–293
records, displaying only selected, 290–293
records, displaying only unique, 824
records, returning maximum number, 825
records, returning number of in, 809–811
records, returning top, 272, 811–812, 830
relational operators in, 293, 370–371
reports, relating to, 299–301, 581, 586, 659–662, 1096–1097
rows, showing/hiding, 287
run permissions, 823, 824
running, 277, 279, 768–769, 780
Rushmore query optimizer, 1295
saving, 78, 273, 277, 294
saving, field rearrangement upon, 817–818
search criteria, entering, 76–77, 290–293
select queries, 271, 369–370
select queries, action queries versus, 775
select queries, converting to append queries, 787–789
select queries, converting to update queries, 779–780
select queries in projects, 1157
simultaneous, maximum, 1116
sorting, 76, 288–290, 765–766, 825
specifications, 1535
speed, optimizing for, 158, 171, 1021, 1294–1295
SQL Server, 1116, 1127
SQL statements, conversion to/from, 826, 1019–1021
SQL statements in, 272, 356, 372–373, 813–817, 826–832
SQL statements, selection for, 830–831
SQL statements, sending to database server, 813, 815–816
standard deviation, returning, 746
subforms, used in, 836, 846–847

Continued

queries *(continued)*
    subqueries, 817, 825
    table joins, creating, 357–360, 803
    table joins, deleting, 358, 360
    table name, destination, 825
    table names, showing/hiding in design
        mode, 821–823
    table relationships, creating in, 174,
        343–345, 349, 351–354, 357–360
    table relationships, overriding, 177
    tables, adding, 75, 275, 277, 349
    tables, adding to views, 1158–1159
    tables, creating using data definition
        queries, 813, 816–817
    tables, displaying names of, 287, 352–353
    tables, involving multiple, 11–13, 343–345,
        351–357
    tables, linked external, 697–698,
        714–715, 716
    tables, opening in, 344
    tables, removing, 275, 349
    tables, updating from, 354–357
    text comparison operations, 377–381
    timeout errors, 824
    total queries, Aggregate, 744, 752–753
    total queries, Aggregate Avg, 746
    total queries, Aggregate Count, 746, 747
    total queries, Aggregate First, 746
    total queries, Aggregate Last, 746
    total queries, Aggregate Max, 746
    total queries, Aggregate Min, 746
    total queries, Aggregate StDev, 746
    total queries, Aggregate Sum, 746, 754–755
    total queries, Aggregate Var, 746
    total queries, categories of, 744–746
    total queries, creating using QBE pane
        Total: row, 742–746
    total queries, described, 271, 741–742
    total queries, expressions in, 744, 745,
        754–756
    total queries, field formatting in, 756
    total queries, Group By, 744, 748–751, 752,
        757, 811–812
    total queries, limiting scope by specified
        criteria, 744, 745, 751–754
    total queries, multi-table, 743
    total queries on all records, 743, 746–748
    total queries on groups of records, 744,
        748–751, 752
    total queries, Total Field Record Limit,
        744, 745
    total queries using aggregate options,
        744, 745–746
    transactions, 825
    type, assigning, 277, 773
    types, 271–272
    union queries, 813–815
    updating, 354–357
    usability hierarchy, in, 5–6
    user input, prompting for, 768
    views, 1158–1161
    Web page creation from, 1186
    wildcards, 377–380
    Yes/No criteria, working with, 382, 778
Query ⇨ Append, 788
Query Builder, 1020–1021
Query by Example (QBE), 88, 244, 245,
    276, 278
Query by Example (QBE) pane
    all-fields reference tag, 282
    columns, hiding/unhiding in, 820–821
    Criteria row, 278, 291
    Delete row, 793
    Field row, 278, 279, 283–284
    fields, working with in, 281–282,
        283–288, 383
    introduced, 276
    or row, 278, 385
    Show row, 278, 287–288, 818
    Sort row, 278, 288–289
    Table row, 278, 823
    Total row, 742–746, 757
Query ⇨ Crosstab, 758
Query ⇨ Delete, 792
Query Design window, 276–278, 345–351
Query Designer, 1159–1160, 1164
Query ⇨ Parameters, 771
Query Parameters dialog box, 771–772
Query Properties dialog box, 765–766
Query ⇨ Remove Table, 275
Query ⇨ Run, 279
Query ⇨ Show Table, 76, 275
Query ⇨ SQL Specific ⇨ Union, 813
Query ⇨ Update, 779
Query window, 275–276, 294
quick fix engineering (QFE), 1116
QuickSort, 242

R

radio buttons. *See* option button controls
random numbers, returning, 333
RDBMS. *See* relational database management
    systems (RDBMS)
Reading Order property, 482

read-only access, 46
real SQL Server data type, 1129
Record Locks property, 442, 824
record management controls, 1223
Record Selector bar, eliminating, 436
record selector column (Datasheet view), 67
Record Selectors property, 436, 1103
Record Source property, 441, 1168, 1169
records
    adding from backup tables, 775
    adding in data access pages (DAPs), 1223
    adding in Datasheet view, 217, 219–220,
        230, 232–233
    adding to external linked tables, 716
    adding using ActiveX Data Objects
        (ADO), 1044–1045
    adding using append queries, 773, 775,
        785–790, 799, 800
    adding using Data Access Objects (DAO),
        1045
    adding using functions, 1172, 1173, 1175
    adding using procedures, 1035, 1044–1048
    backups, appending to, 785–786
    bookmarking, 1023, 1302–1303
    cascading updates/deletes, 181, 183–184,
        233, 790–792
    changes, undoing, 68, 215, 217, 220,
        230–231
    changes, using functions to check for, 1175
    cloning, 1047–1048
    data access pages (DAPs) record
        selectors, 1247–1248
    Datasheet view, 65–69
    deleting, cascade option, 181, 183–184,
        233, 790–792
    deleting, confirming, 919, 922, 932–934
    deleting in data access pages (DAPs), 1223
    deleting in Datasheet view, 217, 229,
        233–234
    deleting, keyboard shortcuts for, 230
    deleting, referential integrity
        considerations, 177, 181–182
    deleting using ActiveX Data Objects
        (ADO), 1048–1047
    deleting using delete queries, 184, 773,
        776, 790–794
    deleting using functions, 1172
    deleting using procedures, 1048–1047
    described, 84
    display height, 237–238
    display options in datasheets, 235–242
    drilling down, 69, 1218
    duplicates, 71, 794, 815

forms, adding in, 441
forms, deleting in, 264, 441
forms, displaying saved records in, 442
forms, locking options in, 442
forms, management from unbound, 1168
forms, saving in, 264
forms, specifying record source, 441
identifiers, unique, 85, 102, 168
identifiers using AutoNumber, 138,
    158, 168
identity, 1130
locked, 230, 442, 800, 824
macros, finding using, 944–947
macros, navigation using, 939, 941–942
macros, using to assign values, 940–941
navigating, 66–69, 224–228, 263, 939,
    941–942
number, 68
number of in query, returning, 809–811
number of in table, returning, 809–811
number of matching criterion, returning,
    810–811
orphan records, 182, 794–798
pointer, 218–219, 1023
printing, 245–247, 1023–1027
queries, displaying only unique
    records in, 824
queries, displaying selected records in,
    290–293
queries, record selection criteria in,
    290–293
queries, returning by top values, 272,
    811–812, 830
queries, returning maximum number, 825
queries, returning number of in, 809–811
record selectors in data access pages
    (DAPs), 1247–1248
rows, relation to, 65, 84
saving in datasheets, 48, 215, 220, 242
saving in forms, 264, 266
saving using functions, 1172, 1174
selector column in datasheets, 67
selectors in dialog boxes, 1103
selectors in subforms, 841
SQL Server, autonumbering in, 1129–1130
subforms, record selectors in, 841
tables, relation to, 212
templates, creating from, 1047–1048
total queries on record groups, 744,
    748–751, 752
values, locating, 225–228
widow records, 182, 794–798
Records ➪ Filter ➪ Advanced Filter/Sort, 245

Records ➪ Remove Filter/Sort, 242
Records ➪ Save, 242
Records ➪ Save Record, 220, 266
RecordSelector property, 1247
RecordSet property, 825
Recordset Type property, 442
recordsets
    ActiveX Data Objects (ADO) recordsets,
        1038, 1039, 1040
    cloning, 1023, 1047–1048
    Data Access Objects (DAO) recordsets,
        1040
    described, 1023, 1038
    updating using functions, 1175–1176
ReDim statements, 1300
ReferenceFromFile function, 1289
References dialog box, 1287, 1438
referential integrity
    AutoNumber fields, using to enforce, 168
    cascading record updates/deletes, 181,
        183–184, 233, 790–792, 933
    data linking, effect on, 694
    Declared Referential Integrity (DRI), 1145
    delete queries, in, 790–791
    described, 177
    enforcing, 181–184
    join lines denoting, 345
    key fields role in, 177
    SQL Server, 1139–1140
    subforms, in, 846
Regional Settings Properties dialog box, 150
registration of OfficeXP/Access, 28, 35–39
*Relational Completeness of Data Base
        Sublanguages* (Codd), 103
relational database management systems
        (RDBMS), 4, 7–8, 83
relational operators, 293, 321–326, 370–371.
        See also specific operators
Relationship builder, 233, 713
relationships. *See* table relationships
Relationships ➪ Show Table, 178
Relationships window, 178–179, 189
/Repair command, 47
Replicable property, 1469, 1470, 1476
ReplicaFilter property, 1478
replication
    Access commands, using, 1470, 1471–1473
    application distribution
        considerations, 1428
    AutoNumber fields, 1469
    Briefcase replication, 59, 1470, 1473
    conflict table, 1467

Data Access Objects (DAO), using, 1471,
        1474–1478
database partitioning for, 1482–1483
database requirements, 1464–1466
database size increased by, 1464, 1470
described, 1463–1464
Design Masters, 1464, 1466–1470,
        1497–1498
fields created by, 1464, 1467, 1469–1470
Jet and Replication Objects (JRO), using,
        1471, 1474
.MDE file considerations, 1330–1331
objects, changes supported, 1464
objects, local, 1469
passwords, removing before, 1464
projects, in, 1471, 1474
replica databases, filtering, 1478
replica databases, partial, 1471, 1474,
        1476–1478, 1482–1483, 1488
replica sets, 1464
replica sets, member IDs, 1466, 1467, 1469,
        1486
replica sets, removing replicas from, 1486
Replication Manager utility, using, 1471,
        1478–1485
system tables added by, 1467–1468, 1472
utilities, 1416
Replication command, 1470
Replication Conflict Viewer dialog box, 1492
Replication Manager, 1416, 1471, 1478–1485,
        1489–1490
replman.exe, 1478
Report Design toolbar, 573–574
Report Design toolbox, 310
Report Design window, 310–311, 979–981
Report Manager Professional (on the CD),
        1554
Report Wizards, 301–311
Report Writer, 11, 576–581
ReportML2DAP.xsl, 1255, 1267
reports. *See also* mail merge reports; mailing
        labels
    AutoFormat, 629, 965
    background shading, 646
    back-version compatibility, 40
    bands, 574
    charts, 302
    closing, 79
    Code Behind Report (CBR), 993
    columns, 296–297, 302, 873–876, 1262
    creating, 298–301, 581–587, 663–664,
        874–875

creating using AutoReport, 218, 302, 312–313
creating using Report Wizards, 301–311
data access pages (DAPs), conversion to, 1261–1265
data assembly step, 299–300, 584–586
dates, displaying, 667, 672–673, 682–684
described, 89, 295
design, 93–100, 298–301, 583–584, 624, 657–658
design, opening, 308
Design View, 303, 310–311, 572
detail headers, 574
detail section, 306, 574, 666–669, 875
detail section, showing/hiding, 306, 580, 616, 948–949
displaying, 78–79
expressions in, 595–596, 667–668, 673–675
Extensible Markup Language (XML), exporting to, 1269–1270
field name changes, 235
fields, adding, 93–97, 303–304, 589–592
fields, grouping, 304–305
filtering, 948, 957
footer controls, 671–674, 678–681, 684–685
footers, report, 574, 577, 578, 580–581, 689
forms conversion to, 470
forms versus, 298
graphs, 302, 534
group footers, 574, 577, 580
group footers, creating, 613–615, 669–670, 675–676
group footers, removing, 616
group headers, 574, 577, 579–580
group headers, creating, 611, 613–615, 669–670, 675–676, 681–682
group headers, removing, 616
group totals, 580, 673
grouping data, 611–615
group/total reports, 295
header controls, 600–601, 670–671, 676–678, 682–684
headers, report, 574, 577, 578–579, 688–689
hyperlinks in, 1212–1214
hyperlinks to, 1212
HyperText Markup Language (HTML), exporting report datasheets to, 1202–1205
images in, 643–644, 966
invoices, 297, 656–659, 661, 679–680
layout, 93, 299, 306–307, 583–584, 587–589

layout preview, 572, 651
lines, creating emphasis using, 644–646, 684
macros, adding conditional text using, 954
macros, formatting using, 952
macros, hiding data using, 957
macros, highlighting data using, 954–957
macros, opening using, 910–911, 948, 1060, 1088
macros, printing using, 1088, 1093–1102
macros, running before layout, 952
macros, running before printing, 952, 953–954
macros, running on return to previous section, 952–953
macros, section data layout using, 952–953
macros, section-level activation/deactivation, 948–949, 951–953, 954
macros, snapshots using, 949–951
mailing labels as, 297–298, 863
margins, 588, 617, 654, 664
menus, assigning to, 1076, 1079
modules behind, 974, 994–995
navigation, 79, 1203
Object Linking and Embedding (OLE) objects in, 643
opening from menu bar items, 1076
opening using macros, 910–911, 948, 1060, 1088
opening using procedures, 1026–1027
option groups, 634–640
page breaks, 613, 617–620
page footers, 574, 577, 578, 579, 580–581
page headers, 574, 579, 592–593
page numbers, 595–596, 684–685
page orientation, 588, 653
paper size, 588, 653
printer setup, 440, 587–589, 651–654
printing, 311, 589, 651–654, 876
printing, designing for, 624, 626
printing, dialog boxes for, 1023–1025, 1087–1088
procedures, opening using, 1026–1027
projects, in, 1127, 1157
queries, relating to, 299–301, 581, 586, 659–662, 1096–1097
rectangles, creating emphasis using, 644–646, 647
reverse video, 624, 647–648
saving, 310, 312, 621
sections, 574–581

Continued

reports *(continued)*
    sections, activation/deactivation using macros, 948–949, 951–953, 954
    sections, formatting using macros, 952–953
    sections, hiding, 616
    sections, sizing, 592–593, 617
    shading effects, 624, 646
    shadow effects, 629–631, 647
    sizing, 589, 592–593, 664
    snapshots, 354, 355, 813, 949–951, 1148–1149
    sorting data, 11, 305–306, 611–613, 664–666
    specifications, 1535–1536, 1537
    speed, optimizing for, 1296–1298
    style, 308, 966
    subreport controls, 397, 839, 841, 843, 850
    summaries, 296
    summaries, group, 673–675
    summaries, percentages, 306, 686
    summaries, showing/hiding detail section, 306, 580, 616, 948–949
    summaries, totals, 306, 580, 686
    summaries using group footer section, 580
    table relationships, 186
    tabular, 296, 302
    test data, 662–663, 668–669
    title, 308
    title page, 688–689
    toggle button controls in, 642
    types, 295–296
    Upsizing Wizard report, 1148–1149, 1155–1156
    usability hierarchy, in, 5–6
    Visual Basic code behind, 974, 994–995
    What You See Is What You Get (WYSIWYG), 10–11
Reports macro condition, 909
Required property, 145
Resolve Window Definition Wizard, 1379–1380
Restore/Maximize button, 57, 63
Resume statements, 1016
reverse video display, 479, 624, 647–648
Rich Text Format (RTF) documents, 692
Right function, 335
Right Margin property, 482
Rnd function, 333
/RO command, 46
RoboHelp, 1399
Rollback Transaction event property, 924

Row Source property, 515, 542, 855, 1019–1021, 1034
Row Source Type property, 508–509, 515, 855
ROWGUID columns, 1130, 1132
rows
    combo box row properties, 515, 858
    deleting, 141–142
    described, 84
    display height, 237–238
    inserting, 141
    list box row properties, 508–509, 1019
    macros, inserting in, 1099, 1100
    navigating, 66–69
    pivot tables, converting to columns in, 563
    queries, showing/hiding in, 287
    records, relation to, 65, 84
RowSource property, 1298
RTF documents. *See* Rich Text Format (RTF) documents
ruler, 260, 414
Run dialog box, installation from, 25
Run Permissions property, 824, 1346
Run ⇨ Run, 902
Run ⇨ Single Step, 913
RunCode action, 47
RunMacro macro action, 905, 913
Running Sum property, 580, 686–688
RunSQL macro action, 933
/Runtime command, 1326–1330, 1406
runtime mode. *See* applications, runtime
Rushmore query optimizer, 1295

S
Save As Data Access Page dialog box, 1224
Save As dialog box, 134, 739, 985–986, 1255
Save As MDE dialog box, 1281
Save Relationships dialog box, 184
Scale property, 1130
schemas, Extensible Markup Language (XML), 1266
screen tips. *See also* tooltips
    forms, in, 438
    Help option, 9, 53, 57, 128
    menu items, assigning to, 1075, 1080
Scroll Bar Align property, 482
Scroll Bars property, 437, 480, 1103
Scroll Tips, 213, 225
scrollbar elevator, 225
search and replace operations, 231–232, 325
Search Manager Professional (on the CD), 1554

searching. *See also* filtering; queries
Boolean (logical) operators, 326–328
case-sensitive, 227
dialog boxes for, 1019–1023
fields, specific, 225–228
files, for, 215–216
forms, from unbound, 1176–1178
functions, using, 1172, 1176–1178
Help system Search tab definition, 1380, 1389–1390
macros, using, 944–947
null values, for, 388–389
pattern matching, 325, 377–378
ranges of values, 329
relational operators, 321–326
speed, optimizing for, 158, 171
Visual Basic Application edition (VBA) code, in, 1522–1523
wildcards, using, 226–227, 326
security. *See also* passwords; permissions
Admin user, 1320, 1333, 1337
Admin user passwords, 1333, 1340, 1351
Admin user, removing permissions from when securing database, 1320, 1325, 1339, 1349
assessment of Access security, 1321–1322, 1414
database secure copies using Security Wizard, 1322, 1353–1360
encryption, 1324, 1325, 1360–1361
form-level, 1322
forms, startup, 1326
Jet, 1115, 1319–1322, 1332
level, choosing, 1322
.MDE files, 1280, 1330–1332
runtime mode, 1326–1328, 1414
source code, protecting, 1414
SQL Server 2000 Desktop Engine, 1115, 1116
startup options, 1328–1330
user profiles, 1334
user-level, 1319–1320
users, adding, 1337–1339
users, creating using Data Access Objects (DAO), 1362
users, default, 1320, 1333, 1337
users, deleting, 1339
users, editing information, 1337
users, group membership assignment, 1339, 1341–1342, 1344–1345
users, group membership removal, 1344–1345

users, personal IDs (PID), 1338–1339
users, security IDs (SID), 1338–1339, 1343
workgroup files, 1320, 1333, 1335–1336, 1357–1359
security IDs (SID), 1338–1339, 1343
Security Wizard, 1322, 1353–1360
Select Bitmap dialog box, 1063
Select Case. . .End Select statements, 1007–1009, 1025
Select Objects tool, 413
SELECT statements, 814, 815, 817, 827, 828–831
Select Unique Record Identifier dialog box, 703
Selected Fields list box, 836–837
Selected property, 1034
Selection behavior property, 415
Selection objects, 1450, 1451
SendKeys macro action, 933, 937, 959
SendKeys syntax, 959
Set statements, 1038, 1439
SetPMeter function, 1309
Setup Wizard, 1420, 1426
SetValue macro action, 939–941, 949, 1095
Seven-Step Design Method, 89–90
s_Generation field, 1467, 1469
s_GUID field, 1467, 1469
Shortcut Menus toolbar, 1078
Shortcut properties, 443, 1080
Show: properties, 287–288
Show Table dialog box, 75, 76, 274–275
ShowAllRecords macro action, 943
ShowDateSelectors property, 567
SID. *See* security IDs (SID)
single data type, 1001
Size command, 419
Size Mode property, 484, 525, 526–527, 542
s_Lineage field, 1467, 1469, 1490
Smalldatetime SQL Server data type, 1129
smallint SQL Server data type, 1129
Smallmoney SQL Server data type, 1129
SmartDrive, 1291
snapshots, 354, 355, 813, 949–951, 1148–1149
snp files, 949
software protection scheme, 28, 35
software requirements, 24, 1117, 1218–1219
Sort By dialog box, 868
sorting
columns, 59
data access pages (DAPs), 1223, 1231
datasheets, in, 242

Continued

sorting *(continued)*
   HyperText Markup Language (HTML)
      pages, in, 1192
   indexes, role of, 158, 173
   introduced, 21
   mailing labels, 867–868
   memo data, 289
   multiple fields, on, 289–290, 611–612
   Object Linking and Embedding (OLE)
      data, 289
   order, ascending, 216, 242, 288–289
   order, default, 160
   order, descending, 216, 242
   order precedence, 289
   primary key considerations, 171
   primary sort, 289
   procedures, using stored, 1162–1163
   queries, in, 76, 288–290, 765–766, 825
   QuickSort, 242
   records, 242
   reports, in, 11, 305–306, 611–613, 664–666
   secondary sort, 289, 611–612
   speed, optimizing for, 158, 171, 173
   SQL Server, 1137–1138
   Structured Query Language (SQL)
      statements, specifying in, 827, 831
   tables, in, 160
   views, adding sort orders to, 1163
Sorting and Grouping box, 611–613, 670
Sounds property, 1457
Source Connect Str property, 824
Source Database property, 824
Special Effect property, 481
Special Effect window, 60–61, 474
Special Offers screen, 37–38
specifications, 1533–1538
speed, optimizing for
   combo boxes, 1297–1298
   data type considerations, 1298–1300
   databases, compacting, 1291, 1312
   databases, opening in exclusive mode,
      1290
   forms, 1296–1298
   hard drive defragmentation, 1292
   indexes, using, 146, 158, 171, 173,
      1292–1294
   list boxes, 1297–1298
   memory, 1275, 1291–1292, 1303
   modules, 1298–1303
   network performance, 1303
   queries, 158, 171, 1021, 1294–1295
   reports, 1296–1298

SmartDrive, 1291
SQL Server 2000 Desktop Engine, using,
   1291
speed, perceived, 1289, 1303–1310
spell checking, 196–197, 554–555
splash screens, 1304–1305, 1408–1410
SQL Server
   forms, connecting to SQL Server database,
      1169–1170
   Jet, as alternative to, 1113
   Jet, using to access SQL Server tables,
      1147, 1151
   queries for, pass-through, 816
   SQL Server 2000 Desktop Engine
      compatibility, 1115
   SQL Server 2000 Desktop Engine relation
      to, 1113–1114
SQL Server 7 technology, 1113
SQL Server 2000 Desktop Engine. *See also*
      projects, Access
   accounts, 1125
   application distribution
      considerations, 1428
   backup recoverability, 1115, 1116
   bootup, starting on, 1120
   client/server model, 1114
   columns, 1130, 1131, 1132, 1141
   connection setup, 1123–1124, 1144
   data entry constraints, 1134, 1135–1137
   data integrity, 1115, 1116
   data types, 1129
   Database Designer, 1138
   database diagrams, working with, 1127,
      1138–1142
   database file, objects stored in, 1126
   databases, creating, 1121–1126
   databases, file extension, 1122
   databases, maximum size, 1116
   databases, naming, 1122–1123
   fault tolerance, 1116
   fields, creating, 1129
   fields, properties, 1129–1130
   hardware requirements, 1117, 1143
   hyperlinks, 1130
   indexes, 1130, 1134
   Input Method Editor (IME) mode, 1130
   installation, 1117–1119
   instance name, 1119
   Jet database engine compared, 1114
   keys, primary/foreign, 1133, 1134–1135
   logon ID, 1124, 1147
   macros, 1127

Microsoft Database Engine (MSDE) databases, accessing, 1121
Microsoft Database Engine (MSDE), removing before installation, 1118
Microsoft Distributed Transaction Coordinator (MSDTC) service, 1120
Microsoft Office XP Developer tools, 1415
modules, 1127
pages, 1127
passwords, 1124, 1147
pausing, 1120–1121
personal computers, application development on, 1114
privileges needed, 1124
queries, maximum simultaneous, 1116
quick fix engineering (QFE) support, 1116
records, autonumbering, 1129–1130
records, identity, 1130
referential integrity, 1139–1140
scalability, 1114, 1116
security, 1115, 1116
server name, 1119, 1124
server-side processing, 1114
Service Manager, 1119–1120
software requirements, 1117
sorting, 1137–1138
speed, 1291
SQL Server Agent service, 1120
SQL Server compatibility, 1115
SQL Server relation to, 1113–1114
SQLServer service, 1120
SQLServer versions accessible to, 1121
starting, 1119–1121
statistics, 1135
stopping, 1120–1121
subdatasheets, 1137–1138
tables, constraints, 1134, 1135–1137
tables, creating, 1128–1130, 1141
tables, deleting, 1141
tables, describing, 1132
tables, displaying ownership, 1131
tables, editing, 1141
tables, file groups, 1132
tables, lookup, 1133
tables, naming, 1131
tables, relationships, 1132–1133, 1139–1140
tables, sort order, 1137–1138
timestamp fields, 1129, 1145
transaction logging, 1116
user ID, 1124, 1147
users, concurrent, 1115–1116

validation, data, 1134, 1135–1136
validation, user, 1124, 1147
Windows NT, integrated security with, 1115, 1116
SQL Server 2000 for Office XP Developer, 1415
SQL Server Service Manager, 1119–1120, 1153
SQL statements. *See* Structured Query Language (SQL) statements
sql_variant SQL Server data type, 1129
Sqr function, 335
Src property, 1251, 1252
standard deviation, 746
starting Access. *See also* startup options
  Access shortcut icon, from, 43
  Office folder, from icon in, 44–45
  Start menu, from, 42–44
  Windows Explorer, from, 45–46
Startup dialog box, 47, 57, 1087
startup options
  Access icon, specifying, 1086
  applications, 1402–1404
  bypassing, 1314, 1330
  command-line parameters, 46–47, 1406
  Database window display, 1403
  databases, opening, 46–47
  databases, passing values to, 47
  forms, 47–48, 438, 455, 906, 1086–1087
  keys, disabling/enabling, 1404
  macros, running, 47–48, 906, 1086
  menu bar, 1086, 1403
  menus, 1403, 1404
  runtime environment, 1406
  shortcut menu display, 1403, 1404
  Startup dialog box, hiding, 47
  status bar display, 1086, 1403
  title bar text, specifying, 1086
  toolbars, 1086, 1404
  user profile options, 46
  username/password options, 46
  Visual Basic (VBA) procedures, running, 47
Startup parameters dialog box, 1402
Startup properties window, 906
Status Bar Text property, 496, 1106
status bars, 57, 213, 496, 1086, 1403
status line messages, 494
Stop Recording window, 1453
StopMacro macro action, 912, 913, 932, 939
Str function, 333
string data type (Visual Basic), 1001
string data types, Access. *See* memo data type; text data type

string manipulation functions, 335. *See also* text, working with

string operators, 323–326. *See also* text, working with

Structured Query Language (SQL) statements. *See also specific statements*

    Active Server Pages (ASP), in, 1202

    conditions, specifying, 831–832

    creating in SQL view window, 826

    database servers, sending commands to, 813, 815–816

    ending, 831–832

    field selection, 814, 815, 817, 827, 828–831

    field values, eliminating duplicates, 829–830

    filters, specifying, 827

    financial functions, 224

    FROM clauses, 830–831

    graphs, in, 542

    indexes, creating, 813, 816–817

    indexes, dropping, 813, 816–817

    Internet resources, 832

    modifying, 826

    ORDER BY clauses, 827, 831, 1157

    queries, conversion to/from, 826, 1019–1021

    queries, in, 272, 356, 372–373, 813–817, 826–832

    query selection, 830–831

    records, displaying based on top values, 830

    sort order, 827, 831

    stored procedures, in, 1161

    subqueries, 817

    table lookup properties, in, 195

    table selection, 827, 830–831

    viewing, 826

    WHERE clauses, 829–830, 831

Style property, 1107

SubDatasheet properties, 440, 825

Subform Wizard, 834

SubKey field, 1525, 1526–1527

subroutines, 1016

subtraction operator, 319

Sum function, 334, 673

Summary Options dialog box, 306, 307

Surgical Strike (on the CD), 1554–1555

Switchboard Manager, 1505–1507

switchboards

    actions possible from, 969

    command buttons, 1049–1050

    creating from forms, 1051

    creating using Database Wizard, 967–969

    creating using Switchboard Manager, 1505–1507

    data-entry forms, as, 1410

    design, 115–116, 967–969

    introduced, 115–116

    page definitions, 968–969

    startup, loading at, 1086

Sybase Server, 692, 718

synchronization

    bidirectional, 1487

    Briefcase synchronization, 59, 1473, 1487

    conflict tables, 1469

    conflicts, resolving, 1490–1497

    Data Access Objects (DAO), using, 1487–1489, 1493–1497

    described, 1463

    error logging, 1469

    forms, using macros, 927–929

    projects, in, 1474

    replicas, partial, 1488–1489

    Replication Manager Synchronizers, 1478–1481, 1489–1490

    Replication menu, using, 1486–1487

    scheduling, 1489–1490

    system tables added by, 1467–1468

    tables, 147

Synchronize Database dialog box, 1486

Synchronize Now dialog box, 1489

SysCmd function, 1306–1307

SYSTEM.MDW, 1320

T

tab controls, 397, 407–408, 1103–1109, 1256

Tab Order dialog box, 453, 1108

Tab properties, 453, 1107

Table Analyzer

    accessing, 187–189

    described, 186–187

    field changes using, 192–196

    installation, 188

    keys, operations on, 194–197

    Looking At the Problem window, 188

    normalization, checking, 186–187

    Relationships window, 189, 192

    reliability, 186, 195, 1292

    Solving the Problem window, 188–189

    spell checking, 196–197

    table changes using, 191, 192–196

    table selection for, 189

table splitting, 191
  tasks accomplished by, 186–187
Table Analyzer DB (on the CD), 187
Table Design window, 134–139, 157,
      1128–1130
table joins. *See* table relationships, joins
Table of Contents Entry dialog box,
      1385–1386
Table Properties dialog box, 207
Table Properties window, 160–161, 1131–1138
table relationships. *See also* keys; referential
      integrity; tables
  analyzing using Table Analyzer, 189–192
  AutoJoin, 822, 823
  conflicts, solving, 182
  creating, 180–186
  deleting, 181, 183–184
  design, 103–108
  displaying, 166, 178–179, 181, 184–185
  editing, 180, 181, 183
  Find Unmatched queries, 182
  join lines, 166, 184–185, 345–346, 1139
  joins, changing properties of, 362–363
  joins, creating in queries, 357–360, 803
  joins, cross-product (Cartesian),
      358, 359, 367
  joins, deleting in queries, 358, 360
  joins, inner (equi-joins), 361–362,
      363–364, 831
  joins, left, 366–367, 831
  joins, meaningless, 359–360
  joins, multiple-field, 360
  joins, outer, 363–367
  joins, right, 364–366, 831
  joins, self, 361
  joins, types of, 360–361
  linked tables, 713
  lookup table relationship, 176
  many-to-many, 176–177
  many-to-one, 176
  one-to-many, 176, 356–357
  one-to-one, 175–176
  parent-child relationship, 177
  primary table, 181
  queries, creating in, 174, 343–345, 349,
      351–354, 357–360
  queries, overridden by, 177
  reports of, printing, 186
  saving, 184
  subforms, layout in, 838–839
  updateability, effect on, 354–355
Table Wizard, 131–132, 961–962

tables. *See also* columns; fields; rows;
      table relationships
  Active Server Pages (ASP), saving as,
      1198–1199
  analyzing using Table Analyzer, 189–192
  background color, 239
  cells, 65
  changing, 162, 192, 197
  closing, 133
  copying, 163–164
  copying structure, 163
  creating by dragging field to empty area,
      193
  creating using make-table action queries,
      719, 773, 776, 781–784
  creating using Table Wizard, 129–134
  data access pages (DAPs), conversion to,
      1255–1256
  data access pages (DAPs) using multiple,
      1220
  data access pages (DAPs) using single,
      1221–1230
  data separation into, 85–86, 100–106
  database, maintaining in separate, 124,
      709–712, 1413–1414
  Database Wizard, using, 964–965
  databases versus, 67
  Datasheet view, 65–69, 132–134
  deleting, 163
  described, 83–84
  design, 85–86, 100–108, 130, 141–144, 161
  Design View, 70–72, 134
  dynasets, based on, 273
  dynasets versus, 273
  fields, adding to, 71, 131, 140–141
  fields, moving, 192–193
  fields, relation to, 212
  file format, 39
  flat-file tables, 190–191
  forms data source, specifying, 254
  forms, multiple-table, 457–463
  forms, updating from, 1035, 1036
  hyperlinks in, 1211, 1213
  HyperText Markup Language (HTML)
      tables, linking, 694, 706–707, 1210
  identifiers, unique, 102
  junction tables, 176–177
  local, 124
  "local" tablename suffix, 1147, 1150
  lookup tables, 109–110, 166–167, 176
  lookup tables in queries, 803–805
  lookup tables in subforms, 852–859
  lookup tables, permanent, 801

Continued

tables *(continued)*
    lookup tables, transient, 801, 803
    lookup tables using DLookUp function, 802–803
    moving linked, 717
    name, changing, 162, 192, 193–194, 716
    naming, 133, 373
    navigating, 65–69
    normalization, 86, 103–106
    opening, 65–66
    Paste As operations, 163–164, 786
    procedures, updating using, 1035–1036
    project objects, as, 1127, 1157
    project tables stored in server database, 1126
    projects, creating in, 1128
    projects, properties in, 1131–1138
    properties, setting, 160–161
    queries, adding to, 75, 275, 277, 349
    queries, displaying table names in, 287, 352–353
    queries, multi-table, 343–345, 351–357
    queries, opening in, 344
    queries, removing from, 275, 349
    queries, updating from, 354–357
    query destination table name, 825
    records, relation to, 212
    records, returning number of in, 809–811
    recordsets as temporary table objects, 1023
    refreshing, 785
    saving, 133–134, 162
    snapshots, 354, 355, 813
    sorting order, 160
    specifications, 1534–1535
    spell checking, 196–197
    splitting using Table Analyzer, 191
    SQL Server, under, 1128–1138, 1139–1140, 1141
    Structured Query Language (SQL) statements affecting, 816
    Structured Query Language (SQL) statements, selection for, 827, 830–831
    subforms, selection for, 836
    synchronization, 147
    upsizing, in, 1144, 1145, 1147, 1149, 1150
    usability hierarchy, in, 5–6
    validation, table-level, 494–495
    views, adding to, 1158–1159
    Web page creation from, 1186, 1190–1192
Tables Container objects, 1365

Tag property, 443
TARGETDIR folder, 1119
task panes, 886–887
Template ⇨ General Templates, 962
Templates dialog box, 121–123
Text Align property, 482
text box controls. *See also* controls
    3-D effects, 481
    alignment, 417, 482
    background color, 481
    borders, 481
    combo boxes, changing to, 512–514
    creating, 409, 410–411, 595
    data access pages (DAPs), in, 1237
    date display properties, 480
    deleting, 598–599
    described, 397, 402
    expressions in, 595–596
    font, 481, 482
    hyperlinks in, 482
    keyboard language, 482
    label placement, 401
    labels attached to, 411, 421, 595
    line spacing, 482
    line wrap, 402
    mail merge reports, in, 882–883
    margins, 482, 609
    memos, in, 453–455, 633
    moving, 450–451, 599–604
    multiple-line, 402, 453–455, 632–633
    number display properties, 480, 482
    positioning, 112, 481
    properties, displaying, 430–431, 479–483, 607–608, 631–632
    reading order, 482
    sizing on text entry, 480, 610–611, 632–633
    sizing to fit, 604–605
    sizing using handles, 449–450, 597
    sizing when creating, 412
    subforms, in, 839, 860
    visibility properties, 480
Text data type
    conversion to/from, 143–144, 333, 672
    data entry, 221, 222
    formats, 147–148
    grouping options in reports, 614
    introduced, 108
    queries, in, 144
    storage size, 136
    type of data stored, 136
    validation, 222
    Visual Basic equivalent, 1003

Text property, 1458
Text Qualifier, 728, 734
text shadow, 477–479, 629–631
Text SQL Server data type, 1129
text, working with. *See also* concatenation
    append queries, 800
    case conversion of data entered, 147, 148,
        153, 221
    case conversion using macros, 940
    comparison operations, 325–326, 377–381
    dates, converting to strings, 672
    fields, joining text with, 672–673
    length of string, returning, 335
    line wrap, 402, 877, 882
    lowercase, returning, 335
    macros, adding conditional text using, 954
    rightmost characters of string,
        returning, 335
    spaces, removing unwanted, 870
    string data type, changing to/from,
        333, 672
    uppercase, returning, 334
    validation rules, 155
Time function, 334
time operations
    current time, returning, 333, 334
    delimiters, 735
    expressions, in, 339
    format, 149–150
    forms, inserting time in, 264
    functions related to, 334
    importing text files, format in, 731–732,
        735
    validation rules, 156
timeout settings, 824
TimerInterval event property, 923
timestamps, 1129, 1145
Tinyint SQL Server data type, 1129
title bar, 56–57, 58, 434–435, 906, 1086
toggle button controls
    creating, 504, 641–642
    datasheets, in, 854
    described, 197
    images in, 504–505, 642–643
    raised, 484
    reports, in, 642
    values returned, 403, 502
    visual display, 403, 504
tokens, HTML template, 1205–1206
Toolbar Properties dialog box, 1070, 1078
Toolbar property, 443, 1084

toolbars. *See also* menu bars
    Access window, 56, 57
    changes, allowing/disallowing, 1404
    commands, adding, 1083
    creating, 57, 1082–1083
    Datasheet window, 215–218
    Formatting toolbar, 448, 472–474
    forms, attaching to, 443, 1084–1085
    icons, 1074, 1082
    items, adding, 1068
    items, creating, 1068
    items, moving, 1068
    items, removing, 1068
    menu bars, changing to, 1071
    pop-up shortcut menus, changing to, 1078
    Query Design window, 277–278
    separator lines, 1083
    startup options, 1086, 1404
    text, customizing, 1075
Toolbars Menu, 1071
Toolbox
    customizing, 535
    Form Toolbox, 74, 398, 410, 412–413
    introduced, 61, 74
    Report Design Toolbox, 310
Tools ➪ Add-Ins, 1499
Tools ➪ Analyze ➪ Documenter, 161
Tools ➪ Analyze ➪ Table, 187
Tools ➪ AutoCorrect, 556
Tools ➪ Database Utilities, 1280, 1331
Tools ➪ Database Utilities ➪ Compact
        Database, 1312
Tools ➪ Database Utilities ➪ Convert
        Database ➪ To, 41
Tools ➪ Database Utilities ➪
        Database Splitter, 711
Tools ➪ Database Utilities ➪ Linked Table
        Manager, 717
Tools ➪ Macro, 905
Tools ➪ Macro ➪ Convert Form's Macros to
        Visual Basic, 989
Tools ➪ Macro ➪ Create Menu, 1065
Tools ➪ Macro ➪ Macros, 1454
Tools ➪ Macro ➪ Record New Macro, 1452
Tools ➪ Options, 56
Tools ➪ Options ➪ Advance, 40
Tools ➪ References, 1438, 1439
Tools ➪ Relationships, 178
Tools ➪ Replication ➪ Create Replica,
        1465, 1471
Tools ➪ Security, 1321
Tools ➪ Security ➪ Encrypt/Decrypt
        Database, 1360, 1362

Tools ➪ Security ➪ Set Database Password,
    1324
Tools ➪ Security ➪ Unset Database Password,
    1325
Tools ➪ Security ➪ User and Group Accounts,
    1337
Tools ➪ Security ➪ User-Level Security
    Wizard, 1353
Tools ➪ Startup, 906
Tools ➪ Startup ➪ Application Title, 58
Tools ➪ Synchronize Now, 1489
tooltips, 57, 128, 1085. *See also* screen tips
Top function, 272, 811–812
Top label property, 481
Top Margin property, 482
TOP query clause, 1163
Top text box property, 481
Top Values property, 824
Topic Files dialog box, 1381
Total Access Analyzer, 1278
transactions, 825, 924
TransferDatabase macro action, 958
TransferSpreadsheet macro action, 958
TransferSQLDatabase macro action, 958
TransferText macro action, 958
transparency, color, 474, 478, 485
Trim function, 870

U

Ucase function, 333, 334, 940
UDFs. *See* user-defined functions (UDFs)
Unbound Form Utilities module (on the CD),
    1172
UNC. *See* Universal Naming Convention
    (UNC)
Undo Batch Edit event property, 924
Unicode Compression property, 146
Uniform Resource Locators (URLs), 1180
Union command, 815
Unique Records property, 824
Unique Values property, 824
uniqueidentifier SQL Server data type, 1129
UniqueTable property, 1230, 1231, 1233,
    1235–1236
Universal Naming Convention (UNC), 1225,
    1248
UpdateCtr controls, 1170
upgrading from earlier versions, 25, 28–29
upsizing
    ActiveX Data Objects (ADO), 1157
    application creation, 1154–1157

    application options, 1147
    backing up before, 1143
    connection information, entering, 1144,
        1153
    Data Access Objects (DAO), 1157
    disk space considerations, 1143
    forms, 1147
    indexes, 1145
    keys, primary, 1145
    login ID, 1144, 1153
    macros, 1147, 1157
    modules, 1147, 1157
    object conversion, 1147, 1157
    permissions needed, 1143
    preparation for, 1143
    printer, default, 1143
    project, creating new, 1147, 1154–1155
    project, default name, 1154
    queries, 1147
    referential integrity error alerts, 1148
    report snapshot, 1148–1149, 1155–1156
    reports, 1147
    tables in, 1144, 1145, 1147, 1149, 1150
    tables, SQL Server attribute selection,
        1146, 1154
    time needed, 1148
    timestamp fields, 1145
    validation, data, 1145
    validation, user, 1147, 1154
Upsizing Wizard, 1142–1150, 1152–1157
usability hierarchy, 5–6
Use Transaction property, 825
Use Triggers option, 1145
User and Group Accounts dialog box,
        1337–1338, 1340, 1343, 1346–1347
/User command, 46
User objects, 1362–1363
user profiles, 46, 1334
user-defined functions (UDFs), 1165–1166
user-defined SQL Server data type, 1129
User-Level Security Wizard. *See* Security
    Wizard
UserName property, 1364
usernames, 46
Users group, 1342, 1357
users, maximum concurrent, 1115–1116
USysRegInfo table, 1525–1529

V

Val function, 333
Valid Row Source Type property, 508–509

validation, data. *See also* data-entry rules
   automatic, 155
   combo boxes, using for data entry,
         505–506, 512–517, 1028–1031
   controls, data-validation, 397
   data entry, with, 222
   data type, automatic validation, 220–221
   date range validation, 156
   Date/Time rules, 156
   expressions, data-validation, 493–496
   form-level, 495, 938–939
   list boxes, using for data entry, 505–512,
         1031–1035
   macros, using, 938–939
   messages, 145, 156, 493, 494, 495
   Number data type, 221, 222
   numeric expressions, 155
   rules, assigning, 145, 155–156
   SQL Server, 1134, 1135–1136
   status line messages, 494
   table-level, 494–495
   text rules, 155
   user-defined, 155
Validation properties, 145, 1029
Value property, 567
varbinary SQL Server data type, 1129
Varchar SQL Server data type, 1129
variables
   ActiveX Data Objects (ADO)
         variables, 1038
   checking in Immediate window, 982
   controls, referencing as, 1301
   controls, unbound, 399
   creating on the fly, 997
   data type assignment, 974, 998,
         1000–1003
   data type, default, 998
   data type, preceding name with, 997
   declaration, 997–998
   declaration, ActiveX Data Objects (ADO)
         variables, 1038
   declaration, explicit, 974, 975
   declaration, implicit, 974
   declaration in modules, 974, 999
   declaration in procedures, 974, 998–1000
   declaration using Dim statement,
         998–999
   declaration using Private statement, 1000
   declaration using Public statement,
         999–1000
   declarations, eliminating unused, 1303

   expression results, assigning to, 996
   fields, referencing as, 1301–1302
   functions, passing variable values to, 1503
   long pointer (lp) variables, 1504
   Microsoft Office XP Developer folder
         variables, 1425–1426
   naming, 997
   object variables, 1438
   private, 1000
   public, 999–1000
   referencing in other modules, 1000
   Response variables, 1031
   storage allocated for, 997
   string variables, 1001
   undeclared, 998
   uses, 996
variant data type, 998, 1002
VBA. *See* Visual Basic Application edition
         (VBA)
versions
   applications, runtime, 1409, 1410, 1424
   back-version compatibility, 12, 39–40, 124
   displaying version info, 27
   file conversion from previous, 39–42, 47
   Jet Database Engine, 1334
   Office component versions, previous, 33
   saving in previous versions, 124
View ➪ Code, 974
View compiled file dialog box, 1390, 1391
View ➪ Conditions, 896, 909
View ➪ Data Outline, 1254
View ➪ Datasheet View, 265
View ➪ Design View, 73, 283
View ➪ Field List, 409
View ➪ Form, 435
View ➪ Form Header/Footer, 468
View ➪ Form View, 266
View ➪ Grid, 260
View ➪ Immediate Window, 982
View ➪ Indexes, 172
View ➪ Layout Preview, 651
View ➪ Macro Names, 896
View ➪ Object Browser, 981
View ➪ Page Header/Footer, 616
View ➪ Pages, 247
View Procedures dialog box, 981
View ➪ Properties, 60, 207
View Query Designer, 1158–1161
View ➪ Report Header/Footer, 616
View ➪ Ruler, 260
View ➪ Sorting and Grouping, 1245

View ➪ SQL View, 372, 826, 1021
View ➪ Tab Order, 452, 1108
View ➪ Table Names, 287, 352–353, 822
View ➪ Toolbars, 57
View ➪ Toolbars ➪ Customize, 1066–1067
View ➪ Toolbars ➪ Web, 1181
View ➪ Toolbox, 398
View ➪ Totals, 742
views
    data access pages (DAPs), conversion to,
        1255–1256
    query views, 1158–1161, 1163
Views Allowed property, 435, 1103
Visible macro action, 1095
Visible property, 480, 939, 955–957, 1106,
    1449–1450
Visual Basic Application edition (VBA). *See
    also* Automation; modules;
    procedures; *specific statements*
    Active Server Pages (ASP), in export
        operations to, 1200
    ActiveX Data Objects (ADO), working with,
        1036–1039
    add-ins, coding custom, 1517–1524
    code, creating in Module window, 975
    code, creating using Command Button
        Wizard, 989–992
    code, creating using Macro Recorder,
        1452–1454
    code, dead, 1303
    code management tools, 1415
    code, text searches in, 1522–1523
    combo boxes using, 1027–1031
    comments, 898, 1415
    conditions, evaluating multiple, 1007–1009
    conditions, evaluating single, 1004–1007
    conditions, repeating commands while
        true, 1010–1012
    controls, hiding/showing using, 1024–1025
    counters, 1013
    Data Access Objects (DAO), working with,
        1037–1041, 1043, 1044–1045,
        1362–1366
    data types, 1001–1003
    described, 16–17, 970
    encrypting databases using, 1361
    error messages, 1017, 1031
    error processing during macro
        conversion, 987, 989
    error trapping, 1017–1018, 1413

    errors, execution redirection on, 1015,
        1016
    errors, handler creation tool, 1415
    errors, ignoring, 1015
    errors, subroutine execution on, 1015,
        1016
    extensibility, 970
    fields, updating using, 1035, 1036–1044
    filtering records, 1018–1027
    forms, in unbound, 1167
    forms, opening using, 978
    GoTo label-name clauses, 1015, 1016
    import operations, automating, 695
    looping, 1009–1014, 1301–1302
    macro conversion to, 985–989
    Macro Recorder, code creation using,
        1452–1454
    macros versus, 983–985
    mathematical operations, 319
    menu bar items, assigning to, 1076
    Microsoft Office XP applications,
        referencing, 1438–1441
    module library, 1057
    modules, password assignment using
        Security Wizard, 1355–1356
    multi-selection list boxes, role in, 512
    object references, 1438
    objects, binding, 1438–1441, 1442
    passwording modules using Security
        Wizard, 1355–1356
    passwords, setting using, 1326
    print dialog boxes using, 1023–1025
    procedures, 971
    processing, conditional, 1003–1009
    records, adding using, 1035, 1044–1046
    records, deleting using, 1035, 1046–1047
    reports, Visual Basic code behind, 974,
        994–995
    startup, running VBA procedures at, 47
    subroutines, 1016
    tables, updating using, 1035–1036
    usability hierarchy, in, 5–6
Visual Basic Code Commenter, 1415
Visual Basic editor, editing macro code
    using, 1454
Visual Basic Error Handler, 1415
Visual Basic for Applications Design
    screen, 1438
Visual Basic Module window, 972, 973, 975
Visual Basic Multi-Code Import/Export, 1416
Visual Basic Scripting code (VBScript), 1202

Visual Basic String Editor, 1416
Visual SourceSafe, 1415
Visual SourceSafe Integration, 1415
voice recognition features, 24

W

Web Browser control, 1215–1216
Web pages. *See also* data access pages;
       hyperlinks; HyperText Markup
       Language (HTML)
    browsing using Web Browser control,
       1215–1216
    data export to dynamic pages, 1198–1201
    data export to static pages, 1186–1187,
       1190–1198, 1202–1205
    displaying after generating, 1197
    dynamic, 1185, 1188–1189
    hyperlinks to, 1212
    queries, creating from, 1186
    source code, viewing, 1197
    static, 1185–1187
    tables, creating from, 1186, 1190–1192
    template files, 1187
Web toolbar, 1181–1183
What You See Is What You Get (WYSIWYG),
       10–11, 626
What's This Button property, 438
What's This? help, custom, 1399
Where macro condition, 898, 1101
WHERE statements, 827, 831
WID. *See* workgroups, ID number (WID)
Width property, 439, 481
wildcards, 226–227, 326, 377–380
Window ⇨ 3 Print Reports: Macro, 1099
Window ⇨ Print Reports Dialog: Form, 1098
Window ⇨ Tile Vertically, 899
Windows Explorer, 45–46
WinPath folder, 1426
WinSysPath folder, 1426
WinZip (on the CD), 1556
Word
    Application object, 1441, 1443–1444
    Automation, working with in, 1440,
       1441–1443, 1444–1454
    class arguments, 1443
    linking Word documents, 1212, 1214
    mail merge reports, in, 884–890
    merge documents, Access support of, 692
    Print Merge, Report Wizard use of, 877,
       884–890

Workflow Designer for Exchange 2000 Server,
       1415
Workflow Designer for SQL Server, 1415
Workgroup Administrator, 1334–1337
workgroup files, 1320, 1333, 1335–1336,
       1357–1359
Workgroup Information File dialog box, 1335
workgroups
    Administrator component removal,
       application reinstallation failure
       from, 1420
    Admins group, 1342–1343
    backup operator groups, 1356
    creating, 1334–1336
    groups, 1341–1342
    groups, adding, 1342–1344
    groups, creating using ActiveX Data
       Objects (ADO), 1363–1364
    groups, default, 1342
    groups, deleting, 1344
    ID number (WID), 1335, 1354–1355
    joining, 1334, 1337
    members, assigning, 1339, 1341–1342,
       1344–1345
    members, removing, 1344–1345
    naming, 1335
    organization, 1335
    project designer groups, 1356
    re-creating, 1335
    Security Wizard groups, 1356
    Users group, 1342, 1357
workspace forms, 427–429
wrap, line, 402, 877, 882
WRKGADM.EXE, 1334
WYSIWYG. *See* What You See Is What You Get
       (WYSIWYG)

X

/X command, 47
x controls, 1169, 1170
XML. *See* Extensible Markup Language (XML)
XML files, 1265
XSD files, 1265, 1266
XSL. *See* Extensible Stylesheet Language
       (XSL)
XSLT. *See* Extensible Stylesheet Language
       Transformation (XSLT)

Y

Year property, 567
Yes! I Can Run My Business (on the CD),
    1550–1551
Yes/No data type
    check box controls, in, 157, 403, 409, 502,
        640–641
    combo box controls, in, 157
    conversion to/from other types, 143–144
    formats, 150–151
    forms, in, 403, 501–505
    introduced, 108
    option button controls, in, 403
    queries, in, 382, 778
    storage size, 137
    text box controls, in, 157, 403, 502
    toggle button controls, in, 403, 641–643
    type of data stored, 137, 138
    validation, automatic, 221
    values returned by, 138, 382
    Visual Basic equivalent, 1003

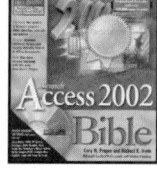

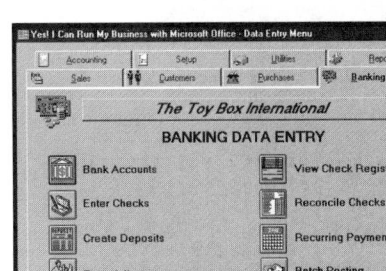

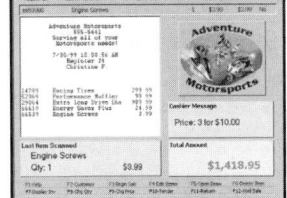

Hungry Minds, Inc.
End-User License Agreement

5. Limited Warranty.

(a) HMI warrants that the Software and Software Media are free from defects in materials and workmanship under normal use for a period of sixty (60) days from the date of purchase of this Book. If HMI receives notification within the warranty period of defects in materials or workmanship, HMI will replace the defective Software Media.

WARRANTIES, EXPRESS OR IMPLIED, INCLUDING WITHOUT LIMITATION IMPLIED WARRANTIES OF MERCHANTABILITY AND FITNESS FOR A PARTICULAR PURPOSE, WITH RESPECT TO THE SOFTWARE, THE PROGRAMS, THE SOURCE CODE CONTAINED THEREIN, AND/OR THE TECHNIQUES DESCRIBED IN THIS BOOK. HMI DOES NOT WARRANT THAT THE FUNCTIONS CONTAINED IN THE SOFTWARE WILL MEET YOUR REQUIREMENTS OR THAT THE OPERATION OF THE SOFTWARE WILL BE ERROR FREE.

(c) This limited warranty gives you specific legal rights, and you may have other rights that vary from jurisdiction to jurisdiction.

6. Remedies.

(a) HMI's entire liability and your exclusive remedy for defects in materials and workmanship shall be limited to replacement of the Software Media, which may be returned to HMI with a copy of your receipt at the following address: Software Media Fulfillment Department, Attn.: *Access 2002 Bible Gold Edition,* Hungry Minds, Inc., 10475 Crosspoint Blvd., Indianapolis, IN 46256, or call 1-800-762-2974. Please allow four to six weeks for delivery. This Limited Warranty is void if failure of the Software Media has resulted from accident, abuse, or misapplication. Any replacement Software Media will be warranted for the remainder of the original warranty period or thirty (30) days, whichever is longer.

(b) In no event shall HMI or the author be liable for any damages whatsoever (including without limitation damages for loss of business profits, business interruption, loss of business information, or any other pecuniary loss) arising from the use of or inability to use the Book or the Software, even if HMI has been advised of the possibility of such damages.

(c) Because some jurisdictions do not allow the exclusion or limitation of liability for consequential or incidental damages, the above limitation or exclusion may not apply to you.

7. U.S. Government Restricted Rights.
Use, duplication, or disclosure of the Software for or on behalf of the United States of America, its agencies and/or instrumentalities (the "U.S. Government") is subject to restrictions as stated in paragraph (c)(1)(ii) of the Rights in Technical Data and Computer Software clause of DFARS 252.227-7013, or subparagraphs (c) (1) and (2) of the Commercial Computer Software - Restricted Rights clause at FAR 52.227-19, and in similar clauses in the NASA FAR supplement, as applicable.

8. General.
This Agreement constitutes the entire understanding of the parties and revokes and supersedes all prior agreements, oral or written, between them and may not be modified or amended except in a writing signed by both parties hereto that specifically refers to this Agreement. This Agreement shall take precedence over any other documents that may be in conflict herewith. If any one or more provisions contained in this Agreement are held by any court or tribunal to be invalid, illegal, or otherwise unenforceable, each and every other provision shall remain in full force and effect.

Installing the Files on Your Computer

All the example .mdb files are Microsoft Access 2002 or 2000 files. They work only in Microsoft Access 2002 or Microsoft Access 2000, and do not work in Microsoft Access 97, 95, 2.0, 1.1, or 1.0.

Installing and Using the Access 2002 Bible Example Files

When you double-click on the SETUP.EXE file in the CD Root, you are prompted to install the example files. To open a file, go to the folder that you installed the example files to and double-click the file that you want to open. If you get an error message when you open an Access database, you either have multiple versions of Microsoft Access on your computer (and Access 2002 is not the default),or you have never told Windows to associate an .MDB files with the program msaccess.exe (Microsoft Access). Follow the instructions in the next section of this appendix to associate all .MDB files with Microsoft Access 2002.

Associating an .MDB file with Microsoft Access

To change which program starts when you open a file:

1. In My Computer or Windows Explorer, click the View menu, and then click Options.

2. Click the File Types tab.

3. In the list of file types, click the one that you want to change (Microsoft Access Databases).

4. The settings for that file type are shown in the File Type Details box.

5. Click Edit.

6. In the Actions box, click Open.

7. Click Edit, and then specify the program (msaccess.exe) you want to use to open files that have this extension.

   Make sure you choose the Access 2002 msaccess.exe if you have other versions of Microsoft Access on your computer.